Architectural Woodwork Standards

1st Edition

A Specification of Qualities, Methods, and Workmanship
Requisite to the Production and Installation of Architectural Millwork

Adopted and Published Jointly, Effective October 1, 2009,
As the Successor, Replacement, and Latest Edition of:
AWI/AWMAC's Quality Standards Illustrated (QSI), and
WI's Manual of Millwork (MM)

By:

Architectural Woodwork Institute (AWI)
46179 Westlake Drive, Suite 120, Potomac Falls, VA 20165
Phone: 571-323-3636 / Fax: 571-323-3630
www.awinet.org

Architectural Woodwork Manufacturers Association of Canada (AWMAC)
516 - 4 Street West, High River, Alberta, T1V 1B6, Canada
Phone: 403-652-7685 / Fax: 403-652-7384
www.awmac.com

Woodwork Institute (WI)
P. O. Box 980247, West Sacramento, CA 95798-0247
Phone: 916-372-9943 / Fax: 916-372-9950
www.woodworkinstitute.com

Joint Standards Committee Members:

Dan Wendell - Chair ● Myron Jonzon - Vice Chair ● Randy Estabrook - Secretary

AWI	WI	AWMAC
Michael Bell - Kentucky	Bill Fenstermacher - California	Myron Jonzon - Alberta
Randy Jensen - Alabama	Mike Hansen - California	Al Sparling - Ontario
Dan Wendell - Kansas	Dick McClure - California	Jim Taylor - British Columbia
William Munyan - North Carolina - Alt.	Bruce Humphrey - California - Alt.	Vince Parolin - Ontario - Alt.

Executive Editor:

Stanley R. (Rob) Gustafson, CAE, CSI, AIA (associate)
CEO - Woodwork Institute

Price: $125.00

INTRODUCTORY STATEMENT

Like all architectural components of the construction process, woodwork design and configuration possibilities are limited only by the creativity of the design professional. We have included architectural wood products which through evolution have become fixtures of our daily lives and have developed a measurable guideline to ensure these products meet these standards.

It is the intent of these standards to assist the design professional to specify a variety of millwork products which meet the functional and esthetic requirements of their clients. Encompassing all products in these standards is not possible; but by understanding and applying these standards and implementing the services provided by the signatory associations, the design professional will best serve their client needs and can be confident their quality criteria will be achieved.

When design professionals reference the Architectural Woodwork Standards for their projects, they also assume the obligation that the quality standards are met.

Disclaimers

The Associations shall not be responsible to anyone for the use of or reliance upon these standards. The Associations shall not incur any obligation nor liability for damages, including consequential damages, arising out of or in connection with the use, interpretation of, or reliance upon these standards.

These Architectural Woodwork Standards provide the minimum criteria for the concept, design, fabrication, finishing, and installation of architectural woodwork. Provisions for mechanical and electrical safety have not been included. References to life-safety requirements are included for information only. Governmental agencies or other national standards-setting organizations provide the standards for life-safety requirements.

Illustrations are intended to assist in understanding the standards and may not include all requirements for a specific product or unit, nor do they show the only method of fabrication. Such partial drawings shall not be used to justify improper or incomplete design and/or construction.

Unless otherwise referenced, Appendixes A and B are not considered an integral part of these standards. The appendixes are provided as an additional resource to the manufacturer, design professional, educators, user, or certifying organization and shall not be interpreted as legal advice or code-compliance language.

If a conflict is found in these standards, the least restrictive requirement shall prevail until addressed by errata.

♦ ♦

Architectural Woodwork Institute (AWI)

The Architectural Woodwork Institute, a not-for-profit trade association of architectural woodwork manufacturers, industry suppliers, and design professionals, was established in 1953 as an expansion of the Millwork Cost Bureau and is dedicated to the goals of:

- Improving architectural woodwork standards
- Providing technical education for members and the design community
- Researching innovative materials and methods of engineering, fabrication, finishing, and installation

The bedrock of the association is its nationwide network of over twenty-five chapters, built on the principle of sharing knowledge, education, and networking that includes:

- Seminars and workshops for AWI members, construction professionals, and design professionals by award of AIA Continuing Education System (CES) credits
- Publications, including:
  - Design Solutions magazine
  - AWI Cost Book
  - Architectural Woodwork Quality Standards Illustrated, Editions 1-8
  - A wide range of member-centric industry information and resources

In 1995, AWI established its Quality Certification Program (QCP) to give the assurance and the expectation to millwork customers that fine woodwork, specified as QCP in construction documents, will comply with the quality grades in these standards. The QCP has been officially adopted by the General Services Administration (GSA) for its woodwork specifications and is endorsed by the American Subcontractors Association (ASA).

46179 Westlake Drive, Suite 120, Potomac Falls, VA 20165 Ph: 571-323-3636 Fax: 571-323-3630 www.awinet.org

Architectural Woodwork Manufacturers Association of Canada (AWMAC)

The Architectural Woodwork Manufacturers Association of Canada (AWMAC)/Association des Manufacturiers de la Menuiserie Architecturale du Canada has its roots in the 1920s millwork industry in Vancouver, Canada. Evolving from regional associations, it has become a nonprofit national registered association. AWMAC's strength is the linkage between the national association, the regional AWMAC Chapters, and the manufacturer, supplier, educational, associate, and design professional members. Today, AWMAC is the national voice of the Canadian architectural woodwork industry and is committed to:

- Partnering with other associations to define and improve architectural woodwork standards
- Collaborating with educational institutions to enhance the apprentice and technical programs and to ensure a quality human resource for the architectural woodwork industry
- Communicating the traditional, new, and innovative architectural woodwork assembly methods and materials to governments, industry, design professionals, and their associations
- Publishing The Sounding Board, a newsletter, and the Salary/Business Conditions Survey

In conjunction with AWMAC, AWMAC Chapters provide:

- Seminars from raw "green" products to installed architectural woodwork for architects, designers, and members
- Annual Awards that celebrate the best in quality, service, and design for manufacturers, associates, and design professionals
- Administration of the Guarantee and Inspection Service (GIS); initiated in 1990, the GIS Program (when specified by the design professional) monitors and guarantees projects that specify AWMAC standards

For further information and correct GIS specification wording, contact your local AWMAC Chapter or AWMAC.
516-4 St. West, High River, Alberta, T1V 1B6, Canada Ph: 403-652-7685 Fax: 403-652-7384 www.awmac.com

♦ ♦

Woodwork Institute (WI)

The Woodwork Institute, a regional, not-for-profit trade association of architectural woodwork manufacturers and industry suppliers, was established in 1951 and is dedicated to the goals of:

- Promoting information relative to the uses, advantages, and utility of architectural millwork products
- Providing the leading architectural woodwork standards
- Providing unbiased industry consultation and quality assurance programs

The basic principals of WI are its dedication to standards setting, quality assurance, recognition, workforce education, and networking that includes:

- Industry-based seminars, offering AIA Continuing Education System (CES) credits
- CE Bernhauer Scholarship Foundation grants
- Bernie B. Barber Awards of Excellence and the Ralph B. McClure Craftsmanship Awards
- Publications, including:
  - *Details* Newsletter
  - *Archetype* magazine
  - *Manual of Millwork*, Editions 1-11
  - A wide range of member-centric industry information and resources

In 1953, WI published its first *Manual of Millwork*, followed in 1959 by the establishment of its Certified Compliance Program (CCP) to give the assurance to millwork customers that the fine woodwork specified in their construction documents will comply with the quality grades in these standards. In 2001, WI expanded its quality assurance options with the establishment of its Monitored Compliance Program (MCP).

P. O. Box 980247, West Sacramento, CA 95798 Ph: 916-372-9943 Fax: 916-372-9950 www.woodworkinstitute.com

THE FOLLOWING ASSOCIATIONS ARE GRATEFULLY ACKNOWLEDGED:

American Institute of Architects (AIA)

American Institute of Architectural Students (AIAS)

American National Standards Institute (ANSI)

American Society of Interior Designers (ASID)

American Society for Testing and Materials (ASTM)

American Subcontractors Association (ASA)

Association for Retail Environments (ARE)

Builders Hardware Manufacturers Association (BHMA)

Canadian Kitchen Cabinet Association (CKCA)

Canadian Window and Door Manufacturers Association (CWDMA)

Composite Panel Association (CPA)

Construction Specifications Canada (CSC)

Construction Specifications Institute (CSI)

The Engineered Wood Association (APA)

Hardwood Plywood & Veneer Association (HPVA)

Interior Design of Canada (IDC)

International Interior Design Association (IIDA)

International Solid Surface Fabricators Association (ISSFA)

International Wood Products Association (IWPA)

Kitchen Cabinet Manufacturers Association (KCMA)

Laminating Materials Association (LMA)

National Electrical Manufacturers Association (NEMA)

National Fire Protection Association (NFPA)

National Hardwood Lumber Association (NHLA)

National Institute of Building Sciences (NIBS)

National Research Council Canada (NRC-CNRC)

Royal Architectural Institute of Canada (RAIG)

Scientific Equipment & Furniture Association (SEFA)

Stair Manufacturer Association (SMA)

Temperate Forest Foundation (TeFF)

Tropical Forest Foundation (TFF)

Western Wood Products Association (WWPA)

Window and Door Manufacturers Association (WDMA)

Wood Moulding and Millwork Producers (WMMPA)

Architectural Woodwork Standards

USER'S GUIDE

USER'S GUIDE

Sponsored by the Architectural Woodwork Institute, the Architectural Woodwork Manufacturers Association of Canada, and the Woodwork Institute (hereinafter called the Associations), these new joint standards represent the best of what all three organizations had to offer in defining the minimum requirements of material and workmanship for the fabrication and installation of architectural woodwork. The joint standards are based on three definitive levels of work: Economy, Custom, and Premium Grade.

These standards are a combination and refinement of what the Associations previously offered individually. They are different and distinctly new in their layout, requirements, etc., and nothing should be assumed to have transferred across unaltered. It is advised, whether you are a design professional, manufacturer, or installer, to thoroughly review these standards.

These standards are both a voluntary and a definitive document, intended to spell out the requirements for satisfactory performance when referenced as part of contract documents. The document is intended to be used in total, not in part. For example, if a project specification requires compliance with Section 10, then compliance with the Preface and the Product, Execution, and Compliance portions of Sections 1-5 (along with Appendix A and the Glossary as referenced) is also required, as applicable. The Introduction, Table of Contents, Suggestion Form, General portions of Sections 1-12, and the Appendixes are generally not part of these standards for compliance purposes.

STANDARDS DOCUMENT is divided as follows:

Introduction
User's Guide
Suggestion Form
Table of Contents
Preface
Section 1 - Submittals
Section 2 - Care & Storage
Section 3 - Lumber
Section 4 - Sheet Products
Section 5 - Finishing
Section 6 - Interior & Exterior Millwork
Section 7 - Stairwork & Rails
Section 8 - Wall Surfacing
Section 9 - Doors
Section 10 - Casework
Section 11 - Countertops
Section 12 - Historic Restoration Work
Appendix A
Glossary
Appendix B

USER'S GUIDE is intended as a tool to enhance your understanding of the philosophy behind the layout of these standards.

SUGGESTION FORM is provided as a common means for the users of these standards to submit comments and suggestions for improvement. The form is located at the end of this User's Guide.

PREFACE covers those areas of importance to be reviewed in advance of using the standards.

SECTION 1 addresses minimum submittal requirements, including shop drawings, samples, etc.

SECTION 2 addresses minimum care and storage (environmental condition) requirements to be maintained before, during, and after the delivery, storage, and installation of product.

USER'S GUIDE

SECTIONS 3-5 address the minimum acceptable performance and appearance characteristics of lumber panel and finishing materials to be used within the standards' product sections (Sections 6-12). These sections do not attempt to establish raw material grades. They define the minimum characteristics for these materials when used in a product governed by Sections 6-12 based on the specified Grade of work (Economy, Custom, or Premium).

SECTIONS 6-12 address minimum acceptable millwork product fabrication and installation requirements based on the specified Grade of work (Economy, Custom, or Premium).

APPENDIX pages provide guidance and information related to the work and should be reviewed in advance of using the standards.

GLOSSARY provides definitions of terms used throughout these standards.

EACH SECTION is organized into four areas of importance:

GENERAL - covers general information about the subject matter, the scope of work, and the requirements applicable to the scope of work in the absence of specifications. The general information portion of Part I contains: Basic Considerations (important information for a design professional), Recommendations (for consideration by design professionals), Acknowledgments (of materials or products relative to this section that might not otherwise be readily known), and Industry Practices (methods of work and material selections applicable to the sections in the absence of specifications).

PRODUCT - covers minimum material, machining, and assembly (manufacturing) requirements for the Grade of work selected or required.

EXECUTION - covers minimum installation requirements for the Grade of work selected or required.

COMPLIANCE - covers ways of verifying compliance with the standards.

SECTION TEXT is laid out in a numerical, indented, outline format, wherein each statement, issue, or rule becomes a specific, uniquely referenced item. Additional discussion or qualifications to an item are indented to the right, immediately below, creating a columnar effect.

In the **PRODUCT** and **EXECUTION** portions of each section, an additional table format illustrates particular requirements that are applicable only to a particular Grade or Grades of work.

The concept of **"UNLESS SPECIFIED OTHERWISE"** is a significant aspect of these standards. When referenced in contract documents, these standards shall establish the minimum contractual compliance requirements for materials, fabrication, installation, and workmanship - in the absence of any specific contractual requirement to the contrary. If there is a conflict between the plans, specifications, and these standards, the **PLANS** and **SPECIFICATIONS SHALL PREVAIL**.

USER'S GUIDE

As a rule of thumb, unless otherwise noted, the statements or rules contained within the **GENERAL, COMPLIANCE**, and the beginning of the **EXECUTION** portions of each section are equally applicable to all Grades of work, as shown in the following format example taken from Section 7:

1.2 **BASIC CONSIDERATIONS**

1.2.1 **ACCEPTABLE REQUIREMENTS** of lumber and/or sheet products used within this woodwork product section are established by Sections 3 and 4, unless otherwise modified herein.

1.2.2 **CONTRACT DRAWINGS** and/or **SPECIFICATIONS**, furnished by the design professional, shall clearly indicate or delineate all material, fabrication, installation and applicable building code/regulation requirements.

1.2.3 **CROSS GRAIN** in band-sawn or laminated members might cause objectionable color variation when finished.

1.2.4 **EDGES** in veneer-laminated members or where multiple layers are exposed by shaping might cause objectionable color variation when finished.

OTHERWISE, within the **PRODUCT or EXECUTION** portions, when a rule applies specifically to a particular Grade or Grades of work, it is shown with a bullet mark in one of the right-hand columns. These columns are both color-coded and headed with an E, C, or P to indicate Economy, Custom, or Premium Grade, respectively. A sample from the Section 7 **PRODUCT** portion is shown below:

DESCRIPTION						E	C	P
⇑ 4.2 MATERIAL	**MATERIAL** (continued)							
	⇑ 4.2.12	At **EXPOSED SURFACES** (continued)						
		⇑ 4.2.12.7	For **TRANSPARENT FINISH** (continued)					
			4.2.12.7.10	Have visible panel **EDGES, REVEALS**, and/or **SPLINES**, when appropriate, that are:				
				4.2.12.7.10.1	Full length.			
				4.2.12.7.10.2	**MILL-OPTION.**	●		
				4.2.12.7.10.3	**MATCH** species of panel face.		●	●
				4.2.12.7.10.4	**COMPATIBLE** for color and grain.		●	
				4.2.12.7.10.5	**WELL-MATCHED** for color and grain.			●
				4.2.12.7.10.6	A minimum of 0.020" (0.5 mm) nominal **THICKNESS** that precludes show-through of core.		●	●
	4.2.13	At **SEMI-EXPOSED SURFACES**:						
		4.2.13.1	For **OPAQUE** finish, permits natural and manufacturing defects, provided the surface is filled solid.					

The **ARROW** in the above example is used on a page-by-page basis to indicate where there is additional coverage of a topic on a previous or a subsequent page. The following description shown is included at the beginning of each table:

ARROWS INDICATE TOPIC IS CARRIED FROM ⇑ OR ONTO ⇓ ANOTHER PAGE.

Where space allows, **VERTICAL TITLES** are also provided within the first three left-hand columns of the tables to help keep track of subject areas.

USER'S GUIDE

UNIQUE to Sections 3, 4, 6, 9, 10, and 11, the numerical outline also incorporates an alpha character to further separate or define the outline string. For example, within **SECTION 3**, the alpha character is used to differentiate between **HARDWOOD** and **SOFTWOOD**, as shown in the following example from Section 3:

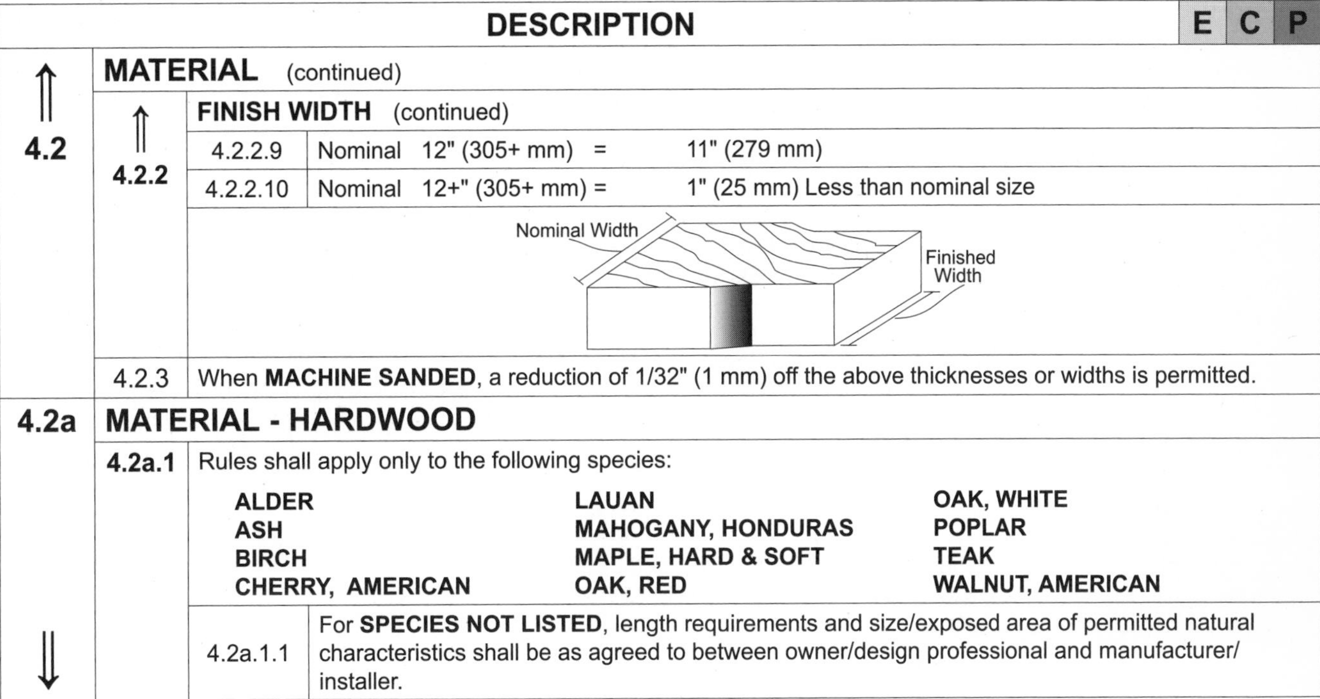

				DESCRIPTION	E C P
⇑ 4.2	**MATERIAL** (continued)				
	⇑ 4.2.2	**FINISH WIDTH** (continued)			
		4.2.2.9	Nominal 12" (305+ mm) =	11" (279 mm)	
		4.2.2.10	Nominal 12+" (305+ mm) =	1" (25 mm) Less than nominal size	
	4.2.3	When **MACHINE SANDED**, a reduction of 1/32" (1 mm) off the above thicknesses or widths is permitted.			
4.2a	**MATERIAL - HARDWOOD**				
	4.2a.1	Rules shall apply only to the following species: **ALDER**, **ASH**, **BIRCH**, **CHERRY, AMERICAN**, **LAUAN**, **MAHOGANY, HONDURAS**, **MAPLE, HARD & SOFT**, **OAK, RED**, **OAK, WHITE**, **POPLAR**, **TEAK**, **WALNUT, AMERICAN**			
⇓		4.2a.1.1	For **SPECIES NOT LISTED**, length requirements and size/exposed area of permitted natural characteristics shall be as agreed to between owner/design professional and manufacturer/installer.		

UNIQUE to Sections 10 and 11, additional specific material, fabrication, and installation requirements have been provided for casework and/or countertops to be used in a laboratory-type setting. These requirements are only applicable if a project's contract documents specifically require compliance to such.

For further clarification or explanation, call your local Association representative.

Architectural Woodwork Standards

Improvement Suggestion Form

I believe that the following suggestion will improve the Architectural Woodwork Standards.

Please look at Section # _______, Page # _______, Item # ___________________

Suggestion (please fully describe the addition, deletion, and/or revision you feel will improve these standards):

____

____

____

____

____

____

____

____

____

____

____

____

____

Please include any additional descriptive sheets, drawings, or product data that may be needed to fully explain your suggestion.

For further clarification or input, you may contact me at:

Company Name: ____
My Name: ____
Address: ________________________ City: __________ State: ____ Zip: ______
Phone: ___________________________ Fax: ___________________________

Fax, mail, or e-mail your completed suggestion form to one of the following sponsor Associations:

AWI
Architectural Woodwork Institute
46179 Westlake Drive, Suite 120
Potomac Falls, VA 20165
Fax: 571-323-3630
www.awinet.org

AWMAC
Architectural Woodwork Manufacturers Association of Canada
516 - 4 Street West
High River, Alberta, T1V 1B6, Canada
Fax: 403-652-7384
www.awmac.com

WI
Woodwork Institute
P. O. Box 980247
West Sacramento, CA 95798-0247
Fax: 916-372-9950
www.woodworkinstitute.com

Architectural Woodwork Standards

TABLE OF CONTENTS

T

INTRODUCTION:
Introductory Statement & Disclaimers 2
Architectural Woodwork Institute (AWI) Introduction 2
Architectural Woodwork Manufacturers of Canada (AWMAC) Introduction 3
Woodwork Institute (WI) Introduction 3
Association Acknowledgements 4

USERS GUIDE:
General. 6
Improvement Suggestion Form 10

PREFACE:
Architectural Woodwork Standards 24
Variations in Natural Wood Products 25
Systems of Measurement. 25
Architectural Woodwork Specifications 26
Architectural Woodwork Drawings 26
Casework Refinishing/Refacing/Refurbishing 28
Moisture and Architectural Woodwork 29
Forest Management Certification 30
Environmental Veneer Considerations 30
Warranty/Guarantee Language 31

SECTION 1 - Submittals:
Grades 34
Basic Considerations
Shop Drawings 34
Mock-ups, Hardware, Moldings, or Finish Samples 34
Code and Regulation Compliance 34
Submittal Approval 35
Recommendations
Submittal Procedure 35
Specification Consideration 35
Acknowledgements 35
Industry Practices. 35
Scope 35
Default Stipulation 35
Product Rules
General 36
Section 6 - Interior & Exterior Millwork 37
Section 7 - Stairwork and Rails. 38
Section 8 - Wall Paneling 38
Section 9 - Doors 39
Section 10 - Casework 40
Section 11 - Countertops 40
Section 12 - Historic Restoration Work 41

SECTION 2 - Care & Storage:
Grades 44
Basic Considerations
Relative Humidity and Moisture Content 44
Dimensional Change Problems. 45
Recommendations 45
Acknowledgements
Responsibility 46
Industry Practices
Off Gases 46
Scope 46
Default Stipulation 46
Product Rules
Delivery 46
Awaiting Installation 47
Interior 47
Exterior 47
After Acceptance 47

SECTION 3 - Lumber:

Grades . . . 50
Lumber Association Grades . . . 50
Lumber Rules . . . 50
Basic Considerations
Availability . . . 50
Fire-Retardant Lumber . . . 50
Preservative Treatment . . . 51
Veneer Construction . . . 51
Photodegradation . . . 51
Oxidation . . . 52
Recommendations
Specification Suggestions . . . 52
Acknowledgments
Engineered Wood Products . . . 52
Industry Practices
Dimensional Conventions . . . 53
Gluing . . . 53
Non-covered Species . . . 53
Scope . . . 53
Default Stipulation . . . 53
Product Rules
General . . . 53
Material . . . 54
Material - Hardwood . . . 55
Material - Softwood . . . 63

SECTION 4 - Sheet Products:

Grades . . . 70
Basic Considerations
Plywood Definition . . . 70
Veneer Grain . . . 70
Figure . . . 70
Special Characteristics . . . 70
Photodegradation . . . 71
Oxidation . . . 71
Fire-Retardant Sheets . . . 71
Panel Adhesives . . . 71
Checking and Warpage . . . 72
Wood Veneer Slicing . . . 72
Matching of Adjacent Wood Veneer Leaves . . . 73
Matching of Wood Veneer Leaves within a Panel Face . . . 74
End-Matching of Wood Veneers . . . 75
Speciality or Sketch Matches of Wood Veneers . . . 76
High Pressure Decorative Laminate (HPDL) . . . 78
Low Pressure Decorative Laminate (LPDL) . . . 78
Vinyl Film . . . 78
Medium Density Overlay (MDO) . . . 78
Hardboard . . . 78
Solid Surface . . . 78
Solid Phenolic . . . 78
Panel Cores
Veneer Core . . . 79
Lumber Core . . . 79
Composite Core . . . 79
Combination Core . . . 79
Core Properties, Performance, and Availability . . . 79
Recommendations
Specification Suggestions . . . 80
Acknowledgements . . . 80
Industry Practices
Panel's Grain Direction . . . 81
Non-covered Species . . . 81
Scope . . . 81
Default Stipulation . . . 81
Product Rules
General . . . 81
Hardwood Veneer . . . 83

SECTION 4 - Sheet Products (continued)
Product Rules (continued)
Hardwood Veneer (continued)
Veneer Face Grade Descriptions . . . 84
Terminology Definitions . . . 85
Allowable Face Grade Characteristics
General . . . 86
Ash, Beech, Birch, Maple, and Poplar . . . 87
Mahogany, Anigre, Makore, and Sapele . . . 88
Red and White Oak . . . 89
Pecan and Hickory . . . 90
Walnut and Cherry . . . 91
Softwood Veneer . . . 92
Face Grade Requirements . . . 92
Allowable Face Grade Characteristics
General . . . 92
Western Red Cedar, White Pine, and Vertical Grain Douglas Fir / Redwood . . . 93
Douglas Fir . . . 94
HPDL . . . 95
LPDL . . . 96
Vinyl Film . . . 96
MDO . . . 97
HDO . . . 97
Hardboard . . . 97
Balance Sheet . . . 97
Backer . . . 97
Solid Surface . . . 98
Solid Phenolic . . . 99
Epoxy Resin . . . 99
Natural and Manufactured Stone . . . 99
Compliance . . . 100

SECTION 5 - Finishing:
Grades . . . 102
Basic Considerations
Purpose . . . 102
Air-Quality Restriction . . . 102
Chemical Resistance . . . 102
Fire-Retardance . . . 102
Sanding . . . 103
Grain . . . 103
Factory or Field Finishing . . . 103
Finishing Systems
General . . . 103
System Listings . . . 104
Comparison Overview . . . 105
Performance Characteristics . . . 106
Recommendations
Include in Division 9 . . . 109
Jobsite Finishing . . . 109
Specification Suggestions . . . 109
Acknowledgements . . . 109
Industry Practices . . . 109
Scope . . . 109
Default Stipulation . . . 110
Product Rules
General . . . 110
Defects and Workmanship . . . 111
Material . . . 113
Application
General . . . 113
Generic Coatings . . . 114
System 1 - Lacquer, Nitrocellulose . . . 115
System 2 & 3 - Lacquer, Pre- and Post-catalyzed . . . 115
System 4 - Latex Acrylic, Water-Based . . . 116
System 5 - Varnish, Conversion . . . 116
System 6 - Oil, Penetrating . . . 116

SECTION 5 - Finishing (continued)

Product Rules (continued)
Application (continued)
System 7 - Vinyl, Catalyzed . . . 117
System 8 - Acrylic, Cross-Linked, Wated-Based . . . 117
System 9 & 10 - UV-Curable, Acrylated Epoxy, Polyester . . . 117
System 11 & 12 - Polyurethane, Catalyzed, or Water-Based . . . 117
System 13 - Polyester, Catalyzed . . . 118
Compliance
General . . . 119
Visual Testing . . . 119
Consistency Testing . . . 119
Sheen Testing . . . 119

SECTION 6 - Interior & Exterior Millwork:

Grades . . . 122
Basic Considerations
Acceptable Requirements . . . 122
Exposed, Semi-Exposed, and Concealed Surfaces . . . 122
Smoothness . . . 122
Radius Work . . . 123
Standing & Running Trim . . . 124
Door Frames and Jambs . . . 125
Window Sash and Frames . . . 125
Blinds and Shutters . . . 126
Screens . . . 127
Ornamental Millwork . . . 127
Recommendations
Include in Division 9 . . . 128
Contract Documents . . . 128
Specification Suggestions . . . 129
Acknowledgements . . . 129
Industry Practices
Structural Members . . . 129
Wall, Floor, and Ceiling Variations . . . 129
Back-Priming . . . 129
Scope . . . 129
Default Stipulation . . . 131
Product Rules
General . . . 131
Material
General . . . 132
Doors and Window Frames . . . 133
Sash . . . 134
Blinds and Shutters . . . 134
Screens . . . 135
Miscellaneous Millwork . . . 135
Glass . . . 136
Machining
General . . . 137
Standing and Running Trim . . . 137
Window Frames . . . 138
Sash . . . 138
Blinds and Shutters . . . 138
Screens . . . 139
Ornamental Millwork . . . 139
Assembly
General . . . 139
Standing and Running Trim . . . 141
Door Frames . . . 141
Window Frames . . . 142
Sash . . . 142
Blinds and Shutters . . . 143
Screens . . . 143
Ornamental Millwork . . . 143
Miscellaneous Millwork . . . 144

SECTION 6 - Interior & Exterior Millwork (continued)

Execution
- Preparation & Qualification 145
- Rules
  - General 146
  - Standing and Running Trim 149
  - Door and Window Frames 150
  - Blinds and Shutters 150
  - Screens 150
  - Ornamental Millwork 150

Compliance
- Smoothness 151
- Gaps, Flushness, and Flatness 151

SECTION 7 - Stairwork & Rails:

Grades 154

Basic Considerations
- Acceptable Requirements 154
- Exposed, Semi-Exposed, and Concealed Surfaces 154
- Stair and Handrail Nomenclature 155
- Handrail Component Nomenclature 155
- Handrail Fabrication 156
- Handrail Joinery 156

Recommendations
- Include in Division 9 156
- Contract Documents 156
- Specification Suggestions 156

Industry Practices
- Structural Members 157
- Wall, Floor, and Ceiling Variations 157
- Back-Priming 157

Scope 157

Default Stipulation 157

Product Rules
- General 158
- Material 158
- Machining 160
- Assembly 162

Execution
- Preparation & Qualification 164
- Rules 164

Compliance
- Smoothness 168
- Gaps, Flushness, and Flatness 168

SECTION 8 - Wall Surfacing:

Grades 172

Basic Considerations
- Acceptable Requirements 172
- Exposed, Semi-Exposed, and Concealed Surfaces 172
- Grade Limitations 172
- Fire-Rated Options and Considerations 172
- Wood Species Selection 173
- Veneer Flitch 174
- Matching of Panels within a Room 175
- Edgebanding Options 178
- Stile and Rail Wall Surfacing 179
- Decorative Laminate Wall Surfacing 180
- Solid Surface Wall Surfacing 181
- Solid Phenolic Wall Surfacing 182

Recommendations
- Include in Division 9 182
- Contract Documents 182
- Specification Suggestions 182

Acknowledgements 182

Industry Practices
- Structural Members 183

SECTION 8 - Wall Surfacing (continued)
Industry Practices (continued)
Wall, Floor, and Ceiling Variations 183
Back-Priming 183
Scope 183
Default Stipulation 183
Product Rules
General 184
Material
General 184
Wood Veneer 185
Solid Stile and Rail Wood 187
Decorative Laminate 188
Solid Surface 189
Solid Phenolic 189
Machining 190
Assembly
General 190
Wood Veneer 192
Solid Stile and Rail Wood 194
Decorative Laminate 194
Solid Surface 195
Solid Phenolic 196
Execution
Preparation & Qualification 196
Rules
General 197
Wood Veneer 200
Decorative Laminate 200
Solid Surface 201
Solid Phenolic 201
Compliance
Smoothness 201
Blueprint Match 202
Gaps, Flushness, Flatness and Alignment 202

SECTION 9 - Doors:
Grades 206
Basic Considerations
Acceptable Requirements 206
Exposed, Semi-exposed and Concealed Surfaces 206
Grade Limitations 206
Warranty 206
NFPA-80 207
Code and Regulations 207
Fire-Rated Doors 207
Transom Panel Options 207
Vertical Meeting Edge Options 208
Dutch Door Options 208
Louver Options 209
Flashing Options 209
Performance Duty Levels 209
Flush Doors
Cores 210
Wood-Face Veneer 210
Edge Types 211
Construction Definitions 212
Examples 213
Pair Match 215
Set Match 215
Transom Match 216
Stile and Rail Doors
General 216
Component Terminology 217
Stiles 217
Rails 217
Mullions 217

SECTION 9 - Doors (continued)
Basic Considerations (continued)
Stile and Rail Doors (continued)
Panels 218
Stile and Rail Construction. 218
Panel Construction. 218
Panel or Glass Retention 219
Panel Layout and Grain Direction 219
Recommendations
Include in Division 9 220
Contract Documents 220
Specification Suggestions. 220
Acknowledgements 220
Industry Practices
Structural Members 221
Wall, Floor, and Ceiling Variations. 221
Handing. 221
Scope 221
Default Stipulation 222
Product Rules
General. 222
Material
Flush Doors 224
Veneer Faced 225
Stand Alone Door Face Veneer Characteristics 226
Ash, Beech, Birch, Maple, and Poplar. 227
Mahogany, Anigre, Makore, and Sapele 228
Red and White Oak. 229
Pecan and Hickory 230
Walnut and Cherry 231
Stile and Rail Doors 231
Machining And Assembly
General 231
WDMA Performance Duties 231
Flush Doors 233
Stile and Rail Doors 236
Execution
Preparation & Qualification 237
Rules. 238
Compliance
Smoothness 241
Gaps, Flushness, and Flatness. 241

SECTION 10 - Casework:
Grades 244
Basic Considerations
Acceptable Requirements 244
Chemical and Stain Resistance. 244
Abrasion Resistance 245
Without Specification to the Contrary. 245
At Presentation Panels 245
Toe-Base Height Variance 245
Exposed. 245
Exposed Exterior Surface 245
Exposed Interior Surface 246
Semi-Exposed 246
Concealed Surfaces 246
Grade Limitations 246
Surface Finish and Surface Definition 246
Illustrations of Surface Terminology 249
Door and Drawer Front Edge Profiles 249
Door Retention Profiles 250
Cabinet Construction Options 250
Cabinet and Door Interface Options 251
Layout Requirements of Cabinet Faces for Grain or Patterns by Grade 251
Cabinet Design Series 253
Adjustable Shelf Loading and Deflection 253

SECTION 10 - Casework (continued)

Basic Considerations (continued)
- Casework Integrity 253
- Cabinet Hardware 254

Recommendations
- Include in Division 9 254
- Contract Documents 254
- Specification Suggestions 254

Industry Practices
- Structural Members 255
- Wall, Floor, and Ceiling Variations 255
- Back-Priming 255
- Nominal Casework Dimensions 255
- Base Cabinet, Stretcher Layout, and Construction 256

Scope 257

Default Stipulation 258

Product Rules
- General 258
  - Hardware 258
- Material
  - General 261
  - Wood Casework 262
  - Decorative Laminate Casework 263
  - Solid Phenolic Casework 264
- Machining
  - General 264
- Assembly
  - General 265
  - Joints 265
  - Edges 267
  - Drawers 267
  - Doors
    - Hinged 269
    - Stile & Rail 270
    - Sliding 272
    - Frameless Glass 273
  - Ends and Divisions 273
  - Tops and Bottoms 274
  - Security and Dust Panels 274
  - Stretchers 275
  - Backs 275
  - Toe Bases, Kicks, and Sleepers 275
  - Shelves
    - Fixed 276
    - Adjustable 276
  - Pullout Shelves 280
  - Clothes Poles and Rods 281
  - Wardrobes 281
  - Anchor Strips 281
  - Moveable Cabinets 281
  - Joinery 281
  - Scribing 282
  - Closure 283
  - Clearances and Tolerances 283
  - Warp and Twist 284
  - Wood Casework 284
  - Decorative Laminate Casework 286
  - Solid Phenolic Casework 286

Execution
- Preparation & Qualification 287
- Rules
  - General 288
  - Anchorage Requirement 291

Compliance
- Smoothness 293
- Gaps, Flushness, Flatness, and Alignment 294

SECTION 11 - Countertops

Grades 296
Basic Considerations
Acceptable Requirements 296
Exposed, Semi-Exposed, and Concealed Surfaces 296
Grade Limitations 296
Chemical or Stain Resistance 296
Abrasion Resistance 297
HPDL. 297
Solid Surface. 297
HPDL Configuration Options. 297
Back and End Splash Construction Options 299
Back and End Splash Assembly Options 299
Wood Configuration Options. 299
Solid Surface Configuration Options. 300
Solid Phenolic, Epoxy Resin, and Natural/Manufactured Stone Configuration Options 301
Recommendations
Include in Division 9 301
Contract Documents 301
Specification Suggestions. 301
Acknowledgements 302
Industry Practices
Structural Members 302
Wall, Floor, and Ceiling Variations. 302
Back-Priming. 302
Scope 302
Default Stipulation 303
Product Rules
General 303
Material
Wood 304
HPDL 304
Solid Surface 305
Solid Phenolic 305
Epoxy Resin 305
Natural and Manufactured Stone 305
Machining
Wood 305
HPDL 306
Solid Surface 306
Solid Phenolic 306
Epoxy Resin 306
Natural and Manufactured Stone 307
Assembly
Wood 308
HPDL 309
Solid Surface 311
Solid Phenolic 311
Epoxy Resin 311
Natural and Manufactured Stone 312
Execution
Preparation & Qualification 312
Rules. 313
Solid or Veneered Wood 316
HPDL 316
Solid Surface 317
Solid Phenolic 318
Epoxy Resin, Natural, and Manufactured Stone 318
Compliance
Smoothness 319
Gaps, Flushness, and Flatness. 319

SECTION 12 - Historic Restoration Work:

Grades 322
Basic Considerations
Rational and Intent 322
Acceptable Requirements. 322

SECTION 12 - Historic Restoration Work (continued)

Basic Considerations (continued)
- Exposed, Semi-Exposed and Concealed Surfaces . . . 323

Recommendations
- Include in Division 9 . . . 324
- Contract Documents . . . 324
- Specification Suggestions . . . 324
- Single Source Responsibility . . . 324

Industry Practices
- Structural Members . . . 325
- Wall, Floor, and Ceiling Variations . . . 325
- Back-Priming . . . 325

Scope . . . 325

Default Stipulation . . . 325

Product Rules
- General . . . 325
- Material . . . 326
- Machining . . . 327
- Assembly . . . 327
- Stripping . . . 328
- Repairs . . . 328
- Finishing . . . 328

Execution
- Preparation & Qualification . . . 329
- Rules . . . 330

Compliance
- Smoothness . . . 332
- Gaps, Flushness, and Flatness . . . 333

APPENDIX - A

Reference Source Directory . . . 337

Reference Source Listings . . . 338

Preservative & Water Repellent Treatments . . . 340

Fire Retardant Coatings . . . 340

Fire Codes . . . 340

ADA Requirements . . . 340

Rated Fire Door Assemblies . . . 340

Building Code Requirements . . . 340

Seismic Fabrication & Installation Requirements . . . 340

Adhesives Guidelines . . . 341

Specific Gravity & Weight of Hardwoods . . . 342

ANSI/BHMA Cabinet Hardware References . . . 343

Typical Joinery Details . . . 347

SEFA Chemical Resistance Guidelines and Testing . . . 349

Cabinet Design Series (CDS)
- General Information . . . 351
- 100 Series - Base Cabinets without Drawers . . . 352
- 200 Series - Base Cabinets with Drawers . . . 355
- 300 Series - Wall Hung Cabinets . . . 357
- 400 Series - Tall Storage Cabinets . . . 359
- 500 Series - Tall Wardrobe Cabinets . . . 363
- 600 Series - Library Cabinets . . . 365
- 700 Series - Moveable Cabinets . . . 367

Casework Integrity
- Structural Integrity Test - Base . . . 371
- Concentrated Load Test . . . 371
- Torsion Test . . . 372
- Submersion Test . . . 372
- Structural Integrity Test - Wall . . . 372
- Door Durability Test . . . 373
- Door Impact Test . . . 373
- Door Hinge Test . . . 373
- Drawer Bottom Impact Test . . . 373
- Drawer Support Test . . . 373
- Drawer and Door Pull Test . . . 374
- Drawer Rolling Load Test . . . 374
- Shelf Load Test . . . 374

T

APPENDIX - A (continued)
Casework Integrity (continued)
Table Structural Integrity Test 375
Fraction / Decimal / Millimeter Conversions 376
Miscellaneous Conversions 377

GLOSSARY. 380

APPENDIX - B
Quality Control Options
AWI - Architectural Woodwork Institute 408
AWMAC - Architectural Woodwork Manufacturers Association of Canada 408
WI - Woodwork Institute 409
Guide Specifications
CSI Division 06 41 00 - Wood & Laminate Casework 411
CSI Division 06 42 00 - Paneling 419
CSI Division 06 46 00 - Wood Trim 425
CSI Division 08 14 00 431
1 - Submittals 437
2 - Care and Storage 439
3 - Lumber 441
Fire Retardance 451
Dimensional Change Problems 453
4 - Sheet Products 455
Core Characteristics 457
Facing Materials. 460
Veneer Cuts 467
Veneer Matching 469
5 - Finishing 477
6 - Interior and Exterior Millwork. 481
Design and Use of Resource 482
Standing and Running Trim Identification 483
Radius Fabrication 484
Design Ideas 485
7 - Stairwork and Rails 527
Design Ideas 530
8 - Wall Surfacing 533
Fire Retardance 535
Veneer Cuts 535
Veneer Matching 538
Joints and Transitions 547
Stile and Rail Paneling 548
Design Ideas 550
9 - Doors. 557
Core Basics 558
Veneer Cuts 560
Veneer Matching 561
Edge and Glazing Options 565
Louver Options 566
Blocking 567
Handing 568
Stile & Rail 570
Design Ideas 573
10 - Casework 579
Shelf Deflection 580
Detail Nomenclature 581
Hardware Selection 583
Design Ideas 585
11 - Countertops 615
HPDL Fabrication and Installation Guidelines 618
HPDL Problems Causes and Prevention 619
Design Ideas 620
12 - Installation 623
13 - Adhesive Summary 629

Architectural Woodwork Standards

PREFACE

PREFACE

1. ARCHITECTURAL WOODWORK STANDARDS

1.1 PURPOSE

1.1.1 Provide design professionals with logical and simple means to comprehensively specify elements of architectural woodwork.

1.1.2 Provide compliance criteria to ensure that all manufacturers/installers bidding on a project compete on an equal basis and are obligated to perform work of equal quality.

1.1.3 Provide industry information, terminology, and test criteria to properly determine compliance.

1.2 OVERVIEW

1.2.1 These standards are based on three Grades of quality that may be mixed within a single project. Limitless design possibilities and a wide variety of lumber and veneer species, along with overlays, high-pressure decorative laminates, factory finishes, and profiles are available in all three Grades.

1.2.1.1 **ECONOMY GRADE** defines the minimum quality requirements for a project's workmanship, materials, or installation and is typically reserved for woodwork that is not in public view, such as in mechanical rooms and utility areas.

1.2.1.2 **CUSTOM GRADE** is typically specified for and adequately covers most high-quality architectural woodwork, providing a well-defined degree of control over a project's quality of materials, workmanship, or installation.

1.2.1.3 **PREMIUM GRADE** is selectively used in the most visible and high-profile areas of a project, such as reception counters, boardrooms, and executive areas, providing the highest level of quality in materials, workmanship, or installation.

1.2.2 These standards cannot address every contingency; however, this document is the most comprehensive architectural woodworking standard available.

1.2.3 When these standards are referenced, the client is protected, and the manufacturer/installer has a clear direction for what is required.

1.2.4 When these standards are referenced as a part of the contract documents and no Grade is specified, Custom Grade will be the **DEFAULT STIPULATION**.

1.2.4.1 In the absence of material specifications, it will be the manufacturer's option to select lumber or veneers suitable for opaque finish.

1.2.5 These standards are not restrictive; they merely establish the rules for what will happen under normal conditions. Issues not set forth in the contract documents or in these standards, when referenced in the specifications, will be resolved by selection, fabrication, finishing, and/or installation at the option of the manufacturer.

1.2.6 In addition to the specific requirements as outlined in these standards, it is intended that all architectural woodwork specified to meet these standards will conform to the generally accepted definitions of "First-Class Workmanship" as defined within these standards and the glossary.

1.3 EXCEPTION

1.3.1 These standards are a guide from which the design professional is free to deviate.

1.3.1.1 When the design professional, as part of the contract documents, deviates from these standards, the contract document takes precedence over the standards.

1.3.1.1.1 Such deviations cannot be adjudicated using the standards as a basis.

1.3.2 These standards are intended for typical commercial/institutional applications and environments and might not perform as expected in abusive environments in which special design considerations should be taken.

1.4 DISCLAIMERS

1.4.1 The sponsors of these standards shall not be responsible to anyone for the use of or reliance upon these standards.

1. ARCHITECTURAL WOODWORK STANDARDS (continued)

1.4 **DISCLAIMERS** (continued)

1.4.2 The sponsors of these standards shall not incur any obligation nor liability for damages, including consequential damages, arising out of or in connection with the use, interpretation of, or reliance upon these standards.

1.4.3 These standards provide the minimum criteria for the concept, design, fabrication, finishing, and installation of architectural woodwork.

1.4.3.1 Provisions for mechanical and electrical safety have not been included. References to life-safety requirements are included for information only.

1.4.3.2 Governmental agencies or other national standards-setting organizations provide the standards for life-safety requirements.

1.4.4 Illustrations are intended to assist in understanding the standards and might not include all requirements for a specific product or unit, nor do they show the only method of fabrication. Such partial drawings shall not be used to justify improper or incomplete design and/or construction.

1.4.5 Unless otherwise stated or referenced, Appendixes A and B are not considered integral parts of these standards. The appendixes are provided as an additional resource to the manufacturer, design professional, educator, user, or certifying organization, and shall not be interpreted as legal advice or code-compliance language.

1.4.6 If a conflict is found in these standards, the least restrictive requirement shall prevail until addressed by errata.

1.5 **IMPROVEMENT**

1.5.1 The Associations encourage your suggestions for changes, revisions, and/or improvements to these standards. A suggestion form is provided just before these prefaces or can be found on each of the Associations' websites (www.awinet.org, www.awmac.com, or www.woodworkinstitute.com). Simply follow the form's instructions.

2. VARIATIONS IN NATURAL WOOD PRODUCTS

2.1 Wood is a natural material with variations in color, texture, and figure.

2.1.1 These variations are influenced by the natural growing process and are uncontrollable by the manufacturer.

2.2 The color of wood within a tree varies between the “sapwood” (the outer layers of the tree that continue to transport sap), which is usually lighter in color, and the “heartwood” (the inner layers in which the cells have become filled with natural deposits).

2.3 Various species produce different grain patterns (figures), which influence the selection process.

2.3.1 There will be variations of grain patterns within any selected species.

2.4 The manufacturer cannot select solid lumber cuttings within a species by grain and color in the same manner in which veneers might be selected.

2.5 Therefore, color, texture, and grain variations may occur in the finest architectural woodworking.

3 SYSTEMS OF MEASUREMENT

3.1 These standards are written with the U.S. Customary System of measurement followed by the metric system in brackets.

3.1.1 The system of measurement used in the original design of a project's architectural drawings will dictate which system of measurement within the standards is used for verification of compliance.

3.1.2 The metric number is typically a “soft” conversion of the U.S. Customary System of measurement.

3.1.3 In order to make the metric number more conceptually coherent and consistent, most conversions for less than 3" (76 mm) in dimension are “soft” converted to the nearest 0.1 mm; for measurements above 3" (76 mm), the “soft” value is converted to the nearest 1 mm.

3.1.4 Exceptions to this convention will occur as, for example, 1220 mm is commonly used for 48", as opposed to 1219 mm.

P

4 ARCHITECTURAL WOODWORK SPECIFICATIONS - GUIDELINES

4.1 Specifications, along with the architectural drawings, are the road map for a project's success.

4.1.1 Budget constraints should be communicated up front so that all parties can work together toward a successful resolution.

4.2 Use of these standards will greatly reduce the text of your specifications and their development time.

4.2.1 They eliminate the need to worry about every fabrication and material detail.

4.2.1.1 Requirements for each **GRADE** are specifically defined within the standards.

4.2.2 However, **SPECIAL REQUIREMENTS** or **UNUSUAL APPLICATIONS** will need to be noted.

4.3 **COMPLIANCE PROGRAMS**, which all sponsor Associations offer, are cost-effective and help enforce your specifications.

4.3.1 They ensure the performance and compliance of your architectural woodwork project's specifications.

4.3.2 Written status reports are issued during the project's progression, affording you timely notification of any noncompliant findings.

4.4 **AVOID CONFLICT** in your specifications that might allow for interpretation other than what was envisioned.

4.4.1 Use of certain words can make a big difference.

4.4.1.1 Requiring compliance to <u>Example A</u> **AND** <u>Example B</u> means that the end result will be in full compliance with both.

4.4.1.2 Requiring compliance to <u>Example A</u> **OR** <u>Example B</u> means that compliance to either is acceptable.

4.5 **ENFORCE** your specifications and their intent; however, be open-minded to proposed changes and cost savings.

4.5.1 Materials and their availability are in constant flux; therefore, listen and be open to change when it does not affect your design intent.

4.6 **PRE-QUALIFY** your bidders to ensure their performance ability.

4.7 Seek out and take advantage of our industry's knowledge and experience.

4.8 The following summarizes the applicable **CSI MASTERFORMAT™ 2004 Edition** Numbers and Titles for which we provide Guide Specifications in the Appendix.

4.8.1 06 20 00 - Finish Carpentry

4.8.2 06 40 00 - Architectural Woodwork

4.8.3 08 14 00 - Wood Doors

4.8.4 09 93 00 - Staining and Transparent Finishing

4.8.5 12 35 00 - Speciality Casework

4.8.6 12 36 00 - Countertops

5 ARCHITECTURAL WOODWORK DRAWINGS - GUIDELINES

5.1 For design professionals, the proper use of these standards will greatly reduce drafting time.

5.1.1 It is not necessary to produce standard joinery details on your drawings.

5.1.2 Requirements for each **GRADE** are defined throughout these standards.

5.1.3 **SPECIAL REQUIREMENTS** or **UNUSUAL APPLICATIONS** need to be noted and detailed.

5.2 Casework and Countertops:

5.2.1 Indicate **CONSTRUCTION TYPE** of casework desired:

5.2.1.1 **TYPE A** - frameless construction.

5 ARCHITECTURAL WOODWORK DRAWINGS (continued)

5.2 Casework and Countertops (continued)

5.2.1 Indicate **CONSTRUCTION TYPE** of casework desired (continued)

5.2.1.2 **TYPE B** - face-frame construction (not recommended for decorative laminate faced casework, and standards are not provided for such).

5.2.2 The standards define the following basic types of casework **CONSTRUCTION TYPES**:

5.2.2.1 Wood Faced - **TYPE A**

5.2.2.2 Wood Faced - **TYPE B**

5.2.2.3 Decorative Laminate Faced - **TYPE A**

5.2.2.4 Solid Phenolic Constructed - **TYPE A**

5.2.3 Casework elevations are not necessary if the **CABINET DESIGN SERIES** numbers are utilized; however, a floor plan indicating each design number selection and relative dimensions is required.

5.2.4 When casework elevations are shown, they should indicate:

5.2.4.1 The basic overall dimensions.

5.2.4.2 Dimensions of those portions that are required to be of predetermined or controlled size.

5.2.4.3 Dimensions required for installation of items of equipment.

5.2.4.4 Whether sliding or hinged doors are desired, including swing if hinged.

5.2.4.5 Thickness of cabinet doors if other than nominal 3/4" (19 mm) is required.

5.2.4.6 Required details not shown in these standards or those that involve installation of unusual equipment.

5.2.4.7 If and where locks are required.

5.2.4.8 Shelf location and whether fixed or adjustable.

5.2.4.8.1 Material and load capacity required.

5.2.4.9 Type of countertop.

5.3 Standing and Running Trim

5.3.1 Elevations should indicate the placement of all standing and running trim, including:

5.3.1.1 Cross section details along with overall dimensions should be shown for all trim types.

5.3.2 If a finish schedule is used in lieu of elevations, it should be comprehensive enough to clearly indicate all of the above.

5.4 Architectural Wall Surfacing

5.4.1 Elevations should indicate the placement of architectural wall surfacing, including each panel size, along with edge, corner, reveal, ceiling, and base treatments.

5.4.1.1 Door and/or other woodwork matching should be so indicated.

5.4.1.2 Reveals should be as specified; however, a minimum of 1/4" (6.4 mm) is recommended.

5.4.2 If a finish schedule is used in lieu of elevations, it should clearly indicate all of the above.

5.5 Wood Doors

5.5.1 Include a comprehensive door schedule indicating the location, type, size, and handling of each door, along with applicable requirements for:

5.5.1.1 Pair and/or transom matching

5.5.1.2 Room and/or panel matching

5 ARCHITECTURAL WOODWORK DRAWINGS (continued)

5.5 Wood Doors (continued)

5.5.1 Include a comprehensive door schedule (continued)

5.5.1.3 Transom panel or Dutch door edge treatment

P

5.5.1.4 Special core blocking

5.5.1.5 Glass and louver cutouts

5.5.1.6 Undercut tolerances

5.5.1.7 Fire, acoustical, x-ray, and/or other ratings/requirements

5.5.1.8 Hardware

5.5.2 Include elevations of typical door types to indicate glass and louver cutout locations.

6 CASEWORK REFINISHING/REFACING/REFURBISHING - GUIDELINES

6.1 The work is typically required to be done in the field.

6.1.1 Refinishing, refacing, and/or refurbishing of casework will not update any **SEISMIC FABRICATION** and/or **INSTALLATION** deficiencies.

6.1.2 Lead and/or toxic material abatement shall not be the responsibility of the woodwork manufacturer/installer.

6.2 **SPECIFICATIONS** shall clearly indicate whether refinishing, refacing, refurbishing, or a combination thereof is required.

6.2.1 **REFINISHING** can be as simple as the application of a new finish over the existing cabinet surfaces or as extensive as the removal of the existing finish, repair or patch of all physical defects, and the application of a new finish; however:

6.2.1.2 Does not include the replacement of hardware, unless so specified.

6.2.2 **REFACING** is usually more involved and very field-labor intensive, and:

6.2.2.1 Existing surfaces, including doors, drawer fronts, cabinet face, and finished ends:

6.2.2.1.1 If **HPDL**, shall be removed with any damaged core areas repaired and core surface suitably prepared for proper adhesion of the new surface material.

6.2.2.1.2 If **PAINT**, shall be stripped to the original surface with any damaged areas repaired and resurfaced with the specified material.

6.2.2.2 Does not include the replacement of hardware, unless so specified.

6.2.3 **REFURBISHING** includes either the refinishing or refacing of the exterior cabinet body, replacement of the cabinet doors and drawer fronts, and replacement of all exposed cabinet hardware, including hinges, pulls, catches, and locks; however:

6.2.3.1 It does not include the repair or replacement of interior components such as shelves, drawer boxes, or drawer slides unless so specified.

6.3 **ARCHITECTURAL PLANS** shall clearly indicate all casework to be refinished, refaced, and/or refurbished. The casework elevations shall also indicate any unusual or special requirements (such as structural repair or component replacement).

6.3.1 It is the design professional's responsibility to specify any and all modifications required for code compliance.

6.3.1.1 Including the means, methods, and materials required to retrofit casework for UBC, Title 24 compliance.

6.3.2 The requirement for reinstallation of existing casework (if needed to be removed), in a manner other than the original, shall be so specified.

6.3.2.1 If new or additional wall blocking is required, it shall be so specified and be the responsibility of the contractor.

6 CASEWORK REFINISHING/REFACING/REFURBISHING (continued)

6.4 All refinishing, refacing, and/or refurbishing of casework governed by these standards shall generally be in accordance with these standards as applicable, with the following exception:

6.4.1 Repair or modification of existing casework shall be in compliance with accepted methods of joinery as contained in these standards.

6.4.1.1 The method of repair used shall be optional with the manufacturer/installer.

6.4.1.2 **NEW COMPONENTS**, such as doors, drawer fronts, drawer boxes, and shelves, shall be compliant to these standards.

6.4.1.3 **GAPS** and **TOLERANCES** shall match that of the existing casework within an elevation and within a room.

6.4.1.4 Hardware replacement for refurbished casework, or when specified to be included with refinishing or refacing, shall include door hinges, door and drawer pulls, and locks (keying requirement to be as specified).

6.4.1.4.1 Drawer slide replacement is not included unless specifically required in the contract documents.

6.4.1.4.2 Match of existing hardware is contingent on the availability of such from a manufacturer's current stock.

6.4.1.4.3 The method of repair or patching of tear-outs used for proper hardware replacement shall be optional with the manufacturer/installer.

6.4.1.5 All work shall meet the requirements of first-class workmanship.

7 MOISTURE AND ARCHITECTURAL WOODWORK

7.1 The moisture content of wood is crucial. If wood is not properly dried and/or seasoned:

7.1.1 The best of **WORKMANSHIP CANNOT PREVENT MOISTURE-RELATED DEFECTS** such as surface checks, cracking, bowing, twisting, and glue-line failure that might occur during production and afterward.

7.1.2 The woodwork product will not have the expected quality and beauty.

7.1.3 In severe cases, a product can even be destroyed.

7.1.4 Unfortunately, **MOST MOISTURE DEFECTS ARE IRREVERSIBLE**.

7.2 Wood is a hygroscopic material, expanding when it takes on moisture, shrinking when it loses moisture.

7.2.1 How much moisture will be absorbed or how fast lumber will dry depends upon the present moisture content of the wood, the wood species, the relative humidity, and the temperature of the surrounding air.

7.2.2 The drying process of lumber has to be slow enough to avoid stress between the surface and the core because too much stress results in surface checks, cracks, split ends, and other drying effects.

7.3 If wet and dry pieces of wood are placed in an area, they will absorb or lose moisture until all pieces have the same final moisture content (Equilibrium Moisture Content or EMC).

7.3.1 For instance, if you make furniture, cabinets, picture frames, or clocks for inside a home, an office, or other heated live-in area, all wooden parts will eventually dry to approximately 6-12% wood moisture (extreme climate zones might have slightly higher or lower values).

7.4 For lasting quality and beauty, use only wood with a moisture content between 6-12%.

7.4.1 Moisture-related defects might occur if only one piece has a higher or lower moisture content than 6-12%.

7.4.2 Without control of the moisture content, there is a greater chance to get moisture-related defects.

7.5 Many manufacturers hope to avoid moisture problems by buying only kiln-dried wood.

7.5.1 **KILN-DRIED WOOD** should have a moisture content between 6-12%.

7 MOISTURE AND ARCHITECTURAL Woodwork (continued)

7.5 Many manufacturers hope to avoid moisture problems (continued)

7.5.2 Even though the wood might be dried properly when it leaves the dry kiln, it can change in moisture content during manufacturing, transportation, or storage.

7.5.3 Manufacturers might inadvertently further complicate the problem by assembling a project with materials that have dissimilar moisture contents.

7.6 To reduce the risk of moisture damage, the U.S. Department of Agriculture, Forest Service, Forest Products Laboratory recommends in their General Technical Report 113 that:

7.6.1 Large assemblies, such as ornamental beams, cornices, newel posts, stair stringers, and handrails, should be built up from comparatively small pieces.

7.6.2 Wide door and window casing and base molding should be hollow-backed.

7.6.3 Backband trim, if mitered at the corners, should be glued and splined before erection.

7.6.4 Large solid pieces, such as wood stile and rail paneling, should be designed and installed so that the panels are free to move across the grain. Narrow widths are preferable.

8 FOREST MANAGEMENT CERTIFICATION: The Associations acknowledge and have adopted the International Wood Products Association's (IWPA) Statement on Certification as modified below.

8.1 We acknowledge the interest in certified timber products and verification of good forest management.

8.2 A number of certification and verification systems are in operation or in development today, and we make no judgment against or endorsement of any single plan.

8.3 Certification can serve as an audit of work already being done toward improved forest management. An absence of certification, however, does not mean there is a lack of quality forest management.

8.4 We wish to recognize the efforts that many countries and companies are making with regard to improved forest management practices. Further, we strongly endorse the right of individual countries and companies that become involved with certification or the verification of forest management to pursue the development of their own internal auditing system or the selection of one that is already established.

8.5 Global consensus has not been reached regarding the scope and viability for any single system of certification to be appropriate for all locations and conditions. Efforts are being made to develop an international framework of mutual recognition between credible and market-oriented sustainable forest management standards and certification systems.

8.6 The development of a mutual recognition process should ensure that these various certification or verification systems:

8.6.1 Do not discriminate against different forest types.

8.6.2 Should be regularly reviewed and updated.

8.6.3 Should be transparent.

8.6.4 Should be cost-effective, recognizing that there is no clear indication that the cost of certification can be incorporated into the pricing of wood products being produced.

8.7 We strongly endorse the development of a mutual recognition system and support any and all efforts that will further enhance management of the world's forests and the growth of global and sustainable trade in wood products.

9 ENVIRONMENTAL VENEER CONSIDERATIONS

9.1 Wood veneer will yield about forty times more surface area than the same log sawn for lumber. Consider using veneered products where feasible in lieu of solid lumber.

9.2 "Environmental" choice is not merely one of species, but of knowing the forest origin and its management status. Good sustainable forestry includes a professionally administered forestry management plan in which timber growth equals or exceeds harvesting rates in both quantity and quality, and ensures adequate regeneration of desired species.

10 Warranty/Guarantee Language

10.1 There have been repeated requests for "industry standard" warranty or guarantee language, both on the part of design professionals and woodwork manufacturers. It is not the purpose or intent of this publication to give legal advice with regard to warranties. Such language varies from governing body to governing body.

10.1.1 **CAUTION**: You might use the following language as a starting point; however, the sponsors of these standards assume no liability whatsoever from its use. **IT IS ADVISED THAT ALL WARRANTY LANGUAGE BE REVIEWED BY COMPETENT COUNSEL FOR THE STATE OR PROVINCE IN WHICH IT IS INTENDED.**

10.1.2 All architectural woodwork is guaranteed to be of good material and workmanship and free from defects that render it unserviceable for the use for which it is intended. Natural variations in the color or texture of the wood are not to be considered defects. The quality of architectural woodwork is safeguarded while it is in the manufacturer's possession. To be protected by this guarantee, products must not be stored in damp warehouses or placed in moist or freshly plastered buildings. The woodwork must not be subjected to abnormal heat or dryness. Permanent-type heat and air conditioning must be in operation a sufficient length of time to "cure" the building before any woodwork or doors are delivered to the site. (Temporary-type heat sources might either add excessive moisture or create excessive dryness, depending upon the type of fuel. Thus, temporary heating can be a source of woodwork problems and should be avoided.)

Adhere to the requirements in Section 2 for range and maintenance of relative humidity. Acclimatize delivered woodwork to the job site for a minimum of 72 hours before installation. Factory-finished woodwork requires up to a week or more on site for acclimatization.

Woodwork must be inspected upon arrival, and all claims or complaints must be filed before painters' finish is applied. All doors must be properly sealed on all surfaces, including top and bottom edges, to prevent absorption of moisture. The manufacturer will not be responsible for defects resulting from neglect of these precautions.

The manufacturer agrees, within a period of _(insert year)_ year(s) after delivery date, to repair or replace (in the white, unfinished, if so furnished originally) without charge any woodwork that is defective within the meaning of this guarantee. The manufacturer does not agree to be responsible for any work that was not originally performed by them. The manufacturer _(insert does or does not)_ agree to pay charges for finishing or installing replaced woodwork. This guarantee is not effective if goods are repaired or replaced without first obtaining the manufacturer's written consent.

NOTES

Architectural Woodwork Standards

SECTION - 1

Submittals

SECTION 1 ✦ SUBMITTALS

(Including: Shop Drawings, Profile and Veneer Flitch Samples, Finish Samples, Hardware Samples)

GENERAL

1 INFORMATION

1.1 **GRADES** - None; shop drawing requirements are the same for all architectural woodwork projects regardless of Grade specified.

1

1.2 **BASIC CONSIDERATIONS**

1.2.1 **SHOP DRAWINGS** are the means by which the design intent is turned into manufacturing information and are essential to a project's control and execution.

1.2.1.1 They serve to assure the design professional of:

1.2.1.1.1 Proper design interpretation and engineering.

1.2.1.1.2 The relationship of woodwork products to other trades for proper coordination.

1.2.1.1.3 Confirmation that the standards and grades are understood and will be conformed to.

1.2.1.2 They are the visual medium and coordinating function by which the manufacturer:

1.2.1.2.1 Communicates and illustrates to the contractor and design professional their interpretation of the contract documents.

1.2.1.2.2 Suggests modifications; the manufacturer is encouraged to make technical suggestions and raise questions based upon working experience; however:

1.2.1.2.2.1 Changes incorporated within shop drawings, in themselves, are not a request for approval.

1.2.1.2.2.2 Changes must be specifically addressed in separate written documentation, requesting approval of the suggested changes.

1.2.1.2.3 Communicates their woodwork engineering and declares their intended method of manufacturing and shows their experience and/or ability.

1.2.1.2.4 Sets forth the intended materials, methods of assembly, and instructions to their staff.

1.2.1.3 They are depended on by others:

1.2.1.3.1 They are the common language between the manufacturer, the design professional, and the contractor.

1.2.1.3.2 They serve as a guide for other trades.

1.2.1.4 They are the property of the manufacturer, and the manufacturer is not responsible for errors caused by their unauthorized use by others.

1.2.2 If **MOCK-UPS** or **HARDWARE**, **MOLDING**, or **FINISH SAMPLES** are desired, they shall be so specified.

1.2.2.1 **MOLDING SAMPLES** are typically not furnished until full-size details (in the shop drawings) have been approved.

1.2.2.2 **FINISH SAMPLES**

1.2.2.2.1 Due to variance in wood color within the same species and even within the same log, a range of color shall be expected on finished wood products.

1.2.2.2.2 **DESIGN PROFESSIONAL** shall provide a sample or paint chip indicating the desired color and transparency as applicable.

1.2.3 **COMPLIANCE** with codes and regulations are to be researched and directed by the design professional and are not the responsibility of the manufacturer.

GENERAL

1.2 **BASIC CONSIDERATIONS** (continued)

1.2.4 It is the role of the contractor to coordinate the manufacturer's shop drawings with work of all other trades and to ensure that hold-to/guaranteed dimensions are actually enforced.

1.2.5 It is the responsibility of the design professional or contractor, depending on contract relationships, to communicate design and field changes to all parties so that if dimensions are changed, each subcontractor can be held responsible for its work.

1.2.6 The **SUBMITTAL APPROVAL** phase is potentially one of the most controversial phases of the relationship between a manufacturer and a design professional.

1.2.6.1 There is always the potential for misunderstanding on both sides.

1.2.6.2 Prompt, thorough review of shop drawings and accurate coordination of multiple trades save time and eliminate problems before construction begins.

1.3 **RECOMMENDATIONS**

1.3.1 That only **TWO** sets of shop drawings are required to be submitted for initial design professional review.

1.3.1.1 If the review is affirmative, the design professional keeps one copy, and a marked set is returned to the manufacturer with a request for the required number of final copies.

1.3.1.2 If the review is not affirmative, the design professional returns one set requesting correction and resubmittal. The other set is kept by the design professional to check the resubmittal against.

1.3.2 **SPECIFY** requirements for:

1.3.2.1 **MOCK-UPS**

1.3.2.2 **HARDWARE SAMPLES**

1.3.2.3 **MOLDING SAMPLES**

1.3.2.4 **FINISH SAMPLES**

1.4 **ACKNOWLEDGEMENTS** - None

1.5 **INDUSTRY PRACTICES**

1.5.1 **SUBMITTALS** are submitted to the contractor, design professional, and/or owner for review prior to fabrication.

PRODUCT

2 SCOPE

2.1 All materials and products covered under the scope of these standards.

3 DEFAULT STIPULATION - Not used or applicable for this section.

4 RULES - The following RULES shall govern unless a project's contract documents require otherwise.

These rules are intended to provide a well-defined degree of control over a project's quality of submittals.

Errata, published on the Associations' websites at www.awinet.org, www.awmac.com, or www.woodworkinstitute.com, shall TAKE PRECEDENCE OVER THESE RULES, subject to their date of posting and a project's bid date.

PRODUCT

SHOP DRAWING RULES (continued)

ARROWS INDICATE TOPIC IS CARRIED FROM ⇑ OR ONTO ⇓ ANOTHER PAGE.

DESCRIPTION					
4.1	**GENERAL** requirements:				
GENERAL	4.1.1	**SUBMITTALS** shall be submitted to the contractor, design professional, and/or owner for review prior to fabrication.			
	4.1.2	**RULES** apply to all Grades equally.			
	4.1.3.	**DRAWING SHEETS** shall be:			
		4.1.3.1	Minimum 11" x 17" (279 x 432 mm)		
			4.1.3.1.1	Door submittals only may be on minimum 8.5" x 11" (216 x 279 mm)	
		4.1.3.2	Numbered		
		4.1.3.3	Dated		
	4.1.4	**COVER** or **TITLE SHEET** is required and shall include as applicable:			
	COVER	4.1.4.1	Project name and address		
		4.1.4.2	Design professional firm and contact information		
		4.1.4.3	Contractor firm and contact information		
		4.1.4.4	Manufacturer firm and contact information		
		4.1.4.5	Installer firm and contact information		
		4.1.4.6	Finisher firm and contact information		
	4.1.5	**MATERIAL LIST** shall include as applicable:			
	MATERIAL	4.1.5.1	The Grade requirements		
		4.1.5.2	Items to be used for exposed, semi-exposed, and/or concealed surfaces, including:		
		LISTINGS	**4.1.5.2.1**	Lumber species and cut for transparent finish	
				4.1.5.2.1.1	Cut is not relevant for items exposed on several sides such as turnings, railings, and some moldings
			4.1.5.2.2	Veneer species, cut, leaf match/balance, panel match, and room match for transparent finish	
			4.1.5.2.3	Lumber and veneer species only for opaque finish	
			4.1.5.2.4	Laminated core type and thickness with any special requirements, such as:	
				4.1.5.2.4.1	Moisture resistant
				4.1.5.2.4.2	Fire retardant
			4.1.5.2.5	Laminates, including grade	
			4.1.5.2.6	Solid phenolic core	
			4.1.5.2.7	Solid surface	
			4.1.5.2.8	Speciality metal work	
			4.1.5.2.9	Special adhesive requirements	
			4.1.5.2.10	Hardware (except fasteners) with manufacturer's specification sheet	
			4.1.5.2.11	Finishing requirements	
	4.1.6	**DRAWINGS** shall:			
		4.1.6.1	Show each item of woodwork in plan, elevation, and section as needed to clearly indicate what is provided where, its methods of construction and attachment, and:		
			4.1.6.1.1	Plan and elevation views shall be drawn in minimum 3/8" (1:30) scale	
			4.1.6.1.2	Detailed section views shall be as required within each product section below	
			4.1.6.1.3	Provide a reference plan showing location(s) of all work to be provided	
⇓	⇓		4.1.6.1.4	Be sufficient in detail scale to clearly indicate all unusual features in construction	

PRODUCT

SHOP DRAWING RULES (continued)

DESCRIPTION

4.1 GENERAL	**GENERAL** requirements (continued)				
	4.1.6 DRAWINGS	**DRAWINGS** shall (continued)			
		4.1.6.2 WALL BLOCKING	Show centerline height and horizontal location of all required internal WALL BLOCKING furnished by others by a standard convention such as:		
			4.1.6.2.1	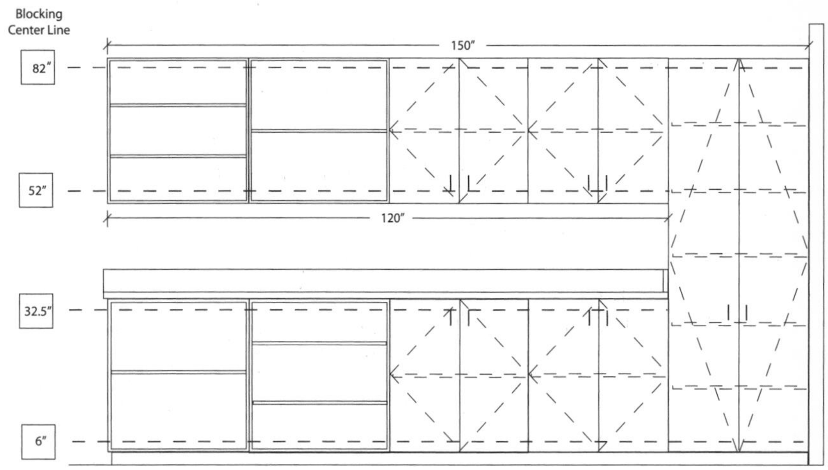 Blocking Center Line; 82"; 52"; 32.5"; 6"; 150"; 120"	
	4.1.7 SAMPLES	**SAMPLES**, if required of:			
		4.1.7.1	**HARDWARE** shall include one sample of each hardware item that will show in normal use when cabinet doors and drawers are closed.		
		4.1.7.2 FINISHING	**FINISHING** shall:		
			4.1.7.2.1	Be a minimum of 12" x 12" (305 mm x 305 mm) for panel products	
			4.1.7.2.2	Be as wide as practical if on lumber by a minimum of 12" (304 mm) in length	
			4.1.7.2.3	Be on material representative of that to be used for the project	
			4.1.7.2.4	Bear a label identifying the date, job name, the design professional, the contractor, and the finish system name and number	
			4.1.7.2.5	For **TRANSPARENT FINISH**, require a minimum of three samples indicating the range of color and grain to be expected for each color selection	
			4.1.7.2.6	For **OPAQUE FINISH**, require a minimum of four samples for each color selection	
	4.1.8	Submittals shall present **FIRST-CLASS WORKMANSHIP** in compliance with these standards.			
4.2	**SPECIFIC SECTION** requirements				
	4.2.1 SECTION 6	**SECTION 6 - INTERIOR & EXTERIOR MILLWORK**			
		4.2.1.1 LISTINGS	**LISTING** requirements shall additionally include:		
			4.2.1.1.1	Related material requirements and specifications	
			4.2.1.1.2	**TRIM SCHEDULE** for each room or area, including as applicable:	
				4.2.1.1.2.1	Detail section reference
			4.2.1.1.3 FRAMES	**FRAME, SASH, SCREEN, BLIND**, and/or **SHUTTER SCHEDULE** for each room or area, including as applicable:	
				4.2.1.1.3.1	Opening number and location
				4.2.1.1.3.2	Elevation and/or section references
				4.2.1.1.3.3	Opening size
				4.2.1.1.3.4	Handing and pre-machining requirements
				4.2.1.1.3.5	Hardware types and locations
				4.2.1.1.3.6	Screen specifications

PRODUCT

SHOP DRAWING RULES (continued)

DESCRIPTION					
4.2 SPECIFIC SECTION REQUIREMENTS	**SPECIFIC SECTION** requirements (continued)				
	4.2.1 SECTION 6	**SECTION 6 - INTERIOR & EXTERIOR MILLWORK** (continued)			
		4.2.1.2 DRAWINGS	**DRAWINGS** requirements shall additionally include as applicable:		
			4.2.1.2.1	**TRIM, FRAME, SASH, SCREEN, BLIND,** and/or **SHUTTER** members, drawn in full (1:1) scale profile.	
				4.2.1.2.1.1	Members too large to fit on a single sheet may be drawn in segments, or at half scale (1:2).
			4.2.1.2..2	**FRAME, SASH, SCREEN, BLIND,** and/or **SHUTTER** construction details drawn to a minimum 3" = 1'-0" (1:5) scale	
			4.2.1.2..3	**FRAMES** in section detail with elevations as necessary for coordination with other crafts	
			4.2.1.2..4	**SASH, SCREEN, BLIND,** and/or **SHUTTERS** in elevation	
			4.2.1.2..5	**BUILT-UP MEMBERS**, drawn in elevation with horizontal and vertical sections	
			4.2.1.2..6	**DETAILED SECTIONS**, minimum 1-1/2" = 1'-0" (1:10) scale, of:	
				4.2.1.2.6.1	Corners
				4.2.1.2.6..2	Joints within the woodwork item
				4.2.1.2.6..3	Joints between the woodwork item and other trim
				4.2.1.2.6..4	Woodwork item meeting features provided by other trades
				4.2.1.2.6..5	Joinery
				4.2.1.2.6..6	Attachment
				4.2.1.2.6..7	Relationships to adjacent trim members or features
	4.2.2 SECTION 7	**SECTION 7 - STAIRWORK & RAILS**, including treads, risers, skirt boards, moldings, newels, and balusters			
		4.2.2.1	**LISTING** requirements shall additionally include:		
			4.2.2.1.1	Related material requirements and specifications	
			4.2.2.1.2	Handrail brackets and other hardware	
		4.2.2.2 DRAWINGS	**DRAWINGS** requirements shall additionally include as applicable:		
			4.2.2.2.1	**RAILS** and **TRIM** members, shown in full-size profile	
				4.2.2.2.1.1	Samples may be substituted for section details at manufacturer's option.
			4.2.2.2.2	**PLAN** and **ELEVATION** views drawn to a minimum 3/4" = 1'-0" (1:20) scale	
				4.2.2.2.2.1	For each run of stair and section of balustrade
			4.2.2.2.3	**DETAILED SECTIONS**, minimum 1-1/2" = 1'-0" (1:10) scale, of:	
				4.2.2.2.3.1	Joinery
				4.2.2.2.3.2	Attachment
				4.2.2.2.3.3	Relationships to adjacent features
	4.2.3 SECTION 8	**SECTION 8 - WALL PANELING**			
		4.2.3.1 LISTINGS	**LISTING** requirements shall additionally include:		
			4.2.3.1.1	Match and balance of panels to adjacent panels	
			4.2.3.1.2	Match and balance of panels within an elevation	
			4.2.3.1.3	Match and balance of panels within a room	
			4.2.3.1.4	Match and balance of panels to adjacent doors or casework	
			4.2.3.1.5	Core type and thickness	
			4.2.3.1.6	Backing or balance sheet	
			4.2.3.1.7	Edgebanding	

PRODUCT

SHOP DRAWING RULES (continued)

DESCRIPTION					
4.2 SPECIFIC SECTION REQUIREMENTS	**SPECIFIC SECTION** requirements (continued)				
	4.2.3 SECTION 8	**SECTION 8 - WALL PANELING** (continued)			
		4.2.3.1	**LISTING** requirements shall; (continued)		
			4.2.3.1.8	Related material specifications	
		4.2.3.2 DRAWINGS	**DRAWINGS** requirements shall additionally include as applicable:		
			4.2.3.2.1	**TRIM** members, shown in full-size profile	
			4.2.3.2.2	**PLAN** and **ELEVATION** views for each panel location	
			4.2.3.2.3	**DETAILED SECTIONS**, minimum 1-1/2" = 1'-0" (1:10) scale, of:	
				4.2.3.2.3.1	Vertical and horizontal sections
				4.2.3.2.3.2	Corner joints, both inside and outside
				4.2.3.2.3.3	Panel to panel joints
				4.2.3.2.3.4	Panel to base or floor joint
				4.2.3.2.3.5	Panel to crown or ceiling joint
				4.2.3.2.3.6	Attachment
				4.2.3.2.3.7	Hardware
	4.2.4 SECTION 9	**SECTION 9 - DOORS**			
		4.2.4.1 LISTINGS	**LISTING** requirements shall additionally include:		
			4.2.4.1.1	Core type and thickness for slab door	
			4.2.4.1.2	Edgebanding	
			4.2.4.1.3	Adhesive type	
			4.2.4.1.4	Match and/or balanced of veneer face to adjacent paneling	
			4.2.4.1.5	Stile and rail construction	
				4.2.4.1.5.1	Solid or veneered core
				4.2.4.1.5.2	Core type and thickness
			4.2.4.1.6	**FRAME SCHEDULE**, including as applicable:	
				4.2.4.1.6.1	Opening number and location
				4.2.4.1.6.2	Elevation and/or section references
				4.2.4.1.6.3	Handing and premachining requirements
				4.2.4.1.6.4	Hardware types and locations
				4.2.4.1.6.5	Glass lite openings with size and location
				4.2.4.1.6.6	Louver openings with type, size, and location
		4.2.4.2 DRAWINGS	**DRAWINGS** requirements shall additionally include as applicable:		
			4.2.4.2.1	**TRIM** members, shown in full-size profile	
			4.2.4.2.2	**MANUFACTURER'S** specifications or cut sheet showing construction.	
			4.2.4.2.3	**DETAILED SECTIONS**, minimum 1-1/2" = 1'-0" (1:10) scale, of:	
				4.2.4.2.3.1	Construction Type, 3-, 5-, or 7-ply for slab doors; solid or veneered for stile and rail
				4.2.4.2.3.2	Core type and thickness
				4.2.4.2.3.3	Diagram of hardware-blocking locations at slab doors
				4.2.4.2.3.4	Stile and rail construction, including stiles, rails, panel raise, and moldings
				4.2.4.2.3.5	Stile and rail joints
				4.2.4.2.3.6	Louvers and/or lites

PRODUCT

SHOP DRAWING RULES (continued)

DESCRIPTION					
4.2 SPECIFIC SECTION REQUIREMENTS	**SPECIFIC SECTION** requirements (continued)				
	4.2.5	**SECTION 10 - CASEWORK**			
	SECTION 10	4.2.5.1	**LISTING** requirements shall additionally include:		
		LISTINGS	4.2.5.1.1	Exposed surface materials and thickness	
			4.2.5.1.2	Semi-exposed surface materials	
			4.2.5.1.3	Concealed surface materials	
			4.2.5.1.4	Inside face of cabinet door material and thickness	
			4.2.5.1.5	Panel core thickness and type	
			4.2.5.1.6	Edgebanding material and thickness	
			4.2.5.1.7	Drawer box material and construction	
			4.2.5.1.8	Drawer slides or guides	
			4.2.5.1.9	Hinges with finish	
			4.2.5.1.10	Adjustable shelf pins, brackets, and/or standards	
			4.2.5.1.11	Miscellaneous finish hardware with finish and manufacturer's cut or spec sheet	
			4.2.5.1.12	Glass type(s) and thickness	
			4.2.5.1.13	Special metal work and/or specialty items	
		4.2.5.2	**DRAWINGS** requirements shall include additionally, as applicable:		
		DRAWINGS	4.2.5.2.1	**REFERENCE PLAN**, so work areas can be located in building	
			4.2.5.2.2	**TRIM** and/or **SCRIBE** shown in full-size profile	
			4.2.5.2.3	**CASEWORK**, shown in plan, elevation, and section view, including:	
				4.2.5.2.3.1	Countertops, per the specific requirements for countertops listed below
				4.2.5.2.3.2	Details need not be drawn if properly referenced to a supplementary document
				4.2.5.2.3.3	Dimensions necessary to construct cabinets
				4.2.5.2.3.4	Widths of face-frame members
				4.2.5.2.3.5	Type and thickness of drawer members, including heights and depths
				4.2.5.2.3.6	Type and thickness of cabinet doors
				4.2.5.2.3.7	Section of each cabinet type or configuration
				4.2.5.2.3.8	Details of all joinery and connections
				4.2.5.2.3.9	Specification and location of special metal work and/or specialty items
				4.2.5.2.3.10	Provision for field dimensions
				4.2.5.2.3.11	Section details showing method of cabinet attachment to walls, floors, and ceilings
			4.2.5.2.4	Blocking or strapping requirements and their locations (blocking to be furnished by others) shown on cabinet elevations with dimension off finished floor	
	4.2.6	**SECTION 11 - COUNTERTOPS**			
		4.2.6.1	**LISTING** requirements shall include, as applicable:		
			4.2.6.1.1	Core thickness and type	
			4.2.6.1.2	Exposed material description and thickness	
			4.2.6.1.3	Backing sheet at top and/or splash	
⇓	⇓	⇓	4.2.6.1.4	Adhesive type	

PRODUCT

SHOP DRAWING RULES (continued)

DESCRIPTION

Number	Description
4.2 SPECIFIC SECTION REQUIREMENTS	**SPECIFIC SECTION** requirements (continued)
4.2.6 SECTION 11	**SECTION 11 - COUNTERTOPS** (continued)
4.2.6.1	**LISTING** requirements shall include (continued)
4.2.6.1.5	Type of sealing compound used to seal sink cutouts and/or splashes
4.2.6.2 DRAWINGS	**DRAWINGS** shall include, as applicable:
4.2.6.2.1	In plan view
4.2.6.2.1.1	Each countertop with field joints
4.2.6.2.1.2	Sink size and location
4.2.6.2.1.3	Support brackets with notation, if furnished by others
4.2.6.2.2	In elevation view
4.2.6.2.2.1	Relationship to casework and support brackets
4.2.6.2.3	In section detail, minimum 3" = 1'-0" (1:5) scale
4.2.6.2.3.1	Front and/or end overhang
4.2.6.2.3.2	Front and/or end edge types
4.2.6.2.3.3	Splash type and height
4.2.6.2.3.4	Drip groove
4.2.6.2.3.5	End splash return
4.2.6.2.3.6	Field joints
4.2.6.2.4	Sink and sink rim types, if included
4.2.6.2.5	Joinery at field joints
4.2.6.2.6	Attachment to casework
4.2.7 SECTION 12	**SECTION 12 - HISTORIC RESTORATION WORK - NOTE:** The above general and specific shop drawing requirements shall prevail for a specific product type.
4.2.7.1	A written **RESTORATION** and **CONSERVATION PROGRAM** shall be developed with a qualified wood conservator and submitted for each phase of the restoration process outlining:
4.2.7.1.1	Where extant wood materials will need to be removed, repaired, and retained, including:
4.2.7.1.1.1	The means and methods to catalog the wood members, remove, crate and protect, store, and reinstall
4.2.7.1.1.2	A plan for protection of surrounding materials, including interface with other trades
4.2.7.1.1.3	A plan to retain toxic and/or offensive off-gassing and provide adequate ventilation
4.2.7.1.1.4	A plan to date-stamp all new work in letters minimum 1/4" (6.4 mm) high noting the month, year, and the installer's or manufacturer's name in an area not exposed to view as a record of when the work was installed
4.2.7.2	**LISTING** requirements shall include, as applicable:
4.2.7.2.1	Items to be repaired, including description, location, original material, and material to be used in repair
4.2.7.2.2	Items to be replaced, including description, location, material to be used, and basis for design
4.2.7.2.3	Specific restoration requirements for:
4.2.7.2.3.1	Removal
4.2.7.2.3.2	Storage

PRODUCT

SHOP DRAWING RULES (continued)

DESCRIPTION

4.2 SPECIFIC SECTION REQUIREMENTS	**SPECIFIC SECTION** requirements (continued)				
	4.2.7 SECTION 12	**SECTION 12 - HISTORIC RESTORATION WORK** (continued)			
		4.2.7.2	**LISTING** requirements shall include (continued)		
			4.2.7.2.3	Specific restoration requirements for (continued)	
				4.2.7.2.3.3	Repair or patching
				4.2.7.2.3.4	Replacement criteria
				4.2.7.2.3.5	Stripping
				4.2.7.2.3.6	Refinishing
			4.2.7.2.4	Material requirements	
				4.2.7.2.4.1	See applicable section above.
		4.2.7.3 DRAWINGS	**DRAWINGS** shall include plan, elevation, and section views, as applicable, of:		
			4.2.7.3.1	See applicable section(s) above.	
			4.2.7.3.2	Reference plan showing location of each item to be repaired or replaced	
			4.2.7.3.3	Relationship of items to be repaired or replaced to building and architectural features	
			4.2.7.3.4	Section details in minimum 1-1/2" = 1'-0" (1:10) scale, of	
				4.2.7.3.4.1	Trim members in full scale
				4.2.7.3.4.2	Fabrication
				4.2.7.3.4.3	Joinery
				4.2.7.3.4.4	Attachment
		4.2.7.4 MOCK-UPS	**MOCK-UPS** shall include:		
			4.2.7.4.1	**DESIGN PROFESSIONAL'S** written acceptance of all representative visual qualities before proceeding with work, including:	
				4.2.7.4.1.1	Any altered or modified methods and techniques used, as required, to achieve intended results
			4.2.7.4.2	Acceptable samples, suitably marked, during the restoration process as a standard for work to be performed	
			4.2.7.4.3	For **NEW WORK**, prepare and have approved samples representative of all:	
				4.2.7.4.3.1	New molding and/or decorative profiles
				4.2.7.4.3.2	Panel, frame, stile and rail door, railing, and/or otherwise unique millwork assemblies
				4.2.7.4.3.3	Typical trim joinery and casework construction
			4.2.7.4.4	For **RESTORATION WORK**, perform sample restoration work of the following general processes on existing materials in an area directed by the design professional, of sufficient scope to demonstrate the effectiveness of proposed materials and techniques of each process:	
				4.2.7.4.4.1	To remove existing finishes
				4.2.7.4.4.2	Of patching, plugging, and/or cut-ins
				4.2.7.4.4.3	Of refinishing

EXECUTION

(Items # 5 & 6 are not applicable to this section)

Compliance

(Item # 7 is not applicable to this section)

Architectural Woodwork Standards

SECTION - 2

Care & Storage

SECTION 2 ✦ CARE & STORAGE

(Including: Care and Moisture Considerations Before, During, and After Installation)

GENERAL

2

1 INFORMATION

1.1 **GRADES** - None; care and storage requirements are the same for all architectural woodwork projects, regardless of Grade specified or required.

1.2 **BASIC CONSIDERATIONS**

1.2.1 Architectural woodwork should be treated like fine furniture, particularly that which is constructed of wood, finished with a transparent finish system.

1.2.2 Except for true oil-rubbed surfaces, modern finishes do not need to be polished, oiled, or waxed.

1.2.2.1 Application of polishing oils, cleaning waxes, or products containing silicone may impede the effectiveness of touch-up or refinishing procedures in the future.

1.2.3 **RELATIVE HUMIDITY AND MOISTURE CONTENT**

1.2.3.1 The space in which architectural woodwork is to be installed needs to be engineered with appropriate humidity controls to maintain its optimum relative humidity.

1.2.3.2 Wood for architectural use needs a moisture content within an optimum range.

1.2.3.2.1 The table and map below (USDA Forest Service, Agriculture Handbook No. 72) shows the Optimum Moisture Content (MC) and the Indoor Relative Humidity required to hold such MC within the general areas of the United States and Canada. NOTE - Some of these areas have additional micro-climates not shown or referenced.

Geographical Location	Optimum Moisture Content (MC)		Optimum Indoor Relative Humidity
	Exterior	Interior	
Most of U.S.; Ontario and Quebec in Canada	9-15%	5-10%	25-55%
Damp Southern Coastal areas of the U.S.; Newfoundland and Canadian Coastal Provinces	10-15%	8-13%	43-70%
Dry Southwestern U.S.	7-12%	4-9%	17-50%
Alberta, Saskatchewan, and Manitoba in Canada	10-15%	4-9%	17-50%

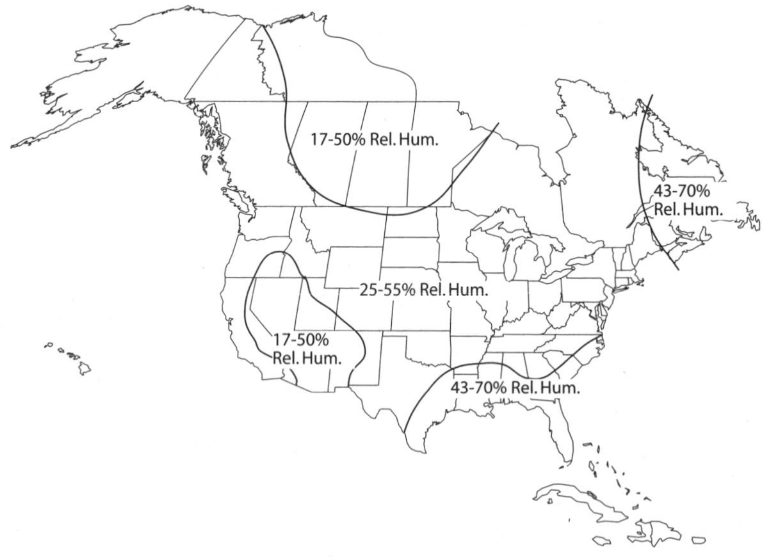

Fig. 2-1

GENERAL

1.2 **BASIC CONSIDERATIONS** (continued)

1.2.4 Architectural woodwork, when properly finished, is relatively durable and resistant to moisture.

1.2.4.1 Prevent direct contact with moisture, and wipe it dry immediately should any occur.

1.2.4.1.1 Allowing moisture to accumulate on, or stay in contact with, any wood surface, no matter how well finished, will cause damage.

1.2.5 **DIMENSIONAL CHANGE PROBLEMS**

1.2.5.1 For centuries, wood has served as a successful, renewable material for architectural woodwork, and as history has shown, wood products perform with complete satisfaction when correctly designed and used.

1.2.5.1.1 Problems directly or indirectly attributed to dimensional change of the wood are usually, in fact, the result of faulty design or improper humidity conditions during site storage, installation, or use.

1.2.5.2 Wood is a hygroscopic material, and under normal use and conditions all wood products contain some moisture. Wood readily exchanges this molecular moisture with the water vapor in the surrounding atmosphere according to the existing relative humidity.

1.2.5.2.1 In high humidity, wood picks up moisture and swells.

1.2.5.2.2 In low humidity, wood releases moisture and shrinks.

1.2.5.3 Oxidation is a reaction of acids in wood (e.g., tannic acid), with iron, oxygen, and moisture, whether this be relative humidity or direct moisture.

1.2.5.3.1 Control of moisture is a simple way to protect wood products from stains as a result of oxidation.

1.2.5.4 Together with proper design, fabrication, and installation, humidity control is an important factor in preventing dimensional change problems.

1.2.5.4.1 As normal minor fluctuations in humidity occur, the resulting dimensional response in properly designed construction will be insignificant.

1.2.5.5 Architectural woodwork products are manufactured as designed from wood that has been kiln dried to an appropriate average moisture content and maintained at this condition up to the time of delivery.

1.2.5.5.1 Subsequent dimensional change in wood is and always has been an inherent natural property of wood.

1.3 **RECOMMENDATIONS**

1.3.1 Maintain an interior relative humidity every hour of every day, within the ranges shown previously in this section.

1.3.1.1 Uncontrolled extremes such as those listed below will likely cause problems:

1.3.1.1.1 Relative humidity, above or below the ranges shown previously in this section.

1.3.1.1.2 Sudden changes in the allowable relative humidity, especially when it is repetitive.

1.3.2 Remove oil or grease deposits; use a mild flax soap, following its directions for dilution.

1.3.3 Do not use abrasives or chemical or ammonia cleaners on fine architectural woodwork surfaces.

1.3.4 Accomplish routine cleaning with a soft, lint-free cloth lightly dampened with water or an inert household dust attractant. Allowing airborne dust, which is somewhat abrasive, to build up will tend to dull a finish over time.

1.3.5 Avoid excessive or repetitive impact, however lightly applied. The cellular structure of the wood will compact under pressure. Many modern finishes are flexible and will show evidence of impact and pressure applied to them.

GENERAL

1.3 **RECOMMENDATIONS** (continued)

1.3.6 Avoid localized high heat, such as a hot pan or plate, or a hot light source, close to or in contact with the finished surface. Exposure to direct sunlight will alter the appearance of fine woodwork over time.

1.3.7 Use the trims, cabinets and fixtures, paneling, shelving, ornamental work, stairs, frames, windows, and doors as they were intended.

1.3.7.1 Abuse of cabinet doors and drawers, for example, may result in damage to them as well as to the cabinet parts to which they are joined.

1.4 **ACKNOWLEDGEMENTS**

1.4.1 **RESPONSIBILITY** for dimensional change problems in wood products resulting from:

1.4.1.1 Improper design rests with the design professional.

1.4.1.2 Improper relative humidity exposure during site storage and installation rests with the contractor.

1.4.1.3 Humidity extremes after occupancy rests with the owner.

1.5 **INDUSTRY PRACTICES**

1.5.1 Raising the temperature in a building for a sustained period of time to eliminate the **OFF GASES** is unacceptable and will negatively affect the appearance and performance of architectural millwork.

1.5.1.1 Open joints, warped paneling/doors, and other defects caused by such are not to be considered a defect.

PRODUCT

2 SCOPE

2.1 All materials and products covered under the scope of these standards.

3 DEFAULT STIPULATION- Not used.

4 RULES - The following RULES shall govern unless a project's contract documents require otherwise.

These rules are intended to provide a well-defined degree of control over a project's quality of materials, workmanship, or installation.

Where E, C, or P is not indicated, the rule applies to all Grades equally.

Errata, published on the Associations' websites at www.awinet.org, www.awmac.com, or www.woodworkinstitute.com, shall TAKE PRECEDENCE OVER THESE RULES, subject to their date of posting and a project's bid date.

ARROWS INDICATE TOPIC IS CARRIED FROM ⇑ OR ONTO ⇓ ANOTHER PAGE.

DESCRIPTION			
4.1	**GENERAL**		
	4.1.1	**DELIVERY** shall be made in accordance with a progress schedule furnished by the contractor; however, only when the:	
		4.1.1.1	Area of operation is enclosed
⇓		4.1.1.2	Wet work is dry
		4.1.1.3	Overhead work is complete
		4.1.1.4	Area is broom clean

PRODUCT

CARE & STORAGE RULES (continued)

DESCRIPTION					
⇑ 4.1	**GENERAL** (continued)				
GENERAL	**4.1.2**	**ARCHITECTURAL WOODWORK**			
	MILLWORK	**4.1.2.1**	While **AWAITING INSTALLATION**, shall be stored:		
			4.1.2.1.1	Flat on a level surface	
			4.1.2.1.2	At least 4" (101.6 mm) off the floor	
			4.1.2.1.3	With a cover to keep it clean, while permitting air circulation	
		4.1.2.2	At **INTERIOR** application, shall be stored and/or installed in an area:		
		INTERIOR	4.1.2.2.1	That is clean	
			4.1.2.2.2	That is dry and well ventilated	
			4.1.2.2.3	That is protected from sunlight and/or excessive heat	
			4.1.2.2.4	That is protected from moisture	
			4.1.2.2.5	That is between 60 - 90 degrees Fahrenheit (15.5 - 32 degrees Celsius) inclusive	
			4.1.2.2.6	That has a maintained Relative Humidity between 25 - 55% inclusive, except in:	
				4.1.2.2.6.1	The damp Southern Coastal areas of the U.S., Newfoundland, and the Canadian Coastal Provinces shall be between 43 - 70% inclusive
				4.1.2.2.6.2	The dry Southwestern U.S., and Alberta, Saskatchewan, and Manitoba in Canada shall be between 17 - 50% inclusive
			4.1.2.2.7	That has a maintained MC (Optimum Moisture Content) between 5 - 10% inclusive, except in:	
				4.1.2.2.7.1	The damp Southern Coastal areas of the U.S., Newfoundland, and Canadian Coastal Provinces shall be between 8 - 13% inclusive
				4.1.2.2.7.2	The dry Southwestern U.S., and Alberta, Saskatchewan, and Manitoba in Canada shall be between 4 - 9% inclusive
			4.1.2.2.8	To which it has been acclimated to for a minimum of 72 hours prior to installation	
		4.1.2.3	At **EXTERIOR** application, shall be stored and/or installed in an area that is:		
			4.1.2.3.1	Clean	
			4.1.2.3.2	Protected from direct moisture	
			4.1.2.3.3	Protected from direct sunlight	
		4.1.2.4	After **ACCEPTANCE**:		
		ACCEPTANCE	**4.1.2.4.1**	At **INTERIOR** application:	
				4.1.2.4.1.1	Shall be maintained in the same environmental conditions as during its storage and/or installation
				4.1.2.4.1.2	Temperature in a building shall not be raised for a sustained period of time to eliminate the **OFF GASES**; it will negatively affect the appearance and performance of architectural millwork
			4.1.2.4.2	At **EXTERIOR** application shall:	
				4.1.2.4.2.1	Have its finish maintained, refinishing as necessary (especially oiled finishes)
				4.1.2.4.2.2	Be protected from excessive moisture and standing water
			4.1.2.4.3	**SEVERE DAMAGE** can result from not adhering to the above rules	
				4.1.2.4.3.1	**FABRICATOR/INSTALLER** shall not be held responsible for the damage caused by not adhering to the above

EXECUTION

(Items # 5 & 6 are not applicable to this section)

Compliance

(Item # 7 is not applicable to this section)

Architectural Woodwork Standards

SECTION - 3

LUMBER

SECTION 3 ✦ LUMBER

(Including: Hardwood and Softwood)

GENERAL

1 INFORMATION

1.1 GRADES

1.1.1 **GRADE CLASSIFICATIONS ECONOMY, CUSTOM**, and **PREMIUM** are used within these standards only in reference to the acceptable quality of workmanship, material, or installation in a completed architectural woodwork product.

1.1.2 **THIS MATERIAL SECTION** deals with lumber, which is a component of finished products covered in sections 6 - 12.

1.1.2.1 **IN THIS SECTION**, the use of these classifications is only for the purpose of identifying lumber that can be used in finished products meeting those Grades.

1.1.2.2 These classifications are not intended to be used as Grades of raw material or to judge a stand-alone board or member.

1.1.3 **LUMBER ASSOCIATION GRADES** shall not be used, since even their highest Grades permit defects unacceptable in architectural woodwork and are not based upon the use of the whole piece, but rather on a percentage of the piece.

1.1.3.1 The appearance of a piece in the end product is of importance, not whether it is cut from a larger board that contained defects that can be eliminated.

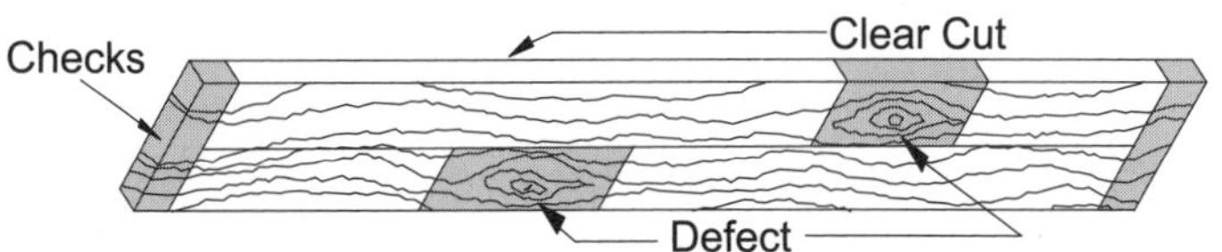

1.1.4 **LUMBER RULES**

1.1.4.1 Apply only to surfaces visible after manufacture and installation.

1.1.4.2 Establish criteria as to which, if any, natural or seasoning characteristics are acceptable.

1.1.4.3 Limit the extent of characteristics that will be permitted based on an exposed area's size and proximity of characteristics to one another.

1.1.4.4 Do not apply to special varieties of species that display unusual characteristics desirable for aesthetic and design reasons.

1.1.5 **MODIFICATIONS** by the contract documents shall govern if in conflict with these standards.

1.2 BASIC CONSIDERATIONS

1.2.1 **AVAILABILITY:** Wide and/or long pieces of clear stock are typically not available.

1.2.1.1 If available, the cost might be substantially higher.

1.2.2 **ECONOMIES** can be realized by detailing and specifying thicknesses and widths within the finish sizes listed herein.

1.2.3 **LUMBER** is furnished plain sawn unless otherwise specified.

1.2.4 **LUMBER GRAIN** might not match veneer grain.

1.2.5 Lumber might not accept **TRANSPARENT FINISHES** in the same manner as plywood; special finishing techniques might be required (see Section 5).

1.2.6 **FIRE-RETARDANT** lumber, with a particular flame-spread classification, is restricted to those species with natural qualities and/or those that will accept treatment using currently available technology.

GENERAL

1.2 **BASIC CONSIDERATIONS** (continued)

1.2.7 **PRESERVATIVE TREATMENT** of lumber will extend its natural life when used in an exterior application and exposed to the elements.

1.2.8 **HARDWOOD** is typically not recommended for exterior use.

1.2.8.1 Exceptions include Apitong, Teak, Tanguile, and Honduras Mahogany.

1.2.9 **QUARTERED** lumber is typically narrower than plain sawn lumber of the same species.

1.2.10 **SPECIAL CHARACTERISTICS,** such as sapwood, heartwood, ribbon stripe, quarter sawn, and rift sawn, if desired, are required to be so specified.

1.2.11 **VENEERED CONSTRUCTION** of lumber can be used to secure wide and thick members in species with limited cutting potential. An acceptable technique is to apply thin lumber or veneer of the faces and edges of a compatible density lumber, structural composite lumber (SCL), or a medium-density fiberboard core.

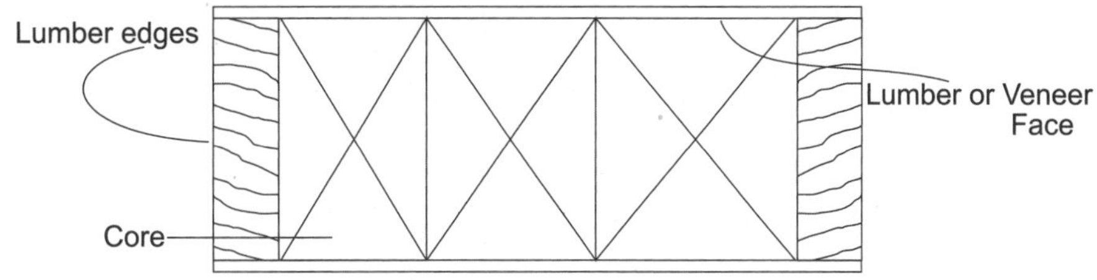

3

1.2.12 **NATURAL** as a type selection of a species allows an unlimited amount of heartwood or sapwood within a face and is the default selection, unless specified otherwise.

1.2.13 **SELECT RED** or **WHITE** means all heartwood or sapwood, respectively, and must be so specified if desired.

1.2.14 **HICKORY, PECAN, BUTTERNUT, KNOTTY PINE, WORMY CHESTNUT, PECKY CYPRESS**, and **WATTLED WALNUT**, for example, exhibit "special and unusual characteristics" and are not covered by these standards.

1.2.14.1 If their use is contemplated, individual ranges of characteristics and availability should be investigated and specified accordingly.

1.2.15 **HONDURAS MAHOGANY** varies in color from a light pink to a light red, reddish brown to a golden brown or yellowish tan, and:

1.2.15.1 Figure or grain includes plain sliced, plain to broken stripe, mottled, fiddleback, swirl, and crotches.

1.2.15.2 It can turn darker or lighter in color after machining.

1.2.16 **LAUAN, TANGUILE**, and other species are native to the Philippine Islands and are sometimes referred to as Philippine Mahogany; however, they are not a true Mahogany.

1.2.16.1 **MAHOGANY** is a generic term and should not be specified without further definition.

1.2.17 **CHERRY, WALNUT**, and certain other hardwood species are required to be specified by origin - such as American Cherry, American Walnut, or English Brown Oak - because they can be significantly different in color and texture.

1.2.18 **PHOTODEGRADATION** is the effect on the appearance of exposed wood faces caused by exposure to both sun and artificial light sources. If an entire face is exposed to a light source, it will photodegrade somewhat uniformly and hardly be noticeable, whereas partially exposed surfaces or surfaces with shadow lines might show nonuniform photodegradation. Some woods, such as American Cherry and Walnut, are more susceptible than others, and extra care should be taken to protect against the effects of nonuniform photodegradation.

GENERAL

1.2 **BASIC CONSIDERATIONS** (continued)

1.2.19 **OXIDATION** is the effect on the appearance of exposed wood faces caused by exposure to atmosphere. This is analogous to browning reactions in freshly cut fruit; for instance, apples. Hardwoods can develop deep yellow to reddish brown discolorations on the surface of the wood when exposed to air immediately after sawing or peeling. These discolorations are especially noticeable on Cherry, Birch, Red Alder, Sycamore, Oak, Maple, and Sweet Gum. Some species, such as Alder, Oak, Birch, and Maple, develop these discolorations during air-seasoning. A related gray stain on several varieties of Southern Oaks also appears to be oxidative in nature. Proper selection, sanding, and finishing can minimize the effects of oxidation. Care should be taken when using filler, as it might not change the same as the wood.

1.3 **RECOMMENDATIONS**

1.3.1 **SPECIFY** requirements for:

1.3.1.1 **UNIFORM COLOR**; special finishing techniques might be required (see Section 5).

1.3.1.2 **SPECIAL CHARACTERISTICS**, such as sapwood, heartwood, ribbon stripe, quarter sawn, rift sawn, or vertical grain.

1.3.1.3 **EXTERIOR APPLICATIONS**, where species selection should take decay resistance into consideration. The following species, when selected for **HEARTWOOD ONLY**, exhibit the listed decay resistance in accordance with the 1999 Wood Handbook by the Forest Products Laboratory:

1.3.1.3.1 **RESISTANT** or **VERY RESISTANT**:

1.3.1.3.1.1 **DOMESTIC** (* indicates extremely high decay resistance):

Baldcypress (Old Growth)
Cedar
Cherry, Black
Chestnut
Cypress, Arizona
Juniper
Locust, Black *
Oak, White
Redwood (Old Growth)
Walnut, Black
Yew, Pacific *

1.3.1.3.1.2 **IMPORT** (* indicates extremely high decay resistance):

Goncalo Alves *
Ipe (lapacho) *
Jarrah *
Lignumvitae *
Mahogany, Honduras
Purpleheart *
Spanish Cedar
Teak (Old Growth) *

1.3.1.3.2 **MODERATELY RESISTANT**:

1.3.1.3.2.1 **DOMESTIC**:

Baldcypress (Young Growth)
Fir, Douglas
Larch, Western
Redwood (Young Growth)
Tamarack

1.3.1.3.2.2 **IMPORT**:

Avodire
Benge
Bubinga
Keruing
Mahogany, African
Meranti, Dark Red
Sapele
Teak (Young Growth)

1.3.1.3.3 If none of the above species is specified, these standards require exterior woodwork to be **TREATED** with an industry-tested and accepted preservative formulation listed by **WDMA**.

1.4 **ACKNOWLEDGEMENTS**

1.4.1 **ENGINEERED WOOD PRODUCTS** are typically manufactured from sliced veneers, which in some cases are stained, then glued up and sawn in such a manner as to imitate a particular species. Use of these engineered products are allowed only if specified and/or approved by the owner and/or design professional.

GENERAL

1.5 **INDUSTRY PRACTICES**

1.5.1 Lumber is **DIMENSIONED** in the following conventional order: thickness, followed by width (across the grain direction), followed by length (with the grain direction); see drawing:

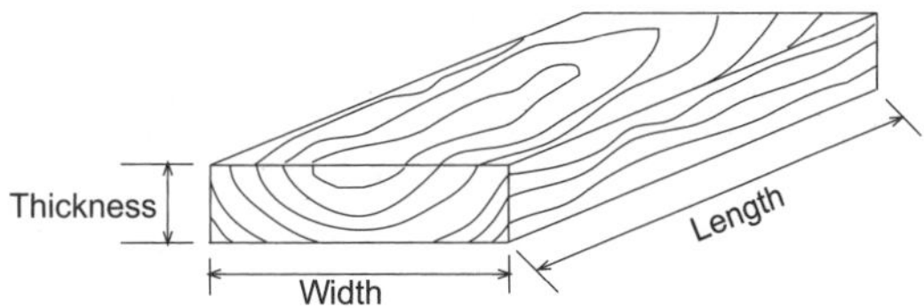

1.5.2 **GLUING** for thickness and/or width is permitted as governed by these standards; see drawing:

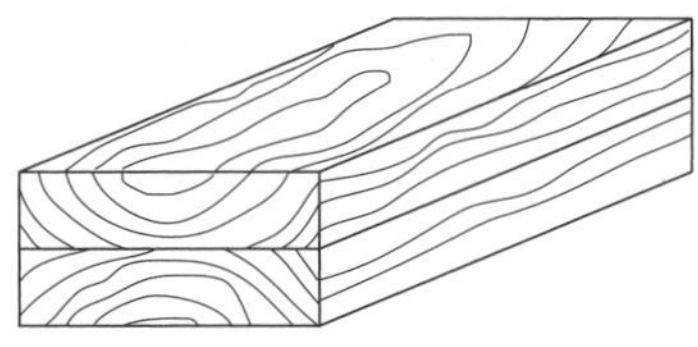

1

2

1.5.3 Specification of **PHILIPPINE MAHOGANY** permits the use of Lauan, Tanguille, and other natural Philippine species.

1.5.4 Specification by the generic term **MAHOGANY** means Genuine Mahogany, such as Honduras or African.

1.5.5 **SPECIES** not specifically covered by these standards shall be as agreed to between owner/design professional and manufacturer/installer as to length requirements and size/exposed area of permitted natural characteristics.

PRODUCT

2 SCOPE

2.1 All hardwood and softwood lumber used for the fabrication or production of the architectural millwork covered by these standards.

3 DEFAULT STIPULATION

3.1 If not otherwise specified or indicated in the contract documents, all lumber shall be natural softwood.

4 RULES - The following RULES shall govern unless a project's contract documents require otherwise.

These rules are not intended to create a lumber grade; they are only intended to establish the acceptable requirements and/or characteristics after the architectural woodwork is completed or installed.

Where E, C, or P is not indicated, the rule applies to all Grades equally.

Errata, published on the Associations' websites at www.awinet.org, www.awmac.com, or www.woodworkinstitute.com, shall TAKE PRECEDENCE OVER THESE RULES, subject to their date of posting and a project's bid date.

ARROWS INDICATE TOPIC IS CARRIED FROM ⇑ OR ONTO ⇓ ANOTHER PAGE.

DESCRIPTION			E	C	P
4.1	**GENERAL**				
	4.1.1	Aesthetic **GRADE RULES** apply only to exposed and semi-exposed surfaces visible after installation.			
⇓	4.1.2	**VISIBLE SURFACES** shall be sound lumber, free of decay, shake, pith, wane, and warp.			
	4.1.3	**"BOARD"** refers to a piece of lumber before gluing for width or thickness.			

PRODUCT

LUMBER RULES (continued)

These rules are not intended to create a lumber grade; they are only intended to establish the acceptable requirements and/or characteristics after the architectural woodwork is completed or installed.

3

		DESCRIPTION	E C P
4.1 GENERAL	**GENERAL** (continued)		
	4.1.4	**"MEMBER"** refers to a piece of lumber after gluing for width or thickness.	
	4.1.5	**LUMBER** shall be plain sawn.	
	4.1.6	**LUMBER** is **DIMENSIONED** by thickness, followed by width (across the grain direction), followed by length (with the grain direction).	
	4.1.7	**SPECIAL CHARACTERISTICS,** such as sapwood, heartwood, ribbon stripe, quarter sawn, rift sawn, and vertical grain, are not required unless specified.	
	4.1.8	**MOISTURE CONTENT** of lumber shall be in compliance with Section 2.	
	4.1.9	**EXTERIOR** use of lumber for architectural millwork requires the lumber to be **PRESERVATIVE TREATED** in accordance with WDMA I.S. 4 (latest edition), unless the lumber is classified as "Resistant or Very Resistant" in accordance with the Forest Products Laboratory (latest edition) Wood Handbook, Table 3-10.	
	4.1.10	**GLUING** for thickness and/or width is permitted as governed by this Section.	
	4.1.11	**ADHESIVE** used to glue for thickness, width, or lay-up of veneered construction shall be for the intended purpose, applied in accordance with the manufacturer's instructions, and be:	
		4.1.11.1 Type I when intended for exterior use.	
		4.1.11.2 Type II when intended for interior use.	
	4.1.12	**PHILIPPINE MAHOGANY** shall permit the use of Lauan, Tanguille, and other natural Philippine species.	
	4.1.13	**SPECIES NOT** specifically **COVERED** by these standards shall be as agreed to between design professional and manufacturer/installer as to length requirements and size/exposed area of permitted natural characteristics.	
4.2 MATERIAL	**MATERIAL**		
	4.2.1 THICKNESS	**FINISHED THICKNESS** of S4S and patterned members shall conform to the following minimum size:	
		4.2.1.1 Nominal 4/4 or 1" (25 mm) = 11/16" (18 mm)	
		4.2.1.2 Nominal 5/4 or 1-1/4" (32 mm) = 15/16" (24 mm)	
		4.2.1.3 Nominal 6/4 or 1-1/2" (38 mm) = 1-3/16" (30 mm)	
		4.2.1.4 Nominal 8/4 or 2" (51 mm) = 1-1/2" (38 mm)	
		4.2.1.5 Nominal 10/4 or 2-1/2" (64 mm) = 2" (51 mm)	
		4.2.1.6 Nominal 12/4 or 3" (76 mm)) = 2-1/2" (64 mm)	
		4.2.1.7 Nominal 16/4 or 4" (102 mm) = 3-1/2" (89 mm)	
		Nominal Thickness / Finished Thickness	
	4.2.2 WIDTH	**FINISHED WIDTH** of S4S and patterned members shall conform to the following minimum size:	
		4.2.2.1 Nominal 1" (25 mm) = 11/16" (18 mm)	
		4.2.2.2 Nominal 2" (51 mm) = 1-1/2" (38 mm)	
		4.2.2.3 Nominal 3" (76 mm) = 2-1/2" (64 mm)	
		4.2.2.4 Nominal 4" (102 mm) = 3-1/2" (89 mm)	
		4.2.2.5 Nominal 5" (127 mm) = 4-1/4" (108 mm)	
		4.2.2.6 Nominal 6" (152 mm) = 5-1/4" (133 mm)	
		4.2.2.7 Nominal 8" (203 mm) = 7" (178 mm)	
		4.2.2.8 Nominal 10" (254 mm) = 9" (229 mm)	

PRODUCT

LUMBER RULES (continued)

These rules are not intended to create a lumber grade; they are only intended to establish the acceptable requirements and/or characteristics after the architectural woodwork is completed or installed.

DESCRIPTION				E C P
4.2	**MATERIAL** (continued)			
	4.2.2	**FINISHED WIDTH** (continued)		
		4.2.2.9	Nominal 12" (305 mm) = 11" (279 mm)	
		4.2.2.10	Nominal 12+" (305+ mm) = 1" (25 mm) less than nominal size	
		Nominal Width / Finished Width		
	4.2.3	When **MACHINE SANDED**, a reduction of 1/32" (1 mm) off the above thicknesses or widths is permitted.		
4.2a	**MATERIAL - HARDWOOD**			
HARDWOOD	**4.2a.1**	Rules shall apply only to the following species: **ALDER**, **ASH**, **BIRCH**, **CHERRY, AMERICAN**, **LAUAN**, **MAHOGANY, HONDURAS**, **MAPLE, HARD & SOFT**, **OAK, RED**, **OAK, WHITE**, **POPLAR**, **TEAK**, **WALNUT, AMERICAN**		
		4.2a.1.1	For **SPECIES NOT LISTED**, length requirements and size/exposed area of permitted natural characteristics shall be as agreed to between owner/design professional and manufacturer/ installer.	
	4.2a.2	**GLUING** for thickness is permitted when finished dimensions exceed 1-1/6" (27 mm).		
	4.2a.3	**GLUING** for width is permitted when finished dimensions exceed 6" (152 mm).		
		4.2a.3.1	Rift sawn White/Red Oak; quarter sawn White/Red Oak, Maple, and Walnut; and select White/Red Birch, White Ash, and Cherry may be glued for width when exceeding 4-1/4" (184 mm).	
		4.2a.3.2	Direction of the end grain of boards glued for width shall be alternated.	
	4.2a.4	Lumber of the **SAME SPECIES** but of **DIFFERENT ORIGINS** shall not be mixed on a project (example: American and European Cherry).		
	4.2a.5	If only the generic term **MAHOGANY** is specified, it shall mean Honduras Mahogany.		
	4.2a.6	Specifications calling for **PHILIPPINE MAHOGANY** shall permit the use of Lauan, Tanguile, and other natural Philippine species of wood.		
	4.2a.7	**OAK, RIFT GRAIN**, shall permit twenty-five percent (25%) of the exposed surface area of each board to contain medullary ray flake.		
	4.2a.8	**ASH, BIRCH**, and **MAPLE** shall permit both sapwood and heartwood in any board.		
	4.2a.9	**MAXIMUM LENGTH REQUIREMENT** for given width up to 1-1/2" (38.1 mm) in thickness shall be:		
		4.2a.9.1	Boards required to be longer than those listed as available may be glued for length or furnished in multiple pieces.	
		4.2a.9.2	ALDER	
			4.2a.9.2.1	2" (51 mm) in width = 9'-10" (2997 mm)
			4.2a.9.2.2	3" (76 mm) in width = 8'-10" (2692 mm)
			4.2a.9.2.3	4" (102 mm) in width = 7'-6" (2286 mm)

PRODUCT

LUMBER RULES (continued)

These rules are not intended to create a lumber grade; they are only intended to establish the acceptable requirements and/or characteristics after the architectural woodwork is completed or installed.

				DESCRIPTION	E	C	P
4.2a HARDWOOD	**MATERIAL - HARDWOOD** (continued)						
	4.2a.9 MAXIMUM LENGTH	**MAXIMUM LENGTH** (continued)					
		4.2a.9.2	**ALDER** (continued)				
			4.2a.9.2.4	5" (127 mm) in width = 6'-10" (2083 mm)			
			4.2a.9.2.5	6" (152 mm) or wider is not usually available.			
		4.2a.9.3	**ASH, NATURAL**				
			4.2a.9.3.1	2" to 3" (51 mm to 76 mm) in width = 15'-6" (4724 mm)			
			4.2a.9.3.2	4" (102 mm) in width = 14'-6" (4420 mm)			
			4.2a.9.3.3	5" (127 mm) in width = 13'-6" (4115 mm)			
			4.2a.9.3.4	6" (152 mm) in width = 12'-6" (3810 mm)			
			4.2a.9.3.5	7" to 8" (178 mm to 203 mm) in width = 10'-6" (3200 mm)			
			4.2a.9.3.6	9" (229 mm) in width = 8'-10" (2692 mm)			
		4.2a.9.4	**ASH, SELECT BROWN** or **WHITE**				
			4.2a.9.4.1	2" to 4" (51 mm to 102 mm) in width = 11'-6" (3505 mm)			
			4.2a.9.4.2	5" to 6" (127 mm to 152 mm) in width = 10'-6" (3200 mm)			
			4.2a.9.4.3	7" (178 mm) in width = 8'-6" (2591 mm)			
			4.2a.9.4.4	8" to 9" (203 to 229 mm) in width = 7'-10" (2388 mm)			
		4.2a.9.5	**BIRCH, NATURAL**				
			4.2a.9.5.1	2" to 4" (51 mm to 102 mm) in width = 10'-6" (3200 mm)			
			4.2a.9.5.2	5" to 6" (127 mm to 152 mm) in width = 9'-6" (2896 mm)			
			4.2a.9.5.3	7" (178 mm) in width = 8'-6" (2591 mm)			
			4.2a.9.5.4	8" to 9" (203 mm to 229 mm) in width = 7'-6" (2286 mm)			
		4.2a.9.6	**BIRCH, SELECT RED** or **WHITE**				
			4.2a.9.6.1	2" to 4" (51 mm to 102 mm) in width = 9'-6" (2896 mm)			
			4.2a.9.6.2	5" to 6" (127 mm to 152 mm) in width = 8'-6" (2591 mm)			
			4.2a.9.6.3	6" (152 mm) or wider is not usually available.			
		4.2a.9.7	**CHERRY, AMERICAN**				
			4.2a.9.7.1	2" to 4" (51 mm to 102 mm) in width = 9'-10" (2997 mm)			
			4.2a.9.7.2	5" to 6" (127 mm to 152 mm) in width = 8'-10" (2692 mm)			
			4.2a.9.7.3	7" (178 mm) in width = 7'-10" (2388 mm)			
			4.2a.9.7.4	8" (203 mm) or wider is not usually available.			
		4.2a.9.8	**LAUAN; MAHOGANY, HONDURAS** and **AFRICAN**				
			4.2a.9.8.1	2" to 9" (51 mm to 229 mm) in width = 15'-10" (4826 mm)			
		4.2a.9.9	**MAPLE, NATURAL**				
			4.2a.9.9.1	2" to 3" (51 mm to 76 mm) in width = 14'-10" (4521 mm)			
			4.2a.9.9.2	4" (102 mm) in width = 13-10" (4216 mm)			
			4.2a.9.9.3	5" (127 mm) in width = 12'-10" (3912 mm)			
			4.2a.9.9.4	6" to 7" (152 mm to 178 mm) in width = 10'-10" (3302 mm)			
			4.2a.9.9.5	8" to 9" (203 mm to 229 mm) in width = 8'-10" (2692 mm)			

PRODUCT

LUMBER RULES (continued)

These rules are not intended to create a lumber grade; they are only intended to establish the acceptable requirements and/or characteristics after the architectural woodwork is completed or installed.

				DESCRIPTION	E C P
4.2a HARDWOOD	**MATERIAL - HARDWOOD** (continued)				
	4.2a.9 MAXIMUM LENGTH	**MAXIMUM LENGTH** (continued)			
		4.2a.9.10	**MAPLE, WHITE**		
			4.2a.9.10.1	2" (51 mm) in width = 14'-10" (4521 mm)	
			4.2a.9.10.2	3" to 4" (76 mm to 102 mm) in width = 11'-10" (3607 mm)	
			4.2a.9.10.3	5" (127 mm) in width = 10'-10" (3302 mm)	
			4.2a.9.10.4	6" to 7" (152 mm to 178 mm) in width = 9'-10" (2997 mm)	
			4.2a.9.10.5	8" (203 mm) or wider is not usually available.	
		4.2a.9.11	**OAK, RED** or **WHITE** (except Rift or Quarter Sawn)		
			4.2a.9.11.1	2" (51 mm) in width = 14'-10" (4521 mm)	
			4.2a.9.11.2	3" to 4" (76 mm to 102 mm) in width = 13'-10" (4216 mm)	
			4.2a.9.11.3	5" to 6" (127 mm to 152 mm) in width = 11'-10" (3607 mm)	
			4.2a.9.11.4	7" (178 mm) in width = 9'-10" (2997 mm)	
			4.2a.9.11.5	8" to 9" (203 mm to 229 mm) in width = 8'-10" (2692 mm)	
		4.2a.9.12	**OAK, RED** or **WHITE, RIFT** or **QUARTER SAWN**		
			4.2a.9.12.1	2" to 3" (51 mm to 76 mm) in width = 13'-10" (4216 mm)	
			4.2a.9.12.2	4" (102 mm) in width = 11'-10" (3607 mm)	
			4.2a.9.12.3	5" to 6" (127 mm to 152 mm) in width = 9'-10" (2997 mm)	
			4.2a.9.12.4	7" (178 mm) in width = 7'-10" (2388 mm)	
			4.2a.9.12.5	8" (203 mm) or wider is not usually available.	
		4.2a.9.13	**POPLAR**		
			4.2a.9.13.1	2" to 6" (51 mm to 152 mm) in width = 15'-10" 4826 mm)	
			4.2a.9.13.2	7" (178 mm) in width = 13'-10" (4216 mm)	
			4.2a.9.13.3	8" to 9" (203 mm to 229 mm) in width = 12'-10" (3912 mm)	
		4.2a.9.14	**TEAK**		
			4.2a.9.14.1	2" (51 mm) in width = 9'-6" (2896 mm)	
			4.2a.9.14.2	3" to 4" (76 mm to 102 mm) in width = 8'-6" (2591 mm)	
			4.2a.9.14.3	5" to 7" (127 mm to 178 mm) in width = 7'-6" (2286 mm)	
			4.2a.9.14.4	8" (203 mm) or wider is not usually available.	
		4.2a.9.15	**WALNUT, AMERICAN**		
			4.2a.9.15.1	2" (51 mm) in width = 9'-6" (2896 mm)	
			4.2a.9.15.2	3" to 4" (76 mm to 102 mm) in width = 8'-6" (2591 mm)	
			4.2a.9.15.3	5" (127 mm) in width = 7'-6" (2286 mm)	
			4.2a.9.15.4	6" (152 mm) in width = 5'-6" (1676 mm)	
			4.2a.9.15.5	7" (178 mm) or wider is not usually available.	
	4.2a.10	**OPAQUE FINISH**			
		4.2a.10.1	**MATCHING** for **COLOR** is not required when glued for thickness or width.		
		4.2a.10.2	**NATURAL CHARACTERISTICS** are allowed only if they are inconspicuous after two coats of finish.		
		4.2a.10.3	**FILLING** of checks, splits, or other open characteristics is the responsibility of the millwork manufacturer.		

PRODUCT

LUMBER RULES (continued)

These rules are not intended to create a lumber grade; they are only intended to establish the acceptable requirements and/or characteristics after the architectural woodwork is completed or installed.

					DESCRIPTION	E	C	P
4.2a HARDWOOD	**MATERIAL - HARDWOOD** (continued)							
	4.2a.10 OPAQUE	**OPAQUE FINISH** (continued)						
		4.2a.10.4 LIMITATIONS	**NATURAL CHARACTERISTIC LIMITATIONS** of any one board's exposed face:					
			4.2a.10.4.1		**NONE** in any face smaller than 200 square inches (5080 square mm), with:	●		
				4.2a.10.4.1.1	**ONE** permitted for each additional 100 square inches (2540 square mm)	●		
				4.2a.10.4.1.2	A maximum of **FIVE** in any board	●		
				4.2a.10.4.1.3	**NO** knots, pitch streaks, or pitch pockets within 18" (452 mm) of one another	●		
			4.2a.10.4.2		**NONE** in any face smaller than 300 square inches (7620 square mm), with:		●	
				4.2a.10.4.2.1	**ONE** permitted for each additional 150 square inches (3810 square mm)		●	
				4.2a.10.4.2.2	A maximum of **FOUR** in any board		●	
				4.2a.10.4.2.3	**NO** knots, pitch streaks, or pitch pockets within 24" (610 mm) of one another		●	
			4.2a.10.4.3		**NONE** in any face smaller than 400 square inches (10160 square mm), with:			●
				4.2a.10.4.3.1	**ONE** permitted for each additional 200 square inches (5080 square mm)			●
				4.2a.10.4.3.2	A maximum of **THREE** in any board			●
				4.2a.10.4.3.3	**NO** knots, pitch streaks, or pitch pockets within 36" (914 mm) of one another			●
		4.2a.10.5 ALLOWANCES	**NATURAL CHARACTERISTIC ALLOWANCES** at interior or exterior use:					
			4.2a.10.5.1		**BARK POCKET** - None			
			4.2a.10.5.2		**BIRDSEYE**, Sound - Unlimited			
			4.2a.10.5.3		**BIRDSEYE**, Checked and Filled - Unlimited			
			4.2a.10.5.4		**BURL**, Sound			
				4.2a.10.5.4.1	< 1" (25 mm) in diameter	●	●	
				4.2a.10.5.4.2	< 3/4" (19 mm) in diameter			●
			4.2a.10.5.5		**CHECK**, Filled			
				4.2a.10.5.5.1	< 3/32" (2 mm) wide x 9" (229 mm) long	●		
				4.2a.10.5.5.2	< 1/16" (2 mm) wide x 6" (152 mm) long		●	
				4.2a.10.5.5.3	< 1/32" (1 mm) wide x 4" (102 mm) long			●
			4.2a.10.5.6		**HONEYCOMB** - None			
			4.2a.10.5.7		**KNOT**, Sound and Tight			
				4.2a.10.5.7.1	< 1" (25 mm) in diameter	●		
				4.2a.10.5.7.2	< 5/8" (16 mm) in diameter		●	
				4.2a.10.5.7.3	< 3/8" (10 mm) in diameter			●
			4.2a.10.5.8		**KNOT**, Checked and Filled			
				4.2a.10.5.8.1	< 3/4" (19 mm) in diameter	●		
				4.2a.10.5.8.2	< 1/2" (13 mm) in diameter		●	
				4.2a.10.5.8.3	< 1/4" (6 mm) in diameter			●

PRODUCT

LUMBER RULES (continued)

These rules are not intended to create a lumber grade; they are only intended to establish the acceptable requirements and/or characteristics after the architectural woodwork is completed or installed.

Section	Description	E	C	P
4.2a	**MATERIAL - HARDWOOD** (continued)			
4.2a.10	**OPAQUE FINISH** (continued)			
4.2a.10.5	**NATURAL CHARACTERISTIC ALLOWANCES** (continued)			
4.2a.10.5.9	**MINERAL STAIN**			
4.2a.10.5.9.1	Unlimited	●		
4.2a.10.5.9.2	< 15% of face		●	
4.2a.10.5.9.3	< 10% of face			●
4.2a.10.5.10	**PATCH** ≤ 1-1/2" (38 mm) wide x 3-1/2" (89 mm) long, and inconspicuous from 60" (1524 mm)			
4.2a.10.5.11	**PITCH POCKET** or **STREAK**, Filled			
4.2a.10.5.11.1	< 1/16" (2 mm) wide x 6" (152 mm) long or 1/8" (3 mm) wide x 4" (102 mm) long	●	●	
4.2a.10.5.11.2	< 1/16" (2 mm) wide x 3" (76 mm) long or 1/8" (3 mm) wide x 2" (51 mm) long			●
4.2a.10.5.12	**SAPWOOD**, in unselected species - Unlimited			
4.2a.10.5.13	**SHAKE**, Filled			
4.2a.10.5.13.1	≤ 1/4" (6 mm) wide x 3" (76 mm) long	●		
4.2a.10.5.13.2	≤ 1/8" (3 mm) wide x 3" (76 mm) long		●	
4.2a.10.5.13.3	≤ 1/16" (2 mm) wide x 2" (51 mm) long			●
4.2a.10.5.14	**SPLIT**, Filled			
4.2a.10.5.14.1	≤ 3/32" (2 mm) wide x 8" (203 mm) long	●		
4.2a.10.5.14.2	≤ 1/16" (2 mm) wide x 6" (152 mm) long		●	
4.2a.10.5.14.3	≤ 1/32" (1 mm) wide x 4" (102 mm) long			●
4.2a.10.5.15	**STICKER BOARD DISCOLORATION** - Unlimited			
4.2a.10.5.16	**WORM HOLE**			
4.2a.10.5.16.1	≤ 1/8" (3 mm) in diameter	●		
4.2a.10.5.16.2	≤ 1/16" (2 mm) in diameter		●	
4.2a.10.5.16.3	None			●
4.2a.11	**TRANSPARENT FINISH**			
4.2a.11.1	**MATCHING**, when glued for thickness or width or when veneered construction is utilized, shall be:			
4.2a.11.1.1	Not required	●		
4.2a.11.1.2	Compatible for color and grain		●	
4.2a.11.1.3	Well matched for color and grain			●
4.2a.11.2	**FILLING** of checks, splits, or other open characteristics is the responsibility of the finisher.	●	●	●
4.2a.11.3	**NATURAL CHARACTERISTIC LIMITATIONS** of any one board's exposed face:			
4.2a.11.3.1	A maximum of **FOUR** with:	●		
4.2a.11.3.1.1	**NO** knots, pitch streaks, or pitch pockets within 24" (610 mm) of one another	●		

PRODUCT

LUMBER RULES (continued)

These rules are not intended to create a lumber grade; they are only intended to establish the acceptable requirements and/or characteristics after the architectural woodwork is completed or installed.

DESCRIPTION					E	C	P
4.2a HARDWOOD	**MATERIAL - HARDWOOD** (continued)						
	4.2a.11 TRANSPARENT	**TRANSPARENT FINISH** (continued)					
		4.2a.11.3 LIMITATIONS	**NATURAL CHARACTERISTIC LIMITATIONS** (continued)				
			4.2a.11.3.2	A maximum of **THREE** with:		●	
			4.2a.11.3.2.1	**NO** knots, pitch streaks, or pitch pockets within 36" (914 mm) of one another		●	
			4.2a.11.3.3	A maximum of **TWO** with:			●
			4.2a.11.3.3.1	**NO** knots, pitch streaks, or pitch pockets within 48" (1219 mm) of one another.			●
			4.2a.11.3.4	For: **ASH**, Natural; **BIRCH**, Natural; **MAHOGANY**, Honduras; **MAPLE**, Hard or Soft, Natural; **RED & WHITE OAK**; **TEAK**			
			4.2a.11.3.4.1	**NONE** in any face smaller than 300 square inches (7620 square mm), with:	●		
			4.2a.11.3.4.1.1	**ONE** permitted for each additional 100 square inches (2540 square mm)	●		
			4.2a.11.3.4.2	**NONE** in any face smaller than 400 square inches (10160 square mm), with:		●	
			4.2a.11.3.4.2.1	**ONE** permitted for each additional 150 square inches (3810 square mm)		●	
			4.2a.11.3.4.3	**NONE** in any face smaller than 600 square inches (15240 square mm), with:			●
			4.2a.11.3.4.3.1	**ONE** permitted for each additional 200 square inches (5080 square mm)			●
			4.2a.11.3.5	For: **ASH**, Select Brown; **BIRCH**, Select Red & White; **MAPLE**, Select White			
			4.2a.11.3.5.1	**NONE** in any face smaller than 200 square inches (5080 square mm), with:	●		
			4.2a.11.3.5.1.1	**ONE** permitted for each additional 100 square inches (2540 square mm)	●		
			4.2a.11.3.5.2	**NONE** in any face smaller than 350 square inches (8890 square mm), with:		●	
			4.2a.11.3.5.2.1	**ONE** permitted for each additional 150 square inches (3810 square mm)		●	
			4.2a.11.3.5.3	**NONE** in any face smaller than 500 square inches (12700 square mm), with:			●
			4.2a.11.3.5.3.1	**ONE** permitted for each additional 200 square inches (5080 square mm)			●

PRODUCT

LUMBER RULES (continued)

These rules are not intended to create a lumber grade; they are only intended to establish the acceptable requirements and/or characteristics after the architectural woodwork is completed or installed.

Section		DESCRIPTION			E	C	P
4.2a (HARDWOOD)		**MATERIAL - HARDWOOD** (continued)					
4.2a.11 (TRANSPARENT)		**TRANSPARENT FINISH** (continued)					
4.2a.11.3		**NATURAL CHARACTERISTIC LIMITATIONS** (continued)					
	4.2a.11.3.6	For: **CHERRY**, American; **WALNUT**, American; **RED & WHITE OAK,** Rift/Quarter Sawn					
		4.2a.11.3.6.1	**NONE** in any face smaller than 150 square inches (3810 square mm), with:		●		
			4.2a.11.3.6.1.1	**ONE** permitted for each additional 75 square inches (1905 square mm)	●		
		4.2a.11.3.6.2	**NONE** in any face smaller than 200 square inches (5080 square mm), with:			●	
			4.2a.11.3.6.2.1	**ONE** permitted for each additional 100 square inches (2540 square mm)		●	
		4.2a.11.3.6.3	**NONE** in any face smaller than 300 square inches (7620 square mm), with:				●
			4.2a.11.3.6.3.1	**ONE** permitted for each additional 150 square inches (3810 square mm)			●
4.2a.11.4 (ALLOWANCES)		**NATURAL CHARACTERISTIC ALLOWANCES** at interior or exterior use:					
	4.2a.11.4.1	**BARK POCKET** - None					
	4.2a.11.4.2	**BIRDSEYE**, Sound - Unlimited					
	4.2a.11.4.3	**BIRDSEYE**, Checked					
		4.2a.11.4.3.1	Unlimited		●		
		4.2a.11.4.3.2	≤ 10% of face			●	
		4.2a.11.4.3.3	None				●
	4.2a.11.4.4	**BURL**, Sound					
		4.2a.11.4.4.1	Unlimited		●		
		4.2a.11.4.4.2	≤ 1" (25 mm) in diameter			●	
		4.2a.11.4.4.3	≤ 1/2" (13 mm) in diameter				●
	4.2a.11.4.5	**CHECK**					
		4.2a.11.4.5.1	≤ 3/32" (2 mm) wide x 8" (203 mm) long		●		
		4.2a.11.4.5.2	≤ 1/16" (2 mm) wide x 6" (152 mm) long			●	
		4.2a.11.4.5.3	≤ 1/32" (1 mm) wide x 4" (102 mm) long				●
	4.2a.11.4.6	**HEARTWOOD**, in Select White Ash, Birch, and Maple - None					
	4.2a.11.4.7	**HONEYCOMB** - None					
	4.2a.11.4.8	**KNOT**, Sound and Tight					
		4.2a.11.4.8.1	≤ 3/8" (10 mm) in diameter		●		
		4.2a.11.4.8.2	≤ 1/4" (6 mm) in diameter			●	
		4.2a.11.4.8.3	≤ 1/8" (3 mm) in diameter				●

PRODUCT

LUMBER RULES (continued)

These rules are not intended to create a lumber grade; they are only intended to establish the acceptable requirements and/or characteristics after the architectural woodwork is completed or installed.

3

DESCRIPTION			E	C	P
4.2a HARDWOOD — **MATERIAL - HARDWOOD** (continued)					
4.2a.11 TRANSPARENT — **TRANSPARENT FINISH** (continued)					
4.2a.11.4 ALLOWANCES — **NATURAL CHARACTERISTIC ALLOWANCES** (continued)					
4.2a.11.4.9	**KNOT**, Checked				
	4.2a.11.4.9.1	≤ 1/2" (13 mm) in diameter	●		
	4.2a.11.4.9.2	≤ 1/4" (6 mm) in diameter		●	
	4.2a.11.4.9.3	None			●
4.2a.11.4.10	**MINERAL STAIN**				
	4.2a.11.4.10.1	Unlimited	●		
	4.2a.11.4.10.2	≤ 10% of face		●	
	4.2a.11.4.10.3	None			●
4.2a.11.4.11	**PATCH**				
	4.2a.11.4.11.1	≤ 1-1/2" (38 mm) wide x 3-1/2" (89 mm) long, and inconspicuous from 60"	●		
	4.2a.11.4.11.1	≤ 1-1/2" (38 mm) wide x 3-1/2" (89 mm) long, and inconspicuous from 36"		●	
	4.2a.11.4.11.2	None			●
4.2a.11.4.12	**PITCH POCKET** or **STREAK**				
	4.2a.11.4.12.1	≤ 1/16" (2 mm) wide x 6" (152 mm) long or 1/8" (3 mm) wide x 4" (102 mm) long	●		
	4.2a.11.4.12.2	None		●	●
4.2a.11.4.13	**SAPWOOD**, in unselected species - Unlimited				
4.2a.11.4.14	**SAPWOOD**, in select Red Birch and Brown Ash - None				
4.2a.11.4.15	**SAPWOOD** in Cherry, and Walnut				
	4.2a.11.4.15.1	Unlimited	●		
	4.2a.11.4.15.2	≤ 10% of face		●	
	4.2a.11.4.15.3	≤ 5% of face			●
4.2a.11.4.16	**SHAKE**				
	4.2a.11.4.16.1	≤ 1/8" (3 mm) wide x 3" (76 mm) long	●		
	4.2a.11.4.16.2	None		●	●
4.2a.11.4.17	**SPLIT**				
	4.2a.11.4.17.1	≤ 3/32" (2 mm) wide x 8" (203 mm) long	●		
	4.2a.11.4.17.2	≤ 1/16" (2 mm) wide x 6" (152 mm) long		●	
	4.2a.11.4.17.3	≤ 1/32" (1 mm) wide x 4" (102 mm) long			●
4.2a.11.4.18	**STICKER BOARD DISCOLORATION**				
	4.2a.11.4.18.1	≤ 10% of face	●		
	4.2a.11.4.18.2	None		●	●
4.2a.11.4.19	**WORM HOLE**				
	4.2a.11.4.19.1	≤ 1/8" (3 mm) in diameter	●		
	4.2a.11.4.19.2	≤ 1/16" (2 mm) in diameter		●	
	4.2a.11.4.19.3	None			●

PRODUCT

LUMBER RULES (continued)

These rules are not intended to create a lumber grade; they are only intended to establish the acceptable requirements and/or characteristics after the architectural woodwork is completed or installed.

				DESCRIPTION	E	C	P
4.2b	**MATERIAL - SOFTWOOD**						
	4.2b.1	Rules shall apply only to the following species: **CEDAR, WESTERN RED**; **FIR, DOUGLAS**; **HEMLOCK**; **PINE, PONDEROSA**; **PINE, SUGAR**; **REDWOOD**					
		4.2b.1.1		For **SPECIES NOT LISTED**, length requirements and size/exposed area of permitted natural characteristics shall be as agreed to between owner/design professional and manufacturer/ installer.			
	4.2b.2	**GLUING** for width is permitted when finished dimensions exceed 7" (178 mm).					
		4.2b.2.1		Direction of the end grain of boards glued for width shall be alternated.			
		4.2b.2.2					
	4.2b.3	**GLUING** for thickness is permitted when finished dimensions exceed 1-1/2" (38 mm).					
	4.2b.4	**VERTICAL GRAIN** shall have a minimum average of 5 growth rings per inch at exposed surfaces.					
	4.2b.5	**MAXIMUM LENGTH REQUIREMENT** for given width up to 1-1/2" (38.1 mm) in thickness shall be:					
SOFTWOOD	LENGTHS	**4.2b.5.1**		**DOUGLAS FIR, HEMLOCK, & WESTERN RED CEDAR**			
			4.2b.5.1.1	4" to 8" (102 mm to 203 mm) in width = 15'-8" (4752 mm)			
			4.2b.5.1.2	10" (254 mm) in width = 13'-8" (4170 mm)			
			4.2b.5.1.3	12" (305 mm) is not usually available.			
		4.2b.5.2		**PONDEROSA** or **SUGAR PINE**			
			4.2b.5.2.1	4" to 12" (102 mm to 305 mm) in width = 15'-8" (4752 mm)			
		4.2b.5.3		**REDWOOD**			
			4.2b.5.3.1	4" to 12" (102 mm to 305 mm) in width = 19'-8" (5994 mm)			
		4.2b.5.4		**BOARDS** required to be **WIDER** than those listed above may be glued for width.			
		4.2b.5.5		**BOARDS** required to be **LONGER** than those listed as available above may be glued or furnished in two pieces for length at the option of the manufacturer.			
	4.2b.6	**OPAQUE FINISH**					
	OPAQUE	4.2b.6.1		**NATURAL CHARACTERISTICS** are allowed only provided they are inconspicuous after two coats of finish are applied.			
		4.2b.6.2		**FILLING** of checks, splits, or other open characteristics is the responsibility of the millwork manufacturer.			
		4.2b.6.3		**NATURAL CHARACTERISTIC LIMITATIONS** of any one board's exposed face:			
			4.2b.6.3.1	**NONE** in any face smaller than 200 square inches (5080 square mm), with:	●		
			4.2b.6.3.1.1	**ONE** permitted for each additional 100 square inches (2540 square mm)	●		
			4.2b.6.3.1.2	A maximum of **FIVE**	●		
⇓	⇓	⇓	4.2b.6.3.1.3	**NO** knots, pitch streaks, or pitch pockets within 18" (457 mm) of one another	●		

3

PRODUCT

LUMBER RULES (continued)

These rules are not intended to create a lumber grade; they are only intended to establish the acceptable requirements and/or characteristics after the architectural woodwork is completed or installed.

Section	Item	DESCRIPTION	E	C	P
4.2b		**MATERIAL - SOFTWOOD** (continued)			
4.2b.6		**OPAQUE FINISH** (continued)			
4.2b.6.3		**NATURAL CHARACTERISTIC LIMITATIONS** (continued)			
4.2b.6.3.2		**NONE** in any face smaller than 400 square inches (10160 square mm), with:		●	
	4.2b.6.3.2.1	**ONE** permitted for each additional 150 square inches (3810 square mm)		●	
	4.2b.6.3.2.2	A maximum of **FOUR**		●	
	4.2b.6.3.2.3	**NO** knots, pitch streaks, or pitch pockets within 24" (610 mm) of one another.		●	
4.2b.6.3.3		**NONE** in any face smaller than 600 square inches (15240 square mm), with:			●
	4.2b.6.3.3.1	**ONE** permitted for each additional 200 square inches (5080 square mm)			●
	4.2b.6.3.3.2	A maximum of **THREE**			●
	4.2b.6.3.3.3	**NO** knots, pitch streaks, or pitch pockets within 36" (914 mm) of one another.			●
4.2b.6.4		**NATURAL CHARACTERISTIC ALLOWANCES** at interior or exterior use:			
4.2b.6.4.1		**BARK POCKET** - None			
4.2b.6.4.2		**BIRDSEYE**, Sound - Unlimited			
4.2b.6.4.3		**BIRDSEYE**, Checked and Filled - Unlimited			
4.2b.6.4.4		**BURL**, Sound			
	4.2b.6.4.4.1	≤ 1" (25 mm) in diameter	●	●	
	4.2b.6.4.4.2	≤ 3/4" (19 mm) in diameter			●
4.2b.6.4.5		**CHECK**, Filled			
	4.2b.6.4.5.1	≤ 3/32" (2 mm) wide x 9" (229 mm) long	●		
	4.2b.6.4.5.2	≤ 1/16" (2 mm) wide x 7" (178 mm) long		●	
	4.2b.6.4.5.3	≤ 1/32" (1 mm) wide x 5" (127 mm) long			●
4.2b.6.4.6		**HONEYCOMB** - None			
4.2b.6.4.7		**KNOT**, Sound and Tight			
	4.2b.6.4.7.1	≤ 1" (25 mm) in diameter	●		
	4.2b.6.4.7.2	≤ 5/8" (16 mm) in diameter		●	
	4.2b.6.4.7.3	≤ 3/8" (10 mm) in diameter			●
4.2b.6.4.8		**KNOT**, Checked and Filled			
	4.2b.6.4.8.1	≤ 3/4" (19 mm) in diameter	●		
	4.2b.6.4.8.2	≤ 1/2" (13 mm) in diameter		●	
	4.2b.6.4.8.3	≤ 1/4" (6 mm) in diameter			●
4.2b.6.4.9		**MINERAL STAIN** - Unlimited			
4.2b.6.4.10		**PATCH**			
	4.2b.6.4.10.1	≤ 1-1/2" (38 mm) wide x 3-1/2" (89 mm) long	●		
	4.2b.6.4.10.2	≤ 1-1/2" (38 mm) wide x 3-1/2" (89 mm) long, and inconspicuous from 60"		●	●

PRODUCT

LUMBER RULES (continued)

These rules are not intended to create a lumber grade; they are only intended to establish the acceptable requirements and/or characteristics after the architectural woodwork is completed or installed.

Section	Subsection	Item	Number	Description	E	C	P
4.2b SOFTWOOD				**MATERIAL - SOFTWOOD** (continued)			
	4.2b.6 OPAQUE			**OPAQUE FINISH** (continued)			
		4.2b.6.4 ALLOWANCES		**NATURAL CHARACTERISTIC ALLOWANCES** (continued)			
			4.2b.6.4.11	**PITCH POCKET** or **STREAK**			
			4.2b.6.4.11.1	≤ 1/8" (3 mm) wide x 9" (229 mm) long	●		
			4.2b.6.4.11.2	≤ 1/8" (3 mm) wide x 6" (152 mm) long		●	
			4.2b.6.4.11.3	≤ 1/8" (3 mm) wide x 3" (76 mm) long			
			4.2b.6.4.12	**SAPWOOD** - Unlimited			
			4.2b.6.4.13	**SHAKE**, Filled			
			4.2b.6.4.13.1	≤ 1/4" (6 mm) wide x 3" (76 mm) long	●		
			4.2b.6.4.13.2	≤ 1/8" (3 mm) wide x 3" (76 mm) long		●	
			4.2b.6.4.13.3	≤ 1/16" (2 mm) wide x 2" (51 mm) long			
			4.2b.6.4.14	**SPLIT**, Filled			
			4.2b.6.4.14.1	≤ 3/32" (2 mm) wide x 9" (229 mm) long	●		
			4.2b.6.4.14.2	≤ 1/16" (2 mm) wide x 7" (178 mm) long		●	
			4.2b.6.4.14.3	≤ 1/32" (1 mm) wide x 5" (127 mm) long			
			4.2b.6.4.15	**STICKER BOARD DISCOLORATION** - Unlimited			
			4.2b.6.4.16	**WORM HOLES,** Filled			
			4.2b.6.4.16.1	≤ 3/16" (5 mm) in diameter	●		
			4.2b.6.4.16.2	≤ 1/8" (3 mm) in diameter		●	
			4.2b.6.4.16.3	≤ 1/16" (2 mm) in diameter			●
	4.2b.7 TRANSPARENT			**TRANSPARENT FINISH**			
		4.2b.7.1		**MATCHING**, when glued for thickness or width or when veneered construction is utilized, shall be:			
			4.2b.7.1.1	Not required	●		
			4.2b.7.1.2	Compatible for color and grain		●	
			4.2b.7.1.3	Well matched for color and grain			●
		4.2b.7.2		**FILLING** of checks, splits, or other open characteristics is the responsibility of the finisher.			
		4.2b.7.3 LIMITATIONS		**NATURAL CHARACTERISTIC LIMITATIONS** of any one board's exposed face:			
			4.2b.7.3.1	**NONE** in any face smaller than 400 sq. in. (10160 sq. mm), with:	●		
			4.2b.7.3.1.1	**ONE** permitted for each additional 200 sq. in. (5080 sq. mm)	●		
			4.2b.7.3.2	**A maximum of FOUR**, with:	●		
			4.2b.7.3.2.1	**NO** knots, pitch streaks, or pitch pockets within 24" (610 mm) of one another	●		
			4.2b.7.3.3	**NONE** in any face smaller than 600 sq. in. (15240 sq. mm), with:		●	
			4.2b.7.3.3.1	**ONE** permitted for each additional 300 sq. in. (7620 sq. mm)		●	
			4.2b.7.3.4	**A maximum of THREE**, with:		●	
			4.2b.7.3.4.1	**NO** knots, pitch streaks, or pitch pockets within 36" (914 mm) of one another		●	

PRODUCT

LUMBER RULES (continued)

These rules are not intended to create a lumber grade; they are only intended to establish the acceptable requirements and/or characteristics after the architectural woodwork is completed or installed.

						E	C	P
4.2b SOFTWOOD	**MATERIAL - SOFTWOOD** (continued)							
	4.2b.7 TRANSPARENT	**TRANSPARENT FINISH** (continued)						
		4.2b.7.3	**NATURAL CHARACTERISTIC LIMITATIONS** (continued)					
			4.2b.7.3.5	**NONE** in any face smaller than 900 sq. in. (22860 sq. mm), with:				●
				4.2b.7.3.5.1	**ONE** permitted for each additional 400 sq. in. (10160 sq. mm)			●
			4.2b.7.3.6	**A maximum of TWO**, with:				●
				4.2b.7.3.6.1	**NO** knots, pitch streaks, or pitch pockets within 48" (1219 mm) of one another			●
		4.2b.7.4 ALLOWANCES	**NATURAL CHARACTERISTIC ALLOWANCES** at interior or exterior use:					
			4.2b.7.4.1	**BARK POCKET** - None				
			4.2b.7.4.2	**BIRDSEYE**, Sound - Unlimited				
			4.2b.7.4.3	**BIRDSEYE**, Checked				
				4.2b.7.4.3.1	Unlimited	●		
				4.2b.7.4.3.2	≤ 10% of face		●	
				4.2b.7.4.3.3	None			●
			4.2b.7.4.4	**BURL**, Sound				
				4.2b.7.4.4.1	≤ 3/4" (19 mm) in diameter	●		
				4.2b.7.4.4.2	≤ 5/8" (16 mm) in diameter		●	
				4.2b.7.4.4.3	≤ 1/2" (13 mm) in diameter			●
			4.2b.7.4.5	**CHECK**				
				4.2b.7.4.5.1	≤ 3/32" (2 mm) wide x 8" (203 mm) long	●		
				4.2b.7.4.5.2	≤ 1/16" (2 mm) wide x 6" (152 mm) long		●	
				4.2b.7.4.5.3	≤ 1/32" (1 mm) wide x 4" (102 mm) long			●
			4.2b.7.4.6	**HONEYCOMB** - None				
			4.2b.7.4.7	**KNOT**, Sound and Tight				
				4.2b.7.4.7.1	≤ 3/4" (19 mm) in diameter	●		
				4.2b.7.4.7.2	≤ 1/2" (13 mm) in diameter		●	
				4.2b.7.4.7.3	≤ 1/4" (6 mm) in diameter			●
			4.2b.7.4.8	**KNOT**, Checked				
				4.2b.7.4.8.1	≤ 1/2" (13 mm) in diameter	●		
				4.2b.7.4.8.2	≤ 1/4" (6 mm) in diameter		●	
				4.2b.7.4.8.3	None			●
			4.2b.7.4.9	**MINERAL STAIN**				
				4.2b.7.4.9.1	Unlimited	●		
				4.2b.7.4.9.2	≤ 10% of face		●	
				4.2b.7.4.9.3	None			●
			4.2b.7.4.10	**PATCH**				
				4.2b.7.4.10.1	≤ 1-1/2" (38 mm) wide x 3-1/2" (89 mm) long, and inconspicuous from 60"	●		
				4.2b.7.4.10.2	≤ 1-1/2" (38 mm) wide x 3-1/2" (89 mm) long, and inconspicuous from 36"		●	
				4.2b.7.4.10.3	None			●

PRODUCT

LUMBER RULES (continued)

These rules are not intended to create a lumber grade; they are only intended to establish the acceptable requirements and/or characteristics after the architectural woodwork is completed or installed.

					DESCRIPTION	E	C	P
4.2b SOFTWOOD	**MATERIAL - SOFTWOOD** (continued)							
	4.2b.7 TRANSPARENT	**TRANSPARENT FINISH** (continued)						
		4.2b.7.4 ALLOWANCES	**NATURAL CHARACTERISTIC ALLOWANCES** (continued)					
			4.2b.7.4.11	**PITCH POCKET** or **STREAK**				
				4.2b.7.4.11.1	≤ 1/16" (2 mm) wide x 6" (152 mm) long or 1/8" (3 mm) wide x 4" (102 mm) long	●		
				4.2b.7.4.11.2	≤ 1/16" (2 mm) wide x 3" (76 mm) long or 1/8" (3 mm) wide x 2" (51 mm) long		●	
				4.2b.7.4.11.3	None			●
			4.2b.7.4.12	**SAPWOOD**, in unselected species - Unlimited				
			4.2b.7.4.13	**SAPWOOD**, in All Heart Redwood - None				
			4.2b.7.4.14	**SHAKE**				
				4.2b.7.4.14.1	≤ 1/8" (3 mm) wide x3" (76 mm) long	●		
				4.2b.7.4.14.2	≤ 1/16" (2 mm) wide x 2" (51 mm) long		●	
				4.2b.7.4.14.3	None			●
			4.2b.7.4.15	**SPLIT**				
				4.2b.7.4.15.1	≤ 1/16" (2 mm) wide x 6" (152 mm) long	●		
				4.2b.7.4.15.2	≤ 1/32" (1 mm) wide x 4" (102 mm) long		●	
				4.2b.7.4.15.3	None			●
			4.2b.7.4.16	**STICKER BOARD DISCOLORATION**				
				4.2b.7.4.16.1	≤ 10% of the face	●		
				4.2b.7.4.16.2	None		●	
				4.2b.7.4.16.3	None			●
			4.2b.7.4.17	**WORM HOLES**				
				4.2b.7.4.17.1	≤ 1/8" (3 mm) in diameter	●		
				4.2b.7.4.17.2	≤ 1/16" (2 mm) in diameter		●	
				4.2b.7.4.17.3	None			●
4.3	**MACHINING -** Not applicable or used for this section.							
4.4	**ASSEMBLY -** Not applicable or used for this section.							

EXECUTION

(Items # 5 & 6 are not applicable to this section)

COMPLIANCE

(Item # 7 is not applicable to this section)

NOTES

Architectual Woodwork Standards

SECTION - 4

Sheet Products

SECTION 4 ✦ SHEET PRODUCTS - WOOD & NON-WOOD FACED

(Including: Hardwood and Softwood Veneer, High-Pressure Decorative Laminate, Thermally Fused Overlays, Vinyl Film, Medium- and High-Density Overlays, Hardboard, Backers, Solid Surface, Solid Phenolic, Epoxy Resin, and Natural/Manufactured Stone)

GENERAL

1 INFORMATION

1.1 GRADES

1.1.1 **GRADE CLASSIFICATIONS ECONOMY, CUSTOM,** and **PREMIUM** are used within these standards only in reference to the acceptable quality of workmanship, material, or installation in a completed architectural woodwork product.

1.1.2 **THIS MATERIAL SECTION** deals with sheet products, which are a component of finished products covered in Sections 6 - 12.

1.1.2.1 **IN THIS SECTION**, the use of Grade classifications is only for the purpose of identifying sheet products that can be used in finished products meeting those Grades.

1.1.2.2 These Grade classifications are not intended to be used as Grades of raw material or to judge a stand-alone sheet.

1.1.3 **PANEL ASSOCIATION GRADES**, by themselves, should not be used for architectural woodwork, because even their highest grades might permit unacceptable defects.

1.1.3.1 The appearance of a piece in the end product is of primary importance, not whether it is cut from a larger sheet that contained characteristics which can be eliminated.

1.1.4 **SHEET REQUIREMENTS**

1.1.4.1 Apply only to surfaces visible after manufacture and installation.

1.1.4.2 Establish criteria as to which, if any, natural characteristics are acceptable.

1.1.4.3 Limit the extent of characteristics that will be permitted based on an exposed area's size and the proximity of characteristics to one another.

1.1.4.4 Do not apply to special varieties of species that display unusual characteristics desirable for aesthetic and design reasons.

1.1.5 **MODIFICATIONS** by the contract documents shall govern if in conflict with these standards.

1.2 BASIC CONSIDERATIONS

1.2.1 **PLYWOOD** is defined as a panel composed of a crossbanded assembly of layers or plies of veneer, or veneers in combination with a lumber core, composite core (MDF or particleboard) or combination core, that are joined with an adhesive. Except for special constructions, the grain of alternate plies is always approximately at right angles, and the thickness and species on either side of the core are identical for balanced effect. An odd number of plies is always used, except when the center two pieces of veneer run parallel; then these are considered one pair of ply.

1.2.2 **VENEER GRAIN** might not match the grain of solid stock, and it might not accept transparent finishes in the same manner; additional finishing steps might achieve similar aesthetic value (see Section 5).

1.2.3 **FIGURE** is not a function of a species grade, and any special desires must be so specified.

1.2.4 **SPECIAL CHARACTERISTICS,** such as sapwood, heartwood, ribbon stripe, birdseye and comb grain, if desired, are required to be specified.

1.2.5 **NATURAL,** as a type of wood species selection, allows an unlimited amount of heartwood or sapwood within a face and is the default selection, unless specified otherwise.

1.2.6 **SELECT RED** or **WHITE** simply means all heartwood or all sapwood, respectively, and must be so specified if desired.

GENERAL

1.2 **BASIC CONSIDERATIONS** (continued)

1.2.7 **SPECIES,** such as Hickory, Pecan, Butternut, or Mahogany, exhibit "special character", and users are advised to thoroughly investigate the expected grain and color of these more exotic species.

1.2.8 **HONDURAS** and **AFRICAN MAHOGANY** vary in color from a light pink to a light red, reddish brown to a golden brown or yellowish tan.

1.2.8.1 Some Mahogany turns darker or lighter in color after machining.

1.2.8.2 The figure or grain runs from plain sliced, plain stripe to broken stripe, mottled, fiddleback, swirl, and crotches.

1.2.9 **LAUAN** (White and Red), **TANGUILE**, and other species are native to the Philippine Islands and are sometimes referred to as Philippine Mahogany; however, they are not a true Mahogany.

1.2.9.1 The generic term **MAHOGANY** should not be specified without further definition.

1.2.10 **CHERRY, WALNUT**, and certain other hardwood species are required to be specified by origin - such as American Cherry, American Walnut, or English Brown Oak - because they can be significantly different in color and texture.

1.2.11 **PHOTODEGRADATION** is the effect on the appearance of exposed wood faces caused by exposure to both sun and artificial light sources. If an entire face is exposed to a light source, it will photodegrade somewhat uniformly and hardly be noticeable, whereas partially exposed surfaces or surfaces with shadow lines might show nonuniform photodegradation. Some woods, such as American Cherry and Walnut, are more susceptible than others, and extra care should be taken to protect against the effects of nonuniform photodegradation.

1.2.12 **OXIDATION** is the effect on the appearance of exposed wood faces caused by exposure to atmosphere. This is analogous to browning reactions in freshly cut fruit; for instance, apples. Hardwoods can develop deep yellow to reddish brown discolorations on the surface of the wood when exposed to air immediately after sawing or peeling. These discolorations are especially noticeable on Cherry, Birch, Red Alder, Sycamore, Oak, Maple, and Sweet Gum. Some species, such as Alder, Oak, Birch, and Maple, develop these discolorations during air-seasoning. A related gray stain on several varieties of Southern Oaks also appears to be oxidative in nature. Proper selection, sanding, and finishing can minimize the effects of oxidation.

1.2.13 **ROTARY-CUT SOFTWOOD SHEETS** are typically manufactured in various grades referring to the appearance of the face, back, and interior plies of the sheet and are intended for exterior (with a fully waterproof glue line) or interior (with a moisture-resistant, but not waterproof, glue line).

1.2.13.1 Clear faces, free of patches, are not typically available.

1.2.14 **SPECIALTY** sheet products, such as plywood with textured faces, prefinished plywood, overlaid plywood, composition sheets, flame-spread-rated plywood, moisture-resistant plywood, lead-lined sheets, projectile resistant armor (bullet proofing), reconstituted veneers, bamboo sheets, acrylic sheets, or PVC sheets are the products of the individual manufacturer, and are covered by their manufacturer's specification - not by these standards.

1.2.15 **FIRE-RETARDANT** sheets are available, but not readily, with various types of treated core, such as veneer, lumber, particleboard, and mineral core.

1.2.15.1 Flame-spread rating will vary for different species of untreated face veneers on treated cores, directly with the density of the untreated face veneers; the higher the density, the higher the flame-spread rating.

1.2.15.1.1 Refer to the latest edition of the Underwriters' Laboratories listings for various flame-spread ratings available bearing U.L. Labels.

1.2.16 **PANEL ADHESIVES** include and are defined as:

1.2.16.1 **TYPE I** Waterproof bond for limited exterior use (2 Cycle Boil Test plus Shear Test).

1.2.16.2 **TYPE II** Water-resistant bond for interior use (3 Cycle Soak Test).

GENERAL

1.2 **BASIC CONSIDERATIONS** (continued)

1.2.17 **CHECKING** or **WARPAGE** of wood-veneered sheets can be avoided by proper environmental maintenance, such as being:

1.2.17.1 Protected from extremes in relative humidity and temperature.

1.2.17.2 Finished on both surfaces to retard moisture movement in and out of the panel.

1.2.17.3 Placed in locations that avoid directly facing air vents and/or radiant heat sources.

1.2.18 **WOOD-VENEER SLICING** is an important factor in the various visual effects obtained. Two veneer slices of the same species will have entirely different visual character, even though their color values are similar. As a log segment is sliced, the leaves of veneer are retained in a sequential flitch. These veneer-sliced options include:

1.2.18.1 **ROTARY SLICED -** The log is mounted centrally in the lathe and turned against a razor-sharp blade, like unwinding a roll of paper. Because this slice follows the log's annular growth rings, a bold variegated grain marking is produced. Rotary-sliced veneer is exceptionally wide.

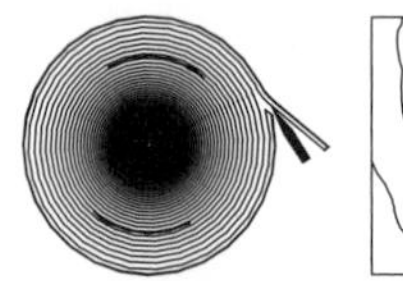
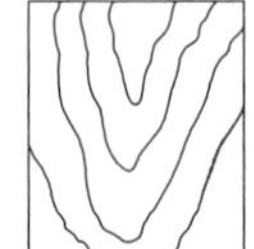

4

1.2.18.2 **PLAIN SLICED (or FLAT SLICED) -** The half log is mounted with the heart side floating against the guide plate of the slicer, and the slicing is done parallel to a line through the center of the log, producing a variegated figure.

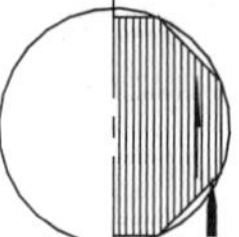
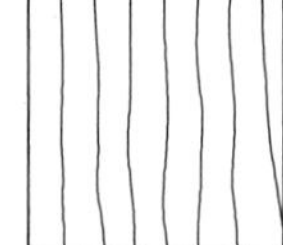

1.2.18.3 **QUARTER SLICED -** The quarter log is mounted on the guide plate so that the growth rings of the log strike at approximately right angles, producing a series of stripes that are straight in some woods and varied in others. In Oak, this slicing can produce unlimited amounts of medullary ray.

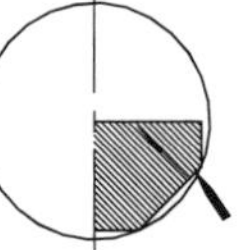
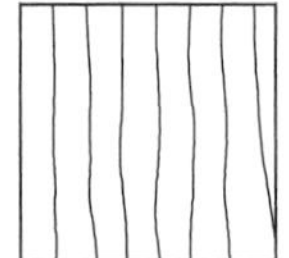

1.2.18.3.1 **VERTICAL GRAIN SLICED -** Unique to some softwoods, the vertical grain effect is produced by slicing perpendicularly to the growth rings.

1.2.18.4 **RIFT SLICED -** Unique to various species of Oak, the rift or comb grain effect is obtained by slicing perpendicular to the Oak's medullary rays on either the lathe or the slicer. Medullary ray cells are distinct characteristics of Oak that radiate from the center of the log like the curved spokes of a wheel. Rift slicing limits the appearance of the medullary ray flake and produces a rather straight grain. Comb grain is a further hybrid selected from the rift slice.

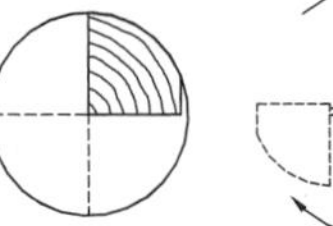
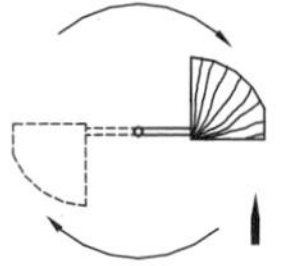
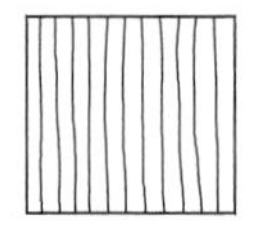

1.2.18.5 **COMMON HARDWOOD VENEER SPECIES** and **CUTS**

SPECIES	ROTARY	PLAIN SLICED (FLAT-CUT)	QUARTERED	RIFT & COMB GRAIN
Anigre		●	●	
Ash	●	●	●	
Beech		●	●	
Birch	●	●		
Cherry	●	●	●	
Hickory	●	●		
Lauan	●		●	
Mahogany, African	●	●	●	

GENERAL

1.2 **BASIC CONSIDERATIONS** (continued)

1.2.18 **WOOD-VENEER SLICING** (continued)

1.2.18.5 **COMMON HARDWOOD VENEER SPECIES** and **CUTS** (continued)

SPECIES	ROTARY	PLAIN SLICED (FLAT-CUT)	QUARTERED	RIFT & COMB GRAIN
Mahogany, Honduras	●	●	●	
Maple	●	●	●	
Meranti	●		●	
Oak, Red	●	●	●	●
Oak, White	●	●	●	●
Pecan		●		
Poplar, Yellow	●	●		
Sapele		●	●	
Walnut, Black	●	●	●	

1.2.19 **MATCHING OF ADJACENT WOOD-VENEER LEAVES,** as with the effect of different veneer cuts, can alter the appearance of a given panel or an entire installation. To create a particular appearance, the veneer leaves of a flitch are edge-glued together in patterns such as:

1.2.19.1 **RANDOM MATCH** - Veneer leaves are joined out of flitch sequence with the intention of creating a casual unmatched effect. Veneers from several logs may be used in the manufacturing of a set of panels.

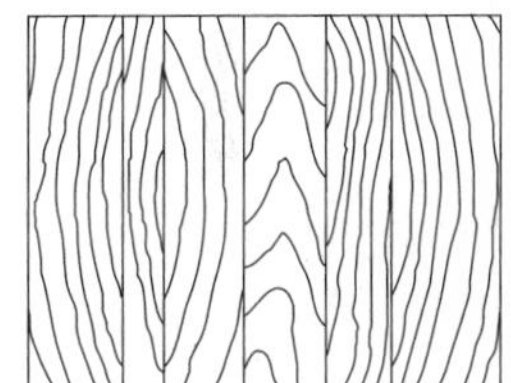

1.2.19.2 **SLIP MATCH** - Veneer leaves are joined side by side, as they are taken in sequence from the flitch, so that the pieces are not matched for color or grain at the joints. This method of matching repeats the same flitch characteristics from piece to piece. Some species of hardwood do not blend well into this pattern. Generally, quarter- and rift-sliced veneers are slip-matched.

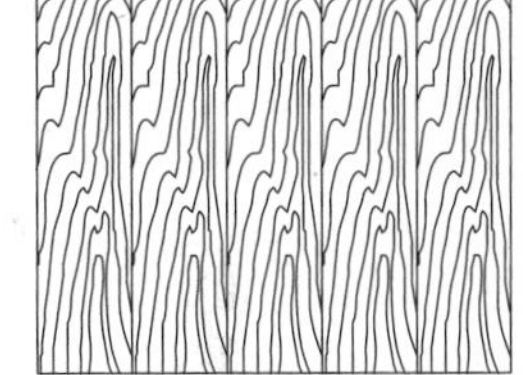

1.2.19.3 **BOOK MATCH** - Every other veneer leaf is turned over as the leaves are taken in sequence from the flitch, similar to turning or unfolding the pages of a book. Since one leaf will be loose-side-up and the next tight-side-up, book-matching produces a color shading, while maintaining a good match for color and grain at the joints. **TIGHT** and **LOOSE LEAVES** might refract light differently and cause a noticeable color variation (barber pole effect) **in** some species. This is a natural characteristic and not a manufacturing defect. It might be possible to minimize this effect utilizing special finishing techniques.

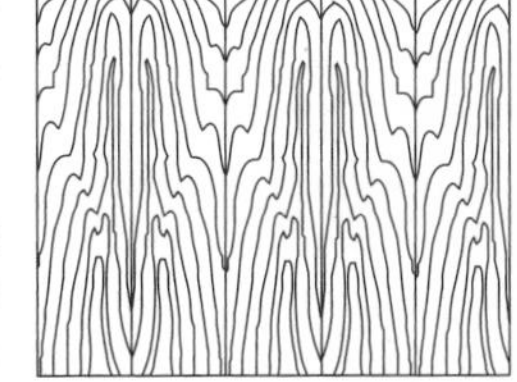

GENERAL

1.2 **BASIC CONSIDERATIONS** (continued)

1.2.20 **MATCHING OF WOOD VENEER LEAVES WITHIN A PANEL FACE** - Individual leaves of veneer in a sliced flitch increase or decrease in width as the slicing progresses. Thus, if a number of panels are manufactured from a particular flitch, the number of veneer leaves per panel face will change as the flitch is utilized. The manner in which these leaves are "laid up" within the panel requires specification, and is classified as follows:

1.2.20.1 **BALANCED MATCH** - Each panel face is assembled from veneer leaves of uniform width before edge trimming. Panels may contain an even or an odd number of leaves, and distribution might change from panel to panel within a sequenced set - shown in Book and Slip match.

1.2.20.2 **CENTER BALANCE MATCH** - Each panel face is assembled from an even number of veneer leaves of uniform width before edge trimming, with a veneer joint in the center of the panel, producing horizontal symmetry. A small amount of figure is lost in this process.

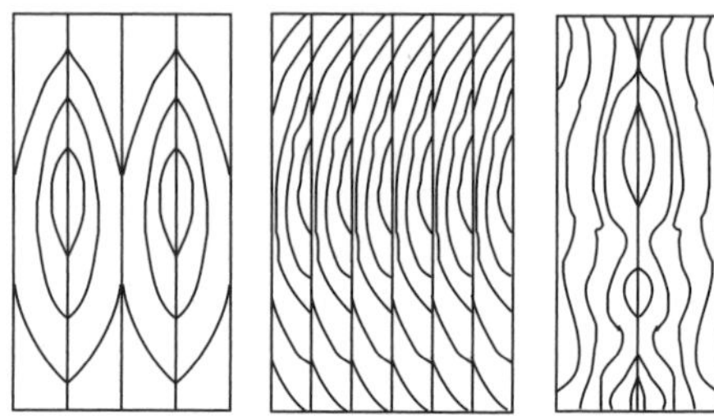

1.2.20.3 **SLIP, CENTER, BOOK MATCH** - Each panel face is assembled of an even (four or more) number of veneer leaves. The veneer leaves are laid out as a slip-matched panel face; then at the center, one half of the leaves are booked to the other half. Quarter- and rift-sliced veneers are generally used for this match, which allows for a pleasing balance of sweep and character marks.

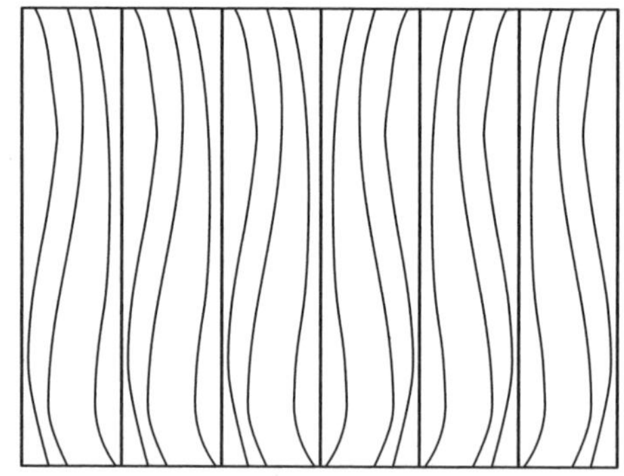

1.2.20.4 **RUNNING MATCH** - Each panel face is assembled from as many veneer leaves as necessary. This often results in an asymmetrical appearance, with some veneer leaves of unequal width. Often the most economical method at the expense of aesthetics, it is the standard for Custom Grade and must be specified for other Grades. Running matches are seldom "sequenced and numbered" for use as adjacent panels. Horizontal grain "match" or sequence cannot be expected.

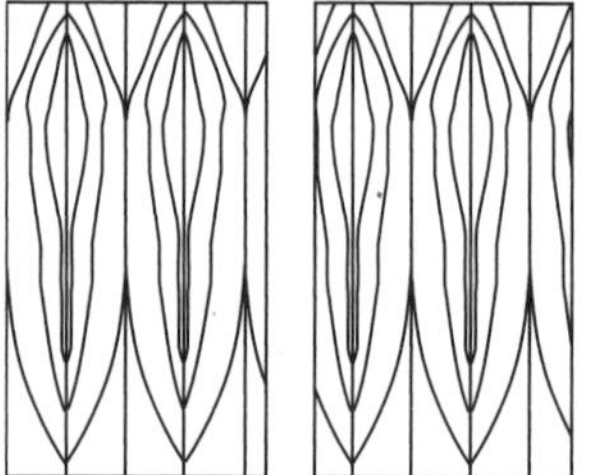

GENERAL

1.2 **BASIC CONSIDERATIONS** (continued)

1.2.21 **END-MATCHING OF WOOD VENEERS -** Often used to extend the apparent length of available veneers for high wall panels and long conference tables. End matching occurs in two types:

1.2.21.1 **ARCHITECTURAL END MATCH -** Leaves are individually book-matched (or slip-matched), first end-to-end and then side-to-side, alternating end and side. It yields the best continuous grain patterns for length as well as width, and minimizes misalignment of grain pattern.

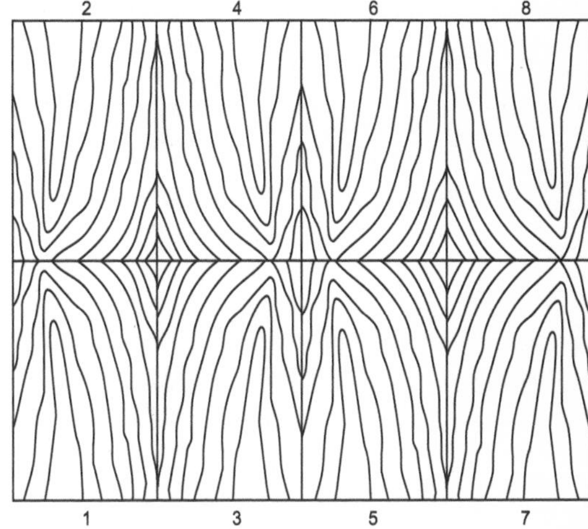

1.2.21.2 **PANEL END MATCH -** Leaves are book-matched (or slip-matched) on panel subassemblies, with sequenced subassemblies end-matched, resulting in some modest cost savings on projects where applicable. For most species, it yields a pleasing, blended appearance and grain continuity. Some misalignment of grain pattern will occur and is not a defect.

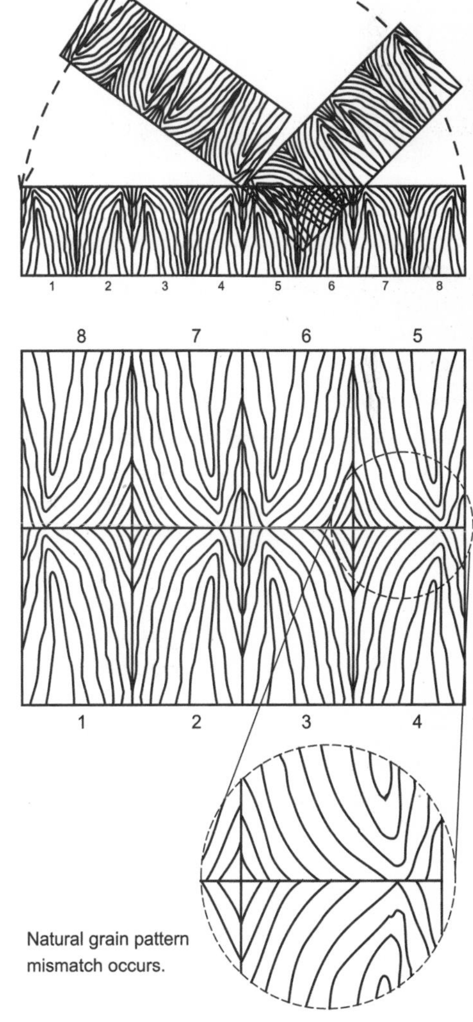

GENERAL

1.2 **BASIC CONSIDERATIONS** (continued)

1.2.21 **END-MATCHING OF WOOD VENEERS** (continued)

1.2.21.3 **CONTINUOUS END MATCH -** Leaves are individually book-matched (or slip-matched). Separate panels are stacked in sequenced order, either horizontally or vertically in the elevation. (Horizontal sequence illustrated.) It yields sequenced grain patterns for elevations, with a pleasing blend of figure horizontally or vertically.

NOTE: Each label represents a full panel from a set.

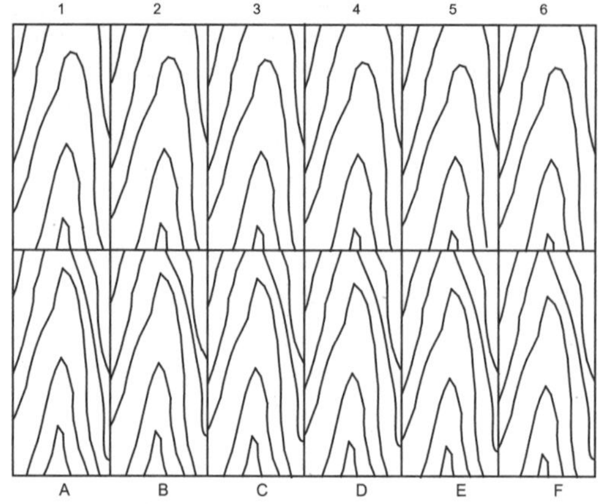

1.2.22 **SPECIALTY OR SKETCH MATCHES OF WOOD VENEERS -** There are regional variations in the "names" of the following veneer leaf-matching techniques, drawn as squares for simplicity. It is strongly recommended that the design professional use both names and drawings to define the desired effect, using a rectangle, polygon, circle, ellipse, or other shape. Rift-sliced, quarter-sliced, and highly figured veneers are generally used for these speciality matches. The different matches of veneer cause the reflection of light to vary from adjoining leaves, bringing "life" to the panel. Due to the inherent nature of the veneering process, alignment at corners might vary.

1.2.22.1 **SUNBURST MATCH -** is made of six or more veneer leaves cut at the appropriate angle with the grain radiating from the center. These veneer leaves are then book-matched, assembled, and trimmed for final size.

1.2.22.2 **BOX MATCH -** is made of four leaves with the grain running parallel to the perimeter of the panel. The leaves are cut at the appropriate angle and end-matched.

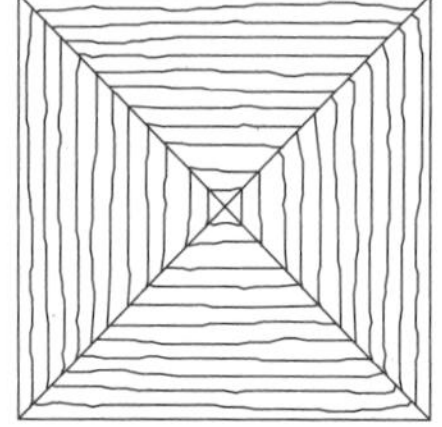

1.2.22.3 **REVERSE OR END GRAIN BOX MATCH -** is made of four leaves with the grain running at right angles to the perimeter of the panel. The leaves are cut at the appropriate angle and book-matched.

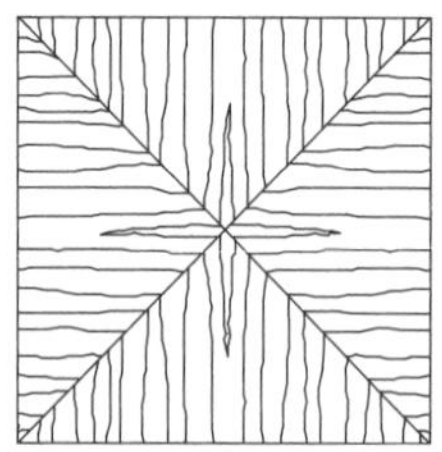

GENERAL

1.2 BASIC CONSIDERATIONS (continued)

1.2.22 SPECIALTY OR SKETCH MATCHES OF WOOD VENEERS (continued)

1.2.22.4 **HERRINGBONE OR V-BOOK MATCH -** is one or more pairs of assembled slipped or booked leaves. Each assembled set of leaves is cut at generally 45 degrees to one edge of the panel. The assembled set of leaves is then end-matched to the adjoining assembled set of leaves.

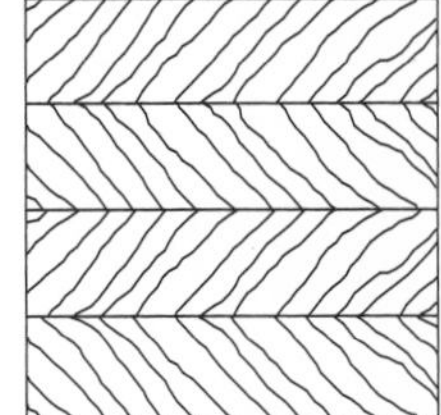

1.2.22.5 **DIAMOND MATCH -** is made of four leaves with the grain running 45 degrees to the perimeter of the panel and surrounding the center. The leaves are cut at the appropriate angle and end-matched.

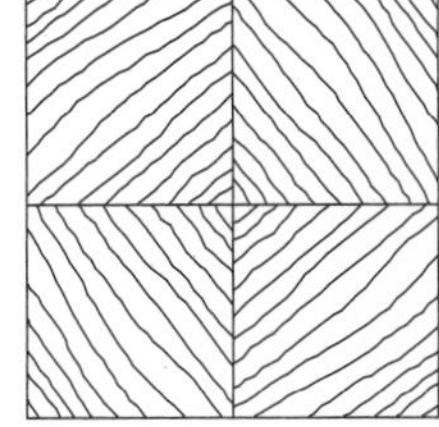

1.2.22.6 **REVERSE DIAMOND MATCH -** is made of four leaves with the grain running 45 degrees to the perimeter of the panel and radiating from the center. The leaves are cut at the appropriate angle and book-matched.

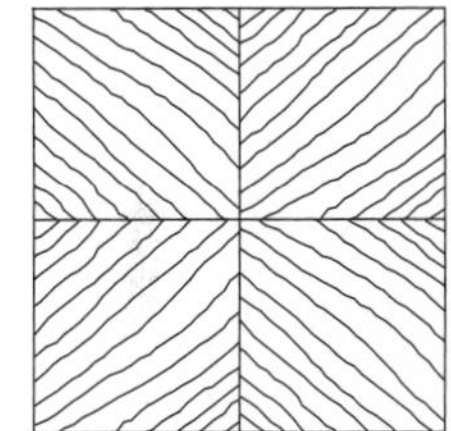

1.2.22.7 **PARQUET MATCH -** is made by dividing the panel into multiple equal-sized pieces and cutting the veneer to the same size. Each veneer leaf is joined at right angles to the adjoining piece of veneer.

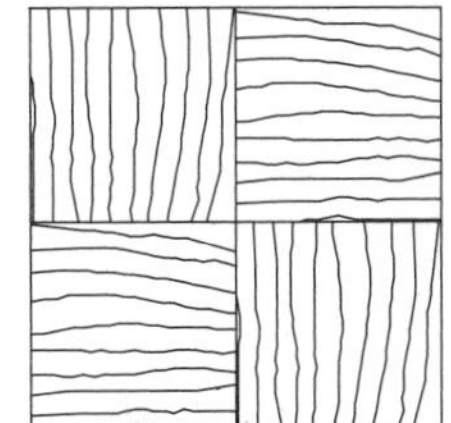

1.2.22.8 **SWING MATCH -** is made by dividing the panel into multiple paired sets. For each paired set, two leaves of veneer are cut at half the width of the set. One of these two veneer leaves is rotated 180 degrees and joined to the other. This pair is then adjoined to the other pairs assembled in the same way.

1.2.22.9 **BOOK** and **BUTT MATCH -** is made by book-matching veneer leaves 1, 3, 5, and 7 (set A) of the 8-leaf sequence. The remaining leaves 2, 4, 6, and 8 (set B) are also book-matched. Set B is then flipped up and over the top end of set A, resulting in an end match.

GENERAL

1.2 **BASIC CONSIDERATIONS** (continued)

1.2.23 **HIGH-PRESSURE DECORATIVE LAMINATE (HPDL)** - is a stand-alone product that can be laminated onto a core as the face of a sheet product or directly onto a structure as a covering. HPDL is produced in a one-step process by fusing together, under heat and pressure, multiple layers of kraft paper saturated with phenolic resin, together with a layer of melamine-saturated decorative paper.

1.2.23.1 **HORIZONTAL GRADE** - Suitable for horizontal surface applications and ranges in thickness from 0.39" to 0.048" (1 mm to 1.22 mm). This is considered a General Purpose Grade.

1.2.23.2 **VERTICAL GRADE** - Suitable for vertical surface applications and ranges in thickness from 0.020" to 0.028" (0.50 mm to 0.71 mm). This is considered a General Purpose Grade.

1.2.23.3 **POST-FORMING** - Can be formed around curved edges by application of heat and restraint. Maximum thickness is approximately 0.039" (1 mm) and can normally be formed to a radius as small as 3/8" (9.5 mm).

1.2.23.4 **BACKER** - Produced without a decorative face and available as standard (slightly thinner than decorative) or regrind (reclaimed HPDL with decorative sheet sanded off).

1.2.23.5 **SPECIALITY** - Special purpose such as cabinet liner, high-wear, fire-rated, electrostatic-dissipative, and chemical-resistant.

1.2.23.6 **NOTE** - Some HPDLs utilize a white background paper to achieve the high-fidelity, contrast, and depth of color in their printed patterns, which leaves a white line at the exposed edges of the laminate and can be extremely noticeable in darker colors.

1.2.24 **LOW-PRESSURE DECORATIVE LAMINATE (LPDL) -** Commonly referred to as TFM (Thermally Fused Melamine), low pressure, direct pressure, or simply as melamine overlays. Thermally fused papers and foils generally weigh between 60 and 130 g/m^2, and are similar to that used in HPDLs. Saturated with reactive resins and partially cured during manufacture to allow for storage and handling, the papers achieve final curing when they are hot-press laminated to a substrate, providing a hard, permanent thermoset bond between the paper and the substrate.

1.2.24.1 **MELAMINE** - impregnated papers, the most common, are noted for their hardness, scratch resistance, and color stability.

1.2.24.2 **POLYESTER** - impregnated papers are noted for their chemical, stain, water, and impact resistance; color clarity; and machinability.

1.2.25 **VINYL FILM -** The solid integrated color, semirigid film is made of polyvinyl chloride (PVC) and is commonly used in drawer-box construction.

1.2.26 **MEDIUM-DENSITY OVERLAY (MDO)** - is a thermosetting phenolic resin-impregnated, cellulose-fiber overlay that provides a smooth, uniformly paintable surface.

1.2.27 **HIGH-DENSITY OVERLAY (HDO)** - is a thermosetting phenolic resin-impregnated, cellulose-fiber overlay that provides a hard, smooth, uniformly textured surface of such character that further finishing is not necessary. Some evidence of underlying grain may appear.

1.2.28 **HARDBOARD** - is a sheet manufactured from interfelted lignocellulosic fibers consolidated under heat and pressure.

1.2.28.1 **APPLICABLE GRADES** - Tempered and Standard

1.2.29 **SOLID SURFACE** - is a manufactured, filled cast polymeric resin panel. The fillers enhance both its performance properties and aesthetics. With a homogeneous composition throughout its thickness, solid surface requires no finish coat and is capable of being fabricated with inconspicuous seams and repaired to its original finish.

1.2.29.1 **COLOR** and **PATTERN MATCH** - Suggest use of same batch material at adjacent sheets.

1.2.30 **SOLID PHENOLIC** - is a sheet product composed of melamine-impregnated decorative surface papers superimposed over a varying number of kraft phenolic core sheets to achieve a desired thickness.

GENERAL

1.2 **BASIC CONSIDERATIONS** (continued)

1.2.31 **PANEL CORES**

1.2.31.1 **VENEER CORE -** is where all plies are veneer, less than 1/4" (6.4 mm) thick, and with always an odd number of plies from 3 or more, except when the center is constructed of two unidirectional plies. The middle ply is called the "center". The plies on either side of the center, but beneath the outer plies, are called "crossbanding." The outer plies are called "faces" and "backs".

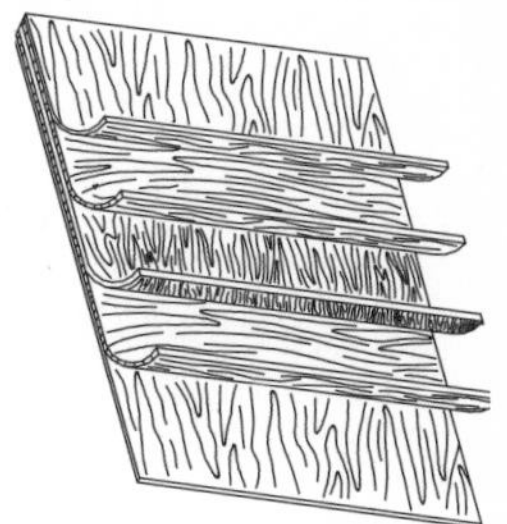

1.2.31.2 **LUMBER CORE -** is where center ply, called the "core" is composed of strips of lumber edge-glued into a solid slab. This type is usually 5-ply, 3/4" (19 mm) thick, but other thickness from 1/2" (12.7 mm) to 1-1/8" (28.6 mm) are manufactured for special uses. There are three main types:

1.2.31.2.1 **STAVED** - is where all the core strips are random length and butt-joined.

1.2.31.2.2 **FULL-LENGTH** - is where all the core strips are one piece in length.

1.2.31.2.3 **BANDED** - is where the outside strips run full-length and the others are random length. Banding may be the same species of lumber as the rest of the core, but it is usually matched to the face and might include all four edges. Banded plywood is typically produced for special uses, such as furniture, desk tops, and cabinet doors.

1.2.31.3 **COMPOSITE CORE -** is made from wood particles and called particleboard or medium-density fiberboard and/or agrifiber (made from agricultural waste products).

It is acceptable, provided it meets or exceeds the performance property requirements of ANSI A208-1 or 2.

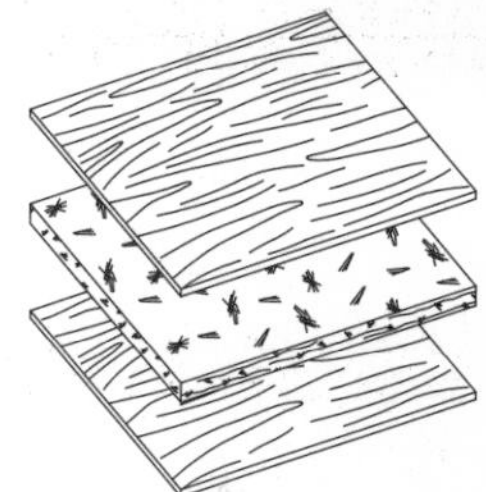

1.2.31.4 **COMBINATION CORE -** is an engineered speciality core, such as random waferboard or oriented strand board developed for specific needs and to increase the utilization of remaining resources. It is typically made from a composition or veneer center core with balanced veneers applied for stability and face veneer uniformity.

It is acceptable, provided it meets or exceeds the performance property requirements of ANSI A208-1 or 2.

1.2.31.5 **CORE PROPERTIES**, **PERFORMANCE,** and **AVAILABILITY** comparison (modified from that developed by HPVA).

1.2.31.5.1 Property and performance characteristics are influenced by the grade, thickness, and species density of the core:

1.2.31.5.1.1 Visual edge quality is rated before treatment and assumes clear "lumber".

1.2.31.5.1.2 Surface uniformity has a direct relationship to the performance of the face veneers.

1.2.31.5.1.3 Dimensional stability relates to the effect of exposure to wide swings in temperature and relative humidity.

GENERAL

1.2 **BASIC CONSIDERATIONS** (continued)

1.2.31 **PANEL CORES** (continued)

1.2.31.5 **CORE PROPERTIES, PERFORMANCE** (continued)

1.2.31.5.1 Property and performance characteristics (continued)

1.2.31.5.1.4 Screw holding and bending strength are influenced by and should be considered in design engineering.

1.2.31.5.2 "**MR**" designates "Moisture Resistant", and "**FR**" stands for "Fire Retardant".

1.2.31.5.3 **COMPARISON TABLE**

Core Type	Flatness	Visual Edge	Surface Uniformity	Dimensional Stability	Screw Holding	Bending Strength	Availability
Particleboard	5	3	5	3	1	3	R
MDF	5	5	5	3	3	3	R
Combination	5	3	5	3	5	5	L
Hardwood Veneer	1	3	3	5	5	5	R
Softwood Veneer	1	3	1	5	5	5	R
Lumber	3	3	3	3	3	5	L
Hardboard - Standard	5	5	5	5	1	3	R
Hardboard - Tempered	5	3	3	3	3	3	L
MR - Particleboard	5	3	3	3	1	3	L
MR - MDF	5	5	3	3	1	3	L
FR - Particleboard	5	1	3	3	1	3	L
Key: 5 = Excellent, 3 = Good, 1 = Fair, R = Readily, and L = Limited							

1.3 **RECOMMENDATIONS**

1.3.1 **SPECIFY** requirements for:

1.3.1.1 **UNIFORM COLOR**, special finishing techniques might be required (see Section 5).

1.3.1.2 **SPECIAL CHARACTERISTICS,** such as sapwood, heartwood, ribbon stripe, quarter sawn, rift sawn, or vertical grain.

1.3.2 **BLEACHED VENEERS** should not be used because of their potential finishing problems.

1.3.3 **VENEER CORE PANELS** should not be used for cabinet doors because they are likely to warp.

1.3.4 **FIRE-RETARDANT** cores should not be used for exteriors because they typically attract moisture.

1.3.5 **FORMALDEHYDE EMISSION REGULATIONS** should be carefully researched before shipping product into an unfamiliar area. Some states, such as California, have significantly reduced their allowable emissions.

1.4 **ACKNOWLEDGEMENTS**

1.4.1 **LOW-DENSITY FIBERBOARD (LDF)** sheets have distinct weight advantages; however, they typically offer substantially less in performance characteristics. LDF is permitted in general paneling products and/or woodwork fabrication, with the exception of casework.

1.4.1.1 **LDF** may be used for casework construction, provided its performance characteristics meet or exceed those required of particleboard.

1.4.1.1.1 Lacking defined standards, on request, the Associations will review individual products and issue approval as appropriate.

GENERAL

1.4 **ACKNOWLEDGEMENTS** (continued)

1.4.2 **COMBINATION CORE** panels are a hybridization of veneer and composition cores offering the advantages of both. Typically these cores are constructed of three or five plies of veneer which are sandwiched between thin laminations of a composite product like MDF, particleboard, hardboard, etc. Other variations utilize a wafer board (randomly oriented wafers) center. Typically these products result in stronger, lighter weight, dimensionally stable panels with increased screw holding ability, and superior surface flatness.

1.4.3 **CONTINUOUS PRESSURE LAMINATES** (melamine or polyester-based) are an alternative to and may be used in lieu of HPDL, provided they conform to the same standards as HPDL.

1.5 **INDUSTRY PRACTICES**

1.5.1 A **PANEL'S GRAIN DIRECTION** is indicated by its size listing; for example, 48" x 96" (1219 mm x 2438 mm) means the grain direction runs with the 96" (2438 mm) direction, whereas a 96" x 48" (2438 mm x 1219 mm) panel's grain direction runs with the 48" (1219 mm) dimension.

1.5.2 **SPECIES** not specifically covered by these standards shall be as agreed to between owner/design professional and manufacturer/installer as to length requirements and size/exposed area of permitted natural characteristics.

PRODUCT

2 SCOPE

2.1 All sheet products used for the fabrication or production of the architectural woodwork covered by these standards.

3 DEFAULT STIPULATION

3.1 If not otherwise specified or indicated in the contract documents, all sheet products shall match the default stipulation of the applicable product sections of these standards.

4 RULES - The following RULES shall govern unless a project's contract documents require otherwise.

These rules are not intended to create a sheet grade; they are only intended to establish the acceptable requirements and/or characteristics after the architectural woodwork is completed or installed.

Where E, C, or P is not indicated, the rule applies to all Grades equally.

ERRATA, published on the Associations' websites at www.awinet.org, www.awmac.com, or www.woodworkinstitute.com, shall TAKE PRECEDENCE OVER THESE RULES, subject to their date of posting and a project's bid date.

ARROWS INDICATE TOPIC IS CARRIED FROM ⇑ OR ONTO ⇓ ANOTHER PAGE.

			DESCRIPTION	E	C	P
4.1	**GENERAL**					
GENERAL	4.1.1		Aesthetic **GRADE RULES** apply only to exposed and semi-exposed surfaces visible after installation.			
	4.1.2		**GRAIN DIRECTION** is indicated by a panel's size listing.			
	4.1.3		**SPECIES** not covered by these standards shall be as agreed to between owner/design professional and manufacturer/installer as to length requirements and size/exposed area of permitted natural characteristics.			
	4.1.4		**REFERENCE STANDARDS**, adopted for the performance, fabrication, and appearance of face veneers, laminates, overlays, backers, and cores:			
		4.1.4.1	Hardwood Plywood - ANSI/HPVA - HP-1 (latest edition)			
		4.1.4.2	Softwood Plywood - U.S. Product Standard - PS-1 (latest edition)			
		4.1.4.3	Medium-Density Overlay (MDO) - APA PS-1 (latest edition)			
⇓	⇓	4.1.4.4	High-Density Overlay (HDO) - APA PS-1 (latest edition)			

PRODUCT

SHEET PRODUCT RULES (continued)

These rules are not intended to create a face grade; they are intended only to establish the acceptable requirements and/ or characteristics after the architectural woodwork is completed or installed.

		DESCRIPTION			E C P
4.1 GENERAL	**GENERAL** (continued)				
	4.1.4	**REFERENCE STANDARDS** (continued)			
		4.1.4.5	Thermally Fused Overlay (Melamine or Polyester) - NEMA - LD-3 (latest edition) for face characteristic only.		
		4.1.4.6	High-Pressure Laminate (HPDL) - NEMA - LD-3 (latest edition)		
		4.1.4.7	Hardboard - ANSI A135.4 (latest edition)		
		4.1.4.8	Particleboard - ANSI 208.1 (latest edition) - Grade M2 or better		
		4.1.4.9	Medium-Density Fiberboard (MDF) - ANSI A208.2 (latest edition)		
		4.1.4.10	Oriented Strand Board (OSB) - APA PS-2 (latest edition)		
	4.1.5	Additional **REQUIREMENTS,** if so specified:			
		4.1.5.1	**FIRE-RETARDANT CORE,** which:		
			4.1.5.1.1	If particleboard, shall be dyed red	
		4.1.5.2	**MOISTURE-RESISTANT CORE,** which:		
			4.1.5.2.1	If particleboard, shall be dyed green	
		4.1.5.3	**WATERPROOF ADHESIVE**		
	4.1.6	**PANEL LAY-UP**			
		4.1.6.1	Shall be for interior use, unless specified otherwise.		
		4.1.6.2	Shall be constructed with an odd number of plies.		
		4.1.6.3	Requires **BALANCED CONSTRUCTION** of faces, thickness, and moisture content to produce a warp-free panel suitable for its intended use.		
		4.1.6.4	Shall have a rigid glue line, and:		
			4.1.6.4.1	**DELAMINATION** or **SEPARATION** shall not occur that exceeds 2" (50.8 mm) in length, 1/4" (6.4 mm) in depth, or 0.003" (0.08 mm) in width.	
		4.1.6.5	Shall **NOT USE CONTACT ADHESIVE** unless there is no other alternative, and if used:		
			4.1.6.5.1	Shall be spray-applied.	
			4.1.6.5.2	Wood face veneers shall have a backer or barrier.	
		4.1.6.6	Requires cores of veneer, lumber, composition, or a combination thereof, and:		
			4.1.6.6.1	Veneer core shall not be used for cabinet-door or drawer-front components.	
		4.1.6.7	**SURFACE** distortions or defects, such as bubbling, blistering, cracking, crazing, telegraphing, or ridges in the exposed face veneer, shall not occur.		
	4.1.7	**THICKNESS TOLERANCE** shall be as established by HPVA.			
		4.1.7.1	+0/-1/32" (0 / 0.8 mm) for nominal thickness up to 1/4" (6 mm)		
		4.1.7.2	+0/-3/64" (0 / 1.2 mm) for nominal thickness of 1/4" (6 mm) or more		
	4.1.8	**SQUARENESS TOLERANCE** shall be as established by HPVA.			
		4.1.8.1	+0/-3/32" (0 / 2.4 mm) for panels larger than 48" x 48" (1220 mm x 1220 mm)		
		4.1.8.2	+0/-1/16" (0 / 1.6 mm) for panels smaller than 48" x 48" (1220 mm x 1220 mm)		
	4.1.9	**STRAIGHTNESS TOLERANCE** shall be as established by HPVA.			
		4.1.9.1	+0/-1/16" (0 / 1.6 mm) for edges up to 96" (2440 mm) in length		
		4.1.9.2	+0/-3/32" (0 / 2.4 mm) for edges longer than 96" (2440 mm) in length		

PRODUCT

SHEET PRODUCT RULES (continued)

These rules are not intended to create a face grade; they are intended only to establish the acceptable requirements and/or characteristics after the architectural woodwork is completed or installed.

		DESCRIPTION	E	C	P
4.1		**GENERAL** (continued)			
	4.1.10	**CATHEDRAL**-type figure shall be achieved by:			
	4.1.10.1	A single component in "AA" and "A" Face Grades.			
	4.1.10.2	The split-heart method in Face Grades "B - D", and:			
	4.1.10.2.1	Each half of a split heart shall be subject to the minimum component width requirements for Face Grade "B".			
4.2a		**MATERIAL - HARDWOOD VENEER**			
HARDWOOD VENEER	4.2a.1	**APPLIES** to the following common species: **ANEGRE, ASH, BEECH, BIRCH, CHERRY, HICKORY, LAUAN, MAHOGANY, African & Honduras, MAKORE, MAPLE, OAK, Red & White, PECAN, POPLAR, SAPELE, WALNUT**			
	4.2a.2	**CORE** shall be at option of manufacturer.			
	4.2a.3	**VENEER** shall be of sufficient thickness so as not to permit show-through of cross-banding after sanding or finishing.			
	4.2a.4	**EDGES** of multi-leaf faces shall appear parallel.			
	4.2a.5	**BACKING SPECIES** shall be manufacturer's option.			
	4.2a.6	**FIGURE** is not a function of a species grade, and any special requirements shall have been so specified.			
	4.2a.7	**NATURAL** allows unlimited heartwood and/or sapwood within a face.			
	4.2a.8	**GRAIN** direction shall be at the option of the manufacturer unless otherwise specified in the contract documents or required within Sections 6 - 12.			
	4.2a.9	**ASH, BIRCH**, and **MAPLE** permit both sapwood and heartwood.			
	4.2a.10	**SELECT RED MAPLE** is not an available species selection.			
	4.2a.11	**RIFT GRAIN OAK** shall allow up to twenty-five percent (25%) of the exposed surface area to contain medullary ray flake.			
	4.2a.11.1	Medullary ray flake to be a maximum of 3/32" (2.4 mm) in width.			
	4.2a.12	For **PRESELECTED FLITCHES,** the following characteristics are not applicable.			
	4.2a.12.1	Owner's representative shall determine, in advance of bid, which characteristics and/or defects are acceptable or are to be eliminated for the total face appearance.			
	4.2a.12.1.1	Yield and leaf width are directly related to this determination.			
	4.2a.13	**VENEER FACE GRADE REQUIREMENT** (based on the following HPVA definitions and characteristics)			
	4.2a.13.1	**OPAQUE FINISH**			
	4.2a.13.1.1	Grade D	●		
	4.2a.13.1.2	Grade C		●	
	4.2a.13.1.3	Grade B			●
	4.2a.13.2	**TRANSPARENT FINISH**			
	4.2a.13.2.1	Grade B	●		
	4.2a.13.2.2	Grade A		●	
	4.2a.13.2.3	Grade AA			●

PRODUCT

SHEET PRODUCT RULES (continued)

These rules are not intended to create a face grade; they are intended only to establish the acceptable requirements and/or characteristics after the architectural woodwork is completed or installed.

<table>
<tr><th colspan="4">DESCRIPTION</th><th>E C P</th></tr>
<tr><td rowspan="5">4.2a
HARDWOOD VENEER</td><td colspan="4">MATERIAL - HARDWOOD VENEER (continued)</td></tr>
<tr><td>4.2a.14</td><td colspan="3">VENEER FACE GRADE DESCRIPTIONS - Range from AA through D, primarily based on appearance features with fewer natural characteristics allowed in higher grades.</td></tr>
<tr><td rowspan="3">DESCRIPTIONS</td><td>4.2a.14.1</td><td colspan="2">GRADE AA - Veneer shall be smooth, tight-cut, and full-length. When the face consists of more than one veneer component or piece, the edges shall appear parallel and be edge-matched. All components of a book- or slip-matched face shall be from the same flitch. Rotary-cut faces may be whole-piece or multi-piece with edge joints tight and no sharp color contrast at the joints. Species specified for natural color will allow color contrasts but shall be book-matched or conform to the type of matching as specified. The components of plain-sliced (flat-cut) and multi-piece rotary faces will be book-matched unless otherwise specified with a running, balanced, or center-matched arrangement. Unless otherwise specified, components in plain-sliced faces will have a matching arrangement selected by themanufacturer. Plain-sliced faces will consist of two or more components with no component less than 6" (152 mm) wide except for outside components, which may be less than 6" (152 mm) to allow for certain types of matching or panel edge loss. No plain-sliced components will have a split-heart. No full quartered-cut is allowed in plain-sliced faces. The width of any single component in quarter-cut, rift-cut, or comb-grain faces shall not be less than 3" (76 mm) except for outside components, which may be less than 3" (76 mm) to allow for certain types of matching or panel edge trim loss.</td></tr>
<tr><td>4.2a.14.2</td><td colspan="2">GRADE A - Veneer shall be smooth, tight-cut, and full-length. When the face consists of more than one veneer component or piece, the edges shall appear parallel and be edge-matched. All components of a book- or slip-matched face shall be from the same flitch. Rotary-cut faces may be whole-piece or multi-piece with edge joints tight; however, no sharp color contrasts are permitted at the joints, and the face will provide a good general appearance. Species specified for natural color will allow color contrasts, but shall be book-matched or conform to the type of matching as specified. The components of plain-sliced (flat-cut) and multi-piece rotary faces will be book-matched, unless otherwise specified with a running, balanced, or center-matched arrangement. Unless otherwise specified, components in plain-sliced faces will have a matching arrangement selected by the manufacturer. Plain-sliced faces will consist of two or more components with no component less than 5" (127 mm) wide except for outside components, which may be less than 5" (127 mm) to allow for certain types of matching or panel edge trim loss. Split-heart is permitted if manufactured cathedral is achieved. No full quarter-cut is allowed in plain-sliced faces. The width of any single component in quarter-cut, rift-cut, or comb-grain faces shall not be less than 3" (76 mm) except for outside components, which may be less than 3" (76 mm) to allow for certain types of matching or panel edge trim loss. In some species, sapwood is permitted; however, in other species, it may be permitted by agreement between buyer and seller.</td></tr>
<tr><td>4.2a.14.3</td><td colspan="2">GRADE B - Veneer shall be smooth, tight-cut, and full-length as described for the various species. All components of a book- or slip-matched face shall be from the same flitch. Slip- or book-matched veneers are available if specified by the buyer. If not specified, multi-piece faces will be pleasingly matched. Sharp color contrasts at the joints are not permitted. Species specified for natural color will allow color contrasts, but shall be book-matched or conform to the type of matching as specified. Plain-sliced faces will consist of two or more components with no component less than 4" (102 mm) wide to allow for certain types of matching or panel edge trim loss. Some full quarter-cut is permitted in plain-sliced faces. For some species, unlimited sapwood is allowed, and in other species, a percentage of sapwood is allowed.</td></tr>
</table>

PRODUCT

SHEET PRODUCT RULES (continued)

These rules are not intended to create a face grade; they are intended only to establish the acceptable requirements and/ or characteristics after the architectural woodwork is completed or installed.

			DESCRIPTION	E C P
4.2a HARDWOOD VENEER	**MATERIAL - HARDWOOD VENEER** (continued)			
	4.2a.14 DESCRIPTIONS	**VENEER FACE GRADE DESCRIPTIONS** (continued)		
		4.2a.14.4	**GRADE C -** Permits unlimited color streaks and spots and color variation. An unlimited number of small burls and pin knots are allowed with no restrictions on the size of the dark pin knot centers, as long as the diameter of pin knots does not exceed 1/4" (6.4 mm) in diameter. The size of sound and repaired knotholes and similar shaped openings cannot exceed 1/2" (9.5 mm) in diameter, with a specified number allowed based on individual species. Faces shall provide a sound face, free of open defects, with only minimal areas of rough grain.	
		4.2a.14.5	**GRADE D -** Permits unlimited color streaks and spots and color variation. An unlimited number of small burls and pin knots are permitted with no restrictions on the size of dark pin knot centers, as long as the diameter of pin knots does not exceed 1/4" (6.4 mm) in diameter. The size of repaired and sound knotholes and similar shaped openings cannot exceed 3/4" (19 mm) (repaired) and 1" (25.4 mm) (sound) diameters, with a specified number based on individual species. Faces shall provide a sound face, free of open defects. The size or percentage of rough grain on the panel surface depends on the species.	
		4.2a.14.6	**OTHER SPECIES -** may be covered by these standards, provided the buyer and seller agree to a species grouping as a basis for the evaluation and grade of the unlisted species. It is obviously not workable to try to develop and include the individual grade requirements for every known species.	
		4.2a.14.7	**SPECIALTY GRADES -** Applicable to veneer in which the features of greatest significance are unusual characteristics that are not covered within grades AA-D. Characteristics shall be as agreed upon between buyer and seller. Species such as Wormy Chestnut, Bird's Eye Maple, and English Brown Oak, which have unusual decorative features, are considered a Speciality Grade.	
		4.2a.14.8	**NOTE** - Variance from these standards might invalidate certain criteria and tests.	
			4.2a.14.8.1 — Example - Strong color contrasts will occur when rotary natural Birch leaves are slip-matched.	
		4.2a.14.9	**PLAIN-SLICED CATHEDRAL FIGURE,** when:	
			4.2a.14.9.1 — Vertically oriented, shall have the crowns pointing up and shall run in the same direction for the entire project.	
			4.2a.14.9.2 — Horizontally oriented, shall have the crowns facing a consistent relative orientation for the entire project.	
	4.2a.15 DEFINITIONS	**TERMINOLOGY DEFINITIONS** for use with following HPVA Characteristic charts:		
		4.2a.15.1	**BARK POCKET:** Bark around which normal wood has grown.	
		4.2a.15.2	**BLENDING**: Color change that is detectable at a distance of 6 - 8 feet (1800 - 2438 mm), but does not distract from the overall appearance of the panel.	
		4.2a.15.3	**BRASHNESS**: Condition of wood characterized by low resistance to shock and by abrupt failure across the grain without splintering.	
		4.2a.15.4	**BURL, BLENDING**: A swirl, twist, or distortion in the grain of the wood that usually occurs near a knot or crotch but does not contain a knot and does not contain abrupt color variation. A blending burl is detectable at 6 - 8 feet (1800 - 2438 mm) as a swirl or a roundel.	
		4.2a.15.5	**BURL, CONSPICUOUS**: A swirl, twist, or distortion in the grain of the wood that usually occurs near a knot or crotch. A conspicuous burl is associated with abrupt color variation and/ or a cluster of small dark piths caused by a cluster of adventitious buds.	
		4.2a.15.6	**COMB GRAIN**: A quality of rift-cut veneer with exceptionally straight grain and closely spaced growth increments resembling the appearance of long strands of combed hair.	

4

PRODUCT

SHEET PRODUCT RULES (continued)

These rules are not intended to create a face grade; they are intended only to establish the acceptable requirements and/or characteristics after the architectural woodwork is completed or installed.

				DESCRIPTION E C P
4.2a HARDWOOD VENEER	**MATERIAL - HARDWOOD VENEER** (continued)			
	4.2a.15 DEFINITIONS	**TERMINOLOGY DEFINITIONS** (continued)		
		4.2a.15.7	**CROSS BAR**: Irregularity of grain resembling a dip in the grain running at right angles, or nearly so, to the length of the veneer.	
		4.2a.15.8	**FLECK, RAY**: Portion of a ray as it appears on the quartered or rift-cut surface. Fleck is often a dominant appearance feature in Oak.	
		4.2a.15.9	**GUM POCKETS**: Well-defined openings between rings of annual growth, containing gum or evidence of prior gum accumulations.	
		4.2a.15.10	**GUM SPOTS AND STREAKS**: Gum or resinous material or color spots and streaks caused by prior resin accumulations sometimes found on panel surfaces.	
		4.2a.15.11	**HAIRLINE SPLITS**: A thin, perceptible separation of wood fibers running parallel to the grain.	
		4.2a.15.12	**HEARTWOOD**: The nonactive or dormant center of a tree generally distinguishable from the outer portion (sapwood) by its darker color.	
		4.2a.15.13	**KNOT:** Cross-section of a tree branch or limb with grain usually running at right angles to that of the piece of wood in which it occurs.	
		4.2a.15.14	**KNOT, CONSPICUOUS PIN**: Sound knots 1/4" (6.4 mm) or less in diameter containing dark centers.	
		4.2a.15.15	**REPAIRS**: A patch, shim, or filler material inserted and/or glued into veneer or a panel to achieve a sound surface.	
		4.2a.15.16	**RIFT-CUT**: A straight grain appearance achieved through the process of cutting at a slight angle to the radial on the half-round stay log or through the use of veneer cut in any fashion that produces a straight grain with minimal fleck.	
		4.2a.15.17	**ROUGH CUT**: Irregularly shaped areas of generally uneven corrugation on the surface of veneer, differing from the surrounding smooth veneer and occurring as the veneer is cut by the lathe or slicer.	
		4.2a.15.18	**RUPTURED GRAIN**: A break or breaks in the grain or between springwood and summerwood caused or aggravated by excessive pressure on the wood by seasoning, manufacturing, or natural process. Grain appears as a single or series of distinct separations in the wood, such as when springwood is crushed, leaving the summerwood to separate in one or more growth increments.	
		4.2a.15.19	**SAPWOOD**: The living wood of lighter color occurring in the outer portion of a tree; sometimes referred to as sap.	
		4.2a.15.20	**SLIGHT**: Visible on observation, but does not interfere with the overall aesthetic appearance with consideration of the applicable grade of the panel face.	
		4.2a.15.21	**SPLITS**: A separation of wood fiber running parallel to the grain.	
		4.2a.15.22	**STREAKS, MINERAL**: Natural discoloration of the wood substance.	
		4.2a.15.23	**VINE MARKS**: Bands of irregular grain running across or diagonally to the grain, which are caused by the growth of climbing vines around the tree.	
		4.2a.15.24	**WORM HOLES OR TRACKS**: Holes or lines resulting from infestation of worms.	
	4.2a.16	The following **SUMMARY CHARTS** of **ALLOWABLE WOOD VENEER FACE GRADE CHARACTERISTICS** are printed with permission from the Hardwood Plywood Veneer Association and their ANSI/HPVA HP1 standards (latest edition).		
		4.2a.16.1	Allowable characteristic tables for **STAND-ALONE DOOR FACES** are in Section 9.	

PRODUCT

SHEET PRODUCT RULES (continued)

These rules are not intended to create a face grade; they are intended only to establish the acceptable requirements and/or characteristics after the architectural woodwork is completed or installed.

4.2a HARDWOOD VENEER

MATERIAL - HARDWOOD VENEER (continued)

4.2a.16 CHARACTERISTICS

SUMMARY CHARTS (continued)

4.2a.16.2 - ASH, BEECH[a], BIRCH, MAPLE, and POPLAR
(ANSI/HPVA - HP1-latest edition)

Cut	Plain-Sliced (Flat Cut), Quarter-Cut, Rotary Cut										
Grade Description	**AA**			**A**			**B**			**C**	**D**
Color and Matching	Sap	Heart	Nat.	Sap	Heart	Nat.	Sap	Heart	Nat.		
Sapwood	Yes	No	Yes	Yes	No	Yes	Yes	No	Yes	Yes	Yes
Heartwood	No	Yes	Yes	No	Yes	Yes	No	Yes	Yes	Yes	Yes
Color Streaks or Spots	Slight			Slight	Yes		Yes			Yes	Yes
Color Variation	Slight	Yes		Slight	Yes		Yes			Yes	Yes
Sharp Color Contrast at Joints	Yes if Slip, Plank, or Random matched			Yes if Slip, Plank, or Random matched			Yes if Slip, Plank, or Random matched			Yes	Yes
Type of Matching Book-Matched Slip-Matched Pleasing-Matched	 Yes Specify --			 Yes Specify --			 Specify Specify Yes			 -- -- --	 -- -- --
Nominal Minimum Width of Face Components[b] — Plain-Sliced / Quarter / Rotary	6" (152 mm) 3" (76 mm) 6" (152 m)			5" (127 mm 3" (76 mm) 5" (127 mm)			3" (76 mm) 3" (76 mm) 4" (102 mm)			No Limit	
Natural Characteristics											
Small Conspicuous Burls & Pin Knots Combined Avg. Number	1 per 5 sq ft (2 per 1 m²) 6 per 32 sq ft			1 per 3 sq ft (4 per 1 m²) 10 per 32 sq ft			1 per 2 sq ft (6 per 1 m²) 16 per 32 sq ft			No Limit	No Limit
Conspicuous Burls - Max. Size	1/4" (6.4 mm)			3/8" (9.5 mm)			1/2" (12.7 mm)			No Limit	No Limit
Conspicuous Pin Knots Avg. Number Max. Size: Dark Part Total	No			1 per 8 sq ft (4 per 3 m²) 4 per 32 sq ft 1/8" (3.2 mm) 1/4" (6.4 mm)			1 per 4 sq ft (3 per 1 m²) 8 per 32 sq ft 1/8" (3.2 mm) 1/4" (6.4 mm)			No Limit	No Limit
Scattered, Sound and Repaired Knots-Combined Avg. Number Max. Size - Sound Max. Size - Repaired Avg. No. - Repaired	No			No			1 per 8 sq ft (4 per 3 m²) 4 per 32 sq ft 3/8" (9.5 mm) 1/8" (3.2 mm) 1 per 8 sq ft (4 per 3 m²)			1 per 4 sq ft (3 per 1 m²) 8 per 32 sq ft 1/2" (12.7 mm) 1/2" (12.7 mm) 1 per 8 sq ft (4 per 3 m²)	1 per 3 sq ft (4 per 1 m²) 10 per 32 sq ft 1" (25.4 mm) 3/4" (19 mm) 1 per 6 sq ft (2 per 1 m²)
Mineral Streaks	No; Maple, Slight			Slight			Slight			Yes	Yes
Bark Pockets	No			No			Few to 1/8" x 1" (3.2 mm x 25.4 mm)			Few to 1/4" x 2" (6.4 mm x 50.8 mm)	1/4" x 2" (6.4 mm x 50.8 mm)
Worm Tracks	Slight			Slight			Slight; Ash, Yes			Yes	Yes
Vine Marks	Slight			Slight			Slight			Yes	Yes
Cross Bars	Slight			Slight			Yes			Yes	Yes
Manufacturing Characteristics											
Rough Cut/Ruptured Grain	No			No			Slight			Two 8" (203 mm) dia. areas or equivalent	5% of panel
Blended Repaired Tapering Hairline Splits	Two 1/32" x 3" (0.8 mm x 76 mm) on panel ends only			Two 1/16" x 6" (1.6 mm x 152 mm)			Four 1/8" x 8" (3.2 mm x 203 mm)			Four 3/16" x 8" (4.8 mm x 203 mm)	Six 1/4" x 10" (6.4 mm x 203 mm)
Repairs	Very small blending			Small blending			Blending			Yes	Yes
Special Characteristics											
Quartered	1" in 12" (25.4 mm in 305 mm) maximum grain slope; 2-1/2" in 12" (63.5 mm in 305 mm) maximum grain sweep										

Open splits, open joints, open bark pockets, or doze not allowed in above grades.

[a] American or European

[b] Outside components will be different size to allow for edge trim loss and certain types of matching.

4

PRODUCT

SHEET PRODUCT RULES (continued)

These rules are not intended to create a face grade; they are intended only to establish the acceptable requirements and/or characteristics after the architectural woodwork is completed or installed.

4.2a HARDWOOD VENEER

MATERIAL - HARDWOOD VENEER (continued)

4.2a.16 CHARACTERISTICS

SUMMARY CHARTS (continued)

4.2a.16.3 - MAHOGANY (African or Honduras), ANIGRE, MAKORE, and SAPELE
(ANSI/HPVA - HP1-latest edition)

Cut	Plain-Sliced (Flat Cut), Quarter-Cut, Rotary Cut				
Grade Description	**AA**	**A**	**B**	**C**	**D**
Color and Matching					
Sapwood	No	No	No	Yes	Yes
Heartwood	Yes	Yes	Yes	Yes	Yes
Color Streaks or Spots	Slight	Slight	Occasional	Yes	Yes
Color Variation	Slight	Slight	Moderate	Yes	Yes
Sharp Color Contrast at Joints	Yes if Slip, Plank, or Random matched	Yes if Slip, Plank, or Random matched	Yes if Slip, Plank, or Random matched	Yes	Yes
Type of Matching Book-Matched Slip-Matched Pleasing-Matched	 Yes Specify --	 Yes Specify --	 Specify Specify Yes	 -- -- --	 -- -- --
Nominal Minimum Width of Face Components [a] Plain-S. / Quarter / Rotary	6" (152 mm) 3" (76 mm) 6" (152 m)	5" (127 mm 3" (76 mm) 5" (127 mm)	3" (76 mm) 3" (76 mm) 4" (102 mm)	No Limit	No Limit
Natural Characteristics					
Small Conspicuous Burls & Pin Knots Combined Avg. Number	1 per 5 sq ft (2 per 1 m^2) 6 per 32 sq ft	1 per 3 sq ft (4 per 1 m^2) 10 per 32 sq ft	1 per 2 sq ft (6 per 1 m^2) 16 per 32 sq ft	No Limit	No Limit
Conspicuous Burls - Max. Size	1/4" (6.4 mm)	3/8" (9.5 mm)	1/2" (12.7 mm)	No Limit	No Limit
Conspicuous Pin Knots Avg. Number Max. Size: Dark Part Total	No	1 per 8 sq ft (4 per 3 m^2) 4 per 32 sq ft 1/8" (3.2 mm) 1/4" (6.4 mm)	1 per 4 sq ft (3 per 1 m^2) 8 per 32 sq ft 1/8" (3.2 mm) 1/4" (6.4 mm)	No Limit	No Limit
Scattered Sound and Repaired Knots-Combined Avg. Number Max. Size - Sound Max. Size - Repaired Avg. No. - Repaired	No	No	1 per 8 sq ft (4 per 3 m^2) 4 per 32 sq ft 3/8" (9.5 mm) 1/8" (3.2 mm) 1 per 8 sq ft (4 per 3 m^2)	1 per 4 sq ft (3 per 1 m^2) 8 per 32 sq ft 1/2" (12.7 mm) 1/2" (12.7 mm) 1 per 8 sq ft (4 per 3 m^2)	1 per 3 sq ft (4 per 1 m^2) 10 per 32 sq ft 1" (25.4 mm) 3/4" (19 mm) 1 per 6 sq ft (2 per 1 m^2)
Mineral Streaks	No	Slight	Slight	Yes	Yes
Bark Pockets	No	No	Few to 1/8" x 1" (3.2 mm x 25.4 mm)	Few to 1/4" x 2" (6.4 mm x 50.8 mm)	1/4" x 2" (6.4 mm x 50.8 mm)
Worm Tracks	No	No	Slight	Few	Yes
Vine Marks	Slight	Slight	Yes	Yes	Yes
Cross Bars	Occasional	Occasional	Yes	Yes	Yes
Manufacturing Characteristics					
Rough Cut/Ruptured Grain	No	No	Slight	Slight	Two 8" dia. areas or equivalent
Blended Repaired Tapering Hairline Splits	Two 1/32" x 3" on (0.8 mm x 76 mm) panel ends only	Two 1/16" x 6" (1.6 mm x 152 mm)	Four 1/8" x 8" (3.2 mm x 203 mm)	Four 3/16" x 8" (4.8 mm x 203 mm)	Six 1/4" x 10" (6.4 mm x 203 mm)
Repairs	Very Small Blending	Small Blending	Blending	Yes	Yes
Special Characteristics					
Unfilled Worm Holes	No	No	No	1/16" (1.6 mm) max. dia.	1/16" (1.6 mm) max. dia.
Quartered	1" in 12" (25.4 mm in 305 mm) maximum grain slope; 2-1/2" in 12" (63.5 mm in 305 mm) maximum grain sweep				

Open splits, open joints, open bark pockets, or doze not allowed in above grades.
[a] Outside components will be different size to allow for edge trim loss and certain types of matching.

PRODUCT

SHEET PRODUCT RULES (continued)

These rules are not intended to create a face grade; they are intended only to establish the acceptable requirements and/or characteristics after the architectural woodwork is completed or installed.

4.2a HARDWOOD VENEER

MATERIAL - HARDWOOD VENEER PANELS (continued)

4.2a.16 CHARACTERISTICS

SUMMARY CHARTS (continued)

4.2a.16.4 - RED and WHITE OAK (ANSI/HPVA - HP1-latest edition)

Cut	Plain-Sliced (Flat Cut), Quarter-Cut, Rotary Cut							
Grade Description	AA		A		B		C	D
	Red	White	Red	White	Red	White		
Color and Matching								
Sapwood	No		5% [a]	Yes [a]	10-20% [b]	Yes	Yes	Yes
Heartwood	Yes		Yes		Yes		Yes	Yes
Color Streaks or Spots	Yes		Yes		Yes		Yes	Yes
Color Variation	Slight		Slight		Yes		Yes	Yes
Sharp Color Contrast at Joints	Yes if Slip, Plank, or Random matched		Yes if Slip, Plank, or Random matched		Yes if Slip, Plank, or Random matched		No	Yes
Type of Matching Book-Matched Slip-Matched Pleasing-Matched	 Yes Specify --		 Yes Specify --		 Specify Specify Yes		 -- -- --	 -- -- --
Nominal Minimum Width of Face Components [c]: Plain-S. Quarter Rotary	6" (152 mm) 3" (76 mm) 6" (152 mm)		5" (127 mm) 3" (76 mm) 5" (127 mm)		3" (76 mm) 3" (76 mm) 4" (102 mm)		No Limit	No Limit
Natural Characteristics								
Small Conspicuous Burls & Pin Knots Combined Avg. Number	1 per 4 sq ft (3 per 1 m^2) 6 per 32 sq ft		1 per 2-2/3 sq ft (4 per 1 m^2) 12 per 32 sq ft		1 per 1-1/3 sq ft (4 per 1 m^2) 24 per 32 sq ft		No Limit	No Limit
Conspicuous Burls - Max. Size	1/4" (6.4 mm)		3/8" (9.5 mm)		1/2" 12.7 mm)		No Limit	No Limit
Conspicuous Pin Knots- Avg. Number Max. Size: Dark Part Total	No		1 per 3 sq ft (4 per 1 m^2) 10 per 32 sq ft 1/8" (3.2 mm) 1/4" (6.4 mm)		1 per 2 sq ft (6 per 1 m^2) 16 per 32 sq ft 1/8" (3.2 mm) 1/4" (6.4 mm)		No Limit	No Limit
Scattered Sound and Repaired Knots - Combined Avg. Number Max. Size - Sound Max. Size - Repaired Avg. No. - Repaired	No		No		1 per 8 sq ft (4 per 3 m^2) 4 per 32 sq ft 3/8" (9.5 mm) 1/8" (3.2 mm) 1 per 8 sq ft (4 per 3 m^2)		1 per 4 sq ft (3 per 1 m^2) 8 per 32 sq ft 1/2" (12.7 mm) 1/2" (12.7 mm) 1 per 8 sq ft (4 per 3 m^2)	1 per 3 sq ft (4 per 1 m^2) 10 per 32 sq ft 1" (25.4 mm) 3/4" (19 mm) 1 per 6 sq ft (2 per 1 m^2)
Mineral Streaks	No		Slight, Blending		Few to 12" (305 mm)		Yes	Yes
Bark Pockets	No		No		Few to 1/8" x 1" (3.2 mm x 25.4 mm)		Few to 1/4" x 2" (4.8 mm x 50.8 mm)	1/4" x 2" (4.8 mm x 50.8 mm)
Worm Tracks	No		No		Slight		Few	Yes
Vine Marks	No		Slight		Yes		Yes	Yes
Cross Bars	Slight		Slight		Yes		Yes	Yes
Manufacturing Characteristics								
Rough Cut/Ruptured Grain	No		No		Slight		Slight	Two 8" (203 mm) dia. areas or equivalent
Blended Repaired Tapering Hairline Splits	Two 1/32" x 3" on (0.8 mm x 76 mm) panel ends only		Two 1/16" x 6" (1.6 mm x 152 mm)		Four 1/8" x 8" (3.2 mm x 203 mm)		Four 3/16" x 8" (4.8 mm x 203 mm)	Six 1/4" x 10" (6.4 mm x 203 mm)
Repairs	Very Small Blending		Small Blending		Blending		Yes	Yes
Special Characteristics								
Ray Fleck [d]	Slight, Blending		Slight, Blending		Slight, Blending		Yes	Yes
Rift and Comb Grain	Rift permits 1" in 12" (25.4 mm in 305 mm) max. grain slope, 2-1/2" in 12" 63.5 mm in 305 mm) max. grain sweep, fleck not to exceed 3/8" (9.5 mm) in width. Comb permits 1/2" in 12" (1`2.7 mm in 305 mm) max. grain slope, 1/2" in 12" (1`2.7 mm in 305 mm) max. grain sweep, fleck not to exceed 3/32" (2.4 mm) in width.							

Unfilled worm holes, open splits, open joints, open bark pockets, or doze not allowed in above grades.

[a] Sap allowed in rotary only unless otherwise specified. [b] 10% sap allowed in rift, comb, and plain-sliced; 20% sap allowed in rotary.

[c] Outside components will be different size to allow for edge trim loss and certain types of matching.

[d] Unless otherwise specified, quartered permits unlimited fleck.

4

PRODUCT

SHEET PRODUCT RULES (continued)

These rules are not intended to create a face grade; they are intended only to establish the acceptable requirements and/ or characteristics after the architectural woodwork is completed or installed.

4.2a HARDWOOD VENEER

MATERIAL - HARDWOOD VENEER PANELS (continued)

4.2a.16 CHARACTERISTICS

SUMMARY CHARTS (continued)

4.2a.16.5 - PECAN and HICKORY (ANSI/HPVA - HP1-latest edition)

Cut	Plain-Sliced (Flat Cut), Quarter-Cut, Rotary Cut				
Grade Description	AA	A	B	C	D
Color and Matching					
Sapwood	Yes	Yes	Yes	Yes	Yes
Heartwood	Yes	Yes	Yes	Yes	Yes
Color Streaks or Spots	Yes	Yes	Yes	Yes	Yes
Color Variation	Yes	Yes	Yes	Yes	Yes
Sharp Color Contrast at Joints	Yes if Slip, Plank, or Random matched	Yes if Slip, Plank, or Random matched	Yes if Slip, Plank, or Random matched	Yes	Yes
Type of Matching Book-Matched Slip-Matched Pleasing-Matched	 Yes Specify --	 Yes Specify --	 Specify Specify Yes	 -- -- --	 -- -- --
Nominal Minimum Width of Face Components [a] Plain-S. Quarter Rotary	 6" (152 mm) 3" (76 mm) 6" (152 mm)	 5" (127 mm) 3" (76 mm) 5" (127 mm)	 3" (76 mm) 3" (76 mm) 4" (102 mm)	No Limit	No Limit
Natural Characteristics					
Small Conspicuous Burls & Pin Knots-Combined Avg. Number	1 per 1 sq ft (11 per 1 m^2) 32 per 32 sq ft	2 per 1 sq ft (22 per 1 m^2) 64 per 32 sq ft	No Limit	No Limit	No Limit
Conspicuous Burls - Max. Size	1/4" (6.4 mm)	3/8" (9.5 mm)	1/2" (12.7 mm)	No Limit	No Limit
Conspicuous Pin Knots [b] Avg. Number Max. Size: Dark Part Total	1 per 2 sq ft (6 per 1 m^2) 16 per 32 sq ft 1/8" (3.2 mm) 1/4" (6.4 mm)	2 per 1 sq ft (22 per 1 m^2) 64 per 32 sq ft 1/8" (3.2 mm) 1/4" (6.4 mm)"	No Limit No Limit 1/8" (3.2 mm) 1/4" (6.4 mm)"	No Limit	No Limit
Scattered Sound and Repaired Knots-Combined Avg. Number Max. Size - Sound Max. Size - Repaired Avg. No. - Repaired	No	No	1 per 8 sq ft (4 per 3 m^2) 4 per 32 sq ft 3/8" (9.5 mm) 1/8" (3.2 mm) 1 per 8 sq ft (4 per 3 m^2)	1 per 3 sq ft (3 per 1 m^2) 10 per 32 sq ft 1/2" (12.7 mm) 1/2" (12.7 mm) 1 per 8 sq ft (4 per 3 m^2)	1 per 3 sq ft (4 per 1 m^2) 10 per 32 sq ft 1" (25.4 mm) 3/4" (19 mm) 1 per 6 sq ft (2 per 1 m^2)
Mineral Streaks	Slight	Slight	Yes	Yes	Yes
Bark Pockets	No	Small, Occasional	Few to 1/4" x 2" (4.8 mm x 50.8 mm)	Few to 3/8" x 4" (9.5 mm x 102 mm)	To 1/2" wide (12.7 mm)
Worm Tracks	No	Slight	Few	Few	Yes
Vine Marks	Slight	Occasional	Yes	Yes	Yes
Cross Bars	Slight	Occasional	Yes	Yes	Yes
Manufacturing Characteristics					
Rough Cut/Ruptured Grain	No	No	Slight	Two 8" (203 mm) dia. areas or equivalent	5% of panel
Blended Repaired Tapering Hairline Splits	Two 1/32" x 3" on (0.8 mm x 76 mm) panel ends only	Two 1/16" x 6" (1.6 mm x 152 mm)	Four 1/8" x 8" (3.2 mm x 203 mm)	Four 3/16" x 8" (4.8 mm x 203 mm)	Six 1/4" x 10" (6.4 mm x 203 mm)
Repairs	Very Small Blending	Small Blending	Blending	Yes	Yes
Special Characteristics					
Bird Peck [c]	No	Slight	Yes	Yes	Yes
Knife Marks	Knife marks might occur in these dense species.				
Quartered	1" in 12" (25.4 mm in 305 mm) maximum grain slope; 2-1/2" in 12" (63.5 mm in 305 mm) maximum grain sweep				

Unfilled worm holes, open splits, open joints, open bark pockets, or doze are not allowed in above grades.
[a] Outside components will be a different size to allow for edge trim loss and certain types of matching.
[b] For Pecan and Hickory, conspicuous pin knots mean sound knots 1/4" (6.4 mm) or less in diameter with dark centers larger than 1/16" (1.6 mm). Blending pin knots are sound knots1/4" (6.4 mm) or less in diameter with dark centers 1/16" (1.6 mm) or less and are allowed in all Grades.
[c] To achieve a more rustic appearance, bird peck shall be specified.

PRODUCT

SHEET PRODUCT RULES (continued)

These rules are not intended to create a face grade; they are intended only to establish the acceptable requirements and/or characteristics after the architectural woodwork is completed or installed.

4.2a HARDWOOD VENEER

MATERIAL - HARDWOOD VENEER (continued)

4.2a.16 CHARACTERISTICS

SUMMARY CHARTS (continued)

4.2a.16.6 - WALNUT and CHERRY (ANSI/HPVA - HP1-latest edition)

Cut	Plain-Sliced (Flat Cut), Quarter-Cut, Rotary Cut				
Grade Description	**AA**	**A**	**B**	**C**	**D**
Color and Matching					
Sapwood [a]	No	No [a]	No [a]	Yes	Yes
Heartwood	Yes	Yes	Yes	Yes	Yes
Color Streaks or Spots	Slight	Slight	Yes	Yes	Yes
Color Variation	Slight	Slight	Yes	Yes	Yes
Sharp Color Contrast at Joints	Yes if Slip, Plank, or Random Match	Yes if Slip, Plank, or Random Match	Yes if Slip, Plank, or Random Match	Yes	Yes
Type of Matching Book-Matched Slip-Matched Pleasing-Matched	 Yes Specify --	 Yes Specify --	 Specify Specify Yes	 -- -- --	 -- -- --
Nominal Minimum Width of Face Components [b] Plain-S. / Quarter / Rotary	6" (152 mm) 3" (76 mm) 6" (152 mm)	5" (127 mm) 3" (76 mm) 5" (127 mm)	3" (76 mm) 3" (76 mm) 4" (102 mm)	No Limit	No Limit
Natural Characteristics					
Small Conspicuous Burls & Pin Knots- Combined Avg. Number	1 per 4 sq ft (3 per 1 m^2) 8 per 32 sq ft	1 per 1-1/3 sq ft (8 per 1 m^2) 24 per 32 sq ft	2 per 1 sq ft (22 per 1 m^2) 64 per 32 sq ft	No Limit	No Limit
Conspicuous Burls - Max. Size	1/4" (6.4 mm)	3/8" (9.5 mm)	1/2" (12.7 mm)	No Limit	No Limit
Conspicuous Pin Knots [c] Avg. Number Max. Size: Dark Part Total	1 per 5 sq ft (3 per 1 m^2) 6 per 32 sq ft 1/8" (3.2 mm) 1/4" (6.4 mm)	1 per 2 sq ft (6 per 1 m^2) 16 per 32 sq ft 1/8" (3.2 mm) 1/4" (6.4 mm)	1 per 1 sq ft (11 per 1 m^2) 32 per 32 sq ft 1/8" (3.2 mm) 1/4" (6.4 mm)	No Limit	No Limit
Scattered Sound and Repaired Knots-Combined Avg. Number Max. Size - Sound Max. Size - Repaired Avg. No. - Repaired	No	No	1 per 8 sq ft (4 per 3 m^2) 4 per 32 sq ft 3/8" (9.5 mm) 1/8" (3.2 mm) 1 per 8 sq ft (4 per 3 m^2)	1 per 4 sq ft (3 per 1 m^2) 8 per 32 sq ft 1/2" (12.7 mm) 1/2" (12.7 mm) 1 per 8 sq ft (4 per 3 m^2)	1 per 3 sq ft (4 per 1 m^2) 10 per 32 sq ft 1" (25.4 mm) 3/4" (19 mm) 1 per 6 sq ft (2 per 1 m^2)
Mineral Streaks	Slight	Slight	Yes	Yes	Yes
Bark Pockets	No	No	Few to 1/8" x 1" (3.2 mm x 25.4 mm)	Few to 1/4" x 2" (6.4 mm x 50.8 mm)	1/4" x 2" (6.4 mm x 50.8 mm)
Worm Tracks	No	No	Slight	Few	Yes
Vine Marks	Slight	Occasional	Yes	Yes	Yes
Cross Bars	Slight	Occasional	Yes	Yes	Yes
Manufacturing Characteristics					
Rough Cut/Ruptured Grain	No	No	Slight	Slight	Two 8" (203 mm) dia. areas or equivalent
Blended Repaired Tapering Hairline Splits	Two 1/32" x 3" (0.8 mm x 76 mm) on panel ends only	Two 1/16" x 6" (1.6 mm x 152 mm)	Four 1/8" x 8" (3.2 mm x 203 mm)	Four 3/16" x 8" (4.8 mm x 203 mm)	Six 1/4" x 10" (6.4 mm x 254 mm)
Repairs	Very Small Blending	Small Blending	Blending	Yes	Yes
Special Characteristics					
Gum Spots and Streaks, Cherry only	Occasional Spots	Occasional Spots	Occasional Spots and Streaks		
Quartered	1" in 12" (25.4 mm in 305 mm) maximum grain slope; 2-1/2" in 12" (63.5 mm in 305 mm) maximum grain sweep				

Unfilled worm holes, open splits, open joints, open bark pockets, or doze are not allowed in above grades.

[a] Sapwood is allowed in Grades A and B; however, the percentage shall be agreed upon between buyer and seller.

[b] Outside components will be a different size to allow for edge trim loss and certain types of matching.

[c] For Walnut and Cherry, conspicuous pin knots mean sound knots 1/4" (6.4 mm) or less in diameter with dark centers larger than 1/16" (1.6 mm). Blending pin knots are sound knots1/4" (6.4 mm) or less in diameter with dark centers 1/16" (1.6 mm) or less and are allowed in all Grades.

4

PRODUCT

SHEET PRODUCT RULES (continued)

These rules are not intended to create a face grade; they are intended only to establish the acceptable requirements and/or characteristics after the architectural woodwork is completed or installed.

	Item	DESCRIPTION	E	C	P
4.2b		**MATERIAL - SOFTWOOD VENEER**			
SOFTWOOD VENEER	4.2b.1	Applies only to the following species: Douglas Fir, Redwood, Western Red Cedar, and White Pine.			
	4.2b.2	Exterior use requires use of waterproof adhesive.			
	4.2b.3	Core shall be at option of manufacturer, within the provisions of these standards.			
	4.2b.4	Vertical Grain shall have a minimum average of five growth rings per inch.			
	4.2b.5	For transparent finish, boat, router, and/or sled patches shall be limited to 12 in any 4' x 8' (102 mm x 2438 mm) panel and proportionately reduced for smaller-size panels.		•	•
	4.2b.6 FACE GRADE	**FACE GRADE REQUIREMENTS** (based on the following Voluntary Product Standard - PS1 [latest edition] and ANSI/HPVA - HP-1 [latest edition] definitions and characteristics as indicated):			
	4.2b.6.1	**WESTERN RED CEDAR** and **WHITE PINE, rotary,** and **knotty-sliced** (ANSI/HPVA - HP-1 [latest edition])			
	4.2b.6.1.1	Grade **B**	•		
	4.2b.6.1.2	Grade **A**		•	•
	4.2b.6.2	**DOUGLAS FIR** and **REDWOOD, vertical grain-sliced** (ANSI/HPVA - HP-1 [latest edition[)			
	4.2b.6.2.1	Grade **A**			
	4.2b.6.3	**DOUGLAS FIR**, rotary sliced (Voluntarily Product Standard - PS1 [latest edition])			
	4.2b.6.3.1	**OPAQUE FINISH**			
	4.2b.6.3.1.1	Grade B	•		
	4.2b.6.3.1.2	Grade A		•	•
	4.2b.6.3.1.3	Medium- or High-Density Overlay may be substituted.			
	4.2b.6.3.2	**TRANSPARENT FINISH**			
	4.2b.6.3.2.1	Grade N			
⇓	**4.2b.7** ⇓	The following **SUMMARY CHARTS** of **ALLOWABLE WOOD VENEER FACE GRADE CHARACTERISTICS** are reprinted with permission from the Hardwood Plywood Veneer Association and their ANSI/HPVA HP-1 standards (latest edition).			

PRODUCT

SHEET PRODUCT RULES (continued)

These rules are not intended to create a face grade; they are intended only to establish the acceptable requirements and/ or characteristics after the architectural woodwork is completed or installed.

DESCRIPTION E C P

4.2b SOFTWOOD VENEER

MATERIAL - SOFTWOOD VENEER (continued)

4.2b.7 CHARACTERISTICS

The following **SUMMARY CHARTS** (continued)

4.2b.7.1 - WESTERN RED CEDAR, WHITE PINE, and VERTICAL GRAIN DOUGLAS FIR/REDWOOD (ANSI/HPVA - HP-1 [latest edition])

Species	Western Red Cedar		White Pine		Douglas Fir	Redwood
Cut	Plain-Sliced (Flat Cut), Quarter-Cut, Rotary Cut				Sliced Vertical Grain	
Grade Description	A	B	A	B	A	A
Color and Matching						
Sapwood	Yes				Limited - No Bright Sapwood	Yes
Heartwood [a]	Yes				Yes [a]	
Color Streaks or Spots	Slight	Yes	Slight	Yes	No	No
Color Variation	No	Slight	No	Yes	Slight	Slight
Stain, Blue or Brown	No	Slight	No	Slight	No	No
Type of Matching						
Book Match	Not Applicable				Yes - Matched for color and grain at the joints	
Random Match	Yes, for pleasing appearance				Not Applicable	
Slip Match	Not Applicable				Yes, for color	
End Match	Specify - Not readily available				Specify - Not readily available	
Natural Characteristics						
Burls	Yes				Small	
Pin Knots	Yes				No	Yes
Sound Knots, maximum size	2" (50.8 mm)		3-1/2" (89 mm)		No	
Spike Knots, maximum size	2" (50.8 mm)	3-1/2" (89 mm)	2" (50.8 mm)	3-1/2" (89 mm)	No	
Repaired Knot Holes, maximum size	3/4" (19 mm)	1-1/2" (38 mm)	3/4" (19 mm)	1-1/2" (38 mm)	No	
Pitch Streaks	Small				Small	No
Pitch Pockets	Few to 1/8" x 1" (3.2 mm x 25.4 mm)	Few to 1/8" x 2" (3.2 mm x 50.8 mm)	Few to 1/8" x 1" (3.2 mm x 25.4 mm)	Few to 1/8" x 2" (3.2 mm x 50.8 mm)	No	
Crow's Foot	Slight	Occasional	Slight	Yes	No	
Manufacturing Characteristics						
Rough Cut	No	Slight	No	Slight	No	
Blended, Repaired, Tapering, Hairline Splits	Yes				Yes	
Repairs	Blending				Blending	
Special Characteristics						
Cross Bar	Not Applicable				No	

Unfilled worm holes, open splits, open joints, or doze are not allowed in above Grades.
[a] Heartwood must have 6 or more annual rings per 1" (25.4 mm).

PRODUCT

SHEET PRODUCT RULES (continued)

These rules are not intended to create a face grade; they are intended only to establish the acceptable requirements and/ or characteristics after the architectural woodwork is completed or installed.

DESCRIPTION | E | C | P

4.2b SOFTWOOD VENEER

MATERIAL - SOFTWOOD VENEER (continued)

4.2b.7 CHARACTERISTICS

The following **SUMMARY CHARTS** (continued)

4.2b.7.2 - DOUGLAS FIR (PS-1 latest edition)

Species	Douglas Fir		
Cut	Rotary Cut		
Grade Description	**N**	**A**	**B**
Color and Matching			
Sapwood	Yes - 100%	Yes	Yes
Heartwood	Yes - 100%	Yes	Yes
Color Streaks or Spots	No	Yes	Yes
Color Variation	Well Matched	Yes	Yes
Stain	No	Yes	Yes
Type of Matching			
Rotary Sliced	Yes		
Natural Characteristics			
Chipped or Depressed Areas	Less then 1/8" x 1/4" (3.2 mm x 6.4 mm)	Less then 1/2" x 2" (12.7 mm x 50.8 mm)	Less then 1/2" x 2" (12.7 mm x 50.8 mm)
Cracks or Checks	Less then 1/32" (0.8 mm) wide	Less then 3/16" (4.8 mm) wide	Less then 3/16" (4.8 mm) wide
Knots, tight	No	No	Yes, maximum 1" (25.4 mm) dia.
Pitch Streaks	Average 3/8" (9.5 mm) wide and blended in color with wood	Average 3/8" (9.5 mm) wide and blended in color with wood	Average 1" (25.4 mm) wide and blended in color with wood
Pitch Pockets	No	No	No
Splits	Repaired - less then 1/16" x 2" (1.6 mm x 50.8 mm)	Repaired - less then 1-1/4" (31.8 mm) x unlimited	Open - less then 1/32" (0.8 mm)
Worm or borer holes	No	No	Yes
Manufacturing Characteristics			
Rough Cut	No	No	Yes, maximum 5% of face
Repairs	Maximum 6, well matched	Maximum 16, excluding shims	Unlimited
Patches	Maximum 3 "Router Patches" 1" x 3-1/2" (25.4 mm x 88.9 mm)	Boat, Router, or Sled, maximum 2-1/4" x 4-1/2" (57.2 mm x 114 mm)	Maximum 4" (102 mm) wide
Shims	Maximum 3/16" x 12" (4.8 mm x 305 mm)	Yes	Yes

PRODUCT

SHEET PRODUCT RULES (continued)

These rules are not intended to create a face grade; they are intended only to establish the acceptable requirements and/or characteristics after the architectural woodwork is completed or installed.

		DESCRIPTION	E C P
4.2c	**MATERIAL - HPDL (High-Pressure Decorative Laminate)** shall:		
	4.2c.1	Be constructed (in conformance with NEMA LD3 [latest edition]) of multiple layers of phenolic resin-saturated kraft paper in combination with a layer of decorative melamine-saturated paper, all fused together under heat and pressure with the following minimum performance properties, and:	
		4.2c.1.1 — Laminate types are abbreviated as "HGS/L" and "VGS/L" for horizontal and vertical general purpose; "HGP" and" VGP" for post-forming; "HGF" for fire-rated, "CLS" for cabinet liner; and "BKL" for backer in accordance with latest NEMA usage.	

4.2c.2

	HGS	HGL	VGS	VGL	HGP	VGP	HGF	CLS	BKL
Nominal thickness inch / (mm)	0.048" (1.2)	0.039" (1.0)	0.028" (0.7)	0.020" (0.5)	0.039" (1.0)	0.028" (0.7)	0.048" (1.2)	0.020" (0.5)	0.020" (0.5)
Thickness tolerance ± inch / (mm)	0.005" (0.12)	0.005" (0.12)	0.004" (0.10)	0.004" (0.10)	0.005" (0.12)	0.004" (0.10)	0.005" (0.12)	0.004" (0.10)	0.004" (0.10)
Wear (cycles, min.)	400	400	400	400	400	400	400	400	—
% Dim change (cross-direction)	0.9	1.0	1.2	1.3	1.4	1.4	0.9	2.0	—
Stain (variety of agents)	No effect 1-10 Moderate effect 11-15							Moderate effect 1-15	—
Cleanability (cycles, maximum)	20								—
Light	Slight effect							Moderate effect	—
High temperature	Slight effect							Moderate effect	—
Radiant heat (seconds, minimum)	125	100	80	60	100	80	75	—	—
Boiling water	No effect				Slight effect		No effect	Moderate effect	—
Impact (inches, min.)	50	35	20	15	30	20	45	10	—

Test procedures and minimum requirements shall comply with NEMA-LD3 (latest edition) for HPDL.

4.2c.3	Have **CORE** optional with manufacturer, within the provisions of these standards.	
4.2c.4	Be within the **THICKNESS** range of:	
	4.2c.4.1	**HORIZONTAL** - 0.028" to 0.048" (0.71 mm to 1.22 mm)
	4.2c.4.2	**VERTICAL** - 0.028" to 0.048" (0.71 mm to 1.22 mm)
	4.2c.4.3	**POST-FORMING** - 0.028" to 0.039" (0.71 mm to 0.99 mm)
	4.2c.4.4	**BACKER -** 0.016" to 0.048" (0.51 mm to 1.22 mm)
	4.2c.4.5	**CABINET LINER** - 0.016" to 0.048" (0.51 mm to 1.22 mm)
4.2c.5	If **FIRE-RATED** required:	
	4.2c.5.1	Be **CLASS 1.**
	4.2c.5.2	Have minimum 0.028" (0.71 mm) thick **BACKING SHEET**.
	4.2c.5.3	Be **BONDED** with a Class 1, ridged set adhesive.

HPDL ⇓

4

PRODUCT

SHEET PRODUCT RULES (continued)

These rules are not intended to create a face grade; they are intended only to establish the acceptable requirements and/ or characteristics after the architectural woodwork is completed or installed.

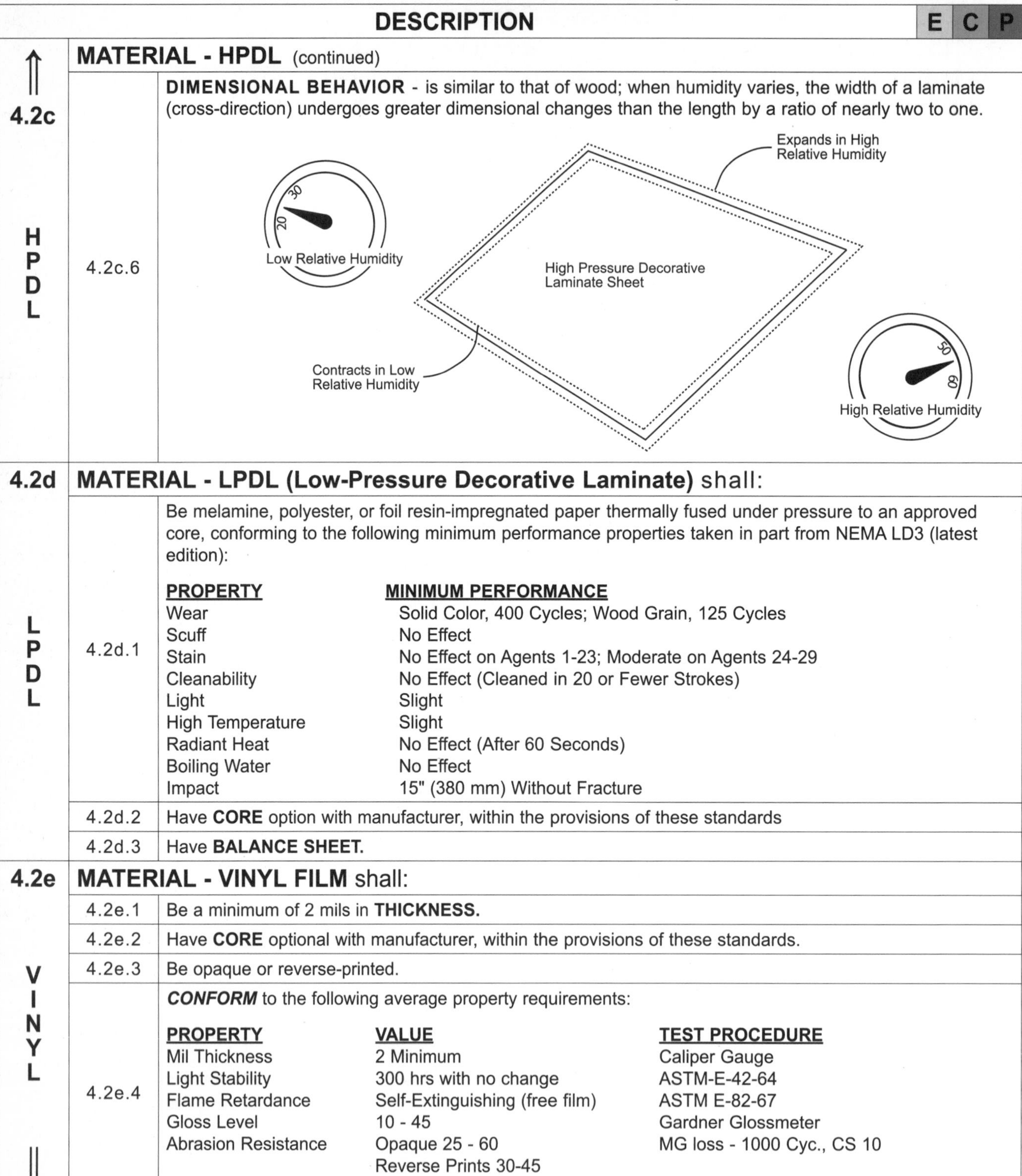

		DESCRIPTION	E	C	P
⇑ 4.2c HPDL	**MATERIAL - HPDL** (continued)				
	4.2c.6	**DIMENSIONAL BEHAVIOR** - is similar to that of wood; when humidity varies, the width of a laminate (cross-direction) undergoes greater dimensional changes than the length by a ratio of nearly two to one.			
4.2d LPDL	**MATERIAL - LPDL (Low-Pressure Decorative Laminate)** shall:				
	4.2d.1	Be melamine, polyester, or foil resin-impregnated paper thermally fused under pressure to an approved core, conforming to the following minimum performance properties taken in part from NEMA LD3 (latest edition):			
	4.2d.2	Have **CORE** option with manufacturer, within the provisions of these standards			
	4.2d.3	Have **BALANCE SHEET.**			
4.2e VINYL ⇓	**MATERIAL - VINYL FILM** shall:				
	4.2e.1	Be a minimum of 2 mils in **THICKNESS.**			
	4.2e.2	Have **CORE** optional with manufacturer, within the provisions of these standards.			
	4.2e.3	Be opaque or reverse-printed.			
	4.2e.4	***CONFORM*** to the following average property requirements:			

4.2d.1 minimum performance properties:

PROPERTY	MINIMUM PERFORMANCE
Wear	Solid Color, 400 Cycles; Wood Grain, 125 Cycles
Scuff	No Effect
Stain	No Effect on Agents 1-23; Moderate on Agents 24-29
Cleanability	No Effect (Cleaned in 20 or Fewer Strokes)
Light	Slight
High Temperature	Slight
Radiant Heat	No Effect (After 60 Seconds)
Boiling Water	No Effect
Impact	15" (380 mm) Without Fracture

4.2e.4 average property requirements:

PROPERTY	VALUE	TEST PROCEDURE
Mil Thickness	2 Minimum	Caliper Gauge
Light Stability	300 hrs with no change	ASTM-E-42-64
Flame Retardance	Self-Extinguishing (free film)	ASTM E-82-67
Gloss Level	10 - 45	Gardner Glossmeter
Abrasion Resistance	Opaque 25 - 60	MG loss - 1000 Cyc., CS 10
	Reverse Prints 30-45	
	Reverse Prints 6000-11000	Cycles to Print Failure, CS 17

PRODUCT

SHEET PRODUCT RULES (continued)

These rules are not intended to create a face grade; they are intended only to establish the acceptable requirements and/ or characteristics after the architectural woodwork is completed or installed.

		DESCRIPTION	E	C	P
⇑ 4.2e	**MATERIAL - VINYL FILM** (continued)				
	4.2e.5	Not have **SURFACE APPEARANCE** affected when exposed to the following agents: Water, Coffee, Olive Oil, Beet Juice, Vinegar, Alcohol, Mustard, Shoe Polish, Mercurochrome, Washable Inks, Crayon, Tea, Household Detergents and Soaps	•	•	
4.2f MDO	**MATERIAL - MDO (Medium-Density Overlay)** shall:				
	4.2f.1	Be (in conformance with APA PS1 [latest edition]) a thermosetting phenolic resin-impregnated cellulose fiber sheet or sheets containing not less than 34% phenolic resin after pressing.			
	4.2f.2	Have **CORE** option with manufacturer, within the provisions of these standards.			
	4.2f.3	Have **BALANCE SHEET**.			
4.2g HDO	**MATERIAL - HDO (High-Density Overlay)** shall:				
	4.2g.1	Be (in conformance with APA PS1 [latest edition]) a thermosetting phenolic resin-impregnated cellulose fiber sheet or sheets, not less than 0.012" (0.30 mm) in thickness after pressing.			
	4.2g.2	Be suitable for painting.			
	4.2g.3	Be allowed in lieu of paint-grade wood veneer for opaque finish.			
	4.2g.4	Have **CORE** option with manufacturer, within the provisions of these standards.			
	4.2g.5	Have **BALANCE SHEET**.			
4.2h HARDBOARD	**MATERIAL - HARDBOARD** shall:				
	4.2h.1	Be (in conformance with CAP/ANSI A135.4 [latest edition]) a panel manufactured of interfelted lignocellulosic fibers, consolidated under heat and pressure to a density of 31 lb/ft^3 or greater with the following minimum performance properties based on 1/4" (6.4 mm) thickness:			
	4.2h.1.1	**STANDARD GRADE:** **PROPERTY** — **PERFORMANCE** Water Absorption — 25% Maximum Thickness Swelling — 20% Maximum Modulus of Rupture — 4500 psi Tensile Strength - Parallel — 2200 psi Tensile Strength - Perpendicular — 90 psi	•		
	4.2h.1.2	**TEMPERED GRADE:** **PROPERTY** — **PERFORMANCE** Water Absorption — 20% Maximum Thickness Swelling — 15% Maximum Modulus of Rupture — 6000 psi Tensile Strength - Parallel — 3000 psi Tensile Strength - Perpendicular — 130 psi		•	•
4.2i	**MATERIAL - BALANCE SHEET** shall be:				
	4.2i.1	**WOOD VENEER** of the same or a compatible species and thickness.			
	4.2i.2	**HPDL** of a compatible thickness.			
	4.2i.3	**OVERLAY** of a compatible thickness.			
4.2j	**MATERIAL - BACKER** shall be:				
	4.2j.1	Brown-colored, minimum 0.002" (0.05 mm) thick, factory-applied, hot-melt coating of blended wax petroleum, copolymer resins, and anti-oxidants with swipe-controlling agents.	•		
⇓	4.2j.2	Polyester or melamine overlay.	•		

4

PRODUCT

SHEET PRODUCT RULES (continued)

These rules are not intended to create a face grade; they are intended only to establish the acceptable requirements and/ or characteristics after the architectural woodwork is completed or installed.

		DESCRIPTION	E	C	P
⇑ 4.2j BACKER	**MATERIAL - BACKER** (continued)				
	4.2j.3	Man-made wood fiber veneers, impregnated with acrylic melamine, fortified, high load resin system, a minimum of 0.020" (0.51 mm).		●	
	4.2j.4	Synthetic polymer-treated backing sheet 0.017" (0.43 mm) - 0.019" (0.48 mm) nominal thickness, designed for use with HPDL.		●	
	4.2j.5	Dark brown-colored, 0.015" (0.38 mm) nominal thickness, phenolic resin impregnated kraft paper.		●	
	4.2j.6	Thermoset resin-treated wood-fiber, brown-colored, 3-ply construction, a minimum of 0.020" (051 mm) in thickness.		●	●
	4.2j.7	Minimum 0.020" (0.51 mm) thick laminate, conforming to NEMA LD3 (latest edition).			●

4.2k	**MATERIAL - SOLID SURFACE** shall:	
SOLID SURFACE	**4.2k.1**	Be a manufactured, filled cast polymeric resin panel. Fillers may be used to enhance both its performance properties and aesthetics. With a homogeneous composition throughout its thickness, solid surface requires no finish coat and is capable of being fabricated with inconspicuous seams and repaired to its original finish - with the following minimum performance properties:
	4.2k.2	**Be COLOR** and **PATTERN MATCHED,** use of same batch materials is required for adjacent sheets.
	4.2k.3	**REPAIRS,** while fully functional might be visible.

4.2k.1.1

PROPERTY	VALUE	TEST PROCEDURE [1]
Abrasion Resistance	Pass	ANSI-Z124.7
Bacterial Resistance	Pass	ASTM-G-22
Boiling Water Surface Resistance	No Visible Effect	NEMA LD3-3.05
Color Stability (200 Hrs.)	No Visible Effect	NEMA LD-3
Fungal Resistance	Pass	ASTM-G-22, or ISO.846
Gloss (60° Gardner)	5-20 minimum	NEMA LD-3
Hardness (Rockwell M)	90 minimum	ASTM-D-785
	50 minimum	Barcol
High Temp. Resistance	No Visible Effect	NEMA LD-3-3.06
Impact Resistance	No Failure	NEMA LD-3-3.08
Izod Impact	0.25 ft.-lbs./in. of notch	ASTM-D-256
Radiant Heat resistance	No Visible Effect	NEMA LD-3-3.010
Specific Gravity [2]	1.5 gram/cm^3 minimum	
Stain Resistance	Pass	ANSI-Z-124
Surface Flammability	Meet or Exceed all applicable code and regulations	
Tensile Strength	4000 psi minimum	ASTM-D-638
Tensile Modulus	500,000 psi minimum, or 25,000 psi minmum at 1/8" Nominal Material	ASTM-D-638
Tensile Elongation	1% maximum, or 10% maximum at 1/8" Nominal Material	ASTM-D-638
Thermal Expansion	2.3 x 10^{-5} in./in./F^{O} maximum	ASTM-D696
Water Absorption	1% maximum	ASTM-D-570 (24 hrs.)

[1] Latest edition

[2] Approximate weight per 12" x 12" (305 x 305 mm): 1/8 (3 mm) 1.02 lbs. (0.544 kg), 1/4" (6 mm) 2.1 lbs. (0.953 kg), 1/2" (13 mm) 4.2 lbs. (1.905 kg), 3/4" (19 mm) 6.2 lbs. (2.812 kg)

PRODUCT

SHEET PRODUCT RULES (continued)

These rules are not intended to create a face grade; they are intended only to establish the acceptable requirements and/or characteristics after the architectural woodwork is completed or installed.

		DESCRIPTION	E C P
4.2l	**MATERIAL - Solid Phenolic** shall:		
SOLID PHENOLIC	4.2l.1	Be a panel composed of melamine-impregnated decorative surface papers superimposed over a varying number of kraft phenolic core sheets to achieve a desired thickness, with the following minimum performance properties:	
	4.2l.1.1	see table below	

PROPERTY	VALUE	TEST PROCEDURE [1]
Compressive Strength	24, 000 psi minimum	ASTM-D-695
Density	90 lbs./ft^3	ASTM-D-792
Flame Test	Self-Extinguishing	ASTM-D-635
Flexural Strength	15,000 psi minimum	ASTM-D-790
High Temp. Resistance	No Visible Effect	NEMA LD-3-3.06
Impact Resistance (1/2 lb. Ball at 120")	No Effect	NEMA LD-3-3.08
Modulus of Elasticity	1,500,000 psi minimum	ASTM-D-638
Screw Pull Out Resistance Based on 1/4" (6.4 mm) Machine Screw	340 lbs. (154 kg) minimum 680 lbs. (308 kg) minimum	At 3/8" (9.5 mm) Penetration At 3/4" (19 mm) Penetration
Shear Strength	2,000 psi minimum	
Tensile Strength	15,000 psi minimum	ASTM-D-638
Thickness Tolerance	± 1/32" (0.8 mm) minimum	
Water Absorption	3% maximum	ASTM-D-570

[1] Latest edition

4.2m	**MATERIAL - Epoxy Resin** shall:	
4.2m.1	Be a panel produced from a composite of epoxy resin, silica, inert fillers, and organic hardeners, cast and cured in ovens at elevated temperatures, homogenous throughout, and nonabsorbent, with the following minimum performance properties:	
4.2m.1.1	see table below	

PROPERTY	VALUE	TEST PROCEDURE [1]
Compressive Strength	30, 000 psi minimum	ASTM-D-695
Density	120 lbs./ft^3	ASTM-D-792
Flexural Strength	11,000 psi minimum	ASTM-D-790
Hardness (Rockwell M)	100(Min.)	ASTM-D-785
Water Absorption	0.05% minimum	ASTM-D-570

[1] Latest edition

4.2n	**MATERIAL - Natural Stone**, shall:	
	4.2n.1	Not be subject to minimum performance properties established by these standards, because it is a natural product.
4.2o	**MATERIAL - Manufactured Stone**, shall:	
	4.2o.1	Be as specified and subject to the manufacturer's instructions and these standards.
4.3	**MACHINING - Not applicable or used for this section.**	
4.4	**ASSEMBLY - Not applicable or used for this section.**	

4

EXECUTION

(Items # 5 & 6 are not applicable to this section)

COMPLIANCE

7 In GENERAL

7.1 **THICKNESS** shall be measured to the nearest 0.001" (0.025 mm) using a dial thickness gage or conventional micrometer.

7.1.1 Sufficient pressure shall be applied to ensure that the anvils of the instruments are in firm and square contact with, but do not compress, the panel surface.

7.1.2 One measurement shall be taken at the mid-width of one end of the panel.

7.1.2.1 This measurement shall represent the panel thickness, unless the measurement is below the minimum or above the maximum requirements.

7.1.2.2 If the measurement is below or above the applicable requirements, three additional measurements shall be taken; one at the approximate mid-width on the opposite end and one at the approximate mid-length on each side of the panel, and the average of the four measurements shall be taken as the thickness of that panel.

7.2 **SQUARENESS** shall be determined by measuring the length of the diagonals of the panel.

7.3 **STRAIGHTNESS** shall be determined by using a straight line along the edge from one corner to the other.

Architectural Woodwork Standards

SECTION - 5

Finishing

SECTION 5 ✦ FINISHING

(Including: Shop and Field Finishing)

GENERAL

1 INFORMATION

1.1 GRADES

1.1.1 **GRADE CLASSIFICATIONS ECONOMY, CUSTOM,** and **PREMIUM** are used within these standards only in reference to the acceptable quality of workmanship, material, or installation in a completed architectural woodwork product.

1.1.2 **THIS FINISHING SECTION** deals with finish application, which is a component of finished products covered in Sections 6 - 12.

1.1.2.1 **IN THIS SECTION**, the use of these classifications is only for the purpose of identifying finish applications that can be used in finished products meeting those Grades.

1.1.2.2 These classifications are not intended to be used as a Grade or to judge a particular finish system.

1.1.3 **FINISHING REQUIREMENTS**

1.1.3.1 Apply to exposed and semi-exposed surfaces visible after manufacture and installation.

1.1.3.2 Establish criteria as to which, if any, application characteristics are acceptable.

1.1.3.3 Address back-priming, when required.

1.1.4 **MODIFICATIONS** in the contract documents shall govern if in conflict with these standards.

1.2 BASIC CONSIDERATIONS

1.2.1 **PURPOSE** of finishing woodwork is twofold.

1.2.1.1 First, the finish traditionally is used as a means to enhance or alter the natural beauty of the wood.

1.2.1.2 Second, the finish protects the wood from potential damage caused by moisture in the atmosphere, contaminants, handling, and day-to-day usage.

1.2.1.3 It is important to understand that a quality finish must offer acceptable performance and also meet the aesthetic requirements of the project.

1.2.1.3.1 Involve your woodwork manufacturer early in the design process to help evaluate the systems in relation to your project requirements.

1.2.1.3.2 In the interest of value engineering, choose performance characteristics that meet, but do not exceed, the needs of your project.

1.2.2 **AIR-QUALITY RESTRICTIONS** can affect the availability and/or use of some finishes, check local jurisdictions, especially in California, which has many different districts regulating VOCs or solvents in coatings.

1.2.3 **CHEMICAL RESISTANCE** - These standards have adopted **SEFA's** (Scientific Equipment and Fixture Association) standard list of 49 chemicals/concentrations, their required methods of testing, and their minimum acceptable results as the minimum acceptable chemical-resistance requirement for finishes used at exposed and semi-exposed surfaces, when such is required by specification.

1.2.3.1 **SEFA's** chemical listing, methods of testing, and minimum acceptable results can be found in **APPENDIX A**.

1.2.4 **FIRE-RETARDANT** or **FIRE-RESISTANT FINISHES** - Subject to applicable codes and regulations, the use of fire-rated substrates in lieu of fire-retardant finishes is recommended.

1.2.5 **PANEL PRODUCTS** require balanced coats of finishing materials for stability and to remain free of warp.

1.2.5.1 At **BOOK-MATCHED** veneers, every other leaf of veneer is turned over as the leaves are taken in sequence from the flitch. Since one leaf will be loose-side-up and the next tight-side-up, it produces a natural color shading. Alternating leaves might refract light differently and cause a noticeable color variation in some species. Proper finishing techniques can minimize this variation.

GENERAL

1.2 **BASIC CONSIDERATIONS** (continued)

1.2.6 **APPLICATION** variances make it very difficult to define "how many coats" of each step in a system are needed.

1.2.6.1 The desired end result is to provide a finish that adds beauty to the wood and gives desirable color, tone, smoothness, and depth.

1.2.7 **PROPER SANDING** is imperative to the final appearance of any finished surface. The quality of sanding dramatically affects the staining process through the topcoat appearance. Improper sanding will cause staining to be blotchy and nonuniform in appearance. In addition, improper sealer sanding can result in scratches and telegraphing topcoats.

1.2.8 **TRANSPARENT** finishes are applied in varying operations, typically consisting of some combination of hand sanding to remove job-handling marks, staining, filling, sealing, sanding, and surface coating.

1.2.9 **SOME EXOTIC SPECIES** have a high natural oil content and do not accept finishes similar to other hardwoods; because of this, the most common finish used is penetrating oil without any filling or sealing dyes or pigments in a stain.

1.2.10 **GRAIN** can significantly impact a finish's visual appearance and smoothness. Close-grain hardwoods and most softwoods do not require a filler to achieve a smooth finish; however, open-grain hardwoods do. Fillers, which are usually light-colored, may be toned to match any intended staining.

1.2.10.1 For finishing purposes, the following hardwoods are classified as:

OPEN GRAIN		CLOSE GRAIN	
Ash Butternut Chestnut Mahogany, African Mahogany, Honduras	Mahogany, Philippine Oak, Red Oak, White Walnut	Alder, Red Beech Birch	Cherry Gum Maple

5

1.2.11 **BIRCH** and **MAPLE** have pores that are large enough to take wood filler effectively when desired, but are small enough, as a rule, to be finished without filler.

1.2.12 **FACTORY** or **FIELD** finishing are permitted, provided there is no violation of applicable codes or regulations.

1.2.12.1 **FACTORY** finishing is usually specified for high-quality work where superior appearance and performance of the finish is desired.

1.2.12.1.1 Benefits of factory finishing include consistency, control of film thickness, environmental compliance, and curing/drying of the finish in a controlled atmosphere.

1.2.12.1.2 Its use assumes a maximum degree of manufacturer prefabrication so that site installation can be performed with a minimum amount of cutting, fitting, and adjustment to facilitate project completion.

1.2.12.2 **FIELD** finishing is typically specified when there is not a demand or specific need for a superior appearance and is not necessarily part of the woodwork contract.

1.2.12.2.1 The **FINISHER** is responsible for examining and accepting the woodwork as supplied prior to the commencement of finishing.

1.2.12.2.2 The **FINISHER** is responsible for meeting or exceeding the control sample for surface performance characteristics (such as color, texture, and sheen), including proper surface preparation, shading, and blending of color, and other requirements as defined in this standard when so referenced.

1.2.13 **FINISHING SYSTEMS**

1.2.13.1 **SPECIFICATIONS** calling for finishes based on samples or guide language from a commodity manufacturer might not be realistic from a custom manufacturer.

1.2.13.2 **INTERMIXING SYSTEMS** will likely cause quality and/or performance problems; they are usually not compatible with each other.

1.2 **BASIC CONSIDERATIONS** (continued)

1.2.13 **FINISHING SYSTEMS** (continued)

1.2.13.3 **APPLICATION** of any finish material in excess of manufacturer's recommendations can cause the finish to fail.

1.2.13.4 **VARYING COSTS** of finish systems typically relate directly to their performing characteristics.

1.2.13.5 **UV** (ultraviolet light) is a method for curing coatings (transparent and opaque) typically used for high-volume, repetitive applications, and is done by a limited number of finishing operations.

1.2.13.6 **COLOR** and **GRAIN ENHANCEMENT** of a system - from the addition of a single stain, to a multiple-step build of one color on another with wash coats in between for added depth and beauty - is not included in the basic systems and needs to be properly specified.

1.2.13.7 **SPECIFICATION** of a system requires listing both the system number and the name, along with any desired enhancements.

1.2.13.8 These standards recognize and offer guidance for the following finishing systems for both transparent or opaque applications, unless otherwise indicated:

1.2.13.8.1 **SYSTEM - 1, LACQUER, NITROCELLULOSE**

1.2.13.8.2 **SYSTEM - 2, LACQUER, PRECATALYZED**

1.2.13.8.3 **SYSTEM - 3, LACQUER, POSTCATALYZED**

1.2.13.8.4 **SYSTEM - 4, LATEX ACRYLIC, WATER-BASED**

1.2.13.8.5 **SYSTEM - 5, VARNISH, CONVERSION**

1.2.13.8.6 **SYSTEM - 6, OIL, SYNTHETIC PENETRATING (available in transparent only)**

1.2.13.8.7 **SYSTEM - 7, VINYL, CATALYZED**

1.2.13.8.8 **SYSTEM - 8, ACRYLIC CROSS LINKING, WATER-BASED**

1.2.13.8.9 **SYSTEM - 9, UV CURABLE, ACRYLATED EPOXY, POLYESTER or URETHANE**

1.2.13.8.10 **SYSTEM - 10, UV CURABLE, WATER-BASED**

1.2.13.8.11 **SYSTEM - 11, POLYURETHANE, CATALYZED**

1.2.13.8.12 **SYSTEM - 12, POLYURETHANE, WATER-BASED**

1.2.13.8.13 **SYSTEM - 13, POLYESTER, CATALYZED**

1.2.14 The following **SYSTEM OVERVIEW TABLES** are intended to give an overview of and help identify the correct standard or specialty finishing system to meet a project's needs; however, they are only relative to the topcoat, not any prior color or filler coats.

1.2.14.1 **TYPICAL USAGE/PERFORMANCE SCORES**

1.2.14.1.1 Differences between systems of 10 points or fewer are not generally considered significant enough to justify the typical added expense of a higher-rated system.

1.2.14.1.2 This systems listing does not imply an endorsement of the materials or compliance with applicable codes and regulations.

1.2.14.1.3 Due to changing environmental regulations and finish technologies, design professionals need to discuss finish options with a manufacturer located in the area of the project.

GENERAL

1.2 **BASIC CONSIDERATIONS** (continued)

1.2.14 The **SYSTEM OVERVIEW TABLES** (continued)

1.2.14.1 **TYPICAL USAGE/PERFORMANCE SCORES** (continued)

1.2.14.1.4 **COMPARISON TABLE** of usages and performance scores:

	Typical Usage	Score	Why and Why Not
1	Interior use for trims, furniture, paneling, and ornamental work	**77-T** **75-O**	**Why** - Repairable; widely available; quick-drying **Why not** - Lack of durability and resistance to most solvents and water; yellows over time
2	Interior use for furniture, casework, paneling, ornamental work, stair parts (except treads), frames, windows, blinds, shutters, and doors	**99-T** **97-O**	**Why** - Repairable; stain-, abrasion-, chemical-resistance **Why not** - Some yellowing; moderate build
3	Interior use for furniture, casework, paneling, ornamental work, stair parts (except treads), frames, windows, blinds, shutters, and doors	**124-T** **123-O**	**Why** - Repairable; finish clarity; stain-, heat-, abrasion-, chemical-resistance **Why not** - Some yellowing; moderate build
4	Interior use for furniture, casework, paneling, ornamental work, stair parts (except treads), frames, windows, blinds, shutters, and doors	**94-T** **94-O**	**Why** - Low VOCs; finish clarity (some formulations); stain resistance; yellowing resistance **Why not** - Low durability; solvent- and heat-resistance; slow drying time
5	Interior use for furniture, casework, paneling, ornamental work, stair parts, frames, windows, blinds, shutters, and doors	**129-T** **129-O**	**Why** - Durable; widely available; good build **Why not** - Occasional lack of finish clarity
6	Interior use on furniture or trims requiring a close-to-the-wood look or very low sheen	**57-T**	**Why** - Close-to-wood, antique look; low sheen **Why not** - Labor-intensive to apply and maintain, refreshing finish required from time-to-time; low resistance properties to most substances
7	Interior use, often on kitchen, bath, office furniture, and laboratory casework	**114-T** **114-O**	**Why** - Durable; widely available; fast drying **Why not** - Occasional lack of finish clarity
8	Interior use for furniture, casework, paneling, ornamental work, stair parts, frames, windows, blinds, shutters, and doors	**99-T** **99-O**	**Why** - Fine durability; excellent abrasion-, solvent-, stain-, and chemical-resistance; moderately fast-drying; resists moisture **Why not** - Possibility of discoloration over time
9	Interior use, doors, paneling, flooring, stair parts, and casework, where applicable; consult your finisher before specifying	**134-T** **133-O**	**Why** - Low VOCs; durable; near 100% solids usage; quick-drying (cure), may qualify as Green Guard **Why not** - Difficult to repair with UV finish, as this requires a handheld UV lamp; availability varies; easy repair with lacquers or conversion varnish
10	Interior use, doors, paneling, flooring, stair parts, and casework where applicable; consult your finisher before specifying	**132-T** **132-O**	**Why** - Low VOCs; quick-drying (cure), maybe Green Guard **Why not** - Difficult to repair with UV finish, requires handheld UV lamp; availability varies; easy repair with lacquers or conversion varnish.
11	Interior use; some formulas available for exterior; floors, stairs, high-impact areas; some doors; generally not good for casework, paneling, windows, blinds, and shutters	**133-T** **132-O**	**Why** - Durable; good build **Why not** - Slow-drying; very difficult to repair; some formulations hazardous to spray-personnel without air make-up suits
12	Interior use for furniture, casework, paneling, ornamental work, stair parts, frames, windows, blinds, shutters, and doors	**112 -T** **112-O**	**Why** - Improved durability; excellent abrasion-, solvent-, stain-, and chemical-resistance; moderately fast-drying; resists moisture **Why not** - Tannins in some wood species may cause discoloration over time
13	Interior use for furniture, casework, paneling, ornamental work, windows, blinds, shutters, and some doors	**131-T** **131-O**	**Why** - Durable; good build; can be polished **Why not** - Not widely available; slow-curing; requires special facilities and skills; very difficult to repair; brittle finish flexibility

T = Transparent and **O** = Opaque

5

1.2 **BASIC CONSIDERATIONS** (continued)

1.2.14 The **SYSTEM OVERVIEW TABLES** (continued)

1.2.14.2 **GENERAL PERFORMANCE CHARACTERISTICS** table:

	SYSTEM NUMBER												
	1	**2**	**3**	**4**	**5**	**6**	**7**	**8**	**9**	**10**	**11**	**12**	**13**
General Durability	2	2	3	2	4	1	4	2	5	5	5	3	5
Repairability	5	4	4	3	3	5	4	4	5	3	2	4	1
Abrasion Resistance	2	4	4	3	4	1	4	4	5	4	5	4	5
Finish Clarity	5	4	5	2	3	5	3	4	5	5	3	4	4
Yellowing in Time	1	2	3	1	4	2	3	4	5	5	4	4	4
Finish Flexibility	1	2	3	3	4	5	4	3	2	3	4	4	1
Moisture Resistance	3	3	4	1	4	1	5	3	5	4	5	4	5
Solvent Resistance	1	2	4	1	5	1	5	3	5	5	5	4	5
Stain Resistance	4	4	5	3	5	1	5	4	5	5	5	4	5
Heat Resistance	1	2	5	1	5	1	5	3	5	5	5	4	5
Household Chemical Resistance	3	4	5	3	5	2	5	4	5	5	5	4	5
Build/Solids	2	3	3	3	4	1	4	3	5	4	4	3	4
Drying Time	5	5	5	2	4	2	5	4	5	5	3	5	2
Affects Wood Flame Spread	Yes	Yes	Yes	No	No	No	No	No	No	No	No	No	Yes

NOTE: 5 = Excellent to 1 = Poor. The numerical ratings are subjective judgments based on the general performance of generic products. Special formulations and facilities will influence some of the performance characteristics.

GENERAL

1.2 **BASIC CONSIDERATIONS** (continued)

1.2.14 The **SYSTEM OVERVIEW TABLES** (continued)

1.2.14.3 **SPECIFIC PERFORMANCE CHARACTERISTICS** table for **TRANSPARENT FINISHES**:

	SYSTEM NUMBER												
	TRANSPARENT FINISHES												
	1	**2**	**3**	**4**	**5**	**6**	**7**	**8**	**9**	**10**	**11**	**12**	**13**
Vinegar	3	4	5	4	5	3	5	4	5	5	5	4	5
Lemon Juice	3	4	5	4	5	3	5	4	5	5	5	4	5
Orange Juice	3	4	5	4	5	3	5	4	5	5	5	4	5
Catsup	3	4	5	4	5	2	5	4	5	5	5	4	5
Coffee	3	4	5	4	5	2	5	4	5	5	5	4	5
Olive Oil	2	3	5	3	5	2	5	4	5	5	5	4	5
Boiling Water	3	4	5	4	5	3	5	4	5	5	5	4	5
Cold Water	5	5	5	5	5	3	5	4	5	5	5	4	5
Nail Polish Remover	1	2	3	2	4	1	2	2	5	5	4	3	4
Household Ammonia	3	4	5	4	5	2	4	2	5	5	5	4	5
VM&P Naphtha	3	4	5	4	5	1	4	4	5	5	5	4	5
Isopropyl Alcohol	1	2	3	1	5	2	4	3	5	5	5	4	5
Wine	3	4	5	4	5	2	4	4	5	5	5	5	5
Windex™	3	3	4	3	5	2	3	2	5	4	5	4	5
409 Cleaner™	3	3	4	4	5	1	4	3	5	5	5	4	5
Lysol™	3	5	5	4	5	2	4	4	5	5	5	4	5
33% Sulfuric Acid	3	4	5	3	5	1	4	4	5	5	5	4	5
77% Sulfuric Acid	1	2	3	1	1	1	2	2	4	3	4	3	4
28% Ammonium Hydroxide	1	2	3	1	5	1	4	2	5	5	5	3	5
Gasoline	1	2	5	2	5	1	4	4	5	5	5	4	4
Murphy's Oil Soap™	5	5	5	5	5	2	4	5	5	5	5	5	5
Vodka 100 Proof	3	4	5	4	5	2	4	4	5	5	5	4	5
1% Detergent	3	4	5	4	5	3	4	4	5	5	5	5	5
10% TSP	3	4	5	4	4	1	5	4	5	5	5	5	5
SUBTOTAL	**65**	**86**	**110**	**82**	**114**	**46**	**100**	**85**	**119**	**117**	**118**	**97**	**117**
Wear	2	3	4	2	5	1	4	4	5	5	5	5	4
Cold Check	5	5	5	5	5	5	5	5	5	5	5	5	5
Adhesion	5	5	5	5	5	5	5	5	5	5	5	5	5
TOTAL SCORE	**77**	**99**	**124**	**94**	**129**	**57**	**114**	**99**	**134**	**132**	**133**	**112**	**131**

NOTE - Testing was evaluated in an ISO 9000-certified laboratory using the following ASTM test criteria: Chemical Resistance Testing - ASTM D1308 (latest edition), Wear Index - Abrasion Resistance Testing - ASTM D4060 (latest edition), Cold Check Resistance - ASTM D1211 (latest edition), Cross Hatch Adhesion - ASTM D3359 (latest edition).
Baseline data for application prior to testing: A. 45-55% humidity at 70-80 degrees Fahrenheit; B. Water-borne coatings must be cured in a dehumidified atmosphere and can be assisted with infrared light and good air movement.
Performance indicator numbers are used, with the following definitions:

For chemical resistance and wear index - abrasion resistance:

- 5 - No effect from the test
- 4 - Minimal effect or slight change and little repair required
- 3 - Some effect; noticeable change, and the coating will recover with minimal repairs
- 2 - Moderate effect, performance adversely affected and repairs required
- 1 - Poor performance and film failure is imminent and repairs difficult

For cross-hatch adhesion:

- 5 - Edges of the cuts are completely smooth; none of the squares of the lattice are detached.
- 4 - Small flakes of the coating are detached at intersections; less than 5% of the area is affected.
- 3 - Small flakes of the coating are detached along the edges and at the intersections of cuts; 5 to 15% of the area is affected.
- 2 - Coating has flaked along the edges and on parts of the squares; 15 to 35% of the area is affected.
- 1 - Coating has flaked along the edges of the cuts in large ribbons and whole squares have detached; 35 to 65% of the area is affected.

1.2 **BASIC CONSIDERATIONS** (continued)

1.2.14 The **SYSTEM OVERVIEW TABLES** (continued)

1.2.14.4 **SPECIFIC PERFORMANCE CHARACTERISTICS** table:

	OPAQUE FINISHES											
	1	**2**	**3**	**4**	**5**	**7**	**8**	**9**	**10**	**11**	**12**	**13**
Vinegar	3	4	5	4	5	5	4	5	5	5	4	5
Lemon Juice	3	4	5	4	5	5	4	5	5	5	4	5
Orange Juice	3	4	5	4	5	5	4	5	5	5	4	5
Catsup	3	4	5	4	5	5	4	5	5	5	4	5
Coffee	3	4	5	4	5	5	4	5	5	5	4	5
Olive Oil	2	3	5	3	5	5	4	5	5	5	4	5
Boiling Water	3	4	5	4	5	5	4	5	5	5	4	5
Cold Water	5	5	5	5	5	5	4	5	5	5	4	5
Nail Polish Remover	1	2	3	2	4	2	2	5	5	4	3	4
Household Ammonia	2	4	5	4	5	4	2	5	5	5	4	5
VM&P Naphtha	3	4	5	4	5	4	4	5	5	5	4	5
Isopropyl Alcohol	1	2	3	1	5	4	3	5	5	5	4	5
Wine	3	4	5	4	5	4	4	5	5	5	5	5
Windex™	3	3	4	3	5	3	2	5	4	5	4	5
409 Cleaner™	3	3	4	4	5	4	3	5	5	5	4	5
Lysol™	3	5	5	4	5	4	4	5	5	5	4	5
33% Sulfuric Acid	3	4	5	3	5	4	4	5	5	5	4	5
77% Sulfuric Acid	1	2	3	1	1	2	2	4	3	4	3	4
28% Ammonium Hydroxide	1	2	3	1	5	4	2	5	5	5	3	5
Gasoline	1	2	5	2	5	4	4	5	5	5	4	4
Murphy's Oil Soap™	5	5	5	5	5	4	5	5	5	5	5	5
Vodka 100 Proof	3	4	5	4	5	4	4	5	5	5	4	5
1% Detergent	3	4	5	4	5	4	4	5	5	5	5	5
10% TSP	3	4	5	4	4	5	4	5	5	5	5	5
SUBTOTAL	**64**	**86**	**110**	**82**	**114**	**100**	**85**	**119**	**117**	**118**	**97**	**117**
Wear	1	1	3	2	5	4	4	4	5	4	4	4
Cold Check	5	5	5	5	5	5	5	5	5	5	5	5
Adhesion	5	5	5	5	5	5	5	5	5	5	5	5
TOTAL SCORE	**75**	**97**	**123**	**94**	**129**	**114**	**99**	**133**	**132**	**132**	**112**	**131**

NOTE - Testing was evaluated in an ISO 9000-certified laboratory using the following ASTM test criteria: Chemical Resistance Testing - ASTM D1308 (latest edition), Wear Index - Abrasion Resistance Testing - ASTM D4060 (latest edition), Cold Check Resistance - ASTM D1211 (latest edition), Cross Hatch Adhesion - ASTM D3359 (latest edition).

Baseline data for application prior to testing: A. 45-55% humidity at 70-80 degrees Fahrenheit; B. Water-borne coatings must be cured in a dehumidified atmosphere and can be assisted with infrared light and good air movement.

Performance indicator numbers are used, with the following definitions:

For chemical resistance and wear index - abrasion resistance:

- 5 - No effect from the test
- 4 - Minimal effect or slight change and little repair required
- 3 - Some effect, noticeable change, and the coating will recover with minimal repairs
- 2 - Moderate effect, performance adversely affected and repairs required
- 1 - Poor performance and film failure is imminent and repairs difficult

For cross-hatch adhesion:

- 5 - Edges of the cuts are completely smooth; none of the squares of the lattice are detached.
- 4 - Small flakes of the coating are detached at intersections; less than 5% of the area is affected.
- 3 - Small flakes of the coating are detached along the edges and at the intersections of cuts; 5 to 15% of the area is affected.
- 2 - Coating has flaked along the edges and on parts of the squares; 15 to 35% of the area is affected.
- 1 - Coating has flaked along the edges of the cuts in large ribbons and whole squares have detached; 35 to 65% of the area is affected.

GENERAL

1.3 **RECOMMENDATIONS**

1.3.1 **INCLUDE IN DIVISION 09 OF THE SPECIFICATIONS:**

1.3.1.1 "Before finishing, all exposed portions of woodwork shall have handling marks or effects of exposure to moisture removed with a thorough, final sanding over all surfaces of the exposed portions, using appropriate grit sandpaper, and shall be cleaned before applying sealer or finish".

1.3.1.2 "Concealed surfaces of all architectural woodwork that might be exposed to moisture, such as those adjacent to exterior concrete walls, shall be back-primed".

1.3.2 For **DECORATIVE LAMINATE** cabinets and countertops, **SPECIFY** the responsibility for finishing (if any) of raw wood parts, such as pulls, trim, applied moldings, banded doors, drawer bodies, and/or wood cabinet interiors.

1.3.3 Avoid **BRUSH-APPLIED** finishes for fine architectural woodwork; they are not covered by these standards.

1.3.4 Avoid **BLEACHED VENEERS** because of potential finishing problems.

1.3.5 Avoid **JOBSITE FINISHING** because a factory-controlled finishing environment offers a superior finished product; however, jobsite finishing is permitted, provided there is no violation of applicable codes and regulations.

1.3.6 Avoid **EXTERIOR WOOD DOORS** when exposed to direct sunlight or without adequate overhead soffit protection finished in a dark color that will absorb heat.

1.3.7 **SPECIFY** requirements for:

1.3.7.1 **FIRE RESISTANCE**

1.3.7.2 **CHEMICAL RESISTANCE**

1.3.7.3 Use of **FILLER**, **WASH COAT**, or **STAIN**

1.4 **ACKNOWLEDGEMENTS**

1.4.1 **LISTING** of a finish system in these standards does not imply an endorsement of such or compliance with applicable codes and regulations.

1.4.2 Some **PREFINISHED WOOD PANELS** or **DECORATIVE OVERLAYS** have aesthetic and performance characteristics that meet or exceed these standards without using a listed or recommended finish system.

1.4.2.1 Such products should be evaluated and/or specified by the design professional.

1.5 **INDUSTRY PRACTICES**

1.5.1 **DOOR MANUFACTURERS** typically offer only their own standard finishes. If one or more acceptable door manufacturers are listed in a project's specifications, it indicates that each manufacturer's standard finish system is acceptable.

1.5.2 **FINISHING** of **RAW WOOD COMPONENTS** on **HPDL** casework (including pulls, trims, moldings, and edgebanding) is typically excluded from the manufacturer's scope of work and is not covered by this finishing section unless required in the project's specifications.

1.5.3 **FINISHING SYSTEMS** are applied per the manufacturer's recommendations.

PRODUCT

2 SCOPE

2.1 All factory or shop finishing of architectural woodwork.

2.2 **TYPICAL INCLUSIONS**

2.2.1 The application of transparent or opaque finish on all architectural woodwork specified to be factory prefinished and/or jobsite finished within the architectural woodwork contract.

5

PRODUCT

2 SCOPE (continued)

2.2 TYPICAL INCLUSIONS (continued)

2.2.2 The application of primer prior to delivery to the jobsite for final paint finish to be applied later by others.

2.2.3 All preparatory work, labor, equipment, materials, and related supplies to produce the specified finish.

2.3 TYPICAL EXCLUSIONS

2.3.1 All painting or priming of building surfaces not specified within the architectural woodwork contract.

2.3.2 All finishing of architectural woodwork specified within the painting specifications.

2.3.3 Jobsite touch-up after delivery or installation.

2.3.4 Raw wood parts on HPDL cabinets, except as specified in the contract documents, such as wood finger-pulls or wood drawer bodies incorporated into the assembly.

2.3.5 Brush-applied topcoat finishes, except as called out under the scope of work for the custom woodwork manufacturer, such as faux finishes.

2.3.6 Items to receive subsequent coats of finish materials by others.

2.3.7 Exterior painting or priming.

3 DEFAULT STIPULATION

3.1 If not otherwise specified or detailed, all work under this section shall meet the same Grade as the item being finished, and/or the finishing system selected shall be optional with the finishing contractor.

4 RULES - The following RULES shall govern unless a project's contract documents require otherwise.

These rules are not intended to create a finishing grade; they are intended only to establish the acceptable requirements and/or characteristics after the architectural woodwork is completed or installed.

Where E, C, or P is not indicated, the rule applies to all Grades equally.

ERRATA, published on the Associations' websites at www.awinet.org, www.awmac.com, or www.woodworkinstitute.com, shall TAKE PRECEDENCE OVER THESE RULES, subject to their date of posting and a project's bid date.

ARROWS INDICATE TOPIC IS CARRIED FROM ⇑ OR ONTO ⇓ ANOTHER PAGE.

				DESCRIPTION	E	C	P
4.1	In **GENERAL**						
GENERAL	**4.1.1**	**FINISHER** shall determine and report the following in writing before the start of any finishing:					
		4.1.1.1	Material or finish system requirements in violation of any applicable codes or regulations.				
			4.1.1.1.1	It shall **NOT** be the responsibility of the finisher to comply with a specification requirement or finishing system that is illegal or otherwise disallowed in a particular area by some regulatory agency.			
		4.1.1.2	Any condition that might affect proper finish application.				
		4.1.1.3	Moisture content of product and/or surrounding wall surfaces, such as drywall or plaster, above 12%.				
	4.1.2	**SAMPLES** shall be submitted and approved before the finishing of any product, and:					
		4.1.2.1	Due to variance in wood color within the same species and even within the same log, a range of color shall be expected on finished wood products.				
			4.1.2.1.1	To establish an acceptable color range, a minimum of three samples shall be submitted.			
⇓	⇓	4.1.2.2	Shall be at least 12" x 12" (305 mm x 305 mm) if on a panel product, and as wide as practical if on lumber by a minimum of 12" (304 mm) in length.				

PRODUCT

FINISHING RULES (continued)

These rules are not intended to create a finishing grade; they are intended only to establish the acceptable requirements and/or characteristics after the architectural woodwork is completed or installed.

				DESCRIPTION	E	C	P
4.1 GENERAL	In **GENERAL** (continued)						
	4.1.2			**SAMPLES** (continued)			
		4.1.2.3		Shall be on material representative of that to be used for the project.			
		4.1.2.4		Shall each bear a label identifying the job name, the design professional, the contractor, and the finish system number.			
	4.1.3			Aesthetic **GRADE RULES** apply only to exposed and semi-exposed surfaces visible after installation.			
	4.1.4			**OVERALL APPEARANCE** shall be:			
		4.1.4.1		Compatible in color and grain.		●	
		4.1.4.2		Well-matched for color and grain.			●
	4.1.5			**APPLICATION VARIANCES** make it difficult to define the number of "coats" needed in each step of a system; regardless, the end result shall provide a finish that adds beauty to the wood and gives desirable color, tone, smoothness, and depth.			
	4.1.6			Some species of wood contain a chemical that reacts unfavorably with certain finishes; it is the responsibility of the finisher to prevent any such reaction.			
		4.1.6.1		When appropriate, a test sample shall be conducted to check for unfavorable reactions.			
		4.1.6.2		The application of a sealer, if required, before finishing to nullify such a chemical reaction, is the responsibility of the finisher.			
	4.1.7			**PANELING** requires a balanced coating on both sides with the same or similar materials.			
		4.1.7.1		Adjacent panels shall be finished together to achieve maximum uniformity of color.			
			4.1.7.1.1	If possible, entire elevations shall be finished together.			
	4.1.8			**TRIM** and **FRAMES** require only the exposed faces and edges to be finished.			
	4.1.9			**DOORS** require all surfaces, including faces, top/bottom edges, and hardware preparation areas at hinge and lock edges to be finished.			
		4.1.9.1		An equal number of coats of the same material shall be applied to each side.			
		4.1.9.2		Pairs of doors and openings with sidelights and transoms shall be finished together to achieve maximum uniformity of color.			
		4.1.9.3		**DOOR FINISHES**, other than those furnished by a door manufacturer, shall be specified to be applied by the woodwork finisher.			
	4.1.10			**CASEWORK** requires all exposed and semi-exposed surfaces to be finished.			
		4.1.10.1		All six faces of cabinet doors shall receive the same number of coats to prevent warping and/or twisting.			
	4.1.11			**DEFECTS** and **WORKMANSHIP**:			
		4.1.11.1		Regardless of requirements otherwise stated in these standards, final sanding prior to the application of finishing materials of any kind is the responsibility of the finisher.			
		4.1.11.2		**HANDLING, MACHINING,** or **TOOL MARKS** are not allowed.			
		4.1.11.3		**INDENTATIONS** and **SCRAPES** shall be for:			
			4.1.11.3.1	Opaque - Filled or patched	●	●	
			4.1.11.3.2	Transparent - Filled or patched	●		
			4.1.11.3.3	Transparent - Steamed out		●	●
		4.1.11.4		**MOISTURE EFFECTS** shall be removed.			
		4.1.11.5		**PARTICLES** and **DUST** shall be removed.			

5

PRODUCT

FINISHING RULES (continued)

These rules are not intended to create a finishing grade; they are intended only to establish the acceptable requirements and/or characteristics after the architectural woodwork is completed or installed.

				DESCRIPTION	E	C	P
4.1 GENERAL	In **GENERAL** (continued)						
	4.1.11 WORKMANSHIP	**DEFECTS** and **WORKMANSHIP** (continued)					
		4.1.11.6	At finish, **SANDING SCRATCHES** shall be:				
			4.1.11.6.1	Inconspicuous beyond 72" (915 mm)	●		
			4.1.11.6.2	Inconspicuous beyond 36" (915 mm)		●	
			4.1.11.6.3	Not permitted			●
		4.1.11.7	**ORANGE PEEL** (slight depressions in the surface similar to the skin of an orange) shall be:				
			4.1.11.7.1	Inconspicuous beyond 72" (915 mm)	●		
			4.1.11.7.2	Inconspicuous beyond 36" (915 mm)		●	
			4.1.11.7.3	Not permitted			●
		4.1.11.8	**RUNS** (running of wet finish film in rivulets) shall be:				
			4.1.11.8.1	Inconspicuous beyond 36" (915 mm)	●		
			4.1.11.8.2	Not permitted		●	●
		4.1.11.9	**SAGS** (partial slipping of finish film creating a curtain effect) shall be:				
			4.1.11.9.1	Inconspicuous beyond 72" (915 mm)	●		
			4.1.11.9.2	Inconspicuous beyond 36" (915 mm)		●	
			4.1.11.9.3	Not permitted			●
		4.1.11.10	**BLISTERING** (small, swelled areas like water blisters on human skin) shall be:				
			4.1.11.10.1	Inconspicuous beyond 36" (915 mm)	●		
			4.1.11.10.2	Not permitted		●	●
		4.1.11.11	**BLUSHING** (whitish haze, cloudy) shall be:				
			4.1.11.11.1	Inconspicuous beyond 36" (915 mm)	●		
			4.1.11.11.2	Not permitted		●	●
		4.1.11.12	**CHECKING** or **CRAZING** (crowfeet or irregular line separation) shall be:				
			4.1.11.12.1	Inconspicuous beyond 36" (915 mm)	●		
			4.1.11.12.2	Not permitted		●	●
		4.1.11.13	**CRACKING** (formation like dried mud) shall be:				
			4.1.11.13.1	Inconspicuous beyond 36" (915 mm)	●		
			4.1.11.13.2	Not permitted		●	●
		4.1.11.14	**PARTICLES** shall be:				
			4.1.11.14.1	Inconspicuous beyond 36" (915 mm)	●	●	
			4.1.11.14.2	Not permitted			●
		4.1.11.15	**ADHESIVE SPOTS** shall be:				
			4.1.11.15.1	Inconspicuous beyond 36" (915 mm)	●		
			4.1.11.15.2	Not permitted		●	●
		4.1.11.16	**FILLED NAIL HOLES** shall be:				
			4.1.11.16.1	Inconspicuous beyond 108" (2745 mm)	●		
			4.1.11.16.2	Inconspicuous beyond 72" (1830 mm)		●	
			4.1.11.16.3	Inconspicuous beyond 36" (915 mm)			●

PRODUCT

FINISHING RULES (continued)

These rules are not intended to create a finishing grade; they are intended only to establish the acceptable requirements and/or characteristics after the architectural woodwork is completed or installed.

Group	Subsection	Item	Sub-item	DESCRIPTION	E	C	P
⇑ 4.1 GENERAL	⇑ 4.1.11	**4.1.11.17**		**FIELD REPAIRS** and **TOUCH-UPS** shall be:			
			4.1.11.17.1	Inconspicuous beyond 108" (2745 mm)	●		
			4.1.11.17.2	Inconspicuous beyond 72" (1830 mm)		●	
			4.1.11.17.3	Inconspicuous beyond 36" (915 mm)			●
	4.1.12 FIRST CLASS			**FIRST-CLASS WORKMANSHIP** is required in compliance with these standards, including but not limited to:			
		4.1.12.1		All joints being tight, true, flush, and securely glued.			
		4.1.2.2		All parts being uniform, square, level, plumb, flush, and in alignment.			
		4.1.2.3		Hardware being neatly installed, free of tear-outs, and adjusted for smooth operation, with all fasteners squarely set.			
		4.1.12.4		Exposed and semi-exposed surfaces free of tear-out, chips, dents, gouges, tool marks, adhesive residue, sand-through, cross-sanding, over/under-filing, sharp edges, poorly fitted edging, or similar defects within the tolerances listed below for any 10 square feet (9290 square cm) of surface area:			
			4.1.12.4.1	Maximum of 8, not exceeding 1/16" (1.6 mm)	●		
			4.1.2.4.2	Maximum of 5, not exceeding 1/32" (0.8 mm)		●	
			4.1.12.4.3	None			●
4.2 MATERIAL	**MATERIAL** requires:						
	4.2.1			**BACK-PRIMING/SEALING**, when factory finishing is required, shall be of a compatible material and conform to the following application requirements:			
		4.2.1.1		**STANDING** and **RUNNING TRIM** shall have one coat at 1 mil dry.		●	●
		4.2.1.2		**WALL SURFACING** shall have two coats at 2 mil dry.		●	●
		4.2.1.3		**CASEWORK** shall have one coat at 1 mil dry.			●
		4.2.1.4		**DECORATIVE LAMINATE** faced woodwork shall have one coat at 1 mil dry.		●	●
	4.2.2			**FLOW** properties capable of drying and/or curing free of streaks, sags, or mottle.			
	4.2.3			If so specified, **CHEMICAL RESISTANCE** at exposed horizontal surfaces shall pass a 24-hour exposure test, whereas exposed vertical surfaces and semi-exposed surfaces shall pass a 1-hour exposure test (ASTM 1308, latest edition).			
4.3 APPLICATION ⇓	**APPLICATION** requires:						
	4.3.1			**SANDING** before and during all finishing procedures and shall include:			
		4.3.1.1		Exposed surfaces being block-sanded parallel with the grain direction and the appropriate grit paper to prevent unacceptable blotchy and/or nonuniform appearance after staining or finishing.			
		4.3.1.2		Removal of handling marks or effects of exposure to moisture.			
		4.3.1.3		Steaming out of deep scratches.			
		4.3.1.4		Easing of sharp edges with a light sanding.			
		4.3.1.5		Removal of all raised grain, cross-sanding, burnishing and machining marks, sanding inconsistencies, and/or defects.			
		4.3.1.6		Light sanding between coats per manufacturer's recommendations.			
	4.3.2			**FACTORY-PRIMING** with one coat of primer applied to appropriate surfaces.			
		4.3.2.1		Sanding of factory-primed surfaces is not required.			
	4.3.3			**VENTILATION**, adequate and continuous, with sufficient heat to maintain temperatures above 65° F for 24 hours before, during, and 48 hours after application of finishes.			
	4.3.4			**OVER-SPRAY** protection to prevent spray or droppings from fouling surfaces not being finished.			
		4.3.4.1		Repair damage as a result of inadequate or unsuitable protection.			

5

PRODUCT

FINISHING RULES (continued)

These rules are not intended to create a finishing grade; they are intended only to establish the acceptable requirements and/or characteristics after the architectural woodwork is completed or installed.

	No.	DESCRIPTION	E	C	P
4.3 APPLICATION		**APPLICATION** (continued)			
	4.3.5	**REMOVAL** of electrical plates, surface hardware, fittings, and fastenings prior to finishing operation.			
	4.3.5.1	Items are to be carefully stored, cleaned, and replaced on completion of work in each area.			
	4.3.5.1.1	Do not use solvent to clean hardwood that might remove permanent finish.			
	4.3.6	The **CLEANING** of surfaces with a dry brush or a tack cloth before applying sealer, stain, or primer.			
	4.3.7	**SCRATCHES**, dents, marks, screw and nail holes, and rough edges shall be properly repaired before finishing.			
	4.3.8	**CONSISTENCY** of each coat shall be as recommended by the manufacturer.			
	4.3.9	**FILM THICKNESS** shall conform to manufacturer's data or recommendation.			
	4.3.10	**FILLER** (including paste types), if required to fill open-pore woods to create a full finish, shall be applied before sealers or topcoats.		●	●
	4.3.11	**THOROUGHLY DRY** each coat before sanding or applying additional coats.			
	4.3.12	**SAPWOOD** treatment:			
	4.3.12.1	At **EXPOSED SURFACES:**			
	4.3.12.1.1	Blending is not required.	●		
	4.3.12.1.2	Sapwood must be blended in the final finish appearance.		●	●
	4.3.12.2	At **SEMI-EXPOSED SURFACES,** blending is not required.			
	4.3.13	**STAINING**:			
	4.3.13.1	For dark stain finishes, the surface shall be wash-coat sealed.			
	4.3.13.2	Oil stain shall be wipe-applied in small areas at a time.			
	4.3.13.3	Non-grain-raising dye stains can be spray-applied.			
	4.3.13.4	Open-grain species shall be stained before applying sealer.			
	4.3.14	At **GENERIC COATING SCHEDULE**, concealed and semi-exposed surfaces require:			
GENERIC	4.3.14.1	**CONCEALED CASEWORK SURFACES,** at factory-finished items that abut walls, floors, and ceilings, shall receive sanding sealer or self-seal system.		●	●
	4.3.14.2	**DRAWER BOX CASE** interior surfaces shall receive sanding sealer or self-seal system.			●
	4.3.14.3	**SEMI-EXPOSED** surfaces, including wood drawer sides and cabinet interiors, shall receive items in [brackets] only if so specified:			
	4.3.14.3.1	[Wash coat]			
	4.3.14.3.2	[Stain]			
	4.3.14.3.3	Sanding sealer			
	4.3.14.3.4	Sand			
	4.3.14.3.5	First topcoat		●	●
	4.3.14.3.6	Second topcoat			●
	4.3.14.4	**EXPOSED** surfaces shall receive items in [brackets] only if so specified:			
	4.3.14.4.1	[Wash coat]			
	4.3.14.4.2	[Stain]			
	4.3.14.4.3	Sanding sealer			
	4.3.14.4.4	Sand			
	4.3.14.4.5	First topcoat			
	4.3.14.4.6	Second topcoat		●	●
	4.3.14.4.7	Third topcoat			●

PRODUCT

FINISHING RULES (continued)

These rules are not intended to create a finishing grade; they are intended only to establish the acceptable requirements and/or characteristics after the architectural woodwork is completed or installed.

Section	Item	DESCRIPTION	E	C	P
4.3		**APPLICATION** (continued)			
4.3.14		At **GENERIC COATING SCHEDULE** (continued)			
	4.3.14.5	**EXCLUDES** wood components on HPDL casework:			
4.3.15		At **SYSTEM COATING SCHEDULE**			
4.3.15.1		**SYSTEM - 1, LACQUER, NITROCELLULOSE** requires items in [brackets] only if so specified:			
4.3.15.1.1		**CLOSE-GRAIN** woods			
	4.3.15.1.1.1	[Wash coat, nitrocellulose]	●	●	
	4.3.15.1.1.2	[Wash coat, vinyl]			●
	4.3.15.1.1.3	[Stain]	●	●	●
	4.3.15.1.1.4	Sealer, nitrocellulose	●	●	
	4.3.15.1.1.5	Sealer, vinyl			●
	4.3.15.1.1.6	First topcoat			
	4.3.15.1.1.7	Second topcoat			●
4.3.15.1.2		**OPEN-GRAIN** woods (including filled finish)			
	4.3.15.1.2.1	Wash coat, nitrocellulose (only at filled finish)		●	
	4.3.15.1.2.2	Wash coat, vinyl (only at filled finish)			●
	4.3.15.1.2.3	[Stain]			
	4.3.15.1.2.4	Filler (only at filled finish)		●	●
	4.3.15.1.2.5	Sealer, nitrocellulose	●	●	
	4.3.15.1.2.6	Sealer, vinyl			●
	4.3.15.1.2.7	First topcoat			
	4.3.15.1.2.8	Second topcoat (only at filled finish)		●	
	4.3.15.1.2.9	Second topcoat			●
4.3.15.2		**SYSTEMS - 2 and 3, LACQUER, PRE- AND POSTCATALYZED** require items in [brackets] only if so specified:			
4.3.15.2.1		**CLOSE-GRAIN** woods			
	4.3.15.2.1.1	[Wash coat, vinyl]			
	4.3.15.2.1.2	[Stain]			
	4.3.15.2.1.3	Sealer, vinyl			
	4.3.15.2.1.4	First topcoat			
	4.3.15.2.1.5	Second topcoat		●	●
4.3.15.2.2		**OPEN-GRAIN** woods (including filled finish)			
	4.3.15.2.2.1	Washcoat, vinyl (only at filled finish)		●	●
	4.3.15.2.2.2	[Stain]			
	4.3.15.2.2.3	Filler (only at filled finish)	●	●	
	4.3.15.2.2.4	Sealer, vinyl			
	4.3.15.2.2.5	First topcoat			
	4.3.15.2.2.6	Second topcoat		●	●

PRODUCT

FINISHING RULES (continued)

These rules are not intended to create a finishing grade; they are intended only to establish the acceptable requirements and/or characteristics after the architectural woodwork is completed or installed.

5

Section				DESCRIPTION	E	C	P
4.3 APPLICATION				**APPLICATION** (continued)			
	4.3.15 SYSTEM COATING SCHEDULE			At **SYSTEM COATING SCHEDULE** (continued)			
		4.3.15.3 SYS 4		**SYSTEM - 4, LATEX ACRYLIC, WATER-BASED** requires items in [brackets] only if so specified:			
			4.3.15.3.1	**CLOSE-** and **OPEN-GRAIN** woods			
			4.3.15.3.1.1	[Stain]	●	●	●
			4.3.15.3.1.2	Sealer, water-reduced	●	●	
			4.3.15.3.1.4	First topcoat, water-reducible acrylic	●	●	
			4.3.15.3.1.5	Second topcoat, water-reducible acrylic		●	
		4.3.15.4 SYSTEM 5		**SYSTEM - 5, VARNISH, CONVERSION** requires items in [brackets] only if so specified:			
			4.3.15.4.1	**CLOSE GRAIN** woods			
			4.3.15.4.1.1	[Wash coat, reduced conversion varnish]	●	●	
			4.3.15.4.1.2	[Wash coat, vinyl]			●
			4.3.15.4.1.3	[Stain]			
			4.3.15.4.1.4	Sealer, reduced conversion varnish	●	●	
			4.3.15.4.1.5	Sealer, vinyl			●
			4.3.15.4.1.6	First topcoat	●	●	●
			4.3.15.4.1.7	Second topcoat			●
			4.3.15.4.2	**OPEN-GRAIN** woods (including filled finish)			
			4.3.15.4.2.1	[Wash coat, reduced conversion varnish] (only at filled finish)		●	
			4.3.15.4.2.2	Wash coat, vinyl (only at filled finish)			●
			4.3.15.4.2.3	[Stain]			
			4.3.15.4.2.4	Filler (only at filled finish)		●	●
			4.3.15.4.2.5	Sealer, reduced conversion varnish	●	●	
			4.3.15.4.2.6	Sealer, vinyl			●
			4.3.15.4.2.7	First topcoat			
			4.3.15.4.2.8	Second topcoat		●	●
		4.3.15.5 SYSTEM 6		**SYSTEM - 6, OIL, PENETRATING** requires items in [brackets] only if so specified:			
			4.3.15.5.1	**CLOSE-** and **OPEN-GRAIN** woods			
			4.3.15.5.1.1	[Simulated oil finish]	●		
			4.3.15.5.1.2	First coat, penetrating oil			
			4.3.15.5.1.3	Brass wool rubdown		●	
			4.3.15.5.1.4	Second coat, penetrating oil		●	
			4.3.15.5.1.5	Wax coat		●	●
			4.3.15.5.1.6	Sealer, catalyzed vinyl	●		
			4.3.15.5.1.7	Scuff sand with appropriate grit	●		

PRODUCT

FINISHING RULES (continued)

These rules are not intended to create a finishing grade; they are intended only to establish the acceptable requirements and/or characteristics after the architectural woodwork is completed or installed.

				DESCRIPTION	E	C	P
4.3 APPLICATION	**APPLICATION** (continued)						
	4.3.15 SYSTEM COATING SCHEDULE	At **SYSTEM COATING SCHEDULE** (continued)					
		4.3.15.6 SYSTEM 7	**SYSTEM - 7, VINYL, CATALYZED** requires items in [brackets] only if so specified:				
			4.3.15.6.1	**CLOSE-GRAIN** woods			
			4.3.15.6.1.1	[Wash coat, vinyl]			
			4.3.15.6.1.2	[Stain]			
			4.3.15.6.1.3	Sealer, vinyl	●	●	
			4.3.15.6.1.4	Sealer, vinyl, catalyzed			●
			4.3.15.6.1.5	First topcoat			
			4.3.15.6.1.6	Second topcoat		●	●
			4.3.15.6.2	**OPEN-GRAIN** woods (including filled finish)			
			4.3.15.6.2.1	[Wash coat, vinyl] (only at filled finish)		●	
			4.3.15.6.2.2	[Wash coat, vinyl, catalyzed] (only at filled finish)			●
			4.3.15.6.2.3	[Stain]			
			4.3.15.6.2.4	Sealer, vinyl	●	●	
			4.3.15.6.2.5	Filler (only at filled finish)		●	●
			4.3.15.6.2.6	Sealer, vinyl, catalyzed			●
			4.3.15.6.2.7	First topcoat			
			4.3.15.6.2.8	Second topcoat		●	●
		4.3.15.7 SYS 8	**SYSTEM - 8, ACRYLIC CROSS-LINKING, WATER-BASED** requires items in [brackets] only if so specified:				
			4.3.15.7.1	**CLOSE-** and **OPEN-GRAIN** woods			
			4.3.15.7.1.1	[Stain]			
			4.3.15.7.1.2	Sealer, water-reduced			
			4.3.15.7.1.3	First topcoat, water-reducible acrylic			
			4.3.15.7.1.4	Second topcoat, water-reducible acrylic		●	●
		4.3.15.8 SYS 9 & 10	**SYSTEM - 9** and **10, UV-CURABLE, ACRYLATED EPOXY, POLYESTER, URETHANE** require items in [brackets] only if so specified; only applicable to Premium Grade:				
			4.3.15.8.1	**CLOSE-** and **OPEN-GRAIN** woods			
			4.3.15.8.1.1	[Stain]			●
			4.3.15.8.1.2	Sealer with B-stage curing			●
			4.3.15.8.1.3	Sealer with full cure			●
			4.3.15.8.1.4	First topcoat with B-stage curing			●
			4.3.15.8.1.5	Second topcoat with full cure			●
		4.3.15.9	**SYSTEM - 11** and **12, POLYURETHANE, CATALYZED,** or **WATER-BASED** require items in [brackets] only if so specified:				
			4.3.15.9.1	**CLOSE-GRAIN** woods			
			4.3.15.9.1.1	[Wash coat, reduced vinyl sealer]			
			4.3.15.9.1.2	[Stain]			
			4.3.15.9.1.3	Sealer, vinyl			
			4.3.15.9.1.4	First topcoat			
			4.3.15.9.1.5	Second topcoat			●

5

PRODUCT

FINISHING RULES (continued)

These rules are not intended to create a finishing grade; they are intended only to establish the acceptable requirements and/or characteristics after the architectural woodwork is completed or installed.

Number	DESCRIPTION	E	C	P
4.3	**APPLICATION** (continued)			
4.3.15	At **SYSTEM COATING SCHEDULE** (continued)			
4.3.15.9	**SYSTEM - 11** and **12, POLYURETHANE, CATALYZED,** or **WATER-BASED** (continued)			
4.3.15.9.2	**OPEN-GRAIN** woods (including filled finish)			
4.3.15.9.2.1	[Wash coat, reduced vinyl sealer] (only at filled finish)		●	●
4.3.15.9.2.2	[Stain]			
4.3.15.9.2.3	Filler (only at filled finish)		●	●
4.3.15.9.2.4	Sealer, vinyl			
4.3.15.9.2.5	First topcoat			
4.3.15.9.2.6	Second topcoat			●
4.3.15.10	**SYSTEM - 13, POLYESTER, CATALYZED** requires items in [brackets] only if so specified; only applicable to Premium Grade:			
4.3.15.10.1	**CLOSE-** and **OPEN-GRAIN** woods			
4.3.15.10.1.1	[Stain]			●
4.3.15.10.1.2	First sealer, polyester			●
4.3.15.10.1.3	Second sealer, polyester			●
4.3.15.10.1.4	Sand with appropriate grit			●
4.3.15.10.1.5	Topcoat, polyester			●
4.3.15.10.1.6	Rub and polish, mechanical			●
4.3.16	**AFTER FINISHING**			
4.3.16.1	Remove all spilled, splashed, or spattered finish materials.			
4.3.16.2	Remove all fingerprints or other marks.			
4.3.16.3	Provide a final dusting of all exterior and interior surfaces, including drawers.			
4.3.16.4	Provide properly labeled touch-up materials to allow for minor touch-up.			
4.3.17	**TOUCH-UP** of:			
4.3.17.1	Factory-finished materials are the responsibility of the installation contractor.			
4.3.17.2	Jobsite-finished materials are the responsibility of the finishing contractor.			

EXECUTION

(Items # 5 & 6 are not applicable to this section)

COMPLIANCE

7 GENERAL

7.1 **VISUAL TESTING** is only applicable to exposed surfaces:

7.1.1 View finished surfaces in the ambient conditions in which they will be installed and used.

7.1.1.1 Perception of color varies with the light source and between individuals.

7.1.2 **TESTS** apply only to new work at the time of installation.

7.1.2.1 They shall not be applied to refinishing conditions, except as agreed in advance between buyer and seller.

7.2 **TESTING** for **CONSISTENCY** of **GRAIN** and **COLOR:**

7.2.1 Compliance with standards for color and grain are highly subjective.

7.2.1.1 Each person's perception of color is unique.

7.2.1.2 The apparent color of a finished wood species is affected by many variables, such as:

7.2.1.2.1 Ambient lighting

7.2.1.2.2 Cellular structure of the individual piece of wood

7.2.1.2.3 Cutting or slicing of the wood

7.2.1.2.4 Machining and sanding of the surface

7.2.1.2.5 Orientation of the surface to the viewer

7.2.2 Compliance shall be evaluated (by comparison to an approved panel, minimum 8" x 12" [200 x 250 mm], that has been signed and dated and protected from light) based on the following conditions:

7.2.2.1 Viewing of the surfaces in the lighting and orientation in which they will be installed.

7.2.2.2 Observing a color and tone blending that is not significantly lighter than the lightest of the range, nor darker than the darkest of the range.

7.2.2.3 Because of natural variations in color and grain, it cannot be expected that all panels will match one particular sample exactly; however, shall match within the sample range submitted.

7.3 **SHEEN TEST**

7.3.1 Listed in point ranges, which might vary by coating supplier and/or by species of wood and the way it takes the topcoat; typically, a spread of 20 points is difficult to observe on installed woodwork.

7.3.2 The following sheen ranges were developed with a 60-degree gloss meter:

7.3.2.1 **FLAT** = 15 to 30

7.3.2.2 **SATIN** = 31 to 45

7.3.2.3 **SEMIGLOSS** = 46 to 60

7.3.2.4 **GLOSS** = 61 or greater

7.3.3 Compliance shall be evaluated (by comparison to a sample panel, minimum 8" x 12" [200 x 250 mm], that has been signed and dated and protected from light) based on the following conditions:

7.3.3.1 Testing of the surfaces with a gloss meter, parallel to the grain, in identical lighting conditions:

7.3.3.1.1 When contract documents call for sheen using the terms Flat, Satin, Semigloss, or Gloss, sheen results falling within the ranges listed above shall be considered in compliance.

COMPLIANCE

7.3 **SHEEN TEST** (continued)

7.3.3 Compliance shall be (continued)

7.3.3.1 Testing of the surfaces with a gloss meter (continued)

7.3.3.1.2 When comparisons of sheen tests between the approved and protected sample panels and the installed work show sheen readings outside of the listed ranges, sheen results within 10 points of each other shall be considered to be in compliance.

7.3.3.2 Testing with a light source (see illustration) does not provide very accurate results; however, it is a general guide:

7.3.3.2.1 A **SATIN FINISH** will deflect direct light.

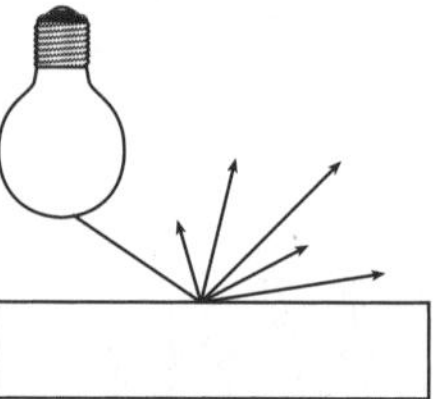

7.3.3.2.2 A highly buffed **GLOSS FINISH** will reflect light.

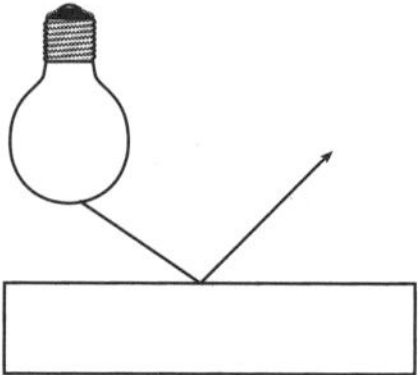

5

Architectural Woodwork Standards

SECTION - 6

INTERIOR & EXTERIOR MILLWORK

SECTION 6 ✦ INTERIOR & EXTERIOR MILLWORK

(Including Standing & Running Trim, Door Frames, Window Frames, Sashes, Blinds & Shutters, Screens, Ornamental & Miscellaneous Millwork Composed of Solid Wood and/or Sheet Products)

GENERAL

1 INFORMATION

1.1 GRADES

1.1.1 These standards are characterized in three Grades of quality that may be mixed within a single project. Limitless design possibilities and a wide variety of lumber and veneer species, along with overlays, high-pressure decorative laminates, factory finishes, and profiles are available in all three Grades.

1.1.2 **ECONOMY GRADE** defines the minimum quality requirements for a project's workmanship, materials, or installation and is typically reserved for woodwork that is not in public view, such as in mechanical rooms and utility areas.

1.1.3 **CUSTOM GRADE** is typically specified for and adequately covers most high-quality architectural woodwork, providing a well-defined degree of control over a project's quality of materials, workmanship, or installation.

1.1.4 **PREMIUM GRADE** is typically specified for use in those areas of a project where the highest level of quality, materials, workmanship, and installation is required.

1.1.5 **MODIFICATIONS** by the contract documents shall govern if in conflict with these standards.

1.2 BASIC CONSIDERATIONS

1.2.1 **ACCEPTABLE REQUIREMENTS** of lumber and/or sheet products used within this woodwork product section are established by Sections 3 and 4, unless otherwise modified herein.

6

1.2.2 **CONTRACT DRAWINGS** and/or **SPECIFICATIONS**, furnished by the design professional, shall clearly indicate or delineate all material, fabrication, installation, and applicable building code/regulation requirements.

1.2.3 **CROSS GRAIN** in band-sawn or laminated members and **EDGES** in veneer-laminated members or where multiple layers are exposed by shaping may cause objectionable color variation when finished.

1.2.4 **WOOD FIRE-RATED DOOR FRAMES** are available in 20-, 45-, 60-, and 90-minute classifications (see Industry Practices [Item 1.5] for additional information).

1.2.5 **EXPOSED SURFACES INCLUDE:**

1.2.5.1 Visible surfaces of standing/running trim, door/window frames, sashes, screens, blinds, shutters, and miscellaneous woodwork, excluding:

1.2.5.1.1 Top horizontal surfaces 80" (2032 mm) or more above the finished floor, unless visible from above.

1.2.5.1.2 Bottom horizontal surfaces 42" (1067 mm) or less above the finished floor.

1.2.6 **SEMI-EXPOSED SURFACES INCLUDE:**

1.2.6.1 Top horizontal surfaces 80" (2032 mm) or more above the finished floor, unless visible from above.

1.2.6.2 Bottom horizontal surfaces 42" (1067 mm) or less above the finished floor.

1.2.7 **CONCEALED SURFACES INCLUDE:**

1.2.7.1 Non-visible surfaces attached to and/or covered by another.

1.2.7.2 Non-visible blocking, spacers, etc., used for attachment.

1.2.8 The **SMOOTHNESS** of:

1.2.8.1 **PLANED** or **MOLDED SURFACES** is directly related to the closeness of the knife cuts.

1.2.8.1.1 The closer the cuts are to each other (i.e., the more knife cuts per inch [KCPI]), the closer the ridges, therefore, the smoother the resulting appearance.

GENERAL

1.2 **BASIC CONSIDERATIONS** (continued)

1.2.8 The **SMOOTHNESS** of (continued)

1.2.8.2 **SANDED SURFACES** is directly related to the grit of the abrasive used.

1.2.8.2.1 Sandpapers come in grits from coarse to fine and are assigned ascending grit numbers. The coarser the grit, the faster the stock removal.

1.2.8.2.2 The surface will show the striations caused by the grit. Sanding with progressively finer-grit papers will produce smoother surfaces.

1.2.9 **RADIUS WORK** is segmented, bent, laminated, and formed or machined to the radius.

1.2.9.1 **SOLID MACHINED** woodwork typically starts with a large, often glued-up piece of material, from which several nested pieces can be machined.

1.2.9.1.1 Characteristically, this method limits the length of pieces that can be developed without a joint.

1.2.9.1.2 It also yields a piece of material with the grain straight on the face, not following the curve.

1.2.9.1.3 Profiles with a flat face can be machined from sheet products with an edgeband applied, yielding larger pieces with more consistent grain.

1.2.9.2 **BLOCK-LAMINATED** woodwork is made of solid machined pieces, glued-up typically in a staggered fashion for width and length.

1.2.9.2.1 This technique is used in radius jambs and often becomes the core for **CORE-VENEERED** woodwork (see 1.2.9.4).

1.2.9.3 **LAMINATED-PLIES** woodwork consists of thin, bendable plies of lumber in a form that will hold its shape without having to be secured to another surface. 6

1.2.9.3.1 The curved piece can then be milled to the desired profile.

1.2.9.3.2 The glue lines follow the edge grain and the curve, thus minimizing their visibility.

1.2.9.3.3 The species of wood and the tightness of the radius determine the maximum thickness of each ply.

1.2.9.4 **CORE-VENEERED** woodwork consists of core machined from lumber or panel product to which finish material is laminated as an exposed face.

1.2.9.4.1 This technique is limited to certain profiles; however, it offers the ability to minimize glue joints and control grain directions.

1.2.9.5 **KERFED** woodwork consists of lumber with repeated saw cuts on the back face of the piece, perpendicular to the bend.

1.2.9.5.1 The tightness of the radius determines the spacing and depth of the kerfs. Kerfing allows the piece to be bent to the required radius and then secured in place to hold the bend. Kerfing could result in "flats" on the face, which show in finishing.

1.2.9.5.2 When dealing with a large radius, it is sometimes possible to stop the kerf prior to going through an exposed edge. In most cases, however, the kerf runs all the way through, and the edge must be concealed.

1.2.9.6 **CHORD SEGMENTATION**, as shown below, is the process of cutting short lengths of straight molding and joining them around a curved substrate and is **NOT** permitted unless specified.

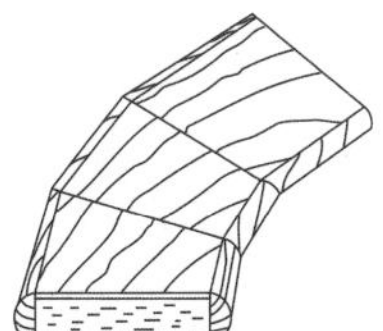

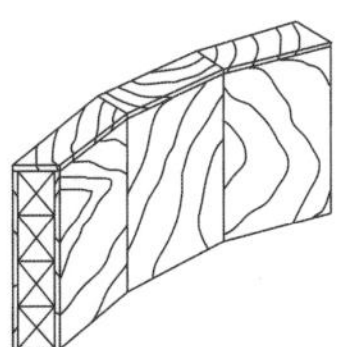

GENERAL

1.2 **BASIC CONSIDERATIONS** (continued)

1.2.9 **RADIUS WORK** (continued)

1.2.9.7 The **METHOD of FABRICATION**, unless specified otherwise, is the manufacturer's option.

1.2.9.7.1 The fabrication method can affect the final appearance, especially regarding the direction of the grain and the visibility of the glue joints. The design professional may wish to specify the method; however, it is recommended that an architectural woodwork firm be consulted before making a particular selection. Mock-ups may be required to visualize the end product.

1.2.10 **STANDING** and **RUNNING** trim nomenclature and examples:

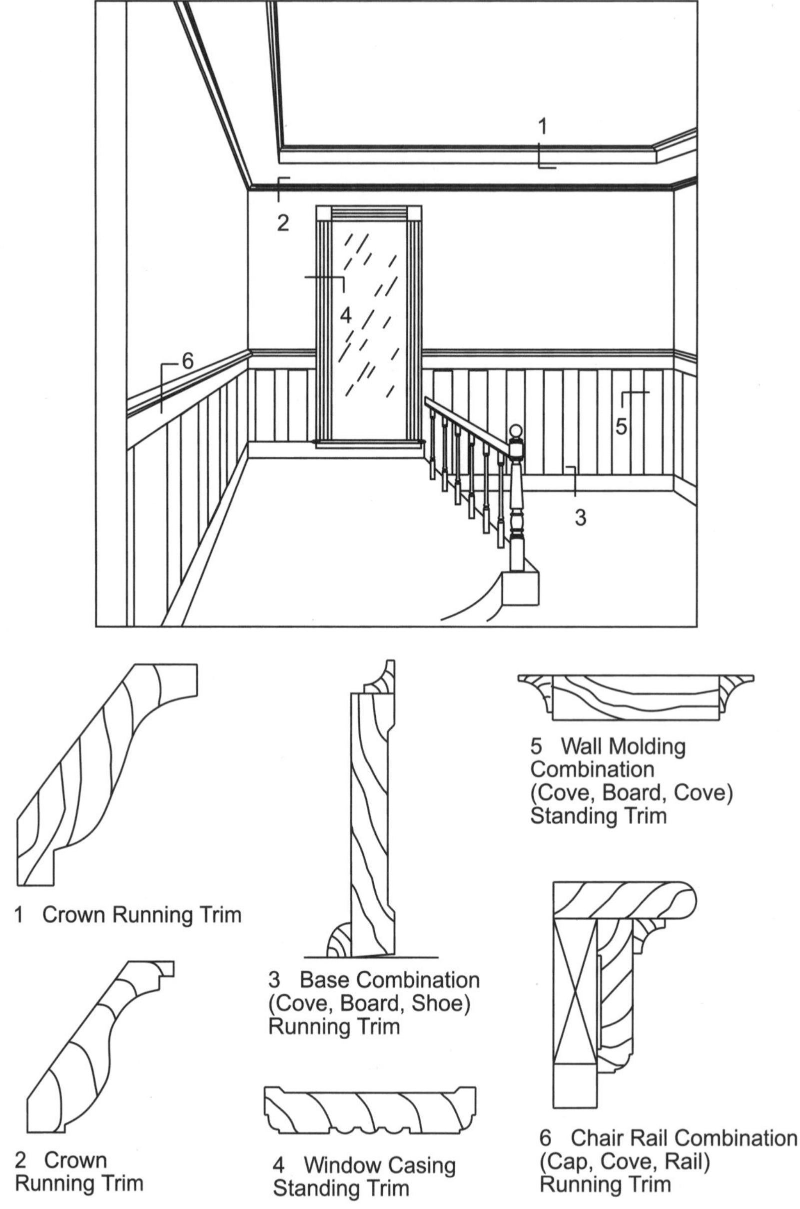

GENERAL

1.2 **BASIC CONSIDERATIONS** (continued)

1.2.11 **DOOR FRAMES** and **JAMBS**

1.2.11.1 Typical **FRAME** and **JAMB** examples:

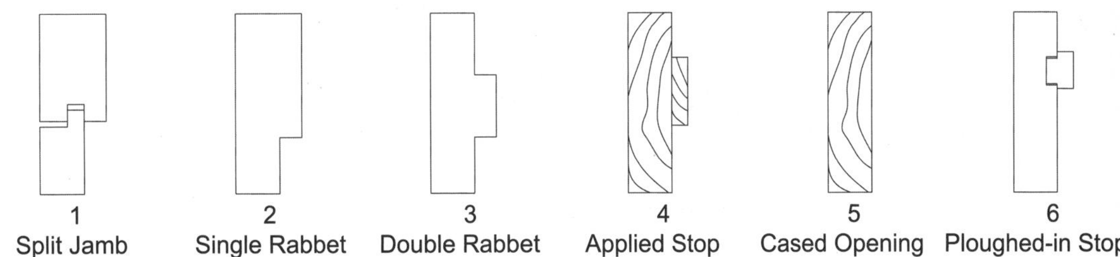

1 Split Jamb | 2 Single Rabbet | 3 Double Rabbet | 4 Applied Stop | 5 Cased Opening | 6 Ploughed-in Stop

1.2.11.2 Typical **FRAME JOINERY** examples:

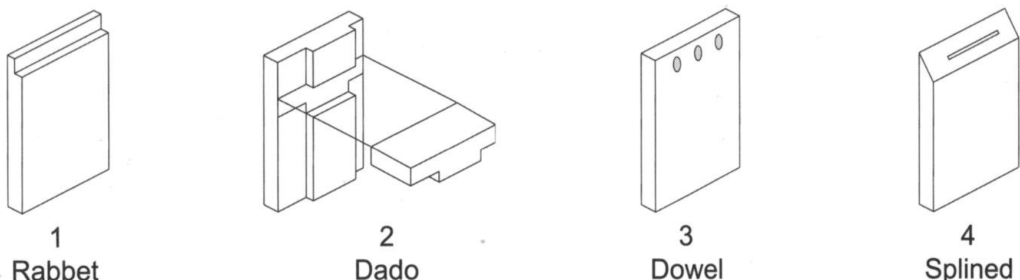

1 Rabbet | 2 Dado | 3 Dowel | 4 Splined

1.2.11.3 **LABELED** (fire-rated) jamb assemblies are available in limited design/ratings/species; however, new designs/ratings are in ongoing development.

1.2.11.3.1 Only firms recognized by applicable code officials are authorized to label a frame assembly. If a label will be required by the applicable code officials, it is the obligation of the design professional to so specify, and the obligation of the manufacturer to assure a properly licensed assembly.

1.2.11.3.2 These standards do not cover **LABELED** frames.

1.2.12 **WINDOW SASH** and **FRAMES**

1.2.12.1 Typical **ASSEMBLY** examples:

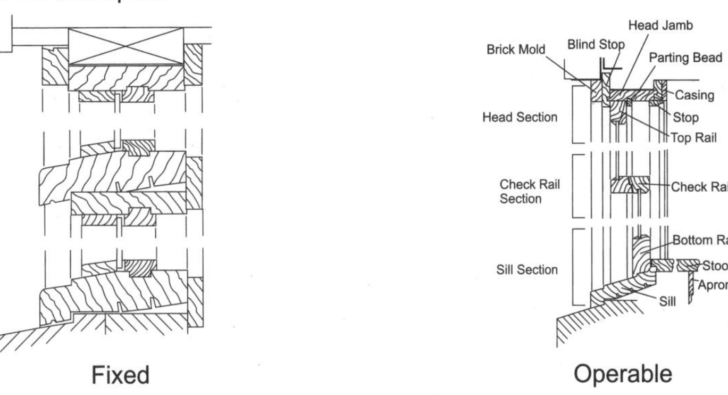

Fixed | Operable

1.2.12.2 Typical **SASH JOINERY** examples:

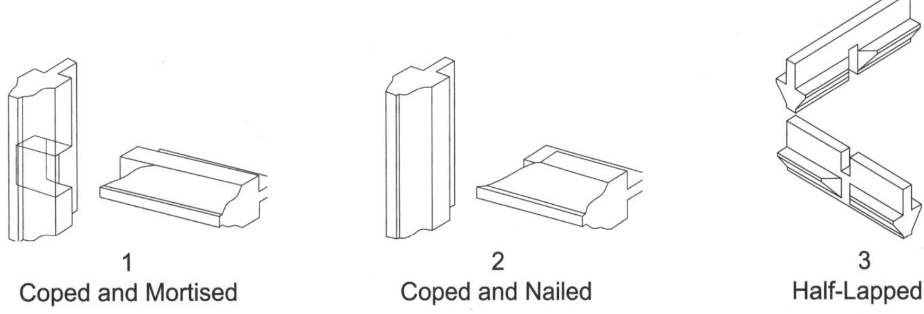

1 Coped and Mortised | 2 Coped and Nailed | 3 Half-Lapped

GENERAL

1.2 **BASIC CONSIDERATIONS** (continued)

1.2.12 **WINDOW SASH and FRAMES** (continued)

1.2.12.2 Typical **SASH JOINERY** examples (continued)

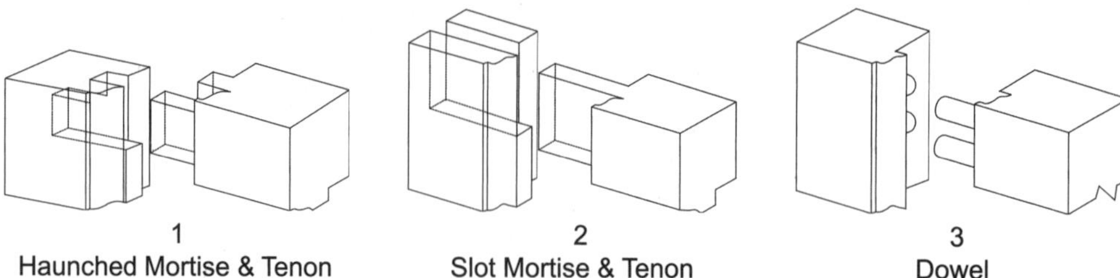

1 Haunched Mortise & Tenon
2 Slot Mortise & Tenon
3 Dowel

1.2.12.3 Typical **GLAZING** examples:

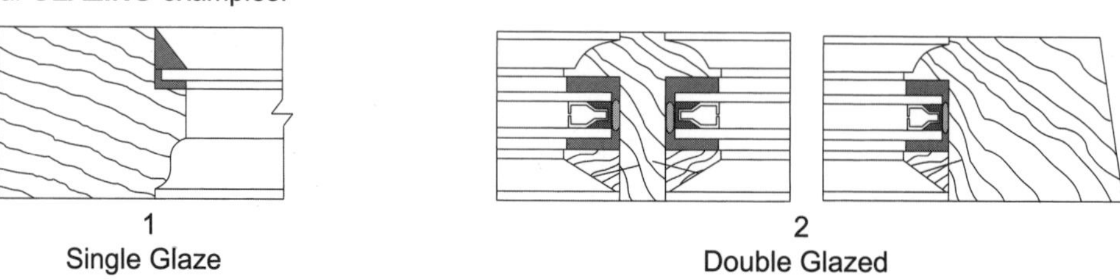

1 Single Glaze
2 Double Glazed

1.2.12.3.1 Paint should lap the glass by 1/16"+ (1.6 mm+) for proper exterior seal:

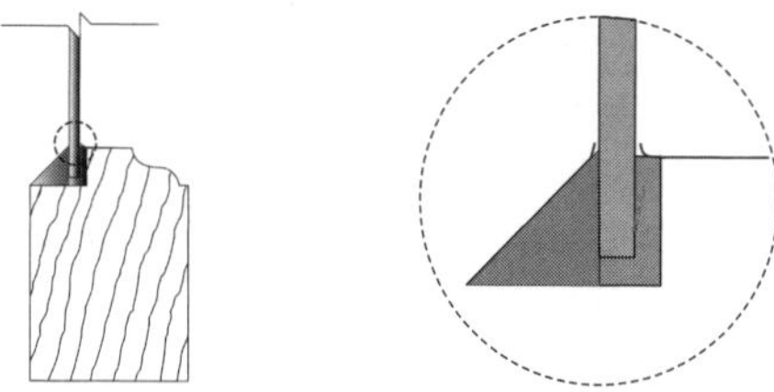

1.2.12.4 **THERMAL INTEGRITY:**

1.2.12.4.1 Wood is a natural insulator that retains heat in winter without a thermal break, resists conductance of cold temperatures 2000 times better than aluminum, and is approximately 30% more thermally efficient than comparable aluminum windows.

1.2.12.4.2 Wood's minimal conduction keeps the inside wood surface of windows warm in the winter and cool in the summer.

1.2.12.4.3 Wood windows are available in single-, double-, and triple-glazing systems, increasing thermal efficiency.

1.2.12.5 **PERFORMANCE TESTING** is applicable only to complete exterior window units and, if required, must be specified and may include all or part of ASTM E 283, Air Infiltration; E 330, Loading; and/or E 547, Water Penetration. ASTM tests must be specified for the current ASTM Grade Level:

1.2.13 **BLINDS** and **SHUTTERS**:

1.2.13.1 **HARDWARE** must be specified, as it dictates the details of construction.

1.2.13.1.1 **MANUFACTURER DOES NOT** typically supply, machine for, or install operating hardware, locking devices, pulls, lifts, etc.

GENERAL

1.2 **BASIC CONSIDERATIONS** (continued)

1.2.13 **BLINDS** and **SHUTTERS** (continued)

1.2.13.2 Typical examples

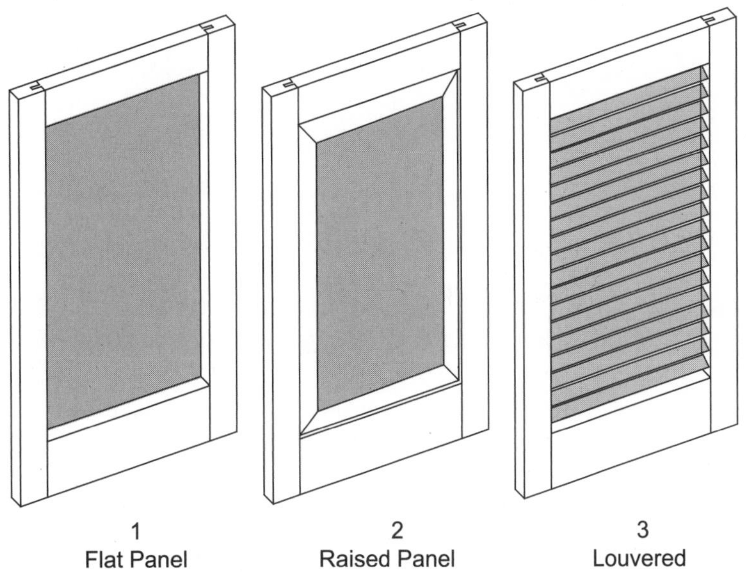

1.2.14 **SCREENS**:

1.2.14.1 **HARDWARE** must be specified, as it dictates the details of construction.

1.2.14.1.1 **MANUFACTURER DOES NOT** typically supply, machine for, or install operating hardware, locking devices, pulls, lifts, etc.

1.2.14.2 Typical bead detail examples:

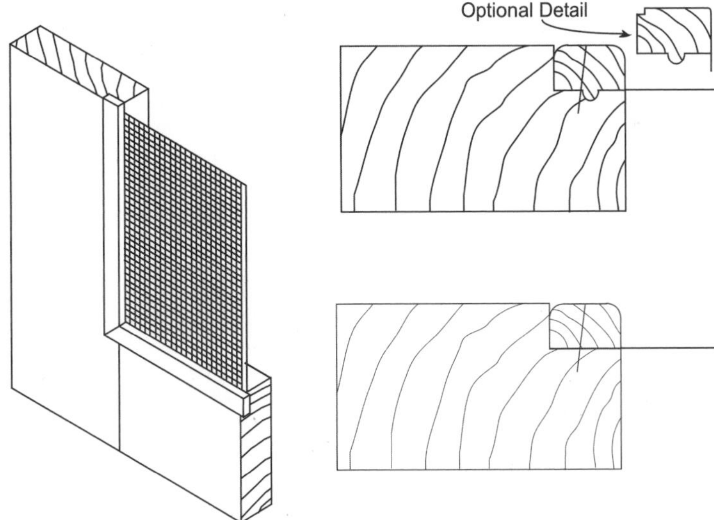

1.2.15 **ORNAMENTAL WOODWORK**:

1.2.15.1 **TYPICAL SOURCES** of wood ornamentation are either mass-produced or custom carved and tooled.

1.2.15.1.1 **MASS-PRODUCED** product is often limited in available species, sizes, and design, and is often a hodgepodge of historic styles, which:

1.2.15.1.1.1 Might lack detail clarity.

1.2.15.1.1.2 Can be appropriate for many applications.

GENERAL

1.2 **BASIC CONSIDERATIONS** (continued)

1.2.15 **ORNAMENTAL WOODWORK** (continued)

1.2.15.1 **TYPICAL SOURCES** (continued)

1.2.15.1.2 **CUSTOM CARVED** or tooled work has a special appearance, with:

1.2.15.1.2.1 Depth and clarity or crispness that machine tooling often cannot achieve.

1.2.15.1.2.2 Slight irregularities because it is done by a skilled artisan; however, this is deemed desirable as it lends character and credence to the work.

1.2.15.1.2.3 Tool-marked surface, which can be sanded smooth or left as a texture.

1.2.15.2 There are four methods of depicting a design in wood:

1.2.15.2.1 **INCISED**: Designs are simply made by shallow grooves in the surface of the material.

1.2.15.2.2 **RELIEF**: Most architectural carving is carved in relief. The degree to which the design is lifted off the surface is described as low or high relief.

1.2.15.2.3 **PIERCED**: Some voids in the design are literally cut through the material and are termed pierced carvings.

1.2.15.2.4 **SCULPTURE**: Carving in-the-round or sculptural works are incorporated into architectural surroundings.

1.2.15.3 **MOLDINGS** have multiple uses but an important one is to visually set apart various elements. For instance, they are transitions between the parts of the entablature.

1.2.15.3.1 They accentuate the trim (architrave) around doors and windows and around an arch (archivolt).

1.2.15.3.2 The various terms depend primarily on the profiles, but there are a few terms that indicate use, location, or size.

1.3 **RECOMMENDATIONS**

1.3.1 **INCLUDE IN DIVISION 09 OF THE SPECIFICATIONS:**

1.3.1.1 For **JOBSITE FINISHING** - BEFORE FINISHING, all exposed portions of woodwork shall have handling marks or effects of exposure to moisture removed with a thorough, final sanding over all surfaces of the exposed portions using an appropriate grit sandpaper, and shall be cleaned before applying sealer or finish.

1.3.1.2 At **CONCEALED SURFACES** - Architectural woodwork that may be exposed to moisture, such as those adjacent to exterior concrete walls, etc., shall be back-primed.

1.3.1.3 At **WOOD SASH** and **WINDOWS**, the finish coats shall be flowed onto the glass area approximately 1/16" (1.6 mm) to properly seal against weather, wind, and rain.

1.3.1.3.1 It is not recommended to use a **RAZOR BLADE** to scrape the glass, as it might break the seal. A broad-blade putty knife is recommended to be used to protect the seal between the glass and the wood members.

1.3.2 **THOROUGHLY REVIEW** Sections 2 and 4, especially Basic Considerations, Recommendations, Acknowledgements, and Industry Practices within Part 1 for an overview of the characteristics and the minimum acceptable requirements of lumber and/or sheet products that might be used herein.

1.3.3 **CONTRACT DOCUMENTS** (plans and/or specifications) shall require that all structural members, grounds, blocking, backing, furring, brackets, or other anchorage which becomes an integral part of the building's walls, floors, or ceilings, required for the installation of architectural woodwork is not to be furnished or installed by the architectural woodwork manufacturer or installer.

GENERAL

1.3 **RECOMMENDATIONS** (continued)

1.3.4 **SPECIFY** requirements for:

1.3.4.1 Fire ratings or special code compliance

1.3.4.2 Window performance testing and/or labeling and hardware

1.3.4.3 Glass type and thickness

1.3.5 **WOOD SPECIES** for:

1.3.5.1 **EXTERIOR SASH** or **FRAME** parts shall be of any species listed in Section 3 as being:

1.3.5.1.1 For **ECONOMY** Grade - **MODERATELY RESISTANT**

1.3.5.1.2 For **CUSTOM** and **PREMIUM** Grade - **RESISTANT** or **VERY RESISTANT**

1.3.6 **CLOSET** and **UTILITY SHELVING**:

1.3.6.1 The design professional shall specify any shelf size, thickness, or support system needed to meet the load-carrying requirements of the project; otherwise, the minimal requirements of the standards shall prevail.

1.3.6.1.1 Shelf-deflection information can be found in Section 10.

1.3.6.2 The design professional shall specify and indicate in the plans any ADA or barrier-free compliance requirements. Actual design for compliance is the responsibility of the design professional.

1.3.6.2.1 **ADA** design information can be found in Appendix A.

1.3.7 **ORNAMENTAL MILLWORK**:

1.3.7.1 **BUILT-UP CONSTRUCTION** can be utilized to improve fire rating.

1.3.7.1.1 Where a **FIRE RATING** is required, members built up by the use of treated cores (fire-rated particleboard or medium-density fiberboard) clad with untreated veneers not thicker than 1/28" (0.9 mm) may help over the use of solid lumber.

1.4 **ACKNOWLEDGEMENTS** - None

1.5 **INDUSTRY PRACTICES**

1.5.1 **FIRE-RATED WOOD DOOR FRAMES** shall be of the manufacturer's standard design and construction, conforming to the requirements of their applicable labeling service.

1.5.2 **STRUCTURAL MEMBERS**, grounds, blocking, backing, furring, brackets, or other anchorage that becomes an integral part of the building's walls, floors, or ceilings, that are required for the installation of architectural woodwork are not furnished or installed by the architectural woodwork manufacturer or installer.

1.5.3 **WALL, CEILING,** and/or opening variations in excess of 1/4" (6.4 mm) or **FLOORS** in excess of 1/2" (12.7 mm) in 144" (3658 mm) of being plumb, level, flat, straight, square, or of the correct size are not acceptable for the installation of architectural woodwork, nor is it the responsibility of the installer to scribe or fit to tolerances in excess of such.

1.5.4 **BACK-PRIMING** of architectural woodwork is not the responsibility of the manufacturer and/or installer, unless the material is being furnished prefinished.

1.5.5 **RADIUS MOLDINGS** are laminated and formed, preshaped, or machined to the radius and fabricated in the longest practical lengths to minimize installer joints.

PRODUCT

2 SCOPE

2.1 All exposed interior and exterior standing and running wood trim members, door frames, window frames, sashes, blinds and shutters, screens, and ornamental and miscellaneous millwork that are not structural in nature.

PRODUCT

MATERIAL, MACHINING, AND ASSEMBLY RULES (continued)

2 SCOPE (continued)

2.2 **TYPICAL INCLUSIONS,** Interior or Exterior:

2.2.1 Base; shoe, casing, picture, ceiling, apron, and stool molds
2.2.2 Thresholds, plinth and corner blocks, and all other exposed wood trim
2.2.3 Wood wainscoting and caps
2.2.4 Wall, ceiling, soffit, or decorative paneling
2.2.5 Decorative columns, pilasters, false beams, screens, or louvers
2.2.6 False or boxed beam members, brackets, corbels, pedestals, finials, drops, and carvings
2.2.7 Buttress wall caps and trim
2.2.8 Band-sawn, turned, or ornamental woodwork
2.2.9 Solid, paneled, or wood-veneered door jambs/frames with sidelights, louvers, transoms, and borrowed lights, including extensions, linings, stops, mullions, transom bars, sills, other components, and fire ratings
2.2.10 Mill-built sliding door and sash pockets, including operating hardware
2.2.11 Cleat and standards/bracket-supported shelves, including hook strips, cleats, poles, and required hardware
2.2.12 Cornice moldings, corner and edge boards, fascia and soffits, water tables, and casing
2.2.13 Metal sash surrounds
2.2.14 Belt and base courses, verge boards, and miscellaneous moldings
2.2.15 Decorative sun screens, trellises, louvers, blinds, and screens
2.2.16 Boxed or solid posts and beams
2.2.17 Corbels, brackets, bolsters, finials, and pediments
2.2.18 Turned and boxed columns
2.2.19 Beam boxing, false rafters, and lookouts when scrolled, turned, or carved
2.2.20 Seat and bench parts, duckboards, and similarly worked wood members
2.2.21 Sheet products applied in the form of multiple boards
2.2.22 High-pressure laminate plastics or decorative sheet products
2.2.23 Staff moldings, blind stops, and parting beads
2.2.24 Attached flashing, sill pans, inside/back linings, and balances
2.2.25 Wood caps, pediments, casing, stucco molds, or stops for exterior door frames
2.2.26 Columns, pilasters, brackets, corbels, paneling, and moldings integral to a frame's design
2.2.27 Elliptical, segment, or full-circle head, arched, peaked, gothic, irregular, and divided entrance specialty units
2.2.28 Frames and sash for double-hung, hopper, tilt/turn, casement, awning, sidelights, clerestory, and fixed windows
2.2.29 Appropriate wood glass stops when indicated
2.2.30 Glass and glazing unless specified otherwise; open sash may be included by agreement
2.2.31 Wood-framed insect screens for window and door openings
2.2.32 Porch screens
2.2.33 Board and cleat, louvered, or paneled blinds or shutters, fixed or active
2.2.34 Ornamental woodwork making use of molded, shaped, and carved elements to create a decorative appearance

2.3 **TYPICAL EXCLUSIONS**

2.3.1 Any structural wood framing, timbers or sheet products, sheathing, siding, decking, or planking and S4S boards or battens
2.3.2 Any composition or plaster wallboards or coverings, lath, shingles, or shakes
2.3.3 Any bucks, grounds, stripping, furring, blocking, reglets, cant strips, or waste molding
2.3.4 Any wood members not exposed
2.3.5 Non-wood, carved, or embossed moldings, including paper-, vinyl-, or foil-wrapped
2.3.6 Commodity frames not governed by these standards
2.3.7 Machining of frames for hardware supplied by others
2.3.8 Any metal stops, frames, or wood cores for metal frames
2.3.9 Hardware, except as noted above
2.3.10 Priming or painting, glass and glazing, weather-stripping, operating hardware, and/or sash balances
2.3.11 Flush or stile and rail doors
2.3.12 Premanufactured or stock window units
2.3.13 Fence posts or fence material where standard stock lumber yard material is indicated
2.3.14 Metal sash, skylights, screens, or weather-stripping/milling for same
2.3.15 Cabinet sash and hardware
2.3.16 Roller screens and hardware

PRODUCT

MATERIAL, MACHINING, AND ASSEMBLY RULES (continued)

2 SCOPE (continued)

2.3 **TYPICAL EXCLUSIONS (continued)**

- 2.3.17 Factory-assembled shelving units
- 2.3.18 Blocking within a wall or ceiling
- 2.3.19 Premanufactured or stock screen units
- 2.3.20 Providing or preparing for any electrical, telephone, mechanical, or plumbing equipment
- 2.3.21 Supplying exposed materials other than those covered herein or specified to be included
- 2.3.22 Factory finish

3 DEFAULT STIPULATION

3.1 If not otherwise specified or indicated in the contract documents, all work shall be unfinished, Custom Grade, solid-stock softwood intended for opaque finish.

4 RULES - The following RULES shall govern unless a project's contract documents require otherwise.

These rules are intended to provide a well-defined degree of control over a project's quality of materials and workmanship.

Where E, C, or P is not indicated, the rule applies to all Grades equally.

ERRATA, published on the Associations' websites at www.awinet.org, www.awmac.com, or www.woodworkinstitute.com, shall TAKE PRECEDENCE OVER THESE RULES, subject to their date of posting and a project's bid date.

ARROWS INDICATE TOPIC IS CARRIED FROM ⇑ OR ONTO ⇓ ANOTHER PAGE.

6

DESCRIPTION					E	C	P
4.1	**GENERAL**						
GENERAL	4.1.1	Aesthetic **GRADE RULES** apply only to exposed and semi-exposed surfaces visible after installation.					
	4.1.2	**WOODWORK** not addressed herein shall be manufactured from solid stock, laminated stock, veneered stock, or a combination thereof.					
	4.1.3	**LUMBER** shall conform to the requirements established in Section 3.					
	4.1.4	**SHEET PRODUCTS** and **BACKING SHEET** shall conform to the requirements established in Section 4.					
	4.1.5	**EXPOSED, SEMI-EXPOSED,** and **CONCEALED** surfaces shall be as listed under item 1.2, Basic Considerations, of this section.					
	4.1.6	**STANDING** and **RUNNING TRIM** shall be furnished as material only, not assembled.					
	4.1.7	Where **MULTIPLE OPTIONS** are permitted, it shall be the manufacturer's choice unless specified otherwise.					
	4.1.8	**FIRE-RETARDANT RATING**, if required, shall be so specified.					
	4.1.9	**SPECIFIC PROFILE**, if required, shall be so specified or drawn.					
	4.1.10	**SPECIAL ORNAMENTAL DETAIL** or joinery, if required, shall be so specified or drawn.					
	4.1.11	At **EXTERIOR** applications:					
		4.1.11.1	**WATERPROOF** Type I adhesive is required.				
		4.1.11.2	**SHEET PRODUCTS** shall be of exterior type.				
		4.1.11.3	**NAILS** and **SCREWS** shall be corrosion-resistant.				
		4.1.11.4	**FRAMES** require:				
			4.1.11.4.1	Preservative treatment of all exposed and concealed exterior members in accordance with Section 3.			
	4.1.12	Where **GLUING** or **LAMINATION** occurs:					
		4.1.12.1	**DELAMINATION** or **SEPARATION** shall not occur beyond that which is allowed in Sections 3 & 4.				
		4.1.12.2	Use of **CONTACT ADHESIVE** is not permitted.				
	4.1.13	**FIRST-CLASS WORKMANSHIP** is required in compliance with these standards.					

PRODUCT

MATERIAL, MACHINING, AND ASSEMBLY RULES (continued)

	DESCRIPTION	E	C	P
4.2	**MATERIAL**			
4.2.1	Shall be lumber or sheet products of the species and Grade specified.			
4.2.2	Shall conform in finish width, thickness, and length of lumber to Section 3.			
4.2.3	Shall not have defects, either natural or manufactured, that exceed those permitted.			
4.2.3.1	Permits unlimited finger-joints.	●		
4.2.4	Requires plain-sawn lumber.			
4.2.5	Permits defects, both natural and manufactured, if covered by adjoining members or otherwise concealed when installed.			
4.2.6	States figure is not a function of a species grade and must be specified in the contract document.			
4.2.7	Permits warp that can be held flat and straight with normal attachment.			
4.2.8 RADIUS	Requires radiused woodwork to be constructed of solid-machined, block-laminated, laminated plies, core-veneered, or kerfed solid stock: Solid-machined, Block-laminated, Laminated Plies, Core-veneered, Kerfed Solid Stock			
4.2.8.1	**CHORD SEGMENTATION** is not permitted.			
4.2.8.2	Members of solid stock or block laminations shall be furnished in such sections as to avoid pronounced cross grain and reduce joints to a minimum.			
4.2.8.3	**GLUE** shall be selected for color to avoid a prominent glue line.			
4.2.9 EXPOSED SURFACES	At **EXPOSED SURFACES**:			
4.2.9.1	Requires end grain be kept to a minimum.	●	●	
4.2.9.2	Requires ends be self-returned with no end grain showing.			●
4.2.9.3	Permits medium-density fiberboard (MDF) for opaque finish.			
4.2.9.4	Requires sheet-product edges to be banded with the same species as the face.		●	●
4.2.9.5	Requires plain-sliced veneer for transparent finish.			
4.2.9.6	Permits mill-option veneer for opaque finish.			
4.2.9.7 TRANSPARENT	For **TRANSPARENT FINISH:**			
4.2.9.7.1	Permits hardwood or softwood.	●		
4.2.9.7.2	Permits only one species for the entire project.		●	●
4.2.9.7.3	Prohibits finger joints.		●	●
4.2.9.7.4	Requires adhesive, used for laminating, to be selected for color to avoid a prominent glue line.		●	●
4.2.9.7.5	Requires lumber (including block segments or veneer of laminated material) and sheet products to be compatible in color and grain.		●	
4.2.9.7.6	Requires lumber (including block segments or veneer of laminated material) to be well-matched for color and grain; sheet products shall be compatible in color with solid stock, and adjacent sheet products shall be well-matched for color and grain.			●
4.2.9.7.7	Requires **INTERSECTIONS** of radius and straight members to be splined or half-lapped, securely glued, and mechanically fastened.		●	●

PRODUCT

MATERIAL, MACHINING, AND ASSEMBLY RULES (continued)

4.2 MATERIAL — 4.2.9 EXPOSED SRFACES — 4.2.9.7 TRANSPARENT FINISH

	DESCRIPTION	E	C	P
4.2	**MATERIAL** (continued)			
4.2.9	At **EXPOSED SURFACES** (continued)			
4.2.9.7	For **TRANSPARENT FINISH** (continued)			
4.2.9.7.8	Requires radius frames to be constructed of laminated plies or core veneered.		●	●
4.2.9.7.9	At **BLOCK LAMINATION:**			
4.2.9.7.9.1	Requires segments to be cut from the same board.			●
4.2.9.7.9.2	Requires segment joints to be staggered.			
4.2.9.7.9.3	Requires adjacent segment ends to have a similar grain angle.		●	●
4.2.9.7.10	At **VENEER LAMINATIONS:**			
4.2.9.7.10.1	Requires exposed layers to be resawn from the same or matched boards.			●
4.2.9.7.10.2	Requires veneer layers to be reassembled in the same order and orientation as cut.		●	●
4.2.9.7.11	Have visible **EDGES**, **REVEALS,** and/or **SPLINES,** when appropriate, that are:			
4.2.9.7.11.1	Full length.			
4.2.9.7.11.2	**MILL-OPTION.**	●		
4.2.9.7.11.3	**MATCH** species of panel face.		●	●
4.2.9.7.11.4	**COMPATIBLE** for color and grain.		●	
4.2.9.7.11.5	**WELL-MATCHED** for color and grain.			●
4.2.9.7.11.6	A minimum of 0.020" (0.5 mm) nominal **THICKNESS** that precludes show-through of core.		●	●
4.2.10	At **SEMI-EXPOSED SURFACES:**			
4.2.10.1	For **OPAQUE** finish, permits natural and manufacturing defects, provided the surface is filled solid.			
4.2.11	At **CONCEALED SURFACES:**			
4.2.11.1	Permits voids, wane, and unfilled knots.			
4.2.11.2	Requires blocking or shims to be of a compatible material.			
4.2.12	At **DOOR** and **WINDOW FRAMES:**			
4.2.12.1	**FLAT-STYLE** cased opening or with applied stop, shall be:			
4.2.12.1.1	Minimum of 11/16" (17 mm) in thickness.	●		
4.2.12.1.2	Minimum of 3/4" (19 mm) in thickness.		●	●
4.2.12.1.3	Minimum of 1-1/16" (27 mm) in thickness at cased opening.			●
4.2.12.1.4	Stops shall be 3/8" (9 mm) in thickness.	●		
4.2.12.1.5	Stops shall be 1/2" (13 mm) in thickness.		●	●
4.2.12.2	**RABBETED STYLE** shall be:			
4.2.12.2.1	Minimum of 1-1/16" (27 mm) in thickness.	●		
4.2.12.2.2	Minimum of 1-5/16" (33 mm) in thickness.		●	
4.2.12.2.3	Minimum of 1-1/2" (38 mm) in thickness.			●

PRODUCT

MATERIAL, MACHINING, AND ASSEMBLY RULES (continued)

	DESCRIPTION	E	C	P
4.2	**MATERIAL** (continued)			
4.2.12	At **DOOR** and **WINDOW FRAMES** (continued)			
4.2.12.3	Of **PLOUGHED STYLE** with T-stop, shall be:			
4.2.12.3.1	Minimum of 3/4" (19 mm) in thickness.	●		
4.2.12.3.2	Minimum of 1-1/16" (27 mm) in thickness.		●	
4.2.12.3.3	Stops shall be minimum 3/4" (19 mm) in thickness set in 1/4" (6 mm) groove.			●
4.2.12.4	Of **SPLIT STYLE** with T-stop, shall be:			
4.2.12.4.1	Minimum of 11/16" (17 mm) in thickness at thin member.	●		
4.2.12.4.2	Minimum of 3/4" (19 mm) in thickness.		●	●
4.2.12.5	Of **VENEERED CONSTRUCTION:**			
4.2.12.5.1	Shall be of the same species.			
4.2.12.5.2	Veneer-wrapped MDF is permitted for interior use only.			
4.2.12.5.3	Veneer-laminated block or MDF core is permitted for interior use only.			
4.2.12.5.3.1	Face veneer shall be of sufficient thickness to prohibit show-through.			
4.2.12.5.3.2	Face veneer shall extend over the edgebands when edgebands exceed 1/8" (3.2 mm) in thickness.			●
4.2.12.6	Requiring **FIRE RATING** shall be of the manufacturer's permitted design and construction in conforming with the requirements of their applicable labeling service.			
4.2.13	At **SASH:**			
4.2.13.1	Shall be **PONDEROSA** or **SUGAR PINE**.			
4.2.13.2	Shall be a minimum of 1-3/8" (35 mm) in thickness.	●	●	
4.2.13.3	Shall be a minimum of 1-3/4" (44 mm) in thickness; however:			●
4.2.13.3.1	Consideration of the size of the window and the applicable codes may require the minimum thickness to be less than this standard.			●
4.2.14	At **BLINDS** and **SHUTTERS:**			
4.2.14.1	Shall be **PONDEROSA** or **SUGAR PINE**.			
4.2.14.2	**STILES** and **RAILS** shall be:			
4.2.14.2.1	Solid stock.			
4.2.14.2.2	Minimum of 3/4" (19 mm) in thickness.			
4.2.14.3	**PANELS** if:			
4.2.14.3.1	**FLAT** shall be:			
4.2.14.3.1.1	**SOLID WOOD**:			
4.2.14.3.1.1.1	Minimum 1/2" (12.7 mm) in thickness and maximum 23-3/4" (603 mm) across the grain in width.	●		
4.2.14.3.1.1.2	Minimum 3/4" (19 mm) in thickness and maximum 13-3/4" (350 mm) across the grain in width.		●	
4.2.14.3.1.1.3	Not permitted.			●
4.2.14.3.1.2	**SHEET PRODUCT**:			
4.2.14.3.1.2.1	Minimum 1/4" (6.4 mm) in thickness.	●		
4.2.14.3.1.2.2	Minimum 1/2" (12.7 mm) in thickness.		●	●

PRODUCT

MATERIAL, MACHINING, AND ASSEMBLY RULES (continued)

Section	DESCRIPTION	E	C	P
4.2	**MATERIAL** (continued)			
4.2.14	At **BLINDS** and **SHUTTERS** (continued)			
4.2.14.3	**PANELS** if (continued)			
4.2.14.3.2	**RAISED** shall be:			
4.2.14.3.2.1	**SOLID WOOD**:			
4.2.14.3.2.1.1	Permitted in any dimension.	●		
4.2.14.3.2.1.2	Minimum 3/4" (19 mm) in thickness and maximum in width 13-3/4" (350 mm) across the grain.		●	
4.2.14.3.2.2	**VENEERED STILES** and **RAILS** or **SHEET PRODUCT**:			
4.2.14.3.2.2.1	Minimum 1/2" (12.7 mm) in thickness.	●		
4.2.14.3.2.2.2	Minimum 3/4" (19 mm) in thickness.		●	●
4.2.15	At **SCREENS:**			
4.2.15.1	Shall be solid lumber.			
4.2.15.2	**LUMBER SPECIES** shall be:			
4.2.15.2.1				
4.2.15.2.1.1	Pine, Fir, Hemlock, or Larch.	●		
4.2.15.2.1.2	Ponderosa Pine, Idaho White Pine, Northern White Pine, Honduras or African Mahogany, or Douglas Fir.		●	
4.2.15.2.1.3	Teak (except at opaque finish), American Mahogany, White Oak, or Western Red Cedar.			●
4.2.15.3	**FRAME THICKNESS** shall be:			
4.2.15.3.1	Mill option.	●		
4.2.15.3.2	Minimum of 3/4" (19 mm).		●	
4.2.15.3.3	Minimum of 1" (25 mm).			●
4.2.15.4	**FRAME PARTS** shall be coped with:			
4.2.15.4.1	Mill-option joinery.	●		
4.2.15.4.2	Mortise and tenon, slot mortise and tenon, or doweled joinery.		●	
4.2.15.4.3	Haunched blind mortise and tenon or doweled joinery.			●
4.2.15.4.4	Half-lap joints permitted at intersecting muntins.		●	●
4.2.15.5	**SCREEN MOLD** shall be of sufficient thickness and width to cover wire edges.			
4.2.15.6	**WIRE CLOTH** shall be:			
4.2.15.6.1	Nylon or fiberglass mesh.	●		
4.2.15.6.2	Aluminum or bronze wire (18 x 14 mesh).		●	
4.2.15.6.3	Bronze wire (18 x 14 mesh).			●
4.2.15.6.4	**SECURED**:			
4.2.15.6.4.1	At mill option.	●		
4.2.15.6.4.2	At a maximum of 3" (76 mm) on center with staples.		●	
4.2.15.6.4.3	By force into a kerf by use of a spline or a projecting bead.			●
4.2.16	At **ORNAMENTAL MILLWORK**			
4.2.17	At **MISCELLANEOUS MILLWORK:**			
4.2.17.1	**CLOSET AND UTILITY SHELVING**			
4.2.17.1.1	Shall be one type of material for each project, project phase, or area, and be:			
4.2.17.1.1.1	Medium-Density Fiberboard (MDF), particleboard, or veneer core product.	●		

PRODUCT

MATERIAL, MACHINING, AND ASSEMBLY RULES (continued)

Section	DESCRIPTION	E	C	P
4.2	**MATERIAL** (continued)			
4.2.17	At **MISCELLANEOUS MILLWORK** (continued)			
4.2.17.1	**CLOSET AND UTILITY SHELVING** (continued)			
4.2.17.1.1	Shall be one type of material for each project (continued)			
4.2.17.1.1.2	Medium-Density Fiberboard (MDF), UV-filled particleboard, or veneer core product.		●	
4.2.17.1.1.3	Medium-Density Fiberboard (MDF), thermoset overlay on particleboard, or veneer core product.			●
4.2.17.1.2	At **ENDS** and **BACK CLEATS**:			
4.2.17.1.2.1	That **RECEIVE** a clothes rod or hooks shall be a minimum of 3/4" x 3-1/2" (19 mm x 89 mm).			
4.2.17.1.2.2	That **DO NOT RECEIVE** a clothes rod or hooks shall be a minimum of 3/4" x 1-1/2" (19 mm x 38 mm).			
4.2.17.1.3	**SHELF THICKNESS** shall be a minimum of 3/4" (19 mm).			
4.2.17.1.4	**WOOD SHELF POLES** shall be a minimum of 1-3/8" (34.9 mm) in diameter.			
4.2.18	At **GLASS**:			
4.2.18.1	Shall conform to all applicable codes and regulations; these standards shall not supersede such regulations.			
4.2.18.2	For **SAFETY** type, shall conform to the Consumer Product Safety Commission's Safety Standard for Architectural Glazing Materials.			
4.2.18.3	**PUTTY** shall conform to Federal Specification TT-P-791a.			
4.2.18.4	For **CLEAR, SINGLE STRENGTH,** shall be furnished within the appropriate size limitation; however:			
4.2.18.4.1	When required because of limitations, double strength shall be furnished.			
4.2.18.5	For **OBSCURE** type, shall be roll-figured sheet glass, 1/8" (3.2 mm) in thickness, of any standard pattern set with the smooth side facing the exterior or corridor, unless otherwise specified.			
4.2.18.6	For **WIRE** type, whether polished or obscure, shall be 1/4" (6.4 mm) in thickness.			
4.2.18.7	For **FLOAT** type, shall be 1/4" (6.4mm) in thickness.			
4.2.18.8	For **BEVELED** type, at exterior openings, shall be set with the beveled face to the outside.			
4.2.18.9	For **LEADED** or **ZINC CANE** installation, shall have the individual light carefully fitted together with cane intersections neatly soldered and the whole assembly watertight. Reinforcing bars shall be provided where necessary.			
4.2.18.10	**INSULATING UNITS** shall have the panes hermetically sealed and separated by a dehydrated air space.			
4.2.19	When **FACTORY FINISHING** is specified, concealed surfaces shall be factory sealed with one coat at 1 mil dry.		●	●

PRODUCT

MATERIAL, MACHINING, AND ASSEMBLY RULES (continued)

Section	DESCRIPTION	E	C	P
4.3	**MACHINING** of:			
4.3.1	**EXPOSED SURFACES** shall comply with:			
4.3.1.1	**SMOOTHNESS REQUIREMENTS** (see 7.1 in **COMPLIANCE**):			
4.3.1.1.1	**SHARP EDGES** shall be eased with a fine abrasive.		●	●
4.3.1.1.2	**TOP FLAT WOOD** surfaces, those that can be sanded with a drum or wide belt sander:			
4.3.1.1.2.1	Minimum 15 KCPI or 100-grit sanding	●		
4.3.1.1.2.2	120-grit sanding		●	
4.3.1.1.2.3	150-grit sanding			●
4.3.1.1.3	**PROFILED** and/or **SHAPED WOOD** surfaces:			
4.3.1.1.3.1	Minimum 15 KCPI or 100-grit sanding	●		
4.3.1.1.3.2	Minimum 20 KCPI or 120-grit sanding		●	
4.3.1.1.3.3	120-sanding			●
4.3.1.1.4	**TURNED WOOD** surfaces:			
4.3.1.1.4.1	Minimum 15 KCPI or 100-grit sanding	●		
4.3.1.1.4.2	120-grit sanding		●	
4.3.1.1.4.3	180-grit sanding			●
4.3.1.1.5	**CROSS-SANDING**, excluding turned surfaces:			
4.3.1.1.5.1	Is not a defect.	●		
4.3.1.1.5.2	Is not allowed.		●	●
4.3.1.1.6	**TEAR-OUTS**, **KNIFE NICKS**, or **HIT-OR-MISS** machining is not permitted.			
4.3.1.1.7	**KNIFE MARKS** are not permitted where sanding is required.			
4.3.1.1.8	**GLUE** or **FILLER**, if used, shall be inconspicuous and match the adjacent surface for smoothness.			
4.3.2	**TRIM** to be applied on flat surfaces shall have the reverse side backed out.		●	●
4.3.2.1	Door and window trim over 2" (50.8 mm) in width with non-exposed ends shall be backed out.		●	●
4.3.3	**SOLID-MACHINED** and **BLOCK-LAMINATED** members shall be divided to minimize the exposure of cross grain in the face of the member, and:			
4.3.3.1	**ANGLE** of **GRAIN** at the face of the curved member shall not exceed 30 degrees, unless a small part size requires otherwise. 30° — Acceptable 90° — Unacceptable		●	●
4.3.4	**INTERSECTIONS** at radius and straight members shall be splined or half-lapped, securely glued, and mechanically fastened.			
4.3.5	**DADOES** shall completely house the male member throughout the entire length of the joint.			
4.3.6	**STANDING & RUNNING TRIM:**			
4.3.6.1	At **EXTERIOR** application, 5-1/4" (133.4 mm) and wider shall require kerfing, 1/8" (3.2 mm) wide by 1/4" (6.4 mm) deep, a maximum of 1-1/2" (38.1 mm) on center.			

6

PRODUCT

MATERIAL, MACHINING, AND ASSEMBLY RULES (continued)

			DESCRIPTION	E	C	P
4.3 MACHINING			**MACHINING** (continued)			
	4.3.7		**WINDOW FRAMES:**			
		4.3.7.1	**SILLS** shall have a drip groove on the underside of the sill.			
		4.3.7.2	**STILES** and/or **RAILS** shall be machined for cords, balances, and any other operating hardware as required.			
		4.3.7.2.1	**STOP** profile is optional.			
	4.3.8 SASH		**SASH:**			
		4.3.8.1	**STILE** and **RAIL PROFILE** is optional.			
		4.3.8.2	For **AWNING TYPE,** stiles and rails shall be machined to accommodate the type of hardware specified and shall be prefit, ready to install.			
		4.3.8.3	For **CIRCLE, GOTHIC,** or **IRREGULAR TYPE,** conform to square-head construction with all irregular joints splined, slot-mortised, or doweled.			
		4.3.8.4	**BOTTOM RAILS** shall be beveled to fit slope of sill.			
	4.3.9 BLINDS & SHUTTERS		**BLINDS** and **SHUTTERS** shall:			
		4.3.9.1	Be of **MORTISE** and **TENON**, or **DOWELED** construction.			
		4.3.9.2	Have **SLATS** overhang each other a minimum of 1/8" (3.2 mm).			
		4.3.9.3 STATIONARY	Have **STATIONARY SLATS** mortised into stiles and set at an angle 45 to 60 degrees from horizontal, and:			
		4.3.9.3.1	**ROUND-EDGE SLATS** shall be set in routed slot.			
		4.3.9.3.2	**FLAT-EDGE SLATS** shall be set in dado slot.	●		
		4.3.9.3.3	**FLAT-EDGE SLATS** shall be set in dado slot with molding applied to face rails to cover dado.		●	●
		4.3.9.4 MOVEABLE	At **MOVABLE SLATS**:			
		4.3.9.4.1	Pivot on a wood, metal, or nylon dowel, and:			
		4.3.9.4.1.1	Pivot pins for damp coastal climates shall be nylon, stainless steel, or brass.			
		4.3.9.4.2	Shall have a vertical control bar set to movable slats with curved staples to allow movement.			

PRODUCT

MATERIAL, MACHINING, AND ASSEMBLY RULES (continued)

Section	Item	No.	DESCRIPTION	E	C	P
4.3 MACHINING			**MACHINING** (continued)			
	4.3.10 SCREENS		**SCREENS** requires:			
		4.3.10.1	**MORTISE** and **TENON**, **SLOT MORTISE,** or **DOWELED** construction.			
		4.3.10.2	**WIRE CLOTH** stretched taut and securely attached to the frame or rolled into a kerf-rabbeted frame.			
		4.3.10.3	**MOLD** neatly mitered and securely attached to the frame.			
		4.3.10.4	**FRAME WIDTH** and **PROFILE** of the manufacturer's option.			
	4.3.11		**ORNAMENTAL MILLWORK** shall:			
		4.3.11.1	Permit cut-sawn edges at **SCROLL WORK**.			
		4.3.11.2	Require **TURNINGS** to be clean, cut, sanded, and well-matched for alignment.			
4.4			**ASSEMBLY** of:			
ASSEMBLY	4.4.1 JOINTS		**JOINTS** at **ASSEMBLED WOODWORK** shall:			
		4.4.1.1	Be neatly and accurately made.			
		4.4.1.2	Be **SECURELY GLUED**, with:			
		4.4.1.2.1	**ADHESIVE** residue removed from all exposed and semi-exposed surfaces.			
		4.4.1.3	Be **REINFORCED** with glue blocks where essential.			
		4.4.1.4	Utilize clamp nail, biscuit spline, butterfly, scarf, or dowel joinery.		●	
		4.4.1.5	Utilize biscuit spline, butterfly, scarf, or dowel joinery.			●
		4.4.1.6	Be **MECHANICALLY FASTENED** with nails or screws, where practical, with:			
		4.4.1.6.1	Fasteners at solid wood countersunk.			
		4.4.1.6.2	Fasteners at solid wood in molding quirks or reliefs where possible.		●	●
		4.4.1.7	**NOT PERMIT** fasteners at exposed surfaces of HPDL or overlay sheet products.			
		4.4.1.8 FLUSHNESS	Require **FLUSHNESS VARIATIONS** at exposed surfaces when mitered or butted not to exceed, at (See Flushness Test illustrations in **COMPLIANCE**):			
		4.4.1.8.1	**INTERIOR**			
		4.4.1.8.1.1	0.025" (0.6 mm)	●		
		4.4.1.8.1.2	0.005" (0.1 mm)		●	
		4.4.1.8.1.3	0.001" (0.03 mm)			●
		4.4.1.8.2	**EXTERIOR**			
		4.4.1.8.2.1	0.05" (1.3 mm)	●		
		4.4.1.8.2.2	0.025" (0.6 mm)		●	
		4.4.1.8.2.3	0.015" (0.4 mm)			●
		4.4.1.9 GAPS	Require **GAPS** at exposed surfaces when mitered or butted not to exceed (see Test A illustrations in **COMPLIANCE**):			
		4.4.1.9.1	**INTERIOR**			
		4.4.1.9.1.1	0.05" (1.3 mm) wide by 20% of the joint length	●		
		4.4.1.9.1.2	0.025" (0.6 mm) wide by 20% of the joint length		●	
		4.4.1.9.1.3	0.015" (0.4 mm) wide by 20% of the joint length			●
		4.4.1.9.2	**EXTERIOR**			
		4.4.1.9.2.1	0.075" (1.9 mm) wide by 30% of the joint length	●		
		4.4.1.9.2.2	0.05" (1.3 mm) wide by 30% of the joint length		●	
		4.4.1.9.2.3	0.025" (0.6 mm) wide by 30% of the joint length			●

6

PRODUCT

MATERIAL, MACHINING, AND ASSEMBLY RULES (continued)

						DESCRIPTION	E	C	P
4.4 ASSEMBLY	**ASSEMBLY** (continued)								
	4.4.1 JOINTS	**JOINTS** at **ASSEMBLED WOODWORK** shall (continued)							
		GAPS	4.4.1.10	Require **GAPS** at exposed surfaces of parallel members not exceed, at (See Test B illustrations in **COMPLIANCE**):					
				4.4.1.10.1	**INTERIOR**				
					4.4.1.10.1.1	0.05" x 8"(1.3 mm x 203 mm) and shall not occur within 48" (1219 mm) of a similar gap.	●		
					4.4.1.10.1.2	0.025" x 6" (0.6 mm x 152 mm) and shall not occur within 60" (1524 mm) of a similar gap.		●	
					4.4.1.10.1.3	0.015" x 3" (0.4 mm x 76 mm) and shall not occur within 72" (1829 mm) of a similar gap.			●
				4.4.1.10.2	**EXTERIOR**				
					4.4.1.10.2.1	0.075" x 10" (1.9 mm x 254 mm) and shall not occur within 24" (610 mm) of a similar gap.	●		
					4.4.1.10.2.2	0.05" x 8" (1.3 mm x 203 mm) and shall not occur within 26" (660 mm) of a similar gap.		●	
					4.4.1.10.2.3	0.025" x 6" (0.6 mm x 152 mm) and shall not occur within 30" (762 mm) of a similar gap.			●
		GAPS	4.4.1.11	Require **GAPS** at exposed surfaces when mitered or butted not exceed, at (See Test C illustrations in **COMPLIANCE**):					
				4.4.1.11.1	**INTERIOR**				
					4.4.1.11.1.1	0.05" (1.3 mm)	●		
					4.4.1.11.1.2	0.025" (0.6 mm)		●	
					4.4.1.11.1.3	0.015" (0.4 mm)			●
				4.4.1.11.2	**EXTERIOR**				
					4.4.1.11.2.1	0.075" (1.9 mm)	●		
					4.4.1.11.2.2	0.05" (1.3 mm)		●	
					4.4.1.11.2.3	0.025" (0.6 mm)			●
			4.4.1.12	Allows **FILLER**:					
				4.4.1.12.1	If inconspicuous when viewed at 36" (914 mm)		●		
				4.4.1.12.2	If inconspicuous when viewed at 24" (610 mm)			●	
				4.4.1.12.3	**NOT ALLOWED**				●
		HPDL	4.4.1.13	At **HPDL** and **PVC,** edges shall be machined flush and filed, sanded, or buffed to remove machine marks and sharp edges, and:					
				4.4.1.13.1	**VISIBLE OVERLAP** (over-filing) shall not exceed:				
					4.4.1.13.1.1	0.005" (0.13 mm) for a maximum length of 2" (50.8 mm) in any 48" (1220 mm) run	●		
					4.4.1.13.1.2	0.005" (0.13 mm) for a maximum length of 1" (25.4 mm) in any 24" (610 mm) run		●	
					4.4.1.13.1.3	**NO VISIBLE OVERLAP**			●
				4.4.1.13.2	**CHIP-OUT** shall be inconspicuous when viewed at:				
					4.4.1.13.2.1	72" (1829 mm)	●		
					4.4.1.13.2.2	48" (1220 mm)		●	
					4.4.1.13.2.3	24" (610 mm)			●

PRODUCT

MATERIAL, MACHINING, AND ASSEMBLY RULES (continued)

No.	DESCRIPTION	E	C	P
4.4	**ASSEMBLY** (continued)			
4.4.1	**JOINTS** at **ASSEMBLED WOODWORK** shall (continued)			
4.4.1.13	At **HPDL** and **PVC,** edges shall be machined flush and filed (continued)			
4.4.1.13.3	**REMOVAL** of color or pattern of face material due to over-machining limited to:			
4.4.1.13.3.1	3/32" x 4" (2.4 mm x 102 mm) and may not occur within 48" (1220 mm) of a similar occurrence.	●		
4.4.1.13.3.2	1/16" x 1-1/2" (1.6 mm x 38.1 mm) and may not occur within 60" (1524 mm) of a similar occurrence.		●	
4.4.1.13.3.3	1/16" x 4" (1.6 mm x 102 mm) and may not occur within 72" (1829 mm) of a similar occurrence.			●
4.4.2	**APPLIED MOLDINGS** shall be spot-glued and mechanically fastened.			
4.4.3	**MITER JOINTS** and **CAPS** shall be well-fitted and cleaned.			
4.4.4	**STILE** and **RAIL ASSEMBLIES** shall be built up in units as large as practical.			
4.4.5	**STILE** and **RAIL MEMBERS** shall be mortised and tenoned, doweled, or splined.		●	●
4.4.6	**SHEET PRODUCTS** shall be allowed to move, float, expand, or contract in reaction to ambient humidity changes.			
4.4.7	**BUILT-UP ITEMS** shall be soundly fabricated with half-lapped, mitered, shoulder-mitered, tonged, or equivalent construction.			
4.4.8	**STANDING & RUNNING TRIM** shall require:			
4.4.8.1	**RADIUS MOLDINGS** to be glued up for length in the longest practical lengths.		●	●
4.4.8.2	**EXTERIOR** trim to be furnished as material only; items required to be assembled shall be so specified.			
4.4.9	**DOOR FRAMES**:			
4.4.9.1	**FIRE RATED** shall be of the manufacturer's standard design and construction, conforming to the requirements of their applicable labeling service.			
4.4.9.2	With **MOLDED EDGES,** other than square or with 1/16" (1.6 mm) or more in radius, shall have mitered joints.		●	●
4.4.9.3	With **SQUARE HEADS** shall have:			
4.4.9.3.1	Jambs furnished machined KD (knocked down).			
4.4.9.3.2	Stops cut to approximate length; however, not mitered or coped.			
4.4.9.3.3	Heads and sills dadoed to receive side jambs, or vice versa.			
4.4.9.4	With **SIDE JAMBS** shall be dadoed into the sills and heads.			
4.4.9.5	With **TRANSOM BARS** shall have them dadoed into side jambs.			
4.4.9.6	With **MULLIONS** shall have them dadoed into sills and heads.			
4.4.9.7	For **EXTERIOR OPAQUE** finished applications, shall have sill and jamb dadoes coated with mastic.		●	●
4.4.9.8	Shall be shipped:			
4.4.9.8.1	As oversize material for installer cutting and joinery.	●		
4.4.9.8.2	As appropriately labeled presized sets with premachined joinery.		●	
4.4.9.8.3	As presized, built-up assemblies in as large as practical sections for safe transportation and installation, with:			●
4.4.9.8.3.1	Joints glued and fit tight, true, and secure.			●
4.4.9.9	At **RADIUS HEADS**:			
4.4.9.9.1	Jambs shall be furnished assembled.	●		
4.4.9.9.2	Curved stops and casing shall be attached to frame.		●	

PRODUCT

MATERIAL, MACHINING, AND ASSEMBLY RULES (continued)

				DESCRIPTION	E	C	P
4.4	**ASSEMBLY** (continued)						
	4.4.9	**DOOR FRAMES** (continued)					
		4.4.9.9	At **RADIUS HEADS** (continued)				
			4.4.9.9.3	Joints at intersection of radiused and straight members shall be splined or half-lapped.			●
	4.4.10	**WINDOW FRAMES:**					
		4.4.10.1		With **MOLDED EDGES,** other than square or with 1/16" (1.6 mm) or more in radius, shall have mitered joints.		●	●
		4.4.10.2		With **TRANSOM BARS** shall have them dadoed into side jambs.			
		4.4.10.3		With **SQUARE EDGE MEMBERS** shall have the heads and sills dadoed to receive side jambs, or vice versa.			
		4.4.10.4		With **GLAZED OPENINGS** shall be trimmed on both sides with wood stops; however, one side shall be removable and the removable stop shall be on exterior side of exterior frames, with:			
		4.4.10.5	4.4.10.5.1	Stops shipped loose as material only.	●		
			4.4.10.5.2	Stops shipped in properly labeled sets, cut to size.		●	
			4.4.10.5.3	Stops tacked in place.			●
		4.4.10.6		Shall include sills and applied exterior trim.			
		4.4.10.7		Shall have **STILES** and/or **RAILS** machined for cords, balances, and any other operating hardware as required.			
		4.4.10.8		Shall have, at **OPAQUE-**finished **EXTERIOR** applications, the sill and jamb dadoes coated with mastic.		●	●
		4.4.10.9		Shall **INCLUDE MACHINING** for:			
			4.4.10.9.1	**OPERATING HARDWARE** (if templates or a physical sample is provided prior to shop-drawing preparation); however, it is not required to be furnished or installed.			
			4.4.10.9.2	**WEATHERSTRIPPING** (provided templates or a physical sample is provided prior to shop-drawing preparation); however, it is not required to be furnished or installed.			
			4.4.10.9.3	**SASH BALANCES** (provided templates or a physical sample is provided prior to shop-drawing preparation); however, it is not required to be furnished or installed.			
		4.4.10.10		Shall **NOT INCLUDE** machining for **NON-OPERATING HARDWARE**, such as locking devices, pulls, lifts, etc., nor is it required to be furnished or installed.			
		4.4.10.11		When **GLASS** is furnished and installed, it shall be bedded in a glazing compound prior to the installation of a face compound or wood bead, and:			
			4.4.10.11.1	**GLAZING MATERIALS** and the method of glazing are optional.			
			4.4.10.11.2	**GLASS** shall be cut slightly scant to prevent binding and set so as to prevent shifting.			
			4.4.10.11.3	**GLAZIER'S POINTS** shall be spaced a maximum of 16" (406 mm) on center with a minimum of one on each edge of each light.			
			4.4.10.11.4	**BEDDING** of glass is required.		●	●
			4.4.10.11.5	When **PUTTY** (excluding primeless putty or glazing compound) is used, glass rabbets shall be primed with linseed oil before glazing.			
	4.4.11	**SASH:**					
		4.4.11.1		Is required and half-lap joints are permitted at intersecting muntins, and:			
			4.4.11.1.1	Bar and muntin alignment shall:			
			4.4.11.1.1.1	Be at right angles to each other and to the sash member.			
			4.4.11.1.1.2	Align with each other vertically and horizontally.			
			4.4.11.1.1.3	Align with similar members on the adjoining sash.			
		4.4.11.2		Requires **MULLIONS** be dadoed into heads and sills.			

PRODUCT

MATERIAL, MACHINING, AND ASSEMBLY RULES (continued)

Section	Description	E	C	P
4.4	**ASSEMBLY** (continued)			
4.4.11	**SASH** (continued)			
4.4.11.3	At **DOUBLE-GLAZED** units requires one stop to be left loose for finishing.			
4.4.11.4	If **GLASS** is furnished and installed, it shall conform to the requirements set herein.			
4.4.12	**BLINDS** and **SHUTTERS** is required, with:			
4.4.12.1	Dadoed or equivalent joinery.			
4.4.13	**SCREENS** is required, with:			
4.4.13.1	Them assembled under pressure and pinned.			
4.4.14	**ORNAMENTAL MILLWORK:**			
4.4.14.1	**WOODWORK** shall be manufacturer-sized except where installer adjustments are required.			
4.4.14.2	**COLUMN** fabrication for opaque finish shall allow finger-joints, with:			
4.4.14.2.1	Maximum of one per 96" (2400 mm) or portion thereof in any individual member.			
4.4.14.2.2	Joints offset a minimum of 3" (76 mm) from adjacent joints.			
4.4.14.2.3	Joints perpendicular to the face of the column resulting in the appearance of a single horizontal line with column upright.			
4.4.14.2.4	Compliance Tests C and Flushness shall apply to such joints.			
4.4.14.3	**SHEET PRODUCTS**			
4.4.14.3.1	Of **SOLID LUMBER** shall be:			
4.4.14.3.1.1	Edge-glued for width.	●		
4.4.14.3.1.2	Maximum 10" (254 mm) in width.		●	
4.4.14.3.1.3	Not permitted.			●
4.4.14.3.2	With **RAISED PANEL RIMS**:			
4.4.14.3.2.1	Mitered and glued to sheet product body.	●	●	
4.4.14.3.2.2	Mitered, splined, or doweled to sheet product body.			●
4.4.14.3.3	With **PANEL PRODUCT CENTERS** require:			
4.4.14.3.3.1	No edge treatment.	●		
4.4.14.3.3.2	Edge covered by veneer or concealed by molding.		●	●
4.4.14.3.4	With **LOOSE JOINTS** between sections require:			
4.4.14.3.4.1	No preparation.	●		
4.4.14.3.4.2	Manufacturer preparation, utilizing mortise and tenon, dowel, or spline joinery.		●	
4.4.14.3.4.3	Manufacturer assembly (if practical), utilizing mortise and tenon, dowel, or spline joinery.			●
4.4.14.3.5	With **OUTSIDE CORNERS** require:			
4.4.14.3.5.1	No preparation.	●		
4.4.14.3.5.2	Manufacturer prepared and shipped loose for installer fitting.		●	
4.4.14.3.5.3	Manufacturer prepared, glued, and braced (if practical).			●
4.4.14.3.6	With **INSIDE CORNERS** require:			
4.4.14.3.6.1	No preparation.	●		
4.4.14.3.6.2	Shipped oversize for installer fitting.		●	●

PRODUCT

MATERIAL, MACHINING, AND ASSEMBLY RULES (continued)

DESCRIPTION	E	C	P
4.4 ASSEMBLY (continued)			
4.4.14 ORNAMENTAL MILLWORK (continued)			
4.4.14.3 SHEET PRODUCTS (continued)			
4.4.14.3.7 With **APPLIED MOLDINGS**, contained wholly within an individual item or used as rim or panel retention members, require:			
4.4.14.3.7.1 Mitered corners.			
4.4.14.3.7.2 No preparation.	●		
4.4.14.3.7.3 Manufacturer application with spot glue and finish nails.		●	
4.4.14.3.7.4 Manufacturer application with spot glue, finish nails, and:			●
4.4.14.3.7.4.1 Filled and sanded.			●
4.4.14.3.8 With **HISTORIC WORK** requires:			
4.4.14.3.8.1 **REPAIRS** to be of the same machining, joinery, and assembly methods as original, reversible adhesives, etc.			
4.4.14.3.8.2 **NEW WORK** match existing, except when hand-made nonuniform profiles occur, a similar profile shall be selected by the design professional.			
4.4.15 MISCELLANEOUS MILLWORK such as:			
4.4.15.1 DECORATIVE SUN SCREENS or **LOUVERS** shall be soundly constructed, with:			
4.4.15.1.1 All members dadoed together and, where design permits, assembled in the mill.			
4.4.15.2 BOXED BEAMS, COLUMNS, PILASTERS, SEATS, BENCHES, and overhead **TRELLISES** shall be soundly constructed, with:			
4.4.15.2.1 Tongued, shoulder-mitered, mortised and tenoned, or doweled joints; securely glued, nailed, and reinforced with glue blocks or metal brackets, as appropriate.			
4.4.15.3 STAVED COLUMNS or **NEWELS** shall be of lock joint, tongue, or spline construction and securely glued with:			
4.4.15.3.1 **CAPS** and **BASES** furnished loose.			
4.4.15.4 **HANDRAILS** and **CROOKS** shall be furnished mill-cut and doweled unless jobsite conditions dictate otherwise.			
4.4.15.5 CLOSET & UTILITY SHELVING, shall have:			
4.4.15.5.1 SHELVES and **DIVIDERS** furnished:			
4.4.15.5.1.1 Unassembled.			
4.4.15.5.1.2 Cut to width.			
4.4.15.5.1.3 In lengths suitable for installer fitting.			
4.4.15.5.2 **CLEATS** furnished as lineal footage.			
4.4.15.5.3 Shelves **EXCEEDING 36"** (914 mm) in length shall:			
4.4.15.5.3.1 Be a minimum of 1" (25.4 mm) in thickness, or:			
4.4.15.5.3.1.1 Have a minimum 3/4" x 3-1/2" (19 mm x 89 mm) applied front-drop cleat.			

PRODUCT

MATERIAL, MACHINING, AND ASSEMBLY RULES (continued)

	DESCRIPTION	E	C	P
4.4 ASSEMBLY	**ASSEMBLY** (continued)			
4.4.15 MISC MILLWORK	**MISCELLANEOUS MILLWORK** (continued)			
4.4.15.5 CLOSET & UTILITY SHELVING	**CLOSET & UTILITY SHELVING**, shall have (continued)			
4.4.15.5.4 EXPOSED EDGES	**EXPOSED EDGES** of sheet good cleats and shelves are defined as visible in normal use position.			
4.4.15.5.4.1	**GAPS** between the end of the shelf and the wall up to 1/4" (6.4 mm) are allowed.			
4.4.15.5.4.2	**ENDS** of shelves held more than 1/4" (6.4 mm) away from a wall shall be banded.			
4.4.15.5.4.3	Do not require any edge work.	●		
4.4.15.5.4.4	Shall be banded to match face with edges eased, with:		●	●
4.4.15.5.4.4.1	Sequence of lamination optional.		●	●
4.4.15.5.4.5	Adjoining adjustable shelves shall have ends banded.			
4.4.15.5.4.6	When **MITER-FOLDED,** shall have no open gaps, and:			
4.4.15.5.4.6.1	Shall be **FILED** or **SANDED** just enough to remove sharpness with minimal exposure of inner layers.			

EXECUTION

5 PREPARATION & QUALIFICATION REQUIREMENTS (unless otherwise specified)

5.1 **CARE, STORAGE, and BUILDING CONDITIONS** shall be in compliance with the requirements set forth in Section 2 of these standards.

5.1.1 Severe damage to the woodwork can result from noncompliance. **THE MANUFACTURER AND/OR INSTALLER OF THE WOODWORK SHALL NOT BE HELD RESPONSIBLE FOR ANY DAMAGE THAT MIGHT DEVELOP BY NOT ADHERING TO THE REQUIREMENTS.**

5.2 **CONTRACTOR IS RESPONSIBLE FOR:**

5.2.1 Furnishing and installing structural members, grounds, blocking, backing, furring, brackets, or other anchorage required for architectural woodwork installation that becomes an integral part of walls, floors, or ceilings to which architectural woodwork shall be installed.

EXECUTION

5 PREPARATION & QUALIFICATION REQUIREMENTS (continued)

5.2 CONTRACTOR IS RESPONSIBLE FOR (continued)

5.2.1 Furnishing and installing structural members (continued)

5.2.1.1 In the absence of contract documents calling for the contractor to supply the necessary blocking/ backing in the wall or ceilings, either through inadvertence or otherwise, the architectural woodwork installer shall not proceed with the installation until such time as the blocking/backing is installed by others.

5.2.1.2 Preparatory work done by others shall be subject to inspection by the architectural woodwork installer and may be accepted or rejected for cause prior to installation.

5.2.1.2.1 **WALL, CEILING,** and/or opening variations in excess of 1/4" (6.4 mm) or **FLOORS** in excess of 1/2" (12.7 mm) in 144" (3658 mm) of being plumb, level, flat, straight, square, or of the correct size are not acceptable for the installation of architectural woodwork, nor is it the responsibility of the installer to scribe or fit to tolerances in excess of such.

5.2.2 Priming and back-priming the architectural woodwork in accordance with the contract documents prior to its installation:

5.2.2.1 If the architectural woodwork is factory-finished, back-priming by the factory finisher is required.

5.3 INSTALLER IS RESPONSIBLE FOR:

5.3.1 Having adequate equipment and experienced craftsmen to complete the installation in a first-class manner.

5.3.2 Checking all architectural woodwork specified and studying the appropriate portions of the contract documents, including these standards and the reviewed shop drawings to familiarize themselves with the requirements of the Grade specified, understanding that:

5.3.2.1 Appearance requirements of Grades apply only to surfaces visible after installation.

5.3.2.2 For transparent finish, special attention needs to be given to the color and the grain of the various woodwork pieces to ensure that they are installed in compliance with the Grade specified.

5.3.2.3 Installation site is properly ventilated, protected from direct sunlight, excessive heat and/or moisture, and that the HVAC system is functioning and maintaining the appropriate relative humidity and temperature.

5.3.2.4 Required priming or back-priming, of woodwork has been completed before its install.

5.3.2.5 Woodwork has been acclimated to the field conditions for a minimum of 72 hours before installation is commenced.

5.3.2.6 Woodwork specifically built or assembled in sequence for match of color and grain is installed to maintain that same sequence.

6 RULES - The following RULES shall govern unless a project's contract documents require otherwise.

These rules are intended to provide a well-defined degree of control over a project's quality of installation.

Where E, C, or P is not indicated, the rule applies to all Grades equally.

ERRATA, published on the Associations' websites at www.awinet.org, www.awmac.com, or www.woodworkinstitute.com, shall TAKE PRECEDENCE OVER THESE RULES, subject to their date of posting and a project's bid date.

ARROWS INDICATE TOPIC IS CARRIED FROM ⇑ OR ONTO ⇓ ANOTHER PAGE.

		DESCRIPTION	E	C	P
6.1 ⇓	In **GENERAL**				
	6.1.1	Aesthetic **GRADE RULES** apply only to exposed and semi-exposed surfaces visible after installation.			

EXECUTION

Area	No.	DESCRIPTION	E	C	P
6.1 GENERAL		**GENERAL** (continued)			
	6.1.2	**TRANSPARENT FINISHED** woodwork shall be:			
	6.1.2.1	Installed with **CONSIDERATION** for color and grain.	●		
	6.1.2.2	**COMPATIBLE** in color and grain.		●	
	6.1.2.3	**WELL-MATCHED** for color and grain.			●
	6.1.2.3.1	**SHEET PRODUCTS** shall be compatible in color with solid stock.			●
	6.1.2.3.2	**ADJACENT SHEET PRODUCTS** shall be well-matched for color and grain.			●
	6.1.3	**REPAIRS** are allowed, provided they are made neatly and are inconspicuous when viewed at:			
	6.1.3.1	72" (1830 mm)	●		
	6.1.3.2	48" (1219 mm)		●	
	6.1.3.3	24" (610 mm)			●
	6.1.4	**INSTALLER MODIFICATIONS** shall comply to the material, machining, and assembly rules within the **PRODUCT** portion of this section and, if applicable, the finishing rules in Section 5.			
WOODWORK	**6.1.5**	**WOODWORK** shall be:			
	6.1.5.1	**SECURELY** fastened and tightly fitted with flush joints, and:			
	6.1.5.1.1	Joinery shall be **CONSISTENT** throughout the project.			
	6.1.5.2	Of **MAXIMUM** available and/or practical lengths.		●	●
	6.1.5.3	**TRIMMED EQUALLY** from both sides when fitted for width.		●	●
	6.1.5.4	**SPLINED** or **DOWELED** when miters are over 4" (100 mm) long.			●
	6.1.5.5	**PROFILED** or **SELF-MITERED** when trim ends are exposed.		●	
	6.1.5.6	**SELF-MITERED** when trim ends are exposed.			●
	6.1.5.7	**MITERED** at outside corners.			
	6.1.5.8	**MITERED** or **BUTTED** for S4S at inside corners.	●	●	
	6.1.5.9	**COPED** at inside corners, except S4S shall be mitered.		●	●
	6.1.5.10	**INSTALLED** plumb, level, square, and flat within 1/8" (3.2 mm) in 96" (2438 mm), and when required:			
	6.1.5.10.1	**GROUNDS** and hanging systems set plumb and true.		●	●
	6.1.5.11	Installed **FREE OF**:			
	6.1.5.11.1	Warp, twisting, cupping, and/or bowing that cannot be held true.			
	6.1.5.11.2	Open joints, visible machine marks, cross-sanding, tear-outs, nicks, chips, and/or scratches.			
	6.1.5.11.3	Natural defects exceeding the quantity and/or size limits defined in Sections 3 & 4.			
	6.1.5.12	**SMOOTH** and **SANDED** without **CROSS SCRATCHES** in conformance to the **PRODUCT** portion of this section.			
	6.1.5.13	**SCRIBED** at:			
	6.1.5.13.1	Flat surfaces		●	●
	6.1.5.13.2	Shaped surfaces			●
GAPS	**6.1.6**	**GAPS** (see Test A-C illustrations in **COMPLIANCE**):			
	6.1.6.1	**CAUSED** by **EXCESSIVE DEVIATIONS** (deviations in excess of 1/4" [6.4 mm] in 144" [3658 mm] of being plumb, level, flat, straight, square, or of the correct size) in the building's walls and ceilings, or 1/2" (12.7 mm) for floors, shall not be considered a defect or the responsibility of the installer.			
	6.1.6.2	Shall not exceed 30% of a joint's **LENGTH** and:			
	6.1.6.2.1	**FILLED** or **CAULKED** allowed	●		
	6.1.6.2.1.1	If color-compatible		●	●

EXECUTION

					DESCRIPTION	E	C	P
6.1	**GENERAL** (continued)							
	6.1.6	**GAPS** (see Test A-C illustrations in **COMPLIANCE**) (continued)						
		6.1.6.3	Of **WOOD** to **WOOD** shall not exceed:					
			6.1.6.3.1	At **FLAT** surfaces:				
				6.1.6.3.1.1	0.050" (1.3 mm) in width.	●		
				6.1.6.3.1.2	0.025" (0.65 mm) in width.		●	
				6.1.6.3.1.3	0.012" (0.3 mm) in width.			●
			6.1.6.3.2	At **SHAPED** surfaces:				
				6.1.6.3.2.1	0.075" (1.9 mm) in width.	●		
				6.1.6.3.2.2	0.050" (1.3 mm) in width.		●	
				6.1.6.3.2.3	0.025" (0.65 mm) in width.			●
		6.1.6.4	Of **WOOD** to **NON-WOOD** shall not exceed:					
			6.1.6.4.1	At **FLAT** and **SHAPED** surfaces:				
				6.1.6.4.1.1	0.100" (2.5 mm) in width.	●		
				6.1.6.4.1.2	0.075" (1.9 mm) in width.		●	
				6.1.6.4.1.3	0.050" (1.3 mm) in width.			●
		6.1.6.5	Of **NON-WOOD** to **NON-WOOD** and/or **ALL ELEMENTS** shall not exceed:					
			6.1.6.5.1	At **FLAT** surfaces:				
				6.1.6.5.1.1	0.100" (2.5 mm) in width.	●		
				6.1.6.5.1.2	0.075" (1.9 mm) in width.		●	
				6.1.6.5.1.3	0.050" (1.3 mm) in width.			●
			6.1.6.5.2	At **SHAPED** surfaces:				
				6.1.6.5.2.1	0.125" (3.2 mm) in width.	●		
				6.1.6.5.2.2	0.100" (2.5 mm) in width.		●	
				6.1.6.5.2.3	0.075" (1.9 mm) in width.			●
	6.1.7	**FLUSHNESS** of joinery (see Flushness Test D illustrations in **COMPLIANCE**):						
		6.1.7.1	Of **WOOD** to **WOOD** shall not exceed:					
			6.1.7.1.1	At **FLAT** surfaces:				
				6.1.7.1.1.1	0.050" (1.3 mm)	●		
				6.1.7.1.1.2	0.025" (0.65 mm)		●	
				6.1.7.1.1.3	0.012" (0.3 mm)			●
		6.1.7.2	Of **WOOD** to **WOOD** shall not exceed:					
			6.1.7.2.1	At **SHAPED** surfaces:				
				6.1.7.2.1.1	0.075" (1.9 mm)	●		
				6.1.7.2.1.2	0.050" (1.3 mm)		●	
				6.1.7.2.1.3	0.025" (0.65 mm)			●
		6.1.7.3	Of **WOOD** to **NON-WOOD** shall not exceed:					
			6.1.7.3.1	At **FLAT** and **SHAPED** surfaces:				
				6.1.7.3.1.1	0.100" (2.5 mm)	●		
				6.1.7.3.1.2	0.075" (1.9 mm)		●	
				6.1.7.3.1.3	0.050" (1.3 mm)			●

EXECUTION

Section	Subsection	Item	Description	E	C	P
6.1 GENERAL			**GENERAL** (continued)			
	6.1.7 FLUSHNESS		**FLUSHNESS** of joinery (continued)			
		6.1.7.4	Of **NON-WOOD** to **NON-WOOD** and/or **ALL ELEMENTS** shall not exceed:			
		6.1.7.4.1	At **FLAT** surfaces:			
		6.1.7.4.1.1	0.100" (2.5 mm)	●		
		6.1.7.4.1.2	0.075" (1.9 mm)		●	
		6.1.7.4.1.3	0.050" (1.3 mm)			●
		6.1.7.4.2	At **SHAPED** surfaces:			
		6.1.7.4.2.1	0.125" (3.2 mm)	●		
		6.1.7.4.2.2	0.100" (2.5 mm)		●	
		6.1.7.4.2.3	0.075" (1.9 mm)			●
	6.1.8 FASTENING		**FASTENING** shall:			
		6.1.8.1	**INCLUDE** the use of construction adhesive, finish nails, trim screws, and/or pins.			
		6.1.8.1.1	Staples, where permitted, shall run parallel to the grain.		●	●
		6.1.8.2	**NOT PERMIT** the use of drywall or bugle-head screws.			
		6.1.8.3	Require exposed fasteners to be countersunk.			
		6.1.8.4	Require exposed fasteners to be set in quirks and reliefs where possible.		●	●
		6.1.8.5	Require exposed fasteners to be inconspicuous when viewed at 24" (610 mm).			●
		6.1.8.6	Allow use of construction adhesive for inconspicuous fastening.			
		6.1.8.7	**NOT PERMIT** exposed fastening through HPDL.			
		6.1.8.8	Require and/or permit fastener holes:			
		6.1.8.8.1	At prefinished materials to be filled by the installer with matching filler furnished by the manufacturer.			
		6.1.8.8.2	At unfinished materials to be filled by the paint contractor or others.			
	6.1.9		**EQUIPMENT CUTOUTS** shall be neatly cut out by the installer, provided templates are furnished in a timely manner.		●	●
	6.1.10		**HARDWARE** shall be:			
		6.1.10.1	Installed neatly without tear-out of surrounding stock.			●
		6.1.10.2	Installed per manufacturer's instructions.			
		6.1.10.3	Installed using all furnished fasteners and fasteners' provisions.			
		6.1.10.4	Adjusted for smooth operation.			
	6.1.11		**AREAS** of installation shall be left broom clean.			
		6.1.11.1	Debris shall be removed and dumped in containers provided by the contractor.			
		6.1.11.2	Items installed shall be cleaned of pencil or ink marks.			
	6.1.12		Entire installation shall present **FIRST-CLASS WORKMANSHIP** in compliance with these standards.			
6.2			**PRODUCT SPECIFIC**			
	6.2.1		Such as **STANDING** and **RUNNING TRIM** shall require:			
		6.2.1.1	Running joints be diagonal scarf or butted with dowel, biscuit, or spline.		●	●
		6.2.1.2	Running joints on multimember trim be staggered from adjacent members.		●	●
		6.2.1.3	Large, one piece or multimember moldings be installed with back blocking as needed.			

EXECUTION

				DESCRIPTION	E	C	P
6.2 PRODUCT SPECIFIC				**PRODUCT SPECIFIC** (continued)			
	6.2.1			Such as **STANDING** and **RUNNING TRIM** shall require (continued)			
		6.2.1.4		**MULTIPLE JOINTS** in running trim shall not be within:			
			6.2.1.4.1	24" (609 mm)	●		
			6.2.1.4.2	36" (914 mm)		●	
			6.2.1.4.3	48" (1220 mm)			●
		6.2.1.5		Base be scribed to the floor, only if so specified.			
		6.2.1.6		Miters over 4" (102 mm) long be joined with spline, dowel, or biscuit.			●
	6.2.2			Such as **DOOR** & **WINDOW FRAMES** shall:			
		6.2.2.1		Have rough wood bucks secured at openings.			
		6.2.2.2		Be set plumb.			
		6.2.2.3		Be seated on the floor.			
		6.2.2.4		Be securely fastened through shims into the framing.			
		6.2.2.5		Have **LEGS** set square with header and parallel to each other within:			
			6.2.2.5.1	3/16" (4.8 mm)	●		
			6.2.2.5.2	1/8" (3.2 mm)		●	
			6.2.2.5.3	1/16" (1.6 mm)			●
		6.2.2.6		Allow horns to be removed before installation.			
		6.2.2.7		Require fire-door frames to be installed per the manufacturers' basic instructions.			
		6.2.2.8		Not permit prehung and precased door/jamb assemblies that are fastened only through the casing.		●	●
	6.2.3			Such as **BLINDS** and **SHUTTERS**			
		6.2.3.1		If installed in a frame, screen, blind, or shutter, shall have a maximum clearance of 1/8" (3.2 mm) at all sides and be set uniformly within 1/8" (3.2 mm) of the frame face.			
	6.2.4			**SCREENS**			
		6.2.4.1		If installed in a frame, screen, blind, or shutter, shall have a maximum clearance of 1/8" (3.2 mm) at all sides and be set uniformly within 1/8" (3.2 mm) of the frame face.			
	6.2.5			**ORNAMENTAL MILLWORK**			
		6.2.5.1		Wood filler strip to cover a maximum of 1-1/2" (38 mm).	●	●	
		6.2.5.2		Scribe/fillers securely fastened with trim screws.	●		
		6.2.5.3		Scribe/fillers securely fastened with sheet goods adhesive, face nails, or pins.		●	●
		6.2.5.4		Exposed surface scribed to the wall with a scribe strip, 1/32" (0.8 mm) maximum gap.			●
	6.2.6			**SHELF POLES** shall be supported at a minimum of 48" (1219 mm) on center.			

COMPLIANCE

7 **FABRICATED** and **INSTALLED** woodwork shall be tested for compliance to these standards as follows:

7.1 **SMOOTHNESS** of exposed surfaces

7.1.1 **KCPI** (Knife Cuts Per Inch) is determined by holding the surfaced board at an angle to a strong light source and counting the visible ridges per inch, usually perpendicular to the profile.

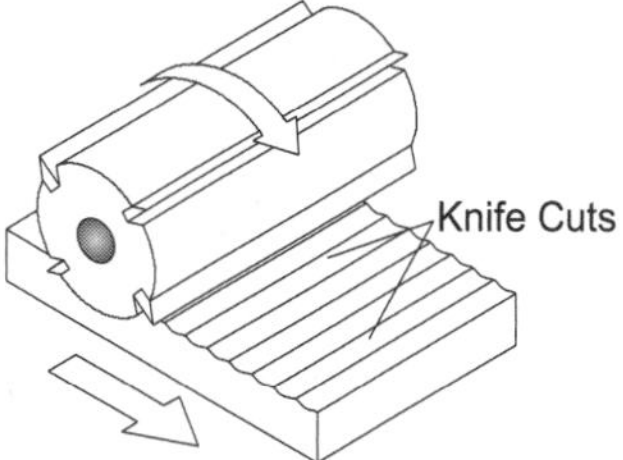

7.1.2 **SANDING** is checked for compliance by sanding a sample piece of the same species with the required grit of abrasive.

7.1.2.1 Observation with a hand lens of the prepared sample and the material in question will offer a comparison of the scratch marks of the abrasive grit.

7.1.2.2 Reasonable assessment of the performance of the finished product will be weighed against absolute compliance with the standard.

7.1.2.3 A product is sanded sufficiently smooth when knife cuts are removed and any remaining sanding marks are or will be concealed by applied finishing coats.

7.1.2.4 Handling marks and/or grain raising due to moisture or humidity in excess of the ranges set forth in this standard shall not be considered a defect.

7.2 **GAPS, FLUSHNESS,** and **FLATNESS** of product and installation:

7.2.1 Maximum gaps between exposed components shall be tested with a feeler gauge at points designed to join where members contact or touch.

7.2.2 Joint length shall be measured with a ruler with minimum 1/16" (1 mm) divisions and calculations made accordingly.

7.2.3 Reasonable assessment of the performance of the finished product will be weighed against absolute compliance with the standards.

(continued)

COMPLIANCE

7 FABRICATED and INSTALLED woodwork shall (continued)

7.2 GAPS, FLUSHNESS, and FLATNESS of product and installation (continued)

7.2.4 The following is intended to provide examples of how and where compliance testing is measured:

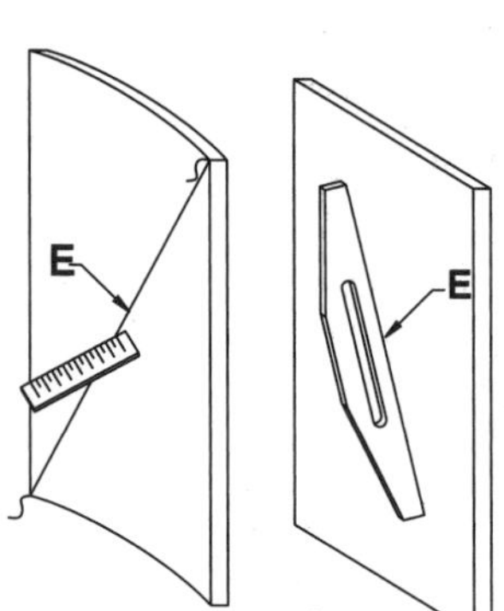

Measured on the concave face

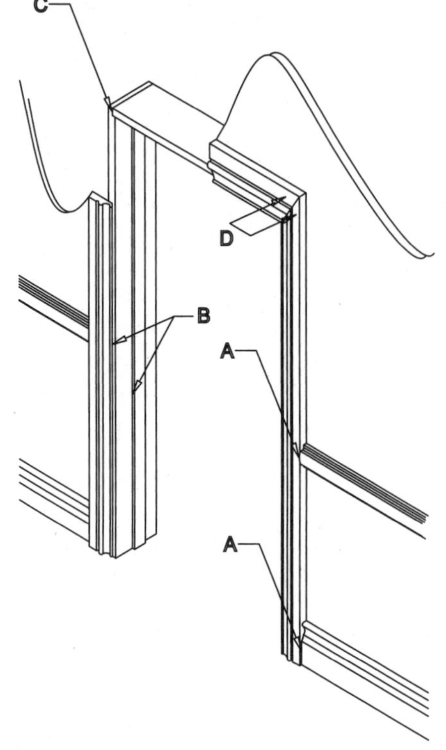

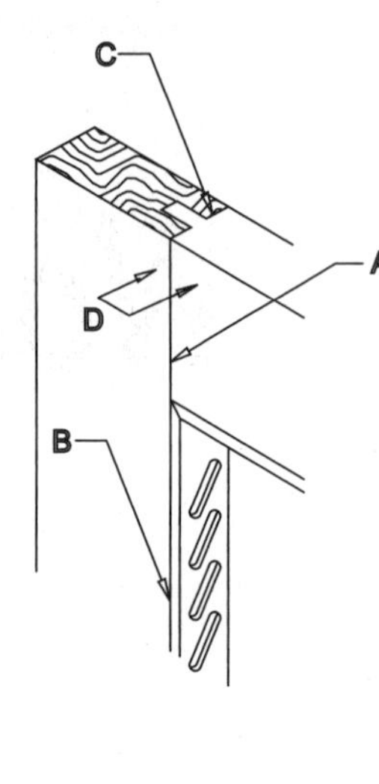

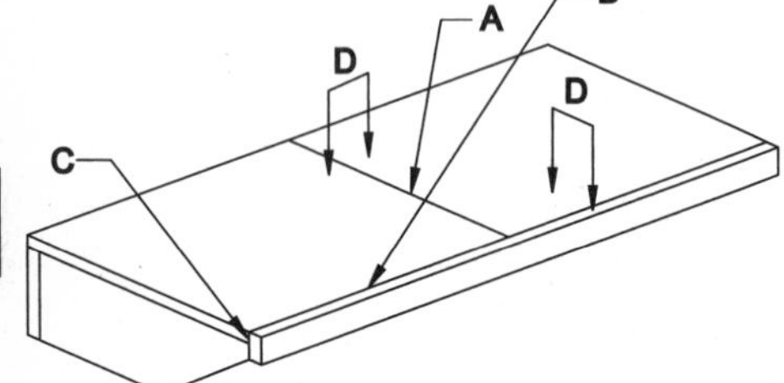

A - Gaps when surfaces are mitered or butted
B - Gaps when parallel pieces are joined
C - Gaps when edges are mitered or butted
D - Flushness between two surfaces
E - Flatness of panel product

Architectural Woodwork Standards

SECTION - 7

STAIRWORK & RAILS

SECTION 7 ✦ STAIRWORK & RAILS

(Including Wood Stairs, Integral Trim, Handrails, and Guardrails)

GENERAL

1 INFORMATION

1.1 GRADES

1.1.1 These standards are characterized in three Grades of quality that may be mixed within a single project. Limitless design possibilities and a wide variety of lumber and veneer species, along with overlays, high-pressure decorative laminates, factory finishes, and profiles are available in all three Grades.

1.1.2 **ECONOMY GRADE** defines the minimum quality requirements for a project's workmanship, materials, or installation and is typically reserved for woodwork that is not in public view, such as in mechanical spaces and utility areas.

1.1.3 **CUSTOM GRADE** is typically specified for and adequately covers most high-quality architectural woodwork, providing a well-defined degree of control over a project's quality of materials, workmanship, or installation.

1.1.4 **PREMIUM GRADE** is typically specified for use in those areas of a project where the highest level of quality, materials, workmanship, and installation is required.

1.1.5 **MODIFICATIONS** by the contract documents shall govern if in conflict with these standards.

1.2 BASIC CONSIDERATIONS

1.2.1 **ACCEPTABLE REQUIREMENTS** of lumber and/or sheet products used within this woodwork product section are established by Sections 3 and 4, unless otherwise modified herein.

1.2.2 **CONTRACT DRAWINGS** and/or **SPECIFICATIONS**, furnished by the design professional, shall clearly indicate or delineate all material, fabrication, installation, and applicable building code/regulation requirements.

1.2.3 **CROSS GRAIN** in band-sawn or laminated members might cause objectionable color variation when finished.

1.2.4 **EDGES** in veneer-laminated members or where multiple layers are exposed by shaping might cause objectionable color variation when finished.

1.2.5 **CURVED MEMBERS**, depending on the Grade, can be band-sawn, block-laminated, or veneer-laminated at the option of the manufacturer.

1.2.5.1 **EDGES** in veneer-laminated members, or where multiple layers are exposed by shaping, might cause objectionable variation in color when finished.

1.2.6 **EXPOSED SURFACES INCLUDE:**

1.2.6.1 All visible surfaces of stringers, skirt boards, treads, risers, and balustrades.

1.2.7 **SEMI-EXPOSED SURFACES** - N/A

1.2.8 **CONCEALED SURFACES INCLUDE:**

1.2.8.1 All non-visible surfaces attached to and/or covered by another.

1.2.8.2 All non-visible blocking or spacers used for attachment.

1.2.9 **DESIGN CONSIDERATIONS** - Stairs, rails, and handrails are subject to building code requirements. Code restrictions apply to rise, run, handrail, and guardrail heights, structural strength and other issues. It is the responsibility of the design professional to comply with applicable building code(s) and regulations.

1.2.9.1 Consultation with an experienced stair builder is strongly recommended.

GENERAL

1.2 **BASIC CONSIDERATIONS** (continued)

1.2.10 **STAIR** and **HANDRAIL NOMENCLATURE:**

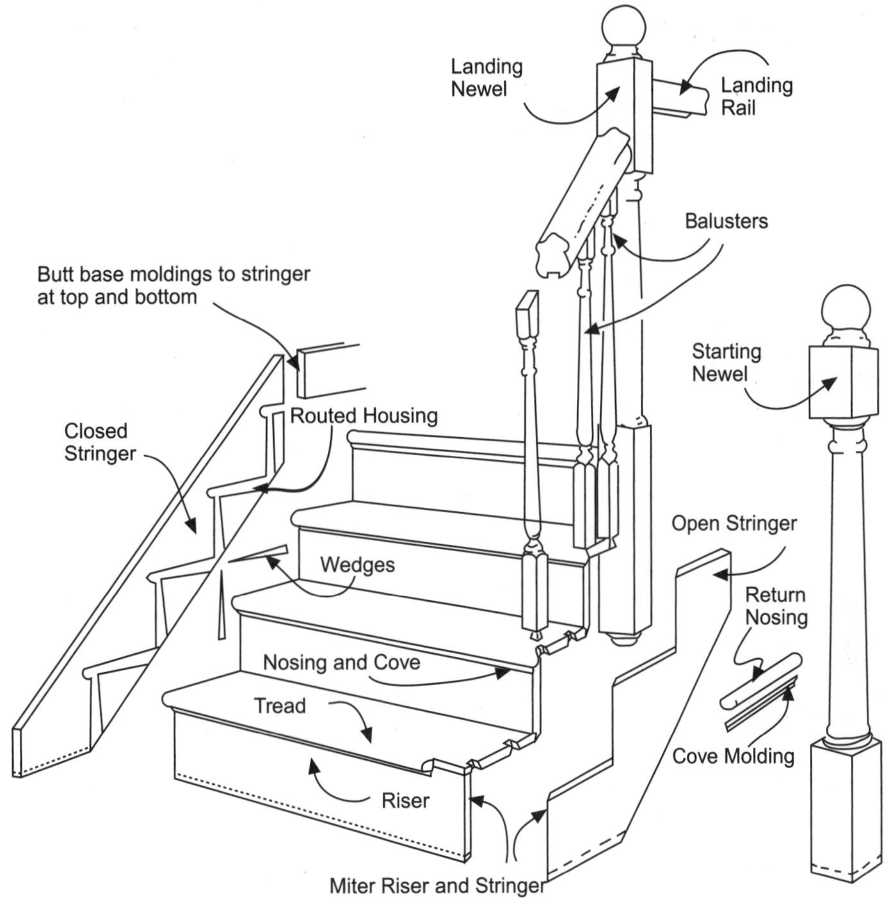

1.2.11 **HANDRAIL COMPONENT NOMENCLATURE:**

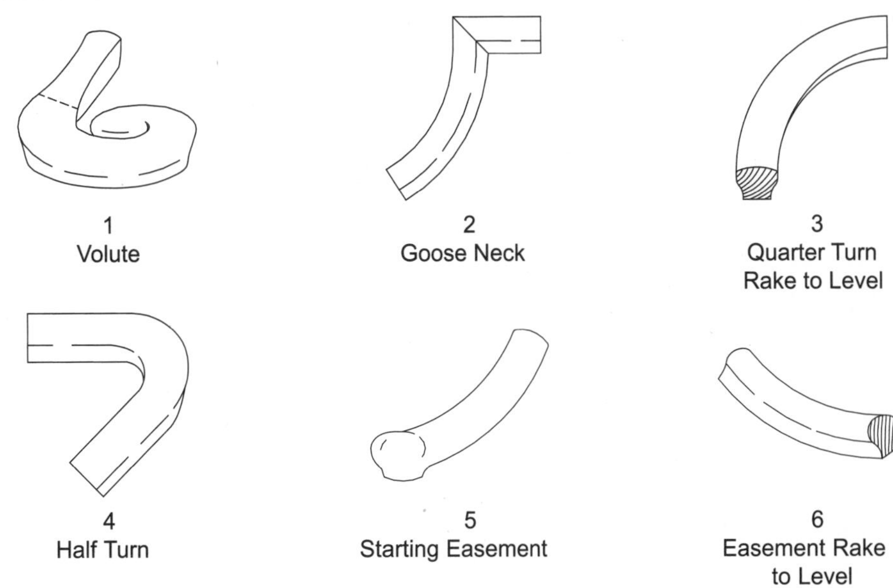

GENERAL

1.2 **BASIC CONSIDERATIONS** (continued)

1.2.11 **HANDRAIL COMPONENT NOMENCLATURE** (continued)

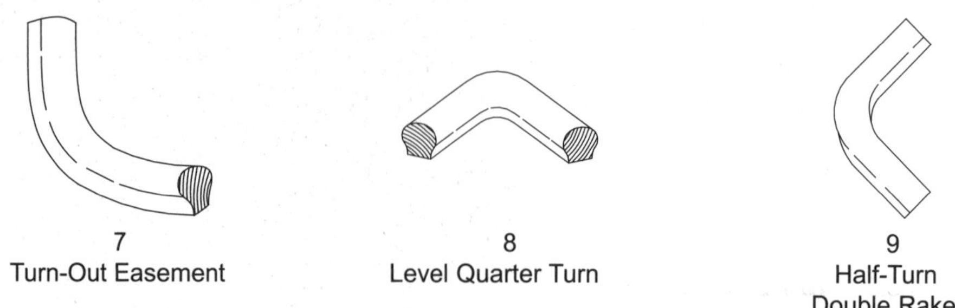

7
Turn-Out Easement

8
Level Quarter Turn

9
Half-Turn
Double Rake

1.2.12 **HANDRAIL FABRICATION:** Large dimension rail fabrication techniques are typically the option of the manufacturer. Lamination on a radius depends on many factors:

1.2.12.1 Typical lamination orientations:

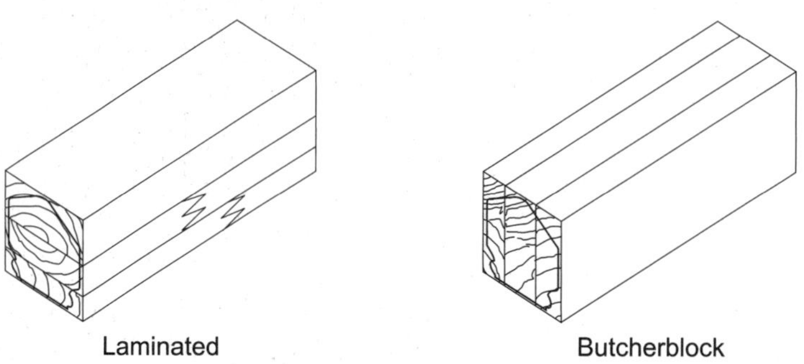

Laminated

Butcherblock

1.2.13 **HANDRAIL JOINERY**:

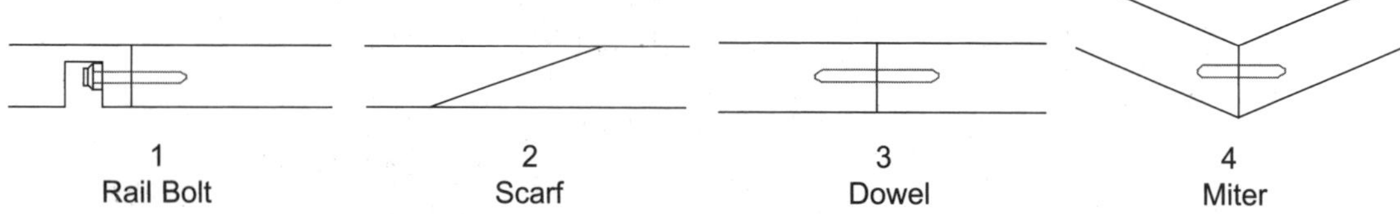

1
Rail Bolt

2
Scarf

3
Dowel

4
Miter

1.3 **RECOMMENDATIONS**

1.3.1 **INCLUDE IN DIVISION 09 OF THE SPECIFICATIONS:**

1.3.1.1 For **JOBSITE FINISHING** - BEFORE FINISHING, all exposed portions of woodwork shall have handling marks or effects of exposure to moisture, removed with a thorough, final sanding over all surfaces of the exposed portions using an appropriate grit sandpaper, and shall be cleaned before applying sealer or finish.

1.3.1.2 At **CONCEALED SURFACES** - Architectural woodwork that might be exposed to moisture, such as those adjacent to exterior concrete walls, shall be back-primed.

1.3.2 **THOROUGHLY REVIEW** Sections 3 and 4, especially Basic Considerations, Recommendations, Acknowledgements, and Industry Practices within **GENERAL** for an overview of the characteristics and the minimum acceptable requirements of lumber and/or sheet products that might be used herein.

1.3.3 **CONTRACT DOCUMENTS** (plans and/or specifications) shall require that all structural members, grounds, blocking, backing, furring, brackets, or other anchorage which becomes an integral part of the building's walls, floors, or ceilings, required for the installation of architectural woodwork is not to be furnished or installed by the architectural woodwork manufacturer or installer.

1.3.4 **SPECIFY** requirements for:

1.3.4.1 Fire ratings.

GENERAL

1.3 **RECOMMENDATIONS** (continued)

1.3.4 **SPECIFY** requirements for (continued)

1.3.4.2 Special code or regulation compliance.

1.4 **ACKNOWLEDGEMENTS - None**

1.5 **INDUSTRY PRACTICES**

1.5.1 **STRUCTURAL MEMBERS**, grounds, blocking, backing, furring, brackets, or other anchorage that becomes an integral part of the building's walls, floors, or ceilings, that are required for the installation of architectural woodwork are not furnished or installed by the architectural woodwork manufacturer or installer.

1.5.2 **WALL, CEILING,** and/or opening variations in excess of 1/4" (6.4 mm) or **FLOORS** in excess of 1/2" (12.7 mm) in 144" (3658 mm) of being plumb, level, flat, straight, square, or of the correct size are not acceptable for the installation of architectural woodwork, nor is it the responsibility of the installer to scribe or fit to tolerances in excess of such.

1.5.3 **BACK-PRIMING** of architectural woodwork is not the responsibility of the manufacturer and/or installer, unless the material is being furnished prefinished.

1.5.4 **RADIUS MOLDINGS** are laminated and formed, preshaped, or machined to the radius and fabricated in the longest practical lengths to minimize installer joints.

PRODUCT

2 SCOPE

2.1 All wood interior stairs and allied wood stair material.

2.2 **TYPICAL INCLUSIONS**

2.2.1 Wood stringers of skirt boards
2.2.2 Treads, risers, nosing, and scotia
2.2.3 Starting steps
2.2.4 All wedges and glue blocks
2.2.5 Newels, balusters, handrails, guard rails, and crooks
2.2.6 Well hole trim
2.2.7 Show rail, fillet, and spandrels
2.2.8 All other wood parts of a stair
2.2.9 Installation; if **UNINSTALLED**, stair materials shall be furnished machined KD (knocked down)

2.3 **TYPICAL EXCLUSIONS**

2.3.1 Any rough horses, structural wood framing, or timbers
2.3.2 Any metal handrail brackets or safety nosing
2.3.3 Any flooring
2.3.4 Priming and/or finishing of any kind

3 DEFAULT STIPULATION

3.1 IF NOT OTHERWISE SPECIFIED OR INDICATED IN THE CONTRACT DOCUMENTS, ALL WORK Shall be unfinished, Custom Grade, solid-stock softwood intended for opaque finish.

4 RULES - The following RULES shall govern unless a project's contract documents require otherwise.

These rules are intended to provide a well-defined degree of control over a project's quality of materials and workmanship.

Where E, C, or P is not indicated, the rule applies to all Grades equally.

PRODUCT

MATERIAL, MACHINING, AND ASSEMBLY RULES (continued)

4 RULES - The following RULES shall govern (continued)

ERRATA, published on the Associations' websites at www.awinet.org, www.awmac.com, or www.woodworkinstitute.com, shall TAKE PRECEDENCE OVER THESE RULES, subject to their date of posting and a project's bid date.

ARROWS INDICATE TOPIC IS CARRIED FROM ⇑ OR ONTO ⇓ ANOTHER PAGE.

		DESCRIPTION		E	C	P
⇑ 4.1 GENERAL	**GENERAL**					
	4.1.1	Aesthetic **GRADE RULES** apply only to exposed and semi-exposed surfaces visible after installation.				
	4.1.2	**LUMBER** shall conform to the requirements established in Section 3.				
	4.1.3	**SHEET PRODUCTS** shall conform to the requirements established in Section 4.				
	4.1.4	**WOODWORK** not addressed herein shall be manufactured from solid stock, laminated stock, veneered stock, or a combination thereof.				
	4.1.5	**BACKING SHEET** shall conform to the requirements established in Section 4.				
	4.1.6	**EXPOSED, SEMI-EXPOSED**, and **CONCEALED** surfaces shall be as listed under the **GENERAL** portion of this section.				
	4.1.7	**STANDING** and **RUNNING TRIM** shall be furnished as material only, not assembled.				
	4.1.8	Where **MULTIPLE OPTIONS** are permitted, it shall be the manufacturer's choice unless specified otherwise.				
	4.1.9	**FIRE-RETARDANT RATING**, if required, shall be so specified.				
	4.1.10	**SPECIFIC PROFILE**, if required, shall be so specified or drawn.				
	4.1.11	**SPECIAL ORNAMENTAL DETAIL** or joinery, if required, shall be so specified or drawn.				
	4.1.12	Radius moldings are laminated and formed, preshaped, or machined to the radius and fabricated in the longest practical lengths to minimize installer joints.				
	4.1.13	For **TRANSPARENT FINISH**, if the **SPECIES** is not specified, the use of either hardwood or softwood (plywood or solid stock) of one species for the entire job is permitted at the manufacturer's option.				
	4.1.14	**STAIRWORK**, including handrails, shall conform to all applicable codes and requirements, and:				
		4.1.14.1	Nothing in these standards shall overrule such.			
	4.1.15	Where **GLUING** or **LAMINATION** occurs:				
		4.1.15.1	**DELAMINATION** or **SEPARATION** shall not occur beyond that which is allowed in Sections 3 & 4.			
		4.1.15.2	Use of **CONTACT ADHESIVE** is not permitted.			
	4.1.16	**BACK-PRIMING** is not the responsibility of the manufacturer and/or installer, unless the material is furnished prefinished.				
	4.1.17	**FIRST-CLASS WORKMANSHIP** is required in compliance with these standards.				
4.2 MATERIAL ⇓	**MATERIAL**					
	4.2.1	Shall be lumber or sheet products of the species and Grade specified.				
	4.2.2	Shall conform in finish width, thickness, and length of lumber to Section 3.				
	4.2.3	Shall not have defects, either natural or manufactured, that exceed those permitted.				
		4.2.3.1	Permits unlimited finger-joints.	●		
	4.2.4	Requires plain-sawn lumber.				
	4.2.5	**TREADS** shall be a minimum of 1" (25.4 mm) in thickness.				
	4.2.6	**CLOSED STRINGERS** shall be a minimum of 3/4" (19 mm) in thickness.				
	4.2.7	Permits defects, both natural and manufactured, if covered by adjoining members or otherwise concealed when installed.				
	4.2.8	States figure is not a function of a species grade and must be specified in the contract document.				
	4.2.9	Permits warp, which can be held flat and straight with normal attachment.				

PRODUCT

MATERIAL, MACHINING, AND ASSEMBLY RULES (continued)

	DESCRIPTION	E	C	P
4.2	**MATERIAL** (continued)			
4.2.10 RADIUS	Requires radiused woodwork to be constructed of solid-machined, block-laminated, laminated plies, core-veneered, or kerfed solid stock and: Solid-machined · Block-laminated · Laminated Plies · Core-veneered · Kerfed Solid Stock			
4.2.10.1	Members of solid stock or block laminations shall be furnished in such sections as to avoid pronounced cross grain and reduce joints to a minimum.			
4.2.10.2	**GLUE** shall be selected for color to avoid a prominent glue line.			
4.2.11	For **SPANDREL** and **SOFFIT PANELS** shall conform to the requirements of Section 8.			
4.2.12 EXPOSED SURFACES	At **EXPOSED SURFACES**:			
4.2.12.1	Requires end grain to be kept to a minimum.	●	●	
4.2.12.2	Requires ends to be self-returned with no end grain showing.			●
4.2.12.3	Permits medium-density fiberboard (MDF) for opaque finish.			
4.2.12.4	Requires sheet product edges to be banded with the same species as the face.		●	●
4.2.12.5	Requires plain-sliced veneer for transparent finish.			
4.2.12.6	Permits mill-option veneer for opaque finish.			
4.2.12.7 TRANSPARENT	For **TRANSPARENT FINISH:**			
4.2.12.7.1	Permits hardwood or softwood.			
4.2.12.7.2	Permits only one species for the entire project.		●	●
4.2.12.7.3	Prohibits finger joints.		●	●
4.2.12.7.4	Requires adhesive, used for laminating, to be selected for color to avoid a prominent glue line.		●	●
4.2.12.7.5	Requires lumber (including block segments or veneer of laminated material) and sheet products to be compatible in color and grain.		●	
4.2.12.7.6	Requires lumber (including block segments or veneer of laminated material) to be well-matched for color and grain; sheet products shall be compatible in color with solid stock, and adjacent sheet products shall be well-matched for color and grain.			●
4.2.12.7.7	Requires **INTERSECTIONS** of radius and straight members to be splined or half-lapped, securely glued, and mechanically fastened.		●	●
4.2.12.7.8	At **BLOCK LAMINATION:**			
4.2.12.7.8.1	Requires segments to be cut from the same board.			●
4.2.12.7.8.2	Requires segment joints to be staggered.			
4.2.12.7.8.3	Requires adjacent segment ends have similar grain angle.		●	●
4.2.12.7.9	At **VENEER LAMINATIONS:**			
4.2.12.7.9.1	Requires exposed layers to be resawn from the same or matched boards.			●
4.2.12.7.9.2	Requires veneer layers to be reassembled in the same order and orientation as cut.			●

 - Architectural Woodwork Standards - 1st Edition, October 1, 2009
As may be updated by errata at www.awinet.org, www.awmac.com, or www.woodworkinstitute.com/awserrata/

PRODUCT

MATERIAL, MACHINING, AND ASSEMBLY RULES (continued)

No.	DESCRIPTION	E	C	P
4.2	**MATERIAL** (continued)			
4.2.12	At **EXPOSED SURFACES** (continued)			
4.2.12.7	For **TRANSPARENT FINISH** (continued)			
4.2.12.7.10	Have visible panel **EDGES**, **REVEALS**, and/or **SPLINES,** when appropriate, that are:			
4.2.12.7.10.1	Full length.			
4.2.12.7.10.2	**MILL-OPTION.**	●		
4.2.12.7.10.3	**MATCH** species of panel face.		●	●
4.2.12.7.10.4	**COMPATIBLE** for color and grain.		●	
4.2.12.7.10.5	**WELL-MATCHED** for color and grain.			●
4.2.12.7.10.6	A minimum of 0.020" (0.5 mm) nominal **THICKNESS** that precludes show-through of core.		●	●
4.2.13	At **SEMI-EXPOSED SURFACES:**			
4.2.13.1	For **OPAQUE** finish, permits natural and manufacturing defects, provided the surface is filled solid.			
4.2.14	At **CONCEALED SURFACES:**			
4.2.14.1	Permits defects such as voids, wane, or unfilled knots.			
4.2.14.2	Requires blocking or shims to be of a compatible material.			
4.2.15	At **BOXED** or **CURB STRINGERS**, shall be of two or more members.			
4.2.16	At **STRINGER TURNOUTS**, including quarter turns, half turns, and the like, shall be of laminated or veneered face construction, and:			
4.2.16.1	Where feasible, such turns shall be a continuous part of the straight stringer.			
4.2.17	At **HANDRAILS**, **GUARD RAILS**, **NEWEL POSTS,** and **BALUSTERS** can be glued up.			
4.2.18	At **RISERS**, bull-nosed or radius, shall be veneered construction with one piece face.			
4.2.19	When **FACTORY FINISHING** is specified, concealed surfaces shall be factory sealed with one coat at 1 mil dry.		●	●
4.3	**MACHINING** of:			
4.3.1	**EXPOSED SURFACES** shall comply with:			
4.3.1.1	**SMOOTHNESS REQUIREMENTS** (see Item 7.1 in **COMPLIANCE**) at:			
4.3.1.1.1	**SHARP EDGES** to be eased with fine abrasive.		●	●
4.3.1.1.2	**TOP FLAT WOOD** surfaces; those that can be sanded with a drum or wide belt sander:			
4.3.1.1.2.1	Minimum 15 KCPI or 100-grit sanding	●		
4.3.1.1.2.2	120-grit sanding		●	
4.3.1.1.2.3	150-grit sanding			●
4.3.1.1.3	**PROFILED** and **SHAPED WOOD** surfaces:			
4.3.1.1.3.1	Minimum 15 KCPI or 100-grit sanding	●		
4.3.1.1.3.2	Minimum 20 KCPI or 120-grit sanding		●	
4.3.1.1.3.3	120-grit sanding			●
4.3.1.1.4	**TURNED WOOD** surfaces:			
4.3.1.1.4.1	Minimum 15 KCPI or 100-grit sanding	●		
4.3.1.1.4.2	120-grit sanding		●	
4.3.1.1.4.3	180-grit sanding			●
4.3.1.1.5	**CROSS-SANDING**, excluding turned surfaces:			
4.3.1.1.5.1	Is not a defect.	●		
4.3.1.1.5.2	Is not allowed.		●	●

PRODUCT

MATERIAL, MACHINING, AND ASSEMBLY RULES (continued)

Section	DESCRIPTION	E	C	P
4.3	**MACHINING** (continued)			
4.3.1	**EXPOSED SURFACES** shall comply with (continued)			
4.3.1.1	**SMOOTHNESS REQUIREMENTS** (continued)			
4.3.1.1.6	**TEAR-OUTS, KNIFE NICKS**, or **HIT-OR-MISS** machining is not permitted.			
4.3.1.1.7	**KNIFE MARKS** are not permitted where sanding is required.			
4.3.1.1.8	**GLUE** or **FILLER**, if used, shall be inconspicuous and match adjacent surface for smoothness.			
4.3.2	**TRIM** to be applied on flat surfaces shall have the reverse side backed out, except at those members that have exposed ends.		●	●
4.3.2.1	Trim over 2" (50.8 mm) in width with unexposed ends shall be backed out.		●	●
4.3.3	**BAND-SAWN** and **BLOCK-LAMINATED** members shall be divided to minimize the exposure of cross grain in the face of the member, and:			
4.3.3.1 (RADIUS)	**ANGLE** of **GRAIN** at the face of curved member shall not exceed 30 degrees, unless a small part size requires otherwise. 30° — Acceptable 90° — Unacceptable		●	●
4.3.4	**INTERSECTIONS** at radius and straight members shall be splined or half-lapped, securely glued, and mechanically fastened.			
4.3.5	**DADOES** shall completely house the male member throughout the entire length of the joint.	●		
4.3.6	**PROFILE** for items such as nosings, handrails, or balusters, if not indicated, shall be optional.			
4.3.7	**FACE STRINGERS** at open-end stairs shall be cut and mitered to receive treads and risers.			
4.3.8	**SHOE RAIL** shall include them being plowed to receive balusters and fillet, unless otherwise indicated.			
4.3.9	**SCOTIA** or **COVE MOLD**, if indicated, shall be provided for each riser; and for open-string stairs, shall be mitered with the end returned.			
4.3.10	**CLOSED STRINGERS** shall include machining to receive the treads, risers, and wedges.		●	●
4.3.11 (TREADS)	**TREADS** at open-string stairs shall include:			
4.3.11.1	Boring or cutting required to receive balusters.	●	●	●
4.3.11.2	Exposed ends of treads **SHAPED** to match nosing.	●		
4.3.11.3	Exposed ends of treads shall have a **MITERED** return nosing, and:		●	●
4.3.11.3.1	Leading corner of the tread return shall be mitered to the leading edge of the tread with a shoulder miter, and:		●	●
4.3.11.3.1.1	Doweled or biscuit joined.		●	●
4.3.12	**RISERS** at open-string stairs shall be mitered.			
4.3.13	**RISERS** shall be rabbetted to receive the back edge of the tread.			
4.3.14	**RAILS** to receive balusters with square or rectangular heads shall be plowed on under-side and provided with fillet.			
4.3.15	Of **NEWEL POSTS**, when built up, shall be of shoulder-miter, lock-joint, tongues, or splined construction.			
4.4	**ASSEMBLY**			
4.4.1	**JOINTS** at **ASSEMBLED WOODWORK** shall:			
4.4.1.1	Be neatly and accurately made.			
4.4.1.2	Be **SECURELY GLUED** with residue removed from all exposed and semi-exposed surfaces, and:			
4.4.1.2.1	Be **REINFORCED** with glue blocks where essential.			

PRODUCT

MATERIAL, MACHINING, AND ASSEMBLY RULES (continued)

	DESCRIPTION	**E**	**C**	**P**
4.4	**ASSEMBLY** (continued)			
4.4.1	**JOINTS** at **ASSEMBLED WOODWORK** shall (continued)			
4.4.1.3	At stringer aprons, fascias, and flat base utilize:			
4.4.1.3.1	Clamp nail, biscuit, spline, butterfly, scarf, or dowel joinery.		●	
4.4.1.3.2	Biscuit, spline, butterfly, scarf, or dowel joinery.			●
4.4.1.4	At **HANDRAILS**:			
4.4.1.4.1	Utilize clamp nails or stair bolts.	●		
4.4.1.4.2	Utilize stair bolts.		●	
4.4.1.4.3	Utilize stair bolts and dowels.			●
4.4.1.4.4	When mitered, utilize screws if stair bolts are impractical.			
4.4.1.4.5	Have holes of stair bolts or screws plugged, unless covered by fillet, and:			
4.4.1.4.5.1	Plugs shall be compatible for color and grain.		●	
4.4.1.4.5.2	Plugs shall be well matched for color and grain.			●
4.4.1.4.5.3	Grain of plugs shall align with handrail grain.			●
4.4.1.5	Be **MECHANICALLY FASTENED** with nails or screws, where practical, with:			
4.4.1.5.1	Fasteners at solid wood countersunk.			
4.4.1.5.2	Fasteners at solid wood in molding quirks or reliefs where possible.		●	●
4.4.1.6	**NOT PERMIT** fasteners at exposed surfaces of HPDL or overlay sheet products.			
4.4.1.7	**FLUSHNESS** — Requires **FLUSHNESS VARIATIONS** at exposed surfaces when mitered or butted (see Test D illustrations in **COMPLIANCE**) not to exceed:			
4.4.1.7.1	**INTERIOR**			
4.4.1.7.1.1	0.025" (0.6 mm)	●		
4.4.1.7.1.2	0.005" (0.1 mm)		●	
4.4.1.7.1.3	0.001" (0.03 mm)			●
4.4.1.7.2	**EXTERIOR**			
4.4.1.7.2.1	0.05" (1.3 mm)	●		
4.4.1.7.2.2	0.025" (0.6 mm)		●	
4.4.1.7.2.3	0.015" (0.4 mm)			●
4.4.1.8	**GAPS** — Requires **GAPS** at exposed surfaces when mitered or butted (see Test A illustrations in **COMPLIANCE**) not to exceed:			
4.4.1.8.1	**INTERIOR**			
4.4.1.8.1.1	0.05" (1.3 mm) wide by 20% of the joint length	●		
4.4.1.8.1.2	0.025" (0.6 mm) wide by 20% of the joint length		●	
4.4.1.8.1.3	0.015" (0.4 mm) wide by 20% of the joint length			●
4.4.1.8.2	**EXTERIOR**			
4.4.1.8.2.1	0.075" (1.9 mm) wide by 30% of the joint length	●		
4.4.1.8.2.2	0.05" (1.3 mm) wide by 30% of the joint length		●	
4.4.1.8.2.3	0.025" (0.6 mm) wide by 30% of the joint length			●
4.4.1.9	Requires **GAPS** at exposed surfaces at parallel members (see Test B illustrations in **COMPLIANCE**) not to exceed:			
4.4.1.9.1	**INTERIOR**			
4.4.1.9.1.1	0.05" x 8" (1.3 mm x 203 mm) and shall not occur within 48" (1219 mm) of a similar gap	●		

PRODUCT

MATERIAL, MACHINING, AND ASSEMBLY RULES (continued)

					DESCRIPTION	E	C	P
4.4	**ASSEMBLY** (continued)							
	4.4.1	**JOINTS** at **ASSEMBLED WOODWORK** shall (continued)						
		4.4.1.9 GAPS	Requires **GAPS** at exposed surfaces at parallel members (continued)					
			4.4.1.9.1	**INTERIOR** (continued)				
				4.4.1.9.1.2	0.025" x 6" (0.6 mm x 152 mm) and shall not occur within 60" (1524 mm) of a similar gap		●	
				4.4.1.9.1.3	0.015" x 3" (0.4 mm x 76 mm) and shall not occur within 72" (1829 mm) of a similar gap			●
			4.4.1.9.2	**EXTERIOR**				
				4.4.1.9.2.1	0.075" x 10" (1.9 mm x 254 mm) and shall not occur within 24" (610 mm) of a similar gap	●		
				4.4.1.9.2.2	0.05" x 8" (1.3 mm x 203 mm) and shall not occur within 26" (660 mm) of a similar gap		●	
				4.4.1.9.2.3	0.025" x 6" (0.6 mm x 152 mm) and shall not occur within 30" (762 mm) of a similar gap			●
		4.4.1.10 GAPS	Requires **GAPS** at exposed surfaces when mitered or butted (See Test C illustrations in **COMPLIANCE**) not exceed:					
			4.4.1.10.1	**INTERIOR**				
				4.4.1.10.1.1	0.05" (1.3 mm)	●		
				4.4.1.10.1.2	0.025" (0.6 mm)		●	
				4.4.1.10.1.3	0.015" (0.4 mm)			●
			4.4.1.10.2	**EXTERIOR**				
				4.4.1.10.2.1	0.075" (1.9 mm)	●		
				4.4.1.10.2.2	0.05" (1.3 mm)		●	
				4.4.1.10.2.3	0.025" (0.6 mm)			●
		4.4.1.11	Allows **FILLER**:					
			4.4.1.11.1		If inconspicuous when viewed at 36" (914 mm).	●		
			4.4.1.11.2		If inconspicuous when viewed at 24" (610 mm).		●	
			4.4.1.11.3		**NOT ALLOWED.**			●
		4.4.1.12 HPDL & PVC	At **HPDL** and **PVC**, edges shall be machined flush and filed, sanded, or buffed to remove machine marks and sharp edges, and:					
			4.4.1.12.1	**VISIBLE OVERLAP** (over-filing) shall not exceed:				
				4.4.1.12.1.1	0.005" (0.13 mm) for a maximum length of 2" (50.8 mm) in any 48" (1220 mm) run.	●		
				4.4.1.12.1.2	0.005" (0.13 mm) for a maximum length of 1" (25.4 mm) in any 24" (610 mm) run.		●	
				4.4.1.12.1.3	**NO VISIBLE OVERLAP.**			●
			4.4.1.12.2	**CHIP-OUT** shall be inconspicuous when viewed at:				
				4.4.1.12.2.1	72" (1829 mm)	●		
				4.4.1.12.2.2	48" (1220 mm)		●	
				4.4.1.12.2.3	24" (610 mm)			●
			4.4.1.12.3	**REMOVAL** of color or pattern of face material due to over-machining limited to:				
				4.4.1.12.3.1	3/32" x 4" (2.4 mm x 102 mm) and shall not occur within 48" (1220 mm) of a similar occurrence.	●		

PRODUCT

MATERIAL, MACHINING, AND ASSEMBLY RULES (continued)

	DESCRIPTION	E	C	P
4.4 ASSEMBLY	**ASSEMBLY** (continued)			
4.4.1	**JOINTS** at **ASSEMBLED WOODWORK** shall (continued)			
4.4.1.12	At **HPDL** and **PVC,** edges shall be machined flush (continued)			
4.4.1.12.3	**REMOVAL** of color or pattern of face material due to (continued)			
4.4.1.12.3.2	1/16" x 1-1/2" (1.6 mm x 38.1 mm) and shall not occur within 60" (1524 mm) of a similar occurrence.		●	
4.4.1.12.3.3	1/16" x 4" (1.6 mm x 102 mm) and shall not occur within 72" (1829 mm) of a similar occurrence.			●
4.4.2	**APPLIED MOLDINGS** shall be spot-glued and mechanically fastened.			
4.4.3	**MITER JOINTS** shall be well fitted and cleaned.			
4.4.4	**BUILT-UP ITEMS** shall be soundly fabricated with half-lapped, mitered, shoulder-mitered, tonged, or equivalent construction.			
4.4.5	**STAIRWORK** shall be furnished KD (knocked down), with:			
4.4.5.1	**TRIM MEMBERS** cut to required length plus allowance for fitting.			
4.4.5.2	**STARTING STEPS** with returned riser assembled ready for installation.			
4.4.5.3	**SCOTIA** and shoe molds temporarily attached.			
4.4.5.4	**BALUSTERS** for open-string stairs shall be provided with dowel or tenon to fit into treads.			
4.4.5.5	**CROOKS** and **RETURNS** shall be doweled and provided with rail bolts ready for assembly.			
4.4.5.6	**GLUE BLOCKS** shall be provided at 12" (305 mm) on center maximum for each riser.			

EXECUTION

7

5 PREPARATION & QUALIFICATION REQUIREMENTS (unless otherwise specified)

5.1 **CARE, STORAGE, and BUILDING CONDITIONS** shall be in compliance with the requirements set forth in Section 2 of these standards.

5.1.1 Severe damage to the woodwork can result from noncompliance. **THE MANUFACTURER AND/OR INSTALLER OF THE WOODWORK SHALL NOT BE HELD RESPONSIBLE FOR ANY DAMAGE THAT MIGHT DEVELOP BY NOT ADHERING TO THE REQUIREMENTS.**

5.2 **CONTRACTOR IS RESPONSIBLE FOR:**

5.2.1 Furnishing and installing structural members, grounds, blocking, backing, furring, brackets, or other anchorage required for architectural woodwork installation that becomes an integral part of walls, floors, or ceilings to which architectural woodwork shall be installed.

5.2.1.1 In the absence of contract documents calling for the contractor to supply the necessary blocking/backing in the wall or ceilings, either through inadvertence or otherwise, the architectural woodwork installer shall not proceed with the installation until such time as the blocking/backing is installed by others.

5.2.1.2 Preparatory work done by others shall be subject to inspection by the architectural woodwork installer, and shall be accepted or rejected for cause prior to installation.

5.2.1.2.1 **WALL, CEILING,** and/or opening variations in excess of 1/4" (6.4 mm) or **FLOORS** in excess of 1/2" (12.7 mm) in 144" (3658 mm) of being plumb, level, flat, straight, square, or of the correct size are not acceptable for the installation of architectural woodwork, nor is it the responsibility of the installer to scribe or fit to tolerances in excess of such.

EXECUTION

5 PREPARATION & QUALIFICATION REQUIREMENTS (continued)

5.2 CONTRACTOR IS RESPONSIBLE FOR (continued)

5.2.2 Priming and back-priming the architectural woodwork in accordance with the contract documents prior to its installation.

5.2.2.1 If the architectural woodwork is factory-finished, back-priming by the factory finisher is required.

5.3 INSTALLER IS RESPONSIBLE FOR:

5.3.1 Having adequate equipment and experienced craftsmen to complete the installation in a first-class manner.

5.3.2 Checking all architectural woodwork specified and studying the appropriate portions of the contract documents, including these standards and the reviewed shop drawings to familiarize themselves with the requirements of the Grade specified, understanding that:

5.3.2.1 Appearance requirements of Grades apply only to surfaces visible after installation.

5.3.2.2 For transparent finish, special attention needs to be given to the color and grain of the various woodwork pieces to ensure that they are installed in compliance with the Grade specified.

5.3.2.3 Installation site is properly ventilated, protected from direct sunlight, excessive heat and/or moisture, and that the HVAC system is functioning and maintaining the appropriate relative humidity and temperature.

5.3.2.4 Required priming or back-priming, of woodwork has been completed before its install.

5.3.2.5 Woodwork has been acclimated to the field conditions for a minimum of 72 hours before installation is commenced.

5.3.2.6 Woodwork specifically built or assembled in sequence for match of color and grain is installed to maintain that same sequence.

6 RULES - The following RULES shall govern unless a project's contract documents require otherwise.

These rules are intended to provide a well-defined degree of control over a project's quality of installation.

Where E, C, or P is not indicated, the rule applies to all Grades equally.

ERRATA, published on the Associations' websites at www.awinet.org, www.awmac.com, or www.woodworkinstitute.com, shall TAKE PRECEDENCE OVER THESE RULES, subject to their date of posting and a project's bid date.

ARROWS INDICATE TOPIC IS CARRIED FROM ⇑ OR ONTO ⇓ ANOTHER PAGE.

		DESCRIPTION	E	C	P
6.1	**GENERAL**				
GENERAL	6.1.1	Aesthetic **GRADE RULES** apply only to exposed and semi-exposed surfaces visible after installation.			
	6.1.2	**TRANSPARENT FINISHED** woodwork shall be:			
	6.1.2.1	Installed with **CONSIDERATION** of color and grain.	●		
	6.1.2.2	**COMPATIBLE** in color and grain.		●	
	6.1.2.3	**WELL-MATCHED** for color and grain.			●
	6.1.2.3.1	**SHEET PRODUCTS** shall be compatible in color with solid stock.			●
	6.1.2.3.2	**ADJACENT SHEET PRODUCTS** shall be well-matched for color and grain.			●
⇓	6.1.3	**INSTALLER MODIFICATIONS** shall comply to the material, machining, and assembly rules within the **PRODUCT** portion of this section and, if applicable, the finishing rules in Section 5.			

EXECUTION

Section	Group	No.	DESCRIPTION	E	C	P
6.1	**GENERAL** (continued)					
		6.1.4	**REPAIRS** are allowed, provided they are neatly made and inconspicuous when viewed at:			
		6.1.4.1	72" (1830 mm)	●		
		6.1.4.2	48" (1219 mm)		●	
		6.1.4.3	24" (610 mm)			●
	WOODWORK	6.1.5	**WOODWORK** shall be:			
		6.1.5.1	**SECURELY** fastened and tightly fitted with flush joints, and:			
		6.1.5.1.1	Joinery shall be **CONSISTENT** throughout the project.			
		6.1.5.2	Of **MAXIMUM** available and/or practical lengths.		●	●
		6.1.5.3	**TRIMMED EQUALLY** from both sides when fitted for width.		●	●
		6.1.5.4	**SPLINED** or **DOWELED** when miters are over 4" (100 mm) long.			●
		6.1.5.5	**PROFILED** or **SELF-MITERED** when trim ends are exposed.		●	
		6.1.5.6	**SELF-MITERED** when trim ends are exposed.			●
		6.1.5.7	**MITERED** at outside corners			
		6.1.5.8	**MITERED** at inside corners	●	●	
		6.1.5.9	**COPED** at inside corners		●	●
		6.1.5.10	**INSTALLED** plumb, level, square, and flat within 1/8" (3.2 mm) in 96" (2438 mm), and when required:			
		6.1.5.10.1	**GROUNDS** and **HANGING SYSTEMS** set plumb and true.		●	●
		6.1.5.11	Installed **FREE OF**:			
		6.1.5.11.1	Warp, twisting, cupping, and/or bowing that cannot be held true.			
		6.1.5.11.2	Open joints, visible machine marks, cross-sanding, tears, nicks, chips, and/or scratches.			
		6.1.5.11.3	Natural defects exceeding the quantity or size limits defined in Sections 3 & 4.			
		6.1.5.12	**SMOOTH** and **SANDED** without **CROSS-SCRATCHES** in conformance to the **PRODUCT** portion of this section.			
		6.1.5.13	**SCRIBED** at:			
		6.1.5.13.1	Flat surfaces		●	●
		6.1.5.13.2	Shaped surfaces			●
	GAPS	6.1.6	**GAPS** (See Test A-C illustrations in **COMPLIANCE**):			
		6.1.6.1	**CAUSED** by **EXCESSIVE DEVIATIONS** (deviations in excess of 1/4" [6.4 mm] in 144" [3658 mm] of being plumb, level, flat, straight, square, or of the correct size) in the building's walls and ceilings, or 1/2" (12.7 mm) for floors, shall not be considered a defect or the responsibility of the installer.			
		6.1.6.2	Shall not exceed 30% of a joint's **LENGTH**, with:			
		6.1.6.2.1	**FILLER** or **CAULKING** allowed:	●		
		6.1.6.2.1.1	If color-compatible		●	●
		6.1.6.3	Of **WOOD** to **WOOD** shall not exceed:			
		6.1.6.3.1	At **FLAT** surfaces:			
		6.1.6.3.1.1	0.050" (1.3 mm) in width.	●		
		6.1.6.3.1.2	0.025" (0.65 mm) in width.		●	
		6.1.6.3.1.3	0.012" (0.3 mm) in width.			●

EXECUTION

						E	C	P
6.1	**GENERAL** (continued)							
	6.1.6	**GAPS** (continued)						
		6.1.6.3	Of **WOOD** to **WOOD** shall not exceed (continued)					
			6.1.6.3.2	At **SHAPED** surfaces:				
				6.1.6.3.2.1	0.075" (1.9 mm) in width.	●		
				6.1.6.3.2.2	0.050" (1.3 mm) in width.		●	
				6.1.6.3.2.3	0.025" (0.65 mm) in width.			●
		6.1.6.4	Of **WOOD** to **NON-WOOD** shall not exceed:					
			6.1.6.4.1	At **FLAT** and **SHAPED** surfaces:				
				6.1.6.4.1.1	0.100" (2.5 mm) in width.	●		
				6.1.6.4.1.2	0.075" (1.9 mm) in width.		●	
				6.1.6.4.1.3	0.050" (1.3 mm) in width.			●
		6.1.6.5	Of **NON-WOOD** to **NON-WOOD** and/or **ALL ELEMENTS** shall not exceed:					
			6.1.6.5.1	At **FLAT** surfaces:				
				6.1.6.5.1.1	0.100" (2.5 mm) in width.	●		
				6.1.6.5.1.2	0.075" (1.9 mm) in width.		●	
				6.1.6.5.1.3	0.050" (1.3 mm) in width.			●
			6.1.6.5.2	At **SHAPED** surfaces:				
				6.1.6.5.2.1	0.125" (3.2 mm) in width.	●		
				6.1.6.5.2.2	0.100" (2.5 mm) in width.		●	
				6.1.6.5.2.3	0.075" (1.9 mm) in width.			●
	6.1.7	**FLUSHNESS** of joinery (See Test D illustrations in **COMPLIANCE**):						
		6.1.7.1	Of **WOOD** to **WOOD** shall not exceed:					
			6.1.7.1.1	At **FLAT** surfaces:				
				6.1.7.1.1.1	0.050" (1.3 mm)	●		
				6.1.7.1.1.2	0.025" (0.65 mm)		●	
				6.1.7.1.1.3	0.012" (0.3 mm)			●
			6.1.7.1.2	At **SHAPED** surfaces:				
				6.1.7.1.2.1	0.075" (1.9 mm)	●		
				6.1.7.1.2.2	0.050" (1.3 mm)		●	
				6.1.7.1.2.3	0.025" (0.65 mm)			●
		6.1.7.2	Of **WOOD** to **NON-WOOD** shall not exceed:					
			6.1.7.2.1	At **FLAT** and **SHAPED** surfaces:				
				6.1.7.2.1.1	0.100" (2.5 mm)	●		
				6.1.7.2.1.2	0.075" (1.9 mm)		●	
				6.1.7.2.1.3	0.050" (1.3 mm)			●
		6.1.7.3	Of **NON-WOOD** to **NON-WOOD** and/or **ALL ELEMENTS** shall not exceed:					
			6.1.7.3.1	At **FLAT** surfaces:				
				6.1.7.3.1.1	0.100" (2.5 mm)	●		
				6.1.7.3.1.2	0.075" (1.9 mm)		●	
				6.1.7.3.1.3	0.050" (1.3 mm)			●

EXECUTION

					DESCRIPTION	E	C	P
⇑ 6.1	**GENERAL** (continued)							
	⇑ 6.1.7	**FLUSHNESS** of joinery (continued)						
		⇑ 6.1.7.3	Of **NON-WOOD** to **NON-WOOD** and/or **ALL ELEMENTS** shall not exceed (continued)					
			6.1.7.3.2	At **SHAPED** surfaces:				
				6.1.7.3.2.1	0.125" (3.2 mm)	●		
				6.1.7.3.2.2	0.100" (2.5 mm)		●	
				6.1.7.3.2.3	0.075" (1.9 mm)			●
	6.1.8	**FASTENING** shall:						
		6.1.8.1	Include the use of construction adhesive, finish nails, trim screws, and/or pins.					
			6.1.8.1.1	Staples where permitted shall run parallel to the grain.			●	●
	F A S T E N I N G	6.1.8.2	**NOT PERMIT** the use of drywall, bugle-head, or case-hardened screws.					
		6.1.8.3	Require exposed fasteners to be countersunk.					
		6.1.8.4	Require exposed fasteners to be set in quirks and reliefs where possible.				●	●
G E N E R A L		6.1.8.5	Require exposed fasteners to be inconspicuous, as defined in the Glossary.					●
		6.1.8.6	Allow use of construction adhesive for inconspicuous fastening.					
		6.1.8.7	Not permit exposed fastening through HPDL.					
		6.1.8.8	Require and/or permit fastener holes:					
			6.1.8.8.1	At prefinished materials to be filled by the installer with matching filler furnished by the manufacturer.				
			6.1.8.8.2	At unfinished materials to be filled by the paint contractor or others.				
	6.1.9	**EQUIPMENT CUTOUTS** shall be neatly cut out by installer, provided templates are furnished in a timely manner.					●	●
	6.1.10	**HARDWARE** shall be:						
		6.1.10.1	Installed neatly without tear-out of surrounding stock.					●
		6.1.10.2	Installed per manufacturer's instructions.					
		6.1.10.3	Installed using all furnished fasteners and fasteners' provisions.					
		6.1.10.4	Adjusted for smooth operation.					
	6.1.11	**AREAS** of installation shall be left broom clean.						
		6.1.11.1	Debris shall be removed and dumped in containers provided by the contractor.					
		6.1.11.2	Items installed shall be cleaned of pencil or ink marks.					
	6.1.12	Entire installation shall present **FIRST-CLASS WORKMANSHIP** in compliance with these standards.						

COMPLIANCE

7 **FABRICATED** and **INSTALLED** woodwork shall be tested for compliance to these standards as follows:

7.1 **SMOOTHNESS** of exposed surfaces

7.1.1 **KCPI** (Knife Cuts Per Inch) is determined by holding the surfaced board at an angle to a strong light source and counting the visible ridges per inch, usually perpendicular to the profile.

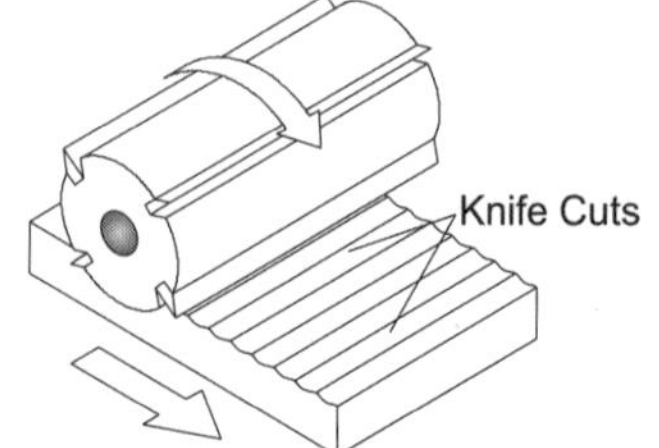

COMPLIANCE

7 FABRICATED and INSTALLED woodwork shall: (continued)

7.1 **SMOOTHNESS** of exposed surfaces (continued)

7.1.2 **SANDING** is checked for compliance by sanding a sample piece of the same species with the required grit of abrasive.

7.1.2.1 Observation with a hand lens of the prepared sample and the material in question will offer a comparison of the scratch marks of the abrasive grit.

7.1.2.2 Reasonable assessment of the performance of the finished product will be weighed against absolute compliance with the standard.

7.1.2.3 A product is sanded sufficiently smooth when knife cuts are removed and any remaining sanding marks are or will be concealed by applied finishing coats.

7.1.2.4 Handling marks and/or grain raising due to moisture or humidity in excess of the ranges set forth in this standard shall not be considered a defect.

7.2 **GAPS, FLUSHNESS, FLATNESS,** and **ALIGNMENT** of product and installation:

7.2.1 Maximum gaps between exposed components shall be tested with a feeler gauge at points designed to join where members contact or touch.

7.2.2 Joint length shall be measured with a ruler with minimum 1/16" (1 mm) divisions and calculations made accordingly.

7.2.3 Reasonable assessment of the performance of the finished product will be weighed against absolute compliance with the standards.

7.2.4 The following is intended to provide examples of how and where compliance testing is measured:

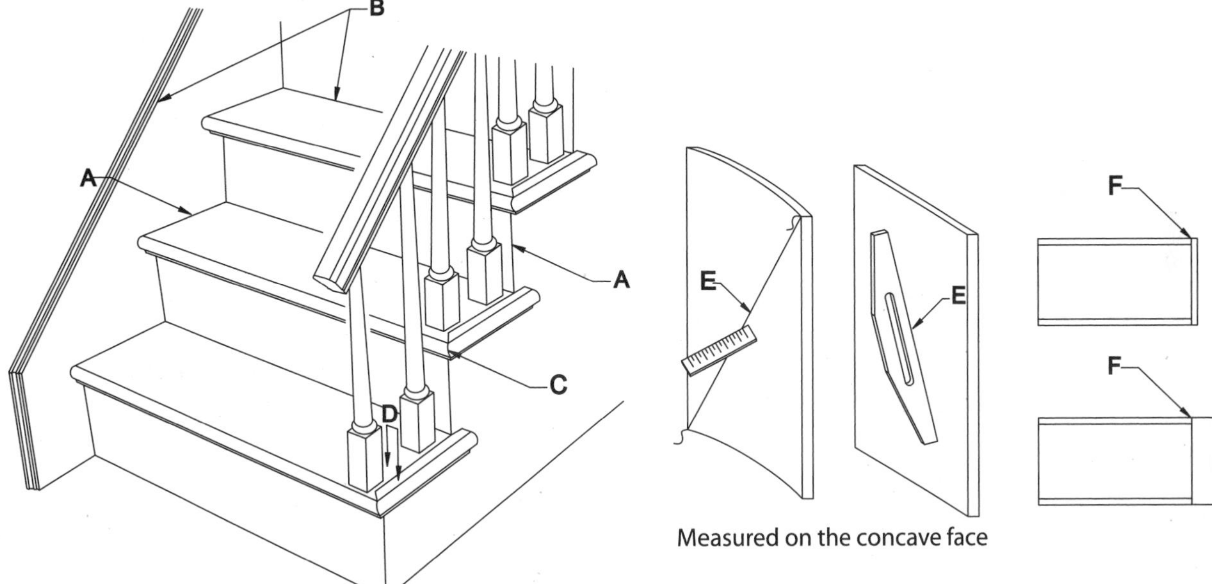

A - Gaps when surfaces are mitered or butted
B - Gaps when parallel pieces are joined
C - Gaps when edges are mitered or butted
D - Flushness between two surfaces
E - Flatness of panel product
F - Flushness of edgebanding

NOTES

Architectural Woodwork Standards

SECTION - 8

WALL SURFACING

SECTION 8 ✦ WALL SURFACING

(Including Wood Veneer, Stile and Rail Wood, Decorative Laminate, Solid Surface, and Solid Phenolic Products)

GENERAL

1 INFORMATION

1.1 GRADES

1.1.1 These standards are characterized in three Grades of quality that might be mixed within a single project. Limitless design possibilities and a wide variety of lumber and veneer species, along with overlays, high-pressure decorative laminates, factory finishes, and profiles are available in all three Grades.

1.1.2 **ECONOMY GRADE** defines the minimum quality requirements for a project's workmanship, materials, or installation and is typically reserved for woodwork that is not in public view, such as in mechanical rooms and utility areas.

1.1.3 **CUSTOM GRADE** is typically specified for and adequately covers most high-quality architectural woodwork, providing a well-defined degree of control over a project's quality of materials, workmanship, or installation.

1.1.4 **PREMIUM GRADE** is typically specified for use in those areas of a project where the highest level of quality, materials, workmanship, and installation is required.

1.1.5 **MODIFICATIONS** by the contract documents shall govern if in conflict with these standards.

1.2 BASIC CONSIDERATIONS

1.2.1 **ACCEPTABLE REQUIREMENTS** of lumber and/or sheet products used within this woodwork product section are established by Sections 3 and 4, unless otherwise modified herein.

1.2.2 **CONTRACT DRAWINGS** and/or **SPECIFICATIONS**, furnished by the design professional, shall clearly indicate or delineate all material, fabrication, installation, and applicable building code/regulation requirements.

1.2.3 **EXPOSED SURFACES**

1.2.3.1 All visible surfaces of architectural wall surfacing.

1.2.4 **SEMI-EXPOSED SURFACES** - N/A

1.2.5 **CONCEALED SURFACES**

1.2.5.1 All non-visible surfaces attached to and/or covered by another.

1.2.5.2 All non-visible blocking or spacers used for attachment.

1.2.6 **GRADE LIMITATIONS**

1.2.6.1 **SOLID-SURFACE** wall surfacing is offered only in **CUSTOM** and **PREMIUM GRADE**.

1.2.6.2 **SOLID-PHENOLIC CORE** wall surfacing are offered only in **PREMIUM GRADE**.

1.2.7 **FIRE-RATED OPTIONS** and **CONSIDERATIONS**

1.2.7.1 **INTUMESCENT COATINGS** for either opaque or transparent wood finishes are formulated to expand or foam when exposed to high heat, and create an insulating effect that reduces the speed of the spread of flame. Improvements are continually being made to these coatings.

1.2.7.1.1 Consequently, the specifier must ascertain whether they will be permitted under the code governing the project, the relative durability of the finish, and the effect of the coating on the desired color of the finished product.

1.2.7.2 **FIRE-RETARDANT TREATED LUMBER** might affect the finishes intended to be used on the wood, particularly if transparent finishes are planned.

1.2.7.2.1 The compatibility of any finish should be tested before it is applied.

GENERAL

1.2 **BASIC CONSIDERATIONS** (continued)

1.2.7 **FIRE-RATED OPTIONS** and **CONSIDERATIONS** (continued)

1.2.7.3 **BUILT-UP CONSTRUCTION**, using a veneer applied to a fire-retardant core in lieu of solid lumber, is often advisable where a fire rating is required.

1.2.7.3.1 The fire rating of the core material determines the rating of the assembled panel. Fire-retardant veneered panels must have a fire-retardant core. Particleboard and medium-density fiberboard (MDF) cores are typically available with a Class I (Class A) rating and can be used successfully with veneer or fire-rated high-pressure decorative laminate faces.

1.2.7.4 **CLASS I FIRE-RATED ARCHITECTURAL WALL SURFACE ASSEMBLIES** are available in veneered wood and HPDL; however, there are misconceptions as to what constitutes a Class I Fire-Rated assembly.

1.2.7.4.1 Wall surfacing certified as a fire-rated assembly (versus having simply been built with a fire-rated surface) shall be specified as a "Class I Fire-Rated Wall Surface Assembly."

1.2.7.4.2 The term "Class I Fire-Rated Wall Surface Assembly" shall mean that the entire wall panel assembly - including surface materials, backer, core, and adhesive - has been tested and is certified as a Class I Fire Rating by an authorized organization, such as Underwriters Laboratories, and must be manufactured by an approved company of the certifying agency.

1.2.7.4.3 Manufacturers of "Class I Fire-Rated Wall Surface Assemblies" require specific methods of installation and trimming in order to label and certify their product.

1.2.7.4.4 Architects/specifiers/design professionals desiring to use Class I Fire-Rated Wall Surface Assembly should coordinate such with an approved manufacturer during the design stage.

1.2.8 Some **HPDLs** utilize a **WHITE BACKGROUND** paper to achieve the high fidelity, contrast, and depth of color of their printed pattern, while leaving a white line at exposed edges, which is extremely noticeable with darker colors.

1.2.9 **WOOD SPECIES SELECTION**

1.2.9.1 The first step in selection starts by looking at "hand samples"; pieces of veneer or lumber representing a particular species, but not necessarily a particular tree or log. 8

1.2.9.1.1 Wood is a natural material (unlike a manufactured product), which varies from tree to tree in its color and texture.

1.2.9.1.1.1 Soil conditions, microclimates, adjacent vegetation and wildlife, genetic heredity, and forestry practice all affect each log.

1.2.9.2 Rather than simply choosing an appropriate wood for its color, one should also consider the size and availability of the species.

1.2.9.2.1 A species that grows in smaller diameter, with shorter logs, lends itself to furniture and smaller projects, whereas an abundant species that grows in large diameter lends itself more to larger public spaces.

1.2.9.2.1.1 Many projects have run into difficulties because the species availability was not compatible with the project's needs.

1.2.9.3 For **OPAQUE** finish, medium-density fiberboard (MDF) is suggested for cost savings and an optimum paintable surface.

1.2.9.3.1 Close-grain hardwood is allowed; however, extra preparation might be required by the finisher, as there might be grain show-through, split veneer joints, and other wood characteristics not present in MDF.

GENERAL

1.2 **BASIC CONSIDERATIONS** (continued)

1.2.10 **WOOD-VENEER WALL SURFACING**

1.2.10.1 Requires the **DESIGN PROFESSIONAL** to specify the desired:

1.2.10.1.1 **SPECIES** of veneer

1.2.10.1.2 Method of **SLICING** (plain, quarter, rotary, or rift)

1.2.10.1.3 **MATCHING OF VENEER LEAVES** (book, slip, or random)

1.2.10.1.4 **MATCHING OF VENEER LEAVES WITHIN A PANEL FACE** (running, balanced, or center-balanced)

1.2.10.1.5 **MATCHING BETWEEN PANELS** (non-sequenced, sequenced, or blueprint)

1.2.10.1.6 **END-MATCHING**

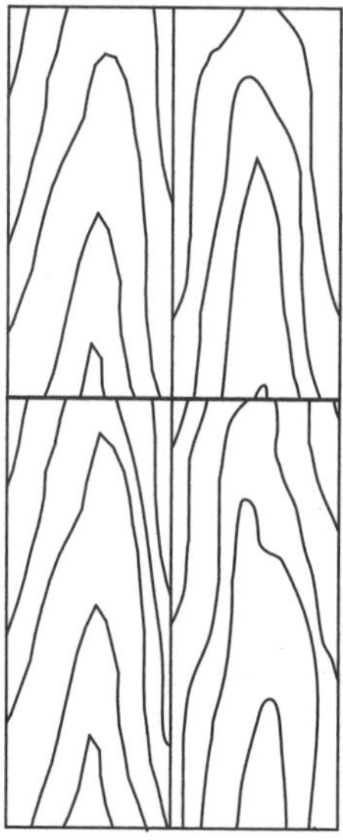

8

1.2.10.1.7 **GRAIN DIRECTION,** if other than vertical

1.2.10.1.8 **FIRE-RETARDANT** rating, if required

1.2.10.1.9 For **SELECTED FLITCHES**, the sources, gross footage of flitches, and cost per square foot

1.2.10.2 **FIGURE** is not a function of a species grade, and any special desires must be specified.

1.2.10.3 **VENEER SLICING** establishes the grain pattern appearance - see **SECTION 4.**

1.2.10.4 **VENEER FLITCH** establishes control of the specific characteristics of the wood veneer.

1.2.10.4.1 A flitch comes from one half of a log (usually 10" [254 mm] to 12" [305 mm] in diameter) sawn open through the center. This half log (cant) is then sliced into thin pieces of veneer (called leaves) and kept in order to form a flitch. When stacked back in order after slicing, the outline of the original log is clearly visible.

1.2.10.4.1.1 Each flitch will be different and will have a distinct identity number called a "flitch number".

1.2.10.4.2 In reviewing flitches, a veneer supplier will show you "live samples". These will be three leaves of veneer pulled from each flitch; one from near the top, one from the middle, and one from near the bottom. By reviewing these three full-length leaves of veneer, you will have a pretty good idea of the color, grain, and character that will appear in that flitch. The live samples will have the flitch number and the total square footage of that flitch written on them.

GENERAL

1.2 **BASIC CONSIDERATIONS** (continued)

1.2.10 **WOOD-VENEER WALL SURFACING** (continued)

1.2.10.4 **VENEER FLITCH** (continued)

1.2.10.4.2 In reviewing flitches (continued)

1.2.10.4.2.1 When a specific flitch is chosen for a project, its source, number, total square footage, and cost allowance need to be included within the project specifications.

1.2.10.4.3 The rule of thumb is that you need 3 sq ft (2787 sq cm) of raw veneer for each square foot of required finished panel. For example, if your project requires 10,000 sq ft (9290304 sq cm) of veneer paneling, you should specify 30,000 sq ft (27870912 sq cm) of raw veneer.

1.2.10.4.3.1 This means finding enough acceptable flitches that total 30,000 sq ft (27870912 sq cm) and incorporating those flitch numbers into the specifications.

1.2.10.4.4 The length of a flitch in relation to a project's requirements is important. The flitch needs to be at least 6" (152 mm) longer than the panel requirements.

1.2.10.4.4.1 On the other hand, choosing a 13' (3962 mm) flitch for a 7' (2134 mm) panel height requirement creates excessive waste and increased cost.

1.2.10.5 **MATCHING** of **WOOD VENEER LEAVES WITHIN A PANEL FACE**: Just as the different veneer-cutting methods can alter grain characteristics, matching can alter the appearance or match of a given panel or an entire installation. There is a wide choice in the types of matches available in hardwoods, and basically, the method of cutting has no bearing in matching. See Section 4 for further information.

1.2.10.6 **MATCHING** of **PANELS WITHIN A ROOM**

1.2.10.6.1 Most plywood distributors maintain an extensive inventory of Architectural Grade flitch stock in all the principal species.

1.2.10.6.1.1 Architectural plywood denotes the use of specially selected veneers and/or special preparation of the faces, normally at an increase in cost.

1.2.10.6.2 Panels shall be laid out and installed in a **RUNNING MATCH.**

1.2.10.6.2.1 If **BALANCED-MATCH** for the layout and installation is specified, all panels in an elevation shall be of the same width.

1.2.10.6.3 Panels might be of a different size in the same elevation.

1.2.10.6.4 The basic varieties of sequence-matched architectural panels and examples of their room layout are as follows (based on the following typical room key):

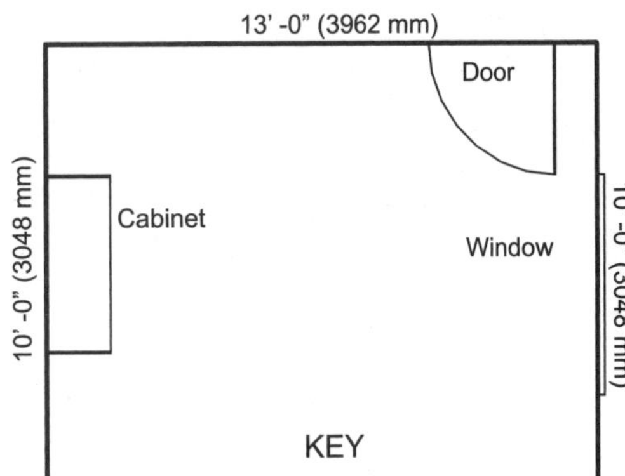

8

GENERAL

1.2 **BASIC CONSIDERATIONS** (continued)

1.2.10 **WOOD-VENEER WALL SURFACING** (continued)

1.2.10.6 **MATCHING of PANELS WITHIN A ROOM** (continued)

1.2.10.6.5 **PREMANUFACTURED PANEL SETS**, with full or selectively reduced width utilization, composed of a specific number of sequence-matched and numbered panels based on a per room basis for net footage selected from a manufacturer's available inventory. Paneling used from room to room may vary in color and grain characteristics.

1.2.10.6.5.1 Premanufactured sequence-matched panels are usually only available in 48" x 96" or 120" (1219 mm x 2438 mm or 3048 mm) sheets in sets varying from 6-12 panels. If more than one set is required, matching between sets cannot be expected. Similarly, doors or components often cannot be fabricated from the same set, resulting in possible mismatch.

1.2.10.6.5.2 **FULL WIDTH** panel utilization.

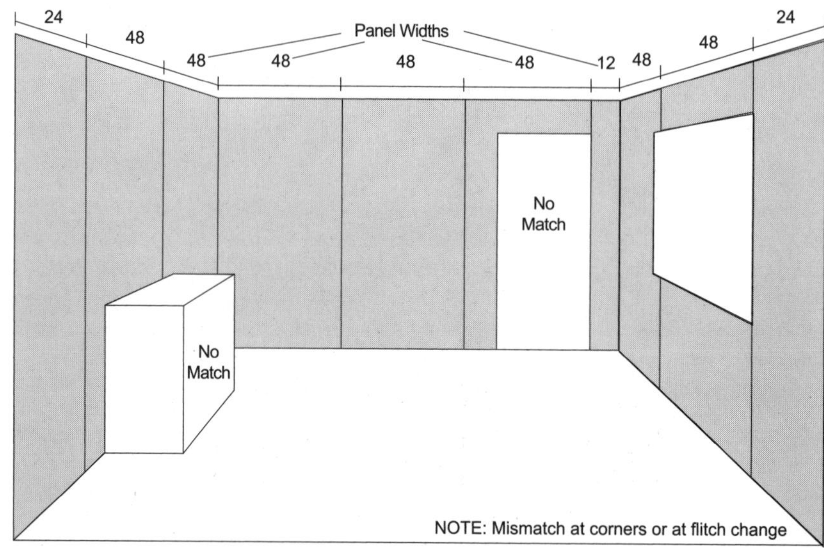

1.2.10.6.5.3 **SELECTIVELY REDUCED** panel utilization.

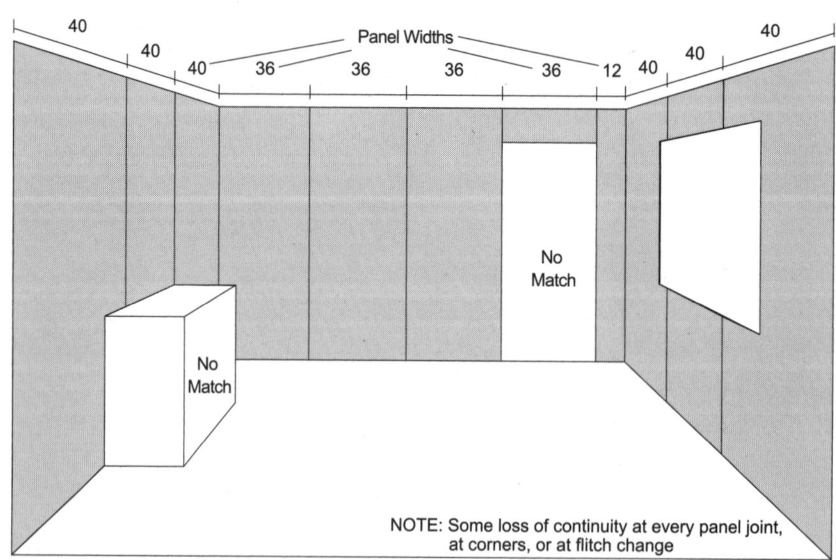

GENERAL

1.2 **BASIC CONSIDERATIONS** (continued)

1.2.10 **WOOD-VENEER WALL SURFACING** (continued)

1.2.10.6 **MATCHING** of **PANELS WITHIN A ROOM** (continued)

1.2.10.6.6 **MADE-TO-ORDER, SEQUENCE-MATCHED PANELS** are manufactured to exact sizes based on the project's net footage and height needs. The customer may request flitch samples from which to select the flitch to be employed, or the supplier may make the flitch selection if so requested; either way, the flitch shall be large enough to do the job.

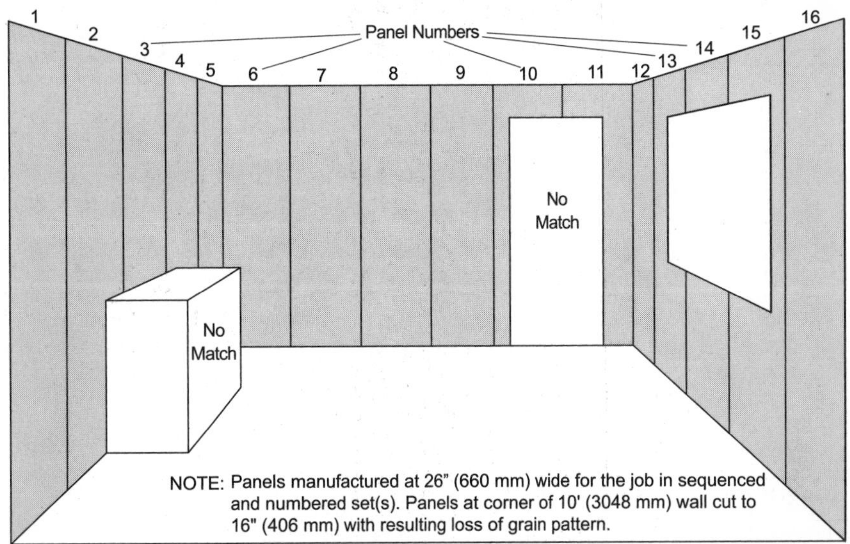

1.2.10.6.7 **MADE-TO-ORDER, BLUEPRINT-MATCHED PANELS** and **COMPONENTS** are manufactured to the exact sizes the manufacturer determines from the blueprints, clipping and matching each individual face to the project's specific needs. Each face will be matched in sequence with adjacent panels, doors, transoms, and cabinet faces as needed to provide for continuity. Again, unless specified otherwise, running match will be furnished.

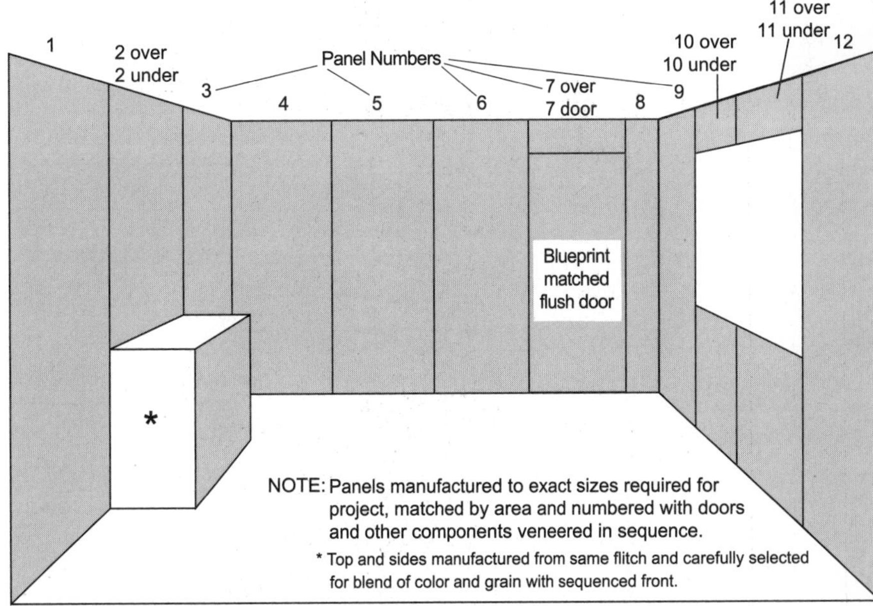

GENERAL

1.2 **BASIC CONSIDERATIONS** (continued)

1.2.10 **WOOD-VENEER WALL SURFACING** (continued)

1.2.10.6 **MATCHING of PANELS WITHIN A ROOM** (continued)

1.2.10.6.7 **MADE-TO-ORDER, BLUEPRINT-MATCHED PANELS** (continued)

1.2.10.6.7.1 Project specifications should require a single source supplier.

1.2.10.6.7.2 Components such as doors, windows, and cabinets plus overall room dimensions are the variables that determine panel width. Balanced-match panels (e.g., 3, 4, 5, 6, or 7 leaves per panel) should be specified rather than center-balanced-match panels (e.g., 4 or 6 leaves per panel) because the former will decrease the leaf-width variable from panel to panel. Therefore, grain continuity is maximized, which enhances the overall aesthetics.

1.2.10.7 **EDGEBANDING** options:

1.2.10.7.1 **VENEER** banded with wrap example:

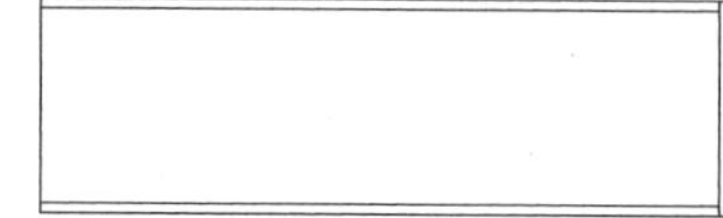

1.2.10.7.2 **INSET SOLID WOOD** banded:

1.2.10.7.3 **APPLIED SOLID WOOD** banded with corner joint options:

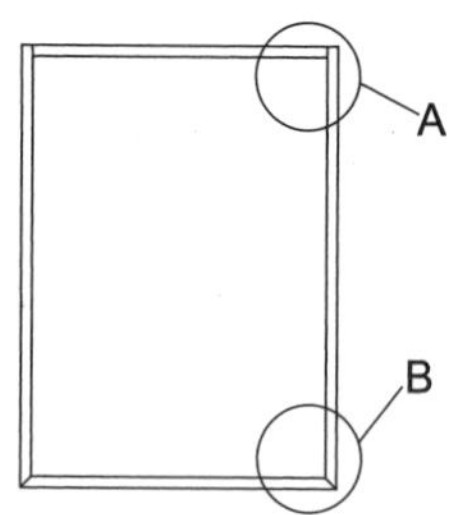

1.2.10.7.4 **APPLIED SOLID WOOD** banding joint options:

1.2.10.7.4.1 Unless specified otherwise, choice is the manufacturer's option.

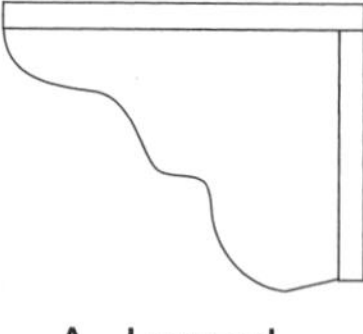

A - Lapped

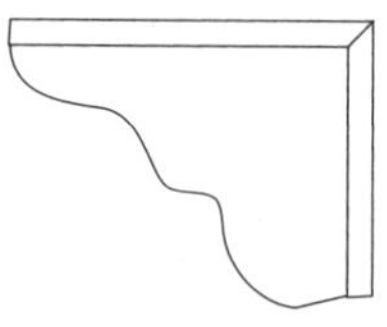

B - Mitered

1.2.10.7.5 **NOTE**: For durability, the bottom edge of veneered wall surfacing is edgebanded and finished.

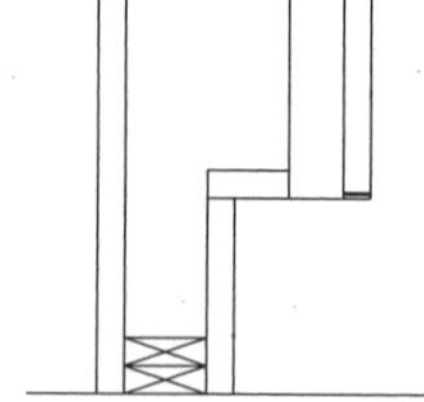

GENERAL

1.2 **BASIC CONSIDERATIONS** (continued)

1.2.10 **WOOD-VENEER WALL SURFACING** (continued)

1.2.10.7 **EDGEBANDING** options (continued)

1.2.10.7.6 **REVEALS** and **REVEAL JOINT** options:

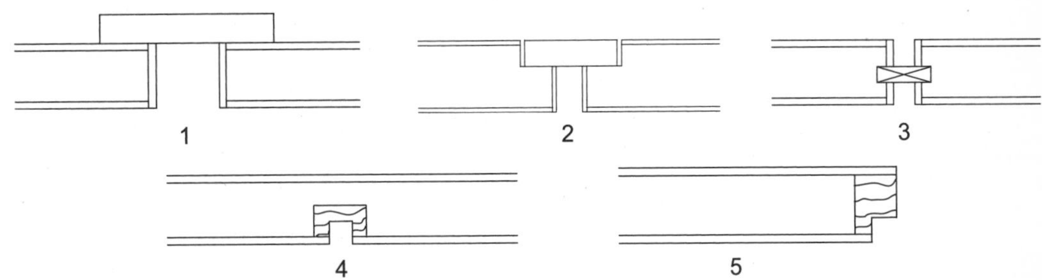

1.2.11 **STILE** and **RAIL WOOD WALL SURFACING**

1.2.11.1 Example of stile and rail wall surfacing:

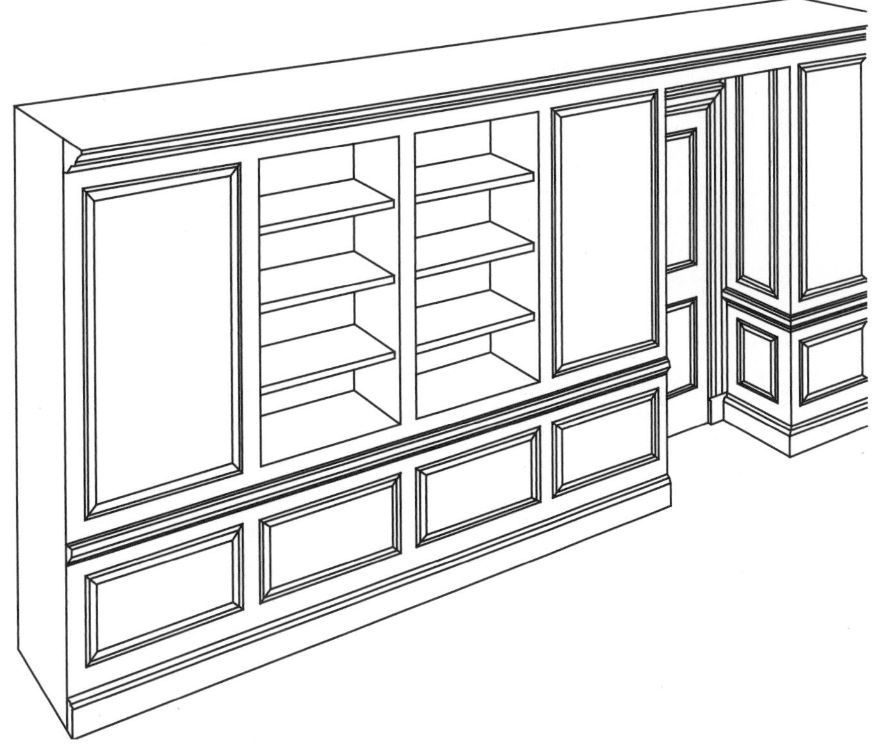

1.2.11.2 Examples of **JOINT** and **TRANSITION** options:

1.2.11.2.1 Loose **PLANT JOINTS** of built-up sections:

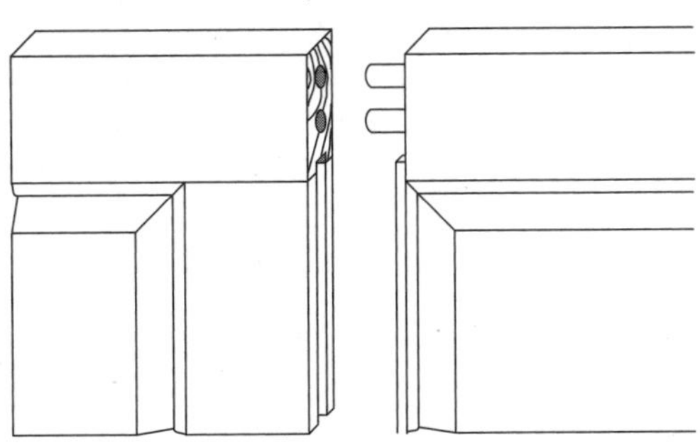

GENERAL

1.2 **BASIC CONSIDERATIONS** (continued)

1.2.11 **STILE** and **RAIL WOOD WALL SURFACING** (continued)

1.2.11.2 Examples of **JOINT** and **TRANSITION** (continued)

1.2.11.2.2 **SOLID WOOD REVEAL CORNERS**:

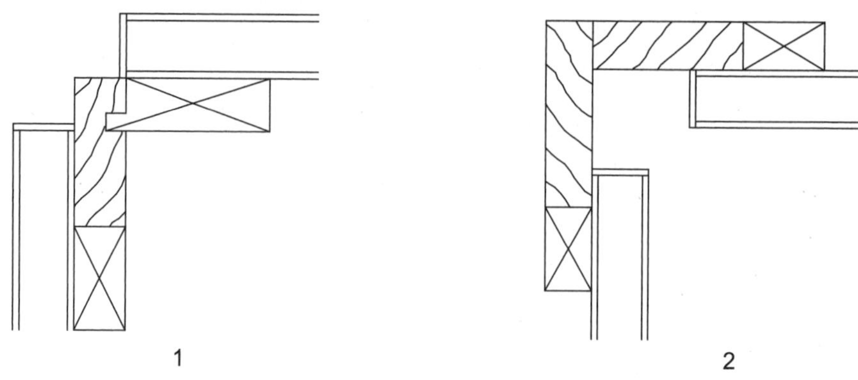

1.2.11.2.3 **SHOP-PREPARED OUTSIDE CORNERS**:

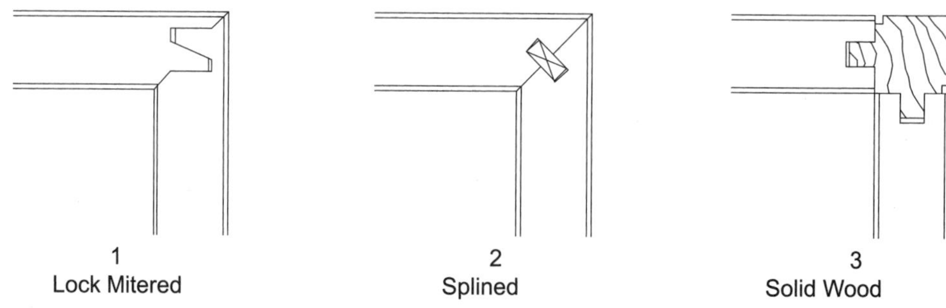

1 Lock Mitered | 2 Splined | 3 Solid Wood

1.2.11.2.4 **CUT TO FIT INSIDE CORNER**:

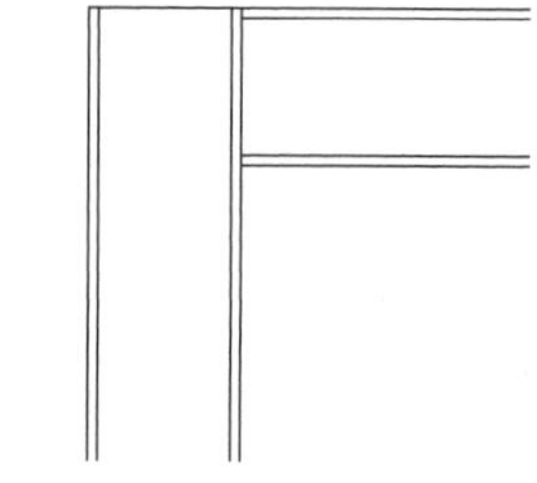

1.2.11.3 Examples of **STILE/RAIL** and **PANEL** buildups:

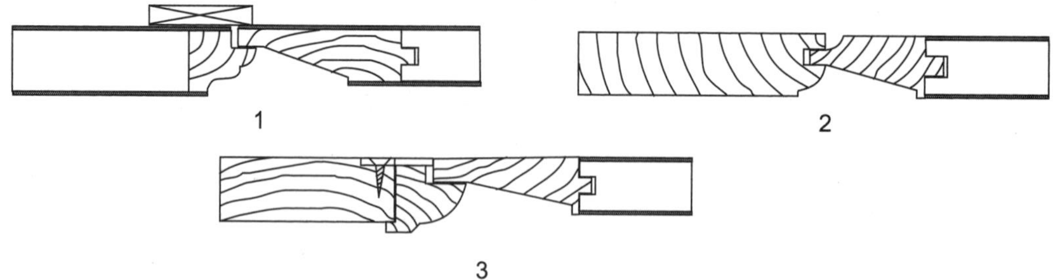

1.2.12 **DECORATIVE LAMINATE WALL SURFACING**

1.2.12.1 **HIGH-GLOSS HPDL** might telegraph minor core and surface imperfections.

1.2.12.2 **HPDL** panels and doors are not recommended for exterior use due to the potential differentials in humidity between the faces.

GENERAL

1.2 **BASIC CONSIDERATIONS** (continued)

1.2.12 **DECORATIVE LAMINATE WALL SURFACING** (continued)

1.2.12.3 Examples of **SHOP-PREPARED** joint and transition options:

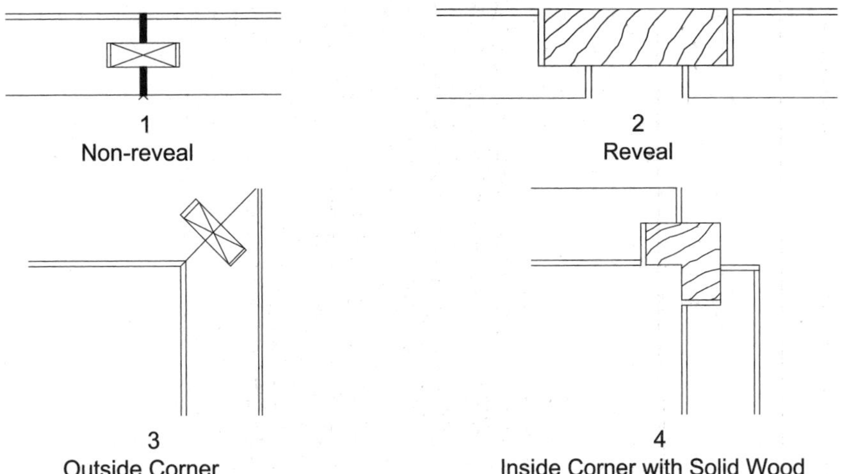

1 Non-reveal

2 Reveal

3 Outside Corner

4 Inside Corner with Solid Wood

1.2.12.4 Examples of **FIELD-PREPARED** joint and transition options:

1.2.12.4.1 **NON-REVEAL JOINTS**:

1.2.12.4.2 **CORNER JOINTS**:

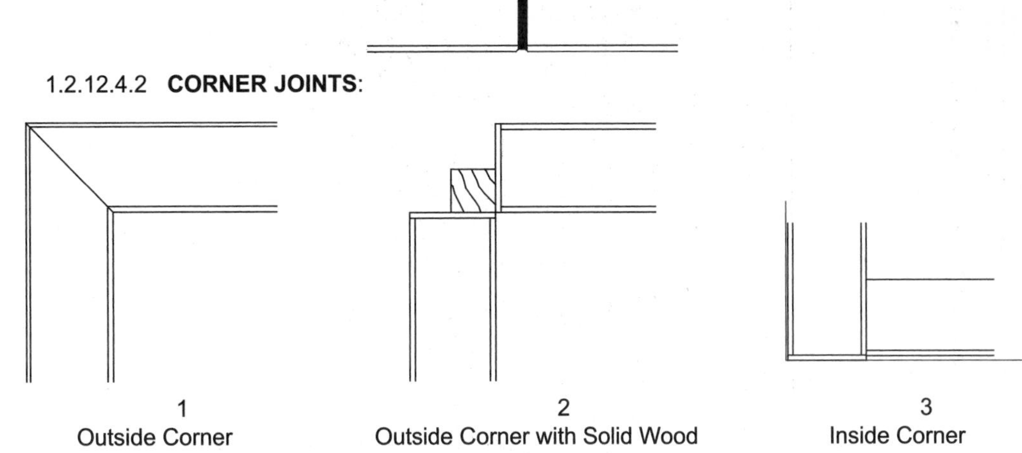

1 Outside Corner

2 Outside Corner with Solid Wood

3 Inside Corner

1.2.12.5 Requires the **DESIGN PROFESSIONAL** to specify the desired:

1.2.12.5.1 **LAMINATE**

1.2.12.5.1.1 Manufacturer

1.2.12.5.1.2 Pattern

1.2.12.5.1.3 Sheen

1.2.12.5.1.4 Pattern direction

1.2.12.5.1.4.1 With lack of specification, pattern direction will be vertical at panels and optional at joints.

1.2.13 **SOLID-SURFACE WALL SURFACING**

1.2.13.1 Is **NOT** recommended for **EXTERIOR USE** by some manufacturers. Design professionals should coordinate material applications within the manufacturer's guidelines.

GENERAL

1.2 **BASIC CONSIDERATIONS** (continued)

1.2.13 **SOLID-SURFACE WALL SURFACING** (continued)

1.2.13.2 Use of the same batch materials is important at adjacent sheets to lessen color variations.

1.2.13.3 Thicknesses are nominal and might be a fabrication concern where thickness is critical.

1.2.14 **SOLID-PHENOLIC WALL SURFACING**

1.2.14.1 Is recommended for **EXTERIOR APPLICATIONS.**

1.3 **RECOMMENDATIONS**

1.3.1 **INCLUDE IN DIVISION 09 OF THE SPECIFICATIONS:**

1.3.1.1 For **JOBSITE FINISHING** - BEFORE FINISHING, all exposed portions of woodwork shall have handling marks or effects of exposure to moisture, removed with a thorough, final sanding over all surfaces of the exposed portions using an appropriate grit sandpaper, and shall be cleaned before applying sealer or finish.

1.3.1.2 At **CONCEALED SURFACES** - Architectural woodwork that might be exposed to moisture, such as those adjacent to exterior concrete walls, shall be back-primed.

1.3.2 **THOROUGHLY REVIEW** Sections 3 and 4, especially Basic Considerations, Recommendations, Acknowledgements, and Industry Practices within Part 1 for an overview of the characteristics and minimum acceptable requirements of lumber and/or sheet products that might be used herein.

1.3.3 **CONTRACT DOCUMENTS** (plans and/or specifications) shall require that all structural members, grounds, blocking, backing, furring, brackets, or other anchorage which becomes an integral part of the building's walls, floors, or ceilings, required for the installation of architectural woodwork is not to be furnished or installed by the architectural woodwork manufacturer or installer.

1.3.4 **SPECIFY** requirements for:

1.3.4.1 Fire ratings

1.3.4.2 Special code compliance

1.3.4.3 Special molding profile

1.3.4.4 Special veneer figure or panel match

1.3.4.5 Special solid surface finish

1.3.5 **BLEACHED VENEERS** might cause finishing problems.

1.3.6 **COMPOSITE CORES** (e.g., particleboard, medium-density fiberboard, agrifiber, or combination core products) are recommended in lieu of veneer core, because these cores produce a smoother exposed face, vary less in thickness, and are less likely to warp.

1.3.7 **HIGH-GLOSS HPDL** might telegraph minor core and surface imperfections.

1.3.8 **HPDL** panels and doors are not recommended for exterior use due to the potential differentials in humidity between the faces.

1.4 **ACKNOWLEDGEMENTS**

1.4.1 Use of **HPDL-BACKED WOOD VENEERS** is permitted, if so specified or otherwise approved.

1.4.2 Use of **CONTINUOUS PRESSURE LAMINATES** (melamine and polyester-based) as an alternative to HPDL is permitted, provided they conform to the same physical properties and thickness as required for HPDL.

1.4.3 **FURRING**, when required, shall be in accordance with Title 8-803.1 of the Uniform Building Code (UBC), which currently requires furring be a maximum of 1-3/4" (44.5 mm) in thickness from the face of the wall to the back of the wall paneling. It also requires that there be fire-blocking at a maximum of 96" (2438 mm) on center or that the voids created by the furring be filled with inert material.

GENERAL

1.5 **INDUSTRY PRACTICES**

1.5.1 **STRUCTURAL MEMBERS**, grounds, blocking, backing, furring, brackets, or other anchorage that becomes an integral part of the building's walls, floors, or ceilings, that are required for the installation of architectural woodwork are not furnished or installed by the architectural woodwork manufacturer or installer.

1.5.2 **WALL, CEILING,** and/or opening variations in excess of 1/4" (6.4 mm) or **FLOORS** in excess of 1/2" (12.7 mm) in 144" (3658 mm) of being plumb, level, flat, straight, square, or of the correct size are not acceptable for the installation of architectural woodwork, nor is it the responsibility of the installer to scribe or fit to tolerances in excess of such.

1.5.3 **BACK-PRIMING** of architectural woodwork is not the responsibility of the manufacturer and/or installer, unless the material is being furnished prefinished.

1.5.4 **RADIUS MOLDINGS** are laminated and formed, preshaped, or machined to the radius and fabricated in the longest practical lengths to minimize field joints.

1.5.5 **WAINSCOT** is defined as being 48" (1219 mm) in height above the finished floor.

1.5.6 **WALL SURFACING** with a defined grain and/or pattern is installed vertically.

PRODUCT

2 SCOPE

2.1 All interior, decorative, solid or veneered wood, laminated plastic, solid-phenolic composite, and solid-surface architectural wall surfacing or coverings.

2.2 **TYPICAL INCLUSIONS**

2.2.1 All exposed decorative solid or veneered wood paneling
2.2.2 All exposed decorative laminated plastic wall covering
2.2.3 All exposed decorative solid-surface wall covering
2.2.4 All wood doors required to be blueprint-matched to wood paneling, not specified otherwise
2.2.4.1 If doors are specified to be furnished by others, the paneling supplier shall control matching
2.2.5 If installed, all furring, blocking, shims, and methods of attachment from the face of the wall out
2.2.6 All exposed decorative solid-phenolic composite wall surface
2.2.7 Class I Fire-Rated HPDL Wall Surfacing Assembly
2.2.8 Class I Fire-Rated Veneered-Wood Wall Surfacing Assembly

2.3 **TYPICAL EXCLUSIONS**

2.3.1 Casework soffits or filler panels
2.3.2 Room, closet, or access doors, unless sequence- and blueprint-matched with paneling
2.3.3 Any bucks or grounds
2.3.4 Composition or plaster wallboards or coverings
2.3.5 Any structural wood framing or plywood
2.3.6 Exposed base other than wood, HPDL, or solid surface

3 DEFAULT STIPULATIONS

3.1 **SOLID-WOOD WALL SURFACING** - unless otherwise specified or detailed, all work shall be **CUSTOM GRADE** of paint-grade hardwood for opaque finish.

3.2 **VENEERED-WOOD WALL SURFACING** - unless otherwise specified or detailed, all work shall be **CUSTOM GRADE** of paint-grade hardwood for opaque finish.

3.3 **DECORATIVE LAMINATE SURFACING** - unless otherwise specified or detailed, all work shall be **CUSTOM GRADE** with retention moldings at all field joints. Colors to be selected from non-premium-priced standard patterns and texture.

PRODUCT

MATERIAL, MACHINING, AND ASSEMBLY RULES (continued)

3 DEFAULT STIPULATIONS (continued)

3.4 **SOLID-SURFACE WALL SURFACING** - unless otherwise specified or detailed, all work shall be **CUSTOM GRADE**, 1/4" (6.4 mm) minimum thickness, directly applied, with 1/4" x 1" (6.4 mm x 25.4 mm) trim bats at vertical butt joints on continuous horizontal runs. Colors to be selected from non-premium-priced standard patterns.

3.5 **SOLID-PHENOLIC WALL SURFACING** - unless otherwise specified or detailed, all work shall be **CUSTOM GRADE**, 1/8" (3 mm) minimum thickness with 1/8" x 1" (3 mm x 25 mm) battens at vertical joints on continuous horizontal runs. Colors to be selected from the manufacturer's standard patterns and colors.

4 RULES - The following RULES shall govern unless a project's contract documents require otherwise.

These rules are intended to provide a well-defined degree of control over a project's quality of materials and workmanship.

Where E, C, or P is not indicated, the rule applies to all Grades equally.

ERRATA, published on the Associations' websites at www.awinet.org, www.awmac.com, or www.woodworkinstitute.com, shall TAKE PRECEDENCE OVER THESE RULES, subject to their date of posting and a project's bid date.

ARROWS INDICATE TOPIC IS CARRIED FROM ⇑ OR ONTO ⇓ ANOTHER PAGE.

			DESCRIPTION	E	C	P
4.1	**GENERAL**					
G E N E R A L	4.1.1		Aesthetic **GRADE RULES** apply only to the faces visible after installation.			
	4.1.2		**LUMBER** shall conform to the requirements established in Section 3.			
	4.1.3		**SHEET PRODUCTS** shall conform to the requirements established in Section 4.			
	4.1.4		**BACKING SHEET** shall conform to the requirements established in Section 4.			
	4.1.5		**EXPOSED, SEMI-EXPOSED**, and **CONCEALED** surfaces shall be as listed under **1.2 BASIC CONSIDERATIONS** of this section.			
	4.1.6		For the purpose of this standard, a **BALANCED PANEL** is one that is free from warp that affects serviceability for its intended purpose.			
	4.1.7		**FURRING** shall be used as required, and:			
		4.1.7.1	It shall be in accordance with applicable codes and regulations for maximum thickness, fire blocking, and void fills.			
	4.1.8		**SURFACING** with a defined grain and/or pattern shall be installed with the grain or pattern direction running vertically.			
	4.1.9		**WAINSCOT** shall be 48" (1219 mm) in height above the finished floor.			
	4.1.10		Where **MULTIPLE OPTIONS** are permitted, it shall be the manufacturer's choice.			
	4.1.11		**FIRE-RETARDANT** requirements shall be specified.			
	4.1.12		**SPECIFIC PROFILE**, if required, shall be specified or drawn.			
	4.1.13		For **TRANSPARENT FINISHED WOOD**, if the species is not specified, use of hardwood or softwood (panel product or solid stock) of **ONE SPECIES FOR THE ENTIRE PROJECT** is permitted.			
	4.1.14		**HOT-MELT-APPLIED** HPDL edgebanding shall be primed before application for proper adhesion, unless:			
		4.1.14.1	Hot-melt adhesive has been especially formulated for the primerless application of HPDL.			
	4.1.15		Where **GLUING** or **LAMINATION** occurs:			
		4.1.15.1	**DELAMINATION** or **SEPARATION** shall not occur beyond that which is allowed in Sections 3 & 4.			
		4.1.15.2	Use of **CONTACT ADHESIVE** is not permitted.			
	4.1.16		**FIRST-CLASS WORKMANSHIP** is required in compliance with these standards.			

8

PRODUCT

MATERIAL, MACHINING, AND ASSEMBLY RULES (continued)

Group	No.	DESCRIPTION	E	C	P
	4.2	**MATERIAL**			
MATERIAL	4.2.1	Shall be lumber or sheet products of the species and Grade specified.			
	4.2.2	Shall conform in finish width, thickness, and length of lumber to Section 3.			
	4.2.3	Shall not have defects, either natural or manufactured, that exceed those permitted.			
	4.2.4	Requires plain-sawn lumber.			
	4.2.5	Permits defects, both natural and manufactured, if covered by adjoining members or otherwise concealed when installed.			
	4.2.6	States figure is not a function of a species grade and must be specified in the contract document.			
	4.2.7	Permits warp that can be held flat and straight with normal attachment.			
	4.2.8	At **EXPOSED SURFACES**:			
EXPOSED	4.2.8.1	Requires end grain to be kept to a minimum.	●	●	
	4.2.8.2	Requires ends to be self-returned with no end grain showing.			●
	4.2.8.3	Permits medium-density fiberboard (MDF) for opaque finish.			
	4.2.8.4	For **TRANSPARENT FINISH**			
	4.2.8.4.1	Permits hardwood or softwood.			
	4.2.8.4.2	Permits only one species for the entire project.		●	●
	4.2.8.4.3	Adjacent veneer and lumber shall be:			
	4.2.8.4.3.1	Mill-option species.	●		
	4.2.8.4.3.2	Compatible for color and grain.		●	
	4.2.8.4.3.3	Well-matched for color and grain.			●
	4.2.9	At **SEMI-EXPOSED SURFACES:**			
	4.2.9.1	For **OPAQUE** finish, permits natural and manufacturing defects, provided the surface is filled solid.			
	4.2.10	At **CONCEALED SURFACES** permits defects, such as voids, wane, or unfilled knots.			
	4.2.11	At **WOOD-VENEER** wall surfacing requires:			
WOOD VENEER	**4.2.11.1**	**CORES** of particleboard or medium-density fiberboard (MDF) shall be:			
CORES	4.2.11.1.1	A minimum of 1/4" (6.4 mm) in thickness.	●		
	4.2.11.1.2	A minimum of 7/16" (11.1 mm) in thickness.		●	
	4.2.11.1.3	A minimum of 11/16" (17.5 mm) in thickness.			●
	4.2.11.1.4	**FIRE-RATED**, when specified, a minimum of 3/8" (9.5 mm) in thickness with a Class I Rating.			
	4.2.11.2	**MATCHING,** such as book-match-and-end match, slip-match-and-end-match, or special sketch faces, to be so specified and detailed.			
	4.2.11.3	For **OPAQUE** finish, face shall:			
OPAQUE	4.2.11.3.1	**NOT** require the selection of color and/or grain.			
	4.2.11.3.2	**PERMIT** the use of paint-grade hardwood, medium-density fiberboard (MDF), or medium-density overlay (MDO).			
	4.2.11.3.2.1	If MDF is used, edgebanding is not required.			
	4.2.11.3.3	Permit mill option of veneer slicing.			
	4.2.11.3.4	**NOT** require matching of veneer leaves.			
⇓	4.2.11.3.5	**NOT** require matching of adjacent panels.			

PRODUCT

MATERIAL, MACHINING, AND ASSEMBLY RULES (continued)

Number	DESCRIPTION	E	C	P
4.2	**MATERIAL** (continued)			
4.2.11	At **WOOD VENEER** (continued)			
4.2.11.3	For **OPAQUE** finish, face shall (continued)			
4.2.11.3.6	Have visible **REVEALS** and **SPLINES** that are:			
4.2.11.3.6.1	Full length.			
4.2.11.3.6.2	Of mill-option species.			
4.2.11.3.7	Have **EDGES**:			
4.2.11.3.7.1	Filled and sanded.	●		
4.2.11.3.7.2	Banded with close-grain material, with:		●	●
4.2.11.3.7.2.1	**FINGER JOINTS** permitted.	●	●	
4.2.11.4	For **TRANSPARENT** finish, shall:			
4.2.11.4.1	Have **FACES** that are:			
4.2.11.4.1.1	**ROTARY**-sliced.	●		
4.2.11.4.1.2	**PLAIN**-sliced.		●	●
4.2.11.4.1.3	Between **ADJACENT LEAVES**:			
4.2.11.4.1.3.1	**MILL-OPTION MATCH**	●		
4.2.11.4.1.3.2	**BOOK-MATCHED**		●	●
4.2.11.4.1.4	Within each **PANEL FACE:**			
4.2.11.4.1.4.1	**MILL-OPTION MATCH**	●		
4.2.11.4.1.4.2	**RUNNING MATCH**		●	
4.2.11.4.1.4.3	**BALANCED-MATCH**			●
4.2.11.4.1.5	Between **ADJACENT PANELS**:			
4.2.11.4.1.5.1	**MILL-OPTION SEQUENCE**	●		
4.2.11.4.1.5.2	**SEQUENCED, NUMBERED, PREMANUFACTURED SET(S)**		●	
4.2.11.4.1.5.3	Custom made to order **SEQUENCED AND NUMBERED SET(S)**			●
4.2.11.4.1.6	Within a **PROJECT AREA**:			
4.2.11.4.1.6.1	**MILL-OPTION SEQUENCE**.	●		
4.2.11.4.1.6.2	**SEQUENCED, NUMBERED, PREMANUFACTURED SET(S)**		●	
4.2.11.4.1.6.3	Custom made to order **SEQUENCED** and **NUMBERED SET(S)**			●
4.2.11.4.2	Have visible **EDGES**, **REVEALS,** and/or **SPLINES,** when appropriate, that are:			
4.2.11.4.2.1	Full length.			
4.2.11.4.2.2	**MILL-OPTION.**	●		
4.2.11.4.2.3	**MATCH** species of panel face.		●	●
4.2.11.4.2.4	**COMPATIBLE** for color and grain.		●	
4.2.11.4.2.5	**WELL-MATCHED** for color and grain.			●
4.2.11.4.2.6	A minimum of 0.020" (0.5 mm) nominal **THICKNESS** that precludes show-through of core.		●	●
4.2.11.4.2.7	**WITHIN A PANEL**, solid wood shall be let into the core before the veneer is applied with the reveal routed through the veneer into the solid wood.		●	●

PRODUCT

MATERIAL, MACHINING, AND ASSEMBLY RULES (continued)

	DESCRIPTION	E	C	P
4.2	**MATERIAL** (continued)			
4.2.12	At **WOOD VENEER** (continued)			
4.2.12.4	For **TRANSPARENT** (continued)			
4.2.12.4.3	Allow **FINGER JOINTS**:			
4.2.12.4.3.1	**MILL OPTION**	●		
4.2.12.4.3.2	One per 96" (2440 mm) of length		●	●
4.2.12.5	Not permit **BLEED-THROUGH** of adhesive at veneer joints that visually affects an applied finish.			
4.2.12.6	At **FIRE-RATED** paneling, require:			
4.2.12.6.1	Class I fire-rated phenolic **BACKING SHEET**, a minimum of .028" (0.7 mm).			
4.2.12.6.2	Class I fire-rated, rigid-set **ADHESIVE**.			
4.2.12	At **SOLID STILE** and **RAIL WOOD** wall surfacing:			
4.2.12.1	**ADHESIVE** bleed-through at joints is not permitted.			
4.2.12.2	**LUMBER** shall be plain-sawn.			
4.2.12.3	**VENEERED** sheet products shall also comply with those requirements spelled out for Veneered Wall Surfacing within this section.			
4.2.12.4	For **OPAQUE** finish:			
4.2.12.4.1	Shall be paint-grade hardwood or softwood at manufacturer's option.	●		
4.2.12.4.2	Shall be paint-grade hardwood.		●	●
4.2.12.4.3	Finger joints are permitted.	●		
4.2.12.4.4	Medium-density fiberboard is permitted.			
4.2.12.5	For **TRANSPARENT** finish, finger joints are permitted.	●		
4.2.12.6	**PANELS**:			
4.2.12.6.1	Shall be solid-stock or veneered construction, at the manufacturer's option.			
4.2.12.6.2	If **FLAT** shall be:			
4.2.12.6.2.1	**SOLID WOOD**:			
4.2.12.6.2.1.1	Minimum 1/2" (12.7 mm) in thickness and maximum 23-3/4" (603 mm) across the grain in width.	●		
4.2.12.6.2.1.2	Minimum 3/4" (19 mm) in thickness and maximum 13-3/4" (350 mm) across the grain in width.		●	
4.2.12.6.2.1.3	Not permitted.			●
4.2.12.6.2.2	**SHEET PRODUCT**:			
4.2.12.6.2.2.1	Minimum 1/4" (6.4 mm) in thickness.	●		
4.2.12.6.2.2.2	Minimum 1/2" (12.7 mm) in thickness.		●	●
4.2.12.6.3	If **RAISED** shall be:			
4.2.12.6.3.1	**SOLID WOOD**:			
4.2.12.6.3.1.1	Permitted in any dimension.	●		
4.2.12.6.3.1.2	Minimum 3/4" (19 mm) in thickness and maximum 13-3/4" (350 mm) across the grain in width.		●	●
4.2.12.6.3.2	**VENEERED STILES** and **RAILS** or **SHEET PRODUCT**:			
4.2.12.6.3.2.1	Minimum 1/2" (12.7 mm) in thickness	●		
4.2.12.6.3.2.2	Minimum 11/16" (17.5 mm) in thickness		●	●

8

PRODUCT

MATERIAL, MACHINING, AND ASSEMBLY RULES (continued)

	DESCRIPTION	E	C	P
4.2	**MATERIAL** (continued)			
4.2.12	At **SOLID STILE** and **RAIL WOOD** (continued)			
4.2.12.6	**PANELS** (continued)			
4.2.12.6.4	**EDGES** of veneered constructed components shall be:			
4.2.12.6.4.1	Veneer-banded with compatible species.	●		
4.2.12.6.4.2	Veneer-banded with same species as face.		●	●
4.2.13	At **DECORATIVE LAMINATE** wall surfacing requires:			
4.2.13.1	**LAMINATE** shall:			
4.2.13.1.1	**CONFORM** to NEMA LD -3 (latest edition).			
4.2.13.1.2	Be of **colors** selected from non-premium-priced standard patterns and texture.			
4.2.13.1.2.1	No minimum thickness	●		
4.2.13.1.2.2	Minimum 0.028" (0.7 mm) in thickness		●	
4.2.13.1.2.3	Minimum 0.048" (1.2 mm) in thickness			●
4.2.13.1.3	When **REQUIRING MORE THAN ONE ADJACENT SHEET**, they shall be prematched by the manufacturer and/or installer to minimize color variation within the scope of the manufacturer's guarantee, and:			
4.2.13.1.3.1	Be fabricated from the longest sheet lengths available.			
4.2.13.1.4	If required to be **FIRE-RATED**, it shall be Class I and:			
4.2.13.1.4.1	Be applied with a rigid-set, Class I fire-rated adhesive.			
4.2.13.1.5	**PATTERNED** or **WOOD GRAIN**:			
4.2.13.1.5.1	Shall **MATCH VERTICALLY**, provided the total height does not exceed the maximum length of the available sheet.			
4.2.13.1.5.2	Is not required to **MATCH HORIZONTALLY.**			
4.2.13.2	**CORE**, when:			
4.2.13.2.1	**APPLIED** to **FURRING STRIPS**, a maximum of 16" (406 mm) on center, shall be hardboard or fine-grained hardwood plywood (a minimum of 1/4" [6.4 mm]) in thickness); or particleboard or medium-density fiberboard (a minimum of 3/8" [9.5 mm] in thickness).			
4.2.13.2.2	**APPLIED** to **FURRING STRIPS**, a maximum of 24" (610 mm) on center shall be particleboard, medium-density fiberboard, or fine-grained hardwood plywood a minimum of 11/16" (17.5 mm) on thickness.			
4.2.13.2.3	**DIRECTLY APPLIED** with retention moldings to sheetrock walls, shall be 3/8" (9.5 mm) thick particleboard, medium-density fiberboard, or fine-grained hardwood plywood.			
4.2.13.2.4	**DIRECTLY APPLIED** with spline or biscuit joints to sheetrock walls, shall be 11/16" (17.5 mm) thick particleboard, medium-density fiberboard, or fine-grained hardwood plywood.			
4.2.13.2.5	**FIRE-RATED,** shall be a minimum of 3/8" (9.5 mm) in thickness and Class I Fire-Rated.			
4.2.13.3	**BACKING SHEET** shall be:			
4.2.13.3.1	A minimum of .020" (0.5 mm) thickness conforming to NEMA LD-3 (latest edition) and:			
4.2.13.3.1.1	Applied to the backside of the core using the same adhesive as the face lamination.			
4.2.13.3.2	When **FIRE-RATED**, a minimum of .028" (0.7 mm) HPDL, Class I Fire-Rated and:			
4.2.13.3.2.1	Applied with a rigid-set, Class I Fire-Rated adhesive.			
4.2.13.3.3	Shall be applied in the same machine or grain direction as the face laminate.			

PRODUCT

MATERIAL, MACHINING, AND ASSEMBLY RULES (continued)

No.	DESCRIPTION	E	C	P
4.2	**MATERIAL** (continued)			
4.2.13 (DECORATIVE LAMINATE)	At **DECORATIVE LAMINATE** (continued)			
4.2.13.4 (REVEALS)	**VISIBLE SPLINES** and **REVEALS** that are:			
4.2.13.4.1	Of 5/64" (2 mm) or less in face dimension by any depth with:			
4.2.13.4.1.1	No treatment of sides or bottom.	●		
4.2.13.4.1.2	Edges and bottom painted to match and preclude show-through of core.		●	●
4.2.13.4.2	Of 5/64" (2 mm) or more in face dimension by any depth with:			
4.2.13.4.2.1	Mill-option banding or painting of edges and bottom to preclude show-through of core.	●	●	
4.2.13.4.2.2	Mill-option banding or painting of bottom to preclude show-through of core.			●
4.2.13.4.2.3	Matching band of partial edges.			●
4.2.13.5 (BANDING)	**EDGEBANDING** of square-edged panel parts:			
4.2.13.5.1	Is required at all exposed vertical and horizontal edges.			
4.2.13.5.2	Shall be color-matched to the exposed face.			
4.2.13.5.3	Shall be HPDL or PVC, a minimum of 0.020" (0.5 mm) in thickness.			
4.2.13.5.4	Shall be applied before or after the face laminate.			
4.2.13.5.5	Does **NOT** require mitering of corners.			
4.2.13.5.5.1	If **MITER-FOLDED**, they shall be machined with the core.			
4.2.14 (SOLID SURFACE)	At **SOLID-SURFACE** wall surfacing:			
4.2.14.1	**DIRECTLY** applied to vertical surfaces shall be a minimum of:			
4.2.14.1.1	1/4" (6.4 mm) in thickness.		●	
4.2.14.1.2	1/2" (12.7 mm) in thickness.			●
4.2.14.2	**INSTALLED ABOVE** the chair-rail height or full-height panels require mechanical fasteners (French cleat, Z-clip, or similar).			
4.2.14.3	**JOINERY** at horizontal shall be:			
4.2.14.3.1	**BUTT-JOINTED** and caulked or covered with a vertical trim batten.		●	
4.2.14.3.2	**HARD-SEAMED,** except:			●
4.2.15.3.2.1	At building expansion joints.			●
4.2.14.4	**COLOR** selection shall be from the manufacturer's:			
4.2.14.4.1	1/4" (6.4 mm) color offering only.		●	
4.2.14.4.2	Full range of color offerings.			●
4.2.14.5	**FINISH** to be manufacturer's standard matt finish unless otherwise specified.			
4.2.14.6	**SEALANTS** and **ADHESIVES** shall comply with each manufacturer's specially developed or recommended products to achieve the proper performance and color match.			
4.2.15	At **SOLID-PHENOLIC** wall surfacing requires:			
4.2.15.1	No **BACKING** or **CORE MATERIAL**.			
4.2.15.2	**THICKNESS** to be a minimum of 1/8" (3.2 mm).			
4.2.15.3	**COLOR** to be selected from the manufacturer's standard product line.			
4.2.15.4	**FINISH** to be selected from the manufacturer's standard product line.			

8

PRODUCT

MATERIAL, MACHINING, AND ASSEMBLY RULES (continued)

No.	DESCRIPTION	E	C	P
4.2	**MATERIAL** (continued)			
4.2.16	At **BACKPRIMING:**			
4.2.16.1	When **FACTORY FINISHING** is specified, concealed surfaces shall be factory-sealed with two coats at 2 mil dry.		●	●
4.2.16.2	When **SITE-APPLIED DECORATIVE LAMINATE** is specified for the face of panels, concealed surfaces shall be factory-sealed with one coat at 1 mil dry.		●	●
4.3	**MACHINING**			
4.3.1	Of **EXPOSED SURFACES** shall comply with:			
4.3.1.1	**SMOOTHNESS REQUIREMENTS** (see Item 7.1 in **COMPLIANCE**):			
4.3.1.1.1	**SHARP EDGES** to be eased with a fine abrasive.		●	●
4.3.1.1.2	**TOP FLAT WOOD** surfaces; those that can be sanded with a drum or wide belt sander:			
4.3.1.1.2.1	Minimum 15 KCPI or 100-grit sanding	●		
4.3.1.1.2.2	120-grit sanding		●	
4.3.1.1.2.3	150-grit sanding			●
4.3.1.1.3	**PROFILED** and **SHAPED WOOD** surfaces:			
4.3.1.1.3.1	Minimum 15 KCPI or 100-grit sanding	●		
4.3.1.1.3.2	Minimum 20 KCPI or 120-grit sanding		●	
4.3.1.1.3.3	120-grit sanding			●
4.3.1.1.4	**TURNED WOOD** surfaces:			
4.3.1.1.4.1	Minimum 15 KCPI or 100-grit sanding	●		
4.3.1.1.4.2	120-grit sanding		●	
4.3.1.1.4.3	180-grit sanding			●
4.3.1.1.5	**CROSS-SANDING**, excluding turned surfaces:			
4.3.1.1.5.1	Is not a defect.	●		
4.3.1.1.5.2	Is not allowed.		●	●
4.3.1.1.6	**TEAR-OUTS**, **KNIFE NICKS**, or **HIT-OR-MISS** machining is not permitted.			
4.3.1.1.7	**KNIFE MARKS** not to be permitted where sanding is required.			
4.3.1.1.8	**GLUE** or **FILLER**, if used, to be inconspicuous and match the adjacent surface for smoothness.			
4.3.1.1.9	At **SOLID SURFACE, SOLID PHENOLIC, EPOXY RESIN,** and **NATURAL STONE** shall be per the manufacturer's recommendations.			
4.4	**ASSEMBLY**			
4.4.1	Of **JOINTS** at **ASSEMBLED WOODWORK** shall:			
4.4.1.1	Be neatly and accurately made.			
4.4.1.2	Be **SECURELY GLUED**, with:			
4.4.1.2.1	**ADHESIVE** residue removed from all exposed and semi-exposed surfaces.			
4.4.1.3	Be **REINFORCED** with glue blocks where essential.			
4.4.1.4	Utilize clamp nail, biscuit spline, butterfly, scarf, or dowel joinery.		●	
4.4.1.5	Utilize biscuit spline, butterfly, scarf, or dowel joinery.			●
4.4.1.6	Shall be **MECHANICALLY FASTENED** with nails or screws, where practical, or with fasteners in solid wood:			
4.4.1.6.1	Countersunk.			
4.4.1.6.2	Located in molding quirks or reliefs where possible.		●	●

PRODUCT

MATERIAL, MACHINING, AND ASSEMBLY RULES (continued)

	DESCRIPTION	E	C	P
4.4	**ASSEMBLY**			
4.4.1	Of **JOINTS** at **ASSEMBLED WOODWORK** shall (continued)			
4.4.1.7	**NOT PERMIT** fasteners at exposed surfaces of **HPDL** or overlay sheet products.			
4.4.1.8	Requires **FLUSHNESS VARIATIONS** at exposed surfaces when mitered or butted (see Test D illustrations in **COMPLIANCE**) not to exceed:			
4.4.1.8.1	**INTERIOR**			
4.4.1.8.1.1	0.025" (0.6 mm)	●		
4.4.1.8.1.2	0.005" (0.1 mm)		●	
4.4.1.8.1.3	0.001" (0.03 mm)			●
4.4.1.8.2	**EXTERIOR**			
4.4.1.8.2.1	0.05" (1.3 mm)	●		
4.4.1.8.2.2	0.025" (0.6 mm)		●	
4.4.1.8.2.3	0.015" (0.4 mm)			●
4.4.1.9	Requires **GAPS** at exposed surfaces when mitered or butted (see Test A illustrations in **COMPLIANCE**) not to exceed:			
4.4.1.9.1	**INTERIOR**			
4.4.1.9.1.1	0.05" (1.3 mm) wide by 20% of the joint length	●		
4.4.1.9.1.2	0.025" (0.6 mm) wide by 20% of the joint length		●	
4.4.1.9.1.3	0.15" (0.4 mm) wide by 20% of the joint length			●
4.4.1.9.2	**EXTERIOR**			
4.4.1.9.2.1	0.075" (1.9 mm) wide by 30% of the joint length	●		
4.4.1.9.2.2	0.05" (1.3 mm) wide by 30% of the joint length		●	
4.4.1.9.2.3	0.025" (0.6 mm) wide by 30% of the joint length			●
4.4.1.10	Requires **GAPS** at exposed surfaces at parallel members (see Test B illustrations in **COMPLIANCE**) not to exceed:			
4.4.1.10.1	**INTERIOR**			
4.4.1.10.1.1	0.05" x 8" (1.3 mm x 203 mm) and shall not occur within 48" (1219 mm) of a similar gap.	●		
4.4.1.10.1.2	0.025" x 6" (0.6 mm x 152 mm) and shall not occur within 60" (1524 mm) of a similar gap.		●	
4.4.1.10.1.3	0.015" (0.4 mm x 76 mm) and shall not occur within 72" (1829 mm) of a similar gap.			●
4.4.1.10.2	**EXTERIOR**			
4.4.1.10.2.1	0.075" x 10" (1.9 mm x 254 mm) and shall not occur within 24" (610 mm) of a similar gap.	●		
4.4.1.10.2.2	0.05" x 8" (1.3 mm x 203 mm) and shall not occur within 26" (660 mm) of a similar gap.		●	
4.4.1.10.2.3	0.025" x 6" (0.6 mm x 152 mm) and shall not occur within 30" (762 mm) of a similar gap.			●
4.4.1.11	Requires **GAPS** at exposed surfaces when mitered or butted (see Test C illustrations in **COMPLIANCE**) not to exceed:			
4.4.1.11.1	**INTERIOR**			
4.4.1.11.1.1	0.05" (1.3 mm)	●		
4.4.1.11.1.2	0.025" (0.6 mm)		●	
4.4.1.11.1.3	0.015" (0.4 mm)			●

PRODUCT

MATERIAL, MACHINING, AND ASSEMBLY RULES (continued)

DESCRIPTION		E	C	P
4.4	**ASSEMBLY** (continued)			
4.4.1	Of **JOINTS** (continued)			
4.4.1.11	Requires **GAPS** at exposed surfaces when mitered or butted (continued)			
4.4.1.11.2	**EXTERIOR**			
4.4.1.11.2.1	0.075" (1.9 mm)	●		
4.4.1.11.2.2	0.05" (1.3 mm)		●	
4.4.1.11.2.3	0.025" (0.6 mm)			●
4.4.1.12	Requires **FLATNESS** of installed and removable sheet products (see Test E illustrations in **COMPLIANCE**) not to exceed:			
4.4.1.12.1	0.050" (1.3 mm) per 12" (305 mm) or portion thereof	●		
4.4.1.12.2	0.036" (0.9 mm) per 12" (305 mm) or portion thereof		●	
4.4.1.12.3	0.027" (0.7 mm) per 12" (305 mm) or portion thereof			●
4.4.1.13	Requires **EDGEBANDING** to be flush with adjacent surfaces (see Test F illustrations in **COMPLIANCE**) not to exceed:			
4.4.1.13.1	0.010" (0.25 mm)	●		
4.4.1.13.2	0.005" (0.13 mm)		●	
4.4.1.13.3	0.003" (0.03 mm)			●
4.4.1.14	Allows **FILLER**:			
4.4.1.14.1	If inconspicuous when viewed at 36" (914 mm).	●		
4.4.1.14.2	If inconspicuous when viewed at 24" (610 mm).		●	
4.4.1.14.3	**NOT ALLOWED.**			●
4.4.1.15	Shall be mitered.			
4.4.1.16	Shall be spot-glued and mechanically fastened:		●	●
4.4.1.16.1	Only to non-panel surfaces; panel is required to float.			
4.4.1.16.2	With a maximum of two positioning nails per 12" (300 mm) of length before a joint.		●	●
4.4.1.16.3	With nails set, filled, and sanded.			●
4.4.2	Of **MITER JOINTS** shall be well-fitted and cleaned.			
4.4.3	Of **BUILT-UP ITEMS** shall be soundly fabricated with half-lapped, mitered, shoulder-mitered, tonged, or equivalent construction.			
4.4.4	At **WOOD-VENEER** wall surfacing:			
4.4.4.1	**PANELS** are to be cut to size by the:			
4.4.4.1.1	Installer.	●		
4.4.4.1.2	Manufacturer and scribed to fit by installer.		●	●
4.4.4.2	**VENEER MATCH** at:			
4.4.4.2.1	Premanufactured **BALANCED-MATCH** panels requires the width of outer leaves after trimming at the edges not to exceed:			
4.4.4.2.1.1	Unlimited.	●		
4.4.4.2.1.2	1-1/2" (38.1 mm) less than the adjoining leaf.		●	
4.4.4.2.1.3	3/4" (19 mm) less than the adjoining leaf.			●
4.4.4.2.2	Custom made-to-order **SEQUENCE BALANCED-MATCH** panels requires the width of outer leaves after trimming at edges not to exceed:			
4.4.4.2.2.1	Unlimited.	●		
4.4.4.2.2.2	1" (25.4 mm) less than the adjoining leaf.		●	

PRODUCT

MATERIAL, MACHINING, AND ASSEMBLY RULES (continued)

No.	DESCRIPTION	E	C	P
4.4	**ASSEMBLY** (continued)			
4.4.4	At **WOOD-VENEER** wall surfacing (continued)			
4.4.4.2	**VENEER MATCH** at (continued)			
4.4.4.2.2	Custom made-to-order **SEQUENCE BALANCED-MATCH** panels (continued)			
4.4.4.2.2.3	1/2" (12.7 mm) less than the adjoining leaf.			●
4.4.4.2.3	Panel to adjoining panel requires **VENEER GRAIN** to align vertically and/or horizontally within a maximum of:			
4.4.4.2.3.1	Unlimited.	●		
4.4.4.2.3.2	1/4" (6.4 mm) variance.		●	
4.4.4.2.3.3	1/8" (3.2 mm) variance.			●
4.4.4.2.4	Panels **WITHIN A ROOM** utilizing:			
4.4.4.2.4.1	The **FULL WIDTH** of **PREMANUFACTURED SETS** are required to be balance-matched with veneer alignment; however:		●	●
4.4.4.2.4.1.1	This requirement does not apply to the trimmed side of a make-up panel.			
4.4.4.2.4.2	**SELECTIVELY REDUCED WIDTH** of **PREMANUFACTURED SETS**, are **NOT** required to be balance-matched or have veneer alignment.			
4.4.4.2.4.3	**CUSTOM-SEQUENCED MATCH** are required to be balance-matched with veneer alignment, including make-up panels.		●	●
4.4.4.2.4.4	**BLUEPRINT MATCH** are required to be balance-matched with veneer alignment at common size panels, make-up panels, and components.		●	●
4.4.4.3	**BUTT JOINTS** shall:			
4.4.4.3.1	**NOT** be shop-prepared.	●		
4.4.4.3.2	Be plant-prepared with edges eased.		●	
4.4.4.3.3	Be plant-prepared and grooved with splines furnished and edges eased.			●
4.4.4.4	**REVEAL JOINTS** and **CORNERS** shall:			
4.4.4.4.1	**NOT** be shop-prepared.	●		
4.4.4.4.2	Be plant-prepared with edges eased and articulation strip(s) furnished.		●	
4.4.4.4.3	Be plant-prepared and machined for furnished articulation strip(s) with edges eased.			●
4.4.4.5	**INSIDE CORNERS** to be shipped oversize for field fitting.			
4.4.4.6	**MITERED** outside corners shall:			
4.4.4.3.6.1	**NOT** be shop-prepared.	●		
4.4.4.3.6.2	Be plant-prepared and shipped loose.		●	
4.4.4.3.6.3	Be plant-prepared, and if site conditions permit, glued and braced prior to shipping.			●
4.4.4.7	**FIELD JOINERY** shall be factory-prepared to the greatest extent possible with feature strips and joint trim furnished oversize, where possible, to allow for jobsite fitting.		●	●
4.4.4.8	**EXPOSED CORNERS** shall be shoulder-mitered, lock-mitered, spline-mitered, or mitered with a biscuit joint, unless specified and/or detailed otherwise.			
4.4.4.9	**MOLDINGS** within an individual panel face shall be:			
4.4.4.9.1	Shipped loose.	●		
4.4.4.9.2	Factory-applied.		●	●

PRODUCT

MATERIAL, MACHINING, AND ASSEMBLY RULES (continued)

					DESCRIPTION	E	C	P
4.4 ASSEMBLY	**ASSEMBLY** (continued)							
	4.4.5	At **SOLID STILE** and **RAIL WOOD** wall surfacing requires:						
		4.4.5.1	**PANELING** shall be factory-assembled in sections as large as practical for field installation.				•	•
		4.4.5.2	At **FIELD JOINTS:**					
			4.4.5.2.1	No factory preparation.		•		
			4.4.5.2.2	Factory preparation to the greatest extent possible with feature strips and joint trim furnished oversize, where possible, to allow for jobsite fitting.			•	•
	4.4.6 DECORATIVE LAMINATE	At **DECORATIVE LAMINATE** wall surfacing:						
		4.4.6.1	The maximum **GAP** at butted edges glued to the same piece of substrate shall not exceed:					
			4.4.6.1.1	3 occurrences of 0.030" x 5" (0.76 mm x 127 mm) in any 65 sq/ft (6 sq/m)		•		
			4.4.6.1.2	2 occurrences of 0.015" x 5" (0.38 mm x 127 mm) in any 65 sq/ft (6 sq/m)			•	
			4.4.6.1.3	1 occurrence of 0.007" x 3" (0.18 mm x 76 mm) in any 65 sq/ft (6 sq/m)				•
		4.4.6.2	The maximum **FLUSHNESS VARIATION** at butted edges shall not exceed:					
			4.4.6.2.1	0.009" (0.23 mm)		•		
			4.4.6.2.2	0.006" (0.15 mm)			•	
			4.4.6.2.3	0.003" (0.08 mm)				•
		4.4.6.3	The maximum **PLUMBNESS VARIANCE** of special patterns shall not exceed:					
			4.4.6.3.1	3/8" (9 mm) in 96" (2440 mm)		•		
			4.4.6.3.2	1/4" (6 mm) in 96" (2440 mm)			•	
			4.4.6.3.3	1/8" (3 mm) in 96" (2440 mm)				•
		4.4.6.4	The maximum **ALIGNMENT VARIATION** of special patterns shall not exceed:					
			4.4.6.4.1	1/4" (6 mm)		•		
			4.4.6.4.2	1/8" (3 mm)			•	
			4.4.6.4.3	1/16" (1.5 mm)				•
		4.4.6.5 EDGES	**EDGES** shall be flush and filed, sanded, or buffed to remove machine marks and sharp edges, and:					
			4.4.6.5.1	**OVERLAP** (over-filing) shall not:				
				4.4.6.5.1.1	Exceed 0.005" (0.13 mm) for a maximum length of 2" (50.8 mm) in any 48" (1220 mm) run.	•		
				4.4.6.5.1.2	Exceed 0.005" (0.13 mm) for a maximum length of 1" (25.4 mm) in any 24" (610 mm) run.		•	
				4.4.6.5.1.3	**BE VISIBLE.**			•
			4.4.6.5.2	**CHIP-OUT** shall be inconspicuous when viewed at:				
				4.4.6.5.2.1	72" (1829 mm)	•		
				4.4.6.5.2.2	48" (1220 mm)		•	
				4.4.6.5.2.3	24" (610 mm)			•
			4.4.6.5.3	**REMOVAL** of color or pattern of face material due to over-machining limited to:				
				4.4.6.5.3.1	3/32" x4" (2.4 mm x 102 mm) and shall not occur within 48" (1220 mm) of a similar occurrence.	•		
				4.4.6.5.3.2	1/16" x 1-1/2" (1.6 mm x 38.1 mm) and shall not occur within 60" (1524 mm) of a similar occurrence.		•	
				4.4.6.5.3.3	1/16" x 4" (1.6 mm x 102 mm) and shall not occur within 72" (1829 mm) of a similar occurrence.			•

PRODUCT

MATERIAL, MACHINING, AND ASSEMBLY RULES (continued)

Section	Item	Sub-item	DESCRIPTION	E	C	P
4.4 ASSEMBLY			**ASSEMBLY** (continued)			
4.4.6 DECORATIVE LAMINATE			At **DECORATIVE LAMINATE** (continued)			
	4.4.6.6		**RETENTION MOLDINGS** are permitted at field joints, and:			
		4.4.6.6.1	Shall be secured to wall studs or blocking.			
	4.4.6.7		**VERTICAL** or **HORIZONTAL JOINTS** shall have a slight "V" and:			
		4.4.6.7.1	Be splined full-length or have biscuit splines at a minimum of 12" (305 mm) on center.			
	4.4.6.8		**PANELS** shall:			
		4.4.6.8.1	**NOT** be shop-prepared; panels are to be shipped as full-size panels for cutting and fitting in the field.	●		
		4.4.6.8.2	Be plant-sized, except where field adjustment is required.		●	●
	4.4.6.9		**BUTT JOINTS** shall:			
		4.4.6.9.1	**NOT** be shop-prepared.	●		
		4.4.6.9.2	Be plant-prepared with edges eased.		●	
		4.4.6.9.3	Be plant-prepared and grooved with splines furnished and edges eased.			●
	4.4.6.10		**REVEAL JOINTS** and **CORNERS** shall:			
		4.4.6.10.1	**NOT** be shop-prepared.	●		
		4.4.6.10.2	Be plant-prepared with edges eased and articulation strip(s) furnished.		●	
		4.4.6.10.3	Be plant-prepared and machined for furnished articulation strip(s) with edges eased.			●
	4.4.6.11		**INSIDE CORNERS** to be shipped oversize for field fitting.			
	4.4.6.12		**MITERED OUTSIDE CORNERS** shall:			
		4.4.6.12.1	**NOT** be shop-prepared.	●		
		4.4.6.12.2	Be plant-prepared and shipped loose.		●	
		4.4.6.12.3	Be plant-prepared, and if site conditions permit, glued and braced prior to shipping.			●
4.4.7			At **SOLID-SURFACE** wall surfacing requires:			
	4.4.7.1		**FABRICATION** to be performed by personnel properly trained to work with specified materials.			
	4.4.7.2		**BUTT JOINT** components to be spaced approximately 1/8 " (3.2 mm) apart to allow satisfactory caulking or seaming:			
		4.4.7.2.1	Shall be **CAULKED** with compatible color-matched sealant.		●	
		4.4.7.2.2	Shall be **SEAMED** with compatible hard-seam adhesive.			●
	4.4.7.3		**VERTICAL JOINTS** in horizontal panel runs to be:			
		4.4.7.3.1	**CAULKED** or trimmed with an **APPLIED** 1/4" x 1" (6.4 mm x 25.4 mm) **BATTEN** using silicone or other manufacturer-approved adhesive.		●	
		4.4.7.3.2	**HARD-SEAMED** with manufacturer-approved hard-seam adhesive.			●
	4.4.7.4		**EXPANSION** joints where required by building design or manufacturer recommendation.			
4.4.8			At **SOLID-PHENOLIC** wall surfacing:			
	4.4.8.1		**FABRICATION** to be performed by personnel properly trained and approved by the applicable solid-phenolic manufacturer.			
	4.4.8.2		**JOINT WIDTH** shall be at least 1/8 " (3.2 mm) to allow satisfactory caulking penetration.			
	4.4.8.3		**VERTICAL JOINTS** shall provide for panel movement in both horizontal and vertical directions, such as by use of:			
		4.4.8.3.1	**TRIMS** or **GASKETS** made of aluminium, PVC, and neoprene.			
	4.4.8.4		At rebated or tongue-and-groove joints, panel thickness shall be a minimum of 3/8" (9.5 mm).			

EXECUTION

INSTALLATION RULES (continued)

5 PREPARATION & QUALIFICATION REQUIREMENTS (unless otherwise specified)

5.1 **CARE, STORAGE, and BUILDING CONDITIONS** shall be in compliance with the requirements set forth in Section 2 of these standards.

5.1.1 Severe damage to the woodwork can result from noncompliance. **THE MANUFACTURER AND/OR INSTALLER OF THE WOODWORK SHALL NOT BE HELD RESPONSIBLE FOR ANY DAMAGE THAT MIGHT DEVELOP BY NOT ADHERING TO THE REQUIREMENTS.**

5.2 **CONTRACTOR IS RESPONSIBLE FOR:**

5.2.1 Furnishing and installing structural members, grounds, blocking, backing, furring, brackets, or other anchorage required for architectural woodwork installation that becomes an integral part of walls, floors, or ceilings to which architectural woodwork shall be installed.

5.2.1.1 In the absence of contract documents calling for the contractor to supply the necessary blocking/backing in the wall or ceilings, either through inadvertence or otherwise, the architectural woodwork installer shall not proceed with the installation until such time as the blocking/backing is installed by others.

5.2.1.2 Preparatory work done by others shall be subject to inspection by the architectural woodwork installer and shall be accepted or rejected for cause prior to installation.

5.2.1.2.1 **WALL, CEILING,** and/or opening variations in excess of 1/4" (6.4 mm) or **FLOORS** in excess of 1/2" (12.7 mm) in 144" (3658 mm) of being plumb, level, flat, straight, square, or of the correct size are not acceptable for the installation of architectural woodwork, nor is it the responsibility of the installer to scribe or fit to tolerances in excess of such.

5.2.2 Priming and back-priming the architectural woodwork in accordance with the contract documents prior to its installation.

5.2.2.1 If the architectural woodwork is factory-finished, back-priming by the factory finisher is required.

5.3 **INSTALLER IS RESPONSIBLE FOR:**

5.3.1 Having adequate equipment and experienced craftsmen to complete the installation in a first-class manner.

5.3.2 Checking all architectural woodwork specified and studying the appropriate portions of the contract documents, including these standards and the reviewed shop drawings to familiarize themselves with the requirements of the Grade specified, understanding that:

5.3.2.1 Appearance requirements of Grades apply only to surfaces visible after installation.

5.3.2.2 For transparent finish, special attention needs to be given to the color and the grain of the various woodwork pieces to ensure they are installed in compliance with the Grade specified.

5.3.2.3 Installation site is properly ventilated, protected from direct sunlight, excessive heat and/or moisture, and that the HVAC system is functioning and maintaining the appropriate relative humidity and temperature.

5.3.2.4 Required priming or back priming of woodwork has been completed before its install.

5.3.2.5 Woodwork has been acclimated to the field conditions for a minimum of 72 hours before installation is commenced.

5.3.2.6 Woodwork specifically built or assembled in sequence for match of color and grain is installed to maintain that same sequence.

6 RULES - The following RULES shall govern unless a project's contract documents require otherwise.

These rules are intended to provide a well-defined degree of control over a project's quality of installation.

Where E, C, or P is not indicated, the rule applies to all Grades equally.

EXECUTION

INSTALLATION RULES (continued)

ERRATA, published on the Associations' websites at www.awinet.org, www.awmac.com, or www.woodworkinstitute.com, shall TAKE PRECEDENCE OVER THESE RULES, subject to their date of posting and a project's bid date.

ARROWS INDICATE TOPIC IS CARRIED FROM ⇑ OR ONTO ⇓ ANOTHER PAGE.

	DESCRIPTION	E	C	P
6.1	**GENERAL**			
6.1.1	Aesthetic **GRADE RULES** apply only to exposed and semi-exposed surfaces visible after installation.			
6.1.2	**TRANSPARENT FINISHED** woodwork shall be installed:			
6.1.2.1	With **CONSIDERATION** of color and grain.	●		
6.1.2.2	**COMPATIBLE** in color and grain.		●	
6.1.2.3	**WELL-MATCHED** for color and grain.			●
6.1.2.3.1	**SHEET PRODUCTS** shall be compatible in color with solid stock.			●
6.1.2.3.2	**ADJACENT SHEET PRODUCTS** shall be well-matched for color and grain.			●
6.1.3	**REPAIRS** are allowed, provided they are neatly made and inconspicuous when viewed at:			
6.1.3.1	72" (1830 mm)	●		
6.1.3.2	48" (1219 mm)		●	
6.1.3.3	24" (610 mm)			●
6.1.4	**INSTALLER MODIFICATIONS** shall comply to the material, machining, and assembly rules within the **PRODUCT** portion of this section and the applicable finishing rules in Section 5.			
6.1.5	**WOODWORK** shall be:			
6.1.5.1	**SECURELY** fastened and tightly fitted with flush joints.			
6.1.5.1.1	Joinery shall be **CONSISTENT** throughout the project.			
6.1.5.2	Of **MAXIMUM** available and/or practical lengths.		●	●
6.1.5.3	**TRIMMED EQUALLY** from both sides when fitted for width.		●	●
6.1.5.4	**SPLINED** or **DOWELED** when miters are over 4" (100 mm) long.			●
6.1.5.5	**PROFILED** or **SELF-MITERED** when trim ends are exposed.		●	
6.1.5.6	**SELF-MITERED** when trim ends are exposed.			●
6.1.5.7	**MITERED** at outside corners.			
6.1.5.8	**MITERED** at inside corners.	●	●	
6.1.5.9	**COPED** at inside corners.		●	●
6.1.5.10	**INSTALLED** plumb, level, square, and flat within 1/8" (3.2 mm) in 96" (2438 mm), and when required:			
6.1.5.10.1	**GROUNDS** and **HANGING SYSTEMS** set plumb and true.		●	●
6.1.5.11	Installed **FREE OF**:			
6.1.5.11.1	Warp, twisting, cupping, and/or bowing that cannot be held true.			
6.1.5.11.2	Open joints, visible machine marks, cross-sanding, tear-outs, nicks, chips, and/or scratches.			
6.1.5.11.3	Natural defects exceeding the quantity or size limits defined in Sections 3 & 4.			
6.1.5.12	**SMOOTH** and **SANDED** without **CROSS SCRATCHES** in conformance to the **PRODUCT** portion of this section.			
6.1.5.13	**SCRIBED** at:			
6.1.5.13.1	Flat surfaces		●	●
6.1.5.13.2	Shaped surfaces			●

GENERAL — WOODWORK ⇓

8

EXECUTION

INSTALLATION RULES (continued)

6.1 GENERAL	DESCRIPTION	E	C	P
	GENERAL (continued)			
6.1.6 GAPS	**GAPS** (see Test A-C test illustrations in **COMPLIANCE**):			
6.1.6.1	**CAUSED** by **EXCESSIVE DEVIATIONS** (deviations in excess of 1/4" [6.4 mm] in 144" [3658 mm] of being plumb, level, flat, straight, square, or of the correct size) in the building's walls and ceilings, or 1/2" [12.7 mm] for floors, shall not be considered a defect or the responsibility of the installer.			
6.1.6.2	Shall not exceed 30% of a joint's length, with:			
6.1.6.2.1	**FILLER** or **CAULKING** allowed:	●		
6.1.6.2.1.1	If color-compatible.		●	●
6.1.6.3	Of **WOOD** to **WOOD** shall not exceed:			
6.1.6.3.1	At **FLAT** surfaces:			
6.1.6.3.1.1	0.050" (1.3 mm) in width.	●		
6.1.6.3.1.2	0.025" (0.65 mm) in width.		●	
6.1.6.3.1.3	0.012" (0.3 mm) in width.			●
6.1.6.3.2	At **SHAPED** surfaces:			
6.1.6.3.2.1	0.075" (1.9 mm) in width.	●		
6.1.6.3.2.2	0.050" (1.3 mm) in width.		●	
6.1.6.3.2.3	0.025" (0.65 mm) in width.			●
6.1.6.4	Of **WOOD** to **NON-WOOD** shall not exceed:			
6.1.6.4.1	At **FLAT** and **SHAPED** surfaces:			
6.1.6.4.1.1	0.100" (2.5 mm) in width.	●		
6.1.6.4.1.2	0.075" (1.9 mm) in width.		●	
6.1.6.4.1.3	0.050" (1.3 mm) in width.			●
6.1.6.5	Of **NON-WOOD** to **NON-WOOD** and/or **ALL ELEMENTS** shall not exceed:			
6.1.6.5.1	At **FLAT** surfaces:			
6.1.6.5.1.1	0.100" (2.5 mm) in width.	●		
6.1.6.5.1.2	0.075" (1.9 mm) in width.		●	
6.1.6.5.1.3	0.050" (1.3 mm) in width.			●
6.1.6.5.2	At **SHAPED** surfaces:			
6.1.6.5.2.1	0.125" (3.2 mm) in width.	●		
6.1.6.5.2.2	0.100" (2.5 mm) in width.		●	
6.1.6.5.2.3	0.075" (1.9 mm) in width.			●
6.1.7 FLUSHNESS	**FLUSHNESS** of joinery (See Test D illustrations in **COMPLIANCE**):			
6.1.7.1	Of **WOOD** to **WOOD** shall not exceed:			
6.1.7.1.1	At **FLAT** surfaces:			
6.1.7.1.1.1	0.050" (1.3 mm)	●		
6.1.7.1.1.2	0.025" (0.65 mm)		●	
6.1.7.1.1.3	0.012" (0.3 mm)			●
6.1.7.1.2	At **SHAPED** surfaces:			
6.1.7.1.2.1	0.075" (1.9 mm)	●		
6.1.7.1.2.2	0.050" (1.3 mm)		●	
6.1.7.1.2.3	0.025" (0.65 mm)			●

EXECUTION

INSTALLATION RULES (continued)

					DESCRIPTION	E	C	P
6.1 GENERAL	**GENERAL** (continued)							
	6.1.7 FLUSHNESS	**FLUSHNESS** of joinery (continued)						
		6.1.7.2	Of **WOOD** to **NON-WOOD** shall not exceed:					
			6.1.7.2.1	At **FLAT** and **SHAPED** surfaces:				
				6.1.7.2.1.1	0.100" (2.5 mm)	●		
				6.1.7.2.1.2	0.075" (1.9 mm)		●	
				6.1.7.2.1.3	0.050" (1.3 mm)			●
		6.1.7.3	Of **NON-WOOD** to **NON-WOOD** and/or **ALL ELEMENTS** shall not exceed:					
			6.1.7.3.1	At **FLAT** surfaces:				
				6.1.7.3.1.1	0.100" (2.5 mm)	●		
				6.1.7.3.1.2	0.075" (1.9 mm)		●	
				6.1.7.3.1.3	0.050" (1.3 mm)			●
			6.1.7.3.2	At **SHAPED** surfaces:				
				6.1.7.3.2.1	0.125" (3.2 mm)	●		
				6.1.7.3.2.2	0.100" (2.5 mm)		●	
				6.1.7.3.2.3	0.075" (1.9 mm)			●
	6.1.8 FASTENING	**FASTENING** shall:						
		6.1.8.1	Use **CONCEALED** fastening wherever possible.					
			6.1.8.1.1	If exposed fastening is required to complete the installation:				
				6.1.8.1.1.1	Fasteners shall be set in quirks or reliefs (where possible), countersunk, and kept to a minimum.			
				6.1.8.1.1.2	**PERMIT** use of construction adhesive, finish nails, trim screws, and/or pins.			
				6.1.8.1.1.3	**DO NOT PERMIT** the use of drywall, bugle-head, or case-hardened screws.			
				6.1.8.1.1.4	Require exposed fasteners to be inconspicuous, as defined in the glossary.			
				6.1.8.1.1.5	**DO NOT PERMIT** exposed fastening through HPDL.			
				6.1.8.1.1.6	**REQUIRE** prefinished materials to be filled by the installer with matching filler furnished by the woodwork supplier.			
				6.1.8.1.1.7	**REQUIRE** unfinished materials to be filled by the paint contractor or others.			
			6.1.8.1.2	Use of an extruded metal Z-mold or clips and/or French dovetail cleats is acceptable for blind installation.				
	6.1.9	**REVEAL STRIPS** that are grooved into paneling are to be left floating and allowed to expand and contract in reaction to changing relative humidity.						
	6.1.10	**EXPANSION JOINTS** shall be provided equivalent to 1/16" (1.6 mm) per 48" (1219 mm) of linear elevation.						
	6.1.11	**PANELING** shall be:						
		6.1.11.1	Of adequate thickness or furred and installed in such a way as to avoid deflection when normal pressure is applied.					
		6.1.11.2	Free of warp exceeding:					
			6.1.11.2.1	1/16" (1.6 mm) per linear foot		●		
			6.1.11.2.2	3/64" (1.2 mm) per linear foot			●	
			6.1.11.2.3	1/32" (0.8 mm) per linear foot				●

8

EXECUTION

INSTALLATION RULES (continued)

				DESCRIPTION	E	C	P
6.1 GENERAL	**GENERAL** (continued)						
	6.1.12	Paneling **JOINTS** shall be:					
		6.1.12.1	Smooth and flush to create a homogenous look.				
		6.1.12.2	Plumb within 1/16" (1.6 mm) in 96" (2438 mm).				
	6.1.13	**BACKS** of wood paneling shall be sealed with at least two coats of sealer.					
	6.1.14	**FLATNESS** of installed and removable sheet products (see Test E illustrations in **COMPLIANCE**) shall not exceed:					
		6.1.14.1	0.050" (1.3 mm) per 12" (305 mm) or portion thereof.		●		
		6.1.14.2	0.036" (0.9 mm) per 12" (305 mm) or portion thereof.			●	
		6.1.14.3	0.027" (0.7 mm) per 12" (305 mm) or portion thereof.				●
	6.1.15	**EQUIPMENT CUTOUTS** shall be neatly cut out by the installer, provided the templates are furnished in a timely manner.				●	●
	6.1.16	**HARDWARE** shall be:					
		6.1.16.1	Installed neatly without tear-out of surrounding stock.				
		6.1.16.2	Installed per the manufacturer's instructions.				
		6.1.16.3	Installed using all furnished fasteners and fastener's provisions				
		6.1.16.4	Adjusted for smooth operation.				
	6.1.17	**AREAS** of installation shall be left broom clean.					
		6.1.17.1	Debris shall be removed and dumped in containers provided by the contractor.				
		6.1.17.2	Items installed shall be cleaned of pencil or ink marks.				
	6.1.18	Entire installation shall present **FIRST-CLASS WORKMANSHIP** in compliance with these standards.					
6.2 PRODUCT SPECIFIC	**6.2.1** VENEER	At **VENEERED** wall surfacing:					
		6.2.1.1	For **TRANSPARENT FINISH**, the installer shall pay special attention to the **COLOR** and the **GRAIN** of the various panels and trim pieces to ensure they are installed in compliance with the **GRADE** specified.				
		6.2.1.2	**PANELS** shall be installed as specified by the architect.				
		6.2.1.3	**GLUING** with construction adhesive is permitted.				
		6.2.1.4	A maximum of 3/4" (19 mm) **REVEAL** at the ceiling to facilitate concealed fasteners is acceptable.				
		6.2.1.5	**EDGES** of core that are not self-edged shall have one coat sealer applied before installation.				
	6.2.2	At **DECORATIVE LAMINATE** wall surfacing:					
		6.2.2.1	**EXPOSED FASTENING** is not permitted, except:				
			6.2.2.1.1	At removable panels.			
		6.2.2.2	**PANELS** shall be installed as specified.				
		6.2.2.3	**GLUING** with construction adhesive is permitted.				
		6.2.2.4	A maximum of 3/4" (19 mm) **REVEAL** at the ceiling to facilitate concealed fasteners is acceptable.				
		6.2.2.5	**EDGES** of core that are not self-edged shall have one coat sealer applied before installation.				
		6.2.2.6	**SCRATCHES** and **CHIP-OUT** shall be inconspicuous beyond:				
			6.2.2.6.1	72" (1830 mm)	●		
			6.2.2.6.2	48" (1220 mm)		●	
			6.2.2.6.3	24" (610 mm)			●

8

EXECUTION

INSTALLATION RULES (continued)

				DESCRIPTION	E	C	P
⇑ 6.2 PRODUCT SPECIFIC				**PRODUCT SPECIFIC**			
	6.2.3 SOLID SURFACE			At **SOLID-SURFACE** wall surfacing:			
		6.2.3.1		**INSTALLATION** shall be performed by personnel properly trained and authorized by the applicable product manufacturer.			
		6.2.3.2		**SEALANTS** and **ADHESIVES** shall be compatible with the individual manufacturer's recommendations or specially developed sealants to achieve the best color match.			
		6.2.3.3		**VERTICAL SURFACING** shall be installed over suitable substrates based on the manufacturer's recommendations.			
		6.2.3.4		**EXPANSION** joints shall be furnished where required by building design or manufacturer recommendations.			
		6.2.3.5		**FIELD SEAMS** within a panel shall be hard-seamed.			
		6.2.3.6		**EXPOSED FASTENING** is not permitted, except:			
			6.2.3.6.1	At removable panels.			
			6.2.3.6.2	Where decorative fasteners are specified.			
		6.2.3.7		For **CONCEALED FASTENING**, a maximum of 3/4" (19 mm) reveal is permitted at the top of panels either under casework or at ceiling.			
		6.2.3.8		**SCRATCHES** and **CHIP-OUTS** shall be inconspicuous beyond:			
			6.2.3.8.1	48" (1220 mm)	●		
			6.2.3.8.2	24" (610 mm)		●	●
	6.2.4 SOLID PHENOLIC			At **SOLID PHENOLIC** wall surfacing:			
		6.2.4.1		**INSTALLATION** shall be performed by personnel properly trained and authorized by the applicable product manufacturer.			
		6.2.4.2		**PANELS** shall be installed as specified.			
			6.2.4.2.1	**GLUING** with construction adhesive is not permitted.			
			6.2.4.2.2	Use **CONCEALED FASTENING** wherever possible.			
			6.2.4.2.3	**EXPANSION CLEARANCE** of at least 3/32" (2.4 mm) for every 120" (305 mm) in length is required. Joints to be caulked shall be at least 1/8" (3.2 mm) wide to allow satisfactory caulking penetration and expansion.			
			6.2.4.2.4	**CAULKED JOINTS** shall be approximately 1/8" (3.2 mm) wide to allow satisfactory caulking penetration and expansion.			
		6.2.4.3		**SEALANTS** and **ADHESIVES** shall be compatible with the individual manufacturer's recommendations or specially developed sealants to achieve the best color match.			

8

COMPLIANCE

7 **FABRICATED** and **INSTALLED** woodwork shall be tested for compliance to these standards as follows:

7.1 **SMOOTHNESS** of exposed surfaces

7.1.1 **KCPI** (Knife Cuts Per Inch) is determined by holding the surfaced board at an angle to a strong light source and counting the visible ridges per inch, usually perpendicular to the profile.

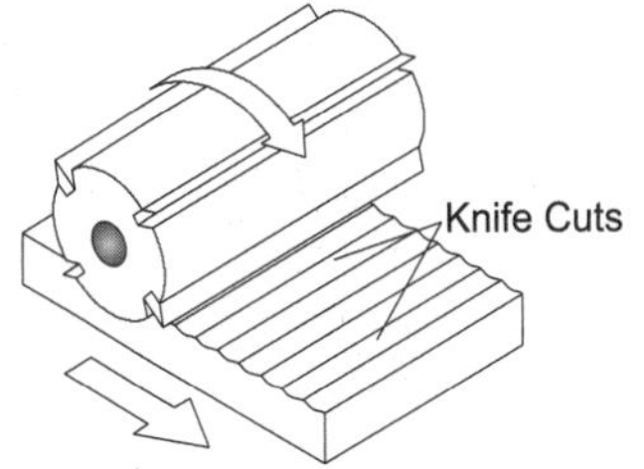

COMPLIANCE

7 FABRICATED and INSTALLED (continued)

7.1 **SMOOTHNESS** of exposed surfaces (continued)

7.1.2 **SANDING** is checked for compliance by sanding a sample piece of the same species with the required grit of abrasive.

7.1.2.1 Observation with a hand lens of the prepared sample and the material in question will offer a comparison of the scratch marks of the abrasive grit.

7.1.2.2 Reasonable assessment of the performance of the finished product will be weighed against absolute compliance with the standard.

7.1.2.3 A product is sanded sufficiently smooth when knife cuts are removed and any remaining sanding marks are or will be concealed by applied finishing coats.

7.1.2.4 Handling marks and/or grain raising, due to moisture or humidity in excess of the ranges set forth in this standard, shall not be considered a defect.

7.2 **TESTS FOR BLUEPRINT-MATCHED PANELS, COMPONENTS, AND RELATED DOORS**

7.2.1 These tests do not apply to flush doors specified under Section 9 or specified using other standards, and they are in addition to those requirements covered above.

7.2.2 At **VENEER JOINT:**

7.2.2.1 **PLUMB** shall not exceed 3/16" (5 mm) in 96" (2440 mm).

7.2.2.2 **TIGHTNESS** disallows any openings or voids of any kind.

7.2.3 At **END-MATCHED JOINTS**, grain loss shall not exceed 1-1/2" (38 mm).

7.2.3.1 Tested by separating end-matched panels 1-1/2" (38 mm) and visually testing grain void for continuity.

7.2.4 At **SIDE-MATCHED JOINTS**, grain loss shall not exceed 1" (25.4 mm).

7.2.4.1 Tested by separating side-matched panels 1" (25.4 mm) and visually testing grain void for continuity.

7.2.5 **HEART FIGURE PROGRESSION** - The full heart figure of plain-sliced veneer shall develop in uniform and natural progression.

7.2.5.1 Split or cut hearts are permitted, provided they are used to maintain sequence or to achieve special effects.

7.2.6 **SAPWOOD** shall be considered a defect except in species and cuts selected for sap appearance.

7.2.7 **VENEER PATCHES,** if required to repair unanticipated voids, shall not be discernible after finishing, when viewed from a distance of 48" (1219 mm) of the installed area in normal light.

7.2.8 **MATCHING** requires all faces to be balanced-match.

7.2.8.1 Center-balance matching must be specified.

7.3 **GAPS, FLUSHNESS, FLATNESS,** and **ALIGNMENT** of product and installation:

7.3.1 Maximum gaps between exposed components shall be tested with a feeler gauge at points designed to join, where members contact or touch.

7.3.2 Joint length shall be measured with a ruler with minimum 1/16" (1 mm) divisions and calculations made accordingly.

7.3.3 Reasonable assessment of the performance of the finished product will be weighed against absolute compliance with the standards.

COMPLIANCE

7 FABRICATED and INSTALLED (continued)

7.3 GAPS, FLUSHNESS, FLATNESS, and ALIGNMENT (continued)

7.3.4 The following is intended to provide examples of how and where compliance testing is measured:

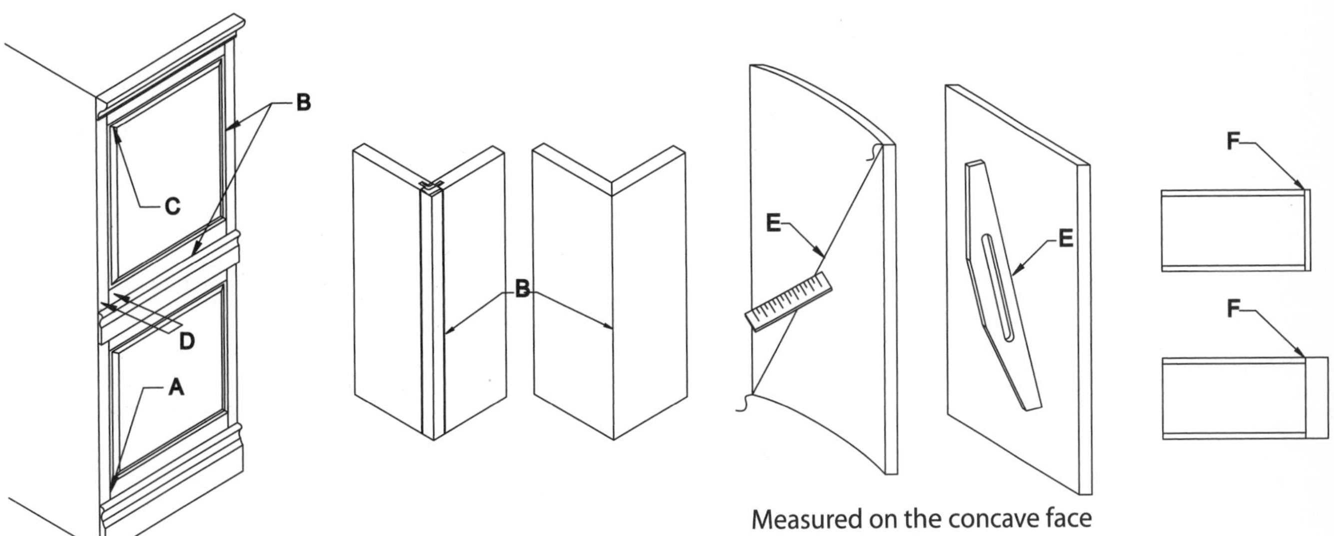

Measured on the concave face

A - Gaps when surfaces are mitered or butted
B - Gaps when parallel pieces are joined
C - Gaps when edges are mitered or butted
D - Flushness between two surfaces
E - Flatness of panel product
F - Flushness of edgebanding
G - Chipout

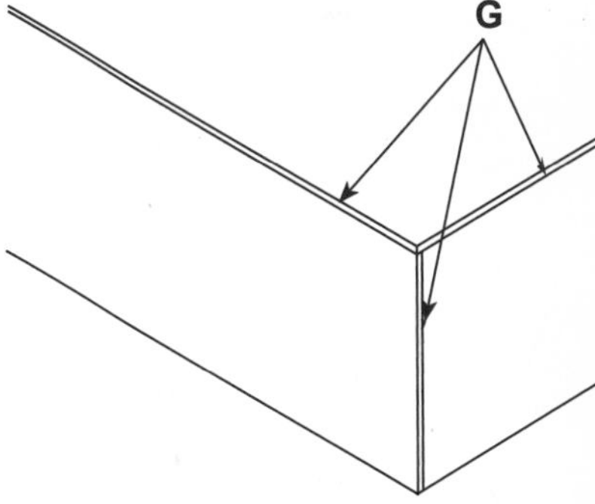

NOTES

Architectural Woodwork Standards

SECTION - 9

DOORS

SECTION 09 ✦ DOORS

(Including Flush and Stile & Rail Construction with Wood, HPDL Faces)

GENERAL

1 INFORMATION

1.1 GRADES

1.1.1 These standards are characterized in three Grades of quality that may be mixed within a single project. Limitless design possibilities and a wide variety of lumber and veneer species, along with overlays, high-pressure decorative laminates, factory finishes, and profiles are available in all three Grades.

1.1.2 **ECONOMY GRADE** is not used for this section.

1.1.3 **CUSTOM GRADE** is typically specified for and adequately covers most high-quality architectural woodwork, providing a well-defined degree of control over a project's quality of materials, workmanship, or installation.

1.1.4 **PREMIUM GRADE** is typically specified for use in those areas of a project where the highest level of quality, materials, workmanship, and installation is required.

1.1.5 **MODIFICATIONS** by the contract documents shall govern if in conflict with these standards.

1.2 BASIC CONSIDERATIONS

1.2.1 **ACCEPTABLE REQUIREMENTS** of lumber and/or sheet products used within this product section are established by Sections 3 and 4, unless otherwise modified herein.

1.2.2 **CONTRACT DRAWINGS** and/or **SPECIFICATIONS**, furnished by the design professional, shall clearly indicate or delineate all material, fabrication, installation, and applicable building code/regulation requirements.

1.2.3 Methods of construction for flush, **EXCLUDING HOLLOW CORE**, and stile and rail doors shown in this section may not represent all types available. Variations of construction and materials are permitted, as long as the appropriate minimum **WDMA DUTY PERFORMANCE LEVELS** are met or exceeded.

1.2.4 **EXPOSED SURFACES**

1.2.4.1 Both visible faces of wood doors, including applied moldings, lights, and louvers.

1.2.5 **SEMI-EXPOSED SURFACES**

1.2.5.1 Both vertical edges of wood doors.

1.2.5.2 Top edge, if visible from above.

9

1.2.6 **CONCEALED SURFACES**

1.2.6.1 Top and bottom edges of wood doors.

1.2.6.1.1 Unless the top edge is visible from above.

1.2.7 **GRADE LIMITATIONS**

1.2.7.1 **FLUSH** and **STILE & RAIL DOORS** are offered only in **CUSTOM** and **PREMIUM GRADES**.

1.2.8 **WARRANTY** shall be to the terms, conditions, and duration of the door manufacturer, unless specified otherwise.

1.2.8.1 Warranties vary between manufacturers and between interior or exterior exposure as to the:

1.2.8.1.1 Coverage.

1.2.8.1.2 Duration.

1.2.8.1.3 Items and conditions that void it.

1.2.8.1.4 Extent of replacement and cost coverage.

GENERAL

1.2 **BASIC CONSIDERATIONS** (continued)

1.2.8 **WARRANTY** (continued)

1.2.8.2 Typically, manufacturers do **NOT** warranty doors with:

1.2.8.2.1 **CUTOUTS EXCEEDING** 40% of the door's area or 54" (1372 mm) of door height, unless approved by authorities with jurisdiction.

1.2.8.2.2 **DIFFERENT:**

1.2.8.2.2.1 Species, face materials, finishes, or laminates on opposite sides.

1.2.8.2.2.2 Temperature and/or humidity conditions on opposite sides.

1.2.8.2.3 **LESS THAN** 5" (127 mm) between cutouts or a cutout and the edge of a door, or:

1.2.8.2.3.1 **LESS THAN** 6" (152.4 mm) at fire-rated doors between cutouts or a cutout and the edge of a door, unless approved by authorities with jurisdiction.

1.2.8.2.4 **EXTERIOR** applications when:

1.2.8.2.4.1 Fire-rated.

1.2.8.2.4.2 Not properly protected from the elements.

1.2.9 **NFPA 80** requires certain design accommodations.

1.2.9.1 Preparation of **FIRE-RATED DOOR ASSEMBLIES** for locks, latches, hinges, remotely operated or monitored hardware, concealed closures, glass lights, vision panels, louvers, astragals, and laminated overlays shall be performed by the manufacturer or its agent in conformance with the manufacturer's **LICENSING** and **LABEL SERVICE AGREEMENT**.

1.2.9.2 Preparation of **SURFACE-APPLIED** hardware, function holes for mortise locks, holes for labeled viewers (a maximum of 3/4" [19 mm]), allowable undercutting, and application of protection plates may be performed at the jobsite.

1.2.10 **APPLICABLE CODES** and **REGULATIONS** may require certain design accommodations, and it is the responsibility of the design professional to employ such within their door designs and schedule.

1.2.11 **FIRE-RATED DOORS**

1.2.11.1 Are **AVAILABLE** in 20-, 45-, 60-, and 90-minute labels.

1.2.11.2 Shall be of **CONSTRUCTION STANDARD** to the door manufacturer and conform with the requirements of all applicable labeling agencies.

1.2.11.3 Shall permit **EDGES** on 45-, 60-, and 90-minute fire-rated doors, regardless of the species of material on the door face; shall be the standard of the door manufacturer; and the species, width, and fire-retardant treatment shall conform to the requirements of the labeling agency acceptable to the authority with jurisdiction for the label specified.

1.2.11.4 **HANGING** shall be compliant with the manufacturer's requirements.

1.2.12 **TRANSOM PANEL** options:

1.2.12.1 **TYPE 1** - requires the bottom edgeband to run the full width of the panel.

1.2.12.2 **TYPE 2** - requires the side edgebands to run through and be visible.

GENERAL

1.2 **BASIC CONSIDERATIONS** (continued)

1.2.12 **TRANSOM PANEL** options (continued)

1.2.12.3 **HORIZONTAL MEETING EDGE** options:

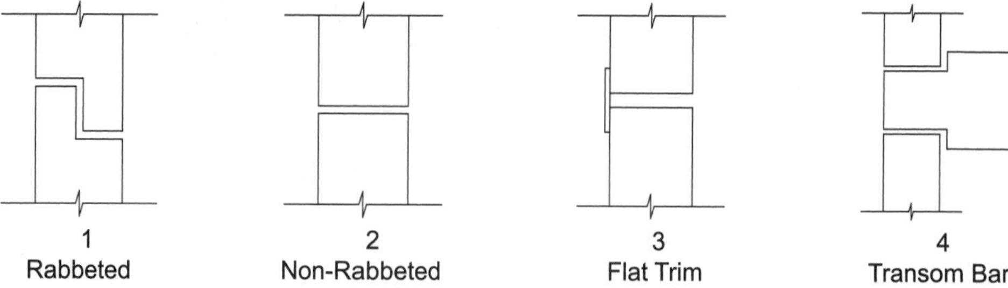

1.2.13 **VERTICAL MEETING EDGE** options:

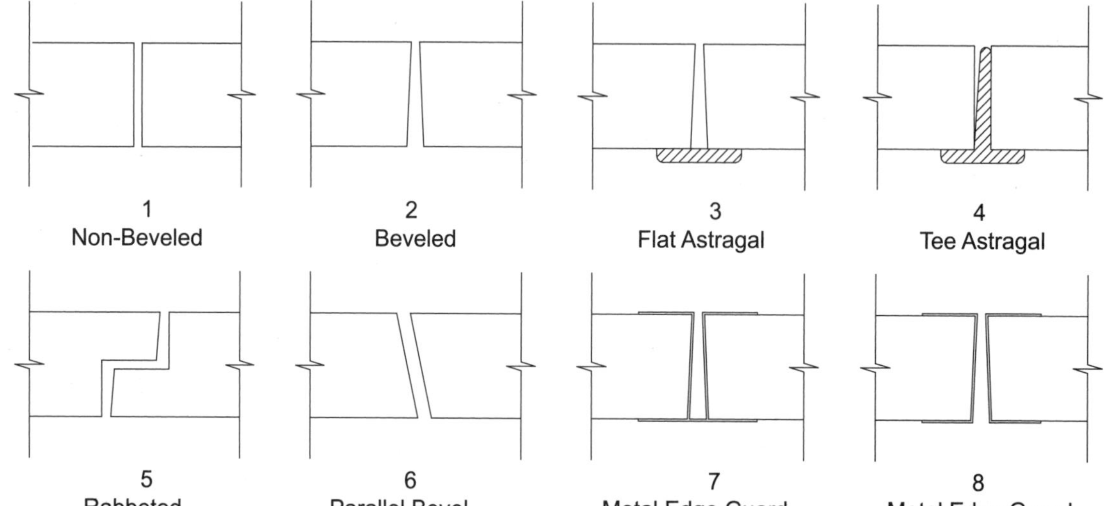

1.2.14 **DUTCH DOOR** options:

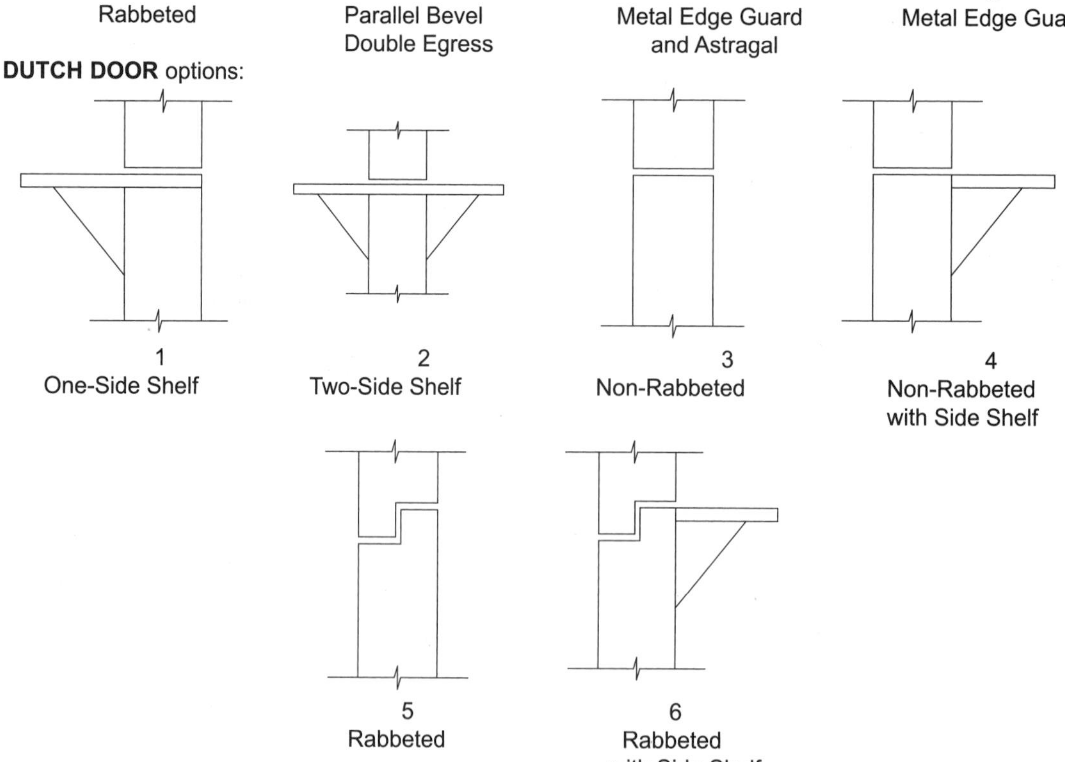

9

GENERAL

1.2 **BASIC CONSIDERATIONS** (continued)

1.2.15 **LOUVER** options:

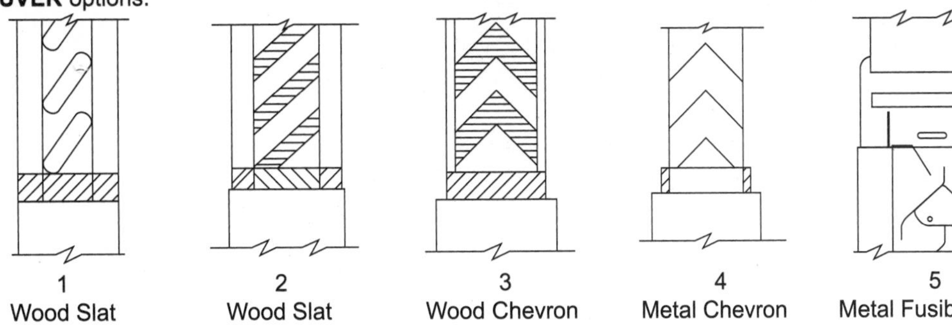

1.2.16 **FLASHING** options:

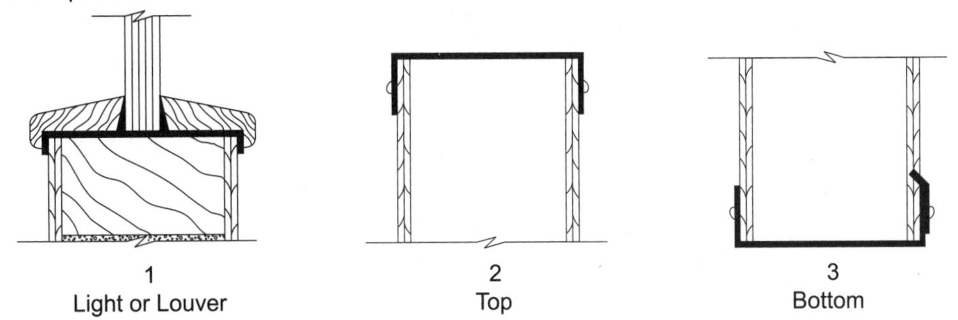

1.2.17 **PERFORMANCE DUTY LEVEL**

1.2.17.1 These standards have adopted the ANSI/WDMA I.S. 1A (latest edition) **HEAVY DUTY** Performance Level for Custom and Premium Grade doors.

1.2.17.1.1 The **HEAVY DUTY** level typically involves doors for moderate usage and requires intermediate minimum performance standards.

1.2.17.1.1.1 Typical **USAGE** examples:

- Assisted living room entry
- Office - Interior passage stairwell
- Mechanical service hallway
- Hotel/motel room entry
- Medical exam room
- Storage
- Apartment/condo entry
- X-ray
- Acoustic

1.2.17.2 If a higher or lower Performance Duty Level is desired, it shall be so specified.

1.2.17.2.1 The **EXTRA HEAVY DUTY** level typically involves doors where use is considered heavy and frequent, and requires the highest minimum performance standards.

1.2.17.2.1.1 Typical **USAGE** examples:

- Classrooms
- Patient rooms
- Bathrooms - Public
- Dorm rooms
- Assembly areas
- Auditorium entry
- Detention/correctional
- Bullet-resistant
- Gym/locker rooms
- Surgical entry
- Trauma centers

1.2.17.2.2 The **STANDARD DUTY** level typically involves doors where frequency of use is low and requires the lowest minimum performance standards.

1.2.17.2.2.1 Typical **USAGE** examples:

- Closet
- Wardrobe
- Bath - Private
- Small, low-usage office

9

GENERAL

.2 **BASIC CONSIDERATIONS** (continued)

1.2.17 **PERFORMANCE DUTY LEVEL** (continued)

1.2.17.2 If a higher or lower Performance Duty Level is desired (continued)

1.2.17.2.3 **DUTY LEVEL** performance requirements are spelled out within the Product portion of this Section.

1.2.18 At **FLUSH** doors:

1.2.18.1 **CORES** shall be particleboard, MDF (medium-density fiberboard), agrifiber, staved lumber, SCL (structural composite lumber), fire-resistant composite, or hollow grid core conforming to the minimum requirements of WDMA - I.S. 1-A.

1.2.18.1.1 **SPECIALITY CORES** for fire-rated, sound-resistant, x-ray, bullet-resistant, or electrostatic-shielded doors shall be properly specified, including the fire rating, sound class, lead thickness, and/or protection rating.

1.2.18.1.1.1 At **FIRE-RATED DOORS**, the type of construction, core type, thickness, edgebands, moldings, blocking, and use of intumescent shall be the standard of the door manufacturer, conforming to the labeling authority granted to them by their fire-labeling agency.

1.2.18.1.1.2 At **SOUND-RESISTANT DOORS**, the type of construction, thickness, edgebanding, applied moldings, special stops, stop adjusters, gaskets, and automatic threshold closing devices shall be the standard of the door manufacturer conforming to the STC (Sound Transmission Class) specified when tested as an opening unit (rather than sealed in place).

1.2.18.1.1.3 At **X-RAY DOORS**, construction, thickness, edgebands, and moldings shall be of the manufacturer's standard.

1.2.18.1.1.4 At **BULLET-RESISTANT** doors, the type of construction, thickness, edgebands, and moldings shall be of the manufacturer's standard.

1.2.18.1.1.5 At **ELECTROSTATIC-SHIELDED** doors, the type of construction, thickness, edgebands, and moldings shall be of the manufacturer's standard.

1.2.18.1.1.6 Cores other than those enumerated herein are manufactured to individual specifications and are not dealt with in these standards for that reason.

1.2.18.1.2 **HARDWARE BLOCKING**, if desired, shall be specified from the following typical options:

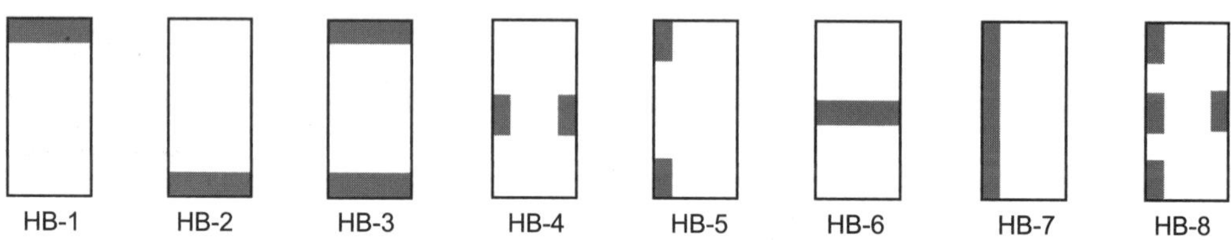

1.2.17.1.2.1 **TOP BLOCKING** may be full or partial width as required by its application.

1.2.18.2 **WOOD-FACE VENEER**

1.2.18.2.1 At **STAND-ALONE** doors with face species of Anigre, Ash, Beech, Birch, Cherry, Hickory, African Mahogany, Honduras Mahogany, Makore, Maple, Red Oak, White Oak, Pecan, Poplar, or Walnut shall conform to the **HPVA DOOR SKIN FACE** tables included within the "product" portion of this section.

1.2.18.2.1.1 Doors of a species not listed above shall conform to the **HPVA DOOR SKIN FACE TABLE** as agreed on between buyer and seller.

GENERAL

1.2 **BASIC CONSIDERATIONS** (continued)

1.2.18 At **FLUSH** doors (continued)

1.2.18.2 **WOOD-FACE VENEER** (continued)

1.2.18.2.2 Doors that are **ADJACENT TO** or **BECOME A COMPONENT OF** other architectural woodwork shall conform to the applicable requirements of **SECTION 4**.

1.2.18.2.3 At **STAND-ALONE, CENTER-BALANCE MATCHED** doors, the width of outer leaves after trimming will not exceed 1" (25.4 mm) less than its adjoining leaf for Custom Grade, or 1/2" (12.7 mm) less than its adjoining leaf for Premium Grade.

1.2.18.2.4 When specifying **NATURAL,** veneers may contain unlimited amounts of **SAPWOOD** and/or **HEARTWOOD.**

1.2.18.2.4.1 If only heartwood or sapwood is desired, it shall be so specified.

1.2.18.2.4.1.1 Before specifying, check with the door manufacturer for availability.

1.2.18.2.5 Special **MATCHING** shall be so specified, such as:

1.2.18.2.5.1 All doors on the same project are to be manufactured using the same or similar flitches.

1.2.18.2.5.2 Sequence-matched face veneers required at pairs or sets of doors and adjacent panels.

1.2.18.2.6 **FIGURE** is not a function of a species grade, and any special requirements must be so specified.

1.2.18.2.7 **SPECIAL CHARACTERISTICS,** such as sapwood, heartwood, ribbon stripe, birdseye, and comb grain, if desired, are required to be specified.

1.2.18.2.8 **VENEER** shall be of sufficient thickness so as not to permit show-through of cross-banding after sanding or finishing.

1.2.18.3 **EDGE TYPE** is the manufacturer's option unless specified otherwise.

1.2.18.3.1 **EDGE TYPE - A - SOLID WOOD** band, face, and cross-band edges show.

1.2.18.3.2 **EDGE TYPE - B - WOOD VENEER** band, face, and cross-band edges covered.

1.2.18.3.3 **EDGE TYPE - C - HPDL or PVC** band, face, and cross-band edges covered.

9

GENERAL

1.2 **BASIC CONSIDERATIONS** (continued)

1.2.18 At **FLUSH** doors (continued)

1.2.18.3 **EDGE TYPE** is the manufacturer's option unless specified otherwise (continued)

1.2.18.3.4 **EDGE TYPE - D - SOLID WOOD** band, veneer face edge shows.

1.2.18.3.5 **EDGE TYPE - E - SOLID WOOD** band, veneer face edge shows.

1.2.18.3.6 **EDGE TYPE - F - SOLID WOOD** band, face, and cross-band edges covered.

1.2.18.4 **CONSTRUCTION DEFINITIONS**

1.2.18.4.1 At **WOOD-FACED** doors:

1.2.18.4.1.1 **5-PLY** consists of a center core field on which is applied to each side a wood veneer or engineered composite cross-band with a face veneer applied over the cross-band.

1.2.18.4.1.2 **7-PLY** consists of a center core field on which is applied to each side 3-ply face skins.

1.2.18.4.2 At **HPDL-FACED** doors:

1.2.18.4.2.1 **3-PLY** consists of a core field with a plastic laminate face applied over both sides of the core field.

1.2.18.4.2.2 **5-PLY** consists of a wood veneer or engineered composite cross-band applied over the core before application of the face laminate.

GENERAL

1.2 **BASIC CONSIDERATIONS** (continued)

1.2.18 At **FLUSH** doors (continued)

1.2.18.5 **EXAMPLES** with component cut-a-ways (the illustration of grain direction is only applicable to wood veneer):

1.2.18.5.1 **WOOD-VENEER FACE** with particleboard, MDF, or agrifiber core (PC-5 / PC-7):

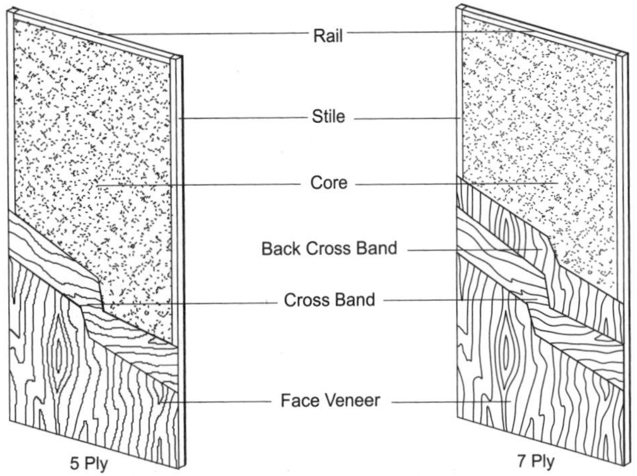

1.2.18.5.2 **HPDL FACE** with particleboard, MDF, or agrifiber core (PC-HPDL-3 / PC-HPDL-5):

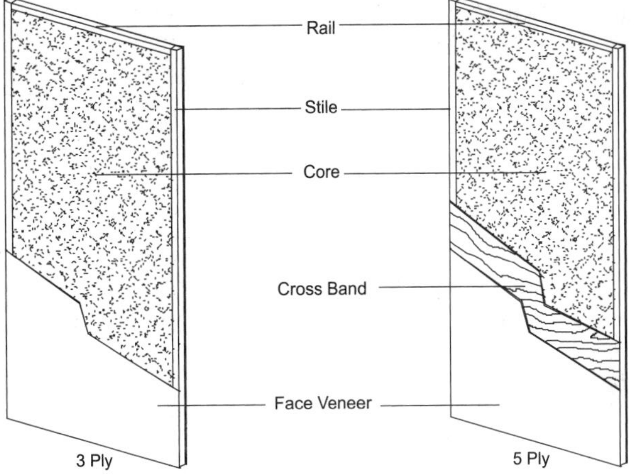

1.2.18.5.3 **WOOD-VENEER FACE** with staved lumber core (SLC-5 / SLC-7):

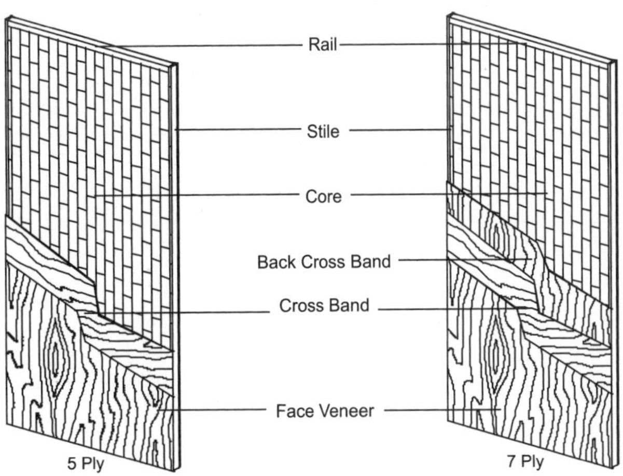

9

GENERAL

1.2 **BASIC CONSIDERATIONS** (continued)

1.2.18 At **FLUSH** doors (continued)

1.2.18.5 **EXAMPLES** with component cut-a-ways (continued)

1.2.18.5.4 **WOOD-VENEER FACE** with structural composite lumber (SCL) core (SCLC-5 / SCLC-7):

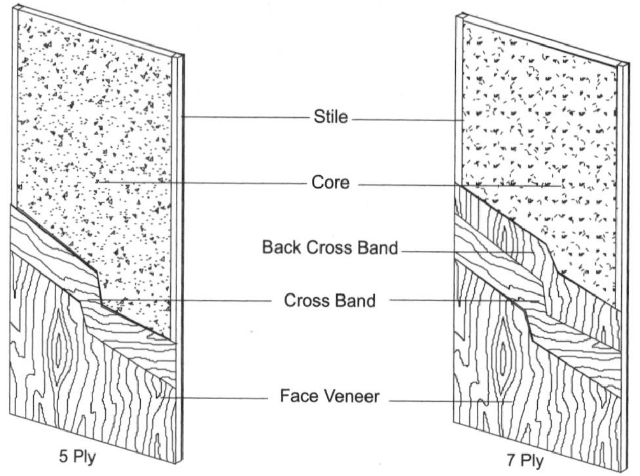

1.2.18.5.5 **WOOD-VENEER FACE** with fire-resistant composite core (FD-5 / FD-7):

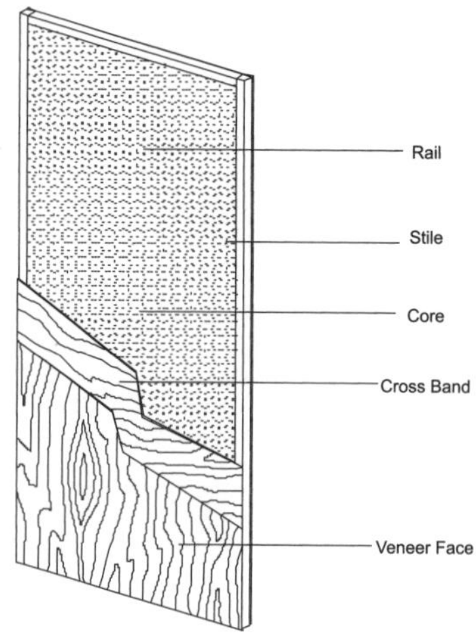

1.2.18.5.6 **HPDL** with fire-resistant composite core (FD-HPDL):

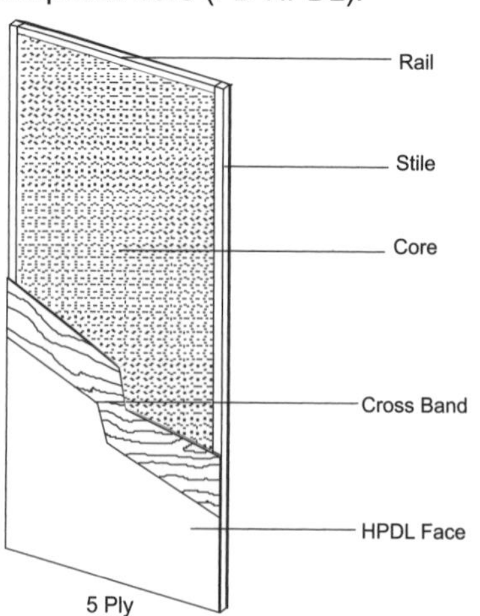

9

GENERAL

1.2 **BASIC CONSIDERATIONS** (continued)

1.2.18 At **FLUSH** doors (continued)

1.2.18.5 **EXAMPLES** (continued)

1.2.18.5.7 **WOOD-VENEER FACE** with hollow core (HC-7):

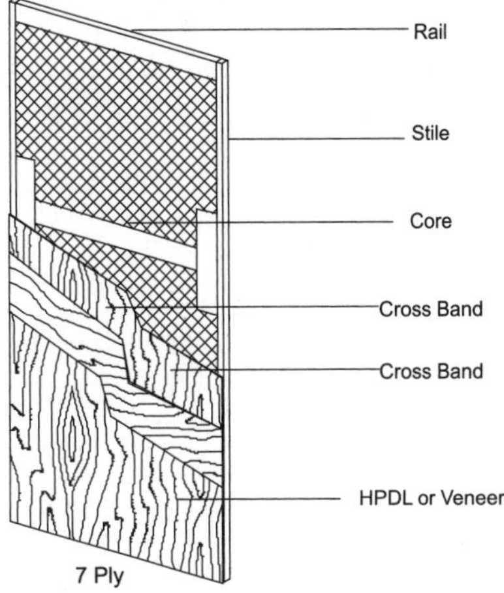

1.2.18.6 **PAIR MATCH** is required; the example below is of book-matched, center-balance matched faces:

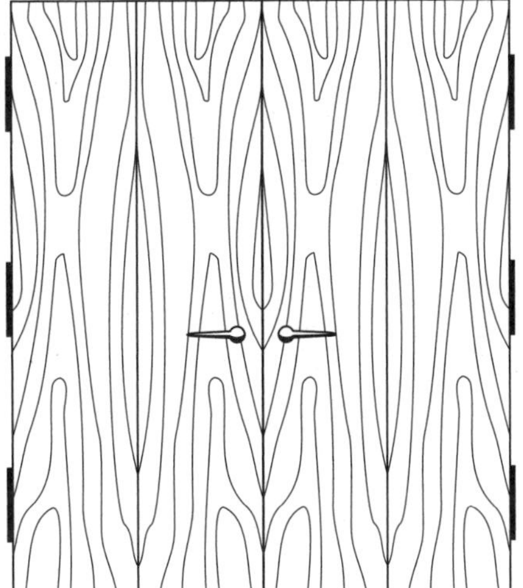

1.2.18.7 **SET MATCH** is required; the example below is of book-matched, center-balance matched faces:

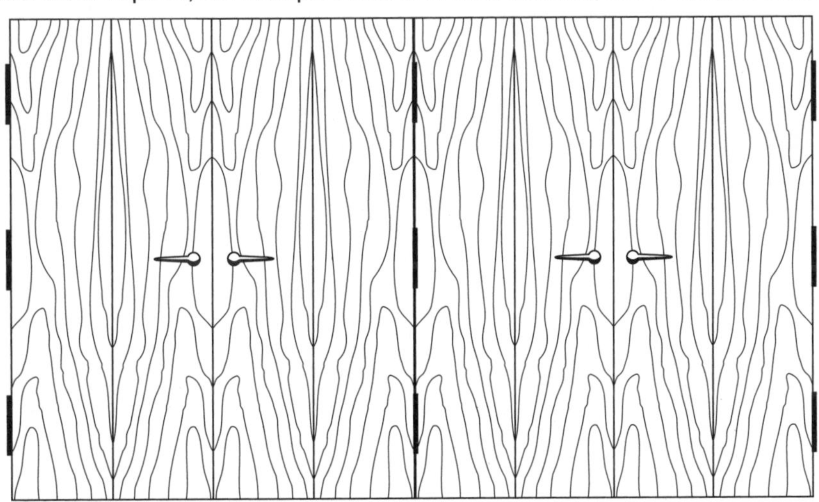

GENERAL

1.2 **BASIC CONSIDERATIONS** (continued)

1.2.18 At **FLUSH** doors (continued)

1.2.18.8 **TRANSOM MATCH** requires a **CONTINUOUS** match at Premium Grade and a **CONTINUOUS** or **END** match at Custom Grade unless specified otherwise - see examples below:

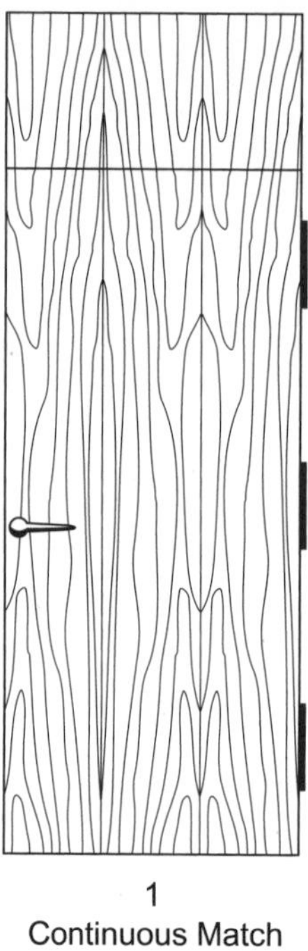

1
Continuous Match

2
End Match

1.2.19 At **STILE AND RAIL** doors:

1.2.19.1 The strength of a stile and rail door is primarily dependent on the shoulders and joints between the stiles and rails; a wide bottom rail will increase significantly the strength and stability of a door far beyond that of a narrow rail.

1.2.19.2 Shall be of **SPECIAL DESIGN** and construction, not a commodity product.

1.2.19.2.1 Care should be taken to ensure that the design of a door's stiles and rails is large enough to structurally accommodate the intended hardware, provide a strong and stable door, and accommodate the usage and size of the opening.

1.2.19.2.2 Because of warpage and twist characteristics of heavy, one-piece, solid hardwood members, that method of construction is not recommended for stile and rail door construction.

1.2.19.2.3 Door panels of either flush (flat) or raised design are typically of the same species as the stiles and rails, and their construction should be left to the experience and option of the manufacturer.

GENERAL

1.2 **BASIC CONSIDERATIONS** (continued)

1.2.19 At **STILE AND RAIL** doors (continued)

1.2.19.3 Component **TERMINOLOGY** is as follows:

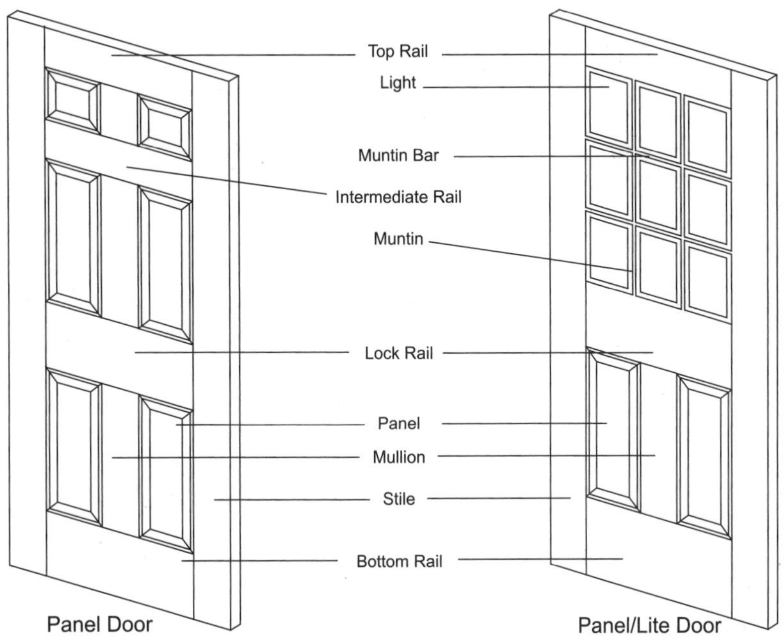

1.2.19.4 **STILES** are the upright or vertical outside members of a door, which:

1.2.19.4.1 May be of **SOLID WOOD** or **VENEERED** construction.

1.2.19.4.2 Typically have **STICKING** profiles of cove and bead, ogee, or ovalo design; however:

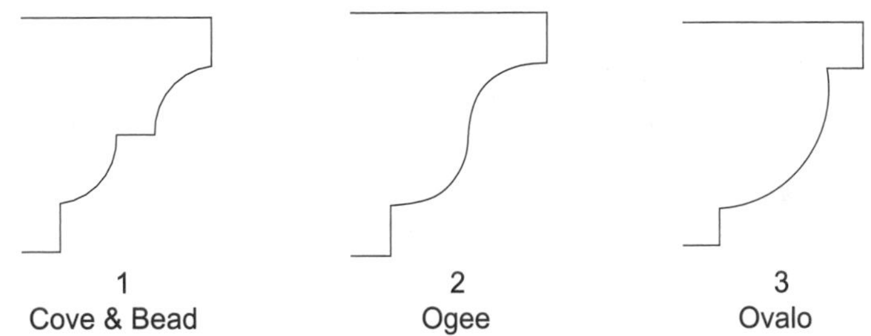

1.2.19.4.2.1 Other profiles may be used.

1.2.19.5 **RAILS** are the cross or horizontal members of the door, which include:

1.2.19.5.1 **BOTTOM RAIL**, the bottom horizontal member and the widest of the rails.

1.2.19.5.2 **TOP RAIL**, the top horizontal member of a door and typically the same width as the stiles.

1.2.19.5.3 **LOCK RAIL**, the horizontal member located at or near lock height.

1.2.19.5.4 **INTERMEDIATE RAIL**, any additional horizontal rail beyond those listed above, but similar to the lock rail.

1.2.19.6 **MULLIONS** are the upright or vertical members (typically larger than a muntin) between panels or lights, similar in function to a cross-rail.

1.2.19.6.1 A variation of the mullion occurs in a door design incorporating the “cross-buck” or “sawbuck,” where the mullions and/or “diagonal rails” are at a 45-degree angle to the bottom rail, forming triangular panels.

GENERAL

1.2 **BASIC CONSIDERATIONS** (continued)

1.2.19 At **STILE AND RAIL** doors (continued)

1.2.19.7 **PANELS** are the members of solid wood, plywood, or composition material that fills the frame formed by the stiles and rails of a door; there are two types:

1.2.19.7.1 **RAISED**, which imparts a three-dimensional effect, may be solid, laminated, rim-banded, or membrane-pressed.

1.2.19.7.1.1 **FLAT** is just that, made of solid, laminated, or composite construction.

1.2.19.8 **MUNTINS** and **MUNTIN BARS** are used at glass openings.

1.2.19.8.1 A muntin bar is a rabbeted molding that extends the total height or width of the glass opening, usually extending from stile to stile or rail to rail, separating lights of glass.

1.2.19.8.2 A muntin is a shorter horizontal or vertical member extending from a muntin bar to a stile, rail, or another muntin bar.

1.2.19.9 **STILE** and **RAIL** construction examples:

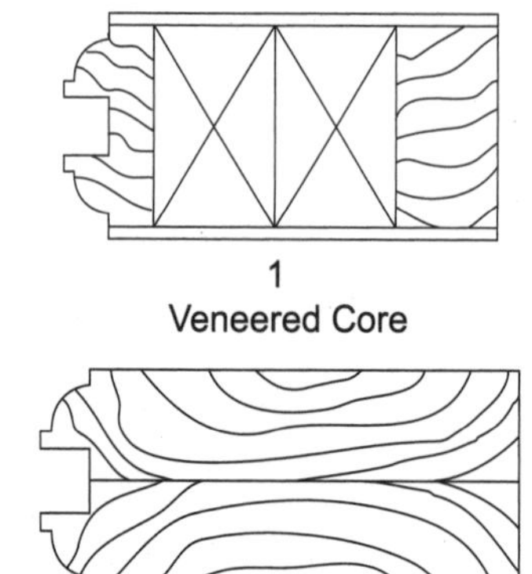

1
Veneered Core

3
Two-Piece Laminated Solid Lumber

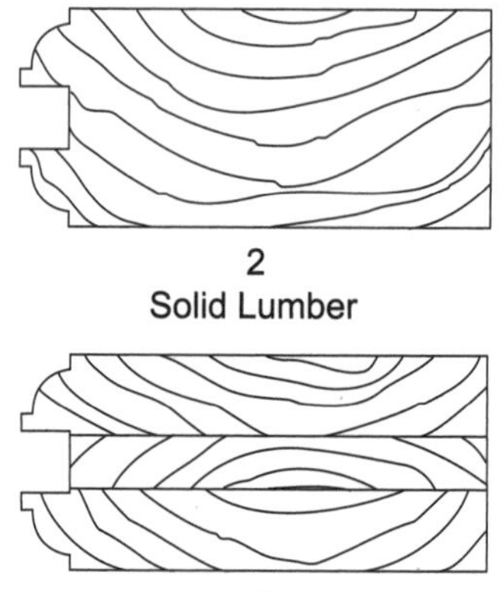

2
Solid Lumber

4
Three-Piece Laminated Solid Lumber

1.2.19.10 **PANEL** construction examples:

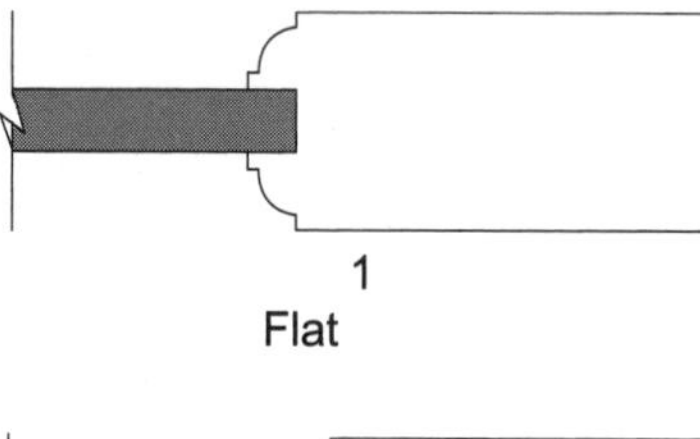

1
Flat

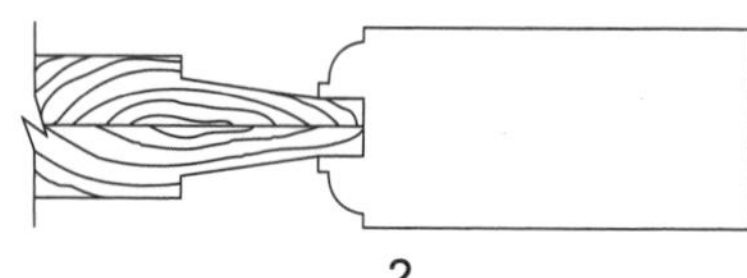

2
Raised, 2-Ply Solid Lumber

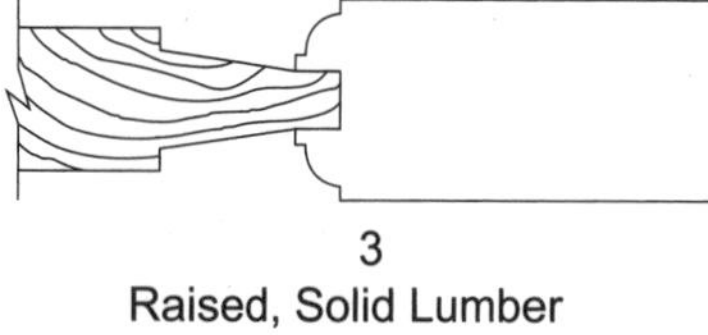

3
Raised, Solid Lumber

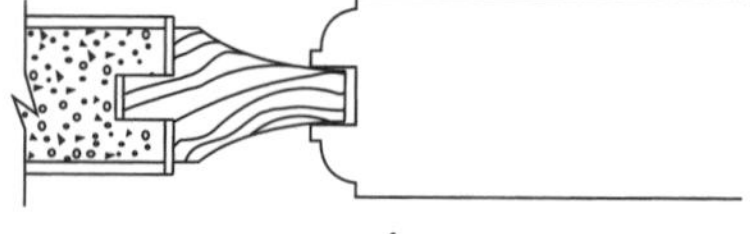

4
Rim-Raised Veneer Panel

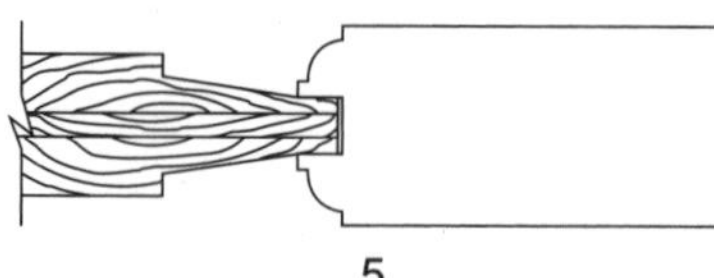

5
Raised, 3-Ply Solid Lumber

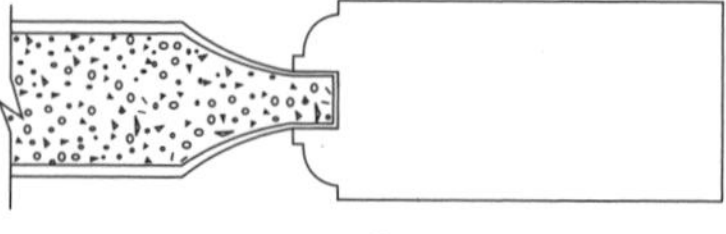

6
Membrane-Pressed Veneer Panel

GENERAL

1.2 **BASIC CONSIDERATIONS** (continued)

1.2.19 At **STILE AND RAIL** doors (continued)

1.2.19.11 Panel or glass **RETENTION** examples:

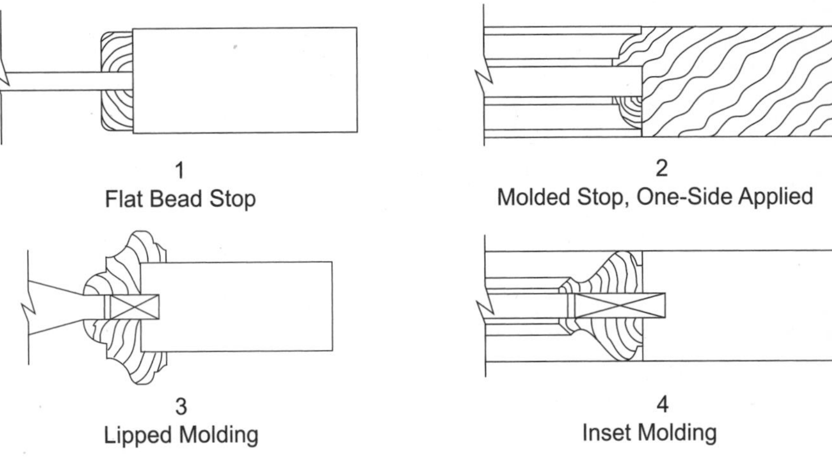

1.2.19.12 **JOINERY** examples:

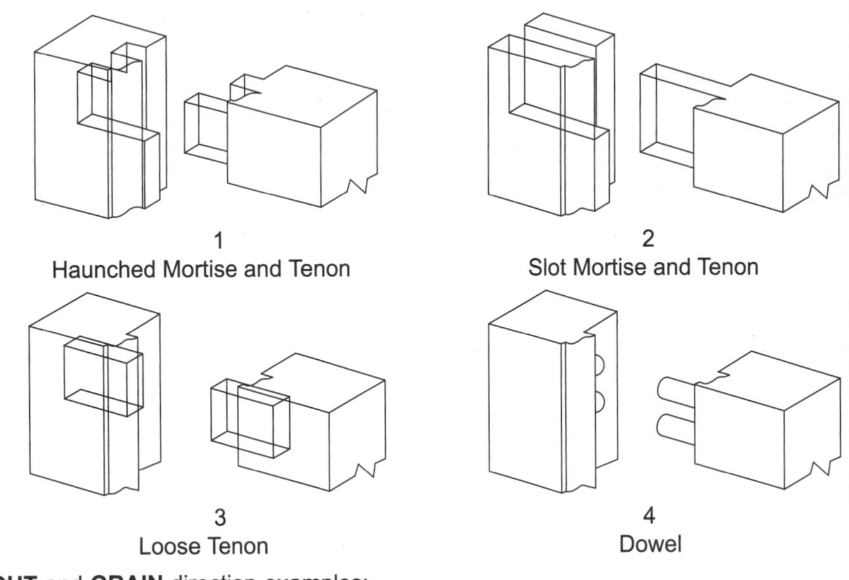

1.2.19.13 Panel **LAYOUT** and **GRAIN** direction examples:

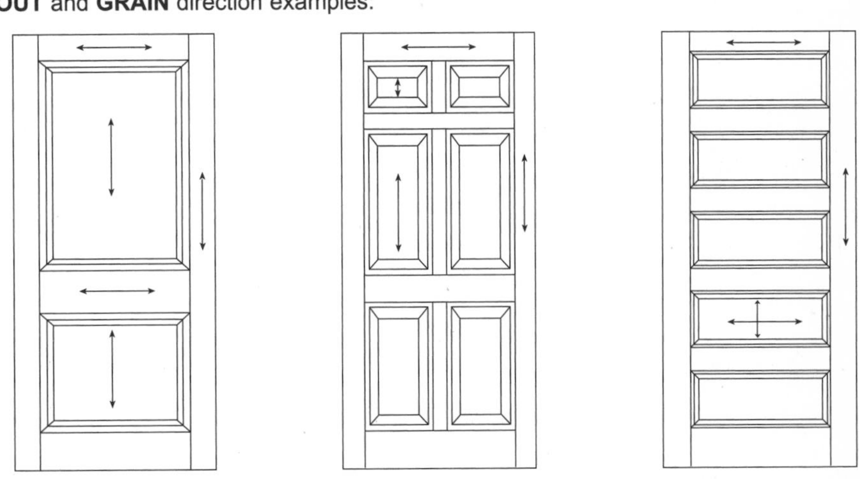

GENERAL

1.3 **RECOMMENDATIONS**

1.3.1 **INCLUDE IN DIVISION 09 OF THE SPECIFICATIONS:**

1.3.1.1 For **JOBSITE FINISHING** - Before finishing, all exposed portions of woodwork shall have handling marks or effects of exposure to moisture removed with a thorough, final sanding over all surfaces of the exposed portions using an appropriate grit sandpaper, and shall be cleaned before applying sealer or finish.

1.3.1.2 At **GLASS LIGHTS** - To create the proper seal against weather, wind, and rain, the finish coats of all doors should be allowed to flow onto the glass area at least 1/16" (1.6 mm), and:

1.3.1.2.1 When **CLEANING**, a razor should not be used to scrape the glass because it will destroy the seal; a broad-blade putty knife should be used to protect the seal between the paint and the glass.

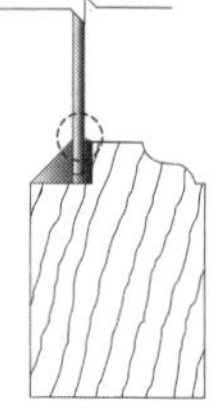

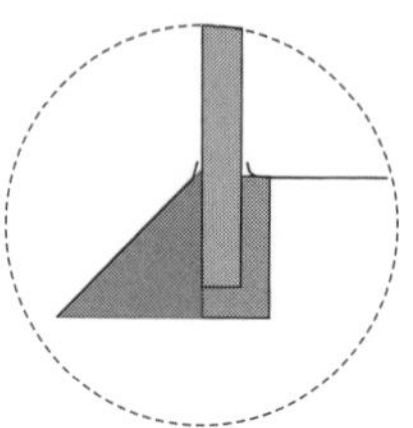

1.3.2 **THOROUGHLY REVIEW** Sections 3 and 4, especially Basic Considerations, Recommendations, Acknowledgements, and Industry Practices within Part 1 for an overview of the characteristics and minimum acceptable requirements of lumber and/or sheet products that might be used herein.

1.3.3 **CONTRACT DOCUMENTS** (plans and/or specifications) shall require that all structural members, grounds, blocking, backing, furring, brackets, or other anchorage which becomes an integral part of the building's walls, floors, or ceilings, required for the installation of architectural woodwork is not to be furnished or installed by the architectural woodwork manufacturer or installer.

1.3.4 **SPECIFY** requirements for:

1.3.4.1 Fire ratings

1.3.4.2 Special code or regulation compliance

1.3.4.3 Special hardware such as kick plates, door closures, hinges, panic hardware, locks, etc.

1.3.4.4 Prohibition of finger-joints otherwise allowed at edges.

1.3.5 **MEDIUM-DENSITY OVERLAY (MDO)** should be specified for **EXTERIOR** opaque applications and as an excellent interior paint-grade surface.

9

1.3.6 Avoid wood doors in **EXTERIOR** applications; however, if needed, they should be:

1.3.6.1 **WATER-REPELLENT** treated.

1.3.6.2 **PROTECTED** according to the manufacturer's requirements from sun and other weather elements by overhangs, deep recesses, and flashings.

1.3.6.3 **PRIMED** with an exterior enamel primer, followed by a minimum of two additional coats of exterior enamel on all surfaces.

1.3.7 At **STILE** and **RAIL** doors, be sure to specify any special:

1.3.7.1 **PANEL** type or configuration

1.3.7.2 **STILE** or **RAIL** widths and/or construction

1.3.7.3 **ORNAMENTAL** detail or joinery

1.4 **ACKNOWLEDGEMENTS**

1.4.1 Use of **HPL-BACKED WOOD VENEERS** is permitted, if specified or otherwise approved.

GENERAL

1.5 **INDUSTRY PRACTICES**

1.5.1 **STRUCTURAL MEMBERS**, grounds, blocking, backing, furring, brackets, or other anchorage that becomes an integral part of the building's walls, floors, or ceilings, that are required for the installation of architectural woodwork are not furnished or installed by the architectural woodwork manufacturer or installer.

1.5.2 **WALL, CEILING,** and/or opening variations in excess of 1/4" (6.4 mm) or **FLOORS** in excess of 1/2" (12.7 mm) in 144" (3658 mm) of being plumb, level, flat, straight, square, or of the correct size are not acceptable for the installation of architectural woodwork, nor is it the responsibility of the installer to scribe or fit to tolerances in excess of such.

1.5.3 **HANDING** of a door is always **DETERMINED FROM THE OUTSIDE**:

1.5.3.1 The outside of an exterior door is the key side.

1.5.3.2 The passage side of an interior door is the key side or imaginary key side.

1.5.3.3 The outside or passage side of a closet door is the key side or imaginary key side.

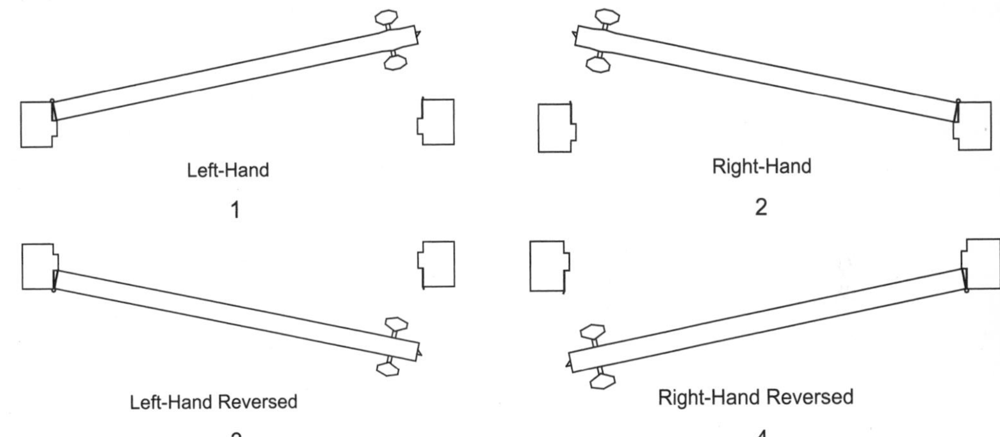

BOTTOM OF DRAWING REPRESENTS OUTSIDE.

PRODUCT

2 SCOPE

2.1 All exterior and interior, flush, and stile and rail wood doors with corresponding and adjacent transoms, fixed panels, and/or side lights. 9

2.2 **TYPICAL INCLUSIONS**

2.2.1 Flush doors, solid, hollow, fire-rated, sound-resistant, x-ray, or bullet-resistant.
2.2.2 Stile and rail doors of veneered, solid, and/or laminated (solid) construction with or without fire-, sound-, or bullet-resistant ratings.
2.2.3 Accessories required to comply with the door manufacturer's fire-rated door approval, including treated or metal edges at pairs of fire-rated doors as required.
2.2.4 Accessories required to comply with the door manufacturer's sound-resistant certification, including gaskets and automatic door bottoms.
2.2.5 Glass stops.
2.2.6 Wood louvers.
2.2.7 **IF SPECIFIED**:
2.2.7.1 Glass or glazing
2.2.7.2 Prefitting and machining for hardware
2.2.7.3 Prehanging and machining for weather-stripping
2.2.7.4 Priming, sealing, and/or finishing
2.2.7.5 Flashing and/or metal edge guards

GENERAL

2 SCOPE (continued)

2.3 TYPICAL EXCLUSIONS

- 2.3.1 Cabinet doors included with casework
- 2.3.2 Wood cores for metal or vinyl clad doors
- 2.3.3 Garage, metal, and fiberglass doors
- 2.3.4 Access doors
- 2.3.5 Metal grills or louvers
- 2.3.6 LPDL or vinyl-faced doors

3 DEFAULT STIPULATION - if not otherwise specified or indicated, flush doors shall be furnished.

3.1 Unless otherwise specified or detailed, all work shall be **CUSTOM GRADE**, solid core, with paint-grade, close-grain hardwood faces and vertical edges.

3.1.1 Core selection is the manufacturer's option.

4 RULES - The following RULES shall govern unless a project's contract documents require otherwise.

These rules are intended to provide a well-defined degree of control over a project's quality of materials and workmanship.

Where E, C, or P is not indicated, the rule applies to all Grades equally.

ERRATA, published on the Associations' websites at www.awinet.org, www.awmac.com, or www.woodworkinstitute.com, shall TAKE PRECEDENCE OVER THESE RULES, subject to their date of posting and a project's bid date.

ARROWS INDICATE TOPIC IS CARRIED FROM ⇑ OR ONTO ⇓ ANOTHER PAGE.

					DESCRIPTION	C	P
4.1					**GENERAL**		
GENERAL	**4.1.1**				These standards are primarily performance-based rather than prescriptive-based, allowing a wide variance of construction methods and/or component configurations, provided the end product meets or exceeds **WDMA's HEAVY DUTY PERFORMANCE DUTY LEVELS** contained within the standards:		
		4.1.1.1			For **FLUSH-VENEERED,** solid-core, fire-rated, sound-resistant, bullet-resistant, lead-lined, and electrostatic-shielded doors - **ANSI/WDMA I.S. - 1A**, (latest edition), **EXCEPT** as **MODIFIED HEREIN.**		
		4.1.1.2			For **STILE** and **RAIL** doors with or without fire-, sound-, or bullet-resistant ratings - **ANSI/WDMA I.S. - 6A**, (latest edition), **EXCEPT AS MODIFIED HEREIN**.		
		4.1.1.3			It is the **RESPONSIBILITY** of the door manufacturer to provide evidence of compliance upon request.		
	4.1.2 TESTING				**IN LIEU OF TESTING** for **WDMA TM-7 & 8**, compliance to the following prescriptive requirements is acceptable:		
		4.1.2.1			If **FACTORY FINISHED**, all four sides shall be finished; top and bottom shall be sealed.		
		4.1.2.2			**FACES** shall be of the same material and construction detail.		
		4.1.2.3			**FLUSH-VENEERED,** solid-core, fire-rated, sound-resistant, bullet-resistant, lead-lined, and electrostatic-shielded doors shall include:		
			4.1.2.3.1		Minimum 5-ply, bonded (stiles and rails securely glued to core) construction.		
			4.1.2.3.2		Minimum WDMA Heavy Duty-rated core. (WDMA TM-10 [latest edition]).		
			4.1.2.3.3		Minimum of 1" (25.4 mm) hardwood stiles and rails.		
			4.1.2.3.4		Blocking for screw-attached hardware at **WDMA** non-heavy duty cores.		
⇓	⇓			4.1.2.3.4.1	Blocking is not required at SCL or staved cores.		

PRODUCT

MATERIAL, MACHINING, AND ASSEMBLY RULES (continued)

	DESCRIPTION	C	P
4.1	**GENERAL** (continued)		
4.1.2	**IN LIEU OF TESTING** (continued)		
4.1.2.4	**STILE** and **RAIL** doors with or without fire-, sound-, or bullet-resistant ratings shall:		
4.1.2.4.1	Be of solid lumber, SCL, LVL, or staved block core construction, with:		
4.1.2.4.1.1	A minimum of 5/8" (15.9 mm) hardwood edgebands and lock and hinge edges, if not solid lumber.		
4.1.2.4.2	Have a minimum of 5" (127 mm) wide stiles, top and intermediate rails.		
4.1.2.4.3	Have a minimum of 8" (203.2 mm) wide bottom rail.		
4.1.2.4.4	Be of dowel, mortise, and tenon joinery, and:		
4.1.2.4.4.1	Dowels shall be a minimum of 1/2" (12.7 mm) in diameter by 5" (127 mm) long, spaced a maximum of 2-1/2" (63.5 mm) on center.		
4.1.2.4.4.2	Top and intermediate rails shall have a minimum of two dowels per joint; and the bottom rail, a minimum of three per joint.		
4.1.2.4.5	Have flat or raised panels a minimum of 5/8" (15.9 mm) in thickness at the tongue of solid lumber or M2 Grade particleboard.		
4.1.3	Aesthetic **GRADE RULES** apply only to the faces visible after installation.		
4.1.4	**LUMBER** shall conform to the requirements established in Section 3.		
4.1.4.1	**HEARTWOOD** or **SAPWOOD** is permitted in Ash, Birch, Maple, Cherry, Elm, and Rotary-Cut Red Oak.		
4.1.4.1.1	If only **HEARTWOOD** or **SAPWOOD** is desired, it shall be so specified.		
4.1.5	**SHEET PRODUCTS** shall conform to the requirements established in Section 4.		
4.1.5.1	Use of **HPDL-BACKED WOOD VENEERS** is permitted if specified or otherwise approved.		
4.1.6	**EXPOSED, SEMI-EXPOSED**, and **CONCEALED** surfaces shall be as listed under **1.2 BASIC CONSIDERATIONS** of this Section.		
4.1.7	For the purpose of this standard, a **BALANCED PANEL** is one that is free from warp that affects serviceability for its intended purpose.		
4.1.8	**EXTERIOR** doors shall be constructed with Type I adhesive.		
4.1.9	**FIRE-RATED** doors shall:		
4.1.9.1	Be of the **FIRE RATING** specified.		
4.1.9.2	Be **CONSTRUCTED** to the manufacturer's standard, conforming with the requirements of their applicable labeling service.		
4.1.9.3	Have **EDGES**, regardless of face species, of manufacturer's approved standard, with species, width, and fire-retardant treatment conforming to the requirements of the applicable labeling service.		
4.1.9.4	Require **PREPARATION**, in accordance with NFPA 80, for locks, latches, hinges, remotely operated or monitored hardware, concealed closures, glass lights, vision panels, louvers, astragals, and laminated overlays to be performed in conformance with the manufacturer's licensing and label service agreement; however:		
4.1.9.4.1	Preparation for **SURFACE-APPLIED HARDWARE**, function holes for mortise locks, holes for labeled viewers, a maximum of 3/4" (19 mm) wood and composite door undercutting, and protection plates may be performed at the jobsite.		
4.1.9.5	Be furnished with the **MANUFACTURER'S** basic hanging and finishing instructions.		
4.1.10	**SOUND-RESISTANT** doors shall:		
4.1.10.1	Be **CONSTRUCTED** to the manufacturer's standard, conforming to the requirements for a minimum STC 50 (Sound Transmission Class) or as specified when tested as an opening unit (versus sealed in place).		
4.1.10.2	Include any required special stops, stop adjusters, gaskets, and automatic threshold-closing devices of the manufacturer's standard.		

9

PRODUCT

MATERIAL, MACHINING, AND ASSEMBLY RULES (continued)

				DESCRIPTION	C	P
⇑ 4.1	**GENERAL** (continued)					
GENERAL	**4.1.11**	**X-RAY** doors shall:				
		4.1.11.1		Be **CONSTRUCTED** to the manufacturer's standard for the type of construction, thickness, edgebands, and moldings.		
		4.1.11.2		**LEAD** thickness shall be a minimum of 1/16" (1.6 mm) or as specified.		
	4.1.12	**BULLET-RESISTANT** doors shall:				
		4.1.12.1		Be constructed to the manufacturer's standard, conforming to the requirements of UL 752 "Bullet-Resisting Equipment" or NIJ (National Institute of Justice) 0108.01 Performance Standards.		
		4.1.12.2		Have a minimum **NIJ** Level 2 protection rating or as specified.		
	4.1.13	**ELECTROSTATIC-SHIELDED** doors shall:				
		4.1.13.1		Be **CONSTRUCTED** to the manufacturer's standard for type of construction, thickness, edgebands, and moldings.		
		4.1.13.2		Have the number and location of electrical leads as specified.		
	4.1.14	**PAIR MATCHING** and **MATCHING IN SETS** is required for flush wood veneer, and shall be:				
		4.1.14.1		**COMPATIBLE** for **COLOR** and **GRAIN**.	●	
		4.1.14.2		**WELL-MATCHED** for **COLOR** and **GRAIN.**		●
	4.1.15	At **STILE** and **RAIL** doors, **PAIR** and **SET MATCH** cannot be achieved and is not required.				
	4.1.16	**EXPOSED FACES** and **EDGES** shall be thoroughly sanded using a minimum of 120-grit sandpaper, and:				
		4.1.16.1		All **EDGES** shall be slightly eased.		
	4.1.17	Overall **DOOR SIZE** for:				
		4.1.17.1		**NON-PREFIT DOORS** (blank) shall be furnished within plus or minus of 1/16" (1.6 mm) for **HEIGHT**, **WIDTH,** and **THICKNESS.**		
		4.1.17.2		**PREFIT DOORS** shall be furnished, sized in:		
			4.1.17.2.1	**WIDTH** within 1/32" (0.8 mm) plus or minus of the specified **FRAME** size, less 1/4" (6.4 mm) in width with a 3-degree bevel on both edges.		
			4.1.17.2.2	**HEIGHT**, within 1/16" (1.6 mm), plus or minus the specified size less the undercut.		
	4.1.18	**BLEED-THROUGH** of glue at a veneer joint that visually affects an applied finish is not permitted.				
	4.1.19	**GLASS** and **GLAZING,** if specified, requires:				
		4.1.19.1		Wood glass stops to be manufacturer-prepared and bundled in appropriately labeled sets, and:		
			4.1.19.1.1	In the absence of specifications or detail, profile shall be optional.		
	4.1.20	**FIRST-CLASS WORKMANSHIP** is required in compliance with these standards.				
4.2	**MATERIAL**					
MATERIAL	4.2.1	Shall be free of **DEFECTS**, both natural and from manufacturing, in excess of those permitted herein.				
	4.2.2	**FIGURE** is not a function of a species grade, and any special desires must be specified.				
	4.2.3	**HARDBOARD** faces shall be 1/8" (3.2 mm) thick, and:				
		4.2.3.1		**TEMPERED** board at **EXTERIOR** locations.		
		4.2.3.2		**STANDARD** board at **INTERIOR** locations.		
	4.2.4	**EXPOSED** surfaces shall be:				
		4.2.4.1		**COMPATIBLE** for color and grain.	●	
		4.2.4.2		**WELL-MATCHED** for color and grain.	●	●
	4.2.5	**CONCEALED** surfaces shall allow nonstructural defects and voids; blocking may be of a compatible species or material other than that of the exposed or semi-exposed surface.				
	4.2.6	At **FLUSH** doors:				
⇓	⇓	4.2.6.1 ⇓		**VENEER FACES** shall be of the species and Grade specified and of sufficient thickness so as not to permit show-through of cross-banding after sanding and/or final finishing.		

9

PRODUCT

MATERIAL, MACHINING, AND ASSEMBLY RULES (continued)

					DESCRIPTION	C	P
4.2 MATERIAL	**MATERIAL** (continued)						
	4.2.6 FLUSH DOORS	At **FLUSH** doors (continued)					
		4.2.6.1 VENEER FACES	**VENEER FACES** shall be of the species and Grade specified (continued)				
			4.2.6.1.1	For **OPAQUE** finish shall be:			
				4.2.6.1.1.1	**SOUND CLOSE-GRAIN** hardwood, **MDO**, **MDF** or **HARDBOARD** at manufacturer's option.	●	
				4.2.6.1.1.2	**MDO**, **MDF** or **HARDBOARD**, at manufacturer's option.		●
			4.2.6.1.2 TRANSPARENT	For **TRANSPARENT** finish:			
				4.2.6.1.2.1	In **SETS** shall be compatible for color and grain.	●	
				4.2.6.1.2.2	With **TRANSOMS** shall be end-matched for color and grain.	●	
				4.2.6.1.2.3	In **SETS** shall be well-matched for color and grain.		●
				4.2.6.1.2.4	**TRANSOMS** shall be continuous-match for color and grain.		●
				4.2.6.1.2.5	Shall be **COMPATIBLE** in **COLOR** and **GRAIN** to the other door faces in the **SAME ROOM** or **AREA**, and:		●
				4.2.6.1.2.5.1	**COORDINATION** of compatibility is the responsibility of the door furnisher.		●
				4.2.6.1.2.6	Doors **ADJACENT** to or that **BECOME A COMPONENT** of other architectural woodwork shall conform to the applicable requirements of **SECTION 4** and **8** for the Grade required.		
				4.2.6.1.2.7	Shall be **HPVA "A" Grade**, with:	●	
				4.2.6.1.2.7.1	**RUNNING-MATCH** and end component less than the HPVA requirement.	●	
				4.2.6.1.2.8	Shall be **HPVA "AA" Grade**, with:		●
				4.2.6.1.2.8.1	**BALANCED CENTER MATCHED.**		●
				4.2.6.1.2.9	Have visible **EDGES** and **REVEALS,** when appropriate, that are:		
				4.2.6.1.2.9.1	**MATCH** species of face.	●	●
				4.2.6.1.2.9.2	**COMPATIBLE** for color and grain.	●	
				4.2.6.1.2.9.3	**WELL-MATCHED** for color and grain.		●
				4.2.6.1.2.9.4	A minimum of 0.020" (0.5 mm) nominal **THICKNESS** that precludes show-through of core.	●	●
				4.2.6.1.2.10	At **STAND-ALONE** doors, face species of Anigre, Ash, Beech, Birch, Cherry, Hickory, African Mahogany, Honduras Mahogany, Makore, Maple, Red Oak, White Oak, Pecan, Poplar, or Walnut shall conform to the following **HPVA DOOR SKIN FACE TABLES** for the allowable veneer characteristics for the Grade required, and:		
				4.2.6.1.2.10.1	**If** not of a species listed above shall conform to **HPVA DOOR SKIN FACE TABLE** as agreed on between the design professional and the manufacturer.		
				4.2.6.1.2.10.2	Including those in **PAIRS** and **SETS.**		
				4.2.6.1.2.10.3	When **CENTER-BALANCE MATCHED**, the width of the outer leaves after trimming shall not exceed 1" (25.4 mm) less than its adjoining leaf.	●	
				4.2.6.1.2.10.4	When **CENTER-BALANCE MATCHED**, the width of the outer leaves after trimming shall not exceed 1/2" (12.7 mm) less than its adjoining leaf.		●

9

PRODUCT

MATERIAL, MACHINING, AND ASSEMBLY RULES (continued)

DESCRIPTION

C P

4.2 MATERIAL (continued)

4.2.6 At **FLUSH** doors (continued)

4.2.6.1 VENEER FACES (continued)

4.2.6.1.2 For **TRANSPARENT** finish (continued)

4.2.6.1.2.11 ANSI/HPVA - HP1 (latest edition) Door skin tables for ASH, BEECH (American or European)**, BIRCH, MAPLE,** and **POPLAR** at stand-alone doors only.

Cut	Plain-Sliced (Flat-Cut), Quarter-Cut, Rotary-Cut					
Grade Description	AA			A		
Color and Matching	Sap (White)	Heart (Red/ Brown)	Natural	Sap (White)	Heart (Red/ Brown)	Natural
Sapwood	Yes	No	Yes	Yes	No	Yes
Heartwood	No	Yes	Yes	No	Yes	Yes
Color Streaks or Spots	Slight			Slight	Yes	
Color Variation	Slight	Yes		Slight	Yes	
Sharp Color Contrast at Joints	Yes, if Slip-, Plank-, or Random-Matched			Yes, if Slip-, Plank-, or Random-Matched		
Type of Matching Book-Matched Slip-Matched Pleasing-Matched	 Yes Specify Not applicable			 Yes Specify Not applicable		
Nominal Minimum Width of Face Components [a] Plain-Sliced Quarter Rotary	 5" (127 mm 3" (76 mm) 5" (127 mm			 4" (102 mm 3" (76 mm) 4" (102 mm)		
Natural Characteristics						
Small Conspicuous Burls & Pin Knots, Combined Average Number	1 per 5 sq ft (2 per 1 m²)			1 per 3 sq ft (4 per 1 m²)		
Conspicuous Burls, Maximum Size	1/4" (6.4 mm)			3/8" (9.5 mm)		
Conspicuous Pin Knots Average Number Maximum Size: Dark Part Total	No			 1 per 8 sq ft (4 per 3 m²) 1/8" (3.2 mm) 1/4" (6.4 mm)		
Scattered Sound and Repaired Knots, Combined Average Number Maximum Size - Sound Maximum Size - Repaired Average No. - Repaired	No			No		
Mineral Streaks	No at Maple, Slight			Slight		
Bark Pockets	No			No		
Worm Tracks	Slight			Slight		
Vine Marks	Slight			Slight		
Cross Bars	Slight			Slight		
Manufacturing Characteristics						
Rough Cut/Ruptured Grain	No			No		
Blended Repaired Tapering Hairline Splits	Two 1/32" x 3" (0.8 mm x 76 mm) on ends only			Two 1/16" x 6" (1.6 mm x 152 mm)		
Repairs	Very small blending			Small blending		
Special Characteristics						
Quartered	1" in 12" (25.4 mm in 305 mm) maximum grain slope; 2-1/2" in 12" (63.5 mm in 305 mm) maximum grain sweep					

Unfilled worm holes, open splits, open joints, open bark pockets, shake, and doze are not allowed in the above Grades.

[a] Outside components will be a different size to allow for edge-trim loss and certain types of matching.

MATERIAL FLUSH DOORS VENEER FACES TRANSPARENT

9

PRODUCT

MATERIAL, MACHINING, AND ASSEMBLY RULES (continued)

DESCRIPTION

C P

4.2 **MATERIAL** (continued)

4.2.6 At **FLUSH** doors (continued)

4.2.6.1 **VENEER FACES** (continued)

4.2.6.1.2 For **TRANSPARENT** finish (continued)

4.2.6.1.2.12 **ANSI/HPVA - HP1 (latest edition) Door skin tables for MAHOGANY** (African or Honduras), **ANIGRE, MAKORE,** and **SAPELE** at stand-alone doors only.

Cut	Plain-Sliced (Flat-Cut), Quarter-Cut, Rotary-Cut	
Grade Description	AA	A
Color and Matching		
Sapwood	No	No
Heartwood	Yes	Yes
Color Streaks or Spots	Slight	Slight
Color Variation	Slight	Slight
Sharp Color Contrast at Joints	Yes, if Slip-, Plank-, or Random-Matched	Yes, if Slip-, Plank-, or Random-Matched
Type of Matching Book-Matched Slip-Matched Pleasing-Matched	 Yes Specify Not Applicable	 Yes Specify Not Applicable
Nominal Minimum Width of Face Components [a] Plain-Sliced Quarter Rotary	 5" (127 mm 3" (76 mm) 5" (127 mm	 4" (102 mm 3" (76 mm) 4" (102 mm)
Natural Characteristics		
Small Conspicuous Burls & Pin Knots, Combined Average Number	1 per 5 sq ft (2 per 1 m^2)	1 per 3 sq ft (4 per 1 m^2)
Conspicuous Burls, Maximum Size	1/4" (6.4 mm)	3/8" (9.5 mm)
Conspicuous Pin Knots Average Number Maximum Size: Dark Part Total	No	 1 per 8 sq ft (4 per 3 m^2) 1/8" (3.2 mm) 1/4" (6.4 mm)
Scattered Sound and Repaired Knots, Combined Average Number Maximum Size - Sound Maximum Size - Repaired Average Number - Repaired	No	No
Mineral Streaks	No	Slight
Bark Pockets	No	No
Worm Tracks	No	No
Vine Marks	Slight	Slight
Cross Bars	Occasional	Occasional
Manufacturing Characteristics		
Rough Cut/Ruptured Grain	No	No
Blended Repaired Tapering Hairline Splits	Two 1/32" x 3" (0.8 mm x 76 mm) on ends only	Two 1/16" x 6" (1.6 mm x 152 mm)
Repairs	Very Small Blending	Small Blending
Special Characteristics		
Quartered	1" in 12" (25.4 mm in 305 mm) maximum grain slope; 2-1/2" in 12" (63.5 mm in 305 mm) maximum grain sweep	

Unfilled worm holes, open splits, open joints, open bark pockets, shake, and doze are not allowed in the above grades.

[a] Outside components will be a different size to allow for edge-trim loss and certain types of matching.

PRODUCT

MATERIAL, MACHINING, AND ASSEMBLY RULES (continued)

DESCRIPTION

C P

4.2 MATERIAL (continued)

4.2.6 At FLUSH doors (continued)

4.2.6.1 VENEER FACES (continued)

4.2.6.1.2 For TRANSPARENT finish (continued)

4.2.6.1.2.13 ANSI/HPVA - HP1 (latest edition) Door skin tables for RED and WHITE OAK at stand-alone doors only.

Cut	Plain-Sliced (Flat-Cut), Quarter-Cut, Rift-and-Comb Grade, Rotary-Cut			
Grade Description	AA		A	
	Red Oak	White Oak	Red Oak	White Oak
Color and Matching				
Sapwood	No		5% [a]	Yes [a]
Heartwood	Yes		Yes	
Color Streaks or Spots	Yes		Yes	
Color Variation	Slight		Slight	
Sharp Color Contrast at Joints	Yes, if Slip-, Plank-, or Random-Matched		Yes, if Slip-, Plank-, or Random-Matched	
Type of Matching Book-Matched Slip-Matched Pleasing-Matched	 Yes Specify Not Applicable		 Yes Specify Not Applicable	
Nominal Minimum Width of Face Components [a, b, c] Plain-Sliced Quarter Rotary	 5" (127 mm) 3" (76 mm) 5" (127 mm		 4" (102 mm 3" (76 mm) 4" (102 mm)	
Natural Characteristics				
Small Conspicuous Burls & Pin Knots, Combined Average Number	1 per 4 sq ft (3 per 1 m²)		1 per 2-2/3 sq ft (4 per 1 m²)	
Conspicuous Burls - Maximum Size	1/4" (6.4 mm)		3/8" (9.5 mm)	
Conspicuous Pin Knots Average Number Maximum Size: Dark Part Total	No		 1 per 3 sq ft (4 per 1 m²) 1/8" (3.2 mm) 1/4" (6.4 mm)	
Scattered Sound and Repaired Knots, Combined Average Number Maximum Size - Sound Maximum Size - Repaired Average No. - Repaired	No		No	
Mineral Streaks	No		Slight, Blending	
Bark Pockets	No		No	
Worm Tracks	No		No	
Vine Marks	No		Slight	
Cross Bars	Slight		Slight	
Manufacturing Characteristics				
Rough Cut/Ruptured Grain	No		No	
Blended Repaired Tapering Hairline Splits	Two 1/32" x 3" on (0.8 mm x 76 mm) at ends only		Two 1/16" x 6" (1.6 mm x 152 mm)	
Repairs	Very Small Blending		Small Blending	
Special Characteristics				
Ray Fleck (Flake)	Slight, Blending Quarter-Cut Unlimited		Slight, Blending Quarter-Cut Unlimited	
Slope and Sweep - Quarter and Rift Comb Grain	1" in 12" (25.4 mm in 305 mm) max. grain slope; 2-1/2" in 12" 63.5 mm in 305 mm) max. grain sweep 1/2" in 12" (12.7 mm in 305 mm) max. grain slope; 1/2" in 12" (12.7 mm in 305 mm) max. grain sweep			

Unfilled worm holes, open splits, open joints, open bark pockets, shake, and doze are not allowed in the above grades.

[a] Sap is allowed in rotary only, unless otherwise specified.

[b] 10% sap is allowed in rift, comb, and plain-sliced; 20% sap is allowed in rotary.

[c] Outside components will be a different size to allow for the edge-trim loss and certain types of matching.

9

PRODUCT

MATERIAL, MACHINING, AND ASSEMBLY RULES (continued)

DESCRIPTION

C P

4.2 **MATERIAL** (continued)

4.2.6 At **FLUSH** doors (continued)

4.2.6.1 **VENEER FACES** (continued)

4.2.6.1.2 For **TRANSPARENT** finish (continued)

4.2.6.1.2.14 **ANSI/HPVA - HP1 (latest edition) Door skin tables for PECAN and HICKORY** at stand-alone doors only.

Cut	Plain-Sliced (Flat-Cut), Quarter-Cut, Rotary-Cut	
Grade Description	**AA**	**A**
Color and Matching		
Sapwood	Yes	Yes
Heartwood	Yes	Yes
Color Streaks or Spots	Yes	Yes
Color Variation	Yes	Yes
Sharp Color Contrast at Joints	Yes, if Slip-, Plank-, or Random-Matched	Yes, if Slip-, Plank-, or Random-Matched
Type of Matching Book-Matched Slip-Matched Pleasing-Matched	 Yes Specify Not Applicable	 Yes Specify Not Applicable
Nominal Minimum Width of Face Components [a] Plain-Sliced Quarter Rotary	 5" (127 mm) 3" (76 mm) 5" (127 mm	 4" (102 mm 3" (76 mm) 4" (102 mm)
Natural Characteristics		
Small Conspicuous Burls & Pin Knots, Combined Average Number	1 per 1 sq ft (11 per 1 m^2)	2 per 1 sq ft (22 per 1 m^2)
Conspicuous Burls - Maximum Size	1/4"	3/8"
Conspicuous Pin Knots [b] Average Number Maximum Size: Dark Part Total	 1 per 2 sq ft (6 per 1 m^2) 1/8" (3.2 mm) 1/4" (6.4 mm)	 2 per 1 sq ft (22 per 1 m^2) 1/8" (3.2 mm) 1/4" (6.4 mm)"
Scattered Sound and Repaired Knots, Combined Average Number Maximum Size - Sound Maximum Size - Repaired Average Number - Repaired	No	No
Mineral Streaks	Slight	Slight
Bark Pockets	No	Small, Occasional
Worm Tracks	No	Slight
Vine Marks	Slight	Occasional
Cross Bars	Slight	Occasional
Manufacturing Characteristics		
Rough Cut/Ruptured Grain	No	No
Blended Repaired Tapering Hairline Splits	Two 1/32" x 3" (0.8 mm x 76 mm) at ends only	Two 1/16" x 6" (1.6 mm x 152 mm)
Repairs	Very Small Blending	Small Blending
Special Characteristics		
Bird Peck [c]	No	Slight
Knife Marks	Knife marks might occur in these dense species.	
Quartered	1" in 12" (25.4 mm in 305 mm) maximum grain slope; 2-1/2" in 12" (63.5 mm in 305 mm) maximum grain sweep	

Unfilled worm holes, open splits, open joints, open bark pockets, and doze are not allowed in the above grades.

[a] Outside components will be a different size to allow for edge-trim loss and certain types of matching.

[b] For Pecan and Hickory, conspicuous pin knots mean sound knots 1/4" (6.4 mm) or less in diameter with dark centers larger than 1/16" (1.6 mm). Blending pin knots are sound knots 1/4" (6.4 mm) or less in diameter with dark centers 1/16" (1.6 mm) or less and are allowed in all grades.

[c] To achieve a more rustic appearance, bird peck shall be specified.

9

PRODUCT

MATERIAL, MACHINING, AND ASSEMBLY RULES (continued)

DESCRIPTION

C P

4.2 MATERIAL (continued)

4.2.6 At FLUSH doors (continued)

4.2.6.1 VENEER FACES (continued)

4.2.6.1.2 For TRANSPARENT finish:

4.2.6.1.2.15 **ANSI/HPVA - HP1 (latest edition) Door skin tables for WALNUT and CHERRY** at stand-alone doors only.

Cut	Plain-Sliced (Flat-Cut), Quarter-Cut, Rotary-Cut	
Grade Description	AA	A
Color and Matching		
Sapwood [a]	No	No [a]
Heartwood	Yes	Yes
Color Streaks or Spots	Slight	Slight
Color Variation	Slight	Slight
Sharp Color Contrast at Joints	Yes if Slip-, Plank-, or Random-Matched	Yes if Slip-, Plank-, or Random-Matched
Type of Matching Book-Matched Slip-Matched Pleasing-Matched	 Yes Specify --	 Yes Specify --
Nominal Minimum Width of Face Components [b] Plain-S. Quarter Rotary	 5" (127 mm) 3" (76 mm) 5" (127 mm)	 4" (102 mm) 3" (76 mm) 4" (102 mm)
Natural Characteristics (except as listed below, natural characteristics are not restricted)		
Small Conspicuous Burls & Pin Knots - Combined Average Number	1 per 4 sq ft (3 per 1 m²)	1 per 1-1/3 sq ft (8 per 1 m²)
Conspicuous Burls - Maximum Size	1/4" (6.4 mm)	3/8" (9.5 mm)
Conspicuous Pin Knots [c] Average Number Maximum Size: Dark Part Total	 1 per 5 sq ft (3 per 1 m²) 1/8" (3.2 mm) 1/4" (6.4 mm)	 1 per 2 sq ft (6 per 1 m²) 1/8" (3.2 mm) 1/4" (6.4 mm)
Scattered Sound and Repaired Knots-Combined Average Number Maximum Size - Sound Maximum Size - Repaired Average No. - Repaired	No	No
Mineral Streaks	Slight	Slight
Bark Pockets	No	No
Worm Tracks	No	No
Vine Marks	Slight	Occasional
Cross Bars	Slight	Occasional
Manufacturing Characteristics		
Rough Cut/Ruptured Grain	No	No
Blended Repaired Tapering Hairline Splits	Two 1/32" x 3" (0.8 mm x 76 mm) on panel ends only	Two 1/16" x 6" (1.6 mm x 152 mm)
Repairs	Very Small Blending	Small Blending
Special Characteristics (except as listed below, natural characteristics are not restricted)		
Gum Spots	Occasional Gum Spots permitted in Cherry	Occasional Gum Spots permitted in Cherry
Quartered	1" in 12" (25.4 mm in 305 mm) maximum grain slope; 2-1/2" in 12" (63.4 mm in 305 mm) maximum grain sweep	

Unfilled worm holes, open splits, open joints, open bark pockets, and doze are not allowed in the above grades.

[a] Sapwood is allowed in Grades A and B; however, the percentage shall be agreed upon between the buyer and the seller.

[b] Outside components will be a different size to allow for edge-trim loss and certain types of matching.

[c] For Walnut and Cherry, conspicuous pin knots mean sound knots 1/4" (6.4 mm) or less in diameter with dark centers larger than 1/16" (1.6 mm). Blending pin knots are sound knots 1/4" (6.4 mm) or less in diameter with dark centers 1/16" (1.6 mm) or less and are allowed in all grades.

MATERIAL — FLUSH DOORS — VENEER FACES — TRANSPARENT

9

PRODUCT

MATERIAL, MACHINING, AND ASSEMBLY RULES (continued)

DESCRIPTION

					C	P
4.2 MATERIAL	**MATERIAL** (continued)					
	4.2.6	At **FLUSH** doors (continued)				
		4.2.6.2	**CROSS-BAND VENEERS** shall be of **WOOD VENEER** or **ENGINEERED COMPOSITE**, and:			
			4.2.6.2.1	**PARTICLEBOARD** cross-band veneers are not permitted.		
		4.2.6.3	**HORIZONTAL** edges shall run the full width between stiles without a gap.			
	4.2.7	At **STILE AND RAIL** doors:				
		4.2.7.1	For **OPAQUE** finish, face and edges shall be solid stock of close-grain hardwood, veneer of sound close-grain hardwood or MDO, at the manufacturer's option.			
		4.2.7.2	For **TRANSPARENT** finish, face and edges shall be:			
			4.2.7.2.1	**SOLID** stock of species specified.		
			4.2.7.2.2	Veneer of **HPVA "A"** Grade.	●	
			4.2.7.2.3	Veneer of **HPVA "AA"** Grade.		●

4.3 MACHINING and ASSEMBLY

4.3.1 **ANSI/WDMA I.S. 1A (latest edition) HEAVY DUTY PERFORMANCE DUTY LEVEL** is the required minimum, and:

- 4.3.1.1 If a higher **EXTRA HEAVY DUTY** or lower **STANDARD DUTY** Performance Duty Level is required, it shall have been specified.
- 4.3.1.2 Wood veneer or HPDL banding requires a minimum 1" (25.4 mm) solid hardwood backing; SCL is not permitted.

4.3.2 Minimum **WDMA PERFORMANCE DUTY VALUES * -** Reprinted with permission from the (Standard), Window & Door Manufacturers Association, Chicago, Il

WDMA PERFORMANCE DUTY

Performance Attribute	Duty Level STANDARD DUTY	 HEAVY DUTY	 EXTRA HEAVY DUTY
Adhesive Bond Durability WDMA TM-6 (latest edition)		Type II	
Cycle Slam WDMA TM-7 (latest edition)	250,000 cycles	500,000 cycles	1,000,000 cycles
Hinge-Loading WDMA TM-8 (latest edition)	400 lbs (2110 N)	475 lbs (2110 N)	550 lbs (2440 N)
Door Finish, Various ASTM test methods	Catalyzed Lacquer	Conversion Varnish	Catalyzed Polyurethane
Screwholding WDMA TM-10 (latest edition) Door Face, unblocked Door Face with optional blocking ** Vertical Door Edge Horizontal Door Edge (with hardware attached)	 400 lbs (2110 N) 700 lbs (3110 N) 400 lbs (2110 N) 180 lbs (1060 N)	 475 lbs (2110 N) 700 lbs (3110 N) 475 lbs (2110 N) 240 lbs (1060 N)	 550 lbs (2440 N) 700 lbs (3110 N) 550 lbs (2440 N) 300 lbs (1330 N)
Telegraph WDMA T-1 (latest edition)		Maximum 0.010" per 3" (0.25 mm per 76 mm) span	
Warp Tolerance WDMA T-2 (latest edition)		Maximum 0.25" per 3'6" x 7'0" (6.35 mm per 1050 mm x 2100 mm) door section	
Squareness WDMA T-3 (latest edition)		Maximum diagonal variance 0.125" (3.17 mm)	

* Other formulations may exhibit similar performance characteristics, but must meet or exceed the performance levels for the systems specified to be considered equal.

** Blocking may be specified in certain hardware applications where the specifier deems the frequency and severity of use so dictates. Blocking is a material used for improved screwholding at hardware attachment points (not required in core types such as SCL or staved lumber).

4.3.3 Of **EXTERIOR** doors require:

- 4.3.3.1 **TYPE I ADHESIVE**.
- 4.3.3.2 **FLASHING**, when specified, to be installed with the ends embedded in a caulking compound.
- 4.3.3.3 **APPLIED MOLDINGS** to be assembled and applied with **TYPE I ADHESIVE.**

4.3.4 Of **INTERIOR** doors require **TYPE I** or **II ADHESIVE** at the manufacturer's option.

9

PRODUCT

MATERIAL, MACHINING, AND ASSEMBLY RULES (continued)

Section	Group	No.	Description	C	P
4.3 MACHINE & ASSEMBLY			**MACHINING and ASSEMBLY** (continued)		
	MOLDINGS	**4.3.5**	Require **APPLIED MOLDINGS**:		
		4.3.5.1	To be solid stuck and free of finger joints.		
		4.3.5.2	To be securely and soundly attached, in contact with the adjacent surface.		
		4.3.5.3	For **OPAQUE** finish:		
		4.3.5.3.1	To be **CLOSE-GRAIN HARDWOOD** of a species of the manufacturer's option.		
		4.3.5.3.2	Require moldings to be **PRIMED** when the doors are factory-primed.		
		4.3.5.4	For **TRANSPARENT** finish:		
		4.3.5.4.1	To be of the **SAME SPECIES** and **GRADE** as the face veneer.		
		4.3.5.4.2	Require molding to be prefinished if doors are factory prefinished.		
		4.3.5.5	At **HPDL**-faced doors:		
		4.3.5.5.1	To be **CLOSE-GRAIN HARDWOOD** at the manufacturer's option.		
		4.3.5.5.2	Require molding to be **STAINED** or **PAINTED** to match the face, if so specified.		
		4.3.6	Require **GLAZING MATERIAL** to be secured in place with mitered wood-glazing beads or clips with glass **BEDDED** in sealant that squeezes out on both sides.		
		4.3.6.1	**GLAZING SEALANTS** shall be a quality, elastic-type compound, which is designed for bedding glazing materials or is recommended for such use by the sealant manufacturer.		
		4.3.6.2	Glazing gaskets.		
	EXPOSED SURFACES	**4.3.7**	Of **EXPOSED SURFACES** shall comply with the following smoothness requirements (see Item 7.1 in **COMPLIANCE**):		
		4.3.7.1	**SHARP EDGES** shall be eased with a fine abrasive.		
		4.3.7.2	**TOP FLAT WOOD** surfaces; those that can be sanded with a drum or wide belt sander:		
		4.3.7.2.1	120-grit sanding	●	
		4.3.7.2.2	150-grit sanding		●
		4.3.7.3	**MOLDED** and **SHAPED WOOD** surfaces:		
		4.3.7.3.1	120-grit sanding		
		4.3.7.4	**TURNED WOOD** surfaces:		
		4.3.7.4.1	120-grit sanding	●	
		4.3.7.4.2	180-grit sanding		●
		4.3.7.5	**CROSS-SANDING**, excluding turned surfaces, is not allowed.		
		4.3.7.6	**TEAR-OUTS**, **KNIFE NICKS**, or **HIT-OR-MISS** machining is not permitted.		
		4.3.7.6.1	**KNIFE MARKS** are not permitted where sanding is required.		
		4.3.7.6.2	**GLUE** or **FILLER**, if used, shall be inconspicuous and match the adjacent surface for smoothness.		
	JOINTS	**4.3.8**	Of **JOINTS** at **ASSEMBLED WOODWORK** shall:		
		4.3.8.1	Be neatly and accurately made.		
		4.3.8.2	Be **SECURELY GLUED**, with:		
		4.3.8.2.1	**ADHESIVE** residue removed from all exposed and semi-exposed surfaces.		
		4.3.8.3	Be **REINFORCED** with glue blocks where essential.		
		4.3.8.4	Utilize clamp nail, biscuit-spline, butterfly, scarf, or dowel joinery.	●	
		4.3.8.5	Utilize biscuit spline, butterfly, scarf, or dowel joinery.		●
		4.3.8.6	Be **MECHANICALLY FASTENED** with nails or screws where practical, with:		
		4.3.8.6.1	Fasteners at solid wood countersunk.		
		4.3.8.6.2	Fasteners at solid wood in molding quirks or reliefs where possible.		
		4.3.8.7	**SHALL NOT PERMIT** fasteners at exposed surfaces of HPDL or overlay sheet products.		

PRODUCT

MATERIAL, MACHINING, AND ASSEMBLY RULES (continued)

DESCRIPTION						C	P
4.3 MACHINE & ASSEMBLY	**MACHINING and ASSEMBLY** (continued)						
	4.3.8 JOINTS	Of **JOINTS** at **ASSEMBLED WOODWORK** (continued)					
		4.3.8.8	Require **FLUSHNESS VARIATIONS** at exposed surfaces when mitered or butted (see Test D illustrations in **COMPLIANCE**) not to exceed:				
			4.3.8.8.1	**INTERIOR**			
				4.3.8.8.1.1	0.005" (0.1 mm)	●	
				4.3.8.8.1.2	0.001" (0.03 mm)		●
			4.3.8.8.2	**EXTERIOR**			
				4.3.8.8.2.1	0.025" (0.6 mm)	●	
				4.3.8.8.2.2	0.015" (0.4 mm)		●
		4.3.8.9 GAPS	Require **GAPS** at exposed surfaces when mitered or butted (see Test A illustrations in **COMPLIANCE**) not to exceed:				
			4.3.8.9.1	**INTERIOR**			
				4.3.8.9.1.1	0.025" (0.6 mm) wide by 20% of the joint length	●	
				4.3.8.9.1.2	0.015" (0.4 mm) wide by 20% of the joint length		●
			4.3.8.9.2	**EXTERIOR**			
				4.3.8.9.2.1	0.050" (1.3 mm) wide by 30% of the joint length	●	
				4.3.8.9.2.2	0.025" (0.6 mm) wide by 30% of the joint length		●
		4.3.8.10 GAPS	Require **GAPS** at exposed surfaces at parallel members (see Test B illustrations in **COMPLIANCE**) not to exceed:				
			4.3.8.10.1	**INTERIOR**			
				4.3.8.10.1.1	0.025" x 6" (0.6 mm x 152 mm) and shall not occur within 60" (1524 mm) of a similar gap.	●	
				4.3.8.10.1.2	0.015" x 3" (0.4 mm x 76 mm) and shall not occur within 72" (1829 mm) of a similar gap.		●
			4.3.8.10.2	**EXTERIOR**			
				4.3.8.10.2.1	0.050" x 8" (1.3 mm x 203 mm) and shall not occur within 26" (660 mm) of a similar gap.	●	
				4.3.8.10.2.2	0.025" x 6" (0.6 mm x 152 mm) and shall not occur within 30" (762 mm) of a similar gap.		●
		4.3.8.11 GAPS	Require **GAPS** at exposed surfaces when mitered or butted (see Test C illustrations in **COMPLIANCE**) not to exceed:				
			4.3.8.11.1	**INTERIOR**			
				4.3.8.11.1.1	0.025" (0.6 mm)	●	
				4.3.8.11.1.2	0.015" (0.4 mm)		●
			4.3.8.11.2	**EXTERIOR**			
				4.3.8.11.2.1	0.050" (1.3 mm)	●	
				4.3.8.11.2.2	0.025" (0.6 mm)		●
		4.3.8.12	With **FILLER** is:				
			4.3.8.12.1	Allowed if inconspicuous when viewed at 24" (610 mm).		●	
			4.3.8.12.2	**NOT ALLOWED.**			●
	4.3.9	Of **FLUSH** doors:					
		4.3.9.1	Shall be **3-, 5-, OR 7-PLY** at the manufacturer's option, unless specified otherwise.				

9

PRODUCT

MATERIAL, MACHINING, AND ASSEMBLY RULES (continued)

	DESCRIPTION	C	P
4.3	**MACHINING and ASSEMBLY** (continued)		
4.3.9	Of **FLUSH** doors (continued)		
4.3.9.2	**CORES**, conforming to the minimum requirements of WDMA - I.S. 1-A (latest edition), at:		
4.3.9.2.1	**SOLID CORE**, shall be particleboard, MDF, agrifiber, staved lumber, SCL, or fire-resistant composite.		
4.3.9.2.2	**HOLLOW CORE**, shall be honeycomb, and the:		
4.3.9.2.2.1	**STILE** and/or **RAIL WIDTHS** remaining after sizing or prefitting to be no less than:		
4.3.9.2.2.1.1	1" (25.4 mm) at **LOCK** and **HINGE** stiles.		
4.3.9.2.2.1.2	6" (152.4 mm) at **TOP**, **BOTTOM,** and intermediate **LOCK** rails.		
4.3.9.3	Require **CUTOUTS:**		
4.3.9.3.1	At **NON-RATED** doors to (unless allowed by individual manufacturer's warranty):		
4.3.9.3.1.1	Not exceed 40% of the door area, for the combined area of all cutouts for lights or louvers.		
4.3.9.3.1.2	Not exceed one-half the door height.		
4.3.9.3.1.3	Be at least 5" (127 mm) from door edges, adjacent cutouts, or hardware mortises.		
4.3.9.3.2	At **RATED** doors:		
4.3.9.3.2.1	Be governed by the individual manufacturer's fire-rated approval and/or NFPA 80 for the combined area and location of cutouts for lights or louvers.		
4.3.9.3.2.2	Be at least 6" (152 mm) from door edges, adjacent cutouts, or hardware mortises.		
4.3.9.3.3	Be **SEALED** with at least two coats of exterior sealer for exterior applications.		
4.3.9.4	Require **TRANSOM PANEL:**		
4.3.9.4.1	**BOTTOM RAILS** to be:		
4.3.9.4.1.1	**TYPE 2**, which allows side rails to run through.	●	
4.3.9.4.1.2	Compatible for color to the vertical edgeband of the door.	●	
4.3.9.4.1.3	**TYPE 1**, full width.		●
4.3.9.4.1.4	Well-matched for color to the vertical edgeband of the door.		●
4.3.9.4.2	**TOP RAILS** of doors with rabbeted transoms to be:		
4.3.9.4.2.1	Compatible in color to the vertical edgeband of the door.	●	
4.3.9.4.2.2	Of the same species as the vertical edgeband of the door.		●
4.3.9.4.3	**FACES**, for transparent finish be:		
4.3.9.4.3.1	End-matched to the door.	●	
4.3.9.4.3.2	Continuous-matched to the door.		●
4.3.9.5	Requires **DUTCH DOORS** without an applied shelf to have the top edge of the bottom leaf and the bottom edge of the top leaf, if rabbeted:		
4.3.9.5.1	For **OPAQUE** finish to be close-grain hardwood of a species of the manufacturer's option.		
4.3.9.5.2	For **TRANSPARENT** finish to be:		
4.3.9.5.2.1	Of a species compatible in color with the face veneer.	●	
4.3.9.5.2.2	The same species as the face veneer.		●

PRODUCT

MATERIAL, MACHINING, AND ASSEMBLY RULES (continued)

Section					DESCRIPTION	C	P
4.3 MACHINE & ASSEMBLY	**MACHINING and ASSEMBLY** (continued)						
	4.3.9 FLUSH DOORS	Of **FLUSH** doors (continued)					
		4.3.9.5	Require **DUTCH DOORS** (continued)				
			4.3.9.5.3	For **HPDL**, to be close-grain hardwood of a species of the manufacturer's option, and:			
				4.3.9.5.3.1	**PAINTED** or **STAINED** to match the face laminate, if edges are so required.		
		4.3.9.6 VERTICAL EDGES	Require **VERTICAL EDGES**:				
			4.3.9.6.1	For **OPAQUE** finished doors:			
				4.3.9.6.1.1	Be **PRIMED,** if doors are factory-primed.		
				4.3.9.6.1.2	Be **CLOSE-GRAIN HARDWOOD** lumber, veneer, or MDO over backer of the manufacturer's option.		
				4.3.9.6.1.3	Permit one **FINGER JOINT** at either veneer edge that is tight, not raised, or not visible from a distance of 48" (1219 mm).	●	
				4.3.9.6.1.4	**FINGER JOINTS** are not permitted.		●
			4.3.9.6.2	For **TRANSPARENT** finished doors:			
				4.3.9.6.2.1	Permit one **FINGER JOINT** at either veneer edge that is tight, not raised, uniform in color and grain, without discoloration, or not visible from a distance of 72" (1829 mm).	●	
				4.3.9.6.2.2	**FINGER JOINTS** are not permitted.		●
				4.3.9.6.2.3	Be **HARDWOOD** lumber or veneer over backer, compatible in color with the face veneer.	●	
				4.3.9.6.2.4	Allow **FLAT-GRAIN DOUGLAS FIR** at VG Douglas Fir-faced doors.	●	
				4.3.9.6.2.5	Be the same species as the face veneer.		●
				4.3.9.6.2.6	Be **PREFINISHED,** if the doors are prefinished.		●
				4.3.9.6.2.7	If the manufacturer's **FIRE-RATED DOOR APPROVAL** prevents the use of matching vertical edges, then the species permitted under their approval shall be allowed.		●
				4.3.9.6.2.8	Require **VG GRAIN DOUGLAS FIR** at VG Douglas Fir-faced doors.		●
			4.3.9.6.3	For **HPDL FACED** doors:			
				4.3.9.6.3.1	Be unfinished **CLOSE-GRAIN HARDWOOD** of manufacturer's option, and:	●	
				4.3.9.6.3.1.1	At opaque finish, permit **FINGER JOINTS** at either edge that are tight, not raised, or not visible from a distance of 48" (1219 mm).	●	
				4.3.9.6.3.1.2	At transparent finish, permit one **FINGER JOINT** at either edge that is tight, not raised, uniform in color and grain, without discoloration, and not visible from a distance of 24" (610 mm).	●	
				4.3.9.6.3.2	Be **HPDL** or **PVC** to match the face laminate or **HARDWOOD** stained and finished to match the face laminate at the manufacturer's option.		●

9

PRODUCT

MATERIAL, MACHINING, AND ASSEMBLY RULES (continued)

DESCRIPTION		C	P
4.3 MACHINE & ASSEMBLY	**MACHINING and ASSEMBLY** (continued)		
4.3.10	**STILE AND RAIL** doors:		
4.3.10.1	For **EXTERIOR** applications shall be glued up with **TYPE I ADHESIVE**.		
4.3.10.2	For **INTERIOR** applications shall be glued up with **TYPE I** or **II ADHESIVE** at the manufacturer's option.		
4.3.10.3	**SPECIAL** stile or rail requirements to accommodate specified hardware shall prevail.		
4.3.10.4	Of **SOFTWOOD** shall be solid-stock or veneer construction.		
4.3.10.5	Of **HARDWOOD** shall be:		
4.3.10.5.1	**SOLID-STOCK** or **VENEER** construction.	●	
4.3.10.5.2	**VENEER** construction.		●
4.3.10.6	The construction of the **STILES** and **RAILS**:		
4.3.10.6.1	If **SOLID STOCK** requires:		
4.3.10.6.1.1	**ONE-PIECE** solid stock.		
4.3.10.6.1.2	**TWO-PIECE** balanced lamination, with opposing grain.		
4.3.10.6.1.3	**THREE-PIECE** lamination, balanced outer pieces, with opposing grain, and:		
4.3.10.6.1.3.1	Face veneers shall be uniform in thickness.		
4.3.10.6.1.4	No **FINGER JOINTS**.		
4.3.10.6.1.5	**EDGE GLUING** in accordance with Section 3.		
4.3.10.6.2	If **VENEERED** requires:		
4.3.10.6.2.1	**CORES** of either **MDF** (medium-density fiberboard), **SCL** (structural composite lumber), edge-glued wood blocks/strips (staved core), particleboard, agrifiber, laminated veneer lumber core, fire-resistant composite core, and speciality door core types.		
4.3.10.6.3	If **STAVED CORE** (edge-glued wood block/strips), it shall be of one species in any one door, and the:		
4.3.10.6.3.1	**STAVES** (block/strips):		
4.3.10.6.3.1.1	Shall not exceed 2" (50.8 mm) in **WIDTH**.		
4.3.10.6.3.1.2	May be of any **LENGTH.**		
4.3.10.6.3.1.3	Shall have **STAGGERED END JOINTS** in adjacent rows.		
4.3.10.6.3.1.4	Shall not permit **VOIDS** between end joints.		
4.3.10.6.3.1.5	Shall not permit open **SURFACE DEFECTS**.		
4.3.10.6.3.1.6	Shall be bonded together under pressure.		
4.3.10.7	With **PANELS** require:		
4.3.10.7.1	They be finished to a uniform thickness and fit snuggly into the stile and rail retention groves, and that:		
4.3.10.7.1.1	They **FLOAT** in their method of retention, and that:		
4.3.10.7.1.1.1	**MECHANICAL FASTENING** is not permitted.		
4.3.10.7.2	**MDF** (medium-density fiberboard) may be used for opaque finish, and:		
4.3.10.7.2.1	At **EXTERIOR** doors, it shall be moisture-resistant.		
4.3.10.7.3	**GRAIN** shall run the long direction of the panel.		

(Side labels: MACHINE & ASSEMBLY; STILE & RAIL DOORS; CONSTRUCTION; PANELS)

PRODUCT

MATERIAL, MACHINING, AND ASSEMBLY RULES (continued)

DESCRIPTION							C	P
4.3 ASSEMBLY	**MACHINING and ASSEMBLY** (continued)							
	4.3.10 STILE & RAIL DOORS	Of **STILE AND RAIL** doors (continued)						
		4.3.10.7 PANELS	With **PANELS** (continued)					
			4.3.10.7.4	At **FLAT** type, they be at least:				
				4.3.10.7.4.1	1/4" (6.4 mm) in thickness at 1-3/8" (35 mm) thick doors.			
				4.3.10.7.4.2	1/2" (12.7 mm) in thickness at 1-3/4" (44 mm) thick doors.			
				4.3.10.7.4.3	5/8" (16 mm) in thickness at 2-1/4" (57 mm) thick doors.			
			4.3.10.7.5 RAISED	At **RAISED** type, they shall be:				
				4.3.10.7.5.1	At least 3/4" (19 mm) in thickness at 1-3/8" (35 mm) thick doors.			
				4.3.10.7.5.2	At least 1-1/8" (28.6 mm) in thickness at 1-3/4" (44 mm) thick doors.			
				4.3.10.7.5.3	At least 1-1/2" (38.1 mm) in thickness at 2-1/4" (57 mm) thick doors.			
				4.3.10.7.5.4	Constructed of either:			
					4.3.10.7.5.4.1	**SOLID STOCK** in opening widths not to exceeding 14" (356 mm).		
					4.3.10.7.5.4.2	**RIM-BANDED** or **MEMBRANE-PRESSED** panel construction.		
				4.3.10.7.5.5	**MITERED** when rim-banded.			
		4.3.10.8	Require **JOINERY:**					
			4.3.10.8.1	To be either **MORTISE** and **TENON** or **DOWELED** and glued under pressure so that the stiles, rails, mullions, and muntins are all bonded together.				
			4.3.10.8.2	At **FACES** to finish true, with stile and rail intersections and other copes well fitted.				
			4.3.10.8.3	**STICKINGS** to be clean cut and smooth.				

EXECUTION

5 PREPARATION & QUALIFICATION REQUIREMENTS (unless otherwise specified)

5.1 **CARE, STORAGE, and BUILDING CONDITIONS** shall be in compliance with the requirements set forth in Section 2 of these standards.

5.1.1 Severe damage to the woodwork can result from noncompliance. **THE MANUFACTURER AND/OR INSTALLER OF THE WOODWORK SHALL NOT BE HELD RESPONSIBLE FOR ANY DAMAGE THAT MIGHT DEVELOP BY NOT ADHERING TO THE REQUIREMENTS.** 9

5.2 **CONTRACTOR IS RESPONSIBLE FOR:**

5.2.1 Furnishing and installing structural members, grounds, blocking, backing, furring, brackets, or other anchorage required for architectural woodwork installation that becomes an integral part of walls, floors, or ceilings to which architectural woodwork shall be installed.

5.2.1.1 In the absence of contract documents calling for the contractor to supply the necessary blocking/backing in the wall or ceilings, either through inadvertence or otherwise, the architectural woodwork installer shall not proceed with the installation until such time as the blocking/backing is installed by others.

5.2.1.2 Preparatory work done by others shall be subject to inspection by the architectural woodwork installer, and may be accepted or rejected for cause prior to installation.

5.2.1.2.1 **WALL, CEILING,** and/or opening variations in excess of 1/4" (6.4 mm) or **FLOORS** in excess of 1/2" (12.7 mm) in 144" (3658 mm) of being plumb, level, flat, straight, square, or of the correct size are not acceptable for the installation of architectural woodwork, nor is it the responsibility of the installer to scribe or fit to tolerances in excess of such.

EXECUTION

INSTALLATION RULES (continued)

5 PREPARATION & QUALIFICATION REQUIREMENTS (continued)

5.2 CONTRACTOR IS RESPONSIBLE FOR (continued)

5.2.2 Priming the architectural woodwork in accordance with the contract documents prior to its installation.

5.3 INSTALLER IS RESPONSIBLE FOR:

5.3.1 Having adequate equipment and experienced craftsmen to complete the installation in a first-class manner.

5.3.2 Checking all architectural woodwork specified and studying the appropriate portions of the contract documents, including these standards and the reviewed shop drawings to familiarize themselves with the requirements of the Grade specified, understanding that:

5.3.2.1 Appearance requirements of Grades apply only to surfaces visible after installation.

5.3.2.2 For transparent finish, special attention needs to be given to the color and grain of the various woodwork pieces to ensure they are installed in compliance with the Grade specified.

5.3.2.3 Installation site is properly ventilated, protected from direct sunlight, excessive heat and/or moisture, and that the HVAC system is functioning and maintaining the appropriate relative humidity and temperature.

5.3.2.4 Required priming of woodwork has been completed before its install.

5.3.2.5 Doors have been acclimated to the field conditions for a minimum of 72 hours before installation is commenced.

5.3.2.6 Doors specifically built or assembled in sequence for match of color and grain are installed to maintain that same sequence.

6 RULES - The following RULES shall govern unless a project's contract documents require otherwise.

These rules are intended to provide a well-defined degree of control over a project's quality of materials, workmanship, or installation.

Where E, C, or P is not indicated, the rule applies to all Grades equally.

ERRATA, published on the Associations' websites at www.awinet.org, www.awmac.com, or www.woodworkinstitute.com, shall TAKE PRECEDENCE OVER THESE RULES, subject to their date of posting and a project's bid date.

ARROWS INDICATE TOPIC IS CARRIED FROM ⇑ OR ONTO ⇓ ANOTHER PAGE.

			DESCRIPTION	C	P
6.1	**GENERAL:**				
	6.1.1		Aesthetic **GRADE RULES** apply only to exposed and semi-exposed surfaces visible after installation.		
G	**6.1.2**		Door **INSTALLERS** shall be furnished with an approved:		
E		6.1.2.1	Hardware schedule and required templates.		
N		6.1.2.2	Set of metal-frame shop drawings, including the locations of the hardware preparations.		
E	6.1.3		**PREFIT** and **PREMACHINED** doors are to be installed in accordance with the manufacturer's data.		
R	**6.1.4**		Doors for **TRANSPARENT FINISH** shall be installed:		
A		6.1.4.1	**COMPATIBLE** in color and grain.	●	
L		6.1.4.2	**WELL-MATCHED** for color and grain.		●
⇓	6.1.5		Doors in **BLUE PRINT MATCHED WALL-PANELED AREAS** shall be installed by the paneling installer.		
	6.1.6		Doors shall not have their **UTILITY** or **STRUCTURAL STRENGTH** impaired in fitting them to the opening, applying hardware, preparing for lights, louvers, or plant-ons, or other detailing.		

EXECUTION

INSTALLATION RULES (continued)

					DESCRIPTION (C P)
6.1 GENERAL	**GENERAL** (continued)				
	6.1.7	Doors at **FIRE-DOOR ASSEMBLIES**, including 20-, 30-, 45-, 60-, and 90-minute rated, shall be prepared for locks, latches, hinges, remotely operated or monitored hardware, concealed closers, glass lights, vision panels, louvers, astragals, and laminated overlays in conformance to the manufacturer's Label Service requirements, and:			
		6.1.7.1	**LABELS** are prohibited from being removed from fire doors.		
	6.1.8	**DOORS** and their **ACCESSORIES** shall be hung plumb and level within 1/16" (1.6 mm) of the height and width of the door assembly.			
	6.1.9	**WHEN INSTALLED**, doors shall operate smoothly and easily without binding, and:			
		6.1.9.1	**PAIRS** of doors, when closed, shall be within 1/16" (1.6 mm) of flush at the meeting edge.		
	6.1.10	**INSTALLER MODIFICATIONS** shall comply to the material, machining, and assembly rules within the **PRODUCT** portion of this section and the applicable finishing rules in Section 5.			
	6.1.11	Door **FACES** shall not extend more than:			
		6.1.11.1	1/16" (1.6 mm) beyond the face of the jamb.		
		6.1.11.2	1/8" (3.2 mm) behind the face of the jamb.		
	6.1.12	**FITTING** for:			
		6.1.12.1	**WIDTH** requires the door to be trimmed equally from both sides; however, on:		
			6.1.12.1.1	**FIRE-RATED DOORS**, in order to preserve the label, they shall be trimmed per the manufacturer's requirements.	
		6.1.12.2	**HEIGHT** requires doors not to have trimmed top or bottom rails more than 3/4" (19 mm), and:		
			6.1.12.2.1	**FIRE-RATED DOORS** shall only be trimmed on the bottom rail.	
			6.1.12.2.2	When cutting to length, extreme care shall be used to prevent chipping of veneer.	
	6.1.13	**CLEARANCE** between the door and frame members shall be a maximum of 1/8" (3.2 mm) on the hinge and lock sides, the top of the door, and between the meeting edges of doors in pairs, and:			
		6.1.13.1	Installer shall not be responsible for clearances in excess of these dimensions if the door manufacturer made an error on prefit widths or locations for mortise hardware.		
		6.1.13.2	Clearance at the bottom of the door shall be as specified on non-rated doors and conform to NFPA 80 on fire-rated doors.		
HARDWARE	**6.1.14**	**HARDWARE** shall be installed:			
		6.1.14.1	In locations and by methods of attachment appropriate for the specific door construction.		
			6.1.14.1.1	Templates for specific hardware preparation and installation are typically available from the manufacturer or the Door Hardware Institute (DHI).	
		6.1.14.2	With appropriate **FASTENERS**, and:		
			6.1.14.2.1	Operate as intended.	
			6.1.14.2.2	Preferably use threaded-to-the-head wood screws on nonrated doors.	
			6.1.14.2.3	Use threaded-to-the-head wood screws on all fire-rated doors.	
			6.1.14.2.4	Require pilot holes to be drilled for all screws.	
			6.1.14.2.5	All screws shall be applied into each piece of hardware.	
	6.1.15	**LEAF HINGES** on:			
		6.1.15.1	**EXTERIOR** or **SOLID-CORE** doors shall require:		
			6.1.15.1.1	A minimum of two hinges for doors up to 60" (1524 mm) in height.	
			6.1.15.1.2	A minimum of three hinges for doors over 60" (1524 mm) in height, and:	
				6.1.15.1.2.1	An additional hinge for each additional 30" (762 mm) or portion thereof in door height.
			6.1.15.1.3	Space between hinges be equal.	

9

EXECUTION

INSTALLATION RULES (continued)

Section	No.	No.	No.	DESCRIPTION	C	P
6.1 GENERAL				**GENERAL** (continued)		
	6.1.15			**LEAF HINGES** on (continued)		
		6.1.15.2		**INTERIOR HOLLOW CORE** doors weighing less than 50 lbs (22.7 kg) and not exceeding 90" (2286 mm) in height shall require only two hinges.		
	6.1.16			**EXTERIOR DOOR CUTOUTS** for lights or louvers shall be protected from water from entering the door core by a satisfactory method such as metal flashing at the bottom of the cutout.		
	6.1.17			**TEMPORARY DISTORTIONS** (warp) will usually disappear when humidity is equalized, and doors seldom need to be replaced.		
	6.1.18			**REPAIRS** are allowed, provided they are made neatly and are inconspicuous when viewed at:		
		6.1.18.1		48" (1219 mm)	●	
		6.1.18.2		24" (610 mm)		●
	6.1.19 WOODWORK			**WOODWORK** such as **APPLIED TRIM** shall be:		
		6.1.19.1		**SECURELY** fastened and tightly fitted with flush joints.		
			6.1.20.1.1	Joinery shall be **CONSISTENT** throughout the project.		
		6.1.19.2		Of **MAXIMUM** available and/or practical lengths.		
		6.1.19.3		**PROFILED** or **SELF-MITERED** when trim ends are exposed.	●	
		6.1.19.4		**SELF-MITERED** when trim ends are exposed.		●
		6.1.19.5		**MITERED** at outside corners.		
		6.1.19.6		**MITERED** at inside corners.	●	
		6.1.19.7		**COPED** at inside corners.		
		6.1.19.8		**INSTALLED** plumb, level, square, and flat within 1/8" (3.2 mm) in 96" (2438 mm).		
			6.1.19.8.1	**GROUNDS** and hanging systems set plumb and true.		
		6.1.19.9		Installed **FREE OF**:		
			6.1.19.9.1	Warp, twisting, cupping, and/or bowing that cannot be held true.		
			6.1.19.9.2	Open joints, visible machine marks, cross-sanding, tear-outs, nicks, chips, and/or scratches.		
			6.1.19.9.3	Natural defects exceeding the quantity and/or size limits defined in Sections 3 and 4.		
		6.1.19.10		**SMOOTH** and **SANDED** without **CROSS SCRATCHES** in conformance to the **PRODUCT** portion of this section.		
	6.1.20 GAPS			**GAPS** (see Test A-C illustrations in **COMPLIANCE**):		
		6.1.20.1		Shall **NOT EXCEED** 30% of a joint's length, with:		
			6.1.20.1.1	**FILLER** or **CAULKING** allowed, if color-compatible.		
		6.1.20.2		Of **WOOD** to **WOOD** shall not exceed:		
			6.1.20.2.1	At **FLAT** surfaces:		
			6.1.20.2.1.1	0.025" (0.65 mm) in width.	●	
			6.1.20.2.1.2	0.012" (0.3 mm) in width.		●
			6.1.20.2.2	At **SHAPED** surfaces:		
			6.1.20.2.2.1	0.050" (1.3 mm) in width.	●	
			6.1.20.2.2.2	0.025" (0.65 mm) in width.		●

EXECUTION

INSTALLATION RULES (continued)

					DESCRIPTION	C	P
⇑ 6.1 GENERAL	**GENERAL** (continued)						
	6.1.21				**FLUSHNESS** of joinery (see Test D illustrations in **COMPLIANCE**):		
	FLUSHNESS	**6.1.21.1**			Of **WOOD** to **WOOD** shall not exceed:		
			6.1.21.1.1		At **FLAT** surfaces:		
				6.1.21.1.1.1	0.025" (0.65 mm)	●	
				6.1.21.1.1.2	0.012" (0.3 mm)		●
			6.1.21.1.2		At **SHAPED** surfaces:		
				6.1.21.1.2.1	0.050" (1.3 mm)	●	
				6.1.21.1.2.2	0.025" (0.65 mm)		●
	6.1.22				**AREAS** of installation shall be left broom clean.		
		6.1.22.1			Debris shall be removed and dumped in containers provided by the contractor.		
		6.1.22.2			Items installed shall be cleaned of pencil or ink marks.		
	6.1.23				Entire installation shall present **FIRST-CLASS WORKMANSHIP** in compliance with these standards.		

COMPLIANCE

7 **FABRICATED** and **INSTALLED** woodwork shall be tested for compliance to these standards as follows:

7.1 **SMOOTHNESS** of exposed surfaces:

7.1.1 **KCPI** (Knife Cuts Per Inch) is determined by holding the surfaced board at an angle to a strong light source and counting the visible ridges per inch, usually perpendicular to the profile.

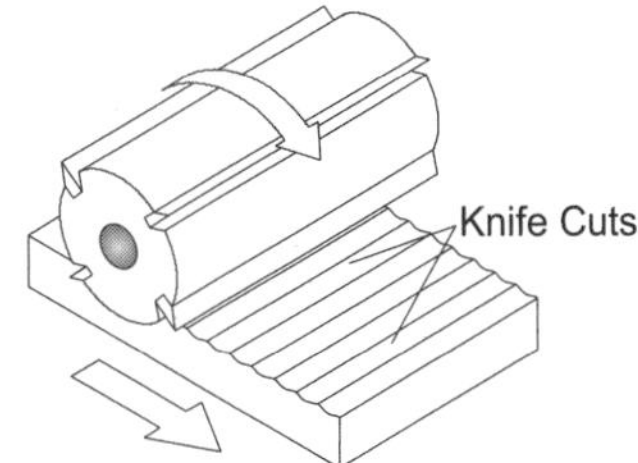

7.1.2 **SANDING** is checked for compliance by sanding a sample piece of the same species with the required grit of abrasive.

7.1.2.1 Observation with a hand lens of the prepared sample and the material in question will offer a comparison of the scratch marks of the abrasive grit.

7.1.2.2 Reasonable assessment of the performance of the finished product will be weighed against absolute compliance with the standard.

7.1.2.3 A product is sanded sufficiently smooth when knife cuts are removed and any remaining sanding marks are or will be concealed by applied finishing coats.

7.1.2.4 Handling marks and/or grain raising due to moisture or humidity in excess of the ranges set forth in this standard shall not be considered a defect.

7.2 **GAPS, FLUSHNESS,** and **FLATNESS** of product and installation:

7.2.1 Maximum gaps between exposed components shall be tested with a feeler gauge at points designed to join where members contact or touch.

9

COMPLIANCE

7 FABRICATED and INSTALLED (continued)

7.2 GAPS, FLUSHNESS, and FLATNESS of product and installation (continued)

7.2.2 Joint length shall be measured with a ruler with minimum 1/16" (1 mm) divisions and calculations made accordingly.

7.2.3 Reasonable assessment of the performance of the finished product will be weighed against absolute compliance with the standards.

7.2.4 The following is intended to provide examples of how and where compliance testing is measured:

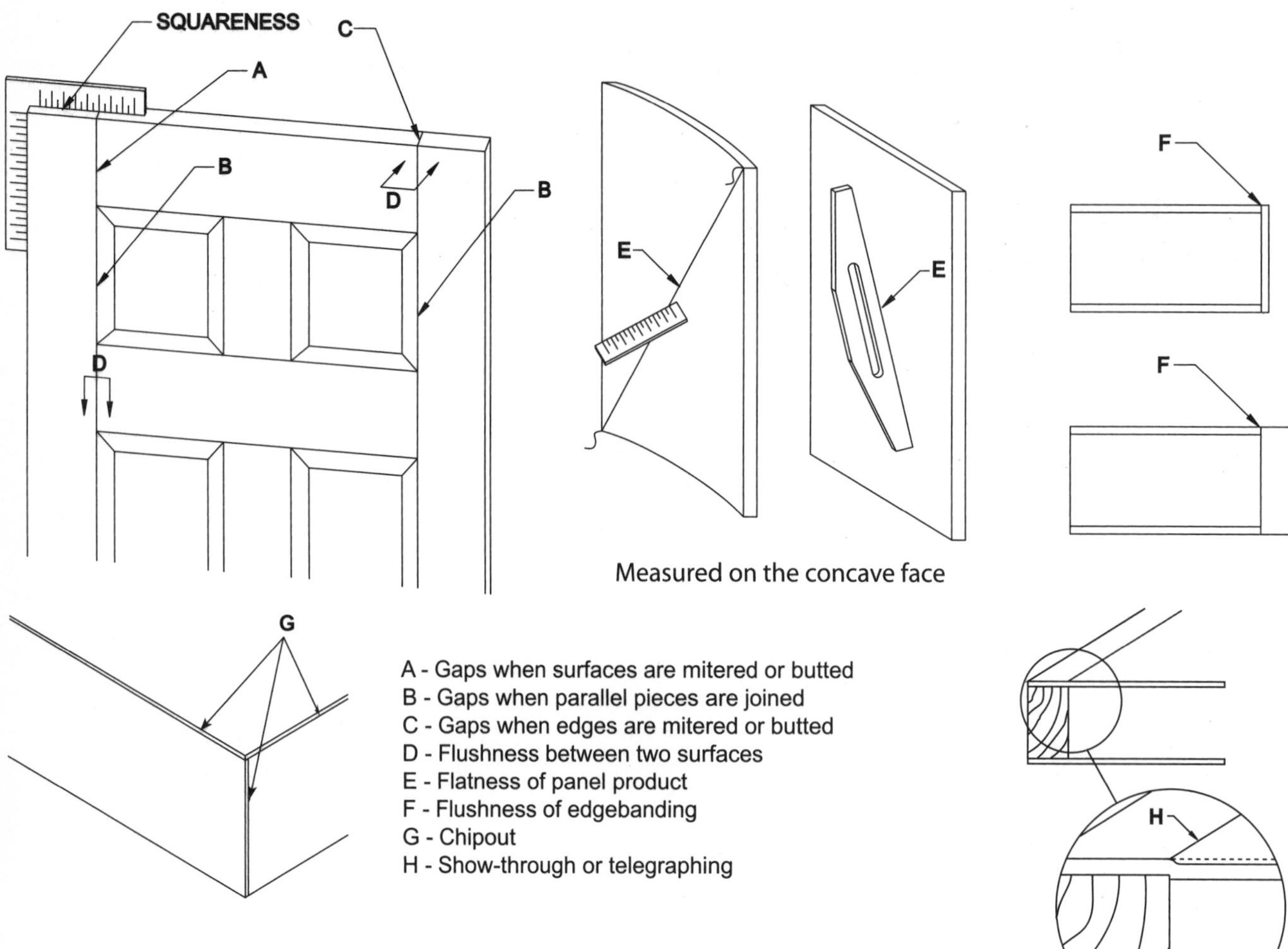

Architectural Woodwork Standards

SECTION - 10

CASEWORK

SECTION 10 ✦ CASEWORK

(Including Wood, Decorative Laminate, and Solid Phenolic-Faced Casework)

GENERAL

1 INFORMATION

1.1 GRADES

1.1.1 These standards are characterized in three Grades of quality that may be mixed within a single project. Limitless design possibilities and a wide variety of lumber and veneer species, along with decorative laminates, factory finishes, and profiles are available in all three Grades.

1.1.2 **ECONOMY GRADE** defines the minimum quality requirements for a project's workmanship, materials, or installation and is typically reserved for woodwork that is not in public view, such as in mechanical rooms and utility areas.

1.1.3 **CUSTOM GRADE** is typically specified for and adequately covers most high-quality architectural woodwork, providing a well-defined degree of control over a project's quality of materials, workmanship, or installation.

1.1.4 **PREMIUM GRADE** is typically specified for use in those areas of a project where the highest level of quality, materials, workmanship, and installation is required.

1.1.5 **MODIFICATIONS** by the contract documents shall govern if in conflict with these standards.

1.2 BASIC CONSIDERATIONS

1.2.1 This section addresses three distinct categories of casework based on the exterior exposed face:

1.2.1.1 **WOOD CASEWORK** with wood faces for transparent or opaque finish.

1.2.1.2 **DECORATIVE LAMINATE CASEWORK** with HPDL or LPDL faces.

1.2.1.3 **SOLID PHENOLIC CASEWORK** with solid phenolic faces.

1.2.2 **ACCEPTABLE REQUIREMENTS** of lumber and/or sheet products used within this woodwork product section are established by Sections 3 and 4, unless otherwise modified herein.

1.2.3 **CONTRACT DRAWINGS** and/or **SPECIFICATIONS**, furnished by the design professional, shall clearly indicate or delineate all material, fabrication, installation, and applicable building code/regulation requirements, and:

1.2.3.1 It is the design professional's responsibility to evaluate the fastening methods required and modify as appropriate to ensure adequate blocking and fasteners are used for the project conditions.

1.2.4 Compliance to **SEISMIC** requirements for casework fabrication and restraint, where required, shall be so specified.

1.2.4.1 Within the United States, the International Building Code (IBC) establishes these minimum requirements; however, some states have expanded on the U.S. requirements.

1.2.4.2 Within Canada, the National Building Code (NBC) establishes these minimum requirements; however, some provinces and cities have expanded on the Canadian requirements.

1.2.5 Any **CHEMICAL-** or **STAIN-RESISTANT** surface requirements must be specified.

1.2.5.1 Consider the chemical and staining agents that might be used on or near the surfaces.

1.2.5.1.1 Chemical resistance and stain resistance are affected by concentration, time, temperature, humidity, housekeeping, and other factors; it is recommended that actual samples are tested in a similar environment with those agents.

1.2.5.2 Common guidelines can be found by referring to:

1.2.5.2.1 NEMA LD3 (latest edition) for chemical resistance.

1.2.5.2.2 ASTM D3023 and C1378 (latest editions) for stain resistance.

1.2.5.2.3 SEFA #3 - Recommendations for Work Surfaces.

GENERAL

1.2 **BASIC CONSIDERATIONS** (continued)

1.2.5 Any **CHEMICAL-** or **STAIN-RESISTANT** surface requirements (continued)

1.2.5.2 Common guidelines can be found by referring to (continued)

1.2.5.2.4 SEFA's Standard Chemical/Concentration list for wood finishing; see Section 5 and Appendix A.

1.2.6 Any **ABRASION-RESISTANT** surface requirements must be specified.

1.2.6.1 Consider the abrasive elements that might be used on or near the surfaces.

1.2.6.2 Common guidelines can be found at:

1.2.6.2.1 ASTM C501 (latest edition).

1.2.6.2.2 NEMA LD3-3.13 (latest edition).

1.2.6.2.3 NEMA LD3.7 (latest edition).

1.2.7 Without **SPECIFICATIONS TO THE CONTRARY**, all:

1.2.7.1 **CORNERS** created by tall, wall, or base casework will create non-usable space.

1.2.7.2 **FINISHED ENDS** shall be **INTEGRAL**, not applied secondarily, except:

1.2.7.2.1 Applied end panels are allowed at Solid Phenolic casework.

1.2.7.2.2 Applied end panels are allowed at teaching wall assemblies.

1.2.7.3 **BASE/TOE** shall be **INTEGRAL** (constructed as an integral part of the cabinet body) or **SEPARATE** (constructed as a separate member) at the option of the manufacturer.

1.2.7.4 **STORAGE**, **JANITOR CLOSET,** and/or **UTILITY ROOM CABINETS** shall be built in conformance to **ECONOMY GRADE**, regardless of the overall project's Grade requirement, unless specified otherwise.

1.2.7.4.1 If material is **SOLID PHENOLIC**, **PREMIUM GRADE** shall be provided.

1.2.8 Surfaces behind **PRESENTATION PANELS** (such as white board or tack board) are treated as:

1.2.8.1 **SEMI-EXPOSED** at Economy Grade and Custom Grade.

1.2.8.2 **EXPOSED** at Premium Grade.

1.2.9 **TOE BASE HEIGHT VARIANCE** due to floor variations is not considered a defect. Casework is required to be installed level; shimming of the toe base, not to exceed 1/2" (12.7 mm), is acceptable. Floor variations exceeding 1/2" (12.7 mm) shall be corrected before cabinets are installed; however, correction of such is not the responsibility of the cabinet installer.

1.2.10 **EXPOSED SURFACES**:

1.2.10.1 **EXPOSED EXTERIOR SURFACES**, defined as all exterior surfaces exposed to view, **INCLUDE**:

1.2.10.1.1 All surfaces visible when doors and drawers are closed, including knee spaces.

1.2.10.1.2 Underside of cabinet bottoms over 42" (1067 mm) above the finished floor, including cabinet bottoms behind light valances and the bottom edge of light valances.

1.2.10.1.3 Cabinet tops under 80" (2032 mm) above the finished floor, or if 80" (2032 mm) and over and visible from an upper building level or floor.

1.2.10.1.4 Visible front edges of stretchers, ends, divisions, tops, bottoms, shelves, and nailers.

1.2.10.1.5 Sloping tops of cabinets that are visible.

GENERAL

1.2 **BASIC CONSIDERATIONS** (continued)

1.2.10 **EXPOSED SURFACES** (continued)

1.2.10.2 **EXPOSED INTERIOR SURFACES**, defined as all interior surfaces exposed to view in open casework or behind transparent doors, **INCLUDE**:

1.2.10.2.1 Shelves, including edgebanding.

1.2.10.2.2 Divisions and partitions.

1.2.10.2.3 Interior face of ends (sides), backs, and bottoms (including pull-outs). Also included are the interior surfaces of cabinet top members 36" (914 mm) or more above the finished floor.

1.2.10.2.4 Interior face of door and applied drawer fronts.

1.2.11 **SEMI-EXPOSED SURFACES**, defined as those interior surfaces only exposed to view when doors or drawers are opened, **INCLUDE**:

1.2.11.1 Shelves, including edgebanding.

1.2.11.2 Divisions.

1.2.11.3 Interior face of ends (sides), backs, and bottoms (including a bank of drawers). Also included are the interior surfaces of cabinet top members 36" (914 mm) or more above the finished floor.

1.2.11.4 Drawer sides, sub-fronts, backs, and bottoms.

1.2.11.5 The underside of cabinet bottoms between 24" (610 mm) and 42" (1067 mm) above the finished floor.

1.2.11.6 Security and dust panels or drawer stretchers.

1.2.12 **CONCEALED SURFACES**, defined as those exterior or interior surfaces that are covered or not normally exposed to view, **INCLUDE**:

1.2.12.1 Toe space unless otherwise specified.

1.2.12.2 Sleepers, stretchers, and solid sub-tops.

1.2.12.3 The underside of cabinet bottoms less than 24" (610 mm) above the finished floor.

1.2.12.4 The flat tops of cabinets 80" (2032 mm) or more above the finished floor, except if visible from an upper floor or building level.

1.2.12.5 The three non-visible edges of adjustable shelves.

1.2.12.6 The underside of countertops, knee spaces, and drawer aprons.

1.2.12.7 The faces of cabinet ends of adjoining units that butt together.

1.2.13 **GRADE LIMITATIONS**:

1.2.13.1 **SOLID PHENOLIC** casework is offered only in **PREMIUM GRADE**.

1.2.14 **FINISH** by surface definition at:

1.2.14.1 **EXPOSED EXTERIOR SURFACES** for:

1.2.14.1.1 **WOOD** casework requires:

1.2.14.1.1.1 For **TRANSPARENT** finish:

1.2.14.1.1.1.1 **WOOD** of specified species, cut, and match.

GENERAL

1.2 **BASIC CONSIDERATIONS** (continued)

1.2.14 **FINISH** by surface definition (continued)

1.2.14.1 **EXPOSED EXTERIOR SURFACES** (continued)

1.2.14.1.1 **WOOD** casework requires (continued)

1.2.14.1.1.2 For **OPAQUE** finish at:

1.2.14.1.1.2.1 **ECONOMY GRADE:**

1.2.14.1.1.2.1.1 Particleboard, MDF, MDO, softwood plywood, hardwood plywood, or solid stock.

1.2.14.1.1.2.2 **CUSTOM GRADE:**

1.2.14.1.1.2.2.1 MDF, MDO, close-grain hardwood plywood, or solid stock.

1.2.14.1.1.2.3 **PREMIUM GRADE:**

1.2.14.1.1.2.3.1 MDF and MDO.

1.2.14.1.2 **DECORATIVE LAMINATE** casework requires at:

1.2.14.1.2.1 **ECONOMY GRADE:**

1.2.14.1.2.1.1 **LPDL** of specified color or pattern.

1.2.14.1.2.2 **CUSTOM** and **PREMIUM GRADE**:

1.2.14.1.2.2.1 **HPDL** of specified color or pattern.

1.2.14.1.3 **SOLID PHENOLIC** casework requires for **PREMIUM GRADE**:

1.2.14.1.3.1 **SOLID PHENOLIC** of specified color or pattern.

1.2.14.2 **EXPOSED INTERIOR SURFACES** for:

1.2.14.2.1 **ECONOMY GRADE** at:

1.2.14.2.1.1 **WOOD** casework requires:

1.2.14.2.1.1.1 For **TRANSPARENT** finish:

1.2.14.2.1.1.1.1 **LPDL** or **WOOD** of the manufacturer's option.

1.2.14.2.1.1.2 For **OPAQUE** finish at:

1.2.14.2.1.1.2.1 Particleboard, MDF, MDO, softwood plywood, hardwood plywood, or solid stock of manufacturer's option.

1.2.14.2.1.2 **DECORATIVE LAMINATE** casework requires:

1.2.14.2.1.2.1 **LPDL** of the manufacturer's option.

1.2.14.2.2 **CUSTOM GRADE** at:

1.2.14.2.2.1 **WOOD** casework requires:

1.2.14.2.2.1.1 For **TRANSPARENT** finish:

1.2.14.2.2.1.1.1 **WOOD** of the same species as the exposed exterior surface.

GENERAL

1.2 **BASIC CONSIDERATIONS** (continued)

1.2.14 **FINISH** by surface definition (continued)

1.2.14.2 **EXPOSED INTERIOR SURFACES** (continued)

1.2.14.2.2 **CUSTOM GRADE** at (continued)

1.2.14.2.2.1 **WOOD** casework requires (continued)

1.2.14.2.2.1.2 For **OPAQUE** finish at:

1.2.14.2.2.1.2.1 MDF, MDO, close-grain hardwood plywood, or solid stock of manufacturer's option.

1.2.14.2.2.2 **DECORATIVE LAMINATE** casework requires:

1.2.14.2.2.2.1 **HPDL** or **LPDL** compatible in color, grain, or pattern of manufacturer's option.

1.2.14.2.3 **PREMIUM GRADE** at:

1.2.14.2.3.1 **WOOD** casework requires:

1.2.14.2.3.1.1 For **TRANSPARENT** finish:

1.2.14.2.3.1.1.1 **WOOD** of same the species and cut as the exposed exterior surface.

1.2.14.2.3.1.2 For **OPAQUE** finish at:

1.2.14.2.3.1.2.1 Use of MDF and MDO of manufacturer's option.

1.2.14.2.3.2 **DECORATIVE LAMINATE** casework requires:

1.2.14.2.3.2.1 **HPDL,** the same as the exposed exterior surface.

1.2.14.2.3.3 **SOLID PHENOLIC** casework requires:

1.2.14.2.3.3.1 **SOLID PHENOLIC,** the same as the exposed exterior surface.

1.2.14.3 **SEMI-EXPOSED SURFACES** for:

1.2.14.3.1 **WOOD** casework require for both **TRANSPARENT** and **OPAQUE** finish at:

1.2.14.3.1.1 **ECONOMY GRADE**:

1.2.14.3.1.1.1 **WOOD** of the manufacturer's option of species, MDO, MDF, particleboard, or **LPDL** of the manufacturer's option of color.

10

1.2.14.3.1.2 **CUSTOM GRADE**:

1.2.14.3.1.2.1 **WOOD** of the manufacturer's option of species, or **LPDL** of the manufacturer's option of color.

1.2.14.3.1.3 **PREMIUM GRADE**:

1.2.14.3.1.3.1 **WOOD** of a compatible species to the exposed.

1.2.14.3.2 **DECORATIVE LAMINATE** casework at all **GRADES** requires:

1.2.14.3.2.1 **LPDL** of the manufacturer's option of color.

1.2.14.3.3 **SOLID PHENOLIC** casework requires:

1.2.14.3.3.1 **SOLID PHENOLIC** of the mill's option of color.

GENERAL

1.2 **BASIC CONSIDERATIONS** (continued)

1.2.14 **FINISH** by surface definition (continued)

1.2.14.4 **CONCEALED SURFACES** for all Grades at:

1.2.14.4.1 **DECORATIVE LAMINATE**, **WOOD**, and **SOLID PHENOLIC** casework require:

1.2.14.4.1.1 The manufacturer's option.

1.2.15 **ILLUSTRATIONS** of cabinet surface terminology:

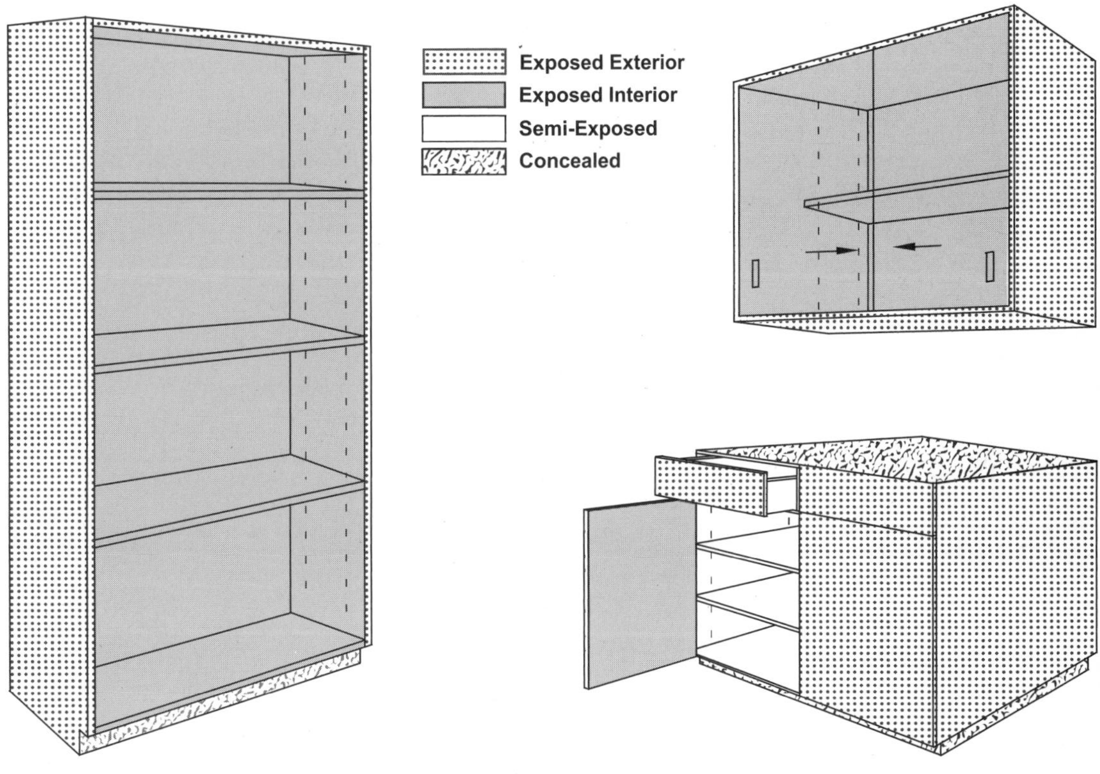

1.2.16 **DOOR** and applied **DRAWER FRONT** profiles are for illustration purposes only and are not intended to be duplicated exactly**:**

1.2.16.1 Common **EDGE PROFILES**:

1.2.16.1.1 Square edge with thin applied band.

1.2.16.1.2 Radius edge with thick applied band.

1.2.16.1.3 Square edge with thick applied band

1.2.16.1.4 Square edge with inset band.

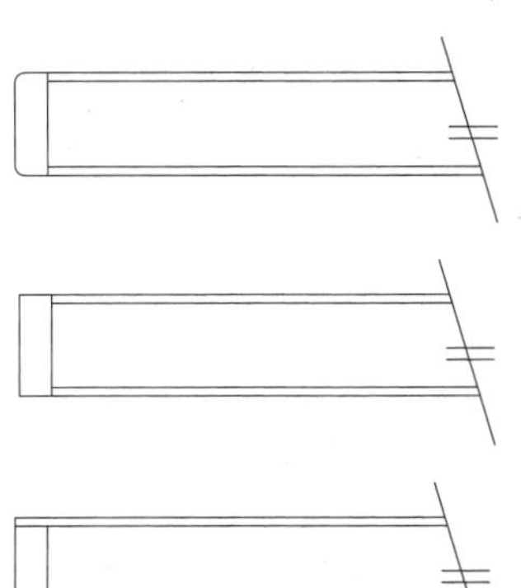

GENERAL

1.2 **BASIC CONSIDERATIONS** (continued)

1.2.16 **DOOR** and applied **DRAWER FRONT** profiles (continued)

1.2.16.1 Common **EDGE PROFILES** (continued)

1.2.16.1.5 Lipped edge with inset band

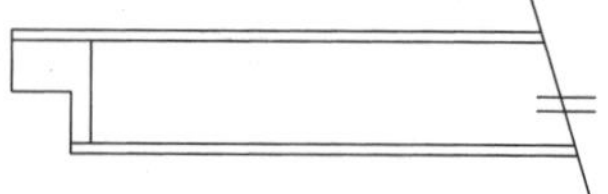

1.2.16.2 Common **RETENTION PROFILES**:

1.2.16.2.1 Fixed panel.

1.2.16.2.2 Removable stop.

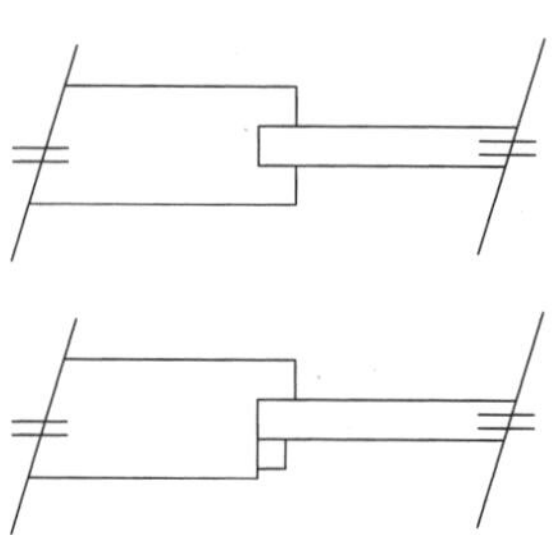

1.2.17 Terminology of casework **CONSTRUCTION TYPE** is delineated as:

1.2.17.1 **TYPE A** - Frameless construction where the front edge of the cabinet body components are edgebanded.

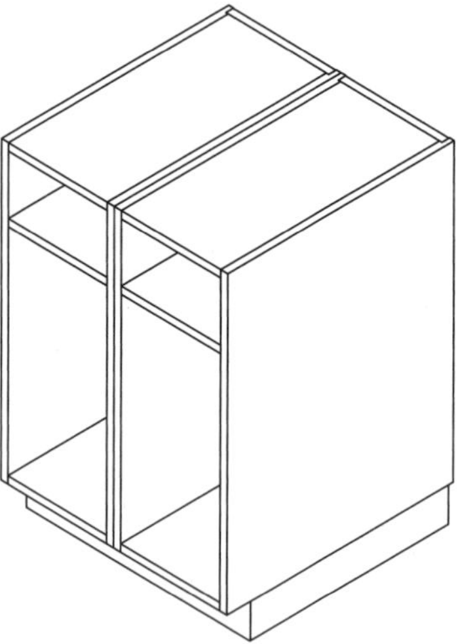

1.2.17.2 **TYPE B** - Face-frame construction where the front edge of the cabinet body components are overlaid with a frame.

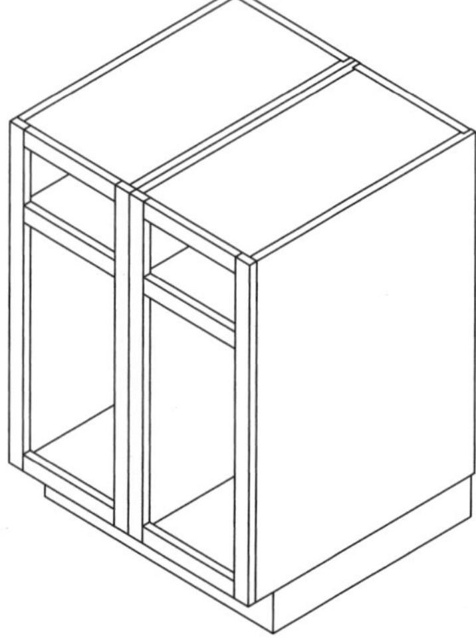

1.2.17.3 **TYPE** selection shall be the **MANUFACTURER'S OPTION**, unless specified otherwise.

GENERAL

1.2 **BASIC CONSIDERATIONS** (continued)

1.2.18 Terminology for the cabinet and door **INTERFACE STYLE** is delineated as:

1.2.18.1 **STYLE 1 - OVERLAY** including flush, reveal, or lipped, as illustrated below:

1.2.18.1.1 **TYPE A CONSTRUCTION:**

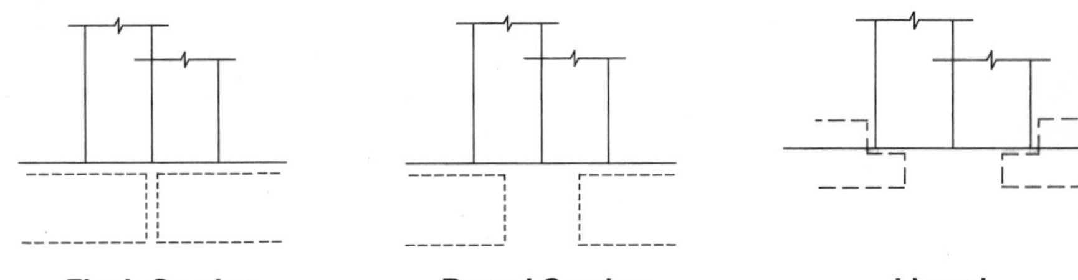

Flush Overlay **Reveal Overlay** **Lipped**

1.2.18.1.2 **TYPE B CONSTRUCTION:**

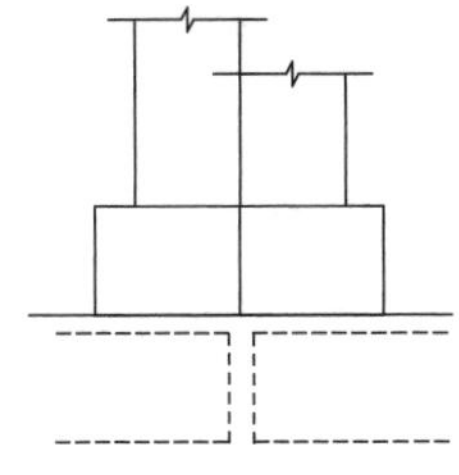

Flush Overlay

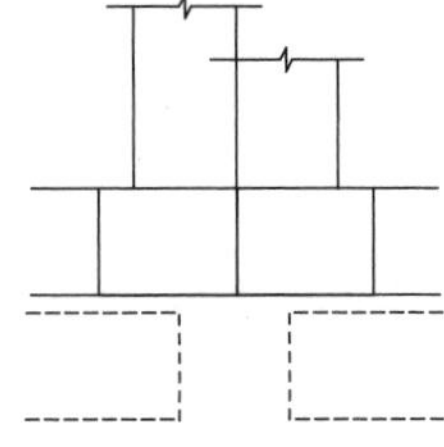

Reveal Overlay

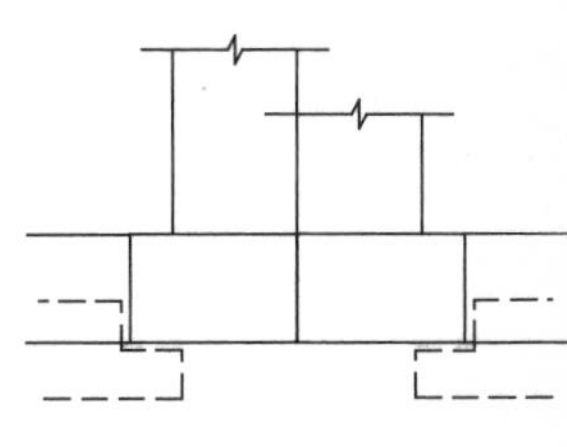

Lipped

1.2.18.2 **STYLE 2 - FLUSH INSET,** as illustrated below:

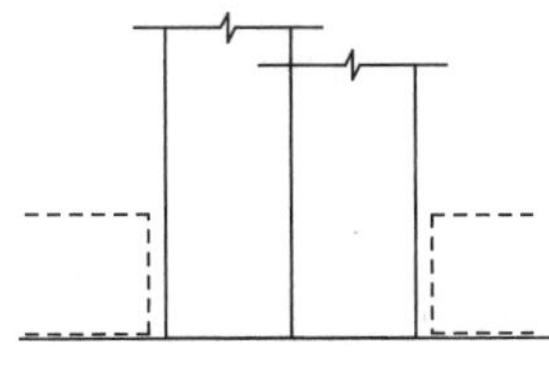

Type A Construction

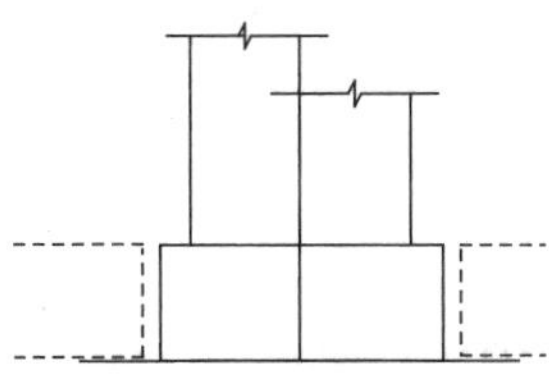

Type B Construction

1.2.18.3 **STYLE 1 - FLUSH OVERLAY** is the default for either **TYPE A** or **B** casework.

1.2.19 **LAYOUT** requirements of grained or patterned faces by Grade:

1.2.19.1 With **STILE-AND-RAIL** doors and drawer fronts for all **GRADES**:

1.2.19.1.1 **DRAWER FRONTS** shall run either vertically or horizontally at the manufacturer's option for the entire project. Doors shall be vertical.

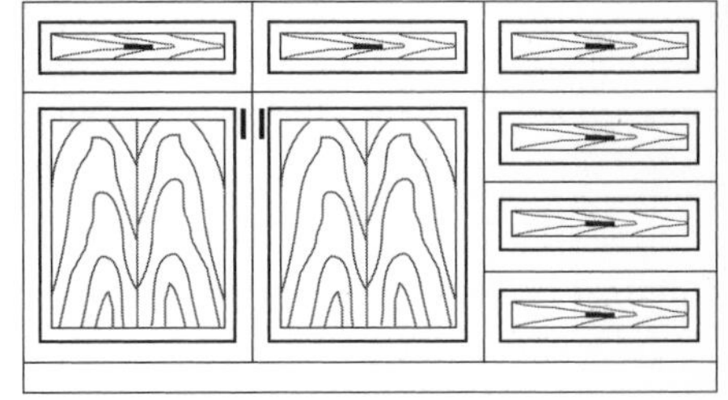

GENERAL

1.2 **BASIC CONSIDERATIONS** (continued)

1.2.19 **LAYOUT** requirements of grained or patterned faces (continued)

1.2.19.2 With **FLUSH PANEL** doors and drawer fronts:

1.2.19.2.1 **ECONOMY GRADE:**

1.2.19.2.1.1 **DRAWER FRONTS** shall run either vertically or horizontally at the manufacturer's option for the entire project. Doors shall be vertical. Mismatch is allowed.

1.2.19.2.2 **CUSTOM GRADE:**

1.2.19.2.2.1 **DOORS, DRAWER FRONTS,** and **FALSE FRONTS** shall run and match **VERTICALLY** within each cabinet unit.

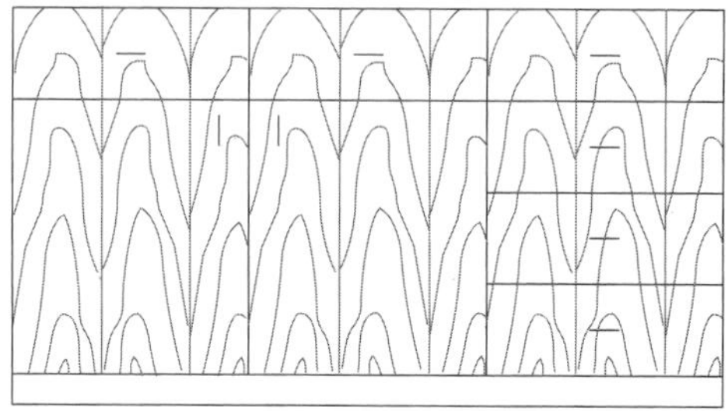

1.2.19.2.3 **PREMIUM GRADE:**

1.2.19.2.3.1 **DOORS, DRAWER FRONTS,** and **FALSE FRONTS** shall run and match **VERTICALLY** within each cabinet unit; and at **CATHEDRAL GRAIN**, the crown shall be pointing up and run in the same direction for the entire project.

1.2.19.2.3.2 **DOORS, DRAWER FRONTS,** and **FALSE FRONTS** shall be well-matched across multiple cabinet faces in one elevation.

1.2.19.2.3.2.1 Requirement for **BLUE PRINT** or **SEQUENCE MATCHING** must be so specified.

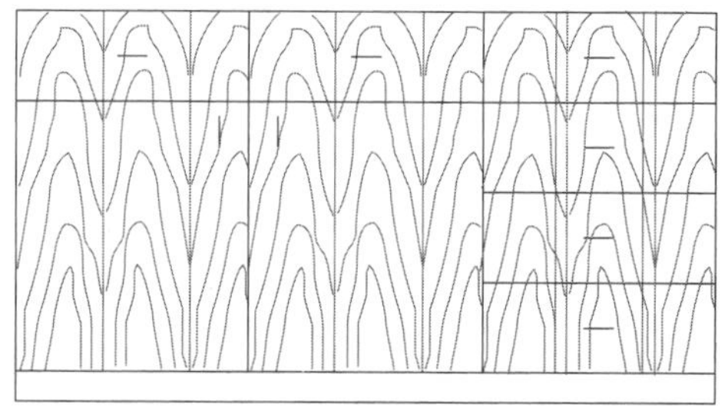

GENERAL

1.2 **BASIC CONSIDERATIONS** (continued)

1.2.20 **CABINET DESIGN SERIES (CDS)**:

1.2.20.1 The industry has developed a series of numbered cabinet designs that are available for ease of specification and drawing.

1.2.20.1.1 A numerical/elevation key to the CDS may be found in **APPENDIX A.**

1.2.20.1.2 Both **AUTODESK REVIT FAMILIES** and **AUTOCAD ".DWG / .DXF"** files of the **CDS** elevations may be found on any of the sponsor Associations' websites:

1.2.20.1.2.1 Architectural Woodwork Institute - www.awinet.org

1.2.20.1.2.2 Architectural Woodwork Manufacturers Association of Canada - www.awmac.com

1.2.20.1.2.3 Woodwork Institute - www.woodworkinstitute.com

1.2.20.1.3 **CDS** cabinets may be specified by number to a specific size requirement on the plan-view drawings without having to draw elevations.

1.2.20.1.4 **CDS** cabinets are drawn as **TYPE A** construction, **FLUSH OVERLAY STYLE 1 INTERFACE**, with integral finished ends and scribes at wall-to-wall installations not exceeding 1-1/2" (38.1 mm) in width.

1.2.21 **ADJUSTABLE SHELF LOADING** and **DEFLECTION:**

1.2.21.1 **PROPER SPECIFICATION** can balance **AESTHETIC** needs with **LOAD** requirements.

1.2.21.2 **LOAD** is the total applied weight, uniformly dispersed on an individual shelf, **NOT TO EXCEED 200 lbs (90.7 kg)** on any one shelf. These standards have adopted the following load capacities:

1.2.21.2.1 50 lbs (22.7 kg) per sq ft/ sq cm for school, hospital, and library or book shelving.

1.2.21.2.2 40 lbs (18.1 kg) per sq ft/ sq cm for all other shelving.

1.2.21.3 Shelving **SPECIFICATION** requires consideration of:

1.2.21.3.1 **DEFLECTION**, the measured distance from a straight line that a shelf will deflect under load.

1.2.21.3.1.1 L/144 (the length of the shelf divided by 144) is the industry standard for the maximum acceptable deflection of a shelf, which permits 1/4" (6.4 mm) deflection in a 36" (914 mm) shelf.

1.2.21.3.2 **CREEP** is the increase in deflection over time, which fluctuates with temperature, humidity, and load stress. **CREEP IS NOT CONSIDERED A DEFECT**; if it is a concern, it can be reduced by:

1.2.21.3.2.1 Reduced loading of shelves.

1.2.21.3.2.2 Use of material with a higher (stiffer) modulus of elasticity (MOE).

1.2.21.3.2.3 Use of alternate construction (support) techniques.

1.2.21.3.2.4 Use of a decreased factor of acceptable deflection.

1.2.22 **CASEWORK INTEGRITY** for casework at applications:

1.2.22.1 These standards have adopted a portion of **SEFA's** (Scientific Equipment and Fixture Association) methods of testing and acceptable results as the minimum acceptable level of integrity for casework, as found in **APPENDIX A**.

GENERAL

1.2 **BASIC CONSIDERATIONS** (continued)

1.2.23 **CABINET HARDWARE:**

1.2.23.1 These standards have adopted **ANSI/BHMA STANDARDS** (latest edition), **GRADE 2**, as the basic minimum requirement.

1.2.23.1.1 For more **SPECIFIC DETAILS,** see the **PRODUCT** portion of this section.

1.2.23.2 Choice of product should be made on the basis of utility, aesthetics, security objectives, and the end use desired.

1.2.23.3 As a general **GUIDE**:

1.2.23.3.1 **GRADE 1** is the highest, suitable for most institutional applications.

1.2.23.3.2 **GRADE 2** is used in most other applications.

1.3 **RECOMMENDATIONS**

1.3.1 **INCLUDE IN DIVISION 09 OF THE SPECIFICATIONS:**

1.3.1.1 For **JOBSITE FINISHING** - Before finishing, all exposed portions of woodwork shall have handling marks or effects of exposure to moisture removed with a thorough, final sanding over all surfaces of the exposed portions using an appropriate grit sandpaper, and shall be cleaned before applying sealer or finish.

1.3.1.2 At **CONCEALED SURFACES** - Architectural casework that may be exposed to moisture, such as those adjacent to exterior concrete walls, etc., shall be back-primed.

1.3.2 **THOROUGHLY REVIEW** Sections 2 and 4, especially Basic Considerations, Recommendations, Acknowledgements, and Industry Practices within Part 1 for an overview of the characteristics and minimum acceptable requirements of lumber and/or sheet products that might be used herein.

1.3.3 **CONTRACT DOCUMENTS** (plans and/or specifications) shall require that all structural members, grounds, blocking, backing, furring, brackets, or other anchorage which becomes an integral part of the building's walls, floors, or ceilings, required for the installation of architectural woodwork is not to be furnished or installed by the architectural woodwork manufacturer or installer.

1.3.4 **SPECIFY** requirements for:

1.3.4.1 Construction **TYPE**.

1.3.4.2 Door and drawer front **INTERFACE STYLE.**

1.3.4.3 **DOOR** and **DRAWER FRONT** edge profile.

1.3.4.4 **TOE BASE** finish.

1.3.4.5 Any specific inside **CLEARANCE** requirements.

1.3.4.6 **SEISMIC** fabrication and/or installation.

1.3.4.7 **FIRE** resistance.

1.3.4.8 **LABORATORY** construction features, such as:

1.3.4.8.1 Removable backs at base cabinets.

1.3.4.8.2 Moisture-resistant base.

1.3.4.8.3 Pipe chase allowance behind base cabinets.

1.3.4.8.4 Removable top ledger at countertop splash.

1.3.4.8.5 **CHEMICAL**-resistant finish or surfaces.

1.3.4.9 At **WOOD CASEWORK:**

1.3.4.9.1 **SPECIES** of veneer.

GENERAL

1.3 **RECOMMENDATIONS** (continued)

1.3.4 **SPECIFY** requirements for (continued)

1.3.4.9 At **WOOD CASEWORK** (continued)

1.3.4.9.2 Method of **SLICING** (plain, quarter, rift, or rotary).

1.3.4.9.3 **MATCHING OF VENEER LEAVES** (book, slip, sketch, or random).

1.3.4.9.4 **MATCHING OF VENEER LEAVES WITHIN A PANEL FACE** (running, balanced, or center-balanced).

1.3.4.9.5 **MATCHING BETWEEN DOORS, DRAWERS,** and **ADJACENT PANELS** (non-sequenced, sequenced, or blueprint).

1.3.4.9.6 **END-MATCHING.**

1.3.4.9.7 **GRAIN DIRECTION,** if other than vertical.

1.4 **ACKNOWLEDGEMENTS** - None

1.5 **INDUSTRY PRACTICES**

1.5.1 **STRUCTURAL MEMBERS**, grounds, blocking, backing, furring, brackets, or other anchorage that becomes an integral part of the building's walls, floors, or ceilings, that are required for the installation of architectural woodwork are not furnished or installed by the architectural woodwork manufacturer or installer.

1.5.2 **WALL, CEILING,** and/or opening variations in excess of 1/4" (6.4 mm) or **FLOORS** in excess of 1/2" (12.7 mm) in 144" (3658 mm) of being plumb, level, flat, straight, square, or of the correct size are not acceptable for the installation of architectural woodwork, nor is it the responsibility of the installer to scribe or fit to tolerances in excess of such.

1.5.3 **BACK-PRIMING** of architectural casework is not the responsibility of the manufacturer and/or installer, unless the material is being furnished prefinished wood.

1.5.4 **WALL SURFACING** with a defined grain and/or pattern is installed vertically.

1.5.5 **CASEWORK DIMENSION RANGES** have developed over time with consideration of materials, ergonomics, construction techniques, and general intended usage. It is the responsibility of the design professional to coordinate accessibility requirements, appliance and equipment sizes, and/or storage requirements with the casework manufacturer and adjust the following dimensions accordingly:

1.5.5.1 **BASE:**

1.5.5.1.1 **HEIGHT** - from the finished floor to the top of the countertop deck ranges from:

1.5.5.1.1.1 34" (864 mm) to 36" (914 mm) at stand-up counters.

1.5.5.1.1.2 31" (787 mm) to 38" (965 mm) at vanities.

1.5.5.1.1.3 28" (711 mm) to 32" (812 mm) at sit-down counters, providing a clear knee space height of 24-1/2" (622 mm).

1.5.5.1.1.4 25-1/4" (641 mm) to 28" (711 mm) at keyboard recesses, providing a clear knee space height of 24-1/2" (622 mm).

1.5.5.1.2 **DEPTH** - from the front of the cabinet door/drawer to the face of the wall ranges from 24" (610 mm) to 30" (762 mm).

1.5.5.2 **WALL-HUNG**:

1.5.5.2.1 **HEIGHT** - including the light apron ranges from 12" (305 mm) to 48" (1219 mm).

1.5.5.2.2 **DEPTH** - from the front of the cabinet door to the face of the wall ranges from 12-1/2" (318 mm) to 14" (356 mm).

GENERAL

1.5 **INDUSTRY PRACTICES** (continued)

1.5.5 **CASEWORK DIMENSION RANGES** (continued)

1.5.5.3 **TALL STORAGE**:

1.5.5.3.1 **HEIGHT** - from the finished floor to the cabinet top ranges from 72" (1829 mm) to 96" (2438 mm).

1.5.5.3.2 **DEPTH** - from the front of the cabinet door to the face of the wall ranges from 12-1/2" (318 mm) to 30" (762 mm).

1.5.5.4 **RECEPTION COUNTER**:

1.5.5.4.1 **HEIGHT** - from the finished floor to the top of the countertop deck ranges from:

1.5.5.4.1.1 34" (864 mm) to 36" (914 mm) at the standing side.

1.5.5.4.1.2 28" (711 mm) to 32" (812 mm) at the sit-down side, providing a clear knee space height of 24-1/2" (622 mm).

1.5.5.4.1.3 25-1/4" (641 mm) to 28" (711 mm) at the sit-down keyboard recesses, providing a clear knee space height of 24-1/2" (622 mm).

1.5.5.4.2 **DEPTH:**

1.5.5.4.2.1 24" (610 mm) to 30" (762 mm) overall countertop on the employee side, plus:

1.5.5.4.2.1.1 An additional 8" (203 mm) of countertop at the customer side.

1.5.5.5 **TELLER COUNTER**:

1.5.5.5.1 **HEIGHT** - from the finished floor ranges from:

1.5.5.5.1.1 50" (1270 mm) to 54" (1372 mm) on the customer side at the security hood.

1.5.5.5.1.2 40" (1016 mm) to 42" (1067 mm) on the teller's side transaction top.

1.5.5.5.2 **DEPTH:**

1.5.5.5.2.1 24" (610 mm) to 32" (813 mm) at the countertop on the employee side, plus:

1.5.5.5.2.1.1 An additional 8" (203 mm) of countertop at the customer side.

1.5.6 **BASE CABINET, STRETCHER, LAYOUT,** and **CONSTRUCTION**:

1.5.6.1 **CASEWORK MANUFACTURER** is responsible for coordinating the following with the **COUNTERTOP MANUFACTURER**, and:

1.5.6.1.1 **COUNTERTOP MANUFACTURER** is responsible for furnishing any filler materials needed in addition to the cabinet top/stretcher necessary for proper setting of their countertops.

1.5.6.1.2 **DOORS**, **DRAWER FRONTS**, and **FALSE FRONTS** creating a 1/4" (6.4 mm) horizontal reveal (+/- 1/8" [3.2 mm]) with the countertop's bottom edge, shall be consistent across elevations, except:

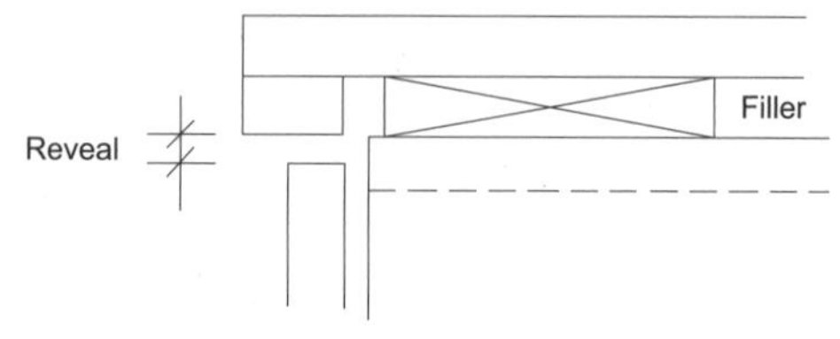

GENERAL

1.5 **INDUSTRY PRACTICES** (continued)

1.5.6 **BASE CABINET, STRETCHER, LAYOUT,** and **CONSTRUCTION** (continued)

1.5.6.1 **CASEWORK MANUFACTURER** is responsible for coordinating (continued)

1.5.6.2.2 **DOORS**, **DRAWER FRONTS**, and **FALSE FRONTS** (continued)

1.5.6.2.2.1 At laboratory applications, reveal shall be 1/4" (6.4 mm) to 1" (25.4 mm) and shall be consistent across elevations.

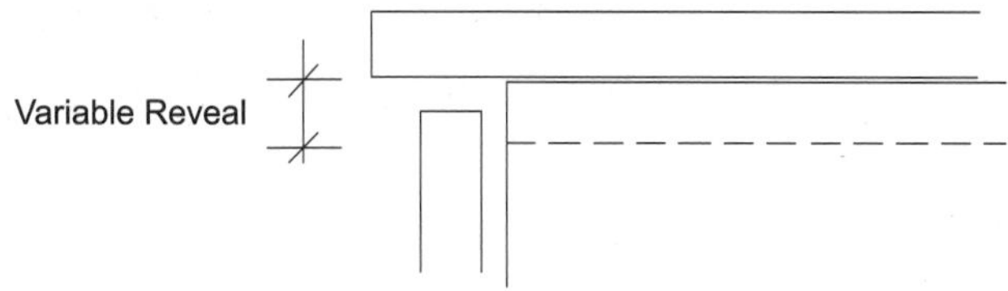

PRODUCT

2 SCOPE

2.1 All wood, high-pressure decorative laminate (HPDL), and/or solid phenolic casework, cabinets, and components of face-frame or frameless construction, fabricated complete in the manufacturer's facilities to field dimensions, as qualified below.

2.2 **TYPICAL INCLUSIONS:**

2.2.1 Altars
2.2.2 Bars and back bars
2.2.3 Bulletin boards, built up
2.2.4 Bookcases, cabinets, carrels, counters, display cases, lecterns, and pulpits
2.2.5 Shelving, built up or machined and knocked down
2.2.6 Wardrobes
2.2.7 Modular cabinets
2.2.8 Cabinet doors
2.2.9 Clothes poles and supports
2.2.10 Shelf standards and rests
2.2.11 Track and hardware for sliding doors
2.2.12 Casters
2.2.13 File drawer rods and followers
2.2.14 Hinges
2.2.15 Drawer guides and slides
2.2.16 Pulls or knobs
2.2.17 Glass, mirrors, and glass doors, with hardware
2.2.18 Trim and moldings necessary for cabinet installation
2.2.19 Filler panels and scribe strips
2.2.20 Rough and finish hardware, which is part of the cabinet
2.2.21 Metal brackets and fittings, which are an integral part of the cabinet, unless specified elsewhere
2.2.22 Cut-outs for sinks or similar units
2.2.23 Linoleum, vinyl, cork, or resilient covering that is a part of the cabinet
2.2.24 Prefinishing, priming, painting, or sealing if so specified

2.3 **TYPICAL EXCLUSIONS:**

2.3.1 Field installation of any kind, unless specified to be included in this scope of work
2.3.2 Cutting of holes for field-applied vents, weeps, or grills, unless part of the cabinet
2.3.3 Fillers, build-up, or sub-tops for countertops, including tile and natural stone
2.3.4 Cutting for field-applied hardware, unless part of the cabinet
2.3.5 Vinyl, rubber, or carpet base

PRODUCT

2.3 **TYPICAL EXCLUSIONS** (continued)

- 2.3.6 Metal support brackets and fittings that are part of the building structure
- 2.3.7 Security panels, unless so specified
- 2.3.8 Tote trays (except at Cabinet Design Series) and base leveling adjusters, unless so specified
- 2.3.9 Furring, stripping, blocking, grounds, or stub walls
- 2.3.10 Mirrors, glass, or glazing, unless part of the cabinet
- 2.3.11 Plumbing, electrical fixtures, and telephone equipment
- 2.3.12 Metal or ceramic tile for countertops
- 2.3.13 Sink rims
- 2.3.14 Special equipment housed in cabinets
- 2.3.15 Work not directly associated with the casework
- 2.3.16 Sliding presentation boards
- 2.3.17 Metal grills
- 2.3.18 Chalkboards and tack boards that are a part of the cabinet, with the necessary trim and trays
- 2.3.19 Easel trays of plastic or metal

3 DEFAULT STIPULATION

3.1 If not otherwise specified or indicated, all work shall be Custom Grade, Type A construction with adjustable shelves and Flush Overlay doors of unfinished close-grain hardwood intended for an opaque finish, non-premium-priced standard pattern, color, and finish decorative laminate or solid phenolic, as covered by Sections 3 and 4.

4 RULES - The following RULES shall govern unless a project's contract documents require otherwise.

These rules are intended to provide a well-defined degree of control over a project's quality of materials and workmanship.

Where E, C, or P is not indicated, the rule applies to all Grades equally.

ERRATA, published on the Associations' websites at www.awinet.org, www.awmac.com, or www.woodworkinstitute.com, shall TAKE PRECEDENCE OVER THESE RULES, subject to their date of posting and a project's bid date.

ARROWS INDICATE TOPIC IS CARRIED FROM ⇑ OR ONTO ⇓ ANOTHER PAGE.

		DESCRIPTION	E	C	P
4.1	**GENERAL**				
GENERAL	4.1.1	Aesthetic **GRADE RULES** apply only to exposed and semi-exposed surfaces visible after installation.			
	4.1.2	**WOODWORK** not addressed herein shall be manufactured from solid stock, laminated stock, veneered stock, or a combination thereof.			
	4.1.3	**LUMBER** shall conform to the requirements established in Section 3.			
	4.1.4	**SHEET PRODUCTS** shall conform to the requirements established in Section 4.			
	4.1.5	**BACKING SHEET** shall conform to the requirements established in Section 4.			
	4.1.6	All materials shall be **SECURELY ATTACHED/FASTENED/BONDED**.			
	4.1.7	**EXPOSED, SEMI-EXPOSED,** and **CONCEALED** surfaces shall be as listed under **BASIC CONSIDERATIONS** of this section.			
	4.1.8	**HARDWARE**:			
		4.1.8.1 Shall conform to **ANSI/BHMA STANDARDS** (latest edition), **GRADE 2** requirements with the exception of requiring "dynamic" load testing for a minimum of 50,000 cycles, and:			
⇓	⇓	⇓ 4.1.8.1.1 For use at **SCHOOLS** and **HOSPITALS**, **HINGES** shall be of all-metal construction, meeting or exceeding the ANSI/BHMA Grade 1 "performance" and "permanent set" test requirements.			

PRODUCT

MATERIAL, MACHINING, AND ASSEMBLY RULES (continued)

DESCRIPTION					E C P
4.1 GENERAL	**GENERAL**				
	4.1.8 HARDWARE	**HARDWARE** (continued)			
		4.1.8.1 ANSI/BHMA	Shall conform to **ANSI/BHMA STANDARDS** (latest edition), **GRADE 2** requirements (continued)		
			4.1.8.1.2	**DRAWER SLIDE** testing shall be based on a drawer box of 22" (559 mm) in depth with a minimum width of 18" (457 mm) for load ratings up to 125 lbs (56.7 kg) and 24" (610 mm) for load ratings of 125 lbs (56.7 kg) and above, using a minimum 22" (559 mm) slide length, and:	
				4.1.8.1.2.1	Slides not manufactured in lengths up to 22" (559 mm) shall be tested in their longest production length.
			4.1.8.1.3	**KEYBOARD TRAYS** shall conform to section 4.13 (Test 12, Drawers and Trays) of ANSI/BHMA A156.9 (latest edition).	
			4.1.8.1.4	**SHELF SUPPORTS** shall meet **ANSI/BHMA GRADE 1** requirements and meet these standards' minimum shelf-load requirements.	
		4.1.8.2	Shall be **FURNISHED** and **INSTALLED** as required to provide a complete casework assembly and installation without:		
			4.1.8.2.1	**IMPAIRMENT** of the cabinet's structural integrity and/or functionality.	
		4.1.8.3	Shall be of a **UNIFORM PLATED BHMA 626** or similar **POWDER-COATED** finish on all exposed surfaces and:		
			4.1.8.3.1	Conform to applicable **ANSI/BHMA** standards (latest edition).	
			4.1.8.3.2	**POWDER-COAT** finish shall be of a chemical family with sufficient chemical/ solvent resistance to not be affected by a rubdown of the solvents or cleaning materials used for final cleanup of the fabricated product, including removal of overspray, glue.	
			4.1.8.3.3	**FINISHES** will vary between manufacturers, and it can be expected to see variations from the same manufacturer between different production runs. These variations are not considered a defect, as long as they are compatible with the overall finish of the installed hardware.	
		4.1.8.4	Shall have the manufacturer's **NAME** or **BRAND**-unique marking stamped on all hinges, slides, and locks for identification purposes.		
		4.1.8.5	Shall be of **FIRST-CLASS WORKMANSHIP**, free of manufacturing imperfections (such as tool or machine marks), and consistent in exposed finish appearance.		
		4.1.8.6	At **LOCKS** shall be furnished when indicated on the architectural drawings, and:		
			4.1.8.6.1	Be **KEYED DIFFERENTLY,** only if so specified.	
			4.1.8.6.2	Be **MASTER-KEYED,** only if so specified.	
		4.1.8.7	At **DRAWER SLIDES** shall conform to the following minimum load capacity requirements:		
			4.1.8.7.1	50 lbs (22.7 kg) at pencil drawers.	
			4.1.8.7.2	75 lbs (34 kg) at general-purpose drawers.	
			4.1.8.7.3	100 lbs (45.4 kg) at file drawers, except:	
				4.1.8.7.3.1	150 lbs (68 kg) at lateral file drawers wider than 24" (610 mm) and less than 30" (762 mm).
				4.1.8.7.3.2	200 lbs (68 kg) at lateral file drawers wider than 30" (762 mm).
		4.1.8.8	At **SHELF SUPPORTS** for bored holes shall either include a minimum of 0.1969" (5 mm) metal pin or double 0.1969" (5 mm) plastic pins (meeting ANSI/BHMA Grade 1 requirements) and:		
			4.1.8.8.1	Meet or exceed these standards' maximum shelf-load requirement of 200 lbs (90.7 kg).	
		4.1.8.9	At **POCKET DOOR HARDWARE** cabinet doors shall be a maximum of 23-5/8" (600 mm) in width. The maximum door height and weight shall be within the manufacturer's listed capacity.		

PRODUCT

MATERIAL, MACHINING, AND ASSEMBLY RULES (continued)

No.	DESCRIPTION	E	C	P
4.1	**GENERAL** (continued)			
4.1.8	**HARDWARE** (continued)			
4.1.8.10	**BASE ADJUSTERS** shall be of the adjustable screw type, having a floor-bearing surface of at least 1-1/8" (28.6 mm) in diameter at each foot, and:			
4.1.8.10.1	Shall provide for **LEVELING** the cabinet from inside of the case through holes in the cabinet bottom.			
4.1.9	Where **MULTIPLE OPTIONS** are permitted, it shall be the manufacturer's choice unless specified otherwise.			
4.1.10	**CASEWORK** shall be:			
4.1.10.1	Assembled complete by the manufacturer, with doors, drawers, and hardware installed.			
4.1.10.2	Assembled with mechanical fasteners and adhesive.			
4.1.10.3	Free of adhesive overspray, fabrication marks, and debris.			
4.1.11	**PANEL COMPONENTS** shall be:			
4.1.11.1	Constructed of particleboard, MDF, or a non-telegraphing core.			
4.1.11.2	Of **BALANCED CONSTRUCTION**, constructed in such a way as not to warp in its intended use.			
4.1.12	At **TYPE A CONSTRUCTION**, self-edging of adjoining units shall be beveled a maximum of 15° for the thickness of the banding. When adjoined, the total beveled "V" shall not exceed 30°.			
4.1.13	**SEPARATELY APPLIED COUNTERTOPS** are required at base cabinets 48" (1219 mm) or less in height.			
4.1.14	**CORNERS** created by tall, wall, or base casework will create non-usable space.			
4.1.15	**STORAGE, JANITOR, CLOSET,** and **UTILITY ROOM CABINETS** shall be of hardboard, particleboard, MDF, or decorative laminate, at the manufacturer's option.	●	●	
4.1.16	**CABINETS OVER 72" (1829 mm) HIGH** (excluding wardrobe cabinets) not abutting a structural wall or another cabinet shall have a fixed shelf approximately mid-height, and:			
4.1.16.1	At **SEISMIC-COMPLIANT** construction, shall have a fixed shelf and anchor strip approximately mid-height, and:			
4.1.16.1.1	**ANCHOR STRIP** and **BACK** shall be securely fastened to the fixed shelf with #10 x 2-1/2" (50.8 mm) screws a maximum of 7" (178 mm) on center.			
4.1.17	At **SLIDING PRESENTATION BOARDS**, an integral stop shall be provided within the top and bottom track to prevent their stopping against the casework.			
4.1.18	**HOT-MELT-APPLIED HPDL** edgebanding shall be primed before application for proper adhesion, unless the hot-melt adhesive used has been specially formulated for the application of HPDL without requiring pre-application of a primer.			
4.1.19	When **PREFINISHING** of wood faced casework is required, wall abutting surfaces shall be back primed with a single coat at 1 mil dry.		●	●
4.1.20	**EXPOSED SURFACES** are divided into two subcategories:			
4.1.20.1	**EXPOSED EXTERIOR SURFACES**, defined as all exterior surfaces exposed to view, include:			
4.1.20.1.1	All surfaces visible when doors and drawers are closed, including knee spaces.			
4.1.20.1.2	The underside of cabinet bottoms over 42" (1067 mm) above the finished floor, including cabinet bottoms behind light valances and the bottom edge of light valances.			
4.1.20.1.3	Cabinet tops under 80" (2032 mm) above the finished floor, or if 80" (2032 mm) and over and visible from an upper building level or floor.			
4.1.20.1.4	Visible front edges of stretchers, ends, divisions, tops, bottoms, shelves, and nailers.			
4.1.20.1.5	Sloping tops of cabinets that are visible.			
4.1.20.2	**EXPOSED INTERIOR SURFACES**, defined as all interior surfaces exposed to view in open casework or behind transparent doors, include:			
4.1.20.2.1	Shelves, including edgebanding.			

10

PRODUCT

MATERIAL, MACHINING, AND ASSEMBLY RULES (continued)

Section	Article	Item	Sub-item	DESCRIPTION	E	C	P
4.1 GENERAL				**GENERAL** (continued)			
	4.1.20			**EXPOSED SURFACES** are divided into two subcategories (continued)			
		4.1.20.2		**EXPOSED INTERIOR SURFACES**, defined as all interior surfaces exposed to view (continued)			
			4.1.20.2.2	Divisions and partitions.			
			4.1.20.2.3	Interior face of ends (sides), backs, and bottoms (even on a bank of drawers). Also included are the interior surfaces of cabinet top members 36" (914 mm) or more above the finished floor.			
			4.1.20.2.4	The interior face of door and applied drawer fronts.			
	4.1.21 SEMI-EXPOSED			**SEMI-EXPOSED SURFACES**, defined as those interior surfaces only exposed to view when doors or drawers are opened, include:			
		4.1.21.1		Shelves, including edgebanding.			
		4.1.21.2		Divisions and partitions.			
		4.1.21.3		Interior face of ends (sides), backs, and bottoms (even on a bank of drawers). Also included are the interior surfaces of cabinet top members 36" (914 mm) or more above the finished floor.			
		4.1.21.4		Drawer sides, sub-fronts, backs, and bottoms.			
		4.1.21.5		The underside of cabinet bottoms between 24" (610 mm) and 42" (1067 mm) above the finished floor.			
		4.1.21.6		Security and dust panels and drawer stretchers.			
	4.1.22 CONCEALED			**CONCEALED SURFACES**, defined as those exterior or interior surfaces that are covered or not normally exposed to view, include:			
		4.1.22.1		Toe space, unless otherwise specified.			
		4.1.22.2		Sleepers, stretchers, and solid sub-tops.			
		4.1.22.3		The underside of cabinet bottoms less than 24" (610 mm) above the finished floor.			
		4.1.22.4		The flat tops of cabinets 80" (2032 mm) or more above the finished floor, except if visible from an upper floor or building level.			
		4.1.22.5		The three non-visible edges of adjustable shelves.			
		4.1.22.6		The underside of countertops, knee spaces, and drawer aprons.			
		4.1.22.7		The faces of cabinet ends of adjoining units that butt together.			
	4.1.23			**FIRST-CLASS WORKMANSHIP** is required in compliance with these standards.			
4.2 MATERIAL				**MATERIAL**			
	4.2.1 GRAIN			**GRAIN** or **DIRECTIONALLY PATTERNED** sheet product:			
		4.2.1.1		Shall run **EITHER** vertically or horizontally at the manufacturer's option, and:	●		
			4.2.1.1.1	**DRAWER FRONTS** shall run either vertically or horizontally for the entire project.	●		
		4.2.1.2		Shall run and match **VERTICALLY** within each cabinet unit, including doors, drawers, false fronts, and finished ends, and:		●	●
			4.2.1.2.1	**CATHEDRAL GRAIN** shall have the crown pointing up and run the same direction for the entire project.			●
			4.2.1.2.2	Shall be well-matched across multiple cabinet faces in each room, and:			●
			4.2.1.2.2.1	Requirement for **BLUE PRINT** or **SEQUENCE MATCHING** must be so specified.			●
		4.2.1.3		At **STILE-AND-RAIL DOOR** and **DRAWER FRONT** panels shall run either vertically or horizontally at the manufacturer's option.			

10

PRODUCT

MATERIAL, MACHINING, AND ASSEMBLY RULES (continued)

Section	Group	No.	DESCRIPTION	E	C	P
4.2 MATERIAL			**MATERIAL** (continued)			
		4.2.2	The **BOTTOM EDGE** of **LIGHT APRONS** shall be considered an exposed surface.			
		4.2.3	**VINYL**-covered material is acceptable for cabinet construction.	●		
		4.2.4	**GLASS SHELVES** shall be tempered or laminated safety glass, with all four edges polished.			
	SEMI EXPOSED	**4.2.5**	At **SEMI-EXPOSED SURFACES,** including **DRAWER BOXES**, requires:			
		4.2.5.1	**CONSISTENT** color or species to be used throughout entire project.			
		4.2.5.2	**MATCHING EXPOSED SURFACE** is only required if so specified.			
		4.2.5.3	**VINYL** overlay is acceptable at **CABINET BACKS** and **DRAWER BOTTOMS**, if matched in color to other semi-exposed materials.	●	●	●
		4.2.5.4	**HARDBOARD** used as vertical or horizontal shelves and/or dividers shall be tempered and smooth on both sides.	●	●	
		4.2.5.4.1	**PAINTED** to match other semi-exposed portions is required only if so specified.	●	●	
		4.2.5.5	**VERTICAL** or **HORIZONTAL SHELVES** and/or **DIVIDERS** shall match other semi-exposed surfaces.			●
		4.2.6	At **CONCEALED SURFACES** shall be the manufacturer's option:			
		4.2.6.1	If specified to have a **MOISTURE-RESISTANT BASE**, all base components shall be any material complying with the **BASE CABINET SUBMERSION TEST**, as explained in **APPENDIX A**.			
	WOOD CASEWORK	**4.2.7**	At **WOOD CASEWORK**:			
	EXPOSED EXTERIOR	**4.2.7.1**	**EXPOSED EXTERIOR** surfaces:			
		4.2.7.1.1	Require **WOOD** of the specified species, cut, and match.			
		4.2.7.1.2	For **TRANSPARENT FINISH** require:			
		4.2.7.1.2.1	Use of one species for the entire project.			
		4.2.7.1.2.2	No use of **ROTARY-CUT VENEER**.		●	●
		4.2.7.1.2.3	Solid stock and/or plywood to be **COMPATIBLE IN COLOR AND GRAIN**.		●	
		4.2.7.1.2.4	Solid stock to be **WELL-MATCHED** for **COLOR** and **GRAIN**; plywood shall be **COMPATIBLE IN COLOR** with solid stock; and adjacent plywood panels shall be **WELL-MATCHED** for **COLOR** and **GRAIN**.			●
		4.2.7.1.3	For **OPAQUE FINISH** permit:			
		4.2.7.1.3.1	Use of particleboard, MDF, MDO, softwood plywood, hardwood plywood, and solid stock.	●		
		4.2.7.1.3.2	Use of MDF, MDO, close-grain hardwood plywood, and solid stock.		●	
		4.2.7.1.3.3	Use of MDF and MDO.			●
		4.2.7.2	**EXPOSED INTERIOR** surfaces, except at doors and drawer fronts, require:			
		4.2.7.2.1	**LPDL** or **WOOD** of the manufacturer's option.	●		
		4.2.7.2.2	**WOOD**, the same species as the exposed exterior surface.		●	
		4.2.7.2.3	**WOOD**, the same species and cut as the exposed exterior surface, and be:			●
		4.2.7.2.3.1	**HPVA GRADE C**.	●		
		4.2.7.2.3.2	**HPVA GRADE B**.		●	
		4.2.7.2.3.3	**HPVA GRADE A**.			●

PRODUCT

MATERIAL, MACHINING, AND ASSEMBLY RULES (continued)

Ref	DESCRIPTION	E	C	P
4.2	**MATERIAL** (continued)			
4.2.7	At **WOOD CASEWORK** (continued)			
4.2.7.2 (EXPOSED INT.)	**EXPOSED INTERIOR** surfaces, except at doors and drawer fronts, require (continued)			
4.2.7.2.4	For **OPAQUE FINISH** permit:			
4.2.7.2.4.1	Use of particleboard, MDF, MDO, softwood plywood, hardwood plywood, and solid stock.	●		
4.2.7.2.4.2	Use of MDF, MDO, close-grain hardwood plywood, and solid stock.		●	
4.2.7.2.4.3	Use of MDF and MDO.			●
4.2.7.2.5	At inside face of **DOOR** and **DRAWER FRONTS**:			
4.2.7.2.5.1	Mill-option species.	●		
4.2.7.2.5.2	**HPVA GRADE B** face of the same species and cut as the exposed exterior surface.		●	
4.2.7.2.5.3	**HPVA GRADE A** face of the same species and cut as the exposed exterior surface.			●
4.2.7.3 (SEMI EXPOSED)	**SEMI-EXPOSED** surfaces (including **DRAWER BOXES**) for both **TRANSPARENT** and **OPAQUE** finishes require:			
4.2.7.3.1	**WOOD** of the manufacturer's option of species, **MDO**, **MDF**, particleboard, or **LPDL** of the manufacturer's option of color.	●		
4.2.7.3.2	**WOOD** of the manufacturer's species option, or LPDL of the manufacturer's color option.		●	
4.2.7.3.3	**WOOD** of compatible species to the exposed:			●
4.2.7.3.3.1	For **OPAQUE** finish, drawer boxes of prefinished hardwood, 7- or 9-ply hardwood plywood with no inner core voids, of manufacturer's species or MDO option.			●
4.2.7.3.3.2	For **TRANSPARENT** finish, drawer boxes of prefinished hardwood, 7- or 9-ply hardwood plywood with no inner core voids, of manufacturer's species option.			●
4.2.7.3.4	**DRAWER SIDES**, **BACK**, and **SUB-FRONTS** be a minimum thickness of:			
4.2.7.3.4.1	7/16" (11.1 mm).	●		
4.2.7.3.4.2	15/32" (12 mm), and a maximum of 5/8" (15.9 mm).		●	●
4.2.8 (LAMINATE)	At **DECORATIVE LAMINATE CASEWORK**:			
4.2.8.1 (EXPOSED EXT.)	**EXPOSED EXTERIOR** surfaces require:			
4.2.8.1.1	**LPDL** of specified color or pattern.	●		
4.2.8.1.2	**HPDL** of specified color or pattern.		●	●
4.2.8.1.3	**MATERIAL**, **PATTERN**, and **COLOR** to be as specified, and:			
4.2.8.1.3.1	If not specified, to be a non-premium-priced, standard pattern or color of manufacturer's option.			
4.2.8.1.3.2	For HPDL, to be a minimum of .028" (0.7 mm) thick.			
4.2.8.1.3.3	To be of one color or pattern per room, with a maximum of **FIVE** different **COLORS** or **PATTERNS** per project.			
4.2.8.2	**EXPOSED INTERIOR** surfaces, except at doors and drawer fronts, require:			
4.2.8.2.1	**LPDL** of the manufacturer's option.	●		
4.2.8.2.2	**HPDL** or **LPDL** compatible in color, grain, or pattern.		●	
4.2.8.2.3	**HPDL**, the same as the exposed exterior surface.			●

10

PRODUCT

MATERIAL, MACHINING, AND ASSEMBLY RULES (continued)

Number	DESCRIPTION	E	C	P
4.2	**MATERIAL** (continued)			
4.2.8	At **DECORATIVE LAMINATE CASEWORK**:			
4.2.8.2	**EXPOSED INTERIOR** surfaces, except at doors and drawer fronts, require:			
4.2.8.2.4	At inside face of **DOOR** and **DRAWER FRONTS**:			
4.2.8.2.4.1	The same material and thickness as the face.	●	●	
4.2.8.2.4.2	The same material, pattern, color, and thickness as the door face.			●
4.2.8.3	**SEMI-EXPOSED** surfaces, including **DRAWER BOXES**, require:			
4.2.8.3.1	**LPDL** of the manufacturer's option of color.			
4.2.8.3.2	At **DRAWER SIDES**, **BACK,** and **SUB-FRONTS** shall:			
4.2.8.3.2.1	Be a minimum thickness of:			
4.2.8.3.2.1.1	7/16" (11.1 mm).	●		
4.2.8.3.2.1.2	15/32" (12 mm), and a maximum of 5/8" (15.9 mm).		●	●
4.2.8.3.2.2	**VENEER-CORE PLYWOOD** with HPDL or LPDL overlay.			●
4.2.8.3.2.3	**PARTICLEBOARD** or MDF with HPDL or LPDL overlay for bottoms only.			●
4.2.9	At **SOLID PHENOLIC CASEWORK**:			
4.2.9.1	**EXPOSED EXTERIOR** surfaces require:			
4.2.9.1.1	**MATERIAL**, **PATTERN,** and **COLOR** to be as specified, and:			
4.2.9.1.1.1	If not specified, to be a non-premium-priced, standard pattern, minimum 3/8" (9.5 mm) thick at the manufacturer's option.			
4.2.9.1.1.2	To be of one color per room, with a maximum of **FIVE** different **COLORS** per project.			
4.2.9.2	**EXPOSED INTERIOR** surfaces be the same as the exposed exterior surface.			
4.2.9.3	At **SEMI-EXPOSED SURFACES,** including **DRAWER BOXES**, require mill-option color.			
4.2.9.4	**SIDES**, **BACK,** and **SUB-FRONTS**, a minimum thickness of 1/2" (12.7 mm).			
4.3	**MACHINING**			
4.3.1	Of **EXPOSED AND SEMI-EXPOSED SURFACES** shall comply with:			
4.3.1.1	**SMOOTHNESS REQUIREMENTS** (see Item 7.1 in **COMPLIANCE**) for:			
4.3.1.1.1	**SHARP EDGES** to be eased with fine abrasive.		●	●
4.3.1.1.2	**TOP FLAT WOOD** surfaces; those that can be sanded with a drum or wide belt sander:			
4.3.1.1.2.1	Minimum 15 KCPI or 100-grit sanding	●		
4.3.1.1.2.2	120-grit sanding		●	
4.3.1.1.2.3	150-grit sanding			●
4.3.1.1.3	**PROFILED** and **SHAPED WOOD** surfaces:			
4.3.1.1.3.1	Minimum 15 KCPI or 100-grit sanding	●		
4.3.1.1.3.2	Minimum 20 KCPI or 120-grit sanding		●	
4.3.1.1.3.3	120-grit sanding			●

PRODUCT

MATERIAL, MACHINING, AND ASSEMBLY RULES (continued)

Item	DESCRIPTION	E	C	P
4.3	**MACHINING** (continued)			
4.3.1	Of **EXPOSED AND SEMI-EXPOSED SURFACES** shall comply with (continued)			
4.3.1.1	**SMOOTHNESS REQUIREMENTS** (see Item 7.1 in **COMPLIANCE**) for (continued)			
4.3.1.1.4	**TURNED WOOD** surfaces:			
4.3.1.1.4.1	Minimum 15 KCPI or 100-grit sanding	●		
4.3.1.1.4.2	120-grit sanding		●	
4.3.1.1.4.3	180-grit sanding			●
4.3.1.1.5	**CROSS-SANDING**, excluding turned surfaces:			
4.3.1.1.5.1	Is not a defect.	●		
4.3.1.1.5.2	Is not permitted.		●	●
4.3.1.1.6	**TEAR-OUTS**, **KNIFE NICKS**, or **HIT-OR-MISS** machining is not permitted.			
4.3.1.1.7	**KNIFE MARKS** are not to be permitted where sanding is required.			
4.3.1.1.8	**GLUE** or **FILLER**, if used, to be inconspicuous and match the adjacent surface for smoothness.			
4.4	**ASSEMBLY**			
4.4.1	Of **JOINTS** at **ASSEMBLED WOODWORK** shall:			
4.4.1.1	Be neatly and accurately made.			
4.4.1.2	Be **SECURELY GLUED**, with:			
4.4.1.2.1	**ADHESIVE** residue removed from all exposed and semi-exposed surfaces.			
4.4.1.3	Require **FLUSHNESS VARIATIONS** at exposed surfaces when mitered or butted (see Test D illustrations in **COMPLIANCE**) not to exceed:			
4.4.1.3.1	At **INTERIOR** use:			
4.4.1.3.1.1	0.025" (0.6 mm)	●		
4.4.1.3.1.2	0.005" (0.1 mm)		●	
4.4.1.3.1.3	0.001" (0.03 mm)			●
4.4.1.3.2	At **EXTERIOR** use:			
4.4.1.3.2.1	0.05" (1.3 mm)	●		
4.4.1.3.2.2	0.025" (0.6 mm)		●	
4.4.1.3.2.3	0.015" (0.4 mm)			●
4.4.1.4	Require **GAPS** at exposed surfaces when mitered or butted (see Test A illustrations in **COMPLIANCE**) not to exceed:			
4.4.1.4.1	At **INTERIOR** use:			
4.4.1.4.1.1	0.05" (1.3 mm) wide by 20% of the joint length.	●		
4.4.1.4.1.2	0.025" (0.6 mm) wide by 20% of the joint length.		●	
4.4.1.4.1.3	0.015" (0.4 mm) wide by 20% of the joint length.			●
4.4.1.4.2	At **EXTERIOR** use:			
4.4.1.4.2.1	0.075" (1.9 mm) wide by 30% of the joint length.	●		
4.4.1.4.2.2	0.05" (1.3 mm) wide by 30% of the joint length.		●	
4.4.1.4.2.3	0.025" (0.6 mm) wide by 30% of the joint length.			●

PRODUCT

MATERIAL, MACHINING, AND ASSEMBLY RULES (continued)

Section					DESCRIPTION	E	C	P
4.4 ASSEMBLY					**ASSEMBLY** (continued)			
	4.4.1 JOINTS				Of **JOINTS** at **ASSEMBLED WOODWORK** shall (continued)			
		4.4.1.5 GAPS			Require **GAPS** at exposed surfaces at parallel members (see Test B illustrations in **COMPLIANCE**) not to exceed:			
			4.4.1.5.1		At **INTERIOR** use:			
				4.4.1.5.1.1	0.05" x 8" (1.3 mm x 203 mm) and shall not occur within 48" (1219 mm) of a similar gap.	●		
				4.4.1.5.1.2	0.025" x 6" (0.6 mm x 152 mm) and shall not occur within 60" (1524 mm) of a similar gap.		●	
				4.4.1.5.1.3	0.015" x 3" (0.4 mm x 76 mm) and shall not occur within 12" (1829 mm) of a similar gap.			●
			4.4.1.5.2		At **EXTERIOR** use:			
				4.4.1.5.2.1	0.075" x 10" (1.9 mm x 254 mm) and shall not occur within 24" (610 mm) of a similar gap.	●		
				4.4.1.5.2.2	0.05" x 8" (1.3 mm x 203 mm) and shall not occur within 26" (660 mm) of a similar gap.		●	
				4.4.1.5.2.3	0.025" x 6" (0.6 mm x 152 mm) and shall not occur within 30" (762 mm) of a similar gap.			●
		4.4.1.6 GAPS			Require **GAPS** at exposed surfaces when mitered or butted (see Test C illustrations in **COMPLIANCE**) not to exceed:			
			4.4.1.6.1		At **INTERIOR** use:			
				4.4.1.6.1.1	0.05" (1.3 mm)	●		
				4.4.1.6.1.2	0.025" (0.6 mm)		●	
				4.4.1.6.1.3	0.015" (0.4 mm)			●
			4.4.1.6.2		At **EXTERIOR** use:			
				4.4.1.6.2.1	0.075" (1.9 mm)	●		
				4.4.1.6.2.2	0.05" (1.3 mm)		●	
				4.4.1.6.2.3	0.025" (0.6 mm)			●
		4.4.1.7			Require **FLATNESS** of installed and removable sheet products (see Test E illustrations in **COMPLIANCE**) not to exceed:			
			4.4.1.7.1		0.050" (1.3 mm) per 12" (305 mm) or portion thereof.	●		
			4.4.1.7.2		0.036" (0.9 mm) per 12" (305 mm) or portion thereof.		●	
			4.4.1.7.3		0.027" (0.7 mm) per 12" (305 mm) or portion thereof.			●
		4.4.1.8			Require **EDGEBANDING** to be flush with adjacent surfaces (see Test F illustrations in **COMPLIANCE**) not to exceed:			
			4.4.1.8.1		0.010" (0.25 mm)	●		
			4.4.1.8.2		0.005" (0.13 mm)		●	
			4.4.1.8.3		0.003" (0.03 mm)			●
		4.4.1.9			Allow **FILLER**:			
			4.4.1.9.1		If inconspicuous when viewed at 72" (1829 mm).	●		
			4.4.1.9.2		If inconspicuous when viewed at 48" (1219 mm).		●	
			4.4.1.9.3		**NOT ALLOWED.**			●
	4.4.2				Fixed **HORIZONTAL** cabinet members shall be either flush or set back a maximum of 1/16" (1.6 mm) at the intersection with vertical members and shall be uniform throughout the room.			

PRODUCT

MATERIAL, MACHINING, AND ASSEMBLY RULES (continued)

		No.	DESCRIPTION	E	C	P
4.4 ASSEMBLY			**ASSEMBLY** (continued)			
		4.4.3	Of **BOTTOM EDGES** of drawer fronts and aprons at knee spaces shall be smoothly sanded with edges eased.		●	●
	EDGES	**4.4.4**	Of **VISIBLE EDGES** requires (see Doors and Drawer Fronts, within this Product portion, for additional requirements):			
		4.4.4.1	At **ADJUSTABLE SHELVES**, only the front edge to be banded.			
		4.4.4.2	The **BOTTOM EDGE** of the end of upper cabinets to be banded.			
		4.4.4.3	When open above, the **TOP EDGE** of the end of cabinets 80" (2032 mm) or more above the floor to are be edgebanded with the manufacturer's option of banding material, unless the edge is considered visible from above; then the banding material shall match the exposed exterior surface.		●	●
		4.4.4.4	**EDGEBANDING** to run parallel to the long direction of the edge regardless of grain and/or pattern.			
		4.4.4.5	**DADOES** or **LOCK JOINTS** shall **NOT** run through the edgeband.		●	●
		4.4.4.6	**TEE-BANDING** must be so specified.			
	DRAWERS	**4.4.5**	Of **DRAWERS** (including trays and sliding bins) requires:			
		4.4.5.1	**COMPONENTS** to be of the same material and color for the entire project, and:			
		4.4.5.1.1	**BOTTOMS** may be vinyl if matching in color.			
	SIDES	**4.4.5.2**	**SIDES** to be, at the option of the manufacturer, and:			
		4.4.5.2.1	**NAILED** to sub-fronts and backs.	●		
		4.4.5.2.2	**MITER FOLDED** at vinyl with integral bottom.	●		
		4.4.5.2.3	**MULTIPLE-DOVETAILED** at solid wood or 7- or 9-ply hardwood veneer core plywood with core showing; mechanical fasteners are not required.		●	●
		4.4.5.2.4	**DOWELED.**		●	●
		4.4.5.2.5	Secured with **DOWEL SCREWS**, which:		●	
		4.4.5.2.5.1	Allows the use of 1/2" (12.7 mm) thick sides with 5/8" (16.1 mm) thick front and back members.		●	
		4.4.5.2.6	**BISCUIT-JOINED.**		●	●
		4.4.5.2.7	**LOCK-JOINTED** and **NAILED.**		●	●
		4.4.5.2.8	**RABBETED** to the fronts or sub-fronts and backs.	●		
		4.4.5.3	At **FLUSH OVERLAY** construction without sub-front, sides to be blind dovetail dadoed to the front.			
		4.4.5.4	Minimum of **TWO MECHANICAL FASTENERS** (dowels, biscuits, nails, screws) per joint, and:			
		4.4.5.4.1	A maximum of 3" (76 mm) on center for **BISCUITS, NAILS,** or **SCREWS**.			
		4.4.5.4.2	A maximum of 1-1/4" (32 mm) on center for joints up to 4" (102 mm) in length and 2-1/2" (64 mm) on center for joints over 4" (102 mm) in length for **DOWELS**.			
		4.4.5.5	**JOINTS** to be securely glued.			
		4.4.5.6	To be properly fitted to the cabinet without excessive play, and:			
		4.4.5.6.1	Fit front to back, less a maximum of 2" (50.8 mm) of interior cabinet depth.			
		4.4.5.6.2	Top to bottom to the greatest extent possible, while remaining fully functional.			
		4.4.5.7	**SLIDES TO OPERATE SMOOTHLY.**			
		4.4.5.8	**CLOSING STOPS** to be provided at the rear of both drawer sides, unless such is built into the slides to prevent the drawer front from impacting the cabinet body.			
		4.4.5.9	**SPRING-LOADED TIP-DOWN STOPS** to be provided (design permitting) to prevent the drawer from pulling out of the cabinet, unless such is built into the drawer slides.			

PRODUCT

MATERIAL, MACHINING, AND ASSEMBLY RULES (continued)

4.4 ASSEMBLY	4.4.5 DRAWERS				DESCRIPTION	E	C	P
ASSEMBLY (continued)								
	Of **DRAWERS** requires (continued)							
		4.4.5.10			At **FILE DRAWERS:**			
			4.4.5.10.1		**FULL-EXTENSION** slides to be provided.			
			4.4.5.10.2		Clear **INSIDE HEIGHT** shall be sufficient for hanging file folder tabs.			
			4.4.5.10.3		**FILE DIRECTION** to be at the option of the manufacturer.			
			4.4.5.10.4		Either a **SYSTEM STAND** or **RAILS** to be provided at the manufacturer's option.			
			4.4.5.10.5		**LEGAL-SIZED DRAWERS** with hanging file suspension bars, provided for both legal- and letter-sized files.			
		4.4.5.11 LOCKS			**LOCKS** to be furnished **ONLY** where shown on contract documents, unless specifications denote specific location requirements, and:			
			4.4.5.11.1		**WITHSTAND** a minimum of 50 lb (22.7 kg) pull force in the locked position.			
			4.4.5.11.2		**STRIKES** are required.			
			4.4.5.11.3		**SECURITY** or **DUST PANELS** are required at locked banks of drawers when each drawer is keyed differently.			
		4.4.5.12			Items such as **TRAYS** and **BINS** shall be similarly constructed.			
		4.4.5.13			**FRONTS** and **FALSE FRONTS**:			
			4.4.5.13.1		Shall match the **CABINET DOORS**, except:			
				4.4.5.13.1.1	Where the drawer and false fronts are too small to allow a match.			
			4.4.5.13.2		**SECURE ATTACHMENT** to sub-front with pan/binder head, countersunk flathead, or ovalhead screws with a minimum of two screws at each end a maximum of 1-1/2" (38.1 mm) from the inside corners of the drawer box and a maximum of 12" (305 mm) on center.			
				4.4.5.13.2.1	Fasteners used to attach drawer pulls or knobs through both the sub-front and drawer front shall be considered a fastener.			
				4.4.5.13.2.2	**FALSE FRONTS** to be securely attached to the cabinet body.			
		4.4.5.14 DRAWER BOTTOMS			**DRAWER BOTTOMS**, excluding integral miter folded:			
			4.4.5.14.1		To be a minimum of 1/4" (6.4 mm) in thickness, except:			
				4.4.5.14.1.1	When exceeding 30" (762 mm) in width, be a minimum of 1/2" (12.7 mm).			
			4.4.5.14.2		With **NO EXPOSED** particleboard or medium-density fiberboard.			
			4.4.5.14.3		With **NO** softwood plywood or hardboard.		●	●
			4.4.5.14.4		Be **PLOWED** into sides, fronts, or sub-fronts, and:			
				4.4.5.14.4.1	Be **SECURELY GLUED** or glue-blocked to form a rigid unit.			
				4.4.5.14.4.2	If 1/2" (12.7 mm) in **THICKNESS**, they are **NOT** required to be plowed into drawer fronts or sub-fronts with the use of integral metal drawer side/slide systems.			
				4.4.5.14.4.3	Shall have a minimum of 3/8" (9.5 mm) shoulder remaining on the sides, front, and back.			
			4.4.5.14.5		Be **SECURELY ATTACHED** to the drawer box back, either by plow or by mechanical fastening (maximum of 4" [102 mm] on center) if run through, and:		●	●
				4.4.5.14.5.1	If surface applied, mechanical fastening (maximum of 4" [102 mm] on center) to the entire box.		●	●

10

PRODUCT

MATERIAL, MACHINING, AND ASSEMBLY RULES (continued)

4.4 ASSEMBLY — DOORS — HINGED — HINGES

Item	DESCRIPTION	E	C	P
	ASSEMBLY (continued)			
4.4.6	Of **DOORS** requires:			
4.4.6.1	**FLUSH OVERLAY** to be the default style.			
4.4.6.2	**VISIBLE EDGES**, after doors and drawers are closed, to match the exposed surface; however:			
4.4.6.2.1	**BANDING** is not required at back beveled doors.	●		
4.4.6.2.2	**BANDING** is required at back beveled doors.		●	●
4.4.6.3	**CORE THICKNESS** to be a minimum of 11/16" (17.5 mm).			
4.4.6.4	**MAXIMUM** cabinet door size shall be 24" (610 mm) in width and 80" (2032 mm) in height.			
4.4.6.5	**1-3/8"** (34.9 mm) or **THICKER** doors to be governed by Section 9.			
4.4.6.6	**STOP SILENCERS** to be installed at the top and bottom of all hinged cabinet doors (on the closing edge) to properly align the door and silence its closing.		●	●
4.4.6.7	**CORE** to be of an approved particleboard, medium-density fiberboard, or otherwise engineered core.			
4.4.6.7.1	**VENEER**, **OSB**, or **LUMBER** cores are not guaranteed against warping, telegraphing, or delamination.			
4.4.6.8	**LOCKS** to be furnished **ONLY** where shown on cabinet elevations of contract documents, unless specifications denote specific location requirements, and:			
4.4.6.8.1	They **WITHSTAND** a minimum of 50 lb (22.7 kg) pull force in the locked position.			
4.4.6.8.2	**STRIKES** are required.			
4.4.6.9	When **HINGED**:			
4.4.6.9.1	Doors shall **STOP,** as applicable, against the cabinet body at the bottom (except at handicapped units), sides, and top stretcher; however:			
4.4.6.9.1.1	At **FLUSH INSET** doors, a positive stop or hardware member acting as such is permitted, and:			
4.4.6.9.1.1.1	**STOPS** shall be provided at both sides of the door opening.			●
4.4.6.9.1.2	At **PAIRED DOORS** below a drawer, a rail, stretcher, or partition (full or partial) shall be provided.		●	●
4.4.6.9.2	**HINGES** shall be installed by the manufacturer, and:			
4.4.6.9.2.1	Operate properly without binding.			
4.4.6.9.2.2	Exposed **ADJACENT HINGES** shall align horizontally.			
4.4.6.9.2.3	Shall be either **SELF-CLOSING** or doors shall be provided with a catch.		●	●
4.4.6.9.2.4	At **GRADE I** hinges, doors:			
4.4.6.9.2.4.1	Under 48" (1219 mm) in height shall have a minimum of two hinges.			
4.4.6.9.2.4.2	48" (1219 mm) to 84" (2134 mm) height shall have a minimum of three hinges.			
4.4.6.9.2.4.3	Over 84" (2134 mm) in height shall have a minimum of four hinges.			
4.4.6.9.2.5	At **GRADE II** hinges, doors:			
4.4.6.9.2.5.1	Under 40" (1016 mm) in height shall have a minimum of two hinges.			
4.4.6.9.2.5.2	40" (1016 mm) to 60" (1524 mm) in height shall have a minimum of three hinges.			

PRODUCT

MATERIAL, MACHINING, AND ASSEMBLY RULES (continued)

DESCRIPTION		E	C	P
4.4	**ASSEMBLY** (continued)			
4.4.6	Of **DOORS** requires (continued)			
4.4.6.9	**HINGES** shall be installed by the manufacturer, and (continued)			
4.4.6.9.2	**HINGES** (continued)			
4.4.6.9.2.5	At **GRADE II** hinges, doors (continued)			
4.4.6.9.2.5.3	60" (1524 mm) to 80" (2031 mm) in height shall have a minimum of four hinges.			
4.4.6.9.2.5.4	Over 80" (2031 mm) in height shall have a minimum of five hinges and an additional hinge for every 18" (457 mm) of additional height.			
4.4.6.9.2.6	**WRAP-AROUND** hinges, as applicable, shall be let into the edge of the door to maintain proper gap tolerance.			
4.4.6.9.2.6.1	Exposed door edges resulting from the **NOTCHING** for hinges are **NOT** required to be finished.	●	●	
4.4.6.9.2.6.2	Exposed door edges resulting from the **NOTCHING** for hinges are required to be painted or stained to match.			●
4.4.6.9.2.7	**CONCEALED** 1-3/8" (35 mm) cup hinge assembly installation, when required to be installed with screws, requires dowel/euro screws or screws recommended by the manufacturer.			
4.4.6.9.3	**LOCKING PAIRS:**			
4.4.6.9.3.1	Shall be equipped with an **ELBOW CATCH** and a **STOP BLOCK** on the inactive leaf, and:			
4.4.6.10.3.1.1	**STOP BLOCK** shall be adequate to prevent the latch of the elbow catch from being defeated by applying vertical pressure on the door.			
4.4.6.9.3.2	**FULL-HEIGHT DOORS** with a **FIXED MID-HEIGHT SHELF** shall have an **ELBOW CATCH** on the inactive leaf at the fixed shelf.			
4.4.6.9.3.3	**FULL-HEIGHT DOORS** (without fixed shelf) shall be equipped with surface-mounted **SLIDE BOLT** or spring-actuated **CHAIN BOLT** with shelf depth adjusted accordingly.		●	●
4.4.6.10	When **STILE** and **RAIL** (see the Hinged and Sliding sub-headings for additional requirements as applicable):			
4.4.6.10.1	**STILES** and **RAILS:**			
4.4.6.10.1.1	**MOLDED PROFILE** (sticking) shall be the manufacturer's option, unless specified otherwise.			
4.4.6.10.1.2	Of **SOLID LUMBER** shall be a minimum of 2-1/2" (63.5 mm) in width.			

PRODUCT

MATERIAL, MACHINING, AND ASSEMBLY RULES (continued)

Number	DESCRIPTION	E	C	P
4.4	**ASSEMBLY** (continued)			
4.4.6	Of **DOORS** requires (continued)			
4.4.6.10	When **STILE** and **RAIL** (continued)			
4.4.6.10.1	**STILES** and **RAILS** (continued)			
4.4.6.10.1.3	Shall be a minimum of 3/4" (19 mm) in **THICKNESS**, and:			
4.4.6.10.1.3.1	To a **TOLERANCE** of +/- 1/32" (0.8 mm) of specified thickness.			
4.4.6.10.1.4	Of **VENEERED** or **OVERLAID** construction shall be **MDF** or **PARTICLEBOARD CORE** a minimum of 3-1/2" (88.9 mm) in width, and:			
4.4.6.10.1.4.1	With approval, framed glass doors may be manufactured from flush panels without stile and rail considerations, provided all other door requirements are met. All exposed edges shall be banded or finished to match adjacent surfaces.			
4.4.6.10.1.5	Doors **OVER** 60" (1524 mm) in height shall have an intermediate rail.			
4.4.6.10.1.6	**STILES** shall run the full height of the door, and:			
4.4.6.10.1.6.1	**TOP**, **CROSS**, and **BOTTOM RAILS** shall run between stiles.		●	●
4.4.6.10.1.6.2	**MULLIONS** shall run between rails.		●	●
4.4.6.10.1.7	**GRAIN** or **DIRECTIONAL PATTERN** shall run vertically on stiles and horizontally on rails.			
4.4.6.10.1.8	**CLEARANCE** shall be a minimum of 3/8" (9.5 mm) between any hardware machining and class cutout.			
4.4.6.10.1.9	**JOINERY** shall be:			
4.4.6.10.1.9.1	The manufacturer's option.	●		
4.4.6.10.1.9.2	Mating male/female sticking glued under pressure.		●	
4.4.6.10.1.9.3	Mortise and tenon, dowels or loose tenon glued under pressure.			●
4.4.6.10.2	**PANEL:**			
4.4.6.10.2.1	**GRAIN** or **PATTERN** direction shall be the manufacturer's option.	●		
4.4.6.10.2.2	**GRAIN** or **PATTERN** direction shall run vertically, and:		●	●
4.4.6.10.2.2.1	Adjacent **DOOR PANELS** for **TRANSPARENT FINISH** shall have a pleasing match for color and grain.		●	●
4.4.6.10.2.3	**CORE** shall be covered by veneer, overlay, or rim banding.			

PRODUCT

MATERIAL, MACHINING, AND ASSEMBLY RULES (continued)

					DESCRIPTION	E	C	P
4.4 ASSEMBLY					**ASSEMBLY** (continued)			
	4.4.6 DOORS				Of **DOORS** requires (continued)			
		4.4.6.10 STILE & RAIL DOOR			When **STILE** and **RAIL** (continued)			
			4.4.6.10.2 PANEL		**PANEL** (continued)			
				4.4.6.10.2.4	When **FLAT** shall be a minimum of 1/4” (6.4 mm) in thickness, and:			
				4.4.6.10.2.4.1	Edge-glued **SOLID LUMBER** is permitted if at least 1/2” (12.7 mm) in thickness and width across grain is 13-3/4” (350 mm) or less.	•	•	
				4.4.6.10.2.4.2	**SOLID LUMBER** is not permitted.			•
				4.4.6.10.2.5	When **RAISED** shall be a minimum of 1/2” (12.7 mm) in thickness, and:			
				4.4.6.10.2.5.1	Edge-glued **SOLID LUMBER** is permitted for panels less than 13-3/4” (350 mm) in width across grain.	•	•	
				4.4.6.10.2.5.2	**SOLID LUMBER** is not permitted for panels.			•
				4.4.6.10.2.5.3	**SOLID LUMBER** is permitted for rimming panels if mitered and glued under pressure.			
				4.4.6.10.2.6	Regardless of **RETENTION** method, shall have the freedom and room to expand and contract in reaction to ambient humidity changes.			
				4.4.6.10.2.7	**APPLIED MOLDINGS** shall be spot-glued and fine finish-nailed.			
			4.4.6.10.3		**GLASS** shall be clear **LAMINATED SAFETY** or **TEMPERED.**			
			4.4.6.10.4		**STOPS** shall:			
				4.4.6.10.4.1	Be continuous and removable, except:			
				4.4.6.10.4.1.1	**GLASS CLIPS** are permitted	•	•	
				4.4.6.10.4.2	For **OPAQUE FINISH**, be synthetic or solid stock of the manufacturer’s option.			
				4.4.6.10.4.3	For **TRANSPARENT FINISH**, be synthetic or solid stock of compatible species to adjacent surface.			
				4.4.6.10.4.4	For **DECORATIVE LAMINATE**, be synthetic or solid stock finished to match adjacent surface.			
				4.4.6.10.4.5	When **SYNTHETIC** only acceptable at the interior face.			
		4.4.6.11 SLIDING			When **SLIDING**:			
			4.4.6.11.1		**THICKNESS** to be a minimum of:			
				4.4.6.11.1.1	1/4” (6.4 mm) for doors 24” (610 mm) and **UNDER** in height.			
				4.4.6.11.1.2	3/4” (19 mm) for doors over 24” (610 mm) in height.			
			4.4.6.11.2		**VERTICAL EDGES** are considered exposed.			
			4.4.6.11.3		**TOP** and **BOTTOM EDGES** are concealed and not required to be banded or filled.			
			4.4.6.11.4		Doors more that 1.5 times as tall as they are wide shall be mounted with overhead metal track and roller hanger to prevent tipping and binding.			

PRODUCT

MATERIAL, MACHINING, AND ASSEMBLY RULES (continued)

	DESCRIPTION	E	C	P
4.4 ASSEMBLY	**ASSEMBLY** (continued)			
4.4.6 DOORS	Of **DOORS** requires (continued)			
4.4.6.11 SLIDING	When **SLIDING** (continued)			
4.4.6.11.5	At **HANGING TRACK** systems, exposed track is acceptable and door heights of:			
4.4.6.11.5.1	36" (914 mm) or less shall be equipped with adequate top and/or bottom guides or runs. Sliding doors in excess of 36" (914 mm) in height shall be installed on hardware of a type optional with the manufacturer.	●		
4.4.6.11.5.2	34" (864 mm) or less shall be installed on the appropriate fiber or metal track, with top guide.		●	●
4.4.6.11.5.3	**OVER** 34" (864 mm) shall be installed on either the overhead metal track with nylon roller hangers, or the metal bottom track with sheaves and top guide.		●	●
4.4.6.11.6	At **TYPE B** construction, a continuous vertical filler strip shall be provided in the opening behind the face frame and in front of the rear sliding door.		●	●
4.4.6.12	When **FRAMELESS GLASS**:			
4.4.6.12.1	Be a **MINIMUM** of 1/4" (6.4 mm) thick.			
4.4.6.12.2	Be clear **TEMPERED SAFETY GLASS**, with:			
4.4.6.12.2.1	Exposed edges **GROUND**.	●	●	
4.4.6.12.2.2	Exposed edges **FLAT-POLISHED**.			●
4.4.6.12.3	Any requirement for **LAMINATED SAFETY GLASS** must be so specified.			
4.4.6.12.4	**CARRIERS** with metal track and top guide, and:			
4.4.6.12.4.1	If needed to **PREVENT SAGGING**, bottoms of upper cabinets shall be increased in thickness, provided with a hardwood track member of sufficient thickness, or provided with a strong back support screwed and glued to the underside.			
4.4.7	**APRONS** require:			
4.4.7.1	A minimum **THICKNESS** of 3/4" (19 mm), and:			
4.4.7.1.1	**BOTTOM EDGE** banded.		●	●
4.4.8 ENDS & DIVISIONS	**ENDS** and **DIVISIONS** require:			
4.4.8.1	**CABINET ENDS** to be furnished, and:			
4.4.8.1.1	**OPEN ENDS** or skeleton frames against walls are **NOT** permitted.			
4.4.8.2	A minimum **THICKNESS** of:			
4.4.8.2.1	3/4" (19 mm), except:			
4.4.8.2.1.1	1/2" (12.7 mm) at face-frame construction.	●		
4.4.8.2.1.2	3/4"(19 mm) at face-frame construction.		●	●
4.4.8.3	**EXPOSED ENDS** be of integral construction, rabbeted or plowed to receive backs, and horizontal members (excluding countertops) shall not extend beyond the exposed end.			
4.4.8.4	**CONCEALED ENDS** allow tops and bottoms to extend past, if applicable.			
4.4.8.5	The **TOP EDGE** of the end of cabinets:			
4.4.8.5.1	If exposed or visible from above be banded with material of matching color and pattern to exposed exterior surface.			
4.4.8.5.2	If open above; however, not visible, at 80" (2032 mm) or more above the floor be banded with the manufacturer's option of edge material.			

PRODUCT

MATERIAL, MACHINING, AND ASSEMBLY RULES (continued)

			DESCRIPTION	E	C	P
4.4 ASSEMBLY			**ASSEMBLY** (continued)			
	4.4.8		**ENDS** and **DIVISIONS** (continued)			
		4.4.8.6	A **SOLID DIVISION** behind all vertical **FACE-FRAME** members or hanging stiles.		●	●
		4.4.8.7	**DRAWER COMPARTMENTS** to be separated from shelf or open compartments by a solid vertical division unless prevented by design or usage.			
		4.4.8.8	At **PANELED CONSTRUCTION**, stiles and rails to be a minimum of 3/4" (19 mm) thickness, with:			
		4.4.8.8.1	A minimum of 1/4" (6.4 mm) **PANEL** thickness.			
		4.4.8.8.2	**HARDBOARD** not permitted for transparent finish.			
		4.4.8.9	**FREE-STANDING** end panels shall provide for concealed installation.			●
	4.4.9 TOPS & BOTTOMS		**TOPS** and **BOTTOMS** require: (Note: Base cabinets with separate countertops are not covered within this heading; see "Stretchers.")			
		4.4.9.1	A minimum **THICKNESS** of 3/4" (19 mm), design permitting.			
		4.4.9.2 BOTTOMS	**BOTTOMS** of wall-hung cabinets:			
		4.4.9.2.1	When **UNSUPPORTED**, not to exceed 48" (1219 mm).			
		4.4.9.2.2	**JOINTS** are permitted where ends are flush with bottoms in each unit.			
		4.4.9.2.3	**EXPOSED EDGES** of the ends shall be banded with the same material as the exposed surfaces.		●	●
		4.4.9.2.4	**CORES** to be subject to a 40 lb (18.1 kg) load capacity of the manufacturer's option.		●	●
		4.4.9.2.5	With a 50 lb (22.7 kg) load capacity at **SCHOOLS**, **HOSPITALS**, and **LIBRARY BOOKSHELVES**.		●	●
		4.4.9.2.6	Be **SECURED** to ends, divisions, and back.		●	●
		4.4.9.2.7	With **THICKNESS** of 1" (25.4 mm) minimum when made with particleboard core and are 42" (1069 mm) and over in length.		●	●
		4.4.9.2.8	If **ENDS EXTEND** below the bottom, the interior exposed surface of the end shall be of the same material as the exposed surface.		●	●
		4.4.9.2.9	When **THICKER** is desired due to heavy loads, they shall be so specified.			
		4.4.9.2.10	At **EXPOSED INTERIOR**, shall be uniform in thickness for the entire elevation or connected elevations, except:		●	●
		4.4.9.2.10.1	When **CONCEALED** behind a minimum 1-1/2" (38.1 mm) face-frame member.		●	●
		4.4.9.3 TOPS	**TOPS** of wall-hung and tall cabinets:			
		4.4.9.3.1	Are not considered **LOAD-BEARING**.			
		4.4.9.3.2	At **TYPE I** construction, permit joints where exposed ends are flush with tops, and:			
		4.4.9.3.2.1	**END** shall be **BANDED** to match other exposed surfaces, except:			
	4.4.10		**SECURITY** and **DUST PANELS** shall:			
		4.4.10.1	Be **FURNISHED** above locked doors and drawers, only if each drawer or door is keyed differently.			
		4.4.10.2	Be a **SOLID PIECE** of plywood, particleboard, medium-density fiberboard, or solid phenolic, a minimum of 1/2" (12.7 m) in thickness, and:			
		4.4.10.2.1	If front and rear **STRETCHERS** are used, a 1/4" (6.4 mm) panel may be let into the stretchers.			

PRODUCT

MATERIAL, MACHINING, AND ASSEMBLY RULES (continued)

4.4 ASSEMBLY		DESCRIPTION	E	C	P
		ASSEMBLY (continued)			
STRETCHERS	**4.4.11**	**STRETCHERS** require: (Note: This is only applicable to base cabinets with separate countertops.)			
	4.4.11.1	They be provided at **BOTH** the front and the back of the cabinet body, except:			
	4.4.11.1.1	At **SINK** compartments, may run front to back.			
	4.4.11.2	**SOLID STOCK** or **PLYWOOD** be a minimum of 3/4" (19 mm) in thickness and 2" (50.8 mm) in width.			
	4.4.11.3	**PARTICLEBOARD** or **MDF** be a minimum of 3/4" (19 mm) in thickness and 3-1/2" (88.9 mm) in width and reinforced as necessary to support the countertop.			
	4.4.11.4	A **PANEL MEMBER**, a minimum of 3/4" (19 mm) in thickness, the full length and depth of the cabinet opening may be used in lieu of stretchers.			
	4.4.11.5	At **DRAWER BANKS**, an intermediate front stretcher when the total drawer opening height exceeds 30" (762 mm).		●	●
BACKS	**4.4.12**	**BACKS**:			
	4.4.12.1	Are required **ONLY** where the cabinet will be set in an unfinished recess or where the back would be exposed to view, and:	●		
	4.4.12.1.1	Be hardboard or plywood a minimum of 1/8" (3.2 mm) in thickness.	●		
	4.4.12.2	Are **REQUIRED** and:		●	●
	4.4.12.2.1	Shall be a minimum of 1/4" (6.4 mm) in thickness.		●	●
	4.4.12.2.2	Shall be of an approved semi-exposed material.		●	●
	4.4.12.2.3	Vinyl is permitted, provided it is of the same color as the other semi-exposed surfaces.			
	4.4.12.3	When **EXPOSED EXTERIOR** shall be a minimum of 1/2" (12.7 mm) in thickness.			
	4.4.12.4	Where **NON-HOUSED** shall be screwed to the case body, divisions, and/or fixed shelves at a maximum of 4" (101.6 mm) on center.			
	4.4.12.5	Where **PLOWED IN**, with a minimum shoulder of 3/8" (9.5 mm), shall be securely nailed or stapled to the case body at a maximum of 4" (101.6 mm) on center.			
	4.4.12.6	**ATTACHMENT** of base, tall, and wall-hung cabinet backs by other than the above requirements for non-housed or plowed-in is permitted, provided it has been independently tested to show compliance to the Wall Cabinet Structural Integrity Test as shown in Appendix A.			
	4.4.12.7	Are **NOT** required to be glued.			
	4.4.12.8	Require **ANCHOR** or **HANGING STRIPS**:			
	4.4.12.8.1	Except when backs are 1/2" (12.7 mm) or thicker.			
	4.4.12.8.2	Are allowed on the interior of the cabinet.	●		
	4.4.12.8.3	Are **NOT** allowed on the interior of the cabinet.		●	●
	4.4.12.9	Shall be rabbeted or dadoed into **EXPOSED ENDS**.			●
	4.4.12.10	**SHALL BE REMOVABLE**, if so specified.			
	4.4.13	**TOE BASES, KICKS,** and **SLEEPERS**:			
	4.4.13.1	Shall be either **SEPARATE** from or **INTEGRAL** to the cabinet body at the manufacturer's option.			
	4.4.13.2	**SEPARATE BASES** shall be mechanically fastened to the cabinet bottom with flat-head screws set flush or slightly recessed.			
	4.4.13.3	Shall be a minimum of 4" (101.6 mm) high.			
	4.4.13.4	Shall be a minimum of 3/4" (19 mm) in thickness.			
	4.4.13.5	**SLEEPERS** shall be provided at a maximum of 36" (86.4 mm) on center.			
	4.4.13.6	If specified for moisture-resistance or laboratory use, **COMPONENTS** within 2" (50.8 mm) of the finish floor to be constructed of solid lumber, exterior plywood, or exterior particleboard.			

PRODUCT

MATERIAL, MACHINING, AND ASSEMBLY RULES (continued)

DESCRIPTION		E	C	P
4.4 ASSEMBLY (continued)				
4.4.13 TOE BASES, KICKS, and SLEEPERS (continued)				
4.4.13.7	**LEVELERS:**			
4.4.13.7.1	May be used at the manufacturer's option.			
4.4.13.7.2	At cabinets over 15-1/2" (394 mm) in depth, shall require four levelers per unit up to 37-1/2" (953 mm) in width and six per unit up to 48" (1219 mm) in width.			
4.4.13.7.3	At cabinets less than 15-1/2" (394 mm) in depth, levelers are only required at the front and shall require two levelers per unit up to 37-1/2" (953 mm) in width and three per unit up to 48" (1219 mm) in width.			
4.4.14	**SHELVES** require:			
4.4.14.1	**CORE** to be a minimum of 3/4" (19 mm) in **THICKNESS**.			
4.4.14.2	When **THICKER SHELVES** or **CENTER SUPPORTS** are desired due to heavy loads, they shall be so specified.			
4.4.14.3	**GRAIN** or **DIRECTIONAL PATTERN** of the face to run the length of the shelf.			
4.4.14.4	**DIVIDERS,** vertical or horizontal, to match the exposed or the semi-exposed surface, as applicable.			●
4.4.14.5	**UNIFORM SHELF THICKNESS** at each elevation or connected elevations at open casework.		●	●
4.4.14.6	**HARDBOARD** used for shelves or vertical or horizontal dividers be smooth on both sides and tempered.		●	●
4.4.14.7	**CABINETS** over 72" (1829) high, not immediately abutting a structural wall or another cabinet, have a fixed shelf at approximate mid-height.			
4.4.14.8	**GLASS** be tempered float glass conforming in thickness to the **MAXIMUM ADJUSTABLE SHELF LENGTHS** listed herein, and:		●	●
4.4.14.8.1	Have all four edges polished.		●	●
4.4.14.9	**FIXED SHELVES:**			
4.4.14.9.1	With a **THICKNESS** of 1" (25.4 mm) minimum when made with particleboard core and are 42" (1069 mm) and over in length.		●	●
4.4.14.9.2	**CORES** to be subject to a 40 lb (18.1 kg) load capacity of the manufacturer's option.		●	●
4.4.14.9.3	With a 50 lb (22.7 kg) load capacity at **SCHOOLS**, **HOSPITALS**, and **LIBRARY BOOKSHELVES**.		●	●
4.4.14.9.4	Be **SECURED** to ends, divisions, and back.			
4.4.14.9.5	**OVER** 48" (1219 mm) in length, be supported as applicable on cleats at the back, or secured through the back.	●		
4.4.14.9.6	**OVER** 48" (1219 mm) have a center support.		●	●
4.4.14.10	**ADJUSTABLE SHELVES:**			
4.4.14.10.1	Shall **CONFORM** in thickness to the listing below of materials and **MAXIMUM PERMITTED LENGTHS**, with:			
4.4.14.10.1.1	**LENGTH** and **GRAIN DIRECTION** running left to right.			
4.4.14.10.1.2	**CREEP** not taken into consideration and not considered a defect.			
4.4.14.10.1.3	**INFORMATION/RATINGS** representing calculations believed to be reliable; however, due to variations in use not known or out of our control, no warranties or guarantees are made as to the end results.			

PRODUCT

MATERIAL, MACHINING, AND ASSEMBLY RULES (continued)

Rule	DESCRIPTION (E C P)
4.4	**ASSEMBLY** (continued)
4.4.14	**SHELVES** require (continued)
4.4.14.10	**ADJUSTABLE SHELVES:**
4.4.14.10.1	Shall **CONFORM** in thickness to the listing below of materials and **MAXIMUM PERMITTED LENGTHS**, with:
4.4.14.10.1.4	**MOE** (Modulus of Elasticity) figures are from published industry standards.
4.4.14.10.1.5	**LAMINATIONS** are based on rigid glue line; contact adhesive is **NOT** permitted.
4.4.14.10.1.6	**TOTAL APPLIED WEIGHT** uniformly dispersed on an individual shelf **NOT EXCEEDING 200 lbs** (90.7 kg) on any one shelf while being subject to load capacities of:
4.4.14.10.1.6.1	50 lbs (22.7 kg) per square foot for **SCHOOL, HOSPITAL, AND LIBRARY OR BOOK SHELVING**.
4.4.14.10.1.6.2	40 lbs (18.1 kg) per square foot for **COMMERCIAL SHELVING**.
4.4.14.10.2	**PARTICLEBOARD**, M-2, 325,000 MOE, with or without LPDL.
4.4.14.10.2.1	At 3/4” (19 mm) in thickness allows for a maximum of:
4.4.14.10.2.1.1	28” (711 mm) in length at a 40 lb/sq ft load.
4.4.14.10.2.1.2	25” (635 mm) in length at a 50 lb/sq ft load.
4.4.14.10.2.2	At 1” (25.4 mm) in thickness allows for a maximum of:
4.4.14.10.2.2.1	37” (940 mm) in length at a 40 lb/sq ft load.
4.4.14.10.2.2.2	34” (866 mm) in length at a 50 lb/sq ft load.
4.4.14.10.3	**PARTICLEBOARD**, M-2, 640,000 MOE, with hardwood veneer on two sides:
4.4.14.10.3.1	At 3/4” (19 mm) in thickness allows for a maximum of:
4.4.14.10.3.1.1	35” (813 mm) in length at a 40 lb/sq ft load.
4.4.14.10.3.1.2	32” (813 mm) in length at a 50 lb/sq ft load.
4.4.14.10.3.2	At 1” (25.4 mm) in thickness allows for a maximum of:
4.4.14.10.3.2.1	46” (1168 mm) in length at a 40 lb/sq ft load.
4.4.14.10.3.2.2	43” (1092 mm) in length at a 50 lb/sq ft load.
4.4.14.10.4	**PARTICLEBOARD**, M-2, 640,000 MOE, with vertical grade HPDL on two sides with rigid or hard glue line.
4.4.14.10.4.1	At 3/4” (19 mm) in thickness allows for a maximum of:
4.4.14.10.4.1.1	40” (1016 mm) in length at a 40 lb/sq ft load.
4.4.14.10.4.1.2	37” (940 mm) in length at a 50 lb/sq ft load.
4.4.14.10.4.2	At 1” (25.4 mm) in thickness allows for a maximum of:
4.4.14.10.4.2.1	53” (1346 mm) in length at a 40 lb/sq ft load.
4.4.14.10.4.2.2	49” (1245 mm) in length at a 50 lb/sq ft load.
4.4.14.10.5	**PARTICLEBOARD**, M-3, 399,000 MOE, with or without LPDL:
4.4.14.10.5.1	At 3/4” (19 mm) in thickness allows for a maximum of:
4.4.14.10.5.1.1	30” (762 mm) in length at a 40 lb/sq ft load.
4.4.14.10.5.1.2	29” (737mm) in length at a 50 lb/sq ft load.

PRODUCT

MATERIAL, MACHINING, AND ASSEMBLY RULES (continued)

DESCRIPTION						E C P
4.4 ASSEMBLY	**ASSEMBLY** (continued)					
	4.4.14 SHELVES	**SHELVES** require (continued)				
		4.4.14.10 ADJUSTABLE	**ADJUSTABLE SHELVES** (continued)			
			4.4.14.10.5	**PARTICLEBOARD**, M-3, 399,000 MOE, with or without LPDL (continued)		
				4.4.14.10.5.2	At 1" (25.4 mm) in thickness allows for a maximum of:	
					4.4.14.10.5.2.1	38" (965 mm) in length at a 40 lb/sq ft load.
					4.4.14.10.5.2.2	36" (914 mm) in length at a 50 lb/sq ft load.
			4.4.14.10.6	**PARTICLEBOARD**, M-3, 1,020,000 MOE, with vertical grade HPDL on two sides with rigid or hard glue line:		
				4.4.14.10.6.1	At 3/4" (19 mm) in thickness allows for a maximum of:	
					4.4.14.10.6.1.1	41" (1041 mm) in length at a 40 lb/sq ft load.
					4.4.14.10.6.1.2	38" (965 mm) in length at a 50 lb/sq ft load.
				4.4.14.10.6.2	At 1" (25.4 mm) in thickness allows for a maximum of:	
					4.4.14.10.6.2.1	54" (1372 mm) in length at a 40 lb/sq ft load.
					4.4.14.10.6.2.2	50" (1270 mm) in length at a 50 lb/sq ft load.
			4.4.14.10.7	MDF (Medium-Density Fiberboard), 525,000 MOE, with or without LPDL:		
				4.4.14.10.7.1	At 3/4" (19 mm) in thickness allows for a maximum of:	
					4.4.14.10.7.1.1	32" (813 mm) in length at a 40 lb/sq ft load.
					4.4.14.10.7.1.2	30" (762 mm) in length at a 50 lb/sq ft load.
				4.4.14.10.7.2	At 1" (25.4 mm) in thickness allows for a maximum of:	
					4.4.14.10.7.2.1	43" (1092 mm) in length at a 40 lb/sq ft load.
					4.4.14.10.7.2.2	40" (1016 mm) in length at a 50 lb/sq ft load.
			4.4.14.10.8	MDF (Medium-Density Fiberboard), 750,000 MOE, with hardwood veneer on two sides.		
				4.4.14.10.8.1	At 3/4" (19 mm) in thickness allows for a maximum of:	
					4.4.14.10.8.1.1	37" (940 mm) in length at a 40 lb/sq ft load.
					4.4.14.10.8.1.2	34" (866 mm) in length at a 50 lb/sq ft load.
				4.4.14.10.8.2	At 1" (25.4 mm) in thickness allows for a maximum of:	
					4.4.14.10.8.2.1	49" (1245 mm) in length at a 40 lb/sq ft load.
					4.4.14.10.8.2.2	45" (1143 mm) in length at a 50 lb/sq ft load.
			4.4.14.10.9	Oriented strand board, 700,000 MOE:		
				4.4.14.10.9.1	At 3/4" (19 mm) in thickness allows for a maximum of:	
					4.4.14.10.9.1.1	36" (914 mm) in length at a 40 lb/sq ft load.
					4.4.14.10.9.1.2	33" (838 mm) in length at a 50 lb/sq ft load.
				4.4.14.10.9.2	At 1" (25.4 mm) in thickness allows for a maximum of:	
					4.4.14.10.9.2.1	48" (1219 mm) in length at a 40 lb/sq ft load.
					4.4.14.10.9.2.2	44" (1118 mm) in length at a 50 lb/sq ft load.
			4.4.14.10.10	Oriented strand board, 1,200,000 MOE, with hardwood veneer on two sides.		
				4.4.14.10.10.1	At 3/4" (19 mm) in thickness allows for a maximum of:	
					4.4.14.10.10.1.1	43" (1092 mm) in length at a 40 lb/sq ft load.
					4.4.14.10.10.1.2	40" (1016 mm) in length at a 50 lb/sq ft load.
				4.4.14.10.10.2	At 1" (25.4 mm) in thickness allows for a maximum of:	
					4.4.14.10.10.2.1	57" (1449 mm) in length at a 40 lb/sq ft load.
					4.4.14.10.10.2.2	53" (1346 mm) in length at a 50 lb/sq ft load.

PRODUCT

MATERIAL, MACHINING, AND ASSEMBLY RULES (continued)

DESCRIPTION		E	C	P

4.4 ASSEMBLY (continued)

4.4.14 SHELVES require (continued)

4.4.14.10 ADJUSTABLE SHELVES (continued)

Number	Description
4.4.14.10.11	Veneer core, (Douglas Fir) plywood, 950,000 MOE:
4.4.14.10.11.1	At 3/4” (19 mm) in thickness allows for a maximum of:
4.4.14.10.11.1.1	40” (1016 mm) in length at a 40 lb/sq ft load.
4.4.14.10.11.1.2	37” (940 mm) in length at a 50 lb/sq ft load.
4.4.14.10.11.2	At 1” (25.4 mm) in thickness allows for a maximum of:
4.4.14.10.11.2.1	53” (1346 mm) in length at a 40 lb/sq ft load.
4.4.14.10.11.2.2	49” (1245 mm) in length at a 50 lb/sq ft load.
4.4.14.10.12	Veneer core, (Douglas Fir) plywood, 1,800,000 MOE, with hardwood veneer on two sides:
4.4.14.10.12.1	At 3/4” (19 mm) in thickness allows for a maximum of:
4.4.14.10.12.1.1	49” (1245 mm) in length at a 40 lb/sq ft load.
4.4.14.10.12.1.2	46” (1168 mm) in length at a 50 lb/sq ft load.
4.4.14.10.12.2	At 1” (25.4 mm) in thickness allows for a maximum of:
4.4.14.10.12.2.1	66” (1676 mm) in length at a 40 lb/sq ft load.
4.4.14.10.12.2.2	61” (1549 mm) in length at a 50 lb/sq ft load.
4.4.14.10.13	Solid Red Oak (Northern) lumber, 1,820,000 MOE:
4.4.14.10.13.1	At 3/4” (19 mm) in thickness allows for a maximum of:
4.4.14.10.13.1.1	49” (1245 mm) in length at a 40 lb/sq ft load.
4.4.14.10.13.1.2	46” (1168 mm) in length at a 50 lb/sq ft load.
4.4.14.10.13.2	At 1” (25.4 mm) in thickness allows for a maximum of:
4.4.14.10.13.2.1	66” (1676 mm) in length at a 40 lb/sq ft load.
4.4.14.10.13.2.2	61” (1549 mm) in length at a 50 lb/sq ft load.
4.4.14.10.14	Solid Birch (Yellow) lumber, 2,010,000 MOE:
4.4.14.10.14.1	At 3/4” (19 mm) in thickness allows for a maximum of:
4.4.14.10.14.1.1	51” (1295 mm) in length at a 40 lb/sq ft load.
4.4.14.10.14.1.2	47” 1194 mm) in length at a 50 lb/sq ft load.
4.4.14.10.14.2	At 1” (25.4 mm) in thickness allows for a maximum of:
4.4.14.10.14.2.1	68” (1727 mm) in length at a 40 lb/sq ft load.
4.4.14.10.14.2.2	63” (1600 mm) in length at a 50 lb/sq ft load.
4.4.14.10.15	Solid phenolic, 1,400,000 MOE:
4.4.14.10.15.1	At 3/8” (9.5 mm) in thickness allows for a maximum of:
4.4.14.10.15.1.1	46” (1168 mm) in length at a 40 lb/sq ft load.
4.4.14.10.15.1.2	44” (1118 mm) in length at a 50 lb/sq ft load.
4.4.14.10.15.2	At 1/2” (12.7 mm) in thickness allows for a maximum of:
4.4.14.10.15.2.1	57” (1448 mm) in length at a 40 lb/sq ft load.
4.4.14.10.15.2.2	54” (1372 mm) in length at a 50 lb/sq ft load.
4.4.14.10.15.3	At 5/8” (15.9 mm) in thickness allows for a maximum of:
4.4.14.10.15.3.1	68” (1727 mm) in length at a 40 lb/sq ft load.
4.4.14.10.15.3.2	63” (1600 mm) in length at a 50 lb/sq ft load.

PRODUCT

MATERIAL, MACHINING, AND ASSEMBLY RULES (continued)

Number	DESCRIPTION	E	C	P
4.4	**ASSEMBLY** (continued)			
4.4.14	**SHELVES** require (continued)			
4.4.14.10	**ADJUSTABLE SHELVES** (continued)			
4.4.14.10.16	Tempered float glass			
4.4.14.10.16.1	At 1/4" (6.4 mm) in thickness allows for a maximum of:			
4.4.14.10.16.1.1	29" (737 mm) in length at a 40 lb/sq ft load.			
4.4.14.10.16.1.2	26" (660 mm) in length at a 50 lb/sq ft load.			
4.4.14.10.16.2	At 5/16" (7.9 mm) in thickness allows for a maximum of:			
4.4.14.10.16.2.1	35" (1960 mm) in length at a 40 lb/sq ft load.			
4.4.14.10.16.2.2	33" (838 mm) in length at a 50 lb/sq ft load.			
4.4.14.10.16.3	At 3/8" (9.5 mm) in thickness allows for a maximum of:			
4.4.14.10.16.3.1	42" (1067 mm) in length at a 40 lb/sq ft load.			
4.4.14.10.16.3.2	39" (991 mm) in length at a 50 lb/sq ft load.			
4.4.14.10.16.4	At 1/2" (12.7 mm) in thickness allows for a maximum of:			
4.4.14.10.16.4.1	51" (1295 mm) in length at a 40 lb/sq ft load.			
4.4.14.10.16.4.2	48" (1219 mm) in length at a 50 lb/sq ft load.			
4.4.14.10.17	Be a maximum of 1/8" (3.2 mm) less than the INSIDE CABINET WIDTH, regardless of the shelf-support system, except where:		●	●
4.4.14.10.17.1	Shelf-support clips require notching; ends may exceed this requirement provided both ends of the shelf are banded and the total clearance between shelf clips is a maximum of 1/8" (3.2 mm).		●	●
4.4.14.10.18	Be a maximum of 1/4" (6.4 mm) less than the **INSIDE CABINET DEPTH**.		●	●
4.4.14.10.19	Be **SUPPORTED** on evenly spaced, cleanly bored holes a maximum of 2" (50.8 mm) on center with shelf rests or on metal shelf standards with metal shelf rests, and:			
4.4.14.10.19.1	**CENTER LINE** of rests shall not exceed a minimum of 1" (25.4 mm) to a maximum of 3" (76.2 mm) from the front and back of the interior cabinet body.			
4.4.14.10.19.2	**SUPPORT** placement shall not conflict with hinge placement.			
4.4.14.10.19.3	The dimension between the **CENTER LINE** of the rests shall not be less than 60% of the shelf's depth.			
4.4.14.10.19.4	With **THREE SUPPORTS** at each end of shelves over 29-3/4" (756 mm) **DEEP**.			
4.4.14.10.20	**METAL SHELF STANDARDS** shall extend vertically the entire interior length of the cabinet body side member, and:			
4.4.14.10.20.1	Be recessed in a plow, slightly proud of the face with the core not visible.			
4.4.14.10.21	**BORED-HOLE SHELF-SUPPORT SYSTEMS** shall extend vertically to within 6" (152.4 mm) of the interior top or bottom of the cabinet body.			
4.4.15	**PULLOUT SHELVES** require:			
4.4.15.1	**BREAD/CUTTING BOARDS** to be solid stock a minimum of 3/4" (19 mm) in thickness, with:			
4.4.15.1.1	**TONGUE** and **GROOVE** bands front and back, all securely glued with **TYPE I** adhesive.			
4.4.15.1.2	Use of **EXTERIOR PLYWOOD** is permitted.	●		

PRODUCT

MATERIAL, MACHINING, AND ASSEMBLY RULES (continued)

DESCRIPTION						E	C	P
4.4 ASSEMBLY	**ASSEMBLY** (continued)							
	4.4.15	**PULLOUT SHELVES** require (continued)						
		4.4.15.2	**PULLOUT BOARDS** be a minimum of 3/4" (19 mm) in thickness and banded three edges, and:					
			4.4.15.2.1	**OPERATE SMOOTHLY** in channels or other rigid guides.				
		4.4.15.3	**WRITING SHELVES** be a minimum of 3/4" (19 mm) in thickness, edgebanded three edges, extending a minimum of 15" (381 mm) or 2/3 of the cabinet depth, and shall be a smooth compatible material to the exposed interior surface.					
	4.4.16 POLES	**CLOTHES POLES** or **RODS** require:						
		4.4.16.1	**WOOD**, a minimum of 1-1/4" (31.8 mm) in diameter, or **METAL,** a minimum of 1-1/16" (27 mm) diameter, at the manufacturers's option, and:					
			4.4.16.1.1	**SUPPORTED** at each end by rosettes or hook strips with bored holes.				
			4.4.16.1.2	**SUPPORTED** at a maximum of 48" (1219 mm) on center.				
	4.4.17	**WARDROBES**:						
		4.4.17.1	60" (1524 mm) or wider require a **HORIZONTAL MEMBER** at the top rail of sliding doors rigidly supported with a vertical 1-3/8" (28.6 mm) round pole or two strips a minimum of 3/4" x 1-1/4" (19 mm x 31.8 mm) forming a "T" member securely positioned behind the door lap.					
	4.4.18 ANCHOR	**ANCHOR STRIPS** are **REQUIRED** and:						
		4.4.18.1	Shall be of solid-stock, plywood, particleboard, or medium-density fiberboard, a minimum of 1/2" (12.7 mm) in thickness, 2-1/2" (63.5 mm) in width, securely glued, and mechanically fastened.					
		4.4.18.2	Where **BACKS,** 1/2" (12.7 mm) or thicker are used, anchor strips are not required.					
		4.4.18.3	Cabinet **HEIGHTS** over 60" (85.4 mm) require an intermediate anchor strip.					
		4.4.18.4	Shall be **PROVIDED** at the top and bottom of the wall side of the cabinet back, or:					
			4.4.18.4.1	At the **INSIDE** if **SEMI-EXPOSED** material is used, provided they are attached to the cabinet body as well as the back and they are flush with the top, bottom, and ends of the cabinet body.				
	4.4.19	**MOVEABLE CABINETS** require:						
		4.4.19.1	**GLIDES** to be metal and adjustable.					
		4.4.19.2	**CASTERS** to have a minimum weight capacity of 90 lbs (40.8 kg).					
		4.4.19.3	Either a **METAL FRAME** or **DIAPHRAGM-TYPE DOUBLE BOTTOM** (see Appendix A, CDS drawings) at cabinets over 42" (10967 mm) in height, with doors and without fixed vertical or horizontal stabilizing partitions.					
		4.4.19.4	**LOCK-JOINT CORNERS** at bottoms or tops be reinforced with a continuous metal angle or wood cleat securely screwed and set with adhesive into the inside of both corner sides.					
	4.4.20 JOINERY	**JOINERY** requires:						
		4.4.20.1	Cabinet members to be **SECURELY FASTENED** together, using one or more of the approved methods, at the manufacturer's option.					
		4.4.20.2	All joints be **SECURELY GLUED**.					
		4.4.20.3	Casework be **ASSEMBLED SQUARE** and **TRUE**, within a tolerance not to exceed 1/32" (0.8 mm) difference in measurement at top versus bottom, and 1/16" (1.6 mm) diagonally.					
		4.4.20.4	**MECHANICAL FASTENERS** for cabinet **BODY**, **BACK,** and/or **DRAWER** construction, a maximum of 4" (101.6 mm) on center with a minimum of two fasteners per joint, and:					
			4.4.20.4.1	At **FACE FRAMES**, a maximum of 8" (203 mm) on center is permitted.				
			4.4.20.4.2	At **EXPOSED SURFACES**, staples, screws, or T-nails are not permitted.				
			4.4.20.4.3	**EXPOSED FASTENERS**, where permitted, be plated, and:				
				4.4.20.4.3.1	**BLACK OXIDE** finish is not permitted.			
				4.4.20.4.3.2	Permitted for access panels.			●

10

PRODUCT

MATERIAL, MACHINING, AND ASSEMBLY RULES (continued)

	DESCRIPTION	E	C	P
4.4	**ASSEMBLY** (continued)			
4.4.20	**JOINERY** requires (continued)			
4.4.20.5	**DADOES, LOCK JOINTS, PLOWS, RABBETS, DOWELS, DOWEL SCREWS,** or **BISCUIT-JOINING PLATES.**			
4.4.20.6	At **DOWEL** joints (see end-view diagram below):			
4.4.20.6.1	**DOWEL** to be a minimum of 5/16" x 1-3/16" (8 mm x 30 mm), and:			
4.4.20.6.1.1	Be **GLUED** and **CLAMPED**.			
4.4.20.6.2	**MINIMUM** of two dowels per joint.			
4.4.20.6.3	**FIRST** dowel to be spaced a maximum of 1-15/16" (37 mm) from each edge or end.			
4.4.20.6.4	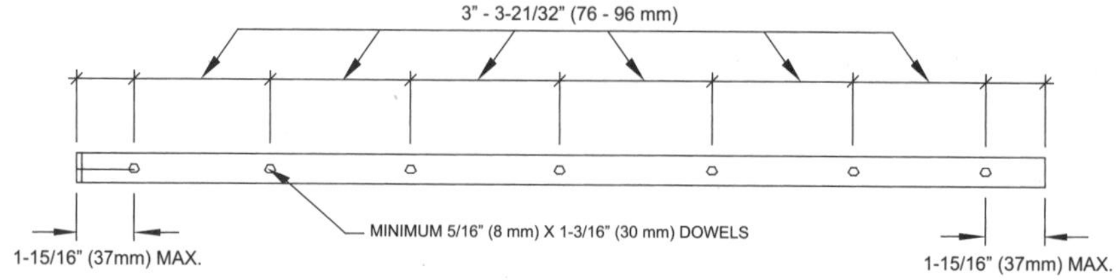 3" - 3-21/32" (76 - 96 mm); MINIMUM 5/16" (8 mm) X 1-3/16" (30 mm) DOWELS; 1-15/16" (37mm) MAX.; 1-15/16" (37mm) MAX.			
4.4.20.7	At **DOWEL SCREW** joints (see end-view diagram below):			
4.4.20.7.1	**DOWEL SCREW** shall be a minimum of 9/32" x 2" (7 mm x 50 mm). 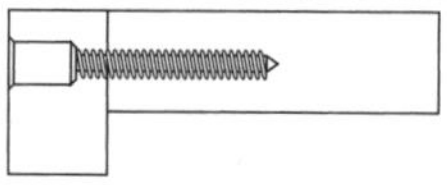			
4.4.20.7.2	**FIRST** dowel screw shall be spaced a maximum of 1-15/16" (37 mm) from each edge or end.			
4.4.20.7.3	**SUBSEQUENT** dowel screws shall be spaced a maximum of 5" (128 mm) on center.			
4.4.20.7.4	**GLUE** is not required.			
4.4.20.7.5	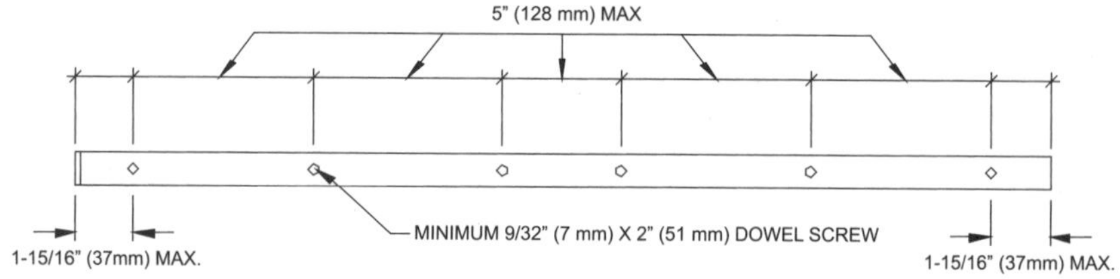 5" (128 mm) MAX; MINIMUM 9/32" (7 mm) X 2" (51 mm) DOWEL SCREW; 1-15/16" (37mm) MAX.; 1-15/16" (37mm) MAX.			
4.4.20.8	At **BISCUIT-JOINING PLATE** joints:			
4.4.20.8.1	**PLATES** shall be a minimum #30 or equal, located a maximum of 2" (51 mm) from each edge or end to the center of the plate, and:			
4.4.20.8.1.1	Be **GLUED** and **CLAMPED**.			
4.4.20.8.2	**SUBSEQUENT** plates shall be spaced a maximum of 6" (152 mm) on center.			
4.4.21	**SCRIBING** requires:			
4.4.21.1	**SCRIBE FILLERS** or **MOLDS** to not exceed 1-1/2" (38.1 mm) in width, and shall:			
4.4.21.1.1	Match exposed surfaces			
4.4.21.1.2	Be furnished in maximum available lengths, given material availability.			
4.4.21.2	**NO** scribing.	●		
4.4.21.3	**SCRIBING** to be furnished by the manufacturer, and:		●	
4.4.21.3.1	**SCRIBE FILLERS** or **MOLDS** are not permitted.			●
4.4.21.3.2	**END JOINTS** of scribing to be beveled.		●	●
4.4.21.3.3	**CORNERS** of scribing to be mitered.		●	●

PRODUCT

MATERIAL, MACHINING, AND ASSEMBLY RULES (continued)

		DESCRIPTION	E	C	P
4.4		**ASSEMBLY** (continued)			
	4.4.21	**SCRIBING** requires (continued)			
	4.4.21.4	**COLOR-COMPATIBLE CAULKING** is permitted, not to exceed 1/8" (3.2 mm).		●	●
	4.4.21.5	The **TRIM MEMBER** used at the inside corner of the adjoining angled cabinets (which is not a scribe or subject to the 1-1/2" [38.1 mm] maximum scribe allowance) be equal and not exceed 2" (50.8 mm) beyond the cabinet front and/or drawer pull.			
	4.4.21.6	**SOFFIT PANELS** to be furnished in maximum available lengths, given material availability, and:		●	●
	4.4.21.6.1	**FASCIA PANEL** directional run (defined as trim taller than 1-1/2" [38.1 mm] and less than 12" [305 mm]) above the cabinets shall be:			
	4.4.21.6.1.1	At the manufacturer's option.	●	●	●
	4.4.21.6.1.2	**VERTICAL** if over 12" (305 mm).			●
	4.4.21.7	**SCRIBING OPTIONS:** 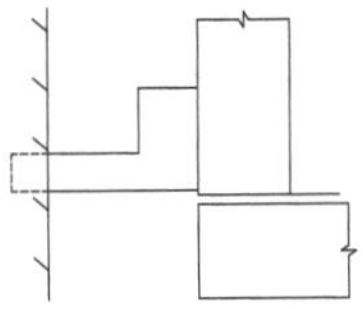 Scribe Filler; 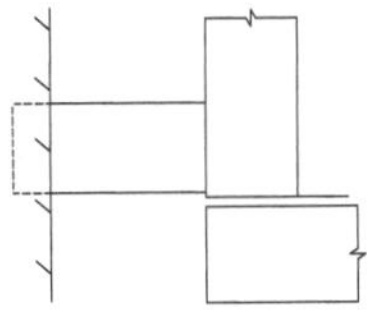 Scribe Filler; 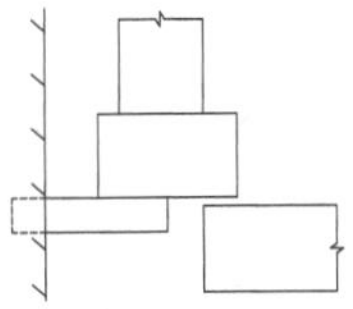 Scribe Mold; 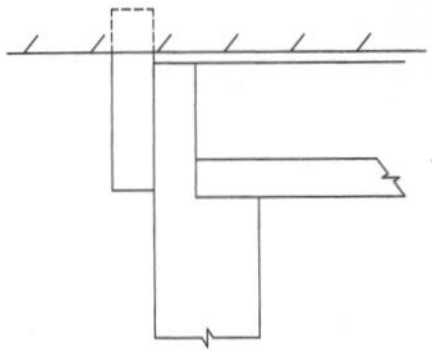 Scribe Mold; 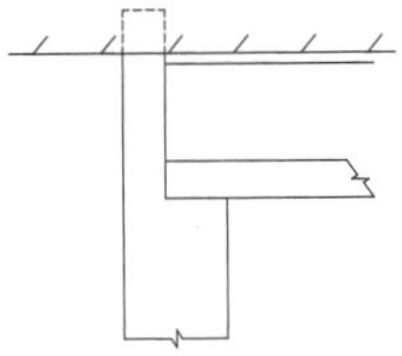 Scribe Allowance; 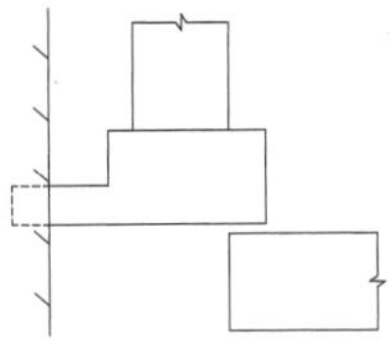 Scribe Allowance			
	4.4.22	A provision for **CLOSURE** is required at all voids or open spaces between cabinets and walls, such as at the top of tall and upper cabinets and the bottom of upper cabinets caused by scribing or angle turns, and:			
	4.4.22.1	At non-visible voids, 1-1/2" (12.7 mm) or less in width, a piece of standard-grade laminate may be used as a closure cap.			
	4.4.22.2	At non visible voids, exceeding 1-1/2" (12.7 mm) in width, a minimum 3/4" (19 mm) closure filler shall be provided of manufacturer's option.			
	4.4.22.3	At visible voids, a minimum 3/4" (19 mm) closure filler shall be provided matching the adjacent surface.			
	4.4.22.4	**CLOSURE OPTIONS:** 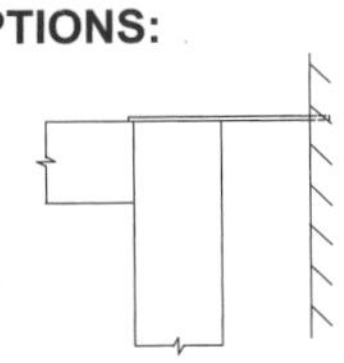 Closure Cap; 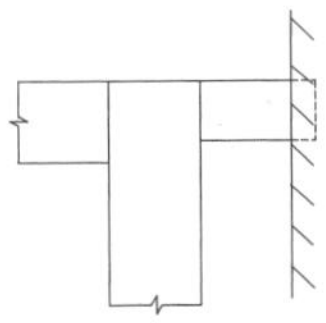 Closure Filler			
	4.4.23	**CLEARANCES** and **TOLERANCES:**			
	4.4.23.1	At **DOORS** and **DRAWERS**, alignment and flushness in both the vertical and horizontal plane (see Test I illustrations in **COMPLIANCE**) shall not exceed:			
	4.4.23.1.1	1/16" (1.6 mm)	●		
	4.4.23.1.2	1/32" (0.8 mm)		●	●
	4.4.23.2	At **REVEAL OVERLAY** construction, shall be as specified or indicated.			

PRODUCT

MATERIAL, MACHINING, AND ASSEMBLY RULES (continued)

				DESCRIPTION	E	C	P
4.4 ASSEMBLY	**ASSEMBLY** (continued)						
	4.4.23 CLEARANCES & TOLERANCES	**CLEARANCES** and **TOLERANCES** (continued)					
		4.4.23.3 FLUSH OVERLAY		At **FLUSH OVERLAY** and **INSET** construction, the maximum uniform gap variance (see Test H illustrations in **COMPLIANCE**) within a cabinet elevation, between any edge of a door and/or drawer and another door and/or drawer or finished end, and doors hung in pairs, shall be (based on the elevations below):			
			4.4.23.3.1	1/8" (3.2 mm) at location **"A"**			
			4.4.23.3.2	1/16" (1.6 mm) at location **"B"**			
			4.4.23.3.3	Subject to a maximum uniform variance of:			
			4.4.23.3.3.1	+/- 3/32" (2.4 mm)	●		
			4.4.23.3.3.2	+/- 1/16" (1.6 mm)		●	
			4.4.23.3.3.3	+/- 1/32" (0.8 mm)			●
			4.4.23.3.4	A, B, A, A, B / A, A, A, A			
			4.4.23.3.5	**DOOR** and **DRAWER FRONTS** shall align vertically and horizontally and be on the same plane as one another.			
	4.4.24 WARP	**WARP** and **TWIST** of cabinet doors less than 1-3/8" (34.9 mm) in thickness shall not exceed that indicated below or a maximum of 1/4" (6.4 mm) in any single door.					
		4.4.24.1		**TOLERANCE** shall not exceed the following per lineal foot:			
			4.4.24.1.1	0.0625" or 1/16" (1.6 mm)	●		
			4.4.24.1.2	0.0469" or 3/64" (1.2 mm)		●	
			4.4.24.1.3	0.0313" or 1/32" (0.8 mm)			●
	4.4.25 WOOD CASEWORK	For **WOOD CASEWORK**:					
		4.4.25.1 VISIBLE EDGES		**VISIBLE EDGES** require:			
			4.4.25.1.1	**VOIDS** to be filled and sanded.	●		
			4.4.25.1.2	No **EDGE FILLING** at medium-density fiberboard.	●		
			4.4.25.1.3	**SHEET PRODUCTS** be edgebanded.		●	●
			4.4.25.1.4	Unless specified otherwise, the sequence of edge/face lamination shall be the manufacturer's option.			
			4.4.25.1.5	**DOOR** and **DRAWER FRONT** edges showing more than 1/4" (6.4 mm) on face shall be mitered, except:			●
			4.4.25.1.5.1	At the ends of wall-hung cabinets, the sequence of edges shall be the bottom edge first.			
			4.4.25.1.6	**FINGER JOINTS** to be:			
			4.4.25.1.6.1	Unlimited.	●		
			4.4.25.1.6.2	Permitted if adjoining pieces are compatible for color and grain.		●	
			4.4.25.1.6.3	Permitted if well-matched for color and grain with a maximum of one in 96" (2438 mm) of length.			●

10

PRODUCT

MATERIAL, MACHINING, AND ASSEMBLY RULES (continued)

		DESCRIPTION	E	C	P
4.4		**ASSEMBLY** (continued)			
4.4.25		For **WOOD CASEWORK** (continued)			
4.4.25.2		**DRAWERS** require (including trays and sliding bins):			
	4.4.25.2.1	**WOOD** shall be finished with a finishing system (see Section 5), at the manufacturer's option.			
	4.4.25.2.2	At **SOLID STOCK**, top edges of sides shall be stop-shaped.			●
	4.4.25.2.3	Permits **HORIZONTAL GRAIN** at stile-and-rail door cabinets.			
	4.4.25.2.4	**FRONT** and **FALSE FRONT:**			
	4.4.25.2.4.1	Be **BANDED** at all four edges, except when back-beveled.			
	4.4.25.2.4.2	For **OPAQUE** finish, have:			
	4.4.25.2.4.2.1	**FILLED** and **SANDED** edges at 7- or 9-ply hardwood plywood and particleboard.	●	●	
	4.4.25.2.4.2.2	**NO BANDING** at medium-density fiberboard.	●	●	
	4.4.25.2.4.2.3	**BANDING** at medium-density fiberboard.			●
	4.4.25.2.4.3	At **TRANSPARENT** finish, have:			
	4.4.25.2.4.3.1	**FILLED** and **SANDED** edges at 7- or 9-ply hardwood plywood and particleboard.	●		
	4.4.25.2.4.3.2	**BANDING** matched to **EXPOSED** surfaces.		●	●
4.4.25.3		**DOORS** require:			
	4.4.25.3.1	**SOLID LUMBER** not be permitted, except at stile-and-rail doors.			
	4.4.25.3.2	At **TRANSPARENT FINISH**, banding on all four edges matching exposed surfaces.			
	4.4.25.3.3	**GLASS STOPS** for transparent finish be of the same species and grade as the exposed surfaces.		●	●
	4.4.25.3.4	When **SLIDING** interior faces shall be of any balancing species.			
4.4.25.4		**FACE FRAMES** require (not applicable to HPDL casework):			
	4.4.25.4.1	**THICKNESS**, a minimum of 3/4" (19 mm).			
	4.4.25.4.2	**SOLID STOCK.**			
	4.4.25.4.3	**GRAIN** to run vertically on stiles and horizontally on rails.			
	4.4.25.4.4	**JOINTS** to be mortised and tenoned, doweled with wood dowels or metal dowel screw, or biscuit-joined, and:			
	4.4.25.4.4.1	To be securely glued.			
	4.4.25.4.5	**FRAMES** to be securely glued to cabinet bodies, and:			
	4.4.25.4.5.1	May be face-nailed.	●	●	
	4.4.25.4.5.2	**EXPOSED NAILING** is not permitted.			●
	4.4.25.4.5.3	**EXPOSED CORNERS** shall be shoulder-mitered, lock-mitered, spline-mitered, or mitered with a biscuit joint.			●
	4.4.25.4.6	**TOPS** and **BOTTOMS**:			
	4.4.25.4.6.1	Minimum of 1/2" (12.7 mm).	●		
	4.4.25.4.6.2	Minimum of 3/4" (19 mm).		●	●

10

PRODUCT

MATERIAL, MACHINING, AND ASSEMBLY RULES (continued)

DESCRIPTION		E	C	P
4.4 (ASSEMBLY)	**ASSEMBLY** (continued)			
4.4.25	For **WOOD CASEWORK** (continued)			
4.4.25.4	**FACE FRAMES** require (continued)			
4.4.25.4.7	At **FLUSH INSET DOORS**:			
4.4.25.4.7.1	Use of a bottom member of the face frame is the manufacturer's option.	●	●	
4.4.25.4.7.2	Use of a bottom member of the face frame is required.			●
4.4.26 (DECORATIVE LAMINATE)	For **DECORATIVE LAMINATE CASEWORK**:			
4.4.26.1	**VISIBLE EDGES** require:			
4.4.26.1.1	Unless specified otherwise, the sequence of the edge/face lamination shall be the manufacturer's option.			
4.4.26.1.2	**HPDL** or **PVC** a minimum of 0.02" (0.5 mm) and maximum of 0.12" (3 mm) at the manufacturer's option, color-matched to the exposed face.			
4.4.26.1.3	**PVC** and **ABS EDGEBANDING** thicker than 0.04" (1 mm) be radiused on edges and corners.			
4.4.26.2	**DRAWERS** require:			
4.4.26.2.1	**FRONT** and **FALSE FRONT:**			
4.4.26.2.1.1	To be **BANDED** at all four edges, except when back-beveled.			
4.4.26.3 (DOORS)	**DOORS** require:			
4.4.26.3.1	**BANDING** on all four edges matching exposed surfaces.		●	●
4.4.26.3.2	**GLASS STOPS** to be hardwood solid stock painted to match plastic or a synthetic (vinyl, neoprene, plastic) gasket/retainer; however:			
4.4.26.3.2.1	**SYNTHETIC** stops are acceptable on the inside only.			
4.4.26.3.3	When **SLIDING:**			
4.4.26.3.3.1	1/4" (6.4 mm) hardboard painted to match adjacent laminate is permitted.	●		
4.4.26.3.3.2	**INTERIOR FACES** shall be a minimum of 0.020" (0.5 mm) thick HPDL balancing sheet.			
4.4.27 (SOLID PHENOLC)	For **SOLID PHENOLIC CASEWORK**:			
4.4.27.1	**EDGEBANDING** is not required.			
4.4.27.2	**DRAWER FRONT** and **FALSE FRONT** thickness to be a minimum of 1/2" (12.7 mm).			
4.4.27.3	**DOOR** thickness to be a minimum of 1/2" (12.7 mm).			
4.4.27.3.1	**GLASS CLIPS** are permitted.			
4.4.27.4	**APRONS** require a minimum thickness of 1/2" (12.7 mm).			
4.4.27.5	**SHELVES** require a minimum thickness of 3/8" (9.5 mm).			
4.4.27.6	**TOPS** and **FIXED BOTTOMS** require a minimum thickness of 1/2" (12.7 mm).			
4.4.27.7	**END** and **DIVISIONS** require a minimum of 1/2" (12.7 mm) in thickness, and:			
4.4.27.7.1	Applied ends are permitted.			
4.4.27.8	**SECURITY** and **DUST PANELS** require a minimum thickness of 1/4" (6.4 mm)			
4.4.27.9	**STRETCHERS** require a minimum of 1/2" (12.7 mm) in thickness and 2" (50.8 mm) in width.			
4.4.27.10	**BREAD/CUTTING BOARDS** require a minimum of 1/2" (12.7 mm) in thickness.			
4.4.27.11	At **SOLID PHENOLIC**, use of a 9/32" x 1-1/4" (7 mm x 32 mm) sheet metal screw is permitted with the first screw 1-15/16" (37 mm) from each edge or end and subsequent screws 5" (128 mm) on center, and:			
4.4.27.11.1	**GLUE** is not required.			

EXECUTION

5 PREPARATION & QUALIFICATION REQUIREMENTS (unless otherwise specified)

5.1 **CARE, STORAGE, AND BUILDING CONDITIONS** shall be in compliance with the requirements set forth in Section 2 of these standards.

5.1.1 Severe damage to the woodwork can result from noncompliance. **THE MANUFACTURER AND/OR INSTALLER OF THE WOODWORK SHALL NOT BE HELD RESPONSIBLE FOR ANY DAMAGE THAT MIGHT DEVELOP BY NOT ADHERING TO THE REQUIREMENTS.**

5.2 **CONTRACTOR IS RESPONSIBLE FOR:**

5.2.1 Furnishing and installing structural members, grounds, blocking, backing, furring, brackets, or other anchorage required for architectural woodwork installation that becomes an integral part of walls, floors, or ceilings to which architectural woodwork shall be installed.

5.2.1.1 In the absence of contract documents calling for the contractor to supply the necessary blocking/ backing in the wall or ceilings, either through inadvertence or otherwise, the architectural woodwork installer shall not proceed with the installation until such time as the blocking/backing is installed by others.

5.2.1.2 Preparatory work done by others shall be subject to inspection by the architectural woodwork installer and shall be accepted or rejected for cause prior to installation.

5.2.1.2.1 **WALL, CEILING,** and/or opening variations in excess of 1/4" (6.4 mm) or **FLOORS** in excess of 1/2" (12.7 mm) in 144" (3658 mm) of being plumb, level, flat, straight, square, or of the correct size are not acceptable for the installation of architectural woodwork, nor is it the responsibility of the installer to scribe or fit to tolerances in excess of such.

5.2.2 Priming and back-priming the architectural woodwork in accordance with the contract documents prior to its installation.

5.2.2.1 If the architectural woodwork is factory-finished, back-priming by the factory finisher is required.

5.3 **INSTALLER IS RESPONSIBLE FOR:**

5.3.1 Having adequate equipment and experienced craftsmen to complete the installation in a first-class manner.

5.3.2 Checking all architectural woodwork specified and studying the appropriate portions of the contract documents, including these standards and the reviewed shop drawings to familiarize themselves with the requirements of the Grade specified, understanding that:

5.3.2.1 Appearance requirements of Grades apply only to surfaces visible after installation.

5.3.2.2 For transparent finish, special attention needs to be given to color and grain of the various woodwork pieces to ensure they are installed in compliance with the Grade specified.

5.3.2.3 Installation site is properly ventilated, protected from direct sunlight, excessive heat and/or moisture, and that the HVAC system is functioning and maintaining the appropriate relative humidity and temperature.

5.3.2.4 Required priming or back-priming of casework has been completed before its install.

5.3.2.5 Casework has been acclimated to the field conditions for a minimum of 72 hours before installation commences.

5.3.2.6 Casework specifically built or assembled in sequence for match of color and grain is installed to maintain that same sequence.

EXECUTION

6 RULES - The following RULES shall govern unless a project's contract documents require otherwise.

These rules are intended to provide a well-defined degree of control over a project's quality of installation.

Where E, C, or P is not indicated, the rule applies to all Grades equally.

ERRATA, published on the Associations' websites at www.awinet.org, www.awmac.com, or www.woodworkinstitute.com, shall TAKE PRECEDENCE OVER THESE RULES, subject to their date of posting and a project's bid date.

ARROWS INDICATE TOPIC IS CARRIED FROM ⇑ OR ONTO ⇓ ANOTHER PAGE.

				DESCRIPTION	E	C	P
6.1	**GENERAL**						
GENERAL	6.1.1			Aesthetic **GRADE RULES** apply only to exposed and semi-exposed surfaces visible after installation.			
	6.1.2			For **TRANSPARENT FINISH,** woodwork shall be installed:			
		6.1.2.1		With **CONSIDERATION** of color and grain.	●		
		6.1.2.2		**COMPATIBLE** in color and grain.		●	
		6.1.2.3		**WELL-MATCHED** for color and grain.			●
	6.1.3			**REPAIRS** are allowed, provided they are neatly made and inconspicuous when viewed at:			
		6.1.3.1		72" (1830 mm)	●		
		6.1.3.2		48" (1219 mm)		●	
		6.1.3.3		24" (610 mm)			●
	6.1.4			**INSTALLER MODIFICATIONS** shall comply to the material, machining, and assembly rules within the **PRODUCT** portion of this section and the applicable finishing rules in Section 5.			
	6.1.5			**CASEWORK** or related items:			
	CASEWORK	**6.1.5.1**		Shall be **SECURELY** fastened and tightly fitted with flush joints.			
			6.1.5.1.1	Joinery shall be **CONSISTENT** throughout the project.			
		6.1.5.2		Such as **SCRIBE MOLDS** shall be of maximum available and/or practical lengths and:			
			6.1.5.2.1	**MITERED** at outside corners			
		6.1.5.3		Shall be **INSTALLED** plumb, level, square, and flat within 1/8" (3.2 mm) in 96" (2438 mm), and when required:			
			6.1.5.3.1	**GROUNDS** and **HANGING SYSTEMS** set plumb and true.		●	●
		6.1.5.4		Shall be Installed **FREE OF**:			
			6.1.5.4.1	Warp, twisting, cupping, and/or bowing that cannot be held true.			
			6.1.5.4.2	Open joints, visible machine marks, cross-sanding, tear-outs, nicks, chips, and/or scratches.			
			6.1.5.4.3	Natural defects exceeding the quantity or size limits defined in Sections 3 and 4.			
			6.1.5.4.4	**EXPOSED FASTENERS** at exposed exterior surfaces.			
		6.1.5.5		Shall be **SMOOTH** and **SANDED** without **CROSS-SCRATCHES** in conformance to the **PRODUCT** portion of this section.			
		6.1.5.6		Shall be **SCRIBED** at:			
			6.1.5.6.1	Flat surfaces.		●	●
			6.1.5.6.2	Shaped surfaces.			●
	6.1.6			**GAPS** (see Test A-C illustrations in **COMPLIANCE**):			
⇓	⇓	6.1.6.1		**CAUSED** by **EXCESSIVE DEVIATIONS** (deviations in excess of 1/4" [6.4 mm] in 144" [3658 mm] of being plumb, level, flat, straight, square, or of the correct size) in the building's walls and ceilings, or 1/2" (12.7 mm) for floors, shall not be considered a defect or the responsibility of the installer.			

EXECUTION

No.	DESCRIPTION	E	C	P
6.1	**GENERAL** (continued)			
6.1.6	**GAPS** (see Test A-C illustrations in **COMPLIANCE**) (continued)			
6.1.6.2	Shall not exceed 30% of a joint's length, with:			
6.1.6.2.1	**FILLER** or **CAULKING** allowed:	●		
6.1.6.2.1.1	If color-compatible.		●	●
6.1.6.3	Of **WOOD** to **WOOD** shall not exceed:			
6.1.6.3.1	At **FLAT** surfaces:			
6.1.6.3.1.1	0.050" (1.3 mm) in width.	●		
6.1.6.3.1.2	0.025" (0.65 mm) in width.		●	
6.1.6.3.1.3	0.012" (0.3 mm) in width.			●
6.1.6.3.2	At **SHAPED** surfaces:			
6.1.6.3.2.1	0.075" (1.9 mm) in width.	●		
6.1.6.3.2.2	0.050" (1.3 mm) in width.		●	
6.1.6.3.2.3	0.025" (0.65 mm) in width.			●
6.1.6.4	Of **WOOD** to **NON-WOOD** shall not exceed:			
6.1.6.4.1	At **FLAT** and **SHAPED** surfaces:			
6.1.6.4.1.1	0.100" (2.5 mm) in width.	●		
6.1.6.4.1.2	0.075" (1.9 mm) in width.		●	
6.1.6.4.1.3	0.050" (1.3 mm) in width.			●
6.1.6.5	Of **NON-WOOD** to **NON-WOOD** and/or **ALL ELEMENTS** shall not exceed:			
6.1.6.5.1	At **FLAT** surfaces:			
6.1.6.5.1.1	0.100" (2.5 mm) in width.	●		
6.1.6.5.1.2	0.075" (1.9 mm) in width.		●	
6.1.6.5.1.3	0.050" (1.3 mm) in width.			●
6.1.6.5.2	At **SHAPED** surfaces.			
6.1.6.5.2.1	0.125" (3.2 mm) in width.	●		
6.1.6.5.2.2	0.100" (2.5 mm) in width.		●	
6.1.6.5.2.3	0.075" (1.9 mm) in width.			●
6.1.7	**FLUSHNESS** of joinery (see Test D illustrations in **COMPLIANCE**):			
6.1.7.1	Of **WOOD** to **WOOD** shall not exceed:			
6.1.7.1.1	At **FLAT** surfaces:			
6.1.7.1.1.1	0.050" (1.3 mm)	●		
6.1.7.1.1.2	0.025" (0.65 mm)		●	
6.1.7.1.1.3	0.012" (0.3 mm)			●
6.1.7.1.2	At **SHAPED** surfaces:			
6.1.7.1.2.1	0.075" (1.9 mm)	●		
6.1.7.1.2.2	0.050" (1.3 mm)		●	
6.1.7.1.2.3	0.025" (0.65 mm)			●

EXECUTION

Section	Item	Description	E	C	P
6.1		**GENERAL** (continued)			
6.1.7		**FLUSHNESS** of joinery (see Test D illustrations in **COMPLIANCE**) (continued)			
6.1.7	**6.1.7.2**	Of **WOOD** to **NON-WOOD** shall not exceed:			
6.1.7	**6.1.7.2.1**	At **FLAT** and **SHAPED** surfaces:			
6.1.7	6.1.7.2.1.1	0.100" (2.5 mm)	●		
6.1.7	6.1.7.2.1.2	0.075" (1.9 mm)		●	
6.1.7	6.1.7.2.1.3	0.050" (1.3 mm)			●
6.1.7	6.1.7.3	Of **NON-WOOD** to **NON-WOOD** and/or **ALL ELEMENTS** shall not exceed:			
6.1.7	**6.1.7.3.1**	At **FLAT** surfaces:			
6.1.7	6.1.7.3.1.1	0.100" (2.5 mm)	●		
6.1.7	6.1.7.3.1.2	0.075" (1.9 mm)		●	
6.1.7	6.1.7.3.1.3	0.050" (1.3 mm)			●
6.1.7	**6.1.7.3.2**	At **SHAPED** surfaces:			
6.1.7	6.1.7.3.2.1	0.125" (3.2 mm)	●		
6.1.7	6.1.7.3.2.2	0.100" (2.5 mm)		●	
6.1.7	6.1.7.3.2.3	0.075" (1.9 mm)			●
6.1.8		**CASEWORK** shall be installed plumb, level, straight, and in plane.			
6.1.9		**DOOR** and **DRAWER GAPS** shall be uniform and show a maximum clearance between adjacent doors or drawers, as set forth in the **PRODUCT** portion of this section, and:			
6.1.9	**6.1.9.1**	**DOOR** and **DRAWER FRONTS** shall align vertically and horizontally, and:			
6.1.9	6.1.9.1.1	Be **FLUSH** (on the same plane) to one another.			
6.1.9	6.1.9.1.2	Minor **ADJUSTMENTS** are the responsibility of the installer.			
6.1.10		**SCRIBING** shall be provided where cabinets contact finished walls or ceiling as elaborated below and in the **PRODUCT** portion of this section, and:			
6.1.10	6.1.10.1	**SCRIBE** strips or scribing is not required.	●		
6.1.10	6.1.10.2	**END JOINTS** of running scribe trim may be butt-jointed.	●		
6.1.10	**6.1.10.3**	**SCRIBING** or **SCRIBE MOLDS** shall be furnished at the manufacturer's option, and:		●	
6.1.10	6.1.10.3.1	**CAULKING** is permitted for a gap of 1/16" (1.6 mm) or less.		●	●
6.1.10	6.1.10.4	**WOOD FILLER STRIPS** are permitted to fill a maximum gap of 1-1/2" (38.1 mm).		●	
6.1.10	**6.1.10.5**	**END JOINTS** of running scribe trim shall be beveled, and:		●	●
6.1.10	6.1.10.5.1	**CORNERS** shall be mitered or coped.		●	●
6.1.10	6.1.10.6	At tall and wall-hung cabinets, **CLOSURE PANELS** shall be provided at top and bottom voids.		●	●
6.1.10	**6.1.10.7**	**ALLOWABLE GAP** at the back bottom edge of wall-hung cabinets shall not exceed that listed below and, when scribing is necessary, the use of a separate scribe mold is permitted.		●	●
6.1.10	6.1.10.7.1	1/2" (12.7 mm)		●	
6.1.10	6.1.10.7.2	1/4" (6.4 mm)			●
6.1.10	6.1.10.8	**SCRIBING** is required to a gap tolerance of 1/32" (0.8 mm).			●
6.1.11		**EXPOSED FASTENERS** are **NOT** permitted at **EXPOSED EXTERIOR** or **EXPOSED INTERIOR** surfaces, except:		●	●
6.1.11	6.1.11.1	At **ACCESS** panels.			

EXECUTION

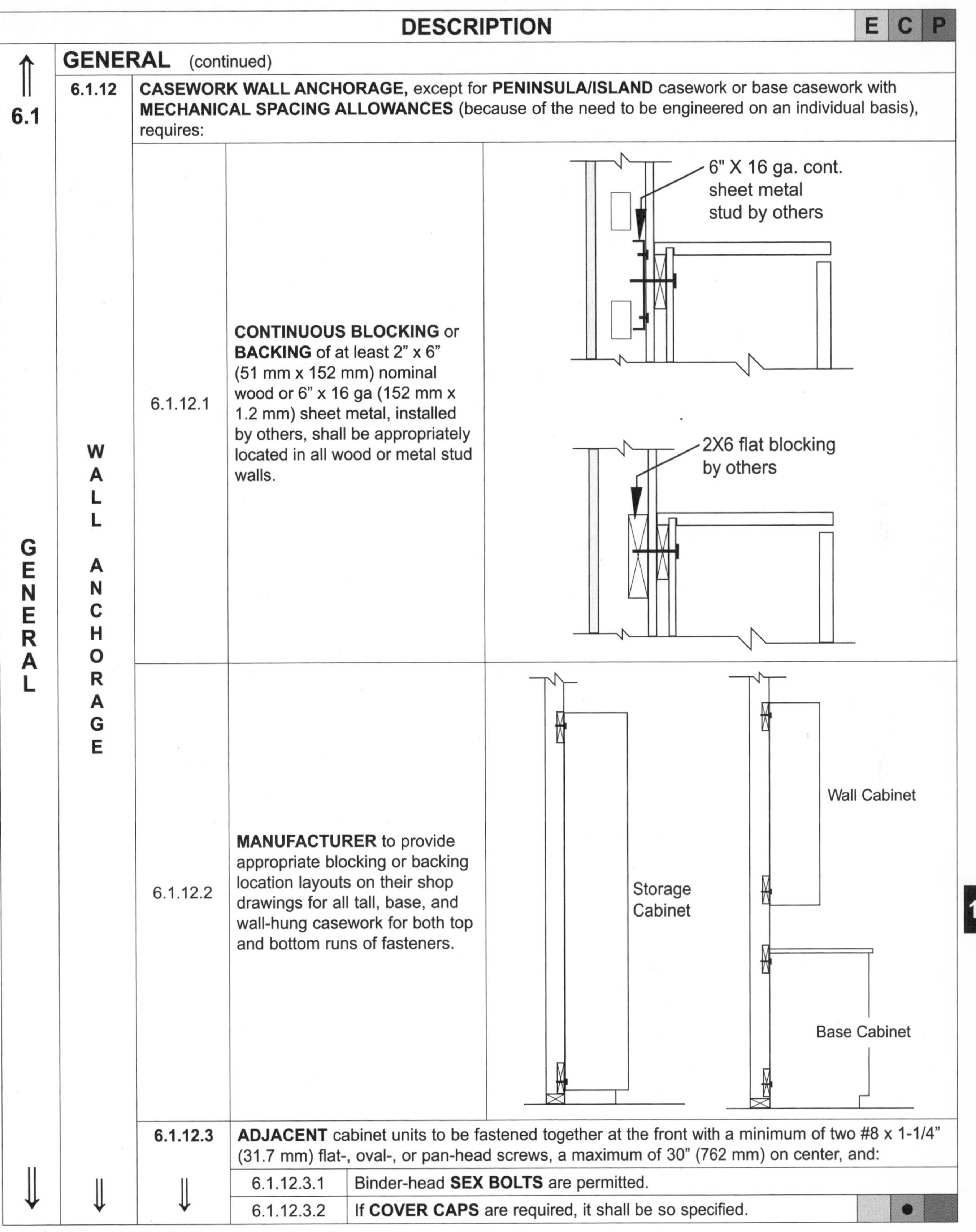

			DESCRIPTION	E C P
6.1 GENERAL	**GENERAL** (continued)			
	6.1.12 WALL ANCHORAGE		**CASEWORK WALL ANCHORAGE,** except for **PENINSULA/ISLAND** casework or base casework with **MECHANICAL SPACING ALLOWANCES** (because of the need to be engineered on an individual basis), requires:	
		6.1.12.1	**CONTINUOUS BLOCKING** or **BACKING** of at least 2" x 6" (51 mm x 152 mm) nominal wood or 6" x 16 ga (152 mm x 1.2 mm) sheet metal, installed by others, shall be appropriately located in all wood or metal stud walls.	
		6.1.12.2	**MANUFACTURER** to provide appropriate blocking or backing location layouts on their shop drawings for all tall, base, and wall-hung casework for both top and bottom runs of fasteners.	
		6.1.12.3	**ADJACENT** cabinet units to be fastened together at the front with a minimum of two #8 x 1-1/4" (31.7 mm) flat-, oval-, or pan-head screws, a maximum of 30" (762 mm) on center, and:	
			6.1.12.3.1 Binder-head **SEX BOLTS** are permitted.	
			6.1.12.3.2 If **COVER CAPS** are required, it shall be so specified.	● (C)

10

EXECUTION

				DESCRIPTION	E	C	P
6.1 GENERAL	**GENERAL** (continued)						
	6.1.12 WALL ANCHORAGE	**CASEWORK WALL ANCHORAGE,** except for **PENINSULA/ISLAND** (continued)					
		6.1.12.3		**ADJACENT** cabinet units to be fastened together at the front with a minimum of two #8 x 1-1/4" (31.7 mm) flat-, oval-, or pan-head screws, a maximum of 30" (762 mm) on center, and:			
			6.1.12.3.3	At **EXPOSED INTERIOR** surfaces, fasteners must be countersunk and covered to match the surface.			●
		6.1.12.4 FASTENERS		**ANCHORAGE FASTENERS** to be neatly installed through the back and anchor strip, at the top and bottom at each cabinet body, and:			
			6.1.12.4.1	**FASTENER** to be a minimum of 3" (76.2 mm) x #10 (4.6 mm) diameter screw with a surface-bearing head.			
			6.1.12.4.2	**EXPOSED INTERIOR** surfaces require screws capable of being recessed and covered with matching cover caps.		●	●
			6.1.12.4.3	Achieve a minimum of 1-1/2" (38.1 mm) **PENETRATION** into the wall studs, blocking, or masonry walls.			
			6.1.12.4.4	Prohibit use of **DRYWALL** or **BUGLE-HEAD** screws.			
		6.1.12.5 CABINET UNITS		Each **CABINET UNIT** or **UNDIVIDED SPAN** shall have a minimum of four anchorage fasteners; two at the top and two at the bottom, subject to:			
			6.1.12.5.1	A maximum horizontal spacing of 16" (406 mm) on center, except:			
			6.1.12.5.1.1	Wall cabinet units over 48" (406 mm) in height shall be 12" (305 mm).			
			6.1.12.5.2	**VERTICALLY**, anchorage fasteners be located within 2" (50.8 mm) of the outside top or bottom of the cabinet unit.			
			6.1.12.5.3	**HORIZONTALLY**, within 2" (50.8 mm) of the outside end.			
			6.1.12.5.4	A **LOCKING HANGING CLEAT**, or other concealed method of installation may be used, provided it has been independently tested to show compliance to the Wall Cabinet Structural Integrity Test shown in Appendix A.			
		6.1.12.6		Bases or toes are not required to be anchored to the floor; however:			
			6.1.12.6.1	Separate bases or toes are required to be fastened to the cabinet to prevent their movement.			
	6.1.13			**NAIL** holes through semi-exposed surfaces shall be countersunk and filled with color matched to the adjacent surface.			
	6.1.14			**GLUE** is not to be permitted on exposed faces.			
	6.1.15			**CAULKING**, when used to fill gaps and/or voids, shall be color-compatible.			
	6.1.16			At **PREFINISHED** woodwork, installer shall do all the filling of nail holes and touch up with matching finish materials furnished by the manufacturer.			

COMPLIANCE

			DESCRIPTION	E	C	P
⇑ 6.1 GENERAL	**GENERAL** (continued)					
	6.1.17	**EQUIPMENT CUTOUTS,** including electrical and plumbing, shall be cut out by the installer, provided any needed templates are furnished prior to installation, and:				
		6.1.17.1	Shall be **NEATLY CUT** and **PROPERLY SIZED** to be covered by standard cover plates or rosettes.			
	6.1.18	**HARDWARE** shall be:				
		6.1.18.1	Installed neatly without tear-out of surrounding stock.			
		6.1.18.2	Installed per the manufacturer's instructions.			
		6.1.18.3	Installed using all mounting holes at hinges.			
		6.1.18.4	Properly fitted and adjusted to ensure correct and smooth operation.			
	6.1.19	**AREAS** of installation shall be left broom clean.				
		6.1.19.1	Debris shall be removed and dumped in containers provided by the contractor.			
		6.1.19.2	Items installed shall be cleaned of pencil or ink marks.			
	6.1.20	Entire installation shall present **FIRST-CLASS WORKMANSHIP** in compliance with these standards.				

COMPLIANCE

7 **FABRICATED** and **INSTALLED** woodwork shall be tested for compliance to these standards as follows:

7.1 **SMOOTHNESS** of exposed surfaces:

7.1.1 **KCPI** (Knife Cuts Per Inch) is determined by holding the surfaced board at an angle to a strong light source and counting the visible ridges per inch, usually perpendicular to the profile.

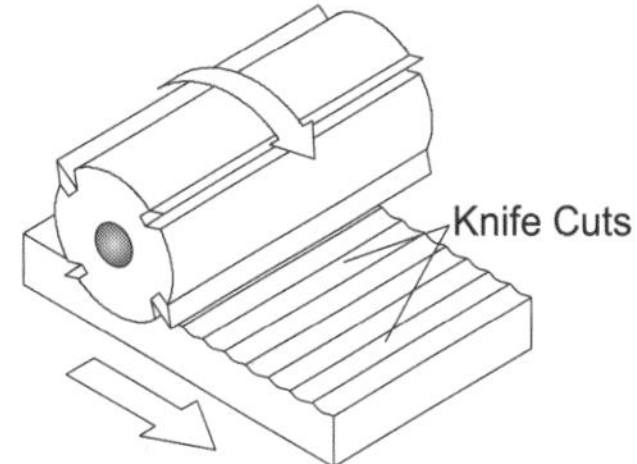

7.1.2 **SANDING** is checked for compliance by sanding a sample piece of the same species with the required grit of abrasive.

7.1.2.1 Observation with a hand lens of the prepared sample and the material in question will offer a comparison of the scratch marks of the abrasive grit.

7.1.2.2 Reasonable assessment of the performance of the finished product will be weighed against absolute compliance with the standard.

7.1.2.3 A product is sanded sufficiently smooth when knife cuts are removed, and any remaining sanding marks are or will be concealed by applied finishing coats.

7.1.2.4 Handling marks and/or grain raising due to moisture or humidity in excess of the ranges set forth in this standard shall not be considered a defect.

COMPLIANCE

7 FABRICATED and INSTALLED (continued)

7.2 **GAPS, FLUSHNESS, FLATNESS,** and **ALIGNMENT** of product and installation:

7.2.1 Maximum gaps between exposed components shall be tested with a feeler gauge at points designed to join where members contact or touch.

7.2.2 Joint length shall be measured with a ruler with a minimum of 1/16" (1 mm) divisions, and calculations will be made accordingly.

7.2.3 Reasonable assessment of the performance of the finished product will be weighed against absolute compliance with the standards.

7.2.4 The following is intended to provide examples of how and where compliance testing is measured:

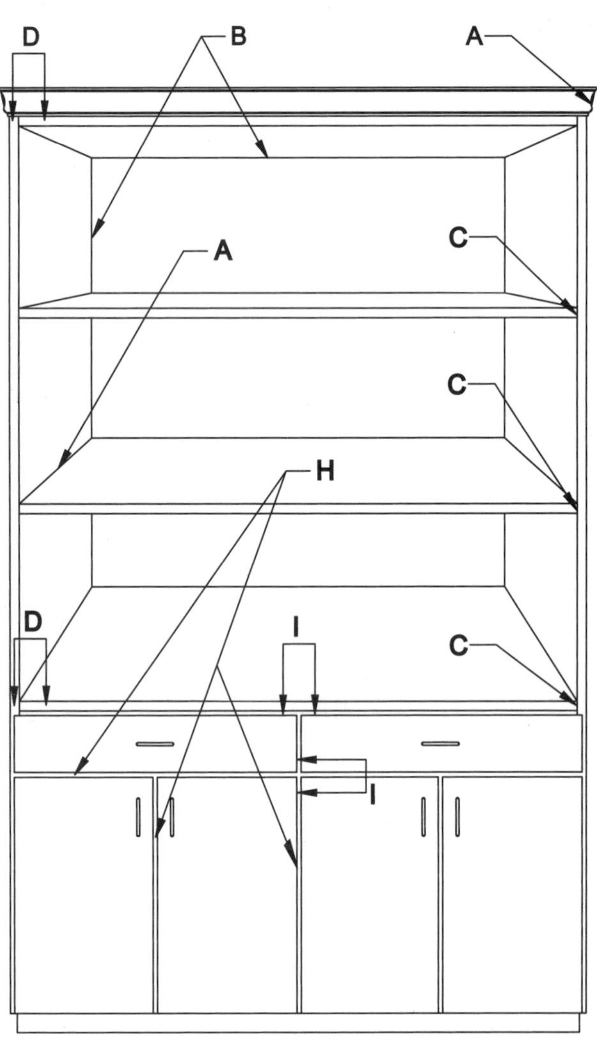

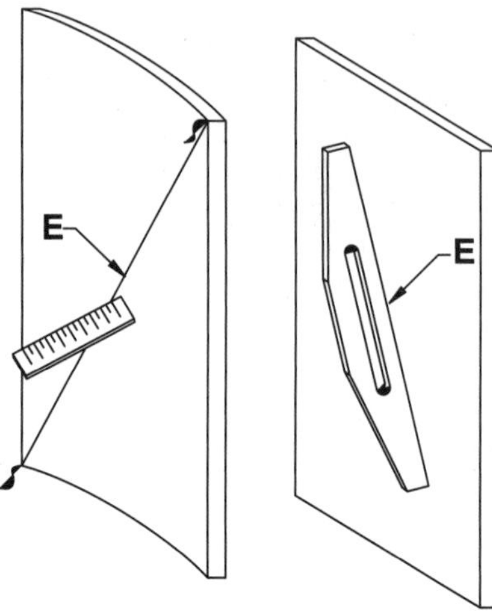

Measured on the concave face

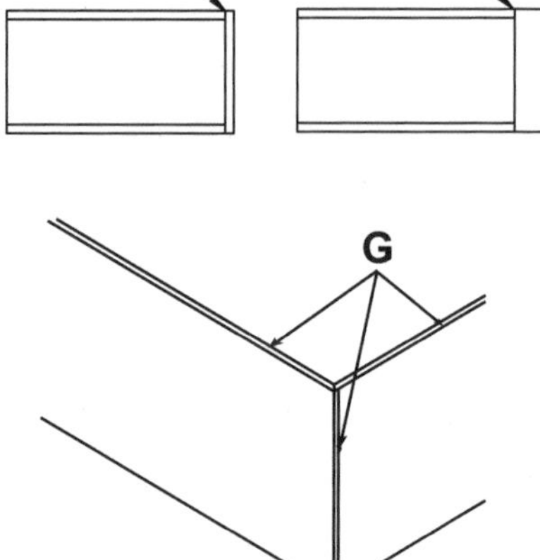

A - Gaps when surfaces are mitered or butted
B - Gaps when parallel pieces are joined
C - Gaps when edges are mitered or butted
D - Flushness between two surfaces
E - Flatness of panel product
F - Flushness of edgebanding
G - Chipout
H - Gaps at doors and drawer fronts
I - Alignment of doors and drawer fronts

Architectural Woodwork Standards

SECTION - 11

COUNTERTOPS

SECTION 11 ✦ COUNTERTOPS

(Including Tops, Wall Caps, Splashes, and Sills of High-Pressure Decorative Laminate, Wood, Solid Surface, Solid Phenolic, Epoxy Resin, and Natural/Manufactured Stone)

GENERAL

1 INFORMATION

1.1 GRADES

1.1.1 These standards are characterized in three Grades of quality that may be mixed within a single project. Limitless design possibilities and a wide variety of lumber and veneer species, along with overlays, high-pressure decorative laminates, factory finishes, and profiles are available in all three Grades.

1.1.2 **ECONOMY GRADE** defines the minimum quality requirements for a project's workmanship, materials, or installation and is typically reserved for woodwork that is not in public view, such as in mechanical rooms and utility areas.

1.1.3 **CUSTOM GRADE** is typically specified for and adequately covers most high-quality architectural woodwork, providing a well-defined degree of control over a project's quality of materials, workmanship, or installation.

1.1.4 **PREMIUM GRADE** is typically specified for use in those areas of a project where the highest level of quality, materials, workmanship, and installation is required.

1.1.5 **MODIFICATIONS** by the contract documents shall govern if in conflict with these standards.

1.2 BASIC CONSIDERATIONS

1.2.1 **ACCEPTABLE REQUIREMENTS** of lumber and/or sheet products used within this woodwork product section are established by Sections 3 and 4, unless otherwise modified herein.

1.2.2 **CONTRACT DRAWINGS** and/or **SPECIFICATIONS**, furnished by the design professional, shall clearly indicate or delineate all material, fabrication, installation and applicable building code/regulation requirements.

1.2.3 **EXPOSED SURFACES**

1.2.3.1 All visible surfaces of an installed countertop.

1.2.4 **SEMI-EXPOSED SURFACES** - N/A

1.2.5 **CONCEALED SURFACES**

1.2.5.1 The underside surface 42" (1067 mm) or less off the finished floor.

1.2.5.2 All non-visible surfaces attached to and/or covered by another.

1.2.5.3 All non-visible blocking, spacers, etc., used for attachment.

1.2.6 **GRADE LIMITATIONS**

1.2.6.1 **SOLID-SURFACE** countertops are offered only in **CUSTOM GRADE** and **PREMIUM GRADE**.

1.2.6.2 **SOLID PHENOLIC, EPOXY RESIN**, and **NATURAL/MANUFACTURED STONE** countertops are offered only in **PREMIUM GRADE**.

1.2.7 **CHEMICAL-** or **STAIN-RESISTANCE** requirements for surfaces must be specified.

1.2.7.1 Consider the chemical and staining agents that might be used on or near the surfaces.

1.2.7.1.1 Chemical and stain resistance is affected by concentration, time, temperature, humidity, housekeeping, and other factors; it is recommended that actual samples are tested in a similar environment with those agents.

1.2.7.2 Common guidelines can be found by referring to:

1.2.7.2.1 NEMA LD3 (latest edition) for chemical resistance.

1.2.7.2.2 ASTM D3023 and C1378 (latest editions) for stain resistance.

1.2.7.2.3 SEFA #3 - Recommendations for work surfaces.

GENERAL

1.2 **BASIC CONSIDERATIONS** (continued)

1.2.8 **ABRASION-RESISTANCE** requirements for countertop surfaces shall be specified.

1.2.8.1 When abrasion-resistance requirements are a concern, users should consider the abrasive elements that might be used on or near the countertop surfaces.

1.2.8.2 Common guidelines can be found in:

1.2.8.2.1 ASTM C501 (latest edition)

1.2.8.2.2 NEMA LD3-3.13 (latest edition)

1.2.8.2.3 NEMA LD3.7 (latest edition)

1.2.9 **HIGH-PRESSURE DECORATIVE LAMINATE (HPDL)** countertops

1.2.9.1 Some HPDLs utilize a **WHITE BACKGROUND** paper to achieve the high-fidelity, contrast, and depth of color of their printed pattern, leaving a white line at exposed edges that is extremely noticeable with darker colors.

1.2.9.2 **FIRE RATED** - Class I Fire-Rated Architectural HPDL countertops are available.

1.2.9.2.1 Countertops desired to be certified as a fire-rated assembly (versus simply having been built with a fire-rated laminate surface) shall be specified as a "Class I Fire-Rated HPDL Countertop."

1.2.9.2.2 The term "Class I Fire-Rated HPDL Countertop" shall mean that the entire countertop assembly -- including surface HPDL, backer, core, and adhesive -- has been tested and certified as to its Class I Fire Rating by an authorized organization, such as Underwriters Laboratories, and must be manufactured by an approved company of the certifying agency.

1.2.9.2.3 Manufacturers of "Class I Fire-Rated Countertop Assemblies" require specific methods of installation and trimming in order to label and certify their product. Design professionals desiring to use a "Class I Fire-Rated Countertop Assembly" should coordinate with an approved manufacturer during the design stage.

1.2.10 **SOLID-SURFACE, NATURAL/MANUFACTURED STONE,** and **EPOXY RESIN** countertops

1.2.10.1 **COLOR** and **PATTERN MATCH:** Some slight color variation may exist from sheet-to-sheet, sheet-to-bowl, or sink products. In sheet stock, use of the same batch material will lessen these variations.

1.2.10.2 **REPAIRS:** When allowed, repairability varies from material to material and may be visible.

1.2.10.3 **PRECAUTIONS:** Product dimensions are nominal. If tolerances are critical, review them with your manufacturer and/or installer.

1.2.10.4 **MACHINABILITY** is an issue with some materials and shall be taken into consideration on selection.

1.2.11 **DESIGN CONSIDERATIONS**

1.2.11.1 Typical **HPDL** countertop configuration options:

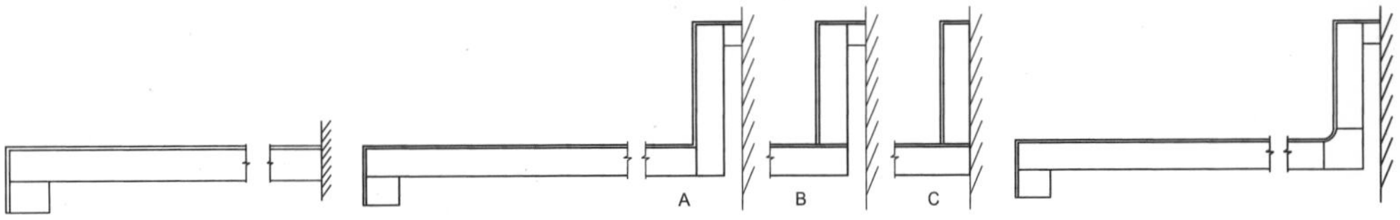

A B C

1
Self-Edged
No Splash

2
Self-Edged w/
Butt Splash

3
Self-Edged w/
Coved Splash

GENERAL

1.2 **BASIC CONSIDERATIONS** (continued)

1.2.11 **DESIGN CONSIDERATIONS** (continued)

1.2.11.1 Typical **HPDL** countertop (continued)

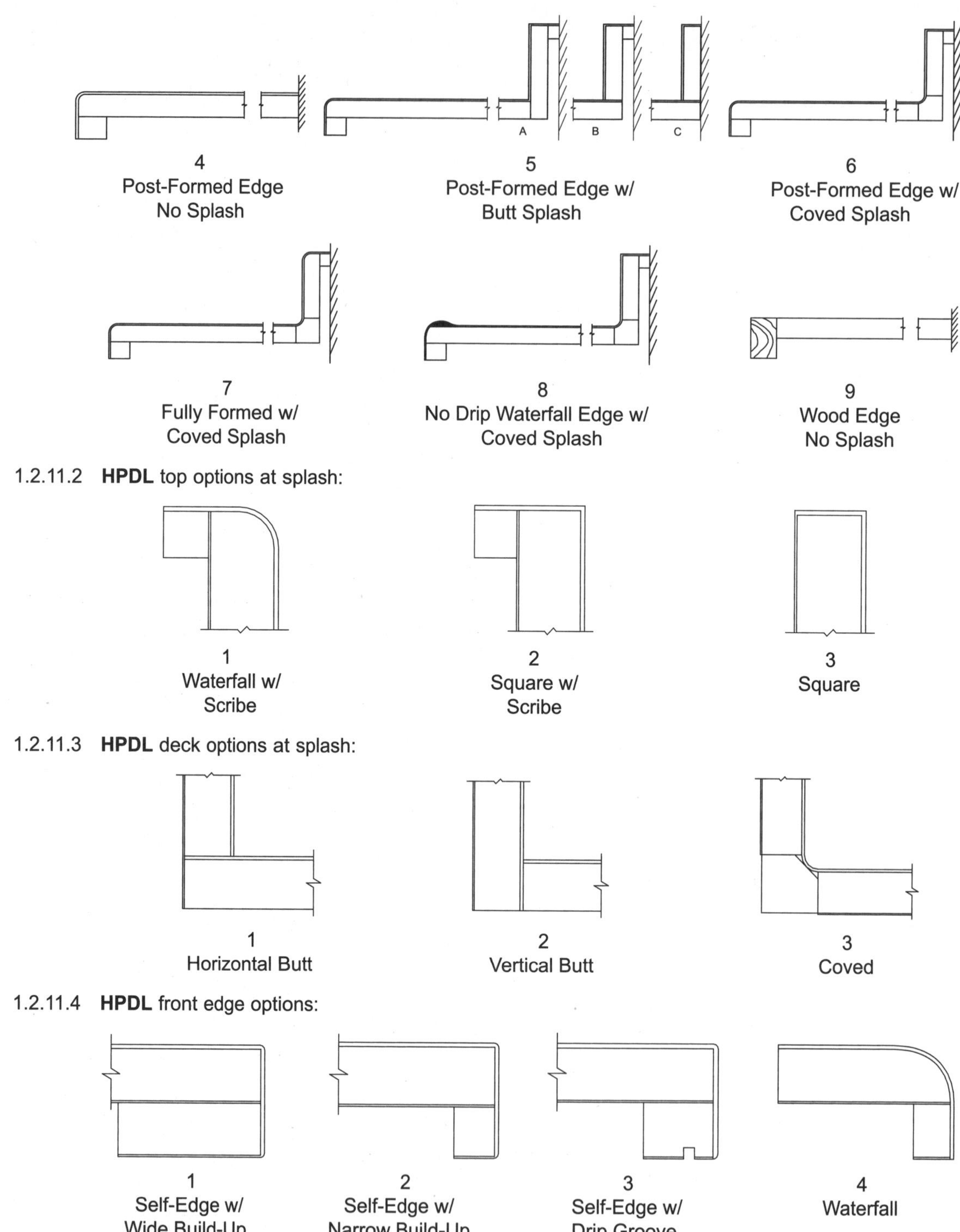

GENERAL

1.2 **BASIC CONSIDERATIONS** (continued)

1.2.11 **DESIGN CONSIDERATIONS** (continued)

1.2.11.4 **HPDL** front edge options (continued)

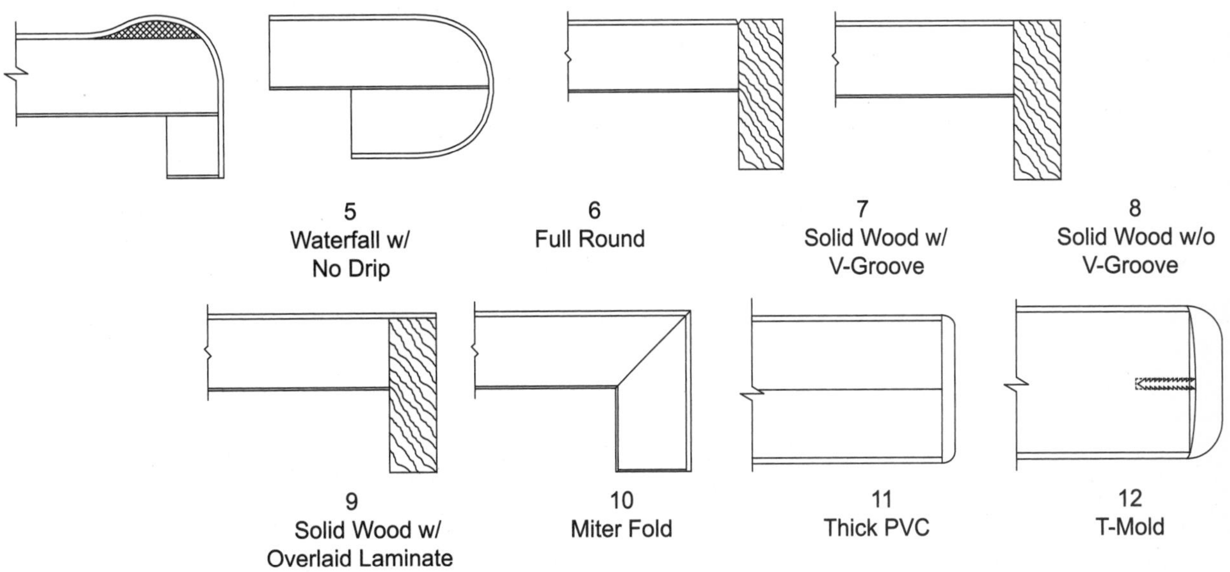

5 Waterfall w/ No Drip

6 Full Round

7 Solid Wood w/ V-Groove

8 Solid Wood w/o V-Groove

9 Solid Wood w/ Overlaid Laminate

10 Miter Fold

11 Thick PVC

12 T-Mold

1.2.11.5 **HPDL BACK** and **END SPLASH** construction types:

1.2.10.5.1 If not otherwise specified, it shall be the manufacturer's option.

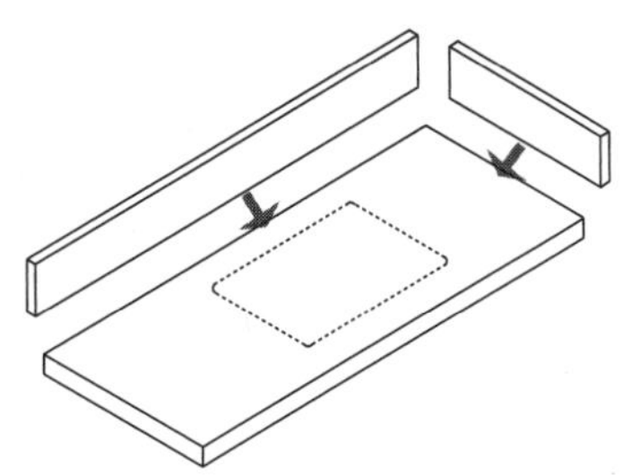

ASSEMBLY 1
Wall Mount, Jobsite Assembled

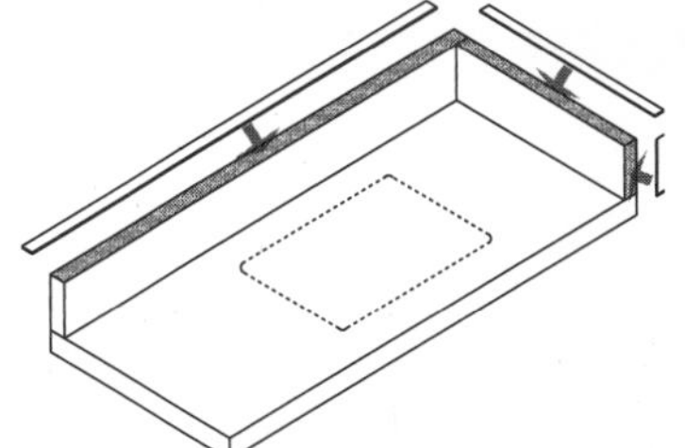

ASSEMBLY 2
Deck Mount, Manufacturer Assembled

1.2.11.6 **MECHANICAL TIGHT JOINT FASTENER**:

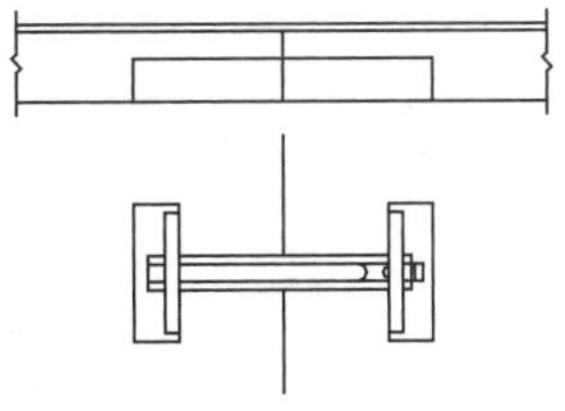

Tight Joint Fastener

1.2.11.7 **WOOD** countertop configuration options:

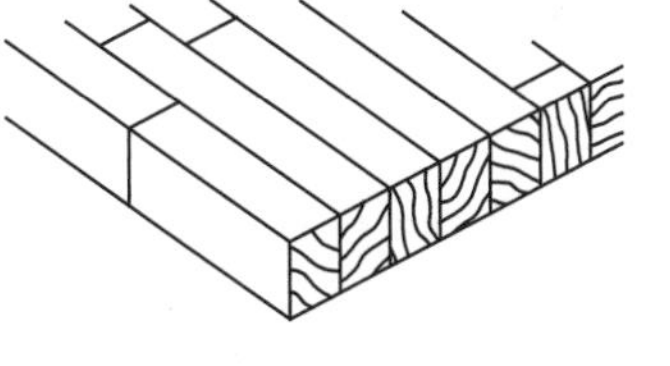

1
Solid Butcher Block

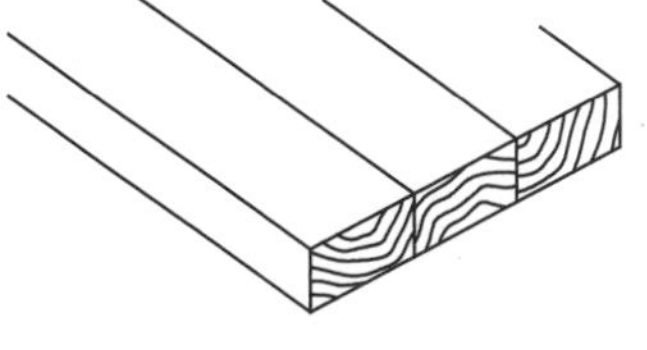

2
Solid Wide Width

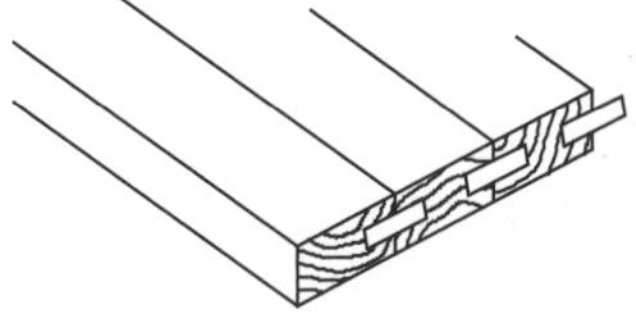

3
Solid, Splined Wide Width

GENERAL

1.2 **BASIC CONSIDERATIONS** (continued)

1.2.11 **DESIGN CONSIDERATIONS** (continued)

1.2.11.7 **WOOD** countertop configuration (continued)

4
Veneer-Banded

5
Solid-Banded

6
Solid-Banded w/ Overlaid Veneer

1.2.11.8 **SOLID-SURFACE** countertop configuration options:

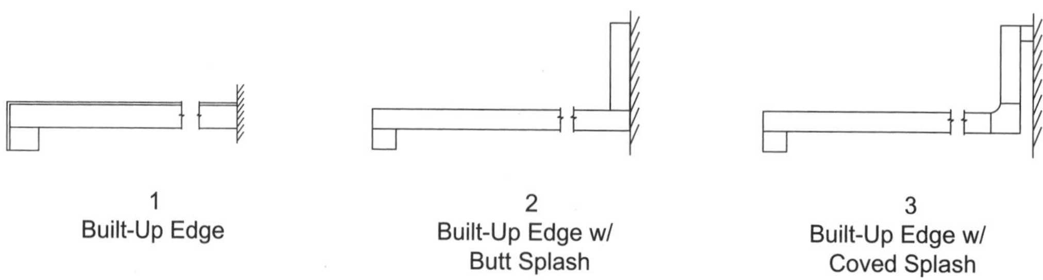

1
Built-Up Edge

2
Built-Up Edge w/ Butt Splash

3
Built-Up Edge w/ Coved Splash

1.2.11.9 **SOLID-SURFACE** top options at splash:

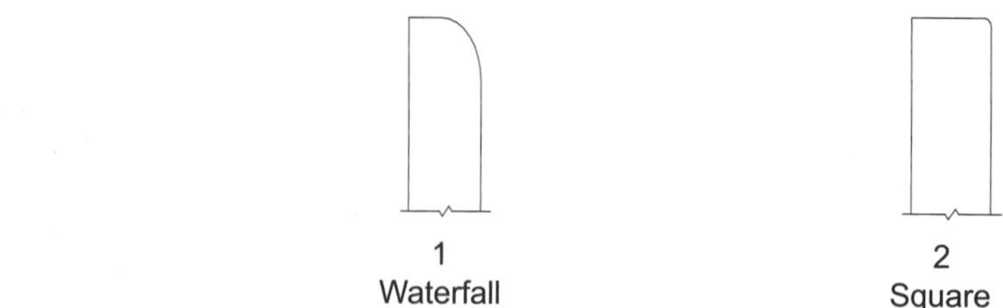

1
Waterfall

2
Square

1.2.11.10 **SOLID-SURFACE** deck options at splash:

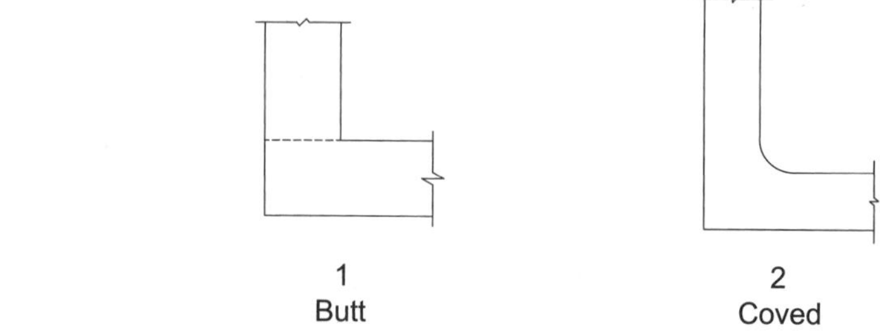

1
Butt

2
Coved

1.2.11.11 **SOLID-SURFACE** edge options:

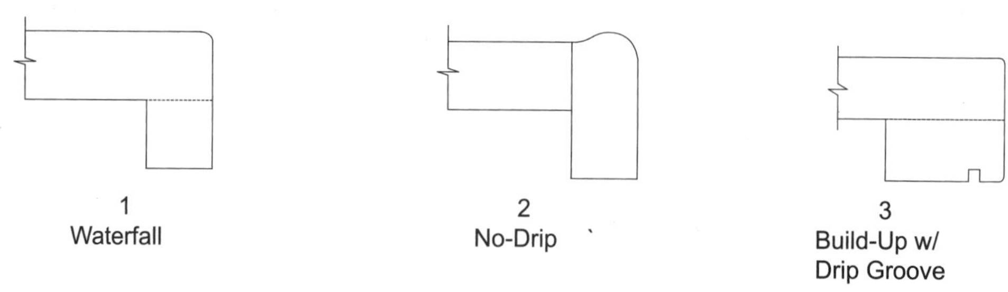

1
Waterfall

2
No-Drip

3
Build-Up w/ Drip Groove

GENERAL

1.2 **BASIC CONSIDERATIONS** (continued)

1.2.11 **DESIGN CONSIDERATIONS** (continued)

1.2.11.12 **SOLID PHENOLIC, EPOXY RESIN,** and **NATURAL/MANUFACTURED STONE** countertop configuration options:

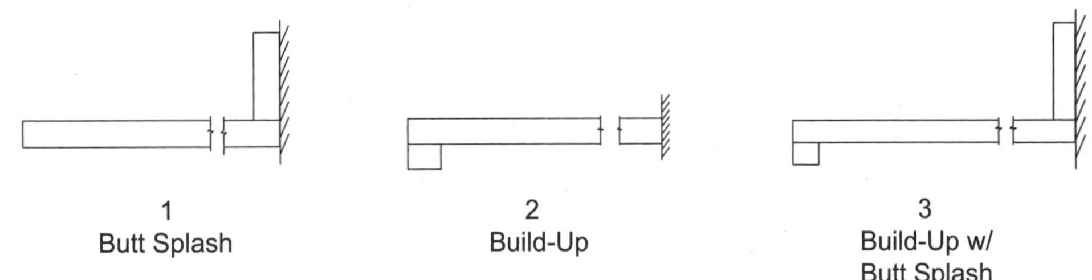

1 Butt Splash — 2 Build-Up — 3 Build-Up w/ Butt Splash

1.2.11.13 **SOLID PHENOLIC, EPOXY RESIN,** and **NATURAL/MANUFACTURED STONE** top and deck options at splash:

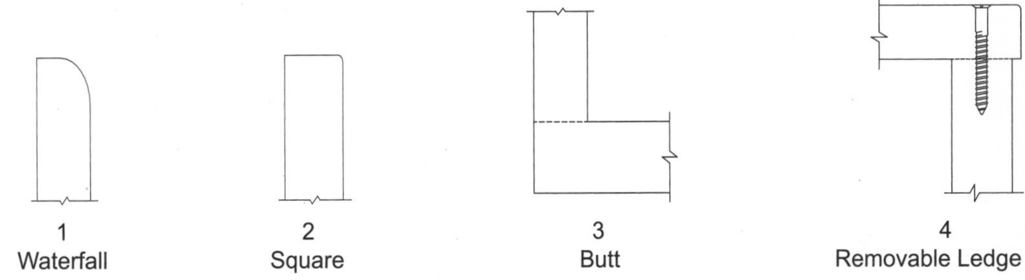

1 Waterfall — 2 Square — 3 Butt — 4 Removable Ledge

1.2.11.14 **SOLID PHENOLIC, EPOXY RESIN,** and **NATURAL/MANUFACTURED STONE** edge options:

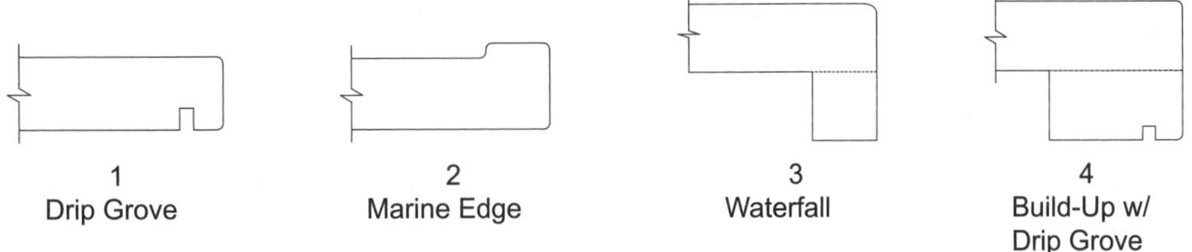

1 Drip Grove — 2 Marine Edge — 3 Waterfall — 4 Build-Up w/ Drip Grove

1.3 **RECOMMENDATIONS**

1.3.1 **INCLUDE IN THE DIVISION 09 OF THE SPECIFICATIONS:**

1.3.1.1 For **JOBSITE FINISHING** - Before finishing, all exposed portions of woodwork shall have handling marks or effects of exposure to moisture removed with a thorough, final sanding over all surfaces of the exposed portions using an appropriate grit sandpaper, and shall be cleaned before applying sealer or finish.

1.3.1.2 At **CONCEALED SURFACES** - Architectural woodwork that may be exposed to moisture, such as those adjacent to exterior concrete walls, etc., shall be back-primed.

1.3.1.3 The underside of all wood countertops shall be sealed with at least one coat of primer or sealer.

1.3.2 **THOROUGHLY REVIEW** Sections 2 and 4, especially Basic Considerations, Recommendations, Acknowledgements, and Industry Practices within Part 1 for an overview of the characteristics and minimum acceptable requirements of lumber and/or sheet products that might be used herein.

1.3.3 **CONTRACT DOCUMENTS** (plans and/or specifications) shall require that all structural members, grounds, blocking, backing, furring, brackets, or other anchorage which becomes an integral part of the building's walls, floors, or ceilings, required for the installation of architectural woodwork is not to be furnished or installed by the architectural woodwork manufacturer or installer.

1.3.4 **SPECIFY** requirements for:

1.3.4.1 Back- and end-splash **ASSEMBLY** type.

GENERAL

1.3 **RECOMMENDATIONS** (continued)

1.3.4 **SPECIFY** requirements (continued)

1.3.4.1 Fire-rating requirements.

1.3.4.2 Laboratory use, such as:
1.3.4.2.1 Chemical-resistant work-surface material requirements or finish.
1.3.4.2.2 Abrasion-resistant work-surface material requirement.
1.3.4.2.3 Removable splash ledger.

1.3.4.3 Special splash/deck or top or edge profiles.

1.3.5 With **HPDL SINK TOPS**, use of under-mount sinks is not recommended because of the potential for moisture problems, even with proper preparation and installation.

1.3.5.1 Use of veneer core plywood with Type II adhesive, industrial-grade particleboard or fiberboard with a 24-hour thickness swell factor of 5% or less, and a 24-hour water-absorption factor of 10% or less is required.

1.3.5.2 Either self-rimming sinks or sinks with surface-mounted metal retention rings are recommended.

1.4 **ACKNOWLEDGEMENTS**

1.4.1 Use of **CONTINUOUS-PRESSURE LAMINATES** (melamine and polyester-based) as an alternative to HPDL is permitted, provided that they conform to the same physical properties and thickness as required for HPDL.

1.4.2 Use of **LOW-PRESSURE DECORATIVE OVERLAY** or other film-finish products is not covered by these standards and Grade rules.

1.5 **INDUSTRY PRACTICES**

1.5.1 **STRUCTURAL MEMBERS**, grounds, blocking, backing, furring, brackets, or other anchorage that becomes an integral part of the building's walls, floors, or ceilings, required for the installation of architectural woodwork is not furnished or installed by the architectural woodwork manufacturer or installer.

1.5.2 **WALL, CEILING**, and/or opening variations in excess of 1/4" (6.4 mm) or FLOORS in excess of 1/2" (12.7 mm) in 144" (3658 mm) of being plumb, level, flat, straight, square, or of the correct size are not acceptable for the installation of architectural woodwork, nor is it the responsibility of the installer to scribe or fit to tolerances in excess of such.

1.5.3 **BACK-PRIMING** of architectural woodwork is not the responsibility of the manufacturer and/or installer, unless the material is being furnished prefinished.

1.5.4 **BUILD-UP** or spacing materials required for installation of a countertop are the responsibility of the countertop manufacturer.

1.5.5 Countertop surfaces with a defined **GRAIN** and/or **PATTERN** are installed running with the length of the top.

1.5.6 At base cabinets with countertops, the **HORIZONTAL REVEAL** between the lower edge of the countertop and the upper edge of the adjacent door or drawer front shall be consistent. Coordination of such is the responsibility of the cabinet manufacturer.

PRODUCT

2 SCOPE

2.1 All HPDL, including Class I Fire-Rated and Chemical-Resistant, Solid-Surface, Natural/Manufactured Stone, Epoxy Resin, Solid Phenolic, and wood facings, tops, splashes, and reagent shelves.

2.2 **TYPICAL INCLUSIONS**

2.2.1 HPDL, Class I Fire-Rated HPDL, Chemical-Resistant HPDL, Solid-Surface, Natural/Manufactured Stone, Epoxy Resin, Solid Phenolic, and Wood Countertops with approved backing sheet, as applicable.
2.2.2 Splashes and reagent shelves.

PRODUCT

MATERIAL, MACHINING, AND ASSEMBLY RULES (continued)

2 SCOPE (continued)

2.2 **TYPICAL INCLUSIONS** (continued)

2.2.3 Solid lumber, metal, or self-edge trim; cutouts for sinks; electrical boxes; and fixtures indicated on drawings.
2.2.4 Installation, if specified.
2.2.5 Solid-surface and/or epoxy sinks.
2.2.6 Window sills.
2.2.7 Support members that are surface-mounted.

2.3 **TYPICAL EXCLUSIONS**

2.3.1 Stripping, furring, blocking, or grounds.
2.3.2 Furnishing or installation sink rims or sinks not listed above.
2.3.3 In-wall support members.
2.3.4 All grounds, backing members, or other items unrelated to the furnishing and installation of countertops and sinks.
2.3.5 Fixtures, plumbing, and data equipment.
2.3.6 Sink outlets and fittings, except at epoxy sinks.

3 DEFAULT STIPULATIONS

3.1 **HPDL COUNTERTOPS** - Unless otherwise specified or detailed, all work shall be **CUSTOM GRADE** (unless the related casework is Premium Grade, then the countertops shall be **PREMIUM GRADE**); of desired HPDL colors selected from the manufacturer's non-premium-priced standard patterns and readily available sheet sizes; with standard self-edge, square butt splash a minimum of 4" (102 mm) above deck of Assembly Type 1 or 2 with square self-edge.

3.2 **WOOD COUNTERTOPS** - Unless otherwise specified or detailed, all work shall be **CUSTOM GRADE** (unless the related casework is Premium Grade, then the countertops shall be **PREMIUM GRADE**) hardwood plywood intended for an opaque finish.

3.3 **SOLID-SURFACE COUNTERTOPS** - Unless otherwise specified or detailed, all work shall be **CUSTOM GRADE** with the manufacturer's option of brand name and edge treatment; desired colors selected from the manufacturer's standard, non-premium-priced line with standard matte finish; a minimum of 1/2" (12.7 mm) thick; with a minimum of a 3" (76 mm) high splash above the deck surface.

3.4 **SOLID PHENOLIC, EPOXY RESIN**, and **NATURAL/MANUFACTURED STONE COUNTERTOPS** - Unless otherwise specified or detailed, all work shall be **CUSTOM GRADE** with the manufacturer's option of brand name and edge treatment; colors to be selected from the manufacturer's standard, non-premium-priced line with standard satin finish, and with compatible sink and accessories.

4 RULES - The following RULES shall govern unless a project's contract documents require otherwise.

These rules are intended to provide a well-defined degree of control over a project's quality of materials and workmanship.

Where E, C, or P is not indicated, the rule applies to all Grades equally.

ERRATA, published on the Associations' websites at www.awinet.org, www.awmac.com, or www.woodworkinstitute.com, shall TAKE PRECEDENCE OVER THESE RULES, subject to their date of posting and a project's bid date.

11

ARROWS INDICATE TOPIC IS CARRIED FROM ⇑ OR ONTO ⇓ ANOTHER PAGE.

		DESCRIPTION	E	C	P
4.1	**GENERAL**				
	4.1.1	**AESTHETIC GRADE RULES** apply only to exposed and semi-exposed surfaces visible after installation.			
	4.1.2	**LUMBER** shall conform to the requirements established in Section 3.			
⇓	4.1.3	**SHEET PRODUCTS** shall conform to the requirements established in Section 4.			
	4.1.4	**BACKING SHEET** shall conform to the requirements established in Section 4.			

PRODUCT

MATERIAL, MACHINING, AND ASSEMBLY RULES (continued)

Section	Item	DESCRIPTION	E	C	P
4.1 GENERAL	4.1.5	**EXPOSED, SEMI-EXPOSED**, and **CONCEALED** surfaces shall be as listed under **BASIC CONSIDERATIONS** of this section.			
	4.1.6	For the purpose of this standard, a **BALANCED PANEL** is one that is free from warp that affects serviceability for its intended purpose.			
	4.1.7	At **SOLID-SURFACE** and **EPOXY RESIN**, fabrication shall be performed by personnel properly trained and approved/certified by the applicable manufacturer.			
	4.1.8	**SURFACING** with grain and/or pattern shall be installed with the grain or pattern direction running length-wise.			
	4.1.9	**EXPOSED FASTENING IS PROHIBITED**, except for access panels.			
	4.1.10	Where **FIRE-RETARDANT** or **MOISTURE-RESISTANT** core is required, documentation shall be furnished, if requested.			
	4.1.11	If **HOT MELT** applied, HPDL edgebanding is not applied with a hot-melt adhesive formulated for its application; the laminate shall be primed before application.			
	4.1.12	Where **GLUING** or **LAMINATION** occurs:			
	4.1.12.1	**DELAMINATION** or **SEPARATION** shall not occur beyond what is allowed in Sections 3 & 4.			
	4.1.13	**FIRST-CLASS WORKMANSHIP** is required in compliance with these standards.			
4.2		**MATERIAL**			
MATERIAL	**4.2.1**	At **EXPOSED SURFACES**:			
EXPOSED SURFACES	4.2.1.1	Shall be free of manufacturing defects.			
	4.2.1.2	**TRANSPARENT FINISHED WOOD:**			
	4.2.1.2.1	Permits hardwood or softwood.			
	4.2.1.2.2	Permits only one species for the entire project.		●	●
	4.2.1.2.3	Adjacent veneer and lumber shall be:			
	4.2.1.2.3.1	Mill option species.	●		
	4.2.1.2.3.2	Compatible for color and grain.		●	
	4.2.1.2.3.3	Well-matched for color and grain.			●
	4.2.1.2.4	Have visible **EDGES, REVEALS**, and/or **SPLINES**, when appropriate, that:			
	4.2.1.2.4.1	Are full length.			
	4.2.1.2.4.2	Are **MILL-OPTION**.	●		
	4.2.1.2.4.3	**MATCH** the species of the panel face.		●	●
	4.2.1.2.4.4	Are **COMPATIBLE** for color and grain.		●	
	4.2.1.2.4.5	Are **WELL-MATCHED** for color and grain.			●
	4.2.1.2.4.6	Are a minimum of 0.020" (0.5 mm) nominal **THICKNESS** that precludes show-through of core.		●	●
	4.2.2	When **FACTORY FINISHING** is specified, concealed surfaces shall be factory sealed with one coat at 1 mil dry.		●	●
	4.2.3	At **CONCEALED SURFACES** shall allow defects, and:			
	4.2.3.1	Blocking, fillers, and shim stock may be of any sound material.			
	4.2.4	At **WOOD** shall be:			
	4.2.4.1	3/4" (19 mm) minimum thickness hardwood (plywood or solid stock) of one species for the entire project.			
	4.2.5	At **HPDL**:			
	4.2.5.1	Shall be general-purpose HPDL, a minimum of .048" (1.2 mm) in thickness, or:			
	4.2..5.1.1	0.042" (1.05 mm) post-forming grade, if required.			

PRODUCT

MATERIAL, MACHINING, AND ASSEMBLY RULES (continued)

				DESCRIPTION	E	C	P
4.2 (MATERIAL)	**MATERIAL** (continued)						
	4.2.5 (HPDL)	At **HPDL**: (continued)					
		4.2.5.2		Use of **CONTINUOUS-PRESSURE LAMINATES** (melamine and polyester-based) as an alternative to HPDL is permitted, provided that they conform to the same physical properties and thickness as required for HPDL.			
		4.2.5.3		**CORE** shall be a minimum of 3/4" (19 mm) particleboard, medium-density fiberboard, veneer core, or otherwise approved engineered core, and:			
			4.2.5.3.1	At **SINK TOPS** and their **SPLASHES**, use of veneer core plywood with Type II adhesive, industrial-grade particleboard or fiberboard with a 24-hour thickness swell factor of 5% or less and a 24-hour water-absorption factor of 10% or less is required for the entire countertop elevation and/or return elevation.			
		4.2.5.4		**FIRE-RATED** countertops require **CLASS I FIRE-RATED HPDL** and:			
			4.2.5.4.1	**CORE**, a minimum of 11/16" (17.5 mm) thick, Class I Fire Rated.			
			4.2.5.4.2	**BACKING SHEET**, a minimum of 0.028" (0.7 mm) high-pressure phenolic Class I Fire-Rated.			
	4.2.6	At **SOLID SURFACE** shall be:					
		4.2.6.1		1/4" (6.4 mm) minimum thickness for use as wall panels, tub enclosures, or other vertical surfaces.			
		4.2.6.2		1/2" (12.7 mm) minimum thickness for countertops and back splashes.			
	4.2.7	At **SOLID PHENOLIC** shall be:					
		4.2.7.1		Minimum 3/4" (19 mm) thick composite of solid phenolic resins molded with a homogenous core of organic fiber-reinforced phenolic and one or more integrally cured surfaces of compatible thermoset nonabsorbent resins.			
	4.2.8	At **EPOXY RESIN** shall be:					
		4.2.8.1		Minimum 1" (25.4 mm) in thickness, uniform mixture throughout of epoxy resin, silica, organic fillers, and inert hardeners with a satin, non-glare finish on the top surface.			
	4.2.9	At **NATURAL/MANUFACTURED STONE** shall be:					
		4.2.9.1		Minimum 3/4"(19 mm) in thickness.			
4.3	**MACHINING**						
	4.3.1	Of **CUTOUTS** within a top, shall be made by either manufacturer or installer, and:					
		4.3.1.1		**SINK** cutouts shall not fall within 18" (457 mm) of a joint.			
	4.3.2	Prohibits **TEAR-OUTS, KNIFE NICKS**, or **HIT-OR-MISS** machining.					
	4.3.3	Prohibits **KNIFE MARKS** where sanding is required.					
	4.3.4	Requires **SHARP EDGES** to be eased with a fine abrasive.					
	4.3.5 (WOOD)	At **WOOD**:					
		4.3.5.1		Occasional patches are allowed.	●		
		4.3.5.2		For **OPAQUE** or **TRANSPARENT FINISH**, finger joints are permitted in solid lumber.	●		
		4.3.5.3		**SMOOTHNESS REQUIREMENTS** (see Item 7.1 in **COMPLIANCE**) require:			
			4.3.5.3.1	**TOP FLAT WOOD** surfaces; those that can be sanded with a drum or wide belt sander:			
			4.3.5.3.1.1	Minimum of 15 KCPI or 100-grit sanding	●		
			4.3.5.3.1.2	120-grit sanding		●	
			4.3.5.3.1.3	150-grit sanding			●

11

PRODUCT

MATERIAL, MACHINING, AND ASSEMBLY RULES (continued)

No.	DESCRIPTION	E	C	P
4.3	**MACHINING** (continued)			
4.3.5	At **WOOD** (continued)			
4.3.5.3	**SMOOTHNESS REQUIREMENTS** (continued)			
4.3.5.3.2	**MOLDED** and **SHAPED WOOD** surfaces:			
4.3.5.3.2.1	Minimum of 15 KCPI or 100-grit sanding	●		
4.3.5.3.2.2	Minimum of 20 KCPI		●	
4.3.5.3.2.3	120-grit sanding			●
4.3.5.3.3	**CROSS-SANDING:**			
4.3.5.3.3.1	Is not a defect.	●		
4.3.5.3.3.2	Is not allowed.		●	●
4.3.6	At **HPDL**:			
4.3.6.1	**CUTOUTS** shall have a minimum of 1/4" (6.4 mm) radius at all inside corners, except at wood or epoxy resin, and:			
4.3.6.1.1	**EDGES** subject to **EXCESSIVE MOISTURE** shall be sealed with a color-toned (for verification), water-resistant sealer before trim or sink rims are installed.			
4.3.6.2	**COVES** at splashes of:			
4.3.6.2.1	1/4" (6.4 mm) radius permits a square cove stick the same thickness as the core material with all voids filled with glue between the HPDL and the cove stick.			
4.3.6.2.2	3/4" (19 mm) radius requires a molded cove stick glued and mechanically fastened a maximum of 12" (305 mm) on center, with no voids permitted between the HPDL or core and the cove stick.			
4.3.6.3	**DRIP GROOVE**, when specified, shall be **CONTINUOUS** and 1/8" x 1/8" (3.2 mm x 3.2 mm) approximately 3/8" (9.5 mm) from the front edge and sealed with a color-toned (for verification), water-resistant sealer:			
4.3.6.3.1	**GROOVE EDGES** shall be smoothly sanded.			
4.3.6.4	**MITER-FOLD** self edge is acceptable.			
4.3.7	At **SOLID SURFACE:**			
4.3.7.1	Shall conform to the manufacturer's recommendations.			
4.3.7.2	**MANUFACTURED JOINTS** shall be precision-machined and glued with the manufacturer's hard seaming material or equal:			
4.3.7.2.1	**SILICONE** is **NOT** permitted at joints, except:			
4.3.7.2.1.1	Where hot areas meet cold areas.			
4.3.7.3	**EDGE** detail requires a:			
4.3.7.3.1	Single drop or build-up with mill-option profile, a minimum of 1" (25.4 mm) thick.		●	
4.3.7.3.2	Build-up with mill-option profile, a minimum of 1-1/2" (38.1 mm) thick.			●
4.3.7.4	**COVED** splash is only required when so specified, with:			
4.3.7.4.1	**ENDS** sent loose without cove.			
4.3.8	At **SOLID PHENOLIC:**			
4.3.8.1	**JOINTS** shall be precision-machined with tight joint fasteners and sealed with a bioside silicon prior to tightening (producing an almost invisible joint).			
4.3.8.2	**FRONT EDGES** shall be built up to a minimum of 1" (25.4 mm) in thickness.			
4.3.9	At **EPOXY RESIN**:			
4.3.9.1	**EXPOSED EDGES** shall be smoothly machined and finished to be compatible with the top face.			
4.3.9.2	**LIPPED TOPS** shall be raised a minimum of 3/16" (4.8 mm) above the work surface, and:			
4.3.9.2.1	Drip groove is not required.			

PRODUCT

MATERIAL, MACHINING, AND ASSEMBLY RULES (continued)

Section	No.	DESCRIPTION	E	C	P
4.3		**MACHINING** (continued)			
	4.3.10	At **NATURAL** and **MANUFACTURED STONE:**			
	4.3.10.1	**EXPOSED EDGES** shall be finished the same as the top surface.			
4.4 ASSEMBLY		**ASSEMBLY**			
	4.4.1	**ADHESIVE** or **JOINT FILLER** material, if used, shall be inconspicuous and match the adjacent surface for smoothness.			
	4.4.2	**SQUARENESS** shall be within ±1/64" (0.4 mm) for each 12" (305 mm).			
	4.4.3	**CUTOUTS** shall be within ±1/8" for locations and +1/8" to 0" (3.2 to 0 mm) for size.			
	4.4.4	**SIZE** shall be within ± 1/8" (3.2 mm) in length and ±1/16" (1.6 mm) in width.			
	4.4.5	**TOPS** requiring more than one sheet of surface material shall be prematched to minimize color variation within the scope of the manufacturer's guarantee and:		●	●
	4.4.5.1	Shall be fabricated from the longest lengths available.		●	●
	4.4.5.2	Top widths exceeding product availability shall have manufacturer-assembled joints.			
	4.4.6	**FILLERS** shall be furnished by the countertop manufacturer.			
	4.4.7	**SEQUENCE** of all edge applications shall be the manufacturer's option, except at HPDL.			
	4.4.8	**REMOVABLE LEDGES** and/or **ACCESS PANELS** shall be attached with flat-head screws, set flush, and:			
	4.4.8.1	If **CHEMICAL RESISTANCE** is required, screws shall be stainless steel.			
	4.4.9 JOINTS	Of **JOINTS** at **ASSEMBLED** work shall:			
	4.4.9.1	Be neatly and accurately made.			
	4.4.9.2	Be **SECURELY GLUED**, with:			
	4.4.9.2.1	**ADHESIVE** residue removed from all exposed and semi-exposed surfaces.			
	4.4.9.3	Be **REINFORCED** with glue blocks where essential.			
	4.4.9.4	**NOT PERMIT** fasteners at exposed surfaces of HPDL or overlay sheet products.			
	4.4.9.5	Require **EDGEBANDING** to be flush with adjacent surfaces not to exceed:			
	4.4.9.5.1	0.010" (0.25 mm).	●		
	4.4.9.5.2	0.005" (0.13 mm).		●	
	4.4.9.5.3	0.003" (0.03 mm).			●
	4.4.9.6	Allows **FILLER** material:			
	4.4.9.6.1	If inconspicuous when viewed at 72" (1829 mm).	●		
	4.4.9.6.2	If inconspicuous when viewed at 48" (1219 mm).		●	
	4.4.9.6.3	If inconspicuous when viewed at 24" (610 mm).			●
	4.4.10	**OVERHANG** shall be:			
	4.4.10.1	**CONSISTENT**, within a minimum of 1/2" (12.7 mm) and a maximum of 1-1/4" (31.8 mm) of cabinet face and/or finished end, and:			
	4.4.10.1.1	Be within 3/8" (9.5 mm) of parallel per elevation.			
	4.4.10.2	If specified, a continuous **DRIP GROOVE** 1/8" x 1/8" (3.2 x 3.2 mm), approximately 3/8" (9.5 mm) in from the front edge, shall be provided.			
	4.4.11	**UNSUPPORTED** countertop **SPANS** shall not exceed 48" (1219 mm), and they shall be reinforced to prevent deflection in excess of 1/4" (6.4 mm) under a 50 lbs (22.7 kg) per square foot (kgs per 305 mm square) load.			
	4.4.12	**EXPOSED EDGES:**			
	4.4.12.1	Shall be neatly and entirely covered.			
	4.4.12.2	Shall be eased.			
	4.4.12.3	**FRONT EDGES** shall be built up to a minimum of 1-1/4" (31.8 mm) in thickness, except at epoxy.			

PRODUCT

MATERIAL, MACHINING, AND ASSEMBLY RULES (continued)

No.	DESCRIPTION	E	C	P
4.4	**ASSEMBLY** (continued)			
4.4.13	**METAL TRIM RIMS** (furnished by others) at sinks or self-rimming sinks must overlap the countertop and/or sink by a minimum of 3/16" (4.8 mm).			
4.4.14	At **WOOD**:			
4.4.14.1	Requires **FLUSHNESS VARIATIONS** at exposed surfaces when mitered or butted (see Test D illustrations in **COMPLIANCE**) not to exceed:			
4.4.14.1.1	0.025" (0.6 mm)	●		
4.4.14.1.2	0.005" (0.1 mm)		●	
4.4.14.1.3	0.001" (0.03 mm)			●
4.4.14.2	Requires **GAPS** at exposed surfaces when mitered or butted (see Test A illustrations in **COMPLIANCE**) not to exceed:			
4.4.14.2.1	0.05" (1.3 mm) wide by 20% of the joint length.	●		
4.4.14.2.2	0.025" (0.6 mm) wide by 20% of the joint length.		●	
4.4.14.2.3	0.015" (0.4 mm) wide by 20% of the joint length.			●
4.4.14.3	Requires **GAPS** at exposed surfaces at parallel members (see test B illustrations in **COMPLIANCE**) not to exceed:			
4.4.14.3.1	0.05" x 8" (1.3 mm x 203 mm) and shall not occur within 48" (1219 mm) of a similar gap.	●		
4.4.14.3.2	0.025" x 6" (0.6 mm x 152 mm) and shall not occur within 60" (1524 mm) of a similar gap.		●	
4.4.14.3.3	0.015" x 3" (0.4 mm x 76 mm) and shall not occur within 72" (1829 mm) of a similar gap.			●
4.4.14.4	Requires **GAPS** at exposed surfaces when mitered or butted (see Test C illustrations in **COMPLIANCE**) not to exceed:			
4.4.14.4.1	0.05" (1.3 mm)	●		
4.4.14.4.2	0.025" (0.6 mm)		●	
4.4.14.4.3	0.015" (0.4 mm)			●
4.4.14.5	Requires **FLATNESS** of installed and removable sheet products (see Test E illustrations in **COMPLIANCE**) not to exceed:			
4.4.14.5.1	0.050" (1.3 mm) per 12" (305 mm) or portion thereof.	●		
4.4.14.5.2	0.036" (0.9 mm) per 12" (305 mm) or portion thereof.		●	
4.4.14.5.3	0.027" (0.7 mm) per 12" (305 mm) or portion thereof.			●
4.4.14.6	**JOINTS:**			
4.4.14.6.1	At L-shaped tops shall have an approximate 45° diagonal joint; butt joints are not permitted.			
4.4.14.6.2	**INSTALLATION JOINTS** shall be fit tight and flush with the use of splines, dowels, or biscuits for alignment, and:			
4.4.14.6.2.1	Be securely fastened with draw-bolt-type mechanical fasteners, if practical.			
4.4.14.6.3	Utilize clamp nail, biscuit, butterfly, scarf, or dowel joinery.		●	
4.4.14.6.4	Utilize biscuit spline, butterfly, scarf, or dowel joinery.			●
4.4.14.7	**CANTILEVER**, with or without a sub-top, shall not exceed 12" (305 mm) from a support, whether in the front, back, or end.			
4.4.14.8	Where **WIDE WIDTH GLUE-UP** is used, boards exceeding 3" (76 mm) in width shall be alternately set with crown up and crown down.			
4.4.14.9	Solid wood edges and applied moldings shall be:			
4.4.14.9.1	Nailed.	●		

11

PRODUCT

MATERIAL, MACHINING, AND ASSEMBLY RULES (continued)

				DESCRIPTION	E	C	P
4.4 ASSEMBLY				**ASSEMBLY** (continued)			
	4.4.14			At **WOOD**: (continued)			
		4.4.14.9		Solid wood edges and applied moldings shall be (continued)			
			4.4.14.9.1	Glued and finish nailed.		●	
			4.4.14.9.2	Pressure glued and splined, biscuited, or doweled without the use of fasteners through the exposed face.			●
	4.4.15 HPDL			At **HPDL**:			
		4.4.15.1		Requires **FLUSHNESS VARIATIONS** at exposed surfaces when mitered or butted (see Test D illustrations in **COMPLIANCE**) not to exceed:			
			4.4.15.1.1	0.075" (1.9 mm)	●		
			4.4.15.1.2	0.035" (0.89 mm)		●	
			4.4.15.1.3	0.020" (0.5 mm)			●
		4.4.15.2		Requires **GAPS** at exposed surfaces when mitered or butted (see Test A illustrations in **COMPLIANCE**) not to exceed:			
			4.4.15.2.1	0.05" (1.3 mm) wide by 20% of the joint length.	●		
			4.4.15.2.2	0.025" (0.6 mm) wide by 20% of the joint length.		●	
			4.4.15.2.3	0.015" (0.4 mm) wide by 20% of the joint length.			●
		4.4.15.3.		Requires **GAPS** at exposed surfaces at parallel members (see Test B illustrations in **COMPLIANCE**) not to exceed:			
			4.4.15.3.1	0.05" x 8" (1.3 mm x 203 mm) and shall not occur within 48" (1219 mm) of a similar gap.	●		
			4.4.15.3.2	0.025" x 6" (0.6 mm x 152 mm) and shall not occur within 60" (1524 mm) of a similar gap.		●	
			4.4.15.3.3	0.015" x 3" (0.4 mm x 76 mm) and shall not occur within 72" (1829 mm) of a similar gap.			●
		4.4.15.4		Requires **GAPS** at exposed surfaces when mitered or butted (see Test C illustrations in **COMPLIANCE**) not to exceed:			
			4.4.15.4.1	0.05" (1.3 mm)	●		
			4.4.15.4.2	0.025" (0.6 mm)		●	
			4.4.15.4.3	0.015" (0.4 mm)			●
		4.4.15.5		Requires **FLATNESS** of installed and removable sheet products (see Test E illustrations in **COMPLIANCE**) not to exceed:			
			4.4.15.5.1	0.050" (1.3 mm) per 12" (305 mm) or portion thereof.	●		
			4.4.15.5.2	0.036" (0.9 mm) per 12" (305 mm) or portion thereof.		●	
			4.4.15.5.3	0.027" (0.7 mm) per 12" (305 mm) or portion thereof.			●
		4.4.15.6		**BACKING SHEET** shall cover the underside of all countertops, the backside of all splashes and be the same for the entire project.			
		4.4.15.7		**LAMINATIONS** shall be made securely to the core with **TYPE II** adhesive applied as recommended by the adhesive manufacturer, and:			
			4.4.15.7.1	**CONTACT ADHESIVE** shall comply with the heat and moisture resistance requirements listed in the glossary.			
			4.4.15.7.2	Adhesive for **SOLID COLOR CORE** laminate application shall conform to the manufacturer's recommendation.			
		4.4.15.8		**FIRE-RATED** countertops require:			
			4.4.15.8.1	Non-formed self-edged.			
			4.4.15.8.2	Screwed-on back splash.			

PRODUCT

MATERIAL, MACHINING, AND ASSEMBLY RULES (continued)

No.	DESCRIPTION	E	C	P
4.4	**ASSEMBLY** (continued)			
4.4.15	At **HPDL**: (continued)			
4.4.15.8	**FIRE-RATED** countertops require (continued)			
4.4.15.8.1	Minimum **CUSTOM GRADE** conformance.			
4.4.15.8.2	**ADHESIVE** be rigid set, Class I Fire-Rated.			
4.4.15.9	**SELF-EDGE:**			
4.4.15.9.1	Permits self-edge applied after top laminate.	●	●	
4.4.15.9.2	Requires self-edge to be applied before top laminate.			●
4.4.15.10	**JOINTS:**			
4.4.15.10.1	At L-shaped **WOOD GRAIN** or **DIRECTIONAL PATTERN** tops shall have an approximate 45° diagonal joint; butt joints are not permitted.			
4.4.15.10.2	**INSTALLATION JOINTS** shall be fit tight and flush with the use of splines, dowels, or biscuits for alignment, and:			
4.4.15.10.2.1	Be securely fastened with draw-bolt-type mechanical fasteners, if practical.			
4.4.15.11	**BOTTOM** of edging and its build-up shall be free of dents, torn grain, glue, etc., and sanded smooth with all sharp edges removed.			
4.4.15.12	**BUILT-UP MEMBERS** shall be of acceptable core material with backing sheet applied, or:		●	●
4.4.15.12.1	The use of moisture-resistant core or a color-coded, water-resistant sealer may be substituted for backing sheet.		●	●
4.4.15.13	**BACK SPLASHES** require end splashes at wall ends.		●	●
4.4.15.14	At **ASSEMBLY 1** (wall mount) **BACK-** and **END-SPLASH** construction, and:			
4.4.15.14.1	**TOP** edge to be banded.			
4.4.15.14.2	**FRONT** edge of end splash to be banded.			
4.4.15.14.3	Splash **MEMBERS** to be bundled and shipped loose to project.			
4.4.15.14.4	**MECHANICAL FASTENERS** are required between splash members and deck.			●
4.4.15.15	At **ASSEMBLY 2** (deck mount) **BACK-** and **END-SPLASH** construction, and:			
4.4.15.15.1	**RAW CORE** at joint between the countertop deck and end splash or butt joint-applied back splash shall be sealed before assembly.			
4.4.15.15.2	**END SPLASHES** at cove or butt back splashes shall be butt-jointed and securely attached with mechanical fasteners, and:			
4.4.15.15.2.1	Mechanical fasteners are not required at wall or cabinet abutments that are not as deep as the countertop return.			
4.4.15.15.2.2	Shall be **CAULKED** with clear or compatible color waterproof caulking so as to leave a visual bead not exceeding 1/8" (3.2 mm).			
4.4.15.15.3	**SCRIBE ALLOWANCE** shall be provided, as appropriate, and:			
4.4.15.15.3.1	**UNBACKED SCRIBE SPAN** shall not exceed 1/2" (12.7 mm) at ends and back walls.			
4.4.15.16	**FINISHED END CAPS** may be applied after top laminate.			
4.4.15.17	**CANTILEVER**, with or without a sub-top, shall not exceed 12" (305 mm) from a support, whether in the front, back, or end.			
4.4.15.18	**REMOVABLE COMPONENTS** shall be attached with flat-head screws, set flush, and:			
4.4.15.18.1	If **CHEMICAL RESISTANCE** is required, the screws shall be stainless steel.			

PRODUCT

MATERIAL, MACHINING, AND ASSEMBLY RULES (continued)

				DESCRIPTION	E	C	P
4.4 ASSEMBLY				**ASSEMBLY** (continued)			
	SOLID SURFACE	4.4.16		At **SOLID SURFACE:**			
			4.4.16.1	Requires **FLUSHNESS VARIATIONS** at exposed surfaces when mitered or butted (see Test D illustrations in **COMPLIANCE**) to be flush.		●	●
			4.4.16.2	Requires **GAPS** at exposed surfaces when mitered or butted (see Test A, B, and C illustrations in **COMPLIANCE**) to be gap-free.		●	●
			4.4.16.3	Requires **FLATNESS** of installed and removable sheet products not to exceed:			
			4.4.16.3.1	0.036" (0.9 mm) per 12" (305 mm) or portion thereof.		●	
			4.4.16.3.2	0.027" (0.7 mm) per 12" (305 mm) or portion thereof.			●
			4.4.16.4	**EXPOSED FINISH** shall be the manufacturer's standard matte finish.			
			4.4.16.5	**SEAM JOINTS** shall be joined with a compatible color-matched adhesive and/or sealant.			
			4.4.16.6	**EXPANSION** clearances of at least 1/8" (3.2 mm) shall be provided.			
			4.4.16.7	**SEALANTS** and/or **ADHESIVES**, as recommended by individual manufacturers, shall be used to achieve the best performance and color match.			
			4.4.16.8	The **MAXIMUM** distance a countertop (with or without a sub-top) may **CANTILEVER** from a support is 12" (305 mm) for 3/4" (19 mm) thick or 6" (152 mm) for 1/2" (12.7 mm) thick material, whether in the front, back, or end.			
	SOLID PHENOLIC	4.4.17		At **SOLID PHENOLIC:**			
			4.4.17.1	Requires **FLUSHNESS VARIATIONS** at exposed surfaces when mitered or butted (see Test D illustrations in **COMPLIANCE**) not to exceed 0.001" (0.03 mm).			●
			4.4.17.2	Requires **GAPS** at exposed surfaces when mitered or butted (see Test A illustrations in **COMPLIANCE**)) not to exceed 0.015" (0.4 mm) wide by 20% of the joint length.			●
			4.4.17.3	Requires **GAPS** at exposed surfaces at parallel members (see Test B illustrations in **COMPLIANCE**) not to exceed 0.015" x 3" (0.4 mm x 76 mm) and shall not occur within 12" (1829 mm) of a similar gap.			●
			4.4.17.4	Requires **GAPS** at exposed surfaces when mitered or butted (see Test C illustrations in **COMPLIANCE**) not to exceed 0.015" (0.4 mm).			●
			4.4.17.5	**FLATNESS** (see Test E illustrations in **COMPLIANCE**) shall be held within ±1/32" (0.8 mm) per 120" (3048 mm) span.			
			4.4.17.6	**EDGE FINISH** shall be the standard black core with a machined satin sheen; polished edges shall be so specified.			
			4.4.17.7	**LIPPED TOPS** shall be raised a minimum of 1/4" (6.4 mm) above the work surface; the width of the raised area shall be determined by the manufacturer.			
			4.4.17.8	**BACK SPLASHES** shall be separate, flat-butted.			
			4.4.17.9	The **MAXIMUM** distance a countertop (with or without a sub-top) may **CANTILEVER** from a support is 12" (305 mm) for 3/4" (19 mm) thick or 6" (152 mm) for 1/2" (12.7 mm) thick material, whether in the front, back, or end.			
	EPOXY RESIN	4.4.18		At **EPOXY RESIN:**			
			4.4.18.1	Requires **FLUSHNESS VARIATIONS** at exposed surfaces when mitered or butted (see Test D illustrations in **COMPLIANCE**) not to exceed 0.050" (0.8 mm).			●
			4.4.18.2	Require **GAPS** at exposed surfaces when mitered or butted shall be per the manufacturer's recommendation and shall be neatly filled with recommended filler material (see Test A, B, and C illustrations in **COMPLIANCE**) and be gap-free.			●
			4.4.18.3	**FLATNESS** (see Test E illustrations in **COMPLIANCE**) shall be held within ±1/16" (1.6 mm) for each 36" (914 mm) span.			
			4.4.18.4	**BACK SPLASHES** shall be separate, flat-butted.			
			4.4.18.5	The **MAXIMUM** distance a countertop (with or without a sub-top) may **CANTILEVER** from a support is 12" (305 mm) for 1" (25.4 mm) thick or 6" (152 mm) for 3/4" (19 mm) thick material, whether in the front, back, or end.			

PRODUCT

MATERIAL, MACHINING, AND ASSEMBLY RULES (continued)

			DESCRIPTION	E	C	P
4.4 ASSEMBLY	**ASSEMBLY** (continued)					
	4.4.19		At **NATURAL** and **MANUFACTURED STONE:**			
	STONE	4.4.19.1	Requires **FLUSHNESS** or **LIPPAGE VARIATIONS** at exposed surfaces when mitered or butted (see Test D illustrations in **COMPLIANCE**) not to exceed 1/32" (0.8 mm) at the center of the joint.			●
		4.4.19.2	Requires **GAPS** at exposed surfaces when mitered or butted (see Test A illustrations in **COMPLIANCE**) not to exceed 0.015" (0.4 mm) wide by 20% of the joint length.			●
		4.4.19.3	Requires **GAPS** at exposed surfaces at parallel members (see Test B illustrations in **COMPLIANCE**) not to exceed 0.015" x 3" (0.4 mm x 76 mm) and shall not occur within 12" (1829 mm) of a similar gap.			●
		4.4.19.4	Requires **GAPS** at exposed surfaces when mitered or butted (see Test C illustrations in **COMPLIANCE**) not to exceed 0.015" (0.4 mm).			●
		4.4.19.5	**THICKNESS** of the material used throughout a project shall not vary in excess of 1/8" (3.2 mm).			
		4.4.19.6	**FLATNESS** (see Test E illustrations in **COMPLIANCE**) shall be held within ±1/16" (1.6 mm) for each 48" (1219 mm) span.			
		4.4.19.7	**BACK SPLASHES** shall be separate, flat-butted.			
		4.4.19.8	The **MAXIMUM** distance a countertop (with or without a sub-top) may **CANTILEVER** from a support is 10" (254 mm) for 3 cm [1-3/16" (30 mm)] or 6" (152 mm) for 2cm [13/16" (20 mm)] thick material, whether in the front, back, or end.			

EXECUTION

5 PREPARATION & QUALIFICATION REQUIREMENTS (unless otherwise specified)

5.1 **CARE, STORAGE, AND BUILDING CONDITIONS** shall be in compliance with the requirements set forth in Section 2 of these standards.

5.1.1 Severe damage to the woodwork can result from noncompliance. **THE MANUFACTURER AND/OR INSTALLER OF THE WOODWORK SHALL NOT BE HELD RESPONSIBLE FOR ANY DAMAGE THAT MIGHT DEVELOP BY NOT ADHERING TO THE REQUIREMENTS.**

5.2 **CONTRACTOR IS RESPONSIBLE FOR:**

5.2.1 Furnishing and installing structural members, grounds, blocking, backing, furring, brackets, or other anchorage required for architectural woodwork installation that becomes an integral part of walls, floors, or ceilings to which architectural woodwork shall be installed.

5.2.1.1 In the absence of contract documents calling for the contractor to supply the necessary blocking/backing in the wall or ceilings, either through inadvertence or otherwise, the architectural woodwork installer shall not proceed with the installation until such time as the blocking/backing is installed by others.

5.2.1.2 Preparatory work done by others shall be subject to inspection by the architectural woodwork installer and may be accepted or rejected for cause prior to installation.

5.2.1.2.1 **WALL, CEILING**, and/or opening variations in excess of 1/4" (6.4 mm) or **FLOORS** in excess of 1/2" (12.7 mm) in 144" (3658 mm) of being plumb, level, flat, straight, square, or of the correct size are not acceptable for the installation of architectural woodwork, nor is it the responsibility of the installer to scribe or fit to tolerances in excess of such.

5.2.2 Priming and back-priming the architectural woodwork in accordance with the contract documents prior to its installation.

5.2.2.1 If the architectural woodwork is factory-finished, back-priming by the factory finisher is required.

EXECUTION

5 PREPARATION & QUALIFICATION REQUIREMENTS (continued)

5.3 INSTALLER IS RESPONSIBLE FOR:

5.3.1 Having adequate equipment and experienced craftsmen to complete the installation in a first-class manner.

5.3.2 Checking all architectural woodwork specified and studying the appropriate portions of the contract documents, including these standards and the reviewed shop drawings, to familiarize themselves with the requirements of the Grade specified, understanding that:

5.3.2.1 Appearance requirements of Grades apply only to the surfaces visible after installation.

5.3.2.2 For transparent finish, special attention needs to be given to the color and grain of the various woodwork pieces to ensure they are installed in compliance with the Grade specified.

5.3.2.3 Installation site is properly ventilated, protected from direct sunlight, excessive heat and/or moisture, and that the HVAC system is functioning and maintaining the appropriate relative humidity and temperature.

5.3.2.4 Required priming or back priming of woodwork has been completed before its install.

5.3.2.5 Countertops have been acclimated to the field conditions for a minimum of 72 hours before installation is commenced.

5.3.2.6 Countertops specifically built or assembled in sequence for match of color and grain are installed to maintain that same sequence.

6 RULES - The following RULES shall govern unless a project's contract documents require otherwise.

These rules are intended to provide a well-defined degree of control over a project's quality of materials, workmanship, or installation.

Where E, C, or P is not indicated, the rule applies to all Grades equally.

ERRATA, published on the Associations' websites at www.awinet.org, www.awmac.com, or www.woodworkinstitute.com, shall TAKE PRECEDENCE OVER THESE RULES, subject to their date of posting and a project's bid date.

ARROWS INDICATE TOPIC IS CARRIED FROM ⇑ OR ONTO ⇓ ANOTHER PAGE.

	No.	DESCRIPTION	E	C	P
6.1		**GENERAL**			
GENERAL	6.1.1	Aesthetic **GRADE RULES** apply only to exposed and semi-exposed surfaces visible after installation.			
	6.1.2	**INSTALLED** plumb, level, square, and flat within 1/8" (3.2 mm) in 96" (2438 mm), and when required:			
	6.1.2.1	**GROUNDS** and hanging systems set plumb and true.		●	●
	6.1.3	**TRANSPARENT FINISHED WOODWORK** shall be installed:			
	6.1.3.1	With **CONSIDERATION** of color and grain.	●		
	6.1.3.2	**COMPATIBLE** in color and grain.		●	
	6.1.3.3	**WELL-MATCHED** for color and grain.			●
	6.1.3.3.1	**SHEET PRODUCTS** shall be compatible in color with solid stock.			●
	6.1.3.3.2	**ADJACENT SHEET PRODUCTS** shall be well-matched for color and grain.			●
	6.1.4	**REPAIRS** are allowed, provided they are neatly made and inconspicuous when viewed at:			
	6.1.4.1	72" (1829 mm)	●		
	6.1.4.2	48" (1220 mm)		●	
⇓	6.1.4.3	24" (610 mm)			●

EXECUTION

	No.	DESCRIPTION	E	C	P
6.1		**GENERAL** (continued)			
	6.1.5	**INSTALLER MODIFICATIONS** shall comply to the material, machining, and assembly rules within the **PRODUCT** portion of this section and the applicable finishing rules in Section 5.			
	6.1.6	**BUILD-UP** or spacing materials required for installation of a countertop are the responsibility of the countertop manufacturer.			
	6.1.7	At base cabinets with countertops, the **HORIZONTAL** reveal between the lower edge of the countertop and the upper edge of the adjacent door or drawer front shall be a consistent 1/4" (6.4 mm) +/- 1/8" (3.2 mm), except:			
	6.1.7.1	At laboratory casework, it shall be 1/4" (6.4 mm) to 1" (25.4 mm) and shall be consistent across elevations, except:			
	6.1.7.1.1	At sink locations.			
	6.1.7.2	Coordination of such is the responsibility of the cabinet manufacturer.			
GENERAL – COUNTERTOPS	**6.1.8**	**COUNTERTOPS** shall be:			
	6.1.8.1	Installed within 1/4" (6.4 mm) plus or minus the industry standard for height specified (see Section 10), except where ADA compliance is required.			
	6.1.8.2	**SECURELY** fastened and tightly fitted with flush joints.			
	6.1.8.2.1	The manufacturer's recommended **CAULK** and **SEALANTS** shall be used to achieve the best performance and color match.			
	6.1.8.2.2	Joinery shall be **CONSISTENT** throughout the project.			
	6.1.8.3	Of **MAXIMUM** available and/or practical lengths.		●	●
	6.1.8.4	**INSTALLED** plumb, level, square, and flat within 1/8" (3.2 mm) in 96" (2438 mm), and when required:			
	6.1.8.4.1	**GROUNDS** and hanging systems set plumb and true.		●	●
	6.1.8.5	Installed **FREE OF**:			
	6.1.8.5.1	Warp, twisting, cupping, and/or bowing that cannot be held true.			
	6.1.8.5.2	Open joints, visible machine marks, cross-sanding, tear-outs, nicks, chips, and/or scratches.			
	6.1.8.5.3	Natural defects exceeding the quantity and/or size limits defined in Sections 3 and 4.			
	6.1.8.6	**SMOOTH** and **SANDED** without **CROSS-SCRATCHES** in conformance to the **PRODUCT** portion of this section.			
	6.1.8.7	**SCRIBED** at:			
	6.1.8.7.1	Flat surfaces.		●	●
	6.1.8.7.2	Shaped surfaces.			●
	6.1.9	**CUTOUTS** and **HOLES** shall be provided for as indicated on the plans.			
	6.1.10	Wall-mounted **MIRRORS** shall not be supported by the countertop or back splash.			
GENERAL – GAPS	**6.1.11**	**GAPS** (see Test A-C illustrations in **COMPLIANCE**):			
	6.1.11.1	**CAUSED** by **EXCESSIVE DEVIATIONS** (deviations in excess of 1/4" [6.4 mm] in 144" [3658 mm] of being plumb, level, flat, straight, square, or of the correct size) in the building's walls and ceilings, or 1/2" (12.7 mm) for floors, shall not be considered a defect or the responsibility of the installer.			
	6.1.11.2	Shall not exceed 30% of a joint's **LENGTH** and:			
	6.1.11.2.1	**FILLED** or **CAULKED**, allowed	●		
		if color-compatible.		●	●
	6.1.11.3	Of **WOOD** to **WOOD** shall not exceed:			
	6.1.11.3.1	At **FLAT** surfaces:			
	6.1.11.3.1.1	0.050" (1.3 mm) in width	●		
	6.1.11.3.1.2	0.025" (0.65 mm) in width		●	
	6.1.11.3.1.3	0.012" (0.3 mm) in width			●

11

EXECUTION

DESCRIPTION		E	C	P
6.1	**GENERAL** (continued)			
6.1.1.1	**GAPS** (continued)			
6.1.11.3	Of **WOOD** to **WOOD** (continued)			
6.1.11.3.2	At **SHAPED** surfaces:			
6.1.11.3.2.1	0.075” (1.9mm) in width	●		
6.1.11.3.2.2	0.050" (1.3 mm) in width		●	
6.1.11.3.2.3	0.025" (0.65 mm) in width			●
6.1.11.4	Of **WOOD** to **NON-WOOD** shall not exceed:			
6.1.11.4.1	At **FLAT** and **SHAPED** surfaces:			
6.1.11.4.1.1	0.100" (2.5 mm) in width	●		
6.1.11.4.1.2	0.075" (1.9 mm) in width		●	
6.1.11.4.1.3	0.050" (1.3 mm) in width			●
6.1.11.5	Of **NON-WOOD** to **NON-WOOD** and/or **ALL ELEMENTS** shall not exceed:			
6.1.11.5.1	At **FLAT** surfaces:			
6.1.11.5.1.1	0.100" (2.5 mm) in width	●		
6.1.11.5.1.2	0.075" (1.9 mm) in width		●	
6.1.11.5.1.3	0.050" (1.3 mm) in width			●
6.1.11.5.2	At **SHAPED** surfaces:			
6.1.11.5.2.1	0.125" (3.2 mm) in width	●		
6.1.11.5.2.2	0.100" (2.5 mm) in width		●	
6.1.11.5.2.3	0.075" (1.9 mm) in width			●
6.1.12	**FLUSHNESS** of joinery (see Test D illustrations in **COMPLIANCE**):			
6.1.12.1	Of **WOOD** to **WOOD** shall not exceed:			
6.1.12.1.1	At **FLAT** surfaces:			
6.1.12.1.1.1	0.050" (1.3 mm)	●		
6.1.12.1.1.2	0.025" (0.65 mm)		●	
6.1.12.1.1.3	0.012" (0.3 mm)			●
6.1.12.1.2	At **SHAPED** surfaces:			
6.1.12.1.2.1	0.075" (1.9 mm)	●		
6.1.12.1.2.2	0.050" (1.3 mm)		●	
6.1.12.1.2.3	0.025" (0.65 mm)			●
6.1.12.2	Of **WOOD** to **NON-WOOD** shall not exceed:			
6.1.12.2.1	At **FLAT** and **SHAPED** surfaces:			
6.1.12.2.1.1	0.075" (1.9 mm)	●		
6.1.12.2.1.2	0.035" (0.89 mm)		●	
6.1.12.2.1.3	0.020" (0.5 mm)			●
6.1.12.3	Of **NON-WOOD** to **NON-WOOD** and/or **ALL ELEMENTS** shall not exceed:			
6.1.12.3.1	At **FLAT** surfaces:			
6.1.12.3.1.1	0.075" (1.9 mm)	●		
6.1.12.3.1.2	0.035" (0.89 mm)		●	
6.1.12.3.1.3	0.020" (0.5 mm)			●

11

EXECUTION

No.	DESCRIPTION	E	C	P
6.1	**GENERAL** (continued)			
6.1.12	**FLUSHNESS** of joinery (continued)			
6.1.12.3	Of **NON-WOOD** to **NON-WOOD** and/or **ALL ELEMENTS** (continued)			
6.1.12.3.2	At **SHAPED** surfaces:			
6.1.12.3.1.1	0.125" (3.2 mm)	●		
6.1.12.3.1.2	0.100" (2.5 mm)		●	
6.1.12.3.1.3	0.075" (1.9 mm)			●
6.1.13	**FASTENING** shall:			
6.1.13.1	**INCLUDE** the use of construction adhesive, finish nails, trim screws, and/or pins.			
6.1.13.2	**NOT PERMIT** the use of drywall or bugle-head screws.			
6.1.13.3	**NOT PERMIT** exposed fastening through **HPDL**.			
6.1.14	**EQUIPMENT CUTOUTS** shall be neatly cut out by the installer, provided templates are furnished in a timely manner.		●	●
6.1.15	**HARDWARE** shall be:			
6.1.15.1	Installed neatly without tear-out of surrounding stock.			●
6.1.15.2	Installed per the manufacturer's instructions.			
6.1.15.3	Installed using all furnished fasteners and fasteners' provisions.			
6.1.15.4	Adjusted for smooth operation.			
6.1.16	**AREAS** of installation shall be left broom clean.			
6.1.16.1	Debris shall be removed and dumped in containers provided by the contractor.			
6.1.16.2	Items installed shall be cleaned of pencil or ink marks.			
6.1.17	Entire installation shall present **FIRST-CLASS WORKMANSHIP** in compliance with these standards.			
6.2	**PRODUCT SPECIFIC**			
6.2.1	WOOD — At **SOLID** or **VENEERED WOOD:**			
6.2.1.1	Front and leading **EDGES** of countertop to withstand a 75-lb (34 kg) pull-up pressure.			
6.2.1.2	Waterproof caulk shall be used at all square butt joints including splashes and return ends.			
6.2.1.3	**CAULKING** shall not exceed 1/16" and shall be furnished by installation contractor, unless otherwise specified.			
6.2.1.4	**INSTALLER-ASSEMBLED JOINTS** shall be fastened together with a mechanical tightening system either routed into or mounted on the bottom side of the countertop.			
6.2.1.5	**SINK CUTOUTS** shall not fall within 18" (457 mm) of discretionary installer joints.			
6.2.1.6	**EDGES** of **CUTOUTS**, subject to excessive moisture, shall be sealed with a color-toned (for verification), water-resistant sealer before trim or sink rims are installed.			
6.2.2	HPDL — At **HPDL**:			
6.2.2.1	**COUNTERTOPS** shall be scribed to walls, and:			
6.2.2.1.1	Securely anchored to base cabinets with proper length screws, and:			
6.2.2.1.1.1	Properly aligned with uniform front edge overhang.			
6.2.2.1.1.2	**INSTALLER ASSEMBLED JOINTS** must be glued and fastened together with a mechanical tightening system either routed into or surface mounted on the bottom side of the countertop.			
6.2.2.1.2	Front and leading **EDGES** of countertop to withstand a 75-lb (34 kg) pull-up pressure.			
6.2.2.2	**WATERPROOF CAULK** shall be used at all square butt joints including wall, splashes, and return ends, and:			
6.2.2.2.1	Caulk shall not exceed 1/4" (6.4 mm).			
6.2.2.2.2	Be furnished by installation contractor, unless otherwise specified.			

EXECUTION

No.	DESCRIPTION	E	C	P
6.2	**PRODUCT SPECIFIC** (continued)			
6.2.2	At **HPDL**: (continued)			
6.2.2.3	At **ASSEMBLY** 1 (wall mount) **BACK-** and **END-SPLASH** (wall mount) construction, all splash components shall be securely adhered to the wall, butt-joined to the countertop, and:			
6.2.2.3.1	Shall be **CAULKED** with clear or compatible-color waterproof caulking (furnished by installer), so as to leave a visual bead not exceeding 1/8" (3.2 mm) between the bottom of the splash and the countertop.			
6.2.2.3.2	Variation in building walls in excess of 1/2" (12.7 mm) in 144" (3658 mm) may result in gaps between splash and walls and shall not be considered a defect or the responsibility of the installer.			
6.2.2.4	At **ASSEMBLY 2** (deck mount) **BACK-** and **END-SPLASH** (deck mount) construction, all exposed top and ends shall be scribed to the wall configuration.			
6.2.2.4.1	**UNBACKED SCRIBE SPANS** shall not exceed 1/2" (12.7 mm) at ends and back walls, and gaps shall:			
6.2.2.4.1.1	Not exceed 1/16" (1.6 mm) and be caulked.		●	
6.2.2.4.1.2	Not exceed 1/32" (0.8 mm) and be caulked.			●
6.2.2.5	**CUTOUTS** shall have a minimum of 1/4" (6.4 mm) radius at all inside corners, except at wood or epoxy resin, and:			
6.2.2.5.1	**SINK CUTOUTS** shall not fall within 18" (457 mm) of discretionary installer joints.			
6.2.2.5.1	**EDGES** of **CUTOUTS**, subject to excessive moisture, shall be sealed with a color-toned (for verification), water-resistant sealer before trim or sink rims are installed.			
6.2.3	At **SOLID SURFACE**:			
6.2.3.1	**INSTALLATION** shall be performed by personnel properly trained and authorized by the applicable product manufacturer.			
6.2.3.2	**SEALANTS** and **ADHESIVES** shall be compatible with the individual manufacturer's recommendations or specially developed sealants to achieve the best color match.			
6.2.3.3	**EXPANSION** joints shall be furnished where required by building design or manufacturer recommendations.			
6.2.3.4	**SUPPORT** shall be adequately furnished to minimize stresses, and:			
6.2.3.4.1	Minimum **FULL PERIMETER** and **JOINT** support is required on all horizontal applications, with:			
6.2.3.4.1.1	A maximum on center separation between supports of 30" (750 mm) for acrylic and 24" (610 mm) for non-acrylic materials.			
6.2.3.4.1.2	A maximum unsupported and unloaded overhang of 12" (305 mm) for 3/4" (19 mm) and 6" (152 mm) for 1/2" (12.7 mm) sheet thickness.			
6.2.3.5	**JOINTS** shall be:			
6.2.3.5.1	Square (butt) rather than mitered near corners to minimize material and facilitate installation.			
6.2.3.5.2	Be fully supported.			
6.2.3.5.3	Edges to be joined shall be straight, smooth, and clean.			
6.2.3.5.3.1	All joints shall be made using the manufacturer's recommended adhesive.			
6.2.3.5.4	L- and U-shaped corners shall have smooth, rounded inside corners, and:			
6.2.3.5.4.1	Seams shall be offset a minimum of 3 times the inside corner radius.			
6.2.3.6	**CUTOUT CORNERS** shall be rounded, 1/4" (6.4 mm) minimum radius, with all edges smoothed, and:			
6.2.3.6.1	At heat-producing areas, corners shall be reinforced per the manufacturer's requirements and protected with approved heat-reflective tape.			

11

EXECUTION

				DESCRIPTION	E C P
6.2 PRODUCT SPECIFIC				**PRODUCT SPECIFIC** (continued)	
	6.2.3 SOLID SURFACE			At **SOLID SURFACE**: (continued)	
		6.2.3.7		**BACK** and **END SPLASHES** shall be securely adhered to the wall, butt-joined to the countertop, and:	
			6.2.3.7.1	Shall be **CAULKED** with clear or compatible-color waterproof caulking (furnished by the installer) so as to leave a visual bead not exceeding 1/8" (3.2 mm) between the bottom of the splash and the countertop.	
			6.2.3.7.2	Variation in building walls in excess of 1/2" (12.7 mm) in 144" (3658 mm) may result in gaps between splash and walls and shall not be considered a defect or the responsibility of the installer.	
			6.2.3.7.3	If specified, **COVED SPLASHES** shall be hard-seamed and integral to the countertop.	
		6.2.3.8		**TOP ADHESION** shall be made using a clear silicone sealant placed a maximum of 12" (12.7 mm) on center.	
		6.2.3.9		**HARD SEAMS** shall be water-tight and gap-free.	
	6.2.4 SOLID PHENOLIC			At **SOLID PHENOLIC:**	
		6.2.4.1		**INSTALLATION SHALL BE PERFORMED** by personnel properly trained and approved/certified by the applicable manufacturer.	
		6.2.4.2		Top shall be **SECURED** to supports with silicone cement or appropriately sized machine screws applied to each corner and along the perimeter edge at not more than 48" (1219 mm) on center.	
		6.2.4.3		**JOINTS** shall be precision-machined with tight joint fasteners and sealed with a bioside silicon prior to tightening.	
		6.2.4.4		**SINKS** shall be stainless steel, polypropylene, or epoxy resin; either lipped or under-mount, and:	
			6.2.4.4.1	**LIPPED** shall be set in a rabbeted cutout in the top.	
			6.2.4.4.2	**UNDER-MOUNT** shall be installed using adjustable metal sink supports for underside installation or fastened directly to the underside of the top using machine screws and silicone adhesive.	
			6.2.4.4.3	**LIPPED** shall be set in a rabbeted cutout in the top.	
		6.2.4.5		**UNDER-MOUNT** shall be installed using adjustable metal sink supports for underside installation or fastened directly to the underside of the top using machine screws and silicone adhesive.	
		6.2.4.6		A bioside silicone adhesive shall be used at the juncture of the sink and countertop to produce a leak-proof joint.	
	6.2.5 EPOXY RESIN & STONE			At **EPOXY RESIN, NATURAL/MANUFACTURED STONE:**	
		6.2.5.1		A 1" (25.4 mm) nominal overhang on the front and ends shall be provided.	
		6.2.5.2		Top shall be **SECURED** to supports with epoxy cement applied to each corner and along the perimeter edge at not more than 48" (1219 mm) on center, and:	
			6.2.5.2.1	Support must be adequate to prevent deflection in excess of 1/4" (6.4 mm) with a 50 lb (22.7 kg) per square foot load or 250 lb (113 kg) at any given point.	
			6.2.5.2.2	Unsupported spans shall not exceed 48" (1219 mm), unless otherwise specified.	
			6.2.5.2.3	The maximum unsupported and unloaded overhang shall not exceed 12" (305 mm) for 3/4" (19 mm) and 6" (152 mm) for 1/2" (12.7 mm) sheet thickness.	
			6.2.5.2.4	**JOINTS** shall be butted and filled with a color-matched epoxy cement.	
		6.2.5.3		**BACK** and **END SPLASHES** shall be securely adhered to the wall, butt-joined to the countertop, and:	
			6.2.5.3.1	Shall be **CAULKED** with clear or compatible-color waterproof caulking (furnished by the installer) so as to leave a visual bead not exceeding 1/8" (3.2 mm) between the bottom of the splash and the countertop.	
			6.2.5.3.2	Variation in building walls in excess of 1/2" (12.7 mm) in 144" (3658 mm) may result in gaps between the splash and the walls and shall not be considered a defect or the responsibility of the installer.	

11

EXECUTION

					DESCRIPTION	E C P
6.2	**PRODUCT SPECIFIC** (continued)					
	6.2.5	At **EPOXY RESIN, NATURAL/MANUFACTURED STONE:** (continued)				
		6.2.5.4	**HARD SEAMS** shall be water-tight and gap-free.			
		6.2.5.5	**SCRIBING** is not required.			
		6.2.5.6	**SINKS** shall be either lipped or under-mounted, and:			
			6.2.5.6.1	**LIPPED** shall be set in a rabbeted cutout in the top.		
			6.2.5.6.2	**UNDER-MOUNT** shall be installed using adjustable metal sink supports, and:		
				6.2.5.6.2.1	An epoxy cement is required at the juncture of the sink and countertop to produce a leak-proof joint.	
				6.2.5.6.2.2	The maximum gap between the top edge of the sink and underside of the countertop shall not exceed 3/16" (4.8 mm).	

COMPLIANCE

7 FABRICATED and INSTALLED woodwork shall be tested for compliance to these standards as follows:

7.1 **SMOOTHNESS** of exposed surfaces

7.1.1 **KCPI** (Knife Cuts Per Inch) is determined by holding the surfaced board at an angle to a strong light source and counting the visible ridges per inch, usually perpendicular to the profile.

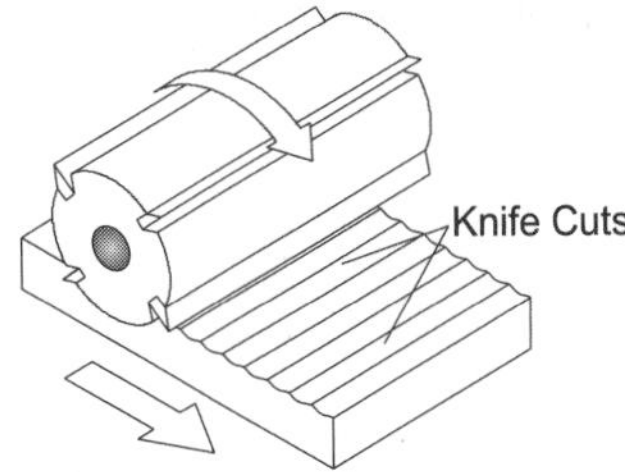

7.1.2 **SANDING** is checked for compliance by sanding a sample piece of the same species with the required grit of abrasive.

7.1.2.1 Observation with a hand lens of the prepared sample and the material in question will offer a comparison of the scratch marks of the abrasive grit.

7.1.2.2 Reasonable assessment of the performance of the finished product will be weighed against absolute compliance with the standard.

7.1.2.3 A product is sanded sufficiently smooth when knife cuts are removed and any remaining sanding marks are or will be concealed by applied finishing coats.

7.1.2.4 Handling marks and/or grain raising due to moisture or humidity in excess of the ranges set forth in this standard shall not be considered a defect. 11

7.2 **GAPS, FLUSHNESS, FLATNESS, AND ALIGNMENT** of product and installation:

7.2.1 Maximum gaps between exposed components shall be tested with a feeler gauge at points designed to join where members contact or touch.

7.2.2 Joint length shall be measured with a ruler with minimum 1/16" (1 mm) divisions and calculations made accordingly.

COMPLIANCE

7 FABRICATED and INSTALLED woodwork shall be tested for compliance (continued)

7.2 GAPS, FLUSHNESS, FLATNESS, and ALIGNMENT of product and installation (continued)

7.2.3 Reasonable assessment of the performance of the finished product will be weighed against absolute compliance with the standards.

7.2.4 The following is intended to provide examples of how and where compliance testing is measured:

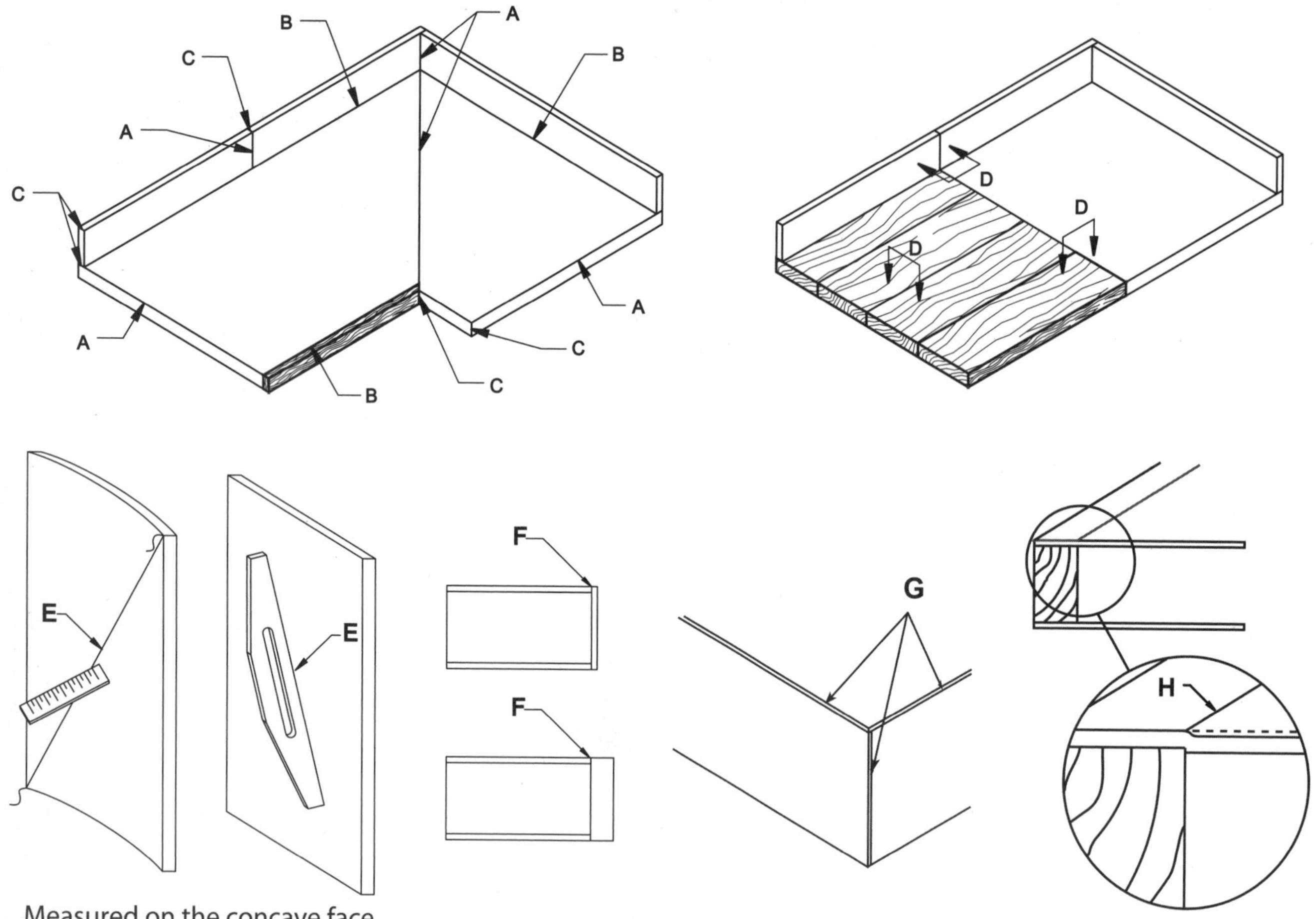

A - Gaps when surfaces are mitered or butted
B - Gaps when parallel pieces are joined
C - Gaps when edges are mitered or butted
D - Flushness between two surfaces
E - Flatness of panel product
F - Flushness of edgebanding
G - Chipout

Architectural Woodwork Standards

SECTION - 12

HISTORIC RESTORATION WORK

SECTION 12 ✦ HISTORIC RESTORATION WORK

Stripping, Repairs, and Finishing

GENERAL

1 INFORMATION

1.1 GRADES

1.1.1 These standards are characterized in three Grades of quality that might be mixed within a single project. Limitless design possibilities and a wide variety of lumber and veneer species, along with overlays, high-pressure decorative laminates, factory finishes, and profiles are available in all three Grades.

1.1.2 Because of the nature of historic woodwork, a specific grade classification is not applicable to this section.

1.1.3 **MODIFICATIONS** by the contract documents shall govern if in conflict with these standards.

1.2 BASIC CONSIDERATIONS

1.2.1 The **RATIONALE** and **INTENT** of this section is to assist in compliance with the U.S. Secretary of the Interior's "**STANDARDS FOR THE TREATMENT OF HISTORIC PROPERTIES** (The Standards) with Guidelines for Preserving, Rehabilitation, Restoring, and Reconstructing Historic Buildings (The Guidelines)" or the **STANDARDS AND GUIDELINES FOR THE CONSERVATION OF HISTORIC PLACES IN CANADA** which spell out requirements such as:

1.2.1.1 The **HISTORIC CHARACTER** of a property will be retained and preserved.

1.2.1.1.1 The removal of distinctive materials or alterations of features, spaces, and spatial relationships that characterize a property will be avoided.

1.2.1.2 Each property will be **RECOGNIZED** as a physical record of its time, place, and use.

1.2.1.2.1 Changes that create a false sense of historical development, such as adding conjectural features or elements from other historic properties, will not be undertaken.

1.2.1.3 **CHANGES** to property that have acquired historic significance in their own right will be retained and preserved.

1.2.1.4 **DISTINCTIVE** materials, features, finishes, and construction techniques or examples of craftsmanship that characterize a historic property will be preserved.

1.2.1.5 **DETERIORATED** historic features will be repaired rather than replaced.

1.2.1.5.1 Where the severity of deterioration requires replacement of a distinctive feature, the new feature will match the old in design, color, texture, and, where possible, materials.

1.2.1.5.2 Replacement of missing features will be substantiated by documentary and physical evidence.

1.2.1.6 Chemical or physical **TREATMENTS**, if appropriate, will be undertaken using the gentlest means possible.

1.2.1.6.1 Treatments that cause damage to historic properties will not be used.

1.2.1.7 New **ADDITIONS**, exterior alterations, or related new construction will not destroy historic materials and spatial relationships that characterize the property.

1.2.1.7.1 The new work shall be differentiated from the old and will be compatible with the historic materials, features, size, scale, proportion, and massing to protect the historic integrity of the property and its environment.

1.2.1.8 New additions and adjacent or related new construction will be undertaken in such a manner that if they are removed in the future, the essential form and integrity of the historic property and its environment will be unimpaired.

1.2.2 **ACCEPTABLE REQUIREMENTS** of lumber and/or sheet products used within this woodwork product section are established by Sections 3 and 4, unless otherwise modified herein.

GENERAL

1.2 **BASIC CONSIDERATIONS** (continued)

1.2.3 **CONTRACT DRAWINGS** and/or **SPECIFICATIONS**, furnished by the design professional, shall clearly indicate or delineate all material, fabrication, installation, and applicable building code/regulation requirements.

1.2.4 **EXPOSED SURFACES**

1.2.4.1 All visible surfaces of standing/running trim and door/window frames.

1.2.4.2 Excluding top horizontal surfaces 72" (1829 mm) or more above the finish grade, deck, or walk, unless visible from above.

1.2.4.3 Excluding bottom horizontal surfaces 48" (1219 mm) or less above the finish grade or walk.

1.2.4.4 All visible surfaces of window and sash members.

1.2.4.5 All visible surfaces of screen, screen door, blind, and shutter members.

1.2.4.6 All visible surfaces of stringers, skirtboards, treads, risers, and balustrades.

1.2.4.7 All visible surfaces of architectural wall surfacing.

1.2.4.8 Both visible faces of wood doors.

1.2.4.9 At casework:

1.2.4.9.1 All surfaces visible when doors and drawers are closed, including knee spaces.

1.2.4.9.2 Underside of cabinet bottoms over 42" (1067 mm) above the finished floor, including bottoms behind light valances.

1.2.4.9.3 Cabinet tops under 80" (2032 mm) above the finished floor, or if they are 80" (2032 mm) and over and visible from an upper building level or floor.

1.2.4.9.4 Visible front edges of web frames, ends, divisions, tops, shelves, and hanging stiles.

1.2.4.9.5 Sloping tops of cabinets that are visible.

1.2.4.9.6 Visible portions of bottoms, tops, and ends in front of sliding doors.

1.2.4.9.7 Visible surfaces in open cabinets or behind glass.

1.2.4.9.8 Interior faces of hinged doors.

1.2.4.9.9 Cabinet and woodwork surfaces behind sliding presentation panels.

1.2.5 **SEMI-EXPOSED SURFACES**

1.2.5.1 Top horizontal surfaces 80" (2032 mm) or more above the finish grade, deck, or walk, unless visible from above.

1.2.5.2 Bottom horizontal surfaces 42" (1067 mm) or less above the finish grade or walk.

1.2.5.3 Both visible edges of wood doors.

1.2.5.4 At casework:

1.2.5.4.1 Shelves.

1.2.5.4.2 Divisions.

1.2.5.4.3 Interior face of ends (sides), backs, and bottoms (even on a bank of drawers). Also included are the interior surfaces of cabinet top members when the top member is 36" (914 mm) or more above the finished floor. 12

1.2.5.4.4 Drawer sides, subfronts, backs, and bottoms.

1.2.5.4.5 The underside of cabinet bottoms between 24" (610 mm) and 42" (1067 mm) above the finished floor.

1.2.5.4.6 In open cabinets or behind glass for all rooms designated as storage, janitor, closet, or utility.

GENERAL

1.2 **BASIC CONSIDERATIONS** (continued)

1.2.6 **CONCEALED SURFACES**

1.2.6.1 All non-visible surfaces attached to and/or covered by another.

1.2.6.2 All non-visible blocking or spacers used for attachment.

1.2.6.3 Top and bottom edges of wood doors.

1.2.6.4 At casework:

1.2.6.4.1 Toe space, unless otherwise specified.

1.2.6.4.2 Sleepers.

1.2.6.4.3 Web frames, stretchers, and solid sub-tops.

1.2.6.4.4 Security panels.

1.2.6.4.5 The underside of cabinet bottoms less than 24" (610 mm) above the finished floor.

1.2.6.4.6 The flat tops of a cabinet 72" (1829 mm) or more above the finished floor, except if visible from an upper building level.

1.2.6.4.7 The three non-visible edges of adjustable shelves.

1.2.6.4.8 The underside of countertops, knee spaces, and drawer aprons.

1.2.6.4.9 The faces of cabinet ends of adjoining units that butt together.

1.3 **RECOMMENDATIONS**

1.3.1 **INCLUDE IN DIVISION 09 OF THE SPECIFICATIONS**:

1.3.1.1 For **JOBSITE FINISHING** - Before finishing, all exposed portions of woodwork shall have handling marks or effects of exposure to moisture removed with a thorough, final sanding over all surfaces of the exposed portions using the appropriate grit sandpaper, and they shall be cleaned before applying sealer or finish.

1.3.1.2 At **CONCEALED SURFACES** - Architectural woodwork that might be exposed to moisture, such as those adjacent to exterior concrete walls, shall be back-primed.

1.3.2 **THOROUGHLY REVIEW** Sections 3 and 4, especially Basic Considerations, Recommendations, Acknowledgements, and Industry Practices within Part 1 for an overview of the characteristics and minimum acceptable requirements of lumber and/or sheet products that might be used herein.

1.3.3 **CONTRACT DOCUMENTS** (plans and/or specifications) shall require that all structural members, grounds, blocking, backing, furring, brackets, or other anchorage which becomes an integral part of the building's walls, floors, or ceilings, required for the installation of architectural woodwork is not to be furnished or installed by the architectural woodwork manufacturer or installer.

1.3.4 **SPECIFY** requirements for:

1.3.4.1 Fire ratings

1.3.4.2 Special code compliance

1.3.5 **HISTORIC WOODWORK RESTORATION,** including stripping, repairs, reconstruction, materials, new fabrication, installation, and finishing, should be of a **SINGLE SOURCE RESPONSIBILITY**.

1.3.5.1 If a **SINGLE SOURCE RESPONSIBILITY** is **NOT REQUIRED**, then the **STRIPPING** and **FINISHING** requirements from the **PRODUCT** portion of this section should be included in the painting section of the specifications.

1.4 **ACKNOWLEDGEMENTS - None**

GENERAL

1.5 **INDUSTRY PRACTICES**

1.5.1 **STRUCTURAL MEMBERS**, grounds, blocking, backing, furring, brackets, or other anchorage that becomes an integral part of the building's walls, floors, or ceilings, that are required for the installation of architectural woodwork are not furnished or installed by the architectural woodwork manufacturer or installer.

1.5.2 **WALL, CEILING,** and/or opening variations in excess of 1/4" (6.4 mm) or **FLOORS** in excess of 1/2" (12.7 mm) in 144" (3658 mm) of being plumb, level, flat, straight, square, or of the correct size are not acceptable for the installation of architectural woodwork, nor is it the responsibility of the installer to scribe or fit to tolerances in excess of such.

1.5.3 **BACK PRIMING** of architectural woodwork is not the responsibility of the manufacturer and/or installer, unless the material is being furnished pre-finished.

PRODUCT

2 SCOPE

2.1 The restoration, fabrication, installation, and finishing of all existing and/or new historic architectural woodwork.

2.2 **TYPICAL INCLUSIONS**

2.2.1 Shall comply with those listed within **Sections 6 - 11**, as applicable.

2.3 **TYPICAL EXCLUSIONS**

2.3.1 Shall comply with those listed within **Sections 6 - 11**, as applicable.

3 DEFAULT STIPULATION

3.1 Unless otherwise specified or detailed, all work shall be **PREMIUM GRADE** of softwood and/or hardwood intended for opaque and/or transparent finish as described in **SECTIONS 3** and **4**.

3.1.1 It is the **RESPONSIBILITY** of the **MANUFACTURER** to observe the project before bid and match all materials for species, grain, and overall appearance.

4 RULES - The following RULES shall govern unless a project's contract documents require otherwise.

These rules are intended to provide a well-defined degree of control over a project's quality of materials and workmanship.

Errata, published on the Associations' websites at www.awinet.org, www.awmac.com, or www.woodworkinstitute.com, shall TAKE PRECEDENCE OVER THESE RULES, subject to their date of posting and a project's bid date.

ARROWS INDICATE TOPIC IS CARRIED FROM ⇑ OR ONTO ⇓ ANOTHER PAGE.

DESCRIPTION		
4.1	**GENERAL**	
G E N E R A L ⇓	4.1.1	Aesthetic **GRADE RULES** apply only to exposed and semi-exposed surfaces visible after installation.
	4.1.2	**LUMBER** shall conform to the requirements established in Section 3.
	4.1.3	**SHEET PRODUCTS** shall conform to the requirements established in Section 4.
	4.1.4	**BACKING SHEET** shall conform to the requirements established in Section 4.
	4.1.5	**EXPOSED, SEMI-EXPOSED**, and **CONCEALED** surfaces shall be as listed under item 1.2, **BASIC CONSIDERATIONS**, of this Section.
	4.1.6	For the purpose of this standard, a **BALANCED PANEL** is one that is free from warp that affects serviceability for its intended purpose.
	4.1.7	**WAINSCOT** shall be 48" (1219 mm) in height above the finished floor.

12

PRODUCT

MATERIAL, MACHINING, AND ASSEMBLY RULES (continued)

DESCRIPTION				
4.1 GENERAL	**GENERAL** (continued)			
	4.1.8	**SURFACING** with a defined grain and/or pattern shall be installed with the grain or pattern direction running vertically.		
	4.1.9	**FURRING** shall be used as required, and:		
		4.1.9.1	It shall be in accordance with applicable codes and regulations for maximum thickness, fire blocking, and void fills.	
	4.1.10	**FIRE-RETARDANT** requirements shall be specified.		
	4.1.11	Where **GLUING** or **LAMINATION** occurs:		
		4.1.11.1	**DELAMINATION** or **SEPARATION** shall not occur beyond that which is allowed in Sections 3 & 4.	
		4.1.11.2	Use of **CONTACT ADHESIVE** is not permitted.	
	4.1.12	**FIRST-CLASS WORKMANSHIP** is required in compliance with these standards.		
4.2 MATERIAL	**MATERIAL**			
	4.2.1	**WOOD** shall match the species, grain, general pattern, and cut of existing, similar, and/or adjacent woodwork.		
	4.2.2	Shall comply with Sections 3 - 11, as applicable, and any modifications by the plans and specifications.		
	4.2.3	**MEMBERS** shall be of the same profile and dimension as existing; however, they may be glued up to achieve this.		
	4.2.4	Shall not have defects, either natural or manufactured, that exceed those permitted.		
	4.2.5	Permits defects, both natural and manufactured, if covered by adjoining members or otherwise concealed when installed.		
	4.2.6	States figure is not a function of a species grade and must be specified in the contract document.		
	4.2.7	Permits warp that can be held flat and straight with normal attachment.		
	4.2.8	**SCREWS, NAILS,** and **ANCHORS**, where exposed, shall match or be equivalent to the existing screws, nails, and anchors.		
	4.2.9	**ANCHORS** and **INSERTS** shall be hot-dipped galvanized.		
	4.2.10 EXPOSED	**EXPOSED SURFACES**		
		4.2.10.1	Require ends to be self-returned with no end grain showing.	
		4.2.10.2	Permit medium-density fiberboard (MDF) for opaque finish.	
		4.2.10.3	For **TRANSPARENT FINISH:**	
			4.2.10.3.1	Permit hardwood or softwood.
			4.2.10.3.2	Permit only one species for the entire project.
			4.2.10.3.3	Adjacent veneer and lumber shall be well-matched for color and grain.
		4.2.10.4	Have visible **EDGES**, **REVEALS**, and/or **SPLINES**, when appropriate, that are:	
			4.2.10.4.1	Full length.
			4.2.10.4.2	**MATCH** species of panel face.
			4.2.10.4.3	**WELL-MATCHED** for color and grain.
			4.2.10.4.4	Minimum 0.020" (0.5 mm) nominal **THICKNESS** that precludes show-through of core.
	4.2.11	**SEMI-EXPOSED SURFACES**		
		4.2.11.1	For **OPAQUE** finish, permit natural and manufacturing defects, provided the surface is filled solid.	
	4.2.12	**CONCEALED SURFACES**		
		4.2.12.1	Permit defects, voids, wane, and unfilled knots.	
		4.2.12.2	Require blocking or shims to be of a compatible material.	
	4.2.13	When **FACTORY FINISHING** is specified, concealed surfaces shall be factory sealed with one coat at 1 mil dry.		

PRODUCT

MATERIAL, MACHINING, AND ASSEMBLY RULES (continued)

				DESCRIPTION
4.3	**MACHINING**			
MACHINING	4.3.1	Shall **COMPLY** with Sections 3 - 11, as applicable, and any modifications by the plans and specifications.		
	4.3.2	Machine new and replacement woodwork to dimensions, profiles, and details to **MATCH EXISTING**.		
	4.3.3	Where **EXISTING MOLDINGS** are hand-made and not necessarily uniform in profile, replacement moldings shall be profiled to an agreed representative sample.		
	4.3.4	All machine work shall be of excellent quality, with all exposed (visible) surfaces **SMOOTHLY SANDED**.		
	4.3.5	Of **EXPOSED SURFACES** shall comply with the following smoothness requirements:		
	EXPOSED	4.3.5.1	**SHARP EDGES** shall be eased with a fine abrasive.	
		4.3.5.2	**TOP FLAT WOOD** surfaces; those that can be sanded with a drum or wide belt sander shall be 150-grit sanded.	
		4.3.5.3	**MOLDED**, **TURNED**, and shaped **WOOD** surfaces shall be 120-grit sanded.	
		4.3.5.4	**CROSS-SANDING**, excluding turned surfaces, is not allowed.	
		4.3.5.5	**TEAR-OUTS**, **KNIFE NICKS**, or **HIT-OR-MISS** machining is not permitted.	
		4.3.5.6	**KNIFE MARKS** are not permitted where sanding is required.	
		4.3.5.7	**GLUE** or **FILLER**, if used, shall be inconspicuous and match the adjacent surface for smoothness.	
4.4	**ASSEMBLY**			
ASSEMBLY	4.4.1	Shall **COMPLY** with Sections 3 - 11, as applicable, and any modifications by the plans and specifications.		
	4.4.2	**PLYWOOD BACKING** may be used in the fabrication of built-up panel assemblies, door and/or window frames, and stacked base trim, provided the exposed profile and configuration matches existing.		
	4.4.3	Of **JOINTS** at **ASSEMBLED WOODWORK** shall:		
	JOINTS	4.4.3.1	Be neatly and accurately made.	
		4.4.3.2	Be **SECURELY GLUED**, with:	
			4.4.3.2.1	**ADHESIVE** residue removed from all exposed and semi-exposed surfaces.
		4.4.3.3	Be **REINFORCED** with glue blocks where essential.	
		4.4.3.4	Be **MECHANICALLY FASTENED** with nails or screws where practical, with:	
			4.4.3.4.1	Fasteners at solid wood countersunk.
			4.4.3.4.2	Fasteners at solid wood in molding quirks or reliefs where possible.
		4.4.3.5	Require **FLATNESS** of installed and removable sheet products (see Test F illustrations in **COMPLIANCE**) not to exceed 0.027” (0.7 mm) per 12” (305 mm) or portion thereof.	
		4.4.3.6	Require **FLUSHNESS VARIATIONS** at exposed surfaces when mitered or butted (see Test D illustrations in **COMPLIANCE**) not to exceed:	
			4.4.3.6.1	At **INTERIOR**, 0.001” (0.03 mm).
			4.4.3.6.2	At **EXTERIOR**, 0.015” (0.4 mm).
		4.4.3.7	Require **GAPS** at exposed surfaces when mitered or butted (see Test A illustrations in **COMPLIANCE**) not to exceed:	
			4.4.3.7.1	At **INTERIOR**, 0.15” (0.4 mm) wide by 20% of the joint length.
			4.4.3.7.2	At **EXTERIOR**, 0.025” (0.6 mm) wide by 30% of the joint length.
		4.4.3.8	Require **GAPS** at exposed surfaces at parallel members (see Test B illustrations in **COMPLIANCE**) not to exceed:	
			4.4.3.8.1	At **INTERIOR**, 0.015” x 3” (0.4 mm x 76 mm) and shall not occur within 72” (1829 mm) of a similar gap.
⇓	⇓		4.4.3.8.2	At **EXTERIOR**, 0.025” x 6” (0.6 mm x 152 mm) and shall not occur within 30” (762 mm) of a similar gap.

PRODUCT

MATERIAL, MACHINING, AND ASSEMBLY RULES (continued)

DESCRIPTION				
⇑ 4.4 ASSEMBLY	**ASSEMBLY** (continued)			
	⇑ 4.4.3	Of **JOINTS** at **ASSEMBLED WOODWORK** shall (continued)		
		4.4.3.9	Require **GAPS** at exposed surfaces when mitered or butted (see Test C illustrations in **COMPLIANCE**) not exceed:	
			4.4.3.9.1	At **INTERIOR**, 0.05” (1.3 mm).
			4.4.3.9.2	At **EXTERIOR**, 0.025” (0.6 mm).
	4.4.4	Of **MOLDINGS** shall be:		
		4.4.4.1	Mitered.	
		4.4.4.2	Spot glued and mechanically fastened.	
			4.4.4.2.1	Only to non-panel surfaces; panels **ARE** required to float.
			4.4.4.2.2	With a maximum of two positioning nails per 12" (300 mm) of length before a joint.
			4.4.4.2.3	With nails set, filled, and sanded.
	4.4.5	Of **MITER JOINTS** shall be well fitted and cleaned.		
	4.4.6	Of **BUILT-UP ITEMS** shall be soundly fabricated with half-lapped, mitered, shoulder-mitered, tonged, or equivalent construction.		
4.5 STRIPPING	**STRIPPING**			
	4.5.1	**COATING STRIPPERS** shall be environmentally approved.		
	4.5.2	**BEFORE STRIPPING** procedures begin, all surfaces shall be tested (with the process and results recorded) to provide the least intrusive and damaging methods, and:		
		4.5.2.1	Approval by the design professional or conservator is required for the selected method.	
		4.5.2.2	**HEAT-BASED** methods of coating removal are permitted, provided the recommendations found in the National Park Service - Preservation Brief 10 *Exterior Paint Problems On Historic Woodwork* are followed.	
	4.5.3	Completely **REMOVE EXISTING FINISH** using multiple applications of stripper and hand scrapers without gouging, splintering, or otherwise damaging sound wood.		
	4.5.4	**STRIPPING RESIDUALS** shall be thoroughly removed, including wax.		
		4.5.4.1	**STRIPPED SURFACES** shall be tested for evidence of **ACID** and **ALKALI**, and:	
			4.5.4.1.1	All stripped surfaces found not to be pH neutral shall be neutralized and retested.
			4.5.4.1.2	A written **SUMMARY REPORT**, including before and after pH levels, shall be submitted to the design professional.
	4.5.5	**SAND** all surfaces by hand with steel wool and the appropriate grit sandpaper to remove all signs of raised grain.		
	4.5.6	**SEAL** all exposed surfaces with an approved sanding sealer.		
4.6	**REPAIRS** shall:			
	4.6.1	**MATCH EXISTING** for recommended methods of repair by governing authorities.		
	4.6.2	For **TRANSPARENT FINISH**, be made with wood of the same species, grade, cut, color tone, and grain pattern.		
	4.6.3	Use the same **CARPENTRY METHODS** exhibited in the existing work.		
	4.6.4	Use nonferrous **FASTENERS**, and:		
		4.6.4.1	Dissimilar metals shall be isolated from one another.	
	4.6.5	Use **WOOD PATCHES** of boat- and/or diamond-shaped so as to minimize those joint surfaces at 90 degrees to the member’s grain direction.		
4.7	**FINISHING** shall:			
	4.7.1	Comply with Section 5 as modified by the plans and specifications.		
	4.7.2	Use **APPLICATIONS** and **TECHNIQUES** best-suited to match the existing and/or desired finish.		

EXECUTION

5 PREPARATION & QUALIFICATION REQUIREMENTS (unless otherwise specified)

5.1 **CARE, STORAGE,** and **BUILDING CONDITIONS** shall be in compliance with the requirements set forth in Section 2 of these standards.

5.1.1 Severe damage to the woodwork can result from noncompliance. **THE MANUFACTURER AND/OR INSTALLER OF THE WOODWORK SHALL NOT BE HELD RESPONSIBLE FOR ANY DAMAGE THAT MIGHT DEVELOP BY NOT ADHERING TO THE REQUIREMENTS.**

5.2 **CONTRACTOR IS RESPONSIBLE FOR:**

5.2.1 Furnishing and installing structural members, grounds, blocking, backing, furring, brackets, or other anchorage required for architectural woodwork installation that becomes an integral part of walls, floors, or ceilings to which architectural woodwork shall be installed.

5.2.1.1 In the absence of contract documents calling for the contractor to supply the necessary blocking/ backing in the wall or ceilings, either through inadvertence or otherwise, the architectural woodwork installer shall not proceed with the installation until such time as the blocking/backing is installed by others.

5.2.1.2 Preparatory work done by others shall be subject to inspection by the architectural woodwork installer and may be accepted or rejected for cause prior to installation.

5.2.1.2.1 **WALL, CEILING,** and/or opening variations in excess of 1/4" (6.4 mm) or **FLOORS** in excess of 1/2" (12.7 mm) in 144" (3658 mm) of being plumb, level, flat, straight, square, or of the correct size are not acceptable for the installation of architectural woodwork, nor is it the responsibility of the installer to scribe or fit to tolerances in excess of such.

5.2.2 Priming and back-priming the architectural woodwork in accordance with the contract documents prior to its installation.

5.2.2.1 If the architectural woodwork is factory-finished, back-priming by the factory finisher is required.

5.3 **INSTALLER IS RESPONSIBLE FOR:**

5.3.1 Having adequate equipment and experienced craftsmen to complete the installation in a first-class manner.

5.3.2 Checking all architectural woodwork specified and studying the appropriate portions of the contract documents, including these standards and the reviewed shop drawings to familiarize themselves with the requirements of the Grade specified, understanding that:

5.3.2.1 Appearance requirements of Grades apply only to surfaces visible after installation.

5.3.2.2 For transparent finish, special attention needs to be given to the color and the grain of the various woodwork pieces to ensure they are installed in compliance with the Grade specified.

5.3.2.3 Installation site is properly ventilated, protected from direct sunlight, excessive heat and/or moisture, and that the HVAC system is functioning and maintaining the appropriate relative humidity and temperature.

5.3.2.4 Required priming or back priming of woodwork has been completed before its install.

5.3.2.5 Woodwork has been acclimated to the field conditions for a minimum of 72 hours before installation is commenced.

5.3.2.6 Woodwork specifically built or assembled in sequence for match of color and grain is installed to maintain that same sequence.

EXECUTION

6 RULES - The following RULES shall govern unless a project's contract documents require otherwise.

These rules are intended to provide a well-defined degree of control over a project's quality of installation and workmanship.

Errata, published on the Associations' websites at www.awinet.org, www.awmac.com, or www.woodworkinstitute.com, shall TAKE PRECEDENCE OVER THESE RULES, subject to their date of posting and a project's bid date.

ARROWS INDICATE TOPIC IS CARRIED FROM ⇑ OR ONTO ⇓ ANOTHER PAGE.

<table>
<tr><th colspan="5">DESCRIPTION</th></tr>
<tr><td>6.1</td><td colspan="4">GENERAL</td></tr>
<tr><td rowspan="24">GENERAL ⇓</td><td>6.1.1</td><td colspan="3">INSTALLATION shall be in compliance with PREMIUM GRADE.</td></tr>
<tr><td>6.1.2</td><td colspan="3">Aesthetic GRADE RULES apply only to exposed and semi-exposed surfaces visible after installation.</td></tr>
<tr><td>6.1.3</td><td colspan="3">INSTALLATION shall comply with Sections 3 - 11, as applicable, and any modifications by the plans and specifications.</td></tr>
<tr><td>6.1.4</td><td colspan="3">At HISTORIC RESTORATION work, where new materials are required to be distressed to blend seamlessly with original, mock-ups shall be approved by the design professional or conservator before proceeding.</td></tr>
<tr><td>6.1.5</td><td colspan="3">GROUNDS, BUCKS, or HANGING SYSTEMS shall be installed plumb and true.</td></tr>
<tr><td>6.1.6</td><td colspan="3">TRANSPARENT finished woodwork shall be installed:</td></tr>
<tr><td rowspan="4"></td><td rowspan="3">6.1.6.1</td><td colspan="2">WELL-MATCHED for color and grain.</td></tr>
<tr><td>6.1.6.1.1</td><td>SHEET PRODUCTS shall be compatible in color with solid stock.</td></tr>
<tr><td>6.1.6.1.2</td><td>ADJACENT SHEET PRODUCTS shall be well-matched for color and grain.</td></tr>
<tr><td>6.1.6.2</td><td colspan="2">INSTALLER shall pay special attention to the color and the grain of the various trim pieces to ensure they are installed in compliance with PREMIUM GRADE.</td></tr>
<tr><td>6.1.7</td><td colspan="3">REPAIRS are allowed, provided they are neatly made and inconspicuous when viewed at 24" (610 mm).</td></tr>
<tr><td>6.1.8</td><td colspan="3">INSTALLER MODIFICATIONS shall comply to the material, machining, and assembly rules within the PRODUCT portion of this section and the applicable finishing rules in Section 5.</td></tr>
<tr><td>6.1.9</td><td colspan="3">WOODWORK shall be:</td></tr>
<tr><td rowspan="11">WOODWORK ⇓</td><td rowspan="2">6.1.9.1</td><td colspan="2">SECURELY fastened and tightly fitted with flush joints.</td></tr>
<tr><td>6.1.9.1.1</td><td>Joinery shall be CONSISTENT throughout the project.</td></tr>
<tr><td>6.1.9.2</td><td colspan="2">Of MAXIMUM available and/or practical lengths.</td></tr>
<tr><td>6.1.9.3</td><td colspan="2">TRIMMED EQUALLY from both sides when fitted for width.</td></tr>
<tr><td>6.1.9.4</td><td colspan="2">SPLINED or DOWELED when miters are over 4" (100 mm) long.</td></tr>
<tr><td>6.1.9.5</td><td colspan="2">SELF-MITERED when trim ends are exposed.</td></tr>
<tr><td>6.1.9.6</td><td colspan="2">MITERED at outside corners.</td></tr>
<tr><td rowspan="2">6.1.9.7</td><td colspan="2">INSTALLED plumb, level, square, and flat within 1/8" (3.2 mm) in 96" (2438 mm), and when required:</td></tr>
<tr><td>6.1.9.7.1</td><td>GROUNDS and HANGING systems set plumb and true.</td></tr>
<tr><td rowspan="3">6.1.9.8</td><td colspan="2">SCRIBED at:</td></tr>
<tr><td>6.1.9.8.1</td><td>Flat surfaces</td></tr>
<tr><td>6.1.9.8.2</td><td>Shaped surfaces</td></tr>
<tr><td>6.1.9.9</td><td colspan="2">SMOOTH and SANDED without CROSS SCRATCHES in conformance to the PRODUCT portion of this section.</td></tr>
</table>

EXECUTION

DESCRIPTION				
6.1 GENERAL	**GENERAL** (continued)			
	6.1.9	**WOODWORK** shall be (continued)		
		6.1.9.10	Installed **FREE OF**:	
			6.1.9.10.1	Warp, twisting, cupping, and/or bowing that cannot be held true.
			6.1.9.10.2	Open joints, visible machine marks, cross-sanding, tear-outs, nicks, chips, and/or scratches.
			6.1.9.10.3	Natural defects exceeding the quantity and/or size limits defined in Sections 3 & 4.
	6.1.10 GAPS	**GAPS** (see Test A-C illustrations in **COMPLIANCE**):		
		6.1.10.1	**CAUSED** by **EXCESSIVE DEVIATIONS** (deviations in excess of 1/4" (6.4 mm) in 144" (3658 mm) of being plumb, level, flat, straight, square, or of the correct size) in the building's walls and ceilings, or 1/2" (12.7 mm) for floors, shall not be considered a defect or the responsibility of the installer.	
		6.1.10.2	Shall not exceed 30% of a joint's length, with:	
			6.1.10.2.1	**FILLER** or **CAULKING** allowed, if color-compatible.
		6.1.10.3	Of **WOOD** to **WOOD** shall not exceed:	
			6.1.10.3.1	At **FLAT** surfaces, 0.012" (0.3 mm) in width.
			6.1.10.3.2	At **SHAPED** surfaces, 0.025" (0.65 mm) in width.
		6.1.10.4	Of **WOOD** to **NON-WOOD** shall not exceed:	
			6.1.10.4.1	At **FLAT** and **SHAPED** surfaces, 0.050" (1.3 mm) in width.
		6.1.10.5	Of **NON-WOOD** to **NON-WOOD** and/or **ALL ELEMENTS** shall not exceed:	
			6.1.10.5.1	At **FLAT** surfaces, 0.050" (1.3 mm) in width.
			6.1.10.5.2	At **SHAPED** surfaces, 0.075" (1.9 mm) in width.
	6.1.11 FLUSHNESS	**FLUSHNESS** of joinery (see Flushness illustrations in **COMPLIANCE**):		
		6.1.12.1	Of **WOOD** to **WOOD** shall not exceed:	
			6.1.11.1.1	At **FLAT** surfaces, 0.012" (0.3 mm)
			6.1.11.1.2	At **SHAPED** surfaces, 0.025" (0.65 mm)
		6.1.11.2	Of **WOOD** to **NON-WOOD** shall not exceed:	
			6.1.11.2.1	At **FLAT** and shaped surfaces, 0.050" (1.3 mm)
		6.1.11.3	Of **NON-WOOD** to **NON-WOOD** and/or **ALL ELEMENTS** shall not exceed:	
			6.1.11.3.1	At **FLAT** surfaces, 0.050" (1.3 mm)
			6.1.11.3.2	At **SHAPED** surfaces, 0.075" (1.9 mm)
	6.1.12	Reveal strips that are grooved into paneling are to be left floating and allowed to expand and contract in reaction to changing relative humidity.		
	6.1.13	Expansion joints shall be provided equivalent to 1/16" (1.6 mm) per 48" (1219 mm) of linear elevation.		
	6.1.14	Paneling shall be:		
		6.1.14.1	Of adequate thickness or furred and installed in such a way as to avoid deflection when normal pressure is applied.	
		6.1.14.2	Free of warp exceeding 1/32" (0.8 mm) per linear foot.	
	6.1.15	Paneling joints shall be:		
		6.1.15.1	Smooth and flush to create a homogenous look.	
		6.1.15.2	Plumb within 1/16" (1.6 mm) in 96" (2438 mm).	

EXECUTION

DESCRIPTION					
6.1	**GENERAL** (continued)				
GENERAL	**6.1.16**	**FASTENING** shall:			
	FASTENING	**6.1.16.1**	Use **CONCEALED** fastening to the fullest extent possible.		
		CONCEALED	**6.1.16.1.1**	If exposed fastening is required to complete the installation:	
			EXPOSED	6.1.16.1.1.1	Fasteners shall be set in quirks or reliefs (where possible), countersunk, and kept to a minimum.
				6.1.16.1.1.2	**PERMIT** the use of construction adhesive, finish nails, trim screws and/or pins.
				6.1.16.1.1.3	**DO NOT PERMIT** the use of drywall, bugle-head, or case-hardened screws.
				6.1.16.1.1.4	**REQUIRE** exposed fasteners to be **INCONSPICUOUS** as defined in the Glossary.
				6.1.16.1.1.5	**DO NOT PERMIT** exposed fastening through HPDL.
				6.1.16.1.1.6	**REQUIRE** prefinished materials to be filled by the installer with matching filler furnished by the manufacturer.
				6.1.16.1.1.7	**REQUIRE** unfinished materials to be filled by the paint contractor or others.
			6.1.16.1.2	Use of an extruded metal Z-mold or clips and/or French dovetail cleats are acceptable for blind installation.	
	6.1.17	**BACKS** of wood paneling shall be sealed with at least two coats of sealer.			
	6.1.18	**FLATNESS** of installed and removable sheet products shall not exceed 0.027" (0.7 mm) per 12" (305 mm) or a portion thereof.			
	6.1.19	**EQUIPMENT CUTOUTS** shall be neatly cut out by the installer, provided templates are furnished in a timely manner.			
	6.1.20	**HARDWARE** shall be:			
		6.1.20.1	Installed neatly without tear-out of surrounding stock.		
		6.1.20.2	Installed per the manufacturer's instructions.		
		6.1.20.3	Installed using all furnished fasteners and fastener's provisions.		
		6.1.20.4	Adjusted for smooth operation.		
	6.1.21	Entire installation shall present **FIRST-CLASS WORKMANSHIP** in compliance with these standards.			

COMPLIANCE

7 **FABRICATED** and **INSTALLED** woodwork shall be tested for compliance to these standards as follows:

7.1 **SMOOTHNESS** of exposed surfaces

7.1.1 **KCPI** (Knife Cuts Per Inch) is determined by holding the surfaced board at an angle to a strong light source and counting the visible ridges per inch, usually perpendicular to the profile.

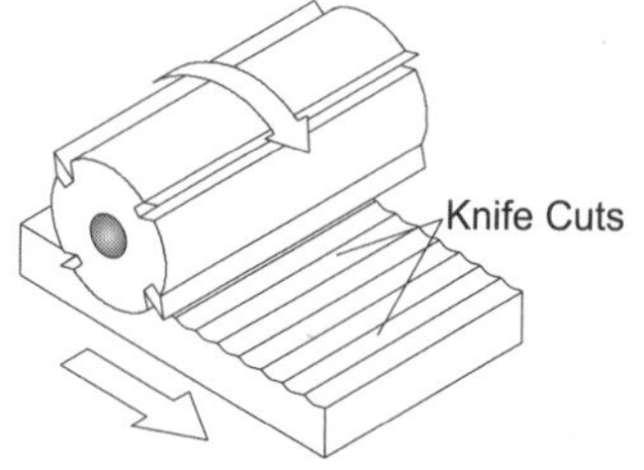

7.1.2 **SANDING** is checked for compliance by sanding a sample piece of the same species with the required grit of abrasive.

7.1.2.1 Observation with a hand lens of the prepared sample and the material in question will offer a comparison of the scratch marks of the abrasive grit.

EXECUTION

7 FABRICATED and INSTALLED (continued)

7.1 SMOOTHNESS of exposed surfaces (continued)

7.1.2 SANDING is checked for compliance (continued)

7.1.2.2 Reasonable assessment of the performance of the finished product will be weighed against absolute compliance with the standard.

7.1.2.3 A product is sanded sufficiently smooth when knife cuts are removed and any remaining sanding marks are or will be concealed by applied finishing coats.

7.1.2.4 Handling marks and/or grain raising due to moisture or humidity in excess of the ranges set forth in this standard shall not be considered a defect.

7.2 GAPS, FLUSHNESS, FLATNESS, and ALIGNMENT of product and installation:

7.2.1 Maximum gaps between exposed components shall be tested with a feeler gauge at points designed to join where members contact or touch.

7.2.2 Joint length shall be measured with a ruler with minimum 1/16" (1 mm) divisions and calculations made accordingly.

7.2.3 Reasonable assessment of the performance of the finished product will be weighed against absolute compliance with the standards.

7.2.4 The following is intended to provide examples of how and where compliance testing is measured:

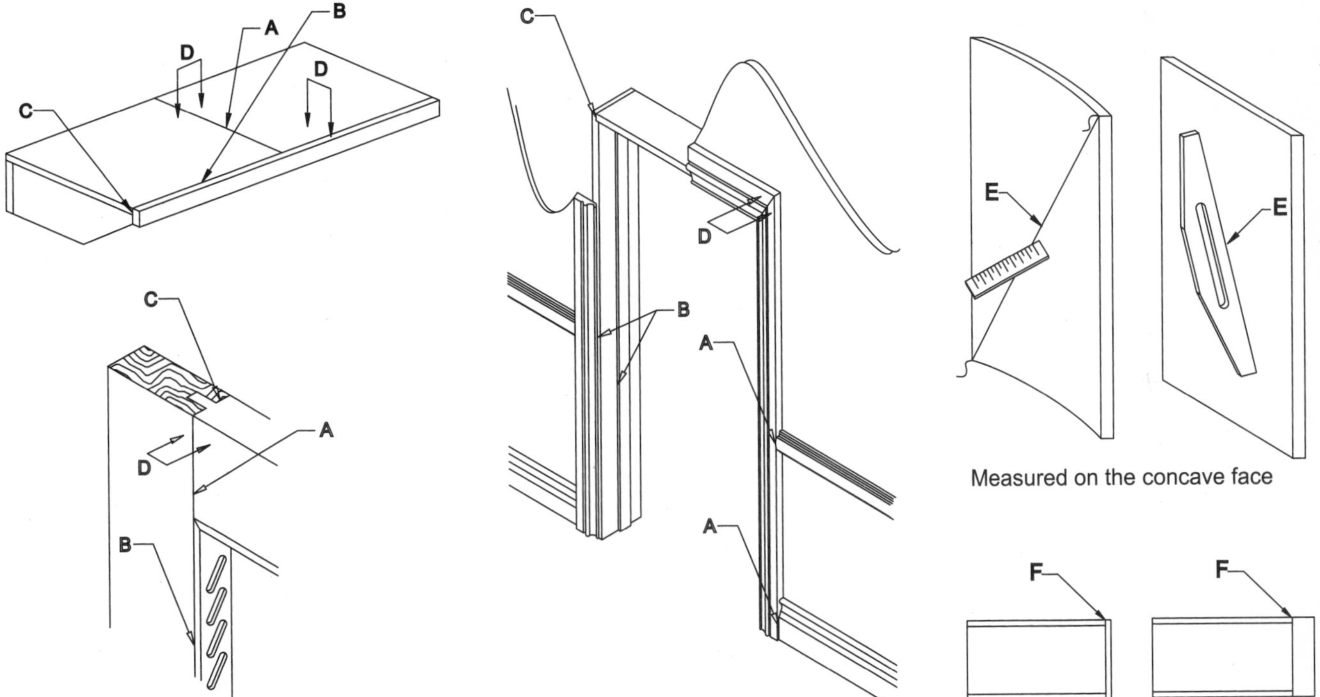

A - Gaps when surfaces are mitered or butted
B - Gaps when parallel pieces are joined
C - Gaps when edges are mitered or butted
D - Flushness between two surfaces
E - Flatness of panel product
F - Flushness of edgebanding

NOTES

Architectural Woodwork Standards

APPENDIX A

TABLE OF CONTENTS

1 Reference Source Directory . . . 337
2 Reference Source Listings . . . 338
3 Preservative & Water-Repellent Treatments . . . 340
4 Fire-Retardant Coatings . . . 340
5 Fire Codes . . . 340
6 ADA Requirements . . . 340
7 Rated Fire Door Assemblies . . . 340
8 Building Code Requirements . . . 340
9 Seismic Fabrication & Installation Requirements . . . 341
10 Adhesives Guidelines . . . 341
11 Specific Gravity & Weight of Hardwoods . . . 342
12 ANSI/BHMA Cabinet Hardware References . . . 343
13 Joinery Details . . . 347
14 SEFA Chemical and Stain Resistance . . . 349
15 Casework Design Series (CDS) . . . 351
16 Casework Integrity . . . 371
17 Fraction/Decimal/Millimeter Conversion Table . . . 376
18 Miscellaneous Conversion Factors . . . 377

REFERENCE SOURCE DIRECTORY

CONTINUING EDUCATION

AIA - American Institute of Architects
AIBD - American Institute of Building Design
BHMA - Builders Hardware Manufacturers Association
CRA - California Redwood Association
IDC - Interior Design of Canada
IIDA - International Interior Design Association
RAIC - Royal Architectural Institute of Canada

STANDARDS & REGULATION

ANSI - American National Standards Institute
ARE - Association for Retail Environments
ASID - American Society of Interior Designers
AWI - Architectural Woodwork Institute
AWMAC - Architectural Woodwork Manufacturers Association of Canada
CSC - Construction Specifications Canada
CSI - Construction Specifications Institute
ICC - International Code Council
IWPA - International Wood Products Association
NFPA - National Fire Protection Association
NHLA - National Hardwood Lumber Association
NIST - National Institute of Standards & Technology
SCS - Scientific Certification Systems (Green Cross)
SEFA - Scientific Equipment & Furniture Association
SFI - Sustainable Forest Initiative
UL - Underwriters' Laboratories
WI - Woodwork Institute
WMMPA - Wood Moulding and Millwork Producers Association
WWPA - Western Wood Products Association

MANUFACTURING

AF&PA - American Forest & Paper Association
AHFA - American Home Furnishings Alliance
CFPC - Certified Forest Products Council
NAM - National Association of Manufacturers
NEMA - National Electrical Manufacturers Association
WDMA - Window & Door Manufacturers Association

TESTING AND GRADING

APA - The Engineered Wood Association
ASTM - American Society for Testing and Materials
ITS - Intertek Testing Services/Warnock Hersey

SUSTAINABLE BUILDING

FSC - Forest Stewardship Council - United States
LEED - Leadership in Energy and Environmental Design
SMART WOOD - The Rainforest Alliance
TFF - Tropical Forest Foundation
USGBC - U.S. Green Building Council

SPECIALIZED PRODUCT

HPVA - Hardwood Plywood & Veneer Association
KCMA - Kitchen Cabinet Manufacturers Association
LMA - Laminating Materials Association, Inc.
NHLA - National Hardwood Lumber Association
WDMA - Window & Door Manufacturers Association
WRCLA - Western Red Cedar Lumber Association

REFERENCE SOURCE LISTINGS

(Page 1 of 3)

AF&PA - American Forest & Paper Association
1111 19th Street NW, Suite 800
Washington, DC 20036
Ph: 800-878-8878 ● Fax: 202-463-2700
www.afandpa.org

AHFA - American Home Furnishings Alliance
Box HP-7
High Point, NC 27261
Ph: 336-884-5000 ● Fax: 336-884-5303
www.ahfa.us

AIA - American Institute of Architects
1735 New York Avenue NW
Washington, DC 20006
Ph: 800-242-3837 ● Fax: 202-626-7547
www.aia.org

AIBD - American Institute of Building Design
7059 Blair Road NW, Suite 201
Washington, DC 20012
Ph: 800-366-2423 ● Fax: 202-249-2473
www.aibd.org

ANSI - American National Standards Institute
25 West 23rd Street, 4th Floor
New York, NY 10036
Ph: 212-642-4900 ● Fax: 212-398-0023
www.ansi.org

APA - The Engineered Wood Association
7011 South 19th Street
Tacoma, WA 98466
Ph: 253-565-6600 ● Fax: 253-565-7265
www.apawood.org

ARE - Association for Retail Environments
4651 Sheridan Street, Suite 407
Hollywood, FL 33021-3657
Ph: 954-893-7300 ● Fax: 954-893-7500
www.are.org

ASID - American Society of Interior Designers
608 Massachusetts Avenue NE
Washington, DC 20002-6006
Ph: 202-546-3480 ● Fax: 202-546-3240
www.asid.org

ASTM - American Society for Testing and Materials
100 Barr Harbor Drive
West Conshohocken, PA 19428-2959
Ph: 610-832-9585 ● Fax: 610-832-9555
www.astm.org

AWI - Architectural Woodwork Institute
46179 Westlake Drive, Suite 120
Potomac Falls, VA 20165
Ph: 571-323-3636 ● Fax: 571-323-3630
www.awinet.org

AWMAC - Architectural Woodwork Manufacturers Association of Canada
516 - 4 Street West
High River, Alberta, Canada, T1V 1B6
Ph: 403-652-7685 ● Fax: 403-762-7384
www.awmac.com

BHMA - Builders Hardware Manufacturers Association
355 Lexington Avenue, 15th Floor
New York, NY 10017
Ph: 212-297-2122 ● Fax: 212-370-9047
www.buildershardware.com

CFPC - Certified Forest Products Council
1306 NW Hoyt Street, Suite 403
Portland, OR 97209
Ph: 503-224-2205 ● Fax: 503-224-2216
www.metafore.org

CPA - Composite Panel Association
19465 Deerfield Avenue, Suite 306
Leesburg, VA 20176
Ph: 703-724-1128 ● Fax: 703-724-1588
www.pbmdf.com

CRA - California Redwood Association
818 Grayson Road, Suite 201
Pleasant Hill, CA 94523
Ph: 925-935-1499 ● Fax: 925-935-1496
www.calredwood.org

CSC - Construction Specifications Canada
120 Carlton Street, Suite 312
Toronto, ON, M5A 4K2, Canada
www.csc-dcc.ca

CSI - Construction Specifications Institute
99 Canal Center Plaza, Suite 300
Alexandria, VA 22314
Ph: 800-689-2900 ● Fax: 703-684-8436
www.csinet.org

DHI - The Door and Hardware Institute
14150 Newbrook Drive, Suite 200
Chantilly, VA 20151-2223
Ph: 703-222-2010 ● Fax: 703-222-2410
www.dhi.org

FSC - Forest Stewardship Council - United States
11100 Wildlife Center Drive, Suite 100
Reston, VA 20190
Ph: 703-438-6401 ● Fax 703-438-3570
www.fscus.org

HPVA - Hardwood Plywood & Veneer Association
1825 Michael Faraday Drive
Reston, VA 20190
Ph: 703-435-2900 ● Fax: 703-435-2537
www.hpva.org

ICC - International Code Council
500 New Jersey Avenue NW, 6th Floor
Washington, DC 20001-2070
Ph: 888-422-7233 ● Fax: 202-783-2348
www.iccsafe.org

IDC - Interior Design of Canada
220-6 Adelaide Street East
Toronto, Ontario, M5C 1H6, Canada
Ph: 416-594-9310 ● Fax: 416-921-3660
www.interiordesigncanada.org

REFERENCE SOURCE LISTINGS

(Page 2 of 3)

IIDA - International Interior Design Association
13-122 Merchandise Mart
Chicago, IL 60654-1104
Ph: 312-467-1950 ● Fax: 312-467-0779
www.iida.org

ITS - Intertek Testing Services
Ph: 800-967-5352
www.intertek-etlsemko.com

IWPA - International Wood Products Association
4214 King Street West
Alexandria, VA 22302
Ph: 703-820-6696 ● Fax: 703-820-8550
www.iwpawood.org

KCMA - Kitchen Cabinet Manufacturers Association
1899 Preston White Drive
Reston VA 20191-5435
Ph: 703-264-1690 ● Fax: 703-620-6530
www.kcma.org

LEED - Leadership in Energy and Environmental Design
(see **USGBC - U.S. Green Building Council**)

NAM - National Association of Manufacturers
1331 Pennsylvania Avenue NW
Washington, DC 20004-1790
Ph: 202-637-3000 ● Fax: 202-637-3182
www.nam.org

NEMA - National Electrical Manufacturers Association
1300 Nrth 17th Street, Suite 1752
Rosslyn, Virginia 22209
Ph: 703-841-3200 ● Fax: 703-841-5900
www.nema.org

NFPA - National Fire Protection Association
P.O. Box 9101
Quincy, MA 02269
Ph: 617-770-3000 ● Fax: 617-770-0700
www.nfpa.org

NHLA - National Hardwood Lumber Association
6830 Raleigh-Lagrange Road
Memphis, TN 38184-0518
Ph: 901-377-1818 ● 901-382-6419
www.natlhardwood.org

NIST - National Institute of Standards & Technology
100 Bureau Drive, Stop 3460
Gaithersburg, MD 20899-3460
Ph: 301-975-6478 ● Fax: 301-926-1630
www.nist.gov

RAIC - Royal Architectural Institute of Canada
330-55 Murray Street
Ottawa, Ontario, K1N 5M3, Canada
Ph: 631-241-3600 ● Fax: 613-241-5750
www.raic.org

SCS - Scientific Certification Systems (Green Cross)
2000 Powell Street, Suite 1350
Emeryville, CA 94608
Ph: 510-452-8003 ● Fax: 510-452-8001
www.scs1.com

SEFA - Scientific Equipment & Furniture Association
1205 Franklin Avenue, Suite 320
Garden City, NJ 11530
Ph: 516-294-54248 ● Fax: 516-294-2758
www.sefalabfurn.com

SFI - Sustainable Forest Initiative
(see AF&PA)
www.aboutsfi.org

Smart Wood - The Rainforest Alliance
Goodwin-Baker Building, 65 Millet Street, Suite 201
Richmond, VT 05477
Ph: 802-434-5491 ● Fax: 802-434-3116
www.smartwood.org

TFF - Tropical Forest Foundation
2121 Eisenhower Avenue, Suite 200
Alexandria, VA 22314
Ph: 703-518-8834 ● Fax: 703-518-8974
www.tropicalforestfoundation.org

UL - Underwriters' Laboratories
333 Pfingsten Road
Northbrook, IL 60062-2096
Ph: 847-272-8800 ● Fax: 847-272-8129
www.ul.com

USGBC - U.S. Green Building Council
1015 18th Street NW, Suite 805
Washington, DC 20036
Ph: 202-828-7422 ● Fax: 202-828-5110
www.usgbc.org

WDMA - Window & Door Manufacturers Association
1400 East Touhy Avenue, Suite 470
Des Plaines, IL 60118
Ph: 800-223-2301 ● Fax: 847-299-1286
www.wdma.com

WH - Warnock - Hersey
(see **ITS - Intertek Testing Services**)
www.warnockhersey.com

WI - Woodwork Institute
P.O. Box 980247
West Sacramento, CA 95798
Ph: 916-372-9943 ● Fax: 916-372-9950
www.woodworkinstitute.com

WMMPA - Wood Moulding and Millwork Producers Association
507 First Street
Woodland, CA 95695
Ph: 530-661-9591 ● Fax: 530-661-9586
www.wmmpa.com

REFERENCE SOURCE LISTINGS

(Page 3 of 3)

WRCLA - Western Red Cedar Lumber Association
1200 - 555 Burrard Street
Vancouver, BC, Canada V7X 1S7
Ph: 604-684-0266 ● Fax: 604-687-4930
www.wrcla.org.

WWPA - Western Wood Products Association
Yeon Building, 522 SW Fifth Avenue
Portland, OR 97204-2122
Ph: 503-224-3930 ● Fax: 503-224-3934
www.wwpa.org

PRESERVATIVE & WATER-REPELLENT TREATMENTS

Within the United States, preservative and water-repellent treatments are governed under I.S. - 4, latest edition, as published by the Window and Door Manufacturers Association (WDMA), www.wdma.com, subject to any applicable EPA or local Air Quality Management District's restrictions on what may be used for the project location. Within Canada, they are governed by the National Building Code of Canada, Section 3.8, Appendix A. Contact the National Research Council Canada at www.nrc.ca.

FIRE-RETARDANT COATINGS

Fire-retardant coatings are typically subject to listing by an accredited testing laboratory and require a registration number for approval recognized by fire inspectors.

FIRE CODES

Within the Untied States, fire codes are primarily governed by the International Code Council, Inc. (ICC), www.iccsafe.org, and the National Fire Protection Association (NFPA), www.nfpa.org. Within Canada, they are governed by the National Building Code of Canada, Section 3.8, Appendix A. Contact the National Research Council Canada at www.nrc.ca.

ADA REQUIREMENTS

Within the Untied States, ADA requirements are governed by the Federal Americans with Disabilities Act (ADA) subject to any applicable state or local requirements that might be more stringent for the project location. For further information regarding national regulations: a) in the United States, contact the Access Board at www.access-board.gov, and b) in Canada, see the National Building Code of Canada, Section 3.8, Appendix A. Contact the National Research Council Canada at www.nrc.ca.

RATED FIRE DOOR ASSEMBLIES

Within the Untied States, rated fire door assemblies are governed in accordance with the National Fire Protection Association's Publication NFPA 80, "Standard for Fire Doors and Fire Windows," subject to any applicable state or local requirements that might be more stringent for the project location. Within Canada, governance is by the National Building Code of Canada, Section 3.8, Appendix A, which can be reviewed at www.nrc.ca.

BUILDING CODE REQUIREMENTS

Within the Untied States, building code requirements are governed by the National Uniform Building Code (UBC), subject to any applicable state or local requirements that might be more stringent for the project location. Within Canada, they are governed by the National Building Code of Canada, Section 3.8, Appendix A. Contact the National Research Council Canada at www.nrc.ca.

SEISMIC FABRICATION & INSTALLATION REQUIREMENTS

Within the Untied States, seismic fabrication and installation requirements are governed by the International Building Code (UBC), subject to any applicable state or local requirements that might be more stringent for the project location. Within Canada, they are governed by the National Building Code of Canada, Section 3.8, Appendix A. Contact the National Research Council Canada at www.nrc.ca.

ADHESIVES GUIDELINES

PERFORMANCE RATINGS:

Type I	Fully Waterproof (Exterior)	Two-Cycle Boil/Shear Test
Type II	Water-Resistant (Interior)	Three-Cycle Soak Test

GENERAL INFORMATION:

GENERIC NAME	BONDING	RATING	CHARACTERISTICS
ALIPHATIC (Carpenter's Glue)	Wood to wood	Type II	Non-toxic; non-flammable; non-staining; water-resistant
CASEIN	Wood to wood	Type II	Water-resistant
CONTACT ADHESIVE	HPDL and wood veneer to wood	Type II	Water-resistant
EPOXY	Wide range; wood; wood to metals	Type I	Two-part system; fully waterproof
HOT-MELT Polyurethane Reactive (PUR)	Wide variety of materials	*	Liquefies when heated; bonds in a liquid state; solidifies as it cools.
PVA (Polyvinyl Acetate)	Wood to wood Wood to HPDL	*	General purpose
PVA (Polyvinyl Acetate - Catalyzed)	Wood to wood	Type I	Fully waterproof
PVC (Polyvinyl Chloride)	Wide variety of materials	*	Crystal clear; fast drying.
RESORCINOL RESIN	Wood to wood and laminates	Type I	Fully waterproof; purple glue line; two-part system; limited pot life (3 hours)
UREA RESIN	Wood to wood	Type II	Mixes with water; must be clamped; 3 to 7 hours of drying time at 70° F (21.1° C).
PANEL/CONSTRUCTION ADHESIVE	Wide variety of materials	Type II	Plastic epoxy base; liquid state; dries fast; difficult to remove; can be used to set adjustment screws in European-type hinges.

* Check manufacturer's rating.

A

SPECIFIC GRAVITY & WEIGHT OF HARDWOODS

SPECIES	SPECIFIC GRAVITY [1]	WEIGHT [2]
ALDER, RED Alnus rubra	.37	28
ASH, WHITE Average of 4 species	.54	41
ASPEN Populus tremuloides	.35	27
AVODIRE Turraeanthus africanus	n/a	36
BASSWOOD Tilia americana	.32	26
BEECH Fagus grandifolia	.56	45
BIRCH, SWEET Betula lenta	.60	46
BIRCH, YELLOW Betula alleghaniensis	.55	43
BUBINGA Guibourtia demeusil	n/a	55
BUTTERNUT Juglans cinerea	.36	27
CATALPA, NORTHERN Catalpa speciosa	.38	29
CATIVO Prioria copaifera	.40	29
CHERRY, BLACK Prunus serotina	.47	35
CHESTNUT Castanea dentata	.40	30
COTTONWOOD, EASTERN Populus deltoides	.37	28
CUCUMBER TREE, YELLOW Magnolia acuminata	.44	34
CYPRESS (BALD CYPRESS) Taxodium distichum	.42	32
DOGWOOD, FLOWERING Cornus florida	.64	51
EBONY (NIGERIAN) Diospyros crassiflora	n/a	63
ELM, AMERICAN Ulmlus Americana	.46	36
SWEETGUM (RED AND SAP) Liquidambar styraciflua	.44	34
TUPELO, WATER Nyssa aquatica	.46	35
HACKBERRY Celtis occidentalis	.49	37
HICKORIES, TRUE Average of 4 species	.65	51
HOLLY Ilex opaca	.50	40
LIMBA Terminalia superba	.45	34
LOCUST, BLACK Robinia pseudoacacia	.66	48
MAHOGANY, AFRICAN Khaya ivorensis	.43	31
MAHOGANY, CUBAN Swietenia mahogany	.57	41
MAHOGANY, CENTRAL AMERICAN Swietenia species	.45	32
MAKORE Tieghemella heckelii		40
MAPLE, RED Acer rubrum	.49	38
MAPLE, SILVER Acer saccharinum	.44	33
MAPLE, SUGAR Acer saccharum	.57	44
MYRTLE Umbellularia Californica	.51	39
NARRA Pterocarpus indicus	.52	42
OAK, COMMERCIAL RED Average of 9 species	.56	44
OAK, COMMERCIAL WHITE Average of 6 species	.59	47
ORIENTAL WOOD Endiandro palmerstoni	n/a	44
OSAGE-ORANGE Maclura pomifera	.76	n/a
PADUAK (AFRICAN) Pterocarpus soyauxii	n/a	43
PADUAK (ANDAMAN) Pterocarpus dalbergioides	.62	45
PADUAK (BURMA) Pterocarpus macrocarpus	.75	54
PALDAO Dracontomelum dao	.59	44
PECAN Carya illinoensis	.60	47
PEARWOOD (EUROPEAN) Purus communis	n/a	43
PHILIPPINE HARDWOODS		
RED LAUAN Shorea negrosensis	.40	36
WHITE LAUAN Pentacme contorta	n/a	36
TANGUILE Shorea polysperma	.53	39
POPLAR, YELLOW (TULIPTREE) Liriodendron tulipifera	.38	28
PRIMAVERA Cybistax donnell-smithii	.40	30
ROSEWOOD (BRAZIL) Dalbergia nigra	n/a	50
SAPELE Entandrophragma cylindricum	.54	40
SATINWOOD (EAST INDIAN) Chloroxylon swientenio	.83	67
SONORA (MANGGASINORO) Shorea philippinensis	.42	31
SYCAMORE Platanus accidentalis	.46	35
TEAK Tectona grandis	.60	43
TIGERWOOD Lavoa klaineana	.45	34
WALNUT, AMERICAN (BLACK) Juglans nigra	.51	39
WILLOW, BLACK Salix nigra	.34	26
ZEBRAWOOD Microberlinia brazzavillensis	.62	48

The data for native species as furnished on this chart are from the U.S. Forest Products Laboratory's Technical Bulletin 158.

[1] Based on green volume and oven dry weight.

[2] Based on pounds per cubic foot at 12% moisture content.

ANSI/BHMA - A156.9-01
CABINET HARDWARE REFERENCES
(Page 1 of 4)

The following illustrations and tables are from ANSI/BHMA's - A156.9-01: Cabinet Hardware Standards (one of a series of standards running from A156.1 through A156.24) and are reproduced with permission as a reference guide.

The following will help you understand the numbering system. Using the first item listed below as an example, "B01011":

B	=	Product class (as designated by BHMA)
0	=	Optional material (predominant base material)
1	=	Hinge (product type)
01	=	Semi-concealed (function/description)
1	=	Grade 1 (performance level)

For further information, clarification, or copies of the ANSI/BHMA Standards, you may contact BHMA at:

Builders Hardware Manufacturers Association
355 Lexington Avenue, Suite 1700, New York, NY 10017
www.buildershardware.com

REFERENCE BY ILLUSTRATION

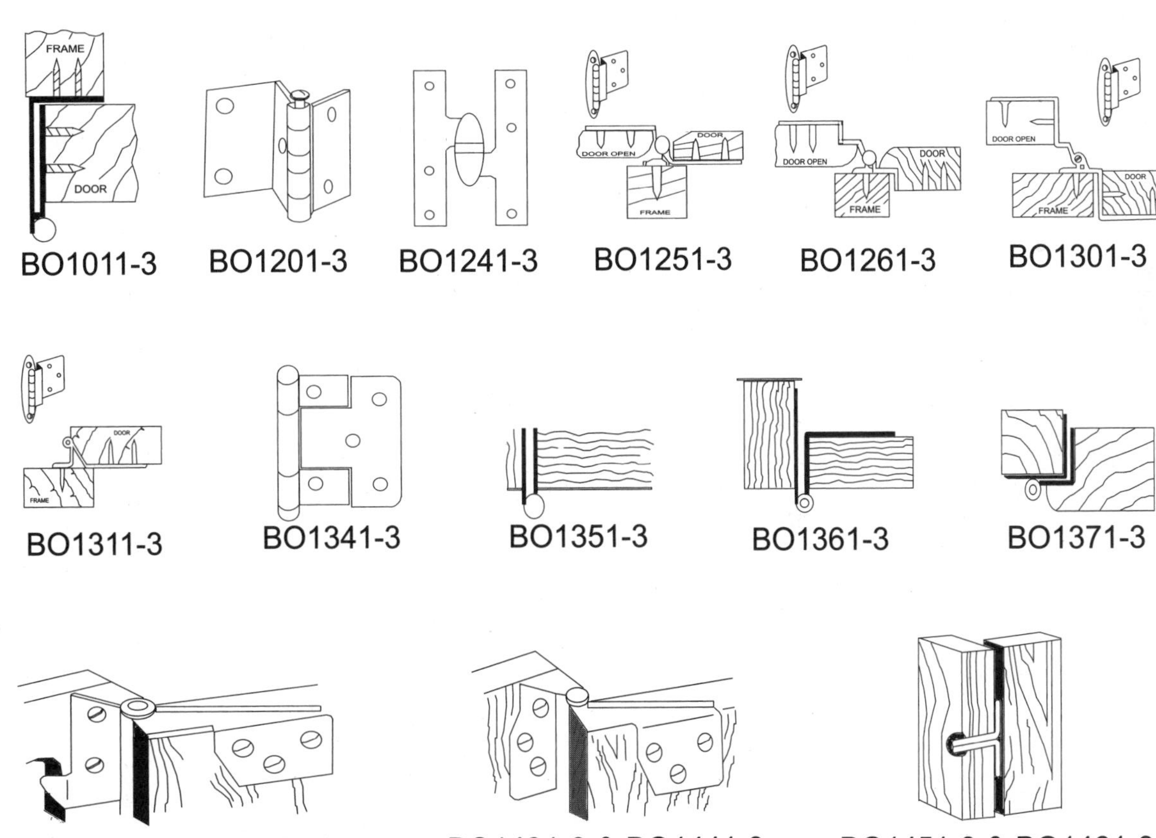

ANSI/BHMA - A156.9-01
CABINET HARDWARE REFERENCES
(Page 2 of 4)

REFERENCE BY ILLUSTRATION (continued)

BO1471-3 & BO1481-3

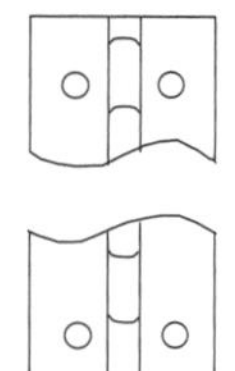
BO1491-3

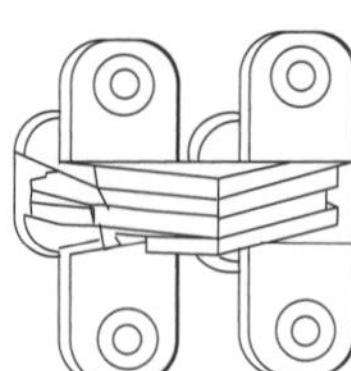
BO1501-3

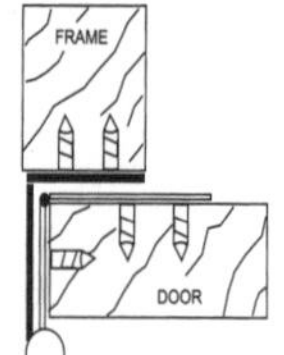

BO1511-3

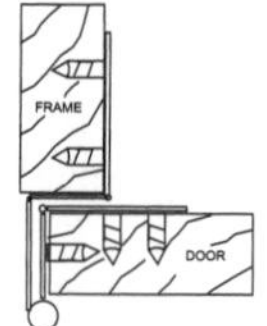

BO1521-3

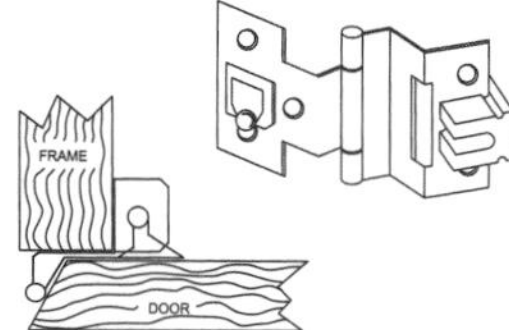

BO1581-3

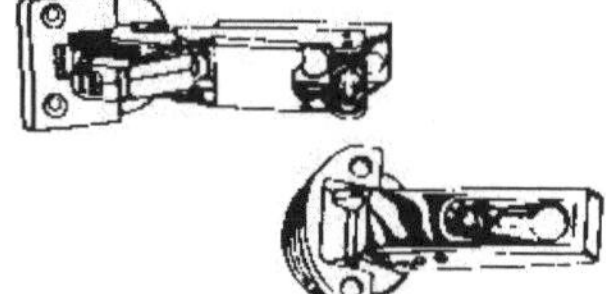
BO1602 & 3

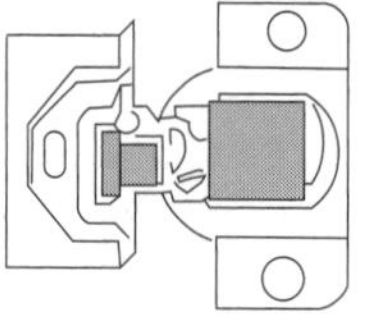
BO1612 & 3

BO2011

BO2031

BO2041

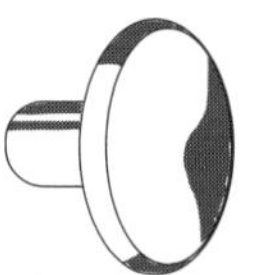
BO2131

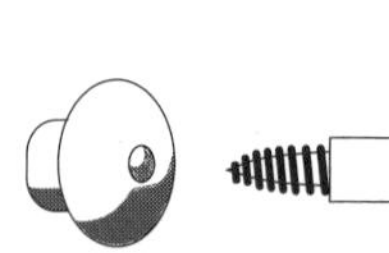
BO2141

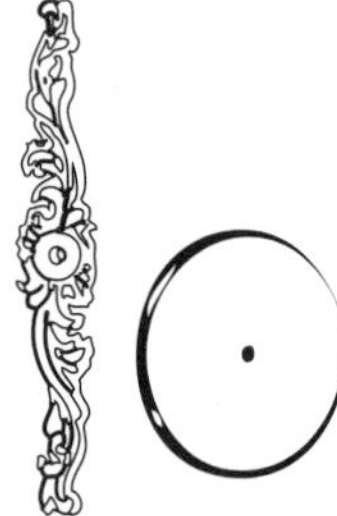
BO2181

BO2191

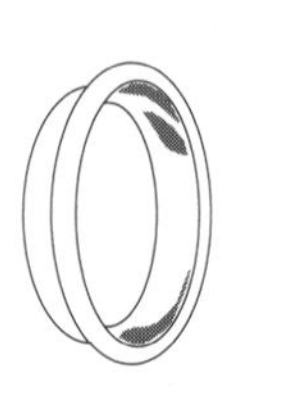
BO2201

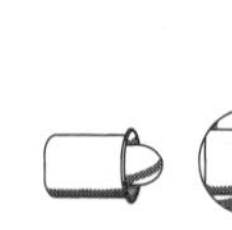
BO3013

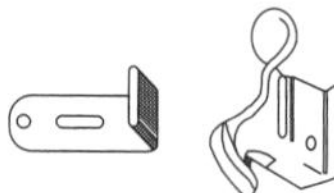
BO3023

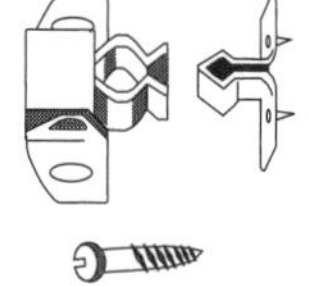
BO3033

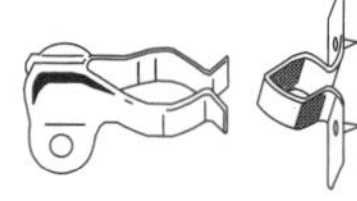
BO3043

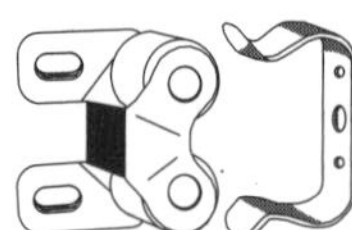
BO3053

A

ANSI/BHMA - A156.9-01
CABINET HARDWARE REFERENCES
(Page 3 of 4)

REFERENCE BY DESCRIPTION

ANSI/ BHMA #	CABINET	DOOR	DESCRIPTION
BO1011-3	Face	Edge	Hinge, Semi-concealed, Overlay Doors, Locked, Knurled or Loose Pin, Rounded or Button Tip
BO1201-3	Edge	Edge/Back	Hinge, Semi-concealed, Flush Door, Loose or Fast Pin
BO1241-3	Face	Face	Hinge, Exposed, Flush Door, Olive Knuckle
BO1251-3	Face	Back	Hinge, Semi-concealed, Overlay Door
BO1261-3	Face	Back	Hinge, Semi-concealed, Inset Lipped Door
BO1301-1	Face	Back	Hinge, Semi-concealed, Flush Door
BO1311-3	Face	Back	Hinge, Semi-concealed, Reverse Bevel Door
BO1331-3	Edge	Back	Hinge, Semi-concealed, Inset Lipped Door
BO1341-3	Face	Back	Hinge, Semi-concealed, Overlay Door
BO1351-3	Edge	Edge	Hinge, Semi-concealed, Flush Door, Locked, Knurled or Loose Pin, Rounded or Button Tip
BO1361-3	Edge	Back	Hinge, Semi-concealed, Flush Door, Locked, Knurled or Loose Pin, Rounded or Button Tip
BO1371-3	Edge	Back	Hinge, Semi-concealed, Inset Lipped Door, Locked, Knurled or Loose Pin, Rounded or Button Tip
BO1411-3	Face	Back	Hinge, Pivot, Overlay Door, Top and Bottom Door Mount, Vertical Frame Mount
BO1421-3	Face	Back	Hinge, Same as Above with Bearing at Joint
BO1431-3	Face	Back	Hinge, Pivot, Overlay Door, Top and Bottom Door Mount, Horizontal Frame Mount
BO1441-3	Face	Back	Hinge, Same as Above with Bearing at Joint
BO1451-3	Edge	Back	Hinge, Pivot, Overlay Door, Mid-Door Edge Mount
BO1461-3	Edge	Back	Hinge, Same as Above with Bearing at Joint
BO1471-3	Edge	Back	Hinge, Pivot, Lipped Door, Mid-Door Edge Mount
BO1481-3	Edge	Back	Hinge, Same as Above with Bearing at Joint
BO1491-3	Face/Edge	Face/Edge/Back	Hinge, Continuous (Piano)
BO1501-3	Edge	Edge	Hinge, Concealed (Soss)
BO1511-3	Face	Edge/Back	Hinge, Semi-concealed, Overlay Door, Locked, Knurled or Loose Pin, Rounded or Button Tip
BO1521-3	Edge	Edge/Back	Hinge, Semi-concealed, Overlay Door, Locked, Knurled or Loose Pin, Rounded or Button Tip
BO1581 & 3	Face/Edge	Back	Hinge, Semi-concealed, Reverse Bevel Door, with Catch
BO1602 & 3	Edge	Back	Hinge, Concealed, European - Frameless
BO1612 & 3	Edge	Back	Hinge, Concealed, European - Face Frame
BO2011	n/a	Back	Pull, 3" (76.2 mm) Center Standard
BO2031	n/a	Back	Pull, Drop, Swing, or Fixed
BO2041	n/a	Face	Pull
BO2131	n/a	Back	Knob

ANSI/BHMA - A156.9-01
CABINET HARDWARE REFERENCES
(Page 4 of 4)

REFERENCE BY DESCRIPTION (continued)

ANSI/ BHMA #	CABINET	DOOR	DESCRIPTION
BO2141	n/a	Face	Knob
BO2181	n/a	n/a	Backing Plate for Knobs
BO2191	n/a	n/a	Backing Plate for Pulls
BO2201	n/a	Face	Flush Pull, Mortised into Door Face
BO3013	Edge	Edge	Catch, Bullet or Ball Friction
BO3023	Edge	Back	Catch, Elbow
BO3033	Edge	Back	Catch, Friction
BO3043	Edge	Back	Catch, Friction
BO3053	Edge	Back	Catch, Roller Spring, Under Shelf Mount
BO3063	Edge	Back	Catch, Friction Spring
BO3071 & 2	Edge	Back	Catch, Roller
BO3091 & 2	Edge	Back	Catch, Roller
BO3112	Edge	Back	Catch, Roller
BO3131 & 2	Face	Back	Catch, Magnetic, Push-In
BO3141 & 2	n/a	Back	Catch, Magnetic, Under Shelf Mount
BO3151-2	n/a	Back	Catch, Magnetic, Door Mount
BO3161-2	n/a	Back	Catch, Magnetic, Under Shelf Mount, Double Door
BO3171-2	Edge	Back	Catch, Magnetic, Heavy Duty
BO3243	Face	Face	Latch, Cupboard
BO3282	Edge		Pusher, for Use with Secret/Touch Latches
BO3333	Edge	Back	Latch, Secret/Touch
BO3343	Edge	Back	Latch, Child-Resistant
BO3352	Face	Face	Latch/Pull, Positive
BO3363	Edge	Back	Latch, Secret/Touch
BO4013			Shelf Rests, Cabinet, for Bored Holes
BO4063	Edge		Shelf Standard, Cabinet, Adjustable, Non-mortising
BO4073	Edge		Shelf Standard, Cabinet, Adjustable, Surface or Mortise Mounted
BO4081 & 3			Shelf Rest, Cabinet, Closed, for Metal Standard
BO4091 & 3			Shelf Rest, Cabinet, Open, for Metal Standard
BO4102 & 3			Shelf Standard, Slotted, Wall, Adjustable
BO4112 & 3			Shelf Bracket, for Slotted Standard
BO5011-3			Drawer Slide, Side Mount Bottom Capture
BO5081-3			Drawer Slide, Center Bottom Mount
BO5061-3			Drawer Slide, Center Top Mount
BO5051-3			Drawer Slide, Side Mount

JOINERY DETAILS

(Page 1 of 2)

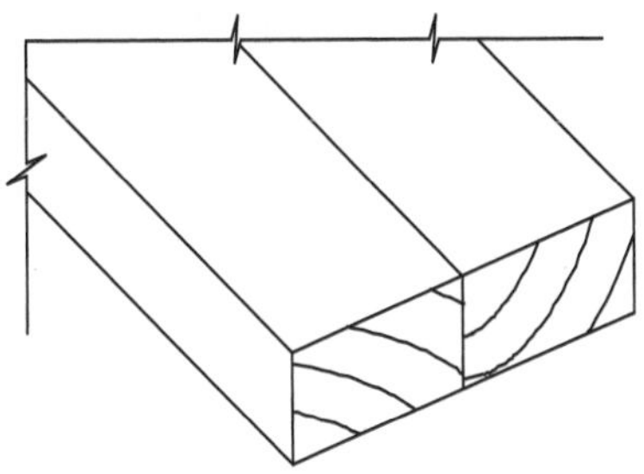

BUTT

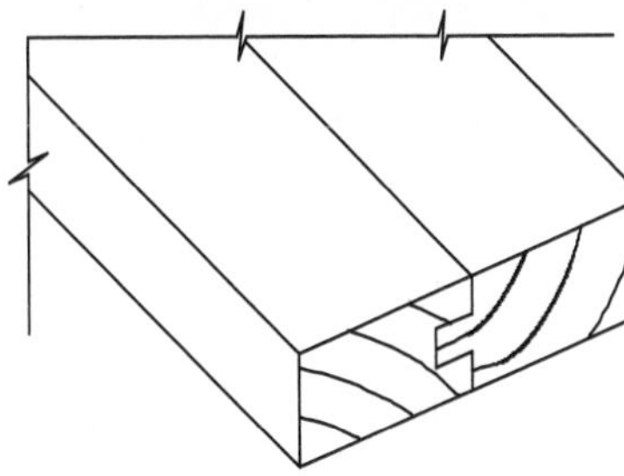

TONGUE & GROOVE

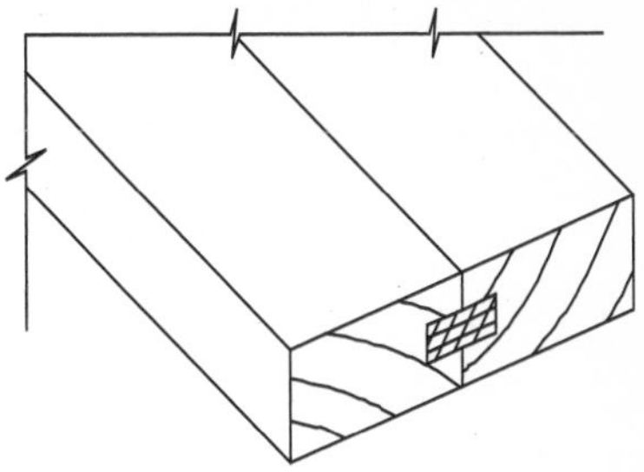

SPLINE

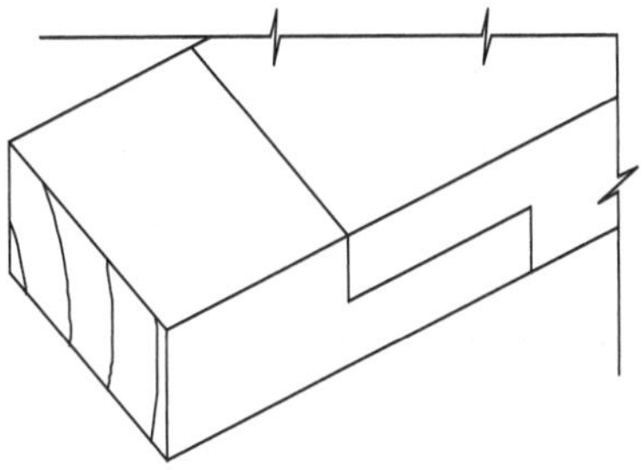

HALF LAP

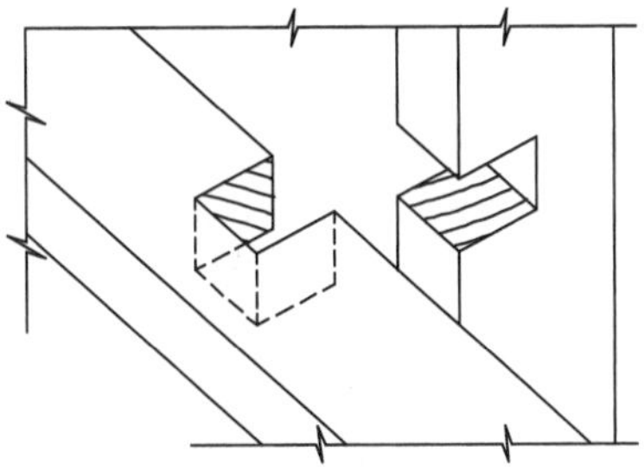

HALF LAP

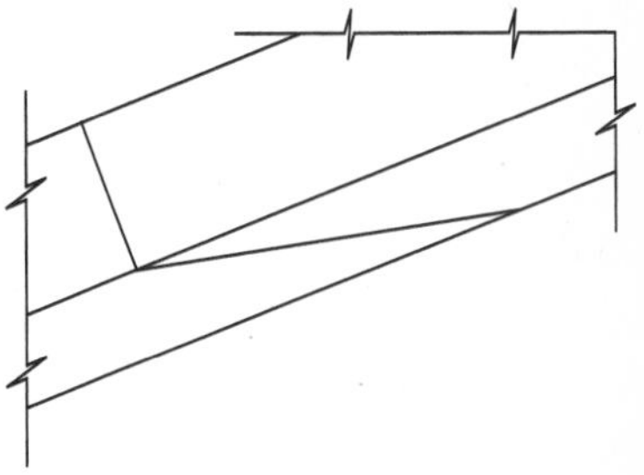

SCARF

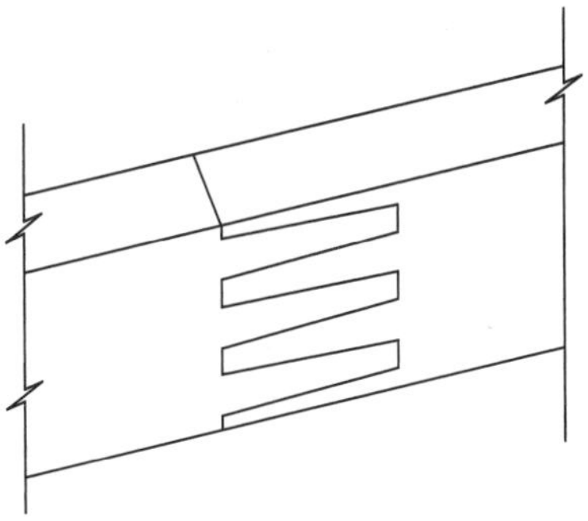

FINGER

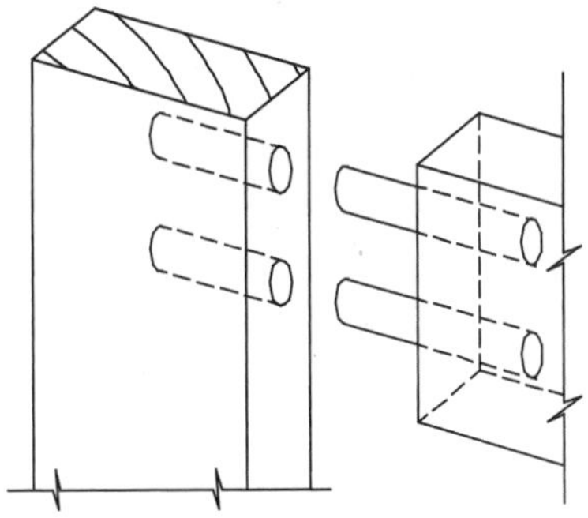

DOWELED

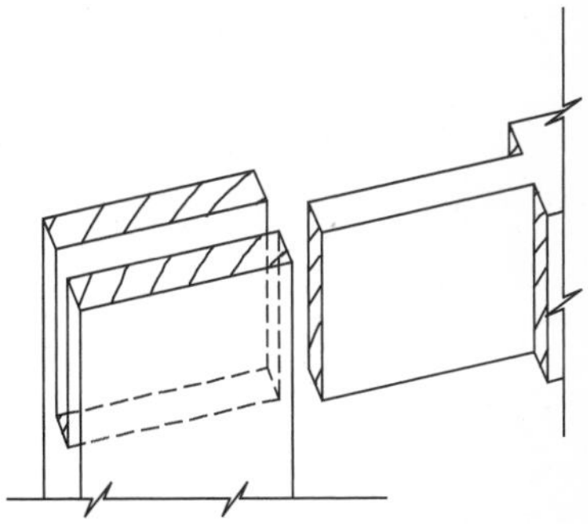

SLOTTED MORTISE & TENON

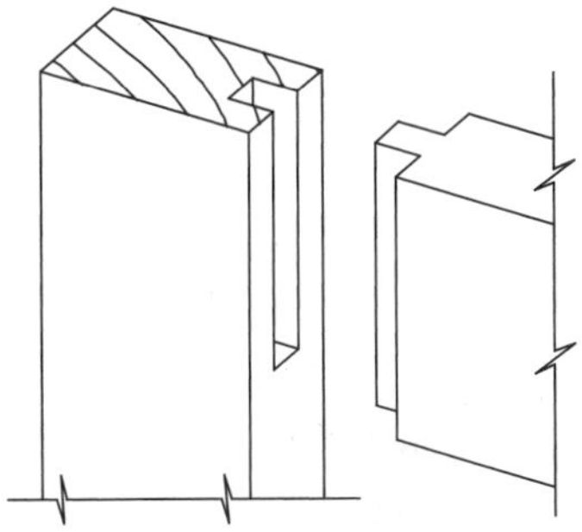

STUB MORTISE & TENON

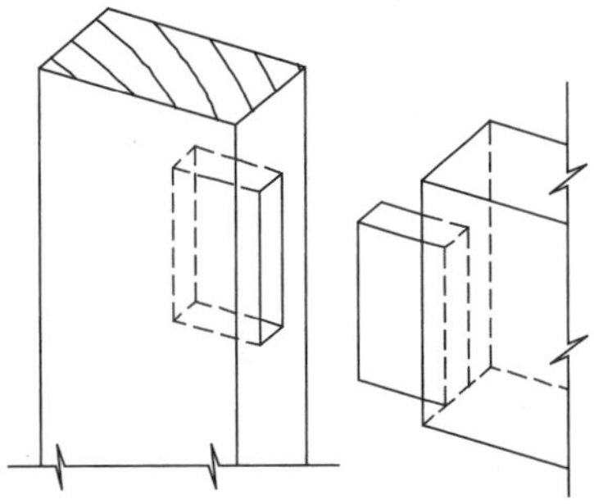

BLIND MORTISE & TENON

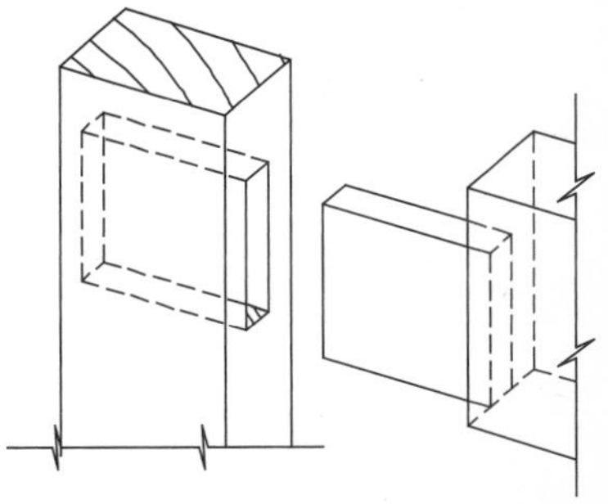

THROUGH MORTISE & TENON

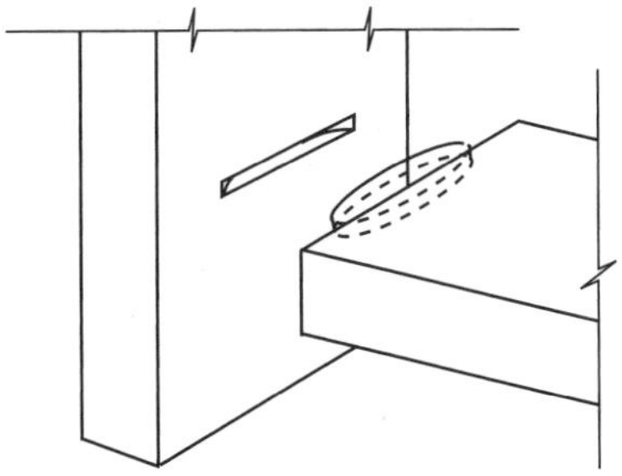

BISCUIT

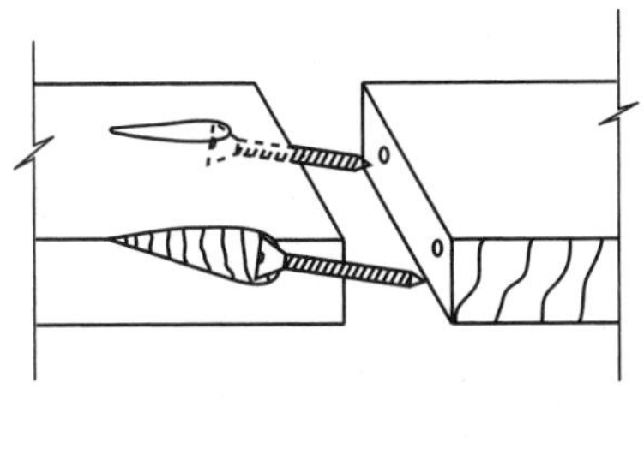

POCKET SCREW

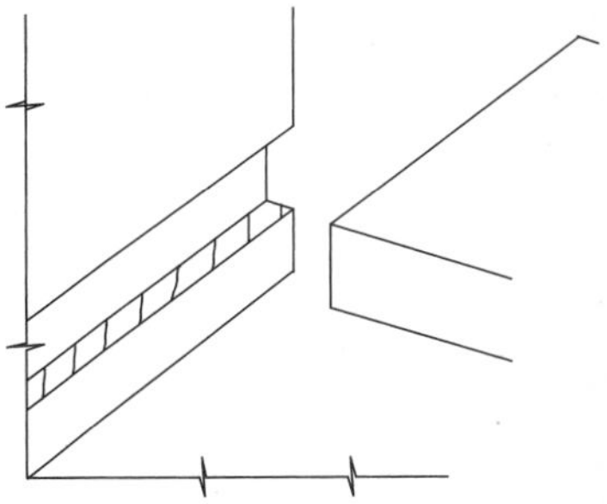

PLOWED IN

JOINERY DETAILS
(Page 2 of 2)

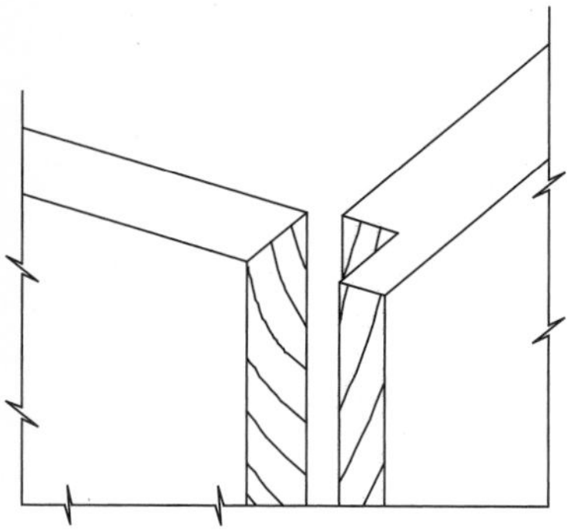

RABBET

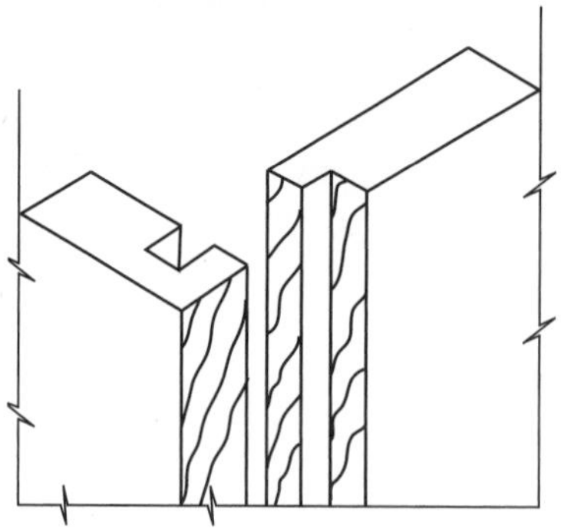

LOCK SHOULDER

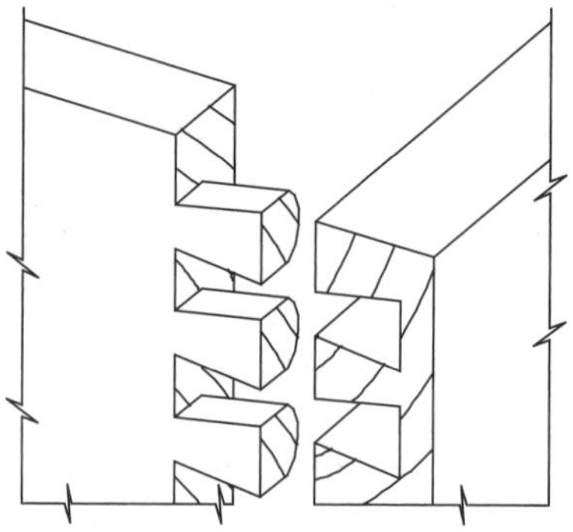

DOVETAIL

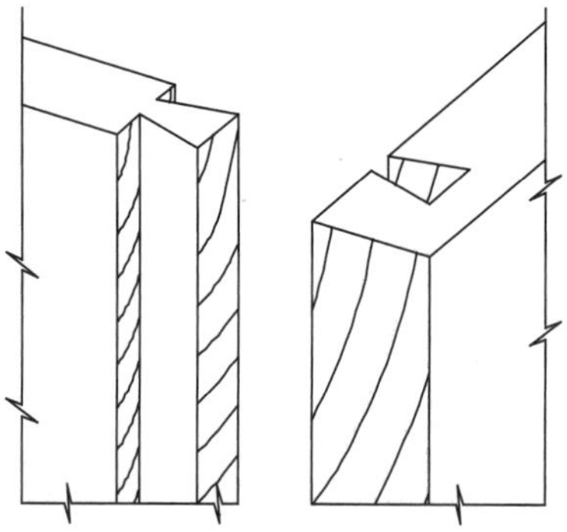

DOVETAIL (French) DADO

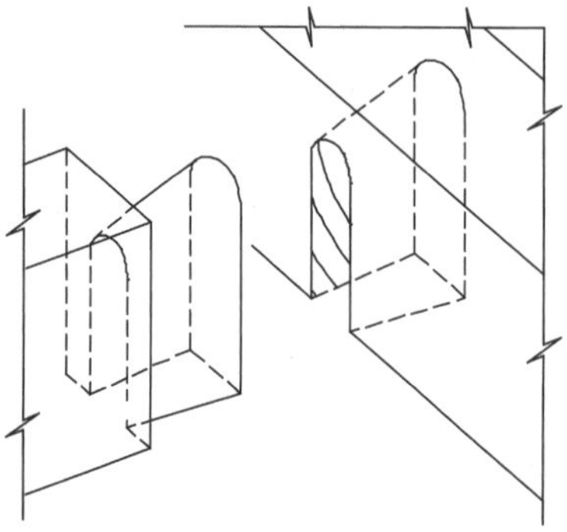

BLIND DOVETAIL

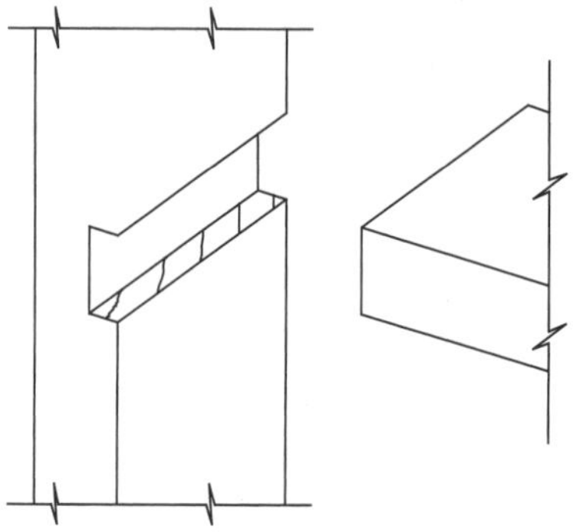

DADO

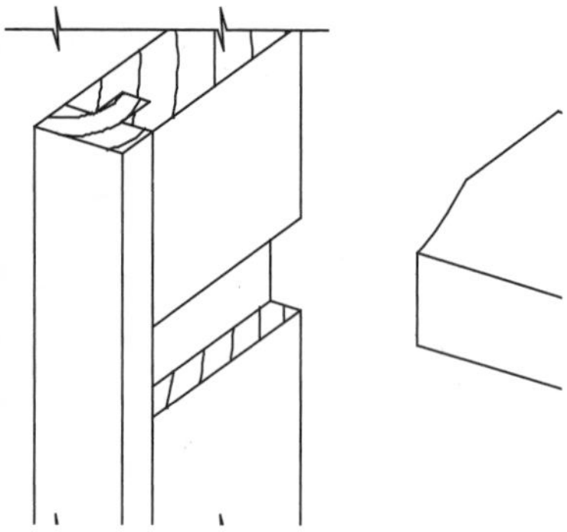

DADO, BLIND OR STOPPED

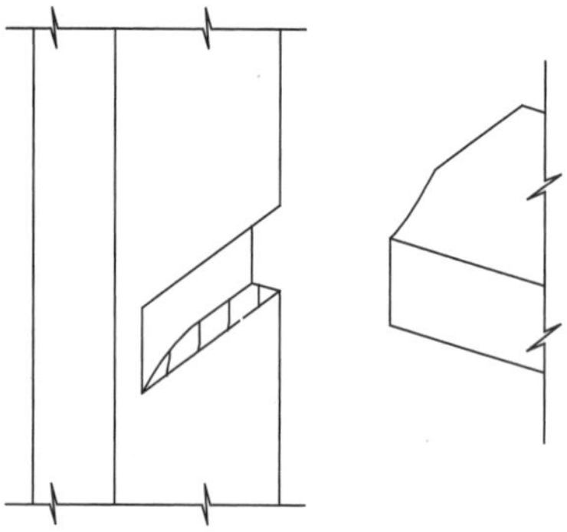

DADO, BLIND OR STOPPED

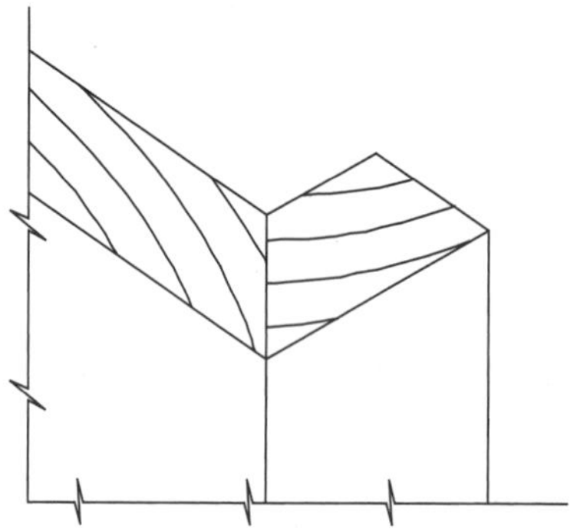

MITER

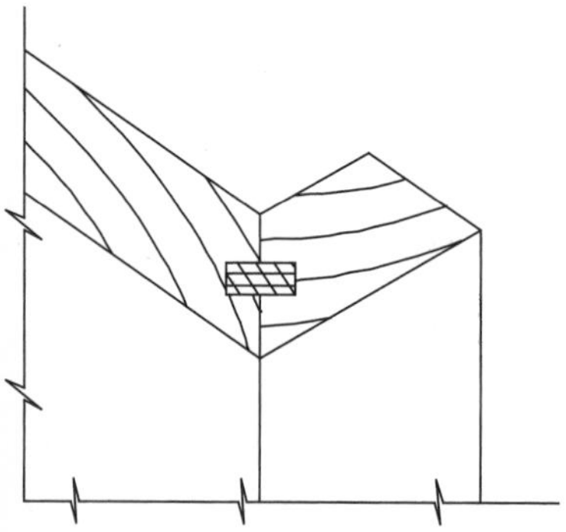

SPLINED MITER

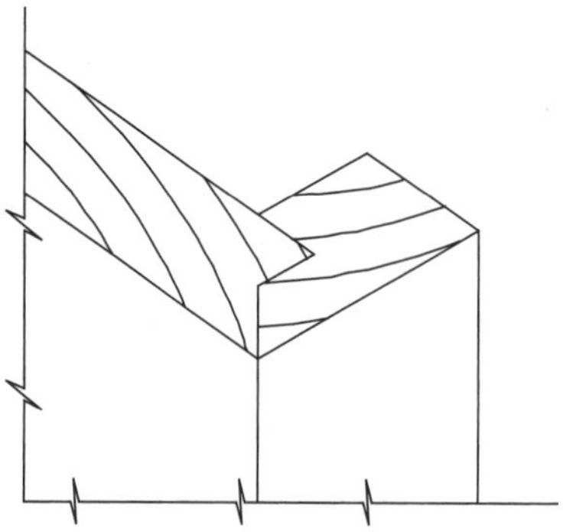

SHOULDER MITER

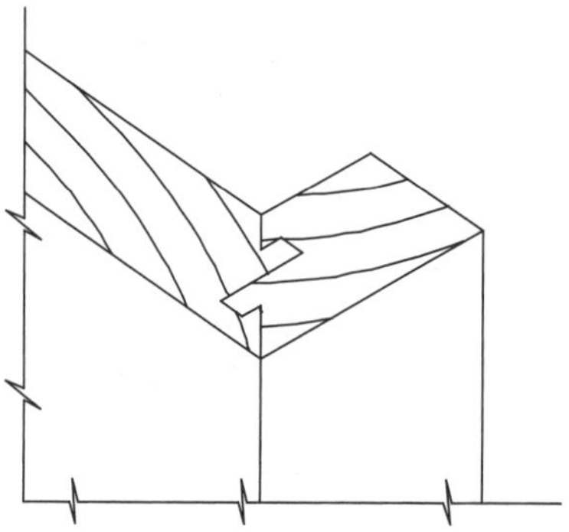

LOCK MITER

SEFA CHEMICAL AND STAIN RESISTANCE

(Page 1 of 2)

If chemical and/or stain resistance is a concern, users should consider the chemical and staining agents that might be used on or near casework or countertop surfaces. Common guidelines can be found in NEMA LD3 (latest edition) for chemical resistance and ASTM D3023 and C1378 (latest editions) for stain resistance. Because chemical and stain resistance is affected by concentration, time, temperature, humidity, housekeeping, and other factors, it is recommended that actual samples are tested in a similar environment with those agents that are of concern.

In lieu of actual sample testing to evaluate the resistance a finish has to chemical spills, these standards have adopted SEFA's (Scientific Equipment and Fixture Association) standard list of 49 chemicals/concentrations, their required methods of testing, and their minimum acceptable results as the means of establishing a minimum acceptable chemical resistance for exposed and semi-exposed surfaces where required by specification.

REQUIREMENT:

Exposed horizontal surfaces, such as countertops, are required to pass a 24-hour exposure test, whereas exposed vertical surfaces and semi-exposed surfaces are required to pass a 1-hour exposure test.

TEST PROCEDURE:

Obtain one sample panel measuring 14" x 24" (356 mm x 610 mm) and test for chemical resistance as described herein:

Place the panel on a flat surface, clean with soap and water, and blot dry. Condition the panel for 48 hours at 73° ±3° F (20° ±2° C) and 50% ±5% relative humidity. Test the panel for chemical resistance using the 49 different chemical reagents (listed on the following page) by one of the following methods:

METHOD A - Test volatile chemicals by placing a cotton ball saturated with reagent in the mouth of a 1-oz. (29.574 cc) bottle and inverting the bottle on the surface of the panel.

METHOD B - Test non-volatile chemicals by placing five drops of the reagent on the surface of the panel and covering with a 24 mm watch glass, convex side down.

For both of the above methods, leave the reagents on the panel for a period of:

One (1) hour for exposed vertical surfaces and semi-exposed surfaces.

Twenty-four (24) hours for exposed horizontal surfaces such as countertops.

Wash off the panel with water, clean with detergent and naphtha, and rinse with deionized water. Dry with a towel and evaluate after 24 hours at 73° ±3° F (20° ±2° C) and 50% ±5% relative humidity using the following rating system:

RESULT CLASSIFICATIONS:

LEVEL 0 - No detectable change.

LEVEL 1 - Slight change in color or gloss.

LEVEL 2 - Slight surface etching or severe staining.

LEVEL 3 - Pitting, cratering, swelling, or erosion of coating; obvious and significant deterioration.

ACCEPTANCE LEVEL:

Results will vary from product to product, and suitability for a given application is dependent upon the chemicals used in a given laboratory setting. Without specification requiring otherwise, an acceptable level of chemical and stain resistance for products requiring such in accordance with these standards and a project's specifications shall be:

FINISHES with test results **SHOWING NO MORE THAN** four of the Level 3 Result Classifications.

SEFA CHEMICAL AND STAIN RESISTANCE

(Page 2 of 2)

	CHEMICAL REAGENT	TEST METHOD
1	Acetate, Amyl	A
2	Acetate, Ethyl	A
3	Acetic Acid, 98%	B
4	Acetone	A
5	Acid Dichromate, 5%	B
6	Alcohol, Butyl	A
7	Alcohol, Ethyl	A
8	Alcohol, Methyl	A
9	Ammonium Hydroxide, 28%	B
10	Benzene	A
11	Carbon Tetrachloride	A
12	Chloroform	A
13	Chromic Acid, 60%	B
14	Cresol	A
15	Dichlor Acetic Acid	A
16	Dimethylformanide	A
17	Dioxane	A
18	Ethyl Ether	A
19	Formaldehyde, 37%	A
20	Formic Acid, 90%	B
21	Furfural	A
22	Gasoline	A
22	Hydrochloric Acid, 37%	B
24	Hydrofluoric Acid, 48%	B
25	Hydrogen Peroxide, 3%	B

	CHEMICAL REAGENT	TEST METHOD
26	Iodine, Tincture of	B
27	Methyl Ethyl Ketone	A
28	Methylene Chloride	A
29	Mono Chlorobenzene	A
30	Naphthalene	A
31	Nitric Acid, 20%	B
32	Nitric Acid, 30%	B
33	Nitric Acid, 70%	B
34	Phenol, 90%	A
35	Phosphoric Acid, 85%	B
36	Silver Nitrate, Saturated	B
37	Sodium Hydroxide, 10%	B
38	Sodium Hydroxide, 20%	B
39	Sodium Hydroxide, 40%	B
40	Sodium Hydroxide, Flake	B
41	Sodium Sulfide, Saturated	B
42	Sulfuric Acid, 33%	B
43	Sulfuric Acid, 77%	B
44	Sulfuric Acid, 96%	B
45	Sulfuric Acid, 77% and Nitric Acid, 70% - equal parts	B
46	Toluene	A
47	Trichloroethylene	A
48	Xylene	A
49	Zinc Chloride, Saturated	B

CASEWORK DESIGN SERIES (CDS)

(Page 1 of 20)

THESE CASEWORK ILLUSTRATIONS ARE PROVIDED TO ASSIST DESIGN PROFESSIONALS AND CASEWORK USERS IN SELECTING TYPICAL DESIGNS. THESE ILLUSTRATIONS ARE NOT INTENDED TO LIMIT OR RESTRICT CREATIVITY, OR TO BE ALL-INCLUSIVE.

When **UTILIZING THE CDS NUMBERING SYSTEM**, it is not necessary to show casework elevations in your architectural drawings. However, it is necessary to show a plan view with each **CDS** number indicated along with the width, height, and depth in inches or millimeters (example: 102-36"x30"x18" [102-914 mm x 762 mm x 457 mm]). Cabinet dimensions indicate the nominal outside dimension (floor to top of countertop for height and face of finished wall to face of cabinet door for depth). Manufacturers are permitted a tolerance of plus/minus 1/2" (12.7 mm) in width only.

When **DESIGNS OTHER THAN THOSE PROVIDED FOR IN THE CDS SYSTEM ARE DESIRED**, they may be indicated by selecting the **CDS** number most closely representing the desired design, followed by the letter "M" and a description or illustration of the design modification (example: 102M - 2 shelves - 36"x30"x18" [102M - 2 shelves - 914 mm x 762 mm x 457 mm] or 102M - no shelves -36"x30"x18" [102M - no shelves -914 mm x 762 mm x 457 mm]). It is suggested that a standard number/ dimension convention similar to that shown below, is used.

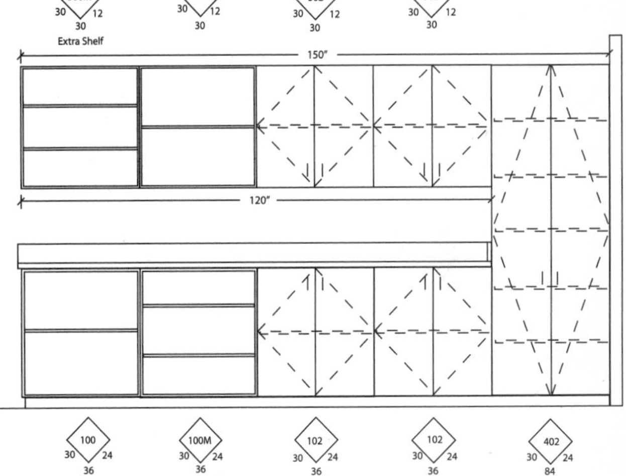

If the **CDS** numbering system is **USED IN CONJUNCTION WITH CABINET ELEVATIONS** on architectural drawings, the cabinet elevations shall govern on any conflict between the requirements of the elevation and the **CDS** number.

CDS cabinets are intended for **TYPE A** construction with integral finished ends and scribes at wall-to-wall installations not exceeding 1-1/2" (38.1 mm) in width.

The following **BASE CASEWORK HEIGHTS** are recommended for various school grades, subject to ADA requirements:

Kindergarten - Grade 1	24" (610 mm)
Grades 2 - 3	27" (686 mm)
Grades 4 - 6	30" (762 mm)
Grades 7 - 9	33" (838 mm)
Grades 10 and above	36" (914 mm)

The **CDS** is subdivided as follows:

Base Cabinets w/o Drawers	100 Series	Tall Wardrobe Cabinets	500 Series
Base Cabinets w/ Drawers	200 Series	Library Cabinets	600 Series
Wall-Hung Cabinets	300 Series	Moveable Cabinets	700 Series
Tall Storage Cabinets	400 Series		

HARDWARE and **ACCESSORIES** shall be as provided for in these standards.

GENERAL NOTES:

1. 100 or 200 Series cabinets may be converted into moveable cabinets by prefixing a "7" to the number. (Example: 7-102-36"x30"x18" [7-102-914 mm x 762 mm x 457 mm]).
2. Moveable cabinets shall be equipped with adequate approved casters for the intended load capacity.
3. CDS #'s 728, 729, 735, 736, 737, 738, and 739 require metal angle reinforced corners.
4. Carts and rolling tall storage cabinets with doors, lacking any horizontal and/or vertical stabilizing dividers, require a diaphragm bottom; specifically CDS #'s 702, 712, 716, 722, 743,744, 746, 747, 750, and 751.
5. Wardrobe cabinets (500 Series) with doors require a framed mirror on one door, and cabinets # 533 and 534 require a paper roller/cutter and slide-out tilting paper shelves.
6. Cart storage cabinets are required to have hardwood side guides, specifically CDS #'s 160, 161, and 162.
7. Ceramics drying cabinets are required to have galvanized metal frame shelves with wire mesh, specifically CDS #'s 198 199, and 459.
8. File drawers require full-extension slides and a file-hanging system, specifically CDS #'s 223, 224, 230, 231, 240, 242, 253, 255, 531, 532, and 533.
9. Wardrobe cabinets are required to have a shelf, pole, and framed mirror when closed with hinged doors, specifically CDS #'s 501, 511, 512, 522, 530, 531, 532, and 552.

CASEWORK DESIGN SERIES (CDS)

(Page 2 of 20)

100 SERIES - BASE CABINETS w/o DRAWERS

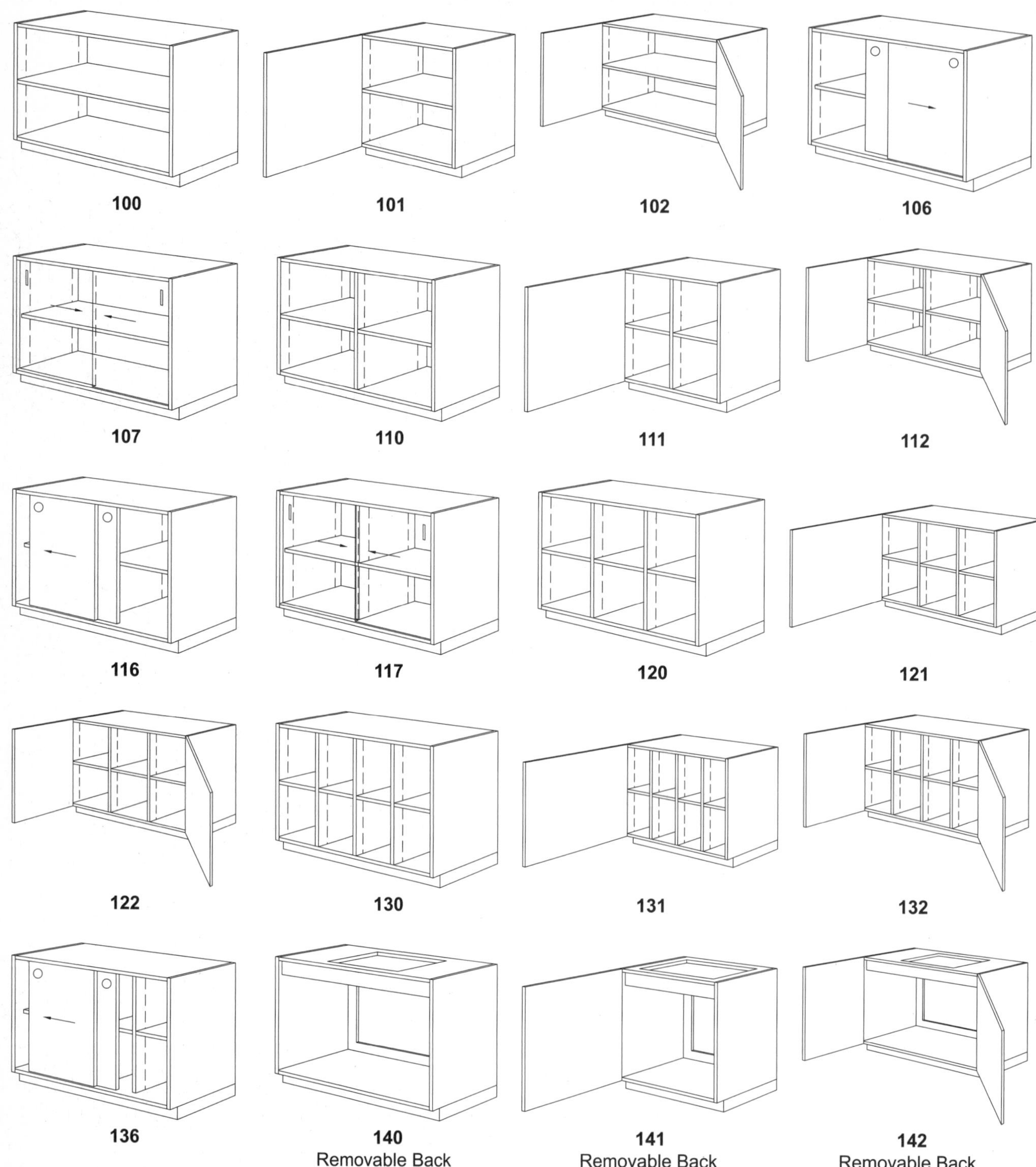

A

CASEWORK DESIGN SERIES (CDS)

(Page 3 of 20)

100 SERIES - BASE CABINETS w/o DRAWERS
(continued)

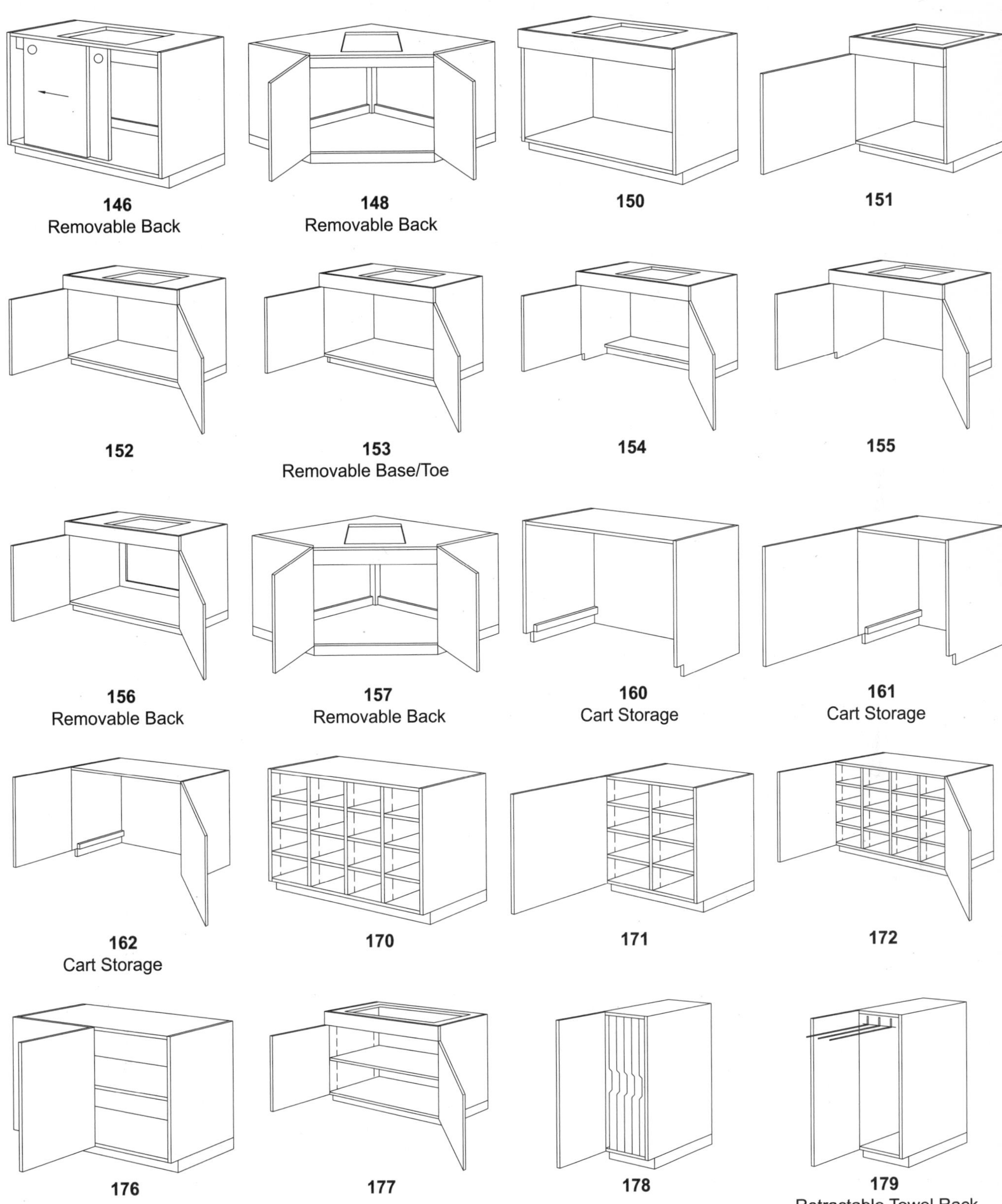

A

CASEWORK DESIGN SERIES (CDS)

(Page 4 of 20)

100 SERIES - BASE CABINETS w/o DRAWERS

(continued)

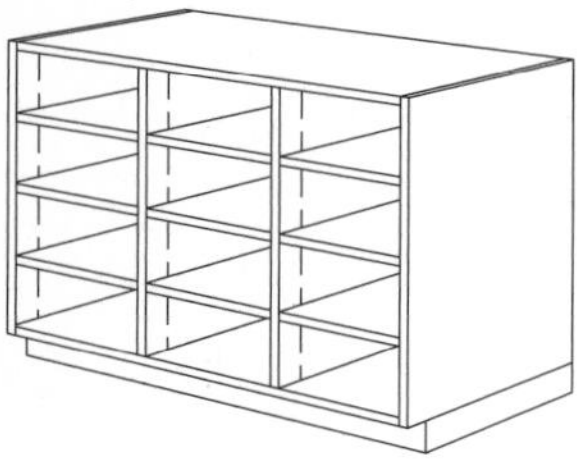

180

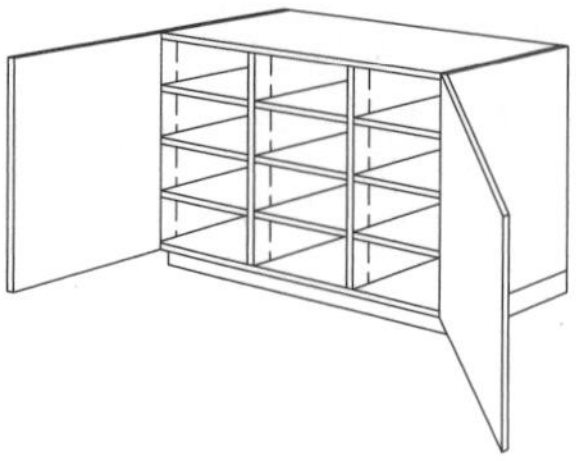

182

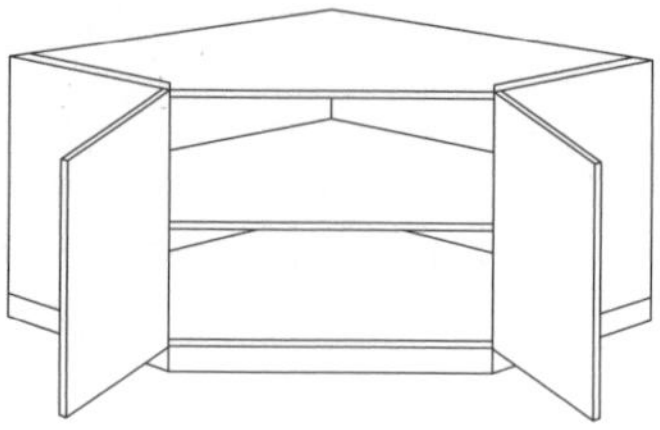

186

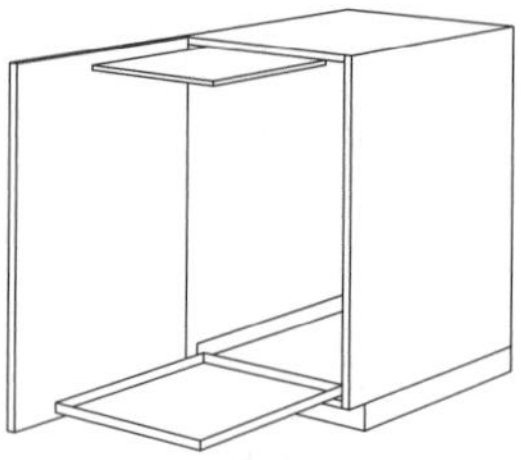

187
Sliding Tray & Lift Shelf

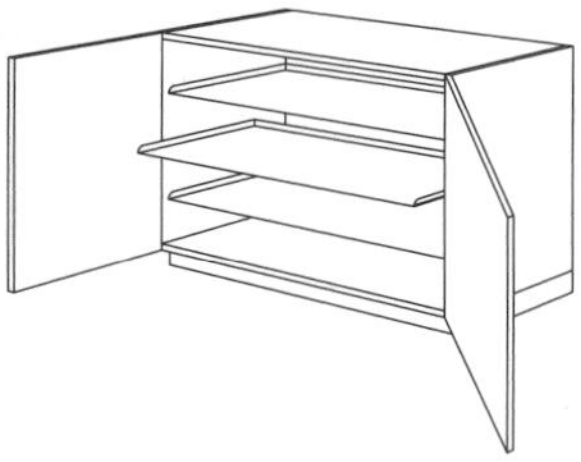

188

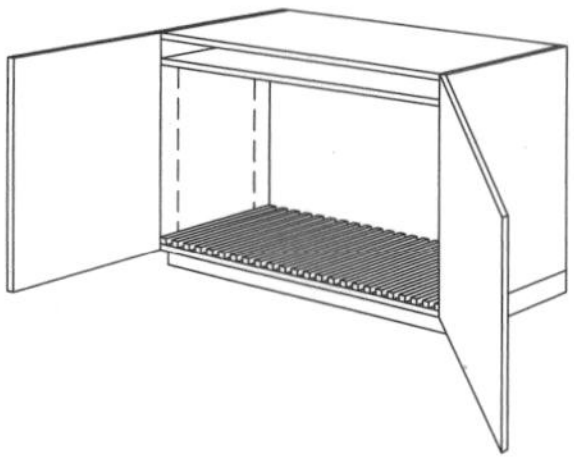

189
Drawing Board Rack

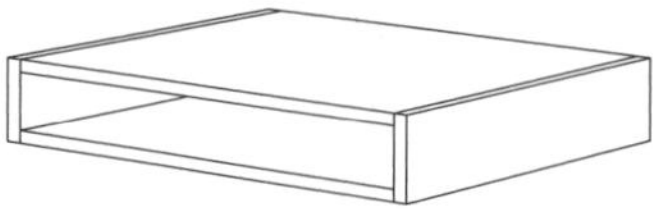

190

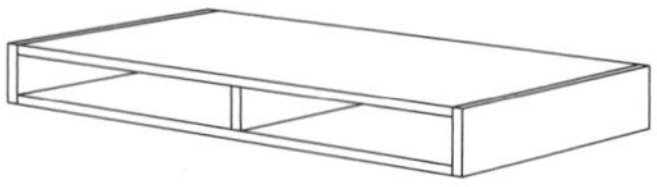

191

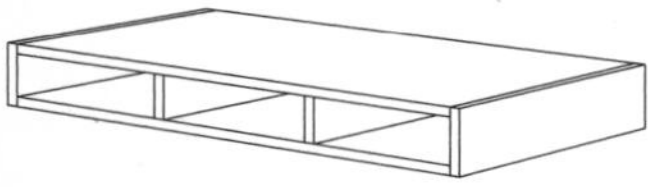

192

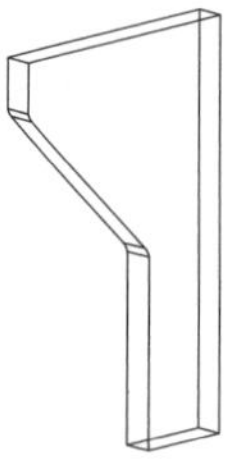

193

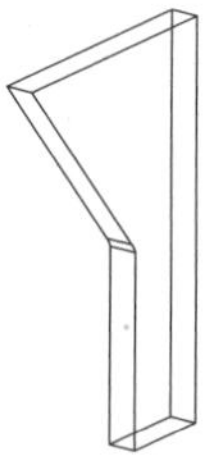

194

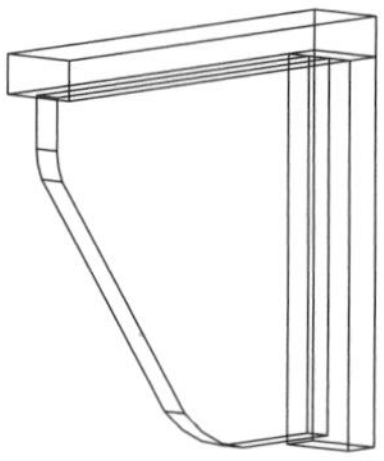

195

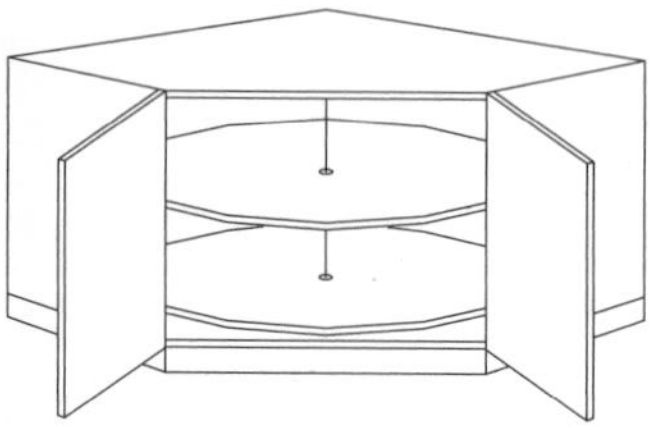

196

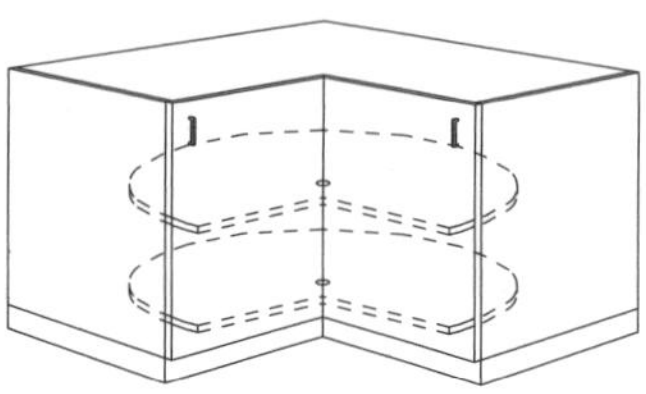

197

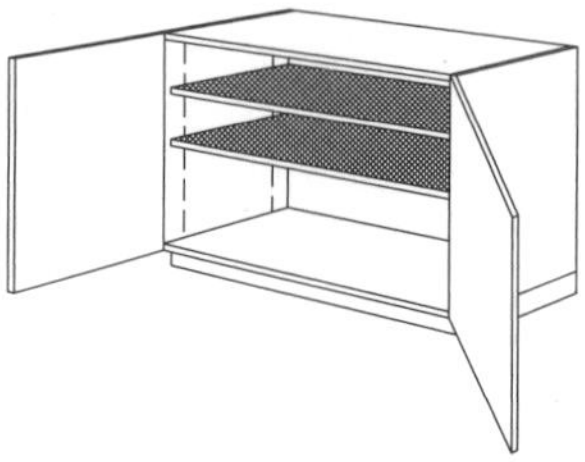

198

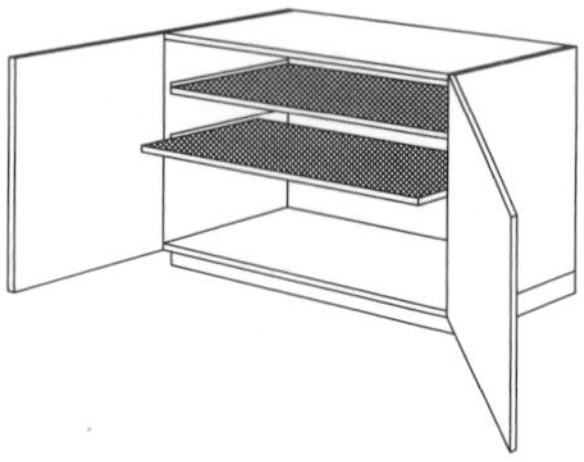

199

CASEWORK DESIGN SERIES (CDS)

(Page 5 of 20)

200 SERIES - BASE CABINETS w/ DRAWERS

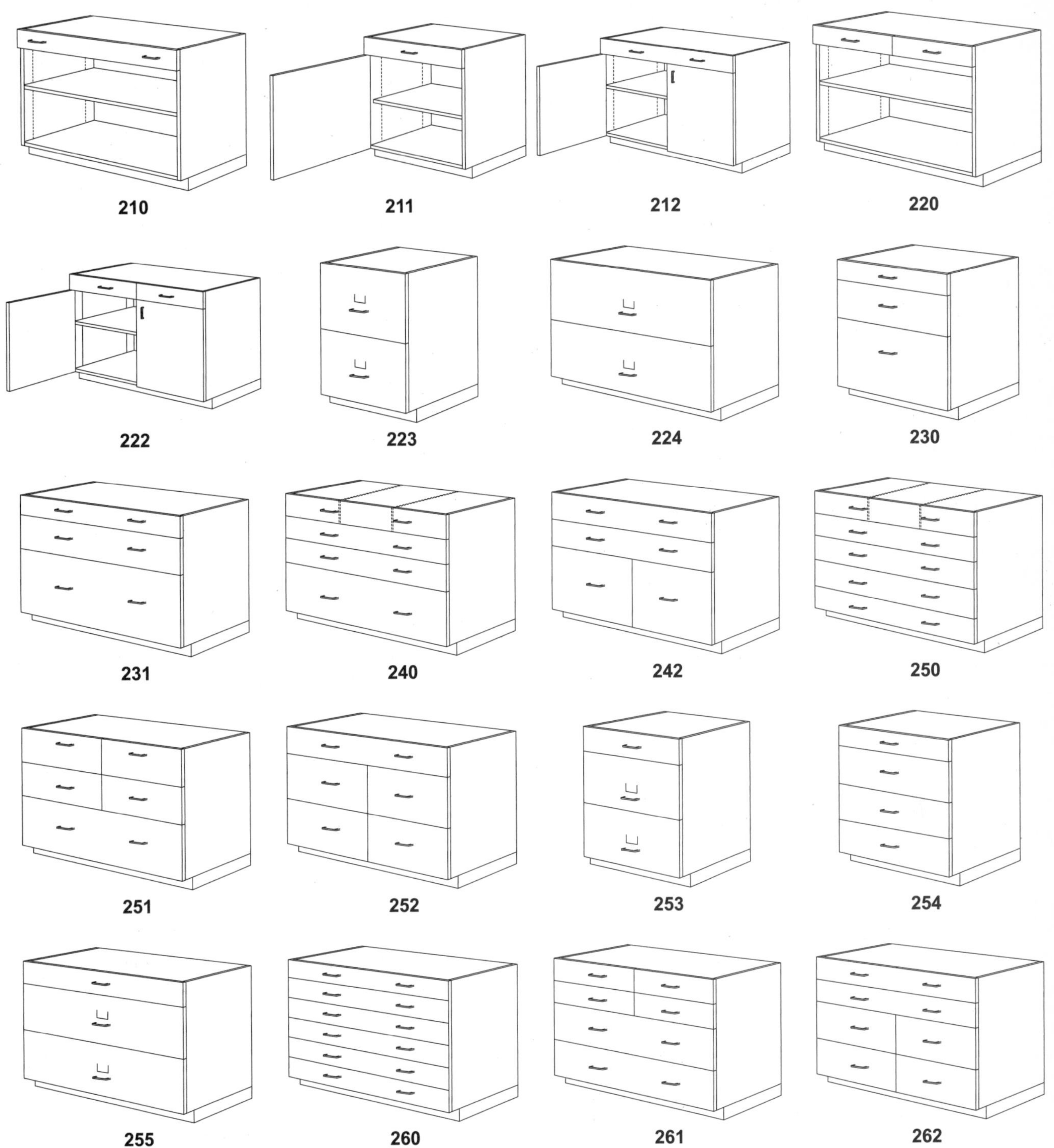

CASEWORK DESIGN SERIES (CDS)

(Page 6 of 20)

200 SERIES - BASE CABINETS w/ DRAWERS

(continued)

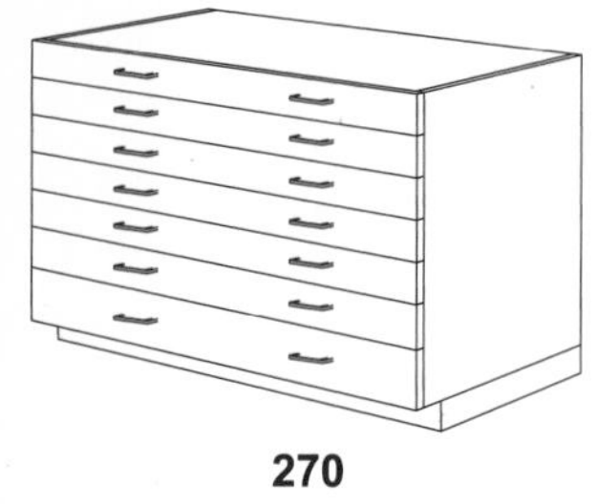

270

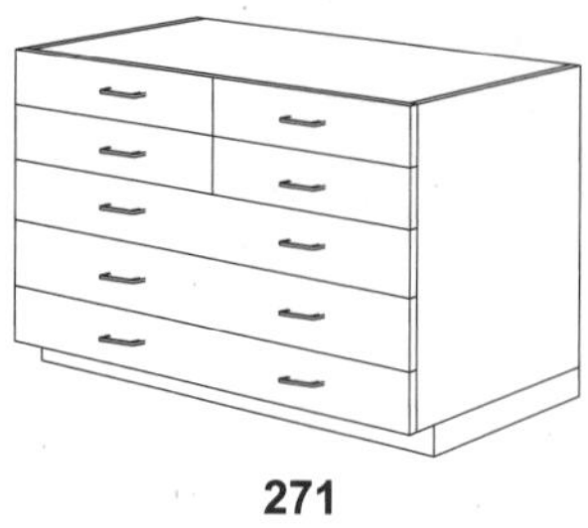

271

272

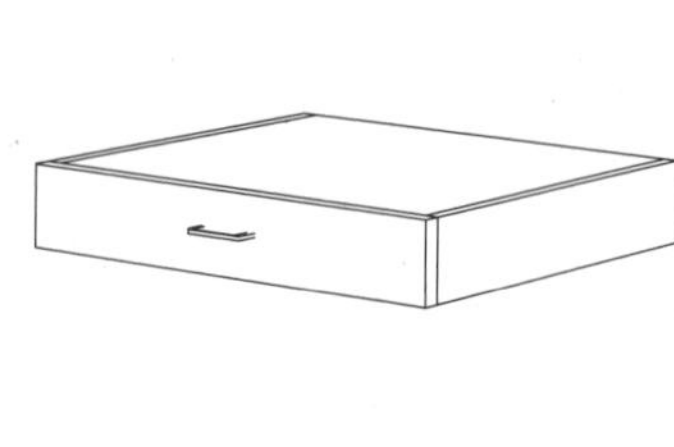

290

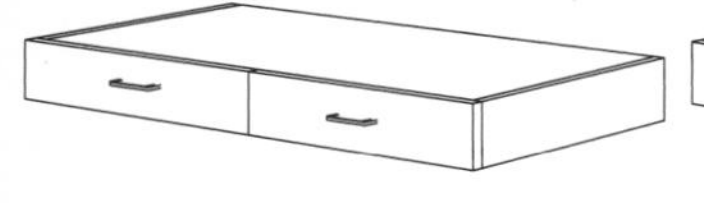

291

292

CASEWORK DESIGN SERIES (CDS)

(Page 7 of 20)

300 SERIES - WALL=HUNG CABINETS

CASEWORK DESIGN SERIES (CDS)

(Page 8 of 20)

300 SERIES - WALL-HUNG CABINETS

(continued)

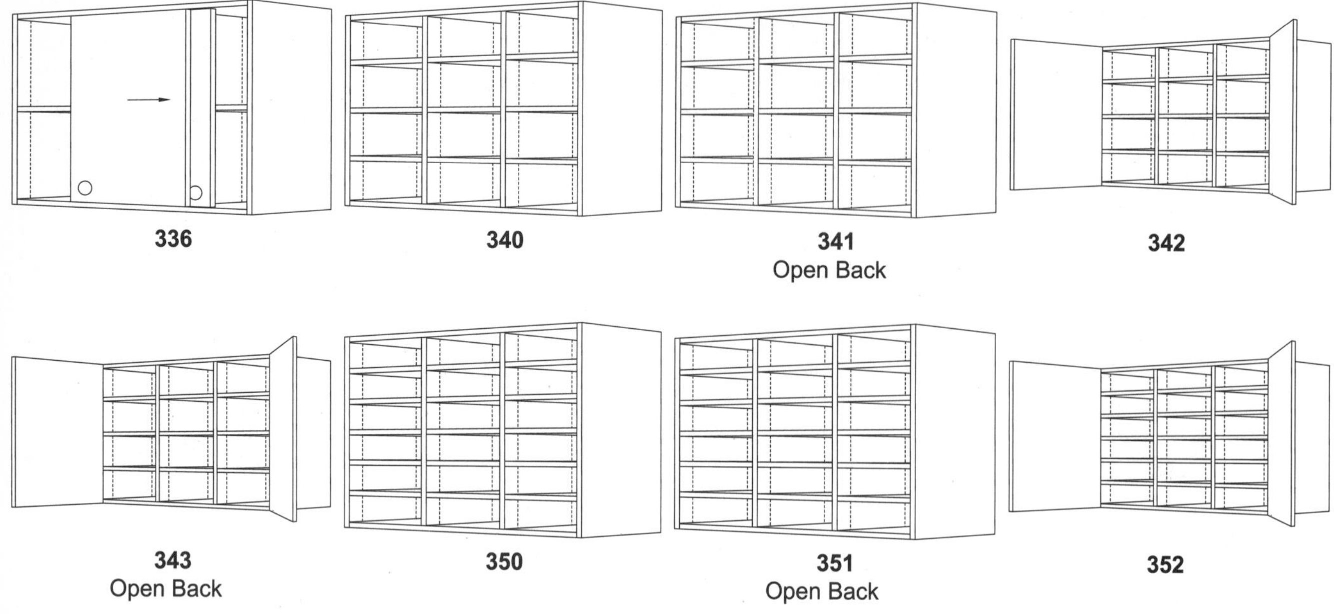

336

340

341
Open Back

342

343
Open Back

350

351
Open Back

352

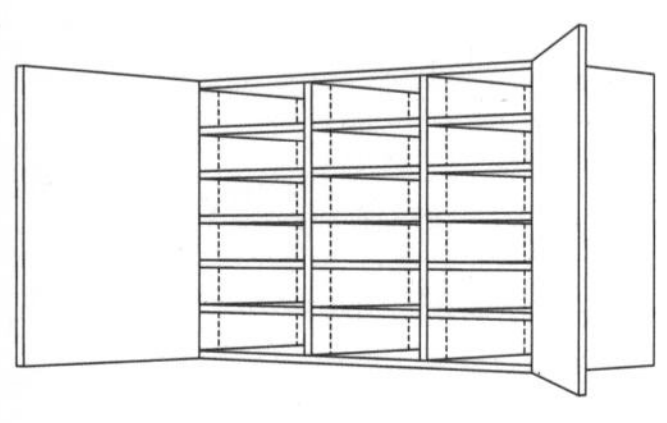

353
Open Back

CASEWORK DESIGN SERIES (CDS)

(Page 9 of 20)

400 SERIES - TALL STORAGE CABINETS

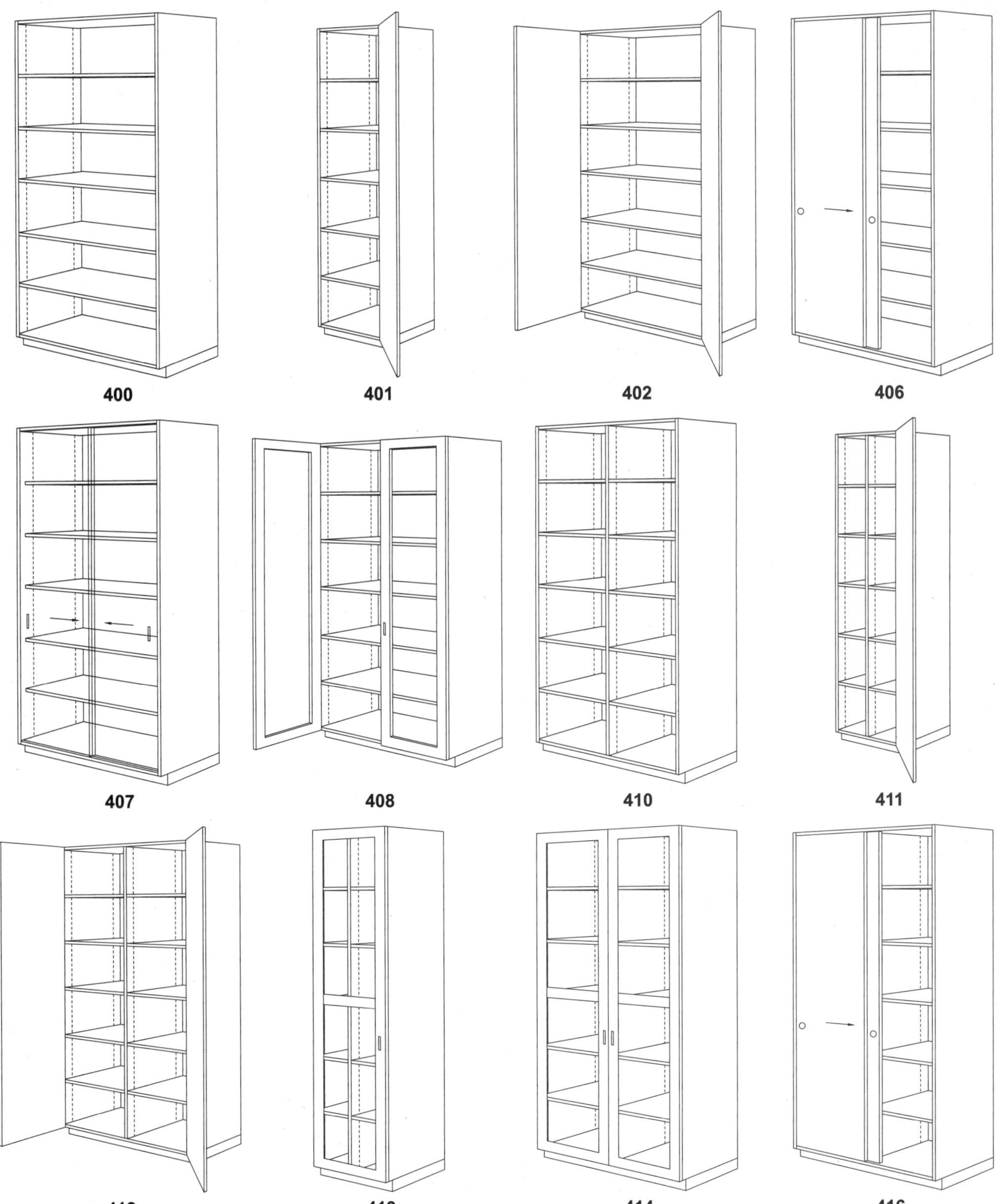

A

CASEWORK DESIGN SERIES (CDS)

(Page 10 of 20)

400 SERIES - TALL STORAGE CABINETS

(continued)

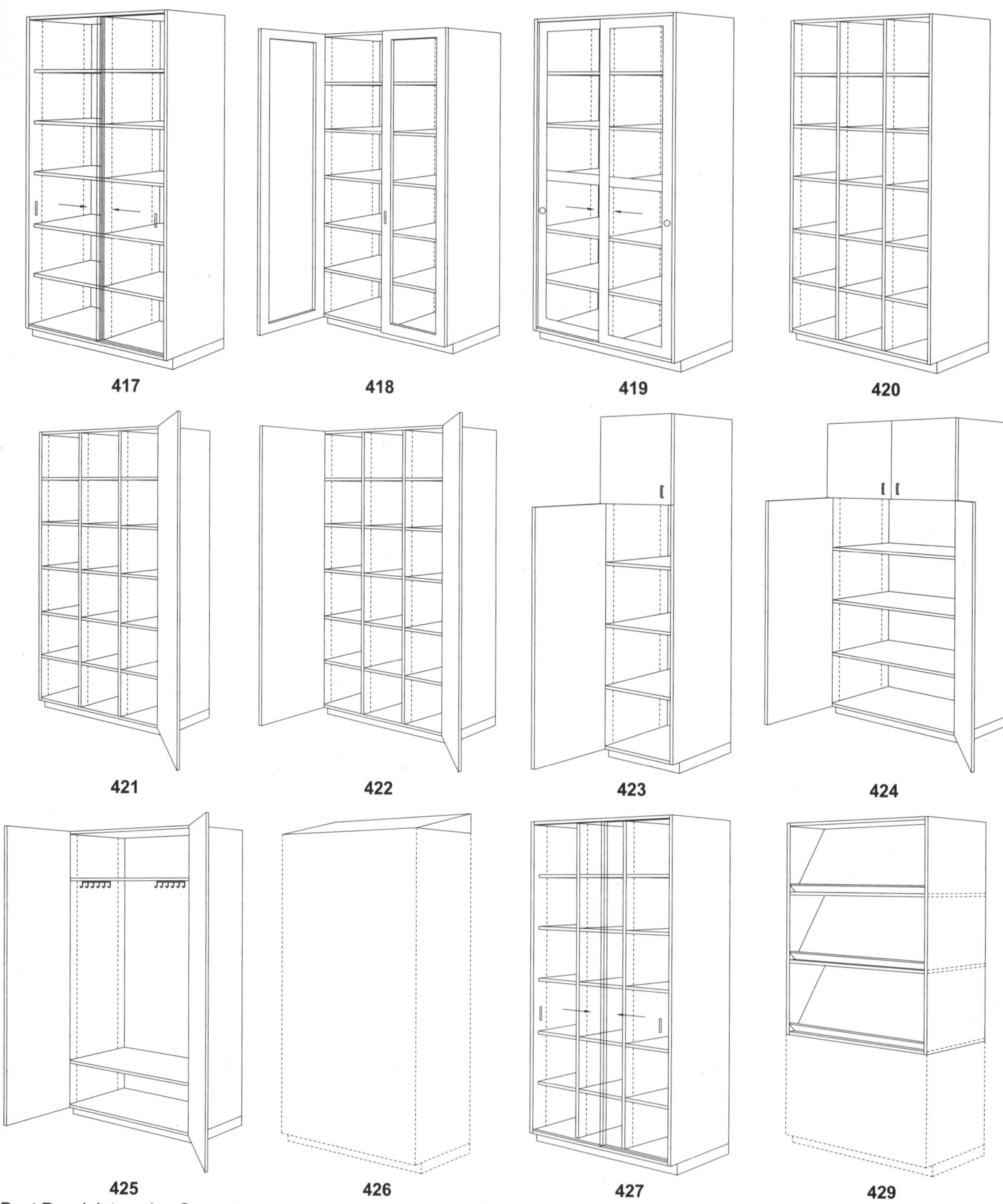

A

CASEWORK DESIGN SERIES (CDS)

(Page 11 of 20)

400 SERIES - TALL STORAGE CABINETS

(continued)

A

CASEWORK DESIGN SERIES (CDS)

400 SERIES - TALL STORAGE CABINETS
(continued)

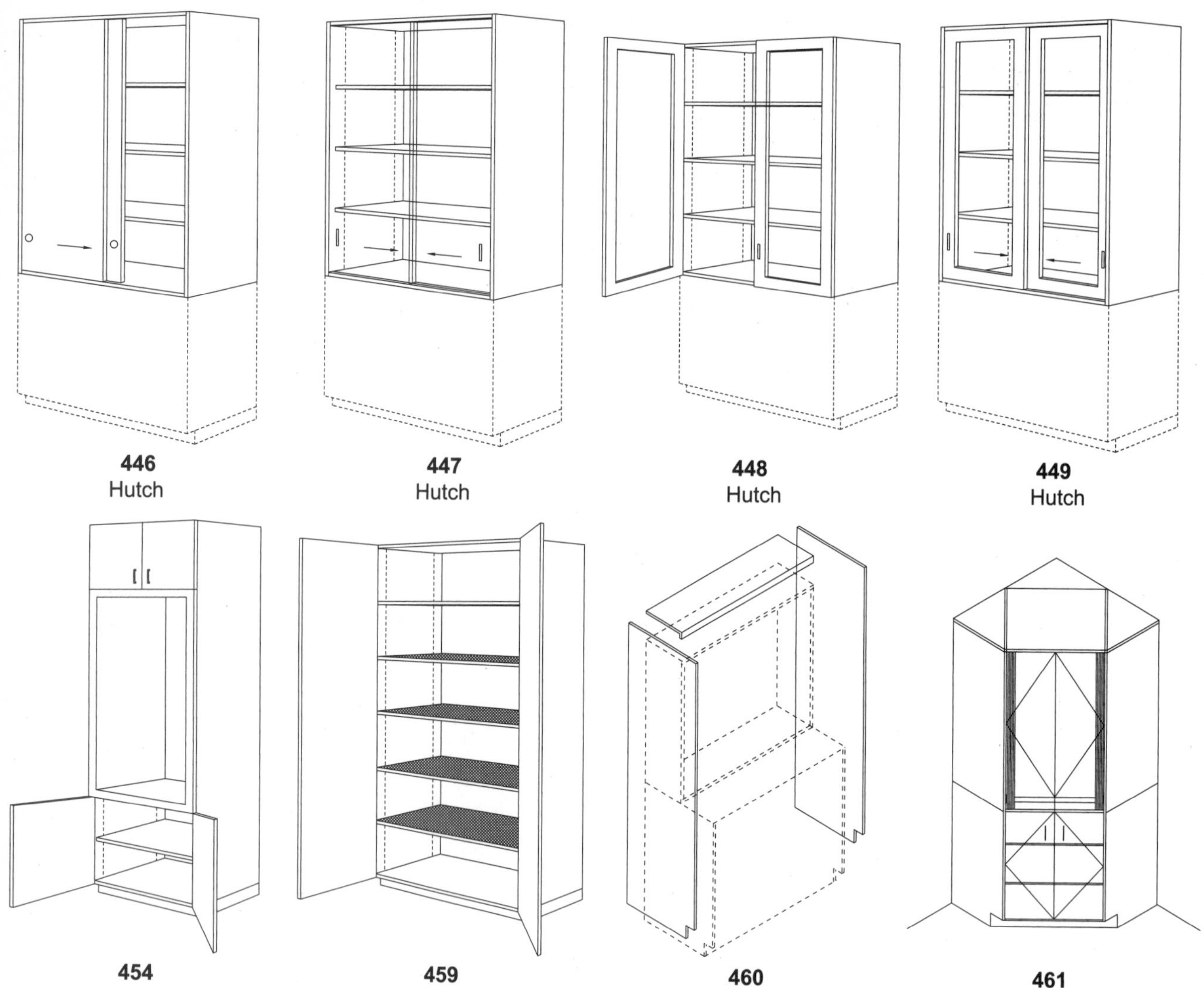

CASEWORK DESIGN SERIES (CDS)

(Page 13 of 20)

500 SERIES - WARDROBE CABINETS

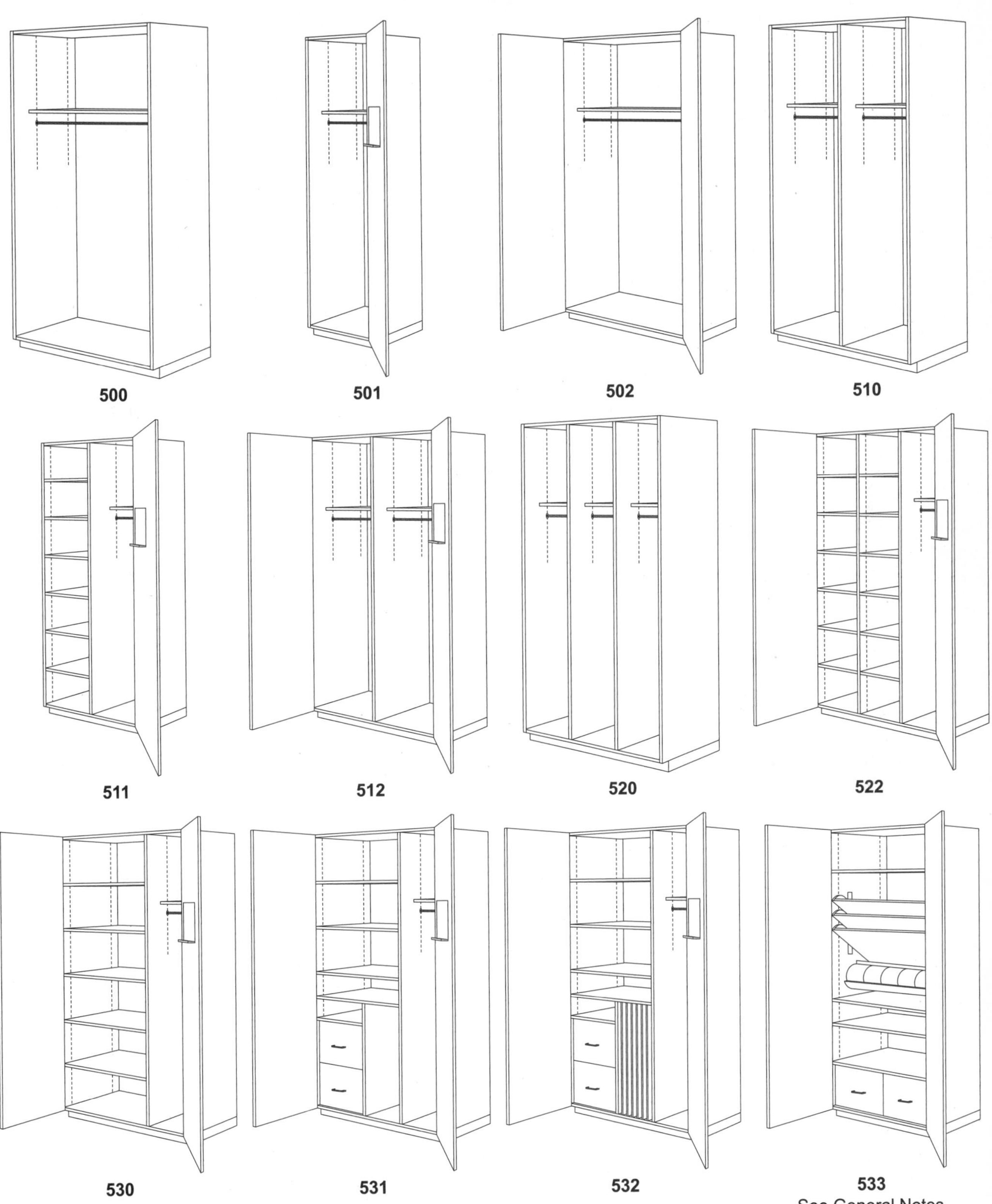

CASEWORK DESIGN SERIES (CDS)

(Page 14 of 20)

500 SERIES - WARDROBE CABINETS
(continued)

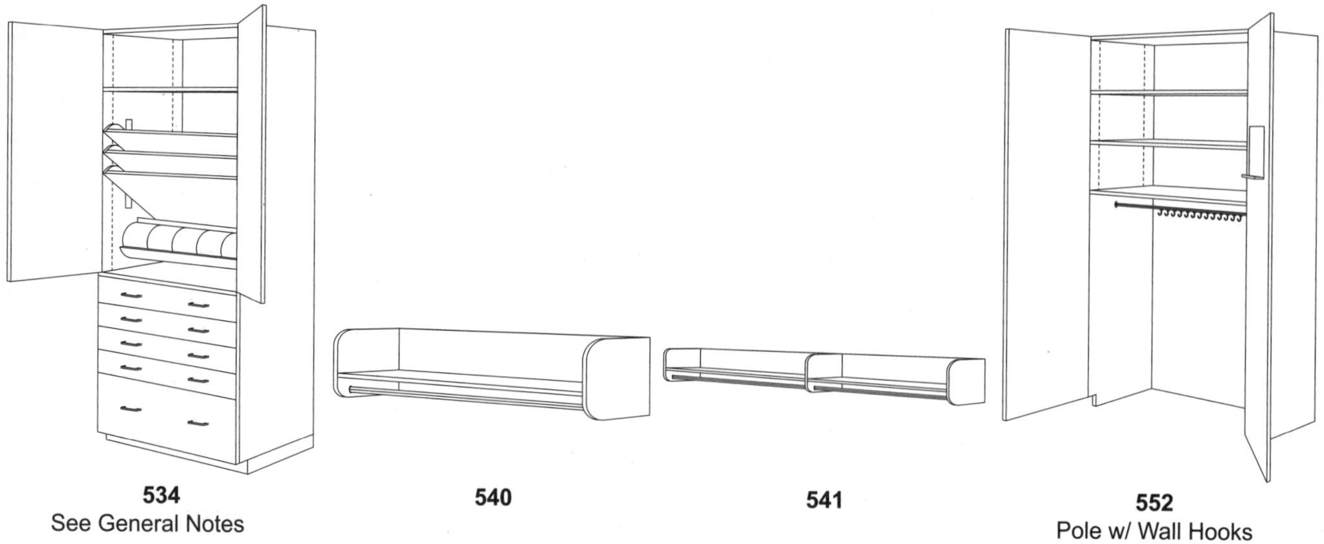

534 See General Notes

540

541

552 Pole w/ Wall Hooks

CASEWORK DESIGN SERIES (CDS)

(Page 15 of 20)

600 SERIES - LIBRARY CABINETS

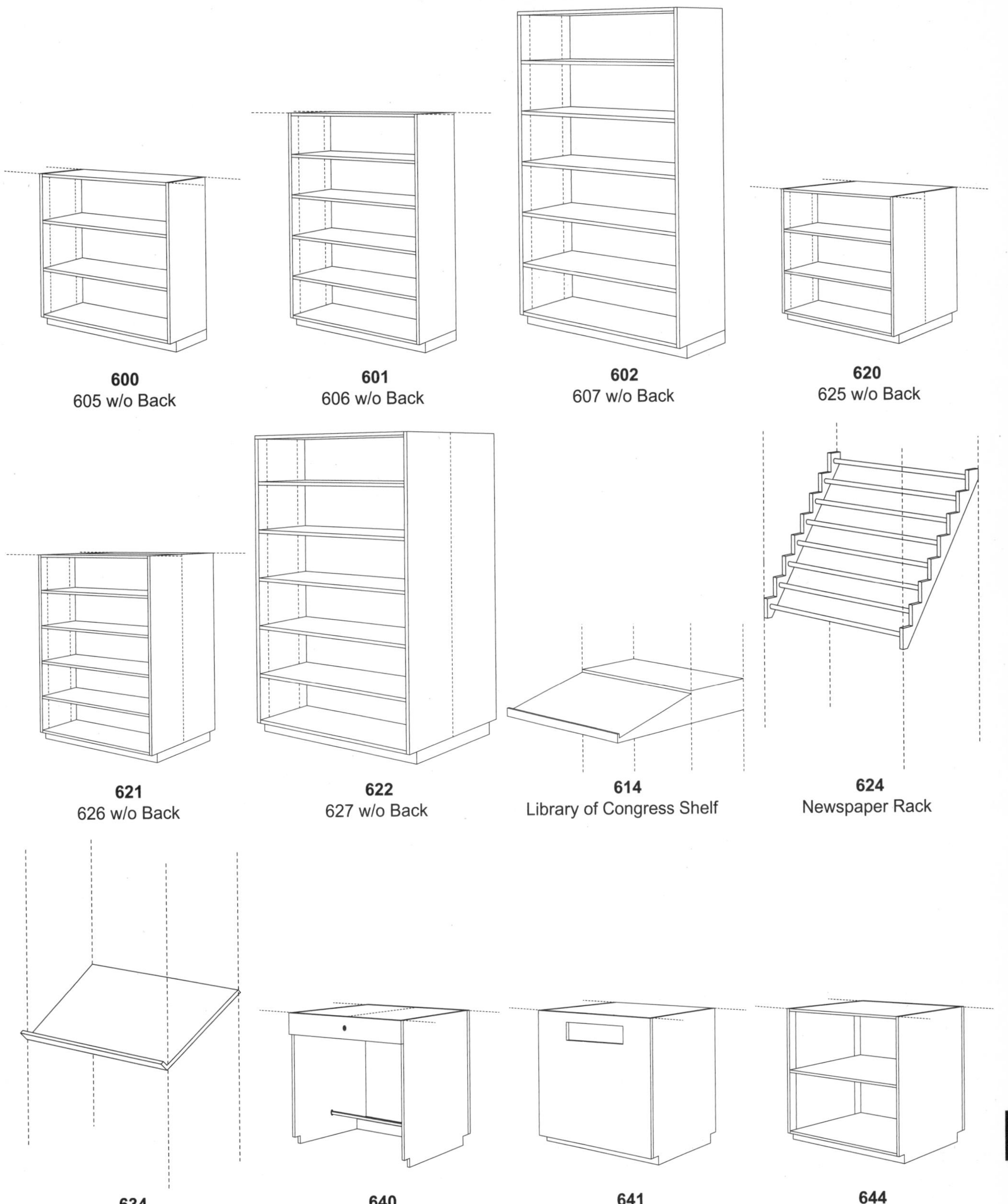

600
605 w/o Back

601
606 w/o Back

602
607 w/o Back

620
625 w/o Back

621
626 w/o Back

622
627 w/o Back

614
Library of Congress Shelf

624
Newspaper Rack

634
Display Shelf

640
Charge Desk

641
Book Return

644

CASEWORK DESIGN SERIES (CDS)

(Page 16 of 20)

600 SERIES - LIBRARY CABINETS
(continued)

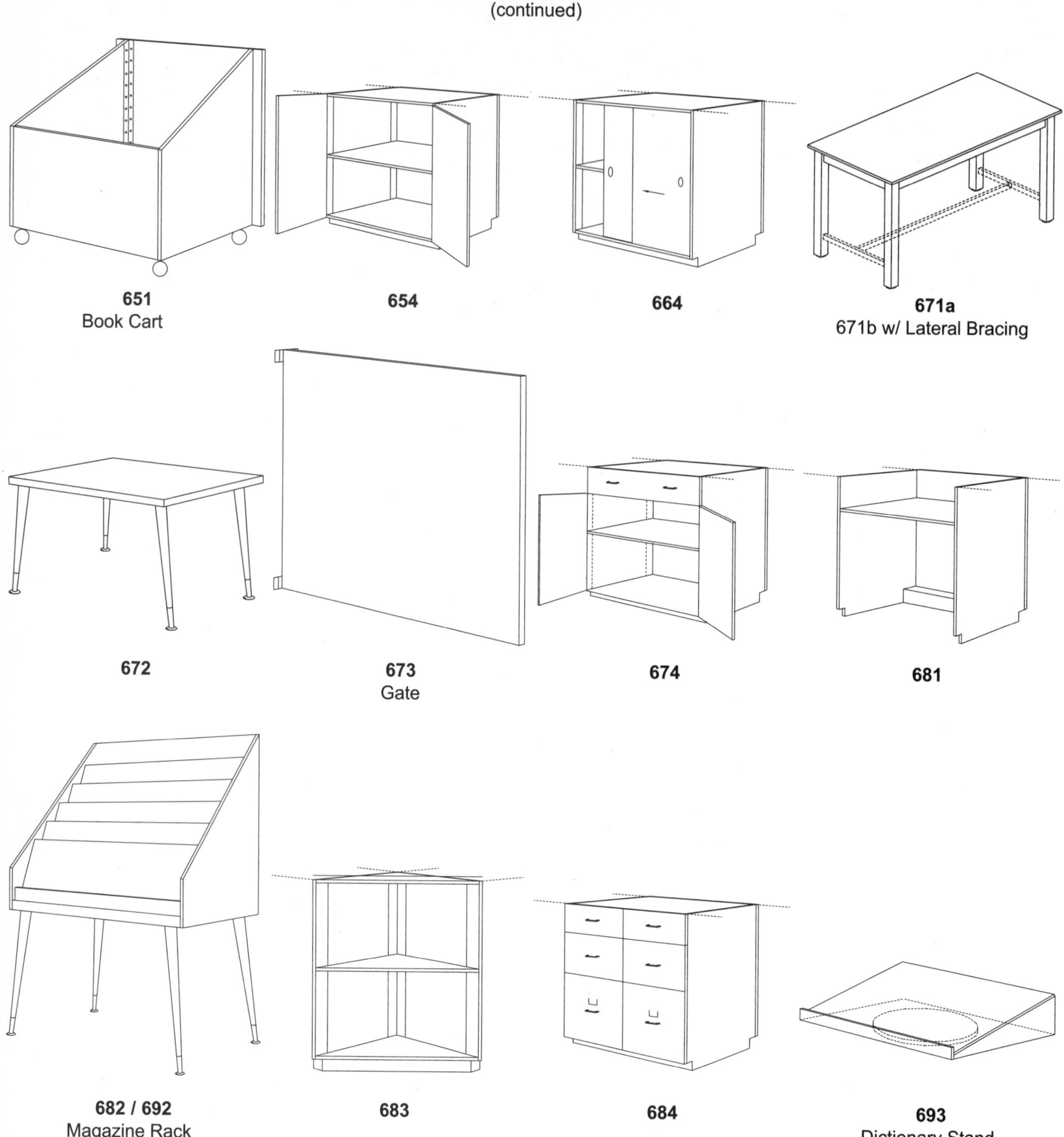

A

CASEWORK DESIGN SERIES (CDS)

(Page 17 of 20)

700 SERIES - MOVEABLE CABINETS

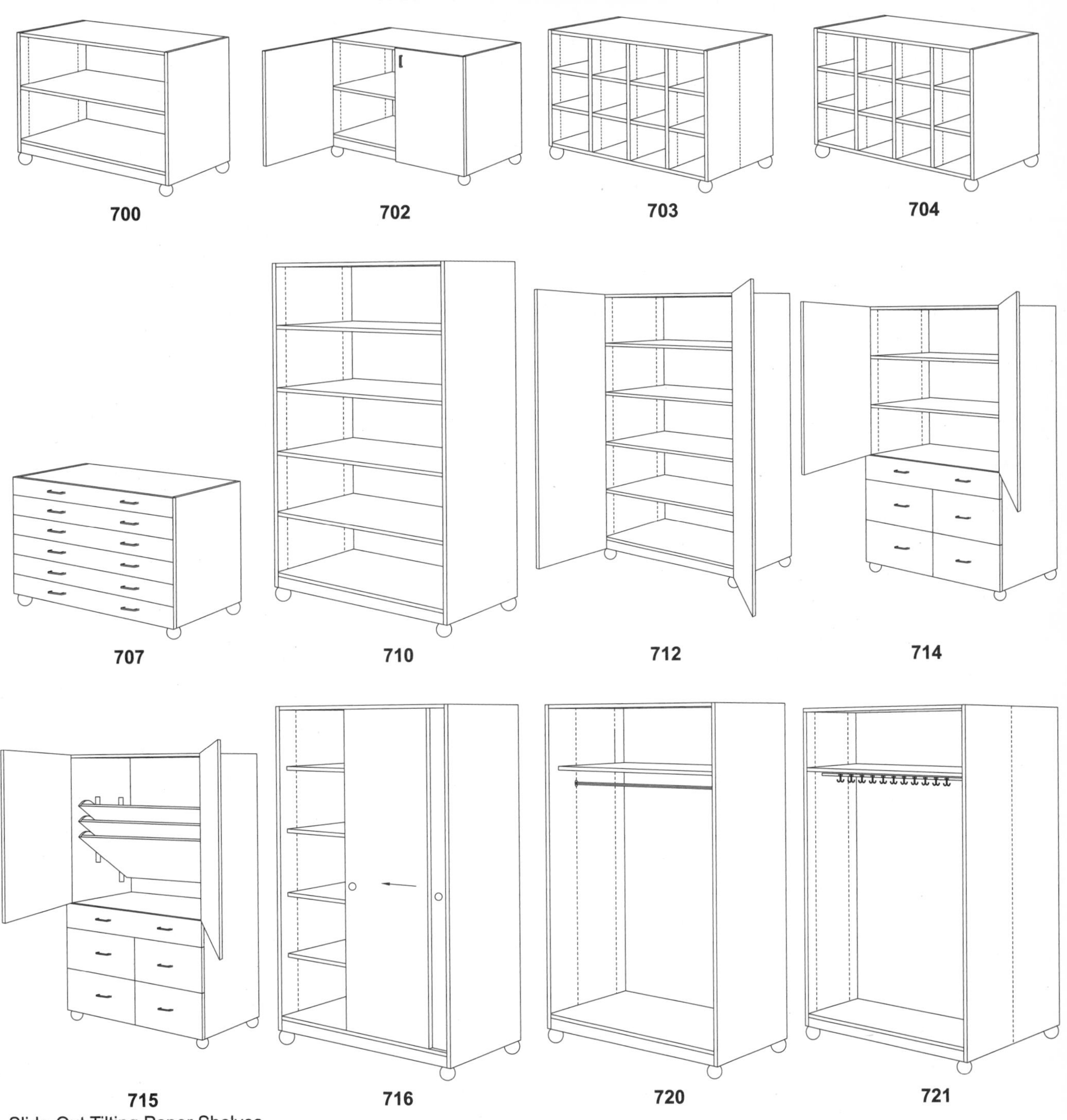

Slide-Out Tilting Paper Shelves

A

CASEWORK DESIGN SERIES (CDS)

(Page 18 of 20)

700 SERIES - MOVEABLE CABINETS
(continued)

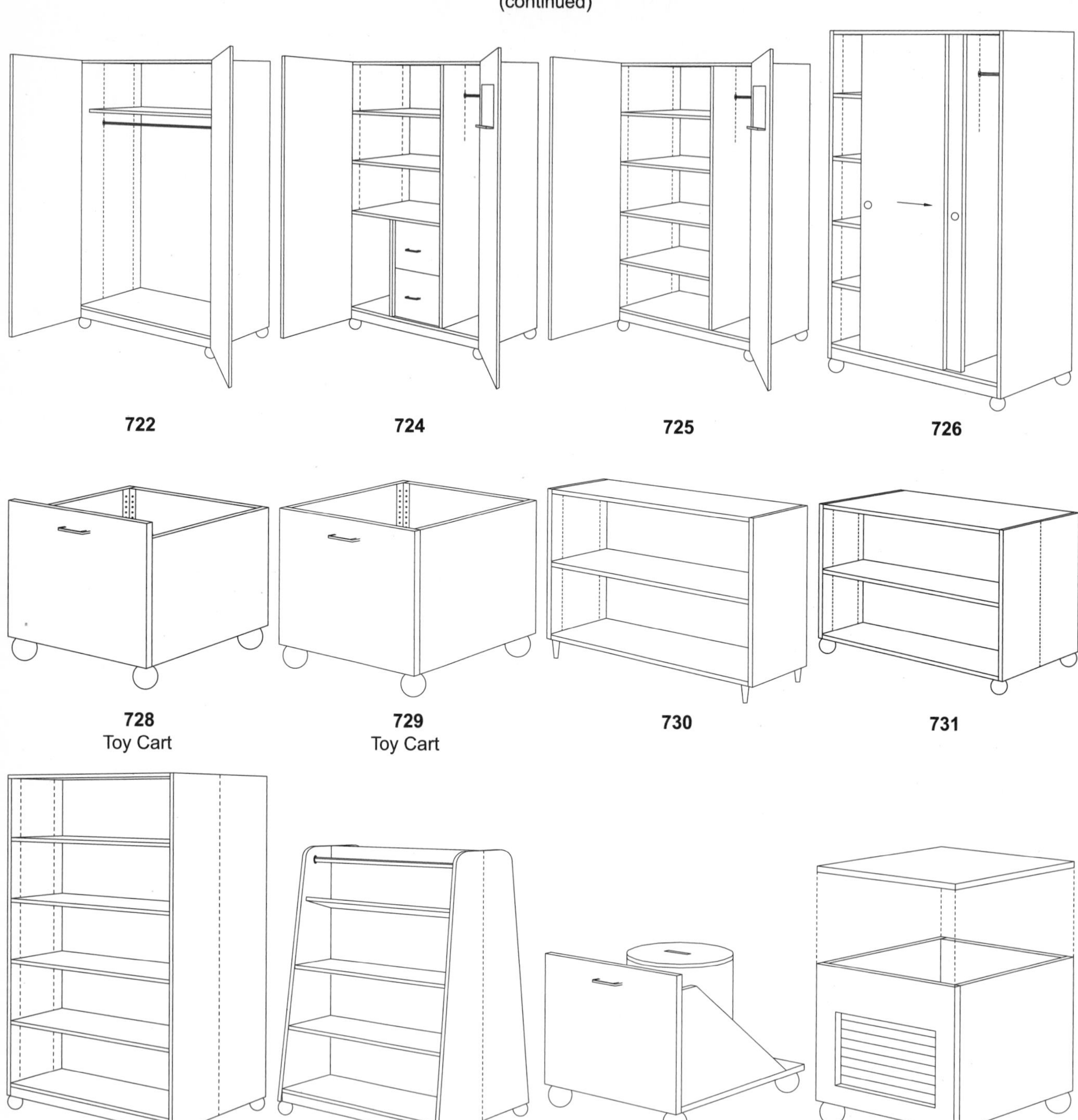

A

CASEWORK DESIGN SERIES (CDS)

(Page 19 of 20)

700 SERIES - MOVEABLE CABINETS
(continued)

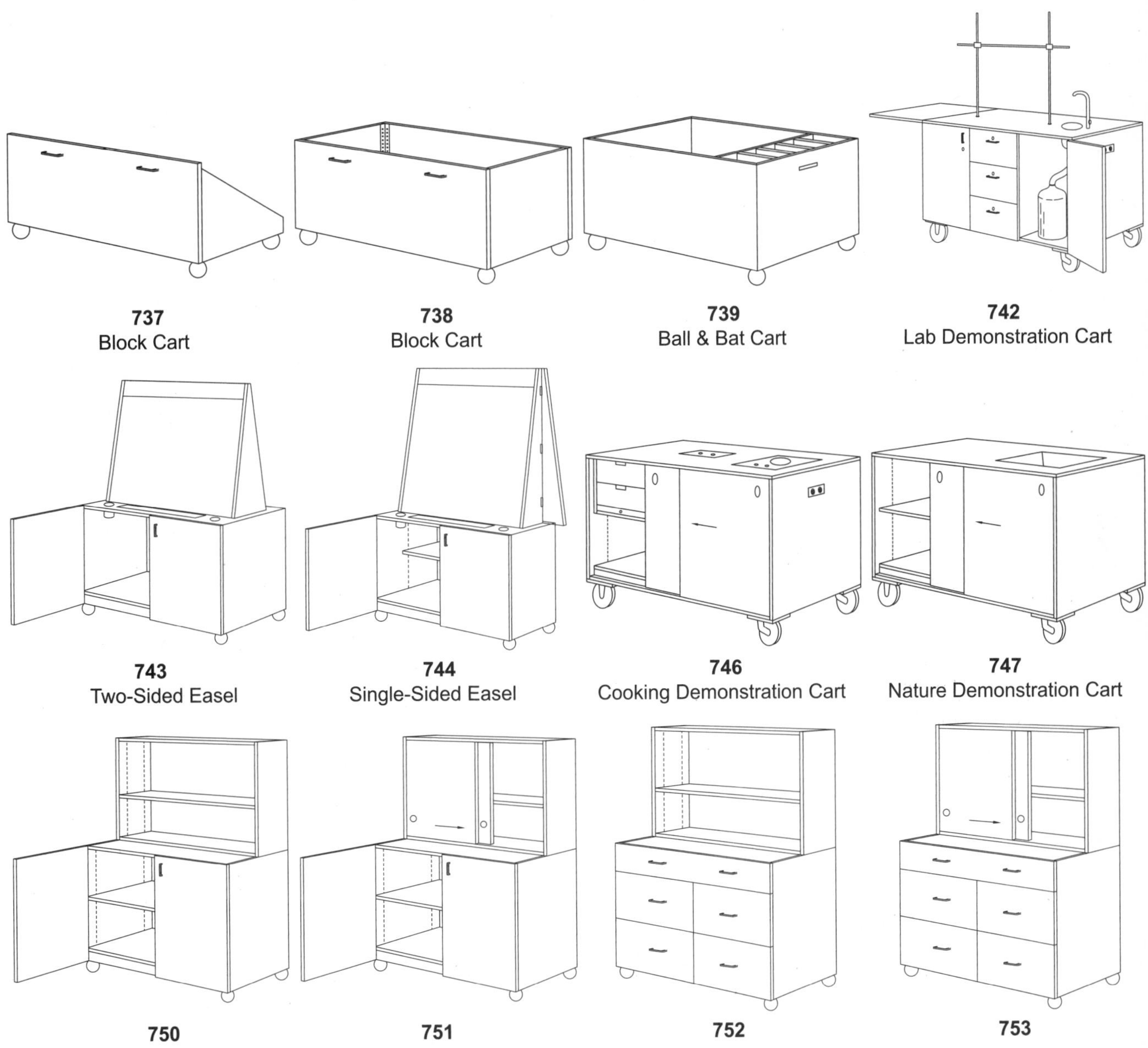

CASEWORK DESIGN SERIES (CDS)

(Page 20 of 20)

700 SERIES - MOVEABLE CABINETS
(continued)

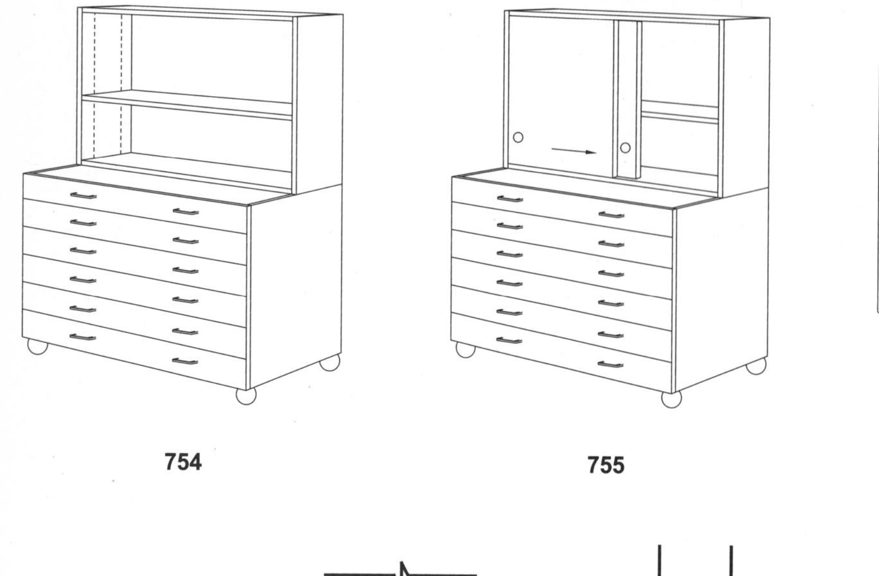

754 **755**

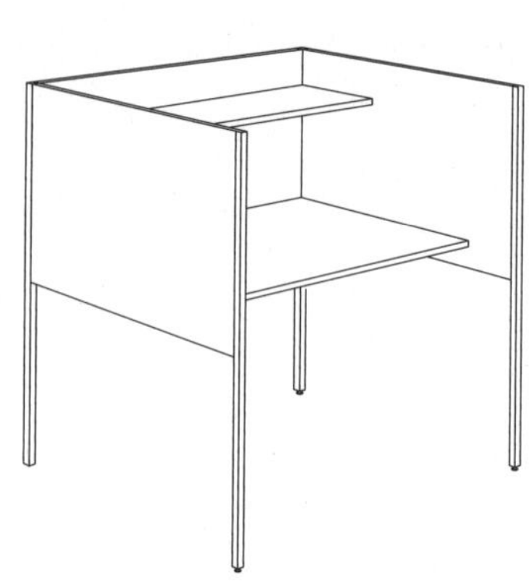

760
Study Carrel

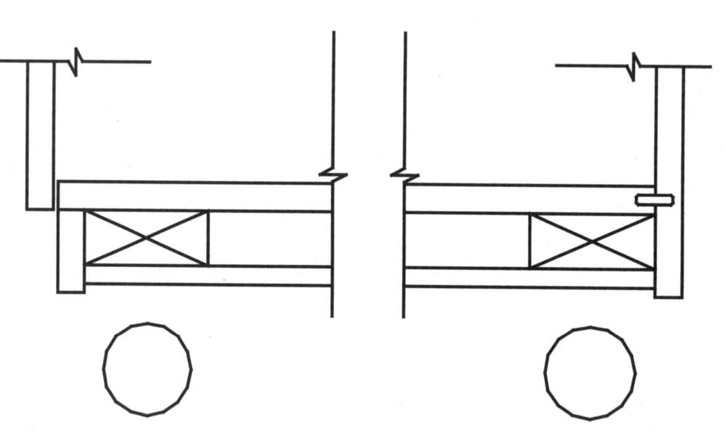

Typical Diaphragm Bottom Detail

CASEWORK INTEGRITY

(Page 1 of 5)

To evaluate the overall integrity of casework, these standards have adopted **SEFA's** (Scientific Equipment and Fixture Association) methods of testing and acceptable results as the minimum acceptable level of integrity for casework conforming to all **GRADES**.

TEST LISTING

- **Structural Integrity - Base Cabinet**
- **Concentrated Load - Base Cabinet**
- **Torsion - Base Cabinet**
- **Base Submersion**
- **Structural Integrity - Wall Cabinet**
- **Door Durability**
- **Door Impact**
- **Door Hinge**
- **Drawer Bottom Impact**
- **Drawer Support**
- **Drawer and Door Pull**
- **Drawer Rolling Load**
- **Drawer Load Cycle**
- **Shelf Load**
- **Structural Integrity - Table**

BASE CABINET TEST UNIT - Shall be 48" (1219 mm) wide, 36" (914 mm) high, and 22" (559 mm) deep with one full-width drawer (approximately one-fourth the height of the cabinet's face opening) and two doors. Cabinet shall be designed to provide unobstructed entry into the cabinet interior with the doors open and shall contain one adjustable shelf. For **LABORATORY USE,** the cabinet back shall be removable and tested with the cabinet back removed.

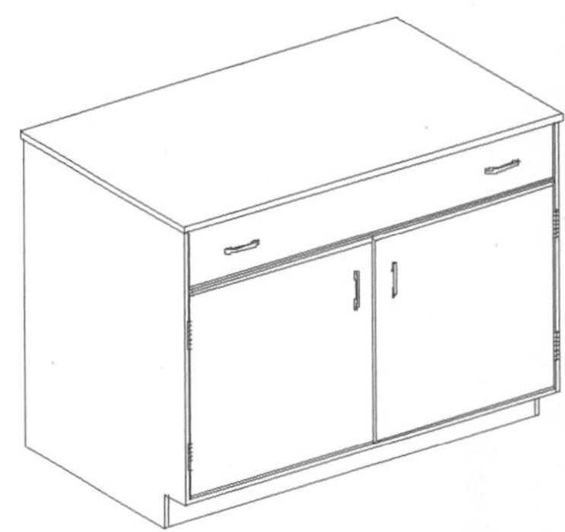

The cabinet shall be free-standing, squared, and set level. A piece of 1" (25.4 mm) thick medium-density fiberboard shall be positioned on the cabinet without glue or fasteners of any kind, of such dimensions that it will overhang the cabinet perimeter by 1" (25.4 mm), and its weight shall be included in the test as live load. Doors and the drawer should be free-moving, and the door shall latch properly.

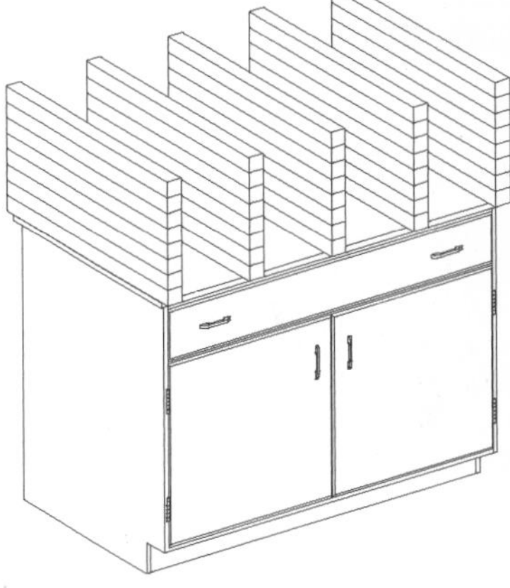

STRUCTURAL INTEGRITY TEST - BASE CABINET

CHALLENGES the load-bearing capability of a cabinet's construction.

PROCEDURE - Load the cabinet top by using 2000 lbs (907 kg) of solid steel bars stacked four high and evenly spaced for a time period of 10 minutes, then unload the cabinet.

ACCEPTANCE LEVEL - Cabinet shall have no signs of permanent failure. If used, inspect the levelers; any deformation shall not interfere with the function of the leveling system.

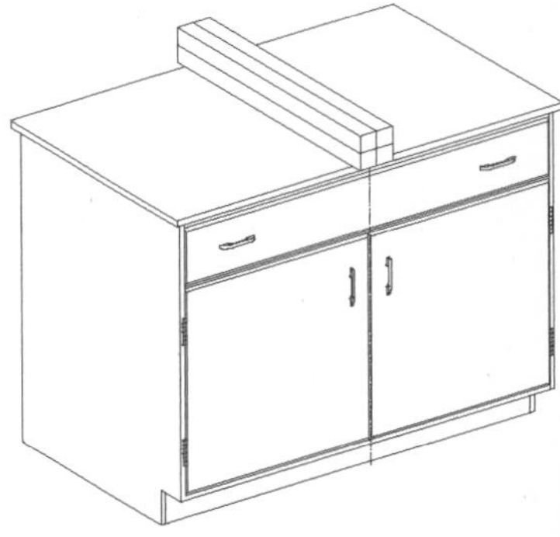

CONCENTRATED LOAD TEST - BASE CABINET

CHALLENGES the functional characteristics of the cabinet when subjected to a concentrated load on the center of the cabinet top.

PROCEDURE - Using solid weights or 10 lb (4.53kg)sand bags, apply a total of 200 lbs (90.7 kg) to the top of the cabinet along the cabinet centerline. Operate the doors and the drawer.

ACCEPTANCE LEVEL - Door and drawer operation shall be normal under condition of test load and there shall be no signs of permanent distortion to the front rail, cabinet joinery, doors, or the drawer after load is removed.

CASEWORK INTEGRITY

(Page 2 of 5)

TORSION TEST - BASE CABINET

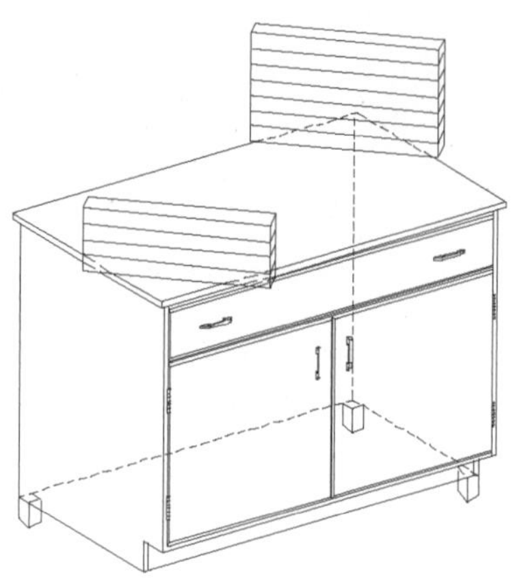

CHALLENGES the structural integrity of the cabinet construction when subjected to a torsional load.

PROCEDURE - The cabinet shall be tested in its normal upright position, raised not less than 4" (101.6 mm) off the floor, and supported on both rear corners and one front corner. The area of support under the cabinet shall be located not more than 6" (152.4 mm) in from each supported corner. Secure the cabinet diagonally from the unsupported corner with seven solid steel bars (350 lbs [159 kg]) on the top of the cabinet to prevent overturning. Apply four solid steel bars (200 lbs [90.7 kg]) to the unsupported corner for a period of 15 minutes. Remove the weight, and place the cabinet on the floor in its normal upright position. Observe the cabinet joinery. Level the cabinet and measure the face and back of the cabinet across the diagonal corners.

ACCEPTANCE LEVEL - When returned to the normal position, the operation of the cabinet shall be normal without any signs of permanent damage. The difference between the two measurements taken from measuring the diagonal corners shall be no more than 1/8" (3.2mm).

SUBMERSION TEST - BASE CABINET

(Only applicable to casework specified for laboratory use)

CHALLENGES the cabinet's resistance to standing water and is only applicable to cabinets whose bases are within 2" (50.8 mm) of the finished floor.

PROCEDURE -The material thickness along the perimeter of the cabinet shall be measured on 6" (152.4 mm) increments. Record the thickness of the material to be submerged in water. Calculate the arithmetic mean of the data taken. Place the entire test cabinet in its upright position so that the cabinet is submerged in a pan filled with 2" (50.8 mm) of water. After 4 hours, remove the unit from the water and immediately measure the thickness of the material at the same points measured initially. Calculate the new arithmetic mean. After the unit has been allowed to dry, inspect for other damage.

ACCEPTANCE LEVEL - The cabinet will show no signs of permanent deformation or deterioration. Any increase in thickness of the base material shall not exceed 4% of the initial mean measurements.

WALL CABINET TEST UNIT - Shall be 48" (1219 mm) wide, 36" (914 mm) high, and 12" (305 mm) deep with two swinging doors and one shelf, and shall be designed in such a way that when the doors are open, access to the cabinet is unobstructed.

STRUCTURAL INTEGRITY TEST - WALL CABINET

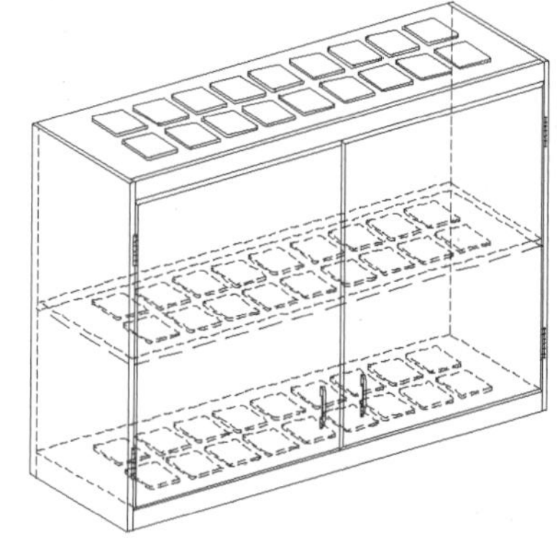

CHALLENGES the strength of the back of the wall cabinet as well as the joinery of the cabinet and the function of the doors when the wall-mounted unit is subjected to load.

PROCEDURE - Using sand or shot bags weighing 10 lbs (4.5 kg) each, load the cabinet bottom, shelf, and top uniformly to a maximum of 200 lbs (90.7 kg) each, with the maximum load not exceeding 600 lbs (272 kg).

ACCEPTANCE LEVEL - With weights in place, operate the doors through full travel to verify the normal operation of the doors. Remove the weights and operate the doors to verify normal operation. Verify that there is no significant permanent deflection of the cabinet top, cabinet back, cabinet bottom, or shelf. After the weights are removed, the cabinet shall show no permanent damage to the cabinet, cabinet bottom, or shelf.

CASEWORK INTEGRITY

(Page 3 of 5)

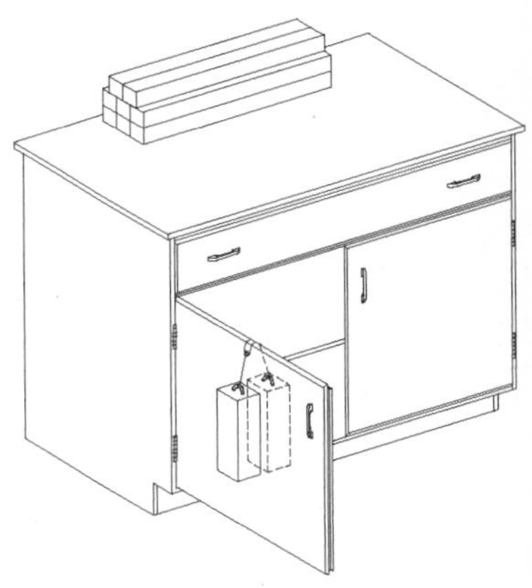

DOOR DURABILITY TEST

CHALLENGES the durability of the door and its hardware (hinge leaf, screws, etc.) to an applied load of 200 lbs (90.7 kg).

PROCEDURE - Remove the shelf for this test. With the unit and top set, add sufficient weight to the top in order to prevent overturning. With the cabinet door open 90 degrees, hang a sling made up of two 100-lb (45.4 kg) weights (shot bags or solid weights) over the top of the door at a point 12" (305 mm) out from the hinge centerline. Slowly move the door through the full cycle of the hinge, up to a 160-degree arc. Remove the weight, swing the door through its full intended range of motion, and close the door.

ACCEPTANCE LEVEL - The open door shall withstand a load of 200 lbs (90.7 kg) when applied at a point 12" (305 mm) from the hinge centerline without significant permanent distortion that will cause binding of the door or hinges or that will adversely affect the operation of the catch.

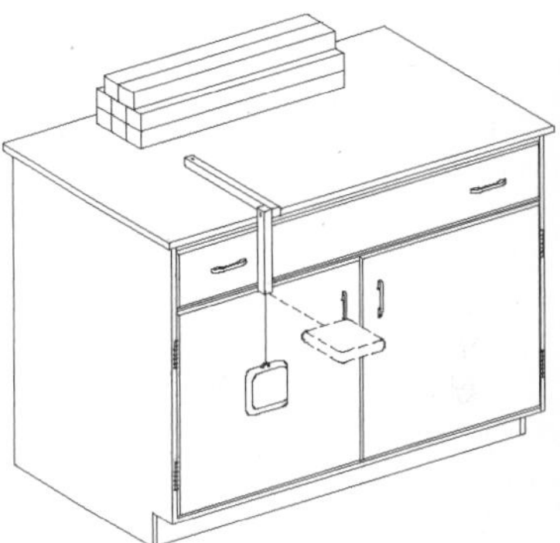

DOOR IMPACT TEST

CHALLENGES the resistance of a 240 inch-pound impact to the door face and is applicable only to cabinet doors that extend below the work surface, excluding glass doors.

PROCEDURE - With the unit and top set, add sufficient weight to the top in order to prevent overturning. A 20-lb (9 kg) sand bag shall be suspended and dropped to provide an impact of 240 inch-pounds at the center of the closed door.

ACCEPTANCE LEVEL - After the test, the door and catch shall operate normally and show no signs of permanent damage.

DOOR HINGE TEST

CHALLENGES the durability of the door hinge hardware to withstand 100,000 cycles as a reliable measure for longevity.

PROCEDURE - This test shall be in conformance to the ANSI test procedure A156.9, Grade 1, requirements for cycle testing of doors. A cycling mechanism shall swing the door 90 degrees. The door shall operate for 100,000 cycles with a speed not greater than 15 cycles per minute.

ACCEPTANCE LEVEL - The door shall operate for the full cycle period without deterioration that will significantly affect the function of the door. The door shall operate freely without binding.

DRAWER BOTTOM IMPACT TEST

CHALLENGES the resistance to impact of the drawer bottom and slide mechanism.

PROCEDURE - Open the drawer to 13" (330 mm) of travel. Drop a 10-lb (4.5 kg) sand or shot bag from a height of 24" (610 mm) into the bottom of the drawer at the center of the width of the drawer and 6" (152 mm) back from the inside face of the drawer. Remove the sand or shot bag.

ACCEPTANCE LEVEL - Operate the drawer through the full cycle. The drawer shall operate normally. Any deformation will not cause binding or interfere with the operation of the drawer.

DRAWER SUPPORT TEST

CHALLENGES the ability to support a point load given to the front of the drawer and will challenge the attachment of the drawer head to the drawer.

PROCEDURE - With the unit and top set, add sufficient weight to the top in order to prevent overturning. Open the drawer to 13" (330 mm) of travel and hang 150 lbs (68 kg) from the drawer head at the centerline of the drawer for 5 minutes. Remove the weight and operate the drawer through the full cycle.

ACCEPTANCE LEVEL - There shall be no interference with the normal operation of the drawer.

CASEWORK INTEGRITY

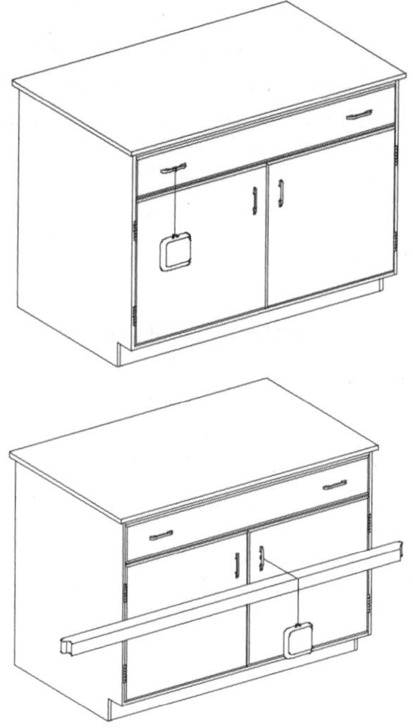

DRAWER AND DOOR PULL TEST

CHALLENGES the strength of the pull hardware.

PROCEDURE - Pulls are to be installed in accordance with the manufacturer's practice, using the specified attaching hardware and method. Block the door and the drawer closed. Using a cable pulley-and-weight assembly, apply a force of 50 lbs (22.7 kg) perpendicular to each pull. Revise the setup to hang weight from each pull.

ACCEPTANCE LEVEL - The pulls shall resist force and support weight without breakage. After completion of the test and removal of the weight, there shall be no significant permanent distortion. Some pull designs will require variations to set up apparatus. These pulls shall be tested in conformance to the applied pull forces.

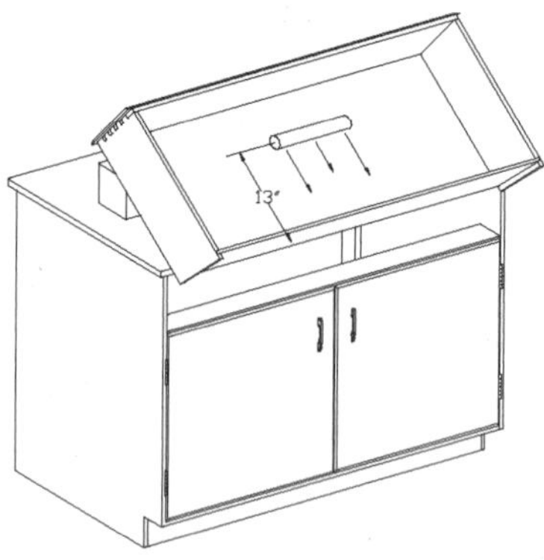

DRAWER ROLLING LOAD TEST

CHALLENGES the strength of the drawer head, bottom, and back as a result of opening and closing the drawer with a rolling load.

PROCEDURE - Position the drawer on a table at a 45-degree angle. Place a 2" (50.8 mm) diameter by 12" (305 mm) long steel rod (approximately 10 lbs [4.5 kg]) 13" (330 mm) from the target impact area (so that the rod will roll freely to impact the back) of the drawer. Subject the back to three impacts, and reverse the drawer to subject the front to three additional impacts.

ACCEPTANCE LEVEL - The drawer shall show no signs (other than minor scratches and dents) of permanent damage. All joinery shall be intact, and the drawer, when replaced in the unit, shall operate normally. Minor scratches and dents are acceptable.

SHELF TEST UNIT - Shelves, both fixed and/or adjustable, regardless of material or application, shall be tested using the following procedure. This is inclusive of shelves in wall cabinets, base cabinets, full-height cabinets, wall-mounted shelves, and free-standing shelves.

SHELF LOAD TEST

CHALLENGES the ability of a shelf and its mounting hardware to support normal loads.

PROCEDURE - The shelf shall be mounted as designed. Measure the distance from the underside of the shelf to a reference point perpendicular to the center of the shelf. Using shot or sand bags weighing 10 lbs (4.5 kg) each, uniformly load the shelf to a maximum of 200 lbs (90.7 kg). Measure the deflection on the shelf by measuring the distance to the reference point and calculating the difference between the two measurements.

ACCEPTANCE LEVEL - The maximum deflection shall be 1/180 of the span, not to exceed 1/4" (6.4 mm).

CASEWORK INTEGRITY

(Page 5 of 5)

TABLE TEST UNIT - Shall be 48" (1219 mm) long, 24" (610 mm) deep, and 36" (914 mm) high. A top of 1"-(25.4 mm) thick medium-density fiberboard shall be positioned on the table so that it will overhang the frame perimeter by 1" (25.4 mm), and its weight shall be included in the test as live load. Tables are represented by a large range of styles and designs, including free-standing tables, desks, aprons mounted between two fixed areas (such as a wall or casework), mobile tables (free-standing tables on wheels or casters), and mobile under-counter units.

TABLE STRUCTURAL INTEGRITY TEST

CHALLENGES the table components to a normal load.

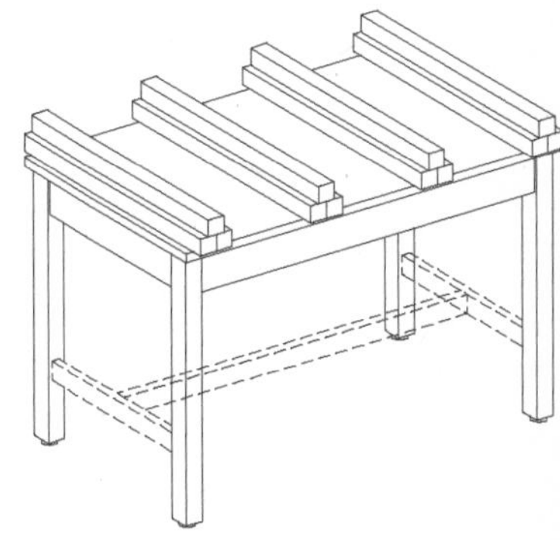

PROCEDURE - Load the table top with an evenly distributed load of no less than 300 lbs (136 kg) for mobile, 600 lbs (272 kg) for free-standing, and 2000 lbs (907 kg) for fixed. Include the weight of the working surface as a live load by using solid steel bars, each weighing 50 lbs (22.7 kg).

ACCEPTANCE LEVEL - No structural breakage shall occur, and the apron rails shall not deflect more than 1/8" (3.2 mm). In the case of a table with a drawer, the deflection of the rail shall not interfere with the function of the drawer.

A

FRACTION/DECIMAL/MILLIMETER CONVERSION TABLE

FRACTION	DECIMAL	MILLIMETER
1/64	0.01563	0.3969
1/32	0.03125	0.7938
3/64	0.04688	1.1906
1/16	0.06250	1.5875
5/64	0.07813	1.9844
3/32	0.09375	2.3813
7/64	0.10937	2.7781
1/8	**0.12500**	**3.1750**
9/64	0.14063	3.5719
5/32	0.15625	3.9688
11/64	0.17188	4.3656
3/16	0.18750	4.7625
13/64	0.20312	5.1594
7/32	0.21875	5.5563
15/64	0.23438	5.9531
1/4	**0.25000**	**6.3500**
17/64	0.26563	6.7469
9/32	0.28125	7.1438
19/64	0.29688	7.5406
5/16	0.31250	7.9375
21/64	0.32813	8.3344
11/32	0.34375	8.7313
23/64	0.35938	9.1281
3/8	**0.37500**	**9.5250**
25/64	0.39063	9.9219
13/32	0.40625	10.3188
27/64	0.42188	10.7156
7/16	0.43750	11.1125
29/64	0.45313	11.5094
15/32	0.46875	11.9063
31/64	0.48438	12.3031
1/2	**0.50000**	**12.7000**

FRACTION	DECIMAL	MILLIMETER
33/64	0.51563	13.0969
17/32	0.53125	13.4938
35/64	0.54688	13.8906
9/16	0.56250	14.2875
37/64	0.57813	14.6844
19/32	0.59375	15.0813
39/64	0.60938	15.4781
5/8	**0.62500**	**15.8750**
41/64	0.64063	16.2719
21/32	0.65625	16.6688
43/64	0.67188	17.0656
11/16	0.68750	17.4625
45/64	0.70313	17.8594
23/32	0.71875	18.2563
47/64	0.73438	18.6531
3/4	**0.75000**	**19.0500**
49/64	0.76563	19.4469
25/32	0.78125	19.8438
51/64	0.79688	20.2406
13/16	0.81250	20.6375
53/64	0.82813	21.0344
27/32	0.84375	21.4313
55/64	0.85938	21.8281
7/8	**0.87500**	**22.2250**
57/64	0.89063	22.6219
29/32	0.90625	23.0188
59/64	0.92188	23.4156
15/16	0.93750	23.8125
61/64	0.95313	24.2094
31/32	0.96875	24.6063
63/64	0.98438	25.0031
1	**1.00000**	**25.4000**

MISCELLANEOUS CONVERSION FACTORS

▼ WHEN KNOWN ▼	▼ MULTIPLY BY ▼	▼ TO FIND ▼
Inches	2.54	Centimeters
Inches	25.4	Millimeters
Square Inches	6.452	Square Centimeters
Feet	30.48	Centimeters
Square Feet	.0929	Square Meters
Yards	.9144	Meters
Square Yards	.8361	Square Meters
Miles	1.6	Kilometers
Square Miles	2.59	Square Kilometers
Acres	.4047	Hectares
Ounces	28.349527	Grams
Pounds	.4536	Kilograms
Pressure	.0703	Bar
Radius	2	Diameter
Diameter	.5	Radius
Diameter	3.1416	Circumference
Diameter	.8862	Side of an Equal Square
Circumference	.31831	Diameter
Circumference	.15915	Radius
Circumference	.2821	Side of an Equal Square
Square of Diameter	.7854	Area of Circle
Square of Diameter	3.1416	Square of Sphere of Globe
Square of Circumference	.07958	Area of Circle
Square of Radius	3.1416	Area of Circle
▲ TO FIND ▲	▲ DIVIDE BY ▲	▲ WHEN KNOWN ▲

▼ WHEN KNOWN ▼	▼ MULTIPLY BY ▼	▼ TO FIND ▼
Fahrenheit	0.556 after subtracting 32	Celsius
Celsius	1.8 and add 32	Fahrenheit

A

NOTES

Architectural Woodwork Standards

GLOSSARY

GLOSSARY

ABRASION RESISTANCE: Resistance to friction wear.

ABS: Abbreviation for "Acrylonitrile butadiene styrene," a synthetic decorative coating or edgebanding.

ACRYLIC COATING CURED WITH RADIATION PROCESS: A coating over particleboard.

ACRYLIC LACQUER: In finishing, a high-quality clear system for finishing furniture.

ADHESION: The degree of attachment between a finish step and the underlying material.

ADHESIVE: A substance capable of bonding materials together by surface attachment. It is a general term and includes all cements and glues.

ADHESIVE, COLD PRESS AND HOT PRESS: "Cold press" means no heat is applied to the press and will include the use of pinch rollers. "Hot press" means heat is applied at the time the press is in operation.

ADHESIVE, TYPE I FULLY WATERPROOF: Forms a bond that will retain practically all of its strength when occasionally subjected to a thorough wetting and drying; bond shall be of such quality that specimens will withstand shear and the two-cycle boil test specified in ANSI/HPVA HP (latest edition).

ADHESIVE, TYPE II WATER-RESISTANT: Forms a bond that will retain practically all of its strength when occasionally subjected to a thorough wetting and drying; bond shall be of such quality that specimens will withstand the three-cycle cold soak test specified in ANSI/HPVA HP (latest edition).

ADJUSTABLE SHELVES: Generally accomplished through the use of multiple holes with either plastic or metal pins to hold the shelves. Some metal or plastic shelf standards are still in use. The adjustment method is the manufacturer's option unless otherwise specified.

AGROFIBER: Refers to core products made from the residual material from a grain crop similar in composition to particleboard.

AIR DRIED: Seasoned by controlled exposure to the atmosphere, in the open or under cover, without artificial heat.

ALL-HEART: Of heartwood throughout; free of sapwood.

ANCHOR STRIPS: Used to mount woodwork; other names include nailers, mounting cleats, hanging strips, and wall cleats.

ANILINE DYE: A synthetic dye often used to impart enhanced clarity of color to wood.

APRON: For purposes of these standards, means a horizontal trim member below the countertop typically at knee spaces or open sink areas.

ARCHITECTURAL WOODWORK: Fine custom woodworking, so varied in design and complexity that it becomes difficult to define; specified for special applications and functions by design professionals and created by manufacturers. It includes all exterior and interior woodwork exposed to view in a finished building (except specialty items of flooring, shingles, exposed roof decking, ceiling, siding, structural wood trusses and rafters, and overhead-type doors), including all exposed wood, plywood, high- and low-pressure decorative laminates, and wood doors. Items made of other materials are included only if called for in the specifications. Finishing may be included if specified. Site installation may also be included if specified.

ARRIS: In architecture, a sharp edge formed by the meeting of two flat or curved surfaces.

ARTICULATED JOINT: In architectural paneling, joint details that allow for field variations.

ASSEMBLY-1: A wall-mounted method of HPDL back and end splash construction.

ASSEMBLY-2: A deck-mounted method of HPDL back and end splash construction.

BACK: The side reverse to the face of a panel, or the poorer side of a panel in any Grade of plywood calling for a face and a back.

BACK-PRIMING: A finish coating typically applied to concealed surfaces of architectural woodwork to minimize moisture penetration.

BACK PUTTY: After the glass has been face-puttied, it is turned over and putty is run into any voids that may exist between the glass and the wood parts.

BACK VENEER: The veneer placed on the semi-exposed or concealed face of a veneered panel construction to balance the construction. Also, the side reverse to the face of a panel, or the poorer side of panel in any Grade calling for a face and a back.

GLOSSARY

BACKED OUT: Wide, shallow area machined on the back surface of wide solid moldings and some frames. Allows the item to span irregular surfaces.

BACKING SHEET: Backing sheet placed on the underside of high-pressure laminate plastic tops to give dimensional stability and to minimize the absorption of moisture into the substrate.

BALANCED CONSTRUCTION: To achieve balanced construction, panels should be absolutely symmetrical from the center line; i.e., use materials on either side that contract or expand, or are moisture-permeable, at the same rate. Balanced finishing coats on the back of veneered panels are also highly recommended. Balancing sheet requirements for HPDL fabrication vary with the product. Doors and free-hanging or freestanding panels should have the same laminate on the back as on the face and be applied in the same machine direction. Tops or cabinet members, on the other hand, merely require some form of balancing material.

BALANCED-MATCH: A common term in book-matching that uses two or more leaves of uniform width on the face of a panel, wherein the two outermost leaves in a panel or face are of the same width.

BALANCING SPECIES: A species of similar density to achieve balance by equalizing the rate of moisture absorption or emission.

BALUSTER: One of the repetitive vertical members below a handrail or guardrail to provide support and a functional barrier.

BALUSTRADE: The assembly of newels, balusters, and rails that make up the safety barrier along balconies and open sides of stairways and ramps.

BANDED: Usually refers to the application of a similar material to the edge of a built-up member to cover or hide the otherwise exposed core, such as on plywood.

BARBER POLE: An effect in book-matching of veneers resulting from tight and loose sides of veneers causing different light reflections when finished.

BARK POCKET: Comparatively small area of bark around which normal wood has grown. Also a patch of bark partially or wholly enclosed in the wood. Classified by size, as with pitch pockets.

BASE BLOCK: The square block terminating a molded baseboard at a doorway; a plinth block.

BASE MOLDINGS OR BASEBOARD: Moldings used to trim the intersection of a wall or cabinet and the floor.

BASE SHOE: A small molding combined with a base molding to complete the trimming of the wall and floor intersection.

BEDDING IN PUTTY: Glazing whereby a thin layer of putty or bedding compound is placed in the glass rabbet, and the glass is inserted and pressed onto this bed.

BELT AND BASE COURSES: Horizontal flat members, either decorative or protective, on the exterior of a building. Typically, a belt course is approximately mid-range in height and a base course is at the bottom of the siding.

BEVEL: A machine angle other than a right angle; e.g., a 3-degree bevel, which is equivalent to a 1/8" (3.2 mm) drop in a 2" (50.8 mm) span. Also, in flooring or wall paneling, a V-shaped groove between strips, planks, or panels.

BEVELED EDGE: An edge of the door that forms an angle of less than 90 degrees with the wide face of the door, such as a 3-degree beveled edge.

BIRD'S EYE: Decorative figure due to small conical depressions in the outer annual rings, which appear to follow the same contour in subsequent growth rings, probably for many years. Rotary slicing cuts the depressions crosswise, exposing a series of circlets called bird's eyes.

BISCUIT SPLINE: A concealed oblong-shaped spline used to join adjacent members.

BLEACHING: The chemical process used to remove color or whiten solid wood or wood-veneered panels. This process may be used to lighten an extremely dark wood or to whiten a lighter-colored wood. Most woods do not turn completely white when bleached.

BLEEDING: When the color of one coating material migrates up through the finishing layer to the succeeding coat, imparting some of it characteristics.

BLENDING: Color change that is detectable at a distance of 6' to 8' (1829 mm to 2438 mm) but that does not detract from the overall appearance of the panel.

GLOSSARY

BLIND CORNER: The space created by abutting cabinets at an approximate 90-degree angle.

BLISTERING: The formation of bubbles on the surface of a coating, caused by trapping air or vapors beneath the surface; an area where veneer does not adhere; a figure resembling an uneven collection of rounded or blister-like bulges caused by the uneven contour of annual growth rings.

BLOCK-FREE: In finishing, when material has dried sufficiently so that finished items do not stick together when stacked.

BLOCKING: Commonly understood as the wooden support material placed within or upon gypsum board and plaster walls to support casework.

BLUEPRINT-MATCHED PANELS AND COMPONENTS: Each panel for walls and components (e.g., desk, doors) is custom-manufactured to the specific size required. All panels are balanced-matched and sequenced-matched to the adjoining panels.

BLUSHING: The whitish, cloud-like haze that occurs in fast-drying finishes, especially lacquer, when they are sprayed in very humid conditions. Blushing is most often due to moisture (water vapor) trapped in the film or to resin precipitating out of solution.

BOARD: A piece of lumber before gluing for width or thickness.

BOARD FOOT: A unit of measurement of lumber represented by a board 12" (305 mm) long, 12" (305 mm) wide, and 1" (25.4 mm) thick. Abbreviated BF, Bf, bf. When stock is less than 1" (25.4 mm) thick, it is usually calculated as if it were a full 1" (25.4 mm) thick.

BOOK-MATCH: Matching between adjacent veneer leaves on one panel face. Every other piece of veneer is turned over so that the adjacent leaves are "opened" as two pages in a book. The fibers of the wood, slanting in opposite directions in the adjacent leaves, create a characteristic light and dark effect when the surface is seen from an angle.

BOOK SIZE: The height and width of a door prior to prefitting.

BOW: A deviation, flatwise, from a straight line drawn from end to end of a piece. It is measured at the point of greatest distance from the straight line.

BOX STRINGER: See *closed stringer.*

BRASHNESS: A condition of wood characterized by a low resistance to shock and by abrupt failure across the grain without splintering.

BRATTISHING: An ornamental crest along a top of a cornice or screen, often carved with leaves and flowers.

BUCKS: Blocking used for the installation of door/window jambs and other woodwork in conjunction with metal framing and/or block walls.

BUGLE-HEAD SCREW: Is similar to countersunk; however, there is a smooth progression from the shaft to the angle of the head, similar to the bell of a bugle. This term is generally used in referencing drywall screws.

BULLNOSE: A convex, rounded shape such as the front edge of a stair step.

BURL: A figure created by abnormal growth or response to injury that forms an interwoven, contorted, or gnarly mass of dense woody tissue on the trunk or branch of the tree. Burls are usually small and characterized by eye-like markings surrounded by swirls and clusters of distorted tissues. The measurement of the burl is the average of the maximum and minimum dimensions of the burl.

BURL, BLENDING: A swirl, twist, or distortion in the grain of the wood that usually occurs near a knot or crotch but does not contain a knot and does not contain abrupt color variation.

BURL, CONSPICUOUS: A swirl, twist, or distortion in the grain of the wood that usually occurs near a knot or crotch. A conspicuous burl can often be associated with abrupt color variation and/or a cluster of small dark piths caused by a cluster of adventitious buds. Burl is also used to describe a figure in wood.

BUTCHER BLOCK: Generally refers to face-laminate hardwoods (usually Maple) forming a work surface in which the edge grain is exposed to wear.

BUTT JOINT: A joint formed by square-edged surfaces (ends, edges, faces) coming together; end butt joint, edge butt joint.

CABINET LINER: As used within these standards, shall describe 0.020" (0.5 mm) high-pressure decorative laminate (HPDL).

GLOSSARY

CANTILEVER: A projecting structure that is attached or supported at only one end, such as an extended countertop.

CANT STRIP: A triangular-shaped or beveled strip of material used to ease the transition from a horizontal plane to a vertical plane.

CASEWORK: Base and wall cabinets, display fixtures, and storage shelves. The generic term for both "boxes" and special desks, reception counters, nurses stations, and the like. Generally includes the tops and work surfaces.

CASING: Generally, a molding placed around a door frame or window frame.

CATALYZED: In finishing, an ingredient added to a basic product to provide additional performance characteristics.

CATHEDRAL GRAIN: A grain appearance characterized by a series of stacked and inverted "V" or cathedral type of springwood (early wood)/summerwood (late wood) patterns common in plain-sliced (flat-cut) veneer.

CAULK: Either the action of making a watertight or airtight seal between two adjacent surfaces by filling the area between the surfaces with a sealant, or the sealant itself.

CENTER-MATCHED: A form of book-matching that uses two or more even-numbered leaves of equal width, matched with a joint occurring in the center of the panel. A small amount of the figure is lost.

CHAIR RAIL: A decorative molding placed at a height on the wall comparable to the place where the back of a chair would impact the wall surface.

CHALK: White or other color chalk marks used by the mills for some form of identification to the mill or for marking defects for repair.

CHAMFER: To cut away the edge where two surfaces meet in an exterior angle, leaving a bevel at the junction.

CHARACTER MARK: As an element of nature, a distinctive feature in a hardwood surface produced by minerals and other elements that are absorbed as a tree grows.

CHARACTERISTICS: The natural irregularities found in wood, whether solid or veneered. Their acceptance is a function of each particular Grade.

CHATTER: Lines appearing across the panel or board at right angles to the grain, giving the appearance of one or more corrugations resulting from bad setting of sanding equipment or planing knives.

CHECKING: Cracks that appear in a finishing film due to lack of cohesion, often caused by too heavy of a coat being applied or a poor grade of finish being used. Also called cold-checking.

CHECKS: Small slits running parallel to the grain of wood, caused chiefly by strains produced in seasoning and drying.

CHICKEN TRACKS: Expression denoting scars that give the particular effect of a chicken's footprint, caused by air roots or vines. Small sections of chicken tracks appear to be part of the wood when highly dense. Chicken tracks that generally follow the grain, and are of an individual line rather than a series of lines merging on each other, are not considered to be a defect.

CHIP CORE: See *particleboard core.*

CHIP MARKS: Shallow depressions or indentations on or in the surface of dressed lumber caused by shavings or chips getting embedded in the surface during dressing.

CHIPPED GRAIN: A barely perceptible irregularity in the surface of a piece caused when particles of wood are chipped or broken below the line of cut.

CLEATS: In closet and utility shelving, the wood members furnished to support the shelf.

CLOSE GRAIN AND OPEN GRAIN: The size and distribution of the cellular structure of the wood influences the appearance and uniformity. Open-grain hardwoods, such as Elm, Oak, Ash, and Chestnut, are "ring-porous" species. These species have distinct figure and grain patterns. Close-grain hardwoods, such as Cherry, Maple, Birch, and Yellow Poplar, are "diffuse-porous" species. Most North American diffuse-porous woods have small, dense pores resulting in less distinct figure and grain. Some tropical diffuse-porous species (e.g., Mahogany) have rather large pores.

CLOSED STRINGER: In stairwork, a stringer that boxes in the treads and risers.

GLOSSARY

CLUSTERED: When a defect described in the grading rule is sufficient in number and sufficiently close together to appear to be concentrated in one area.

COFFER: A sunken, decorative panel in a ceiling.

COMB GRAIN: Comb grain is selected from rift for its exceptionally straight grain and closely spaced growth increments. Allowable medullary ray flake is limited.

COMBINATION CORE: Typically, these cores are constructed of three or five plies of veneer sandwiched between thin laminations of a composite product such as MDF, particleboard, hardboard, etc. Another variation utilizes a wafer board (randomly oriented wafers, typically Aspen) center. Typically, these cores result in a lightweight, strong, dimensionally stable panel with increased screwholding ability compared to particleboard and superior surface flatness compared to typical veneer core panels.

COMPATIBLE EDGEBAND (CE): When relating the door edge to face appearance, the edge is not the same species as the face; however, it must be similar in overall color, grain, character, and contrast to the face. See self-edge (SE).

COMPATIBLE FOR COLOR AND GRAIN: For purposes of these standards, means members shall be selected so that: a) lighter-than-average color members will not be adjacent to darker-than-average color members, and there will be no sharp contrast in color between the adjacent members, and b) the grain of adjacent members shall not vary widely or be dissimilar in grain, character, and figure.

COMPATIBLE SPECIES: For purposes of these standards, means different species which are able to exist in a harmonious combination of color and grain.

COMPONENT (OF FACE): An individual piece of veneer that is jointed to other pieces to achieve a full length and width face. The terms "piece" and "leaf" are used interchangeably with "component" in the context of face.

COMPOSITION FACE PANELS: A door face panel composed of a wood derivative.

CONCEALED SURFACE: Surface not normally visible after installation.

CONSPICUOUS: Detectable; readily visible with the naked eye when observed in normal light at a distance stated within these standards.

CONSTRUCTION, TYPE A: Frameless construction, where the front edge of the cabinet body components are simply edgebanded.

CONSTRUCTION, TYPE B: Face-frame construction, where the front edge of the cabinet body components is overlaid with a frame.

CONTACT ADHESIVE: Normally used for bonding high-pressure decorative laminates to a substrate.

CONTRACTOR: A general contractor, normally holding the legal agreement for construction of an owner's building project.

CONVERSION VARNISH: In finishing, a class of coatings that are tough and exhibit excellent resistance to household chemicals.

COPE/COPED: To cut the end of one member to match the profile of another molded member.

CORE: The material (typically, veneer, lumber, particleboard, medium-density fiberboard, or a combination of these) on which an exposed surface material (typically, veneer or HPDL) is applied.

CORE, HOLLOW: A core assembly of strips or other units of wood, wood derivative, or insulation board with intervening hollow cells or spaces that support the outer faces.

CORE, MINERAL: A fire-resistant core material generally used in wood doors requiring fire ratings of 3/4 hours or more.

CORE, SOLID: The innermost layer or section in flush door construction. Typical constructions are as follows:

> **PARTICLEBOARD** - A solid core of wood or other lignocellulose particles bonded together with a suitable binder, cured under heat, and pressed into a rigid panel in a flat-platen press.
>
> **STAVE** - A solid core of wood blocks or strips.
>
> **WOOD BLOCK, LINED** - A solid core of two parts; a central wood block core bonded to two core liners of wood or other lignocellulose materials.

GLOSSARY

CORNICE: A finishing detail along the top edge of a piece of furniture or a building.

COVE MOLDINGS: Similar to crown moldings, often smaller in size and less decorative.

CRATERING: The formation of small depressions in a finish, sometimes called fish eye. Often caused by the contamination of the finish material or the substrate with silicone, oil, or other substances.

CRAWLING: The tendency of a wet film to creep or crawl away from certain areas of a substrate. Very sharp corners or contamination is often the cause (see *cratering*).

CREEP: Is the increase in shelf deflection over time, which fluctuates with temperature, humidity, and load stress.

CROOK: A deviation, edgewise, from a straight line drawn from end to end of a piece. It is measured at the point of greatest distance from the straight line.

CROSSBANDING: A ply placed between the core and face veneer in 5-ply construction, or a ply placed between the back and face of a 3-ply skin in 7-ply construction. When the crossbanding has directional grain, it is placed at right angles to the grain of the face veneer. When used with laminate face doors, crossbanding may consist of more than one ply.

CROSS BAR: Irregularity of grain resembling a dip in the grain running at right angles, or nearly so, to the length of the veneer, caused chiefly by strains produced in seasoning.

CROSS BREAK: Separation (break) of the wood cells across the grain. Such breaks may be due to internal strains resulting from unequal longitudinal shrinkage, or to external forces.

CROSS FIGURE: A series of naturally occurring figure effects characterized by mild or dominant patterns across the grain in some faces. For example, a washboard effect occurs in fiddle-back cross figure; and cross wrinkles occur in the mottle figure.

CROSSFIRE: Figure extending across the grain, such as fiddleback, raindrop, and mottle.

CROSS GRAIN: Applied to wood in which the grain is not running lengthwise of the material in one direction. The irregularity is due to interlocked fiber, uneven annual rings, or to the intersection of branch and stem.

CROTCH: Comes from the portion of a tree just below the point where it forks into two limbs. The grain is crushed and twisted, creating a variety of plume and flame figures, often resembling a well-formed feather. The outside of the block produces a swirl figure that changes to full crotch figure as the cutting approaches the center of the block.

CROWN MOLDINGS: Used to accent ceiling intersections and traditional pediments and casework tops.

CUP: A deviation in the face of a piece from a straight line drawn from edge to edge of that piece. It is measured at the point of greatest distance from the straight line.

CURB STRINGER: See *closed stringer*.

CURING: The complete drying of a finish to the ultimate development of its properties.

CURLY: Figure that occurs when the fibers are distorted, producing a wavy or curly effect in the lumber or veneer. Primarily found in Maple or Birch.

CUSTOM GRADE: The middle or normal Grade in both material and workmanship, and intended for high-quality, conventional work.

CUSTOM SEQUENCE-MATCHED PANELS: All panels are custom manufactured to a uniform width and/or height according to each elevation. All panels are balanced-matched and sequence-matched to the adjoining panels.

DADO, BLIND, OR STOPPED JOINT: A dado that is not visible when the joint is completed.

DADO JOINT: A rectangular groove across the grain of a wood member into which the end of the joining member is inserted; also a housed joint. Variations include “mortise and tenon” and “stopped or blind dado” joints.

DART: A conventionalized arrowhead shape, often alternating with egg or other forms in moldings.

DEAD KNOTS (OPEN KNOTS): Openings where a portion of the wood substance of the knot has dropped out or where cross checks have occurred to present an opening.

GLOSSARY

DECAY: Disintegration of wood due to the action of wood-destroying fungi; "doze", "rot", and "unsound wood" mean the same as "decay."

DECORATIVE COMPOSITE PANELS: For the purposes of these standards, a thermally fused panel flat-pressed from a thermoset polyester or melamine resin-impregnated paper (minimum 30%); see *low pressure decorative laminates*.

DEFECT: Fault that detracts from the quality, appearance, or utility of the piece. Handling marks and/or grain raising due to moisture shall not be considered a defect.

DEFECT, OPEN: Open joints, knotholes, cracks, loose knots, wormholes, gaps, voids, or other openings interrupting the smooth continuity of the wood surface.

DEFLECTION: Is the measured distance from a straight line that a shelf will deflect under load.

DELAMINATION: Separation of plies or layers of wood or other materials through failure of the adhesive joint.

DESIGN PROFESSIONAL: An architect, interior designer, specification writer, or other individual qualified by virtue of education and/or training to provide services for the design of buildings, interiors, and furnishings.

DIMENSION LUMBER: Material that is precut in width and thickness to a standard size.

DISCOLORATIONS: Stains in wood substances. Common veneer stains are sap stains, blue stains, stains produced by chemical action caused by the iron in the cutting knife coming in contact with the tannic acid of the wood, and those resulting from exposure of natural wood extractives to oxygen and light, to chemical action of vat treatments or the adhesive components, and/or to the surface finish.

DISTRESSING: In finishing, either a mechanical or chemical special effect.

DISTRIBUTOR: A person or organization that provides products on a wholesale basis to a manufacturer of woodwork.

DOVETAIL, BLIND JOINT: A dovetail joint that is not visible when the joint is completed.

DOVETAIL JOINT: A joint formed by inserting a projecting wedge-shaped member (dovetail tenon) into a correspondingly shaped cut-out member (dovetail mortise); variations include the "dovetail dado" and the "blind dovetail dado."

DOWEL: Cylindrical peg or a metal screw used to strengthen a wood joint.

DOWELED JOINT: A joint using "dowels" (doweled construction); also "doweled edge joint."

DOWEL SCREW: For purposes of these standards, means a smooth shouldered screw used in lieu of wood dowels for casework joinery.

DOZE: A form of incipient decay characterized by a dull and lifeless appearance of the wood, accompanied by a loss of strength and softening of the wood substance.

DRAWINGS: Part of the project documents put in place by the owner and/or design professionals, which, in combination with written specifications, define the scope, quality assurance, requirements, submittals, field dimensions, product handling, and product specifications to the manufacturer. Shop drawings are detailed engineering drawings produced by the manufacturer for the fabrication of the architectural woodwork products, and are often submitted to the owner and/or design professional for approval.

EASED EDGES: For the vast majority of work, a sharp arris or edge is not permitted. Such edges are traditionally "eased" by lightly striking the edge with a fine abrasive. Less often, or as a design element, such edges are machined to a small radius.

EASEMENTS: Short curved segments of handrail that provide for changes in pitch, elevation, or direction.

ECONOMY GRADE: The lowest Grade in both material and workmanship, and intended for work where price outweighs quality considerations.

EDGEBAND, CONCEALED: Not more than 1/16" (1.6 mm) of the band shall show on the face or edge of the plywood or particleboard.

EDGE GRAIN (EG) OR VERTICAL GRAIN (VG): A piece or pieces sawn at approximately right angles to the annual growth rings so that the rings form an angle of 45 degrees or more with the surface of the piece.

EDGE JOINT: When the edges of boards are glued together to increase the width.

GLOSSARY

EFFECT: The final result achieved in a finished wood surface, after the application of a clearly specified series of finishing procedures (steps) have been completed. Successfully achieving a specified "effect" requires the active participation of the design professional and the woodwork finisher.

END BUTT JOINT: 1. When one end is glued to an edge or face of another board to form an angle (e.g., stiles and rails of a face frame). 2. When the end of one board is fastened to the end of another to increase its length (e.g., running trim).

END GRAIN: The grain seen in a cut made at a right angle to the direction of the fibers in a board.

END MATCH: Matching between adjacent veneer leaves on one panel face. Veneer leaves are book-matched end to end as well as side to side. Generally used for very tall panels or for projects in which only short length veneers are available.

ENGINEERED VENEER: Veneers that are first peeled, normally from Obeche or Poplar logs. The peeled veneer leaves are dyed to a specified color, then glued together in a mold to produce a large laminated block. The shape of the mold determines the final grain configuration. The block is then sliced into leaves of veneer with a designed appearance that is highly repeatable.

EQUILIBRIUM MOISTURE CONTENT: The moisture content at which wood neither gains nor loses moisture when surrounded by air at a given relative humidity and temperature.

ESCUTCHEON: A protective fitting around a keyhole; also a shield-like ornament.

EVOLUTE: A design of recurrent waves used for borders or other linear elements.

EXPIRE: To lapse or become inactive without cause of termination or cancellation.

EXPOSED EXTERIOR SURFACES: For purposes of these standards, specifically casework, means all exterior surfaces exposed to view.

EXPOSED FASTENERS: Any mechanical fastening device, filled or unfilled, that can be seen on exposed or semi-exposed surfaces of woodwork.

EXPOSED INTERIOR SURFACES: For purposes of these standards, specifically casework, means all interior surfaces exposed to view in open casework or behind transparent doors.

EXPOSED SURFACES: Surfaces normally visible after installation.

FACE: The better side of any panel in which the outer plies are of different veneer grades; also either side of a panel in which there is no difference in veneer grade of the outer plies.

FACE-FRAME CONSTRUCTION: Construction Style B.

FACE JOINT: When the faces of boards are glued together to increase the thickness.

FACE VENEER: The outermost exposed wood veneer surface of a veneered wood door, panel, or other component exposed to view when the project is completed.

FASTENER, MECHANICAL: The generic term for securing devices that are used in the fabrication and/or installation of architectural woodwork, such as dowels, dowel screws, splines, nails, screws, bolts, shot pins, etc.

FEATHERED SHEETS: The top outer sheets of some flitches, generally containing sapwood, that do not run full length.

FEW: A small number without regard to their arrangement in the panel.

FIBER: One of the long, thick-walled cells that give strength and support to hardwoods.

FIBERBOARD CORE: Manufactured from wood reduced to fine fibers mixed with binders and formed by the use of heat and pressure into panels.

FIDDLEBACK: A fine, strong, even ripple figure as frequently seen on the backs of violins. The figure is found principally in Mahogany and Maple, but occurs sometimes in other species.

FIELD: With reference to work location, meaning in the field or jobsite versus in the manufacturing plant or shop.

FIGURE: The natural pattern produced in the wood surface by annual growth rings, rays, knots, and natural deviations from the normal grain, such as interlocked and wavy grain, and irregular coloration.

GLOSSARY

FILL (PUTTY REPAIRS): A repair to an open defect, usually made with fast-drying plastic putty. Should be well-made with nonshrinking putty of a color matching the surrounding area of the wood. To be flat and level with the face and panel and to be sanded after application and drying.

FILLER: In finishing, ground inert solids specifically designed to fill pores or small cavities in wood as one step in the overall finishing process. In casework, paneling, ornamental work, stairwork, frames, and some other architectural woodwork applications, an additional piece of trim material between woodwork members or between woodwork and some other material used to create a fill or transition between the members.

FINGER JOINT: When the ends of two pieces of lumber are cut to an identically matching set. Used most commonly to increase the length of the board. A series of interlocking fingers are precision-cut on the ends of two pieces of wood that mesh together and are held rigidly in place with adhesive.

FIRE RATED: Fire-retardant particleboard is available with an Underwriters' Laboratory (UL) stamp for Class 1 fire rating (Flame Spread 20, Smoke Developed 25). Fire-rated doors are available with particleboard and mineral cores for ratings up to 1-1/2 hours. It is the responsibility of the specifier to indicate which fire-retardant classification is required for a particular product. In the absence of such a specified rating, the manufacturer may supply unrated product.

FIRE-RATED DOOR: A door that has been constructed in such a manner that when installed in an assembly and tested will pass ASTM E-152 "Fire Test of Door Assemblies," and can be rated as resisting fire for 20 minutes (1/3 hour), 30 minutes (1/2 hour), 45 minutes (3/4 hour) (C), 1 hour (B), or 1-1/2 hours (B). The door must be tested and carry an identifying label from a qualified testing and inspection agency.

FIRE-RETARDANT TREATMENT: Only a few species are treated with chemicals to reduce flammability and retard the spread of flame over the surface. This usually involves impregnation of the wood, under pressure, with salts and other chemicals. White Oak is untreatable.

FIRST-CLASS WORKMANSHIP: For architectural woodwork, the finest or highest class of workmanship for the Grade specified, and shall be free of manufacturing and natural defects covered under grading rules in these standards.

FLAKE: More properly called "fleck," and sometimes referred to as "silver grain." Created when the veneer knife of saw passes through the medullary rays, wood rays, or pith rays in such a manner as to reveal the natural wavy, pencil-like stripes in the wood.

FLAKEBOARD: See *particleboard*.

FLAMESPREAD CLASSIFICATION: The generally accepted measurement for fire rating of materials. It compares the rate of flamespread on a particular species with the rate of flame spread on untreated Red Oak.

FLAT GRAIN (FG) OR SLASH GRAIN (SG): A piece or pieces sawn approximately parallel to the annual growth rings so that all or some of the rings form an angle of less than 45 degrees with the surface of the piece.

FLAT SLICING: See *plain slicing*.

FLECK, RAY: Portion of a ray as it appears on the quartered or rift-cut surface. Fleck is often a dominant appearance feature in oak.

FLITCH: A hewn or sawn log made ready for veneer production or the actual veneer slices of one half log, kept in order, and used for the production of fine plywood panels.

FLUSH CONSTRUCTION: Cabinet construction in which the door and drawer faces are set within and flush with the body members or face frames of the cabinet with spaces between face surfaces sufficient for operating clearance.

FLUSH OVERLAY: Cabinet construction in which door and drawer faces cover the body members of the cabinet with spaces between face surfaces sufficient for operating clearance.

FLUTE: One of a series of parallel, lengthwise channels or grooves in a column, cornice molding, band, or furniture leg.

FRAMELESS CONSTRUCTION: Construction Style A.

FRETWORK: A repeated, symmetrical, interlaced design of small bars.

FURRING: Material added to a wall surface to create a true plane.

GLOSSARY

GABLE: Aside from the traditional usage referring to the end of a building, in casework the end or side of a cabinet.

GAP: An unfilled opening in a continuous surface or between adjoining surfaces.

GARLAND: A sculptural ornament, usually in relief, in the form of a swag or festoon of flowers or fruit.

GENERAL CONTRACTOR: See *contractor.*

GLAZING: In finishing, an added step for achieving color or to heighten grain appearance.

GLOSS: See *sheen.*

GLUE BLOCK: A wood block, usually triangular in cross-section, securely glued to an angular joint between two members for a greater glue bond area.

GLUE SPOTS: The discoloration or barrier to finish penetration caused by the bleedthrough or unremoved glue on an exposed or semi-exposed wood surface.

GLUED, SECURELY: The bonding of two members with an adhesive forming a tight joint with no visible delamination at the lines of application.

GRADE: Unless otherwise noted, this term means Grade rules for Economy, Custom, and/or Premium Grade.

GRADING RULES: Most hardwoods are graded utilizing the rules established by the National Hardwood Lumber Association. Softwoods, on the other hand, are graded by several grading associations. The three primary softwood grading associations are Western Wood Products Association, Southern Pine Inspection Bureau, and Redwood Inspection Service.

Although lumber must be purchased by the manufacturer according to these grading rules, these rules should not be used to specify lumber for architectural woodwork. Specify the Grade of Work for the fabricated products under these standards.

Softwood plywood is graded by the American Plywood Association (APA, The Engineered Wood Association). Grade markings are stamped on the back or edge of each sheet. Hardwood plywood is made under the standards of the Hardwood Plywood and Veneer Association (HPVA). These Grades are rarely marked on the panels.

GRAIN: The fibers in wood and their direction, size, arrangement, appearance, or quality. When severed, the annual growth rings become quite pronounced and the effect is referred to as "grain".

> **FLAT GRAIN (FG) or SLASH GRAIN (SG) -** lumber or veneer is a piece sawn or sliced approximately parallel to the annual growth rings so that some or all of the rings form an angle of less than 45 degrees with the surface of the piece.
>
> **MIXED GRAIN (MG) -**is any combination of vertical or flat grain in the same member. Vertical grain lumber or veneer is a piece sawn or sliced at approximately right angles to the annual growth rings so that the rings form an angle of 45 degrees or more with the surface of the piece.
>
> **QUARTERED GRAIN -** is a method of sawing or slicing to bring out certain figures produced by the medullary or pith rays, which are especially conspicuous in Oak. The log is flitched in several different ways to allow the cutting of the veneer in a radial direction. Rift or comb grain is lumber or veneer that is obtained by cutting at an angle of about 15 degrees off of the quartered position. Twenty-five percent (25%) of the exposed surface area of each piece of veneer may contain medullary ray flake.

GRAIN CHARACTER: A varying pattern produced by cutting through growth rings, exposing various layers. It is most pronounced in veneer cut tangentially or rotary.

GRAIN FIGURE: The pattern produced in a wood surface by annual growth rings, rays, knots, or deviations from natural grain, such as interlocked and wavy grain and irregular coloration.

GRAIN SLOPE: Expression of the angle of the grain to the long edges of the veneer component.

GRAIN SWEEP: Expression of the angle of the grain to the long edges of the veneer component over the area extending one-eighth of the length of the piece from the ends.

GROOVE: Rectangular slot of three surfaces cut parallel with the grain of the wood.

GROUND: A narrow strip of wood that serves as a guide for plaster as well as a base to which trim members are secured. Grounds are applied to rough interior openings especially doors and windows; along interior walls at the finish floor line; and wherever wainscot may be installed. The thickness of a ground is that of the combined lath and plaster, while the width varies from 1" (25.4 mm) to 3" (76.2 mm), which is often called plaster grounds (around interior or exterior openings) and base grounds (when used around base of rooms).

GLOSSARY

GROWTH RINGS: The layer of wood added by a tree in a single growing season, the markings of which contribute to the figure in finished woods.

GUM POCKETS: Well-defined openings between rings of annual growth, containing gum or evidence of prior gum accumulations.

GUM SPOTS AND STREAKS: Gum or resinous material or color spots and streaks caused by prior resin accumulations sometimes found on panel surfaces.

HAIRLINE: A thin, perceptible line showing at the joint of two pieces of wood.

HALF LAP JOINT: A joint formed by extending (lapping) the joining part of one member over the joining part of another.

HALF ROUND: A method of cutting veneers on an off-center lathe that results in modified characteristics of both rotary and plain-sliced veneers; often used in Red and White Oak.

HANDLING MARKS: Scratches, dents, blemishes, mars, or scuffs left or created by physical handling or packaging

HANDRAIL: In stairwork, the member that follows the pitch of the stair for grasping by the hand.

HAND-RUBBED FINISH: In finishing, a manual step performed to smooth, flatten, or dull the topcoat.

HARDBOARD: A generic term for a panel manufactured primarily from inter-felted lignocellulose fibers consolidated under heat and pressure in a hot press and conforming to the requirements of ANSI/AHA A 135.4 (latest edition).

HARDBOARD, TEMPERED: Hardboard that has been coated or impregnated with an oil and then baked to give it more impact resistance, hardness, rigidity, tensile strength, and more resistance to scratches and moisture. Tempered hardboard is typically smooth on both sides and may have a dark smooth finish.

HARDNESS: The property of a coating that causes it to resist denting or penetration by a hard object.

HARDWOOD: General term used to designate lumber or veneer produced from temperate zone deciduous or tropical broad-leaved trees in contrast to softwood, which is produced from trees that are usually needle-bearing or coniferous. The term does not imply hardness in its physical sense.

HEARTWOOD: The wood extending from the pith or the center of the tree to the sapwood, usually darker in color than sapwood.

HEAT-RESISTANCE TEST: A sample of the laminated plastic approximately 12" x 12" (305 x 305 mm), glued to the substrate for a minimum of 21 days shall be used for this test. A hot-air gun rayed at 14 amperes, 120 volts, with a nozzle temperature of 500° F or 274° C shall be directed at the test panel. A thermometer set at the panel surface shall register 356° F or 180° C for an exposure time of 5 minutes. The formation of a blister or void between the overlay and the substrate shall constitute a failure of the adhesive. A metal straightedge shall be used to determine if a blister has occurred. This determination shall be made within 30 seconds of heat removal.

HIGH-DENSITY OVERLAY: The standard grades of high-density overlay shall be as listed in PS 1, latest edition. The surface of the finished product shall be hard, smooth, or uniformly textured, although some evidence of underlying grain may appear. The surface shall be of such a character that further finishing by paint or protective coating is not necessary.

HIGH-PRESSURE CABINET LINER: Conforms to NEMA LD-3 (latest edition), has a color or pattern sheet to enhance its appearance, and is intended for use in cabinet interiors.

HIGH-PRESSURE DECORATIVE LAMINATE (HPDL): Laminated thermosetting decorative sheets intended for decorative purposes. The sheets consist essentially of layers of a fibrous sheet material, such as paper, impregnated with a thermosetting condensation resin and consolidation under heat and pressure. The top layers have a decorative color or a printed design. The resulting product has an attractive exposed surface that is durable and resistant to damage from abrasion and mild alkalies, acids, and solvents, meeting the requirements of the National Electrical Manufacturers Association (NEMA) LD-3 (latest edition).

HOLE: Applies to holes from any cause.

HOLES, WORM: Holes resulting from infestation by worms greater than 1/16" (1.6 mm) in diameter.

HPDL: See high-pressure decorative laminate.

HPDL COMPACT: See *solid phenolic*.

GLOSSARY

HUMIDITY: The common term for relative humidity; the amount of moisture in an atmosphere in relation to temperature.

INCONSPICUOUS: Not readily visible without careful inspection (as a measurement of natural or machining characteristics).

INDENTATIONS: Areas in the face that have been compressed as the result of residue on the platens of the hot press or handling damage through the factory.

INLAY: A surface decoration composed of small pieces of contrasting woods or other materials set flush with a wood surface.

INNER PLIES: Plies other than face or back plies in a panel construction. Crossbands and centers are classed as inner plies (see core).

INSTALLER: A person or organization that regularly engages in the practice of installing architectural woodwork.

INTARSIA: A surface decoration of wood consisting of wood inlays in contrasting colors.

INTUMESCENT COATINGS: Can be applied to the surface of flammable products to reduce flammability.

JOINT: The line of juncture between the edges or ends of two adjacent pieces of lumber or sheets of veneer, such as butt, dado (blind, stopped), dovetail, blind dovetail, finger, half lap, lock, miter (shoulder, lock, spline), mortise and tenon (blind-slotted, stub, or through), rabbet, scarf, spline, and tongue-and-groove joint.

JOINT, OPEN: Joint in which two adjacent pieces of lumber or veneer do not fit tightly together.

JOINTS TIGHT, FACTORY: Any joints or a combination of joints and/or mechanical fasteners, that are used to join two members in the shop. Distance between members shall not exceed those set forth in these standards.

JOINTS TIGHT, FIELD: Any joints or a combination of joints and/or mechanical fasteners that are used to join two members in the field. Distance between members shall not exceed those set forth in these standards.

KCPI: Stands for "knife cuts per inch"; generally used when describing the result of molded profiles or S4S materials.

KERF: The groove or notch made as a saw passes through wood; also the wood removed by the saw in parting the material.

KILN-DRIED: Lumber dried in a closed chamber in which the removal of moisture is controlled by artificial heat and usually by controlled relative humidity.

KNIFE MARKS: The imprints or markings of the machine knives on the surface of dressed lumber.

KNOCKED DOWN (KD): Unassembled, as contrasted to assembled.

KNOT: A portion of a branch/limb whose growth rings are partially or completely intergrown on the board's face, with the growth shaped so that it will retain its place in the piece. The average dimension of the exposed knot surface shall be used in determining the size.

KNOT, CONSPICUOUS PIN: Sound knots 1/4" (6.4 mm) or less in diameter containing dark centers.

KNOT HOLES: Openings produced when knots drop from the wood in which they were embedded.

KNOT, OPEN: Opening produced when a portion of the wood substance of a knot has dropped out, or where cross-checks have occurred to produce an opening.

KNOTS, SOUND TIGHT: Knots that are solid across their face and fixed by growth to retain their place.

KNOTS, SPIKE: Knots cut from 0º to 45º to the long axis of limbs.

LACQUER: A coating composed of synthetic film forming materials such as nitrocellulose, ethylcellulose, natural and synthetic resins, which are dissolved in organic solvents and are dried by solvent evaporation.

LEAF: The individual pieces of wood veneer that make up a flitch.

LIFTING: In finishing, the softening of a dried film by the solvents of a succeeding coat, which causes raising and wrinkling of the first coat.

LIGHTS (LITES): In door construction, beaded openings to receive glazing.

GLOSSARY

LINENFOLD: In decorative woodwork, a carved surface that imitates drapery.

LOCK BLOCK: A concealed block the same thickness as the door stile or core that is adjacent to the stile at a location corresponding to the lock location and into which a lock is fitted.

LOCK JOINT: Interlocking machine joint between two members.

LOCKING JOINT: There are many variations of this joint. The joint is produced when the adjoining pieces are machined into a locking form.

LONGWOOD: Wood produced from the bole or stem, from stump to first branch or fork, where the majority of wood is taken from the tree.

LOOSE SIDE: In knife-cut veneer, that side of the leaf that was in contact with the knife as the veneer was being cut, and containing cutting checks (lathe checks) because of the bending of the wood at the knife edge.

LOUVERS: In door construction, openings fitted with metal or wood louver panels.

LOW-PRESSURE DECORATIVE LAMINATE: A general term referring to a variety of melamine or polyester-enhanced surface papers and foils laminated to a core, typically referred to as melamine or polyester overlays.

LPDL: See *low-pressure decorative laminate*.

LUMBER: Pieces of wood no further manufactured than by sawing, planing, crosscutting to length, and perhaps edge-machining.

LUSTER: See *sheen*.

MACHINE BITE: A depressed cut of the machine knives at the end of a piece.

MACHINE BURN: A darkening of the wood due to overheating by machine knives or rolls when pieces are stopped in the machine.

MAHOGANY: The term "Mahogany" should not be specified without further definition. It must be understood that there are different species of Mahogany that should be specified.

African, Central and South American, or Tropical American, including Honduras Mahogany, are genuine and true Mahoganies. True or genuine Mahogany varies in color from light pink to light red; reddish brown to golden brown or yellowish tan. Some Mahogany turns darker and some lighter in color after machining.

The figure or grain in genuine Mahogany runs from plain-sliced, plain stripe to broken stripe, mottled, fiddleback, swirl, and crotches. As uniform color is not a natural characteristic of this species, if a uniform color is desired it is recommended that the finishing specification include a statement that toner or tint must be applied so that color variation shall be kept to a minimum.

Lauan White and Red, Tanguile, and other species are native to the Philippine Islands and are sometimes referred to as Philippine Mahogany. Those species are not a true Mahogany.

When only the word "Mahogany" is specified, it usually (but not always) means a true Mahogany as selected by the manufacturer unless a specific species is called for in the specifications. When Philippine Mahogany is specified, it nearly always means Lauan, Tanguile, and other natural Philippine species of wood.

MANUFACTURER: A person or organization that regularly engages in the practice of manufacturing, prefinishing, and/or installing architectural woodwork.

MARQUETRY: A mosaic of multicolored woods, sometimes interspersed with other materials, such as mother-of-pearl.

MATCHING EDGEBAND: See *self-edge*.

MATCHING WITHIN PANEL FACE: The individual leaves of veneer in a sliced flitch increase or decrease in width as the slicing progresses. Thus, if a number of panels are manufactured from a particular flitch, the number of veneer leaves per panel face will change as the flitch is utilized.

MECHANICAL FASTENER: The generic term for securing devices that are used in the fabrication and/or installation of architectural woodwork such as dowels, dowel screws, spline, nails, screws, bolts, pinks, shot pins, etc.

MEDIUM-DENSITY FIBERBOARD (MDF): See particleboard for a basic description. As used in these standards, whether as MDF alone or as core material, the MDF shall meet the requirements of ANSI A-208.2 (latest edition).

GLOSSARY

MEDIUM-DENSITY OVERLAY (MDO): A panel product particularly well-suited for opaque (paint) finishes; most versions are highly weather-resistant.

MEDIUM-DENSITY PARTICLEBOARD: Generally refers to particleboard manufactured to an approximate density of 45 lbs per cubic foot (20.41 kg per cubic cm); the type of particleboard used for architectural woodworking substrates.

MEDULLARY RAY: Extends radially from the center of a log toward the outer circumference. These rays serve primarily to store food and transport it horizontally. These rays vary in height from a few cells in some species to an excess of 4" (102 mm) in Oaks. In Oak, it produces the flake effect common to quarter-sawn lumber.

MELAMINE: Resin-impregnated paper used in decorative composite panel products (see *thermally fused decorative laminate panel*).

MEMBER: An individual piece of solid stock or plywood that forms an item of woodwork.

METAMERISM: An apparent change in color when exposed to differing wavelengths of light; the human perception of color.

MILL RUN: Molding run to pattern only, not assembled, machined for assembly, or cut to length. The terms "material only" and "loose and long" mean the same as "mill run."

MILLWORK: See *architectural woodwork*.

MINERAL STREAK: An olive to greenish-black or brown discoloration of undetermined cause in hardwoods.

MIRROR POLISH FINISH: In finishing, several steps of wet sanding, mechanical buffing, and polishing.

MISMATCH: An uneven fit in worked lumber when adjoining pieces do not meet tightly at all points of contact or when the surfaces of adjoining pieces are not in the same plane.

MITERFOLD: Made from a single panel in one machining process; includes placement of tape, machining, application of adhesive, folding, glue, clamp, and clean.

MITER JOINT: The joining of two members at an angle that bisects the angle of junction.

MITER, LOCK JOINT: A miter joint employing a tongue and groove to further strengthen it.

MITER, SHOULDER JOINT: Any type of miter joint that presents a shoulder, such as a lock miter or a splined miter.

MODULAR CASEWORK: Casework produced from a manufacturer's standard details adapted to use for a particular project.

MODULUS OF ELASTICITY: Deformations produced by low stress are completely recoverable after loads are removed. Plastic deformation or failure occurs when loaded to higher stress levels.

MOISTURE CONTENT: The weight of the water in the wood expressed in percentage of the weight of the oven-dry wood.

MOLDED EDGE: Edge of piece machined to any profile other than a square or eased edge.

MOLDING: A decorative strip, usually having a curved or projecting surface. Some common moldings include:

> **ANGLE BEAD -** A vertical molding that protects or decorates the projecting angle of a wall or partition.
>
> **ASTRAGAL -** A molding with a half-round profile; also the strip covering the junction of a pair of doors.
>
> **BACKBAND -** The outer molding element of a door window casing.
>
> **BAGUETTE -** A simple, narrow, convex molding.
>
> **BASE CAP -** A molding used to trim a baseboard.
>
> **BEAD -** A narrow half-round molding that is continuous or divided into bead-like forms.
>
> **BEAD AND REEL -** A molding with a profile of half a circle or more, in which beads form alternate design forms seen edge-on.
>
> **BILLET -** A molding made of several bands of raised cylinders or rectangular segments.
>
> **BOLECTION MOLDING -** Unusually designed with large and broad convex projection.

G

GLOSSARY

CABLE MOLDING - Carved spirally to resemble a rope or cable.

CHAIR RAIL - Applied along a wall for protection or as a design element between wall treatments, such as paneling, wallpaper, or paint.

COVE MOLDING - Features a quarter round channel along the face and a square back.

CROWN MOLDING - The decorative molding that conceals the joint between the wall and ceiling.

CYMA MOLDING - Has an S-shaped profile.

DENTIL MOLDING - Composed of a series of small rectangular blocks.

DOVETAIL MOLDING - Carved with interlocked triangles.

EGG AND ANCHOR MOLDING - Composed of alternating oval and anchor-like shapes.

EGG AND DART MOLDING - Composed of alternating egg and arrowhead shapes.

EGG AND TONGUE MOLDING - Composed of alternating egg and pointed elements.

FILLET - A thin molding used to separate or decorate larger moldings.

LATTICE - A thin, flat molding, rectangular in cross-section, used to build decorative screening or conceal joinery.

LEAF AND DART MOLDING - Composed of alternating leaf-like and arrowhead shapes.

OGEE - A molding with reverse-curved face that is concave above and convex below.

PEARL MOLDING - Carved to imitate a string of pearls.

PELLET MOLDING - Carved in a series of discs, with the flat surfaces facing the viewer.

QUARTER ROUND - A molding with a convex, quarter-cylindrical shape.

REED, REEDING - A molding made of closely spaced, parallel, half-round convex profiles.

ROPE MOLDING - Carved to imitate the twisted strands of cordage.

ROUNDEL - One of the series of elements in a bead molding.

SCOTIA MOLD - A deep concave molding, more than a quarter round in section, also called a “cove mold.”

SHOE MOLDING - A small molding with a concave channel and a square back.

THUMB MOLDING - A convex molding with a flattened cross-section.

MORTISE AND TENON, BLIND JOINT: A mortise and tenon joint in which the tenon does not extend through the mortise and does not remain visible once the joint is completed; also “blind tenoned.”

MORTISE AND TENON, SLOTTED JOINT: A mortise and tenon right-angle joint in which the tenon is visible on two edges once the joint is completed.

MORTISE AND TENON, STUB JOINT: A short tenon inserted in a plow or groove.

MORTISE AND TENON, THROUGH JOINT: A mortise and tenon joint in which the inserted tenon extends completely through the mortise and the end of the tenon remains visible once the joint is completed.

MOTTLE: Broken wavy patches across the face of the wood that give the impression of an uneven, although smooth, surface caused by a twisted interwoven grain with irregular cross figure, which is the mottle. The effect is due to reflected light on the uneven arrangement of the fibers. Other terms used to describe variations include bee’s wing, fiddle, peacock, plum, ram, block, or stop mottle.

NAILED: Members secured together with nails, including power-driven nails or staples. On exposed surfaces, staples and tee nails shall run parallel to the grain.

NATURAL: When referring to color and matching, veneers containing any amount of sapwood and/or heartwood.

GLOSSARY

NEWEL POST: In stairwork, an upright post that supports or receives the handrail at critical points of the stair, such as starting, landing, or top; the central vertical support of a spiral staircase.

NGR STAINS: Refers to non-grain-raising stains.

NOMINAL: The average sizes (width and thickness) of lumber just out of the sawmill before being processed into usable board stock. Always larger than "finished" dimensions. Also, a term that designates a stated dimension as being approximate and subject to allowances for variation.

NOSING: A rounded convex edge, as on a stair step.

OCCASIONAL: A small number of characteristics that are arranged somewhat diversely within the panel face.

OPAQUE FINISH: A paint or pigmented stain finish that hides the natural characteristics and color of the grain of the wood surface and is not transparent.

OPEN GRAIN AND CLOSE GRAIN: The size and distribution of the cellular structure of the wood influences the appearance and uniformity. Open-grain hardwoods, such as Elm, Oak, Ash, and Chestnut are "ring-porous" species. These species have distinct figure and grain patterns. Close-grain hardwoods, such as Cherry, Maple, Birch, and Yellow Poplar, are "diffuse-porous" species. Most North American diffuse-porous woods have small, dense pores resulting in less distinct figure and grain. Some tropical diffuse-porous species (e.g., Mahogany) have rather large pores.

ORANGE PEEL: The description of a coating that does not flow out smoothly, exhibiting the texture of an orange.

ORIENTED STRAND BOARD (OSB): is an engineered wood product formed by layering strands (flakes) of wood in specific orientations. In appearance it may have a rough and variegated surface with the individual strips lying unevenly across each other.

OVERLAP: A condition where the veneers comprising plywood are so misplaced that one piece overlaps the other and does not make a smooth joint.

OVERLAY: To superimpose or laminate a wood veneer of various species or a decorative item, such as melamine, polyester, or high-pressure decorative laminate to one or both sides of a given substrate, such as plywood, particleboard, or medium-density fiberboard.

OVERSPRAY: The dry, pebble-like surface caused when the sprayed finish begins to dry in the air before it hits the surface.

PANEL MATCH: Establishes the leaf layout in each individual panel.

PANELWORK: Includes stile-and-rail paneling and all kinds of flush-panel work made of lumber, panel products, and high-pressure decorative laminates.

PARTICLEBOARD: A generic term for a panel manufactured from lignocellulosic materials (usually wood), primarily in the form of discrete pieces of particles, as distinguished from fibers, combined with a synthetic resin or other suitable binder, and bonded together under heat and pressure in a hot-press by a process in which the entire interparticle bond is created by the added binder, and to which other materials may have been added during manufacturing to improve certain properties. Particles are further defined by the method of pressing. When pressure is applied in the direction perpendicular to the faces as in a conventional multi-platen hot-press, they are defined as flat-platen pressed; and when the applied pressure is parallel to the faces, they are defined as extruded.

PARTICLEBOARD, FIRE-RETARDANT TREATED: Particleboard treated to obtain Class I or Class II fire rating.

PATCH: A repair made by inserting and securely gluing a sound piece of wood of the same species in place of a defect that has been removed. The edges shall be cut clean and sharp and fit tight with no voids. "Boat" patches are oval-shaped with sides tapering in each direction to a point or to a small rounded end; "router" patches have parallel sides and rounded ends; "sled" patches are rectangular with feathered ends.

PECKY: Pockets of disintegrated wood caused by localized decay or wood areas with abrupt color change related to localized injury such as bird peck. Peck is sometimes considered a decorative effect, such as bird peck in Pecan and Hickory or pecky in Cypress.

PEDIMENT: A triangular ornament above a cornice.

PENETRATING OIL: In finishing, an oil-based material designed to penetrate the wood.

GLOSSARY

PERFORMANCE-BASED: With reference to these standards, and in contrast to prescriptive-based, refers to the lack of dictated or specifically required technical processes in lieu of a concept that allows innovation as long as the required outcomes are achieved.

PHENOL FORMALDEHYDE RESIN: Typically used for exterior-type construction. Plywood and doors bonded with this adhesive have a high resistance to moisture. The most common types require high temperatures during pressing to aid in the curing process.

PHOTODEGRADATION: The effect on the appearance of exposed wood faces caused by exposure to both sun and artificial light sources. Obviously, if an entire face is exposed to a light source, it will photodegrade somewhat uniformly and hardly be noticeable; whereas partially exposed surfaces or surfaces with shadow lines may show nonuniform photodegradation. Some woods, such as American Cherry and Walnut, are more susceptible than others to photodegradation.

PILASTER: A fluted or carved, flat, decorative column attached to a building or furniture.

PIN HOLES: All circular or nearly circular holes in the exposed surface.

PITCH: An accumulation of resin that occurs in separations in the wood or in the wood cells themselves.

PITCH POCKET: A well-defined opening between the annual growth rings that contains pitch.

PITCH STREAK: A well-defined accumulation of pitch in the wood cells in a more or less regular streak.

PITH: A small, soft core occurring in the center of the log.

PLAIN-SAWN: A hardwood figure developed by sawing a log lengthwise at a tangent to the annual growth rings. It appears as U-shaped or straight markings in the board's face.

PLAIN SLICING: Most commonly used for hardwood plywood. The log is cut in half, and one half is placed onto a carriage and moved up and down past a fixed knife to produce the veneers. Veneer is sliced parallel to the pith of the log and approximately tangent to the growth rings to achieve flat-cut veneer. Each piece is generally placed in a stack and kept in order. One half log, sliced this way, is called a "flitch."

PLANK: A board, usually between 1-1/2" to 3-1/2" (38.1 to 88.9 mm) thick and 6" (152 mm) or more wide, laid with its wide dimension horizontal and used as a bearing surface.

PLASTIC BACKING SHEET: A thin sheet, usually phenolic, applied under pressure to the back of a laminated plastic panel to achieve balance by equalizing the rate of moisture absorption or emission.

PLASTIC LAMINATE FINISH: See *high-pressure decorative laminate.*

PLEASING-MATCHED: A face containing components that provide a pleasing overall appearance. The grain of the various components need not be matched at the joints, but will not be widely dissimilar in character and/or figure. Sharp color contrasts at the joints of the components are not permitted. Members are selected so that lighter-than-average color members are not placed adjacent to darker-than-average members.

PLOW: A rectangular groove or slot of three surfaces cut parallel to the grain of a wood member, in contrast to a dado, which is cut across the grain.

PLY: A single sheet of veneer or several strips laid with adjoining edges that may or may not be glued, which forms one veneer laminate in a glued panel (see layer). In some constructions, a ply is used to refer to other wood components such as particleboard or MDF.

PLYWOOD: A panel composed of a crossbanded assembly of layers or plies of veneer, or veneers in combination with a lumber core or particleboard core, that are joined with an adhesive. Except for special constructions, the grain of alternate plies is always approximately at right angles, and the thickness and species on either side of the core are identical for balanced effect. An odd number of plies is always used.

POLYESTER: In finishing, a very high solids-content plastic coating, leaving a deep, wet look.

POLYURETHANE: A very hard and wear-resistant finish, which is very difficult to repair. Most commonly used as a two-component system, comprising multifunctional isocyanate or moisture-cured urethane, with a higher solids content than lacquers. Single component (excluding moisture-cured) products are usually composed of precatalyzed urethane.

POMELE: A trade term for a small blister figure in Mahogany and Sapele.

GLOSSARY

PREMANUFACTURED SETS: Each panel, usually 4' x 8' (1219 mm x 2438 mm) or 4' x 10' (1219 mm x 3048 mm), is part of a sequenced set of balanced-matched, premanufactured panels to be installed full width with the sequencing maintained. The panel's balanced-match becomes unequal at the start, end, and any other opening or change in plane when trimmed.

PREMIUM GRADE: The highest Grade available in both material and workmanship intended for the finest work. This is naturally the most expensive Grade.

PREQUALIFICATION: Prior review and approval of a bidder's qualifications to perform specified work.

PRESCRIPTIVE-BASED: With reference to these standards, and in contrast to performance-based, refers to the manner in which regulations are expressed that dictate the technical processes by which the required outcomes are to be achieved.

PRESERVATIVE: (n.) A treating solution that prevents decay in wood; (adj.) having the ability to preserve wood by inhibiting the growth of decay fungi.

PROFILE: A trim that has a shaped detail along one or more edges. Eased edges are included in profiles. Ends or faces may also have profiles.

PUTTIED: See *fill*.

PUTTY SMEAR: Where putty has been incorrectly placed in a surrounding area of wood as well as into the open defect that the putty was intended to repair. Putty smears are not allowed where the expression "well-puttied" is used.

PVC: Abbreviation for "polyvinyl chloride," a synthetic decorative coating or edgebanding.

PVC EDGING: A polyvinyl chloride edging, usually in seamless rolls, typically applied by edgebanding machines using hot-melt adhesives. Available in a variety of solid colors, patterns, and wood-grain designs, in both textured and smooth finish.

QUARTER-SAWN (QUARTERED LUMBER): Refers to solid lumber cutting. Available in limited amounts in certain species. Yields straight-grain, narrow boards with "flake" or figure in some species (particularly in Red and White Oak).

QUARTER SLICING: Produces a striped grain pattern, straight in some woods, varied in others. Veneer produced by cutting in a radial direction to the pith to the extent that fleck or ray flake is produced, and the amount may be unlimited. In some woods, principally Oak, fleck results from cutting through the radial medullary rays.

QUARTERS: The commercial thicknesses usually associated with the purchase or specification of hardwoods, such as "five quarter" (5/4's of 1"), meaning 1-1/4" (31.8 mm) in thickness.

QUILTED: A highly figured pattern of folds or waves, somewhat resembling the appearance of rectangular blisters.

QUIRK: For purpose of these standards, means a sharp incision in moldings or trim that can hide the use of a mechanical fastener.

RABBET: Rectangular cut on the edge of a member; a "rabbet" has two surfaces, and a "plow" has three.

RABBET JOINT: A groove cut across the grain of the face of a member at an edge or end to receive the edge or end thickness of another member.

RAIL: The cross or horizontal pieces of a stile-and-rail assembly or the cross pieces of the core assembly of a wood flush door or panel.

RAILING: In stairwork, the member that follows the pitch of the stair for grasping by the hand.

RAISED GRAIN: Roughened condition of the surface of dressed lumber on which hard summerwood is raised above the softer springwood, but is not torn loose from it.

RAISED PANEL: Traditional door or wall panel with a bevel edge captured in a stile-and-rail frame.

RANDOM MATCH: Matching between adjacent veneer leaves on one panel face. Random selection in the arrangement of veneer leaves from one or more flitches producing a deliberate mismatch between the pieces of veneer.

RAY: One of the radial structures in a tree that stores nourishment and transports it horizontally through the trunk. In quarter-sawn Oak, the rays form a figure called fleck.

RED/BROWN: When referring to color and matching, veneers containing all heartwood, ranging in color from light to dark.

GLOSSARY

RED BIRCH: The heartwood of the Yellow Birch tree.

REGLET: Defines a flat, narrow molding, used chiefly to separate the parts or members of compartments or panels from one another.

RELIEF: Defined as the difference in elevation between the high and the low parts of an area or where a form is raised (or alternatively lowered) from a flattened background without being disconnected from it.

REPAIRS, BLENDING: Wood or filler insertions similar in color to adjacent wood so as to blend well.

RESORCINOL FORMALDEHYDE RESIN: For woodworking, formulated into highly water-resistant glues, usually purple in color and difficult to work.

RETURN: Continuation in a different direction of a molding or projection, usually right angles.

REVEAL OVERLAY: Cabinet construction in which the door and drawer faces partially cover the body members or face frames of the cabinet with spaces between face surfaces creating decorative reveals.

RIFT CUT: Usually referring to veneers, but can be applied to solid lumber (usually as rift-sawn); this method is similar to quarter slicing, but accentuates the vertical grain and minimizes the fleck of the finished material. Veneer produced by cutting at a slight right angle to the radial to produce a quartered appearance.

RING, ANNUAL GROWTH: The growth layer put on in a growth year.

RISER: The board at the back of a tread that "rises" to the bottom of the next tread above. In an "open riser" stair, this element is left out, and the gap between the treads is open. Open-riser stairs are prohibited by code in many circumstances.

ROOM MATCH: Refers to the matching of panel faces within a room.

ROTARY SLICING: Most common method for preparing veneers for softwood plywood. The log is placed in a lathe and rotated against a stationary knife. This produces a more-or-less continuous sheet of veneer, similar to pulling a long sheet off a roll of paper towels.

RUBBER MARKS: A raised or hollowed cross-grain cut caused by a sliver between the knife and pressure bar when slicing veneers.

RUNNING MATCH: Each panel face is assembled from as many veneer leaves as necessary. Any portion left over from one panel may be used to start the next.

RUNNING TRIM: Generally combined in the term "standing and running trim" and refers to random, longer length trims delivered to the jobsite (e.g., baseboard, chair rail, crown molding).

RUNS: The result of spraying a heavier coat on a vertical, or nearly vertical, surface than the viscosity of the finish will allow to hold without movement; when in close multiples are also called "sags".

RUPTURED GRAIN: A break or breaks in the grain or between springwood and summerwood caused or aggravated by excessive pressure on the wood by seasoning, manufacturing, or natural processes. Ruptured grain appears as a single or a series of distinct separations in the wood, such as when springwood is crushed, leaving the summerwood to separate in one or more growth increments.

S4S: Means "Surfaced Four Sides", and generally refers to the process of reducing nominal-sized rough lumber to finished widths and thicknesses.

SAGS: In finishing, partial slipping of finish film creating a "curtain" effect.

SAND-TROUGH: A defect on the exposed visible surface, such as depressions, bumps, marks, or core usually caused by thin veneers or over-sanding.

SANDED, CROSS: Sanded across, rather than parallel to, the grain of a wood surface.

SANDED, MACHINE: Sanded by a drum or equivalent sander to remove knife or machine marks. Handling marks and/or grain raising due to moisture shall not be considered a defect.

GLOSSARY

SANDED, SMOOTHLY: Sanded sufficiently smooth so that all machining, machine-sanding marks, cross-sanding, and other sanding imperfections will be concealed by the painter's applied finish work. The proper sanding grit varies with the species of material; however, it generally runs in the 120- to 150-grit range. Handling marks and/or grain raising due to moisture shall not be considered a defect.

SAPWOOD: The outer layers, or living wood, that is between the bark and the heartwood of a tree. Sapwood is generally lighter in color than heartwood.

SASH: A single assembly of stiles and rails into a frame for holding glass, with or without dividing bars, to fill a given opening. It may be either open or glazed.

SCARF JOINT: When the ends of two boards are cut on an angle and glued together to increase the length of the board.

SCL: See *structural composite lumber.*

SCRIBE: To mark and cut an item of woodwork so that it will abut an uneven wall, floor, or other adjoining surface.

SEALERS: Compounds that provide a sandable coating and a smooth surface for final topcoat application, provide system toughness and holdout, provide moisture resistance, and contribute to build and clarity.

SECURELY ATTACHED: The attachment of one member to another by means of approved joinery, adhesive, mechanical fasteners, or by a combination of these means. Members shall not be considered securely attached if they disassemble during standard usage and stress.

SECURELY FASTENED OR BONDED: See *securely attached.*

SELECT: A lumber grading term. Also, in architectural specifications, the term "select" is frequently used to describe, clarify, or qualify specific characteristics of the hardwood lumber being specified; for example, Select White Maple or Select White Birch -- by using "select" as a descriptor, Natural, Brown, and Red Maple/Birch are excluded.

SELF-EDGE: Application of an edge that matches the face.

SEMI-EXPOSED SURFACES: Surfaces that are only visible under closer examination.

SEQUENCE - MATCHED: When referring to paneling, the veneer matching of one panel to another.

SERPENTINE: A wave-like design alternating concave and convex lines.

SHADING: In finishing, transparent color used for highlighting and uniform color.

SHAKE: A separation or rupture along the grain of wood in which the greater part occurs between the rings of annual growth (see ruptured grain).

SHARP CONTRAST: For the purpose of this standard, this term applies to woodwork such as veneer of lighter-than-average color joined with the veneer of darker-than-average color. Two adjacent pieces of woodwork should not be widely dissimilar in grain, figure, and natural character markings.

SHEEN: Finish shine or brightness; luster, patina, and radiance. The sheen or gloss level of a cured finish is traditionally measured with a 60-degree gloss meter. The words used to describe various sheens are not standardized between companies.

SHELF DEFLECTION: Shelf deflection is the deviation from true flat of a shelf when placed under load.

SHELLAC: A coating made from purified lac, a secretion from an insect (laccifera lacca) that is dissolved in alcohol and often bleached white. It was first used in 1590 and was most popular in the 1920s and 1930s.

SHIM SHEETS: One or more sheets of veneer in a flitch where one side varies significantly in thickness from the other.

SHOP DRAWINGS: See *drawings.*

SHOW-THROUGH: Irregular surfaces visible on the face of a veneered panel (such as depressions, bumps, mechanical marks, or core or frame outlines).

SKIN: The hardwood plywood (usually 3-ply), hardboard, or composition panel, whether flat or configured, that is used for facings for flush wood doors, bending laminations, finished end panels, and the like.

GLOSSARY

SKIRT BOARD: A trim member similar to base, run on the rake along the wall adjoining a stairway. The skirt board covers the joint between the treads and risers and the wall. Also, the similar member below the treads at the open side of a stairway. A wall routed to receive the treads and risers may replace a skirt board.

SLEEPER, BASE: A support member, usually vertical in placement, between the front and rear members of a non-integral toe base or kick assembly.

SLICED: Veneer produced by thrusting a log or sawed flitch into a slicing machine that shears off the veneer in sheets.

SLIGHT: Barely perceptible, but not to the extent as to detract from the overall appearance of the product (as a measurement of natural or machining characteristics).

SLIP-MATCHED: A sheet from a flitch is slid across the sheet beneath and, without turning, spliced at the joints.

SMOOTH, TIGHT CUT: Veneer cut to minimize lathe checks.

SOFTWOOD: General term used to describe lumber or veneer produced from needle- and/or cone-bearing trees (see hardwood).

SOLID PHENOLIC: A composite of solid phenolic resins molded with a homogenous core of organic fiber-reinforced phenolic and one or more integrally cured surfaces of compatible thermoset nonabsorbent resins.

SOLID STOCK: Solid, sound lumber (as opposed to plywood), that may be more than one piece of the same species, securely glued for width or thickness.

SOUND: Absence of decay.

SP: See *solid phenolic.*

SPANDREL: The triangular element in a staircase between the stringer and the baseboard.

SPECIES: A distinct kind of wood.

SPECIFIC GRAVITY: The ratio of the weight of a certain volume of a substance to the weight of an equal volume of water, the temperature of which is 39.2 degrees Fahrenheit (4 degrees Celsius).

SPLINE: A thin narrow strip forming a key between two members, usually of plywood, inserted into matching grooves that have been machined in abutting edges of panels or lumber to ensure a flush alignment and a secure joint.

SPLINE JOINT: A joint formed by the use of a "spline." Splines customarily run the entire length of the joint.

SPLIT: A separation of the wood due to the tearing apart of the wood cells.

SPLIT HEART: A method of achieving an inverted "V" or cathedral type of springwood (earlywood)/summerwood (latewood), plain-sliced (flat-cut) figure by joining two face components of similar color and grain.

SPLITS: Separations of wood fiber running parallel to the grain.

STAIN: A variation (normally blue or brown) from the natural color of the wood. It should not be confused with natural red heart. In finishing, produces the desired undertone color with proper distribution, depth, and clarity of grain. Selection of the type of stain used is governed by the desired artistic result. In natural wood, a variation in the color tending toward blue or brown, but not to be confused with naturally occurring heartwood.

STAINING: An optional operation in wood finishing to achieve the desired undertone color and complement the wood with proper distribution of color, depth of color, and clarity of grain.

STAIRWORK: Wood material to form a stair or to clad stair parts constructed of materials other than wood, and that are custom-manufactured to a design for a particular project.

STANDARD LACQUER: In finishing, a nitrocellulose-based lacquer without additives.

STANDING TRIM: Generally combined in the term "standing and running trim" and refers to the trims of fixed length delivered to the jobsite (e.g., door jambs and casings, premachined window stools).

GLOSSARY

STAPLED: Members secured together with nails, including power-driven nails or staples. On exposed surfaces, staples shall run parallel to the grain.

STAVED CORE: Typically refers to a core used in flush doors made up of end- and edge-glued wood blocks.

STICKING: A term used to describe shaped or molded solid wood members.

STILE-and-RAIL CONSTRUCTION: A technique often used in the making of doors, wainscoting, and other decorative features for cabinets and furniture. The basic concept is to capture a panel within a frame, and in its most basic form it consists of five members: the panel and the four members that make up the frame. The vertical members of the frame are called stiles, while the horizontal members are known as rails.

STILES/VERTICAL EDGES: The upright or vertical pieces of stile-and-rail assemblies; the vertical members of the core assembly of a wood flush door.

STOPS: Generally a molding used to "stop" a door or window in its frame.

STREAKS, MINERAL: Natural colorations of the wood substance.

STRETCHER: An upper support member of base cabinet fabrication, used in lieu of a solid top, to space the end panels.

STRINGER: A diagonal element supporting the treads and risers in a flight of stairs.

STRINGER TURNOUT: In stairwork, that portion of a stringer that curves or angles away from the basic run, typically used at the beginning tread.

STRIPE: Stripe figure is a ribbon grain:

> **BROKEN STRIPE** - A modification of ribbon stripe. The figure markings taper in and out, due to twisted or interlocked grain, so that the ribbon stripe is not continuous as it runs more or less the full length of the flitch.
>
> **PLAIN STRIPE** - Alternating darker and lighter stripes running continuously along the length of a piece, due to cutting wood with definite growth rings on the quarter.
>
> **ROE** - Also called "roey". Short, broken ribbon or stripe figure in quarter-sliced or -sawn wood, due to the spiral formation of the fibers, or interlocked grain, in the growth rings. The irregular growth produces alternate bands of varying shades of color and degrees of luster.
>
> **RAINDROP** - When the waves of the fibers occur singly or in groups with considerable intervals between, the figure looks like streaks made by raindrops striking a window pane at a slant.
>
> **RIBBON STRIPE** - In some wood with interwoven grain, such as Mahogany, wide unbroken stripes can be produced by cutting on the quarter.

STRIPPING: For purposes of these standards, means the process of removing an old or existing finish from a surface.

STRUCTURAL COMPOSITE LUMBER (SCL): A man-made composite that utilizes stranded wood fibers from a variety of tree species, providing an alternative to dimension lumber. The material is engineered for strength and stability. While not really "lumber", it is marketed as a lumber substitute to be used in place of stave lumber core materials.

SUB-FRONT: A front drawer box member over which another front is placed.

SUBSTRATE: Generally used to describe a panel product (see also core) upon which a decorative finish material is applied.

SUBTOP: A separate support member for countertops.

SUGAR: Color streaks or spots attributed to discoloration involving sap in Maple veneer.

SURFACE CHECK: The separation of a wood, normally occurring across the rings of annual growth; usually as a result of seasoning, and occurring only on one surface of the piece.

SWIRL: Figure obtained from that part of a tree where the crotch figure fades into the figure of the normal stem.

TAMBOUR: A rolling top or front in casework enclosing a storage space. It consists of narrow strips of wood fastened to canvas or a similar material.

GLOSSARY

TANNIN BLEED: The tendency of waterborne coatings to turn Maple and Red Oak pink. Naturally occurring tannic acids are water soluble, and the higher pH of waterborne coatings will tend to create this problem. One can get tannin bleed with solvent-based coatings as well, but it is more prevalent in waterborne coatings.

TAPE: Strips of gummed paper or cloth sometimes placed across the grain of large veneer sheets to facilitate handling and sometimes used to hold the edges of veneer together at the joint prior to gluing.

TELEGRAPH OR TELEGRAPHING: In veneer or laminated work, the variations in surface refraction as a result of the stile, rail, core, core laps, glue, voids, or extraneous matter show through to the face of a panel or a door. The selection of high-gloss laminates and finishes should be avoided because they tend to accentuate natural telegraphing.

TENON: The projecting tongue-like part of a wood member to be inserted into a slot (mortise) of another member to form a mortise-and-tenon joint.

TEXTURE: A term used to describe relative size and distribution of the wood elements. Coarse texture in veneer is associated with fast growth and harder, more difficult wood to cut. Soft or fine texture in veneer is associated with slower growth and with less summerwood, resulting in wood fibers that are easier to cut.

THERMALLY FUSED DECORATIVE LAMINATE PANEL: A polyester or melamine resin-impregnated paper, thermally fused under pressure to a composite core.

THICK PHENOLIC: See *solid phenolic*.

TIGHT: Set together so that there is no opening between members.

TIGHT SIDE: In knife-cut veneer, that side of the leaf that was farthest from the knife as the veneer was being cut and containing no cutting checks (lathe checks).

TONERS: Transparent or semitransparent colors used in wood finishing to even the color or tone of the wood.

TONGUE: Projection on the edge or end of a wood member that is inserted into the groove or plow of a similar size to form a joint.

TONGUE-AND-GROOVE JOINT: A joint formed by the insertion of the “tongue” of one wood member into the “groove” of the other.

TOPCOAT: The final protective film of a finish system. There are various topcoats with different properties.

TOP FLAT SURFACE: The flat surface that can be sanded with a drum sander.

TORN GRAIN: A roughened area caused by machine work in processing.

TRANSPARENT FINISH: A stain or a clear finish that allows the natural characteristics and color of the grain of the wood surface to show through the finish.

TREAD: The horizontal surface of a staircase step.

TREAD RETURN: A narrow piece of tread stock applied to the open end of a tread so that the end grain is not exposed. The leading corner of the return is mitered to the leading edge of the tread with a shoulder miter.

TREENAIL: A hardwood pin, peg, or spike used to fasten beams and planking, usually made of dry compressed lumber so that it will expand when moistened; sometimes pronounced and spelled “trunnel.”

TWIST: A distortion caused by the turning or winding of the edges of the surface, so that the four corners of any face are no longer in the same plane.

UNDRESSED: Lumber that is not planed smooth.

UREA FORMALDEHYDE RESIN: Commonly used for Type I assemblies; relatively water-resistant. Often requires curing by heat, but will cure at room temperature over time.

V-GROOVED: Narrow and shallow V- or U-shaped channels machined on a surface to achieve a decorative effect. V-grooving is most commonly encountered in mismatched or random-matched wall panels as the grooves fall on the edge joints of the pieces of veneer, making the face appear as planking.

GLOSSARY

VARNISH: An oil-based finished used to coat a surface with a hard, glossy film.

VENEER: A thin sheet or layer of wood, usually rotary cut, sliced or sawn from a log or flitch. Thickness may vary from 1/100" (0.3 mm) to 1/4" (6.4 mm).

VENEER CORE: Plywood constructed using a core of an odd number of veneer plies, with face and back veneers of overlays adhered thereto.

VENEER, RIFT CUT: Veneer in which the rift or comb grain effect is obtained by cutting at an angle of about 15 degrees off of the quartered position. Twenty-five percent (25%) of the exposed surface area of each piece of veneer may contain medullary ray flake.

VENEER, ROTARY CUT: Veneer in which the entire log is centered in a lathe and is turned against a broad cutting knife that is set into the log at a slight angle.

VENEER, SLICED: Veneer in which a log or sawn flitch is held securely in a slicing machine and is thrust downward into a large knife that shears off the veneer in sheets.

VENEERING: Veneering and laminating thin pieces of wood dates back to the Egyptian pyramid-building era. Since that period, this area of woodworking has become a highly technical business. Veneering is still common today, but production techniques have changed considerably. Modern adhesives, for example, are used instead of hard-to-handle glues. See rotary slicing, plain slicing, rift cut, quarter slicing, and half round.

VERGE BOARD: An exposed member attached along the rake of a gable-end roof open cornice; also implies the larger rake member of an exterior cornice; sometimes referred to as a "barge board".

VERTICAL GRAIN: Produced by cutting perpendicular to a log's growth rings, where the member's face is no more than 45 degrees to the rings. This produces a pleasing straight grain line. Vertical grain is defined as having no less than an average of five growth rings per inch on its exposed face.

VINE MARK: Bands of irregular grain running across or diagonally to the grain, which are caused by the growth of climbing vines around the tree.

VINYL: Heavy film, minimum of 4 mils in thickness, opaque or reverse printed.

VINYL LACQUERS: In finishing, catalyzed lacquers with a plastic rather than a nitrocellulose base.

VISCOSITY: The property of a fluid that causes it to resist flowing.

VOLUTE: The spiral decorative element terminating the lower end of a stair rail.

WAFERBOARD: See *particleboard.*

WAINSCOT: A lower interior wall surface that contrasts with the wall surface above it. Unless otherwise specified, it shall be 48" (1219 mm) in height above the floor.

WANE: Defect in lumber defined as bark or lack of wood from any cause on the edge or corner, except eased edges.

WARP: Any deviation from a true or plane surface, including bow, crook, cup, twist, or any combination thereof. Warp restrictions are based on the average form of warp as it occurs normally, and any variation from this average form, such as short kinks, shall be appraised according to its equivalent effect. Pieces containing two or more forms of warp shall be appraised according to the combined effect in determining the amount permissible.

> **BOW** - A deviation flatwise from a straight line drawn from end to end of a piece. It is measured at the point of greatest distance from the straight line.
>
> **CROOK** - A deviation edgewise from a straight line drawn from end to end of a piece. It is measured at the point of greatest distance from the straight line.
>
> **CUP** - A deviation in the face of a piece from a straight line drawn from edge to edge of a piece. It is measured at the point of greatest distance from the straight line.
>
> **TWIST** - A deviation flatwise, or a combination of flatwise and edgewise, in the form of a curl or spiral, and the amount is the distance an edge of a piece at one end is raised above a flat surface against which both edges at the opposite end are resting snugly.

In passage doors, any distortion in the door itself and not its relationship to the frame or jamb in which it is to be hung, measured by placing a straight edge or a taut string on the concave face.

GLOSSARY

WASH COATS: Thin solutions applied as a barrier coat to wood. Used prior to wiping stains for color uniformity.

WATER-REPELLENT: A wood-treating solution that deposits waterproof or water-resistant solids on the walls of wood fibers and ray cells, thereby retarding their absorption of water; having the quality of retarding the absorption of water by wood fibers and ray cells.

WAVY: Curly grain with large undulations; sometimes referred to as "finger roll" when the waves are about the width of a finger.

WAX FINISH: Wax finishes are designed for cosmetic purposes only and provide no long-term protection. They are commonly used for low-performance, low-abuse parts and in some areas for Pine furniture as a specialty appearance. No test data has been established.

WELL HOLE: In stairwork, the open space in which the stair is set.

WELL-MATCHED FOR COLOR AND GRAIN: For the purpose of these standards, means that the members that make up the components of an assembly and components of an adjacent assembly are: a) similar and nearly uniform in color, and b) have similar grain, figure, and character. Adjacent members must be of the same grain type whether flat grain (plain-sliced), vertical grain (quarter-cut), rift grain, or mixed grain.

WHITE: When referring to color and matching, veneers containing all sapwood ranging in color from pink to yellow.

WHITE BIRCH: Term used to specify the sapwood of the Yellow Birch tree.

WINDOWS: In architectural woodwork, all frames and sashes for double-hung, casement, awning, sidelights, clerestory, and fixed windows. Stock and name-brand units are not included.

WIPING STAINS: Refers to pigmented oils or solvents applied to wood.

WOOD FILLER: An aggregate of resin and strands, shreds, or flour of wood, which is used to fill openings in wood and provide a smooth, durable surface.

WOOD FLUSH DOOR: An assembly consisting of a core, stiles and rails, and/or edgebands, with two or three plies of overlay on each side of the core assembly. All parts are composed of wood, wood derivatives, or high-pressure decorative laminates.

WOODWORK: See *architectural woodwork.*

WOODWORKER: See *manufacturer.*

WORKMANSHIP: See *first-class workmanship.*

WORMHOLES: Holes resulting from infestation of worms or marks caused by various types of wood attacking insect and beetle larvae. Often appears as sound discolorations running with or across the grain in straight to wavy streaks. Sometimes referred to as "pith flecks" in certain species of Maple, Birch, and other hardwoods because of a resemblance to the color of pith.

WORM TRACK OR SCAR: The groove or resulting scar tissue in the wood caused by worms or other borers. Often appears as sound discolorations running with or across the grain in straight to wavy streaks. Sometimes referred to as pith flecks in certain species of Maple, Birch, and other hardwoods because of a resemblance to the color of pith.

AWS
Additional Resources

Appendix B

TABLE OF CONTENTS

These additional resources are provided to assist in the use and understanding of the *Architectural Woodwork Standards*; however, none of what is included within this Appendix is to be interpreted as part of the *Architectural Woodwork Standards* for compliance purposes.

Association Quality Control Enforcement Options
- Architectural Woodwork Institute (AWI) . . . 408
- Architectural Woodwork Manufacturers Association of Canada (AWMAC) . . . 408
- Woodwork Institute (WI) . . . 409

CSI Guide Specifications
- Section 06 41 00 - Wood & Laminate Casework . . . 411
- Section 06 42 00 - Paneling . . . 419
- Section 06 46 00 - Wood Trim . . . 425
- Section 08 14 00 - Wood Doors . . . 431

1 - Submittals . . . 437

2 - Care and Storage . . . 439

3 - Lumber . . . 441

4 - Sheet Products . . . 455

5 - Finishing . . . 479

6 - Interior and Exterior Millwork . . . 483
- Design Ideas . . . 485

7 - Stairwork and Rails . . . 527
- Design Ideas . . . 530

8 - Wall Surfacing . . . 533
- Design Ideas . . . 550

9 - Wood Doors . . . 557
- Design Ideas . . . 573

10 - Casework . . . 579
- Design Ideas . . . 585

11 - Countertops . . . 615
- Design Ideas . . . 620

12 - Installation . . . 623

13 - Adhesive Summary . . . 629

Quality Control Enforcement Options

Architectural Woodwork Institute
Quality Certification Program (QCP)

Your reputation depends on others when you specify architectural woodwork. The Quality Certification Program (QCP) provides the means to ensure that the quality you specify is the quality you get.

The AWI Quality Certification Corporation (AWI QCC) is a fully independent, international credentialing body and is the sole administrator of the QCP. To fulfill its mission, which is to Verify, inspect, report and enforce architectural woodwork standards compliance, the QCP:

- Performs more than 500 inspections annually;
- Inspects firms and projects throughout Asia, Africa, Europe, and North America.
- Is ISO 65 compliant;
- Retains a highly experienced team of inspectors, each of whom must possess a minimum of 15 years experience in the architectural woodwork industry; they must pass the 150 question written test, adhere to a strict conflict of interest policy, and undergo extensive training by the QCP.

Established in 1995, the QCP provides design professionals and owners a means of verifying the skills and competence of the architectural woodwork manufacturers on a project-specific basis. As a design professional or project owner, you are protected if the woodwork delivered to a QCP project does not meet specifications. One of the major benefits of the quality certification program is that it provides the resources to prevent noncompliant woodwork from being installed on the job site.

The QCP accredits eligible woodworking firms to certify that their work complies with the project specifications and the Architectural Woodwork Standards (*AWS*). QCP verifies compliance with the specifications and the standards through the inspection process. This includes all certified projects registered to new program participants, all projects for which it receives an inspection-request from the design professional and/or the owner, and dozens of randomly chosen projects each year.

Woodworking firms earn certification credentials through comprehensive testing, rigorous inspections, and the submittal of 10 trade references. Moreover, they must demonstrate the ability to fabricate, finish, and/or install work in accordance with the quality grade criteria set forth in the Architectural Woodwork Standards (*AWS*).

QCP suggested specification language 1 — Quality Standard: Unless otherwise indicated, comply with "Architectural Woodwork Standards" for grades of interior architectural woodwork, construction, finishes, and other requirements.
Provide AWI Quality Certification Program [labels] [certificates] indicating that woodwork [including installation] complies with requirements of grades specified. This project has been registered as AWI/QCP Number ________
OR, the contractor, upon award of the work, shall register the work under this Section with the AWI Quality Certification Program. (800-449-8811)

The QCP is endorsed by every leading organization that values quality, including the U.S. General Services Administration (GSA) and the American Subcontractors Association (ASA). Put the QCP to work for you. For more information, please visit our website www.awiqcp.org, or call (800) 449-8811.

♦ ♦

Architectural Woodwork Manufacturers Association of Canada
Guarantee and Inspection Service (GIS)

AWMAC regional chapters manage the GIS monitoring program, initiated in 1990. AWMAC GIS Certified Inspectors review, inspect and report on pretender specifications if requested, sample units when specified and shop drawings. Inspectors also perform a comprehensive final inspection of the architectural woodwork for the project owner. The AWMAC GIS program offers, through its members in good standing, a two year AWMAC Guarantee Certificate on projects which have the recommended GIS wording specified in the tender documents.

GIS MANDATE
In order to ensure that the quality of materials and workmanship of the architectural woodwork specified are in compliance with the current AWMAC Architectural Woodwork Standards (*AWS*), the AWMAC Guarantee and Inspection Service program (GIS) must be specified and be considered an integral component of the scope of work.

GIS OBJECTIVE
The objectives of the Guarantee and Inspection Service are:

1. To assist the design authority in achieving "good architectural woodwork".
2. To offer the owner, customer, design authority, and woodwork contractor an assurance that strict monitoring of the architectural woodwork requirements on a given project will meet the specified AWMAC standards.

GIS WORDING FOR SPECIFICATIONS

Architectural woodwork shall be manufactured and/or installed to the current AWMAC Architectural Woodwork Standards and shall be sub¬ject to an inspection at the plant and/or site by an appointed AWMAC Certified Inspector. Inspection costs shall be included in the tender price for this project. (Contact your local AWMAC Chapter for details of inspec¬tion costs). Shop drawings shall be submitted to the AWMAC Chapter office for review before work commences. Work that does not meet the AWMAC Architectural Woodwork Standards, as specified, shall be replaced, reworked and/or refinished by the architectural woodwork contractor, to the approval of AWMAC, at no additional cost to the owner.

If the woodwork contractor is an AWMAC Manufacturer member in good standing, a two (2) year AWMAC Guarantee Certificate will be issued. The AWMAC Guarantee shall cover replacing, reworking and/or refinishing any deficient architectural woodwork due to faulty workmanship or defective materials supplied and/or installed by the woodwork contractor, which may appear during a two (2) year period following the date of issuance.

If the woodwork contractor is not an AWMAC Manufacturer member they shall provide the owner with a two (2) year maintenance bond, in lieu of the AWMAC Guarantee Certificate, to the full value of the architectural woodwork contract.

For more information about AWMAC and the GIS Program visit our website at www.awmac.com and contact your local AWMAC Chapter office or phone the GIS office at: 1-866-447-7732.

♦ ♦

Woodwork Institute

- Assurance Options -
Certified and Monitored Compliance Programs

One of the greatest joys of being a design/specification professional is seeing your ideas become reality. The Woodwork Institute (WI) has been sharing your vision since 1951.

Currently over 10,000 design/specification professionals use our *Architectural Woodwork Standards* (*AWS*). The *AWS* establishes a minimum standard of quality, while giving you the flexibility to pair your vision with your customer's desires. The *AWS* is offered free of charge to members of the design/specification community in our service area.

Our Directors of Architectural Services (DAS), are employed throughout our service area, and provide knowledge from significant years of first-hand experience in the millwork industry. Their primary focus is compliance verification (inspection service); however, as registered AIA/CES instructors, they also provide numerous hours of standards/quality assurance/industry-based education. Additionally, our DAS's are available as an unbiased, industry consultation service. Education, consultation, and inspection services (when specified through one of our quality assurance programs), are provided free of cost to the design/specification community.

In conjunction with the *AWS*, WI also offers two distinct quality assurance options:

CERTIFIED COMPLIANCE PROGRAM (CCP)

A discipline of quality control used in conjunction with the *AWS,* providing a non-biased means of confirming conformance to your plans and specifications. Requiring Certified Compliance informs others of the expected specifications, without bidder discrimination. When receiving certified shop drawings, you are assured they conform to your specifications and *AWS* requirements, leaving verification of your design intent as your primary concern. Evidence of Certification is provided primarily by issuance of a Certified Compliance Certificate, listing the items certified, the applicable Grade, and whether installation is included. Additionally, shop drawings and each elevation of casework and/or countertops shall bear an individually serial-numbered "Certified Compliance Label," if so specified. The CCP started in 1959, and now certifies over 1,700 projects annually.

MONITORED COMPLIANCE PROGRAM (MCP)

A discipline of quality affirmation used in conjunction with the *AWS,* providing non-biased reviews/inspections of your project from its beginning through completion with WI Certification, without bidder discrimination. Requiring Monitored Compliance informs others of the quality demanded in what you have designed and specified for your client. The Institute will issue written progress reports throughout the duration of the project. The shop drawings, millwork products, and installation (of all involved parties), will progressively be inspected for compliance to your specifications and the specified Grade per the *AWS*. Evidence of Monitored Compliance is provided by issuance of a Monitored Compliance Certificate, listing the items certified, the applicable Grade, and whether installation is included. Additionally, shop drawings and each elevation of casework and/or countertops shall bear an individually serial-numbered "Certified Compliance Label." The MCP started in 2001, and has now become the premier quality control option.

For more information, please visit our website at www.woodworkinstitute.com, or call 916-372-9943.

NOTES

CSI Guide Specification
Section 06 41 00
Wood & Laminate Casework

CSI Section 06 41 00
Wood and Plastic Laminate Casework

This guide specification covers the materials and methods you would want to specify for wood or laminated plastic casework. It is strongly recommended that you read the "Cabinet Section" of *Architectural Woodwork Standards* before using this guide spec. Many of the items you would ordinarily specify are governed by your choice of Grade.

In this guide spec, choices are [**bold, in brackets**]. Comments are shaded.

PART 1 - GENERAL

1.01 SUMMARY

A. Section Includes:

1. [**Wood Casework**] [**Plastic Laminate Casework**].
2. [**Plastic Laminate**] [**Solid Surface**] [**Wood**] countertops.
3. Hardware typically furnished by the casework manufacturer.
4. Shelving.
5. [**Decorative metalwork incorporated into wood casework.**]
6. Structural supports incorporated into wood casework.
7. [**Factory finishing.**]

Factory finishing is strongly recommended. It is extremely difficult to get a quality finish under job site conditions.

B. Excluding:

1. Metal support brackets and fittings that are part of the building structure.
2. Plumbing, electrical fixtures, and telephone equipment.

C. Related Sections:

1. Rough Carpentry: Wood blocking or grounds inside finished walls or above finished ceilings.
2. Plumbing: Fixtures and fittings installed in countertops.
3. Wood Doors.

1.02 REFERENCES

A. Minimum standards for work in this Section shall be in conformity with the *Architectural Woodwork Standards*.

All of the other standards are referenced within the *AWS*.

1.03 SUBMITTALS

A. Shop Drawings:

1. Submit shop drawings in conformance with the requirements of the *Architectural Woodwork Standards*.
2. Submit two copies, one of which will be returned with reviewed notations. Make corrections noted (if any), and distribute required copies prior to the start of work.

B. Samples:

1. Submit four [**finished**] samples of each species and cut of wood to be used. Lumber samples to be minimum 6" by 12", and plywood samples to be minimum 12" by 12". Samples shall represent the range of color and grain expected to be provided.

Include Item 1 if there is any factory finished wood or veneer included in this Section.

Include Item 2 if any wood is to be provided for job site finishing.

2. Submit a sample in the specified finish of each hardware item that will be visible at exposed surfaces when the job is complete.

CSI Section 06 41 00
Wood and Plastic Laminate Casework

C. [**Mockups:**

Mockups shouldn't be necessary for most projects. Include this item if full sized samples are desired.

1. **Provide mockups of one base cabinet, one wall hung cabinet, and one countertop. Base cabinet shall have at least one drawer. Mockup shall be of the material and finish to be provided. The Approved Mockup may be incorporated in the project.**]

1.04 QUALITY ASSURANCE

A. Work shall be in accordance with the Grade or Grades specified of the *Architectural Woodwork Standards*.

B. [**Association Quality Assurance Program.**]

Association quality assurance programs provide a pre qualification for the sub contractor. Bidders will be Association program participants or they will understand that their work will be inspected by an Association program representative. For better quality assurance, it's recommended that an Association assurance program is used.

C. Qualification:

1. Firm (woodwork manufacturer) with no less than 5 years of production experience similar to a specific project, whose qualifications indicate the ability to comply with the requirements of this Section.
2. The woodwork manufacturer must have at least one project in the past 5 years where the value of the woodwork was within 20 percent of the cost of woodwork for this Project.

D. Single Source Responsibility: A single manufacturer shall provide and install the work of described in this Section.

1.05 DELIVERY STORAGE AND HANDLING

A. Deliver materials only when the project is ready for installation and the general contractor has provided a clean storage area.

1. Delivery of architectural millwork shall be made only when the area of operation is enclosed, all plaster and concrete work is dry and the area broom clean.
2. Maintain indoor temperature and humidity within the range recommended by the *Architectural Woodwork Standards* for the location of the project.

1.06 SCHEDULING

A. Coordinate fabrication, delivery, and installation with the general contractor and other applicable trades.

PART 2 - PRODUCTS

2.01 COMPONENTS

A. Lumber shall be in accordance with the *Architectural Woodwork Standards* Grade specified for the product being fabricated. Moisture Content shall be 6% to 12% for boards up to 2" (50.8 mm) inch nominal thickness, and shall not exceed 19% for thicker pieces.

B. Veneers shall be in accordance with the *Architectural Woodwork Standards* requirements for its use and the Grades.

C. Core shall be [**MDF**] [**particleboard**] meeting the requirements of *Architectural Woodwork Standards*.

Particleboard or MDF are recommended as core materials.

D. Veneer core plywood shall be a non-telegraphing hardwood manufactured with exterior glue.

E. Plastic Laminate shall meet the requirements of the *Architectural Woodwork Standards* for its intended use.

CSI Section 06 41 00
Wood and Plastic Laminate Casework

F. [**Cabinet Liner shall be type CLS.**]

> Include this Item if you intend to use cabinet liner at semi-exposed surfaces.

G Edgeband

1. Veneer of the same species and cut as the exposed surfaces.
2. [**PVC**] [**ABS**] [**high pressure decorative laminate**].

> PVC and ABS edgeband are available to match many laminate patterns. PVC is more durable than laminate and it is less subject to glue failure. PVC is available in 3mm and 0.5mm thicknesses. 0.5mm is generally used at case bodies, and 3mm may be used at doors, drawer fronts, and false fronts. ABS is a new product that claims to have the positive qualities of PVC without the environmental down side.

H Adhesives used shall be [**type I**] [**type II**].

> Type I glue is water proof; Type II is water resistant. Type II is satisfactory except in a very wet environment.

I Hardware:

1. Pulls: [__________].
2. Drawer Guides shall be [**full extension**] [**¾ extension**] *AWS* approved.

> If you specify brand and model of drawer guides, specify for pencil drawers, box drawers, file drawers, and lateral file drawers, as applicable.

3. Hinges: [**five knuckle Grade 1 hinges**] [**concealed European style Grade II hinges minimum 120° opening**] Brand, Model. Hinges shall be *AWS* compliant.

> The *AWS* requires Grade I hinges for schools, hospitals and recommends such for police and fire facilities, and other high usage applications.

4. Door Catches: [__________]

> If self closing hinges are selected catches will not be required. Self closing Grade I hinges are not available.

5. Shelf Supports: Shelf supports for adjustable shelves in wall-hung cabinets and the upper half of tall cabinets shall be designed to prevent shelves from sliding forward in a seismic event.

> Bored hole shelf support systems and metal shelf ladders have both been determined to provide satisfactory support.

6. Locks
   a. Door locks: [___________].
   b. Drawer locks: [___________].
   c. Glass door locks: [__________].
   d. [_____________].
   e. Provide [___________] keys per lock.
   f. Elbow Catches: [____________].

> Elbow catches will only be necessary at the inactive leaf of locking pairs of doors. If no door locks are required, elbow catches will not be necessary.

7. Sliding glass door hardware: [__________].

> Sliding glass doors that are more than 1 ½ times as tall as they are wide should be installed using top hung hardware. Tall, thin glass doors on bottom roller systems will tip and bind.

8. Etc.

> Other hardware items may include wire grommets, keyboard trays, and other specialty items.

2.02. FABRICATION

A. Wood Casework

1. Casework shall meet the requirements of the *Architectural Woodwork Standards* [**Premium Grade**] [**Custom Grade**] [**Grades shown on plans**].

> The *AWS* allows the use of Economy Grade for custodian's closets and utility rooms regardless of the Grade specified for the project as a whole (unless otherwise specified). This is usually the only application for Economy Grade.

CSI Section 06 41 00
Wood and Plastic Laminate Casework

2. Casework shall be *Architectural Woodwork Standards* CONSTRUCTION TYPE [**A, frameless**] [**B, face frame**] and cabinet and door INTERFACE STYLE [**1, overlay**] [**2, flush inset**].

   > Typically TYPE A and STYLE 1 go together while TYPE B goes with either STYLE 1 or 2. Almost all plastic laminate casework is TYPE A and STYLE 1.

3. Exposed Surfaces shall be [[**species**], [**cut**]], [[**book**][**slip**] **matched**] [**material suitable for opaque finish**]] meeting the requirements of the *AWS* for the Grade specified.

   > The species is the species of tree, such as Oak or Maple. The cut used is the angle of the face of the board to the growth rings. Flat sawn or plain sliced is the most common cut. Quarter sawn or Rift cut lumber is cut with the face at right angles to the growth rings, giving a vertical grain appearance. Match refers to the way veneer leaves are matched within a panel. Book match is the most common.

   a. **[Blueprint Match: veneers at room(s) [__________] shall be blueprint matched.**

   > This item is only necessary if there is an area where a blueprint match is desired. Similar language must be inserted in the Sections specifying wood paneling, wood trim, and wood doors.

      1. **All work in this/these area(s) shall be AWS Premium Grade.**
      2. **Casework, paneling, doors and wood trim shall be provided by the same manufacturer.**
      3. **Veneers shall be taken from the same flitch, to be selected by the architect.**
      4. **Faces at cabinet doors, drawer fronts and false fronts shall be sequence matched, shall run and match vertically, and shall be sequence matched with adjacent wall paneling and/or doors.**
      5. **Faces at exposed ends of cabinets shall be selected from the same flitch, and shall be well matched to the adjacent paneling and to the cabinet fronts.**
      6. **All components including casework, paneling, doors, and trim shall be factory finished at the same time in the same facility.**]

4. Exposed interior surfaces shall be [**per the requirements of the AWS**] [**veneer of the same species as the exposed faces**] [**low pressure melamine overlay**].

   > The default choices in the *AWS* are very well thought out. It should only be necessary to call out a material here if you wish for something special.

5. Semi-exposed surfaces shall be [**per the requirements of the AWS**] [**veneer of the same species as the exposed faces**] [**low pressure melamine overlay**].

   > The default choices in the *AWS* are very well thought out. It should only be necessary to call out a material here if you wish for something special.

6. Doors, drawer fronts, and false fronts shall be [**flush overlay**] [**reveal overlay**] [**lipped**] [**flush inset**].

   > STYLE 1 flush overlay is the most common door style and usually goes with TYPE A construction. The other door styles are generally used with face frame construction.

B. Plastic Laminate Casework:

1. Shall be *Architectural Woodwork Standards* [**Custom**] [**Premium**] Grade.

   > The *AWS* allows the use of Economy Grade for custodian's closets and utility rooms regardless of the Grade specified for the project as a whole (unless otherwise specified). This is usually the only application for Economy Grade.

2. Exposed interior surfaces shall be [**low pressure melamine overlay**] [**low pressure melamine overlay of a color and pattern compatible with exposed surfaces**] [**high pressure laminate matching exposed surfaces**].

   > The *AWS* default choices for exposed interiors and semi exposed surfaces are well matched with the *AWS* Grades. The items above and below are not necessary unless you have specific desires.

3. Semi-exposed surfaces shall be [**low-pressure melamine overlay**] [**cabinet liner**] [**laminate matching exposed surfaces**].

4. Doors, drawer fronts, and false fronts shall be [**flush overlay**] [**reveal overlay**].

   > STYLE 1 flush overlay is the most common door style and usually goes with TYPE A construction. The other door styles usually go with face frame construction. Plastic Laminate casework is not usually constructed with face frames.

   a. **[Edgeband at doors, drawer fronts, and false fronts shall be 3mm** [**PVC**] [**ABS**].]

   > PVC and ABS edgeband come in 3mm and 0.5mm thicknesses. 3mm edgeband on doors and drawer fronts is more durable, but the thicker edge will be more noticeable if the laminate is a wood grain or other pattern rather than a solid color.

CSI Section 06 41 00
Wood and Plastic Laminate Casework

C. Drawers shall meet the requirements of the *AWS* for the Grade or Grades specified.

> The *AWS* does an excellent job of matching drawer materials and construction methods to the casework Grade. If something special is desired, modify this Item.

D. Laminated Plastic Countertops:

1. Laminate shall be [**Manufacturer**] [**Pattern**].
2. Core material shall be [**particleboard**] [**MDF**] [**exterior grade hardwood plywood with a non-telegraphing grain**].

> Particleboard and MDF are satisfactory in most environments. The *AWS* requires water resistant Particleboard or MDF at tops with sinks. Plywood is recommended only in the most abusive wet environments.

3. Back splashes shall be ASSEMBLY [**1-Wall mount, jobsite assembled**] [**2-Deck mount, manufacturer assembled**].

> If a preference is desired it shall be so specified, otherwise the Assembly method shall be manufacturers option.

4. Back splashes shall be [**butt joint**] [**cove**] [**per drawings**] and shall be [____] inches (millimeters) high.

> If several backsplash details are used, label “per drawing”, and be sure all tops are clearly detailed in the plans.

5. Front edges shall be [**self edge**] [**no drip bullnose edge**] [**waterfall edge**] [**no drip tilt edge**] [**three millimeter PVC edge**] [**wood edge**].

> As mentioned above, if several details are to be used, make sure they are clearly shown or labeled on the plans.

E. Solid Surface Countertops:

1. Solid surface shall be [**brand**] [**pattern**] [**color**].
2. Back splashes shall be [butt joint] [cove] [per details] and shall be [____] inches (millimeters) high.

> If several backsplash details are used call out “per details,’ and be sure all tops are clearly detailed in the plans.

F. Front edges shall be [self edge] [no drip bullnose edge] [waterfall edge] [no drip tilt edge].

> As above, if several details are to be used make sure they are clearly shown or labeled on the plans.

G Factory Finishing

1. All products provided in this Section shall be factory finished using *Architectural Woodwork Standards* finish system [_____].
2. Finish shall be *AWS* [**Premium**] [**Custom**] Grade.

> As noted above, Factory Finishing is strongly recommended. In addition to getting a better finish, you are moving the air quality problems off site where a proper spray booth will protect the environment and the health of the finishers. It is still worth while to select a low VOC finishing system, as some touch up will be required at the job site.

PART 3 - EXECUTION

3.01. EXAMINATION

A. Verify the adequacy and proper location of any required backing or support framing.

B. Verify that mechanical, electrical, plumbing, and other building components affecting work in this Section are in place and ready.

3.02. INSTALLATION

A. Install all work in conformance with the *Architectural Woodwork Standards,* latest edition.

1. Installation shall conform to the *AWS* Grade of the items being installed.

B. All work shall be secured in place, square, plumb, and level.

CSI Section 06 41 00
Wood and Plastic Laminate Casework

C. All work abutting other building components shall be properly scribed.

D. Mechanical fasteners used at exposed and semi-exposed surfaces, excluding installation attachment screws and those securing cabinets end to end, shall be countersunk.

E. Equipment cutouts shown on plans shall be cut by the installer.

3.03. ADJUSTING & TOUCH UP

A. Before completion of the installation, the installer shall adjust all moving and operating parts to function smoothly and correctly.

B. All nicks, chips, and scratches in the finish shall be filled and retouched. Damaged items that cannot be repaired shall be replaced.

3.04. CLEANUP

A. Upon completion of installation, the installer shall clean all installed items of pencil and ink marks and broom clean the area of operation, depositing debris in containers provided by the general contractor.

END OF SECTION

NOTES

CSI Guide Specification
Section 06 42 00
Paneling

CSI Section 06 42 00
Paneling

This guide specification covers the materials and methods you would want to specify for wood or laminated plastic casework. It is strongly recommended that you read the "Cabinet Section" of *Architectural Millwork Standards* before using this guide spec. Many of the items you would ordinarily specify are governed by your choice of Grade.

In this guide spec, choices are in [**bold, in brackets**]. Comments are in shaded background.

PART 1 - GENERAL

1.01. SUMMARY

A. Section Includes:

Select the applicable items from the list below

1. [**Solid or Veneered Wood Paneling.**]
2. [**High Pressure Decorative Laminate Wall Covering.**]
3. [**Solid Surface Wall Covering.**]
4. [**Solid Phenolic Wall Covering.**]
5. [**All furring, blocking, shims, and methods of attachment from the face of the wall out.**]

Include Item 5 if installation is included.

6. [**Factory finishing.**]

Factory finishing is strongly recommended. It is extremely difficult to get a quality finish under job site conditions.

B. Excluding:

1. Casework, Soffits or other Filler Panels.
2. Room, Closet, or Access Doors.
3. Any structural wood framing of plywood.
4. Exposed base.

C. Related Sections:

1. Rough Carpentry: Wood blocking or grounds inside finished walls or above finished ceilings.
2. Casework.
3. Wood Doors.
4. Wood Trim.

1.02. REFERENCES

A. Minimum standards for work in this Section shall be in conformity with the *Architectural Woodwork Standards*, latest edition, published jointly by the Architectural Woodwork Institute, the Architectural Woodwork Manufacturer Association of Canada, and the Woodwork Institute.

All of the other standards you would reference are within the *AWS*.

1.03. SUBMITTALS

A. Shop Drawings:

1. Submit shop drawings in conformance with the requirements of the *Architectural Woodwork Standards.*
2. Submit two copies, one of which will be returned with reviewed notations. Make corrections noted (if any), and distribute required copies prior to the start of work.

B. Samples:

1. Submit four [**finished**] samples of each species and cut of wood to be used. Lumber samples to be minimum 6" by 12", plywood samples to be minimum 12" by 12". Samples shall represent the range of color and grain expected to be provided.

CSI Section 06 42 00
Paneling

2. [**Submit four additional samples of each material for the use of the paint trade.**]

> Include this Item if materials are to be finished at the job site.

C. [**Mockups:**

> Mockups shouldn't be necessary for most projects. Include this Item if full sized samples are desired.

1. **Provide a mockup of one Section of paneling, including an outside and an inside corner. The mockup shall be of the material and finish to be provided.**]

1.04. QUALITY ASSURANCE

A. Work shall be in accordance with the Grade or the Grades Specified of the *Architectural Woodwork Standards.*

B. [**Association Quality Assurance Program.**]

> Association quality assurance programs provide a pre qualification for the sub contractor. Bidders will be Association program participants or they will understand that their work will be inspected by an Association program representative. For better quality assurance, it's recommended that an Association assurance program is used.

C. Qualification:

1. Firm (woodwork manufacturer) with no less than 5 years of production experience similar to this Project, whose qualifications indicate the ability to comply with the requirements of this Section.
2. The woodwork manufacturer must have had at least one project in the past 5 years where the value of the woodwork was within 20 percent of the cost of woodwork for this Project.
3. Single Source Responsibility: A single manufacturer shall provide and install the work of this Section.

1.05. DELIVERY, STORAGE, AND HANDLING

A. Deliver materials only when the project is ready for installation and the general contractor has provided a clean storage area.

1. Delivery of architectural millwork shall be made only when the area of operation is enclosed, all plaster and concrete work is dry, and the area broom clean.
2. Maintain indoor temperature and humidity within the range recommended by the *Architectural Woodwork Standards* for the location of the project.

1.06. SCHEDULING

A. Coordinate fabrication, delivery, and installation with the general contractor and other applicable trades.

PART 2 - PRODUCTS

2.01. COMPONENTS

A. Meeting the requirements of the *Architectural Woodwork Standards.*

1. Lumber shall be sound and kiln dried.
   a. Exposed lumber shall be [[**species**], [**cut**]] [**closed grained hardwood**].

> The species is the species of tree, such as birch or oak. The cut is the angle of the face to the grain, such as plain sliced or rift. Book match is the most common. Use closed grain hardwood for painted wood paneling.

2. Veneer shall be [**species**] [**cut**] [[**book**] [**slip**]] matched.

> The match is the way the veneers are arranged on the panel. Book match is the most common.

3. Panels for opaque finish shall be [**MDO**] [**MDF**] [**closed grain hardwood veneer**].
4. Core material for laminated panels shall be [**MDF**] [**Particleboard**].
5. Laminate shall be [**manufacturer**] [**pattern**].

CSI Section 06 42 00
Paneling

6. Solid surface shall be **[manufacturer] [pattern]**.
    a. All solid surface at any room or area shall be from the same batch to prevent color mismatch.

7. Solid Phenolic shall be **[manufacturer] [pattern]**.

2.02 FABRICATION

Select the appropriate items below

A. Paneling shall be *Architectural Woodwork Standards* **[Economy] [Custom] [Premium]** Grade.

B. Stile and Rail Wood Paneling:
1. Stiles and rails shall be **[3/4] [1]** inch thick.
2. Joints at stiles and rails shall be securely fastened with dowels or biscuits.
3. Panels shall be **[flat] [raised]**.

C. Flat Veneered Paneling:
1. Panels shall be **[full width] [selectively reduced] [balanced sequence matched panels] [blueprint matched]**.
2. Visible edges and reveals shall be **[filled and painted] [match faces] [per details]**.
3. Outside corners shall be **[lock mitered] [mitered and splined] [per detail]**.
4. **[Blueprint Match: Work at room(s) [__________] shall be blueprint matched.**

This item is only necessary if there is an area where a blueprint match is desired. This could apply if there is transparent finish flat wood paneling adjacent to Wood Doors and Wood Casework. Similar language must be inserted in the Sections specifying casework, wood trim, and wood doors.

a. All work in this/these area(s) shall be AWS Premium Grade.

b. Casework, paneling, doors and wood trim shall be provided by the same manufacturer.

c. Veneers shall be taken from the same flitch, to be selected by the architect.

d. Faces at cabinet doors, drawer fronts, and false fronts shall be sequence matched, shall run and match vertically, and shall be sequence matched with adjacent wall paneling and/or doors.

e. Faces at exposed ends of cabinets shall be selected from the same flitch, and shall be well matched to the adjacent paneling and to the cabinet fronts.

f. All components including casework, paneling, doors, and trim shall be factory finished at the same time in the same facility.]

D. High Pressure Decorative Laminate Paneling:
1. Panels shall be **[full width -OR- selectively reduced]**.
2. Visible edges and reveals shall be **[filled and painted] [match faces] [per details]**.
3. Outside corners shall be **[lock mitered] [mitered and splined] [per detail]**.

E. Solid Surface Paneling:
1. Panels shall be **[manufacturer], [pattern]**.
2. Reveals shall be provided for expansion a maximum of 96" (2438 mm) on center.
3. Reveals shall be **[butt jointed and caulked] [covered with a trim batten] [splined with a loose spline]**.
4. Outside corners shall be **[hard seamed] [per details]**.

F. Solid Phenolic Core Paneling:
1. Reveals or slip joints shall be provided for expansion a maximum of 96" (2438 mm) on center.
2. Reveals shall be **[butt jointed and caulked] [be provided with a trim batten]**.
3. Outside corners shall be **[butt jointed] [trimmed with a metal corner mold] [per details]**.

CSI Section 06 42 00
Paneling

G. [**Factory Finishing:**

> This Item will not apply to HPDL, Solid Surface, or SPC paneling. As noted above, Factory Finishing is strongly recommended. In addition to getting a better finish, you are moving the air quality problems off site, where a proper spray booth will protect the environment and the health of the finishers.

1. **All products provided in this Section shall be factory finished using Architectural Woodwork Standards finishing system [_____].**
2. **Finish shall be AWS [Premium] [Custom] Grade.**]

PART 3 - EXECUTION

3.01. EXAMINATION

A. Verify the adequacy and proper location of blocking and support framing.

B. Verify that mechanical, electrical, plumbing, and other building components (supplied by others), affecting work in this Section are in place and ready.

3.02. INSTALLATION

A. Install all work in conformance with the *Architectural Woodwork Standards*, latest edition.

1. Installation shall conform to the *AWS* Grade of the items being installed.

B. All work shall be secured in place, square, plumb, and level.

C. All work abutting other building components shall be properly scribed.

D. Mechanical fasteners at exposed and semi-exposed surfaces shall be countersunk and filled.

3.03. ADJUSTING & TOUCH UP

A. All nicks, chips, and scratches shall be [**sanded smooth**] [**filled and retouched**]. Damaged items that cannot be repaired shall be replaced.

> Use “sanded smooth” if the work is to be finished at the job site. Use “filled and retouched” if the materials are to be factory finished.

3.04. CLEANUP

A. Upon completion of installation, the installer shall clean all installed items of pencil and ink marks, and broom clean the area of operation, depositing debris in containers provided by the general contractor.

END OF SECTION

NOTES

CSI Guide Specification
Section 06 46 00
Wood Trim

CSI Section 06 46 00
Wood Trim

This guide specification covers the materials and methods you would want to specify for wood or laminated plastic casework. It is strongly recommended that you read the "Cabinet Section" of *Architectural Millwork Standards* before using this guide spec. Many of the items you would ordinarily specify are governed by your choice of Grade.

In this guide spec, choices are in [**bold, in brackets**]. Comments are in shaded background.

PART 1 - GENERAL

1.01 SUMMARY

A. Section Includes:

Select the applicable items from the list below.

1. [**Interior Wood Door Frames.**]
2. [**Wood Door and Window Casings.**]
3. [**Wood Aprons.**]
4. [**Wood Base and Shoe Moldings.**]
5. [**Wood Chair Rails.**]
6. [**Wood Cornices.**]
7. [**Wood Fascia and Soffits.**]
8. [**Wood Stops, Stools, and Sills.**]
9. [**Factory finishing.**]

Factory finishing is strongly recommended. It is extremely difficult to get a quality finish under job site conditions.

B. Related Sections:

1. Rough Carpentry: Wood blocking or grounds inside finished walls or above finished ceilings.
2. Wood Paneling.
3. Wood and Plastic Laminate Casework.
4. Wood Doors.

1.02 REFERENCES

A. Minimum standards for work in this Section shall be in conformity with the *Architectural Woodwork Standards*, latest edition, published jointly by the Architectural Woodwork Institute, the Architectural Woodwork Manufacturer Association of Canada, and the Woodwork Institute.

All of the other standards you would reference are within the *AWS*.

1.03 SUBMITTALS

A. Shop Drawings:

1. Submit shop drawings in conformance with the requirements of the *Architectural Woodwork Standards.*
2. [**Furnish a AWS Certified Compliance Label on the first page of the shop drawings.**]
3. Submit two copies, one of which will be returned with reviewed notations. Make corrections noted (if any), and distribute required copies prior to the start of work.

B. Samples:

1. Submit four [**finished**] samples of each species and cut of wood to be used. Lumber samples to be minimum 6" by 12", plywood samples to be minimum 12" by 12". Samples shall represent the range of color and grain expected to be provided.
2. [**Submit four additional samples of each material for the use of the paint trade.**]

Include this Item if materials are to be finished at the job site.

CSI Section 06 46 00
Wood Trim

1.04 QUALITY ASSURANCE

A. Work shall be in accordance with the Grade or the Grades Specified of the *Architectural Woodwork Standards*.

B. [**Association Quality Assurance Program.**]

> Association quality assurance programs provide a pre qualification for the sub contractor. Bidders will be Association program participants or they will understand that their work will be inspected by an Association program representative. For better quality assurance, it's recommended that an Association assurance program is used.

C. Qualification:

1. Firm (woodwork manufacturer) with no less than 5 years of production experience similar to this Project, whose qualifications indicate the ability to comply with the requirements of this Section.
2. The woodwork manufacturer must have had at least one project in the past 5 years where the value of the woodwork was within 20 percent of the cost of woodwork for this Project.

D. Single Source Responsibility: A single manufacturer shall provide and install the work of this Section.

1.05 DELIVERY, STORAGE, AND HANDLING

A. Deliver materials only when the project is ready for installation and the general contractor has provided a clean storage area.

1. Delivery of architectural millwork shall be made only when the area of operation is enclosed, all plaster and concrete work is dry and the area broom clean.
2. Maintain indoor temperature and humidity within the range recommended by the *Architectural Woodwork Standards* for the location of the project.

1.06 SCHEDULING

A. Coordinate fabrication, delivery, and installation with the general contractor and other applicable trades.

PART 2 - PRODUCTS

2.01 COMPONENTS

A. Lumber shall be sound, kiln dried, and in accordance with the *Architectural Woodwork Standards* requirements for its use and the Grade specified.

B. Particleboard, MDF, and Plywood shall meet the requirements of the *AWS* for the Grade specified and their intended use.

C. Veneered components shall be in accordance with the *Architectural Woodwork Standards* requirements for the Grade specified.

1. [**Core shall be** [**particleboard**] [**MDF**].]

> If this item is not included, core is at the manufacturer's option, subject to requirements of the *AWS*. Particleboard or MDF are recommended as core materials.

2. Adhesives used shall be [**Type I**] [**Type II**].

> Type I glue is water proof; Type II is water resistant. Type II is satisfactory except in a very wet environment.

2.02 FABRICATION

A. Interior Millwork shall be *Architectural Woodwork Standards* [**Custom**] [**Premium**] Grade.

B. Door Jambs shall be [**flat jamb with applied stop**] [**Plowed jamb with a T stop**] [**rabbeted**].

C. Wainscot height shall be [___] inches above finish floor.

CSI Section 06 46 00
Wood Trim

D. Trim for opaque finish.

1. Moldings shall be [**MDF**] [**closed grain hardwood**].
2. Flat trim items shall be [**MDF**] [**MDO**] [**closed grain hardwood veneer**].
   a. Exposed edges shall be [**sanded and filled if necessary**] [**edge banded with closed grain hardwood veneer**].

E. Trim for transparent finish:

1. Moldings shall be [[**species**], [**cut**]] [**as indicated in the finish schedule**].
2. Exposed faces of veneered items shall be [[**species**] [**cut**] [**match**]] [**as indicated in the finish schedule**].

F. [**Blueprint Match: Work at room(s) [__________] shall be blueprint matched:**

Include this Item if there is a room or area where a blueprint match is desired.

1. All work in this/these area(s) shall be AWS Premium Grade.
2. Casework, paneling, doors, and wood trim shall be provided by the same manufacturer.
3. Veneers shall be taken from the same flitch, to be selected by the architect.
4. Faces at cabinet doors, drawer fronts, and false fronts shall be sequence matched, shall run and match vertically, and shall be sequence matched with adjacent wall paneling and/or doors.
5. Faces at exposed ends of cabinets shall be selected from the same flitch, and shall be well matched to the adjacent paneling and to the cabinet fronts.
6. Solid wood elements such as base, casing, and frames shall be well matched for color and grain, and shall be compatible in color and grain with veneered elements.
7. All components including casework, paneling, doors, and trim shall be factory finished at the same time in the same facility.]

G. [**Factory Finishing**

1. [All products provided in this Section shall be factory finished using "Architectural Woodwork Standards" finish system [_____].]
2. [Finish shall be AWS [Premium Grade] [Custom Grade] [the same Grade as the items being finished.]

As noted above, Factory Finishing is strongly recommended. In addition to getting a better finish, you are moving the air quality problems off site, where a proper spray booth will protect the environment and the health of the finishers. It is still worth while to select a low VOC finishing system, as some touch up will be required at the job site.

PART 3 - EXECUTION

3.01 EXAMINATION

A. Verify the adequacy and proper location of any required backing or support framing.

B. Verify that mechanical, electrical, plumbing, and other building components effecting work in this Section are in place and ready.

3.02 INSTALLATION

A. Install all work in conformance with the *Architectural Woodwork Standards*, latest edition.

1. Installation shall conform to the *AWS* Grade of the items being installed.

B. All work shall be secured in place, square, plumb, and level.

C. All work abutting other building components shall be properly scribed.

D. Mechanical fasteners used at exposed and semi-exposed surfaces shall be countersunk.

CSI Section 06 46 00
Wood Trim

3.03 ADJUSTING & TOUCH UP

A. All nicks, chips and scratches shall be [**sanded out**] [**filled and re-touched**]. Damaged items which cannot be repaired shall be replaced.

> Use "sanded out" if material is to be finished at the job site. Use "filled and retouched" if the materials are factory finished.

3.04 CLEANUP

A. Upon completion of installation, the installer shall clean all installed items of pencil and ink marks, and broom clean the area of operation, depositing debris in containers provided by the general contractor.

END OF SECTION

NOTES

CSI Guide Specification
Section 08 14 00
Wood Doors

CSI Section 08 14 00
Wood Doors

This guide specification covers the materials and methods you would want to specify for wood or laminated plastic casework. It is strongly recommended that you read the "Cabinet Section" of *Architectural Millwork Standards* before using this guide spec. Many of the items you would ordinarily specify are governed by your choice of Grade.

In this guide spec, choices are in [**bold, in brackets**]. Comments are in shaded background.

PART 1 - GENERAL

1.01 SUMMARY

A. Section Includes:

Select the applicable Items from the list below.

1. [**Flush Wood Doors**] [**Transom Panels**]
2. [**Stile and Rail Wood Doors.**]
3. [**Fire-Rated Wood Doors.**]
4. [**Wood Doors with HPDL faces.**]
5. [**Sound Rated Wood Doors including gaskets and automatic door bottoms.**]
6. [**X-ray Resistant Wood Doors.**]
7. [**Bullet Resistant Wood Doors.**]
8. [**Wood Louvers, Glass Stops, and Astragals.**]
9. [**Glazing.**]

If glazing is included here, delete it below. If it is not included here, show it under "Excluding".

10. [**Factory finishing.**]

Factory finishing is strongly recommended. It is extremely difficult to get a quality finish under job site conditions.

B. Excluding:

1. Cabinet doors.
2. Metal or Vinyl doors with wood cores.
3. Garage, Metal, and Fiberglass doors.
4. Metal grills or Louvers.
5. [Glazing.]

C. Related Sections:

1. Rough Carpentry: Wood blocking or grounds inside finished walls or above finished ceilings.
2. Door Hardware.
3. Door Frames.

1.02 REFERENCES

A. *Architectural Woodwork Standards*, latest edition, published jointly by the Architectural Woodwork Institute, the Architectural Woodwork Manufacturer Association of Canada, and the Woodwork Institute.

The other standards you would reference are within the *AWS*.

B. ANSI/WDMA I.S. 1A, latest edition.

C. ANSI/WDMA I.S. 6A, latest edition.

1.03 SUBMITTALS

A. Shop Drawings:

1. Submit shop drawings in conformance to the requirements of the *Architectural Woodwork Standards*.
2. Submit two copies, one of which will be returned with reviewed notations. Make corrections noted (if any), and distribute required copies prior to the start of work.

CSI Section 08 14 00
Wood Doors

B. Samples:

1. Submit four [**finished**] samples of each species and cut of wood to be used. Veneer samples to be minimum 12" (305 mm) by 12" (305 mm) . Samples shall represent the range of color and grain expected to be provided.

Samples may not be necessary for painted or LP covered doors.

2. [**Submit four additional samples of each material for the use of the paint trade.**]

1.04 QUALITY ASSURANCE

A. Work shall be in accordance with the Grade or the Grades Specified of the *Architectural Woodwork Standards*.

B. [**Association Quality Assurance Program.**]

Association quality assurance programs provide a pre qualification for the sub contractor. Bidders will be Association program participants or they will understand that their work will be inspected by an Association program representative. For better quality assurance, it's recommended that an Association assurance program is used.

C. Qualification:

1. Firm (woodwork manufacturer) with no less than 5 years of production experience similar to this Project, whose qualifications indicate the ability to comply with the requirements of this Section.
2. The woodwork manufacturer must have had at least one project in the past 5 years where the value of the woodwork was within 20 percent of the cost of woodwork for this Project.

D. Single Source Responsibility: A single manufacturer shall provide and install the work of this Section.

1.05 DELIVERY, STORAGE, AND HANDLING

A. Deliver materials only when the project is ready for installation and the general contractor has provided a clean storage area.

1. Delivery of architectural millwork shall be made only when the area of operation is enclosed, all plaster and concrete work is dry and the area broom clean.
2. Maintain indoor temperature and humidity within the range recommended by the *Architectural Woodwork Standards* for the location of the project.

1.06 SCHEDULING

A. Coordinate fabrication, delivery, and installation with the general contractor and other applicable trades.

PART 2 - PRODUCTS

2.01 COMPONENTS

A. Flush Wood Doors:

Select below the types of doors that are required.

1. [**Doors shall meet the requirements of ANSI/WDMA Extra Heavy Duty performance level.**]

AWS requires ANSI/WDMA Heavy Duty performance level for all doors. Require Extra Heavy Duty for doors that will see frequent and heavy use such as classrooms, patient rooms, and public restrooms. See Section 9 of the *AWS* for more discussion of duty levels.

2. Faces of wood veneered doors intended for transparent finish shall be [**species**] [**cut**], with [**book**] [**slip**] veneer match.

Veneer may be plain sliced, quarter sliced, rift, or rotary cut. The match is the system of matching veneer leaves on the panel. Book matched is the most common system; slip match is also frequently used. Rotary cut veneers may be wide enough to make single leaf faces.

3. Faces at Plastic Laminate faced doors shall be [**manufacturer**] [**pattern**].
4. Faces at doors for opaque finish shall be [**closed grain hardwood -OR- MDO -OR- MDF**].

CSI Section 08 14 00
Wood Doors

5. Core shall be [**hollow grid**] [**Particleboard**] [**staved lumber**] [**structural composite lumber**] [**per door schedule**].

Particleboard or SCL are recommended as core materials.

B. Stile and Rail Doors:

1. [**Doors shall meet the requirements of ANSI/WDMA Extra Heavy Duty performance standard.**]

AWS requires ANSI/WDMA Heavy Duty performance level for all doors. Require Extra Heavy Duty for doors that will see frequent and heavy use such as classrooms, patient rooms, and public restrooms. See Section 9 of the *AWS* for more discussion of duty levels.

2. Lumber shall be [**species, cut**] [**closed grain hardwood**].

Select closed grain hardwood for opaque finish.

3. Core material for panels shall be [**MDF**] [**water resistant MDF**] [**SCL**] [**exterior grade hardwood plywood**].

Custom Grade allows solid lumber panels. Include this Item if Premium Grade is specified and you prefer one core material over another.

4. Core material for stiles and rails shall be [**MDF**] [**SCL**] [**stave core**].

Custom Grade allows solid lumber stiles and rails. Include this Item if Premium Grade is specified and you prefer one core material over another.

5. Type I adhesives shall be used at exterior doors.
6. [**Lights shall be** [**tempered**] [**laminated**] safety glass.

Include this Item if glazing is included in this Section.

A. Lights at exterior doors shall be [________].

Insert your preferred insulated or low e glazing.

2.02 FABRICATION

A. Slab doors shall be *Architectural Woodwork Standards* [**Custom**] [**Premium**] Grade:

1. Doors shall be [**3**] [**5**] [**7**] ply construction.

Three ply construction is only used for Laminate faced doors.

2. Exterior doors shall be assembled with Type 1 glue.
3. Size of doors; type, size, and location of lights and louvers; astragals, edging, flashing, and specialty hardware; X-ray and sound requirements, and transom panels shall be as indicated on the door schedule.
4. Fire-rated doors shall be of the construction standard of the manufacturer and conform with the requirements of all applicable labeling agencies.
5. Provide blocking as required for surface mounted hardware to prevent the need for through bolting.

Specify a blueprint match if there is an area where casework, doors, and panels should all be sequence matched. Similar language must be inserted in the Sections specifying wood paneling, wood trim, and casework.

6. [**Blueprint Match: Work at room(s)** [__________] **shall be blueprint matched:**
   a. **All work in this/these area(s) shall be AWS Premium Grade.**
   b. **Casework, paneling, doors and wood trim shall be provided by the same manufacturer.**
   c. **Veneers shall be taken from the same flitch, to be selected by the architect.**
   d. **Faces of cabinet doors, drawer fronts and false fronts shall be sequence matched, shall run and match vertically, and shall be sequence matched with adjacent wall paneling and/or doors.**
   e. **Faces at exposed ends of cabinets shall be selected from the same flitch, and shall be well matched to the adjacent paneling and to the cabinet fronts.**
   f. **All components including casework, paneling, doors and trim shall be factory finished at the same time in the same facility.**]

B. Stile and Rail Doors shall be *Architectural Woodwork Standards* [**Custom**] [**Premium**] Grade.

1. Panels:
   A. Shall be [**1/2 (12.7 mm)**] [**3/4 (19 mm)**] [**1 3/8 (34.9)**] [**1 ¾ (44.5 mm)**] inches thick.

Use ½" or ¾" panels for flat panel construction. Use thicker panels for raised panels.

CSI Section 08 14 00
Wood Doors

B. [**Veneered panels shall be [book] [slip] matched.**]

Use this item if Premium Grade is specified.

2. Sticking and panel edge details shall be **[per plans] [per manufacturer's standard details as selected by architect]**.

C. Factory Finishing:

As noted above, Factory Finishing is strongly recommended. In addition to getting a better finish, you are moving the air quality problems off site, where a proper spray booth will protect the environment and the health of the finishers. It is still worth while to select a low VOC finishing system, as some touch up will be required at the job site.

1. All products provided in this Section shall be factory finished using *Architectural Woodwork Standards* finishing system [_____].
2. Finish shall be *AWS* [**Premium -OR- Custom**] Grade.

PART 3 - EXAMINATION

3.01 EXAMINATION

A. Verify that frames are set square, plumb, level, and in plane.
   1. Report openings that are not within tolerance to the General Contractor for correction before hanging doors.

3.02 INSTALLATION

A. Install all work in conformance with the Architectural Woodwork Standards, latest edition.
   1. Installation shall conform to the *AWS* Grade of the items being installed.

B. Doors shall be secured in place, square, plumb, and level.

C. Hardware shall be installed complete and as recommended by the manufacturer.

3.03 ADJUSTING & TOUCH UP

A. Before completion of the installation, the installer shall adjust all moving and operating parts to function smoothly and correctly.

B. All nicks, chips, and scratches in the finish shall be filled and retouched. Damaged items which cannot be repaired shall be replaced.

3.04 CLEANUP

A. Upon completion of installation, the installer shall clean all installed items of pencil and ink marks, and broom clean the area of operation, depositing debris in containers provided by the general contractor.

END OF SECTION

NOTES

1
Submittals

1 - Submittals

WHAT TO EXPECT

"The Woodworker shall submit shop drawings, samples, brochures, etc. on all items of architectural woodwork. Shop drawings shall be of sufficient detail in scale to determine compliance with the intent of the Quality Standard Grade specified." - from an office Master Specification

In commonly used Guide Specifications, the scale, level of detail and quantity of shop drawings actually required for custom architectural woodwork are described rather broadly. The key to achieving the most detailed and useful set of drawings is clear and continual communication between the architect/designer and the woodwork manufacturer, from the earliest stage of design.

PURPOSE

Shop drawings are the means by which the design intent is turned into reality, serving as the primary instructions for woodwork engineering and fabrication, and as a guide for other trades. As the primary communication among woodworker, general contractor and design professional, shop drawings serve a valuable coordinative function. Good shop drawings are the extension of the design into the area of engineering. They should indicate methods of construction, exact material selections, finishes, method of attachment and joinery, exact dimensions and should include the woodworker's technical suggestions.

LEVEL OF DETAIL

The level of detail required on shop drawings is established by the Quality Grade and complexity of the project. The specifier is at liberty to specify any level of detail as a requirement of the project and of the contract documents. It should be noted that requirements for local codes and utilization of fire retardant wood products are to be researched and directed by the design professional and are not the responsibility of the woodworker.

What constitutes the minimum expectation for a set of shop drawings? The answer is not simple, since there are many variables as to the complexity, quality and type of work being specified.

A suggested level of detail and scale of drawings has been established in tabular form and is provided on the following pages to be used as a guideline.

APPROVALS

The approval stage provides the architect/designer a final opportunity, prior to fabrication, to make changes or correct mistakes. Shop drawings, however, are not an extension of the design development process; therefore, changes of intent made during shop drawing review will in many cases involve an increase in cost and time.

During the review process the design professional should consider the following:

• Only two copies are necessary for checking purposes. After being reviewed, one marked copy should be returned to the woodworker with a request for the required number of prints or a sepia from which the owner's representative may make prints.

• Those charged with review of shop drawings should be completely familiar with woodwork fabrication, and be responsible for insuring compliance with referenced Standards as well as design intent.

• Deviations from the original plans are often recommendations for improvement, and not necessarily a "flying in the face" of instructions. It is as wrong for a checker to arbitrarily stamp "Redraw and Resubmit" on a shop drawing that proposes a change as it is wrong to automatically accept a folio of drawings because they contain duplicates of the original plans.

The four common levels of approval are:

- Approved
- Approved As Noted
- Redraw and Resubmit
- Disapproved

Approvals are generally indicated by a stamp on each of the drawings. When selecting "Approved As Noted" rather than "Redraw and Resubmit," the design professional can often save weeks of production time provided the intent and all changes are clearly marked on the drawings.

SCHEDULING

Most projects are encumbered by a tight production schedule, especially for the finish trades such as woodworking, painting, carpeting and wall coverings. Prompt review of shop drawings and accurate coordination of multiple trades can save weeks of time and eliminate problems before construction begins.

We recommend the design professional work with the woodwork manufacturer to determine the maximum "approval-to-fabrication" timeline needed to keep the job on schedule (e.g., "Shop drawings must be returned approved to fabricate seven (7) days after submittal.")

SCHEDULES VS. DRAWINGS

In some cases shop drawings are not required to communicate the necessary quality, type, quantity and details of an item. Tabular schedules are used instead, generally for such items as doors, frames, stock factory cabinets, closet shelves, and furniture items.

THE PROCESS

It is the role of the design professional and the contractor to coordinate the woodworker's shop drawings with work of all other trades and to insure the "hold" dimensions are actually held. It is also the responsibility of the architect or contractor to give field changes to all parties so that if dimensions are changed, each subcontractor and material supplier can be held responsible for his work.

2
Care and Storage

2 - Care and Storage

PERMANENT FURNITURE

Architectural woodwork should be treated like fine furniture, particularly that which is constructed of wood finished with a transparent finish system.

Fine architectural work is finished with a commercial finish which is durable and resistant to moisture. Allowing moisture to accumulate on, or stay in contact with, any wood surface, no matter how well finished, will cause damage. Prevent direct contact with moisture, and wipe dry immediately should any occur.

TREATMENT

With the exception of true oil-rubbed surfaces, modern finishes do not need to be polished, oiled, or waxed. In fact, applying some polishing oils, cleaning waxes, or products containing silicone may impede the effectiveness of touch-up or refinishing procedures in the future.

CLEANING

No abrasives or chemical or ammonia cleaners should be used to clean fine woodwork surfaces.

Routine cleaning is best accomplished with a soft, lint-free cloth lightly dampened with water or an inert household dust attractant. Allowing airborne dust, which is somewhat abrasive, to build up will tend to dull a finish over time.

Remove oil or grease deposits with a mild flax soap, following the directions for dilution on the container.

IMPACT

Avoid excessive or repetitive impact, however lightly applied. The cellular structure of the wood will compact under pressure. Many modern finishes are flexible, and will show evidence of impact and pressure applied to them.

HEAT

Avoid localized high heat, such as a hot pan or plate, or a hot light source, close to or in contact with the finished surface. Exposure to direct sunlight will alter the appearance of fine woodwork over time.

HUMIDITY

Maintain the relative humidity around the woodwork in accordance with the guidelines published in this standard, every hour of every day, to minimize wood movement.

ABUSE

Use the trims, cabinets and fixtures, paneling, shelving, ornamental work, stairs, frames, windows, and doors as they were intended. Abuse of cabinet doors and drawers, for example, may result in damage to them as well as to the cabinet parts to which they are joined.

REPAIR AND REFINISHING

Contact a local woodworking firm, or the offices of the associations, to explore the options for repair or refinishing. It is often cost effective to replace damaged woodwork elements rather than attempting large scale, on site refinishing.

3
Lumber

3 - Lumber

LUMBER used in architectural woodwork is divided into two groups:

HARDWOODS: Lumber obtained from angiosperms, usually deciduous trees (broadleaf trees). There are more angio sperms on Earth than any other plant group, over 200,000 species. About 900 of those species are commonly available for lumber or veneer throughout the world.

SOFTWOODS: Lumber obtained from gymnosperms, about 600 of which are coniferous trees such as pine, spruce, and fir. The gymnosperms are among the largest and oldest living plants.

NOTE: The above groups have **NO** relationship to the density or "hardness" within or between various species. Some softwoods are harder than some hardwoods, and hardness varies greatly between species within each group.

AWS lumber grades will always be referenced when specifying architectural woodwork. Selection of the ***AWS*** Grade for the finished product (Premium, Custom, or Economy) will define both materials and workmanship for that product. Lumber grades defined by the lumber manufacturers' associations allow some defects which the architectural woodworker must remove (cut out), or otherwise work around (by gluing, etc.).

The selection of the proper wood species for an architectural design can be the end result of a number of contributing factors and conditions. Intended use, costs, hardness, and relative stability are among many important considerations.

The architect and designer may make his selection from a large variety of foreign and domestic species, now commercially available. The unique quality that wood imparts to design is that each species has its own distinguishing characteristics. Once the species is chosen, its effectiveness may vary according to the manner in which it is sawn, sliced as veneer, treated, and finished.

This Section is designed to counsel the architect and designer in the comparisons, considerations, and species which should be evaluated before decisions are made and specifications are written. This Section will help you correlate and tabulate the information needed. An informed choice will reward the owner with the best possible performance by a natural building material.

WOOD AS A PLANT

The trunk and its branches: The cross section of a tree shows the following well-defined features in succession from the outside to the center: (1) bark and cambium layer; (2) wood, which in most species is clearly differentiated into sapwood and heartwood; and (3) pith, the small central core. The pith and bark, of course, are excluded from finished lumber.

Most branches originate at the pith, and their bases are intergrown with the wood of the trunk as long as they are alive. These living branch bases constitute intergrown or tight knots. After the branches die, their bases continue to be surrounded by the wood of the growing trunk and therefore loose or encased knots are formed. After the dead branches fall off, the stubs become overgrown, and subsequently clear wood is formed.

All growth in thickness takes place in the cambium layer by cell division. No growth in either diameter or length takes place in wood already formed; new growth is purely the addition of new cells, not the further development of existing cells.

ANNUAL RINGS

Most species grown in temperate climates produce well-defined annual growth rings, which are formed by the difference in density and color between wood formed early and late in the growing season. The inner part of the growth ring formed first is called "spring wood," and the outer part formed later in the growing season is called "summer wood."

Spring wood is characterized by cells having relatively large cavities and thin walls. Summer wood cells have smaller cavities and thicker walls, and consequently are more dense than spring wood. The growth rings, when exposed by conventional methods of sawing, provide the grain or characteristic pattern of the wood. The distinguishing features of the various species are thereby enhanced by the differences in growth ring formation.

Some tropical species, on the other hand, experience year long even growth which may result in less obvious growth rings.

SOFTWOODS AND HARDWOODS

Native species of trees and the wood produced by these trees are divided into two botanical classes: hardwoods, which have broad leaves; and softwoods, which have needle-like or scale-like leaves. This botanical classification is sometimes confusing, because there is no direct correlation between calling a species a hardwood or softwood and the hardness or softness of the wood itself. Generally, hardwoods are more dense than softwoods, but some hardwoods are softer than many softwoods. If hardness is a desired characteristic, refer to the Comparative Table of Wood Species later in this section.

HEARTWOOD

Heartwood consists of inactive cells formed by changes in the living cells of the inner sapwood rings, presumably after their use for sap conduction and other life processes of the tree have largely ceased. The cell cavities of heartwood may also contain deposits of various materials that frequently provide a much darker color. Not all heartwood, however, is darker. The infiltrations of material deposited in the cells of heartwood usually make lumber cut therefrom more durable when exposed to weather. All wood, with the possible exception of the heartwood of Redwood and Western Red Cedar, should be preservative-treated when used for exterior applications.

SAPWOOD

Sapwood contains living cells and performs an active role in the life processes of the tree. It is located next to the cambium and functions in sap conduction and storage of food. Sapwood commonly ranges from 1" to 2" (25-50 mm) in thickness. The Maples, Hickories, Ashes, and some of the Southern Yellow Pines and Ponderosa Pine may have sapwood 3" to 6" (76-152 mm) in thickness, especially in second growth trees.

3 - Lumber

MEDULLARY RAYS

Medullary rays extend radially from the pith of the log toward the circumference. The rays serve primarily to store food and transport it horizontally. They vary in height from a few cells in some species to four or more inches in the oaks, and produce the fleck (sometimes called flake) effect common to the quarter-sawn lumber in these species.

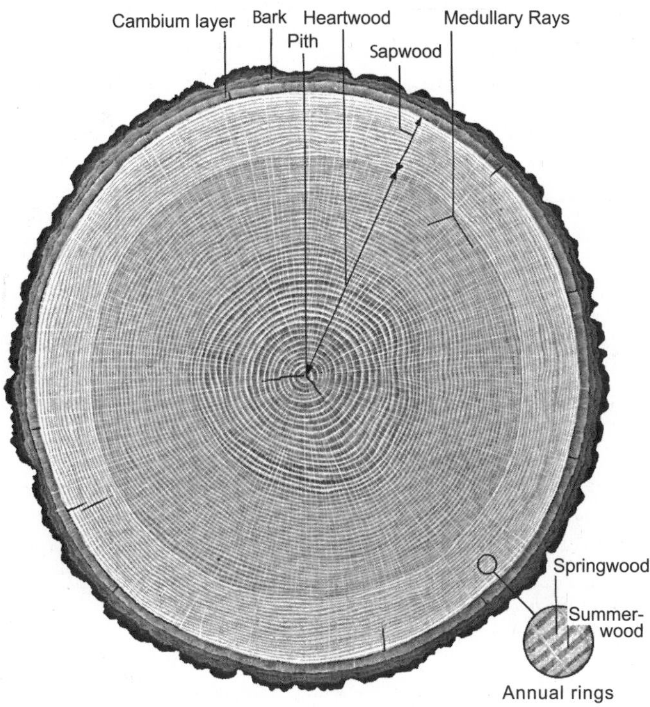

COMPARATIVE TABLE OF WOOD SPECIES

In order to simplify species selection, the Comparative Table of Wood Species (pg. 436) has been prepared showing pertinent characteristics of some species of domestic and foreign woods used by the architectural woodwork industry. The table can quickly confirm or deny the wisdom of a species selection by the architect or designer or conversely lead to a proper selection after studying the characteristics.

COST has been broken into both Lumber and Plywood headings, with data divided into Low, Moderate, High, and Very High [V. High]. (Important: Market conditions cause these relationships to vary. Current ratios are likely to be different.) The reason for cost variations in the two products is obvious when we consider the physical differences. Generally, the prices of veneered products reflect the relatively high labor and equipment cost and relatively low material cost in their manufacture. On the other hand, the price of lumber in most species reflects cost factors that are exactly the opposite. In spite of their physical differences, the two products are always compatible, and both are essential to complete design freedom in contemporary buildings.

End use determines the importance of Hardness in selecting a species for each particular type of application. Counters, door frames, wall treatments in high-traffic areas, etc., are obvious uses of wood products where hardness and resistance to abrasion must be considered. In many other applications these factors, relatively speaking, are not of great importance.

The **DIMENSIONAL STABILITY** column is helpful in selecting woods for use where humidity conditions may vary widely and where design or fabrication of a wood product does not allow free movement or the use of plywood. The column figures indicate extreme conditions and show the maximum amount of movement possible in a 12" (305 mm) wide piece of unfinished wood where its moisture content increases or decreases from 10% to 5%. The possible change in dimension demonstrates that unfinished interior woodwork must be carefully protected prior to finishing by keeping it in rooms where relative humidity is between 25% and 55%. The column also shows the variation between species, and between flat grain and edge grain where such cuts are available commercially.

Careful analysis of the table will make it possible for an architect, designer or specification writers (who may have only a limited knowledge of architectural wood species) to make an informed selection. It is our intent that this tool will enhance understanding between the manufacturer of the woodwork you have designed and your profession, thereby enabling the building industry to better service the client.

3 - Lumber

COMPARATIVE TABLE OF WOOD SPECIES

Species	Costs (1)		Practical Size Limits (2)			Hardness	Dimensional Stability (3)
	Lumber	Plywood	Thick-ness	Width	Length		
Ash	Moderate	Moderate	2-1/2"	5-1/2"	12'	Hard	10/64"
Basswood	Low	No data	2-1/2"	5-1/2"	10'	Soft	10/64"
Beech	Low	No data	1-1/2"	5-1/2"	12'	Hard	14/64"
Birch, Yellow - natural	Moderate	Moderate	1-1/2"	5-1/2"	12'	Hard	12/64"
Birch, Yellow - select red	Moderate	Moderate	1-1/2"	4-1/2"	11'	Hard	12/64"
Birch, Yellow - select white	Moderate	Moderate	1-1/2"	4"	11'	Hard	12/64"
Butternut	High	V. High	1-1/2"	4-1/2"	8'	Soft	8/64"
Cedar, Western Red	High	Moderate	3-1/4"	11"	16'	Soft	10/64"
Cherry, American Black	High	High	2-1/2"	4"	7'	Hard	9/64"
Chestnut - wormy	High	No data	3/4"	5-1/2"	10'	Medium	9/64"
Cypress, Yellow	Low	No data	2-1/2"	7-1/2"	16'	Medium	8/64"
Fir, Douglas - flat grain	High	Moderate	3-1/4"	11"	16'	Medium	10/64"
Fir, Douglas - vertical grain	High	No data	1-1/2"	11"	16'	Medium	6/64"
Hickory	Low	Moderate	1-1/2"	4-1/2"	12'	Very Hard	11/64"
Mahogany, African - plain sawn	High	High	2-1/2"	9"	15'	Medium	7/64"
Mahogany, African - quarter sawn	V. High	V. High	2-1/2"	5-1/2"	15'	Medium	5/64"
Mahogany, Genuine (American)	High	V. High	2-1/2"	11"	15'	Medium	6/64"
Maple, Hard - natural	Moderate	Moderate	3-1/2"	7-1/2"	12'	Very Hard	12/64"
Maple, Hard - select white	Moderate	High	2-1/2"	5-1/2"	12'	Very Hard	12/64"
Maple, Soft - natural	Moderate	No data	3-1/2"	7-1/2"	12'	Medium	9/64"
Oak, English Brown	V. High	V. High	1-1/2"	4-1/2"	8'	Hard	No data
Oak, Red - plain sawn	Moderate	Moderate	2-1/2"	7-1/4"	12'	Hard	11/64"
Oak, Red - rift sawn	High	High	1-1/16"	3-1/2"	8'	Hard	7/64"
Oak, Red - quarter sawn	High	High	1-1/16"	5-1/2"	8'	Hard	7/64"
Oak, White - plain sawn	Low	High	1-1/2"	5-1/2"	10'	Hard	11/64"
Oak, White - rift sawn	High	High	3/4"	3"	8'	Hard	7/64"
Oak, White - quarter sawn	High	High	3/4"	4"	8'	Hard	7/64"
Pecan	Low	Moderate	1-1/2"	4-1/2"	12'	Hard	11/64"
Pine, Eastern or Northern White	Moderate	No data	1-1/2"	9-1/2"	14'	Soft	8/64"
Pine, Idaho	Moderate	No data	1-1/2"	9-1/2"	16'	Soft	8/64"
Pine, Ponderosa	Moderate	Moderate	1-1/2"	9-1/2"	16'	Soft	8/64"
Pine, Sugar	Moderate	No data	3-1/4"	11"	16'	Soft	7/64"
Pine, Southern Yellow	Low	No data	1-1/2"	7-1/2"	16'	Medium	10/64"
Poplar, Yellow	Low	No data	2-1/2"	7-1/2"	12'	Medium	9/64"
Redwood, flat grain heartwood	Moderate	No data	2-1/2"	11"	16'	Soft	6/64"
Redwood, vert. grain heartwood	Moderate	No data	2-1/2"	11"	16'	Soft	3/64"
Teak	V. High	V. High	1-1/2"	5-1/2"	8'	Hard	6/64"
Walnut, American Black	Moderate	High	2-1/2"	4"	6'	Hard	10/64"
Walnut, Nogal	Moderate	No data	3/4"	9-1/2"	9'	Medium	12/64"
Zebrawood, African - quarter sawn	V. High	V. High	1-1/2""	7"	14'	Hard	7/64"

(1) Market conditions will cause these relationships to vary. These are raw costs without consideration of labor.
(2) Maximum practical sizes without lamination/gluing. Only 10% of any order is required to be at maximum sizes.
(3) These figures represent possible width change in a 12" (304.8 mm) board when moisture content is reduced from 10% to 5%. Figures taken are for plain sawn unless indicated otherwise in the species column.

3 - Lumber

Plainsawn Lumber

Riftsawn Lumber

Quartersawn Lumber

ASH, WHITE (Fraxinus americana)

While White Ash has always enjoyed widespread use for industrial products where hardness, shock resistance, stability and strength were important, its acceptance for architectural woodwork is increasing. It is open grained and has a strong and pronounced grain pattern. The heartwood is light tan or brown and its sapwood creamy white. Color contrast between the two is minor and its blond effect makes it particularly appealing when a light or near natural finish is desired. Finished with darker tones it presents a very forthright, honest, and virile effect. Its cost is moderate and it is readily available in lumber form. In veneered form some size limitation may be experienced but it can be easily produced on special order.

BIRCH, YELLOW - "Natural" (Betula alleghaniensis)

BIRCH, YELLOW - "Select Red" (heartwood) (Betula alleghaniensis)

BIRCH, YELLOW - "Select White" (sapwood) (Betula alleghaniensis)

Yellow Birch has been and continues to be one of the prominent wood species used for architectural woodwork. This is due not only to its attractive appearance but also to its general availability both as lumber and as veneered products, its adaptability to either paint or transparent finish, and its abrasion resistance. The heartwood of the tree varies in color from medium to dark brown or reddish brown while its sapwood, which comprises a better than average portion of the tree, is near white. Despite its wide usage some confusion exists as to the common terms used to describe Birch lumber and/or veneer. Virtually all commercially used Birch is cut from the Yellow Birch tree, not from the White Birch tree, which botanically is a distinct species. The term "Natural" or "Unselected" Birch means that the lumber or veneer may contain both the sapwood, or white portion, as well as the heartwood, or dark portion, of the tree in unrestricted amounts. The term "Select Red" Birch describes the lumber or veneer produced from the heartwood portion of the tree, and the term "Select White" Birch describes the lumber or veneer produced from the sapwood portion of the tree. To obtain "Red" or "White" Birch exclusively requires selective cutting with corresponding cost premium as well as considerable restriction on the width and length availability in lumber form. Birch, in veneer form, is readily available in all "selections" and is usually rotary cut. While some sliced veneer is produced which simulates the same grain effect as lumber, its availability and cost reflect the same cutting restrictions that are incurred in producing the "select" forms of Birch lumber.

CHERRY, AMERICAN BLACK (Prunus serotina)

Wild Black American Cherry is a fine and especially stable close grained cabinet and veneer wood. Its heartwood color ranges from light to medium reddish brown. Its sapwood, which is a light creamy color, is usually selectively eliminated from the veneer and lumber. In some respects it resembles Red Birch, but has a more uniform grain and is further characterized by the presence of small dark gum spots which, when sound, are not considered as defects but add to its interest. Cherry is available in moderate supply as lumber and architectural paneling and is usually plain sawn or sliced. Exceptionally rich appearance is achieved with transparent finishes which, together with its fine machining characteristics, justifies its identity with Early American cabinetry and furniture manufacturing, thus adding to its prestige as one of our most desirable native woods.

3 - Lumber

CYPRESS, YELLOW (Taxodium distichum)

While Cypress is still prevalent throughout the south, distinction should be made between the type now generally available and what was once known as "Tidewater Red Cypress." The latter, once the "premium" wood for exterior applications, is now virtually extinct and subject to limited usage. The currently available Cypress lumber, while similar in appearance, does not contain the heartwood of inherently high decay resistance once associated with the species, and in lumber form contains a high percentage of sapwood. Thus, like most softwoods, preservative treatment is imperative if used on the exterior. While this does not preclude its exterior application, it is perhaps more generally utilized for paneling where its strong, bold grain is best displayed.

FIR, DOUGLAS (Flat Grain) (Pseudotsuga taxifolla)

Douglas Fir is a large, fast-growing species and is native to the northwest. It accounts for much of the lumber produced in North America. While the preponderance of its production is developed for structural and construction type products, some of its upper grades are used for stock millwork and specialized woodwork. Its heartwood is reddish tan while its sapwood is creamy yellow. Since its growth rings are conspicuous, a rather bold grain pattern develops when either plain sawn for lumber or rotary cut as is common in plywood. Some lumber and veneer is cut edge or vertical grain, producing a superior form of the product since the tendency to "grain-raise" is greatly reduced.

MAHOGANY, AFRICAN (plain sawn) (Khaya ivorensis)

This, one of the true Mahoganies, is perhaps the most widely used of the several Mahogany species. This is due to its excellent cutting and working characteristics and versatility. While its use has been largely for interior purposes, its innate stability and moderate decay resistance justifies its consideration for selected and demanding exterior applications. It has a very pleasing open grain, with its heartwood ranging in color from light to medium dark reddish brown. In lumber form it is more readily available as plain sawn and selectively so as quartersawn. In veneer form the quarter or "ribbon striped" cut predominates, but plain sliced, as well as many of the exotic "figure" cuts, can be produced on special order.

MAHOGANY, GENUINE OR AMERICAN (Swietenia macrophylla)

This Mahogany species is commonly known as "Honduras Mahogany," but actually encompasses all of this species that grow throughout Mexico, Brazil, Peru, and Central America. Its traditional identity with fine cabinetry and furniture justifies its position as one of the finest woods for this purpose. Its stability, workability, warm appearance, and firm grain make it a favorite of all woodworking craftsmen. It is a semi-open grain wood, with its heartwood color ranging from light tan to a rich golden brown depending to some extent on the country of its origin. Its outstanding stability and decay resistance expands its potential to include exterior applications for "monumental" projects. It is most generally available as plain sawn lumber and plain sliced veneer with different veneer cuts available on special order.

MAPLE, HARD - "Natural" (Acer saccharum)

MAPLE, HARD - "Select White" (Sapwood) (Acer saccharum)

Hard Maple is very similar in general characteristics to Yellow Birch. It is heavy, hard, strong, and resistant to shock and abrasion. The heartwood of the tree is reddish brown and its sapwood is near white with a slight reddish-brown tinge. Another natural characteristic is the prevalence of dark mineral streaks (predominantly in the heartwood), which can be minimized in the sapwood by selective cutting. Like Birch, common usage of descriptive terms does occasion some confusion. The term "Natural" or "Unselected" Maple indicates that the lumber or veneer may contain both the white sapwood and the darker heartwood. The term "White" Maple means that the lumber or veneer is selected and separated from the pieces containing the dark heartwood. Unlike Birch, the heartwood is so low in content that no comparable selection is available. Maple's close identity with furniture and specialized industrial use overshadows its potential for architectural woodwork. Its modest cost, and pleasing, mild grain pattern warrants its consideration, especially on items subject to hard usage.

ENGLISH BROWN OAK (Quercus robur)

The English Brown Oak, or Pollard Oak is a tree which varies in height from 18-40 m [60'-130'] depending on soil conditions. It varies in color from a light tan to a deep brown with occasional black spots. It produces burls and swirls which are very brittle and fragile, but beautiful work can be obtained with their use. English Brown Oak is considered one of the finest woods in use today.

English Brown Oak is obtained from trees which have had their tops cut out before reaching maturity. This pruning leads to the production of a number of new branches around the cut, and if these are subsequently lopped off, more new branches are formed.

This wood is difficult to season and to work, tending to warp and twist in drying and to tear in working. The best figure is obtained from trees which have been cut over regularly every few years, the branches never being left sufficiently long for the production of large knots. The constant exposure of freshly cut surfaces promotes attack from parasites, the result being that a considerable portion of these trees become decayed sooner or later. This has made the timber relatively scarce and costly.

OAK, RED (plain sawn) (Quercus rubra)

OAK, RED (rift sawn) (Quercus rubra)

Red Oak is one of the most abundant of our domestic hardwoods. Its moderate cost, strength, wearability, and appealing grain characteristics make its use widespread. It is open grained and in its plain sawn or sliced form expresses a very strong "cathedral" type grain pattern. The heartwood is reddish tan to brown and very uniform in color. Its sapwood is lighter in color and minimal in volume, making its elimination by selective cutting very easy. Red Oak is also available in rift sawn or sliced form, which produces a very uniform straight-grained effect. Less frequently it is quarter sawn or sliced, still producing a straight grain but with the fleck (sometimes called flake) of the medullary ray accented. Some sacrifice in width and length availability occurs when producing either rift or quarter sawn lumber.

3 - Lumber

OAK, WHITE (plain sawn) (Quercus alba)

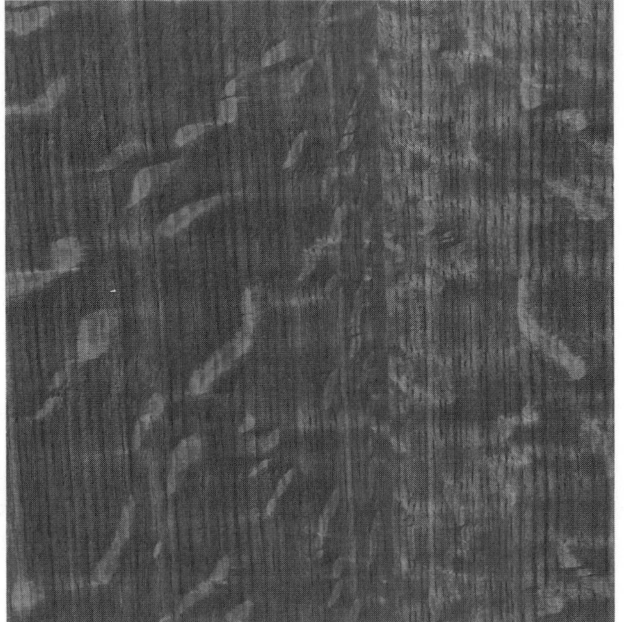

OAK, WHITE (quarter sawn) (Quercus alba)

White Oak, like Red Oak, is perhaps one of the best-known hardwoods in the world, and its use for architectural woodwork is widespread. It is hard and strong. Its heartwood has good weathering characteristics, making its use for selected exterior applications appropriate. It is open grained and in its plain sawn form is highly figured. The heartwood varies considerably in color from light grayish tan to brown, making the maintenance of color consistency difficult. Its sapwood is much lighter in color, is fairly prevalent, and its elimination is accomplished by selective ripping. White Oak is often rift sawn or sliced, producing a very straight-grained effect or frequently quarter sawn or sliced, producing straight grain, but with the fleck (sometimes called flake) of the medullary ray greatly pronounced. The special cuts mentioned are more readily attained in veneer form since the solid lumber cutting techniques greatly restrict its width and length potential.

PINE, PONDEROSA (Pinus ponderosa)

Ponderosa Pine is said to be the softwood species most commonly used for exterior and interior woodwork components. Its heartwood is tannish pink, while its sapwood is a lighter creamy pink. Its supply is extensive; found in commercial quantities in every state west of the Great Plains. Ponderosa Pine grows in pure stands and is abundant in mixed stands. Also, like most Pines, the proportion of sapwood is high and its heartwood has only a moderate natural decay resistance. Fortunately, its receptivity to preservative treatment is high, and since all Pines should be so treated when used on the exterior, it can be used interchangeably with them.

PINE, SOUTHERN YELLOW (Short Leaf) (Pinus echinata)

Southern Yellow Pine, commonly called Short Leaf Pine, is commercially important in Arkansas, Virginia, Missouri, Louisiana, Mississippi, Texas, and South and North Carolina, and is found in varying abundance from New York and south central Pennsylvania, south and westerly to eastern Texas and Oklahoma.

The yellowish wood is noticeably grained, moderately hard, strong, and stiff. A cubic foot of air-dried Southern Yellow Pine weighs 36 to 39 pounds. It is used extensively in house building, including framing, ceiling, weather boarding, panels, window and door frames, casing, and carved work. The grain shows well in natural finish or when stained. Frames of overstuffed furniture, chairs, desks, agricultural machinery, wood pulp, mine props, barrels, and crates are also made of this Pine.

POPLAR, YELLOW (Liriodendron tulipfera)

Yellow Poplar, sometimes incorrectly called "Whitewood," is an extremely versatile and moderately priced hardwood that is well adapted to general interior woodwork usage. It is even textured, close grained, stable, of medium hardness, and has an inconspicuous grain pattern. The heartwood is pale greenish yellow while the sapwood is white. Occasional dark purple streaks also occur. The tight, close grain results in outstanding paintability, while its modest figure and even texture permits staining to simulate more expensive hardwood. Due to its indistinct grain figure, Poplar is seldom used for decorative veneered products. Its white sapwood is not appropriate for use in exterior applications.

REDWOOD, FLAT GRAIN (Heartwood) (Sequoia sempervirens)

Redwood is the product of one of nature's most impressive accomplishments. The enormous size and unique inherent characteristics of this tree produce a material ideally suited for exterior applications. Its heartwood color is a fairly uniform brownish red, while its very limited sapwood is lemon colored. In its plain sawn form medium "cathedral" type figure develops, while in the vertical grain a longitudinal striped figure results. Its availability in "all heartwood" form with its outstanding natural resistance to decay accounts for its wide usage for exterior purposes. It is considered a very stable wood and its paint retention qualities are excellent. Redwood's principal identity with painted exterior application should not preclude its consideration for either exterior or interior use with transparent finish. Its pleasing and uniform color lends itself to a variety of such finishes suggesting the warmth and honesty of wood in its natural state. The enormous size of the trees yields lumber of unusually character-free widths and lengths.

TEAK (Tectona grandis)

Teak is one of the most versatile and valuable woods and has attained great prestige value. The figure variations are extensive and it is available in both lumber and veneered products. Adding to its appeal is its distinctive tawny yellow to green to dark brown color, often with light and dark accent streaks. It is perhaps most appealing in plain sawn or sliced cuts. While it has unique stability and weathering properties, making it ideal for exterior applications, its high cost usually limits its use to decorative interior woodwork, most often in veneer form. Its great beauty and interest dictate it being finished in its near "natural state."

3 - Lumber

AMERICAN BLACK WALNUT (Juglans nigra)

American Black Walnut is perhaps our most highly prized domestic wood species. Its grain pattern variations are extensive and in veneered form produces, in addition to its normal plain sliced cut, quartered or "pencil striped" as well as specialty cuts such as crotches, swirls, burls, and others. Its heartwood color varies from gray brown to dark purplish brown. The sapwood, which is very prevalent in solid lumber, is cream colored and its complete elimination by selective cutting is very costly. Fortunately, if this natural effect is felt to be undesirable, its appearance can be neutralized by sap staining in the finishing process. The growth conditions of Walnut result in significant width and length limitations in its lumber form. Its potential is best expressed in veneered products.

ZEBRAWOOD, AFRICAN (quarter sawn) (Brachystegea fleuryana)

The Zebrawood tree is an equatorial tree of medium size, obtaining a height of about 65' (20 m) with a diameter of about 3' (1 m). The sapwood is pale in color and distinct from the heartwood, which is of a creamy yellow color veined or striped with very dark brown or black. The striped effect is seen at its best when the wood is quarter sawn.

The wood is reported to be easy to saw but somewhat difficult to work with other tools. It is claimed that there is little tendency for the wood to "work" after seasoning. It has been used for a number of years for cabinet work, fine joinery, fancy turnings, and veneers. By careful selection of veneered material, the skilled craftsman can obtain very beautiful effects in paneled work. In large panels, a very striking and attractive result may be obtained when using Zebrawood.

OTHER SPECIES

There are many other species, both domestic and imported, used in fine woodworking. Nearly all are ecologically sound and appropriate for use. Using fine hardwoods for architecture gives value to the species, encouraging improved forest management techniques and the continuation of the species. As of March 2001, there are only four tree species listed on the Convention on International Trade in Endangered Species (CITES) Appendix I restricted table: Brazilian Rosewood, Monkey Puzzle Tree, Guatemalan Fir, and Alerce. Contact your local woodwork manufacturer for up-to-date information or visit www.cites.org.

USE OF RECLAIMED TIMBER

Interest in timber salvaged or reclaimed from old logs cut from old growth forests has increased recently.

Logs harvested over 100 years ago and transported by water often sank en-route to mills. The resulting "lost underwater forest" lay on the bottoms of rivers and lakes until recently as proper environmental and mechanical procedures for retrieving them have been developed.

Reclaimed submerged materials are utilized in all aspects of construction of fine furniture, architectural woodwork and musical instruments. Submerged lumber is generally processed in both solid lumber, plain sliced and rotary veneer.

The uniqueness of the harvesting procedures, the high quality of the material and unusual aesthetic qualities are a few of desirable traits associated with this special material.

Some of the characteristics unique only to reclaimed submerged timber are:

- Greater density due to tighter growth rings than currently harvested stock;
- Beautiful variance of color gained from the transfer of mineral absorption found naturally in bottom sediments and water;
- Substantial increase of ease in milling due to sap replacement;
- Superior tonal qualities;
- A more pristine appearance;
- Aspects of Historical importance as well as environmental consciousness is added to any project;
- Complete use of the harvested resource.

Check availability and differences in aesthetic qualities before selecting.

ENGINEERED PRODUCTS

Structural Composite Lumber (SCL) — A man-made composite that utilizes grain oriented wood strands from a variety of tree species, providing an alternative to dimension lumber. The material is engineered for strength and stability. While SCL is not really "lumber," it is marketed as a lumber substitute. SCL can be specified as core, stile backers, and core for stiles and rails, so long as all other criteria of the AWS are met in relation to its use.

ÆSTHETIC CHARACTERISTICS

One of the qualities which contributes to the widespread use of wood is the option offered for æsthetic selection. It varies between species, between two logs of the same species, and between two boards from the same log. Æsthetic considerations in specifying wood are influenced by the following characteristics:

COLOR - The basic hue of the species, which may be further enhanced by the finishing process employed.

Sapwood and heartwood - The color of wood within a tree varies between the "sapwood" (the outer layers of the tree that continue to transport sap), which is usually lighter in color than the "heartwood" (the inner layers in which the cells have become filled with natural deposits). If desired, sapwood may be stained in the finishing process to blend with the heartwood. This difference in color is so pronounced in certain species that the sapwood is marketed under a different nomenclature from the heartwood. Some examples are:

- Select White Birch - sapwood of Yellow or Paper Birch
- Select Red Birch - heartwood of Yellow Birch
- Natural Birch - both sapwood and heartwood of any Birch
- Select White Ash - sapwood of White or Green Ash
- Select Brown Ash - heartwood of Black Ash
- Natural Ash - both sapwood and heartwood of any Ash
- Select White Maple - sapwood of the Sugar Maple

3 - Lumber

GRAIN

The appearance produced by the arrangement of wood fibers and pores of the species. Open grain woods are said to be ring-porous and usually show a distinct grain pattern. Close grain woods are said to be diffuse-porous with even grain.

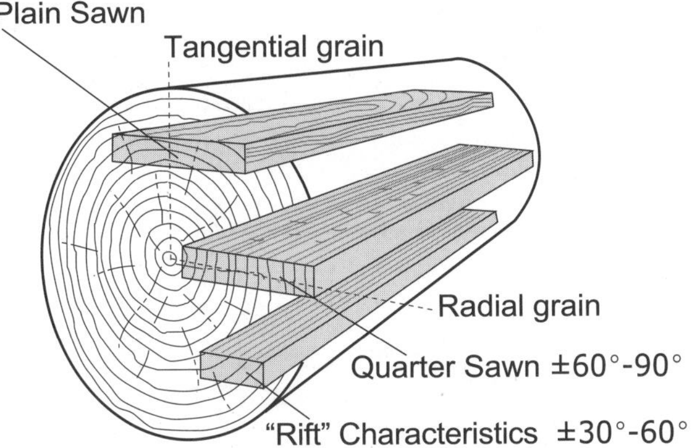

OPEN GRAIN AND CLOSE GRAIN

The size and distribution of the cellular structure of the wood influences the appearance and uniformity. Open grain hardwoods, such as Elm, Oak, Ash, and Chestnut are ring-porous species. These species have distinct figure and grain patterns. Close grain hardwoods, such as Cherry, Maple, Birch, and Yellow Poplar, are diffuse-porous species. Most North American diffuse-porous woods have small, dense pores resulting in less distinct figure and grain. Some tropical diffuse-porous species (e.g., Mahogany) have rather large pores.

FIGURE

Various species produce different grain patterns (figures), which influence the selection process. There will be variations of grain patterns within any selected species. The architectural woodworker cannot select solid lumber cuttings within a species by grain and color in the same manner in which veneers may be selected.

METHODS OF SAWING

The sawing method, and the selection of boards after sawing the log will produce the following types of lumber:

PLAIN SAWN

Plain sawing, the most common type of lumber sawing, yields broad grain, the widest boards and least waste. The annular rings are typically 30 degrees or less to the face of the board.

QUARTER SAWN

Most often cut as Rift-and-Quartered, and then sorted for appearance, quarter sawn lumber is available in certain species, yields a straight grain, narrow boards, and fleck (sometimes called flake) or figure which runs across the grain in some species (notably the oaks). Dimensional stability across the grain is the best. The annular rings run approximately 60 to 90 degrees to the face of the board, with the optimum being 90 degrees. Quartered lumber is generally more expensive than plain sawn.

RIFT SAWN

Rift sawing produces small flecks caused by cutting through the wood rays. Only certain species produce these flecks, primarily Red and White Oak. Rift cutting reduces yield and increases cost. The annular rings run about 30 to 60 degrees to the face of the board, with the optimum being 45 degrees.

FINISHING CHARACTERISTICS

The many species of wood vary considerably in their receptivity to the multitude of finishing processes on the market. Some woods, because of their open pores, will accept fillers while tighter grained woods will not. Some will show greater contrast between the "early wood" and the "late wood" when stained than others. Design professionals should take into consideration the finish that will be applied when selecting a particular species. Consult with a woodworker about finishing prior to selection or specification. Providing large samples of the desired finish to woodworkers during the design phase and bidding process will assure the designer of obtaining an acceptable final product, while enabling the woodworker to be aware of exactly what is required.

AVAILABILITY

The supply of lumber is in constant flux throughout the world. It is affected by many factors such as current demand, export regulations of the country of origin, natural forces of weather, fire, disease, political situations, etc. Consult a woodworker before specifying uncommon species, as well as large quantities of a species, thickness, width, or long length.

SIZE LIMITATIONS

Certain trees (species) naturally grow larger, thus producing longer and wider lumber. Other trees are smaller and produce narrow and shorter boards. The architectural woodworker must work with the available lumber, which must be considered when selecting any species.

COST

The cost of lumber, as with other commodities, is influenced by supply and demand, both of which are constantly changing. For current comparative costs consult a woodworker.

STRENGTH, HARDNESS, DENSITY

Always a consideration is the ability of the selected lumber species to sustain stress; resist indentation, abuse, and wear; and to carry its anticipated load in applications such as shelving and structural members. *The Wood Handbook*, published by the U.S. Forest Products Society, contains comprehensive data on the mechanical properties of wood.

3 - Lumber

DIMENSIONAL STABILITY, RELATIVE HUMIDITY, AND MOISTURE CONTENT

All woods are affected significantly by moisture and to a lesser degree by heat. Lumber swells and shrinks primarily in two directions: thickness and width. There is insignificant change in length. The changes in dimension due to moisture vary with different species, thus influencing the selection of lumber to use and the design elements.

Prevention of dimensional problems in architectural woodwork products as a result of uncontrolled relative humidity is possible. Wood products perform, as they have for centuries, with complete satisfaction when correctly designed and used. Problems directly or indirectly attributed to dimensional change of the wood are usually, in fact, the result of faulty design or improper humidity conditions during site storage, installation, or use.

Wood is a hygroscopic material, and under normal conditions all wood products contain some moisture. Wood readily exchanges this moisture with the water vapor in the surrounding atmosphere according to the relative humidity. In high humidity, wood picks up moisture and swells. In low humidity, wood releases moisture and shrinks. As normal minor changes in humidity occur, the resulting dimensional response in properly designed construction will be insignificant. To avoid problems, it is recommended that relative humidity be maintained within the range of 25% and 55%. Uncontrolled extremes - below 20% or above 80% relative humidity - are likely to cause problems. Together with proper design, fabrication, and installation, humidity control is the important factor in preventing dimensional change problems. The book *Understanding Wood* by Bruce Hoadley contains excellent data of wood and moisture.

SHRINKAGE

Due to Drying

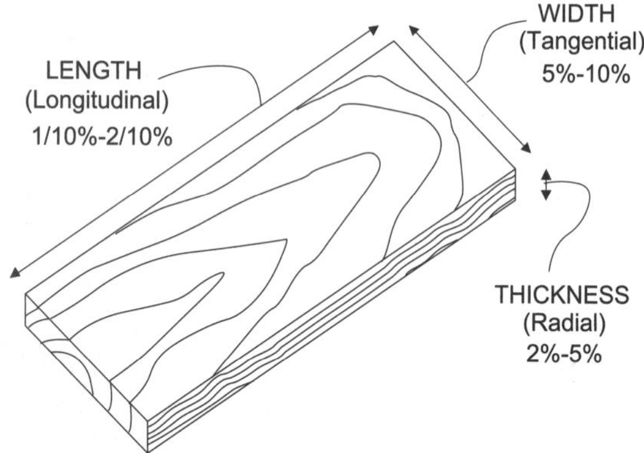

TS=2RS
Tangential Shrinkage
Approximates Twice
the Radial Shrinkage

Shrinkage of 1" x 8" x 10'
Dried from Green to Oven Dry
Approximates: 3/64" in thickness
3/4" in width
1/8" in length

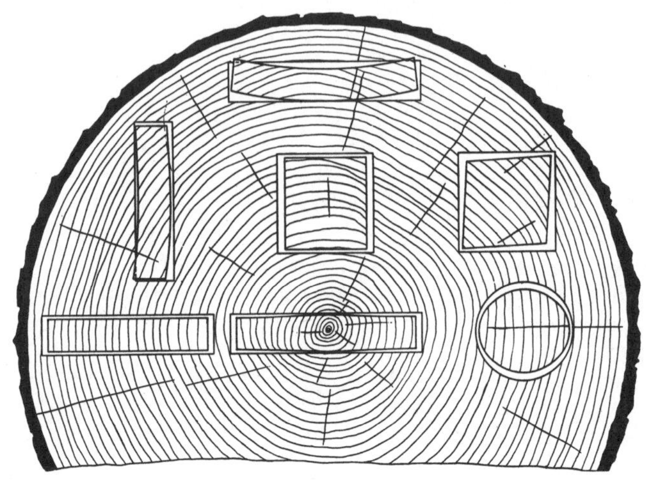

Wood is anisotropic in its shrinkage characteristics. It shrinks most in the direction of the annual rings when it loses moisture from the cell walls. This illustration from the USDA *Wood Handbook* shows the typical distortion of cuts from various parts of a log.

EXPANSION

Due to Moisture in the Air

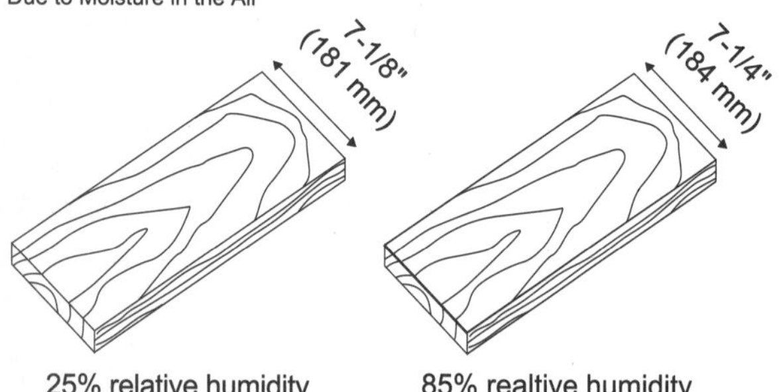

25% relative humidity

85% realtive humidity

Expansion of 1" x 8" x 10' when relativity Humidity increases from 25% to 85%

Moisture can also cause iron stain (oxidation) in wood, also referred to as blue/black stain. Iron stain is a natural reaction of acids with iron, oxygen, and moisture (either high relative humidity or direct moisture) in wood. Control of moisture is a simple way to protect wood products from iron stain.

ADAPTABILITY FOR EXTERIOR USE

Years of performance have shown certain species to be more durable for exterior applications. Heartwood shall be furnished when these species are designated for external use, excluding the sapwood. The following is a list of species generally considered acceptable for exterior use, from the *Wood Handbook* (USDA):

Eastern and Western Red Cedar
Cherry, black
Douglas, Fir
Mahogany, Genuine
Chestnut
Oak, white
Teak, old growth
Redwood, heartwood
Locust, black
Spanish Cedar

3 - Lumber

BALDCYPRESS (Taxodium distichum) has a long tradition as a species resistant to decay, but beware! There are at least nine other species of four different genus which are marketed under the common name cypress. Only the heartwood of T. distichum, often marketed as Tidewater or Red Cypress, is decay resistant. Sinker Cypress, that is old trees which have been brought up from below water in which they have been submerged for some time and properly cured and dried, is also resistant. None of this Cypress will come from new cutting, but as salvaged wood.

FIRE-RETARDANT WOOD

The natural fire-retardant qualities and acceptability of treatments vary among the species. Where items of architectural woodwork are required to have a flame spread classification to meet applicable building and safety codes, the choice of lumber species must be a consideration. Most treated species are structural softwoods. Following are some references to assist in making these choices. Additional data on various species may be available from the U.S. Department of Agriculture Forest Service, Fire Safety of Wood Products Work Unit — (608) 231-9269.

Flame Spread Classification: This is the generally accepted measurement for fire rating of materials. It compares the rate of flame spread on a particular species with the rate of flame spread on untreated Oak. Most authorities accept the following classes for flame spread:

Class I or A.	0-25
Class II or B.	26-75
Class III or C.	76-200

Built-up Construction to Improve Fire Rating: In lieu of solid lumber, it is often advisable, where a fire rating is required, to build up members by using treated cores clad with untreated veneers not thicker than 1 mm [1/28"]. Some existing building codes, except where locally amended, provide that facing materials 1 mm [1/28"] or thinner finished dimension are not considered in determining the flame spread rating of the woodwork.

In localities where basic model building codes have been amended, it is the responsibility of the specifier to determine whether the application of the facing material specified will meet the code.

Fire-Retardant Treatments (FRT): Some species may be treated with chemicals to reduce flammability and retard the spread of flame over the surface. This usually involves impregnating the wood, under pressure, with salts suspended in a liquid. The treated wood must be redried prior to fabrication. FRT wood may exude chemicals in relative humidity above 85%, damaging finishes and corroding metals in contact with the FRT surface. Consult with a woodworker about the resulting appearance and availability of treated woods prior to specification.

Hardwoods currently being treated (Flame spread less than 25) include 4/4 Red Oak, and 4/4 to 8/4 Poplar. These woods can be machined after treatment, although machining may void the label classification. Fire retardant treatment does affect the color and finishing characteristics of the wood.

According to the traditional model codes in the USA and subject to local code modifications, untreated wood and wood products can usually be used in up to 10% of the combined surface area of the walls and ceiling. Cabinetry, furniture, and fixtures are rarely fire rated, and can be built of combustible materials.

The National Building Code of Canada (1995), states:
3.1.5.7.1 - Combustible millwork including interior trim, doors and door frames, aprons, and backing, handrails, shelves, cabinets and counters is permitted in a building required to be of noncombustible construction.

Code requirements are reviewed and updated regularly. The design authority shall check document publication dates and local amendments to national codes, and shall inform the woodworker of requirements.

Face veneers are not fire-retardant treated, and combining untreated veneers with treated lumber will usually result in color and finishing contrasts.

Finishing of Fire-Retardant Treated Lumber: Fire-retardant treatments may affect the finishes intended to be used on the wood, particularly if transparent finishes are planned. The compatibility of any finishes should be tested before they are applied.

Intumescent Coatings for Wood: It is possible to reduce flammability by using intumescent coatings in either opaque or transparent finishes. These are formulated to expand or foam when exposed to high heat, and create an insulating effect, which reduces the speed of flame spread. Improvements are continually being made on these coatings. Consequently, the specifier must ascertain whether they will be permitted under the code governing the project. The relative durability of the finish and the effect of the coating on the desired color of the finished product vary from manufacturer to manufacturer. In general, the coatings are less durable, softer, and more hygroscopic than standard finishes.

3 - Lumber

Wood Species (a)	Flame Spread Index (b)	Smoke Developed Index (b)	Source (c)
ASTM E 84 flame-spread indexes for various wood species of 19 mm thick [3/4"] solid lumber as reported in the literature.			
Birch, Yellow	105-110	no data	UL
Cedar, Western Red	70	213	HPVA
Cedar, Alaska (Pacific Coast yellow)	78	90	CWC
Cottonwood	115	no data	UL
Baldcypress (Cypress)	145-150	no data	UL
Fir, Douglas	70-100	no data	UL
Fir, Pacific silver	69	58	CWC
Sweetgum (Gum, red)	140-155	no data	UL
Hemlock. western (West Coast)	60-75	no data	UL
Maple, Sugar (maple flooring)	104	no data	CWC
Oak, Red	100	100	UL
Oak, White	100	100	UL
Pine, red	142	229	CWC
Pine, Eastern White	85	122	CWC
Pine, Western White	75	no data	UL
Pine, Northern White	120-215	no data	UL
Pine, Ponderosa	105-230	no data	UL
Pine, Southern Yellow	130-195	no data	UL
Pine, Lodgepole	93	210	CWC
Poplar, Yellow	170-185	no data	UL
Redwood	70	no data	UL
Spruce, Eastern (Northern, White)	65	no data	UL, CWC
Spruce, Sitka (Western, Sitka)	100, 74	no data, 74	UL, CWC
Walnut, Black	130-140	no data	UL
No reliable data is available on other species at the time of this printing.			
(a)-In cases where the name given in the source did not conform to the official nomenclature of the Forest Service, the probable official nomenclature name is given and the name given by the source is given in parentheses. (b)-Data area as reported in the literature (dash where data do not exist). (c)-CWC, Canadian Wood Council (CWC 1996); HPVA, Hardwood Plywood & Veneer Association (Tests); UL, Underwriters Laboratories, Inc. (UL 527, 1971) from the Wood Handbook, Forest Products Society, 1999 - FPS catalog no. 7269			

PRESERVATIVE TREATMENTS

Modern technology has developed methods of treating certain species to extend their life when exposed to the elements. Some lumber species used for exterior architectural woodwork may be treated with an industry tested and accepted formulation. One such formulation is a liquid containing 3-iodo-2-propynyl butyl carbamate (IPBC) as its active ingredient, which must be used according to manufacturer's directions.

The Window & Door Manufacturers Association (WDMA), through the treatments and coatings committee, has reviewed information from third party testing laboratories which indicates that the number of formulations at the stated in-use concentration meet the requirements of WDMA I.S.4, latest edition. The formulations are acceptable for use under the WDMA Hallmark Water-Repellent Non-Pressure Preservative Treatment Certification Program and are adopted to meet all requirements.

3 - Lumber

IMPORTANT PRODUCT ADVISORY REGARDING DIMENSIONAL CHANGE PROBLEMS IN ARCHITECTURAL WOODWORK

This advisory concerns prevention of dimensional problems in architectural woodwork products as the result of uncontrolled relative humidity. It is further intended as a reminder of the natural dimensional properties of wood and wood-based products such as plywood, particleboard, and high pressure decorative laminate (HPDL) and of the routine and necessary care—and responsibilities—which must be assumed by those involved.

For centuries, wood has served as a successful material for architectural woodwork, and as history has shown wood products perform with complete satisfaction when correctly designed and used. Problems directly or indirectly attributed to dimensional change of the wood are usually, in fact, the result of faulty design, or improper humidity conditions during site storage, installation, or use.

Wood is a hygroscopic material, and under normal use and conditions all wood products contain some moisture. Wood readily exchanges this molecular moisture with the water vapor in the surrounding atmosphere according to the existing relative humidity. In high humidity, wood picks up moisture and swells. In low humidity, wood releases moisture and shrinks. As normal minor fluctuations in humidity occur, the resulting dimensional response in properly designed construction will be insignificant. To avoid problems, it is recommended that relative humidity be maintained within the range of 25-55%. Uncontrolled extremes—below 20% or above 80% relative humidity—can likely cause problems.

Oxidation is a reaction of acids in wood (e.g., tannic acid), with iron, oxygen, and moisture, whether this be relative humidity or direct moisture. Control of moisture is a simple way to protect wood products from stains as a result of oxidation.

Together with proper design, fabrication, and installation, humidity control is obviously the important factor in preventing dimensional change problems.

Architectural woodwork products are manufactured as designed from wood that has been kiln dried to an appropriate average moisture content and maintained at this condition up to the time of delivery. Subsequent dimensional change in wood is and always has been an inherent natural property of wood. These changes cannot be the responsibility of the manufacturer or products made from it. Specifically:

- Responsibility for dimensional change problems in wood products resulting from improper design rests with the designer/architect/specifier.
- Responsibility for dimensional change problems in wood products resulting from improper relative humidity exposure during site storage and installation rests with the general contractor.
- Responsibility for dimensional change problems in wood products resulting from humidity extremes after occupancy rests with engineering and maintenance.

NOTES

4
Sheet Products

4 - Sheet Products

There are a great variety of panels manufactured with differences in core materials, adhesives or binders, forming techniques, surface treatments, etc., which affect characteristics of the panels.

In addition, constant research gives rise to the production of new panel products. These new products are usually accompanied by data on test results of important characteristics for end-use purposes. In selecting new panel products for architectural woodworking, such data should be considered with reference to the AWS.

Many prefinished wood panels and decorative overlays have aesthetic and performance characteristics that meet or exceed the AWS, and should be evaluated, approved, and specified by the design professional when desired.

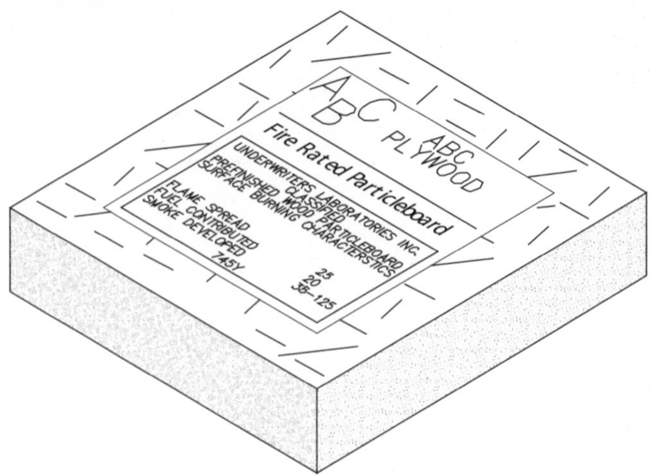

TYPES OF PANEL CORES

There are a wide range of core materials available for the fabrication of architectural woodwork. The primary core materials are covered in the AWS as follows:

INDUSTRIAL GRADE PARTICLEBOARD CORE - wood particles of various sizes that are bonded together with a synthetic resin or binder under heat and pressure.

Medium Density Industrial Particleboard is used in the broadest applications of architectural woodwork. It is especially well suited as a substrate for high quality veneers and decorative laminates.

When used as panels without any surface plies, the product is referred to as particleboard. *When used as an inner core with outer wood veneers, the panel is referred to as particle core plywood.* Industrial particleboard is commercially classified by "density," which is measured by the weight per cubic foot of the panel product.

• Low Density [LD series] = generally less than 640 kg per m^3 (40 pounds per ft^3).

• Medium Density [M series] = generally between 640-800 kg per m^3 (40-50 pounds per ft^3).

• High Density [H series] = generally above 800 kg per m^3 (50 pounds per ft^3). Rarely used for woodwork.

MOISTURE RESISTANT PARTICLEBOARD CORE

Some Medium Density Industrial Particleboard is bonded with resins more resistant to swelling when exposed to moisture. The most common grades are ANSI 208.1-1999 Type M-2-Exterior Glue and M-3-Exterior Glue. Availability to the architectural woodworker is limited in some markets.

FIRE-RETARDANT PARTICLEBOARD CORE

Some Medium Density Industrial Particleboard has been treated during manufacture to carry a UL stamp for Class I fire rating (Flame spread 20, Smoke developed 450). This material is often used as a substrate for paneling requiring a Class I rating. Fire-retardant Medium Density Fiberboard is also available in some markets.

MEDIUM DENSITY FIBERBOARD (MDF) CORE - wood particles reduced to fibers in a moderate pressure steam vessel, combined with a resin, and bonded together under heat and pressure.

Due to the finer texture of the fibers used in manufacturing Medium Density Fiberboard (MDF) it is smoother than Medium Density Particleboard. The uniform texture and density of the fibers create a homogenous panel that is very useful as a substrate for paint, thin overlay materials, veneers and decorative laminates. MDF is among the most stable of the mat-formed panel products. When used as an inner core with outer wood veneers, the panel is referred to as MDF core plywood.

Some MDF is made to meet the ANSI 208.2-2002 reduced thickness swell criteria. Availability to the architectural woodworker is limited in some markets.

VENEER CORE - three or more layers (plies) of wood veneers pressed and glued into a single sheet.

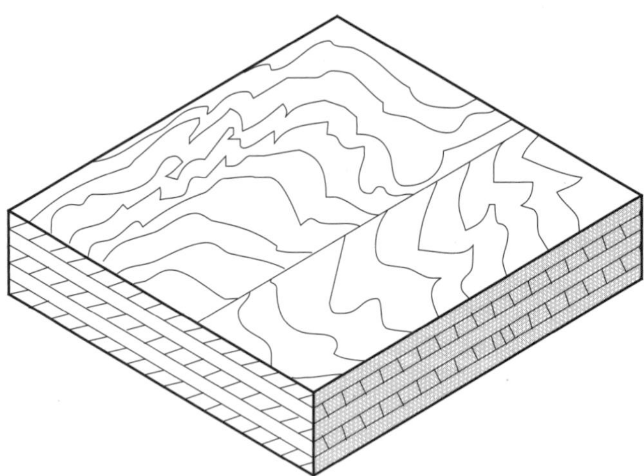

What many think of as traditional "plywood," a panel made up of alternating layers of thin veneers, is called veneer core. Adhesive is placed between the veneer layers, and the panels are assembled under heat and pressure until the adhesive is set. The two outside layers of veneer are often selected for species, grain, and appearance; and are called the "face veneers."

4 - Sheet Products

COMBINATION CORE - A balanced blend of particleboard or fiberboard with veneer layers.

A combination of veneer core and particleboard/fiberboard core technologies, utilizing some of the advantages of each. This material should be evaluated and approved by the customer. Many products will meet the AWS.

HARDBOARD CORE - Hardboard is defined as inter-felted fibers consolidated under heat and pressure to a density of 500 kg per m^3 (31 pounds per cubic foot) or greater.

Often used for casework backs, drawer bottoms, and divider panels, hardboard is available with either one side (S1S) or two sides (S2S) smooth. There are typically two types of hardboard core used by architectural woodworkers: Standard (untempered) and Tempered, which is standard hardboard subjected to a curing treatment increasing its stiffness, hardness, and weight.

AGRIFIBER/AGROFIBER CORE - Panel products made from straw and similar fiber are appearing in the marketplace. Boards which meet the ANSI 208.1 or 208.2 standards for Medium Density are acceptable for use under the AWS.

The characteristics of agrifiber/agrofiber core material performance vary by manufacturer, and are not included in the following table.

CHARACTERISTICS OF CORE MATERIAL PERFORMANCE

NOTE: It is important for the reader to understand the difference between "flatness" and "dimensional stability" characteristics. Particleboard and MDF are the recommended substrates for high pressure decorative laminate and wood veneer work because of their excellent flatness. Fair dimensional stability (expansion/contraction in panel size) is acceptable unless the product is exposed to wide swings in relative humidity, generally below 20% or above 80% with swings of more than 30 points.

Panel Core Type	Flatness	Visual Edge Quality	Surface Uniformity	Dimensional Stability	Screw Holding	Bending Strength	Availability
Industrial Particleboard (Medium)	Excellent	Good	Excellent	Fair	Fair	Good	Readily
Medium Density Fiberboard (MDF)	Excellent	Excellent	Excellent	Fair	Good	Good	Readily
Veneer	Fair	Good	Fair	Excellent	Excellent	Excellent	Readily
Lumber	Good	Good	Good	Good	Excellent	Excellent	Limited
Combination Core with composite crossbands	Excellent	Good	Excellent	Good	Excellent	Excellent	Limited
Combination Core with composite inner ply	Good	Fair	Good	Good	Good	Good	Limited
Moisture Resistant Particleboard	Excellent	Good	Good	Fair	Fair	Good	Limited
Moisture Resistant MDF	Excellent	Excellent	Excellent	Fair	Good	Good	Limited
Fire Rated Particleboard	Excellent	Fair	Good	Fair	Fair	Good	Limited

Notes: Various characteristics above are influenced by the grade and thickness of the core and specific gravity of the core species. Visual Edge Quality is rated before treatment with edge bands or fillers and Visual Edge Quality of lumber core assumes the use of "clear edge" grade. Surface Uniformity has a direct relationship to the performance of fine veneers placed over the surface. Dimensional Stability is usually related to exposure to wide swings in relative humidity. Screwholding and Bending Strength are influenced by proper design and engineering.

4 - Sheet Products

PLYWOOD

The term "plywood" is defined as a panel manufactured of three or more layers (plies) of wood or wood products (veneers or overlays and/or core materials), generally laminated into a single sheet (panel). Plywood is separated into two groups according to materials and manufacturing:

HARDWOOD PLYWOOD - manufactured of hardwood or decorative softwood veneers over a core material, such as medium density particleboard, medium density fiberboard, low density lumber, and/or other veneers.

SOFTWOOD PLYWOOD - Panels manufactured with softwood face veneers are described in standards published by the APA - The Engineered Wood Association. Softwood plywood is seldom incorporated into finished architectural woodworking projects, except to achieve specific design aesthetics. Softwood (construction) plywood is not recommended for use as a core material due to poor stability and core voids.

PANEL CONSTRUCTION BALANCE

To achieve balanced construction, panels must be an odd number of layers (plies) symmetrical from the center line; e.g., all inner plies, except the innermost ply, should occur in pairs, using materials and adhesives on both sides that contract and expand, or are moisture permeable, at the same rate. A ply may consist of a single veneer, particleboard, medium density fiberboard, or hardboard. Each pair of inner plies should be of the same thickness and direction of grain. Each ply of each pair is placed on opposite sides of the innermost ply or layer, alternating grain directions from the center out. (Particleboard and MDF do not have a specific grain orientation.)

Balanced Construction

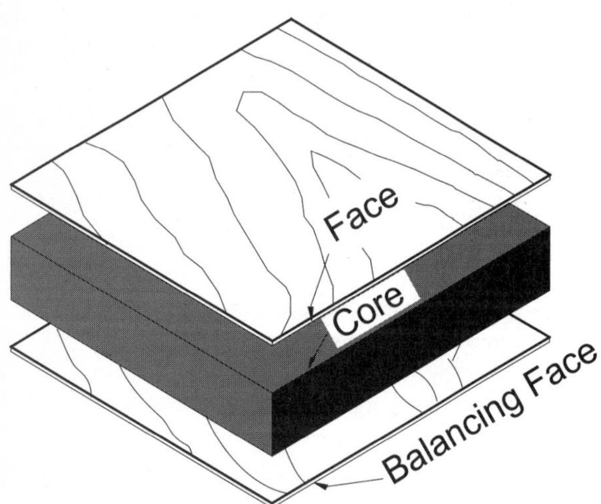

GENERAL RULES: The thinner the facing material, the less force it can generate to cause warping. The thicker the substrate, the more it can resist a warping movement or force.

TYPES OF PLYWOOD

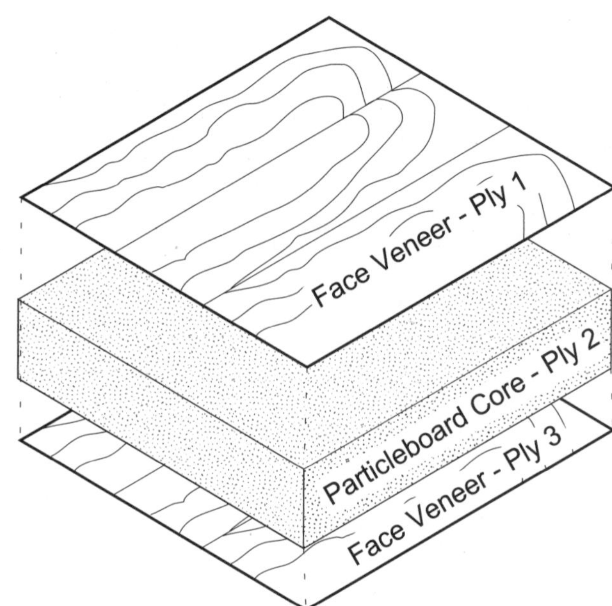

Particleboard Core Plywood

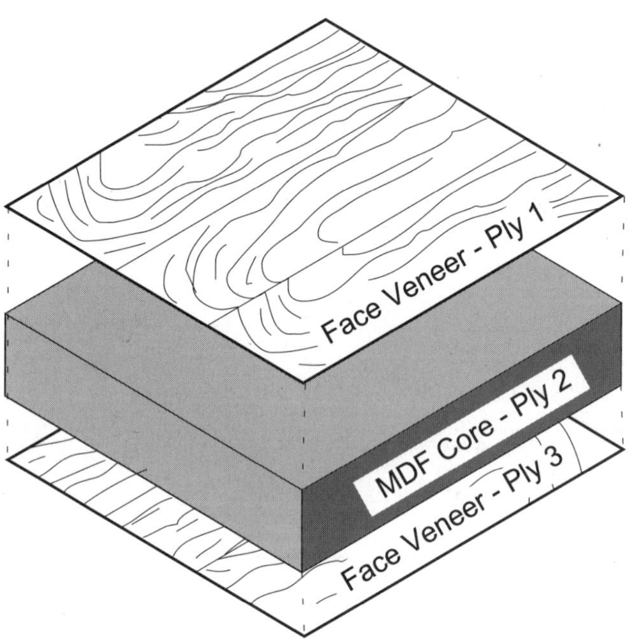

Medium Density Fiberboard Core Plywood

4 - Sheet Products

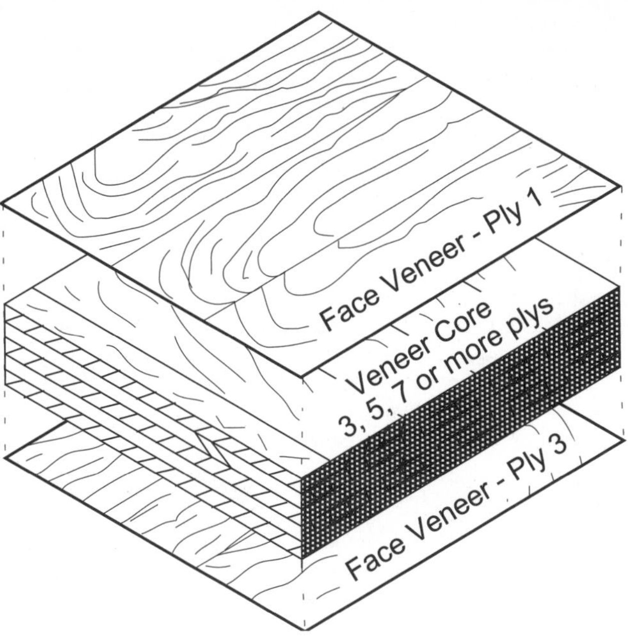

Veneer Core Plywood

Face Veneer - Ply 1
Random Waferboard Core
with Thick Wood Veneer Crossbands
Face Veneer - Ply 2

Combination Core Plywood

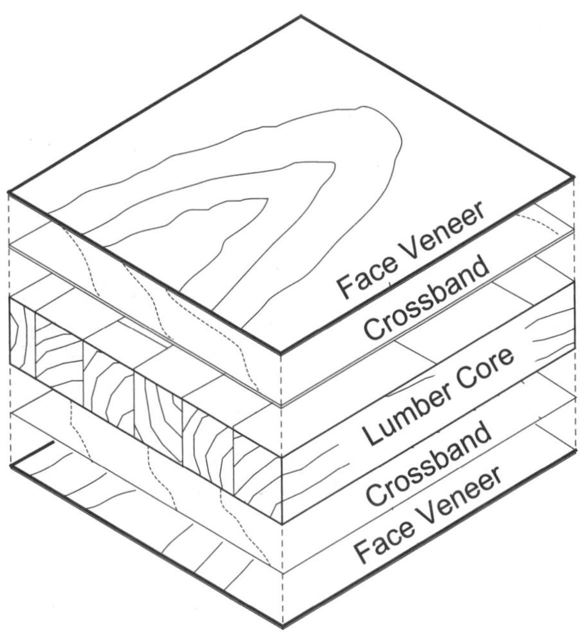

Lumber Core Plywood

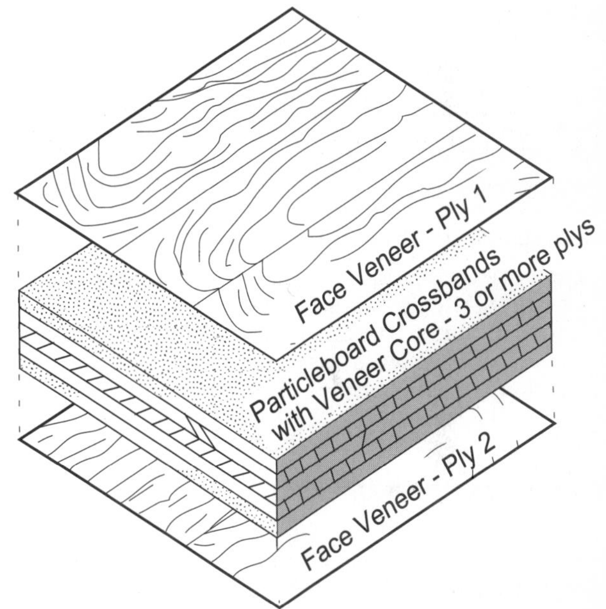

Combination Core Plywood

4 - Sheet Products

TYPES OF FACING MATERIALS

WOOD VENEERS

Wood veneer is produced by veneer manufacturers in a variety of "industry standard" thicknesses. The slicing process is controlled by a number of variables. The thickness of the raw veneer has little bearing on the ultimate quality of the end product so long as show-through and sand-through is avoided.

HARDWOOD VENEER - Species: Available in many domestic and imported wood species.

Cut: Normally cut as plain sliced. Rift sliced and quarter sliced available in certain species at additional cost. Some species available as rotary cut.

SOFTWOOD VENEER - Species: Most common is Douglas fir; Pines are available; other softwoods in limited supply.

Cut: Most softwood veneer is Rotary cut. Plain sliced softwood veneer and "vertical grain" (quarter sliced) softwood veneer are limited in availability with the long lead times and higher prices associated with special orders.

DECORATIVE LAMINATES, OVERLAYS, AND PREFINISHED PANEL PRODUCTS

Decorative surfacing materials are often applied to wood product substrates such as industrial particleboard, fiberboard, hardboard, etc. Terminology and definitions of these overlay products follow, broadly grouped as:

THERMOSET DECORATIVE OVERLAY

Decorative thermally fused panels flat pressed from a thermoset polyester or melamine resin-impregnated web. Most products are pre-laminated to Industrial Particleboard or Medium Density Fiberboard substrates when they arrive at the woodwork fabricator. Performance characteristics are similar to High Pressure Decorative Laminate.

MEDIUM DENSITY OVERLAYS

Pressed resin-impregnated paper overlays, highly resistant to moisture, applied to suitable cores for both interior and exterior uses. The seamless panel face and uniform density furnishes a sound base for opaque finishes and paint.

THERMOPLASTIC SHEET

Semirigid sheet or roll stock extruded from a nonporous acrylic/polyvinyl chloride (PVC) alloy solid color throughout. Withstands high impact. Minor scratches and gouges are less conspicuous due to the solid color. Thickness ranges from 0.7 mm [.028"] to 6.4 mm [.250"]. Not recommended for horizontal surfaces where hot items may be placed and in areas near heat sources.

FOILS

These papers are generally referred to as "finished foils" in Europe. In the United States they have been called melamine papers, intermediate weight foils and impregnated foils. Not all foils are finished, nor are they all impregnated. Therefore foils vary in bond strength, porosity, cutting qualities and machinability. (Of limited use in custom architectural woodworking.)

VINYL FILMS

Polyvinyl chloride (PVC) film, either clear or solid color, used extensively for decorative vertical surfaces in mobile homes, recreational vehicles, commercial panels and movable walls. Product thicknesses range from0.02" to .03 (0.5 mm to 0.8 mm). Some films are available with scuff-resistant top coatings. (Of limited use in custom architectural woodworking.)

BASIS WEIGHT PAPERS

Sometimes referred to as "micro-papers" or "rice papers," these overlays are printed paper coated with polyurethane, urea, polyester, acrylic, or melamine resins. They offer an economical alternative for low-wear surfaces. (Of limited use in custom architectural woodworking.)

H PRESSURE DECORATIVE LAMINATES

Resin-impregnated kraft paper substrates with decorative plastic face materials and a clear protective top sheet, formed under heat and pressure. The assembly offers resistance to wear and many common stains and chemicals. Common uses include casework exteriors, countertops, and wall paneling.

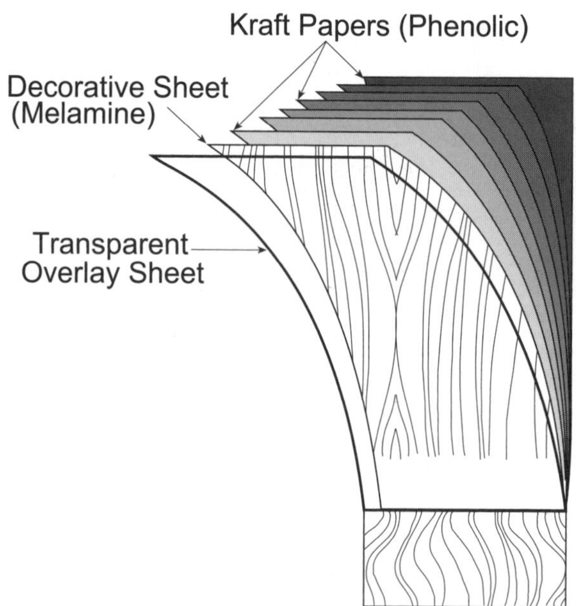

HPDL Elements

4 - Sheet Products

HPDL TYPES MOST COMMONLY USED

BASIC TYPES

Five basic types form the majority of applications of high pressure decorative laminate in North America: They are General Purpose, Vertical, Postforming, Cabinet Liner and Balancing Sheet laminates.

General Purpose (HGS and HGL) Used for most horizontal applications, such as desk tops and self-edged kitchen countertops, "HG" laminates offer durability, resistance to stains, and resistance to heat.

Vertical (VGS and VGL) A slightly thinner material, "VG" laminates are produced for areas which will receive less wear and impact than typical horizontal materials. They are an excellent choice for cabinet doors, the sides of casework, primarily decorative display shelves and vertical panels.

Postforming (HGP and VGP) Specifically for applications where a radiused surface is desirable, "P" laminates offer strong performance in both horizontal and vertical applications. A major advantage of formed surfaces on the exposed corners of casework and service counters is the edge's resistance to chipping damage. Most chip damage occurs at sharp 90° corners. Surfaces are thermoformed under controlled temperature and pressure. Not all manufacturers have post-forming machinery.

Flame Retardant (SGF, HGF, and VGF) These laminates are capable of providing flame retardant characteristics as determined by test methods required by the authority having jurisdiction. HGF is the most common type used.

Cabinet Liner (CLS) A thin vertical sheet, this type is designed for areas where the surface must be decorative, but will need to withstand little wear, such as the inside surfaces of cabinets and closets.

Backing Sheet (BKL) Backing materials are essential in the fabrication of most HPDL clad surfaces to prevent warping and to protect against dimensional instability of both laminate and substrate in conditions of changing temperature and humidity. Backing sheets are non-decorative, and both economical and effective in the creation of a successful application.

In summary, these types have the limitations of all high pressure decorative laminate:

• They are for interior use only, and may not be successfully used outdoors or under heavy exposure to the ultraviolet rays of the sun.

• They should not be used as cutting surfaces, because knives and other sharp tools will readily deface the surface and lower its other performance capabilities.

• They should not be exposed to caustic chemicals, such as drain and toilet bowl cleaners, which can permanently etch the surface.

• While they offer outstanding heat resistance, exposure to constant heat - from a curling iron, an electric skillet or coffee pot, for example - can harm the surface and may cause it to discolor or blister.

• Finally, basic HPDL types are veneering, and not structural materials. They must be adhered to satisfactory substrates for successful use.

SPECIALTY TYPES

The technological development of new high pressure decorative laminate products has multiple application opportunities for designers in every area from residential to contract, institutional, light industrial and custom commercial planning.

Variations in manufacturing technique, as well as in materials used, have created many new high pressure decorative laminate products. Some of these products offer enhancement of a basic characteristic; for example, heightened resistance to wear, impact or staining, or static dissipation.

Since these special materials in every case represent significant value added to basic HPDL, their cost is usually higher. Actual cost varies by material chosen, quantity specified, and manufacturer; you should work closely with your woodworker for material's cost on individual projects.

Specialty types available from several producers are summarized here. New types, and those offered by only one producer, appear constantly. Professional publications and manufacturers' literature will help keep you abreast of these new developments.

COLOR-THROUGH DECORATIVE LAMINATES. The interest in specifying solid color decorative laminates and the resurgence of interest in very pale pastels and neutral shades have caused increasing concern with the brown line visible at glued HPDL edges.

Color-through decorative laminates were formulated specifically to provide light colors without this brown line.

Color-through HPDL is produced in thicknesses of 0.050" to 0.060" (1.3 to 1.5 mm) and may be applied to substrates in three basic ways:

• As sheets, to form a decorative face with a true monolithic look;

• As edge trims, to match a face of conventional HPDL or to accent a natural material such as wood or leather;

• As decorative inlays.

Color-through HPDL may also be layered, in the same or several different colors, then sliced, routed or sandblasted for decorative dimensional and sculptural effects.

Color-through HPDL is produced with multiple layers of decorative papers, rather than the decorative-plus-kraft composition of conventional laminate. As a result, this material is slightly stiffer and slightly more brittle when flexed.

Selection of adhesive must take into consideration that a visible glue line will detract from the beauty of a fabricated piece. Adhesive should be untinted.

The bond created must be strong, too. Colorthrough HPDL contains a high level of melamine resin, and can generate considerable force when temperature and humidity fluctuate.

4 - Sheet Products

The substrate choice must be appropriate to resist this dimensional movement. Also, the substrate must sustain all anticipated tensile and flexural load, and must supply all needed screw-holding properties.

STATIC-DISSIPATIVE LAMINATES. High pressure decorative laminate is a good electrical insulator—in fact, it was for the specific purpose of electrical insulation that the product was originally developed.

HPDL does not store static electricity, and it is therefore a suitable material for use in hospital operating rooms, X-ray rooms, and computer room controlled environments where the accumulation and retention of static electricity must be avoided.

However, the growing need for work surfaces in areas such as electronic clean rooms, where electrostatic charges must be actively, continuously channeled away, has triggered the development of specifically conductive (static-dissipative) laminates.

These HPDL sheets have a conductive layer enclosed in, or backing, the sheet. Connected to suitable grounding, they create a decorative, sturdy, practical work surface. Applications include electronic workbench tops and work areas around instrument monitoring devices, in lab testing environments, around photo equipment and on computer desktops.

Antistatic laminates are produced in a number of compositions, thicknesses, colors and patterns. Consult manufacturers' literature for details.

CHEMICAL-RESISTANT DECORATIVE LAMINATES. For intermediate laboratories, the need for a work surface impervious to strong chemicals (acids and bases; dental, medical and photographic supplies), has long been met by drab industrial materials such as stainless steel, slate and soapstone.

There is a growing need for alternatives. High costs, both of materials and, in the case of stones, of support structures, are serious concerns, especially in construction and remodeling of schools and hospitals.

Chemical-resistant decorative laminates offer the familiar advantages of HPDL: resistance to wear, conductive and radiant heat, and impact; as well as ease in cleaning, color fastness, and relatively light weight.

These laminates may be applied on vertical as well as horizontal surfaces, to extend protection to cabinet doors and sides. And they may be postformed for seamless edges.

They may be specified in both vertical and forming thicknesses, and in a number of colors and patterns.

Adhesives should be specified carefully. Edges which may be exposed to chemical attack should be glued with chemical-resistant adhesives.

Formulation of chemical-resistant HPDL differs from producer to producer. Consult product literature to make sure the material you specify meets the needs of your projects.

FIRE-RATED DECORATIVE LAMINATES. Safer interiors are a primary concern for commercial, contract and institutional designers across North America. The threat of fire—and its concomitant hazard of smoke—has created a critical need for interior materials that address this concern without aesthetic sacrifice.

Every major manufacturer of HPDL materials offers fire- and smoke-retardant grades for interior application. The addition of fire retardant does not affect the performance characteristics of HPDL; wear and stain resistance, ease of maintenance, and color stability remain very strong.

Fire-rated high pressure decorative laminates are evaluated and certified according to ASTM-E-84 test procedures (cataloged as ASTM-E-84 Tunnel Test; and as Test No. 723 by Underwriters Laboratories, Inc. Similar Canadian testing is cataloged as CAN4-512-79).

With appropriate choices of substrate and adhesive, panels clad with fire-rated HPDL may be produced to comply with Class 1, I, or A, fire codes. Finished panels, already certified, may also be specified from some HPDL manufacturers.

Major applications of fire-rated HPDL include door, wall, and wainscot cladding in corridors, stairwells, entries, and elevators; as well as surfacing on fixtures and cabinetry. These materials are supplied in both horizontal and vertical types, in a wide range of colors and patterns.

They may not be postformed; the special formulation that produces fire retardant is not compatible with heat forming.

Adhesive choice for fire-rated HPDL is important. As with many types of FR particleboard, some PVA adhesives are incompatible with the fire-retardant chemical composition of the HPDL material. Resorcinol adhesives are best for both chemical compatibility and fire rating of the end product. Contact adhesives do surprisingly well in some cases. Verify test ratings with your HPDL manufacturer.

THICK LAMINATES. High pressure decorative laminate is produced by several manufacturers in thicknesses adequate to preclude the use of a substrate.

These HPDL products range in thickness from $^{1}/_{10}$" to 1" (2.5 mm - 25.4 mm), and have decorative faces on both sides for balance. Unlike conventional sheets, thick laminates may be drilled and tapped, and offer significant screw-holding capacity. Screw holes must be centered at least 1-$^{1}/_{2}$ times the diameter of the screw in from any edge, horizontal or vertical.

Depending on thickness, these laminates may be used for many flat applications, such as toilet and dressing room partitions, workbenches, shelving, and table tops. Thick laminates are also used in cladding interior doors, where their special properties can eliminate the need for cross banding.

Durability and impact resistance of thick laminates exceed these same properties in comparably thick panels fabricated with an HPDL + medium density fiberboard + HPDL assembly.

Dimensional stability is slightly less predictable, because of the time required for humidity changes to affect movement through the many plies.

4 - Sheet Products

Panels are heavy for their size—an asset in sturdiness of the end application, but a factor which must be considered when planning for time and cost of labor and transportation as well as for support structures.

DIMENSIONAL LAMINATES are conventional high pressure decorative laminates with deeply embossed finishes. These laminates are manufactured in a very broad range of colors and patterns, and add to the visual and tactile appeal of HPDL in both horizontal and vertical applications. Some dimensional laminates may be successfully postformed.

Typical embossed finishes include versions of leather, slate, woven fabric and reed. Selection and individual texture vary from one producer's line to another—these finishes are proprietary. Manufacturers can provide actual product samples.

Dimensional laminates are frequently specified for bar and restaurant tabletops, for retail fixtures and display walls, and for countertops.

Dimensional laminates offer the æsthetic and performance characteristics of conventional laminates; low points require a bit more attention in cleaning. Deeply embossed finishes are not recommended for high wear areas, because the highest points receive all the wearing force and may show wear more rapidly than matte-finish laminates.

HPDL-CLAD DECORATIVE TAMBOURS extend the wide choice of color and finish, as well as the long wear and easy care attributes, of high pressure decorative laminate to flexible tambours for both architectural cladding and functional closure systems.

These tambours are produced by several major HPDL manufacturers; actual configurations vary from traditional flat slats and half-rounds to flexible grids, horizontal rectangles, and triangular slats. They may be specified in literally hundreds of color or pattern and finish combinations. Each producer's line should be carefully examined to give you a full grasp of the options open to you.

Tambours clad with high pressure decorative laminate are perhaps most important because of their capability for exact coordination with HPDL sheets. Thus, one color scheme can be effectively continued throughout the surfaces of a cabinet, a piece of furniture, even a room.

HPDL clad tambours provide visually appealing surfaces for walls and wainscoting, vertical areas of reception desks and bank counters, and flexible wraps around table pedestals and columns. They create exciting graphic effects on cabinet doors and drawer panels, as well as on full-size interior doors.

Tambours are relatively light in weight and may be easily installed with construction mastic; but, like conventional high pressure decorative laminate sheets, they are not structural materials, and must be adhered to an appropriate substrate.

Functional tambours, which slide along tracks or grooves, extend the color, finish and wear benefits of HPDL to roll-top desks, appliance garages and other storage areas.

NATURAL WOOD LAMINATES are one excellent example of the ongoing evolution of the high pressure decorative laminate process. Presently, natural wood laminates may be specified in two formats; both feature thin veneers of fine woods bonded under high pressure and heat to a core of kraft papers and phenolic resins. One process leaves the face of the wood untreated, and ready to finish. The other adds a protective face of melamine resin.

Performance characteristics vary with the presence or absence of the melamine resin.

In both cases, the ease of cutting and bonding, as well as the wear resistance, improve in comparison to raw wood veneer. With the melamine face, the natural wood assumes all the easy care and long wear properties of conventional high pressure decorative laminate.

Applications of these products involve public spaces, such as banks and reception areas of hotels, where the full beauty of fine wood is an important aesthetic asset.

METAL-FACED LAMINATES. Several manufacturers of high pressure decorative laminates now produce metal veneers with a backer of kraft paper and phenolic resin, and at least one product with a thermoplastic core between two metal sheets is presently available.

The material used for most metal laminates is interior-type anodized aluminum. Other materials, including copper and nickel alloys, may be specified in various formats.

The primary advantage of metal-clad laminates lies in their relative ease of fabrication, as compared to conventional metals. Such sheets may be cut, formed and machined with standard woodworking equipment. And the laminate backer makes for ease in gluing; the adhesives and techniques used for HPDL are appropriate. Metal laminates add light and visual drama for interior vertical surfaces. Walls, wainscoting, stairwells, columns and accent trims around ceilings are appropriate for their application. Inset trims, reveals and base moldings around furniture and casework can be very effectively accented with metal laminates. Freestanding panels faced with metal laminates should have similar veneer on their reverse sides, to control warping.

Metal faced laminates are recommended for vertical surfaces where resistance to abuse is not a major concern. These materials have largely replaced metallic foil-faced laminates, because of the greater beauty, increased durability, and generally higher quality of sheets with solid metal surfacing. Note: metal laminates will conduct electricity.

FLOORING LAMINATES are formulated specifically for surfacing panels used for access, or raised, floors. These laminates, available from several major producers of high pressure decorative laminate, combine the good looks and easy maintenance of conventional HPDL with greatly enhanced wear resistance, and feature the capability for permanent static dissipation.

Such flooring offers outstanding performance in areas such as hospitals, for cardiac and intensive care areas; electronic clean rooms and computer facilities; and high traffic areas, where heavy wear from both pedestrian and wheeled traffic is predictable.

4 - Sheet Products

These laminates can be maintained with regular damp mopping, using water and a mild, nonflammable, organic cleaner. They do not require sealing, varnishing, buffing or waxing.

Stock selection of patterns is limited to frequently specified neutral colors and patterns; custom colors and patterns can be made available.

ENGRAVING STOCK for indoor signs and nameplates is available from some HPDL producers. It offers the resistance to stain, wear and impact of conventional laminates, and makes up easily into attractive, easy to clean, long lasting signage.

This material may be specified with a black, white, or red core, with two decorative faces, in many colors, patterns, and finishes.

CUSTOM LAMINATE PRODUCTS. Many architectural designers are unaware of the custom capabilities of high pressure decorative laminate manufacturers.

These capabilities extend from production of specially developed colors and patterns to individual layups of surfaces to custom silk screening.

Typical uses include horizontal and vertical surfaces for games and sports from backgammon to bowling; custom lamination of maps, menus and charts; table tops and wall panels with logotypes or special graphics; hand inlaid patterns; laminated textiles; and special matches for corporate colors.

Your HPDL manufacturer will be happy to consult with you when custom services are needed for effective realization of a design.

Your woodworker will be an excellent partner for your design team when your designs call for custom treatments.

VOLUNTARY STANDARDS

Voluntary standards for the production of these overlay products are available from: National Electrical Manufacturers Association (NEMA), Rosslyn, VA; Laminating Materials Association (LMA), Oradell, NJ.

SPECIAL PRODUCTS

Included in this classification are special panel products such as lead-lined panels for X-ray areas; bullet-resistant panels for armor protected areas; honeycomb-core panels when light weight is a consideration, etc.

LEAD-LINED PANELS

Usually a sheet of lead of a specified thickness, to meet X-ray shield requirements, is laminated between 2 layers of core material. A decorative overlay and balancing sheet can then be applied as required.

PROJECTILE RESISTANT ARMOR (BULLET PROOFING)

Available as steel plate-, glass-, polycarbonate-, acrylic- or fiberglass-reinforced material which can offer protection against most available small-arms fire, depending upon the thickness specified. These panels are usually built into the interior of the structure of the counter, teller's lines, judge's benches, etc. Standards and tests for bullet resistance are set by both Underwriters Laboratories (UL. 752) and the National Institute of Justice (N.I.J.-0108.01).

SOLID SURFACING MATERIALS

Solid surfacing materials are available and can be fabricated and/or supplied by many woodworkers. The products (and manufacturer's warranties) vary and must be fabricated according to manufacturer's recommendations, including the use of unique fasteners and adhesives. Many decorative inlays are available. Consult your woodworker about performance issues, materials, colors, and patterns.

COMPOSITE VENEERS

Composite veneers are slices of blocks or "flitches" made from pre-dyed veneer which has been laminated, and in some cases deformed, to produce a special grain and color characteristic.

Composite veneer has both advantages and limitations. The woodworker and the design professional may choose to use composite veneers for economical and/or æsthetic reasons.

Composite veneers are not meant as a substitute for real wood veneer. Each has its own place and proper application. The design professional, in consultation with a woodwork manufacturer, will determine which product to use on a specific project.

ACRYLIC AND METHACRYLATE SHEETS

Overlay materials typically 3.2 mm [$^1/_8$"] thick with a high-gloss finish. Individual products should be evaluated and specified or approved by the design professional when desired. Manufacturer's performance test data is available for review.

SOLID PHENOLIC

A composite of solid phenolic resins molded with a homogeneous core of organic fiber reinforced phenolic and one or more integrally cured surfaces of compatible thermoset nonabsorbent resins. SPC has seen some use in recent years as wall surfacing, casework parts, and countertops.

4 - Sheet Products

THERMOSET DECORATIVE OVERLAY SUMMARY TABLE

Tests for Resistance to:	Test Description [1]	Minimum Requirements		NEMA LD3-2000 VGL [2]
		Solid Colors	Wood Grains	
Wear	A measure of the ability of a decorative overlaid surface to maintain its design or color when subjected to abrasive wear.	400 cycles	125 cycles	400 cycles
Scuff	A measure of the ability of a decorative overlaid surface to maintain its original appearance when exposed to scuffing.	No effect		<---Same
Stain	A measure of the ability of a decorative overlaid surface to resist staining or discoloration from contact with 29 common household substances.	No effect 1-10 Moderate 11-15		<---Same
Clean-ability	A measure of the ability of a decorative overlaid surface to be cleaned using a sponge.	No effect. Surface cleaned in 20 or fewer strokes		<---Same
Light [3]	A measure of the ability of a decorative overlaid surface to retain its color after exposure to a light source having a frequency range approximating sunlight.	Slight		<---Same
High temperature	A measure of the ability of a decorative overlaid surface to maintain its color and surface texture when subjected to a high temperature [180° C (356° F)].	Slight		<---Same
Radiant heat	A measure of the ability of a decorative overlaid surface to resist spot damage when subjected to a radiant heat source.	No effect up to 60 seconds		<---Same
Boiling water [4]	A measure of the ability of a decorative overlaid surface to maintain its color and surface texture when subjected to boiling water.	No effect		<---Same
Impact	A measure of the ability of a decorative overlaid surface to resist fracture due to spot impact by a steel ball dropped from a measured height.	380 mm [15"] without fracture		<---Same

[1] These test procedures are identical to those used by the National Electrical Manufacturers Association (NEMA) for testing high pressure decorative laminates. The minimum requirements to comply for SOLID COLORS meet or exceed NEMA Standard LD3-(latest edition for high pressure decorative laminates).
[2] This standard applies to decorative panel faces only.
[3] Environmental regulations have caused certain colors to be subject to changes in appearance and the manufacturer should be consulted.
[4] Melamine panels, when produced under conditions for optimum panel performance, may show slight effect.
A shipment meeting 95% of the minimum requirements of the performance standard is in conformance.

4 - Sheet Products

WOOD VENEER SPECIES - General characteristics of selected species:

Species	Cut and Details	Width to	Length	Flitch Size	Cost (1)	Availability
Mahogany	Plain Sliced Honduras Mahogany	457 mm [18"]	3658 mm [12']	Large	Moderate	Good
	Quartered Honduras Mahogany	305 mm [12"]	3658 mm [12']	Large	High	Moderate
	Plain Sliced African Mahogany	457 mm [18"]	3658 mm [12']	Large	Moderate	Moderate
	Quartered African Mahogany	305 mm [12"]	3658 mm [12']	Large	High	Good
Ash	Plain Sliced American White Ash	305 mm [12"]	3048 mm [10']	Medium	Moderate	Good
	Quartered American White Ash	203 mm [8"]	3658 mm [12']	Small	High	Good
	Quartered or Plain Sliced European Ash	254 mm [10"]	3048 mm [10']	Medium	High	Limited
Anegre	Quartered or Plain Sliced Anegre	305 mm [12"]	3658 mm [12']	Large	High	Good
Avodire	Quartered Avodire	254 mm [10"]	3048 mm [10']	Large	High	Limited
Cherry	Plain Sliced American Cherry	305 mm [12"]	3353 mm [11']	Medium	Moderate	Good
	Quartered American Cherry	102 mm [4"]	3048 mm [10']	V. Small	High	Moderate
Birch	Rotary Cut Birch (Natural)	1220 mm [48"]	3048 mm [10']	Large	Low	Good
	Rotary Cut Birch (Select Red or White)	914 mm [36"]	3048 mm [10']	Medium	Moderate	Moderate
	Plain Sliced Birch (Natural)	254 mm [10"]	3048 mm [10']	Small	Moderate	Limited
	Plain Sliced Birch (Select Red or White)	127 mm [5"]	3048 mm [10']	Small	High	Limited
Butternut	Plain Sliced Butternut	305 mm [12"]	3048 mm [10']	Medium	High	Limited
Makore	Quartered or Plain Sliced Makore	305 mm [12"]	3658 mm [12']	Large	High	Good
Maple	Pl. Sl. (Half Round) American Maple	305 mm [12"]	3048 mm [10']	Medium	Moderate	Good (2)
	Rotary Birdseye Maple	6096 mm [20"]	3048 mm [10']	Medium	V. High	Good
Oak	Plain Sliced English Brown Oak	305 mm [12"]	3048 mm [10']	Medium	V. High	Limited
	Quartered English Brown Oak	254 mm [10"]	3048 mm [10']	Medium	V. High	Limited
	Plain Sliced American Red Oak	4877 mm [16"]	3658 mm [12']	Large	Moderate	Good
	Quartered American Red Oak	203 mm [8"]	3048 mm [10']	Small	Moderate	Good
	Rift Sliced American Red Oak	254 mm [10"]	3048 mm [10']	Medium	Moderate	Good
	Comb Grain Rift American Red Oak	203 mm [8"]	3048 mm [10']	Small	V. High	Limited
	Plain Sliced American White Oak	305 mm [12"]	3658 mm [12']	Medium	Moderate	Good
	Quartered American White Oak	203 mm [8"]	3048 mm [10']	Small	Moderate	Good
	Rift Sliced American White Oak	203 mm [8"]	3048 mm [10']	Medium	High	Good
	Comb Grain Rift American White Oak	203 mm [8"]	3048 mm [10']	Small	V. High	Limited
Hickory or Pecan	Plain Sliced American Hickory or Pecan	305 mm [12"]	3048 mm [10']	Small	Moderate	Good
Sapele	Quartered or Plain Sliced Sapele	305 mm [12"]	3658 mm [12']	Large	High	Good
Sycamore	Plain Sliced English Sycamore	254 mm [10"]	3048 mm [10']	Medium	V. High	Limited
	Quartered English Sycamore	152 mm [6"]	3048 mm [10']	Medium	V. High	Limited
Teak	Plain Sliced Teak	305 mm [12"]	3658 mm [12']	Large	V. High	Limited (3)
	Quartered Teak	305 mm [12"]	3658 mm [12']	Medium	V. High	Limited (3)
Walnut	Plain Sliced American Walnut	305 mm [12"]	3658 mm [12']	Medium	Moderate	Good
	Quarter Sliced American Walnut	152 mm [6"]	3048 mm [10']	V. Small	High	Rare

(1) Cost reflects raw veneer costs weighted for waste or yield characteristics and degree of labor difficulty.
(2) Seasonal factors may affect availability.
(3) Availability of blond Teak is very rare.
When Quartered or Plain Sliced (Pl. Sl.) are listed on the same line, the width dimensions are Plain Sliced; Quartered is narrower.

4 - Sheet Products

TYPES OF VENEER CUTS

The manner in which a log segment is cut with relation to the annual rings will determine the appearance of the veneer. When sliced, the individual pieces of veneer, referred to as leaves, are kept in the order in which they are sliced, thus permitting a natural grain progression when assembled as veneer faces. The group of leaves from one slicing is called a flitch and is usually identified by a flitch number and the number of gross square feet of veneer it contains. The faces of the leaves with relation to their position in the log are identified as the tight face (toward the outside of the log) and the loose face (toward the inside or heart of the log). During slicing the leaf is stressed on the loose face and compressed on the tight face. When this stress is combined with the natural variation in light refraction caused by the pores of the wood, the result is a difference in the human perception of color and tone between tight and loose faces.

The principal methods of slicing veneers and the general visual characteristics of the grain are:

PLAIN SLICING (OR FLAT SLICING)

This is the slicing method most often used to produce veneers for high quality architectural woodworking. Slicing is done parallel to a line through the center of the log. A combination of cathedral and straight grain patterns results, with a natural progression of pattern from leaf to leaf.

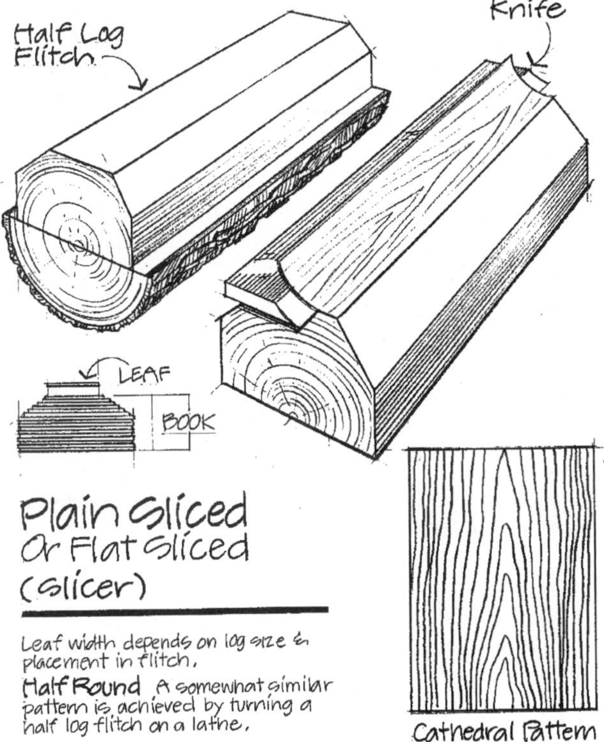

QUARTER SLICING (OR QUARTER CUT)

Quarter slicing simulates the quarter sawing process of solid lumber, roughly parallel to a radius line through the log segment. In many species the individual leaves are narrow as a result. A series of stripes is produced, varying in density and thickness from species to species. "Fleck" (sometimes called flake) is a characteristic of this slicing method in Red and White Oak.

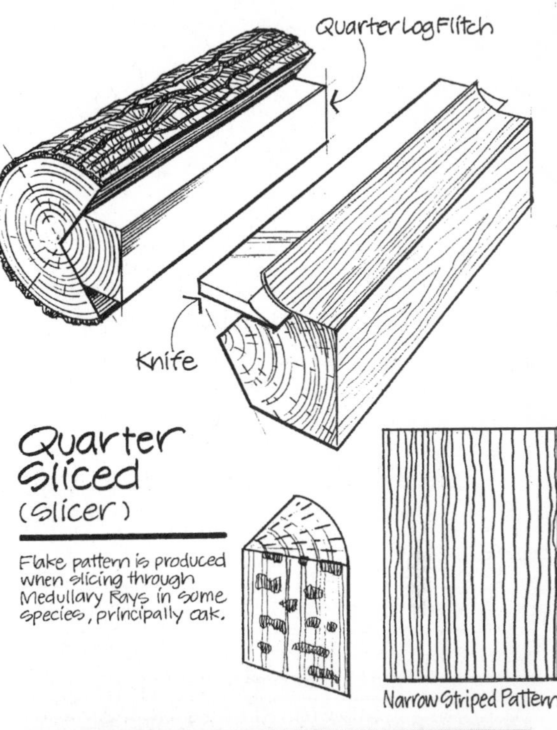

4 - Sheet Products

RIFT SLICING (OR RIFT CUT)

Rift veneers are produced most often in Red and White Oak, rarely in other species. Note that rift veneers and rift sawn solid lumber are produced so differently that a "match" between rift veneers and rift sawn solid lumber is highly unlikely. In both cases the cutting is done slightly off the radius lines minimizing the "fleck" (sometimes called flake) associated with quarter slicing.

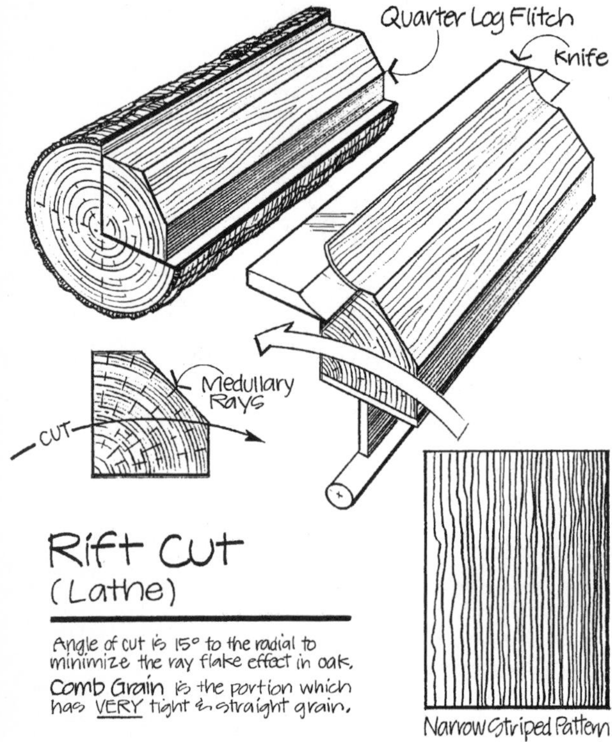

COMB GRAIN

Limited in availability, comb grain is a select product of the Rift process distinguished by tight, straight grain along the entire length of the veneer. Slight angle in the grain is allowed. Comb grain is restricted to Red and White Oak veneers.

ROTARY

The log is center mounted on a lathe and "peeled" along the general path of the growth rings like unwinding a roll of paper, providing a generally bold random appearance. Rotary cut veneers may vary in width and matching at veneer joints is extremely difficult. Almost all softwood veneers are cut this way. Except for a specific design effect, rotary veneers are the least useful in fine architectural woodwork.

Rotary sliced fine hardwood veneers are used in a limited way, and usually for special figure and cut, in the manufacture of Premium Grade woodwork. Careful consideration, specification, and communication are recommended when rotary cut is contemplated.

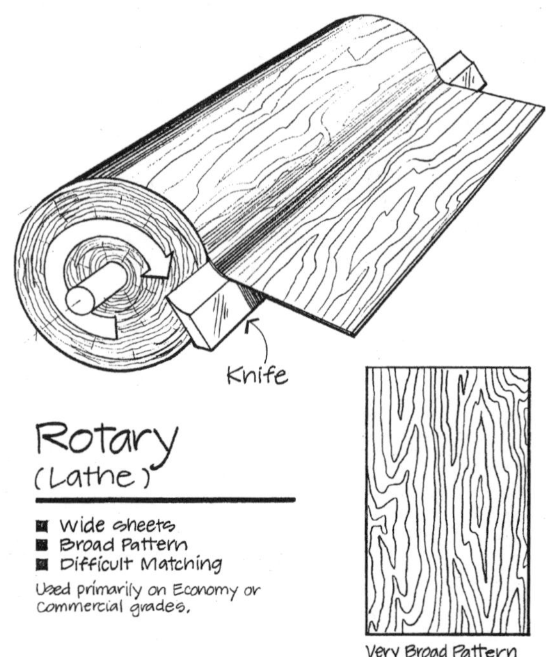

COMPOSITE VENEERS

Sliced from fast-growing trees, these veneers are dyed and then reglued in molds to create "grain" patterns. The color is established during manufacture because the high percentage of glue lines resist staining by the woodworker. Must be specified by brand name and manufacturer's designation. "Matching" between components may not be possible.

4 - Sheet Products

MATCHING ADJACENT VENEER LEAVES

It is possible to achieve certain visual effects by the manner in which the leaves are arranged. As noted, rotary cut veneers are difficult to match; therefore most matching is done with sliced veneers. The matching of adjacent veneer leaves must be specified. Special arrangements of leaves such as "diamond" and "box" matching are available. Consult your woodworker for choices. The more common types are:

BOOK MATCHING

The most commonly used match in the industry. Every other piece of veneer is turned over so adjacent pieces (leaves) are opened like the pages of a book.

Visual Effect - Veneer joints match, creating a symmetrical pattern. Yields maximum continuity of grain. When sequenced panels are specified, prominent characteristics will ascend or descend across the match as the leaves progress from panel to panel.

Barber Pole Effect in Book Match - Because the tight and loose faces alternate in adjacent pieces of veneer, they may accept stain differently, and this may result in a noticeable color variation. Book matching also accentuates cell polarization, causing the perception of different colors. These natural characteristics are often called barber pole, and are not a manufacturing defect.

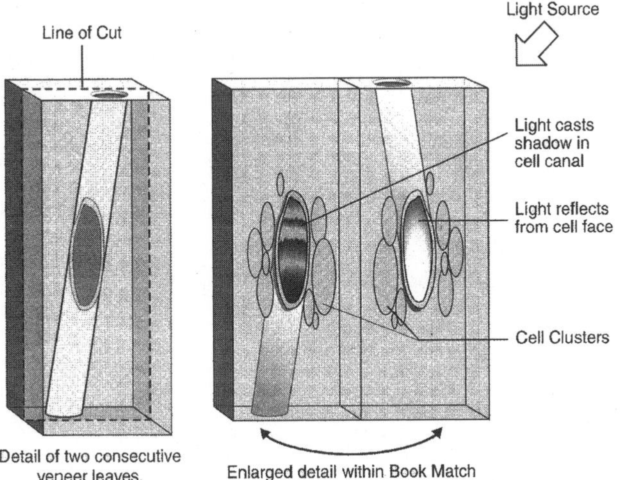

SLIP MATCHING

Often used with quarter sliced and rift sliced veneers. Adjoining leaves are placed (slipped out) in sequence without turning, resulting in all the same face sides being exposed.

Visual Effect - Grain figure repeats; but joints do not show visual grain match.

Note: The lack of grain match at the joints can be desirable. The relatively straight grain patterns of quartered and rift veneers generally produce pleasing results and a uniformity of color because all faces have the same light refraction.

RANDOM MATCHING

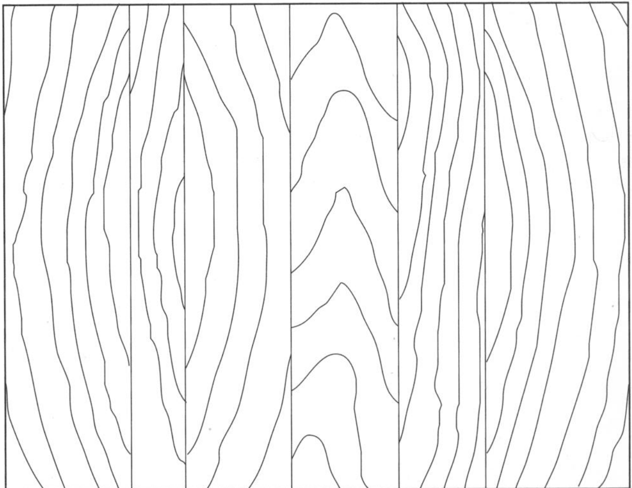

Veneer leaves are placed next to each other in a random order and orientation, producing a "board-by-board" effect in many species.

Visual Effect - Casual or rustic appearance, as though individual boards from a random pile were applied to the product. Conscious effort is made to mismatch grain at joints.

Degrees of contrast and variation may change from panel to panel. This match is more difficult to obtain than book or slip match, and must be clearly specified and detailed.

4 - Sheet Products

END MATCHING

Often used to extend the apparent length of available veneers for high wall panels and long conference tables. End matching occurs in three types:

ARCHITECTURAL END MATCH

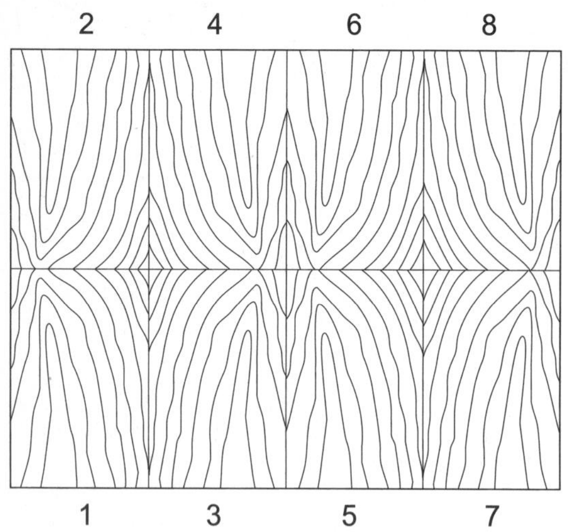

Leaves are individually book (or slip) matched, first end-to-end and then side-to-side, alternating end and side.

Visual Effect - Yields best continuous grain patterns for length as well as width. Minimizes misalignment of grain pattern.

CONTINUOUS END MATCH

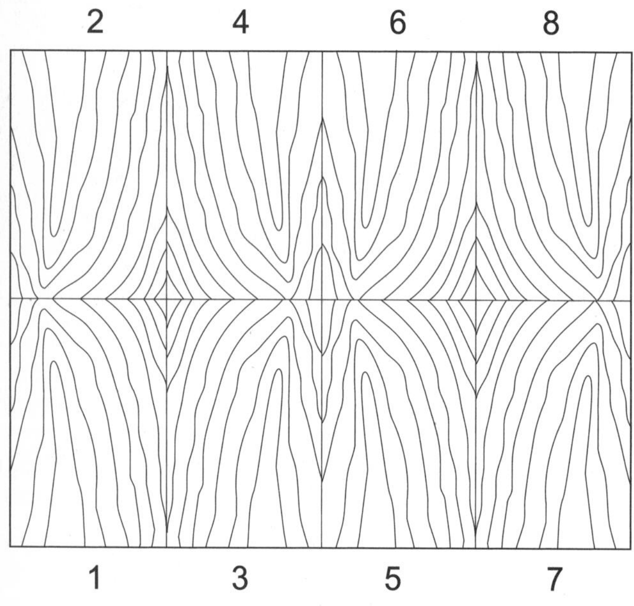

Leaves are individually book (or slip) matched, separate panels are stacked in sequenced order, either horizontally or vertically in the elevation. (Horizontal sequence illustrated.)

Visual Effect - Yields sequenced grain patterns for elevations, with pleasing blend of figure horizontally or vertically.

PANEL END MATCH

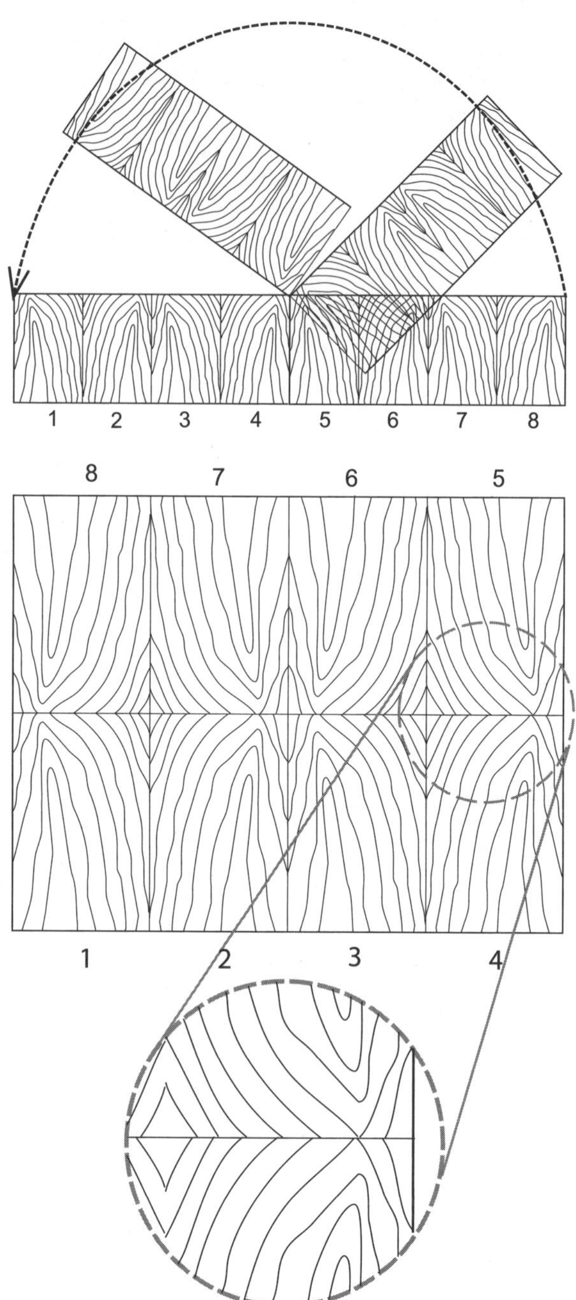

Natural Grain Pattern Mismatch Occurs

Leaves are book (or slip) matched on panel subassemblies, with sequenced subassemblies end matched, resulting in some modest cost savings on projects where applicable.

Visual Effect - For most species, yields pleasing, blended appearance and grain continuity. Some misalignment of grain pattern will occur, and is not a defect.

4 - Sheet Products

MATCHING WITHIN INDIVIDUAL PANEL FACES

The individual leaves of veneer in a sliced flitch increase or decrease in width as the slicing progresses. Thus, if a number of panels are manufactured from a particular flitch, the number of veneer leaves per panel face will change as the flitch is utilized. The manner in which these leaves are "laid up" within the panel requires specification, and is classified as follows:

RUNNING MATCH

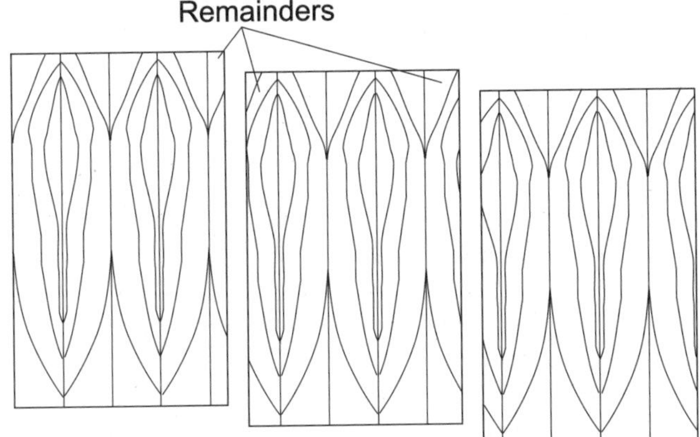

Each panel face is assembled from as many veneer leaves as necessary. This often results in a non-symmetrical appearance, with some veneer leaves of unequal width. Often the most economical method at the expense of æsthetics, it is the standard for Custom Grade and must be specified for other Grades. Running matches are seldom "sequenced and numbered" for use as adjacent panels. Horizontal grain "match" or sequence cannot be expected.

BALANCE MATCH

Each panel face is assembled from veneer leaves of uniform width before edge trimming. Panels may contain an even or odd number of leaves, and distribution may change from panel to panel within a sequenced set. While this method is the standard for Premium Grade, it must be specified for other Grades, and it is the most common assembly method at moderate cost.

BALANCE AND CENTER MATCH

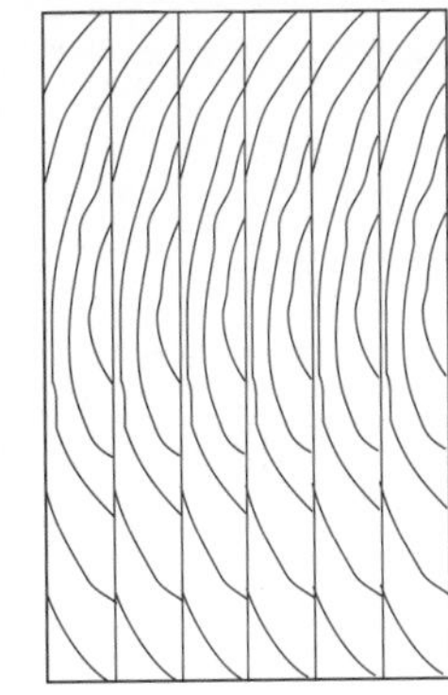

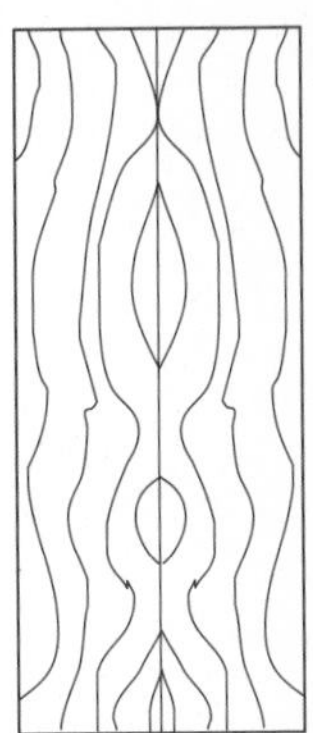

Each panel face is assembled of an even number from veneer leaves of uniform width before edge trimming. Thus, there is a veneer joint in the center of the panel, producing horizontal symmetry. A small amount of figure is lost in the process. Considered by some to be the most pleasing assembly at a modest increase in cost over Balance Match.

FIRE-RETARDANT PANELS

FLAME SPREAD CLASSIFICATION

The various codes utilize flame spread classifications for wood and other materials. It is the responsibility of the specifier to determine which elements, if any, of the woodwork require special treatment to meet local codes. In most codes, the panel products used to fabricate casework and furniture are not regulated.

FLAME SPREAD FACTORS

CORE - The fire rating of the core material determines the rating of the assembled panel. Fire-retardant veneered panels must have a fire-retardant core. Particleboard core is available with a Class I (Class A) rating and can be used successfully with veneer or rated high pressure decorative laminate faces. MDF (Medium Density Fiberboard) is available with a fire rating in some markets.

FACE - Some existing building codes, except where locally amended, provide that facing materials $^{1}/_{28}$" (0.9 mm)or thinner are not considered in determining the flame spread rating of the panel. If state and local codes move toward adoption of the International Building Code provisions, it is possible that the $^{1}/_{28}$" (0.9 mm) exemption may not be available. In localities where basic panel building codes have been amended it is the responsibility of the specifier to determine whether the application of the facing material specified will meet the code. Traditionally, face veneers are not required to be fire-retardant treated, and such treatment will adversely affect the finishing process.

4 - Sheet Products

SPECIAL MATCHES

There are regional variations in the "names" of the following veneer leaf matching techniques. It is strongly recommended the design professional use both names and drawings to define the effect desired.

8 Piece Sunburst

Box Match

Reverse or End Grain Box

Herringbone or V-Book Match

Diamond Match

Reverse Diamond Match

Parquet Match

Swing Match

Book & Butt Match w/ Border

4 - Sheet Products

METHODS OF MATCHING PANELS

Veneered panels used in casework or paneling in the same area may be matched to each other. This important component of the project must be carefully detailed and specified. The natural growth patterns of the tree will cause the figure on the sequential panels to ascend, descend, or show a "grain progression" as the eye moves from panel to panel. These illustrations were developed in Imperial measure and have not been converted for this edition. The four common methods are:

PRE-MANUFACTURED SETS - FULL WIDTH

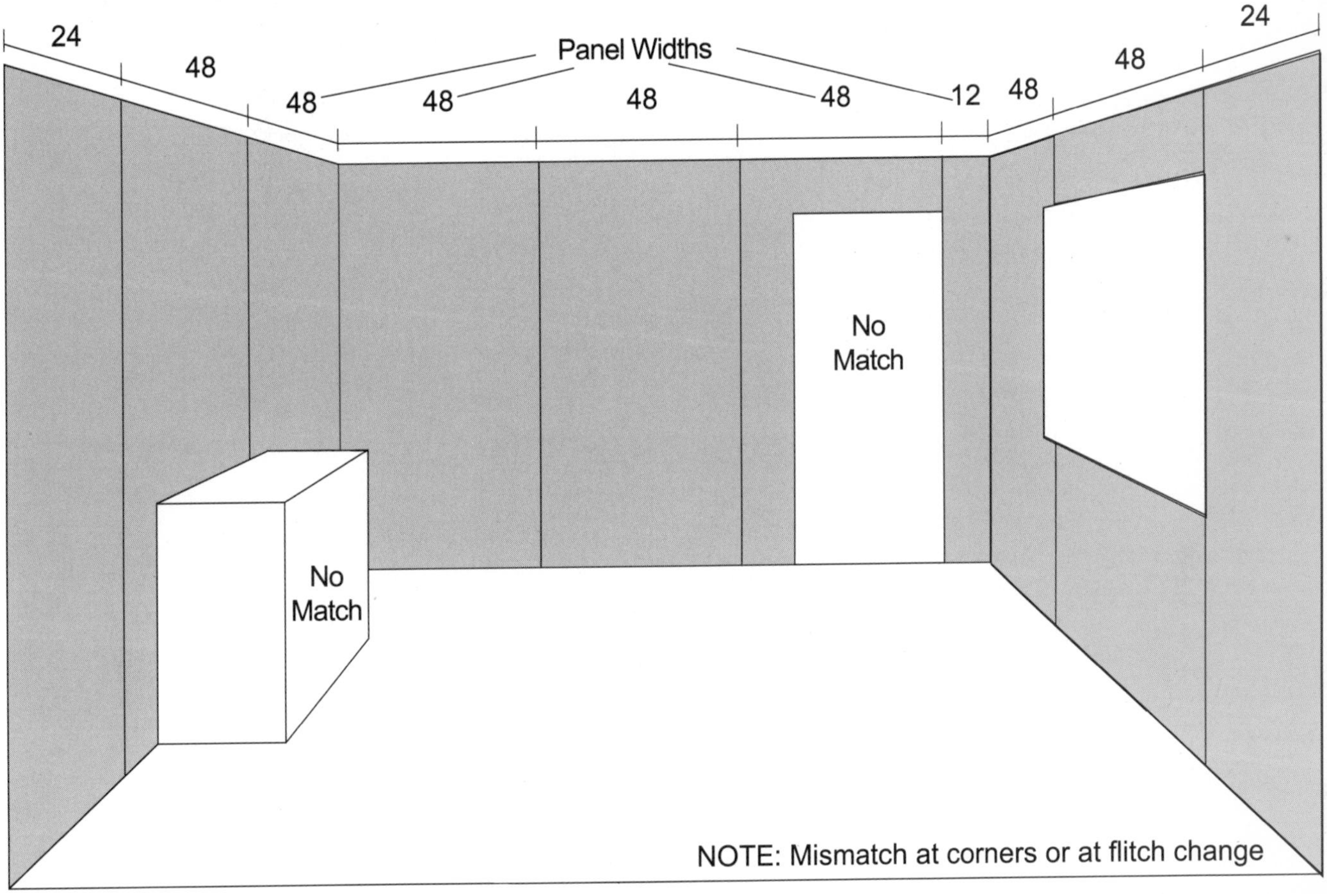

Panel Widths
24 48 48 48 48 48 12 48 48 24
No Match
No Match
NOTE: Mismatch at corners or at flitch change

These are one step above stock plywood panels, usually made and warehoused in 4' x 8' or 4' x 10' sheets in sequenced sets. They may be produced from a single flitch or a part of a flitch, usually varying in number from 6 to 12 panels. If more than one set is required, matching between the sets cannot be expected. Similarly, doors or components often cannot be fabricated from the same flitch materials, resulting in noticeable mismatch. This is often the most economical type of special panel products.

FLOOR PLAN KEY

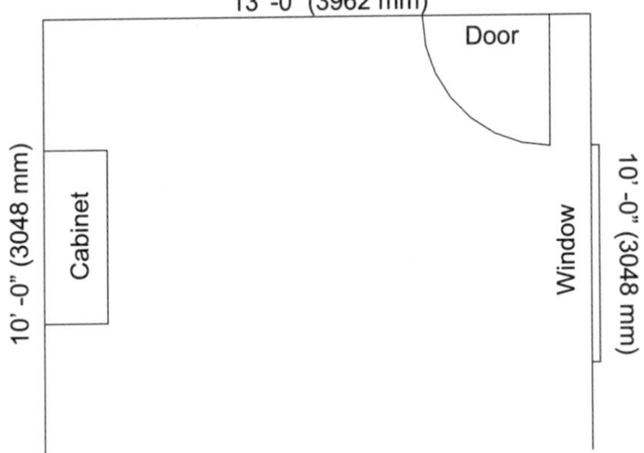

4 - Sheet Products

PRE-MANUFACTURED SETS - SELECTIVELY REDUCED IN WIDTH

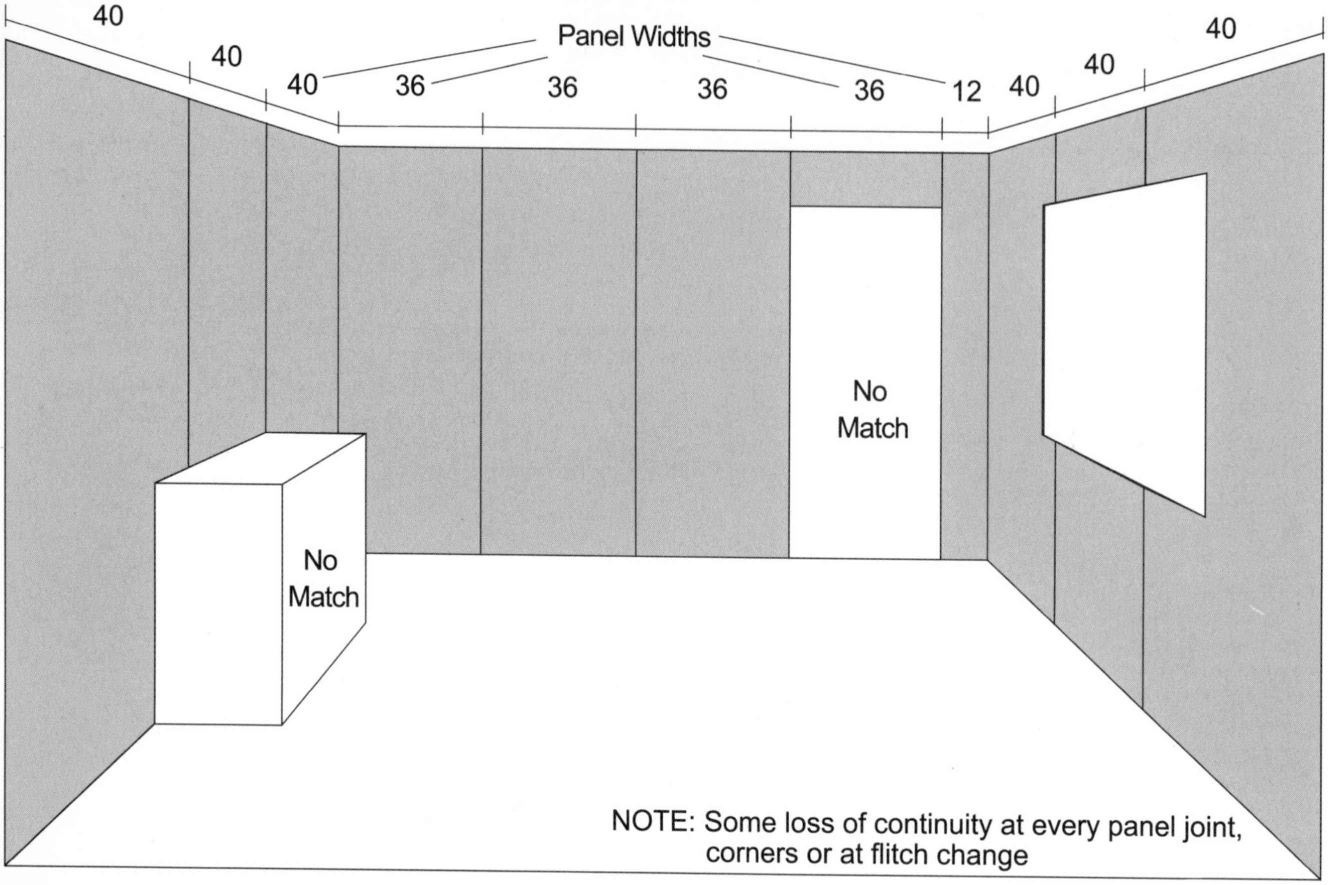

40
40
40
Panel Widths
36
36
36
36
12
40
40
40
No Match
No Match
NOTE: Some loss of continuity at every panel joint, corners or at flitch change

These are panels just like those in the previous illustration, usually made and warehoused in 4' x 8' or 4' x 10' sheets in sequenced sets. They are often selected for continuity, recut into modular widths, and numbered to achieve the appearance of greater symmetry. If more than one set is required, matching between the sets cannot be expected. Similarly, doors or components often cannot be fabricated from the same flitch materials, resulting in noticeable mismatch.

FLOOR PLAN KEY

13' -0" (3962 mm)
Door
10' -0" (3048 mm)
Cabinet
Window
10' -0" (3048 mm)

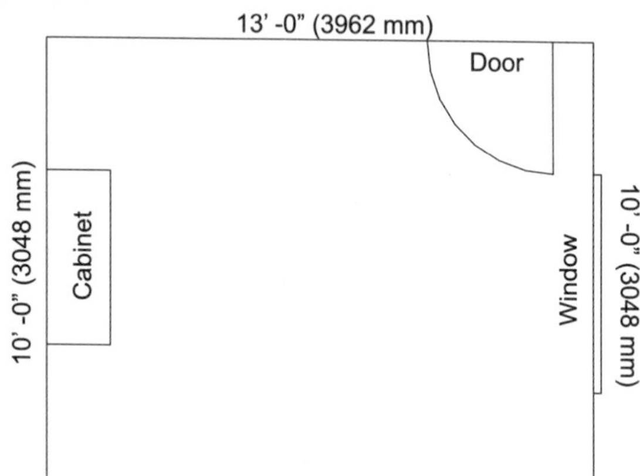

SE-

4 - Sheet Products

QUENCE-MATCHED UNIFORM SIZE SET

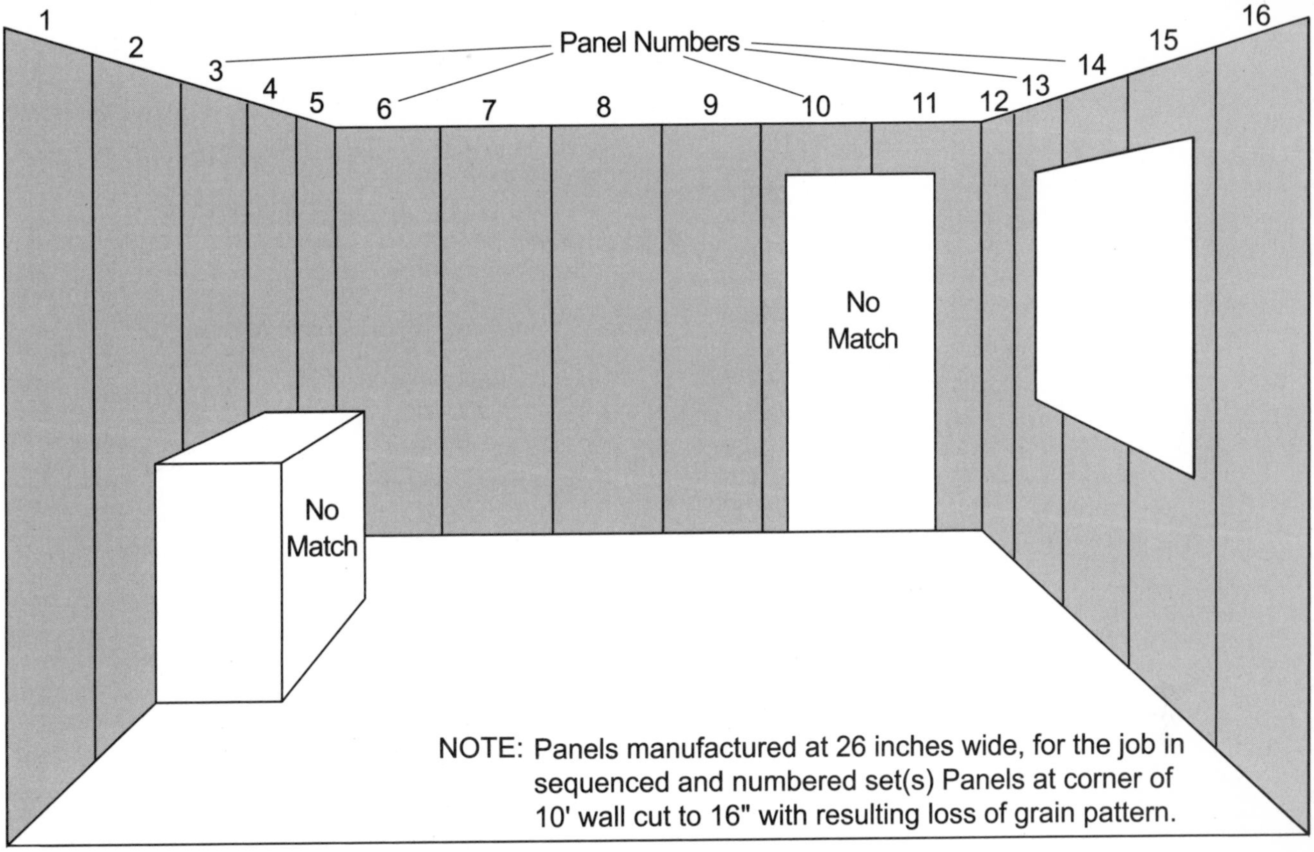

1
2
3
4
5
6
7
8
9
10
11
12
13
14
15
16
Panel Numbers
No
Match
No
Match
NOTE: Panels manufactured at 26 inches wide, for the job in sequenced and numbered set(s) Panels at corner of 10' wall cut to 16" with resulting loss of grain pattern.

These sets are manufactured for a specific installation to a uniform panel width and height. If more than one flitch is required to produce the required number of panels, similar flitches will be used. This type of panel matching is best used when panel layout is uninterrupted, and when the design permits the use of equal-width panels. Some sequence will be lost if trimming is required to meet field conditions. Doors and components within the wall cannot usually be matched to the panels. Moderate in cost, sequenced uniform panels offer a good compromise between price and æsthetics.

FLOOR PLAN KEY

13' -0" (3962 mm)
Door
10' -0" (3048 mm)
Cabinet
Window
10' -0" (3048 mm)

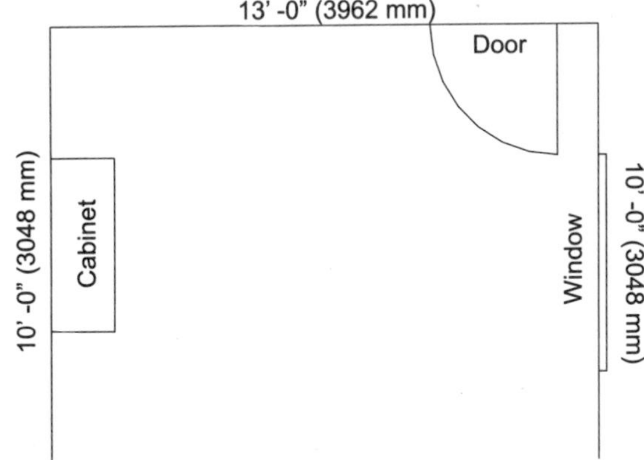

BLUE-

4 - Sheet Products

PRINT-MATCHED PANELS AND COMPONENTS

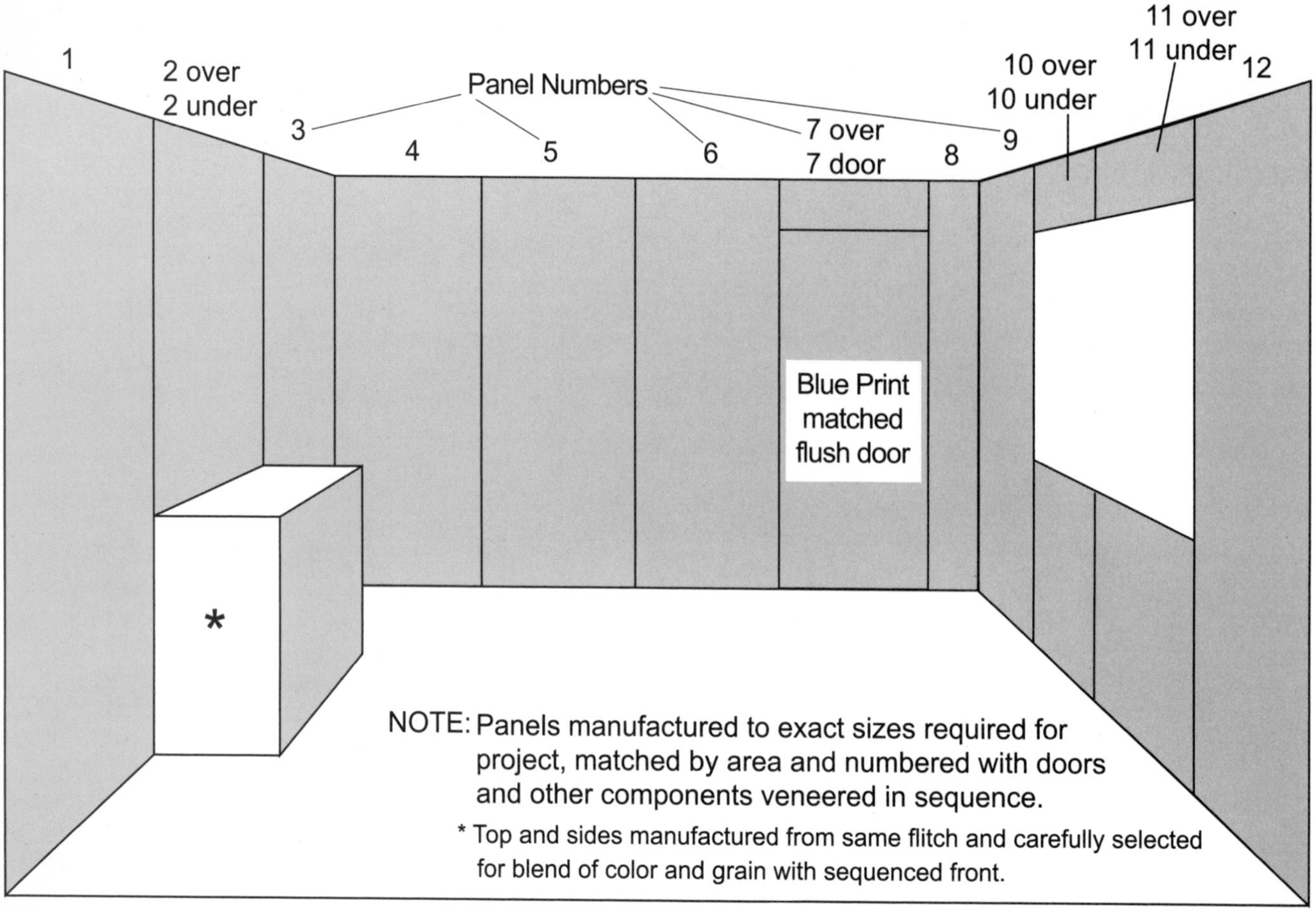

1
2 over
2 under
Panel Numbers
3
4
5
6
7 over
7 door
8
9
10 over
10 under
11 over
11 under
12
Blue Print
matched
flush door
*
NOTE: Panels manufactured to exact sizes required for project, matched by area and numbered with doors and other components veneered in sequence.
* Top and sides manufactured from same flitch and carefully selected for blend of color and grain with sequenced front.

This method of panel matching achieves maximum grain continuity since all panels, doors, and other veneered components are made to the exact sizes required and in the exact veneer sequence. If possible, flitches should be selected that will yield sufficient veneer to complete a prescribed area or room. If more than one flitch is needed, flitch transition should be accomplished at the least noticeable, predetermined location. This method requires careful site coordination and relatively long lead times. Panels cannot be manufactured until site conditions can be accurately measured and detailed. This panel matching method is more expensive and expresses veneering in its most impressive manner.

FLOOR PLAN KEY

13' -0" (3962 mm)
Door
10' -0" (3048 mm)
Cabinet
Window
10' -0" (3048 mm)

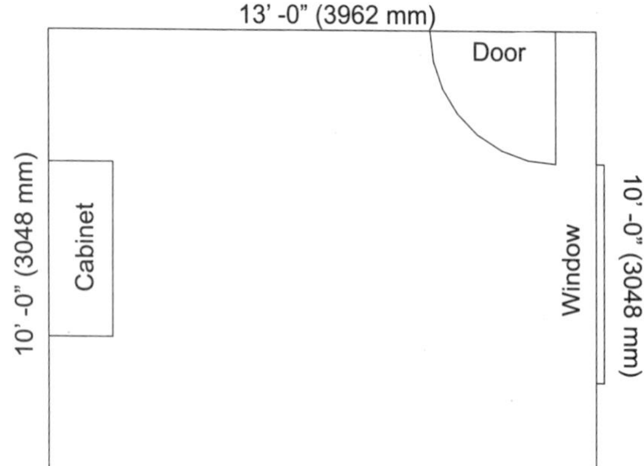

5
Finishing

5 - Finishing

DESCRIPTION AND PURPOSE

Specifying of factory finish is usually selected for high-quality work where superior appearance and performance of the finish is desired. Benefits of factory finishing include consistency, control of film thickness, environmental compliance, and the curing of the finish in a controlled atmosphere. Its use assumes a maximum degree of shop prefabrication so that site installation can be performed with a minimum amount of cutting, fitting, and adjustment to facilitate project completion.

The purpose of finishing woodworking is twofold. First, the finish is used traditionally as a means to enhance or alter the natural beauty of the wood. Second, the finish must protect the wood from damage by moisture, contaminants, and handling. It is important to understand that a quality finish must offer acceptable performance and also meet the aesthetic requirements of the project.

The AWS illustrates a number of finishing systems. The finishing system provides a protective surface for the product. Some of these systems are in general use; others are intended for special conditions and can only be applied under a strictly controlled environment. The cost of the systems vary, the higher performing finishes usually being more costly than the lower performing finishes. Unnecessary cost could be added to a project through over-specification.

- Systems are usually not compatible with each other. Trying to intermix systems could cause quality and/or performance problems.
- Old fashioned or consumer-oriented brush applied finishes are not recommended for factory finished fine architectural woodwork, and are not covered by the AWS.
- Finish systems often fail because too much top coat material is applied. Check with the finish system supplier for advice.

When specifying, please use the system name as set forth in the AWS. Involve your woodwork manufacturer early in the design process to evaluate the systems in relation to your project requirements. Choose performance characteristics which meet, but do not exceed, the needs of your project in the interest of value engineering.

Many prefinished real wood panels and decorative overlays have aesthetic and performance characteristics which meet or exceed the AWS, and shall be evaluated, approved and specified by the design professional when desired.

The listing of a finish system in the AWS does not imply an endorsement of the materials and/or methods or compliance with federal and/or local Environmental Protection Agency or other requirements. Some finishing professionals have, for example, found that polyurethanes and/or polyesters require special finishing procedures for a quantity of laboratory casework. Check with the finishing supplier for recommendations in the use of these products. In cases like these, catalyzed vinyl shall be the topcoat of choice.

WOOD FINISHES, STEPS AND COLOR

A variety of finishes are available for wood products. Aesthetically, systems may vary from no stain, to a single stain, to a multiple step application. Some samples will require multiple color and finish steps in order to meet the architect's requirements. The existing system specified may not include all steps necessary to match the architect's example or requirements. Color and grain enhancement of some finishes require the build of one color step on another. This will sometimes require an additional step of a protective wash coat between color steps. Generally, this procedure adds to the depth and beauty of the finish. Each added step increases costs and shall be specified.

Special consideration should be given to raw wood parts on high pressure decorative laminate-clad (HPDL) cabinets such as wood pulls, wood trims, applied moldings, banded doors, drawer bodies, and wood cabinet interiors. Specifications regarding the responsibility for finishing (if any) shall be clarified by the design professional.

NOTE TO SPECIFIER

Too often, specifications call for finishes based on samples or guide language from a specialty manufacturer.

Examples include the over-specification of polyurethane or polyester top coats when they are neither necessary or available from the custom fabricator.

FINISH CURING

There are a variety of ways to cure a finish. For the most part the method should not concern the design professional or specification writer. It is the performance of the top coat which is important. Select the performance criteria which best meets the needs of your client from the finish tables. Finish chemistry, performance, value-to-performance ratio, and your finisher's abilities should be considered.

UV (ultraviolet light) curing is one of the methods for curing topcoats. It is typically used for high volume, repetitive applications, and requires special reactors to cure. It is currently done by a limited number of finishing operations. The process is environmentally friendly. A number of prefinished panel products are coated with materials designed specifically for UV curing. While UV cured top coats are not all alike, most are very high performance finishes. Consult with the fabricator for performance tests and details

All factory finish systems utilize top coats with spray or flat line application that air dry within one hour, as is common practice, with the exception of waterborne polyesters, and two-component urethanes which may extend these time limits but will be dust free within 24 hours. Finishing materials will be selected for chemical compatibility with each other and with the substrate by the finishing professional.

COLOR "MATCH" AND CONSISTENCY

The term "color match" is often misleading. The best case achievable using a natural product like wood in a wide variety of lighting conditions is a good "blend" of color and tone throughout the project area. The natural color of the wood product is altered by the application of even a clear topcoat. Further alteration is achieved through the use of stains, glazes, bleaches, etc. All wood changes color; especially Cherry, Fir, genuine and African Mahogany, Walnut, Teak, and others. Filled nail holes will not

5 - Finishing

change with wood. The apparent consistency of the color is a combination of light reflectance, cellular structure, natural characteristics, applied colors, and sheen.

Color and "matching" of a sample are often highly subjective. Individual perception, ambient lighting, and reflectivity influence judgement. Design professionals are encouraged to consult directly with a woodworker during the design and selection phase of each project.

PREFINISHED WOOD PANELS

Many prefinished real wood panels and decorative overlays have aesthetic and performance characteristics which meet or exceed the AWS, and should be evaluated, approved and specified by the design professional when desired.

VENEER FINISHING

The fundamental construction of flush wood doors and hardwood veneered panel products is very similar. Both products use various substrates, or plies, with a top ply of hardwood veneer. As a result, the following observations and considerations apply equally to flush wood doors and hardwood veneered panel product

BLOTCHY APPEARANCE OF THE FINISHED SURFACE

Blotching occurs because some wood species exhibit an uneven distribution of large and small pores in their structure. The occurrence of this is readily apparent in such hardwood species as Maple and Birch and, to a lesser degree, in Cherry. This irregular distribution of pores usually causes an uneven absorption of stain, hence, an apparent blotchy appearance in the finish. Reduction of the blotching condition can sometimes be achieved by proper sanding, wash coating (prior to staining) or by choosing non-penetrating pigments, such as dyes, alcohol stains or glaze. When these steps are required or desired, they shall be specified in addition to finish system selection.

BARBER POLE, OR CANDY STRIPING

This effect is most evident when veneer leaves are book matched. Because book matched veneer panel or door faces are made up by turning every other piece (leaf) of veneer over, like the pages of a book, the face of one leaf and the back of the next leaf is exposed. This exposes the "tight" and "loose" face of the leaves. One of the most striking examples of Barber Pole effect can be seen in book matched rift and quarter cut oak. Check with your woodworker when you are considering specifying rift or quartered veneers.

TECHNIQUES TO CONSIDER

While a blotchy appearance and the "barber pole effect" may occur in any species, due to the natural characteristics of wood, there are steps that can be taken to reduce these effects. The following are two of the techniques that are of particular importance.

SANDING

While the selection of species, cut and match are major factors in the final appearance of any project, the first step, in controlling the quality of finished appearance, is proper sanding.

An important element of this standard is the statement "just prior to staining." Specifications that indicate "factory shall finish sand prior to shipment" do not provide a correct solution for proper surface preparation. Such a directive fails to take into account the length of time panels will be stored at the job site, potential damage from handling and the effects of changes in the relative humidity. Proper sanding can only be done, just prior to staining/finishing.

The successful sanding of panels, or flush doors, is best accomplished with a hand block, powered pad sander, wide belt sander or stroke sander, exerting uniform pressure over the entire surface. Depending upon the condition of the surface it may be necessary to use successively finer grits of abrasive to properly prepare the surface, brushing off the surface between grits. The AWS sets forth the smoothness requirement for all Grades of work. Proper and complete surface preparation is the key factor in the successful finish procedure.

WASH COAT

A washcoat is a thin coat of material, usually clear lacquer or vinyl sealer (6 to 10 parts thinner to one part sealer, topcoat). A washcoat can fulfill several purposes such as: to stiffen the small wood fibers that are raised by the staining operation, so they can be cut off easily with fine sand paper (320 grit), to seal the stain, particularly if it is a bleeding type, to aid in the wiping and clean up of filler, and to minimize excessive penetration of stain or filler to minimize blotchiness. As with any finish process, samples should always be prepared to ensure that the desired finish is achieved.

BLUE STAIN

Blue stain occurs in Oak veneers when natural tannic acid in the wood comes in contact with iron and or moisture. Enough moisture may occur during heavy rains or high humidity in buildings not yet temperature controlled. The following is from a door manufacturer's care and handling brochure.

"To prevent blue stain, never use steel wool on the bare wood. Fine particles of the wool will cling to the door and cause trouble later. If you use shellac (a solvent for iron), it should not be stored in iron containers. To remove blue stain prior to finishing doors, we recommend a solution of oxalic acid crystals. The solution is made by dissolving 12 ounces of crystals in one gallon of lukewarm water. Use a plastic or rubber container. Wear rubber gloves while working with the solution. Apply it to the stained areas with a brush or sponge; allow the door to dry and sand with 150 to 180 grit sandpaper. The entire door surface should be treated to avoid spotting. Important: Failure to rinse the treated area adequately may have a damaging effect on the finish subsequently applied, or may cause damage to nearby glass, porcelain or other surfaces in confined areas. Damage may not result immediately, but may result during storage or after installation."

5 - Finishing

FIRE-RETARDANT TREATED LUMBER AND COATINGS

Fire retardant treatments may affect the finishes intended to be used on the wood, particularly if transparent finishes are planned. The compatibility of any finishes should be tested before they are applied.

"Fire-retardant" coatings usually are of the intumescent type. They may be water-based or solvent-based, but both contain ingredients which, under the influence of heat, produce gases and char-like products, resulting in the formation of a thick nonflammable crust that effectively insulates combustible substrates from heat and flame. However, these ingredients are for the most part water-sensitive and therefore reduce durability and range of usage of the coatings.

These coatings only delay the spread of fire and help contain it to its origin. To be of any appreciable value, fire-retardant coatings must be applied in strict conformance with the manufacturer's instructions. These finishes are not particularly durable and their use should be restricted to application over interior surfaces.

The need for, and effectiveness of, fire-retardant and fire-resistant finishes depends on the type of construction, nature of occupancy, and other technical features of the building. Because these finishes are considerably more expensive and have reduced durability, their use should be carefully limited to those areas where confining fire spread is the overwhelming consideration; for example, interior entrances, hallways, stairwells and ceilings.

STRIPPING RECOMMENDATION (WHEN SPECIFIED)

While them AWS does not cover the removal of existing finishes on woodwork, the methods and skill involved in large measure determines the quality of preservation, conservation, and restoration during Historical Work. Stripping is usually performed by specialists trained in historic work, but there are some architectural woodworkers who have such specialists on the staff. Regardless of the assignment of responsibility for existing finish removal, the following guidelines should be inserted in the contract documents by the design team:

- Strippers shall be environmentally sound, solvent based. Alkaline based products are not acceptable. All strippers shall be neutral based, not requiring additional neutralization treatment.
- Before stripping begins, all surfaces shall be tested (with the process and results recorded) to provide the least intrusive and damaging methods. Approval of the architect, design professional or conservator is required before execution of the work.
- Completely remove existing finish using multiple applications of the approved methods without gouging, splintering or otherwise damaging sound surfaces.
- Thoroughly remove all stripping residuals, include wax, before proceeding.
- Stripped surfaces shall be tested for evidence of acid or alkali, reworking the surface until it tests pH neutral.
- Carefully sand all surfaces by hand with no coarser than 220 grit garnet or aluminum oxide sandpaper to remove all signs of raised grain.

6
Interior and Exterior Millwork

6 - Interior and Exterior Millwork

METHODS OF PRODUCTION

Flat Surfaces:

- Sawing - This produces relatively rough surfaces that are not utilized for architectural woodwork except where a "rough sawn" texture or finish is desired for design purposes. To achieve the smooth surfaces generally required, the rough sawn boards are further surfaced by the following methods:
- Planing - Sawn lumber is passed through a planer or jointer, which has a revolving head with projecting knives, removing a thin layer of wood to produce a relatively smooth surface.
- Abrasive Planing - Sawn lumber is passed through a powerful belt sander with tough, coarse belts, which remove the rough top surface.

Moulded Surfaces:

Sawn lumber is passed through a moulder or shaper that has knives ground to a pattern which produces the moulded profile desired.

SMOOTHNESS OF FLAT AND MOULDED SURFACES

Planers and Moulders: The smoothness of surfaces which have been machine planed or moulded is determined by the closeness of the knife cuts. The closer the cuts to each other (i.e., the more knife cuts per inch [KCPI]) the closer the ridges, and therefore the smoother the resulting appearance.

Sanding and Abrasives: Surfaces can be further smoothed by sanding. Sandpapers come in grits from coarse to fine and are assigned ascending grit numbers. The coarser the grit, the faster the stock removal. The surface will show the striations caused by the grit. Sanding with progressively finer-grit papers will produce smoother surfaces.

DESIGN AND USE OF RESOURCES

Moldings should be cut from lumber approximately the same size as the finished piece to make the best use of our natural resources. Designing moldings with the size of typical boards in mind has several advantages.

The typical 1" x 4" (25.4 mm x 101.6 mm) will yield a very nice 3/4" (19 mm) thick molding, but will not be thick enough to develop a molding which is a full 1" (25.4 mm) thick in finish dimension. The typical 2" x 4" (50.8 mm x 101.6 mm) piece of lumber can be made into moldings about 1-3/4" (44.5 mm) thick in a similar manner.

Deep or large moldings are often best cut from more than one piece and built up to make the final profile. Just as in the manufacturing of single moldings, this process minimizes waste and reduces the tendency of the finished profiles to twist, warp, cup, or bow as a result of removing too much material from either side of the initial board.

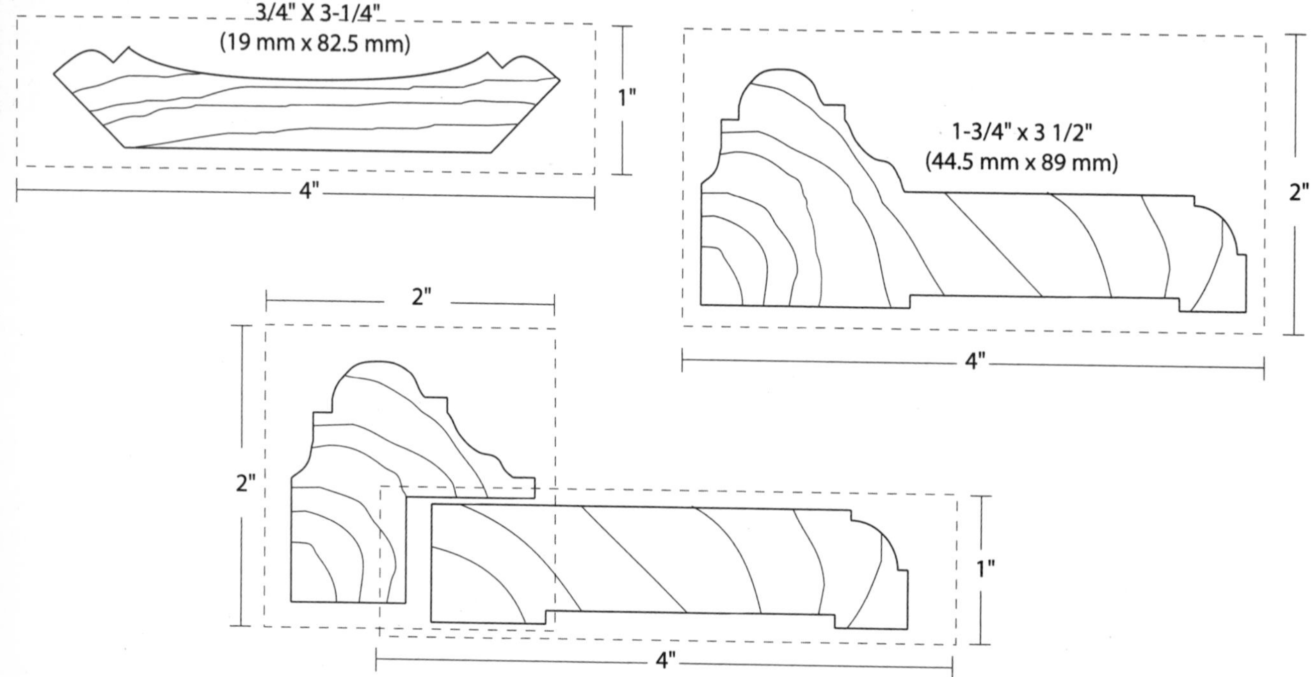

(Appendix B is not part of the AWS for compliance purposes)

6 - Interior and Exterior Millwork

IDENTIFICATION OF STANDING AND RUNNING TRIM AND RAIL PARTS

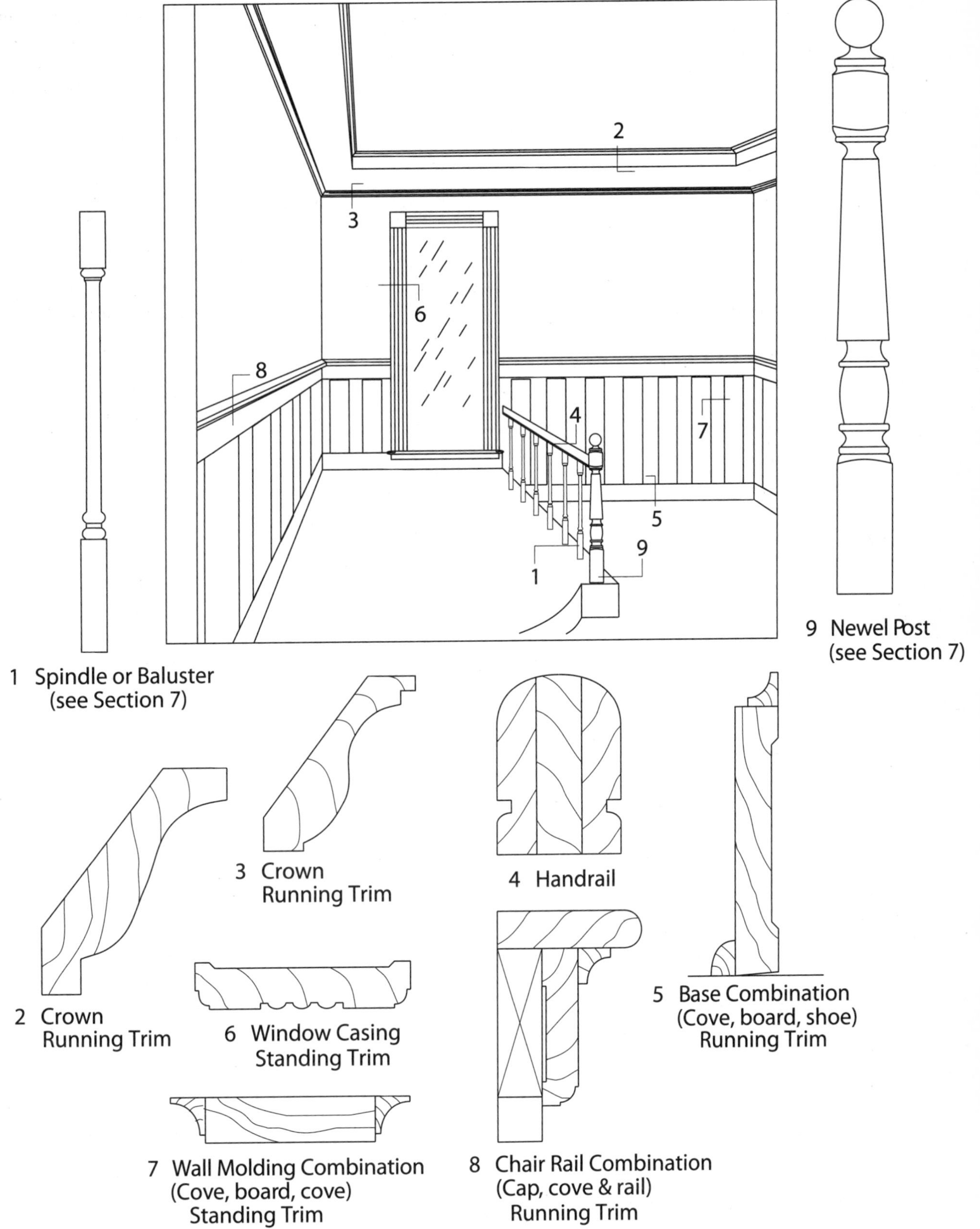

6 - Interior and Exterior Millwork

RADIUS MOLDINGS

Both traditional and nontraditional architectural styles often call for radius standing and running trim either in plan, elevation, or both. In situations where the size of the molding and the radius to which it is to be formed is such that a straight molding will not conform to the substrate, the architectural woodworker can use several methods to fabricate radius moldings. Moldings applied to radii can be segmented, bent, laminated and formed, pre-shaped, or machined to the radius. Woodworkers will fabricate the moldings in the longest practical lengths, with the purpose of minimizing the field joints.

The architectural woodworker frequently uses band sawing for fabricating radius moldings. With this technique, the woodworker starts with a large, often glued-up piece of material and band s*AWS* to get a curved piece. In order to cut down on waste, the woodworker tries to get several curved pieces from one large piece by nesting, as shown in Illustration A. Characteristically, this method of fabricating radius moldings limits the length of pieces that can be developed without a joint. It also yields a piece of material with grain straight on the face, not following the curve.

When dealing with profiles with a flat face (see Illustration B), the woodworker may saw the pieces from a sheet of plywood and then apply an edge band. This will yield larger pieces with more consistent grain.

Another technique for fabricating a radius mould involves laminating thin, bendable plies of lumber in a form (see Illustration C). Laminated pieces hold their shape without being secured to another surface. This curved piece will then be milled to the desired profile. The glue lines follow the edge grain and the curve, thus minimizing their visibility. The species of wood and the tightness of the radius determine the maximum thickness of each ply.

When dealing with some cross Sections, it can be advantageous to combine band sawing and laminating. The woodworker band s*AWS* a core of common lumber and laminates finish material to the exposed faces. From looking at Illustration D, it is apparent that this technique must be limited to certain profiles. It does, however, offer the ability to minimize glue joints and control grain directions. Finally, the simplest method for obtaining a radius molding is kerfing.

As seen in Illustration E, kerfing consists of making repeated saw cuts on the back face of the piece, perpendicular to the bend. The tightness of the radius determines the spacing and depth of the kerfs. Kerfing allows the piece to be bent to the required radius, and then secured in place to hold the bend. Kerfing almost always results in "flats" on the face which show in finishing. When dealing with a large radius, it is sometimes possible to stop the kerf prior to going through an exposed edge. In most cases, however, the kerf runs all the way through, and the edge must be concealed .

Unless specifically called out, the architectural woodworker will have the option of which method to use for fabricating radius molding. Since the fabrication method determines the final appearance of the pieces, especially regarding the direction of grain and visibility of glue joints, the architect or designer may wish to specify the method. It is recommended that an architectural woodwork firm be consulted before making a selection. Mock-ups may be required to visualize the end product.

Some acceptable methods of radius fabrication

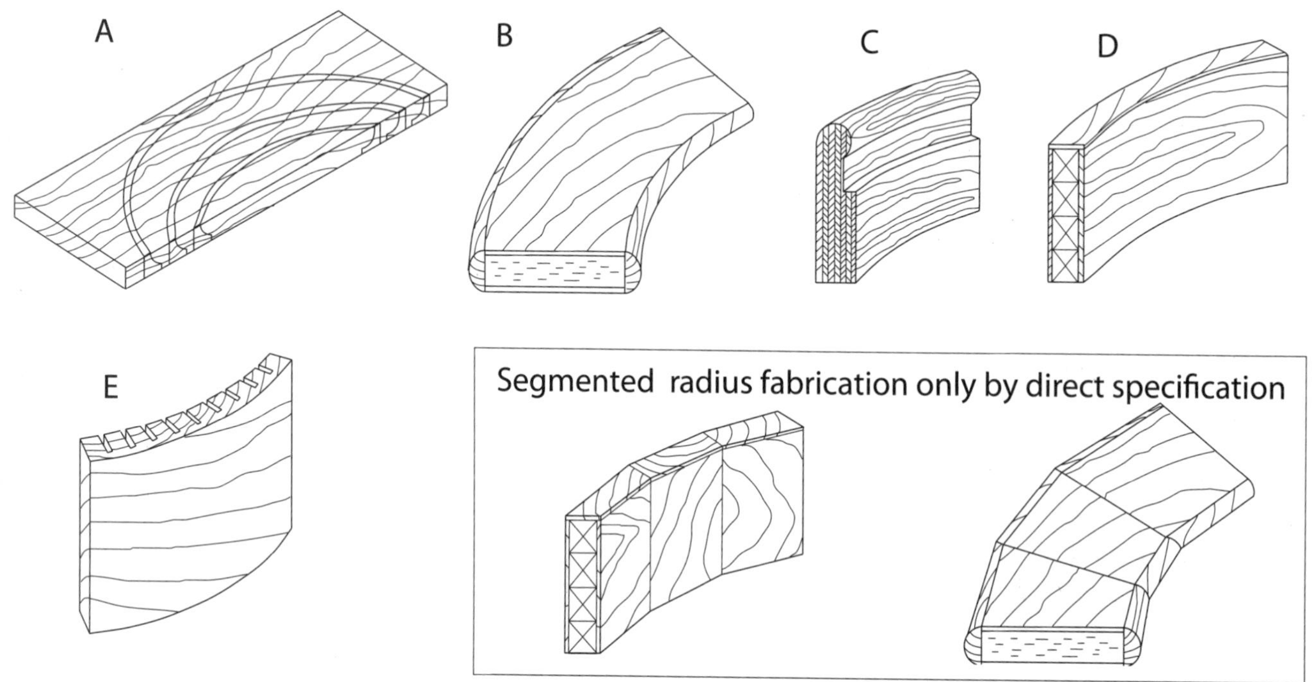

(Appendix B is not part of the AWS for compliance purposes)

6 - Interior and Exterior Millwork

Solid Lumber Paneling Patterns

The variety of solid lumber paneling is only limited by the imagination of the design professional. Virtually any machinable profile can be custom manufactured. The following profiles are some of the traditional patterns associated with solid board paneling. They are not dimensioned intentionally, allowing the design professional to determine the scale and proportions most appropriate for the project.

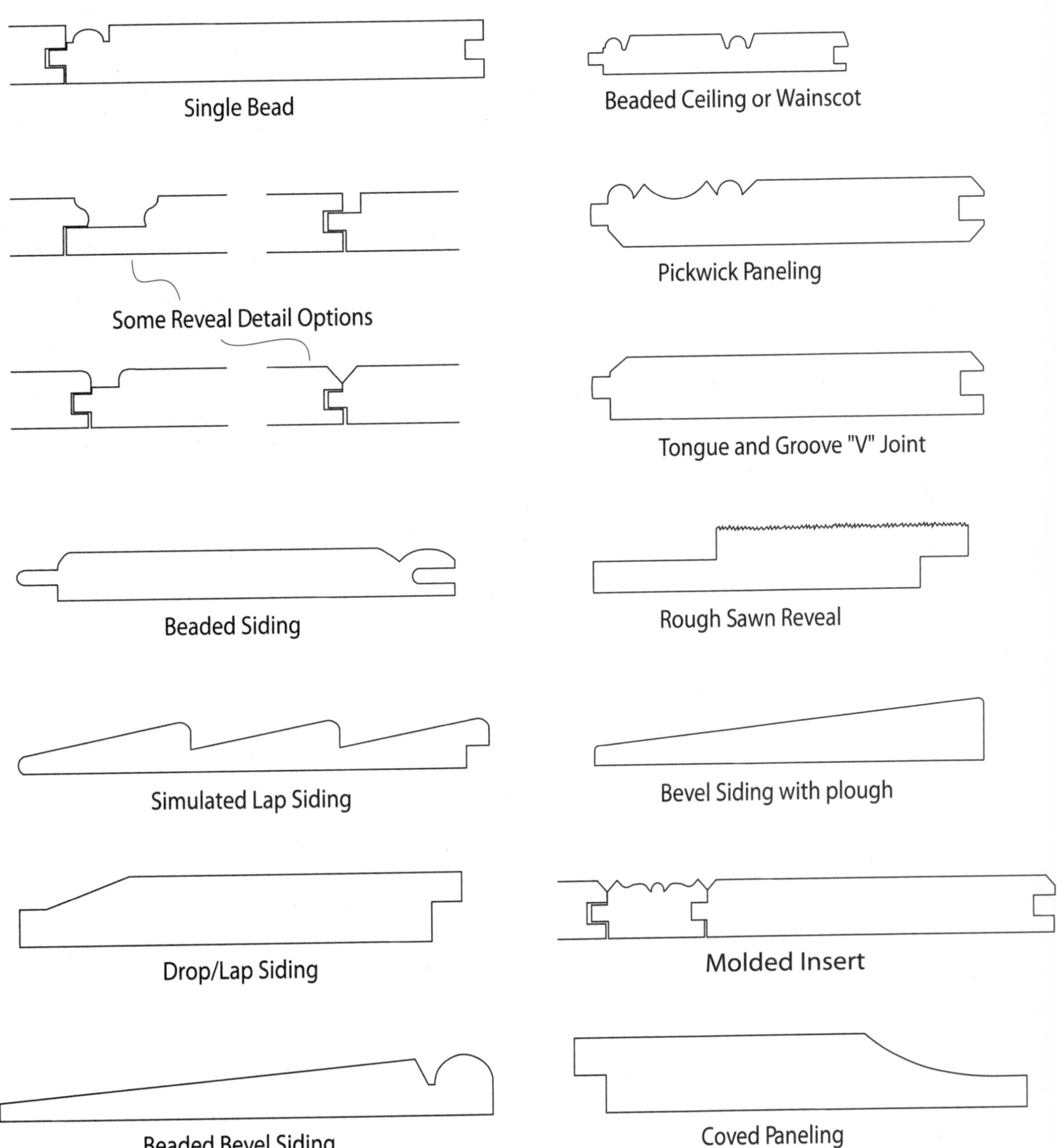

6 - Interior and Exterior Millwork

TYPICAL USES OF STANDING AND RUNNING TRIM AND RAILS

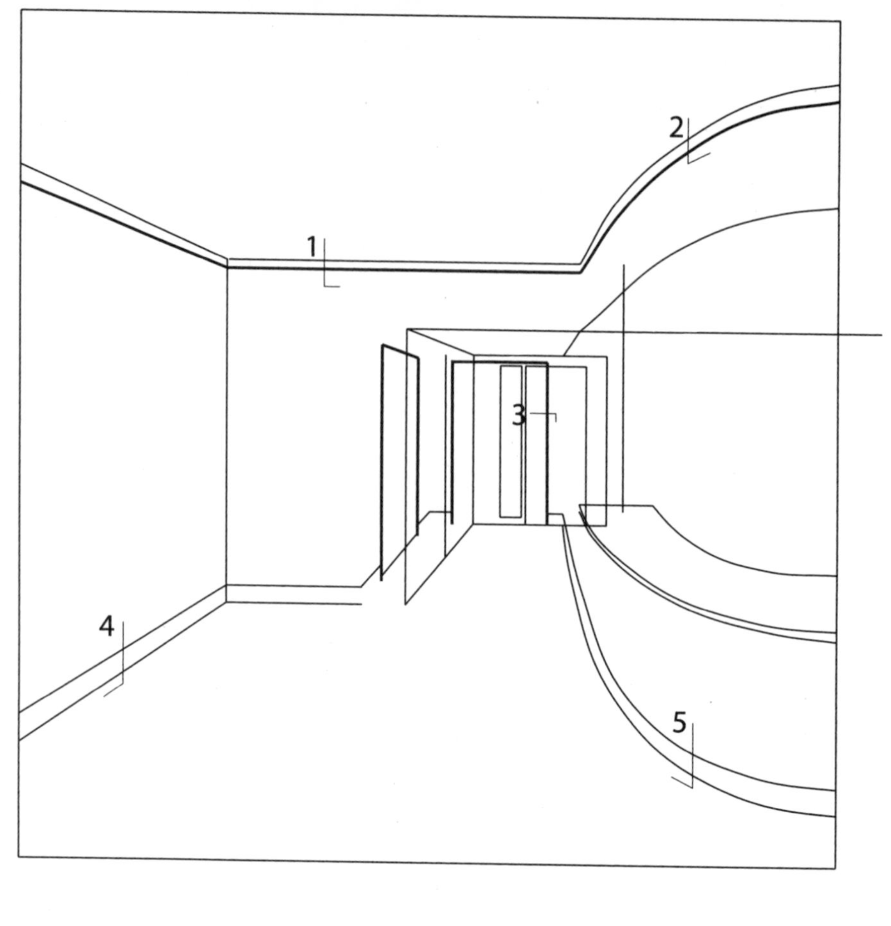

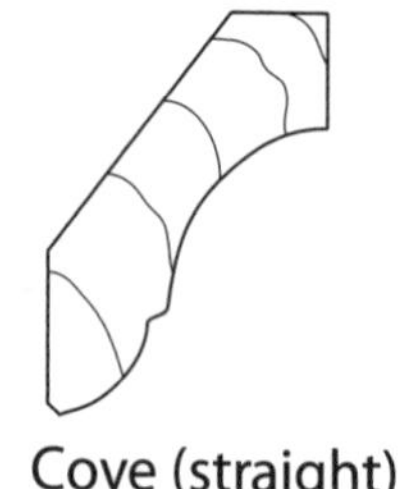

1 Cove (straight)

Loose

Large Radius field bend;
Small Radius machined
to approximate curve

2 Cove (radius)

H.M Frame

3 Back band

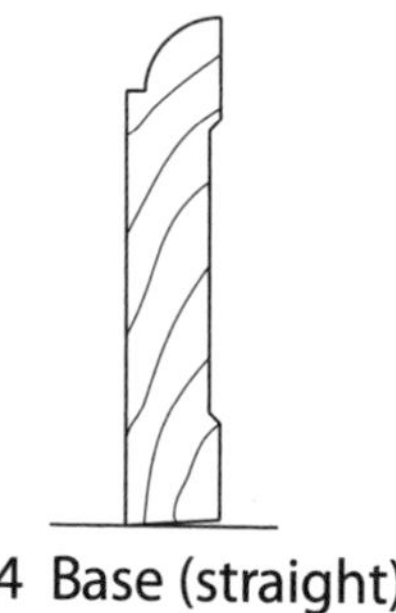

4 Base (straight)

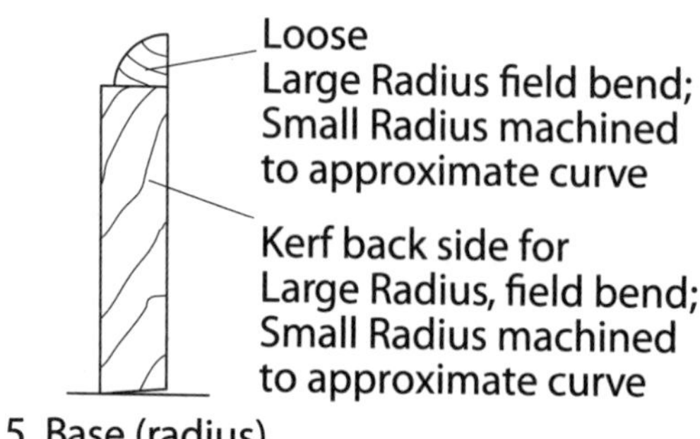

5 Base (radius)

6 - Interior and Exterior Millwork

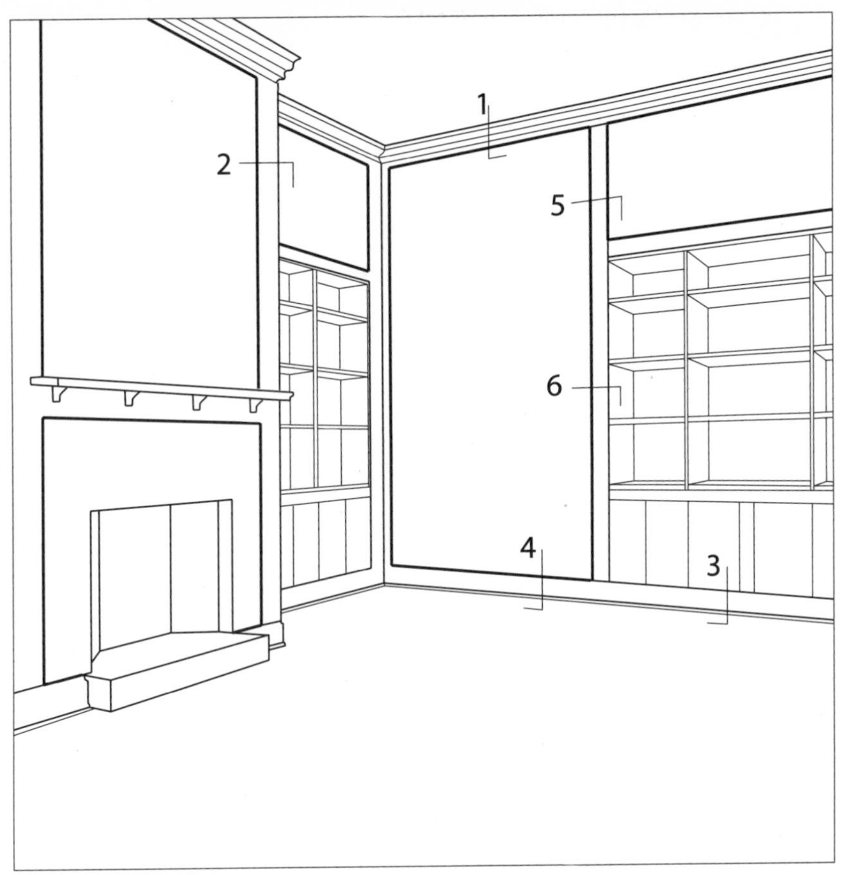

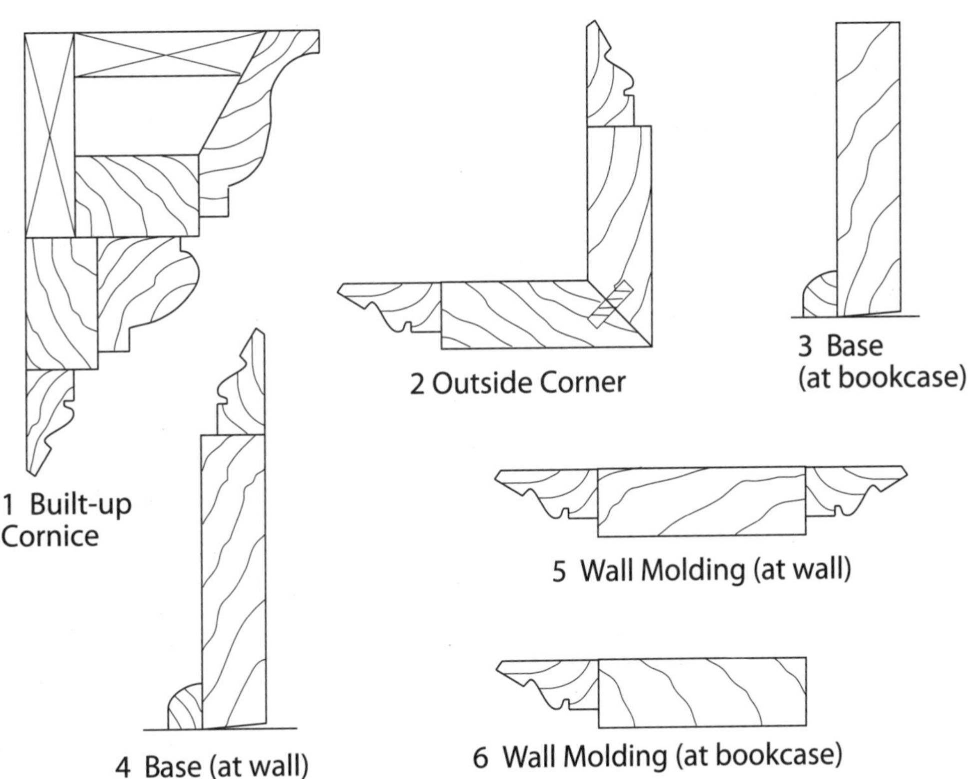

6 - Interior and Exterior Millwork

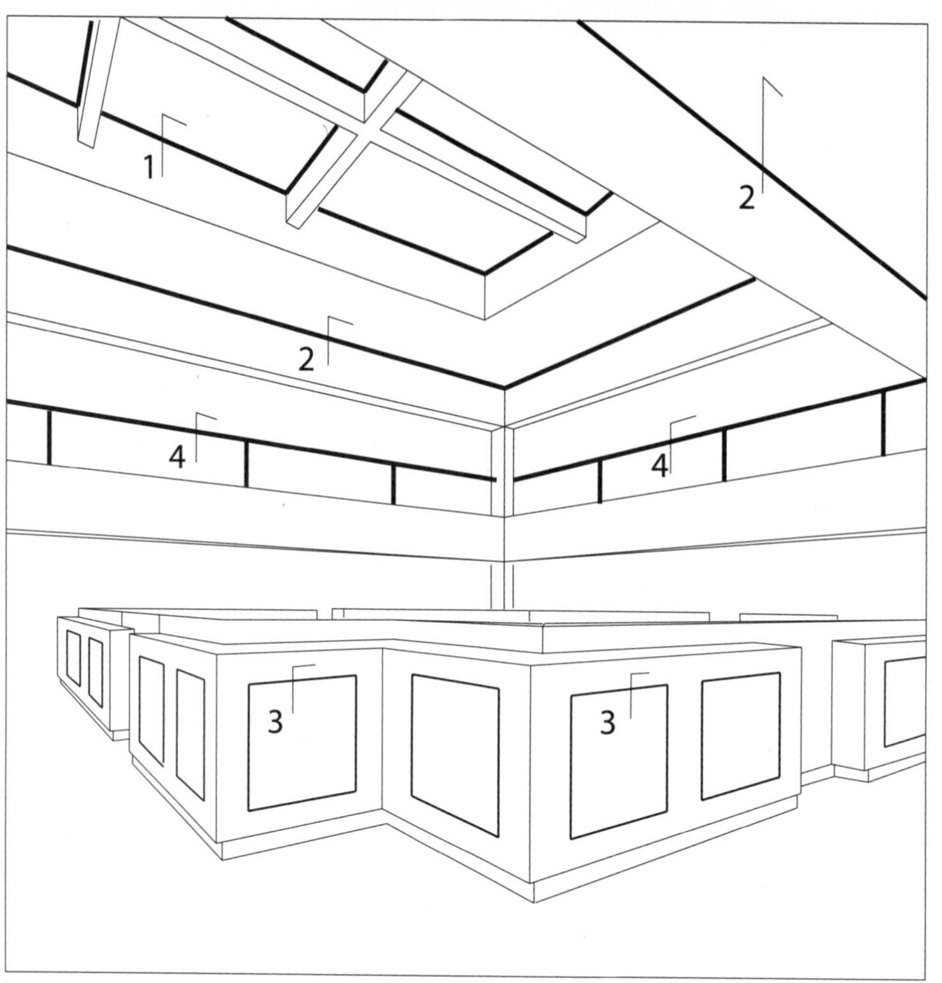

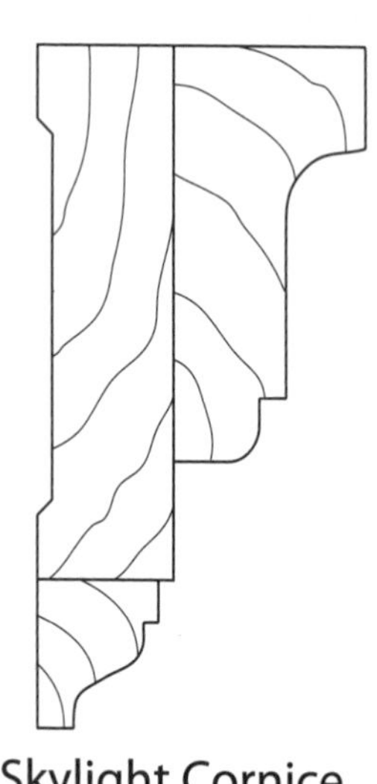

1 Skylight Cornice

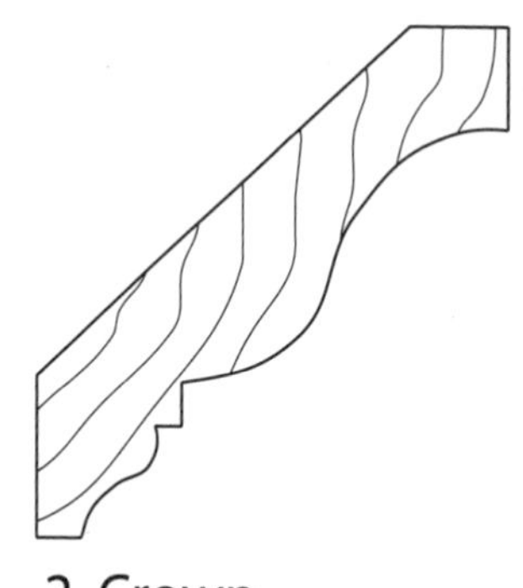

2 Crown

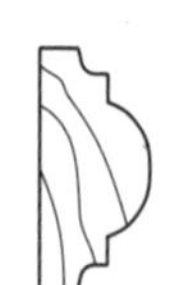

3 Panel Molding

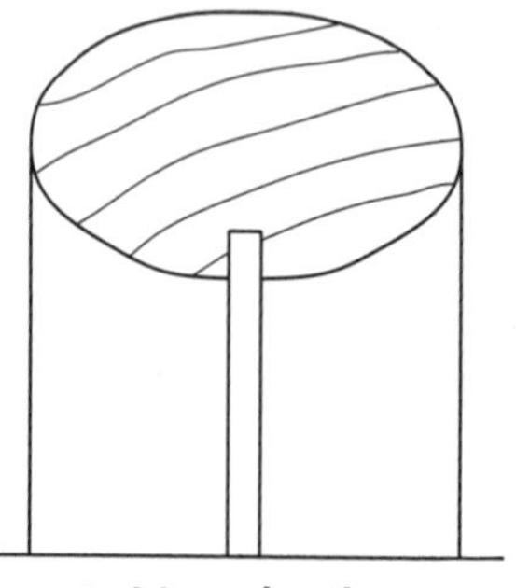

4 Handrail

6 - Interior and Exterior Millwork

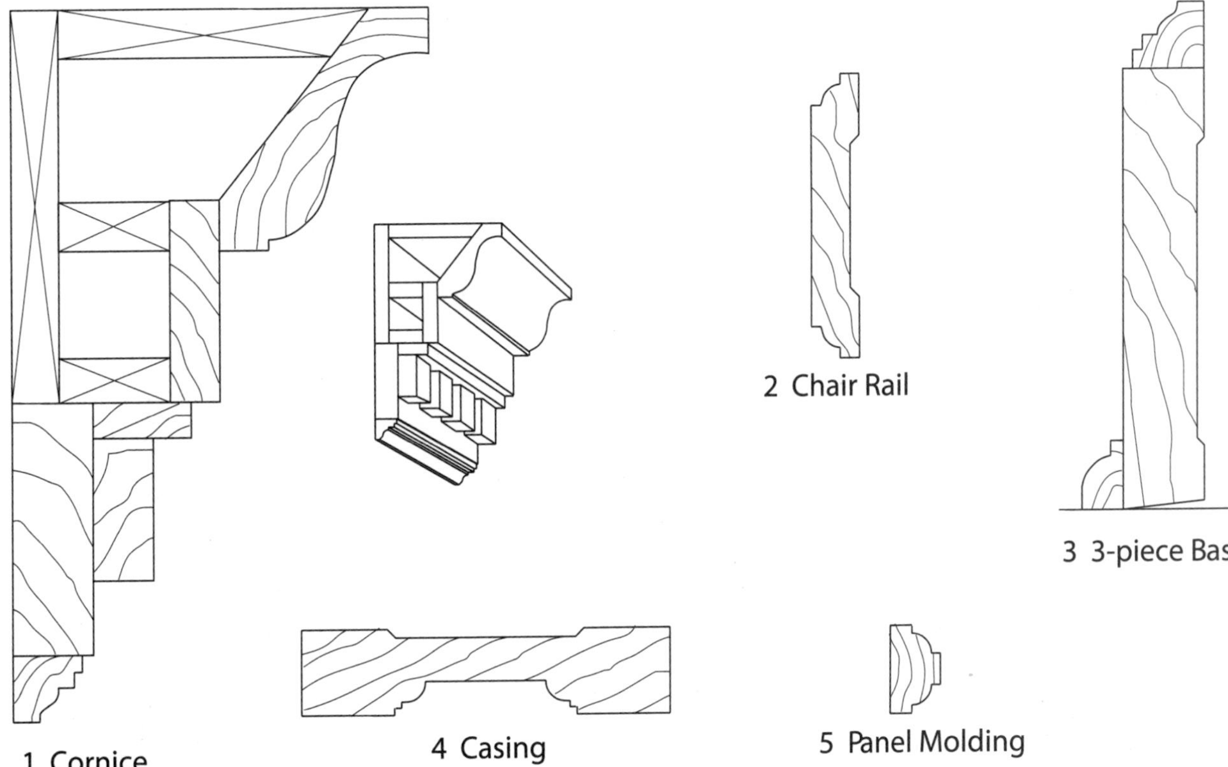

6 - Interior and Exterior Millwork

"BUILT-UP" MOLDINGS FOR LARGER PROFILES

(Used with permission of the Wood Molding and Millwork Producers Association.)

Ceilings

The most obvious area for "built-up" moldings is where the walls meet the ceiling. This is primarily true of rooms with high ceilings. In low-ceiling rooms (8' (2438 mm)), single molding profiles usually work best. A series of "built-up" moldings would have a tendency to make a low ceiling appear even lower. But if your ceilings are high (10' (2540 mm) or higher), there is no limit to the rich three-dimensional elegance you can add to the room's appearance with the creative application of moldings. Below are several suggested combinations. Let your imagination create your own combinations and designs.

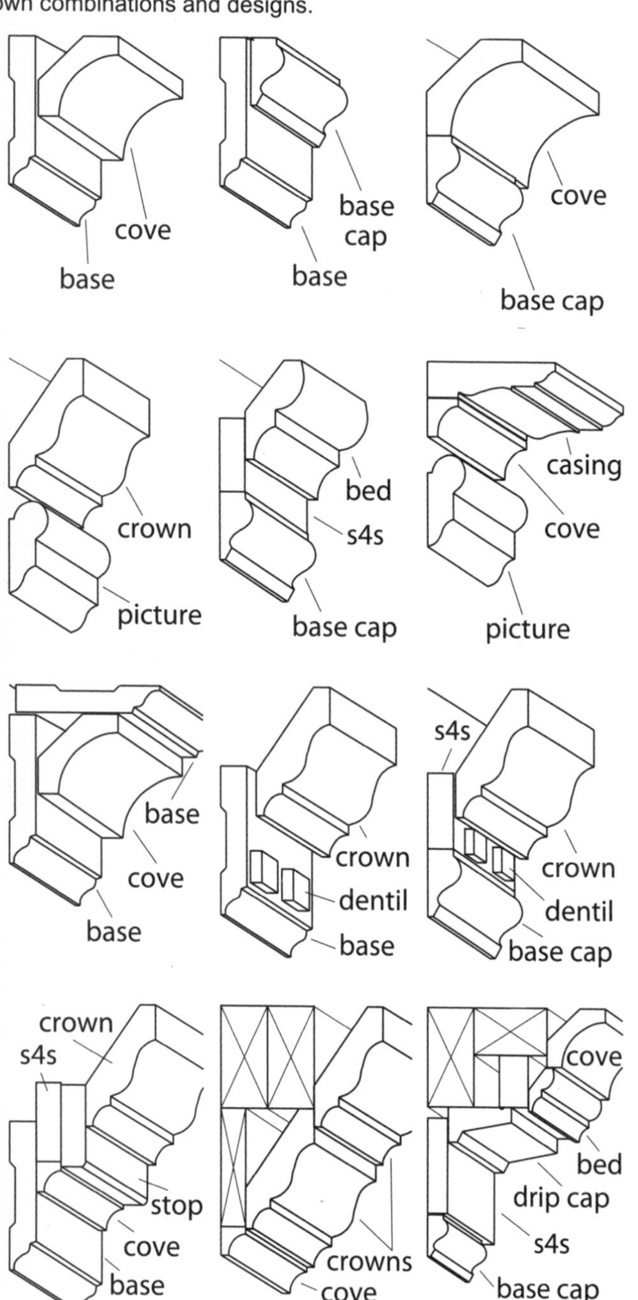

Chair Rails

Adding chair rails to a room is a very traditional method of breaking up walls, adding both interest and protection. They prevent the wall from being bumped or scuffed by chairs and can also be used to separate two types of decorating material such as paneling, wallpaper, and paint. Following are some variations of "built-up" chair rail combinations.

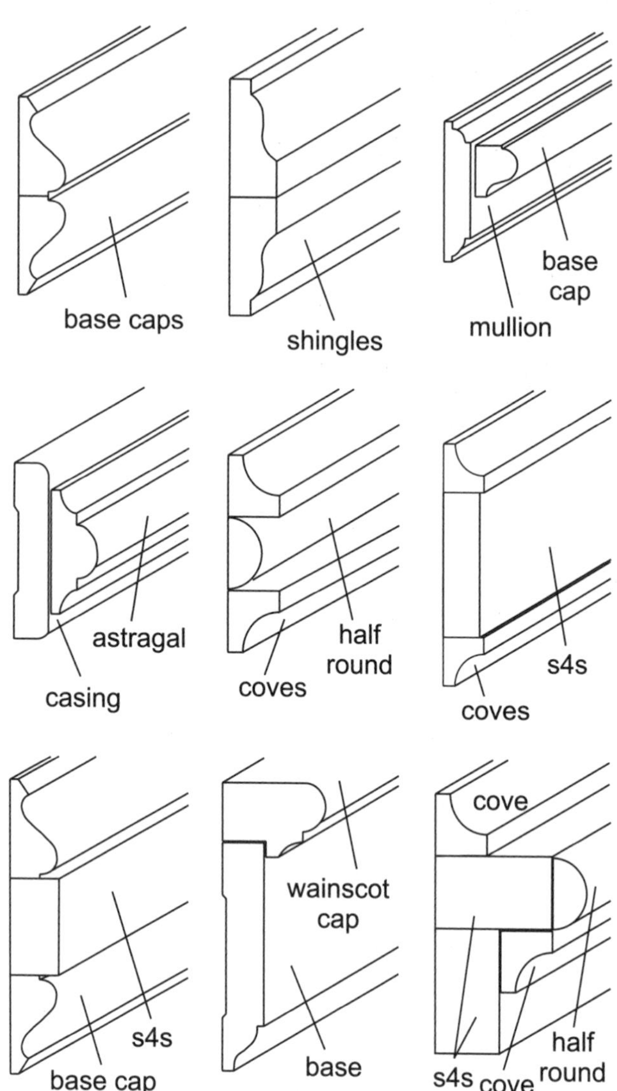

6 - Interior and Exterior Millwork

Fireplaces

The use of "built-up" moldings is also an excellent way to highlight or frame a fireplace or add depth and richness to the fireplace mantel. Below are a few creative but simple-to-install profile combinations.

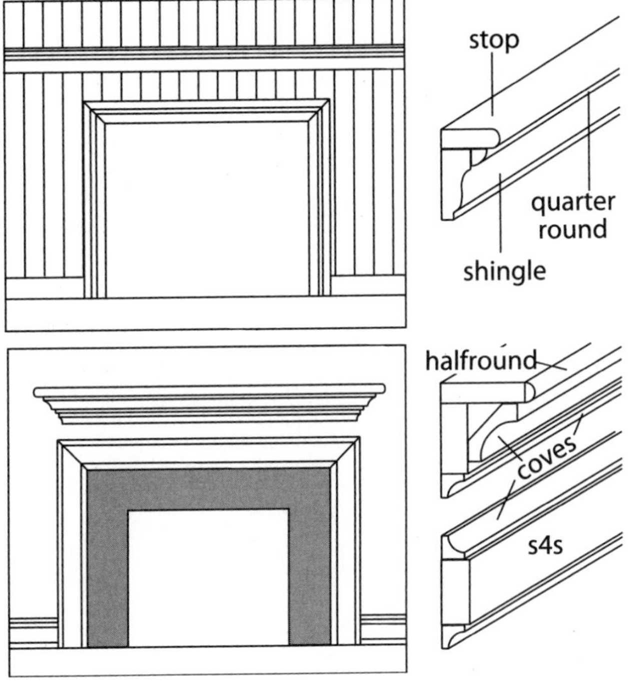

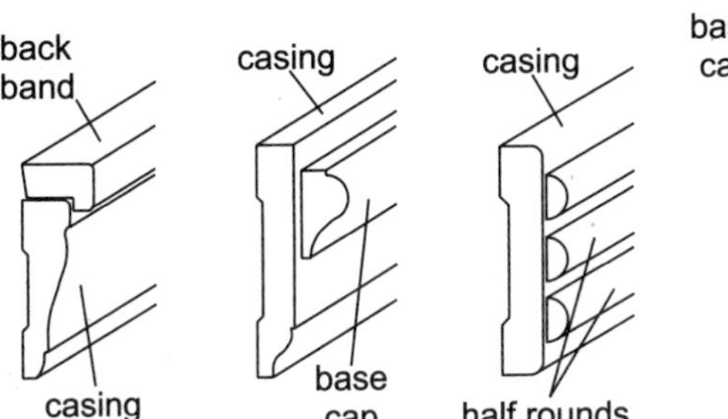

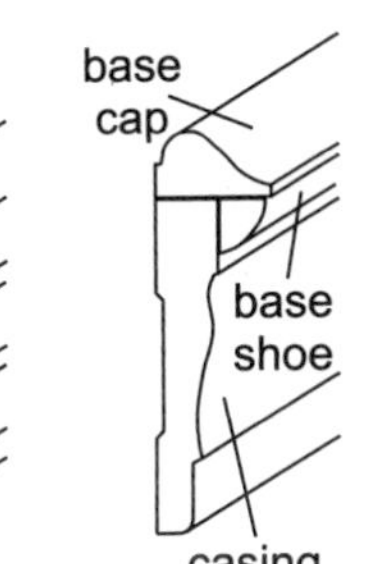

Doors and Windows

The framing of doors and windows is most commonly done with single molding profiles, but by adding other patterns, the basic trim can easily be transformed into a window or door casing of classical depth and beauty. Installing plinth blocks at the bottom of casing further enhances the traditional look.

Base

The elaborate look of elegance can even be carried through to base moldings where the wall meets the floor, as illustrated in the following variations.

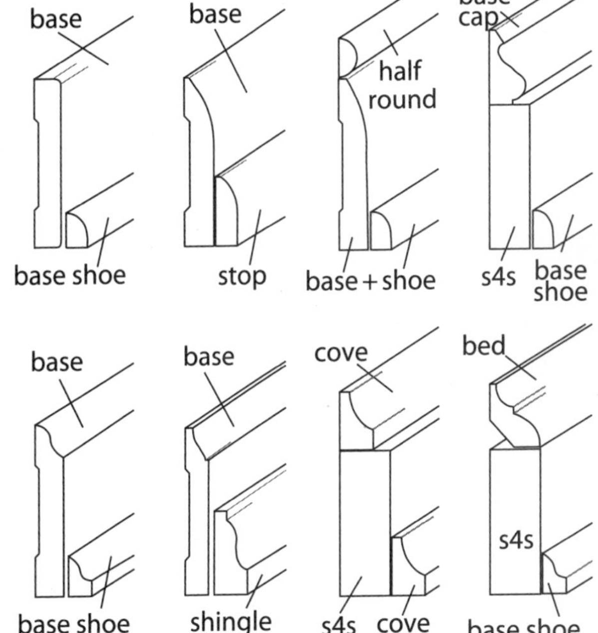

6 - Interior and Exterior Millwork

COMBINATION CORNICES AND WALL TRIMS

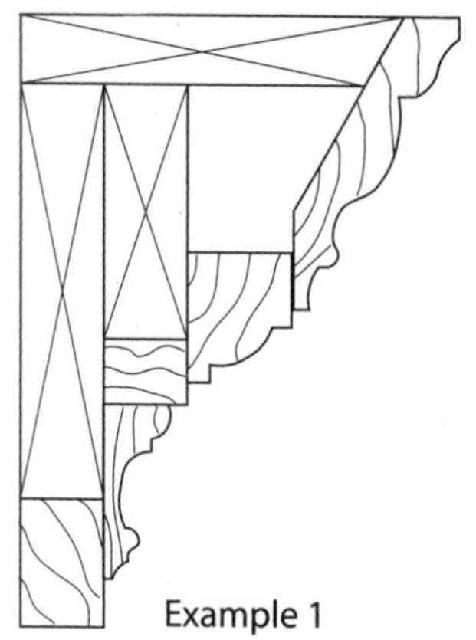
Example 1

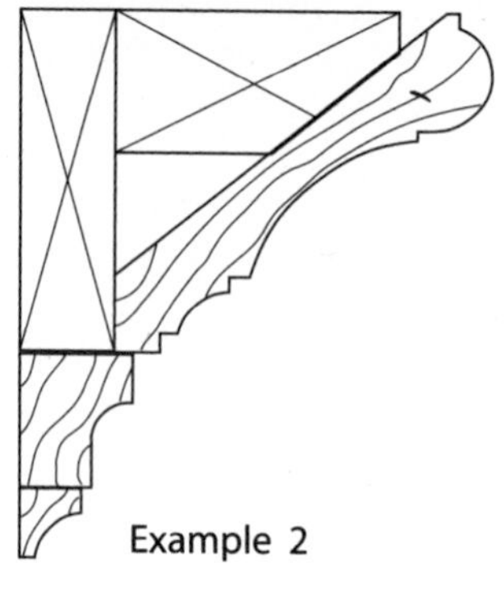
Example 2

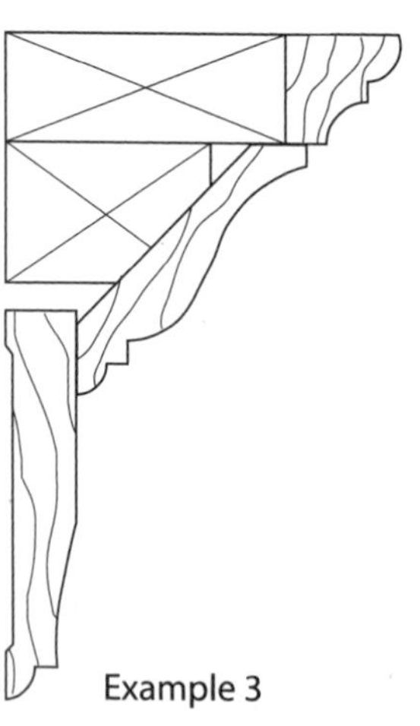
Example 3

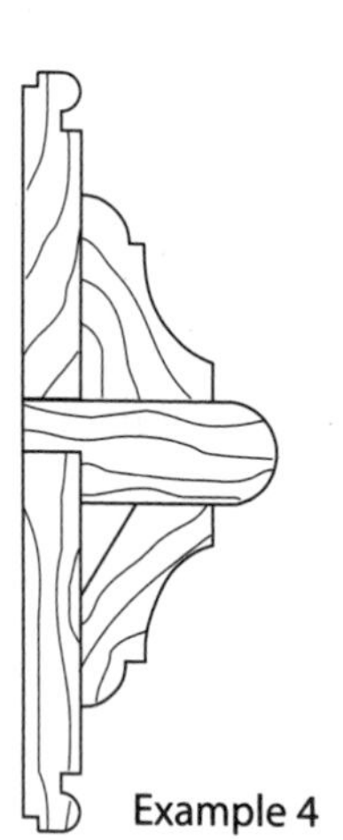
Example 4

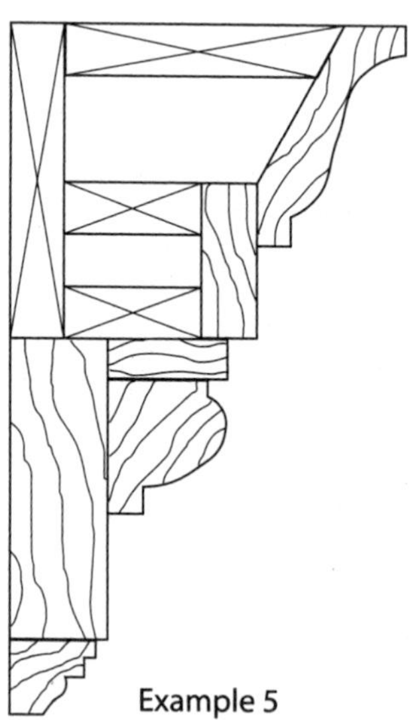
Example 5

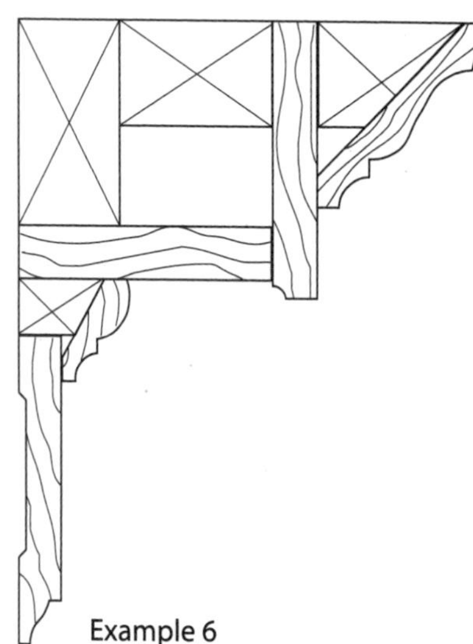
Example 6

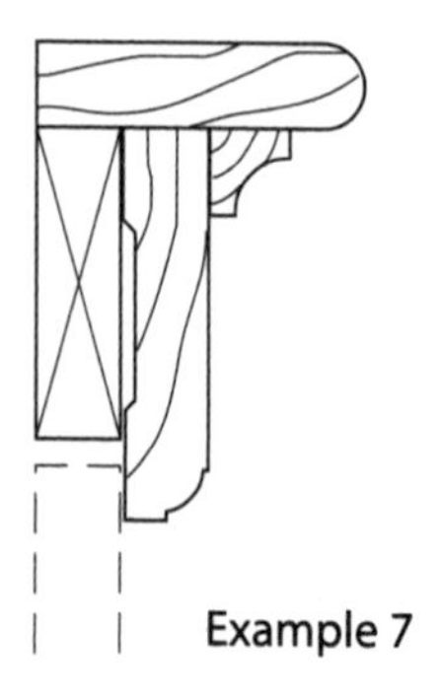
Example 7

6 - Interior and Exterior Millwork

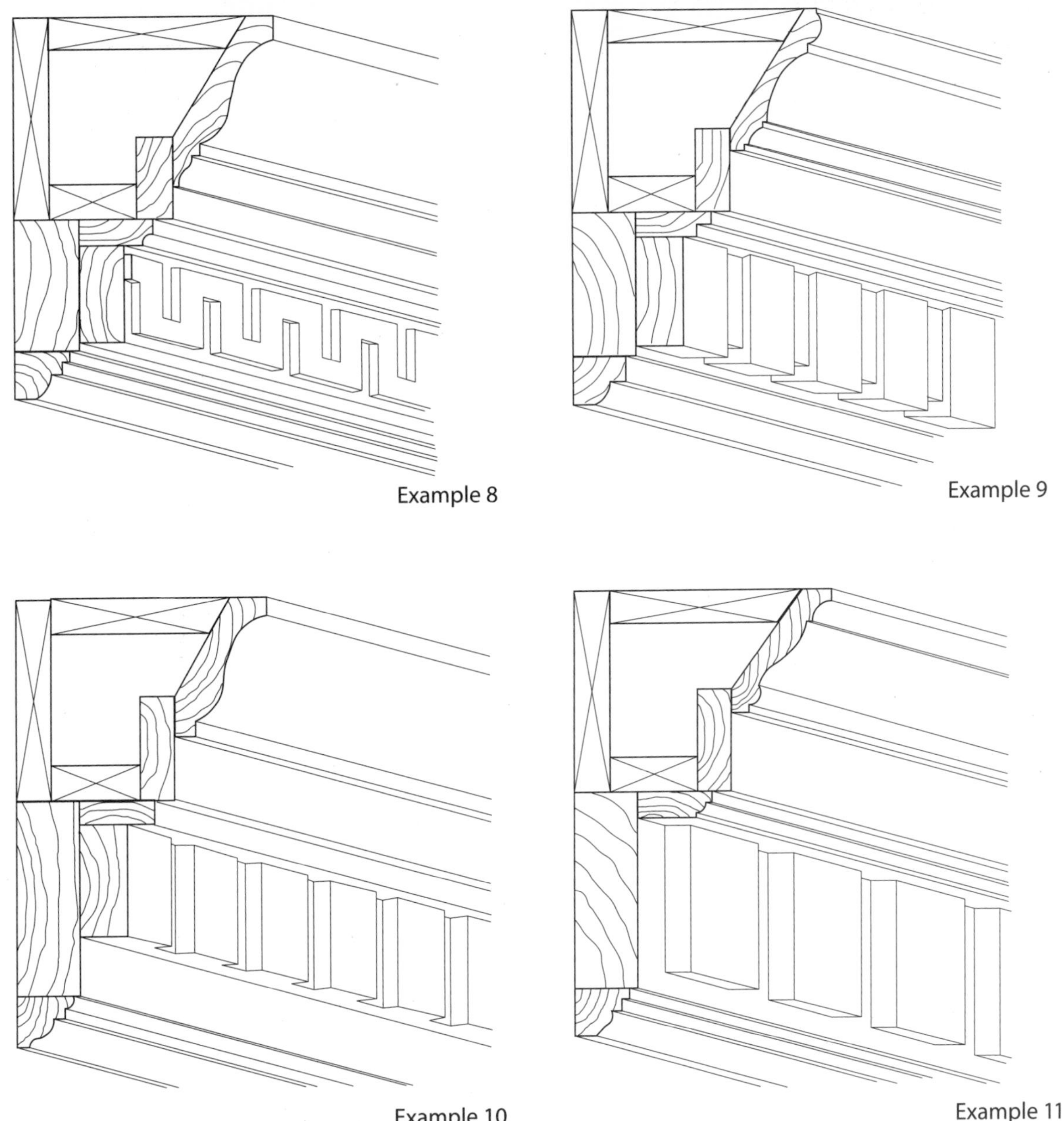

IMPORTANT NOTE: The following drawings are illustrations, not measured or engineered. They are offered for general profile shape only. Some manufacturers may vary the profile or sizes. They are not dimensioned intentionally, allowing the design professional to determine the scale and proportions most appropriate for the project.

6 - Interior and Exterior Millwork

Base Caps and Bases

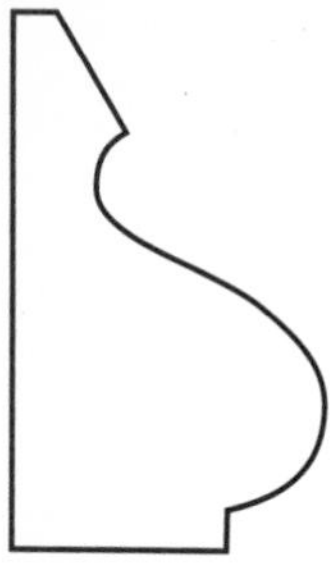
BAS-1000

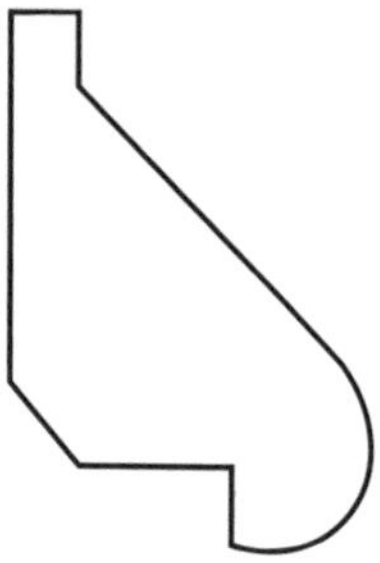
BAS-1001

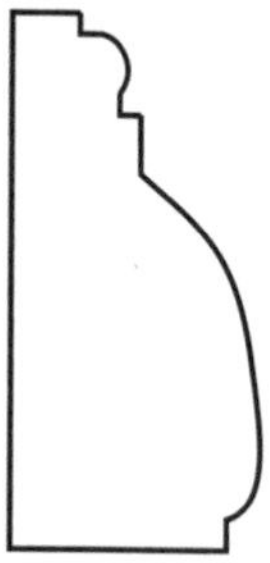
BAS-1002

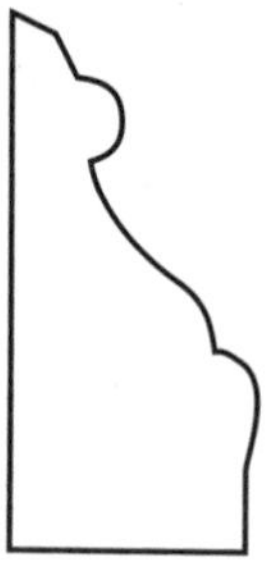
BAS-1003

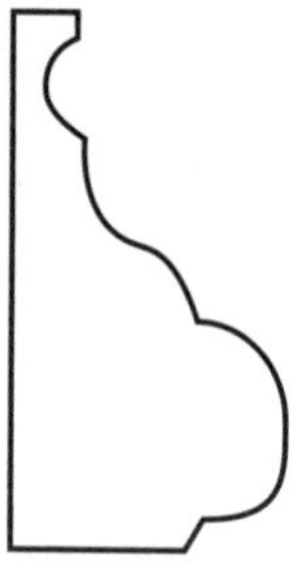
BAS-1004

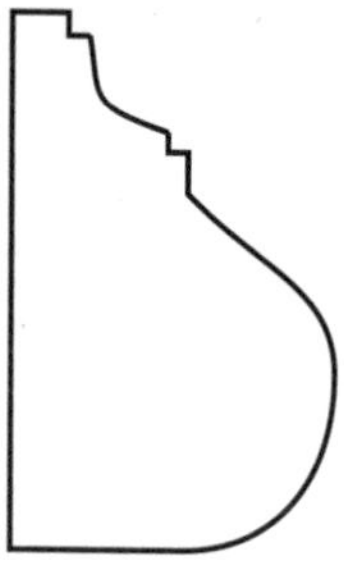
BAS-1005

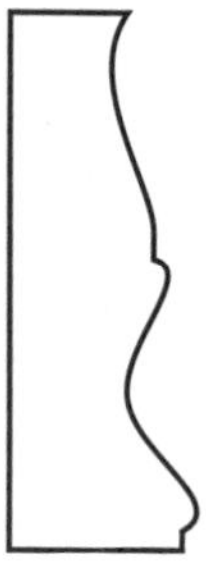
BAS-1006

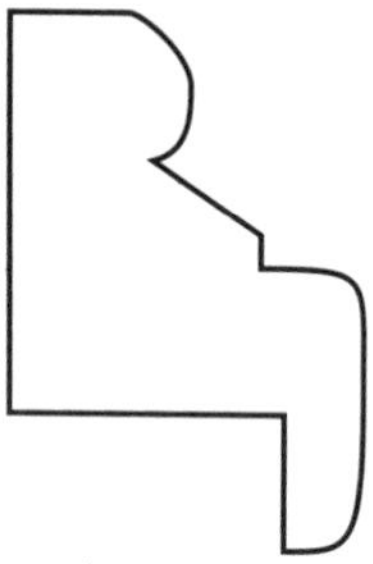
BAS-1007

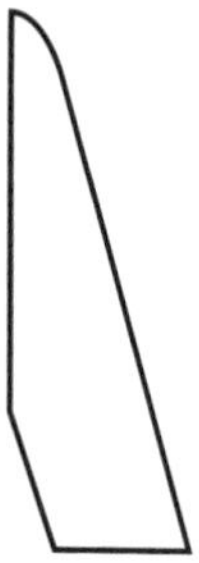
BAS-1008

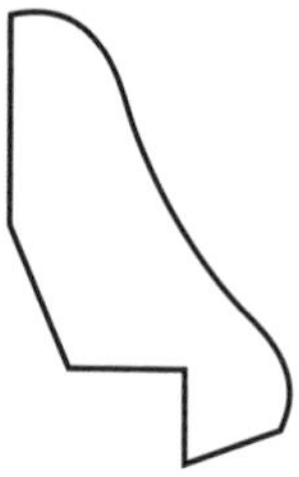
BAS-1009

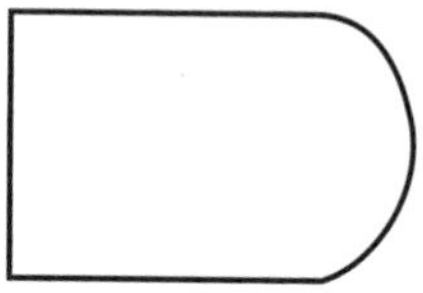
BAS-1010

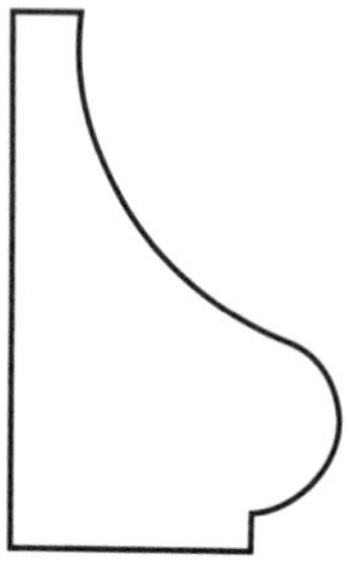
BAS-1011

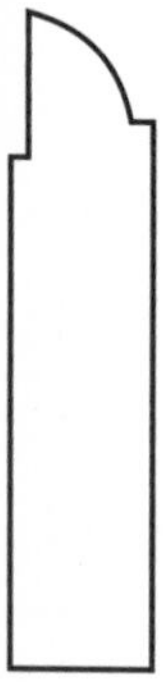
BAS-1012

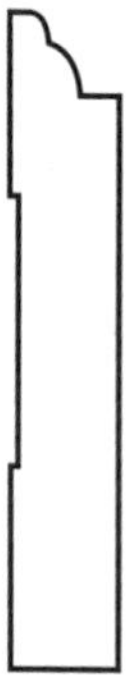
BAS-1013

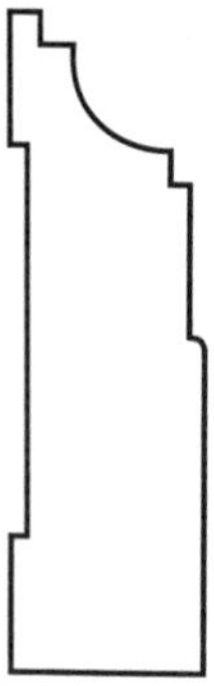
BAS-1014

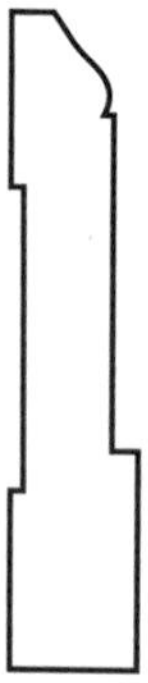
BAS-10015

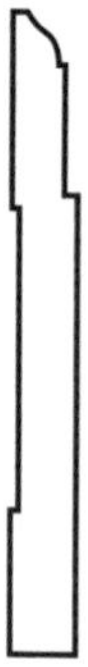
BAS-1016

BAS-1017

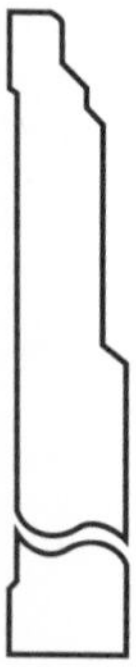
BAS-1018

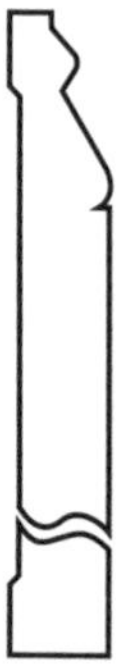
BAS-1019

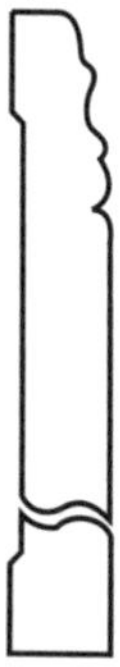
BAS-1020

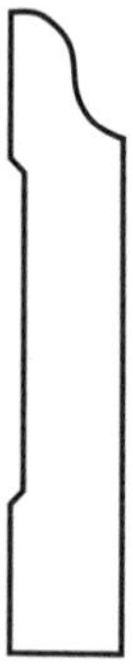
BAS-1021

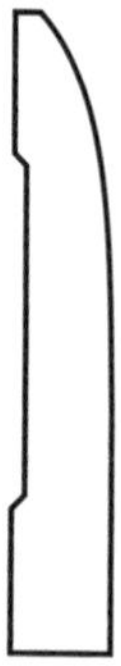
BAS-1022

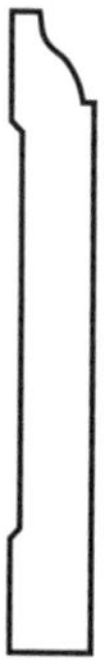
BAS-1023

(Appendix B is not part of the AWS for compliance purposes)

6 - Interior and Exterior Millwork

Base Caps and Bases

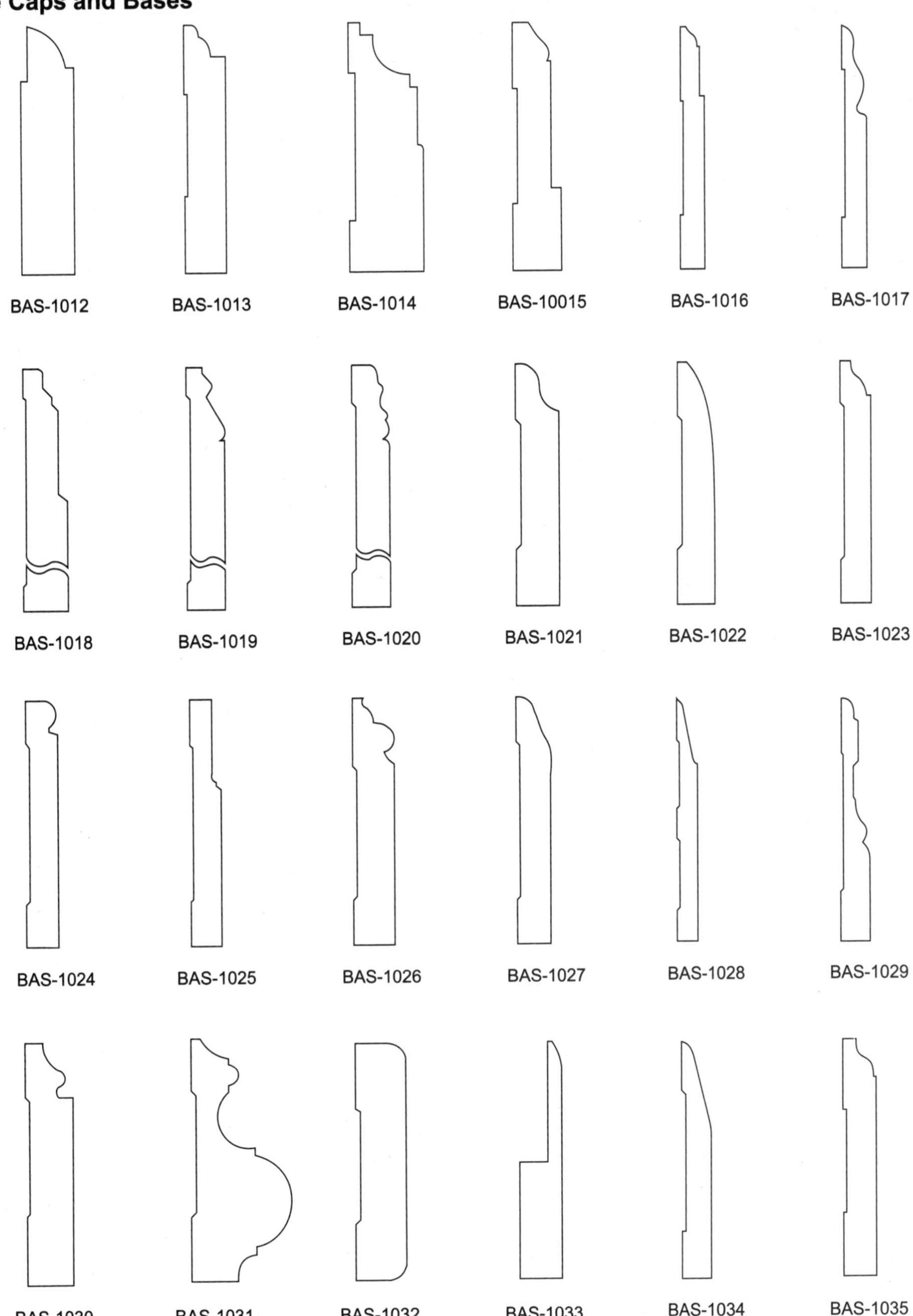

6 - Interior and Exterior Millwork

Base Caps and Bases

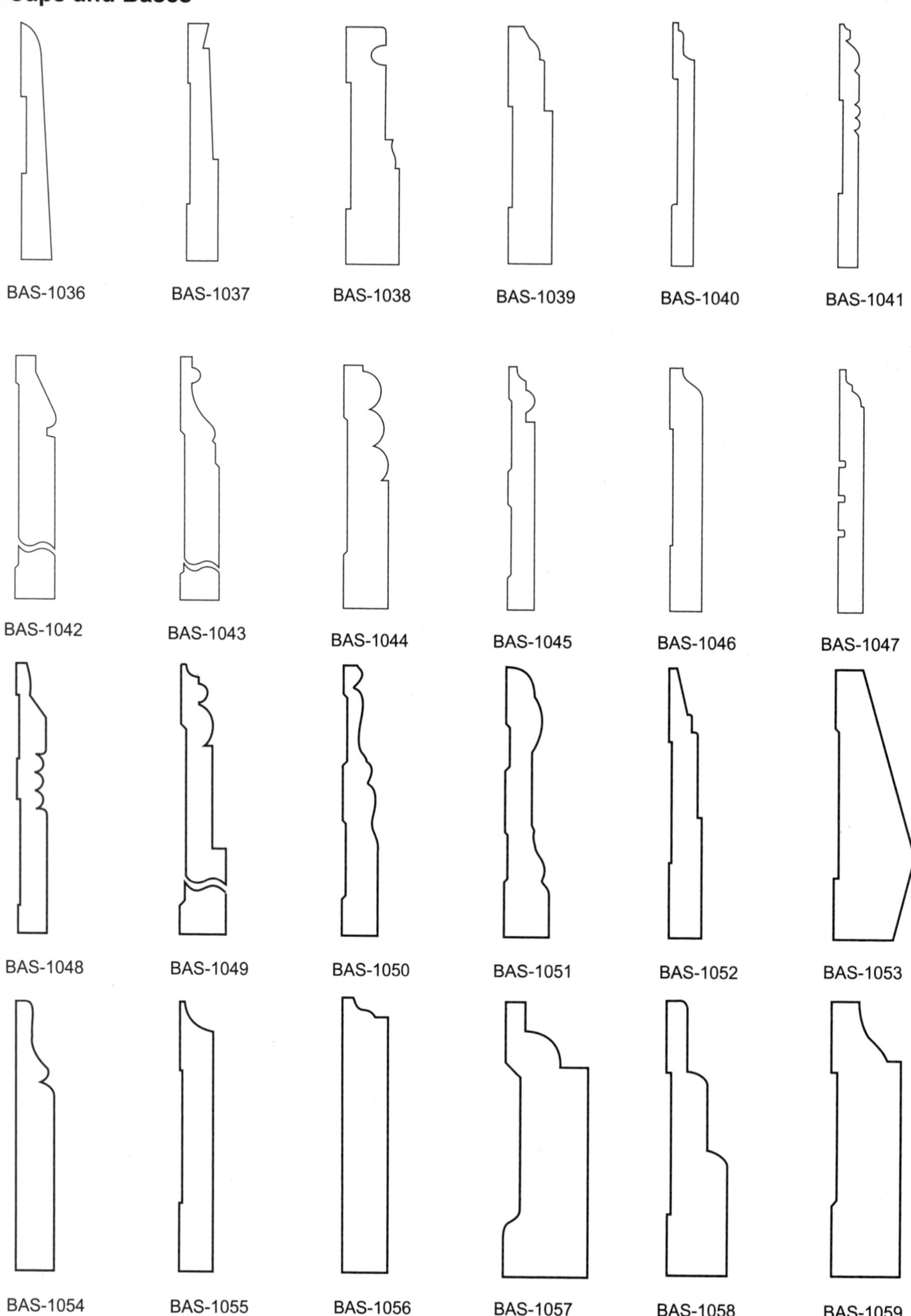

6 - Interior and Exterior Millwork

Base Caps and Bases

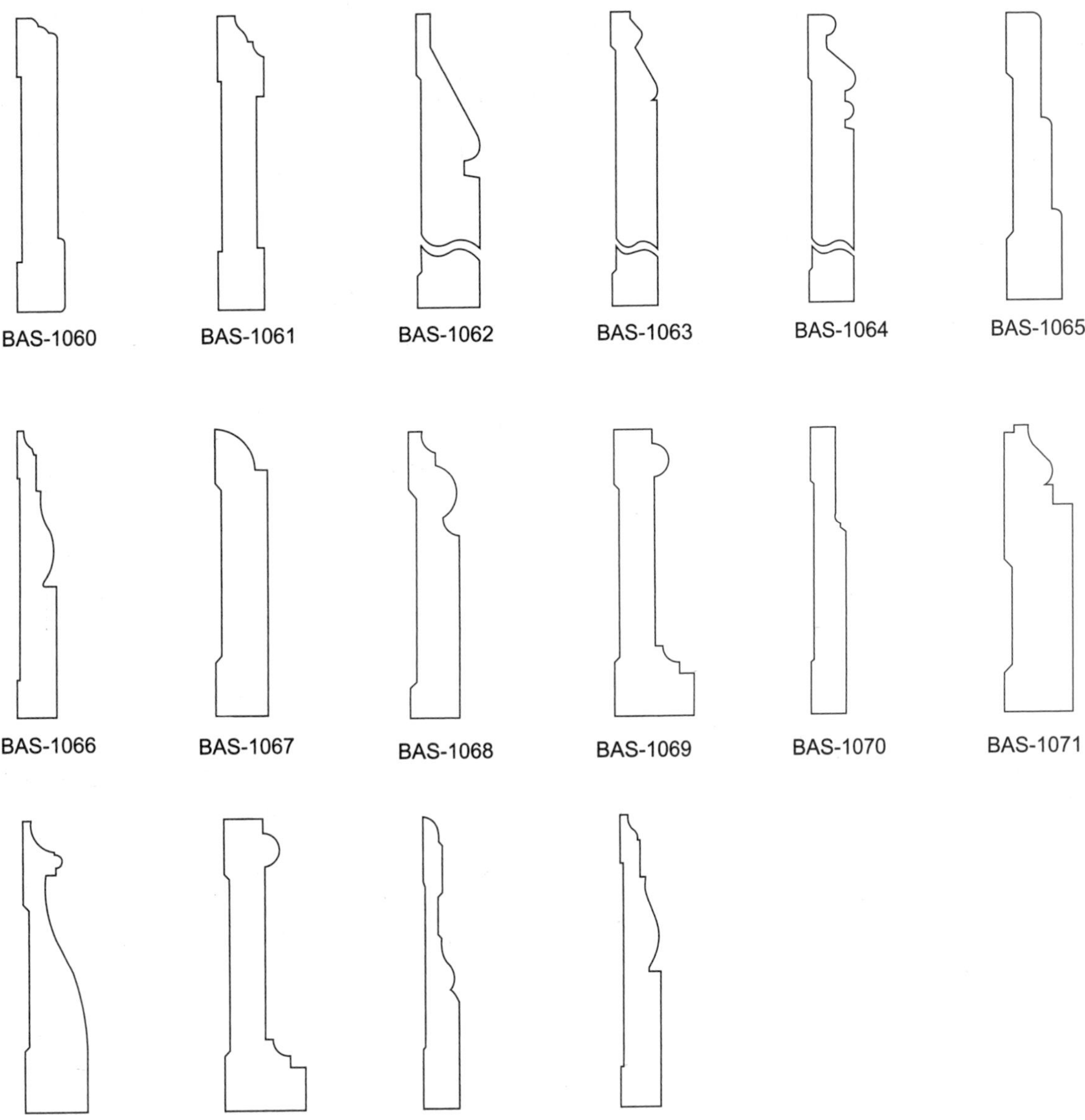

6 - Interior and Exterior Millwork

Casings

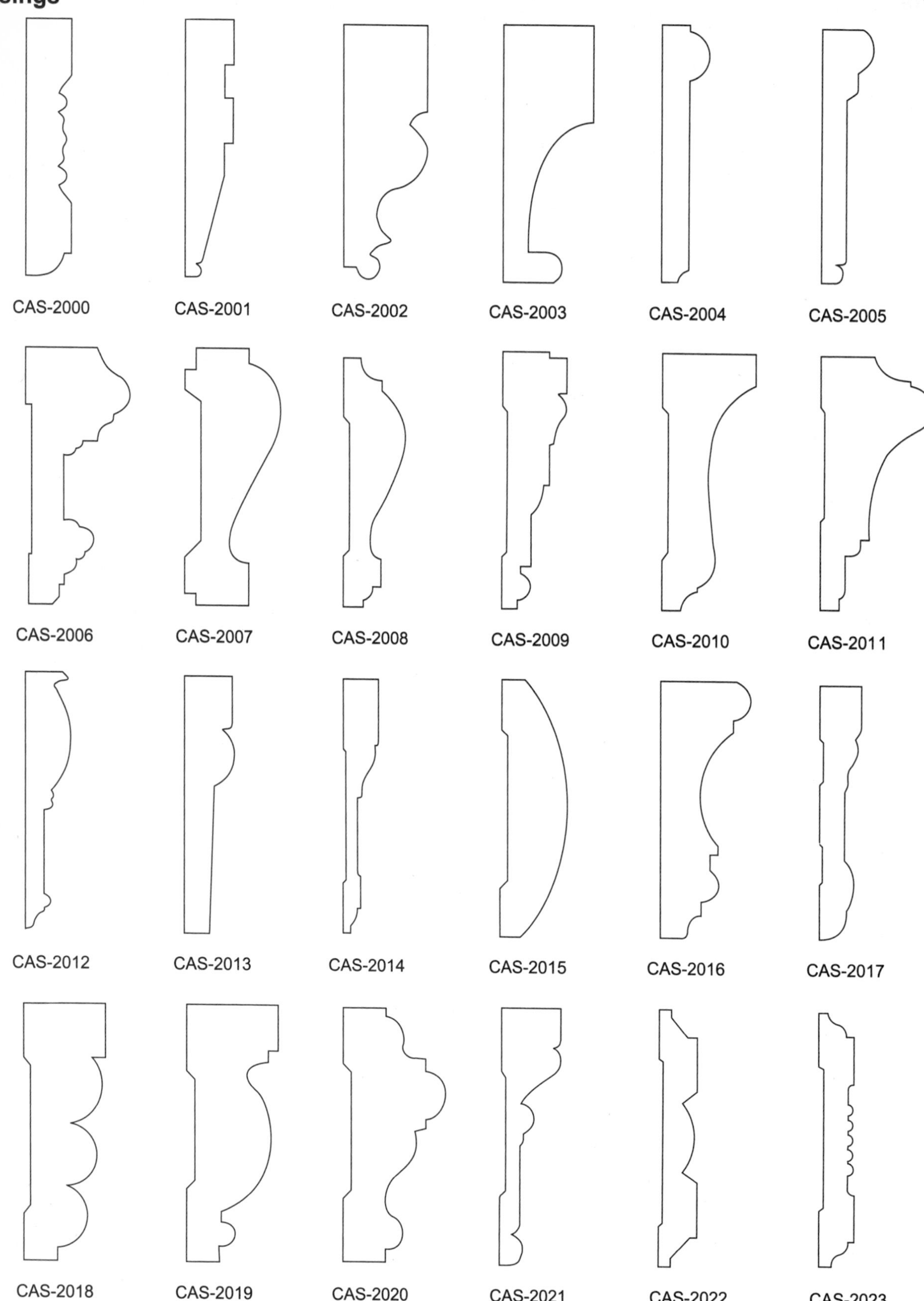

6 - Interior and Exterior Millwork

Casings

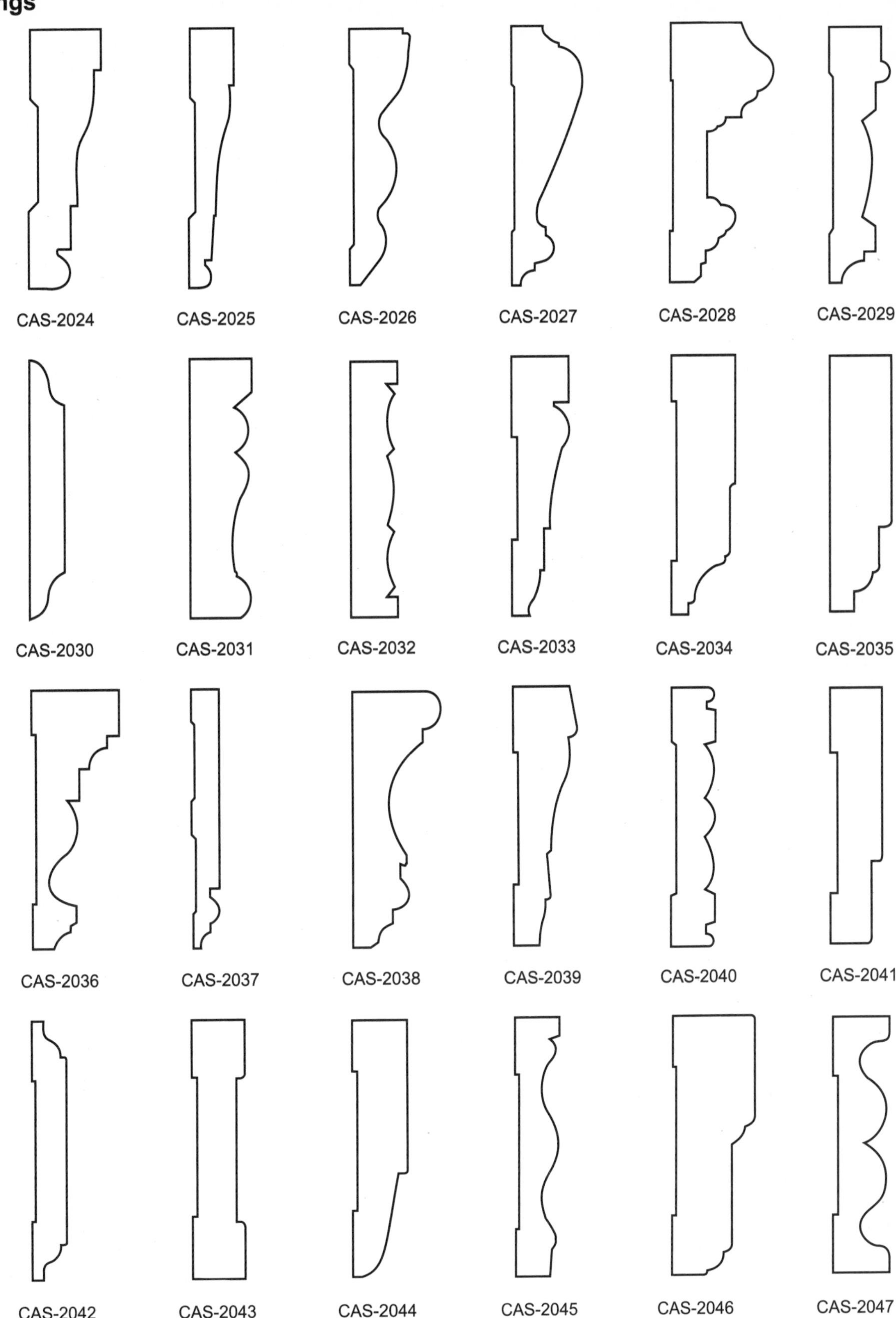

6 - Interior and Exterior Millwork

Casings

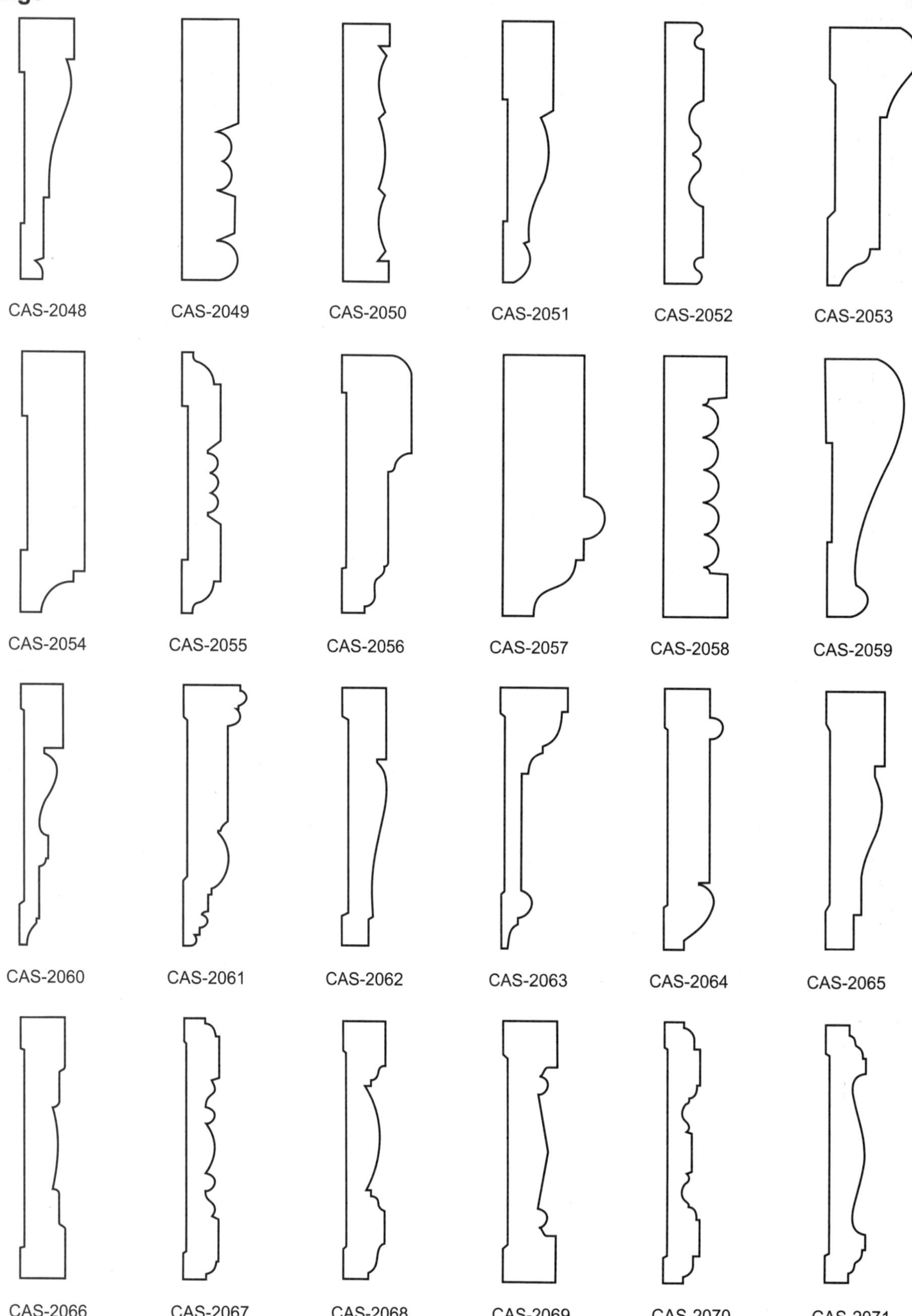

6 - Interior and Exterior Millwork

Casings

CAS-2072  CAS-2073  CAS-2074 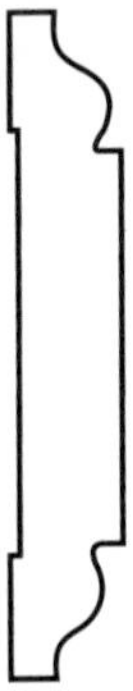 CAS-2075  CAS-2076  CAS-2077

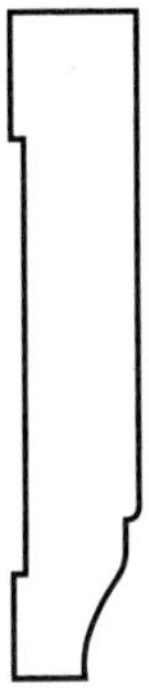

CAS-2078  CAS-2079 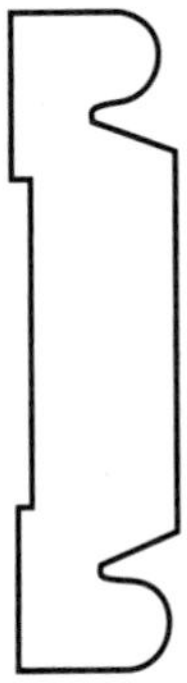 CAS-2080  CAS-2081  CAS-2082  CAS-2083

CAS-2084  CAS-2085  CAS-2086 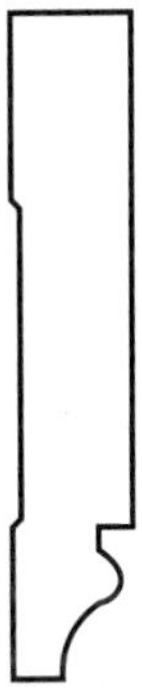 CAS-2087  CAS-2088  CAS-2089

CAS-2090  CAS-2091  CAS-2092  CAS-2093  CAS-2094  CAS-2095

6 - Interior and Exterior Millwork

Casings

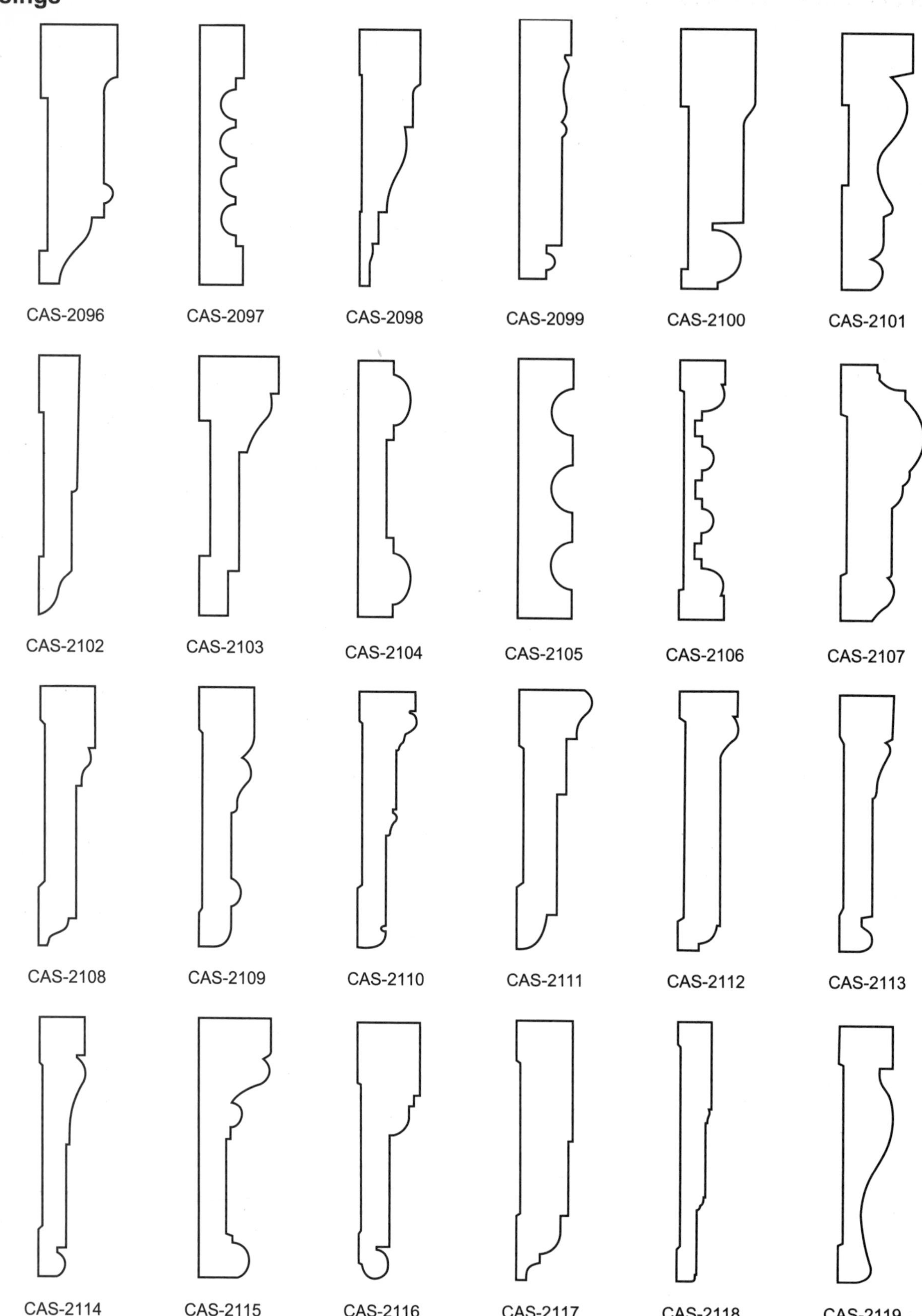

6 - Interior and Exterior Millwork

Casings and Panel Moldings

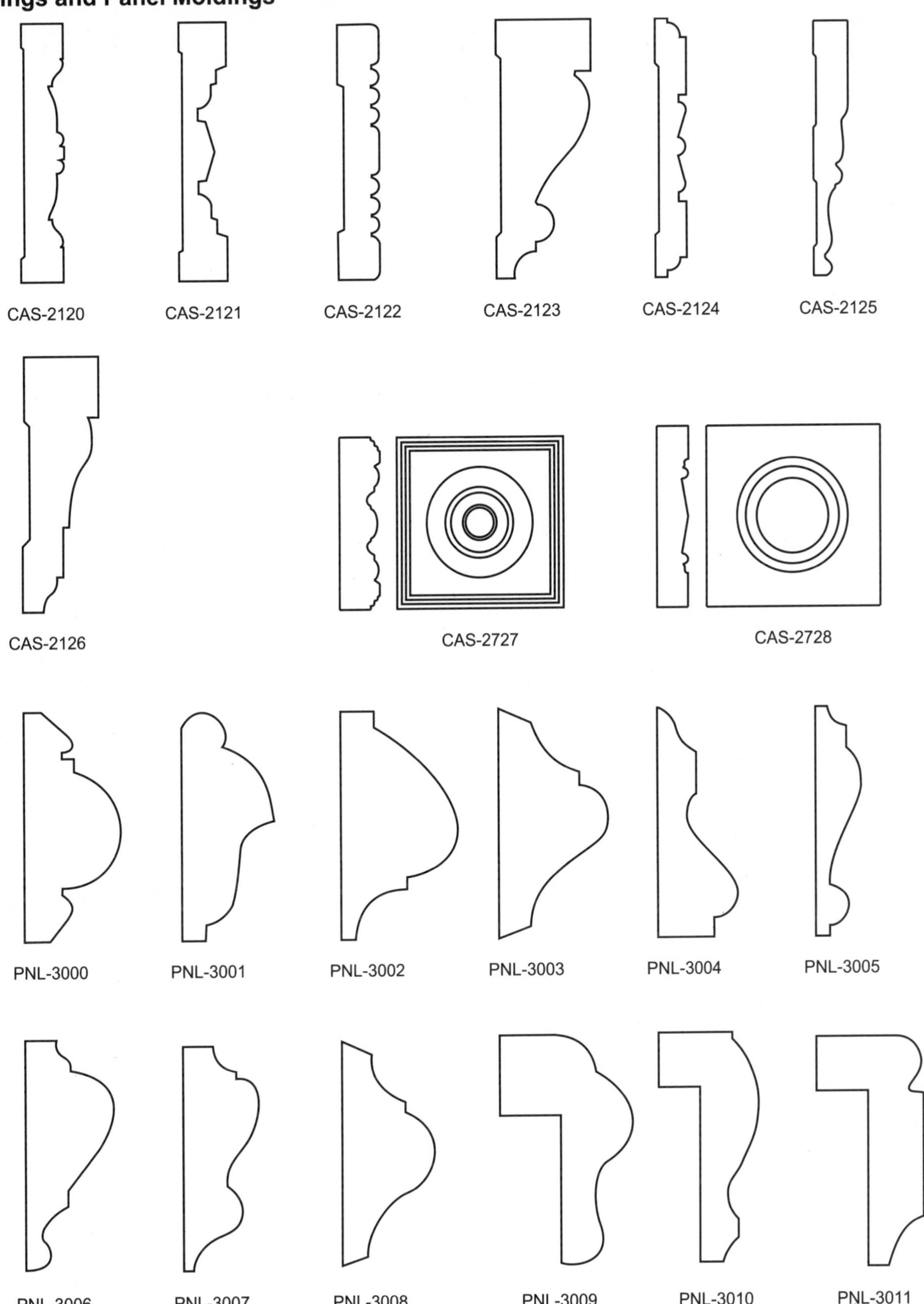

6 - Interior and Exterior Millwork

Crown Moldings

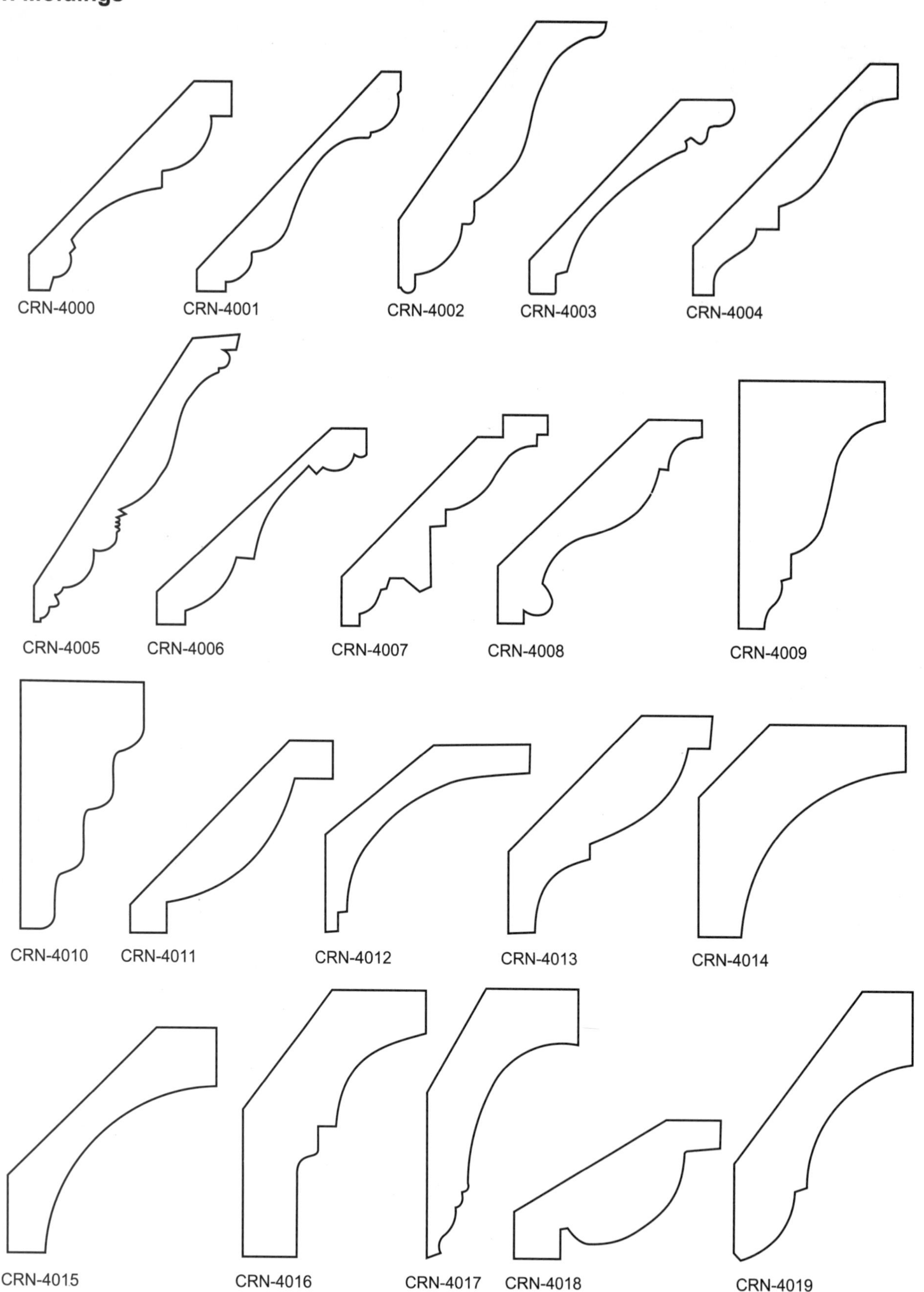

6 - Interior and Exterior Millwork

Crown Moldings

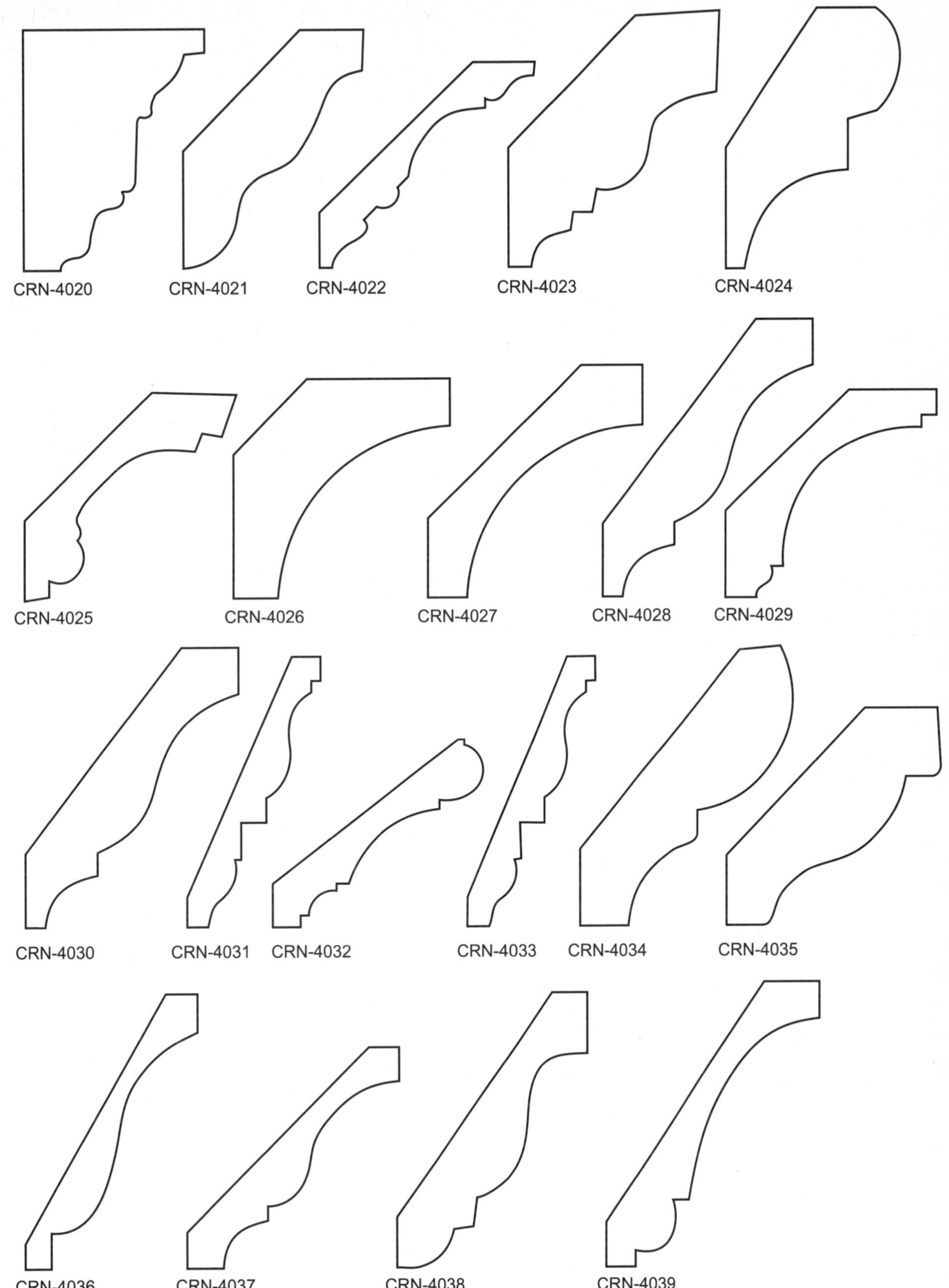

6 - Interior and Exterior Millwork

Handrails

6 - Interior and Exterior Millwork

Chair Rails

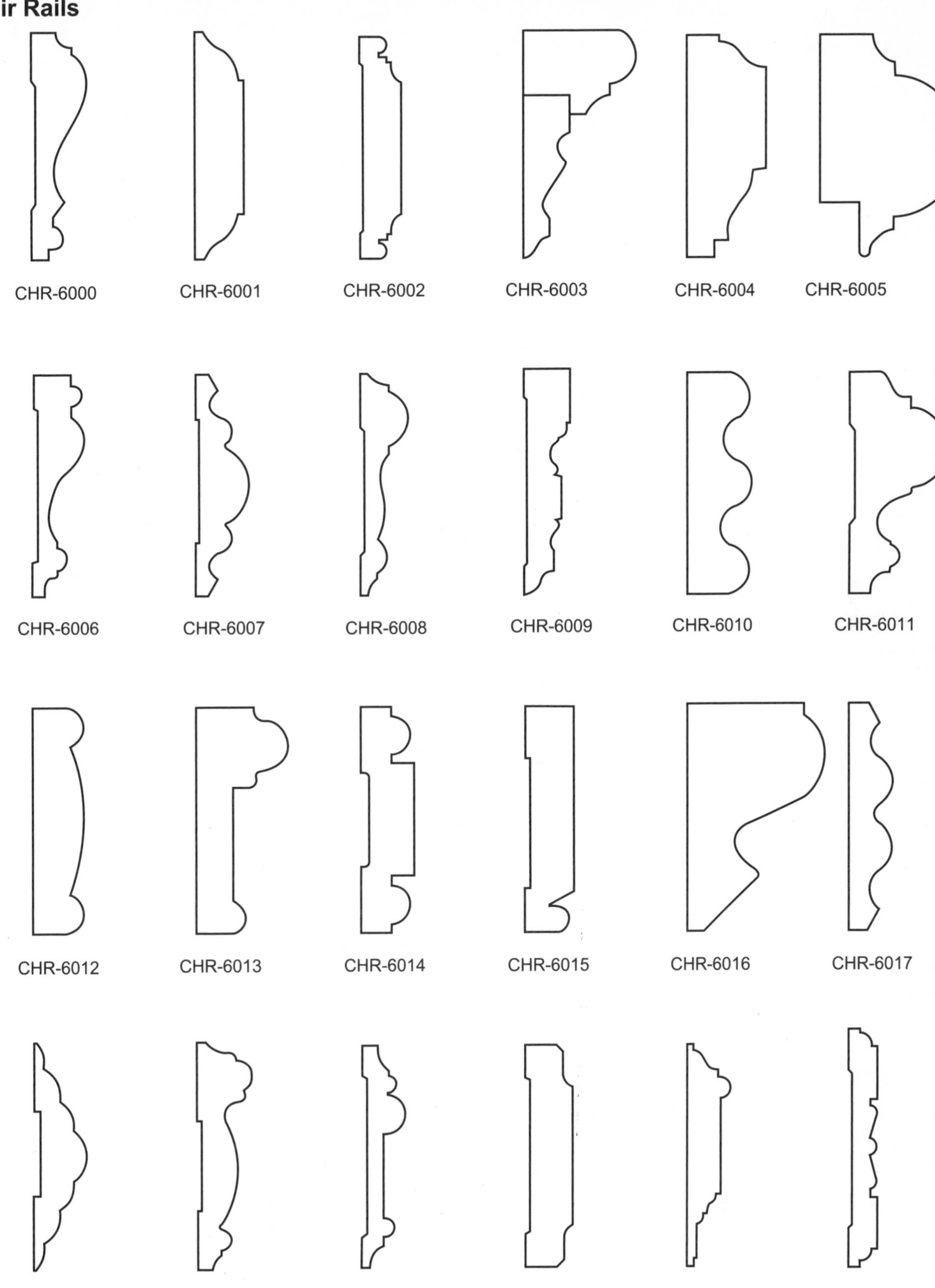

6 - Interior and Exterior Millwork

Chair Rails

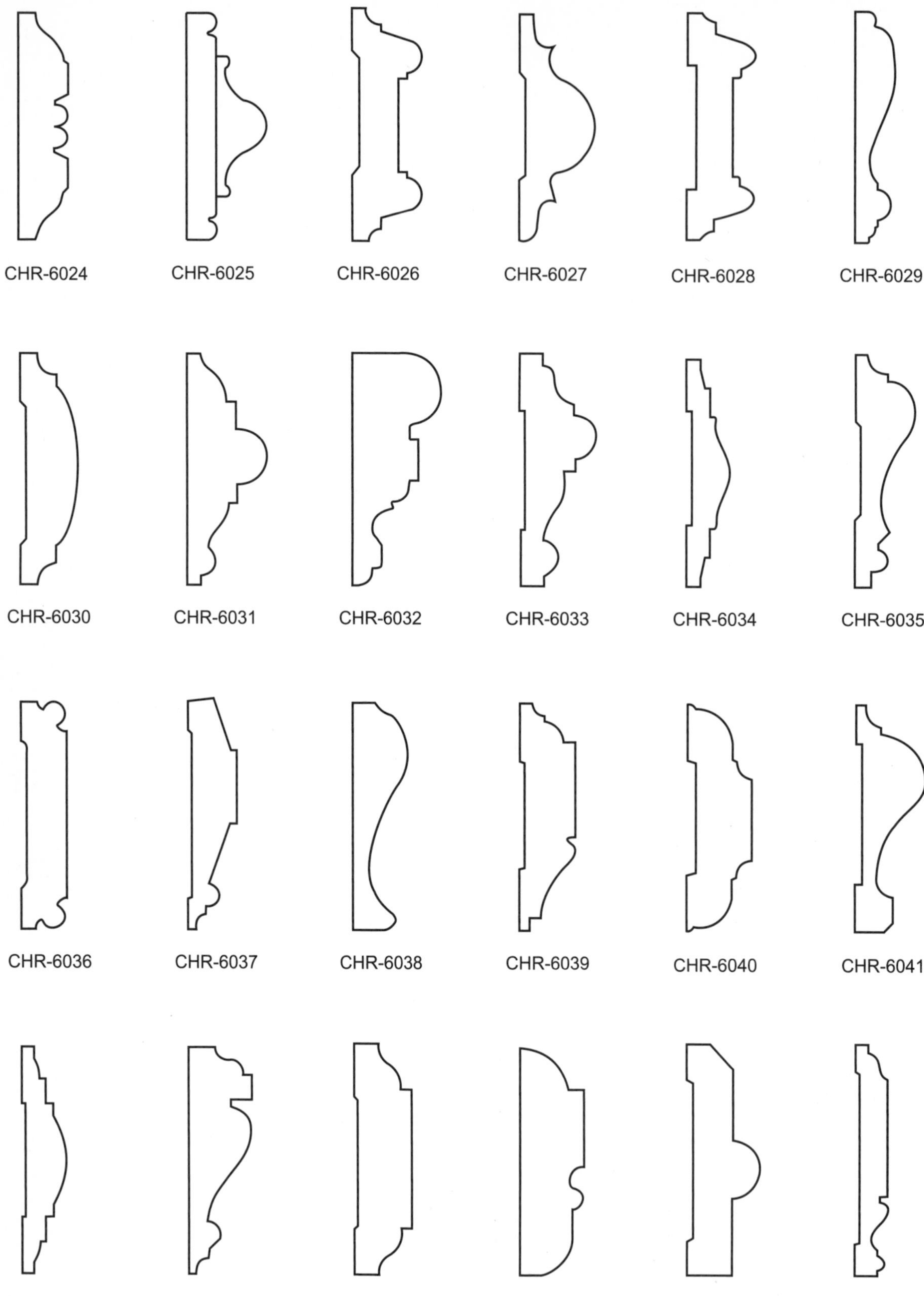

6 - Interior and Exterior Millwork

Picture Moldings

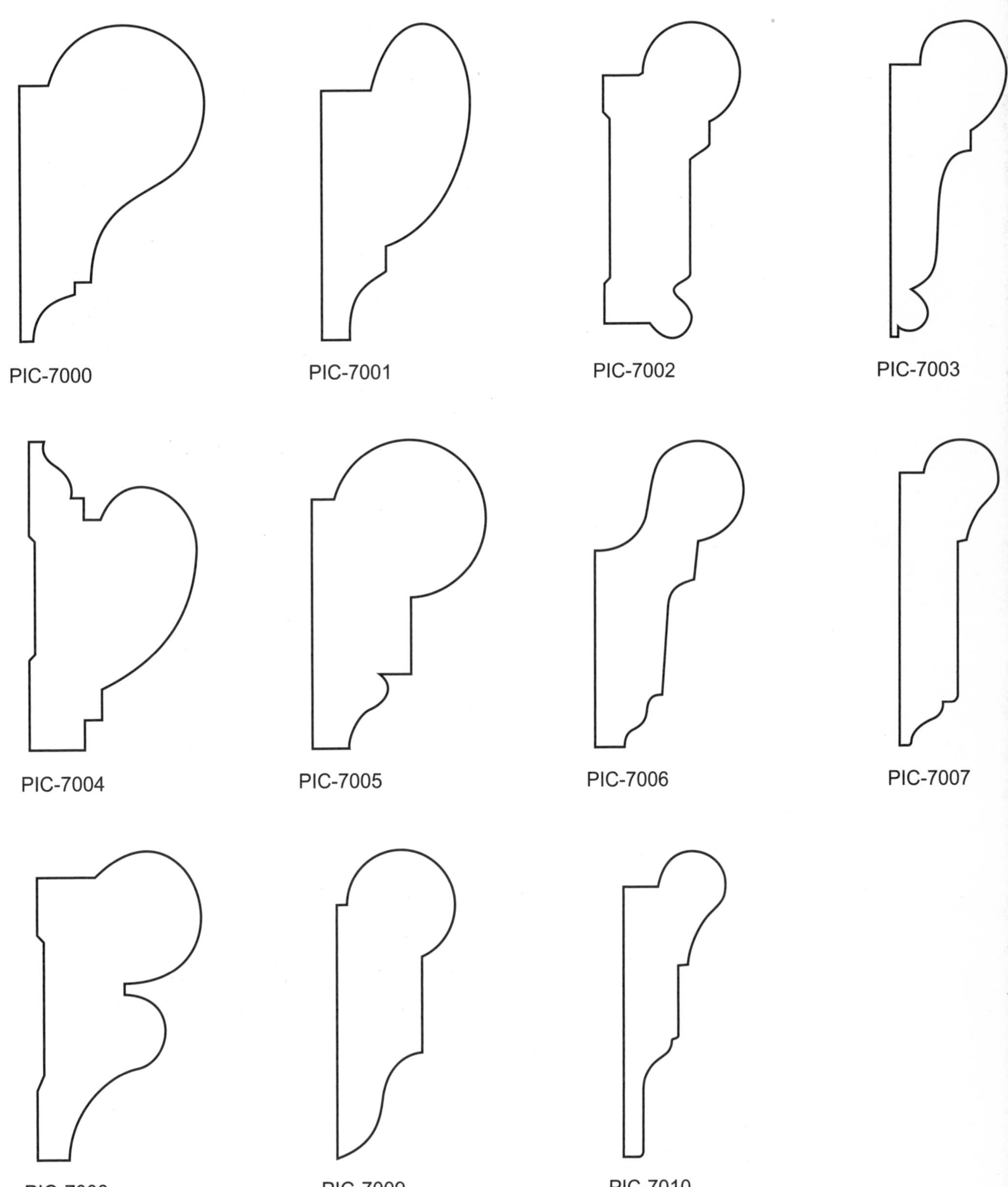

6 - Interior and Exterior Millwork

Ornamental woodwork can be considered any addition to the purely functional and may partly rely on context for its aesthetic appeal. Among various definitions, the one pertinent here is: "Something that lends grace or beauty; a manner or quality that adorns." Ornamentation is defined as a decorative device or embellishment. A good example is the molding which can have functional uses such as covering joints, or with a profile, can be a design element. The profile can be further embellished or enriched by decorative carving. Architectural carving combines the flat surfaces and clearly defined lines of geometry with the interpretive modeling of naturalistic forms.

Historic preservation, conservation and restoration disciplines are extensions of ornamental woodwork. Aspects of this work include, but are not limited to, stripping, repair, reconstruction, reuse of historic material, addition of new material, and special documentation for the work.

The United States Department of the Interior (www.doi.gov/), the National Park Service (www.nps.gov/), and the Historic Sites and Monuments Board of Canada (www.parkscanada.gc.ca/) publish documents related to work under their jurisdiction. The most recent publications from these entities will provide valuable information for the design professional and the woodwork fabrication, finishing, and installation.

There are a number of related arts which are incorporated into wood constructions, such as stained glass, ceramic tiles, mosaic, fabric, plaster or composition ornament, faux finishes, metal hardware and stone inlays.

Excludes:

Standing and running trim except as incorporated as integral parts of elements.

Unless required by the details and/or woodwork specifications, the woodworker shall not:

• provide or prepare for any electrical, telephone, mechanical, or plumbing equipment;

• install woodwork or furnish common blocking, furring or hanging devices for the support or attachment of the woodwork;

• supply exposed materials other than wood or plastic laminate;

• factory finish; or

• supply "stock" or specialty products. If they are to be supplied, they must be specified by a brand name or manufacturer.

6 - Interior and Exterior Millwork

FIRE-RETARDANT SOLID LUMBER

Finishing of Fire-Retardant-Treated Lumber: Fire retardant treatments may affect the finishes intended to be used on the wood, particularly if transparent finishes are planned. The compatibility of any finishes should be tested before they are applied.

Built-up Construction to Improve Fire Rating: In lieu of solid lumber, it is often advisable, where a fire rating is required, to build up members by using treated cores (Fire rated particleboard or medium density fiberboard) clad with untreated veneers not thicker than $^{1}/_{28}$" (0.9 mm). Some existing building codes, except where locally amended, provide that facing materials $^{1}/_{28}$" (0.9 mm) or thinner finished dimension are not considered in determining the flame spread rating of the woodwork.

SOURCES FOR WOOD ORNAMENTATION

There are two possible sources for wood ornamentation: machine-produced elements and the custom carver.

A. The mass-produced product is often limited in available species, sizes and design, which is often a hodge-podge of historic styles. Often the detail lacks clarity because of the tooling, sanding or finish. However, the product is relatively inexpensive, consistent in appearance and appropriate for many applications.

B. On the other hand, there are a number of reasons to contact a custom carver.

1. When the pieces required are impractical or impossible to shape on conventional shop machinery. Examples are tapering profiles as in keystones, acute (interior) corners such as in Gothic tracery and compound curves as in stair handrails.
2. When small quantities are specified which are impractical or too expensive to fabricate by computerized methods.
3. When there is a need to replicate missing (hand carved) elements for restoration or renovation.
4. When elements of specified dimensions are required and unavailable otherwise.
5. When a particular wood species is required.
6. When customized logos or lettering is desired.
7. When patterns are required for casting in another material such as plaster, metal, or glass.
8. When uniqueness is valued by the customer.

Hand tooled and carved work has a special appearance. It has a depth and clarity or crispness which machine tooling often cannot achieve. Because it is done by a skilled artisan there will be slight irregularities, but this is deemed desirable as it lends character and credence to the work. Whether the surface is sanded smooth or the texture of tool marks is left, is one of the points of discussion between the millwork company and carver.

WORKING WITH THE ARTISAN

The custom carver usually works by him- or herself in a studio situation, but this does not necessarily indicate limitations either in quality, production time or fabrication capability. Work is done on a commission basis, so it is common to expect reasonable lead times.

A. What the woodcarver will need to know (from millwork specifier or customer):

1. Type of element - molding, capital, bracket, etc.
2. Sizes - drawings showing elevations and Sections are absolutely necessary for accurate cost estimates, whether provided by the millwork company or drawn by the carver. Often the carver will redraw computer-generated designs or ones not full sized.
3. Species of wood and who will supply the "blanks.". Finishes (paint grade, gilding, faux finish) should also be discussed.
4. Context and/or installed location should be made clear in order to understand lighting and the degree of detail necessary.
5. Intended schedule or completion date.
6. Budget if available as the carver can propose subtle changes in order to oblige a tight budget.

The millwork company should make reasonable efforts to provide as much information as possible as to design, and material. If providing blanks, effort should be made to fabricate them as accurately as possible. Material should be straight grained and contain a minimum of glue lines and therefore, grain directional changes. Consultation concerning what should be provided (sizes, species, special fabrication such as turning) with the carver is essential.

B. What to expect from the carver

1. The carver provides skill and knowledge through experience. The cost is in labor not material. Carving is a unique product which adds immeasurably to the character and attractiveness of the overall project.
2. The carving should closely resemble what is represented in drawings and verbal descriptions.
3. The product should be cleanly carved without distracting irregularities and chips or fuzz in the recesses. The agreed upon surface treatment: sanded, tool textured, primed or gilded, etc. should be consistent throughout.
4. Work should be done in a timely manner as agreed upon.

Quality in artistic handwork is often a subjective matter, but proper communication and agreement among parties should reduce variance of interpretation.

6 - Interior and Exterior Millwork

ARCHITECTURAL ORNAMENTATION

Discussing ornamental style is a difficult endeavor because it is historically complex and subject to interpretation. North America is made up of ethnic groups from around the world and each has brought its own cultural history to the mix. The notes here do not intend to exclude any style of ornamentation, but concentrate on the predominant influence of Western Art and Architecture. Risking over-simplification, style tends to vacillate over time between two extremes — formal, restrained classicism and emotional and vivacious Romanticism.

Much of Western Architecture derives from the art and architecture of ancient Greece and Rome. Classicism is based on symmetry and proportion providing mathematical relationships among all elements of the building. One characteristic is the use of columns for support, though engaged columns and pilasters were used, sometimes in conjunction with arches. The *orders* of architecture, have been codified and reinterpreted ever since Vitruvious wrote a treatise on architecture in 30 BCE. In reality there was wide variation and great adaptability over a thousand years of evolution in many disparate geographical areas. The Parthenon in Athens, the Maison Carée in Nîmes, France, or the Pantheon in Rome are familiar examples. In succeeding revivals an abundance of government and academic building reflect these archetypes - the United States Capital building, many state and county courthouses, and Jefferson's University of Virginia.

Romanticism, on the other hand, is subjective, derived from the randomness of nature, *spiritual*, and introduces asymmetry, exuberance, and complex lines. Many designs are eclectic, fantastic and mix a number of exotic motifs. Though there are many of the same mathematical concerns in Romanesque and Gothic buildings as there are in Classical buildings, the ornamentation conveys a different feeling. The achievement of Gothic architecture was the introduction of the pointed arch which solved some structural limitations of Romanesque vaulting. While classicism appears to be simple in concept, romanticism seems to relish complexity. A Gothic cathedral when viewed from any angle except frontally does not seem to have much order, with flying buttresses and pinnacles and windows complicating one's perception of the form of the building.

Reacting to Gothic embellishments, Renaissance architects rediscovered classicism, but in time the classical tenets were corrupted (Mannerism) and the Baroque, which emphasized undulating surfaces, complicated interior spaces and dramatic decoration, permeated Europe. As a reaction to the flamboyance of the Baroque, interest in Classicism reemerged in the 18th Century. But in this era the Rococo style and the "Chinese" style, (Chinoiserie), especially in furniture, were also in vogue. The 19th Century saw continued classicism, but also an eclectic mix of revivals - Romanesque, Gothic and Eastern styles.

CLASSICAL ORDERS

The *orders* of architecture refer to the configurations and relationship of parts of Greek and Roman buildings. (See illustrations on the following pages.) Over the centuries, the relationship of parts of the classical building have been systematized, but one should keep in mind that Greek and Roman architecture had many variations and evolved through time. Generally, the orders refer to the proportions of the building; some being squarish or heavy, while others are taller and therefore lighter. The trabeated or post and lintel system of building consists of columns and a superstructure supporting the roof. This entablature is made up of the architrave, the frieze and the cornice. The architrave is the beam, which spans from column to column. The frieze is derived from the band covering the joist ends, while the cornice creates the eaves. The columns have base moldings (except the Doric order) a shaft, plain or fluted, and a capital, which supports the architrave. Because the capitals are very different in appearance for each order it is an easy way to distinguish among them. Because the roof line ran the length of the building the triangular area above the entablature is called the pediment.

There are three Greek orders and two Roman ones.

The Doric column has no base but rests directly on the stylobate or *floor*, of the building, is fluted and has a simple turned bowl-like capital. The bulging shape is the echinus. The frieze of the Doric is divided into triglyphs and metopes; the latter often decorated with sculptural figures (as on the Parthenon). This order appears sturdy and well planted, having a horizontal appearance.

The Ionic order has a column which has several rounds of base moldings, usually consisting of two tori or half-round moldings, divided by a scotia or concave recess, a shaft which is fluted and a capital with distinctive scrolls or volutes. The frieze is relatively plain, or contains sculptural figures in an uninterrupted procession. Above the frieze is the characteristic dentil molding.

The Corinthian order proportionally is similar to the Ionic though some examples have very slender proportions. The column is similar, but the capital has acanthus leaves, and volutes spring like sprouts from the foliage. The entablature is similar to the Ionic, but the use of modillions or brackets in the eaves (separating rosettes in the soffit) sets this order apart.

The Roman orders are the Tuscan and the Composite.

The first is derived from native antecedents and is a relatively plain style with unfluted columns, simply echinus capital and entablature like the Ionic without the dentil course.

The Composite has a capital, which is an amalgamation of the Ionic volutes, and the Corinthian acanthus leaves. The entablature is similar to the Corinthian. The Romans introduced several building innovations, but the use of the arch (the arcuated system), and therefore vaults and domes, changed architecture immeasurably.

6 - Interior and Exterior Millwork

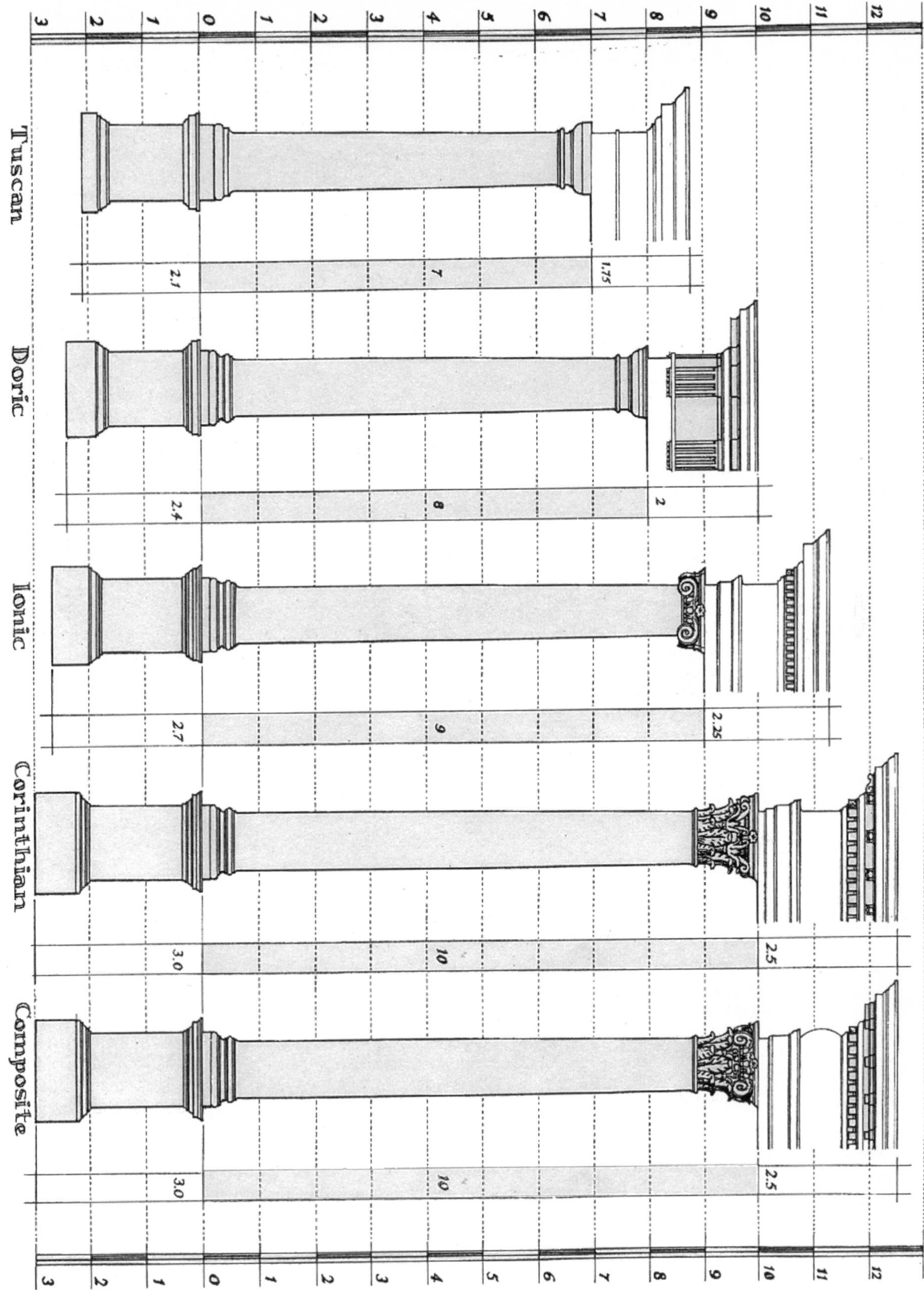

The Five Orders - Chitham, Robert. The Classical Orders of Architecture; used with permission.

6 - Interior and Exterior Millwork

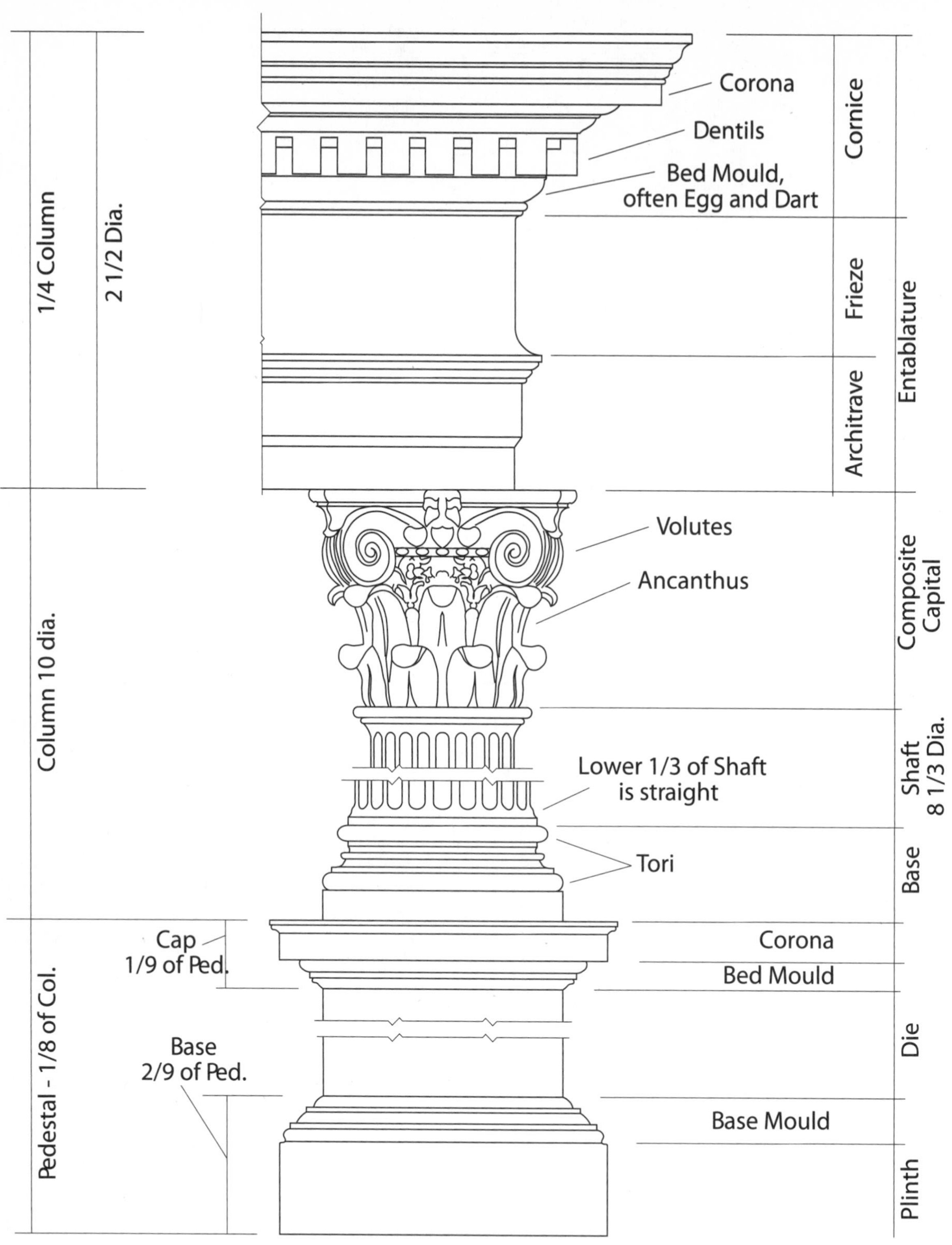

The columns of the classical orders of Greek and Roman architecture are often adapted for modern construction. These orders are Tuscan, Doric, Ionic, Corinthian, and Composite. The Composite figure (above) names the basic features of a classical order and gives some of the proportions of the column in relation to the shaft diameter as a basic unit of measurement. Pilasters are rectangular in plan, without taper from top to bottom. If used structurally they are usually referred to as piers, but are treated architecturally as columns. The typical pilaster extends a third or less of its width from the wall surface behind it.

6 - Interior and Exterior Millwork

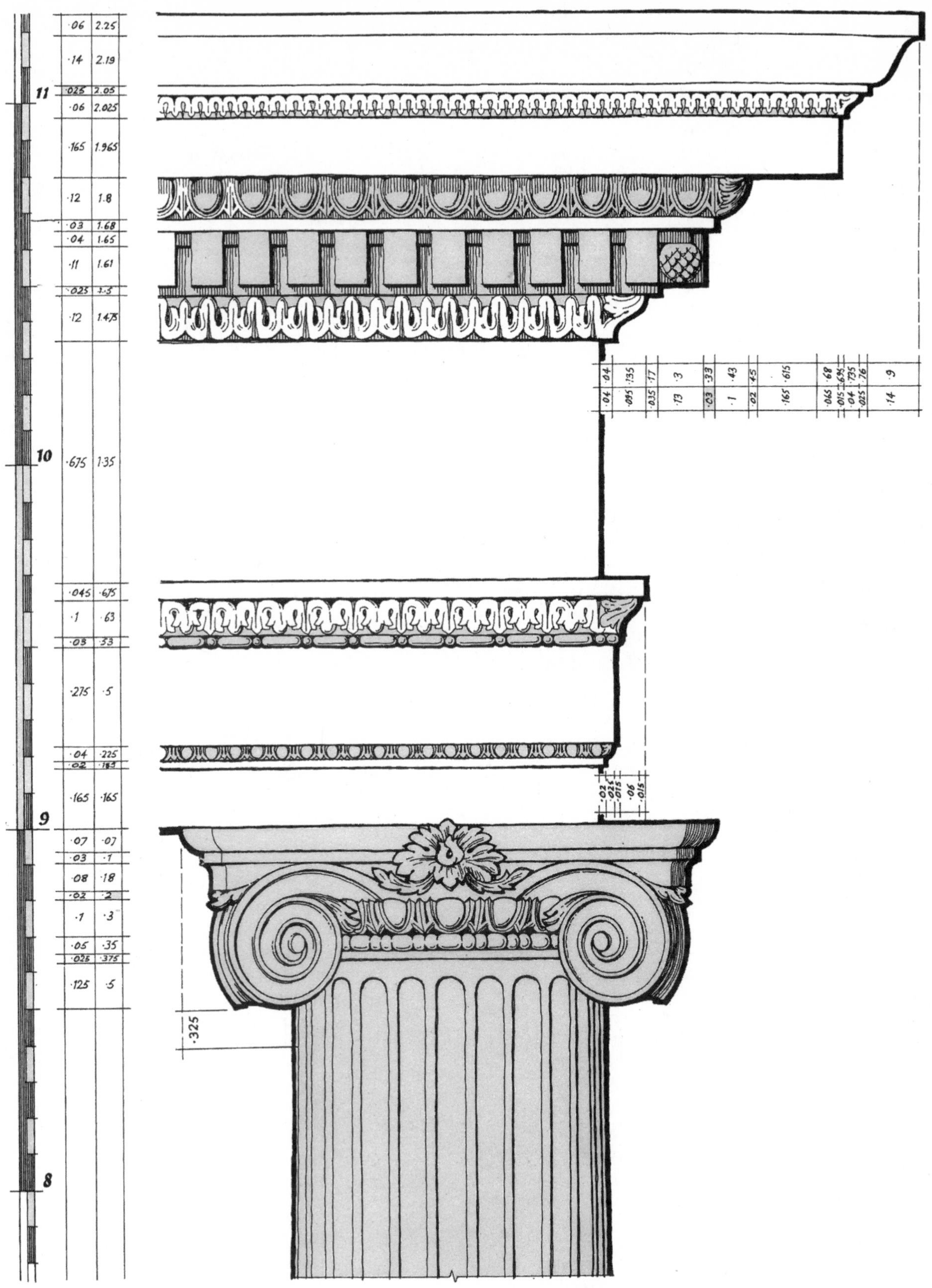

Ionic Capital and Entablature - Chitham, Robert. The Classical Orders of Architecture; used with permission.

6 - Interior and Exterior Millwork

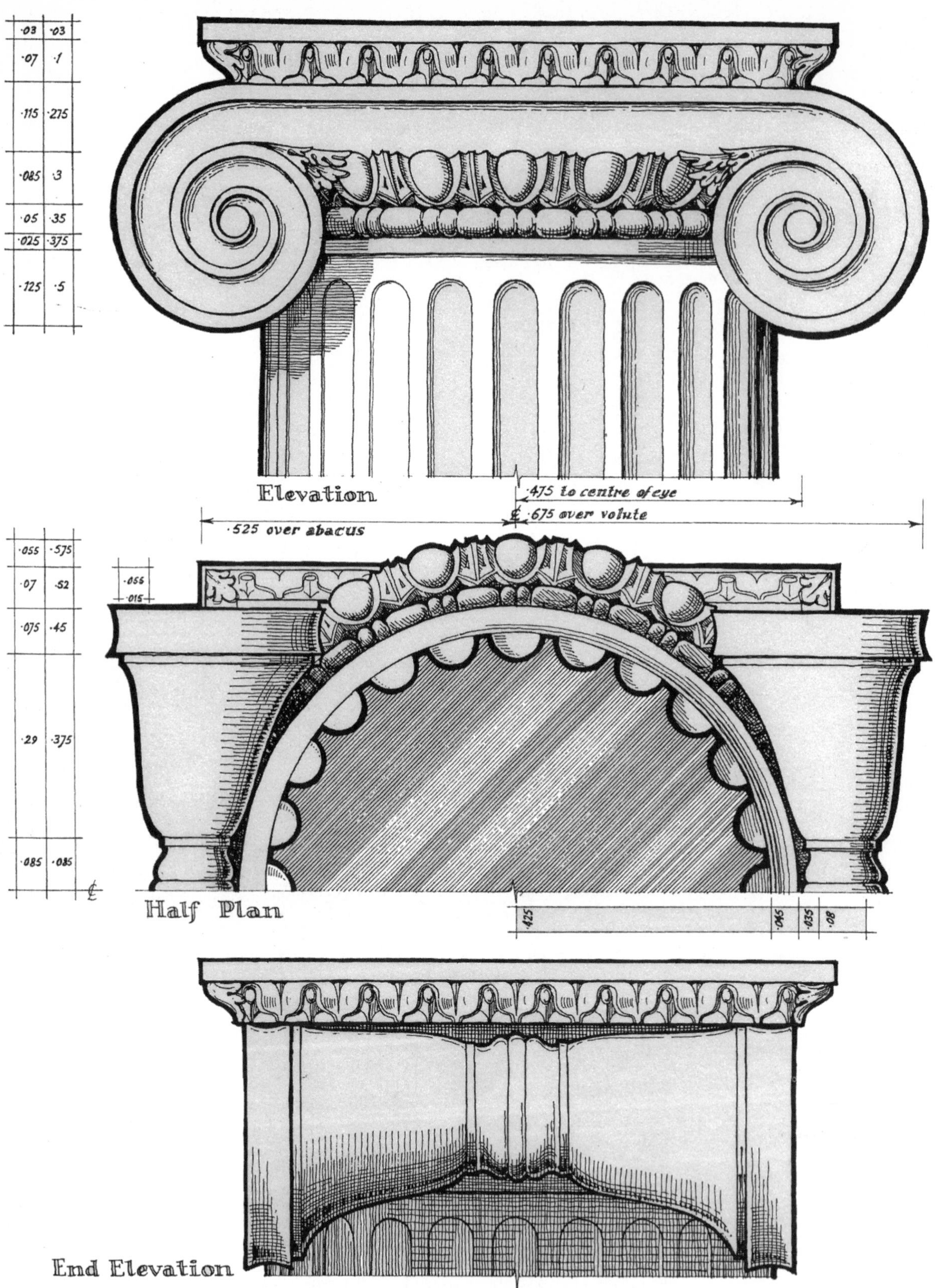

Ionic Capital detail - Chitham, Robert. The Classical Orders of Architecture; used with permission.

6 - Interior and Exterior Millwork

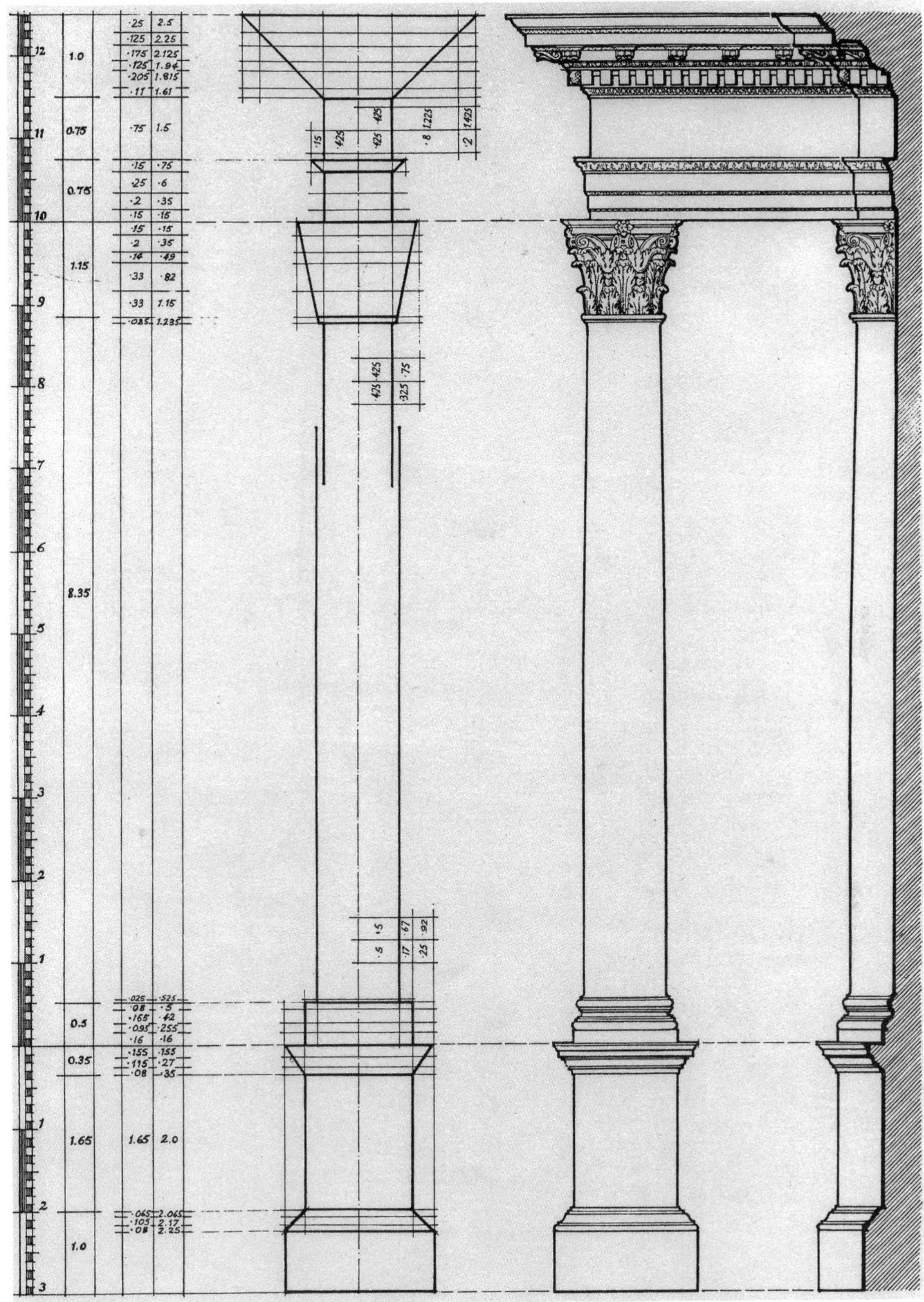

CORINTHIAN ORDER PROPORTIONS - CHITHAM, ROBERT. THE CLASSICAL ORDERS OF ARCHITECTURE; USED WITH PERMISSION.

6 - Interior and Exterior Millwork

Corinthian Capital detail - Chitham, Robert. The Classical Orders of Architecture; used with permission.

6 - Interior and Exterior Millwork

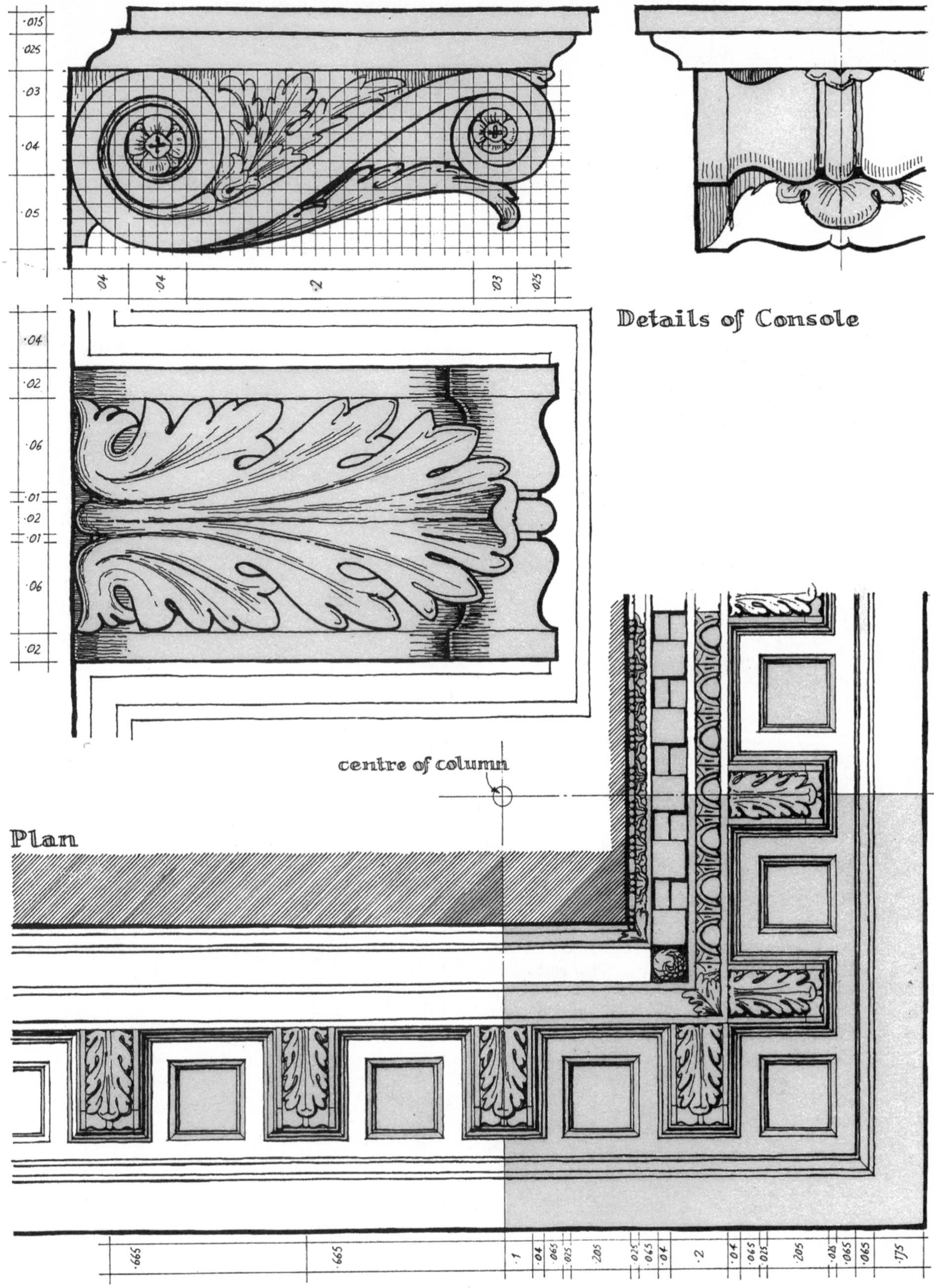

Corinthian Entablature detail - Chitham, Robert. The Classical Orders of Architecture; used with permission.

6 - Interior and Exterior Millwork

TERMINOLOGY OF ORNAMENTATION

A rudimentary explanation of some carving terms will assist the millwork specifier in communicating with the custom carver.

There are four methods of depicting a design in wood.

- *Incised*: Incised designs are simply made by shallow grooves in the surface of the material.
- *Relief*: Most architectural carving is carved in relief. The degree to which the design is *lifted*, off the surface is described as *low*, or *high*, relief.
- *Pierced*: Some voids in the design are literally cut through the material and are termed pierced carvings.
- *Sculpture*: Carving in-the-round or sculptural works are also incorporated into architectural surroundings.

Moldings have multiple uses but one important one is to visually set apart various elements. For instance, they are transitions between the parts of the *entablature*. They accentuate the trim (*architrave*) around doors and windows, and around an arch (*archivolt*). The various terms depend primarily on the profiles, but there are a few terms which indicate use, location or size.

The curving profiles are often separated or off set by a relatively small flat called a *fillet*.

The small half round is an *astragal*, often decorated with *beads* or *bead and billet*. A larger half round, usually associated with the base of a column or base of a structure is called a *torus* (plural *tori*) molding, sometimes decorated with *ribbon-bundled* bay laurel, oak leaves, or reeds.

The *ovolo* is a quarter ellipse (Greek) or quarter round (Roman) profile, most often carved with *egg and dart* design, but many other possibilities make it a very popular molding.

The *cyma recta* is a double-curved molding with the concave curve on the outside of the molding, pointing toward the viewer as if *reaching*, outward. The *cyma reversa* is the opposite, the convexity nearer the viewer and seems to support or bolster the element to which it is attached. Both profiles are often carved with foliage, generically termed *acanthus leaf*. Both of these profiles as well as the ovolo often have the curved portion separated from the fillet by deep valleys or *quirks*.

Medieval moldings were often made of a number of closely placed profiles, often with deep hollows and repeated rounds.

Romanesque architecture continued many of the same principles of classical architecture, though much of the decoration; such as column capitals became more idiosyncratic and depicted the profusion of natural foliage. The innovation of the pointed arch (loosely called the Gothic arch), ubiquitous in Gothic architecture, allowed buildings to soar to great heights and to redistribute weight. This allowed larger windows and the lacy stone work termed *tracery*. The designs of this tracery are geometrically derived from, for the most part, overlapping and intersecting circles. The circular voids are called *foils* and the pointed interSections *cusps*; thus a three lobbed design is a trefoil, while one of four is a quatrefoil, one of five is a cinquefoil. Tracery was found incorporated into the woodwork of choir stalls, paneling and memorial structures.

Much decoration was derived from nature in depictions of vines and animals. Of course, religious figures and symbols were also a primary motif. Foliage climbing the edges of pinnacles and spires consists of the leaves, called *crockets*, and the terminating leaves, a *finial* or (especially on pew ends) *poppyhead*. Moldings were made of multiple profiles and combined with running vines and crestings, or stylized leaves. Square flowers and ballflowers were often spaced along moldings. At interSections of the ribbed vaults were *bosses*, which depict foliage (like a *rosette*), figures, or heraldic devises. A selected partially illustrated glossary related to ornament and architecture follows.

ORNAMENTAL WOODWORK GLOSSARY

abacus

The uppermost member of the **capital** of a **column**; often a plain square slab, but sometimes moulded or carved. The plate or bearing surface at the top of a column upon which the **architrave** rests.

acanthus

An indigenous plant of the Mediterranean area depicted on the **Corinthian capital** and used as a decorative motif on many objects throughout history. Today nearly a generic term for any multi-leafleted foliage.

arch

A curved construction which spans an opening; usually consists of wedge-shaped blocks called **voussoirs** and a keystone, or a curved or pointed structural member which is supported at the sides or ends (often contrasted to **trabeated** construction of post and lintel).

architrave

1. In the classical **orders**, the lowest members of the **entablature**; the beam that spans from column to column, resting directly on their **capitals**. 2. The ornamental moldings around the faces of the jambs and lintel of a doorway or other opening.

archivolt

The face molding of an arch (the **architrave** of an **arch**).

astragal

1. a **bead**, usually half-round, with a **fillet** on one or both sides. It may be plain, but the term is more correctly used to describe the classical molding decorated with a string of beads or bead-and-reel shapes. A small molding of half round Section, often carved with beads; often referred to as a ***bead*** by furniture-makers.

bead

1. A bead molding. 2. A narrow wood strip, moulded on one edge, against which a door or window sash closes; a stop bead. 3. A pearl-shaped carved decoration on moldings or other ornaments, usually in a series, or in conjunction with other shapes; a beading.

bead-and-reel

A semiround convex molding carved with a pattern of disks alternating with round or elongated beads.

6 - Interior and Exterior Millwork

bolection molding
A molding which covers the joint between panel and stile and projects above the surface of stile; a molding applied to a flat ground.

boss
1. A projecting, usually richly carved ornament, decorative rosette, portrait, heraldic devise or similar motif, placed at the interSection of ribs, groins, beams, etc., or at the termination of a molding. 2. In masonry, a roughly shaped stone set to project for carving in place.

bracket
A general term for an element projecting from a wall or other surface to support another element such as a beam or **cornice**.

capital
The topmost member, usually decorated, of a **column** or **pilaster**, etc., it provides a larger bearing surface for the **architrave**; different in appearance according to the order of the building.

cavetto
A cove; a molding profile whose arc is a segment of a circle, (unlike **scotia** whose profile has two centers).

cinquefoil
A five-lobed pattern divided by **cusps;** in Gothic **tracery** a geometric design with five round open areas.

column
1. In structures, a relatively long, slender structural compression member such as a post, pillar, or strut; usually vertical, supporting a load which acts in (or near) the direction of its longitudinal axis. 2. In classical architecture, a cylindrical support of the **entablature**, consisting of a base (except Greek Doric), shaft, and capital.

Composite order
One of the five classical orders. A Roman order of classical architecture which has proportions close to the **Corinthian** order, but the capital is a combination of the **Ionic** and the Corinthian capitals. The entablature is also similar or identical with the Corinthian entablature.

console
A scrolled bracket used to support an architectural element such as a **cornice**, **entablature** over a door, mantel shelf or in furniture, a table top.

corbel
A projection from a wall which supports a beam, **arch** or vault ribbing.

Corinthian order
One of the Greek orders characterized by slender proportions; the column shaft is fluted, with a **capital** depicting **acanthus** leaves and scrolled *sprouts* (caulicoli) and with an **entablature** with **dentil** course and **modillions** under the soffit. Roman adaptations often highly decorated.

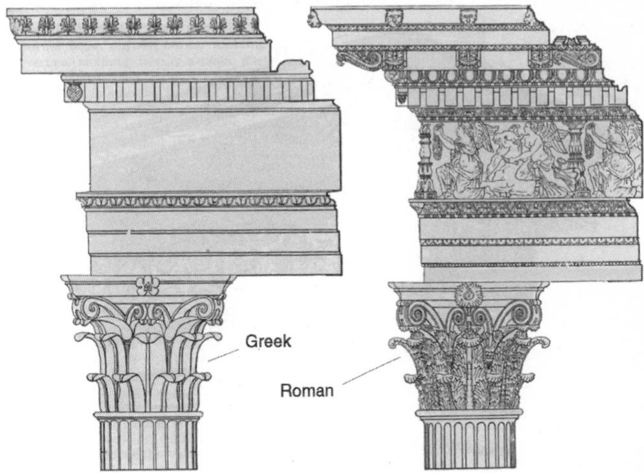

Cornice
1. Any moulded projection which crowns or finishes the parts to which it is affixed. 2. The third or uppermost division of an **entablature**, resting on the **frieze** consisting of **corona** and **cymatium**. 3. An ornamental molding, usually of wood or plaster, running round the walls of a room just below the ceiling; a crown molding; the molding forming the top member of a door or a window frame.

corona
The overhanging vertical member of a **cornice**.

crockets
Regularly spaced leaves projecting along the gable of a Gothic arch, spire, or pinnacle. Sometimes as terminations of the interior **cusps** of an arch or **trefoil**, **quartrefoil**, etc.

cusp
In Gothic **tracery**, the intersection or termination of arcs which define foliations or spaces.

cyma recta
A molding with an S curve Section; orientation is with concave curve foremost toward viewer. Example is **cymatium** of **cornice**; opposite of cyma reversa.

cyma reversa
A molding with a S curve Section; orientation is with convex curve foremost toward viewer. Example is panel (**bolection**) molding.

cymatium
The top molding of the cornice; usually a cym profile, but can be an ovolo or (rarely) a cavetto.

6 - Interior and Exterior Millwork

dentil
One of a band or small, square, tooth-like blocks forming part of the characteristic ornamentation of the Ionic, Corinthian, and Composite orders.

Doric order
One of the Greek orders; the sturdiest order with stout proportions; the **column** has no base, is fluted and has a relatively simple flaring **capital**; the **frieze** of the **entablature** is divided into **triglyphs** and **metopes.** Example is the Parthenon.

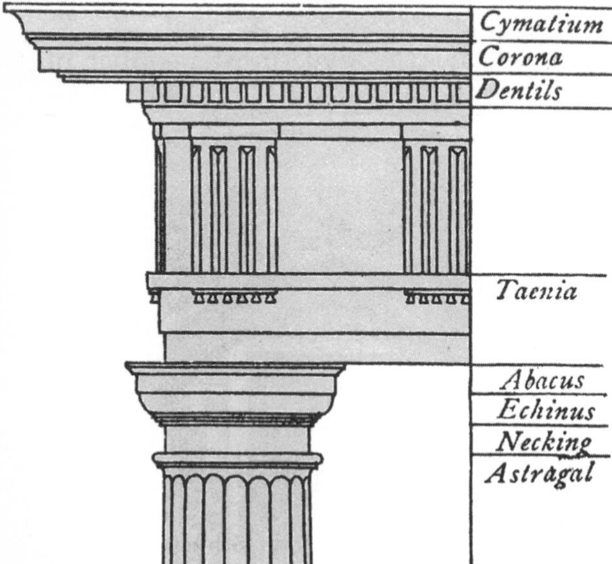

echinus
The bulging or flaring of a **capital**; of elliptical Section as in the **Doric** order, often an **ovolo** molding.

egg and dart
The egg-shaped ornament alternating with a dart-like ornament, used to enrich **ovolo** and other moldings.

entablature
In classical architecture, the elaborated beam member carried by the **columns**, horizontally divided into **architrave** (below), **frieze**, and **cornice** (above).

entasis
The intentional slight convex curving of the vertical profile of a tapered column used to overcome the optical illusion of concavity that characterized straight-sided columns.

fillet
A molding consisting of a narrow flat band, often square in Section; the term is loosely applied to almost any rectangular molding used to visually separate molding profiles.

finial
An ornament which terminates the point of a spire, pinnacle, etc., often turned or carved (downward pointing decorations are called *drops*).

foil
In **tracery**, any of several lobes, circular or nearly so, tangent to the inner side of a larger arc, as of an **arch**, and meeting each other in points, called **cusps**, projecting inward from the arch, or circle. Five foils make a **cinquefoil**.

frieze
1. The middle horizontal member of a classical **entablature**, above the **architrave** and below the **cornice**. 2. A similar decorative band near the top of an interior wall below the **cornice**. 3. Any broad horizontal band near the top of the wall or element (such as a mantelpiece).

fret
An essentially two-dimensional geometric design consisting of shallow bands; example is Greek key.

gadroon
Elongated bulbous shapes in series, as on decorative urns and turnings; a molding of repeated tear-drop shaped elements, often on a thumbnail profile.

Gothic arch
A loose term denoting a pointed arch consisting of two (or more centers) as opposed to Roman or Romanesque arch which is semicircular.

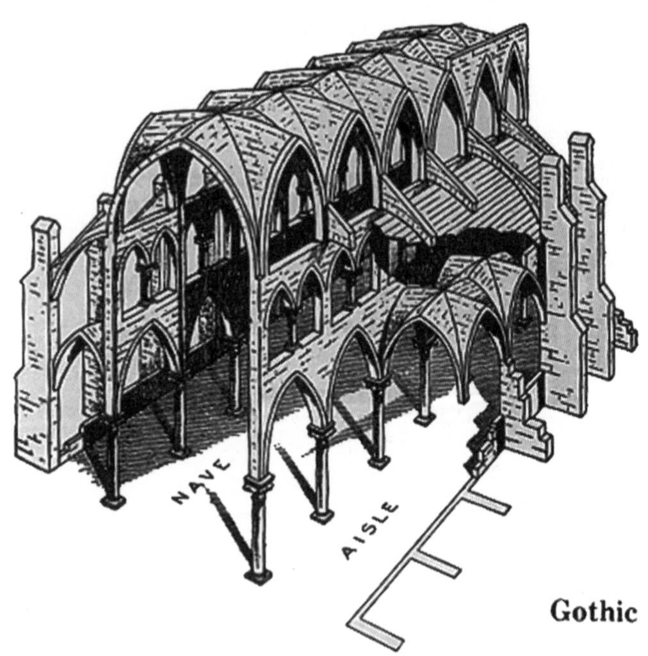

groin
The ridge, edge, or curved line formed by the interSection of the surfaces of two intersecting **vaults**.

6 - Interior and Exterior Millwork

guillouche

Shallow design of overlapping circles, sometimes in-filled with **rosettes**.

Ionic order

The classical order originated by the Ionian Greeks, characterized by its **capital** with large **volutes**, a fasciated **entablature**, continuous **frieze**, usually **dentils** in the **cornice**, and by its elegant detailing.

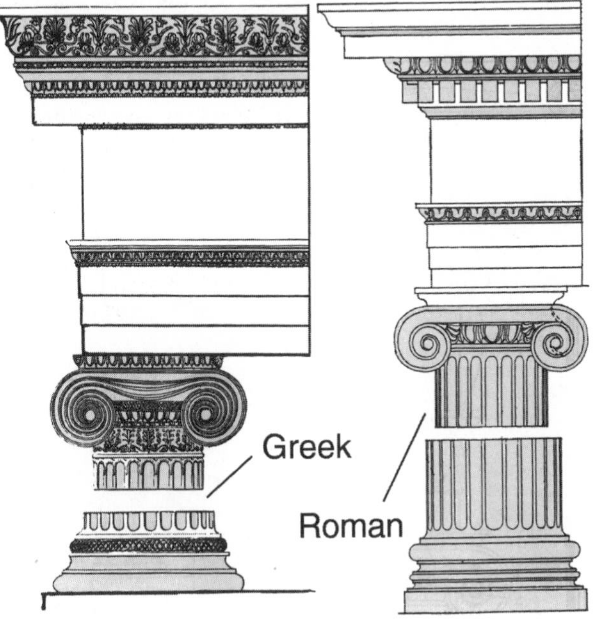

metopes

The panel between the **triglyphs** in the **Doric** frieze, often carved.

modillions

A horizontal bracket or console, usually in the form of a scroll with acanthus, supporting the **corona** under a **cornice**.

mutule

A sloping flat block on the soffit of the **Doric cornice**

order

1. An arrangement of **columns** with an **entablature**. 2. In classical architecture, a particular style of **column** with its **entablature**, having standardized details. The Greek orders were the **Doric**, **Ionic**, an **Corinthian**; the Romans added the **Tuscan** and **Composite** orders.

ovolo

A convex molding, less than a semicircle in profile; usually a quarter of a circle or approximately a quarter-ellipse in profile, often decorated with egg and dart design.

pediment

1. In classical architecture, the triangular gable end of the roof above the horizontal cornice, often filled with sculpture. 2. In later work, a surface used ornamentally over doors or windows; usually triangular but may be curved.

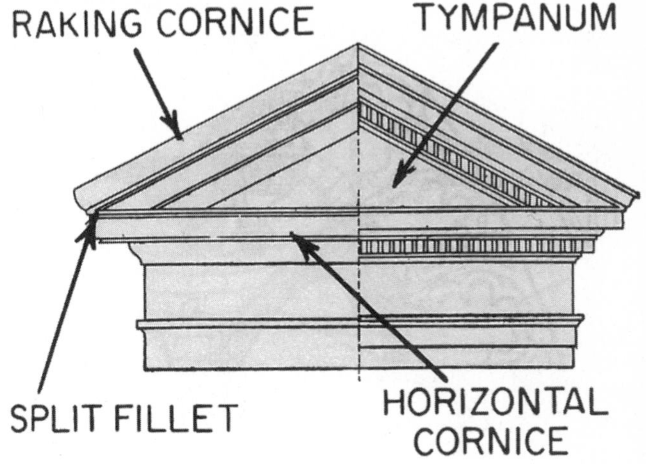

pilaster

An engaged pier or pillar, often with capital and base.

poppyhead

A carved foliage ornament generally used for the finials of pew ends and similar pieces of church furniture.

plinth

1. A square or rectangular base for column, pilaster, or door framing. 2. A solid monumental base, often ornamented with moldings, etc.

quatrefoil

A four-lobed pattern divided by **cusps**.

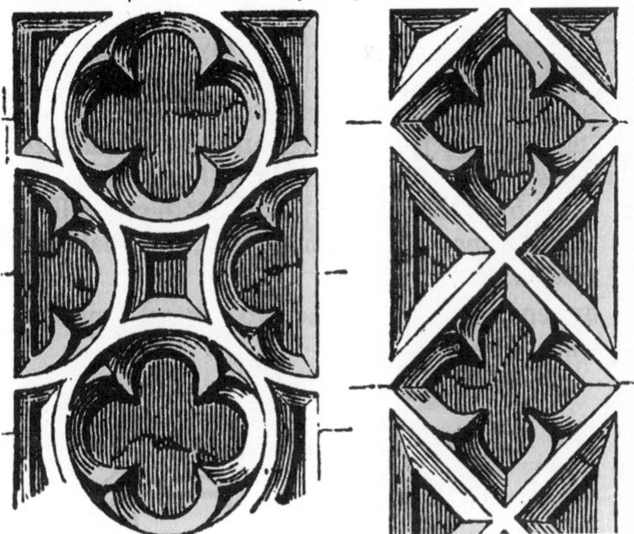

quirk

An indentation separating one element from another, as between moldings; a valley between fillet and profile of a molding; between abacus and echinus of **Doric** capital.

6 - Interior and Exterior Millwork

Romanesque

The style emerging in Western Europe in the early 11th century, characterized by massive articulated wall structures, round arches, and powerful vaults, and lasting until the advent of Gothic architecture in the middle of the 12th century (illustration follows).

rosette

1. A round pattern with a carved or painted conventionalized floral and/or foliage design where petals/leaves radiate from center.

2. A circular or oval decorative wood plaque used in joinery, such as one applied to a wall to receive the end of a stair rail.

scotia

A deep concave molding defined by two varying arcs, especially one at the base of a **column** in Classical architecture.

shaft

The portion of a **column** or **pilaster** between the **base** and the **capital**.

soffit

The exposed undersurface of any overhead component of a building, such as an **arch**, balcony, beam, **cornice**, lintel, etc.

stylobate

The *floor* of classical temple; top step of crepidoma.

torus, tori

A bold projecting molding, convex in shape, generally forming the lowest member of a base over the **plinth**.

trabeated

1. Descriptive of construction using beams or lintels, following the principle of post and lintel construction, as distinguished from construction using arches and vaults. 2. Furnished with an **entablature**.

tracery

The pierced designs of window mullions in the Medieval period consisting of geometrically derived curving shapes; the same designs on furniture panels, walls and the decorative arts.

trefoil

A three-lobed pattern divided by **cusps**.

Tracery with Trefoils

triglyph

The characteristic ornament of the **Doric frieze**, consisting of slightly raised blocks of three vertical bands separated by V-shaped grooves. The triglyphs alternate with plain or sculptured panels called **metopes**.

6 - Interior and Exterior Millwork

Tuscan order

A simplified version of the Roman **Doric** order, having a plain **frieze** and no **mutules** in the **cornice**.

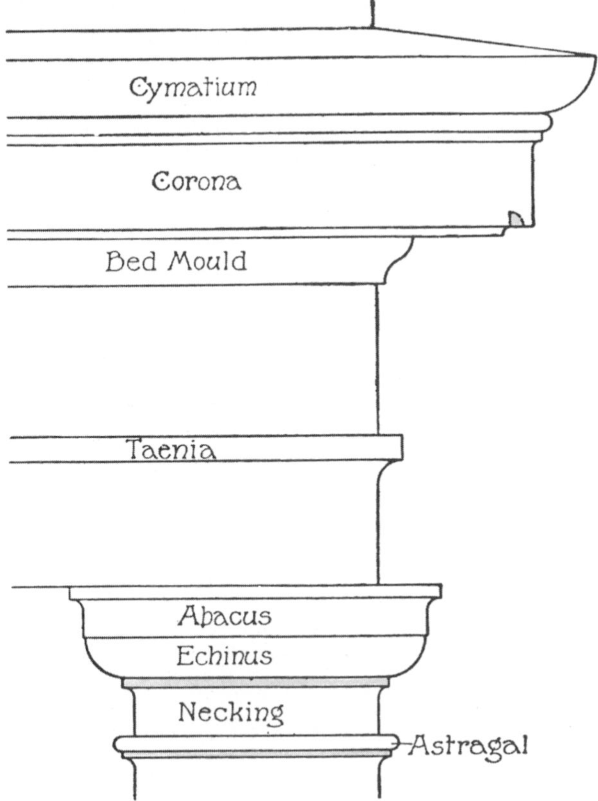

Tuscan order entablature and capital

volutes

1. A spiral scroll, as on **Ionic**, **Corinthian**, or **Composite capitals**, etc.

2. A stair crook having an easement with a spiral section of stair rail.

voussoir

A wedge-shaped masonry unit in an arch or vault whose converging sides are cut as radii of one of the centers of the arch or vault.

Resources and References

A. Museums with period rooms

There are many historic houses around the country which are open to the public. Eighteenth Century homes such as Gunston Hall in VA, and Drayton Hall, near Charleston, SC, along the Eastern Seaboard and Neoclassical houses as one moves West. There are museums with *period* rooms as well. The Metropolitan Museum in New York, the Philadelphia Museum of Art, and Colonial Williamsburg are only a few.

B. Publications

Dover Publications, Inc.
31 East Second Street
Mineola , NY 11501

Dover Publications has an incomparable listing of books which, for the most part, are reprintings of older publications; from Andrea Palladio's *Four Books of Architecture* to Augustus Charles Pugin's *Gothic Ornament* as well as handbooks and specialized subjects.

One invaluable Dover handbook is *Illustrated Dictionary of Historic Architecture* by Cyril M. Harris. It is from Harris that the definitions and many of the illustrations in the Glossary have been used with permission.

Three others which offer good illustrations are:

Colling, James K. *Medieval Decorative Ornament*, New York, (Reprint of 1874 edition); Dover Publications, Inc. 1995.

Griesbach, C.B. *Historic Ornament: A Pictorial Archive,* New York, Dover Publications, Inc., 1975.

Speltz, Alesander. *The Styles of Ornament,* (Reprint of German Edition of 1906), New York, Dover Publications, Inc., 1959.

Several books explaining in detail the orders of architecture are:

Adam, Robert. *Classical Architecture: A Comprehensive Handbook to the Tradition of Classical Style*, New York: Harry N. Abrams, Inc., Publishers, 1990.

Chitham, Robert. *The Classical Orders of Architecture*, New York: Rizzoli International Publications, Inc., 1985 (may be out of print).

Ware, William R. *The American Vignola: A Guide to the Making of Classical Architecture,* New York: Dover Publications, Inc., 1994.

A definitive history of architecture is:

Fletcher, Sir Banister. *A History of Architecture on the Comparative Method*, 20th edition ed., Dan Cruickshank and Andrew Saint, Oxford: Architectural Press, 1996.

For carving classical architectural elements:

Wilbur, Frederick. *Carving Architectural Detail in Wood: the Classical Tradition*, Lewes, UK: Guild of Master Craftsmen Publications, Ltd. 2000.

NOTES

7

Stairwork and Rails

7 - Stairwork and Rails

DESIGN SUMMARY

This short summary is a collection of hints and illustrations about the challenges of designing and building safe stairs. The *AWS* cannot and does not offer these data as advice on code compliance. Safe stairs and design and engineering to meet local codes remains the responsibility of the design professional.

The three critical steps in stair design are:

- check local code;
- consult with an experienced stair builder to double-check your geometry; and
- pre-clear your stair design with the local building officials.

NET STAIR WIDTH

The minimum width of a normal stairway is 44" (1118 mm) when expected occupant load is 50 or more. Otherwise, the minimum width is usually 36" (915 mm).

RISER HEIGHT

For stairways serving an occupant load of greater than 10 persons, the typical maximum riser height is about 7" (178 mm). For stairways serving an occupant load of fewer than 10, the maximum riser height varies from 7-3/4" (197 mm) to 8-1/4" (210 mm) depending on local code. All codes agree that the height of each riser must be consistent with the others. Riser height is measured from the finished top of a tread to the finished top of the adjacent tread.

TREAD LENGTH (RUN)

For stairways serving an occupant load of greater than 10, the minimum tread length is usually 11" (279 mm). For stairways serving fewer than 10, the minimum is usually 9-1/2" (241 mm). Just as the rise must be consistent, so must the run.

RATIO OF RISER TO TREAD

There are some well established Imperial guidelines for stair layout. Three rules of thumb for a good relation between the height of a riser and the width of a tread are: (1) the tread width multiplied by the riser height in inches should equal between 72 and 75; (2) the tread width plus twice the riser height should equal about 25; or rise + run = about 17" (432 mm), remembering that the rise and run must work together. It is the pitch of the stair which makes it functional and safe. A stair which meets two of the three guidelines should be easy to use.

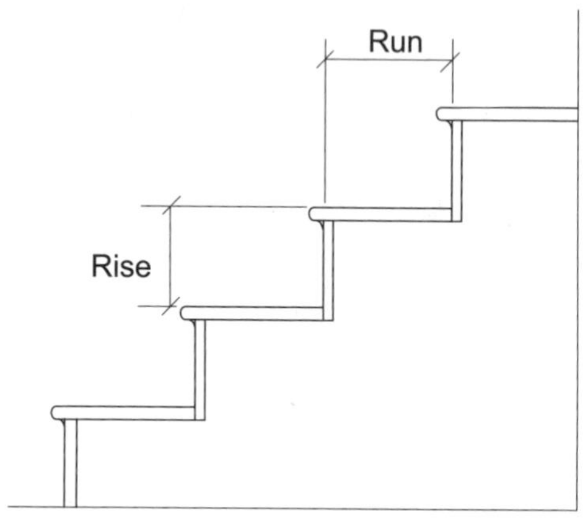

HEADROOM - A minimum of 2032 mm [80"] must be allowed for headroom measured from a plane parallel and tangent to the nose of the treads to all overhead points.

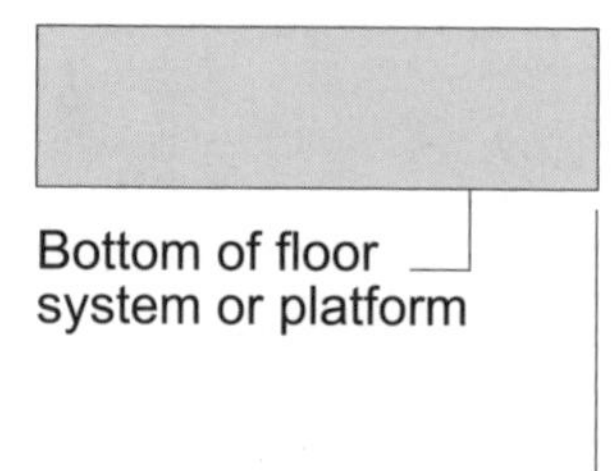

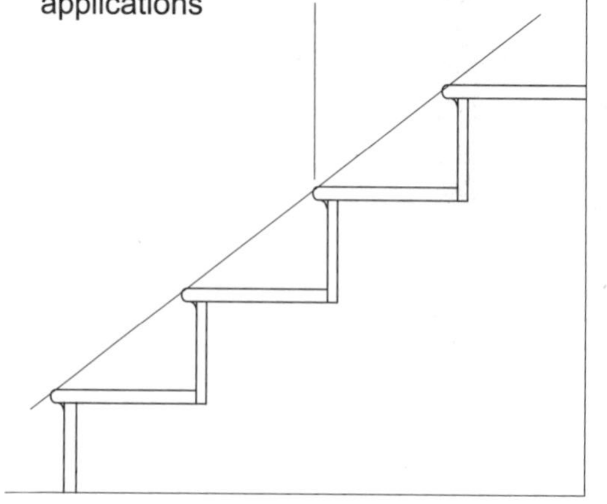

7 - Stairwork and Rails

HANDRAILS - Stair handrails should be mounted in such a manner that the top of the handrail be no less than 34" (864 mm) and no more than 38" (965 mm) above tread and landing noses. Stairways wider than 44" (1118 mm) should include a handrail on both sides of the stair. Handrails should clear walls and other obstructions by no less than 1-1/2" (38 mm) to allow for adequate finger clearance, but should not project more than about 4-1/2" (115 mm). Consult all codes and requirements.

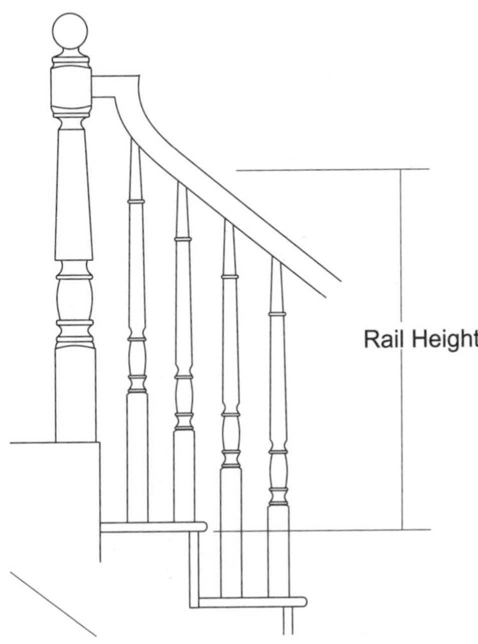

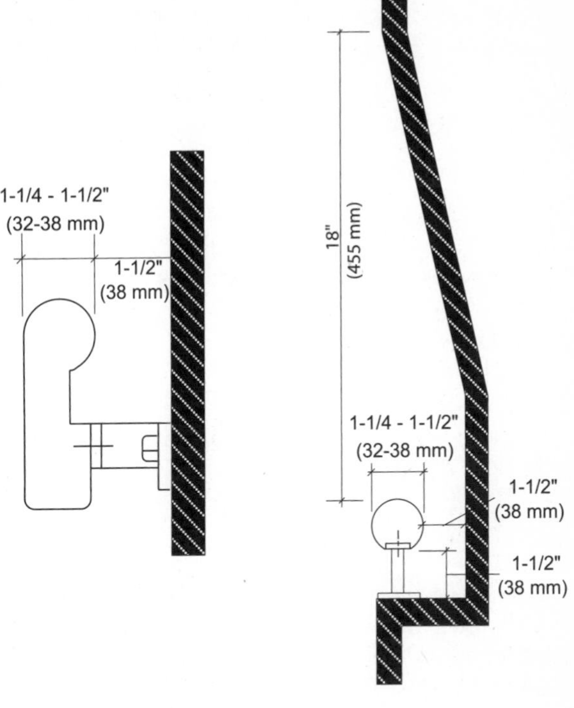

LEVEL BALUSTRADE - Balustrade at balconies or landings must be at least 36" (915 mm) above the finish floor for most residential applications and at least 42" (1067 mm) above the finish floor for most commercial applications. Some jurisdictions require the use of a guardrail in addition to the handrail on the stair.

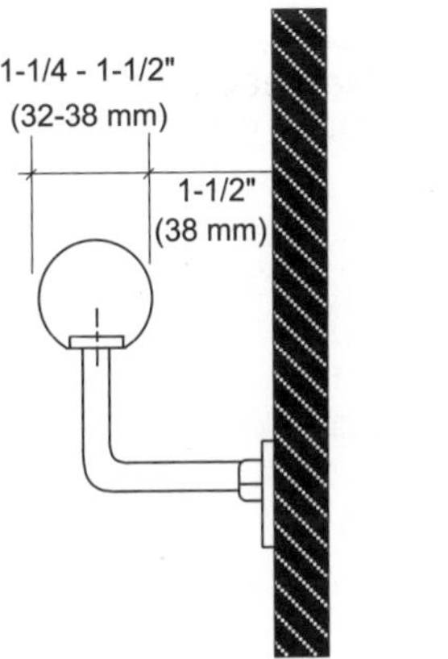

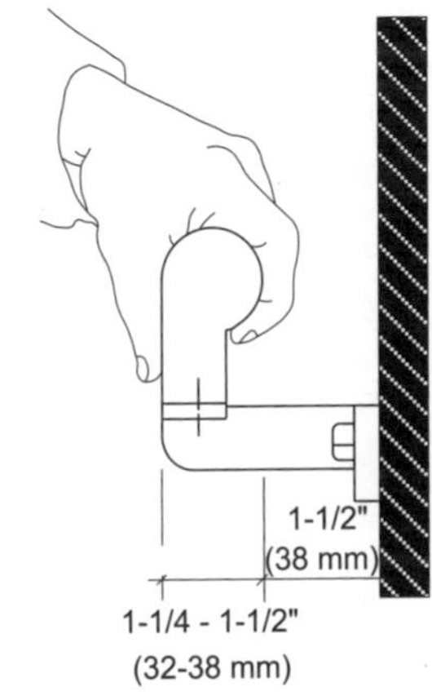

CURVED/CIRCULAR STAIRS - In most regional codes, a circular stair must have an inside radius that is no less than twice the width of the stair. Most books also specify a minimum tread run of 6" (152 mm) at the most restrictive point, but this is not always practical or possible Curved stairways with tighter radii and more limited tread run are usually allowed under stair codes. As a guide, the required tread run should be no less than 10" (254 mm) , measured at a point 12"-18" (305-457 mm) from the most restrictive (narrow) side of the stair.

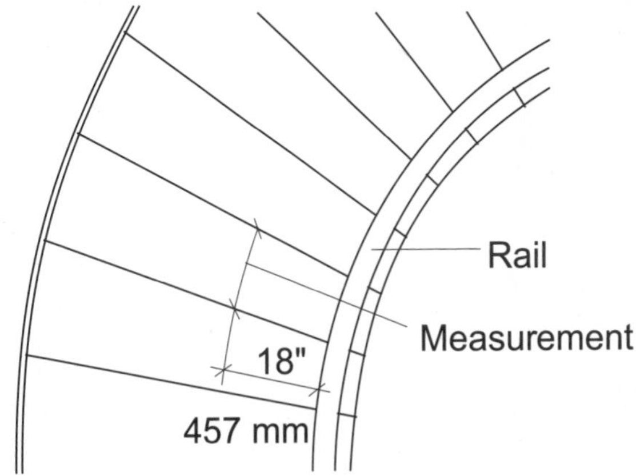

Please consult with the local building department before committing a stair space to design details and project documents.

7 - Stairwork and Rails

FREEDOM OF EXPRESSION

Custom-designed woodwork gives you complete freedom of expression.

• Design flexibility: The use of custom-designed woodwork in a building allows the design professional freedom of expression while meeting the functional needs of the client. A custom-designed building is enhanced by the use of custom-designed woodwork.

• Cost effective: Custom woodwork does compete favorably with mass-produced millwork, and offers practically limitless variations of design and material. Most woodwork lasts the life of the building - quality counts.

• Complete adaptability: By using custom woodwork, the architect or designer can readily conceal plumbing, electrical and other mechanical equipment without compromising the design criteria.

• No restrictions: Custom architectural woodwork permits complete freedom of selection of any of the numerous hardwoods and softwoods available for transparent or opaque finish. Other unique materials available from woodwork manufacturers require no further finishing at all, such as plastic laminates and decorative overlays. These materials can be fashioned into a wide variety of profiles, sizes, and configurations. The owner and design professional have the best of both worlds - high quality and freedom of choice.

• Dimensional flexibility: Since custom woodwork is normally produced by a specialty architectural woodwork firm, dimensions can easily be changed prior to actual fabrication, if required by job conditions. Special situations such as designing for the disabled can readily be accommodated by the custom architectural woodwork manufacturer.

STRAIGHT RUNS

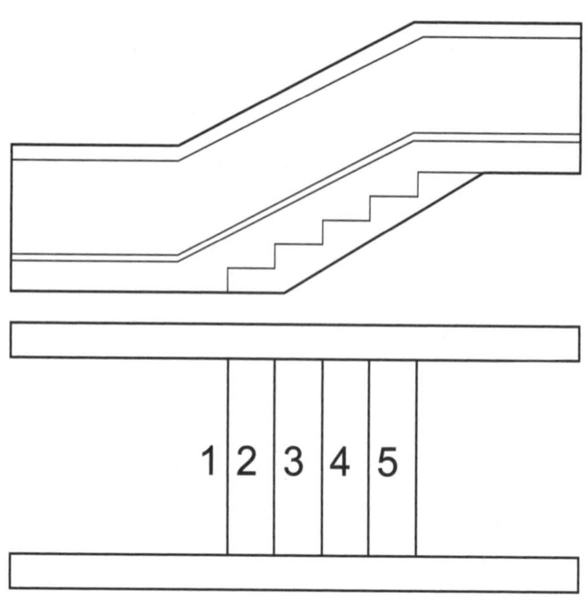

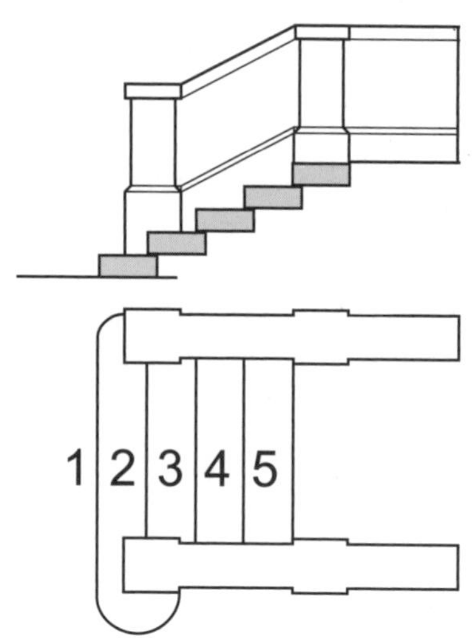

7 - Stairwork and Rails

TURNING RUNS

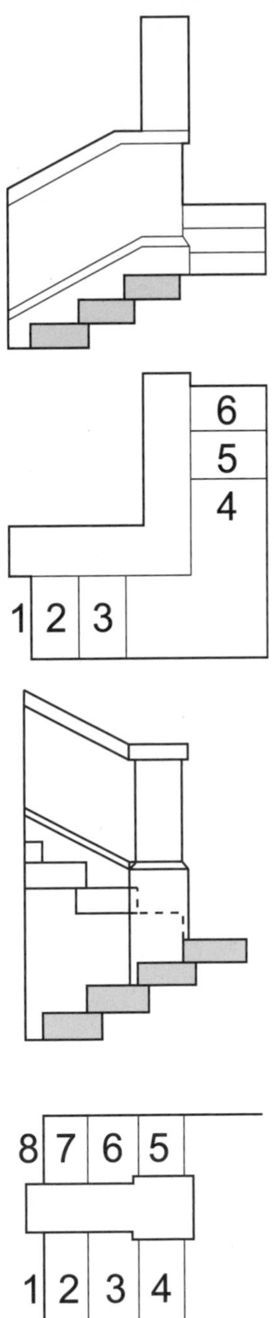

BACKPITCH EXAMPLE

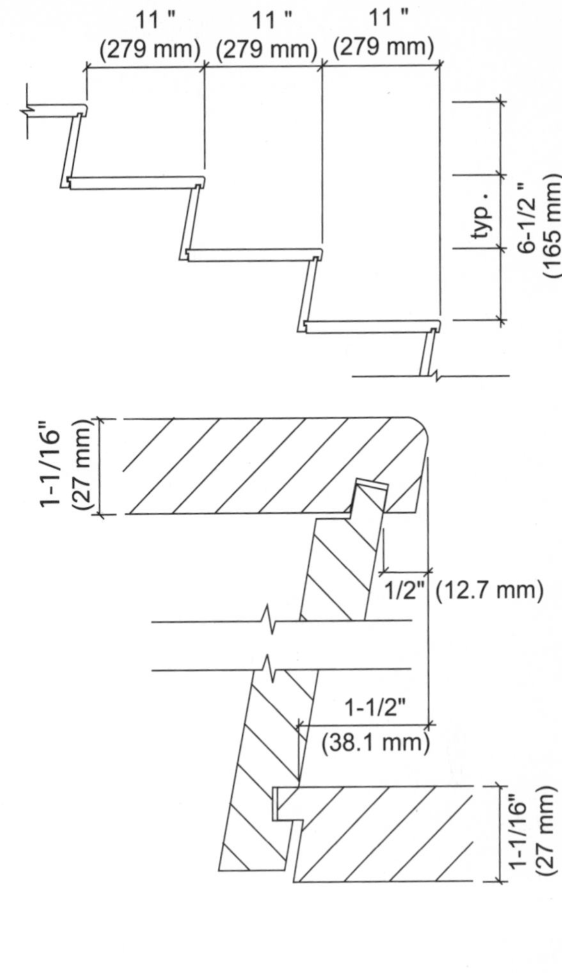

7 - Stairwork and Rails

WINDING RUN

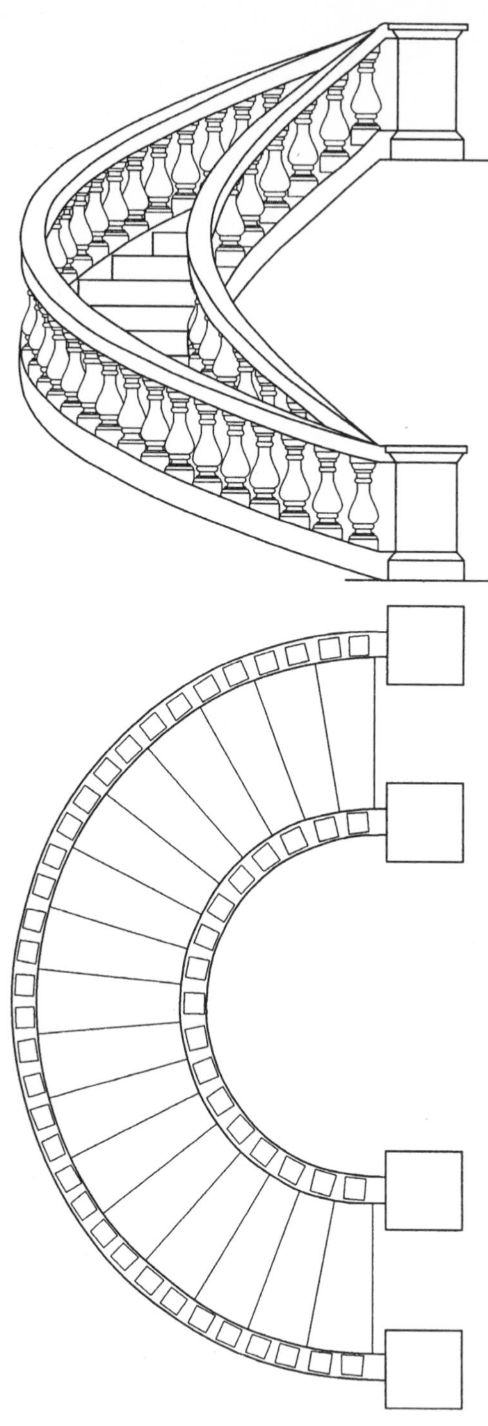

8

Wall Surfacing

8 - Wall Surfacing

Smoothness of Flat and Moulded Surfaces

Planers and Moulders: The smoothness of surfaces that have been machine planed or moulded is determined by the closeness of the knife cuts. The closer the cuts to each other (i.e., the more knife cuts per inch [KCPI]), the closer the ridges, and therefore the smoother the resulting appearance.

Sanding and Abrasives: Surfaces can be further smoothed by sanding. Sandpapers come in grits from coarse to fine and are assigned ascending grit numbers. The coarser the grit, the faster the stock removal. The surface will show the striations caused by the grit. Sanding with finer grit papers will produce smoother surfaces.

Standing and Running Trim

Site-applied cornice, chair rail, base, trim, and mouldings are governed by the areas of the *Architectural Woodwork Standards* covering Standing and Running Trim.

Installation Recommendation

This section does not cover field installation of paneling and doors; however, the methods and skill involved in the installation of paneling and doors in large measure determine the final appearance of the project. The design, detailing, and fabrication should be directed toward achieving installation with a minimum of exposed face fastening. The use of interlocking wood cleats or metal hanging clips combined with accurate furring and shimming will accomplish this. Such hanging of panels has the additional advantage of permitting panel movement that results from humidity changes or building movement. Depending upon local practice, many woodworkers will perform the wall preparation and installation of the paneling and related wood doors.

Finishing Recommendation

This Section does not cover finishing. However, site conditions and air quality regulations for finishing are rarely conducive to good results. Poor lighting, dust-laden air, and techniques available are limiting factors. Depending upon local practice, many woodworkers will factory finish, yielding better results than can be achieved from field finishing. Unless specified in the Contract Documents, the manufacturer is not responsible for the appearance of field finished panels or doors.

Material Selections

Design professionals shall specify the following:

A. Veneers for Transparent Finishes - The Big 5!

1. Species: There are numerous foreign and domestic species available. Involve your woodworker early in the design and selection process.
2. Slicing: Select either plain sliced, quarter sliced, or (in the case of Oak only), rift sliced.
3. Matching of individual leaves: Select either book matched (most appropriate for plain sliced), slip matched (most appropriate for quartered and rift sliced), or random matched (for a rustic look, usually more expensive). Specify end matching for tall elevations.
4. Matching on each panel face: Select either running match, balance match, or center balance match. Specify type of end matching for tall elevations.
5. Matching between panels: Select either no sequence, premanufactured sets - full width, premanufactured sets - selectively reduced in width, sequence matched uniform size set(s), or blueprint matched panels and components.

B. Materials for Opaque Finishes

1. Medium Density Overlay (MDO) - This provides the optimum paintable surface for architectural panels and doors. The thermosetting resin overlay is designed to take and hold paint. Opaque finish sheens above 40 Satin require special manufacturing procedures.
2. Close Grain Hardwood - Extra preparation may be required by the finisher as there may be grain show-through, split veneer joints, and other wood characteristics in this Grade.
3. Mill Option - Face materials are determined by the manufacturer.

C. High Pressure Decorative Laminates (HPDL)

1. Virtually any high pressure decorative laminate color and texture can be used in the manufacture of architectural panels and doors with the following cautions:
2. High gloss HPDL will highlight minor core and surface imperfections, often unacceptably.
3. HPDL panels and doors are not recommended for exterior use due to the potential differentials in humidity between the faces.

Variations in Natural Wood Products

Wood is a natural material, with variations in color, texture, and figure. These variations are influenced by the natural growing process and are uncontrollable by the woodworker. The color of wood within a tree varies between the "sapwood" (the outer layers of the tree which continue to transport sap), which is usually lighter in color than the "heartwood" (the inner layers in which the cells have become filled with natural deposits). Various species produce different grain patterns (figures), which influence the selection process. There will be variations of grain patterns within any selected species. The architectural woodworker cannot select solid lumber cuttings within a species by grain and color in the same manner in which veneers may be selected. Color, texture, and grain variations will occur in the finest architectural woodworking.

Shop Drawings and Engineering

Shop drawings are the means by which the design intent is turned into reality. They shall indicate methods of construction, exact material selections, grain direction(s), methods of attachment and joinery, and exact dimensions. They should also include the woodworker's technical suggestions. Unless specified, sequence of lamination and assembly is determined by the woodworker.

8 - Wall Surfacing

Fire-Retardant Ratings

Fire-Retardant Solid Lumber

The natural fire-retardant qualities and acceptability of treatments vary among the species. Where certain items of architectural woodwork are required to have a flame spread classification to meet applicable building and safety codes, the choice of lumber species must be a consideration. Additional data on various species may be available from U.S. Department of Agriculture Forest Service, Fire Safety of Wood Products Work Unit at (608) 231-9265.

Flame Spread Classification: This is the generally accepted measurement for fire rating of materials. It compares the rate of flame spread on a particular species with the rate of flame spread on untreated Oak.

Most authorities accept the following classes for flame spread:

Class I or A	0-25
Class II or B	26-75
Class III or C	76-200

Fire-Retardant Treatments: Some species may be treated with chemicals to reduce flammability and retard the spread of flame over the surface. This usually involves impregnating the wood, under pressure, with salts suspended in a liquid. The treated wood must be redried prior to fabrication. Consult with your woodworker about the appearance and availability of treated woods prior to specification.

The sizes and species currently being treated (flame spread less than 25), are very limited, and not available in all markets. Fire-retardant treatment does affect the color and finishing characteristics of the wood.

Subject to local codes, untreated wood and wood products can usually be used in up to 10% of an area, according to the traditional model codes:

BOCA - Basic National Building Code

ICBO (UBC) - Uniform Building Code

SBCCI (SBC) - Standard Building Code

NFPA - 101 Life Safety Code

Face veneers are not fire retardant treated, and combining untreated veneers with treated lumber can result in color and finishing contrasts.

Intumescent Coatings for Wood: It is possible to reduce flammability by using intumescent coatings in either opaque or transparent finishes. These are formulated to expand or foam when exposed to high heat, and create an insulating effect that reduces the speed of spread of flame. Improvements are continually being made on these coatings. Consequently, the specifier must ascertain whether they will be permitted under the code governing the project, the relative durability of the finish, and the effect of the coating on the desired color of the finished product.

Finishing of Fire-Retardant-Treated Lumber: Fire-retardant treatments may affect the finishes intended to be used on the wood, particularly if transparent finishes are planned. The compatibility of any finishes should be tested before they are applied.

Built-up Construction to Improve Fire Rating: In lieu of solid lumber, it is often advisable, where a fire rating is required, to build up members by using treated cores clad with untreated veneers not thicker than 1 mm [$^1/_{28}$"]. Existing building codes, except where locally amended, provide that facing materials 1 mm [$^1/_{28}$"] or thinner finished dimension are not considered in determining the flame spread rating of the woodwork.

Fire-Retardant Panel Products

Flame Spread Factors:

A. Core - The fire rating of the core material determines the rating of the assembled panel. Fire-retardant veneered panels must have a fire-retardant core. Particleboard core is available with a Class I (Class A) rating and can be used successfully with veneer or rated high pressure decorative laminate faces. MDF (Medium Density Fiberboard) is available with a fire rating in some markets.

B. Face - Some existing building codes, except where locally amended, provide that facing materials 1 mm [$^1/_{28}$"] or thinner are not considered in determining the flame spread rating of the panel. If state and local codes move toward adoption of the International Building Code provisions, it is possible that the 1 mm [$^1/_{28}$"] exemption may not be available.

Note: The International Code is rapidly replacing the traditional codes. In localities where basic panel building codes have been amended, it is the responsibility of the specifier to determine whether the application of the facing material specified will meet the code.

Face veneers are not required to be fire-retardant treated, and such treatment will adversely affect the finishing process.

If a Class I panel assembly is specified with a decorative laminate face, the fire-rated decorative laminate and the laminate balancing sheet must be applied to a Class I core material (usually particleboard), with the laminate manufacturer's recommended adhesive for rated assemblies.

It is the responsibility of the specifier to indicate what fire-retardant rating, if any, is required for the paneling. In the absence of such a specified rating, the woodworker shall supply unrated paneling.

Types of Veneer Cuts

The manner in which a log segment is cut with relation to the annual rings will determine the appearance of the veneer. When sliced, the individual pieces of veneer, referred to as *leaves*, are kept in the order in which they are sliced, thus permitting a natural grain progression when assembled as veneer faces. The group of leaves from one slicing is called a *flitch,* and is usually identified by a flitch number and the number of gross square feet of veneer it contains.

8 - Wall Surfacing

The faces of the leaves with relation to their position in the log are identified as the *tight face* (toward the outside of the log), and the *loose face* (toward the inside or heart of the log). During slicing the leaf is stressed on the loose face and compressed on the tight face. When this stress is combined with the natural variation in light refraction caused by the pores of the wood, the result is a difference in the human perception of color and tone between tight and loose faces.

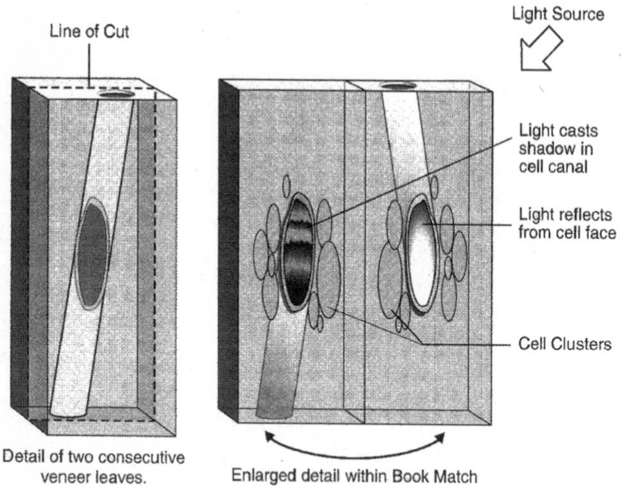

The principal methods of slicing veneers and the general visual characteristics of the grain are:

Plain Slicing (or Flat Slicing)

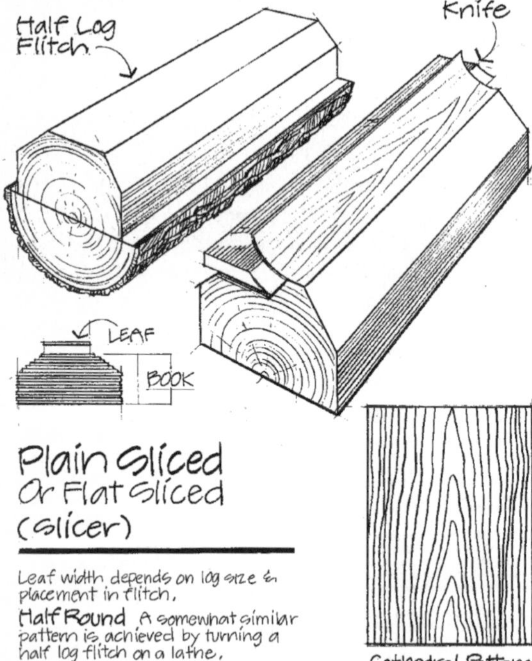

This is the slicing method most often used to produce veneers for high quality architectural woodworking. Slicing is done parallel to a line through the center of the log. A combination of cathedral and straight grain patterns results, with a natural progression of pattern from leaf to leaf.

Plain Slicing (Flat Slicing)

Quarter Slicing (or Quarter Cut)

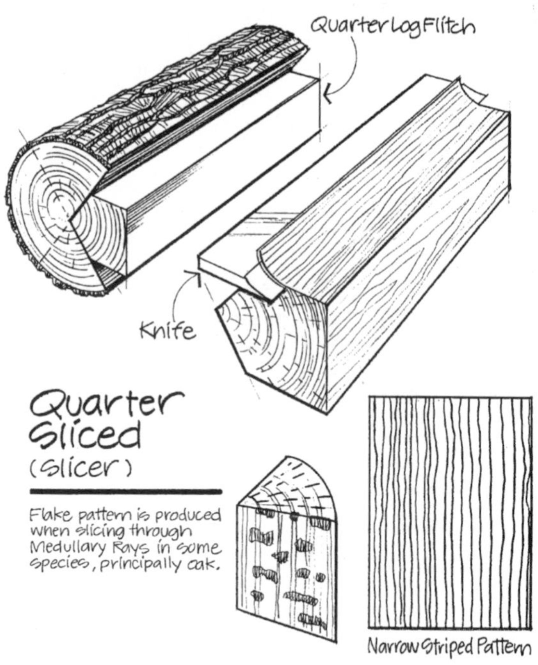

Quarter slicing simulates the quarter sawing process of solid lumber, roughly parallel to a radius line through the log segment. In many species the individual leaves are narrow as a result. A series of stripes is produced, varying in density and thickness from species to species. Flake is a characteristic of this slicing method in Red and White Oak.

8 - Wall Surfacing

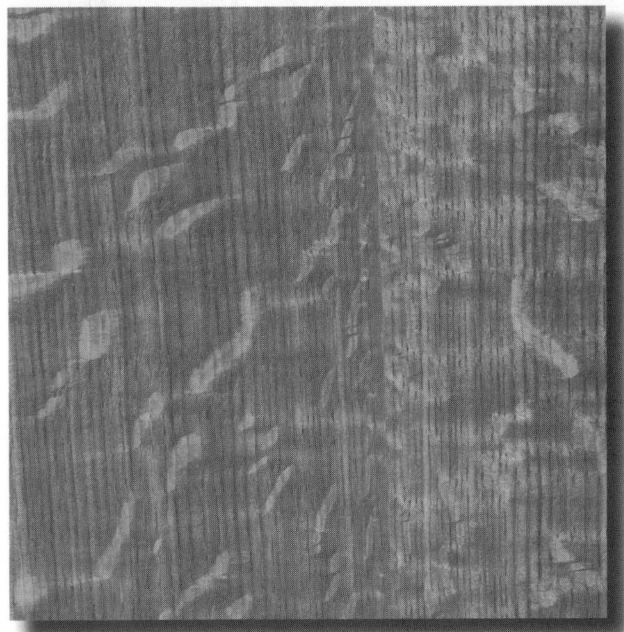

Quarter Slicing (Oak)

Rift Slicing

Rift Slicing (or Rift Cut)

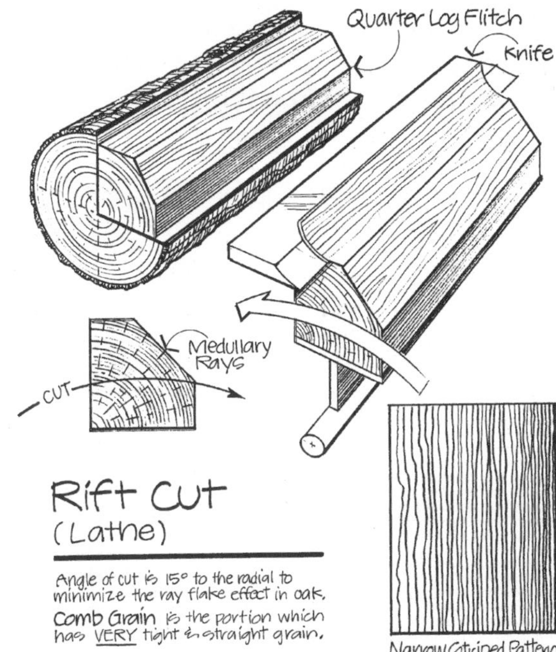

Rift veneers are produced most often in Red and White Oak, rarely in other species. Note that rift veneers and rift sawn solid lumber are produced so differently that a *match* between rift veneers and rift sawn solid lumber is highly unlikely. In both cases the cutting is done slightly off the radius lines minimizing the fleck or flake associated with quarter slicing.

Comb Grain

Limited in availability, comb grain is a select product of the Rift process distinguished by tight, straight grain along the entire length of the veneer. Slight angle in the grain is allowed. Comb grain is restricted to Red and White Oak veneers.

Rotary

Knife

Rotary
(Lathe)

- Wide sheets
- Broad Pattern
- Difficult Matching

Used primarily on Economy or Commercial grades.

Very Broad Pattern

The log is center-mounted on a lathe and *peeled* along the general path of the growth rings like unwinding a roll of paper, providing a generally bold random appearance. Rotary cut veneers may

8 - Wall Surfacing

vary in width and matching at veneer joints is extremely difficult. Almost all softwood veneers are cut this way. Except for a specific design effect, rotary veneers are the least useful in fine architectural woodwork.

NOTE: Rotary sliced fine hardwood veneers are used in a limited way, and usually for special figure and cut, in the manufacture of Premium Grade woodwork. Careful consideration, specification, and communication are recommended when rotary cut is contemplated.

Composite Veneers

Sliced from fast-growing trees, these veneers are dyed and then re-glued in molds to create "grain patterns." The color is established during manufacture because the high percentage of glue-line resists staining by the woodworker. Must be specified by brand name and manufacturer's designation. *Matching* between components may not be possible.

Matching Between Adjacent Veneer Leaves

It is possible to achieve certain visual effects by the manner in which the leaves are arranged. As noted, rotary cut veneers are difficult to match, therefore most matching is done with sliced veneers. The matching of adjacent veneer leaves must be specified. These are the more common types:

Book Matching

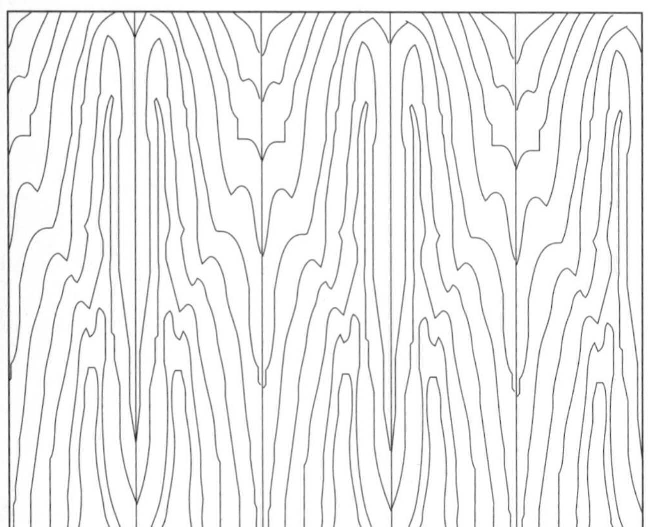

This is the most commonly used match in the industry. Every other piece of veneer is turned over so adjacent pieces (leaves) are "opened" like the pages of a book. and May be used with plain, quarter, or rift sliced veneers.

Visual Effect - Veneer joints match, creating a symmetrical pattern. Book matching yields the maximum continuity of grain. When sequenced panels are specified, prominent characteristics will ascend or descend across the match as the leaves progress from panel to panel.

Barber Pole Effect in Book Match

Because the "tight" and "loose" faces alternate in adjacent pieces of veneer, they may accept stain differently, and this may result in a noticeable color variation. Book matching also accentuates cell polarization, causing the perception of different colors. These natural characteristics are often called barber pole, and are not a manufacturing defect. It is possible, in some instances, to minimize this effect with special finishing techniques.

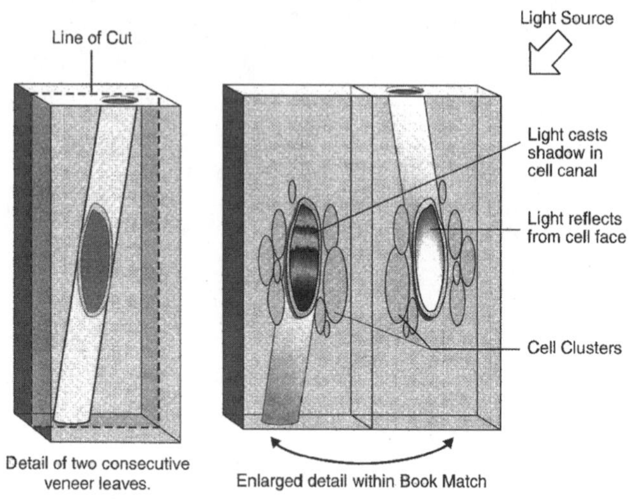

Detail of two consecutive veneer leaves.

Enlarged detail within Book Match

Slip Matching

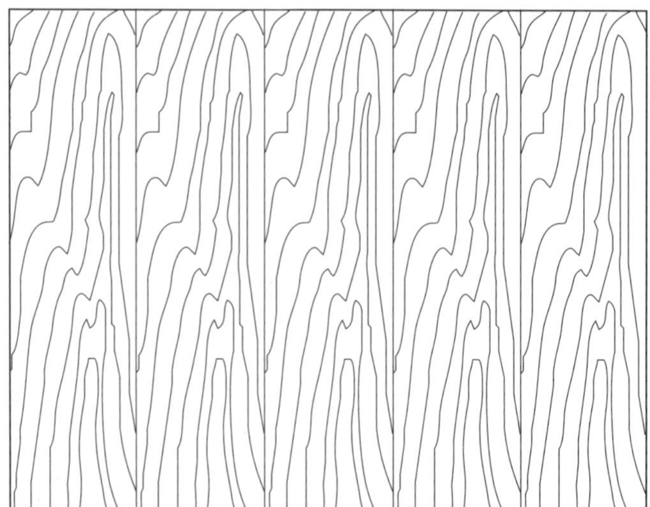

Often used with quarter sliced and rift sliced veneers. Adjoining leaves are placed (slipped out) in sequence without turning, resulting in all the same face sides being exposed.

Visual Effect - Grain figure repeats but joints do not show grain match. When sequenced panels are specified, prominent characteristics will ascend or descend across the match as the leaves progress from panel to panel. The lack of grain match at the joints can be desirable. The relatively straight grain patterns of quartered and rift veneers generally produce pleasing results and a uniformity of color because all faces have the same light refraction.

8 - Wall Surfacing

Random Matching

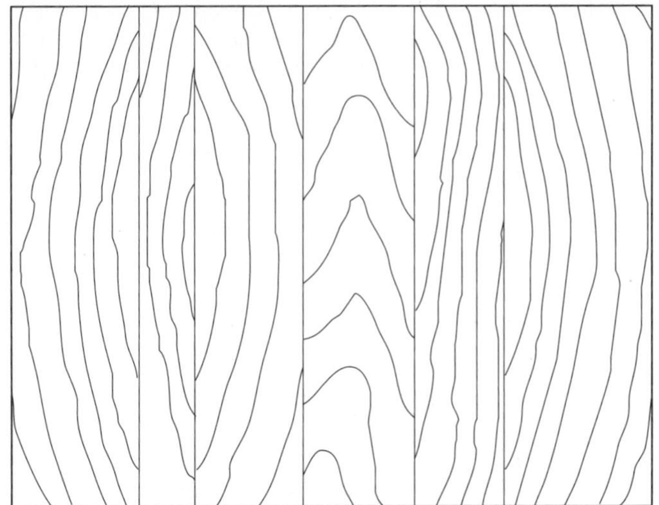

Veneer leaves are placed next to each other in a random order and orientation, producing a "board-by-board" effect in many species.

Visual Effect - Casual or rustic appearance, as though individual boards from a random pile were applied to the product. Conscious effort is made to mismatch grain at joints. Degrees of contrast and variation may change from panel to panel. This match is more difficult to obtain than Book or Slip Match, and must be clearly specified and detailed.

End Matching

Often used to extend the apparent length of available veneers for high wall panels and long conference tables. There are two types of end matching:

A. Architectural End Match. - Leaves are individually book (or slip) matched, first end-to-end and then side-to-side, alternating end and side. (Book and butt match illustrated.)

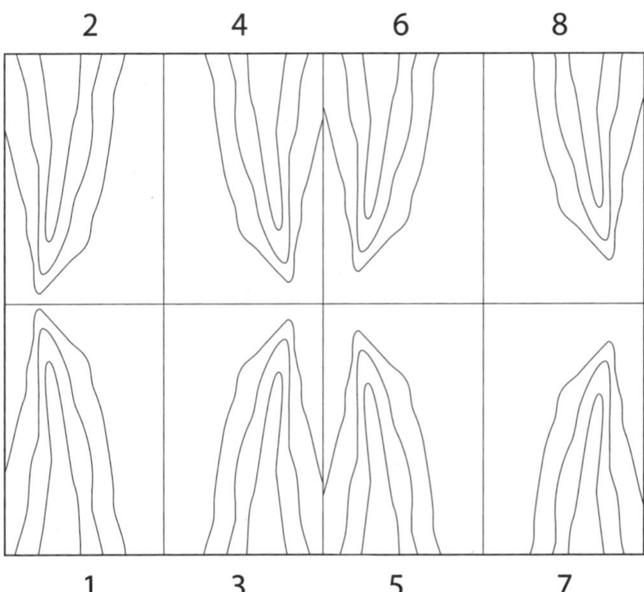

Visual Effect - Yields best continuous grain patterns for length as well as width.

B. Continuous Sequenced Match

Leaves are individually book (or slip) matched, separate panels are stacked in sequenced order, either horizontally or vertically in the elevation (Horizontal sequence illustrated.)

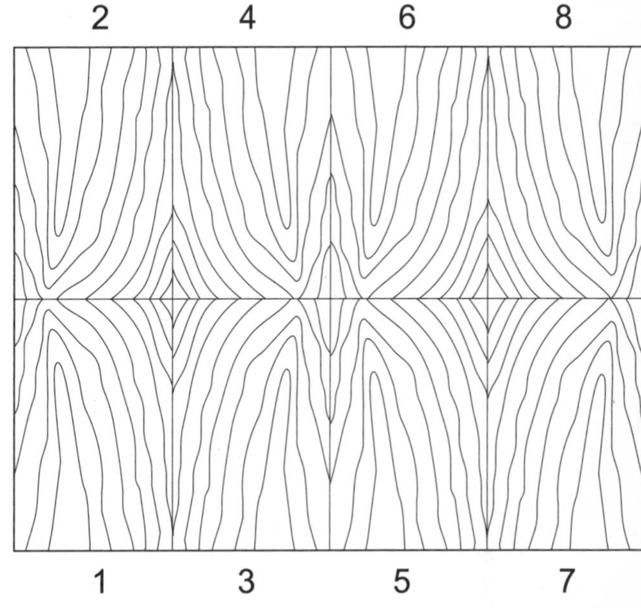

Visual Effect Yields sequenced grain patterns for elevations, with pleasing blend of figure horizontally and vertically.

C. Panel End Match Leaves are book (or slip) matched on panel sub-assemblies, with sequenced sub-assemblies end matched, resulting in some modest cost savings on projects where applicable.

8 - Wall Surfacing

Natural Grain Pattern Mismatch Occurs

Visual Effect - For most species, yields pleasing, blended appearance and grain continuity. Some misalignment of grain pattern will occur, and is not a defect.

Matching within Individual Panel Faces

The individual leaves of veneer in a sliced flitch increase or decrease in width as the slicing progresses. Thus, if a number of panels are manufactured from a particular flitch, the number of veneer leaves per panel face will change as the flitch is utilized. The manner in which these leaves are laid up within the panel requires specification, and are classified as follows:

Running Match

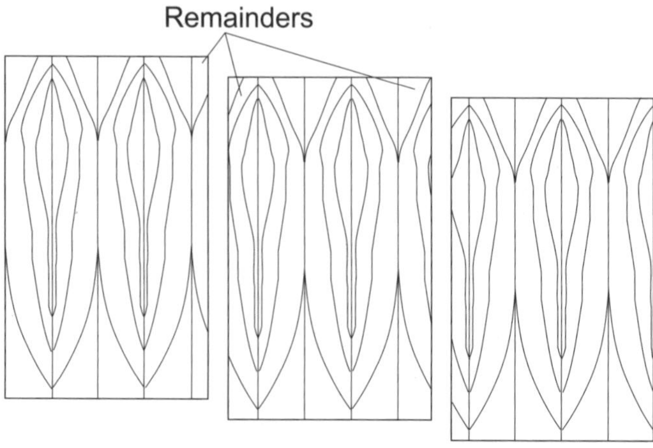

Each panel face is assembled from as many veneer leaves as necessary. This often results in a nonsymmetrical appearance, with some veneer leaves of unequal width. Often the most economical method at the expense of æsthetics, it is the standard for Custom Grade, and must be specified for other grades. Running matches are seldom sequenced and numbered for use as adjacent panels. Horizontal grain match or sequence cannot be expected.

Balance Match

Each panel face is assembled from veneer leaves of uniform width before edge trimming. Panels may contain an even or odd number of leaves, and distribution may change from panel to panel within a sequenced set. While this method is the standard for Premium Grade, it must be specified for other Grades. It is the most common assembly method.

8 - Wall Surfacing

Center Balance Match

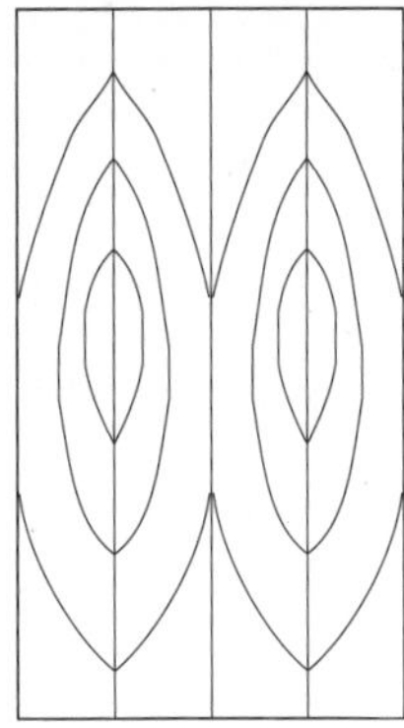
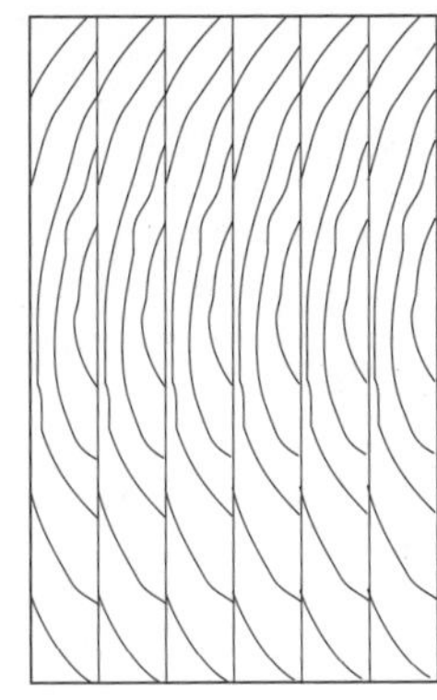
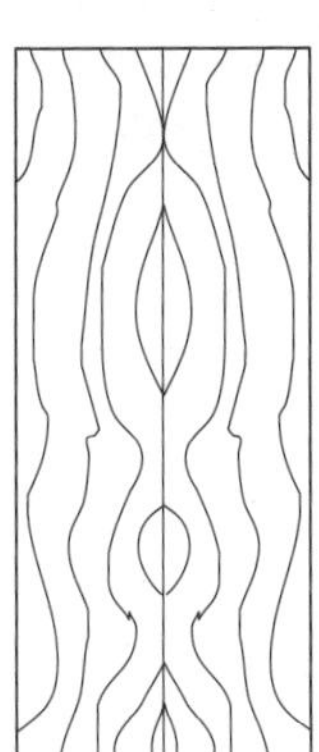

Each panel face is assembled of an even number of veneer leaves of uniform width before edge trimming. Thus, there is a veneer joint in the center of the panel, producing horizontal symmetry. In some instances a small amount of figure is lost in the process. Considered by some to be the most pleasing assembly at a modest increase in cost over Balance Match.

8 - Wall Surfacing

Special Matches

There are regional variations in the names of the following veneer leaf matching techniques. It is strongly recommended the design professional use *both* names and drawings to define the effect desired.

8 Piece Sunburst

Box Match

Reverse or End Grain Box

Herringbone or V-Book Match

Diamond Match

Reverse Diamond Match

Parquet Match

Swing Match

Book & Butt Match w/ Border

8 - Wall Surfacing

Matching of Panels Within an Area

Veneered panels used in casework or paneling in the same area may be matched to each other. This important component of the project must be carefully detailed and specified. The natural growth patterns of the tree will cause the figure on the sequential panels to ascend, descend, or show a grain progression as the eye moves from panel to panel. The four common methods are:

1 - Premanufactured Sets - Full Width

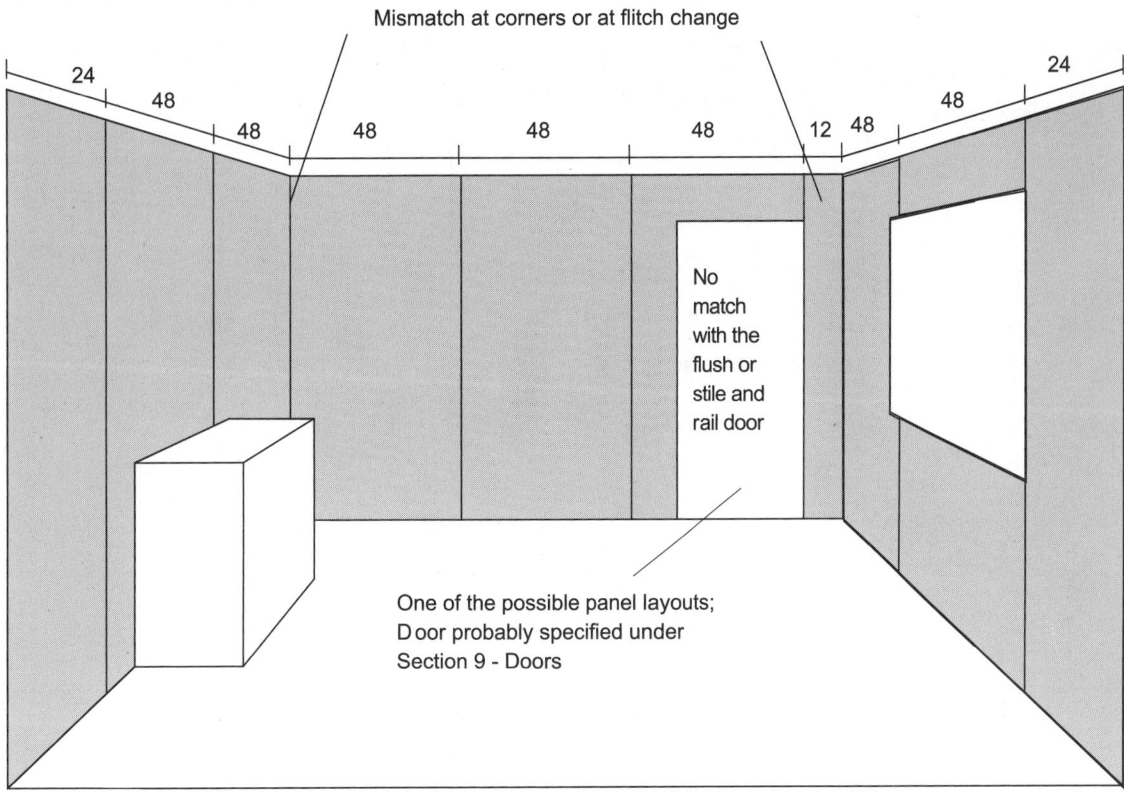

FLOOR PLAN KEY

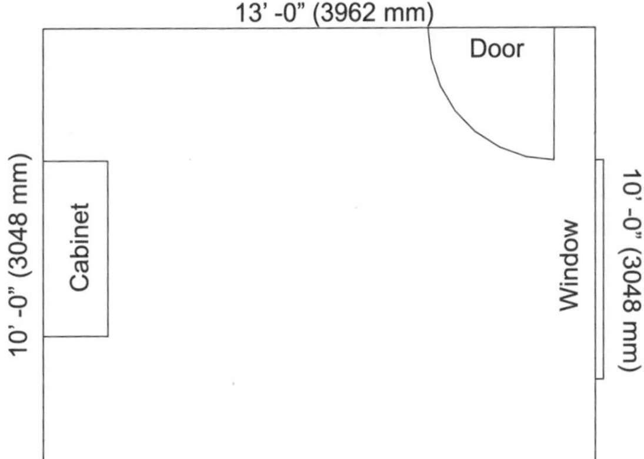

These are one step above stock plywood panels, usually made and warehoused in 4' x 8' (1219 mm x 2032 mm), or 4' x 10' (1219 mm x (2540 mm) sheets in sequenced sets. They may be produced from a single flitch or a part of a flitch, usually varying in number from 6 to 12 panels. If more than one set is required, matching between the sets cannot be expected. Similarly, doors or components often cannot be fabricated from the same flitch materials, resulting in noticeable mismatch. This is often the most economical type of special panel products.

8 - Wall Surfacing

2 - Premanufactured Sets - Selectively Reduced in Width

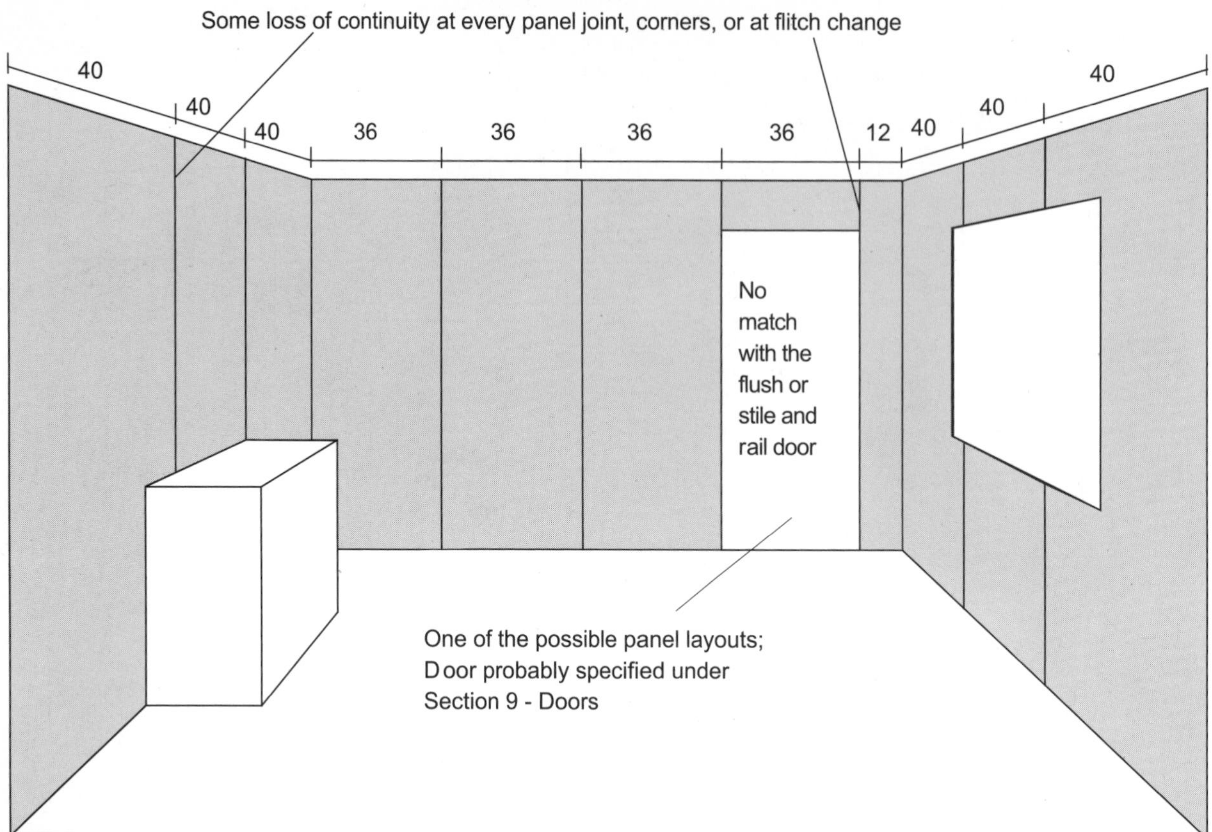

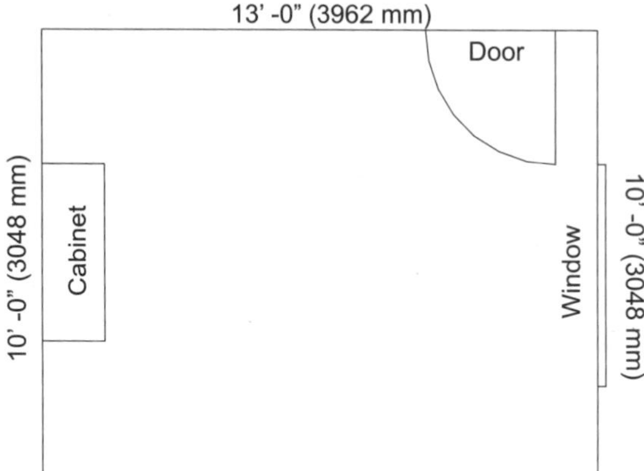

These are panels just like those in the previous illustration, usually made and warehoused in 4' x 8' (1219 mm x 2032 mm), or 4' x 10' (1219 mm x (2540 mm), sheets in sequenced sets. They are often selected for continuity, recut into modular widths, and numbered to achieve the appearance of greater symmetry. If more than one set is required, matching between the sets cannot be expected. Similarly, doors or components often cannot be fabricated from the same flitch materials, resulting in noticeable mismatch.

8 - Wall Surfacing

3 - Sequence Matched Uniform Size Set

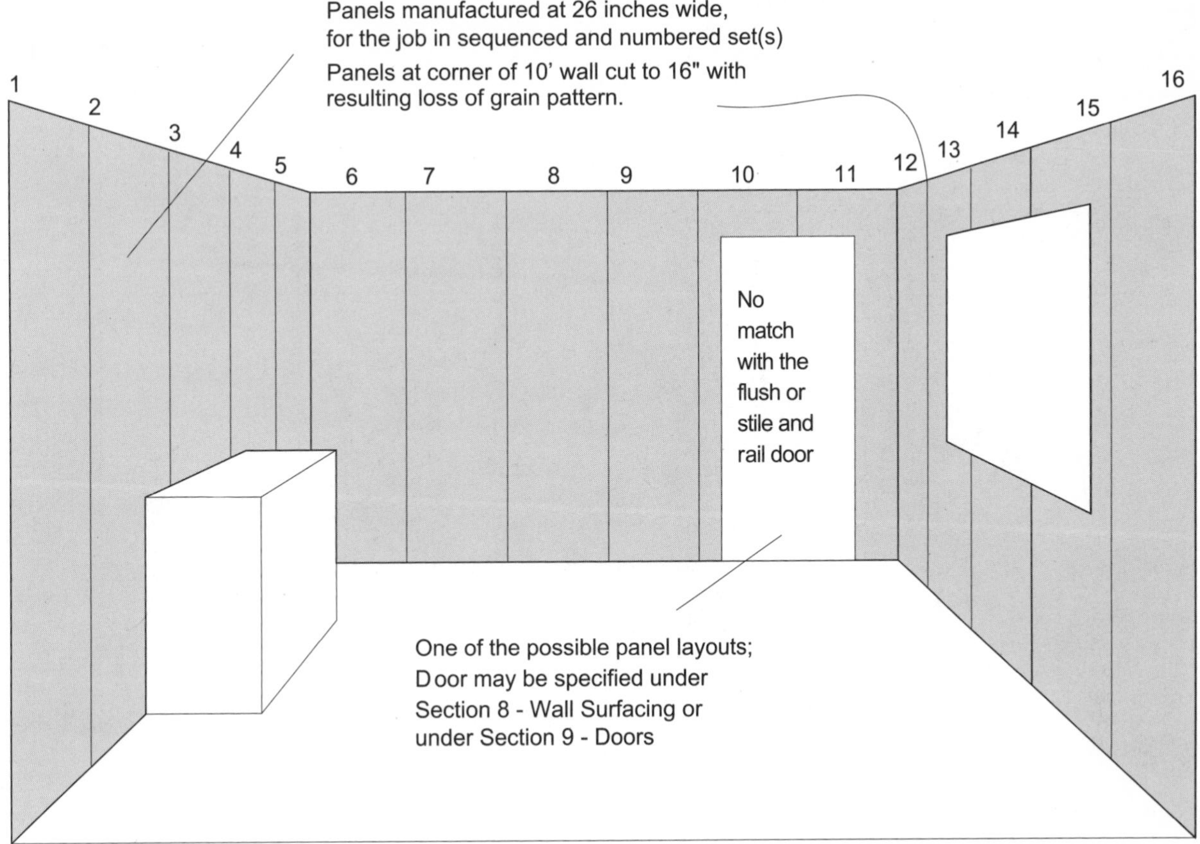

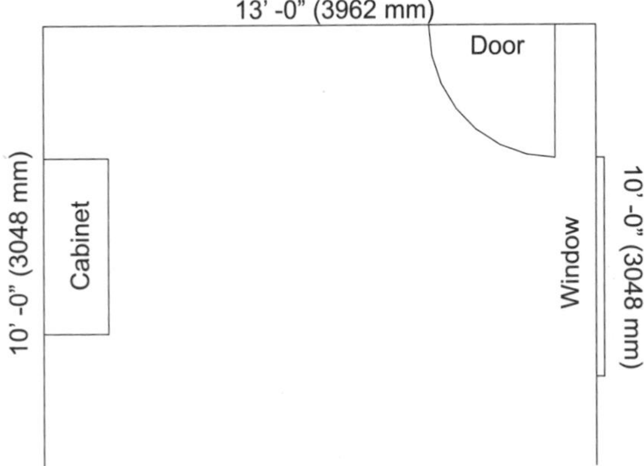

These sets are manufactured for a specific installation to a uniform panel width and height. If more than one flitch is required to produce the required number of panels, similar flitches will be used. This type of panel matching is best used when panel layout is uninterrupted, and when the design permits the use of equal-width panels. Some sequence will be lost if trimming is required to meet field conditions. Doors and components within the wall cannot usually be matched to the panels. Moderate in cost, sequenced uniform panels offer a good compromise between price and aesthetics.

8 - Wall Surfacing

4 - Blueprint Matched Panels and Components

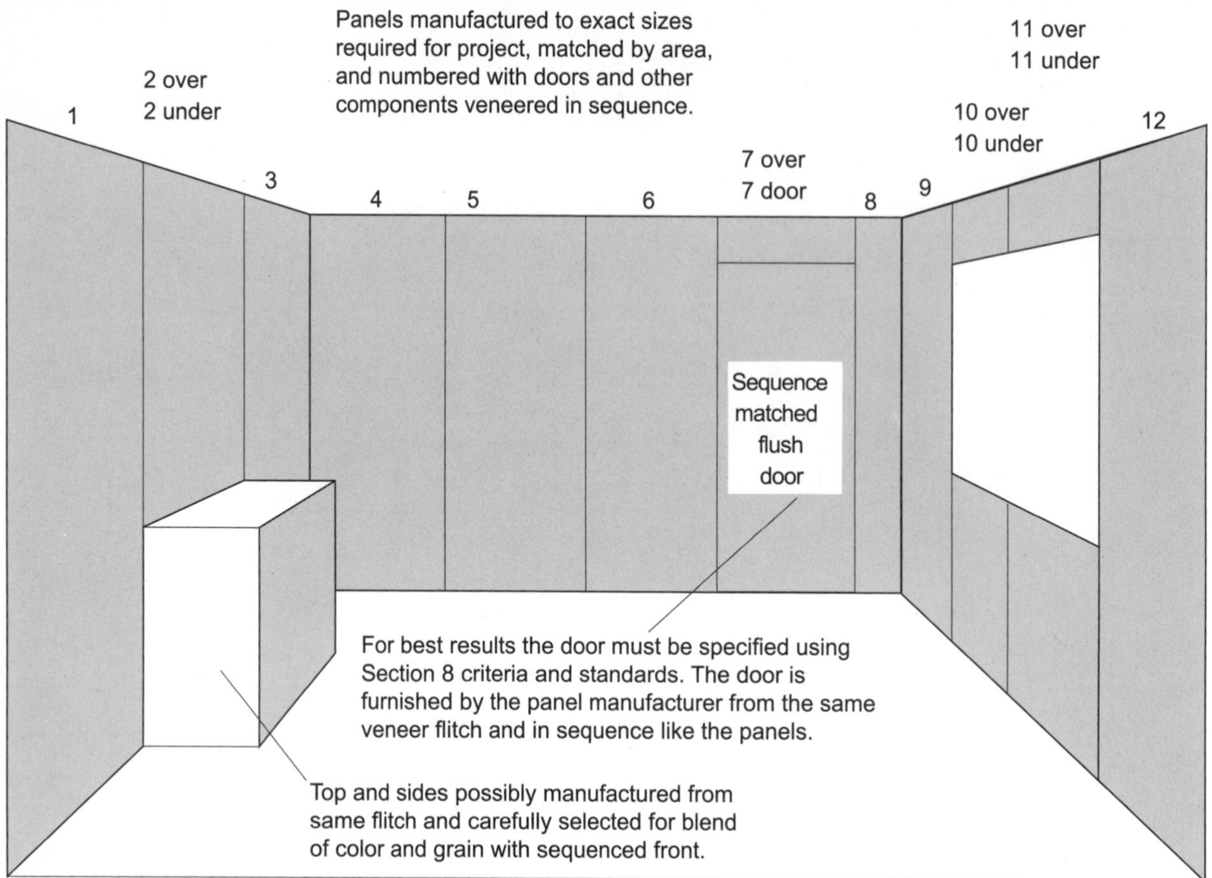

FLOOR PLAN KEY

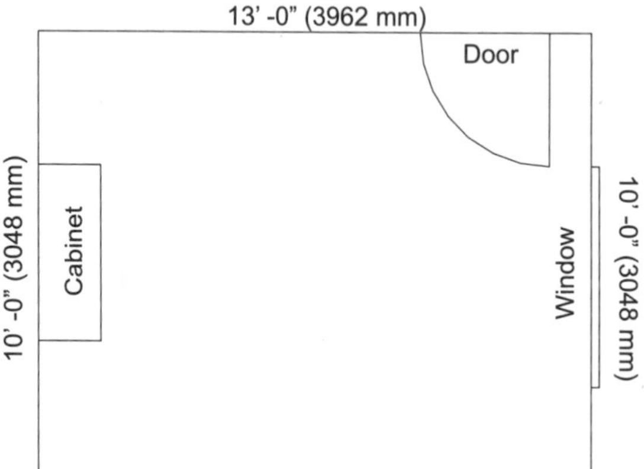

This method of panel matching achieves maximum grain continuity since all panels, doors, and other veneered components are made to the exact sizes required and in exact veneer sequence. If possible, flitches should be selected that will yield sufficient veneer to complete a prescribed area or room. If more than one flitch is needed, flitch transition should be accomplished at the least noticeable, predetermined location. This method requires careful site coordination and relatively long lead times. Panels cannot be manufactured until site conditions can be accurately measured and detailed. This panel matching method is more expensive and expresses veneering in its most impressive manner.

8 - Wall Surfacing

Joints and Transitions

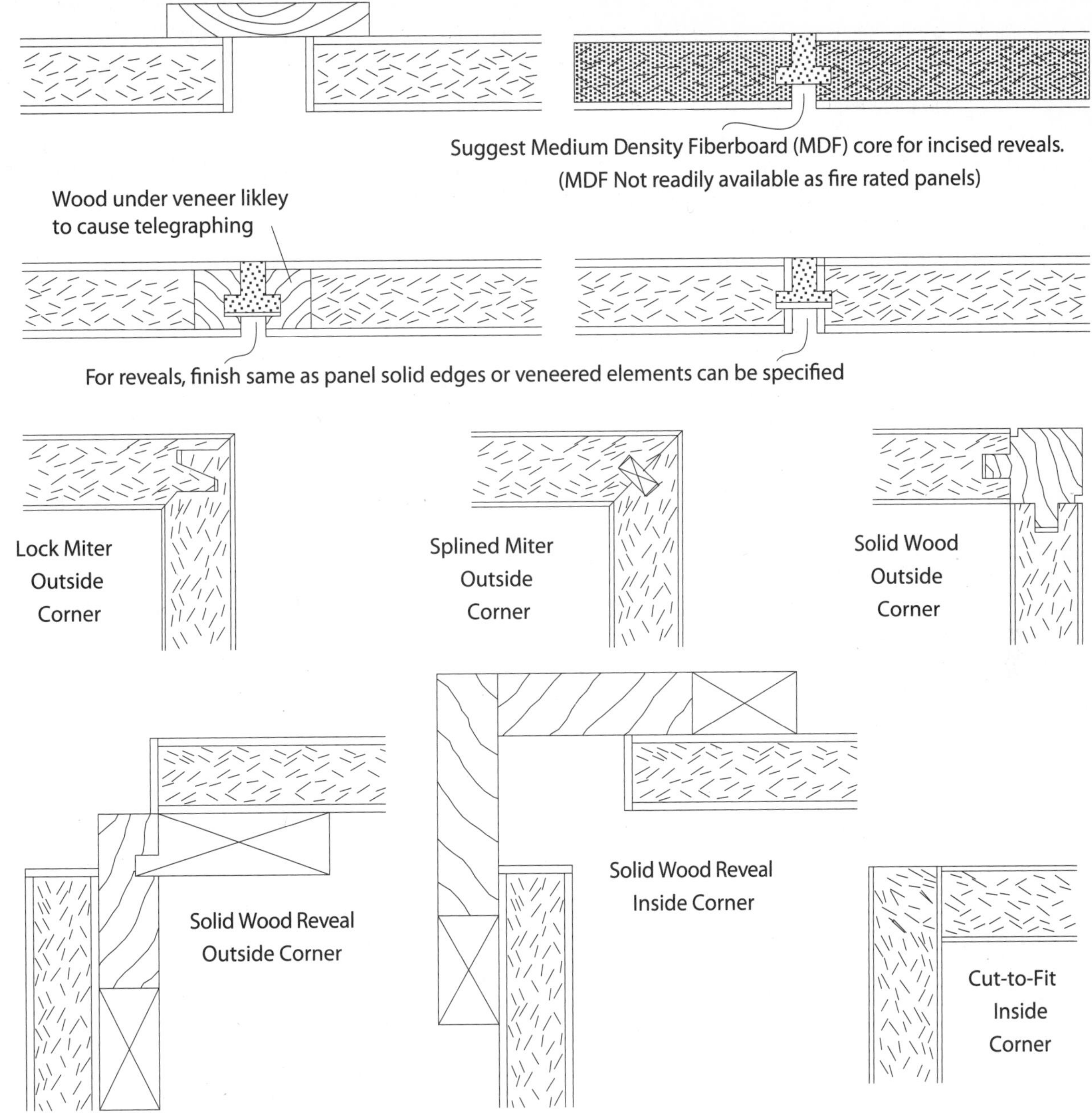

Flitch Selection

NOTE: The architect or designer may choose to see samples of veneer flitches to evaluate color and grain characteristics for other than premanufactured sets. This must be specified. Unless specified, sequence of lamination is determined by the woodworker.

When it is determined that the use of pre-manufactured panel sets is not adequate for the scope of the project, then selecting specific veneer flitches is an option to consider.

When sliced from a log, the individual pieces of veneer are referred to as leaves. These leaves are kept in order as they are sliced and then dried. As the leaves come out of the dryer, the log is literally reassembled. This sliced, dried and reassembled log or parital log is called a flitch. The flitch is given a number and the gross square footage of the flitch is tallied.

To select specific veneer flitches for a project:

1. Determine the net square footage of face veneer required for the project. This should include paneling, casework, built-in furniture items, and when specifying a sequence to a blueprint matched project, the flush doors.

8 - Wall Surfacing

2. Multiply the net square footage times three (this is the average ratio. Some species require a higher multiplier). Example: 5,000 (net square feet) x 3 = 15,000 square feet; this is the gross square footage that should be sampled for this project.

While this may sound like a daunting quantity of veneer to look through, there is an established process that simplifies the task. When a numbered flitch is sampled, typically, three leaves of veneer are removed from the flitch and numbered sequentially. Starting from the top of the flitch, a leaf is removed from one-third of the way down, then from one-half, and then from two-thirds down in the flitch. These three sequentially numbered leaves of veneer form a representative sample of that flitch.

3. To view a sampling of veneer that will meet the project needs, one should request samples from numbered flitches, that will represent thirty to forty-five thousand square feet of veneer. This means that if the average size of the flitches which are sampled is 2,500 square feet, there will be about 36 to 54 leaves of veneer, representing 12 to 18 flitches of architectural quality veneers.

Since it will take at least 6 flitches, with a gross square footage of 2500 square feet, to meet the project needs, give careful consideration to the following key criteria:

Length - Is the length adequate for the requirements?

Width - What will the net yield for width be from each flitch?

Gross square footage of each flitch - total yield must be 15,000 square feet

Color and grain compatibility - While exact matching is not possible, from flitch to flitch, this is the opportunity to select the range of color and grain compatibility that will enhance the visual continuity of the entire project.

NOTE: The reality of this process is that the square footage of individual flitches of veneer will probably range from 1,200 square feet up to 3,000 square feet. This means that one may end up selecting 9 or 10 flitches, instead of just 6. But the goal remains the same as in the example: selecting flitches that will satisfy the æsthetic needs, while fulfilling the face veneer requirements for the project.

It is recommended that specifications be written with the foregoing objective in mind. Then, when the project has been awarded to a qualified woodworker, talk directly to the woodworker and be involved in one of the most exciting aspects of bringing the design concepts to reality.

Stile and Rail Paneling

Flat or raised panels with wood veneer faces or of solid lumber, combined with stiles and rails. Design may encompass face application of mouldings. Joints between panels, stiles, rails, and other members to be as designed for functional or decorative purposes.

(Appendix B is not part of the AWS for compliance purposes)

8 - Wall Surfacing

Veneered stile and rail with concealed stile and rail edges and panel rim

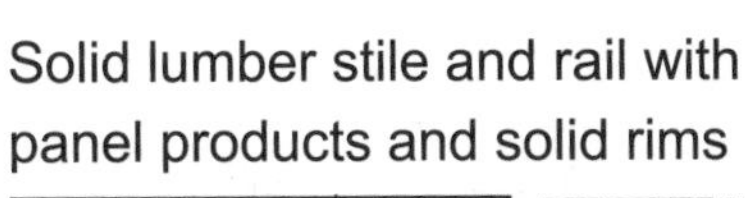

Likely to cause telegraphing through face veneer at lumber joint

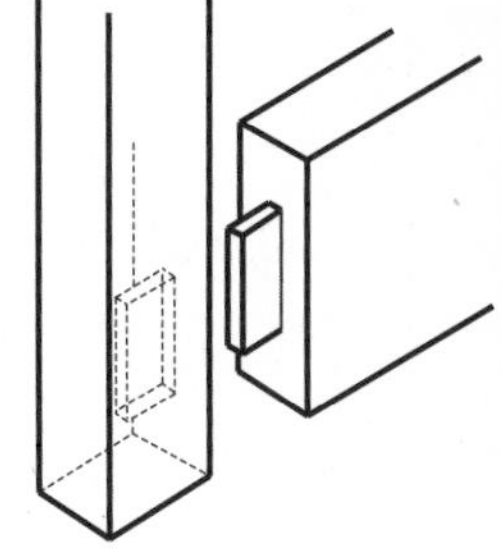

Mortise and Tenon construction

Solid lumber stile and rail with panel products and solid rims

Solid stile and rail with lip moulding and panel product with solid rim

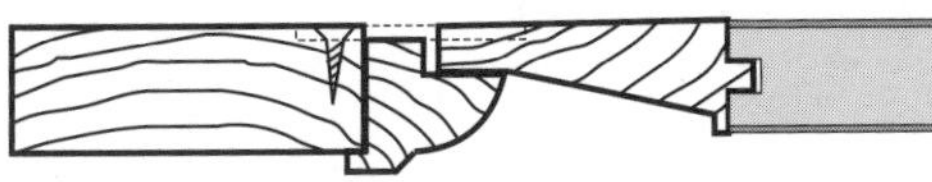

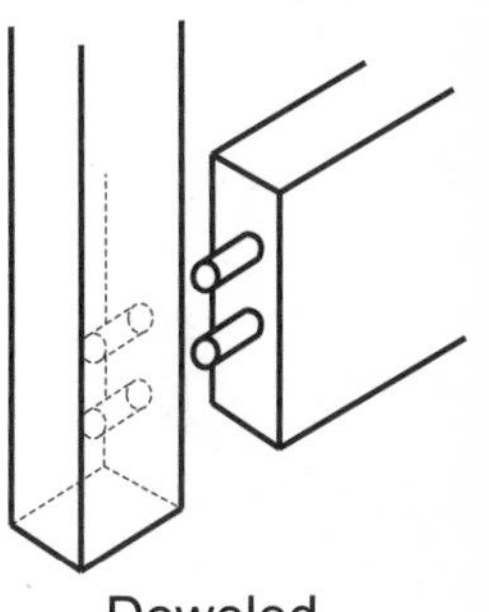

Doweled construction

Medium density fiberboard (MDF) for stiles, rails and panels

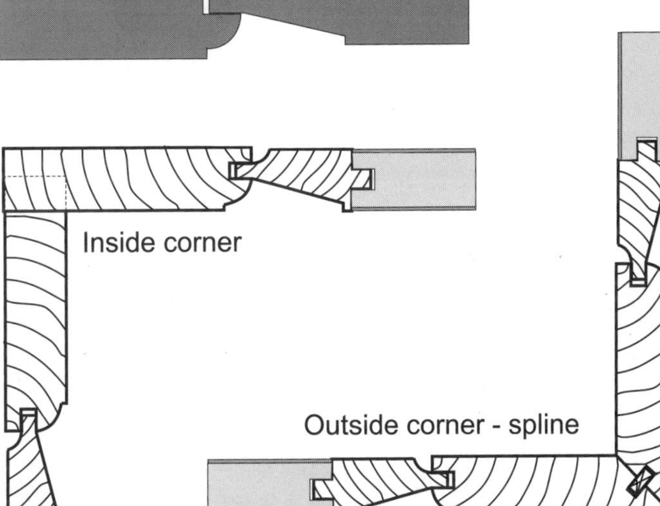

Inside corner

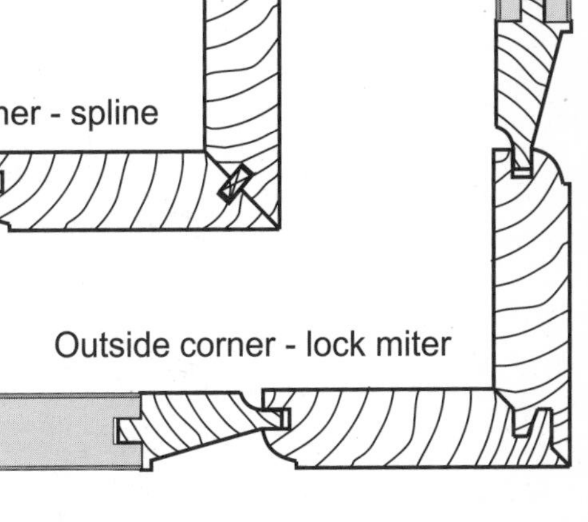

Outside corner - spline

Outside corner - lock miter

8 - Wall Surfacing

Freedom of Expression

Custom-designed woodwork gives you complete freedom of expression.

• Design flexibility: The use of custom-designed woodwork in a building allows the design professional freedom of expression while meeting the functional needs of the client. A custom-designed building is enhanced by the use of custom-designed woodwork.

• Cost effective: Custom woodwork does compete favorably with mass-produced millwork, and offers practically limitless variations of design and material. Most woodwork lasts the life of the building – quality counts.

• Complete adaptability: By using custom woodwork, the architect or designer can readily conceal plumbing, electrical and other mechanical equipment without compromising the design criteria.

• No restrictions: Custom architectural woodwork permits complete freedom of selection of any of the numerous hardwoods and softwoods available for transparent or opaque finish. Other unique materials available from woodwork manufacturers require no further finishing at all, such as plastic laminates and decorative overlays. These materials can be fashioned into a wide variety of profiles, sizes, and configurations. The owner and design professional have the best of both worlds – high quality and freedom of choice.

• Dimensional flexibility: Since custom woodwork is normally produced by a specialty architectural woodwork firm, dimensions can easily be changed prior to actual fabrication, if required by job conditions. Special situations such as designing for the disabled can readily be accommodated by the custom architectural woodwork manufacturer.

• Quality assurance: Adherence to the *AWS* and specifications will provide the design professional a quality product at a competitive price.

8 - Wall Surfacing

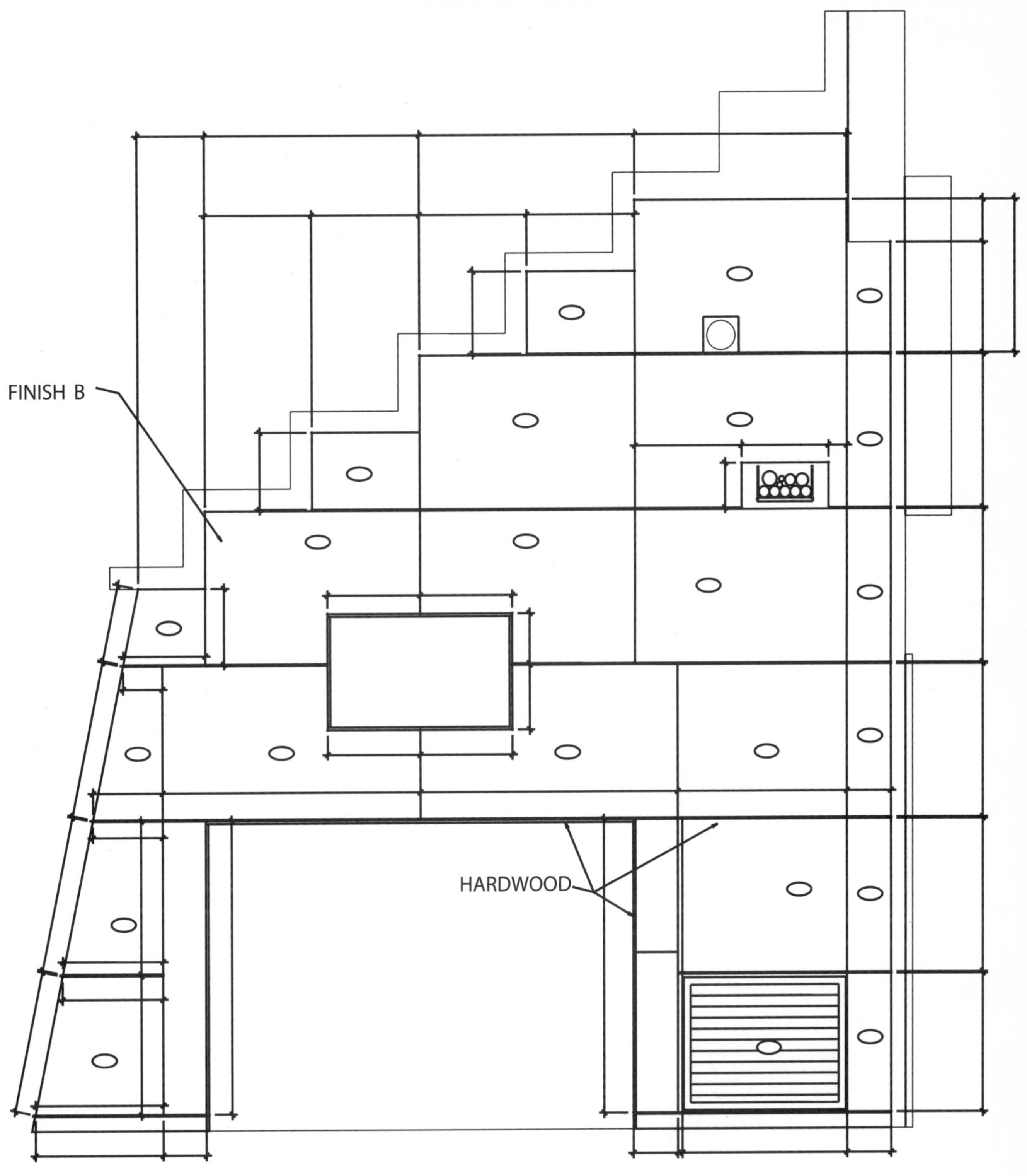

8 - Wall Surfacing

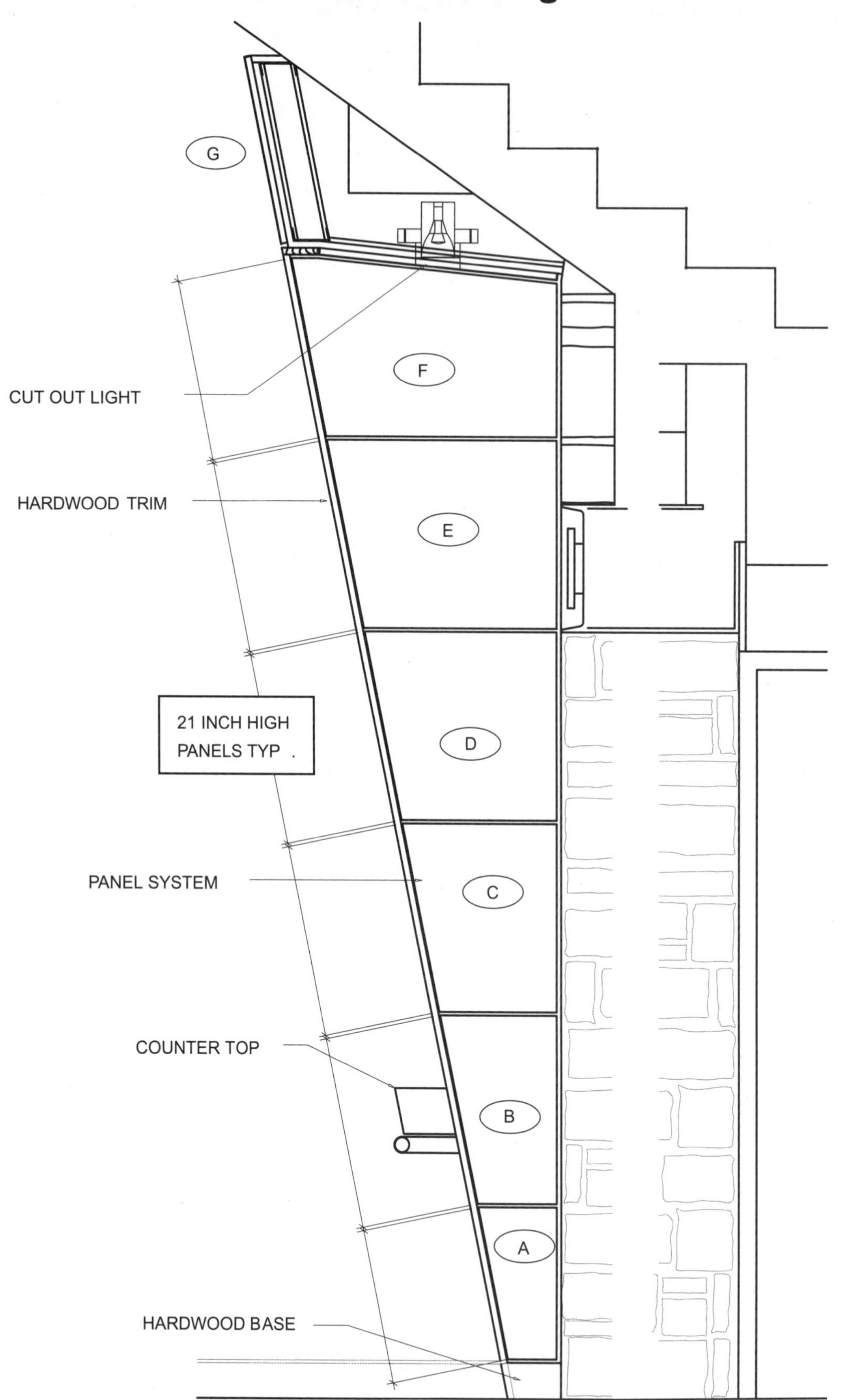

8 - Wall Surfacing

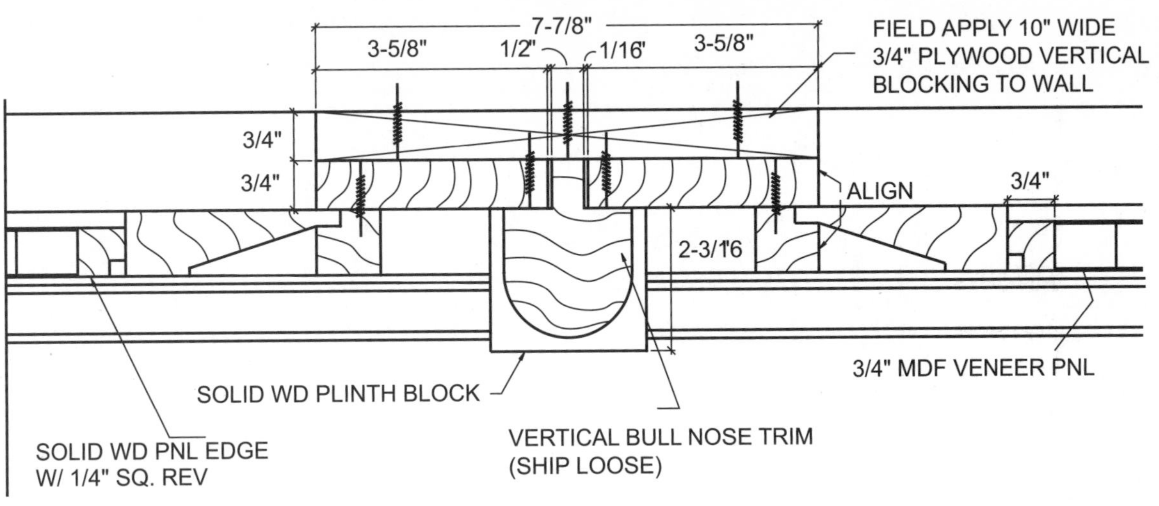

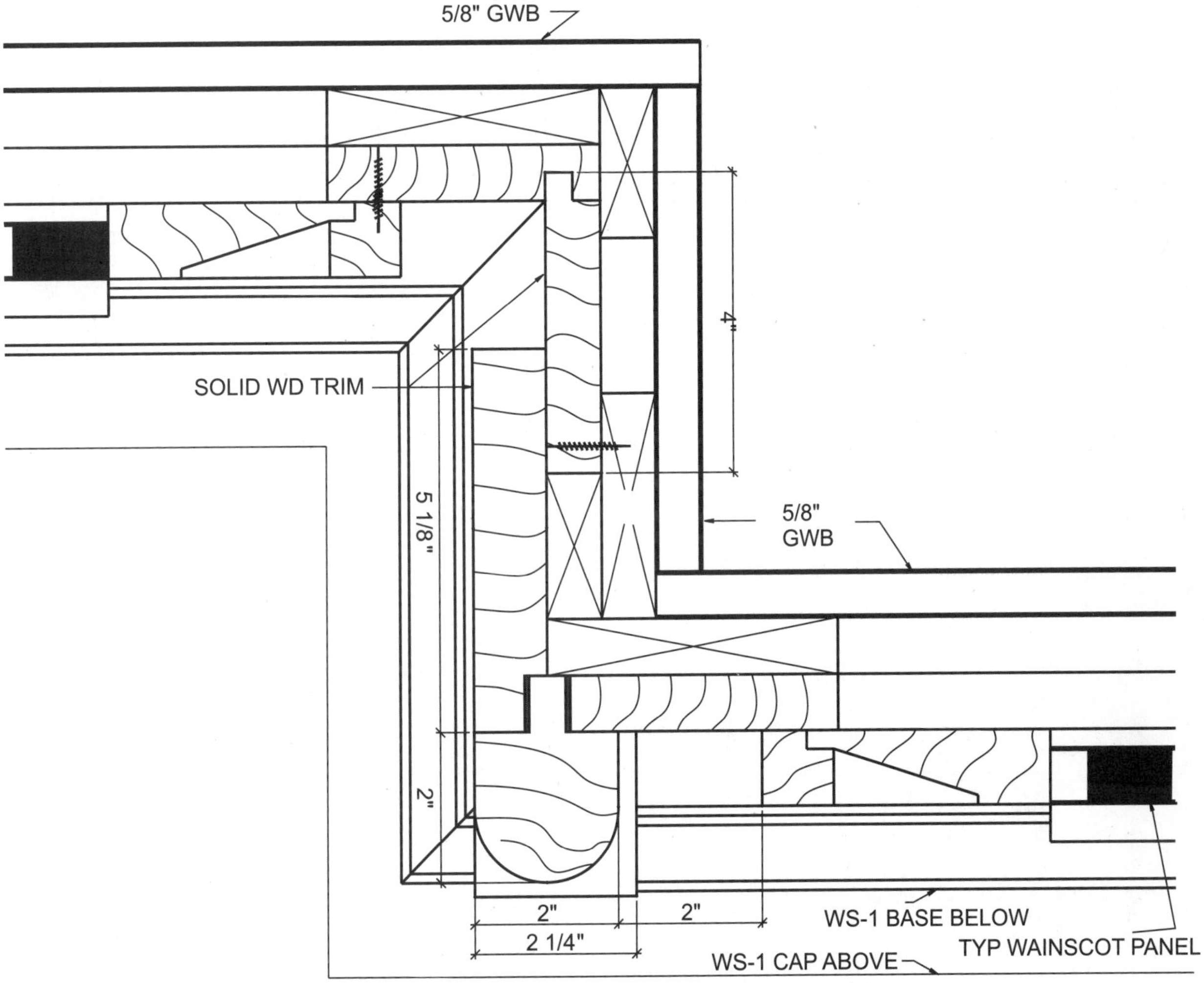

5/8" GWB

4"

SOLID WD TRIM

5 1/8"

5/8"
GWB

2"

2"

2"

2 1/4"

WS-1 BASE BELOW

TYP WAINSCOT PANEL

WS-1 CAP ABOVE

8 - Wall Surfacing

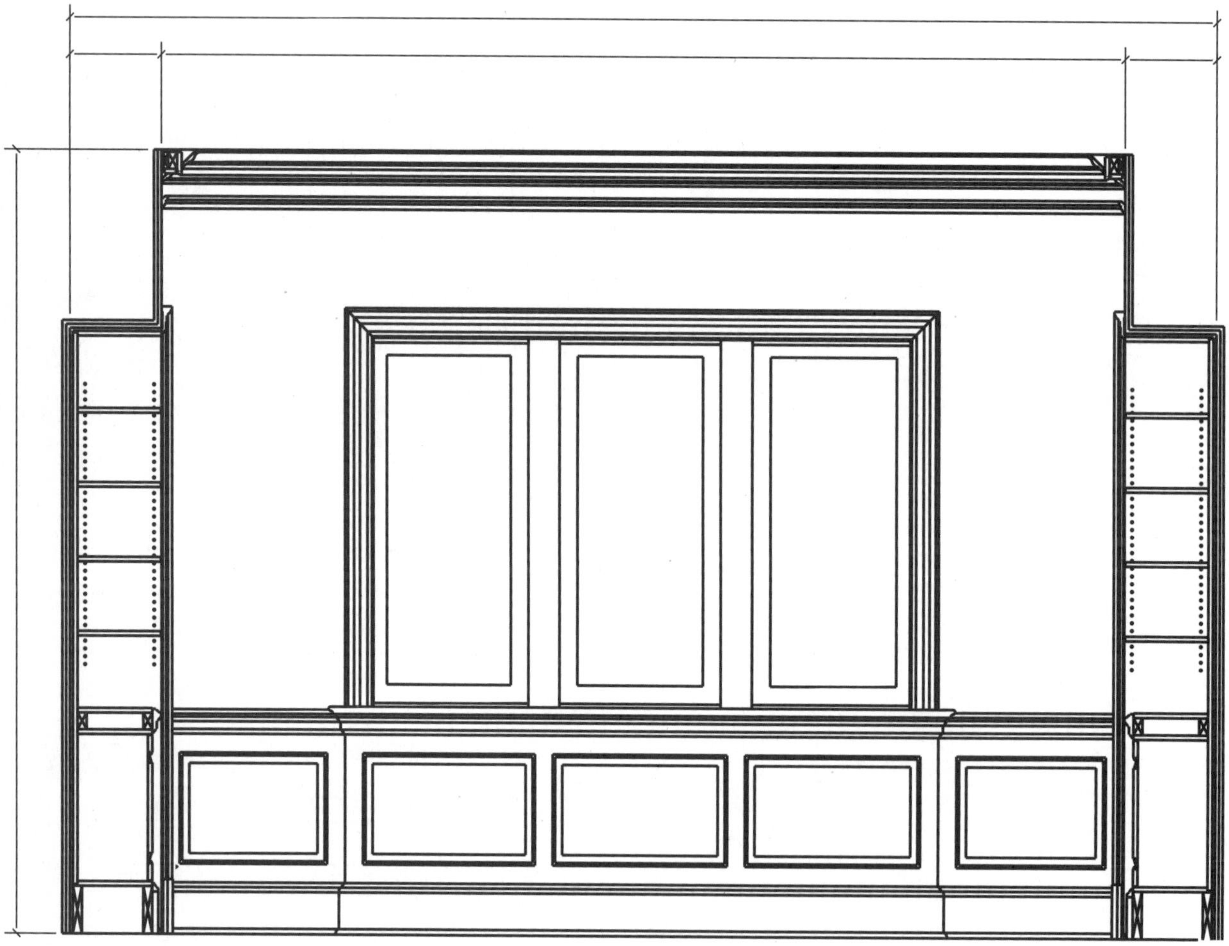

8 - Wall Surfacing

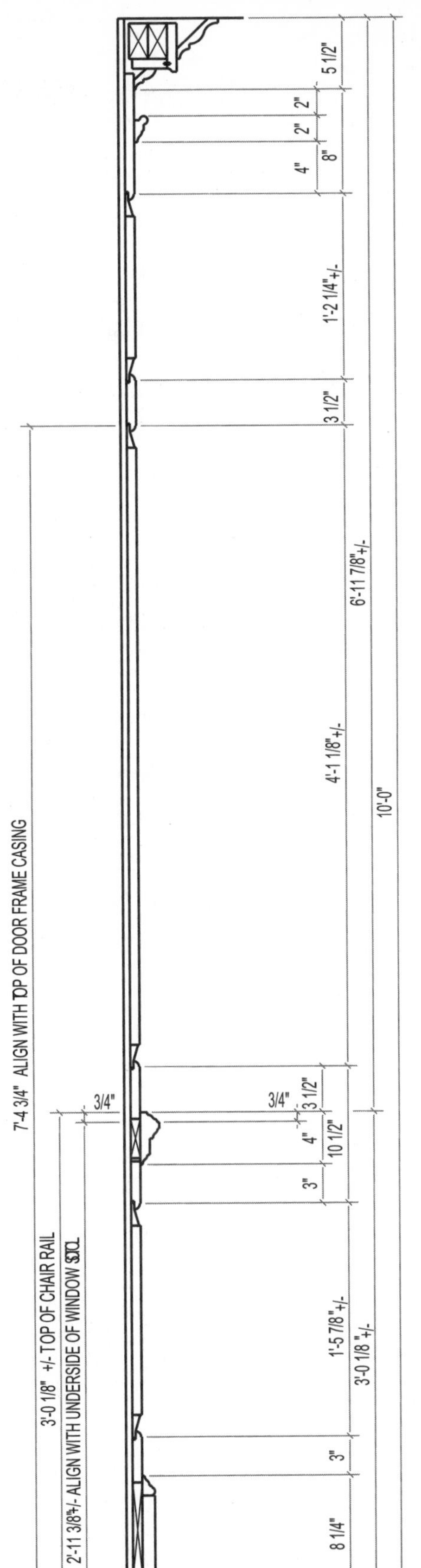

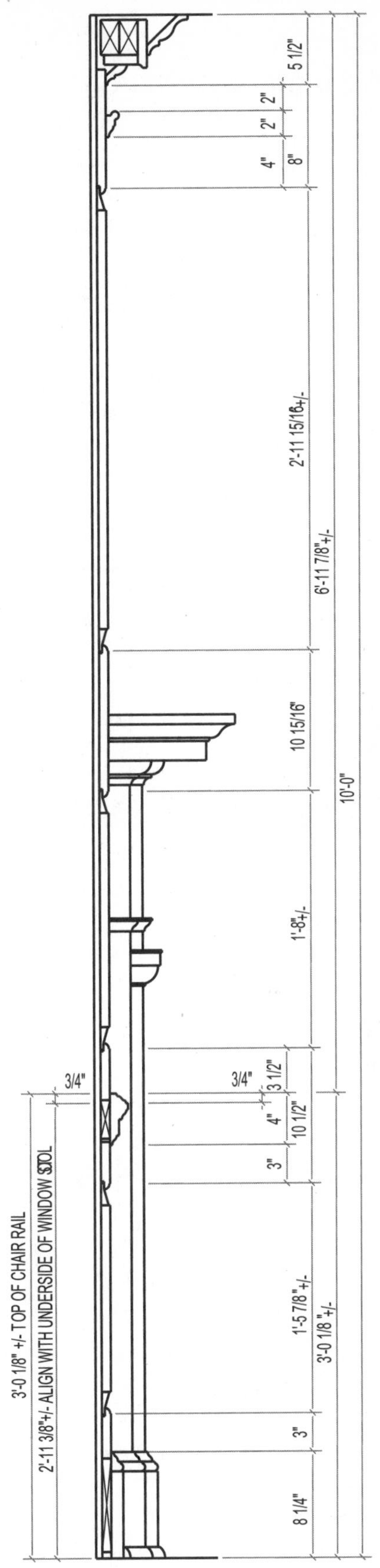

8 - Wall Surfacing

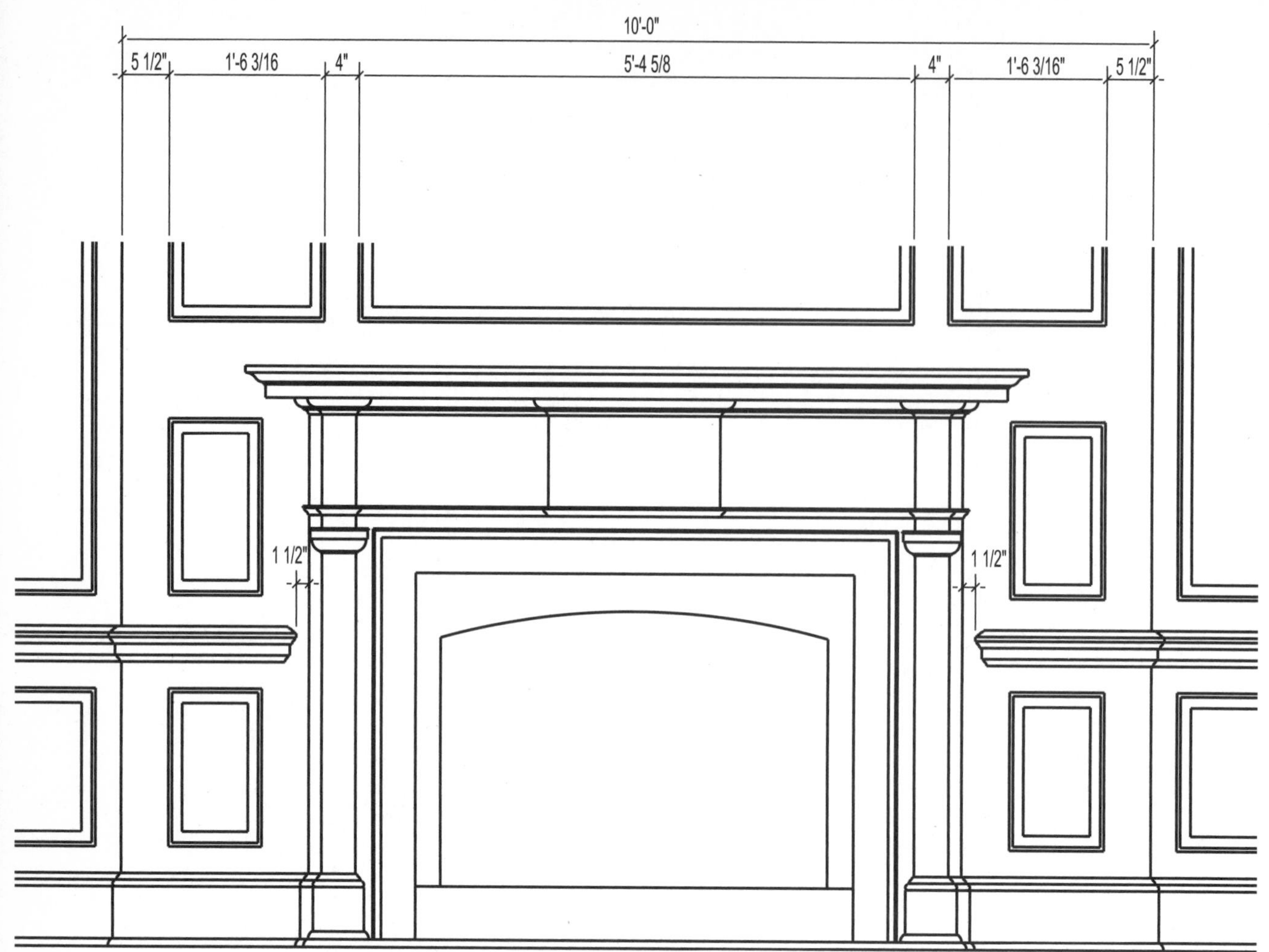

9
Wood Doors

9 - Wood Doors

EXTERIOR DOORS

Wood doors are not recommended for exterior use. Most flush doors no longer have extended exterior use warranties and most have no warranty at all. Refer to manufacturers' written warranty for specifics.

Exterior doors shall be water repellent treated at the factory after manufacturing. Protect doors according to manufacturers' requirements, which may include flashing of top, bottom and cut outs.

Wood doors shall be protected from the sun and other weather elements by overhangs, deep recesses, etc.

Medium density overlay faced doors shall be used for severe exposure conditions.

All surfaces of exterior doors shall be primed with an exterior enamel primer, followed by a minimum of two additional coats of exterior enamel on all surfaces.

CODE and RULE REQUIREMENTS

The design professional shall be responsible for contract documents which clearly detail products which will comply with applicable codes and rules including, but not limited to, NFPA 80 requirements; ADA national and federal guidelines; local, state, and federal building codes; positive pressure requirements and labeling; glass or glazing; prefitting and/or machining for hardware; prehanging and/or machining for weatherstripping; priming, sealing and/or transparent finishing; and flashing and/or metal edge guards. The door manufacturer is often a valuable assistant in these matters.

Contract documents shall:

- Specify neutral pressure or positive pressure compliance.
- If positive pressure, specify the category of door: A or B assembly.
- Specify whether the smoke and draft label (S label) is validated or not.

FACE MATERIAL SELECTION

The panel face veneer standards of the Hardwood Plywood & Veneer Association HP-1, latest edition, is adopted as the minimum standard for face veneers.

Specifiers need to determine and specify the following:

VENEERS FOR TRANSPARENT FINISHES

SPECIES: There are numerous foreign and domestic species available. Involve your member woodworker early in the design and selection process.

MATCHING: Many different visual effects can be obtained by face veneer matching.

Appearance and layout of individual pieces of veneer

Matching between pieces (leaves) of veneer

Orientation of spliced veneer on a door face

Appearance of doors in pairs or sets

Appearance of doors with transoms

MATERIALS FOR OPAQUE FINISHES

Medium Density Overlay. This provides the optimum paintable surface for architectural doors. The resin saturated paper overlay is designed to paint well and provide an even sheen.

Close Grain Hardwood. Extra preparation will be required by the finisher as there will be grain show-through, open-appearing veneer joints, and other wood characteristics when using this product for a painted finish.

Mill Option. Face materials are determined by the manufacturer.

HIGH PRESSURE DECORATIVE LAMINATES (HPDL)

Virtually any high pressure decorative laminate color and texture can be used in the manufacture of architectural doors with the following cautions:

• High gloss and Vertical Grades of HPDL will highlight minor core and surface imperfections, often unacceptably.

• HPDL doors are not recommended for exterior use due to the potential differences in lineal expansion between the faces and wood components when exposed to the elements.

CORE CONSTRUCTION

The design professional or specification writer has the opportunity to select the door core type. In the absence of specification, particle core (PC) shall be furnished, complying with particleboard standard ANSI A208.1 Particleboard, Grade LD-1 or LD-2. If a specific grade of particleboard is desired, it must be specified. When not specified the manufacturer has the option to use either LD-1 or LD-2 particleboard as core material.

BASIC CORE TYPES

The five most common core types are particleboard core, stave lumber (glued block) core (SLC), structural composite lumber core (SCLC), hollow core, and fire-resistant door core.

Specify one, or a combination of, solid core, hollow core, or fire-resistant core, and acoustical, ballistic resistant, or lead lining when required. The requirements for each core type are illustrated in Section 9. In the absence of clear specifications, the core shall be the option of the manufacturer. Structural composite lumber (SCLC) may be specified in any Grade.

• When solid core is selected, specify one of the following: particleboard (PC), stave lumber (SLC), or structural composite lumber (SCLC). When the weight of the door is a design factor, consult the door manufacturer to determine the differences between PC, SLC, and SCLC core types.

• When hollow core, specify the honeycomb, with the minimum cell size required, grid core, or ladder construction.

• When fire-resistant core is required beyond the 20-minute label level, consult your door manufacturer for code-compliant core types, blocking options, metal edges, cut outs, and astragals.

NOTE: This standard recommends limiting the use of structural composite lumber (SCLC) to interior applications. The use of

9 - Wood Doors

structural composite lumber (SCLC) for top and/or bottom rails, and blocking is acceptable. SCLC is proving to have excellent performance characteristics as a replacement for stave core, as it often minimizes or eliminates telegraphing of the lumber blocks through the face veneers or overlays. When the edge of an SCL-core door will be visible after installation, design professionals may wish to specify a fill-and-paint treatment, or the application of a veneer edgeband to conceal the coarse texture of the edge of the SCL material. It is the responsibility of the design professional to make a selection in the best interests of the client.

Special Core Types

Special cores for X-ray doors, acoustical doors, electrostatic shield doors, ballistic resistant, and others are available. Consult your door manufacturer for information.

CORE TO EDGE ASSEMBLY

These standards provide for multiple types of assembly between the core and the vertical and horizontal edges in solid core doors:

PC, SCLC, SLC or FD: Stiles and rails securely glued to core, abrasively planed flat prior to application of faces.

FPC, FSCLC or FSLC: Stiles and rails not bonded to core prior to application of faces.

IHC or SHC: Stiles and rails placed around hollow core inserts.

FIRE RATINGS

The Model Codes have established a fire door rating and operating classification system for use in protecting door openings in fire-resistive-rated wall constructions. All fire doors must meet certain requirements and bear certifying labels of an independent testing agency approved by the building official. The type of fire-rating (Positive Pressure or Neutral Pressure), and the label required (20, 45, 60 or 90 minute), must be specified. If Positive Pressure is required, the Category of door and validation of the Smoke and Draft Control Label shall be specified and all appropriate fire and smoke gaskets shall be added to the hardware schedule by the design professional.

CRITICAL NOTE and WARNING:

The status of fire-resistant doors and openings is in the process of change. The design professional shall contact the architectural hardware consultant to verify that the total opening complies with both international and local code requirements before finalizing the specification for fire-rated doors, hardware, and openings.

SPECIAL FUNCTION DOORS

Sound retardant (acoustical), lead lined (X-ray), ballistic resistant, and electrostatic shield doors are manufactured by some companies to meet these special needs. Refer to manufacturer's literature for details.

Transom panels and special function doors are available and should be specified carefully, with particular attention to the meeting edge details, operational functions and accessories, and veneer match options. In the absence of clear and complete specifications, fabrication details will be at the option of the manufacturer.

DOOR SELECTION and PERFORMANCE CRITERIA

Manufacturers have relied on the natural strength of hardwood lumber and veneer to assure long term performance. The construction minimums required in previous editions of our standards have proved to have superior performance over the long term. Two things have occurred to require a closer look at the performance properties of door parts and incorporate some minimum physical property requirements to all door grades.

Many new engineered wood products are now replacing traditional hardwood to reduce cost and improve production efficiency. Some of these are as good or better than natural hardwood. However, the risk of look-alike and substandard products that do not perform as well is great. Some have no grain direction, increasing the chance of failure due to excessive linear expansion. Some have less than sufficient strength properties.

The materials and construction methods used determine how well a door will resist high use and abuse. With the introduction of materials that are not the traditional hardwood lumber and veneer, this becomes more important. Wood products, whether natural or engineered, have a wide range of strength characteristics.

9 - Wood Doors

APPEARANCE OF INDIVIDUAL PIECES OF VENEER

VENEER CUTS

The way in which a log is cut in relation to the annual rings determines the appearance of veneer. The beauty of veneer is in the natural variations of texture, grain, figure, color, and the way it is assembled on a door face.

Faces will have the natural variations in grain inherent in the species and cut. Natural variations of veneer grain and pattern will vary from these illustrations.

These are representative drawings of real wood veneers. Involve your woodworker early in the design and selection process.

Flat Cut (Plain Sliced)

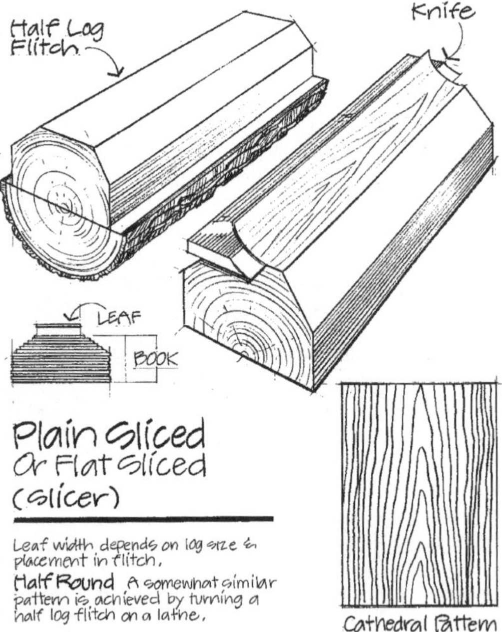

Slicing is done parallel to a line through the center of the log. Cathedral and straight grained patterns result. The individual pieces of veneer are kept in the order they are sliced, permitting a natural grain progression when assembled as veneer faces.

Quarter Cut

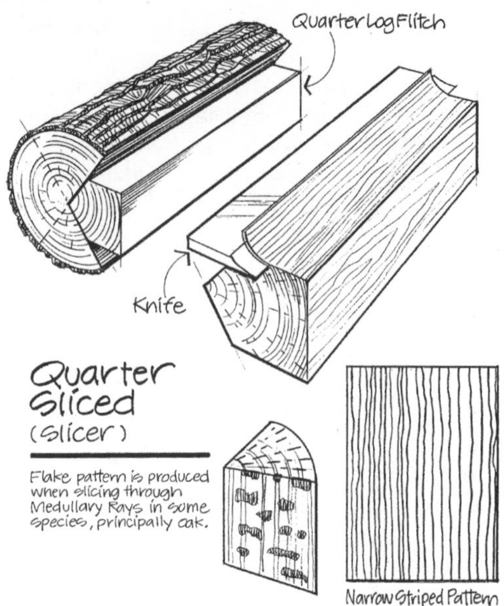

A series of stripes is produced. These stripes vary in width from species to species. A natural distribution of ray fleck (flake), is a characteristic of this cut in Red Oak and White Oak.

Rift Cut

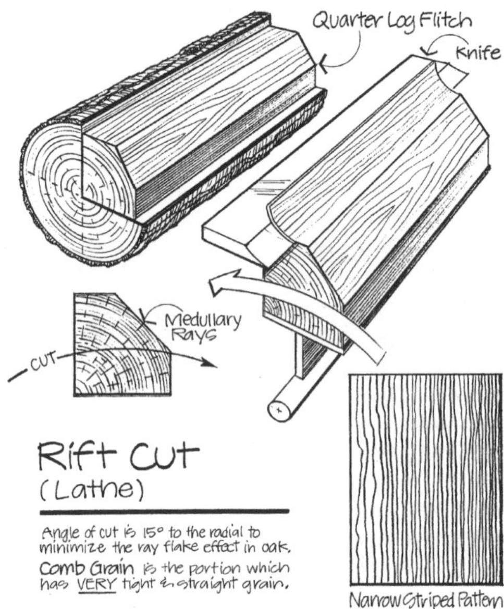

The cut slices slightly across the medullary rays, accentuating the vertical grain and minimizing the "fleck." Rift grain is restricted to Red Oak and White Oak.

Comb Grain

Limited availability. This is a rift cut veneer distinguished by the tightness and straightness of the grain along the entire length of the veneer. Slight angle in the grain is allowed. Comb grain is restricted to Red Oak and White Oak. There are occasional cross bars and fleck is minimal.

9 - Wood Doors

Rotary

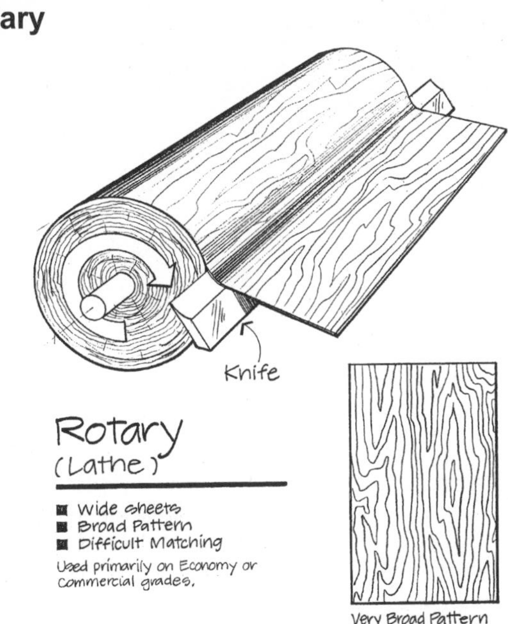

This cut follows the log's annual growth rings, providing a generally bold random appearance.

MATCHING BETWEEN INDIVIDUAL PIECES OF VENEER

Leaf Matching

The way in which the individual cuts are placed next to each other during the fabrication of the veneer face is the next factor affecting the appearance of the doors. The type of match at the joint line must be specified.

Natural variations in the leaves and the progression of the grain pattern across the face are the hallmarks of real wood doors.

Book Match

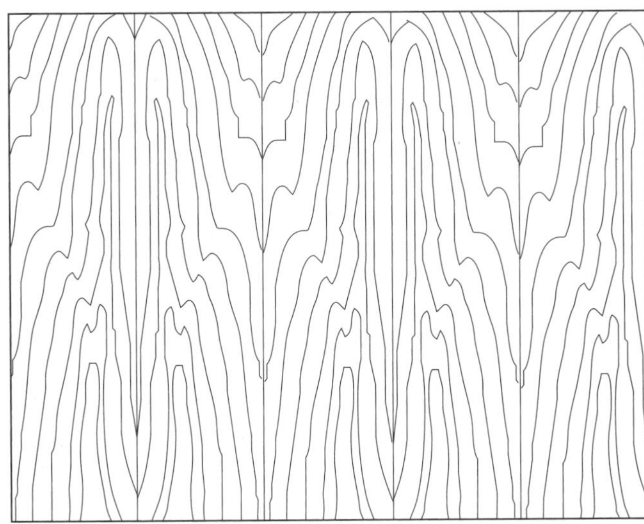

This is the most commonly used match in the industry. Every other piece of veneer is turned over so adjacent pieces are opened like two adjacent pages in a book. The veneer joints match and create a mirrored image pattern at the joint line, yielding a maximum continuity of grain. Book matching is used with plain sliced, and less often with other cuts of veneers.

Barber Pole Effect in Book Match

Because the "tight" and "loose" faces alternate in adjacent pieces of veneer, they may accept stain differently, and this may result in a noticeable color variation. Book matching also accentuates cell polarization, causing the perception of different colors. These natural characteristics are often called barber pole, and are not a manufacturing defect. It is possible, in some instances, to minimize this effect with special finishing techniques.

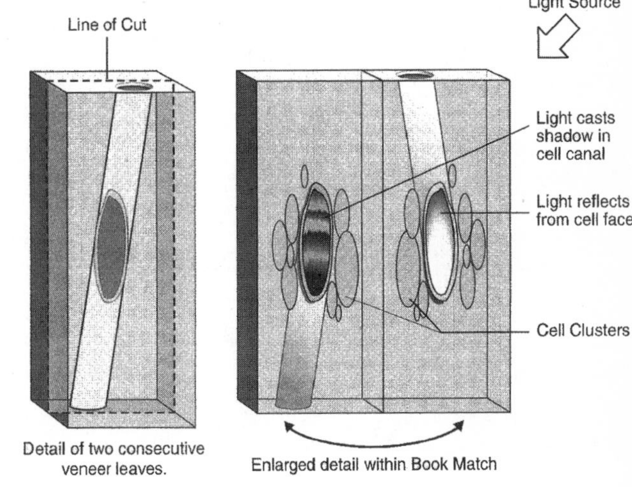

Slip Match

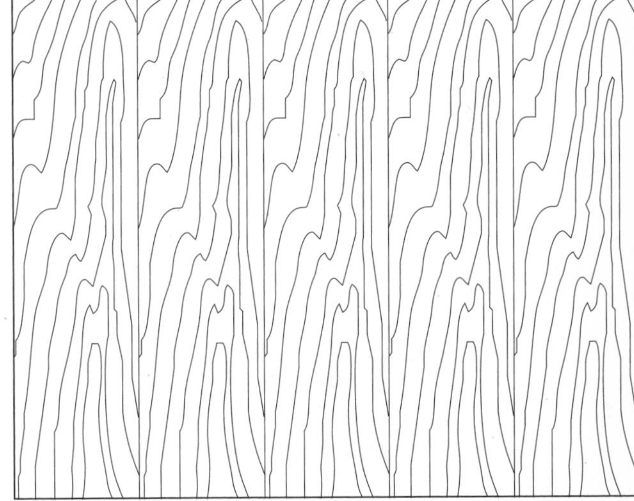

Adjoining pieces of veneer are placed in sequence without turning over every other piece. The grain figure repeats, but joints won't show mirrored effect. Slip matching is often used in quarter cut, rift cut, and comb grain veneers to minimize the barber pole effect.

9 - Wood Doors

Random Match

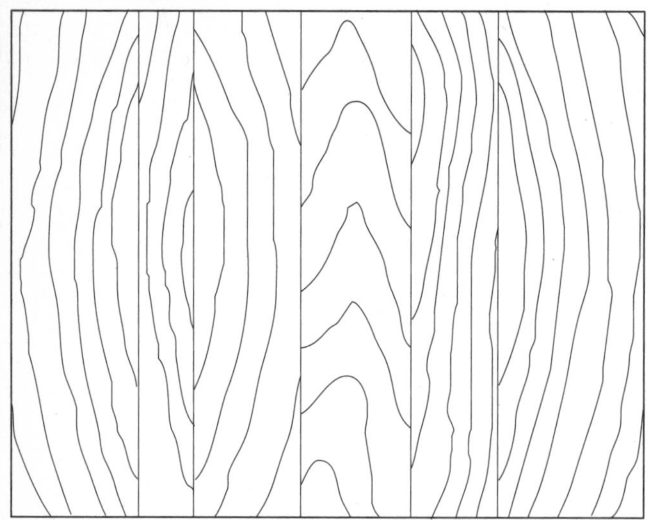

A random selection of individual pieces of veneer from one or more logs. Produces a "board-like" appearance.

ASSEMBLY OF SPLICED VENEER ON A FACE

The type of "assembly match" must be specified to obtain a desired appearance. Any sequence matching from opening to opening must be specified. The following three face assembly methods give a wide range of flexibility and cost control to the design professional.

Balance Match

Symmetrical appearance. Each face is assembled from an even or odd number of pieces of uniform width before trimming. This match reduces veneer yield.

Center Balance Match

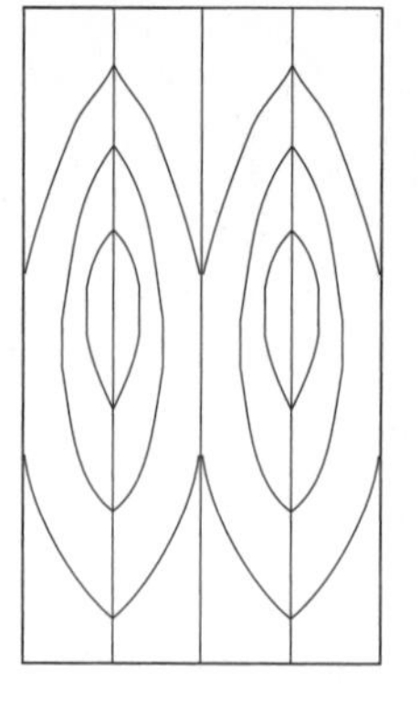

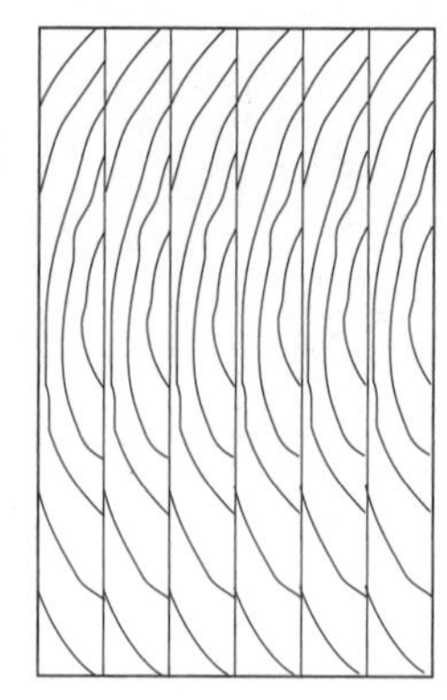

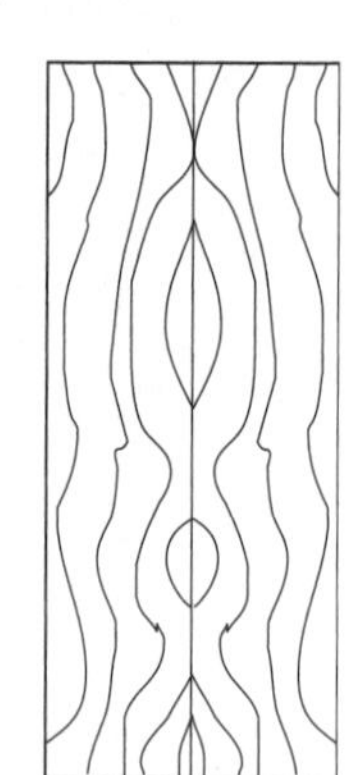

Symmetrical appearance. Each face is assembled from an even number of veneer pieces of uniform width before trimming. Thus, there is a veneer joint in the center of the panel. This match further reduces veneer yield.

Running Match

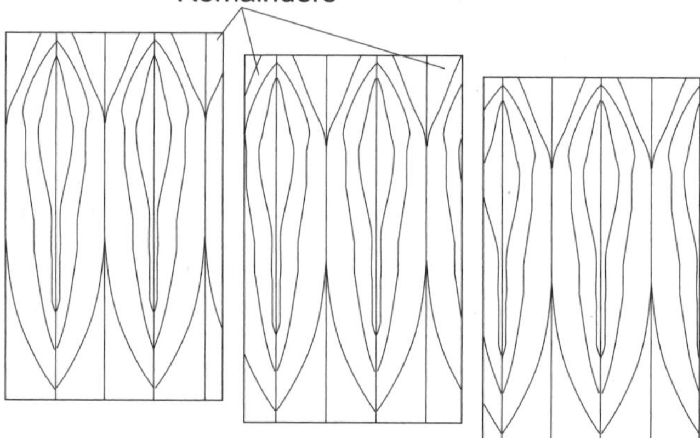

Nonsymmetrical appearance on any single door face. Veneer pieces of unequal width are common. Each face is assembled from as many veneer pieces as necessary.

9 - Wood Doors

DOORS IN PAIRS OR SETS

Pair Match

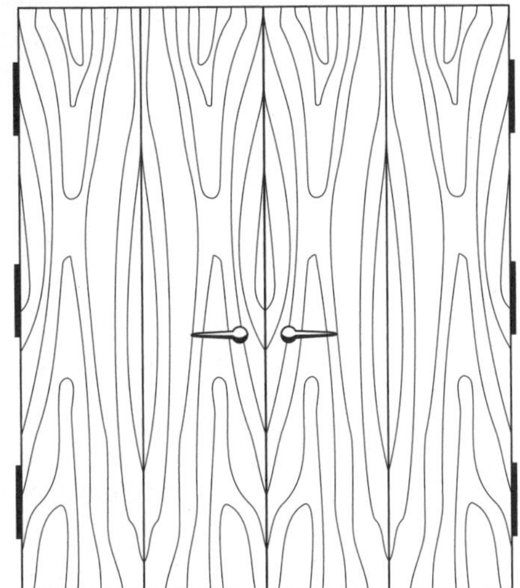

Doors hung in adjacent sets or in close proximity may be (and in some Grades, must be), specified as pair matched where appropriate. Note to specifiers: The illustration shows book-matched, center balance matched faces. The *AWS* does not require this condition.

Set Match

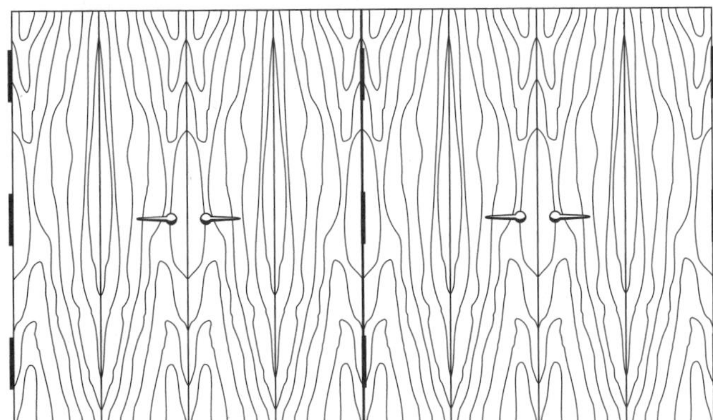

Doors hung in adjacent sets may be (and in some Grades, must be), specified as set matched where appropriate.

Note to specifiers: The illustration shows book-matched, center balance matched faces. The *AWS* does not require this condition.

Doors with Transoms

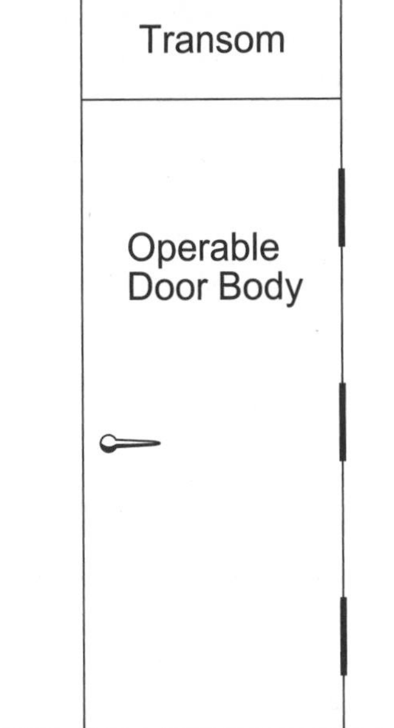

The use of the transom increases the apparent height of the wood door and often enhances the appearance of the opening. The type of match should be specified, and a slight misalignment of veneer grain may occur between the transom and the door. Industry practice allows a variation in grain alignment from side to side of 3/8" (9.5 mm) on a single door, and 1/2" (12.7 mm) on pairs of doors with a single transom. Tighter tolerances must be specified as a part of Premium Grade doors.

Continuous Match

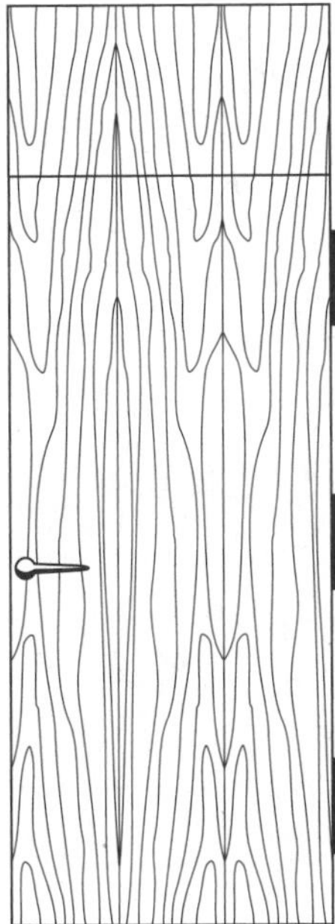

Provides optimum veneer utilization as each single piece of veneer extends from the top of the transom to the bottom of the door. Available veneer length in the species may limit this option.

9 - Wood Doors

End Match

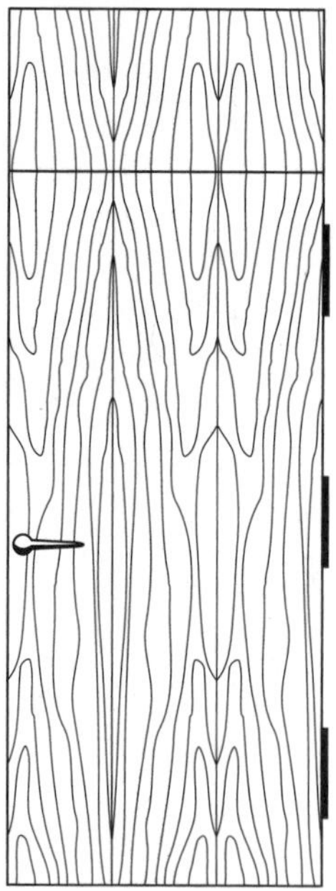

A single piece of veneer extends from the bottom to the top of the door with a mirror image at the transom.

No Match

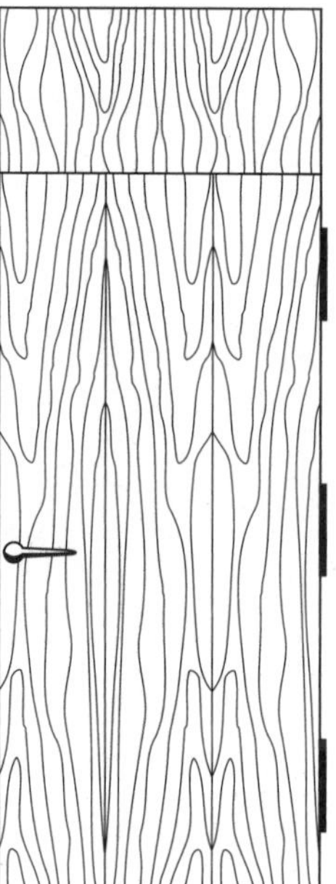

Alignment Criteria

Grain pattern alignment between the door and transom, even when cut from the same panel, will vary to some extent. This is due to the natural progression of the annual rings which create the figure in the wood. Misalignment will be more apparent in doors veneered with open grain species than with close grain.

Misalignment of up to 3/8" (9 mm) is permitted in every Grade.

Hardwood Veneer Face Grade Summary

Read Section 4 for the complete description of veneer face grades.

NOTE: When veneers are specified as "natural," they may contain any amount or combination of sapwood and heartwood, with the resultant contrast in color in many species.

The industry recognizes that cost is an important factor, and having lower veneer standards can result in some savings. Specifying *Architectural Woodwork Standards* Custom Grade meets that need. However, when doors are a part of an overall design scheme and/or are adjacent to other fine architectural woodwork specified under these standards, the level of quality of those doors must be consistent with other millwork components.

9 - Wood Doors

Construction Details

General Moulding Requirements

Species shall match or be compatible with face veneer or laminate.

Specify transparent or opaque finish.

Moulding shall be free of open defects, shake, splits, or doze.

Moulding must be smooth and free of visible knife, saw, or sanding marks. Specify from following options:

MEETING EDGE OPTIONS

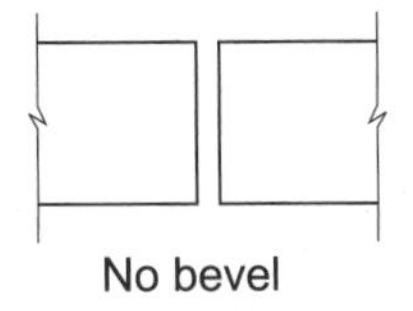

No bevel

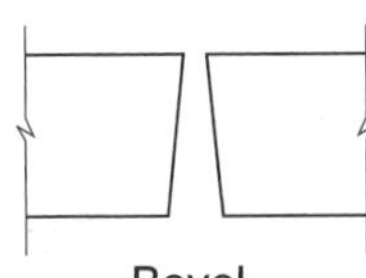

Bevel

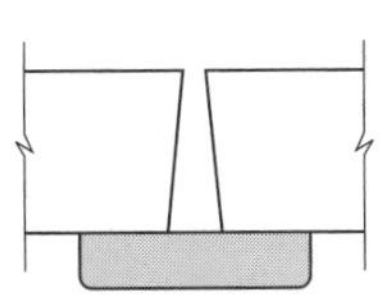

Flat astragal

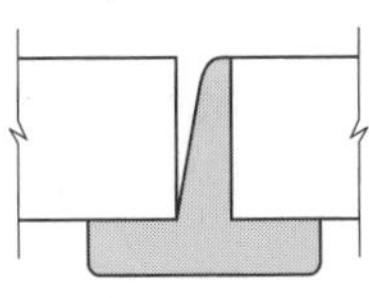

Tee astragal

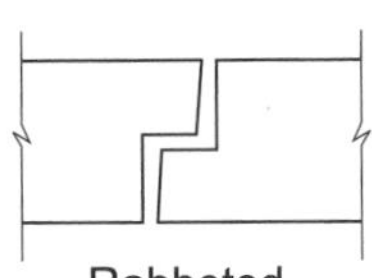

Rabbeted

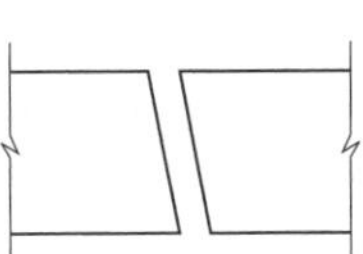

Parallel bevel
Double egress

Metal edge guards and astragal

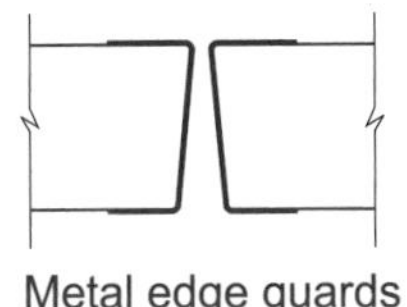

Metal edge guards

TRANSOM MEETING EDGE OPTIONS

Non-rabbeted

Rabbeted

Glazing Options

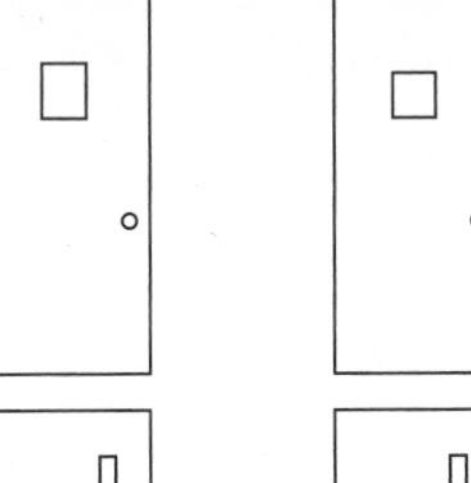

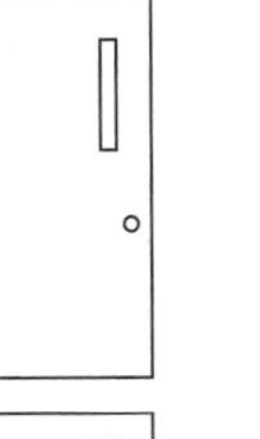

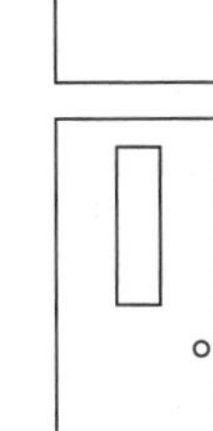

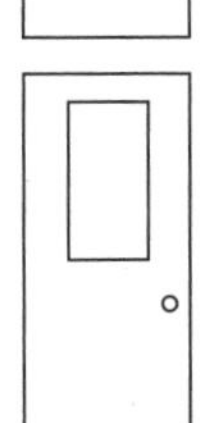

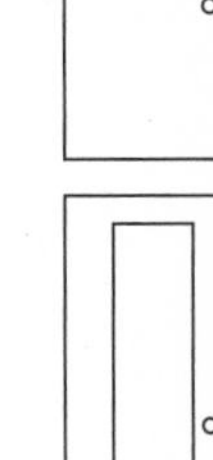

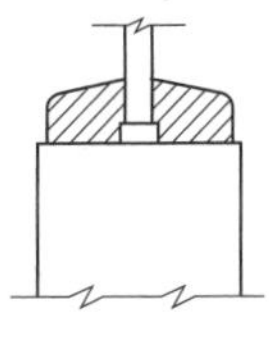

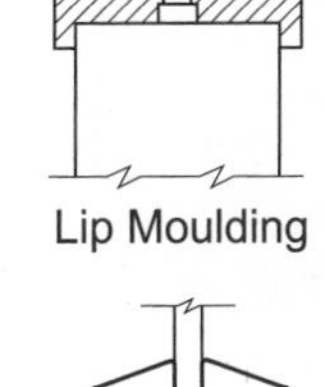

Lip Moulding

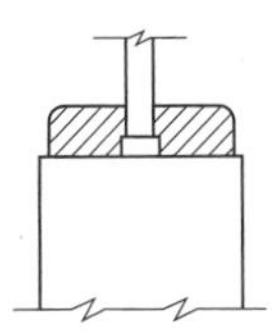

Flush Mouldings

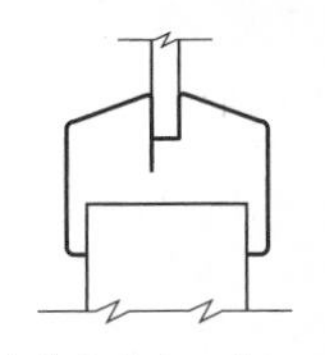

Metal vision frame

W = Wood mouldings

M = Metal vision frames

All cutouts for metal or wood vision panels must be a minimum of 6" (152 mm) from the edge of the door and/or other cutouts for louvers, locks, closers, or other hardware for 45-minute though 90-minute doors. 20-minute PC and SLC doors must be a minimum of 5" (127 mm) [5"], and 20 minute SCLC doors must be a minimum of 1-1/2" (38 mm).

These distances must be maintained or the fire label and warranty will be voided.

Using a 10" (254 mm) margin between the edge of the door and the edge of any cutout near the lock area will eliminate most label and warranty conflicts.

9 - Wood Doors

Louver Options

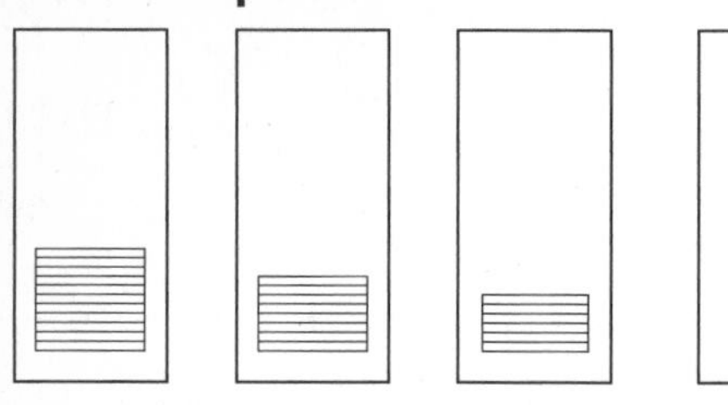

Variety of sizes

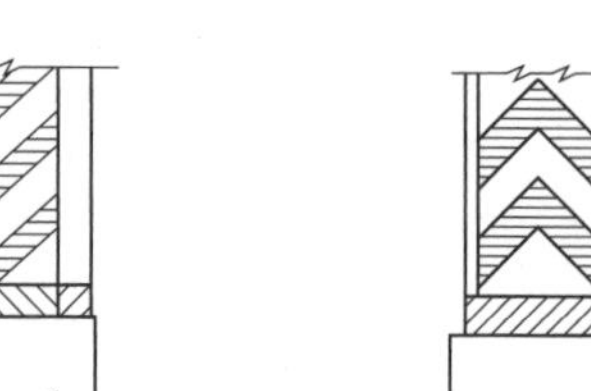

Wood slats

Wood chevrons

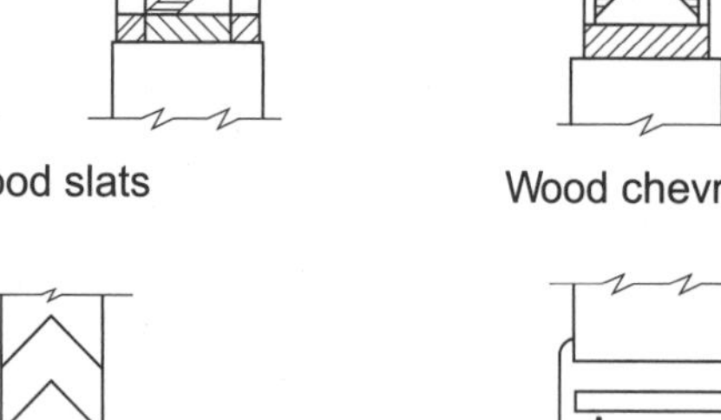

Metal chevrons

Fusible link

WL = Wood louver. Not allowed by NFPA 80 in fire-rated doors.

FL = Fusible link louver.

Not allowed by NFPA 80 in means-of-egress fire doors. Generally, fusible link louvers installed in 45, 60, and 90 minute fire-rated doors must comply with individual fire door authorities and ADA requirements.

All fusible link louvers must be minimum 8" (203 mm) from the bottom of the door to the bottom of the louver cutout, and 6" (152 mm) from the edge of the louver cutout to the edge of the door and/or other cutouts for vision panels, locks, closers, or other hardware.

These minimum dimensions must be maintained or the fire rating label and warranty will be voided.

Sizes and details other than those illustrated are available.

Flashings

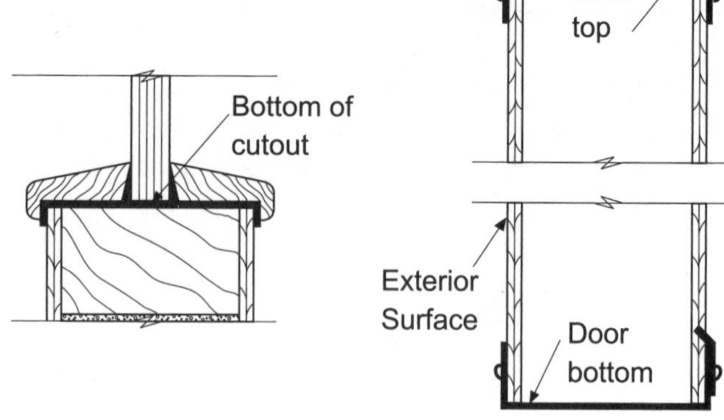

If the woodworker is to flash the top of the door or the bottom edge of cutouts for exterior doors, it must be specified.

Dutch Door Options

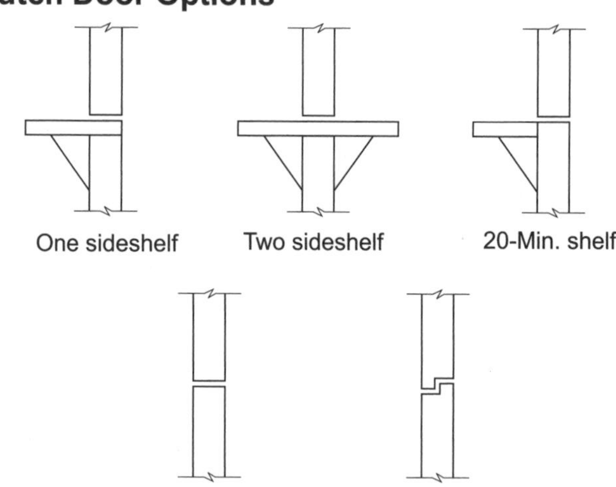

9 - Wood Doors

Blocking Options (Particle Core and Fire-Resistant Core)

For undercutting flexibility and specialized hardware applications, a number of internal blocking options are available from most manufacturers. Among them are such options as 5" (127 mm) top rail, 5" (127 mm) bottom rail, 5" x 18" (127 x 457 mm) lock blocks (may be one side only), 2-1/2" (64 mm) cross blocking. Other options may be available. Consult your manufacturer early in the design process to determine availability.

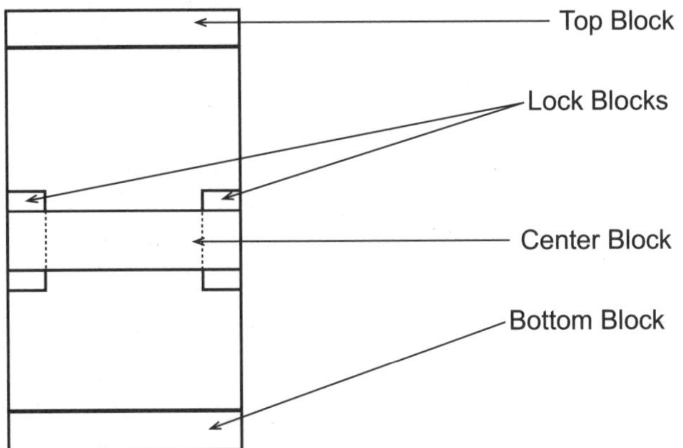

Dimensional Tolerances

NOTE: These dimensions given as typical industry tolerances.

The dimensions usually apply in the absence of specifications.

Doors Not Prefit

- Width, Height, Thickness: ± 1/16" (1.6 mm)
- Out of Square: max. 1/8" (3.2 mm) measured from corner to corner on the diagonal

Doors Machined for Hardware

- Width: ± 1/32" (0.8 mm)
- Height: ± 1/16" (1.6 mm)
- Thickness: ± 1/16" (1.6 mm)
- Hardware location: ± 1/32" (0.8 mm)
- Locks and hinges: ± 1/32" (0.8 mm)

Typical Prefit Clearances

- Top and hinge edges: 1/8" (3.2 mm)
- Single door, lock edge: 1/8" (3.2 mm)
- Pair meeting edge: 1/16" (1.6 mm) per leaf
- Bottom (rated or nonrated): 1/2" (13 mm) from top of decorative floor covering; 3/4" (19 mm) maximum from top of non-combustible floor; 3/8" (10 mm) maximum from top of non-combustible sill or threshold.

Sample Submission

Woodwork manufacturers will provide standard colors for selection.

To specify nonstandard colors and sheens, the architect shall provide two or more samples at least 8" x 10" (200 x 250 mm) showing the desired finish effect on the wood species and cut to be used.

Samples are to bear identification of the project, architect, general contractor, and door supplier. The manufacturer may elect to submit samples in sets of two or more, illustrating the possible range of variations. The finished sample sets then become the final criteria for evaluating color and finish appearance conformity. However, variations can be expected due to the nature of wood.

Sample Protection

Approved samples must be protected from the effect of light. Cover faces and place samples in closed storage during the period between approval and fabrication, finishing, and delivery of the finished product.

Care and Installation at Job Site

In the absence of specific requirements from the door manufacturer, the criteria shall prevail.

Storing

- Store at least 4" (101.6 mm) off floor, flat on a level surface in a clean, dry, well-ventilated area protected from sunlight, wide swings in relative humidity, and abnormal heat or cold. Relative humidity should not be less than 25% or more than 55%.
- Store doors in closed-in building with operational HVAC system.
- Cover doors to keep clean, but allow air circulation.
- Seal at earliest possible moment. Edge sealing is particularly important.
- Lift or carry door. Do not drag one door against another.
- Handle doors with clean hands or clean gloves.

Installation

- Allow doors to become acclimated to finished building heat and humidity before fitting and hanging.
- Utility or strength of doors must not be impaired by fitting to the opening, applying hardware, plant-ons, louvers, or other detailing.
- In fitting for width, trim equally from both sides.
- In fitting for height, do not trim top or bottom edge more than 3/4" (19 mm), unless accommodated by additional blocking.
- Threaded-to-the-head wood screws are preferable for fastening all hardware on nonrated doors and required on all rated doors. Pilot holes must be drilled for all screws to avoid splitting.
- Use two hinges for doors up to 60" (1524 mm) in height, three hinges for doors up to 90" (2286 mm) in height, and an additional hinge for every additional 30" (762 mm) of door height or portion thereof.
- Light or louver cuts in exterior doors must be treated or flashed to prevent moisture from entering the door core.

9 - Wood Doors

Fire Door Requirements

Install doors as required by NFPA Pamphlet 80.

All 45-, 60-, and 90-minute rated doors may be hung with either half surface or full mortise hinges. Core reinforcements (blocking) can be specified to permit hardware to be surface mounted with screws. Labels shall not be removed from fire-rated doors.

Preparation of Labeled Door

Preparation of 20-, 45-, 60-, and 90-minute rated doors must be done under label service in accordance with the manufacturer's service procedure. This includes trimming for size except a maximum of 3/4" (19 mm) off the bottom of the door. Preparation of locks, latches, hinges, closers, lights, louvers, astragals, and any fabrication must be done under licensed label service. Refer to NFPA 80, Standards for Fire Doors and Fire Windows for requirements and exceptions.

Fire-Retardant Salts

The edge and crossbands of some rated doors contain salts which attract moisture. When exposed to high humidity, they appear on the surfaces as white crystals. Clear finishes will highlight these crystals. Remove the crystals by light sanding after the doors are thoroughly dried. If the crystal build-up is heavy, clean with a damp sponge and allow to dry before sanding. At that point, seal and refinish. Avoid the use of steel wool on fire-rated wood doors.

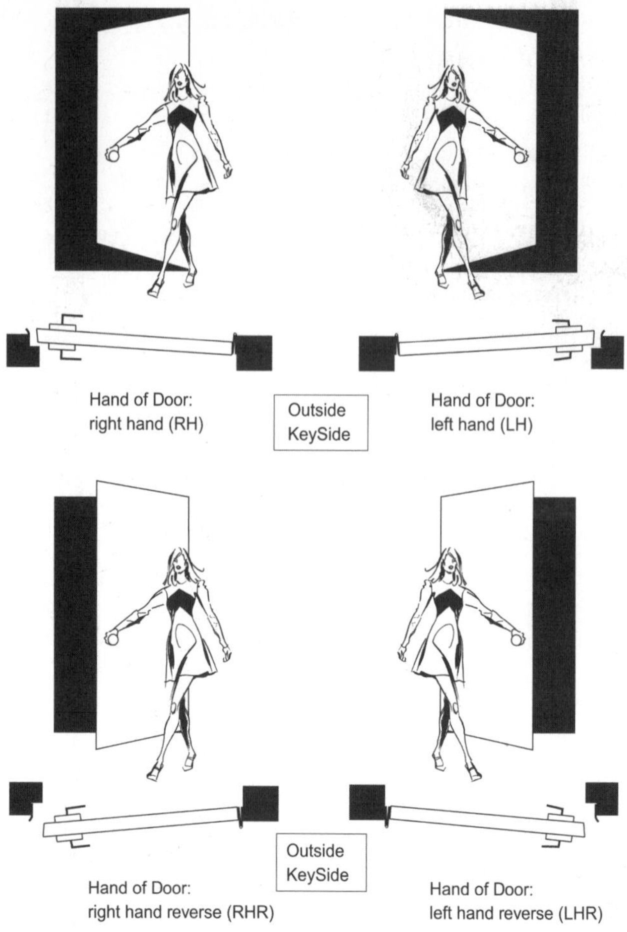

Hand and Bevel of Doors

The "hand" of a door is always determined from the outside. The outside of an exterior door is the street or entrance (key) side. The outside of an interior room or auditorium door is the corridor or hall (key or imaginary key) side. The outside of a closet door is the side opposite the closet; the room, corridor or hall side. The outside of a single communicating door is the side from which the butts are invisible when the door is closed. The outside of twin communicating doors is the space between the two doors.

Standard-handed doors push away from the person standing on the outside/key side. Reverse-handed doors pull toward the person standing on the outside/key side.

Door Symbols and Abbreviations

Door style descriptors were assigned in previous editions to facilitate specifying. They were found to be more confusing than helpful. They have been discontinued. The following short list of abbreviations applies to some door companies:

ME = Matching edges; i.e., vertical edges same as decorative faces.

CE = Compatible edges; i.e., vertical edges selected for compatibility with decorative faces.

PC = Particleboard core, solid core door with stiles and rails bonded to the core and abrasive planed flat prior to the application of the faces.

PC-5 = Core with 2 layers on each side

PC-7 = Core with 3 layers on each side

PC-HPDL-3 = Core with laminate to each side

PC-HPDL-5 = Core with crossband and laminate each side

SCLC = Structural composite lumber core, solid core door with stiles and rails bonded to the core and abrasive planed flat prior to the application of the faces.

SCLC-5 = Core with 2 layers on each side

SCLC-7 = Core with 3 layers on each side

9 - Wood Doors

SCLC-HPDL-5 = Core with crossband and laminate each side

SLC = Staved lumber core, solid core door with stiles and rails bonded to the core and abrasive planed flat prior to the application of the faces.

SLC-5 = Core with 2 layers on each side

SLC-7 = Core with 3 layers on each side

SLC-HPDL-5 = Core with crossband and laminate each side

FPC = Floating particleboard core, solid core placed within a stile and rail frame, bonded together by the faces.

FPC-5 = Core with 2 layers on each side

FPC-7 = Core with 3 layers on each side

FSLC = Floating staved lumber core, solid core placed within a stile and rail frame, bonded together by the faces.

FSLC-7 = Core with 3 layers on each side

FD = Fire-resistant core, fire-resistant materials assembled to stiles and rails according to methods prescribed by the testing agency to meet rigorous smoke, flame, and pressure tests.

Labeled fire doors are specified by their resistance ratings.

FD-5 = Core with 2 layers on each side

FD-7 = Core with 3 layers on each side

FD-HPDL-3 = Core with laminate to each side

FD-HPDL-5 = Core with crossband and laminate each side

IHC-7 = Institutional hollow core, honey comb, ladder, or grid type cores inside stiles and rails, bonded together by the faces.

SHC-7 = Standard hollow core, honey comb, ladder, or grid type cores inside stiles and rails, bonded together by the faces.

SR = Sound retardant doors, specified by their performance characteristics.

LL = Lead lined doors, designed to resist penetration by radiation of various types, and specified by their performance.

ES = Electrostatic shielded doors.

BR = Ballistic resistant doors.

NOTE: Your door manufacturer is the best source of specific guidance when writing door specifications.

Exterior Doors

Careful consideration must precede specification of wood doors for exterior use. The selection of a wood species suited for exterior exposure is critical. Exterior doors shall be water repellent treated at the factory after manufacturing. Protect doors according to manufacturers' requirements, which may include flashing of top, bottom and cut outs. Exterior doors shall be properly sealed immediately after sizing and machining for fit in the field. Wood doors shall be protected from the sun and other weather elements by overhangs, deep recesses, etc. While wood stile and rail entry doors have performed well for centuries, the selection of a wood door places a burden on the owner to maintain the door be keeping it painted or sealed, protected from moisture, and properly adjusted in the opening.

Some door companies limit their warranties on exterior doors; some will provide no warranty.

Flashing

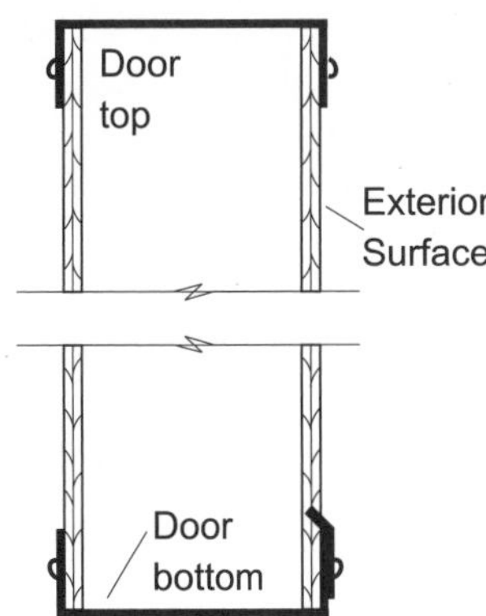

If the woodworker is to flash the top of the door or the bottom edge of cutouts for exterior doors, it must be specified.

Fire Ratings (when specified)

The traditional model codes have established a fire door rating and operating classification system for use in protecting door openings in fire-resistive-rated wall constructions. All fire doors must meet the requirements of current codes and bear certifying labels of an independent testing agency approved by the building official.

Code and Rule Requirements

The design professional shall be responsible for contract documents which clearly detail products which will comply with applicable codes and rules including, but not limited to, NFPA 80 requirements; ADA national and federal guidelines; local, state, and federal building codes; positive pressure requirements and labeling; glass or glazing; prefitting and/or machining for hardware; prehanging and/or machining for weatherstripping; priming, sealing and/or transparent finishing; and flashing and/or metal edge guards. The door manufacturer is often a valuable assistant in these matters.

Factory Finishing (when specified)

Firms differ in the variety of factory finishes offered. Some finishes may not be available from all manufacturers.

Finishes protect wood from moisture, handling, or harsh chemicals. The sooner moisture is restricted from entering or leaving, the longer wood lasts and the finer it looks.

Transparent finishes without stain provide a protective coating for the wood, maintaining its natural look. Transparent finishes with stain provide the architect or designer an opportunity to create a striking visual effect by modifying color, texture, and sheen.

Finishing Options

Section 5 of the *AWS* defines the finishing systems and performance characteristics.

Note: Carefully study Section 5, and consult with your woodworker early in the design phase can result in both high quality and cost savings.

Factory finishing is generally specified when a project requires high quality performance and superior appearance.

9 - Wood Doors

Factory finishing offers many benefits, including:

- State-of-the-art equipment in a well-lighted, dust-free environment (conditions normally not available in the field), which provides uniform color, texture, and sheen.
- Proper sanding prior to the application of stains and finishes. Field conditions often hinder surface preparation resulting in a lack of clarity and uniformity in finish and color.
- Protection from unfavorable relative humidity conditions at the earliest possible time.
- Cost savings (in most cases) over the total cost of field-applied finishes by a separate contractor.
- Shorter installation time on the job site, resulting in faster project completion.

Stile and Rail Door Construction Details

Stiles

Stiles are the vertical outside members. They may be solid wood or veneered. Stiles usually have solid sticking (solid stuck, solid moulded). Sticking is usually of two profiles: "cove and bead" or "ovolo." Other profiles may be used. The stiles are ploughed or grooved along the edge to receive the panels, rails, and/or glass. If the door is to be assembled by dowelled construction, the stiles are bored to receive the dowels. If the door is to be assembled by lag screw construction, the stiles shall be solid hardwood lumber. The stiles will contain much of the hardware for the door, and must be sized and fabricated to fit the intended hardware, locks, and latches.

Rails

Rails are the cross or horizontal members of the door. They may be solid wood or veneered. Rails are coped on both ends to fit the sticking of the stile. Tenons or dowels are machined into the rails to fit mortises or dowel boring in the stiles.

The top and bottom rails are required, with the addition of intermediate cross rails or lock rails as appropriate. The bottom rail is usually the widest of the members, made of edge glued lumber or veneered, depending on the door construction. The top rail is often the same face dimension as the stiles.

The lock rail, if there is one, is usually a wide member located at lock height. In the case of narrow stiles or large hardware, this rail serves to house the lock and latch mechanisms.

Mullions

The mullion is an upright or vertical member between panels. It is similar to a cross rail in the way it is fit and machined.

Panels

The door panels are either solid lumber or panel products that fill the frame formed by the stiles, rails, and mullions. When the figure of the wood is visible in the finished product, the grain direction of the panels usually runs along their longest dimension; vertical for tall panels and horizontal for wide (or laying) panels.

Muntins and Bars

Stile and rail door with glass panels often utilize muntins and bars, which are smaller in section than mullions. A bar is a rabbeted moulding, which extends the total height or width of the glass opening. A muntin is a short bar, either horizontal or vertical, extending from a full bar to a stile, rail, or another bar. Muntins and bars are traditionally coped and mortised joinery.

Custom-designed stile and rail doors offer many opportunities for creativity and choice. Some of the variables include:

- Panel layout
- Grain patterns and relationships
- Stile and rail construction
- Moulding details
- Panel construction
- Joinery techniques

Selection among these variables requires some knowledge of their relative performance characteristics. The following drawings illustrate some of the options. Many woodworkers feel veneered and laminated constructions offer the lowest risk of warp for most species of wood. Consult your woodworker early in the design process for assistance in making selections.

9 - Wood Doors

Door Thickness, Panel Layout, and Grain Patterns

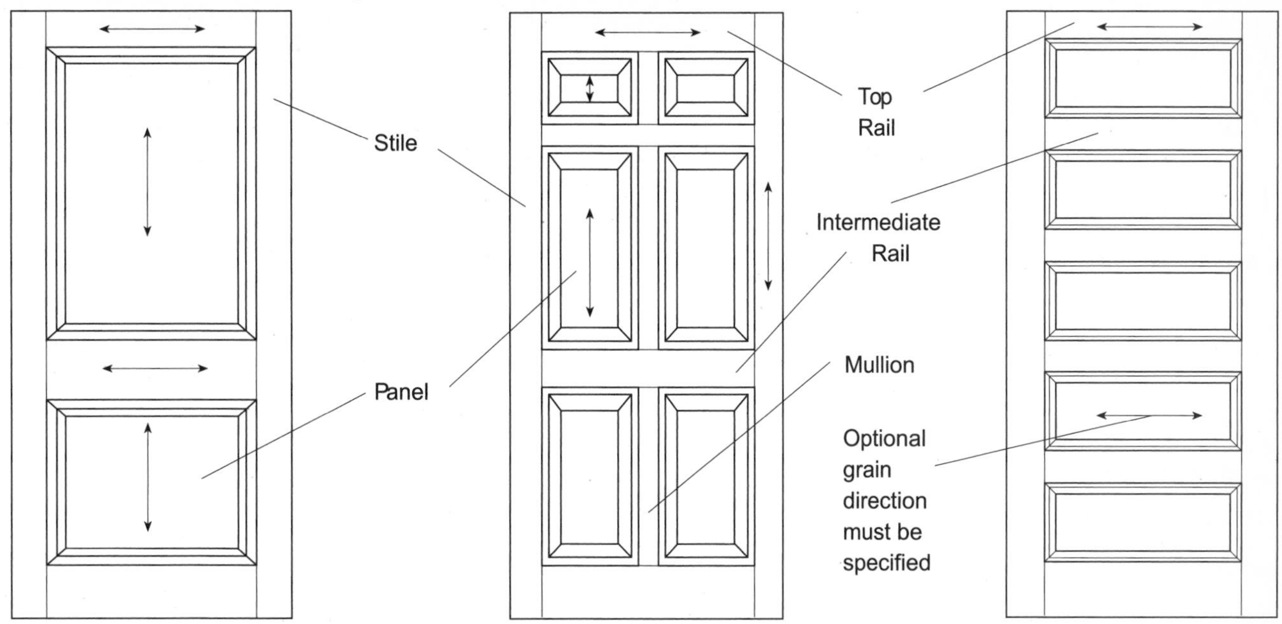

Stile and rail doors are usually 44 mm [1-3/4"] thick. For doors over 1067 mm [3'-6"] in width or 2440 mm [8'-0"] in height, 57 mm [2-1/4"] minimum thickness is required. Doors over maximum width or height and required by specification to be less than 57 mm [2-1/4"] in thickness shall not be subject to the *AWS* test for warp. Traditionally, the grain direction flows with the longest dimension of the stile, rail, or panel. Panel grain direction can sometimes be altered for design purposes, and must be specified. If raised panels are to be rim-raised veneered construction, the grain of the rims will flow around the panel with the long dimension of the rim material.

Stile and Rail Construction

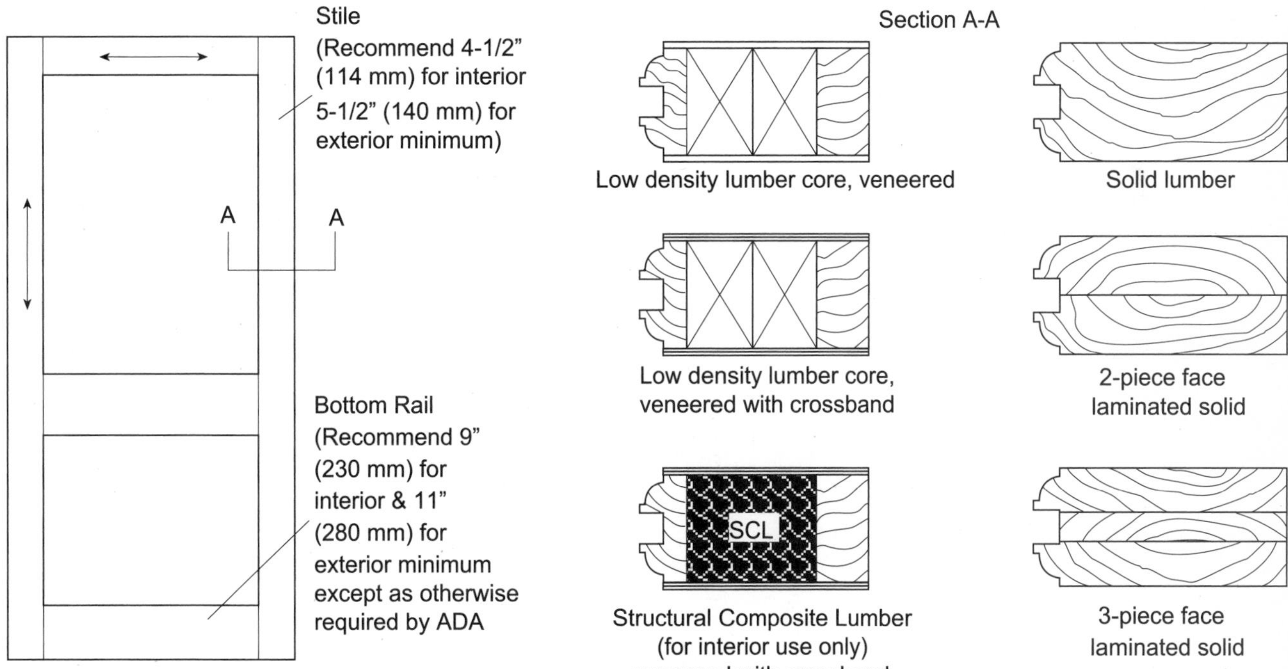

There are a variety of methods of stile and rail fabrication. It is possible to fabricate stile and rail doors that will perform within the tests established in this Standard using any of the illustrated techniques and others.

9 - Wood Doors

Panel Construction

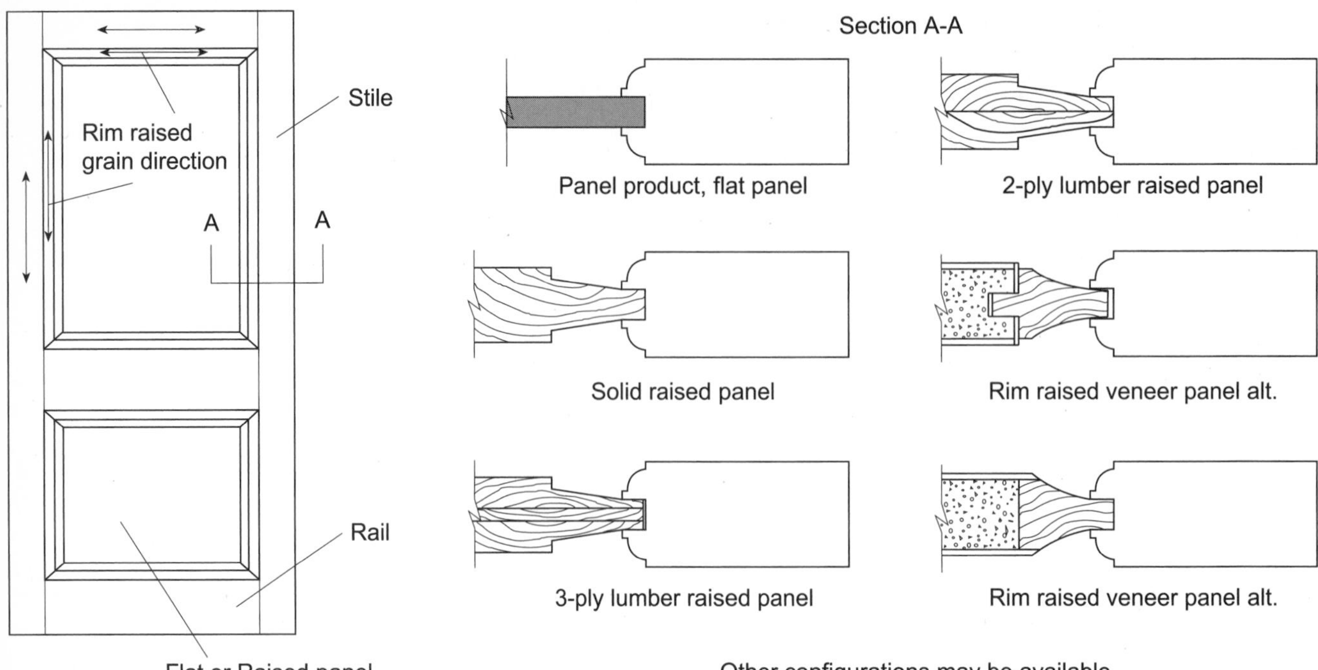

Flat or Raised panel

Other configurations may be available

There are a variety of methods of flat panel and raised panel fabrication. Review the *AWS* for maximum allowable widths in solid or edge-glued lumber. It is possible to fabricate stile and rail doors that will perform within the tests established in the compliance criteria of the *AWS* using any of the illustrated techniques and others.

Panel and Glass Retention

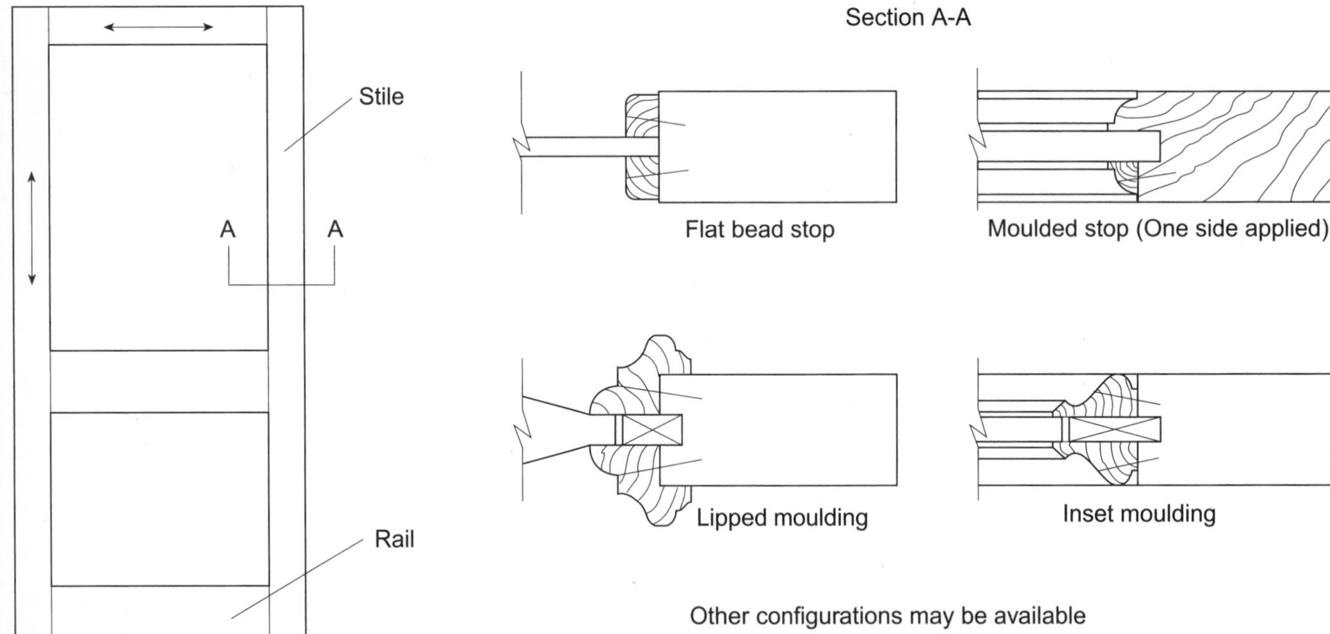

Other configurations may be available

A wide variety of design choices are available from woodworkers. The illustrations are intended as guidelines for the design professional and should not limit the potential for creative solutions. Glass cannot always be centered on stiles and rails, depending on the thickness. Mouldings and stop are usually applied with small brads or finish nails.

9 - Wood Doors

FREEDOM OF EXPRESSION

This section is a sample of design ideas. It makes no pretense of being complete. It's here for the reader to use as a starting point. The exercise of personal creativity is the essence of fine architectural woodworking.

Custom-designed woodwork gives you complete freedom of expression.

- Design flexibility: The use of custom-designed woodwork in a building allows the design professional freedom of expression, while meeting the functional needs of the client. A custom-designed building is enhanced by the use of custom-designed woodwork.
- Cost effective: Custom woodwork does compete favorably with mass-produced millwork, and offers practically limitless variations of design and material. Most woodwork lasts the life of the building – quality counts.
- Complete adaptability: By using custom woodwork, the architect or designer can readily conceal plumbing, electrical and other mechanical equipment without compromising the design criteria.
- No restrictions: Custom architectural woodwork permits complete freedom of selection of any of the numerous hardwoods and softwoods available for transparent or opaque finish. Other unique materials available from woodwork manufacturers require no further finishing at all, such as plastic laminates and decorative overlays. These materials can be fashioned into a wide variety of profiles, sizes, and configurations. The owner and design professional have the best of both worlds - high quality and freedom of choice.
- Dimensional flexibility: Since custom woodwork is normally produced by a specialty architectural woodwork firm, dimensions can easily be changed prior to actual fabrication, if required by job conditions. Special situations such as designing for the disabled can readily be accommodated by the custom architectural woodwork manufacturer.
- Quality assurance: Adherence to the *AWS* and specifications will provide the design professional a quality product at a competitive price. Use of a qualified industry member firm will help ensure the woodworker's understanding of the quality level required.

9 - Wood Doors

Fig. 1400-D-1 Fig. 1400-D-2 Fig. 1400-D-3 Fig. 1400-D-4

Fig. 1400-D-5 Fig. 1400-D-6 Fig. 1400-D-7 Fig. 1400-D-8

Fig. 1400-D-9 Fig. 1400-D-10 Fig. 1400-D-11 Fig. 1400-D-12

Fig. 1400-D-13 Fig. 1400-D-14 Fig. 1400-D-15 Fig. 1400-D-16

9 - Wood Doors

Fig. 1400-D-17
Fig. 1400-D-18
Fig. 1400-D-19
Fig. 1400-D-20
Fig. 1400-D-21
Fig. 1400-D-22
Fig. 1400-D-23
Fig. 1400-D-24
Fig. 1400-D-25
Fig. 1400-D-26
Fig. 1400-D-27
Fig. 1400-D-28
Fig. 1400-D-29
Fig. 1400-D-30
Fig. 1400-D-31
Fig. 1400-D-32

9 - Wood Doors

Fig. 1400-D-33
Fig. 1400-D-34
Fig. 1400-D-35
Fig. 1400-D-36
Fig. 1400-D-37
Fig. 1400-D-38
Fig. 1400-D-39
Fig. 1400-D-40
Fig. 1400-D-41
Fig. 1400-D-42
Fig. 1400-D-43
Fig. 1400-D-44
Fig. 1400-D-45
Fig. 1400-D-46
Fig. 1400-D-47

9 - Wood Doors

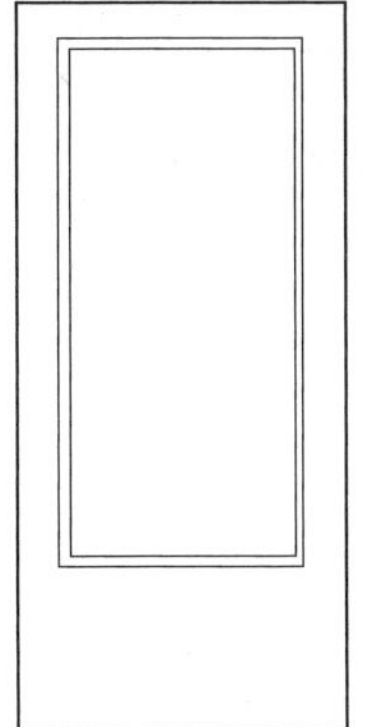

Fig. 1400-D-48

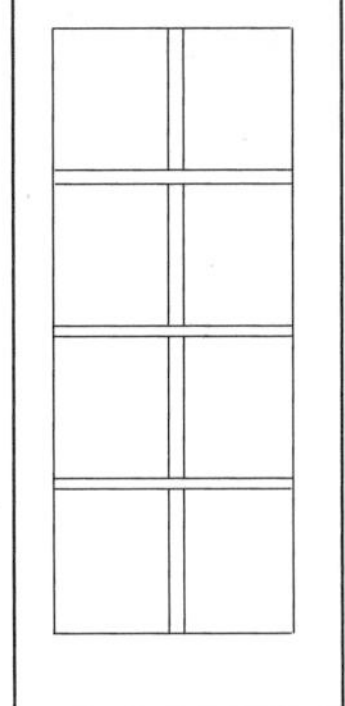

Fig. 1400-D-49

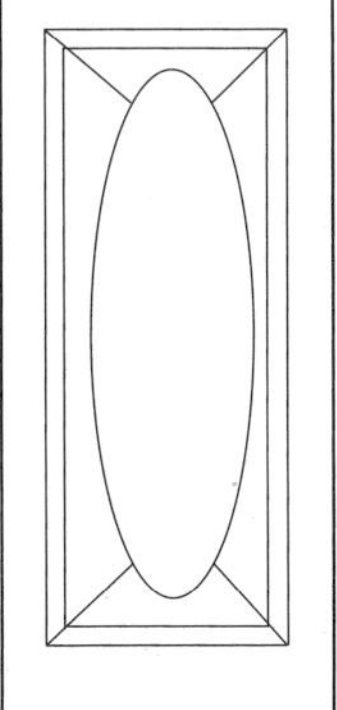

Fig. 1400-D-50

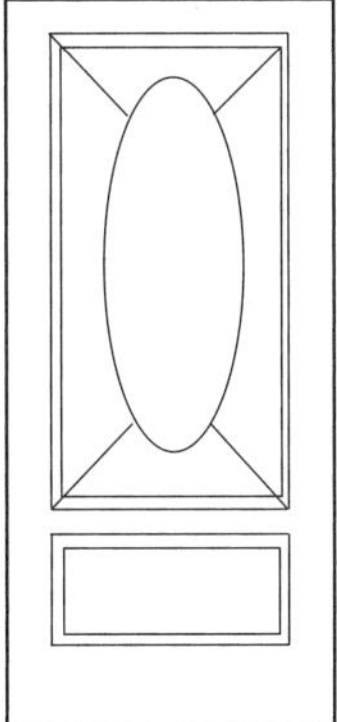

Fig. 1400-D-51

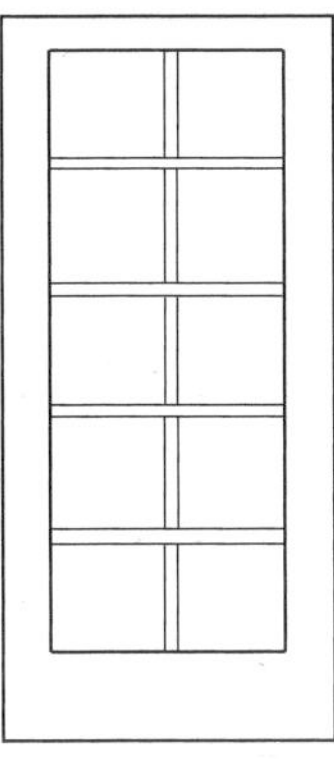

Fig. 1400-D-52

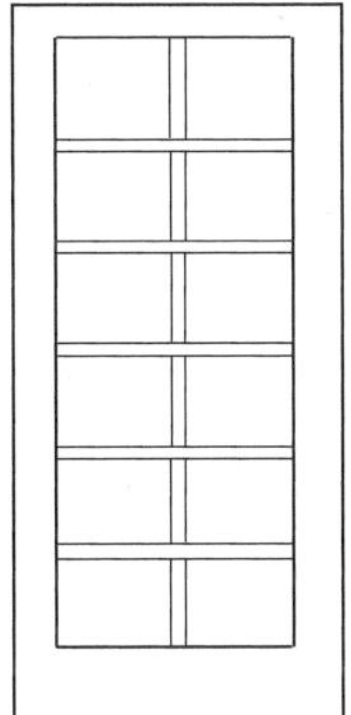

Fig. 1400-D-53

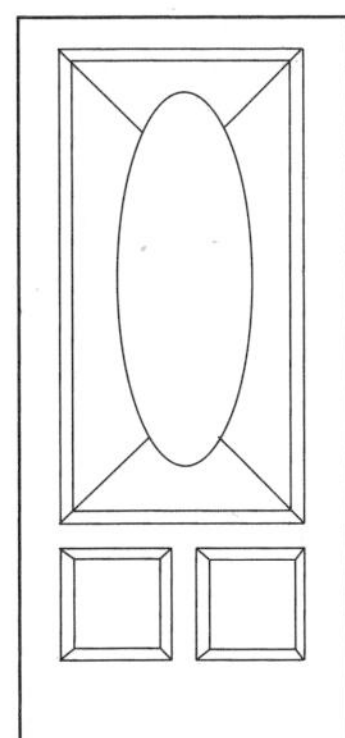

Fig. 1400-D-54

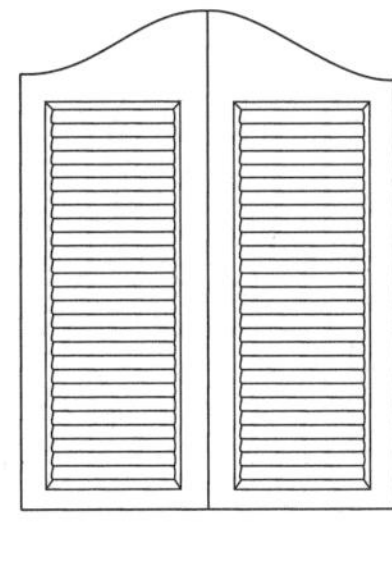

Fig. 1400-D-55

NOTES

10
Casework

10 - Casework

SHELF DEFLECTION INFORMATION

The Department of Wood Science in the Division of Forestry at West Virginia University, conducted a study for the Architectural Woodwork Institute regarding the deflection of wood shelving materials under various amount of stress. The following table represents their findings with the various products tested. The study was developed in the inch-pound method and is not converted to metric for this example.

The table shows total uniformly distributed load requirements necessary to cause deflection of 1/4 inch in shelves 8 and 12 inches wide with spans (i.e., unfixed, supported at each end) of 30, 36, 42, and 48 inches. Load required to deflect shelves more or less than 1/4 inch may be estimated by direct proportion. For example, the uniformly distributed load required to cause a deflection of 1/8 inch is one-half that of the value in the table. For widths different than 8 or 12 inches (the values used in the table), load required to cause a 1/4 inch deflection may also be determined by direct proportion. A 6 inch wide shelf, for example, will deflect twice as much as a 12 inch wide shelf under the same load.

The following equation shows how deflection is related to shelf dimensions, width, thickness, span, load per inch of span and E-value, a material property which measures stiffness or resistance to deflection. The higher the E-value, the less the deflection. When a shelf is made with several materials, each with its own E-value, a composite E-value must be determined.

To compute deflection:

$$D=\frac{0.1563wl^4}{Ebh^3}$$

In which the values are:

D = deflection (in inches)

w = load per lineal inch of span

l = span (length)

E = modulus of elasticity

b = base (width)

h = depth (thickness)

Shelf Deflection of 1/4" by Estimated Total Distributed Load in Pounds

Material	Thickness		Span: 30"		36"		42"		48"	
		Width	8"	12"	8"	12"	8"	12"	8"	12"
Yellow-Poplar Red Gum Sweet Gum	lumber	3/4"	322 lbs.	483 lbs.	189 lbs.	284 lbs.	117 lbs.	175 lbs.	78 lbs.	117 lbs.
		1-1/16"	912	1368	528	790	332	498	221	332
Hard Maple Pecan Red Oak	lumber	3/4"	356 lbs.	534 lbs.	209 lbs.	313 lbs.	133 lbs.	206 lbs.	88 lbs.	133 lbs.
		1-1/16"	1021	1536	592	888	373	560	249	374
Birch Hickory	lumber	3/4"	400	600	232	348	146	219	98	146
		1-1/16"	1134	1701	660	990	414	621	277	415
Medium density particleboard (raw or covered with "melamine")		3/4"	78	117	46	69	29	43	19	28
		1"	185	277	109	164	69	102	45	66
Medium density fiberboard (raw or covered with "melamine")		3/4"	100	150	58	87	36	54	25	38
		1"	237	356	137	206	85	128	59	90
Birch faced plywood, veneer core		3/4"	145	218	86	129	54	81	36	54
Birch faced plywood, medium density particleboard core		3/4"	125	188	72	109	46	68	31	46
Medium density particleboard covered two sides and one edge with nominal 0.028" high pressure decorative laminate		3/4" (core)	174	261	100	139	64	96	42	63
Medium density particleboard covered two sides and one edge with nominal 0.050" high pressure decorative laminate		3/4" (core)	234	350	137	205	86	129	58	87
Medium density particleboard with 1/8" solid lumber edge		3/4"	89	139	53	79	33	50	22	33
Medium density particleboard with 3/4" solid lumber edge		3/4"	100	150	60	90	42	63	25	38
Medium density particleboard with 3/4" x 1-1/2" solid lumber dropped edge		3/4"	384	435	216	241	132	152	92	107

NOTE: All medium density particleboard is ANSI 208.1- (ltest edition), Type M-2
The information and ratings stated here pertain to material currently offered and represent results of tests believed to be reliable. However, due to variations in handling and in methods not known or under our control, no warantee or guarantee as to the end results can be made.

10 - Casework

DETAIL NOMENCLATURE

Familiarity with the labeled details on this page will facilitate communication between architects, designers, specifiers, and woodwork manufacturers by establishing common technical language.

Spline Joint: Used to strengthen and align faces when gluing panels in width or length, including items requiring site assembly.

Stub Tenon: Joinery method for assembling stile and rail type frames that are additionally supported, such as web or skeleton case frames.

Haunch Mortise and Tenon Joint: Joinery method for assembling paneled doors or stile and rail type paneling.

Conventional Mortise and Tenon Joint: Joinery method for assembling square-edged surfaces such as case face frames.

Dowel Joint: Alternative joinery method serving same function as Conventional Mortise and Tenon.

French Dovetail Joint: Method for joining drawer sides to fronts when fronts conceal metal extension slides or overlay the case faces.

Conventional Dovetail Joint: Traditional method for joining drawer sides to fronts or backs. Usually limited to flush or lipped type drawers.

Drawer Lock-Joint: Another joinery method for joining drawer sides to fronts. Usually used for flush type installation, but can be adapted to lip or overlay type drawers.

Exposed End Details: Illustrates attachment of finished end of case body to front frame using a butt joint and a lock mitered joint.

Through Dado: Conventional joint used for assembly of case body members. Dado not concealed by application of case face frame.

Blind Dado: Variation of Through Dado with applied edge "stopping" or concealing dado groove.

Stop Dado: Another method of concealing dado exposure. Applicable when veneer edging or solid lumber is used. Exposed End Detail illustrates attachment of finished end of case body to front frame using butt joint.

Dowel Joint: Fast becoming an industry standard assembly method, this versatile joinery technique is often based on 1-14" (32 mm) spacing of dowels.

Edge Banding: Method of concealing plies or inner cores of plywood or particleboard when edges are exposed. Thickness or configuration will vary with manufacturers' practices.

Paneled Door Details: Joinery techniques when paneled effect is desired. Profiles are optional as is the use of flat or raised panels. Solid lumber raised panels may be used when width does not exceed the standard. Rim-raised panels recommended for Premium Grade or when widths exceed the *AWS* or when transparent finish is used.

Spline Joint

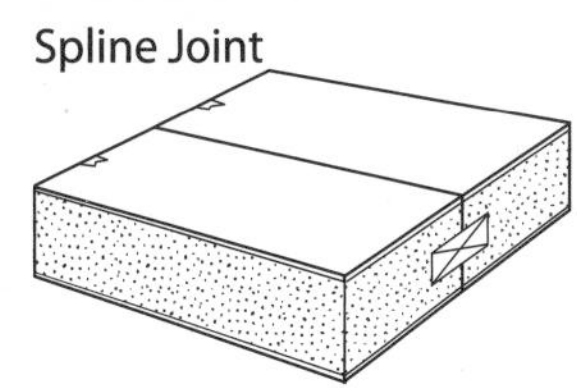

Stub Tenon

Haunch Mortise and Tenon Joint

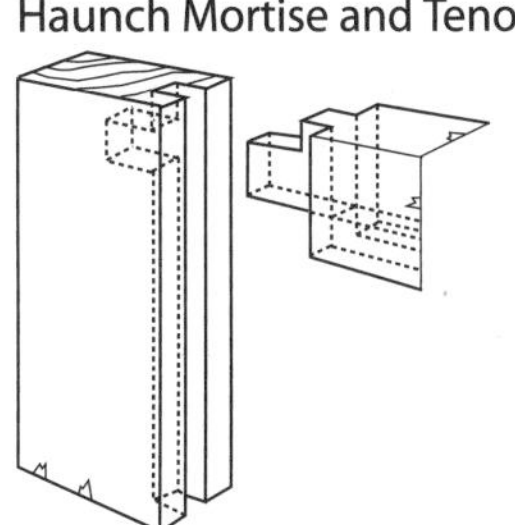

Conventional Mortise and Tenon Joint

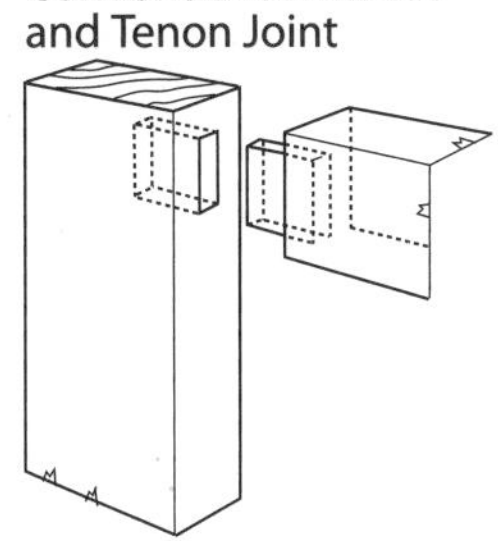

Dowel Joint

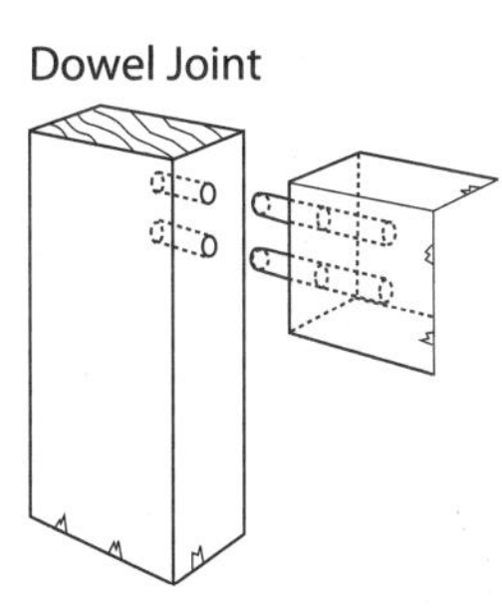

French Dovetail Joint

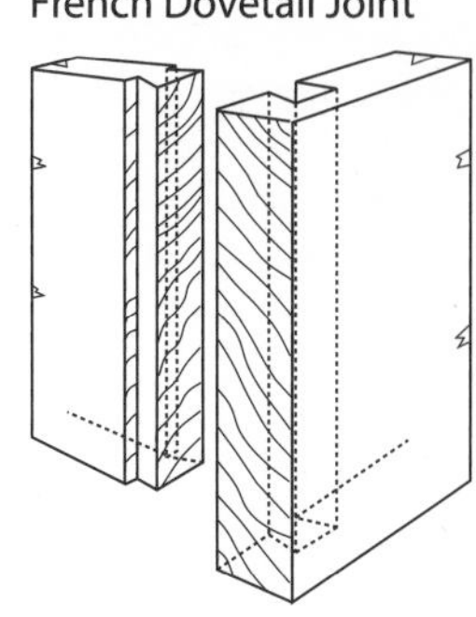

Conventional Dovetail Joint

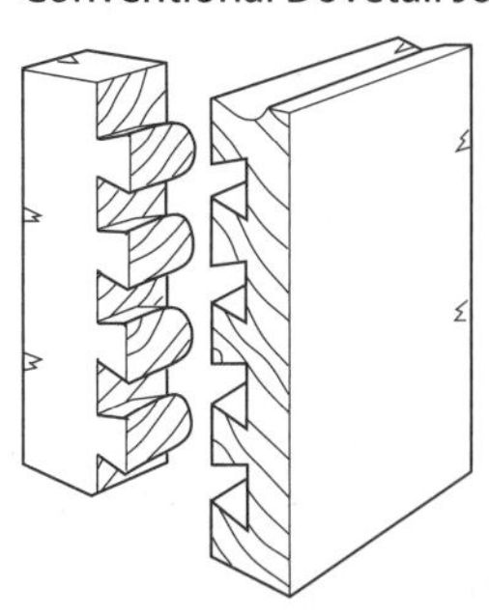

Drawer Lock-Joint

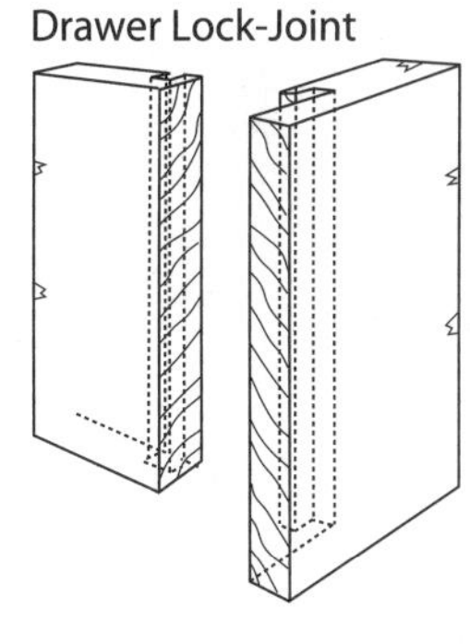

Exposed End Details

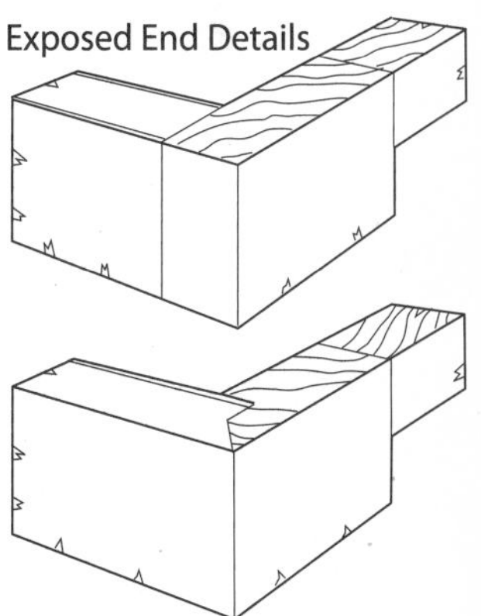

10 - Casework

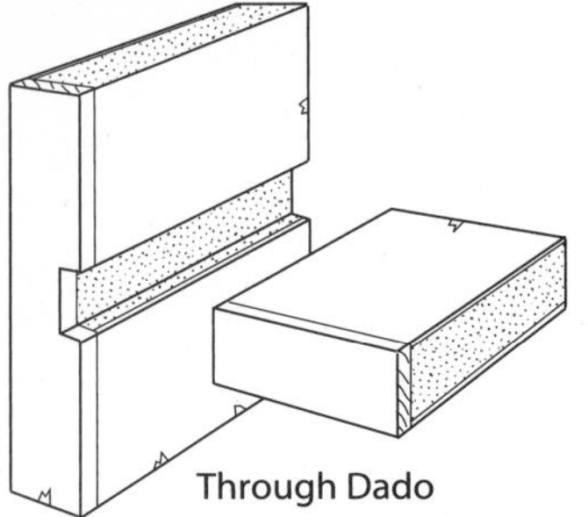
Through Dado

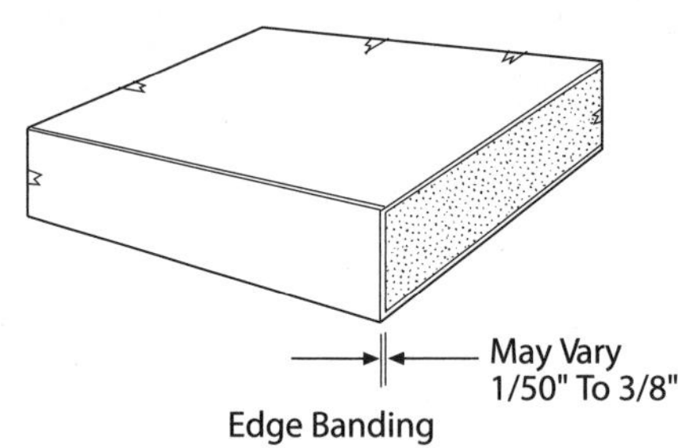
May Vary
1/50" To 3/8"
Edge Banding

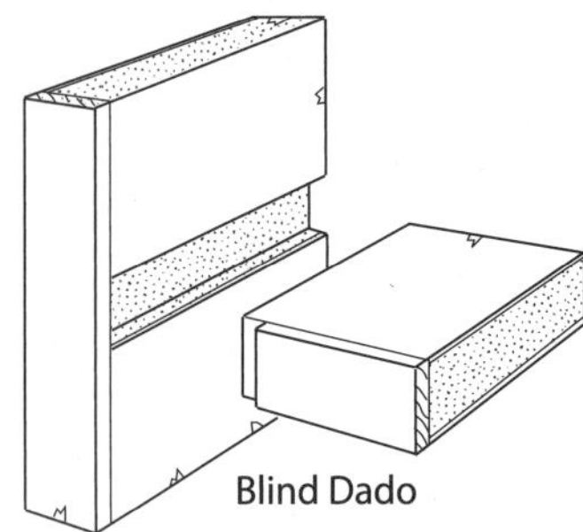
Blind Dado

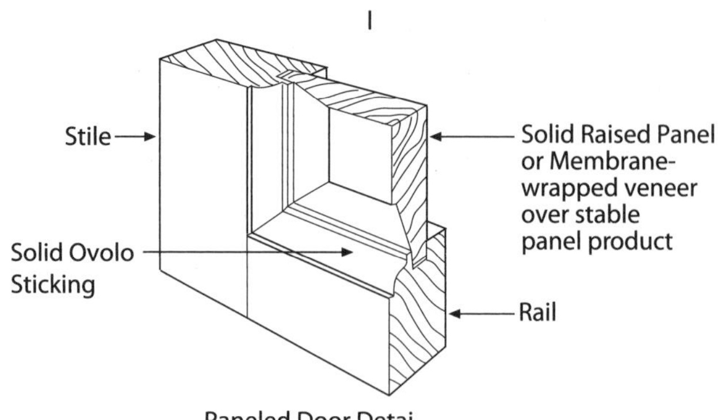
Stile
Solid Raised Panel
or Membrane-
wrapped veneer
over stable
panel product
Solid Ovolo
Sticking
Rail
Paneled Door Detai

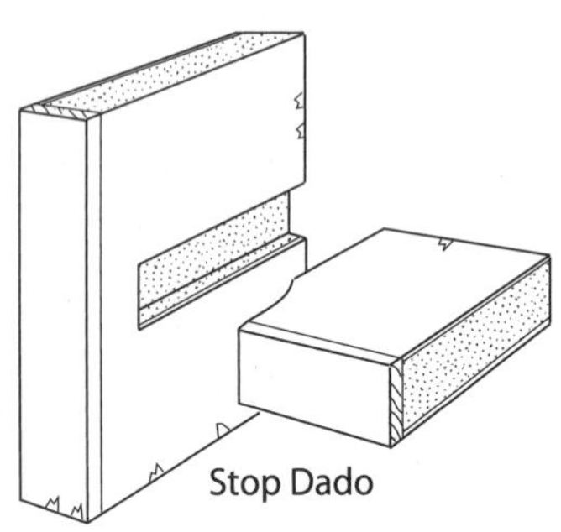
Stop Dado

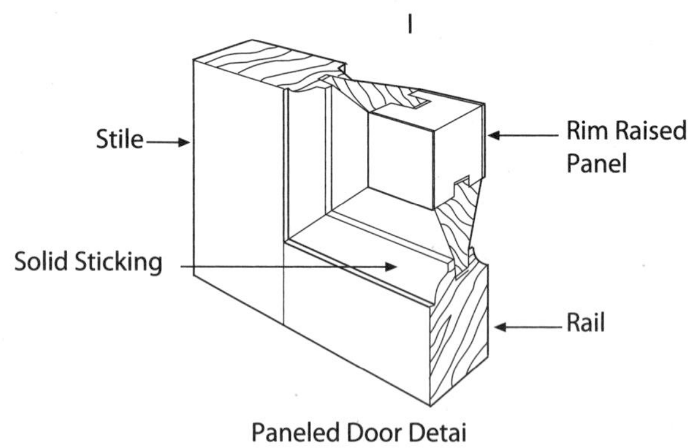
Stile
Rim Raised
Panel
Solid Sticking
Rail
Paneled Door Detai

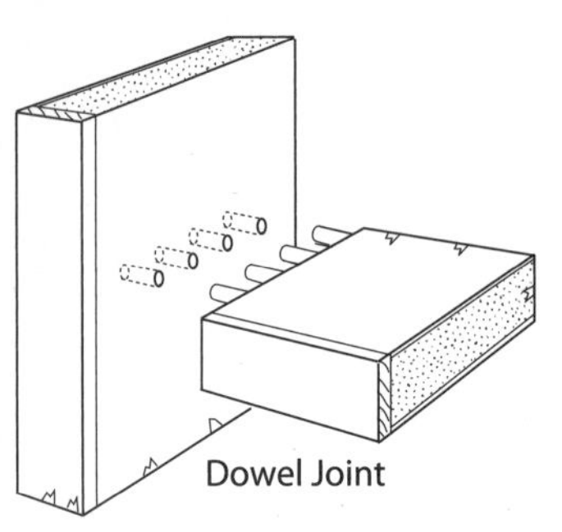
Dowel Joint

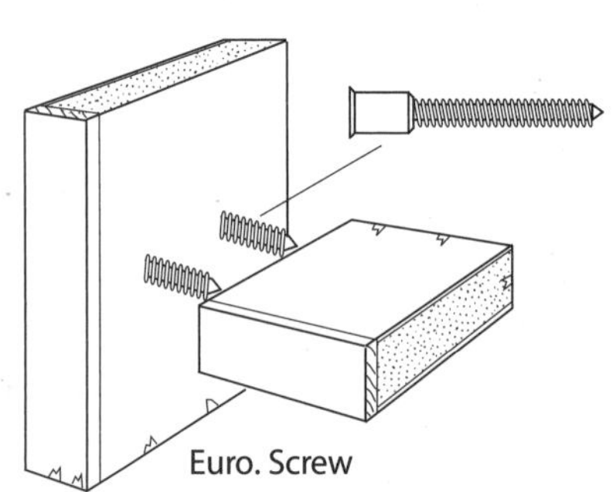
Euro. Screw

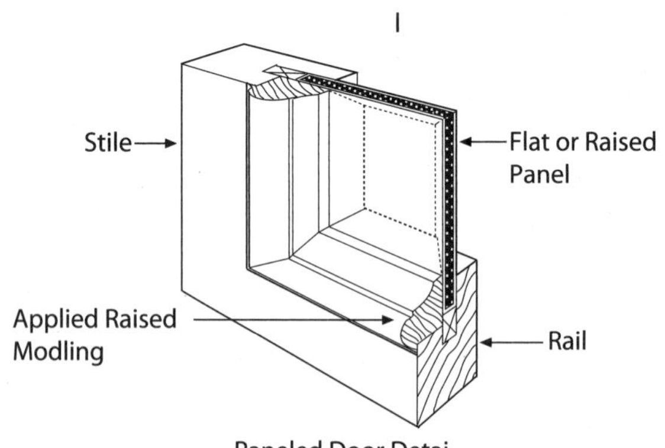
Stile
Flat or Raised
Panel
Applied Raised
Modling
Rail
Paneled Door Detai

10 - Casework

Hinge Selection Guide

Architectural cabinet hinges will usually be furnished from the manufacturer's stock unless otherwise specified. The four most common hinge types are illustrated below, along with a brief table to assist in selection.

European hinges with the screws set in synthetic inserts are fast becoming industry standard. These hinges have been found to be cost-effective alternatives to the more traditional hinges shown below. Follow hinge manufacturers' recommendations on number and spacing of hinges. There are conditions, however, in which the use of butt or wraparound hinges will continue to be the best solution. Pivot hinges often require a cut-in center hinge. Consult manufacturer's recommendations.

Hinge Type	Butt	Wraparound	Pivot	European Style
		Frame Door		
Applications	Conventional Flush with Face Frame	Conventional Reveal Overlay	Reveal Overlay Flush Overlay	Conventional Flush without Face Frame Reveal Overlay Flush Overlay
Strength	High	Very High	Moderate	Moderate
Concealed when closed	No	No	Semi	Yes
Requires mortising	Yes	Occasionally	Usually	Yes
Cost of hinge	Low	Moderate	Low	Moderate
Ease of installation	Moderate	Easy	Moderate	Very Easy
Easily adjusted after installation	No	No	No	Yes
Remarks	Door requires hardwood edge	Exposed knuckle and hinge body	Door requires hardwood edge	1. Specify degree of opening 2. No catch required on self-closing styles

10 - Casework

Drawer Slide Selection Guide

The following table serves as both a checklist and a starting point for the discussion of a wide variety of drawer slide systems. While by no means exhaustive, the characteristics described below are often considered the most important by the client, the design professional, and the woodwork manufacturer. The selection of the slide characteristics will affect the usefulness of the cabinets. Careful consideration should be given to avoid "over-specifying" for the purpose intended.

The owner and the design professional will be wise to involve a manufacturer in the design and selection process early in the project. Dimensions use the inch-pound convention.

Degree of Extension	☐ STANDARD EXTENSION—All but 4-6" of drawer body extends out of cabinet ☐ FULL EXTENSION—Entire drawer body extends out to face of cabinet ☐ FULL EXTENSION WITH OVERTRAVEL—Entire drawer body extends beyond the face of cabinet
Static Load Capacity	☐ 50 Pounds—Residential/Light Commercial ☐ 75 Pounds—Commercial ☐ 100 Pounds—Heavy Duty ☐ Over 100 Pounds—Special Conditions, Extra Heavy Duty
Dynamic Load Capacity	☐ 30 Pounds; 35,000 cycles—Residential/Light Commercial ☐ 50 Pounds; 50,000 cycles—Commercial ☐ 75 Pounds; 100,000 cycles—Heavy Duty
Removal Stop	☐ INTEGRAL STOP—Requires ten times the normal opening force to remove drawer ☐ POSITIVE STOP—Latch(es) which must be operated/opened to remove drawer
Closing	☐ SELF CLOSING/STAY CLOSED—Drawer slides will self-close with their related dynamic load when the drawer is 2" from the fully closed position and not bounce open when properly adjusted
Metal Sided Systems	In recent years several hardware manufacturers have developed "drawer systems" of one type or another, nearly all proprietary. In addition to the above criteria, the following should be considered for these systems prior to approval for use: ☐ POSITIVE STOP—-Drawer must stop within itself and not rely on the drawer front to stop it ☐ PULLOUT STRENGTH—System must demonstrate sufficient strength of attachment of front to sides - design professional should evaluate and approve individually

10 - Casework

Ideas in Groups

The subdivisions of this Section are an ever-growing collection of design ideas with an additional level of detail. While these ideas are grouped by (admittedly somewhat arbitrary) classifications, the design professional should never hesitate to adopt and adapt from one group to another.

Most importantly, the *Architectural Woodwork Standards* presents these ideas as a *starting point* for creative design and fabrication. They are not intended as an illustration of the only way to accomplish a design solution, nor are they intended to establish firm recommendations on dimensions or fabrication techniques.

NOTE: There are projects, such as credenzas, which benefit from having the grain or pattern carried on to the toe space. Toe kicks with exposure to moisture are often specified to be solid hardwood, with the grain running horizontally. Such special considerations shall be clearly noted on the design drawings and in the specifications. Base/toe on cabinets shall be integral (constructed as an integral part of the cabinet body), or separate (constructed as a separate member), at the option of the manufacturer.

Stile and rail doors and drawer fronts, and face frames on some cabinets, require careful attention to details regarding material selection for compatibility of grain and color as well as grain direction.

When transparent finish is specified for exposed surfaces, semi-exposed surfaces are not required to be transparent finish.

The advice and suggestions of all the members of the construction team, from the customers through the designers through the contractors and subcontractors, can and should be evaluated.

The classifications to follow are:

Schools and Libraries

Banks and Courts

Corporate Woodwork

Furniture and Fixtures

Reception

Church Fittings

Basic Cabinetry

10 - Casework

Schools and Libraries

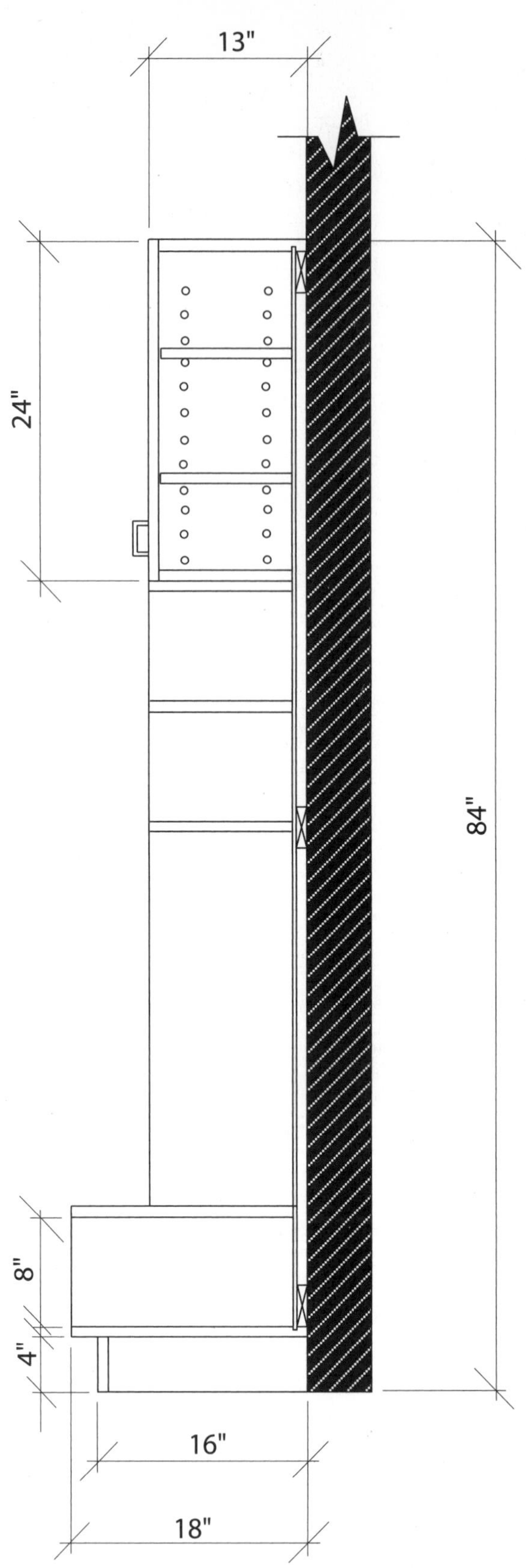

10 - Casework

Schools and Libraries

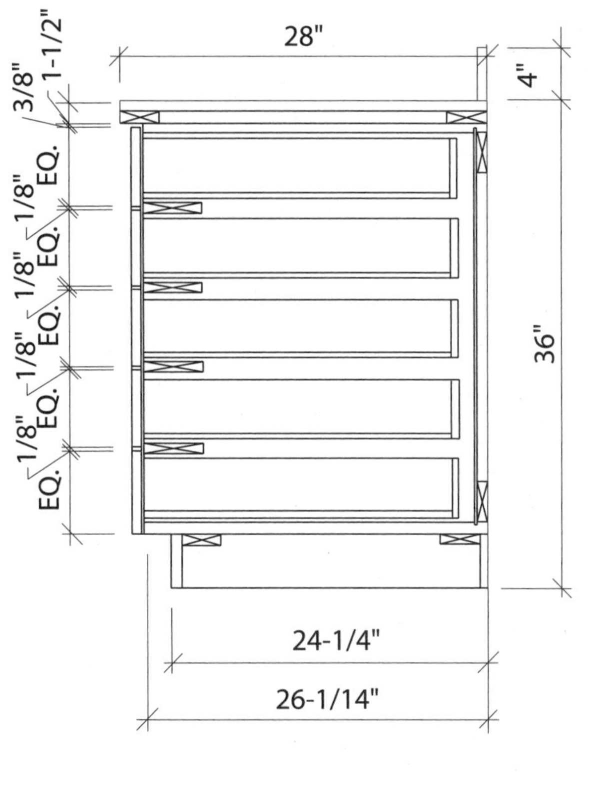

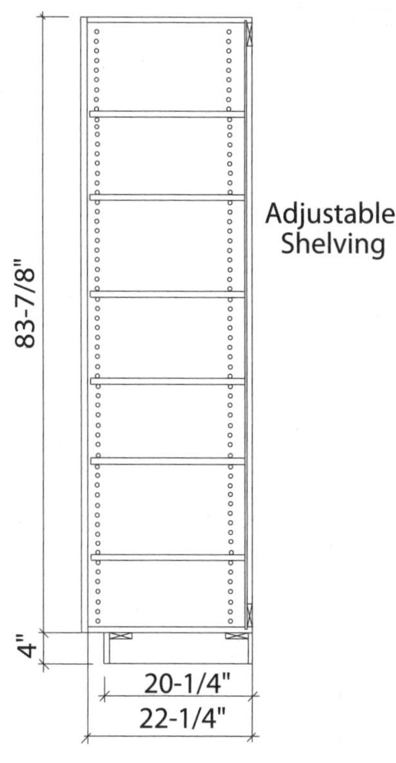

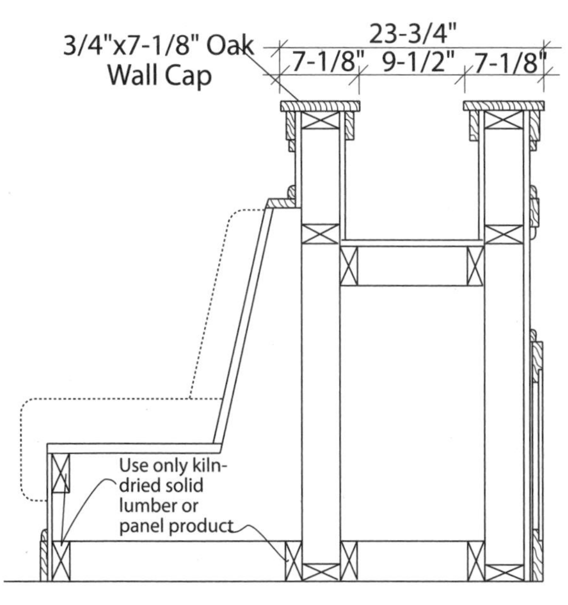

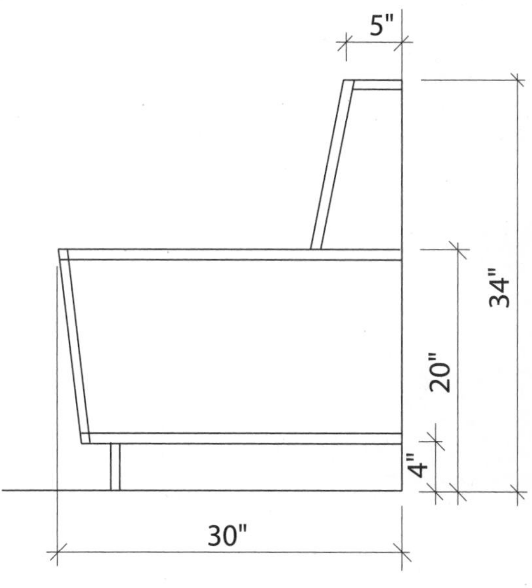

10 - Casework

Schools and Libraries

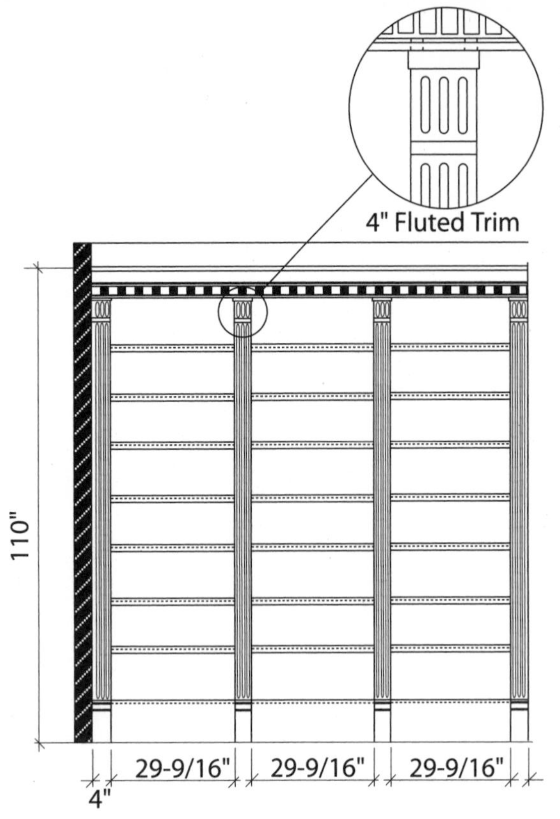

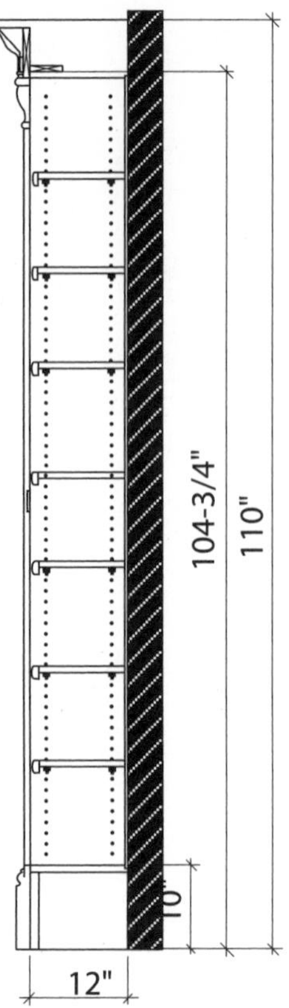

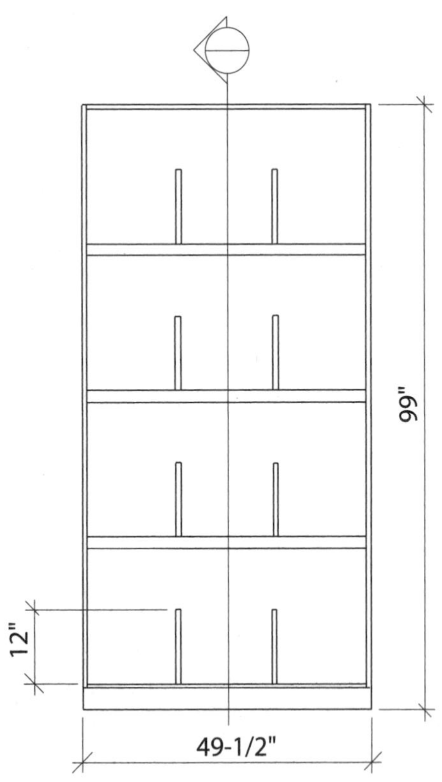

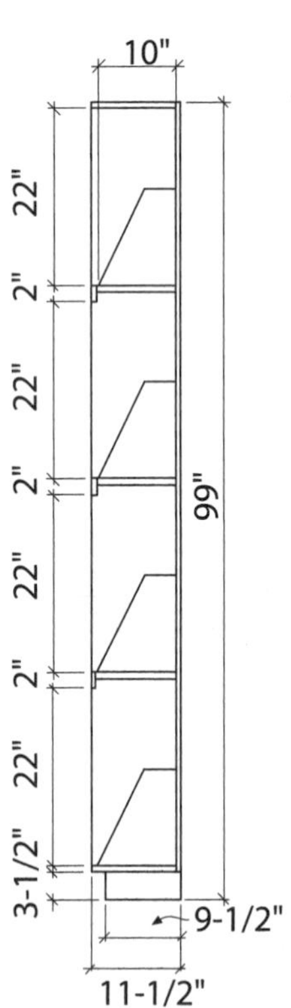

(Appendix B is not part of the AWS for compliance purposes)

10 - Casework

Schools and Libraries

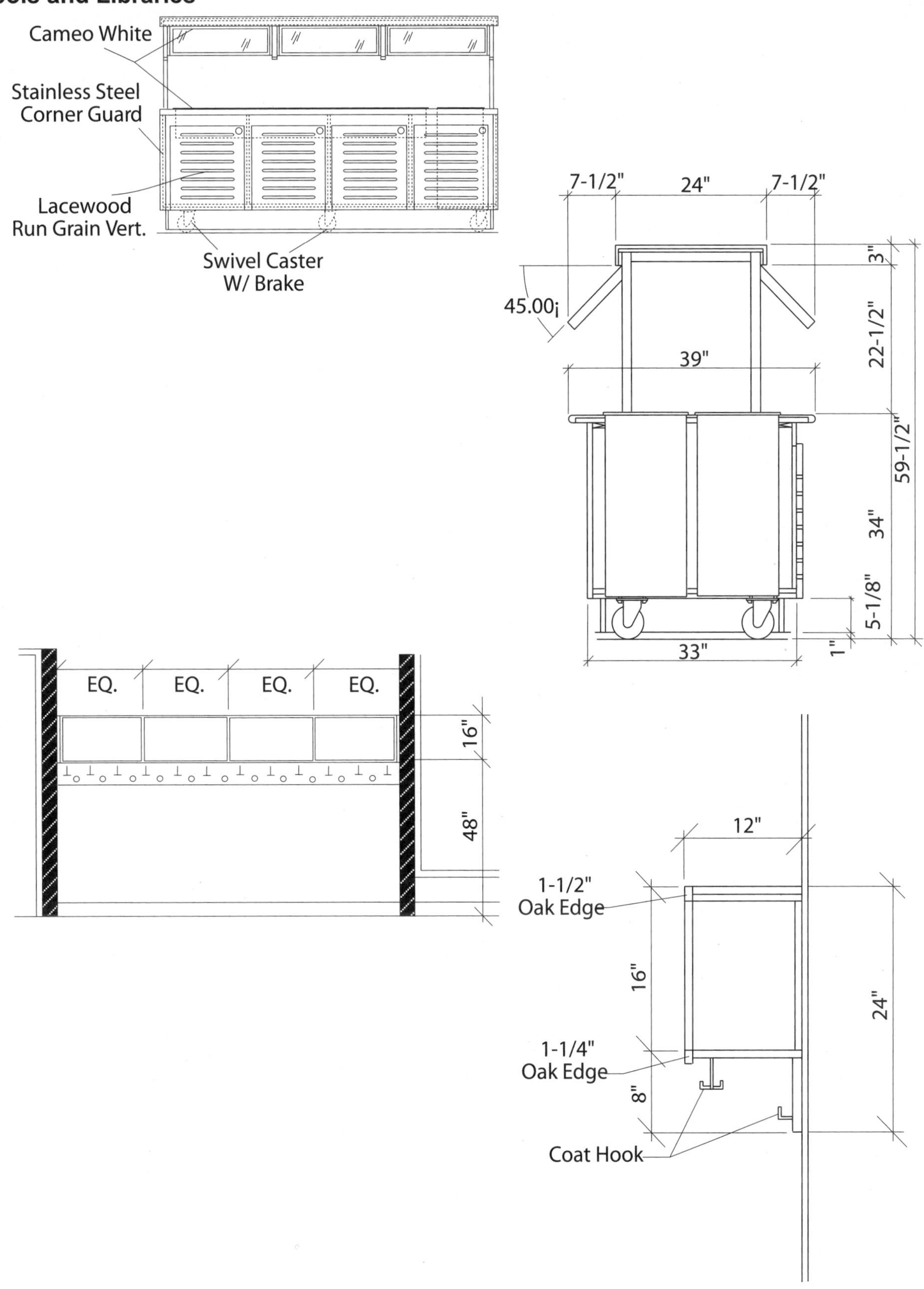

10 - Casework

Banks and Courts

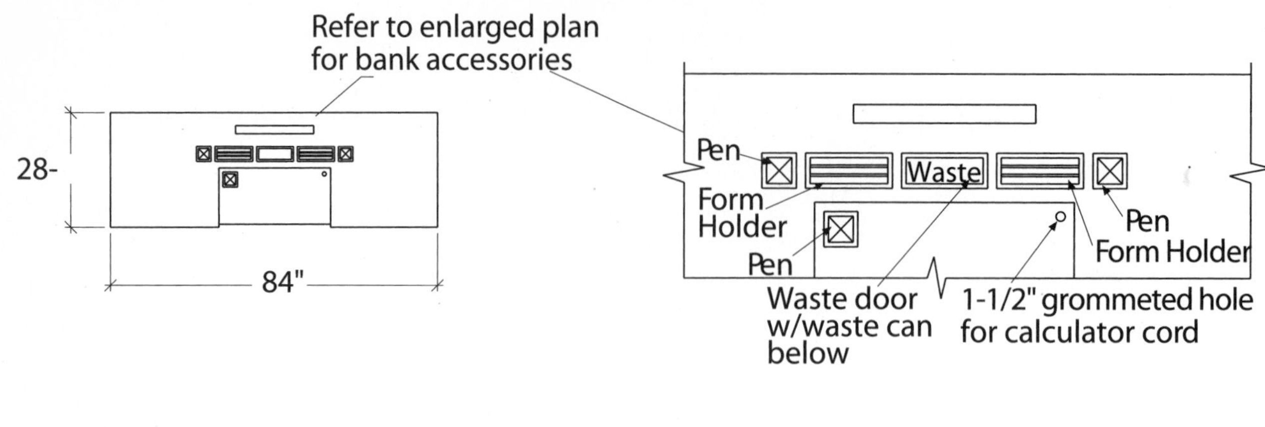

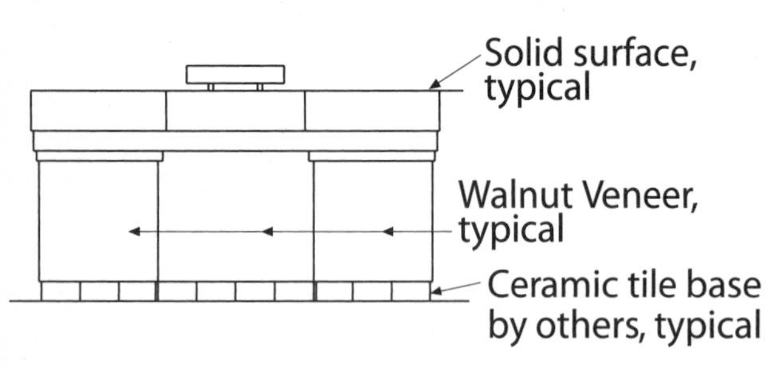

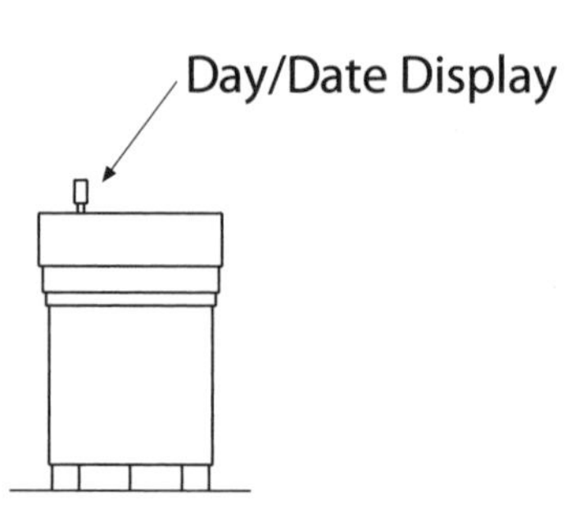

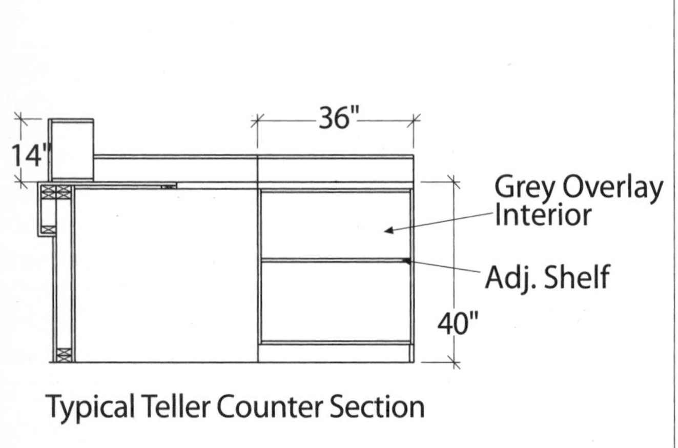

Typical Teller Counter Section

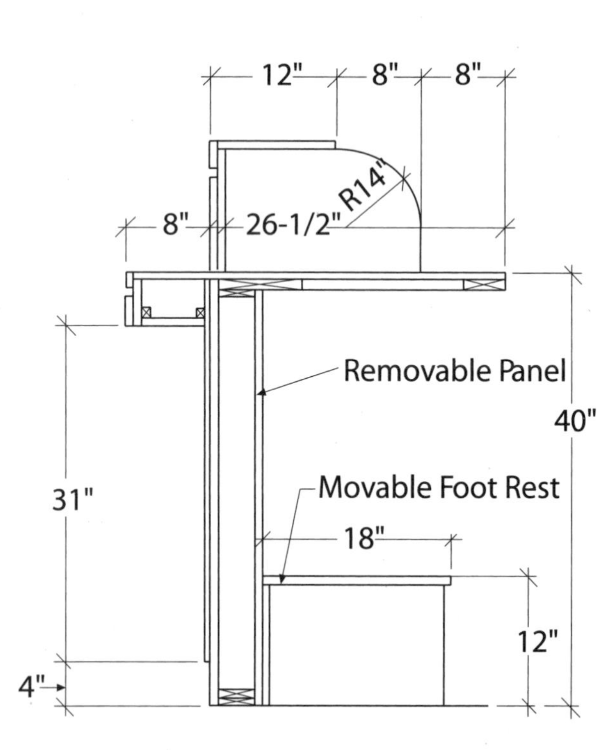

(Appendix B is not part of the AWS for compliance purposes)

10 - Casework

Banks and Courts

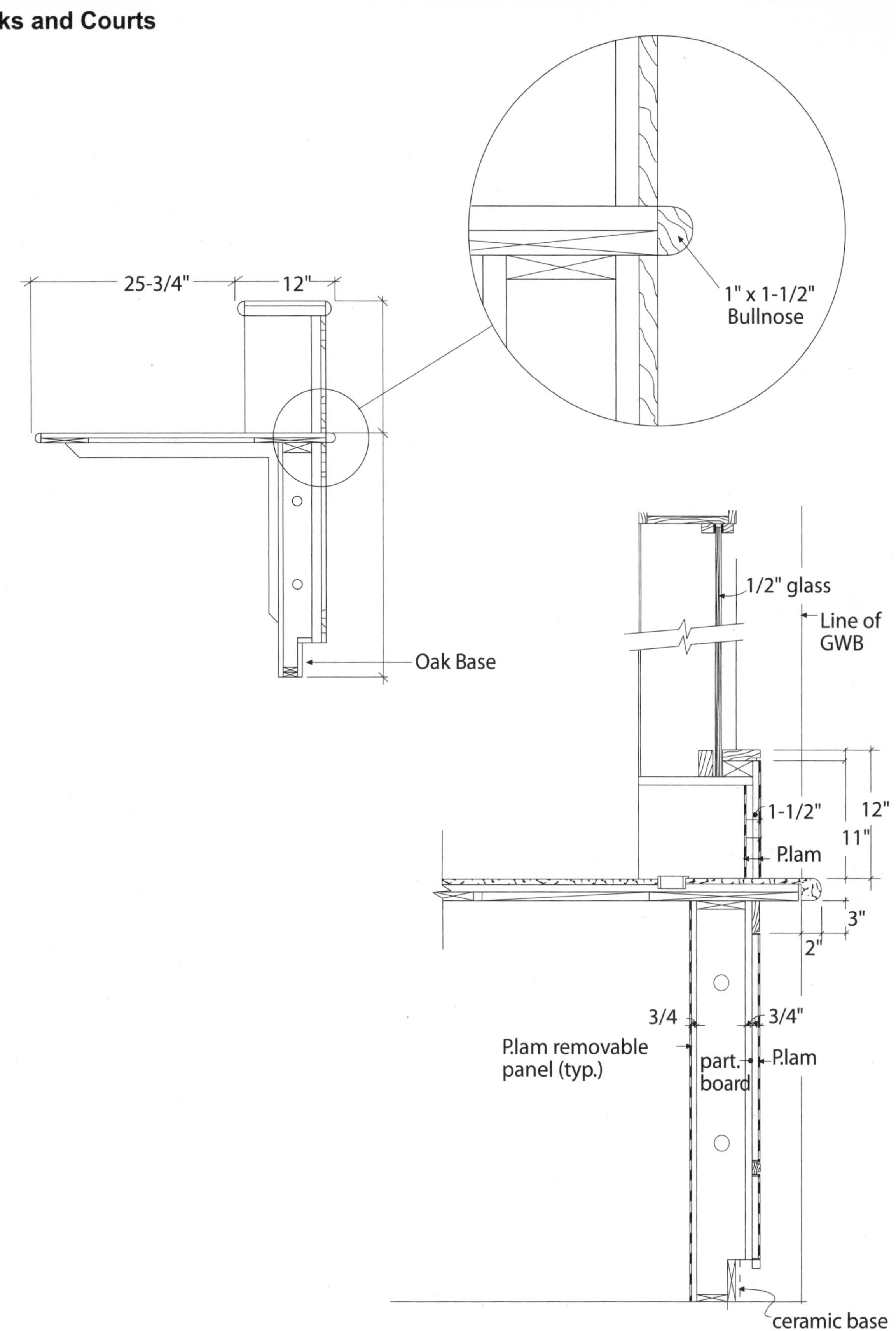

10 - Casework

Banks and Courts

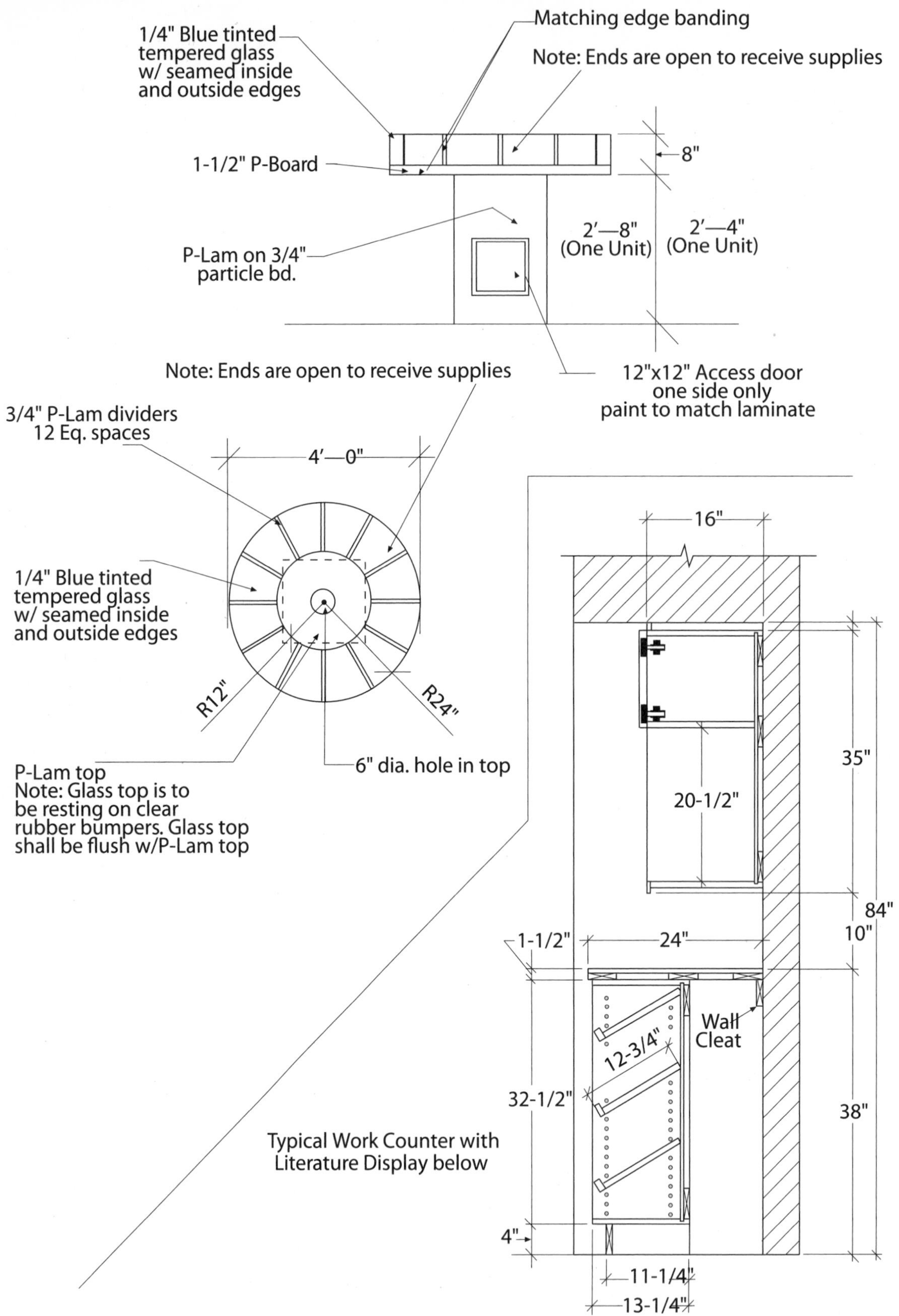

Typical Work Counter with Literature Display below

10 - Casework

Judge's Bench

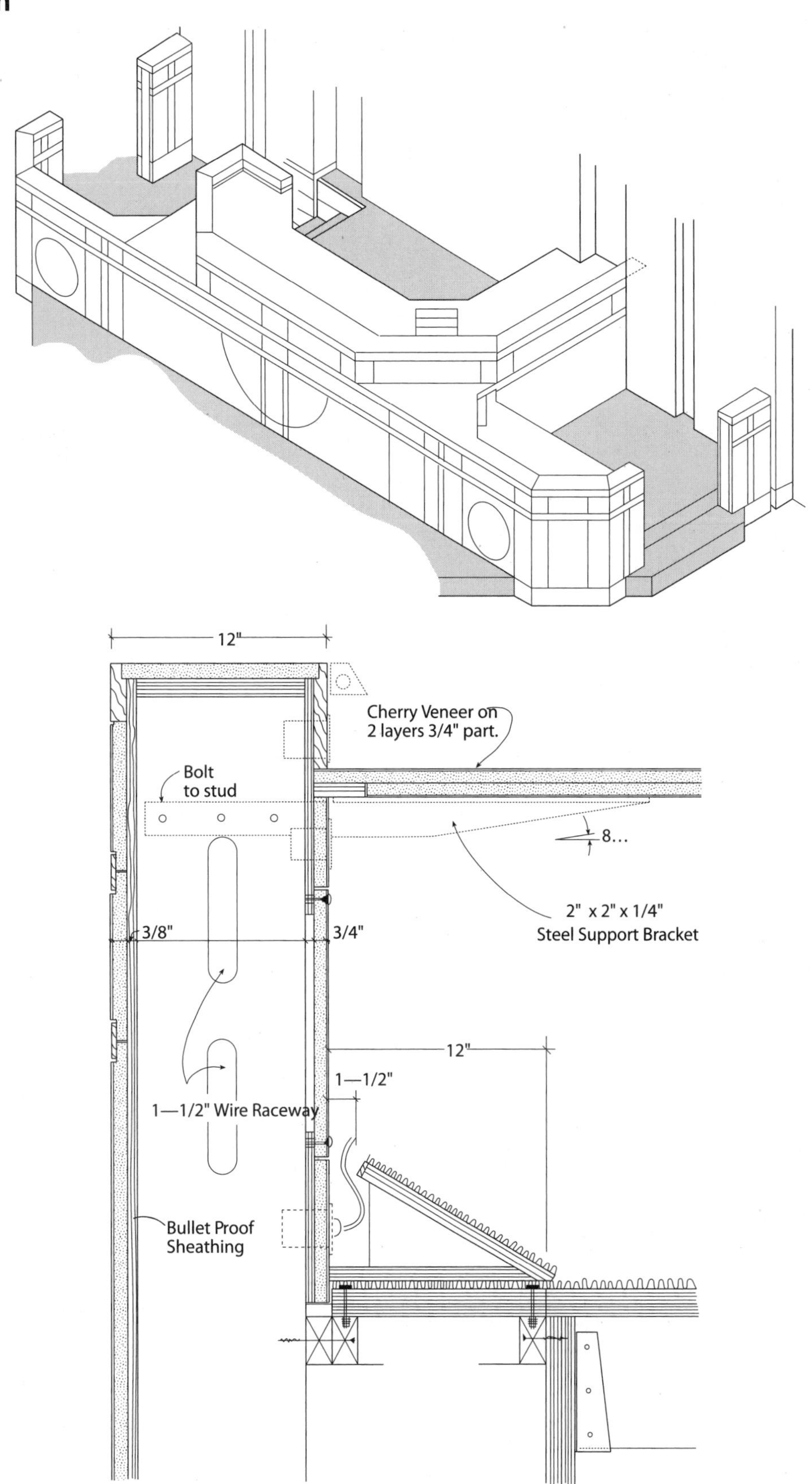

10 - Casework

Corporate Woodwork

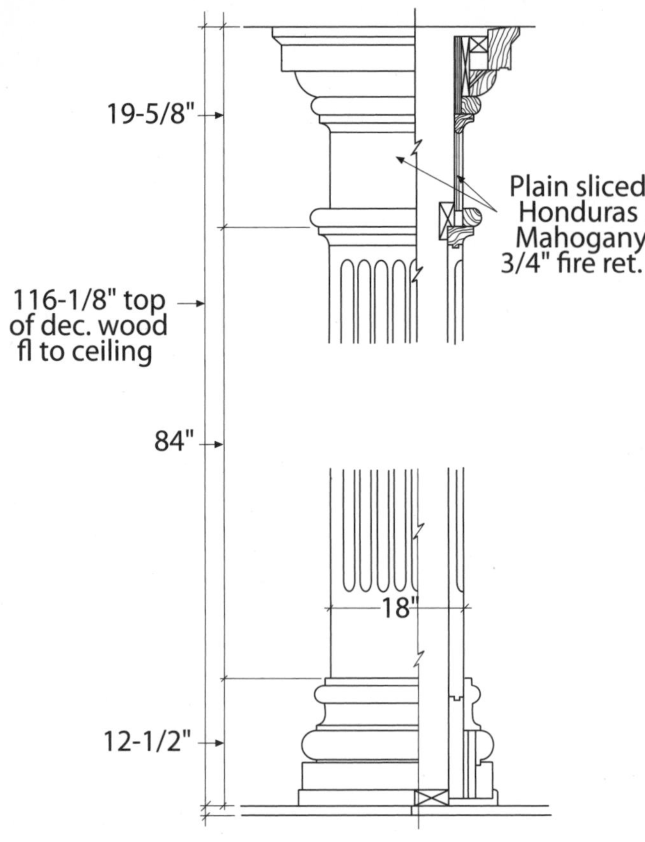

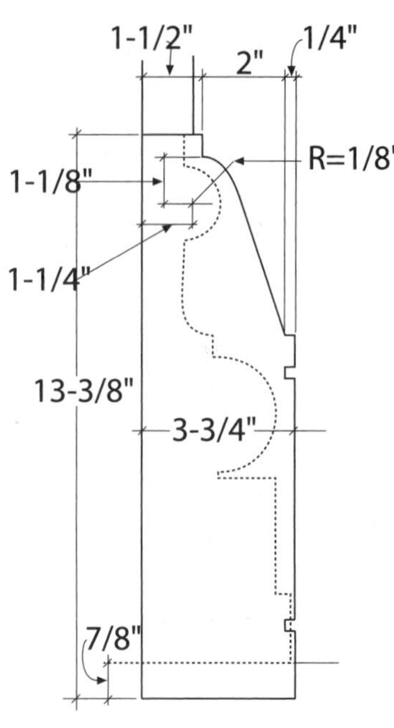

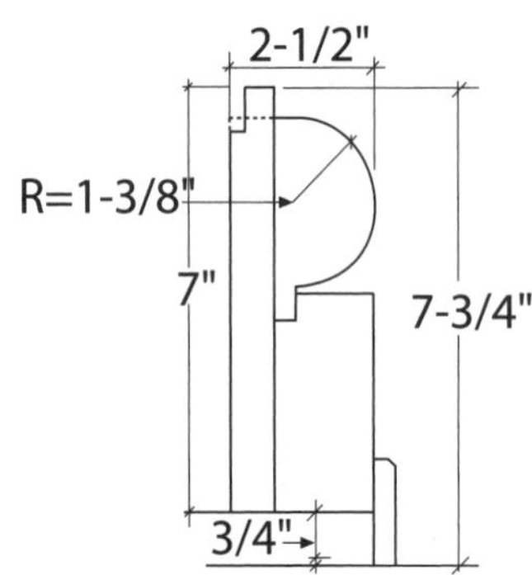

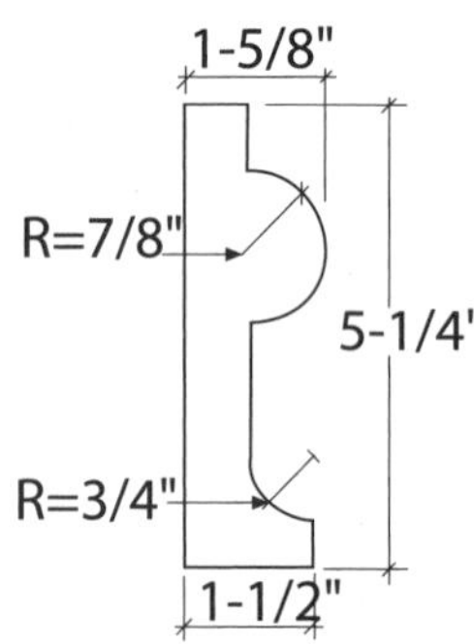

10 - Casework

Corporate Woodwork

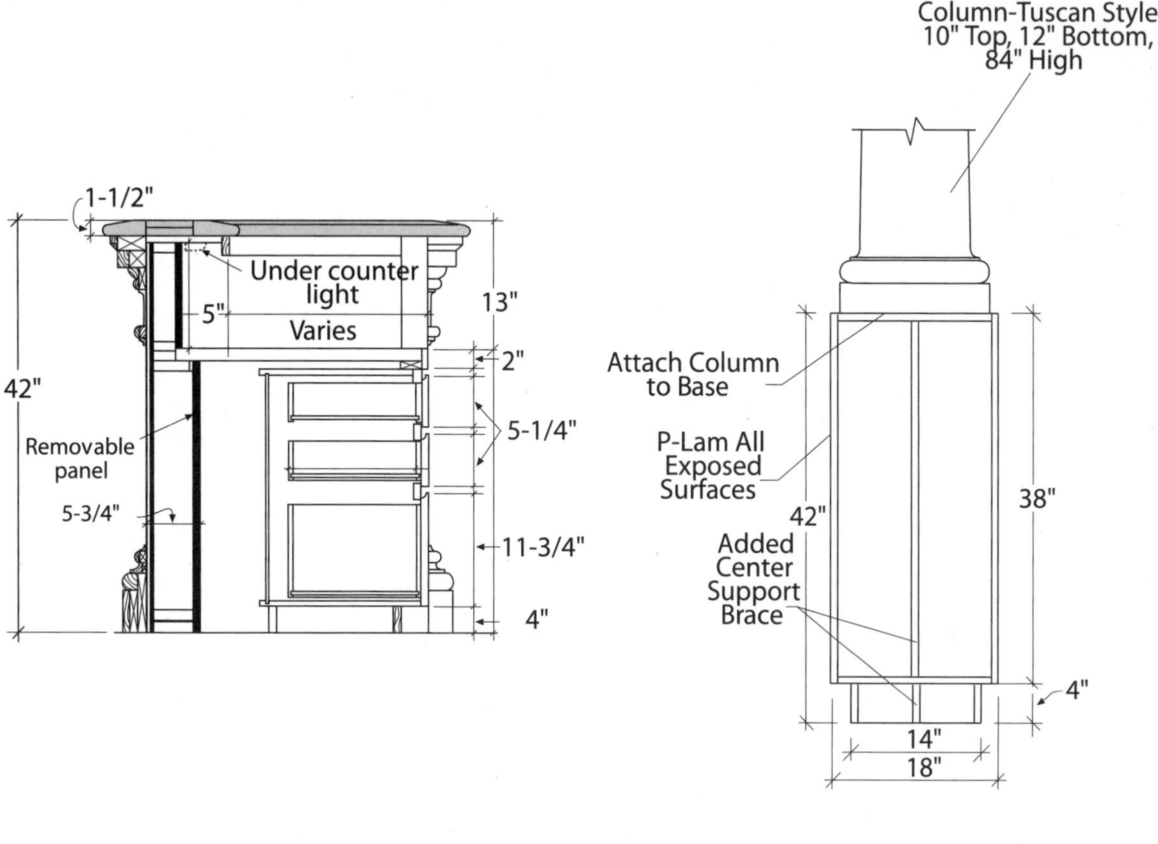

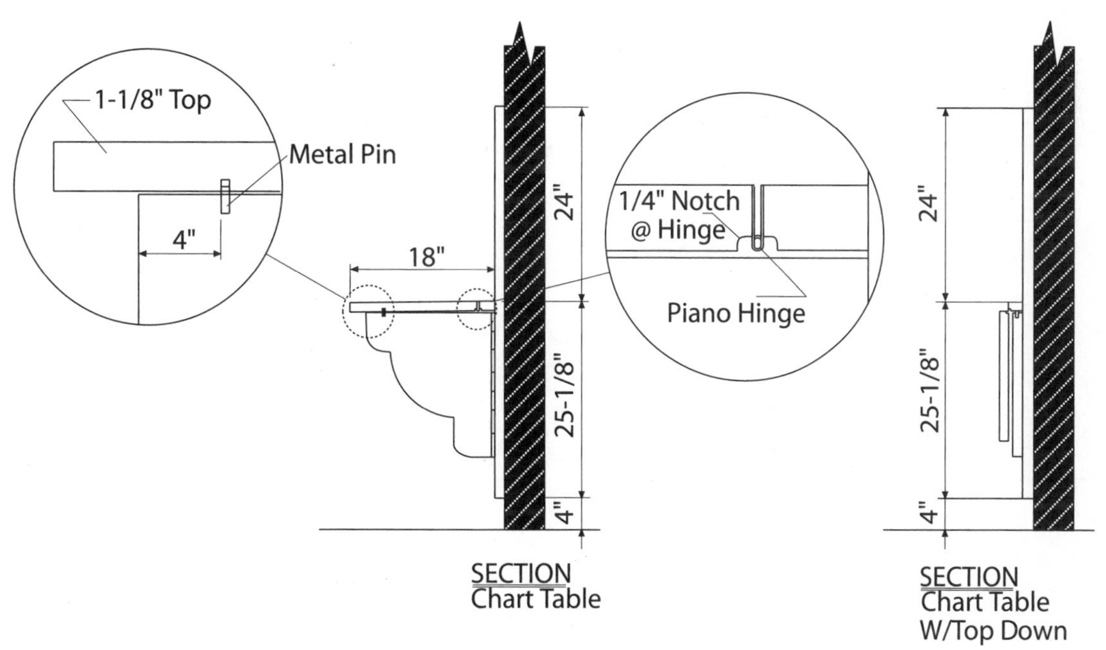

10 - Casework

Corporate Woodwork

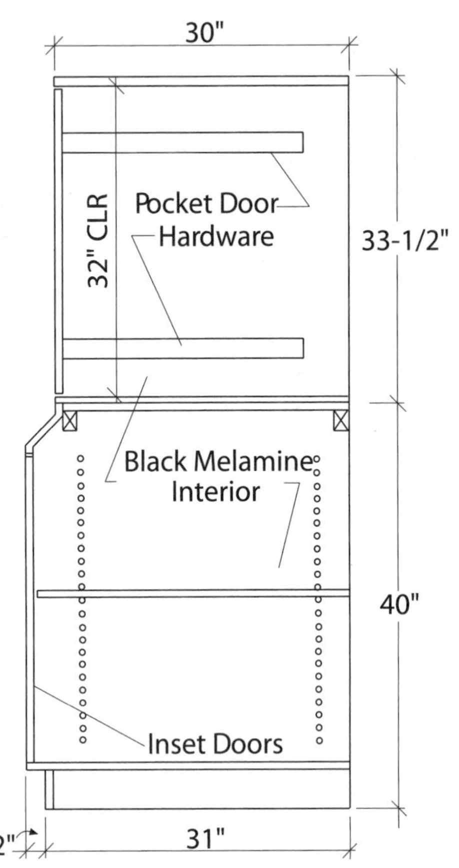

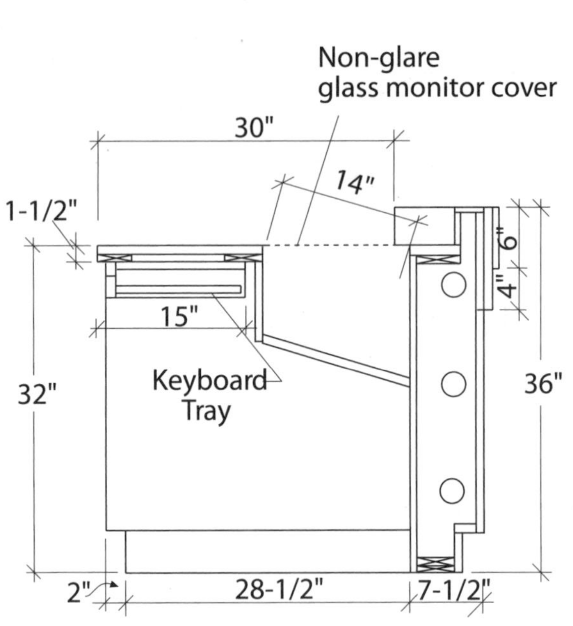

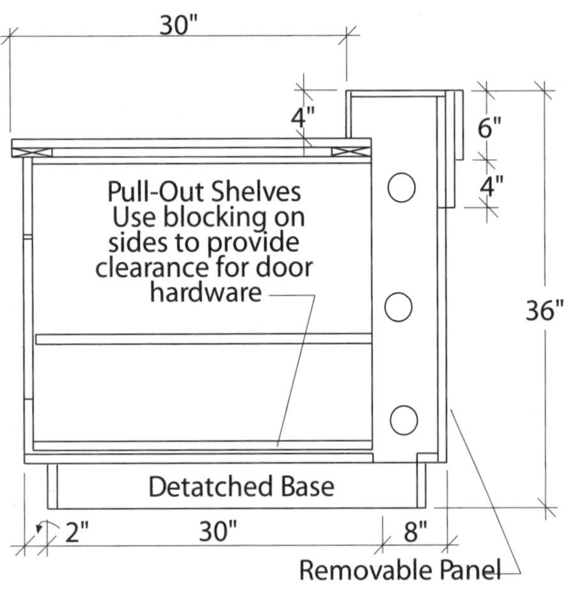

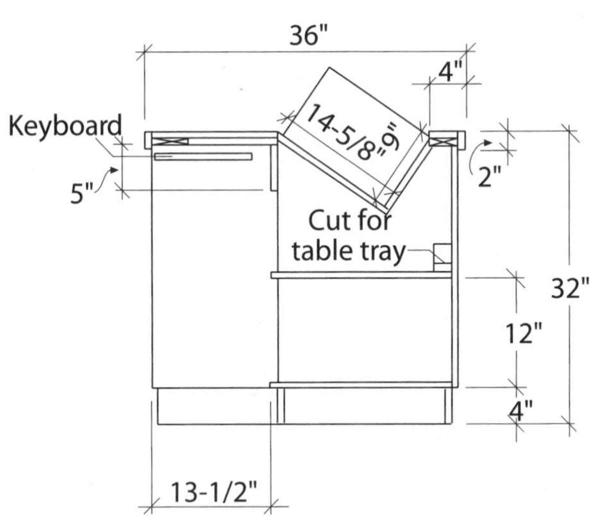

10 - Casework

Corporate Woodwork

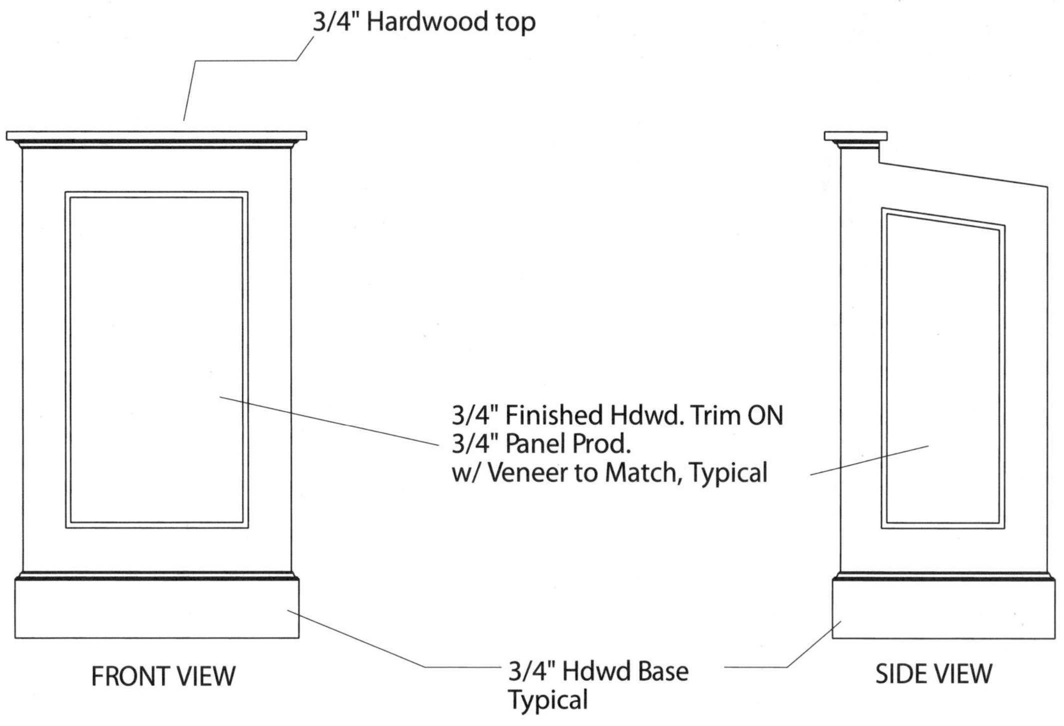

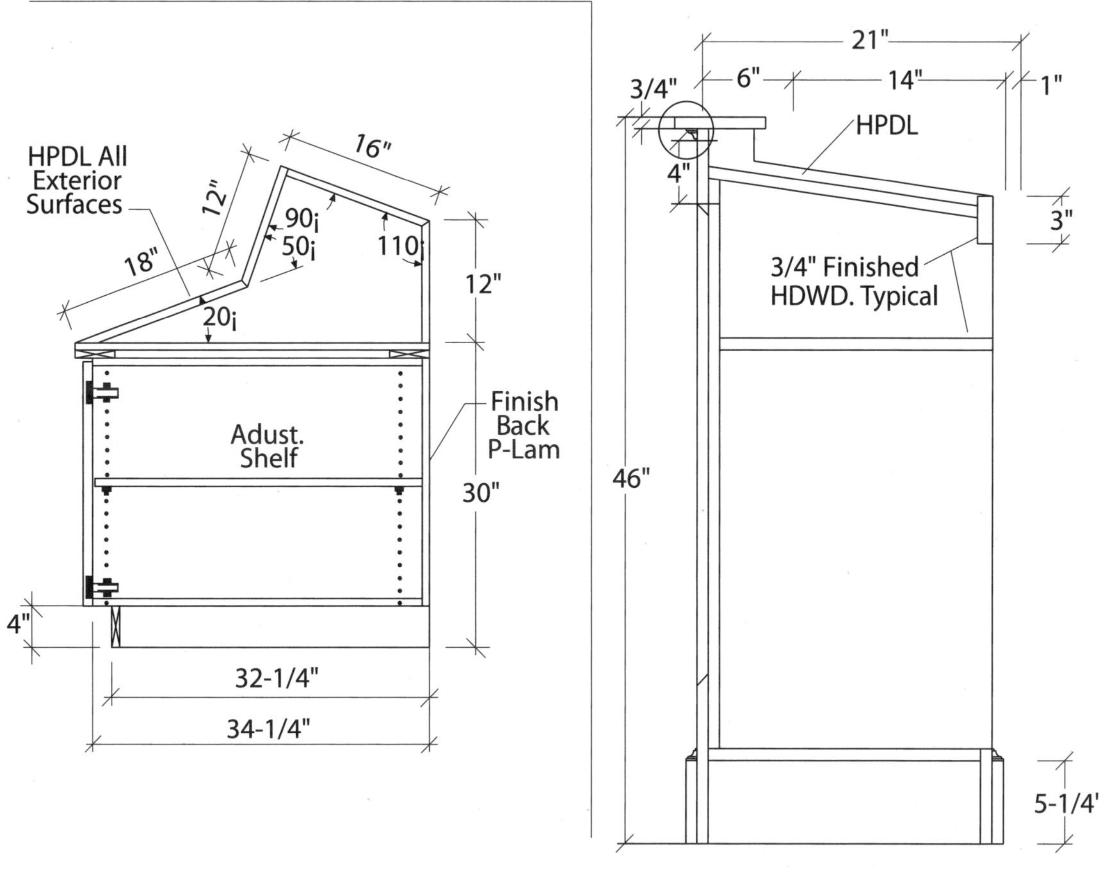

10 - Casework

Corporate Woodwork

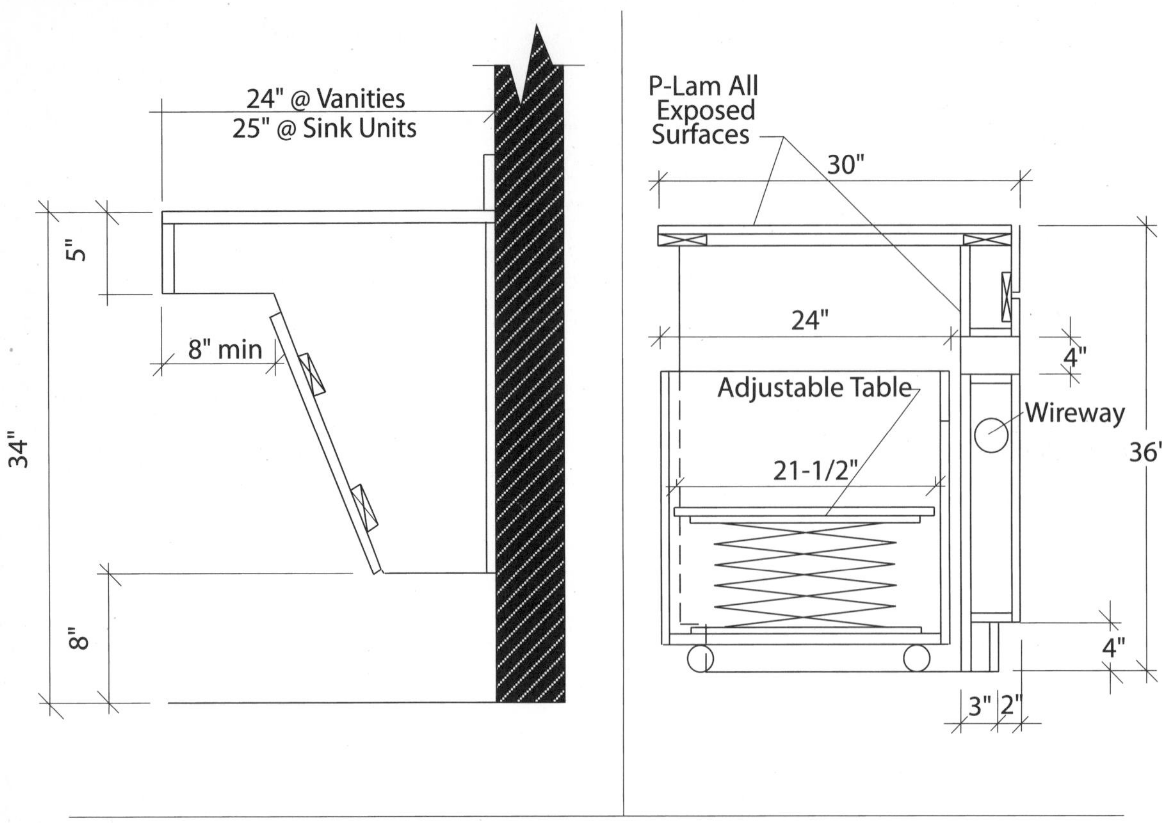

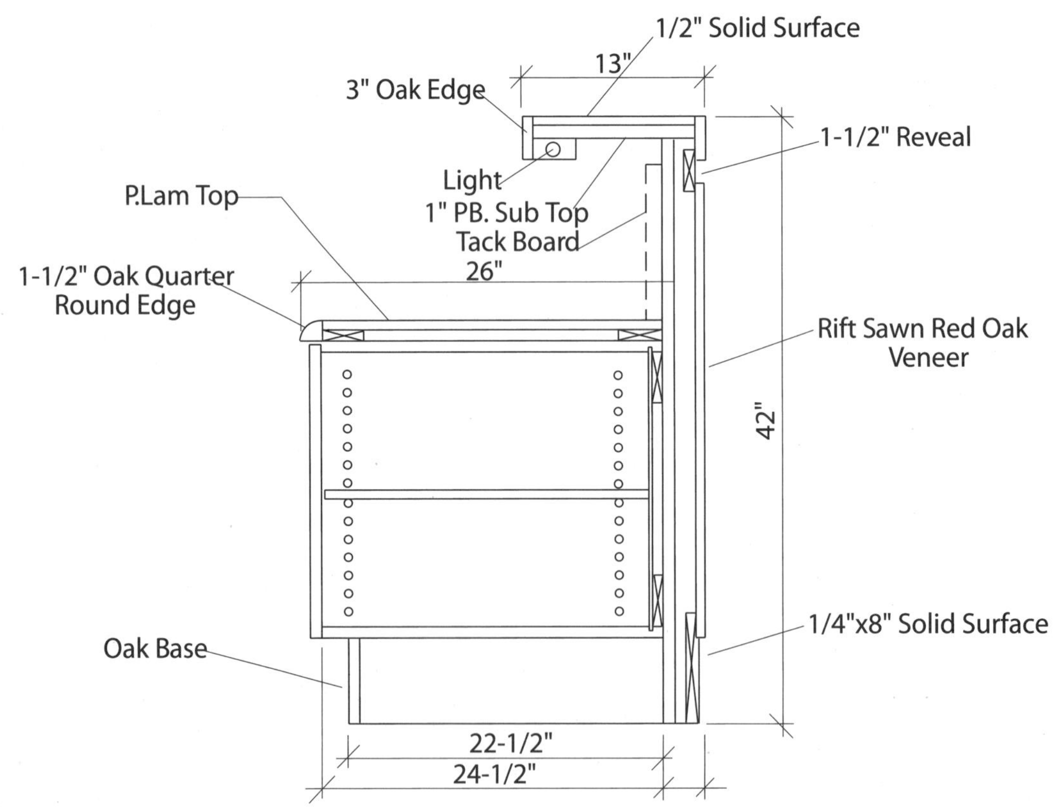

10 - Casework

Furniture and Fixtures

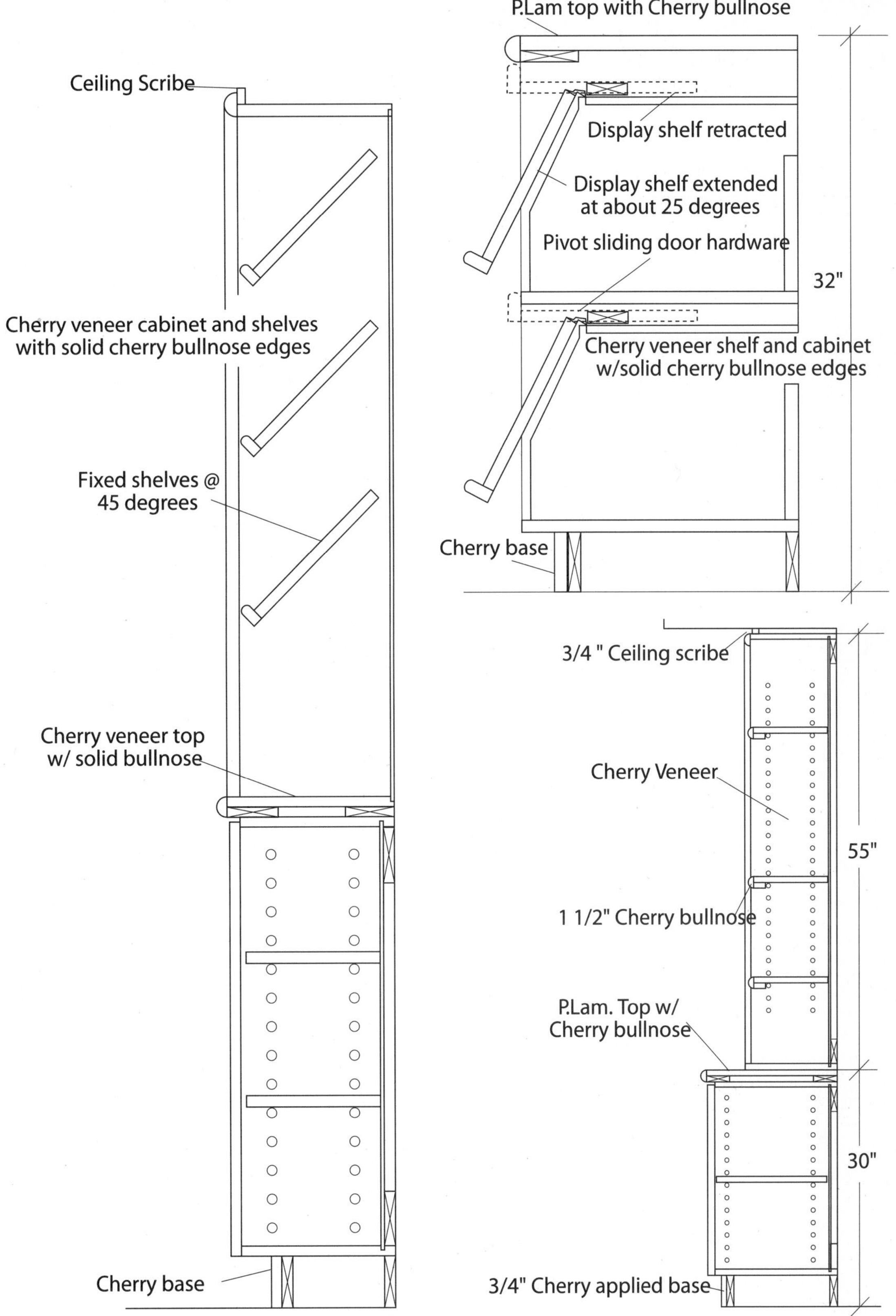

10 - Casework

Furniture and Fixtures

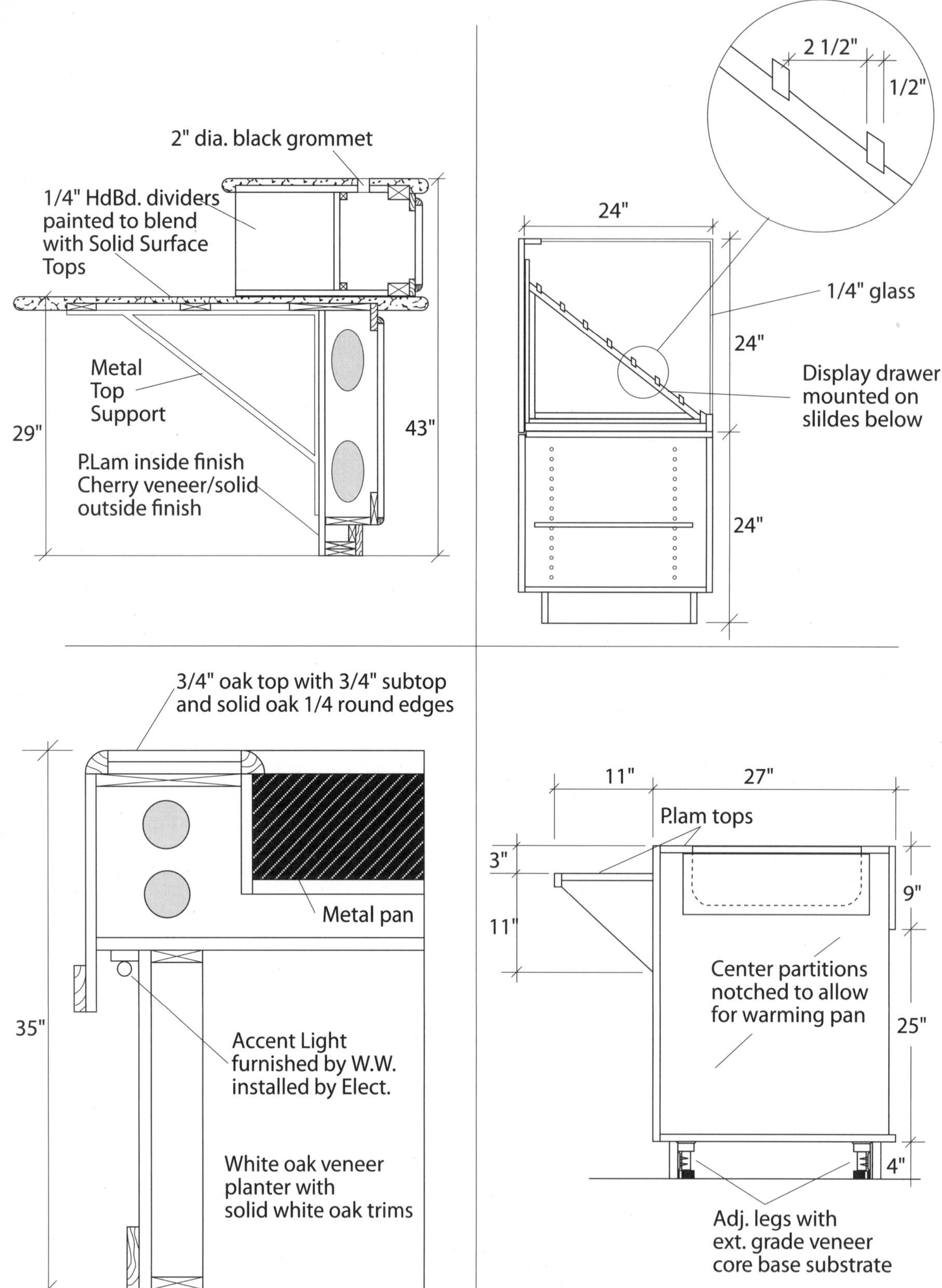

10 - Casework

Furniture and Fixtures

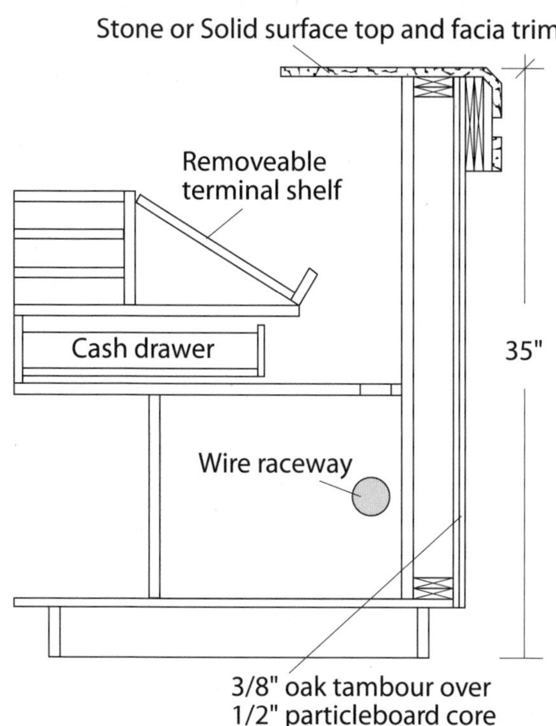

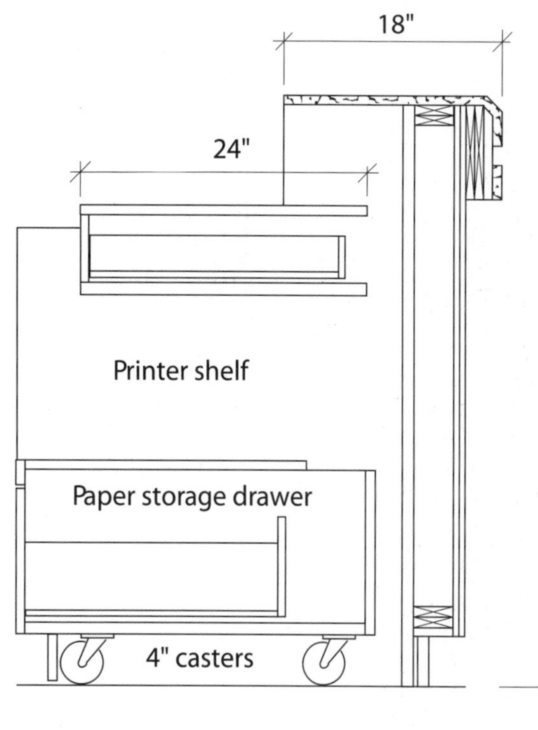

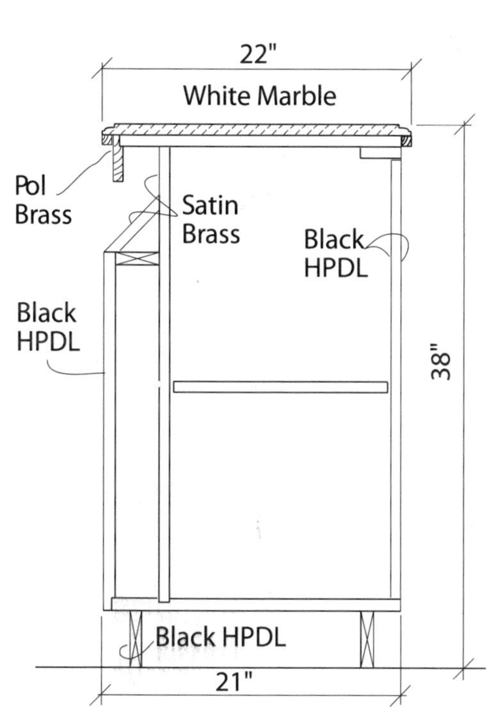

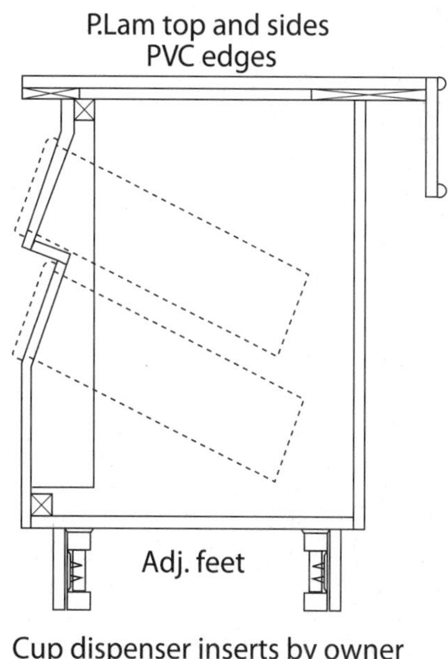

10 - Casework

Furniture and Fixtures

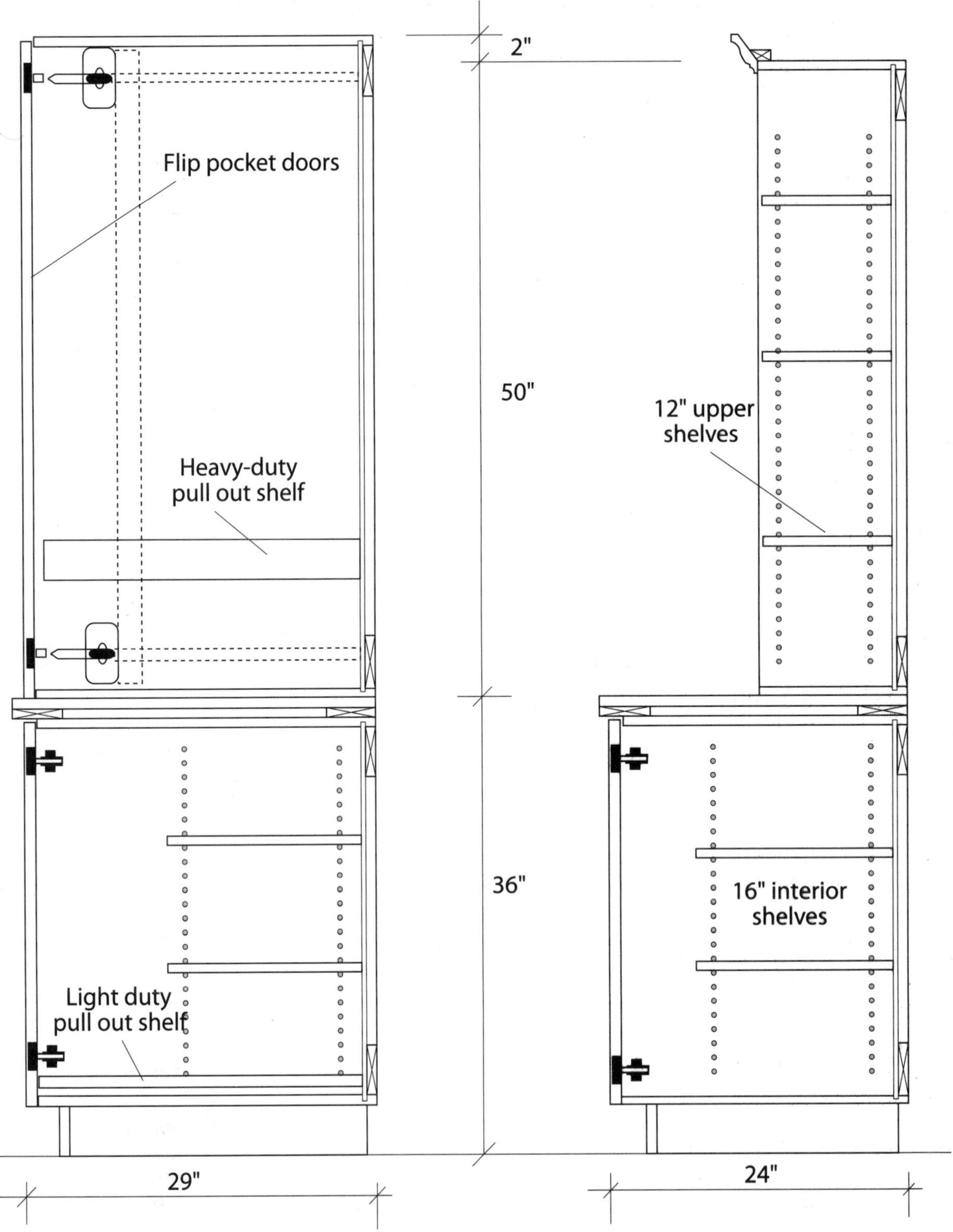

(Appendix B is not part of the AWS for compliance purposes)

10 - Casework

Furniture and Fixtures

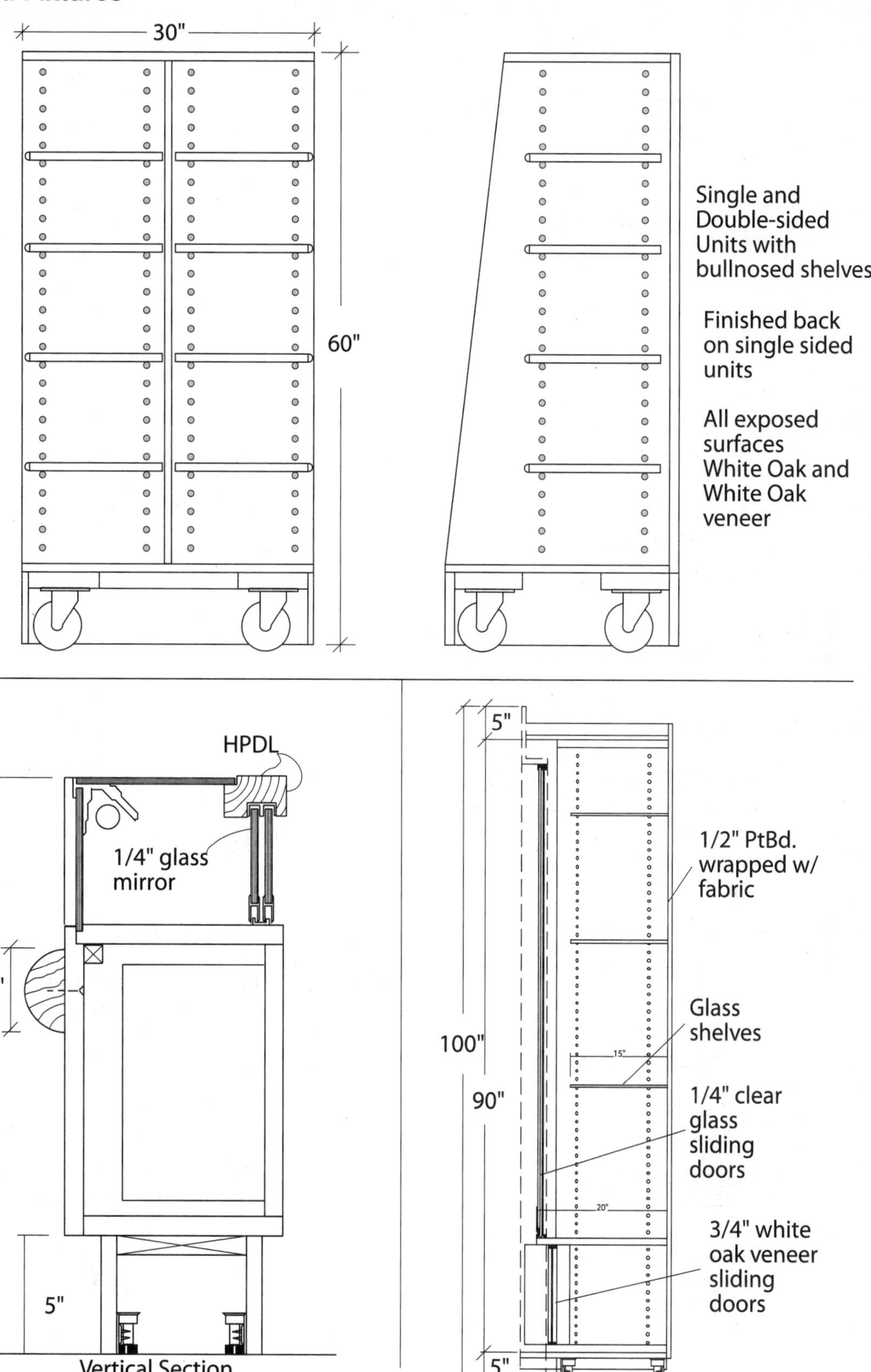

10 - Casework

Furniture and Fixtures

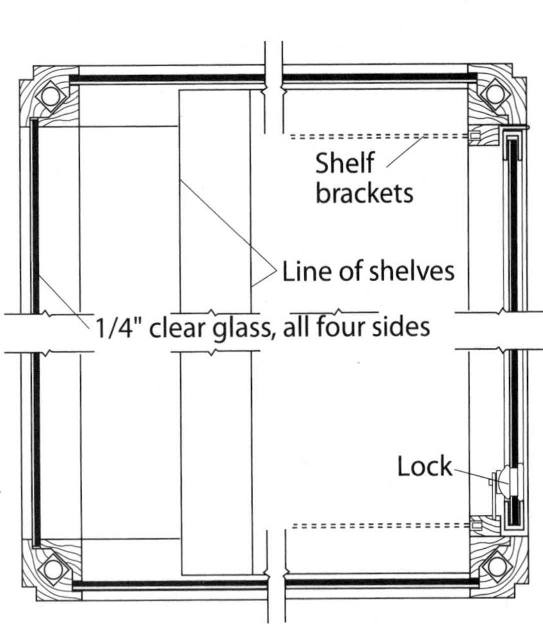

Plan Section

Isometric

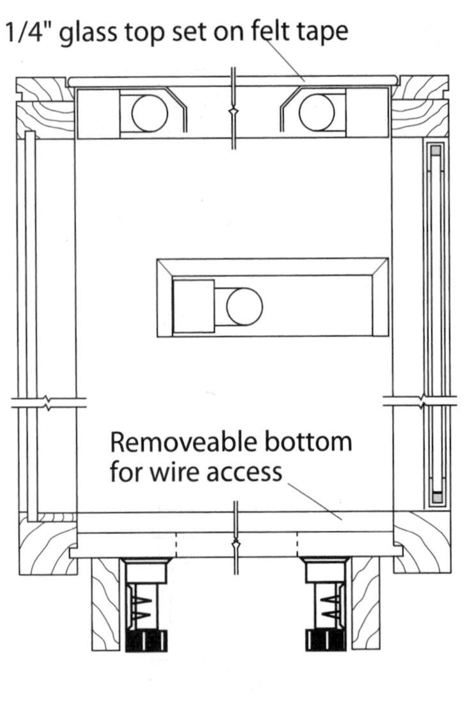

Vertical Section

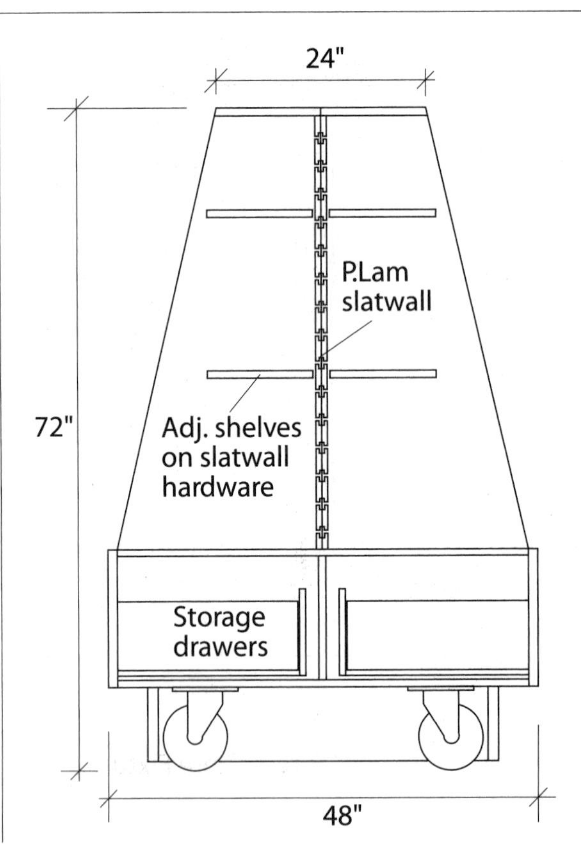

10 - Casework

Furniture and Fixtures

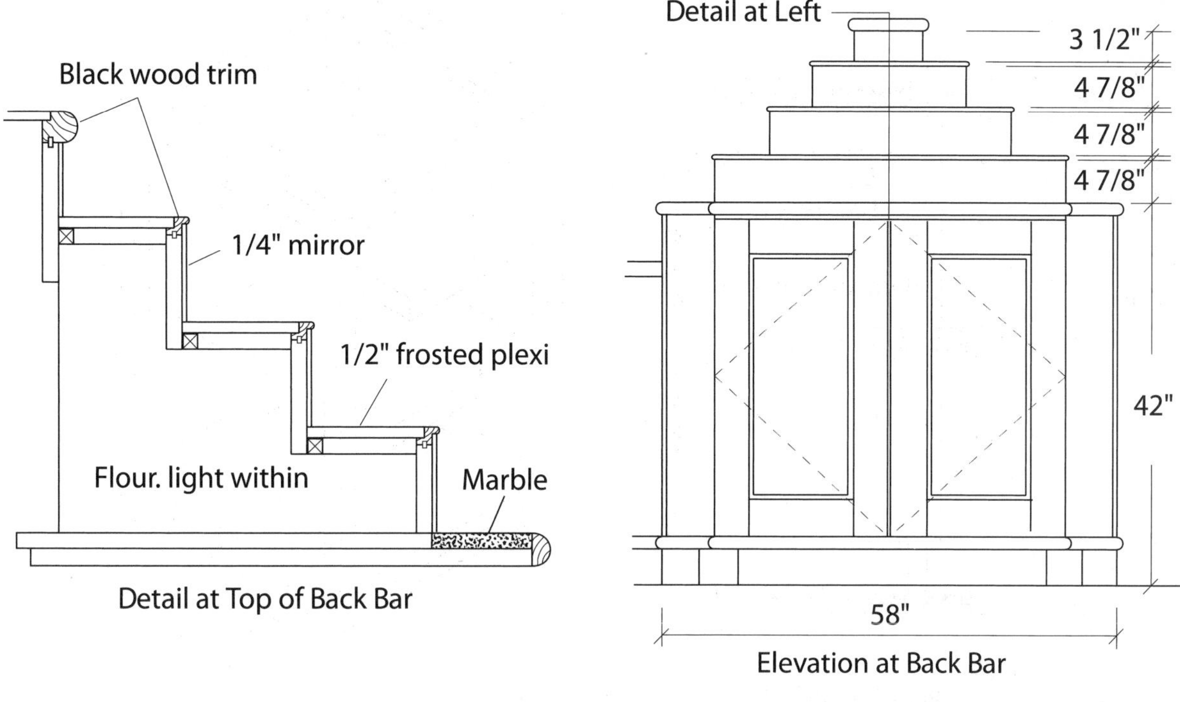

Detail at Top of Back Bar

Elevation at Back Bar

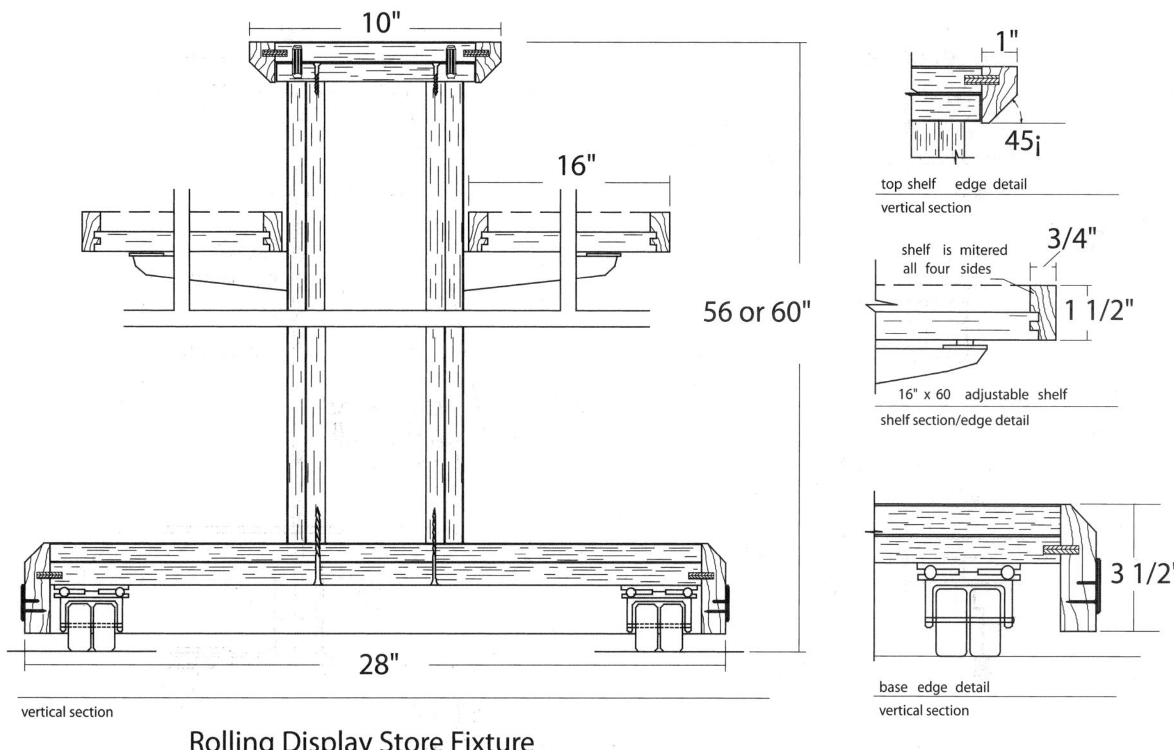

Rolling Display Store Fixture

10 - Casework

Furniture and Fixtures

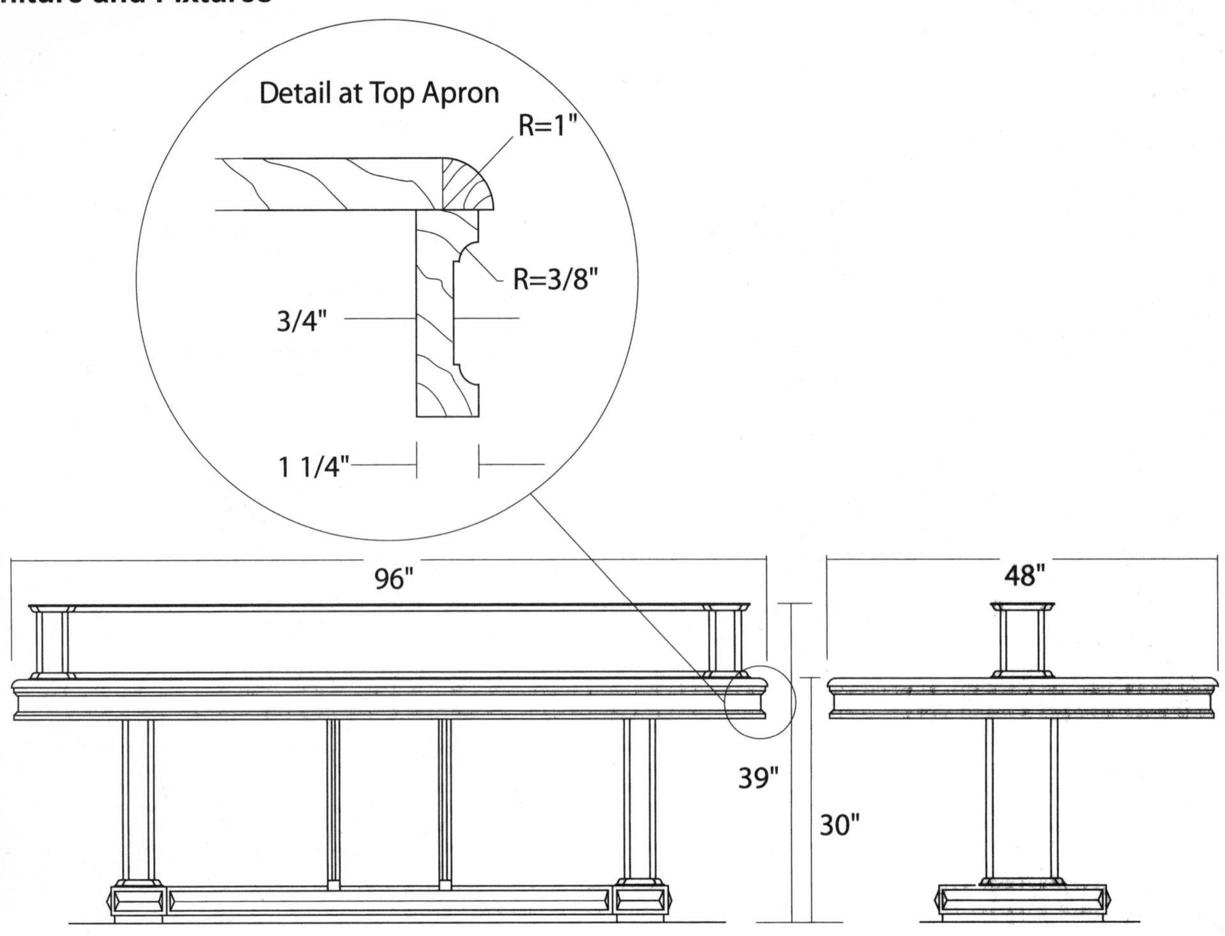

10 - Casework

Reception

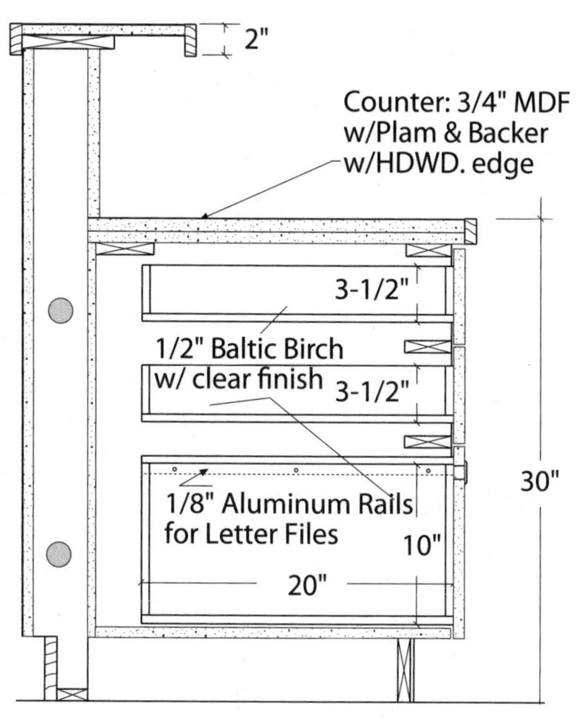

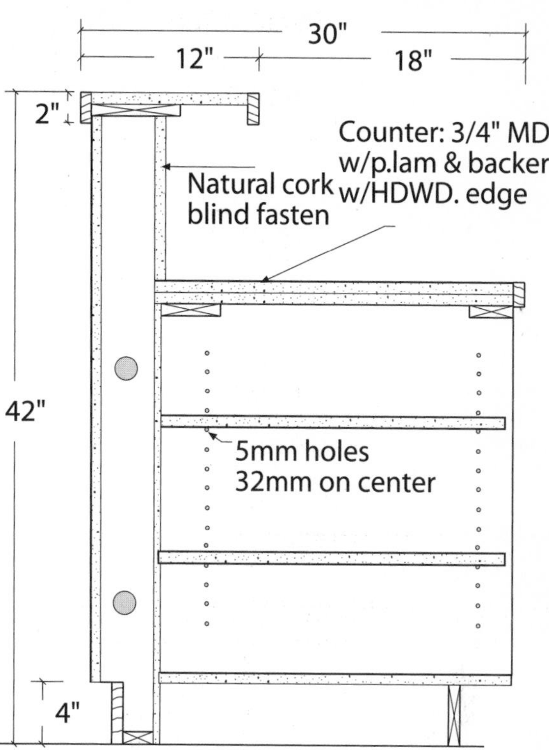

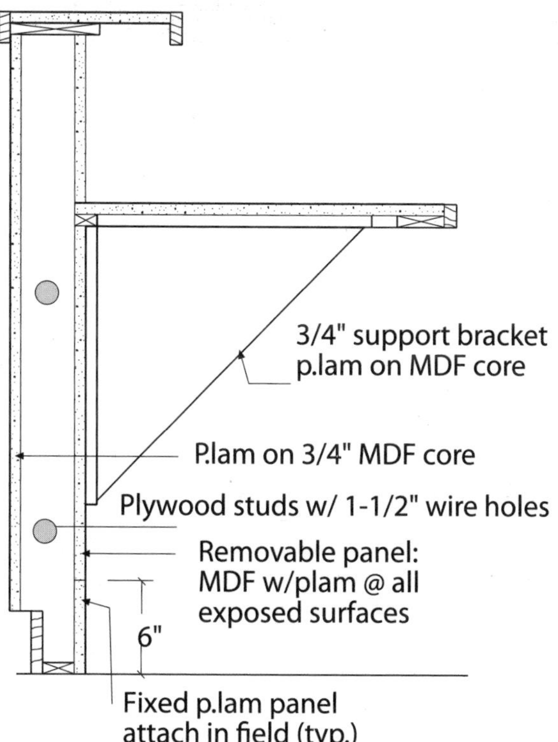

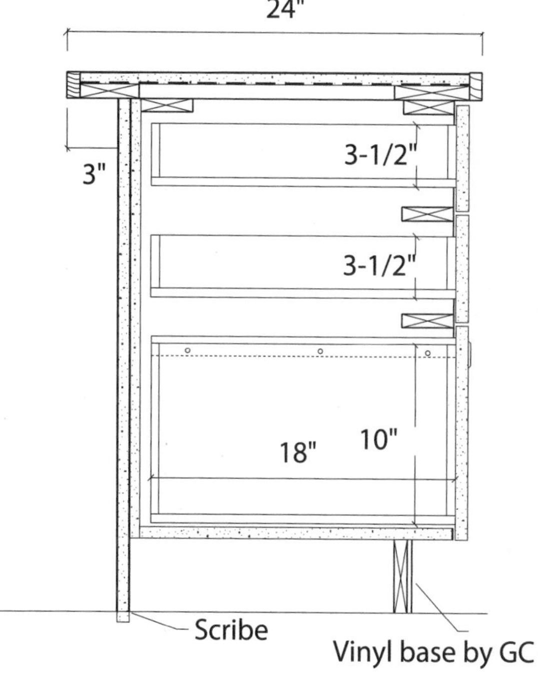

10 - Casework

Reception

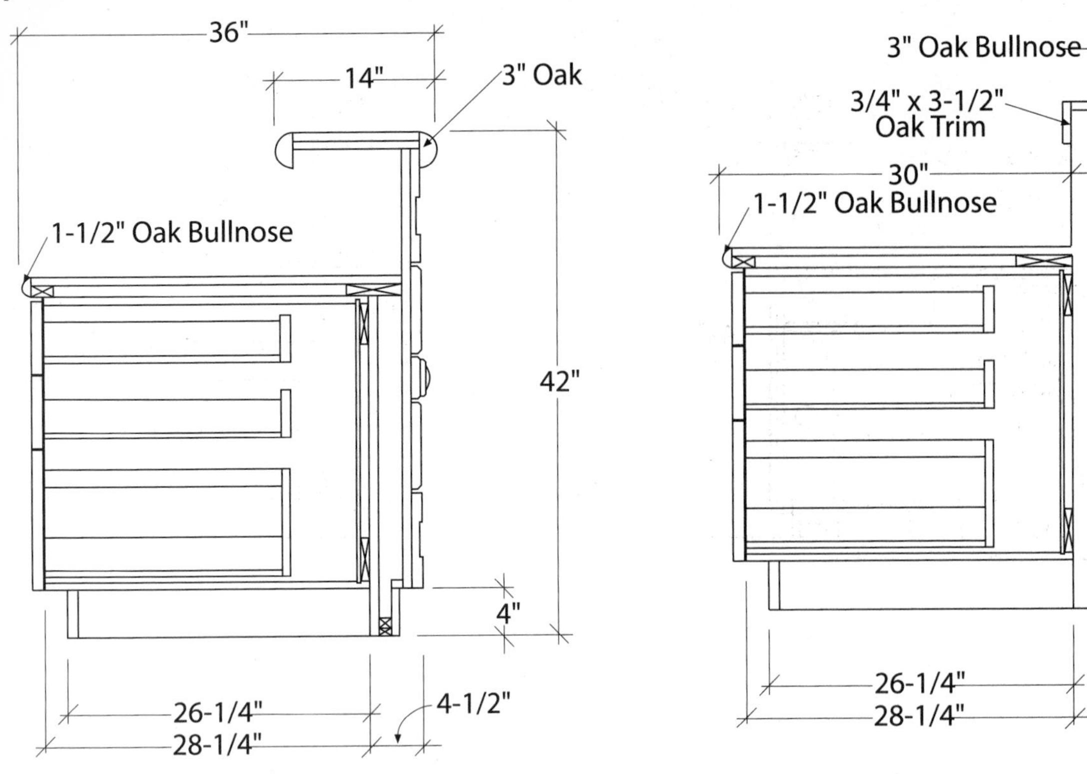

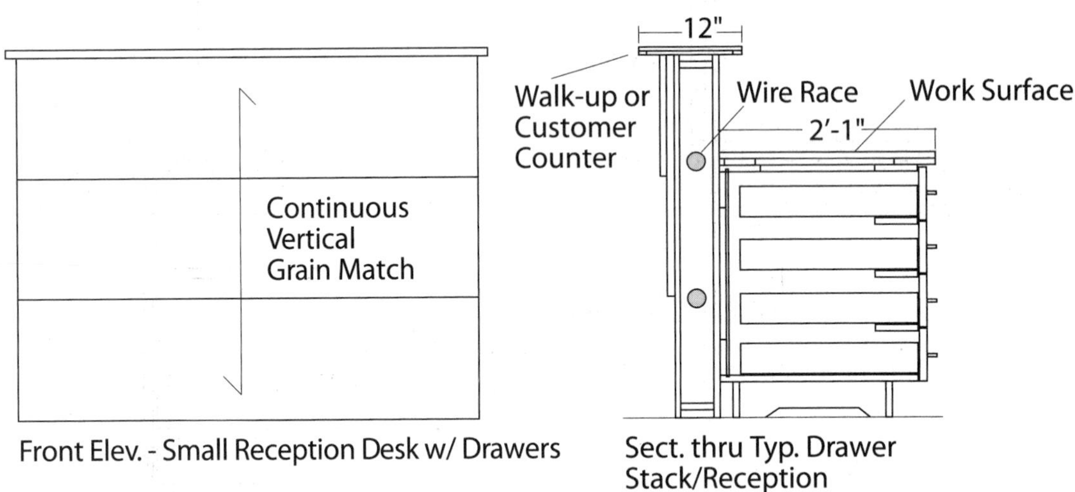

Front Elev. - Small Reception Desk w/ Drawers

Sect. thru Typ. Drawer Stack/Reception

10 - Casework

Reception

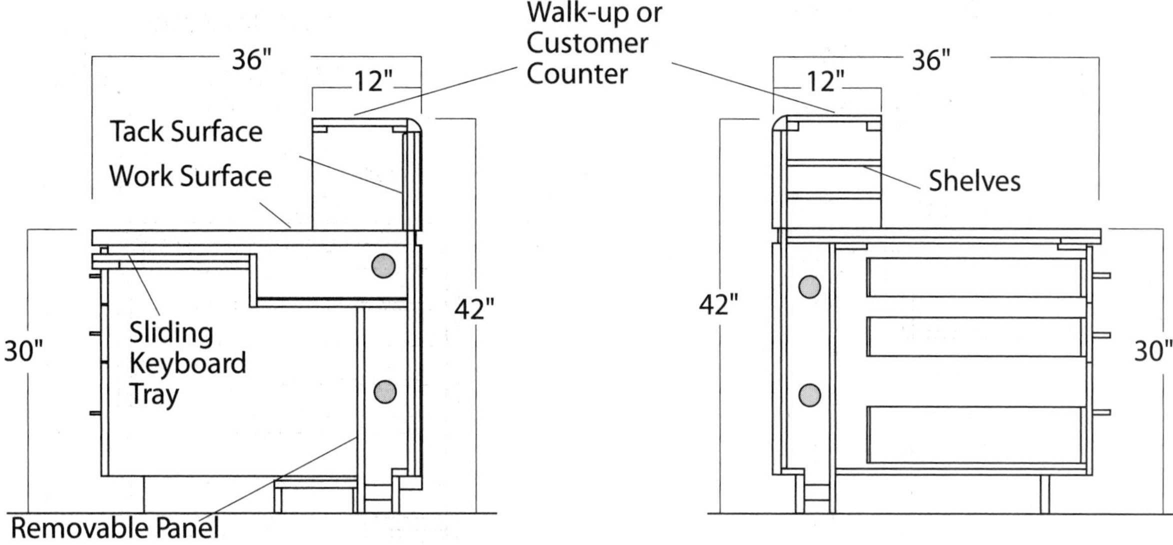

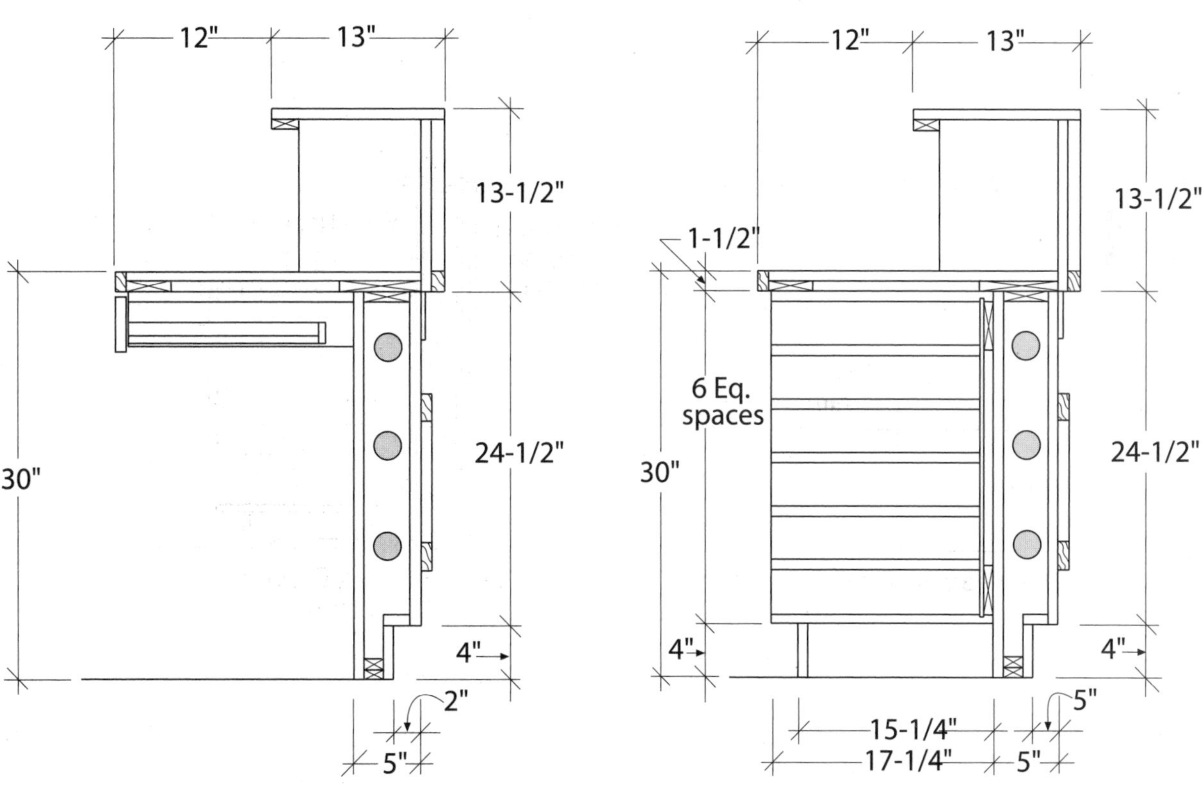

10 - Casework

Reception

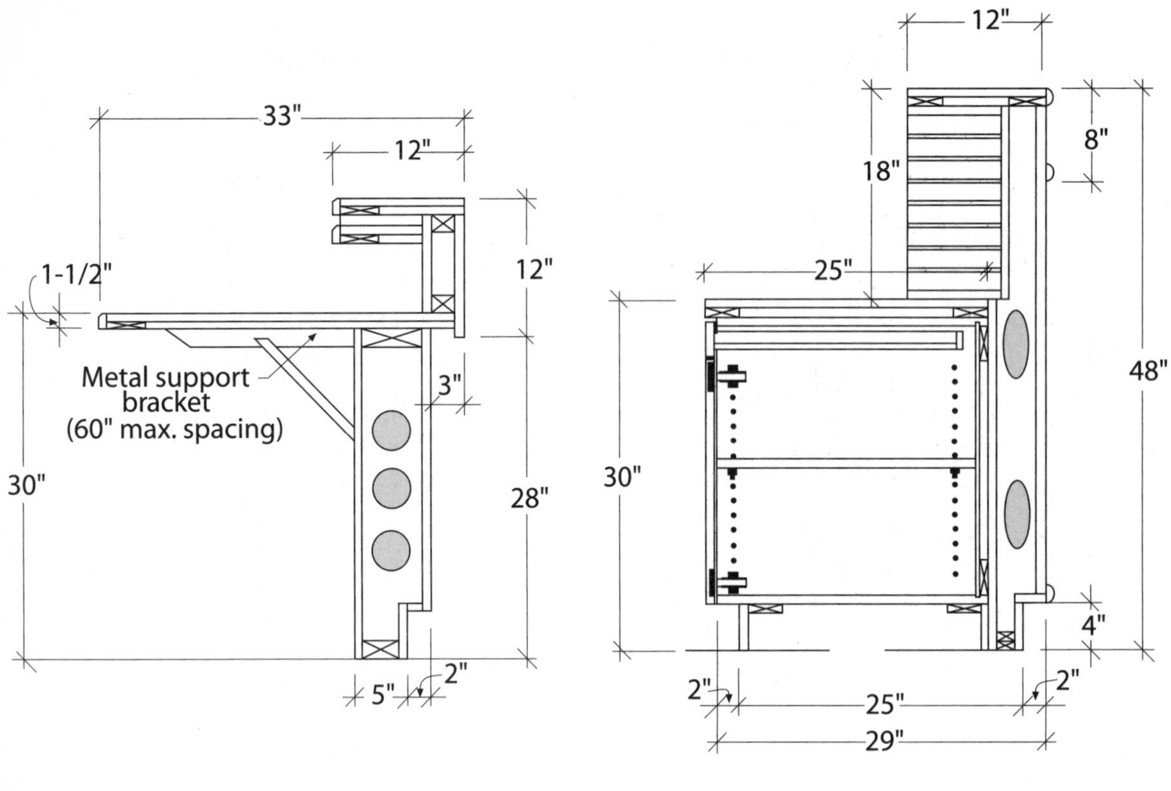

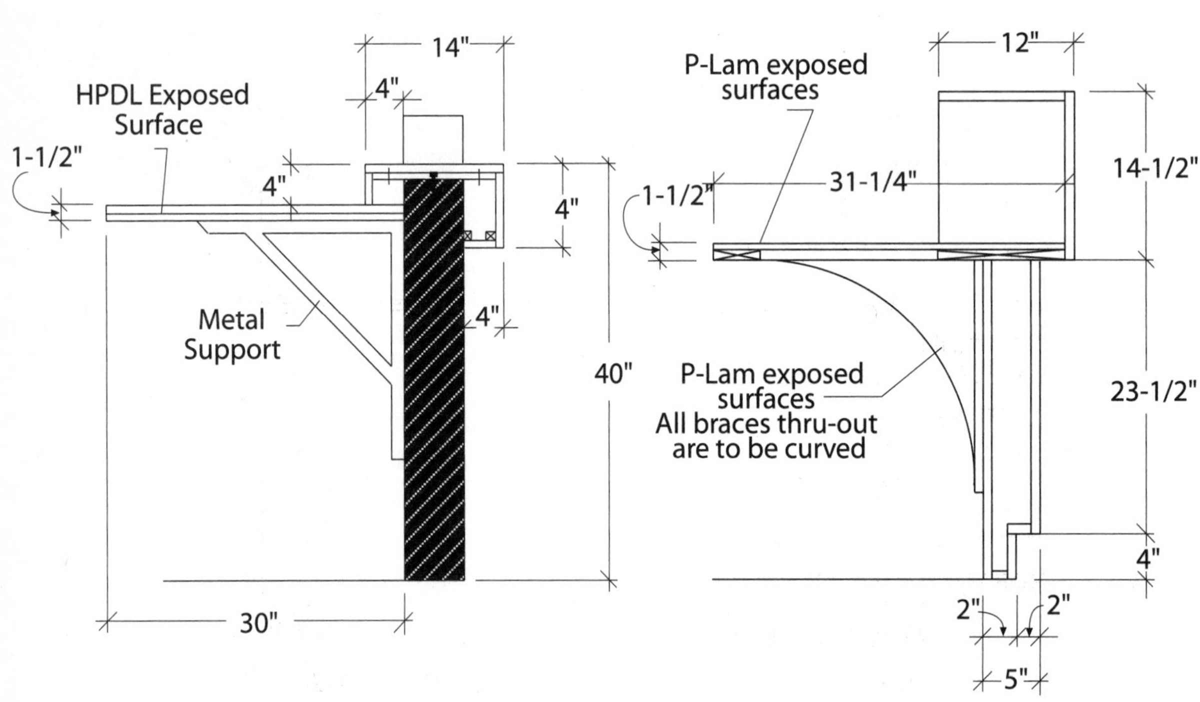

(Appendix B is not part of the AWS for compliance purposes)

10 - Casework

Reception

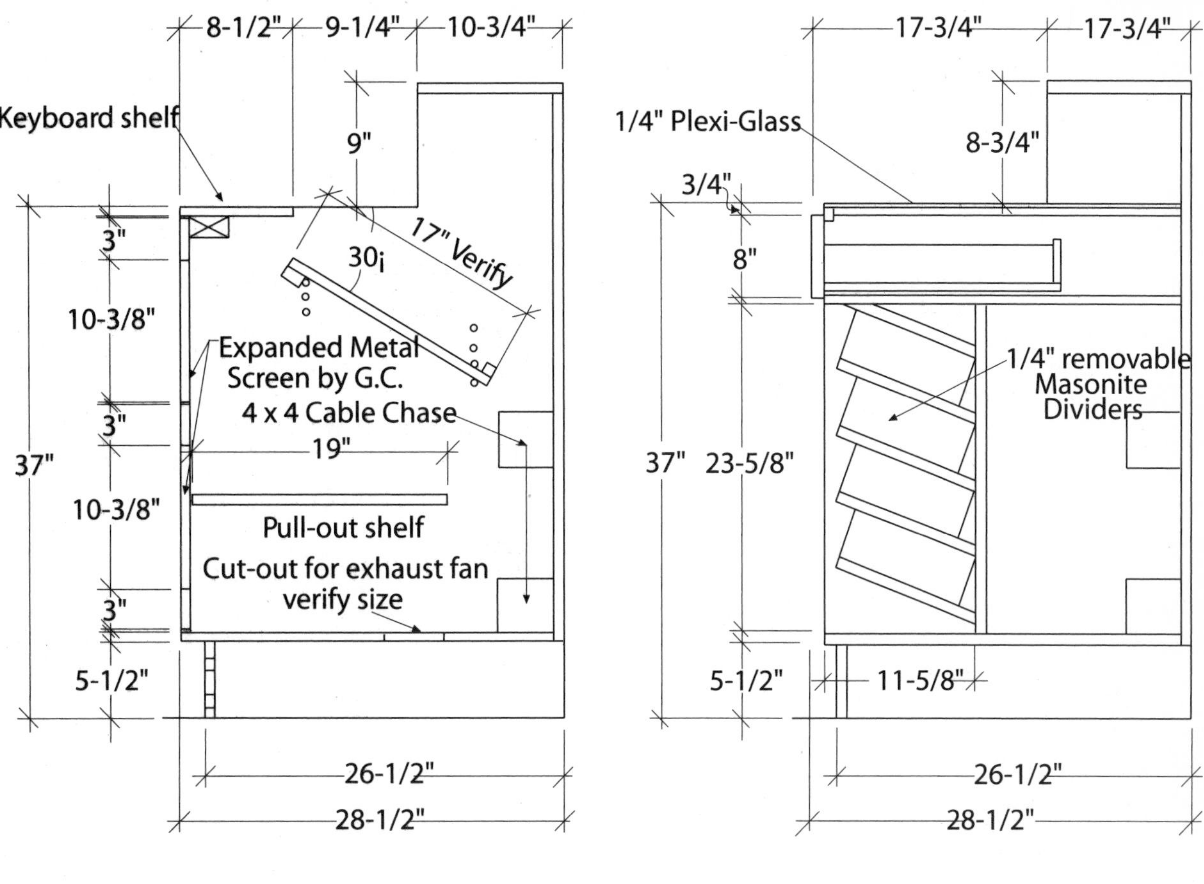

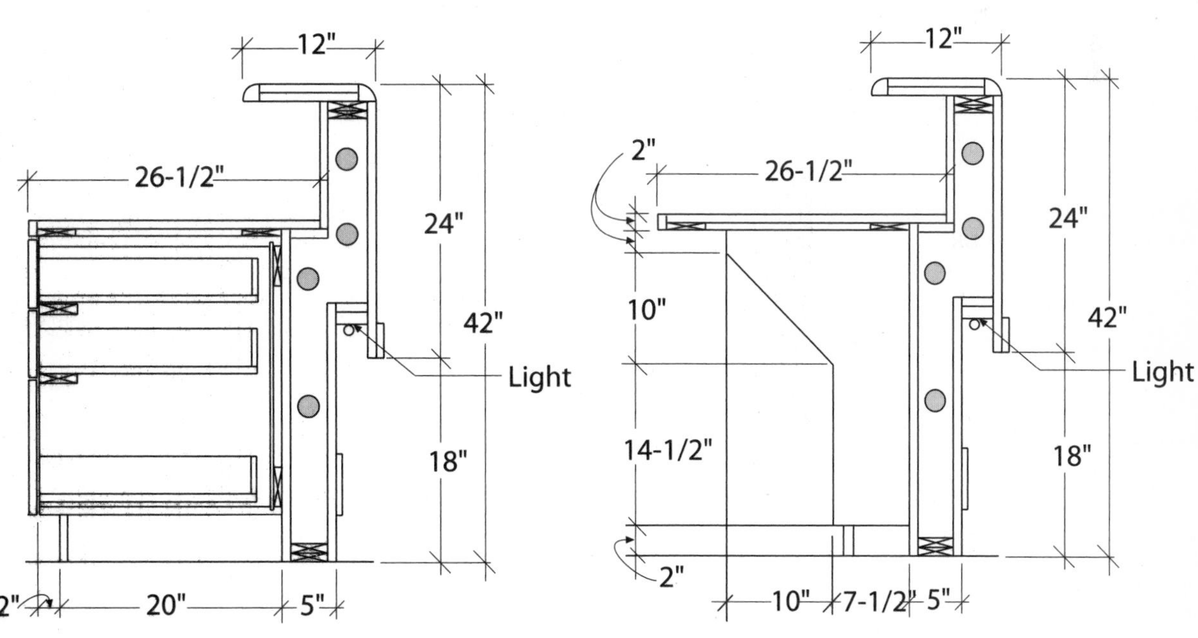

10 - Casework

Church Fittings

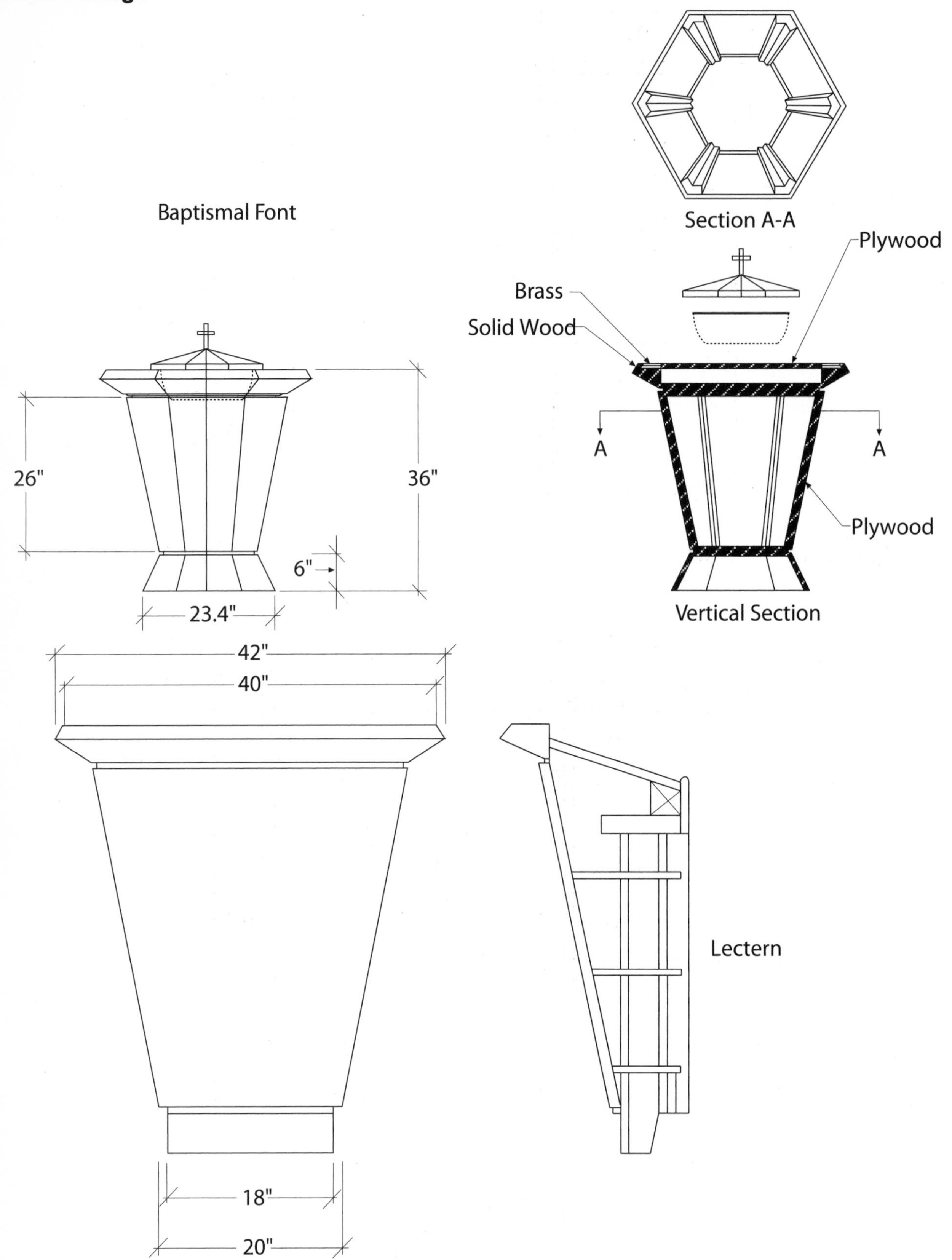

10 - Casework

Basic Cabinetry

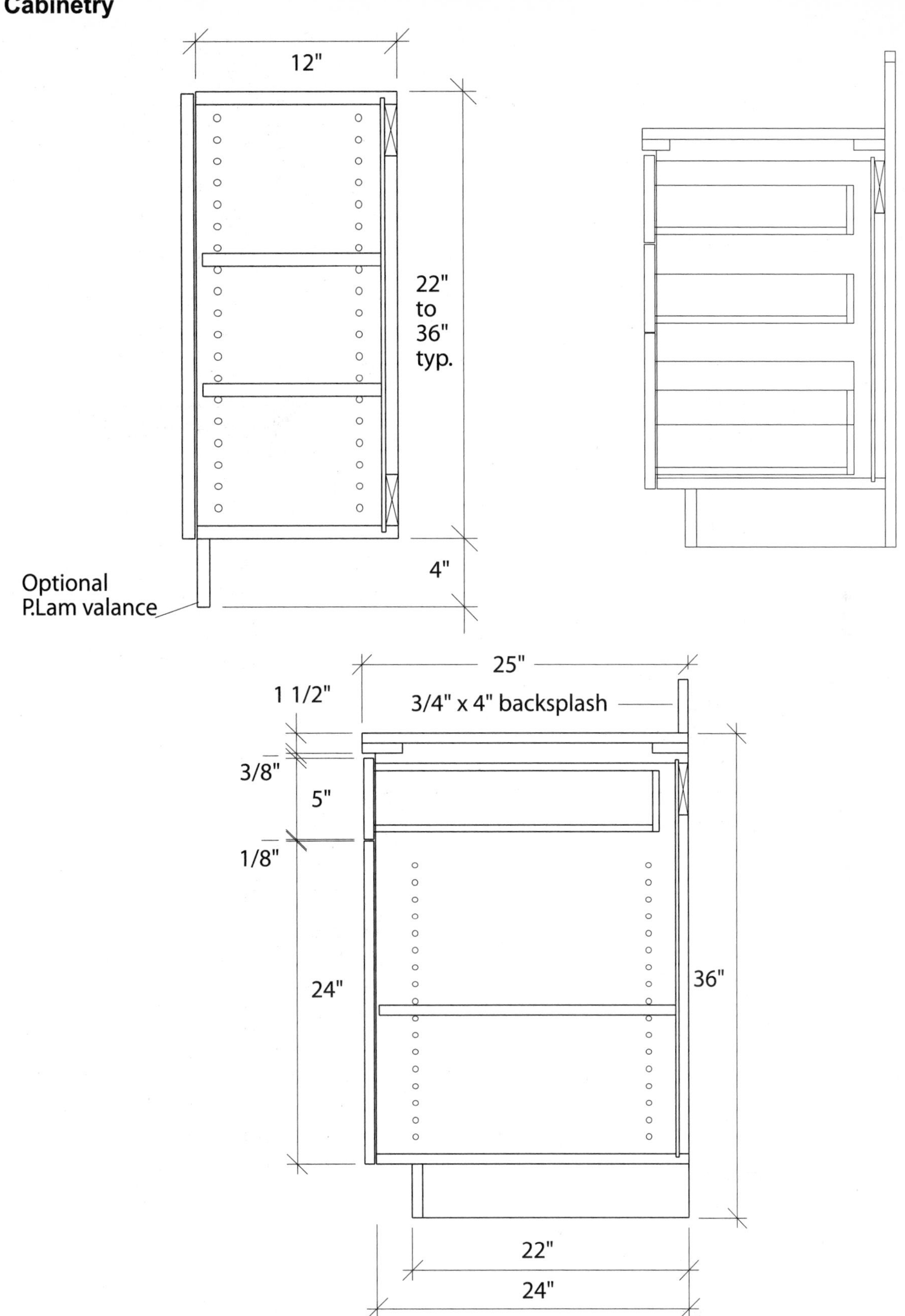

10 - Casework

Basic Cabinetry

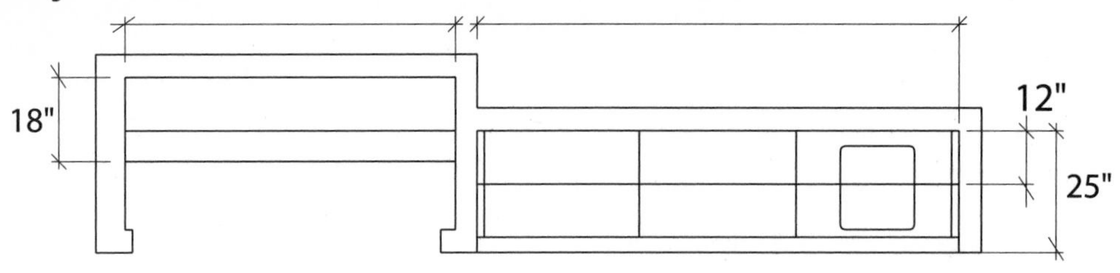

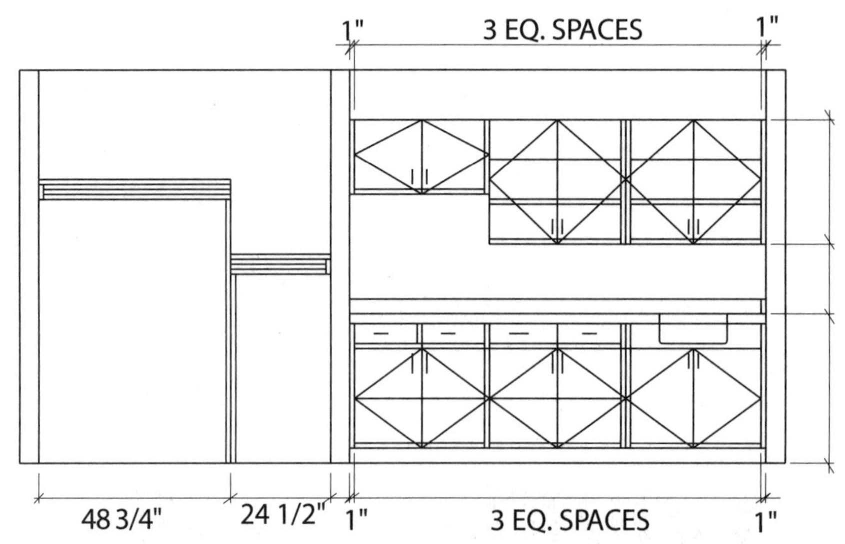

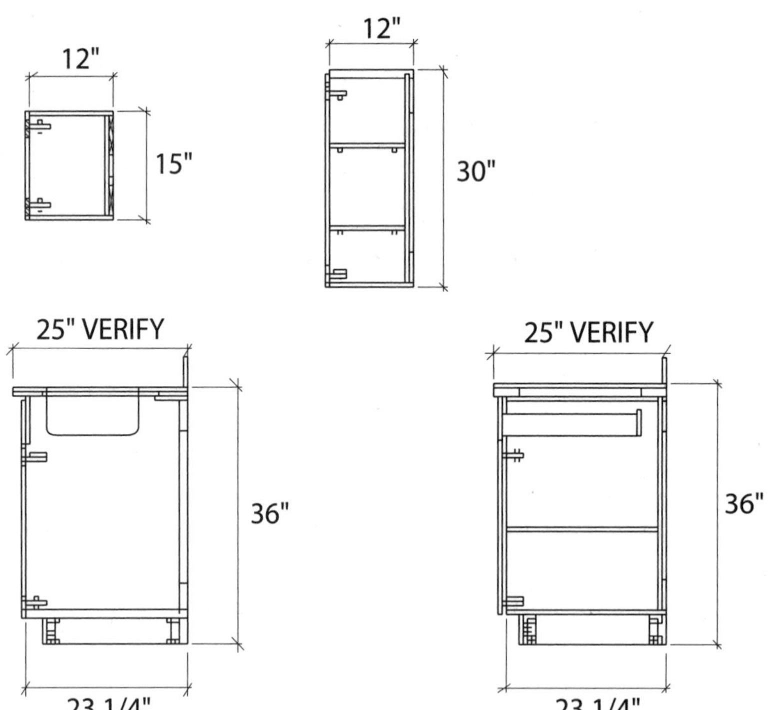

11 Countertops

11 - Countertops

Typical Countertop Configurations:

A. Panel Product Tops - This type of top consists of wood veneer over a stable substrate, veneer edge banded or with an applied decorative edge of another material as specified.

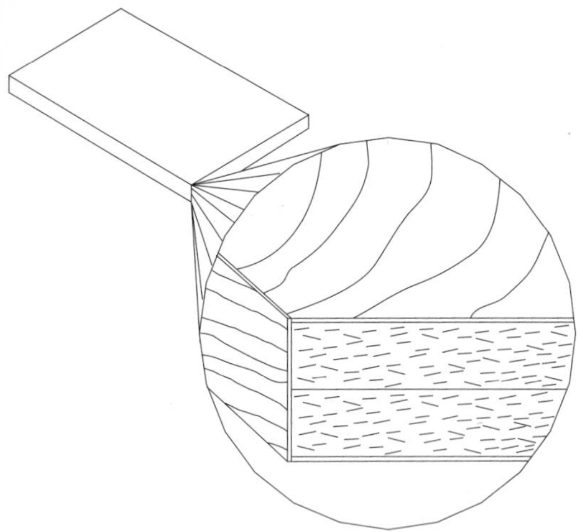

B. High Pressure Decorative Laminate (HPDL) Tops - This type of top consists of plastic laminate over a stable substrate, self edge banded or with an applied decorative edge of another material as specified.

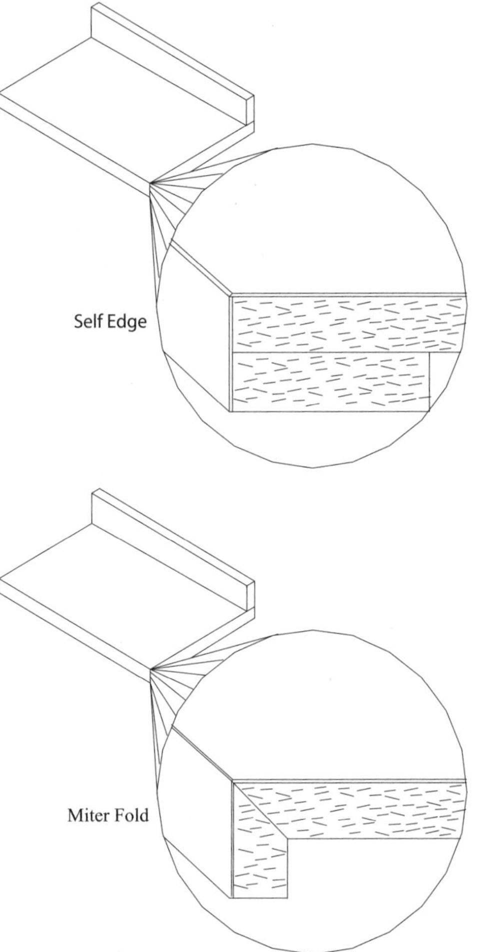

C. Post-formed High Pressure Decorative Laminated Tops - This type of top consists of plastic laminate formed with heat and pressure over a stable substrate and must be specified.

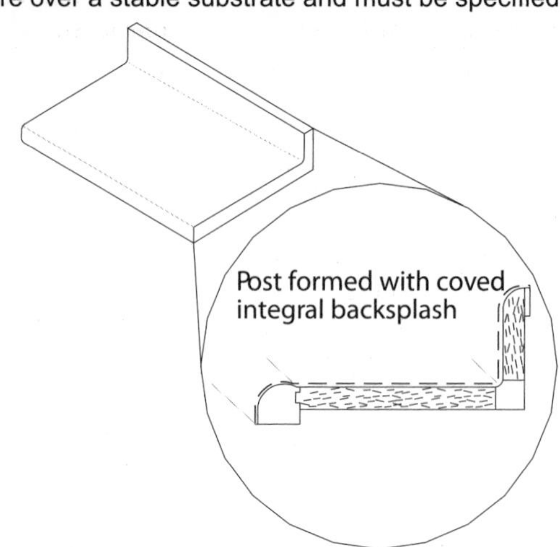

D. Combination Material Tops - This type of top may consist of a mixture of materials, such as wood, high pressure decorative laminate, inlays, etc.

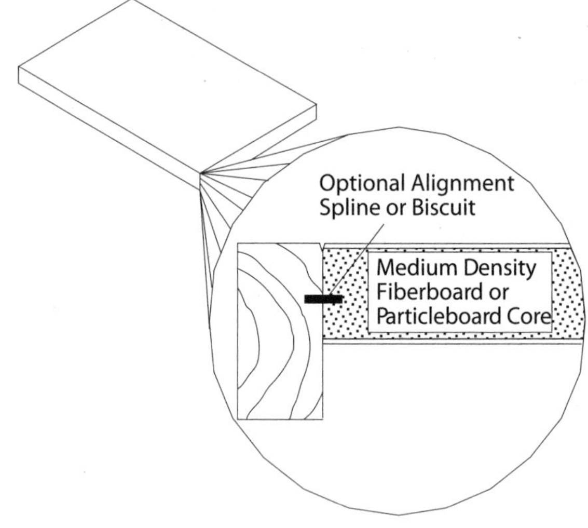

11 - Countertops

E. Solid Surfacing Materials - This type of top requires special fabrication techniques, depending upon the composition of the product. Many woodworkers fabricate and install the products. Must be specified by brand name and manufacturer.

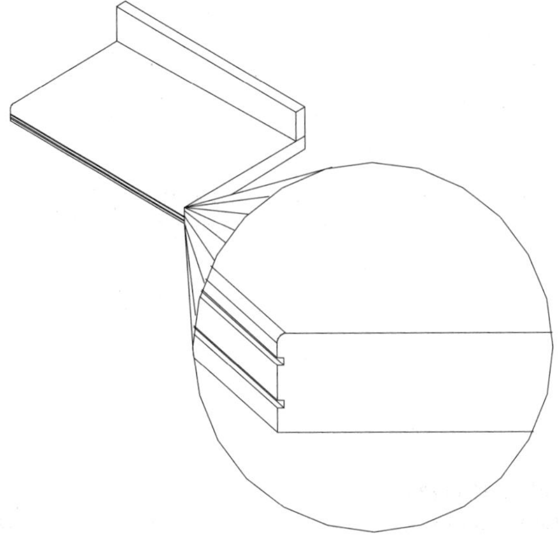

F. Solid Laminated Tops - This type of top consists of narrow strips of wood, face glued together, similar to "butcher block," but custom manufactured to specifications.

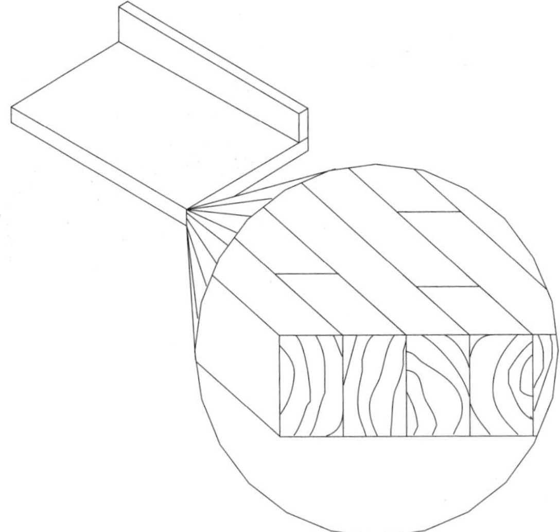

G. Solid Wood Tops - This type of top consists of boards edge glued to a desired width. In this kind of top there is no assurance of matching grain or color at the edges or individual ends of the boards.

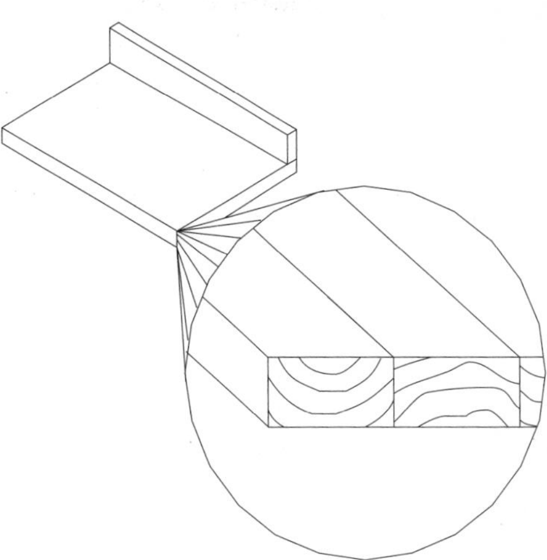

H. Epoxy Resin Laboratory Tops and Splashes - Specially formulated resin tops designed to resist harsh chemicals. Must be specified by brand name and manufacturer.

11 - Countertops

General Guidelines for Fabrication and Installation for HPDL

Data was taken in part from the National Electrical Manufacturers Association (NEMA), and is used with permission.

When making any cutout (as for electrical receptacles, ranges, sinks, grills, windows, chopping blocks, L-shaped counter tops, and so forth), all inside corners should be smoothly rounded using a minimum comer radius of $^1/_8$" [3 mm]. A router is an ideal tool for making cutouts. (1)

When removing large areas from a sheet of laminate (e.g., a sink cutout), the connecting strips between the remaining areas should be left as wide as possible. (2)

Factory-trimmed sheet edges and saw-cut edges should be routed or filed. Original edges on factory-cut laminates are not finished edges since oversized laminates are supplied to allow for proper fabrication.

All chips, saw marks, and hairline cracks should be removed from cuts by filing, sanding, or routing.

Backsplash seam areas on countertops which are exposed to spilled water or other fluids should be *sealed with caulking* to ensure a tight seal.

When laminate is bonded to a substrate, precaution should be taken to prevent warping of the assembly. Laminates used on shelves or in long unsupported spans should make use of a backer. A thick backer (approximately the same thickness as the face sheet), can provide more stability than a thin backer. Thicker laminates can offer better dimensional stability and resistance to stress (corner) cracking. Paint, varnish, vinyl film, and fiber backers will not balance HPDL.

Before using nails or screws, oversized holes should be drilled through the laminate with a sharp drill bit.

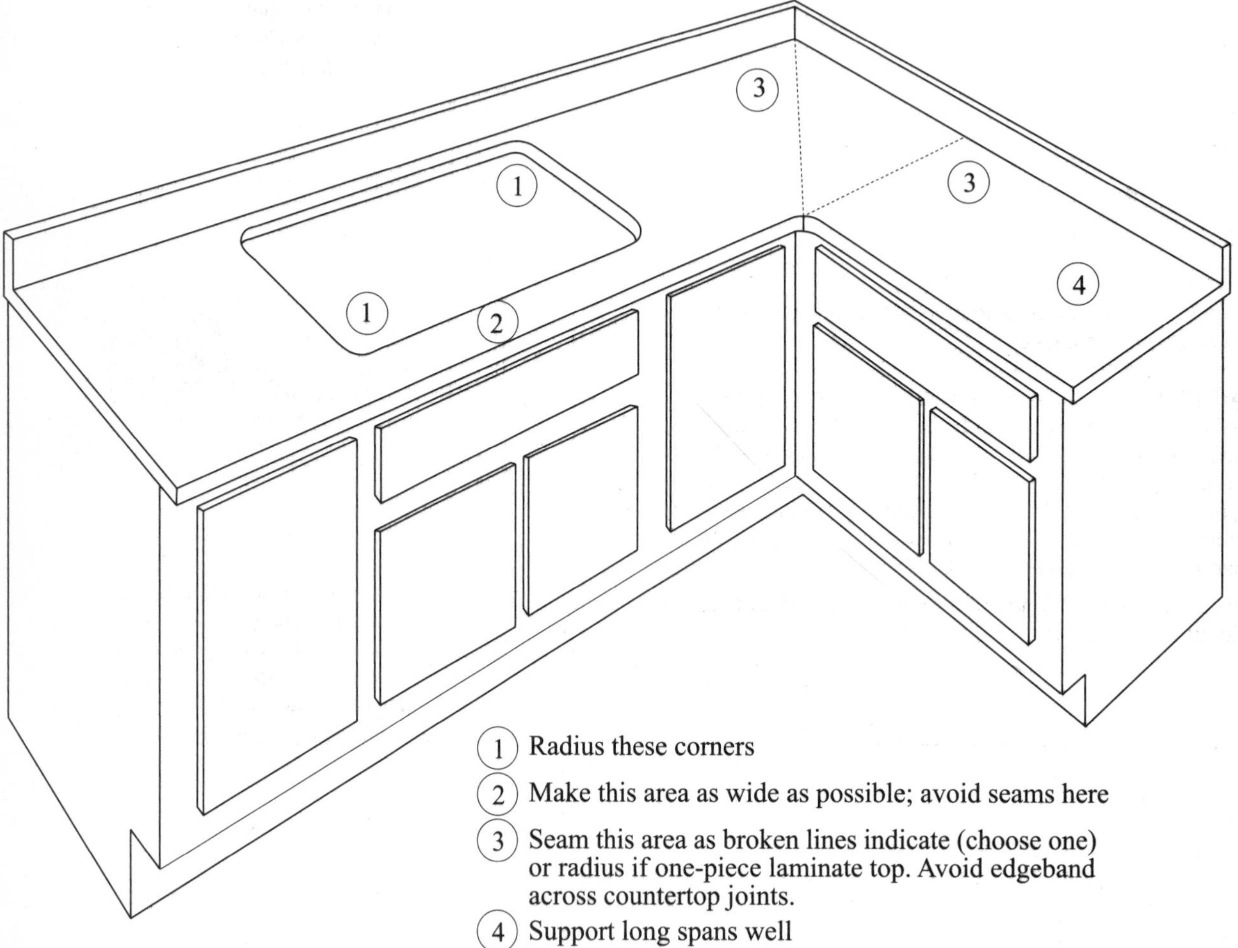

11 - Countertops

Typical Problems - Causes and Prevention

Some of the problems that may arise after laminates have been fabricated and installed are the following:

CRACKING of the laminate at corners and around cutouts may be caused by improper conditioning, improper bonding and, sometimes, poor planning, or any combination of these reasons. Cracking may be caused by shrinkage; conditioning helps to prevent it. Rough edges, inside corners that have not been rounded, binding and/or forced fits can contribute to cracking.

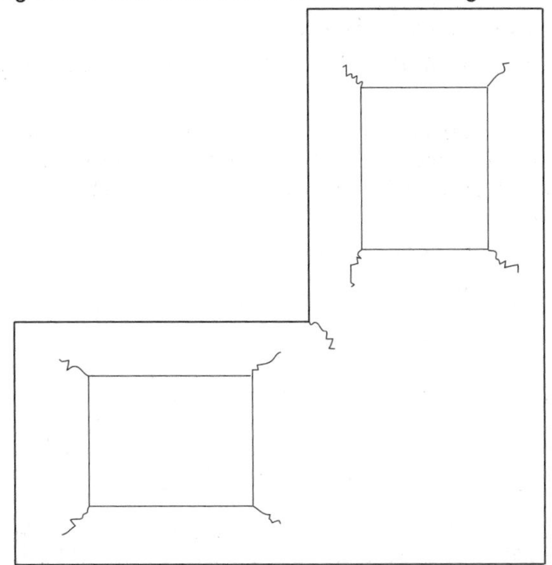

If the seams are properly placed in the layout of the laminate, stresses can be minimized.

SEPARATION of the laminate from the substrate may generally be caused by a poor adhesive bond. The bonding procedure should be reviewed with close attention to uniform glue line, uniform pressure and cleanliness of mating surfaces. If the edges fail to bond, extra adhesive may be applied and the product reclamped. Contact adhesives can often be reactivated by heat and rebonded by adequate pressure if the glue line is not starved.

NOTE: Some cleaning agents, excess heat, and moisture can contribute to bond failure at joints and edges.

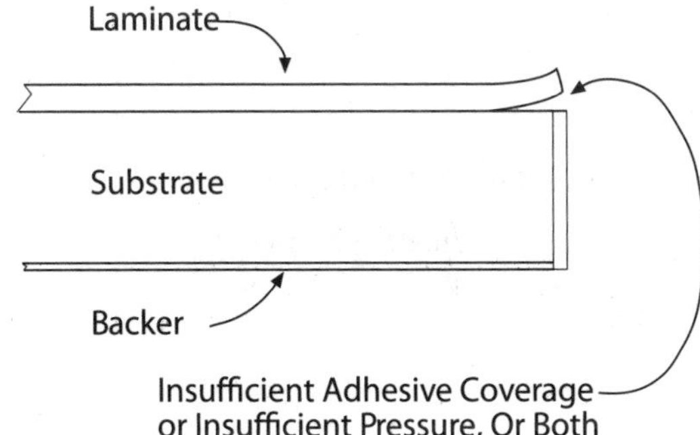

BLISTERING or **BUBBLING** of the laminate surface away from the substrate can be caused by excessive heat, starved glue line, improper conditioning, and inadequate pressure or drying. When contact adhesive is used, the condition can sometimes be corrected by applying heat and pressure. But uniform glue lines and pressure over clean conditioned laminates and substrate might have prevented the problem.

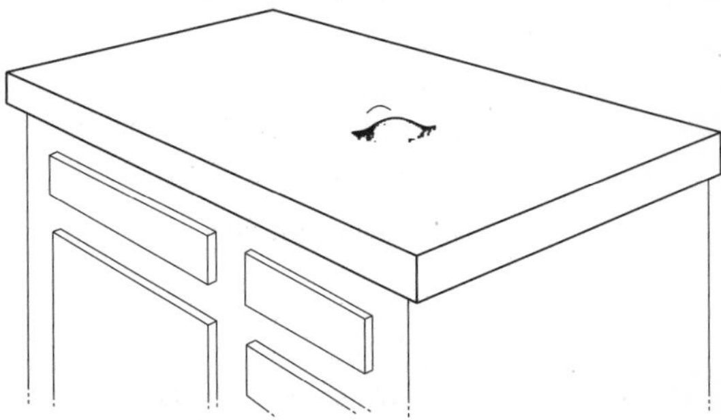

The forming of a blister or bubble over a small area, often accompanied by a darkening of the laminate can be caused by continual exposure to a source of heat. Electrical appliances which produce heat and light bulbs should not be placed in contact with or close proximity to laminate surfaces.

REPEATED HEATING may cause the laminate and adhesive to react and finally deteriorate after continual exposure to temperatures above 66° C [150° F].

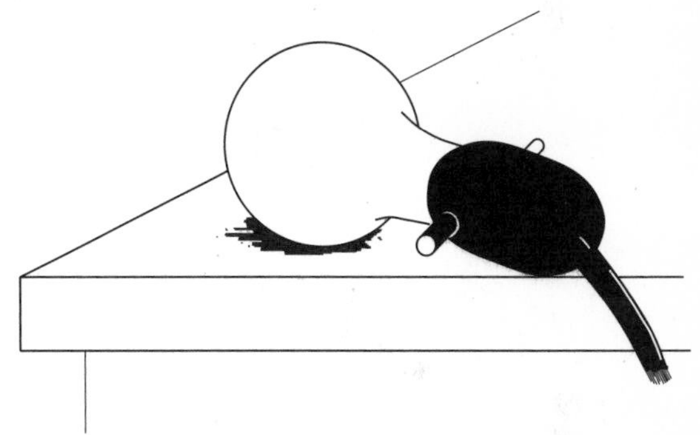

CRACKING of the laminate in the center of the sheet may be caused by flexing of the substrate when it covers a wide span or by spot gluing. Wide spans call for sturdy framework, and special attention should be given to the uniformity of glue lines and gluing pressures. Also, care should be taken to avoid trapping foreign objects between the laminate and the substrate.

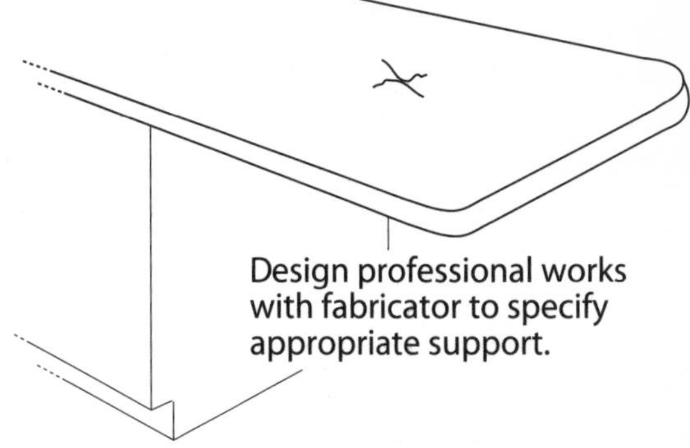

11 - Countertops

LONG, UNSUPPORTED SPANS are generally avoided. Most manufacturers limit spans to between 760 to 915 mm [30 to 36"] before the addition of a support of some type. A wide variety of engineering solutions are available.

WARPING of the assembly may be generally caused by unbalanced construction or unbalanced glue lines. Proper HPDL backer sheets should be chosen and aligned so that their grain direction is parallel to that of the face laminate. Proper gluing is also important. If the substrate is secured to a framework, the framework should be designed to hold the assembly to a flat plane. Conditioning is also helpful.

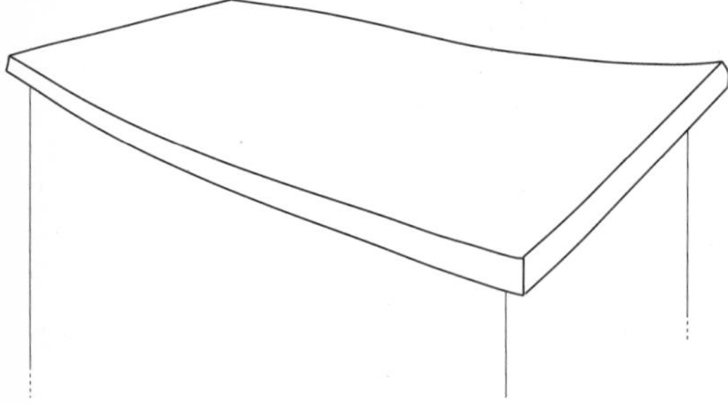

FREEDOM OF EXPRESSION

This Section is a sample of design ideas. It makes no pretense of being complete. It's here for the reader to use as a starting place. The exercise of personal creativity is the essence of fine architectural woodworking.

Custom-designed woodwork gives you complete freedom of expression.

- Design flexibility: The use of custom-designed woodwork in a building allows the design professional freedom of expression while meeting the functional needs of the client. A custom-designed building is enhanced by the use of custom-designed woodwork.
- Cost effective: Custom woodwork does compete favorably with mass-produced millwork, and offers practically limitless variations of design and material. Most woodwork lasts the life of the building - quality counts.
- Complete adaptability: By using custom woodwork, the architect or designer can readily conceal plumbing, electrical and other mechanical equipment without compromising the design criteria.
- No restrictions: Custom architectural woodwork permits complete freedom of selection of any of the numerous hardwoods and softwoods available for transparent or opaque finish. Other unique materials available from woodwork manufacturers require no further finishing at all, such as plastic laminates and decorative overlays. These materials can be fashioned into a wide variety of profiles, sizes, and configurations. The owner and design professional have the best of both worlds - high quality and freedom of choice.
- Dimensional flexibility: Since custom woodwork is normally produced by a specialty architectural woodwork firm, dimensions can easily be changed prior to actual fabrication, if required by job conditions. Special situations such as designing for the disabled can readily be accommodated by the custom architectural woodwork manufacturer.
- Quality assurance: Adherence to the *AWS* and specifications will provide the design professional a quality product at a competitive price. Use of a qualified industry member firm will help ensure the woodworker's understanding of the quality level required.

11 - Countertops

These illlustrations are not intended to be all inclusive. Other engineering solutions may be acceptable. In the absence of specifications, fabrication methods are at the option of the woodwork manufacturer.

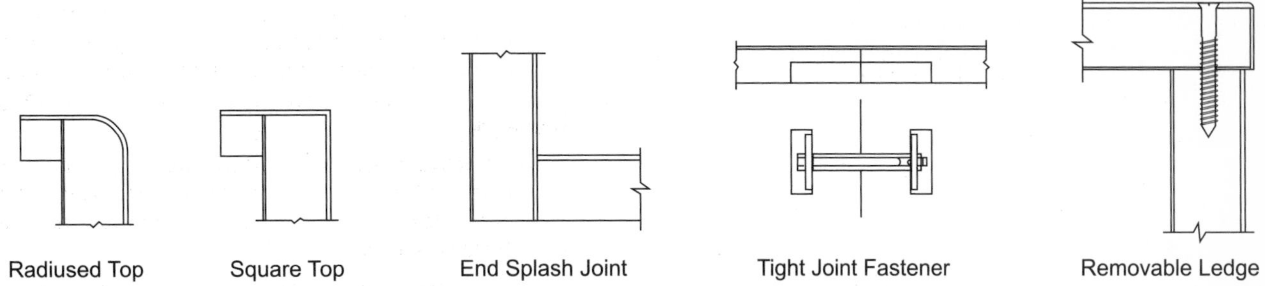

Radiused Top | Square Top | End Splash Joint | Tight Joint Fastener | Removable Ledge

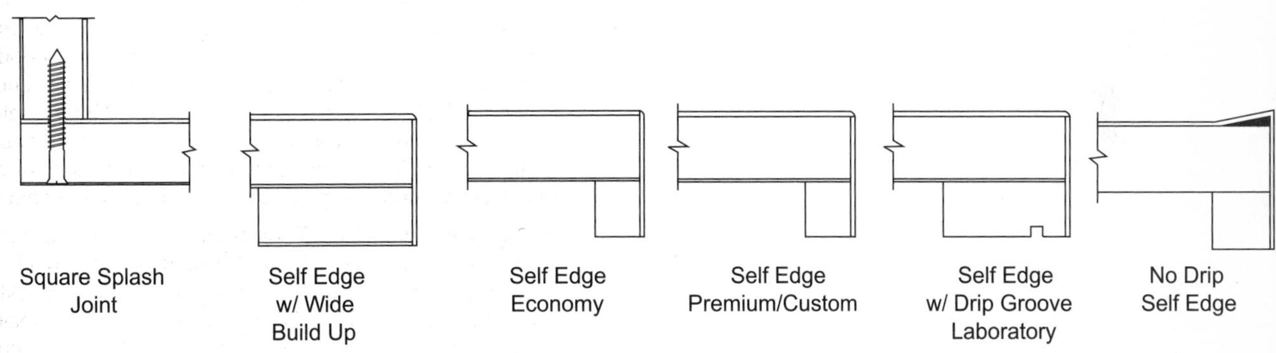

Square Splash Joint | Self Edge w/ Wide Build Up | Self Edge Economy | Self Edge Premium/Custom | Self Edge w/ Drip Groove Laboratory | No Drip Self Edge

The details below cannot be made on radiused counter tops:

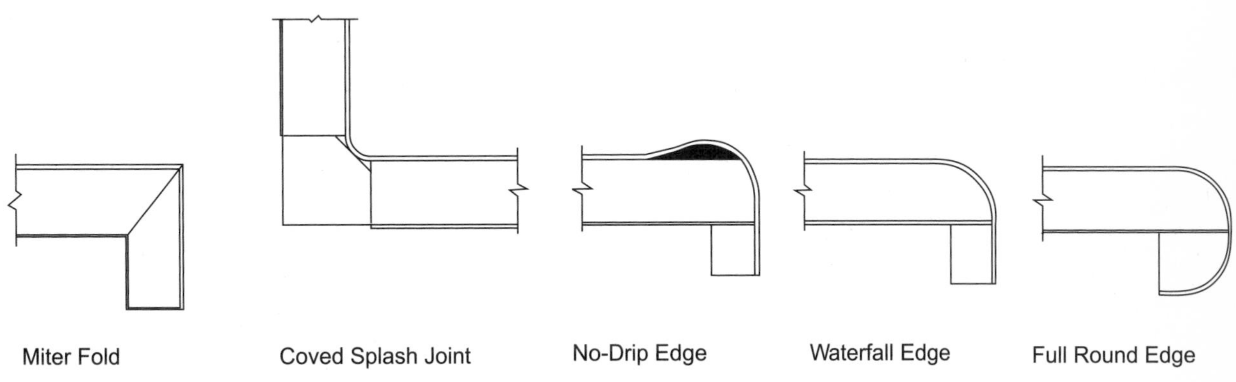

Miter Fold | Coved Splash Joint | No-Drip Edge | Waterfall Edge | Full Round Edge

Details courtesy of The Woodwork Institute of California
Used with permission.

NOTES

12
Installation

12 - Installation

Site Conditions, Materials, and Preparation

It is the responsibility of the general contractor to insure the following site conditions which are required for the installation to meet the *AWS*.

A. Walls, ceilings, floors, and openings must be level, plumb, straight, in-line, and square.

NOTE: In the absence of floor tolerances in the contract documents, variance of a cabinet's toe base height due to floor variations is not a defect. Casework is required to be installed level. Shimming of toe base, not to exceed 12.5 mm [1/2"], is acceptable. Floor variations exceeding 12.5 mm [1/2"] shall be corrected before cabinets are installed. Wall panel installations are subject to the same tolerances at wall or ceiling. Correction is not the responsibility of the manufacturer or installer.

B. Prior to delivery and installation of architectural woodwork, casework and related woodwork, to the job site, the building environment shall be stabilized to provide condition that will maintain a relative humidity of not less than 25%, nor more than 55%.

NOTE: These parameters apply for most of North America. In any event, relative humidity during the time of installation shall remain within the range to be maintained during occupancy.

All woods are affected by humidity, which is the water/moisture, in vapor form, in the atmosphere, but not appreciably by heat. Lumber swells and shrinks, primarily in two directions only, thickness and width, and insignificantly in length. These changes in dimension, due to effects of humidity, vary with different species. Providing and maintaining a stable environment, from the time of delivery, through installation, and on through building occupancy, is the key to minimizing the effects of humidity.

C. Areas to receive architectural woodwork must be fully enclosed with windows installed and glazed, exterior doors in place, HVAC systems operational, and temporary openings closed. All plaster, wet grinding, and concrete work shall be fully dry.

D. A secure storage area must be provided within the building that is flat and level, clean, dry, well ventilated, protected from direct sunlight, and broom clean.

E. Unless specified as part of the installer's contract, it is the responsibility of the general contractor to furnish and install structure, grounds, and blocking, or other anchorage which become part of the walls, floors, or ceilings, required for architectural woodwork installation.

F. All metal backing strips welded to steel studs shall be as specified and/or detailed on architectural/design drawings to show locations and gauge of thickness of these items.

G. Should the architect, designer, or engineer omit details calling for the general contractor to supply necessary blocking or backing strips in the wall, either through inadvertence or otherwise, the architectural woodwork installer shall not proceed with the installation until such time as the blocking is installed by others. The owner or owner's general contractor is responsible for placing blocking acceptable to the woodwork installer prior to installation, with no penalty to the woodwork manufacturer or installer.

H. All preparatory work done by others shall be subject to inspection by the architectural woodwork installer, and may be accepted or rejected prior to commencing installation.

I. Rough openings which are installed by others prior to commencement of installation shall be built square, in plane, and to the proper dimensions.

Architectural woodwork is a "finish" trade, and should be installed after ceilings, plumbing, flooring, etc. The fabricator of the work shall not be held responsible for any damage that might develop by others not adhering to the above procedures.

Delivery and Storage Requirement

Architectural woodwork shall be delivered to the jobsite only after all painting, wet work, grinding, and similar operations are completed. For most areas of North America, the ambient relative humidity at the site, including both the storage and the installation areas, should be maintained between 25% and 55% prior to delivery and through the life of the installation. In any event, the range of relative humidity change should not exceed 30 percentage points. Relative humidity below 20% and above 80% is particularly harmful to wood and wood products, not to mention fabrics, ceiling materials, and flooring, wall coverings and the human inhabitants.

Installation (when specified)

The methods and skill involved in the installation of woodwork in large measure determine the final appearance of the project. Architectural woodwork shall be allowed to come to equilibrium on site prior to installation. A minimum of 72 hours shall be allowed for best results. Factory finished woodwork will require a week or more to acclimatize. The design, detailing and fabrication should be directed toward achieving installation with a minimum of exposed face fastening. The use of interlocking wood cleats or metal hanging clips combined with accurate furring and shimming will accomplish this. Such hanging of woodwork has the additional advantage of permitting movement that results from humidity changes or building movement.

Finishing (when specified)

This Section does not cover finishing. However, site conditions for finishing are rarely conducive to good results. Poor lighting, dust-laden air, and available techniques are limiting factors. In many areas woodworkers will factory finish, yielding better results than can be achieved from field finishing.

Priming and back priming are the responsibility of the general contractor unless specified otherwise.

When projects are factory finished under Section 9, field touch-up is the responsibility of the installing contractor, and includes the filling and touch-up of exposed job-made nail or screw holes, refinishing of raw surfaces resulting from job fitting, repair of job-inflicted scratches and mars, and final cleaning of the finished surfaces. The prefinisher may be contracted to supply touch-up materials by special arrangement and agreement between the finisher and the general contractor.

12 - Installation

Fire-Retardant Ratings (when specified)

It is the responsibility of the specifier to research local codes and to indicate what fire-retardant rating, if any, is required for the specific items and classifications of the woodwork.

In the absence of such a specified rating, the woodworker shall supply, and the installer shall install unrated woodwork.

Recommendations which follow

Illustrations do not represent the only possible, practical, or appropriate engineering solutions for the issues shown. Design professionals and woodworking professionals often work together to create innovative solutions for installation. Solutions proposed by responsible parties shall not be deemed inappropriate merely because they are not shown herein. Variance from compliance with the *AWS* can be, and often is, granted by the design authority or owner.

Hanging Cleat Recommendations

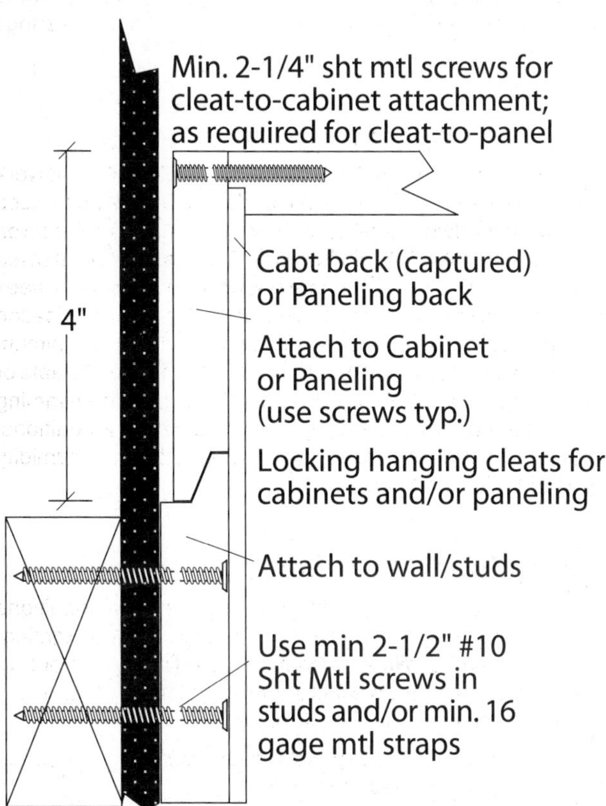

CABINET OR PANEL HANGING

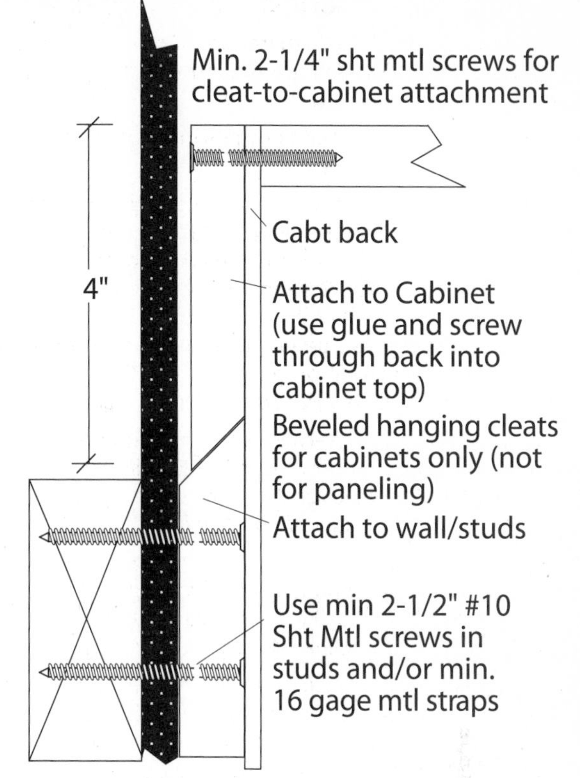

CABINET HANGING

Interlocking wood wall cleat system.

1) Cleats typically constructed of panel products.

2) Blocking typically installed by others.

3) An instrument is required for proper field layout to level and plumb panels. Shims are installed behind wall-mounted members.

4) Number and placement of cleats to be determined in consultation with installation team.

Dim. 13-19 mm (1/2 - 3/4")

WOOD INTERLOCK

12 - Installation

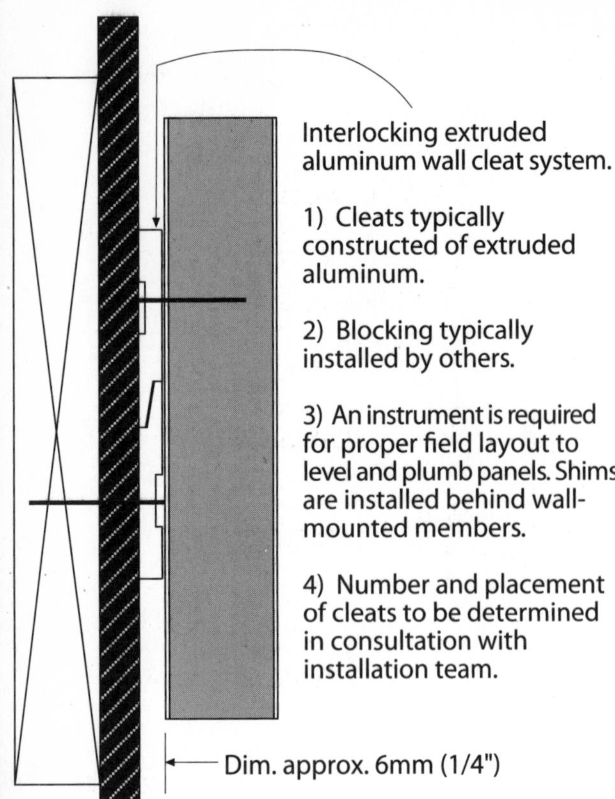

ALUMINUM INTERLOCK

12 - Installation

Cabinet Fastening Recommendations

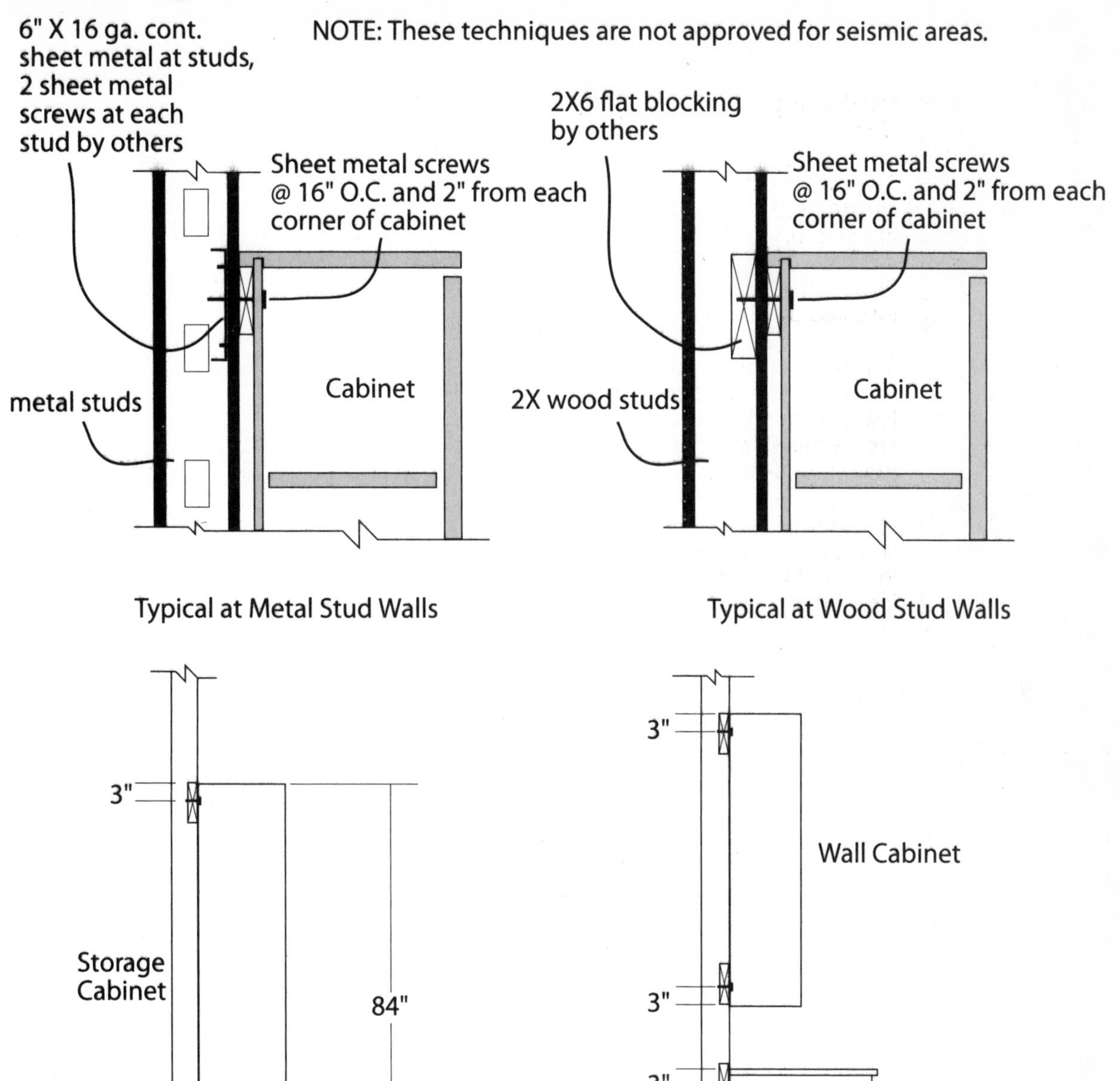

Typical at Metal Stud Walls

Typical at Wood Stud Walls

Typical Cabinet Fastening Details - In-wall Blocking usually by General Contractor

12 - Installation

HPDL Countertop Requirements

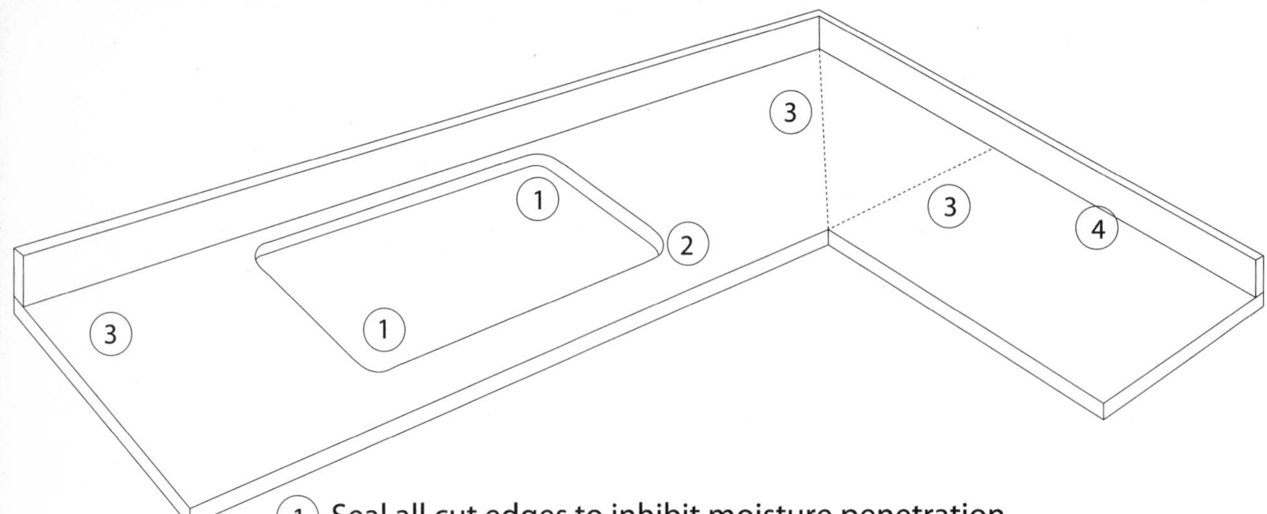

(1) Seal all cut edges to inhibit moisture penetration
NOTE: Use of pigment in the sealant will facilitate confirmation.

(2) Radius cut outs to minimize stress fractures

(3) Locate joints in HPDL and substrate at least 18" (460 mm) from sink, unless design criteria locates sink within this dimension of corner joint or change of direction of top. Seal joints watertight when within 48" (1220 mm) of sink cut outs for any Grade of work.

(4) Seal backsplash to top with caulk or silicone:
Required at fabrication when factory assembled Premium Grade
Required at installation for Premium and Custom Grade
Mill/Installer's option for Economy Grade

13
Adhesive Summary

Adhesive Summary

Adhesives

Adhesives have been used to bond wood for centuries, but until about 1930, the choice was limited to a relatively few resinous substances with adhesive properties derived from plants and animals.

The following table describes some of the characteristics of modern adhesives. Most adhesives will adhere to wood, but satisfactory performance depends on careful consideration of these factors:

1. Physical and chemical compatibility of the glue and the wood;
2. Processing requirements (open time/closed time, etc.);
3. Mechanical properties; durability in the expected service conditions;
4. Ease of use;
5. Color and cost.

Plastics and metals are generally more difficult to bond successfully than wood. When they are bonded to wood, it is necessary to choose an adhesive capable of bonding the more difficult material.

Adhesive Summary

Class	ANSI/HPVA WDMA Type	Form	Properties	Typical uses for wood bonding
Urea resin	Type II	Dry powders or liquids; may be blended with melamine or other resins	High in both wet and dry strength; moderately durable under damp conditions; moderate to low resistance to temperatures in excess of 120° F; white or tan	Hardwood plywood for interior use and furniture; interior particleboard; flush doors; furniture core stock
Phenol resin*	Type I	Dry powders or liquids	High in both wet and dry strength; very resistant to moisture and damp conditions; dark red in color	Primary adhesive for exterior softwood plywood and flakeboard
Resorcinol resin and phenol-resorc-inol resins	Type I	Liquid; hardener supplied separately	High in both wet and dry strength; very resistant to moisture and damp conditions; dark red	Primary adhesive for laminated timbers and assembly joints to withstand severe service conditions
Polyvinyl acetate resin emulsions	Slight moisture resistance	Liquid; ready to use	Generally high in dry strength; low resistance to moisture and elevated temperatures; joints tend to yield under continued stress; white or yellow	Furniture assembly, flush doors, bonding of plastic laminates, architectural woodworking
Crosslinkable polyvinyl acetate resin emulsions	Type I	Similar to polyvinyl acetate resin emulsions but includes a resin capable of forming linkage (catalyzed)	Improved resistance to moisture and elevated temperatures; improved long-term performance in moist or wet environments; color varies	Interior and exterior doors, moulding and architectural woodworking
Contact adhesives	Type II	Typically an elastomer base in organic solvents or water emulsion	Initial joint strength develops immediately upon pressing, increases slowly over a period of weeks; dry strengths generally lower than those of conventional woodworking glues; water resistance and resistance to severe conditions variable; color varies	For some nonstructural bonds; high pressure decorative laminates to substrates. Useful for low strength metal and some plastic bonding.
Mastics (elastomeric construction adhesives)	Type II	Puttylike consistency, synthetic or natural elastomer base, usually in organic solvents	Gap filling; develop strength slowly over several weeks; water resistance and resistance for severe conditions variable; color varies	Lumber and plywood to joists and studs; gypsum board; styrene and urethane foams
Thermoplastic synthetic resins (hot melts)	Not tested for moisture resistance	Solid chunks, pellets, ribbons, rods, or films; solvent-free	Rapid bonding; gap filling; lower strength than conventional woodworking adhesives; minimal penetration; moisture resistant; white to tan	Edge banding of panels; films and paper overlays
Epoxy resins	Type I	Chemical polymers, usually in two parts, both liquid; completely reactive, no solvents	Good adhesion to metals, glass, certain plastics, and wood products; permanence in wood joints not adequately established; gap-filling	Used in combination with other resins for bonding metals, plastics, and materials other than wood; fabrication of cold molded wood panels

*Most types used in the United States are alkaline-catalyzed. The general statements refer to this type.
Above data summarized from Table 9-2, Wood Handbook, U.S. Dept. of Agriculture, Forest Service, Agriculture Handbook 72, 1987

Generic Name	ANSI/HPVA WDMA Type	Form	Properties	Typical uses for wood bonding
Aliphatic (Carpenter's Glue)	Type II	Liquid; ready to use	Non-toxic; non-flammable; non-staining Highly water resistant for interior use	Furniture assembly, flush doors, bonding of plastic laminates, architectural woodworking
Casein	Type II	Dry powder form, or prepared from raw materials	Highly water resistant, not waterproof	Doors for interior use, laminated timber, some architectural woodworking

Type data similar to ANSI/HPVA/WDMA testing as follows (no testing done by the Architectural Woodwork Institute):
-- Type I: Fully waterproof (exterior) 2 Cycle Boil/Shear test
-- Type II: Water resistant (interior) 3 Cycle Soak test

NOTES